D1557176

THEOLOGY OF THE NEW TESTAMENT

THEOLOGY OF THE NEW TESTAMENT

Udo Schnelle

Translated by M. Eugene Boring

BakerAcademic
a division of Baker Publishing Group
Grand Rapids, Michigan

Originally published as *Theologie des Neuen Testaments*

Published by Baker Academic
a division of Baker Publishing Group
PO Box 6287, Grand Rapids, MI 49516-6287
www.bakeracademic.com

Printed in the United States of America

Library of Congress Cataloging-in-Publication Data

Schnelle, Udo.
[Theologie des Neuen Testaments. English]
Theology of the New Testament / Udo Schnelle ; translated by M. Eugene Boring.
p. cm.
Includes bibliographical references and index.
ISBN 978-0-8010-3604-0 (cloth)
1. Bible. N.T.—Theology. I. Title.
BS2397.S4613 2009
225.6—dc22 2009018422

09 10 11 12 13 14 15 7 6 5 4 3 2 1

Contents

Translator's Preface

Udo Schnelle has established himself as a scholar of international reputation especially by his works on Paul and John.[1] His comprehensive introduction to New Testament studies has become the standard work in German-speaking countries.[2] He is editor of a multivolume collection of texts from the Hellenistic world that illuminate the context and interpretation of the New Testament.[3] In the present volume, he integrates, updates, and expands his previous work into a full-scale theology of the New Testament that brings together detailed individual studies under a single overarching perspective. His command of primary sources from the Hellenistic world and of the vast secondary literature of New Testament exegesis and interpretation is documented in the footnotes and bibliography, but that the volume is rooted in careful study of the New Testament itself is manifest in the more than 10,000 biblical references. Udo Schnelle presents his own point of view with clarity, in the context of a discussion of alternatives addressed with fairness and respect. He is an active churchman, has served as the pastor of a congregation, and writes as one concerned to allow the New Testament authors to speak their own messages,

1. On Paul, see especially his major work Udo Schnelle, *Apostle Paul: His Life and Thought* (trans. M. Eugene Boring; Grand Rapids: Baker Academic, 2005). His valuable and readable commentary on John (*Das Evangelium nach Johannes* [THKNT 4; Leipzig: Evangelische Verlagsanstalt, 1998]) has not yet been translated into English, but see his Habilitationsschrift, *Antidocetic Christology in the Gospel of John* (trans. Linda M. Maloney; Minneapolis: Fortress, 1992). For a selection of Schnelle's other works, see the bibliography of this volume.

2. Udo Schnelle, *Einleitung in das Neue Testament* (6th ed.; Göttingen: Vandenhoeck & Ruprecht, 2007), the 2nd edition of which is available in English as Udo Schnelle, *The History and Theology of the New Testament Writings* (trans. M. Eugene Boring; Minneapolis: Fortress, 1998).

3. Udo Schnelle, ed. *Neuer Wettstein: Texte zum Neuen Testament aus Griechentum und Hellenismus* (Berlin: de Gruyter, 1996–).

and to equip modern readers to perceive their theological breadth and depth. This book not only informs, it also generates dialogue—with the author, with his conversation partners past and present, and with the New Testament itself. These are among the reasons I am glad to have a part in commending it to the English-speaking world.

At the author's and the publisher's request, I have augmented the bibliography with English books and articles, mostly listing books and articles comparable to the ample German bibliography already present, for the benefit of students who do not read German, and I have combined the author's original sectional bibliographies into a single comprehensive bibliography in the back of the book. I have also complied with the author's and publisher's request that I occasionally provide translator's notes on the German text reflecting the European context with which the reader might not be familiar. In both cases, I have kept my own contributions to a minimum. (My notes are generally in square brackets and signed with my initials.)

For biblical citations, I have generally followed the NRSV, sometimes adjusting it to accommodate the emphasis or particular nuance of the German text cited or translated by the author. For translations of literature from the Hellenistic world, I have generally followed the Loeb Classical Library.

The translation has been read by the author, Udo Schnelle, and by James Ernest of Baker Academic. Each made helpful suggestions that contributed to a more readable and accurate translation, and to each I express my deep gratitude.

M. Eugene Boring
Fort Worth, TX
March 29, 2009

Author's Preface to the German Edition

The goal of this *Theology of the New Testament* is a comprehensive presentation of the variety and riches of the New Testament world of thought. Each author and each text of the New Testament focuses on their common center, Jesus Christ—each from their own perspective. It is precisely this plurality of perspectives that opens up new vistas for faith, facilitating a new level of thinking and acting.

I here express my gratitude to Prof. Dr. Friedrich Wilhelm Horn (Mainz), who has read particular chapters of this book and has given helpful responses. I would also like to thank my academic assistant Markus Göring (Halle), and Martin Söffing, theology student at Halle, for their help in correcting the proofs.

Udo Schnelle
Halle
August 2007

Abbreviations

Bibliographic and General

AASFDHL	Annales Academiae scientiarum fennicae: Dissertationes humanarum litterarum
AAWGPH	Abhandlungen der Akademie der Wissenschaften in Göttingen: Philologisch-historische Klasse
AB	Anchor Bible
ABG	Arbeiten zur Bibel und ihrer Geschichte
ABRL	Anchor Bible Reference Library
AGJU	Arbeiten zur Geschichte des antiken Judentums und des Urchristentums
AJEC	Ancient Judaism and Early Christianity
AKG	Antike Kultur und Geschichte
ALGHJ	Arbeiten zur Literatur und Geschichte des hellenistischen Judentums
AMT	Athenäums Monografien: Theologie
AnBib	Analecta biblica
ANRW	*Aufstieg und Niedergang der römischen Welt: Geschichte und Kultur Roms im Spiegel der neueren Forschung.* Edited by H. Temporini and W. Haase. Berlin: de Gruyter, 1972–
ARGU	Arbeiten zur Religion und Geschichte des Urchristentums
ARW	*Archiv für Religionswissenschaft*
ASE	Abhandlungen zum Staatskirchenrecht und Eherecht
AT	Arbeiten zur Theologie
ATANT	Abhandlungen zur Theologie des Alten und Neuen Testaments
BALK	Beiträge zur Archäologie der literarischen Kommunikation
BBB	Bonner biblische Beiträge
BET	Beiträge zur biblischen Exegese und Theologie
BETL	Bibliotheca ephemeridum theologicarum lovaniensium
BEvT	Beiträge zur evangelischen Theologie
BFCT	Beiträge zur Förderung christlicher Theologie
BG	Biblische Gestalten

BHT Beiträge zur historischen Theologie
Bib *Biblica*
BIS Biblical Interpretation Series
BiS Biblische Studien
BiTS Biblical Tools and Studies
BK *Bibel und Kirche*
BKP Beiträge zur klassischen Philologie
BN *Biblische Notizen*
BTB *Biblical Theology Bulletin*
BTS Biblisch-theologische Studien
BU Biblische Untersuchungen
BVB Beiträge zum Verstehen der Bibel
BWANT Beiträge zur Wissenschaft vom Alten und Neuen Testament
BWM Bibelwissenschaftliche Monographien
BZ *Biblische Zeitschrift*
BZAW Zeitschrift für die alttestamentliche Wissenschaft
BZNW Beihefte zur Zeitschrift für die neutestamentliche Wissenschaft
ca. circa
CBET Contributions to Biblical Exegesis and Theology
CBQ *Catholic Biblical Quarterly*
CBQMS Catholic Biblical Quarterly Monograph Series
chap(s). chapter(s)
ConBNT Coniectanea biblica: New Testament Series
COQG Christian Origins and the Question of God
CTM Calwer theologische Monographien
DDD *Dictionary of Deities and Demons in the Bible*. Edited by K. van der Toorn, B. Becking, and P. W. van der Horst. 2nd ed. Leiden: Brill, 1999
diss. dissertation
ed(s). editor(s), edited by
EdF Erträge der Forschung
EDNT *Exegetical Dictionary of the New Testament*. Edited by H. Balz and G. Schneider. Translated by James W. Thompson and John W. Medendorp. 3 vols. Grand Rapids: Eerdmans, 1990–93
EF Erträge der Forschung
e.g. *exempli gratia,* for example
EHS Europäische Hochschulschriften
EKKNT Evangelisch-katholischer Kommentar zum Neuen Testament
EKL *Evangelisches Kirchenlexikon*. Edited by Erwin Fahlbusch et al. 3rd ed. 5 vols. Göttingen: Vandenhoeck & Ruprecht, 1985–97
enl. enlarged
esp. especially
ET English translation
et al. *et alii,* and others

ETL	*Ephemerides theologicae lovanienses*
ETS	Erfurter theologische Studien
EvT	*Evangelische Theologie*
exp.	expanded
f(f).	and the following one(s)
frg.	fragment
FRLANT	Forschungen zur Religion und Literatur des Alten und Neuen Testaments
FTS	Frankfurter theologische Studien
FzB	Forschung zur Bibel
FZPT	*Freiburger Zeitschrift für Philosophie und Theologie*
GBS	Grove Biblical Series
GCS	Die griechischen christlichen Schriftsteller der ersten Jahrhunderte
GH	Grundzüge einer Historik
GNT	Grundrisse zum Neuen Testament
GSTR	Giessener Schriften zur Theologie und Religionspädagogik
GTA	Göttinger theologischer Arbeiten
GuL	*Glaube und Lernen*
HAW	Handbuch der Altertumswissenschaft
HBS	Herders biblische Studien
Hermeneia	Hermeneia—A Critical and Historical Commentary on the Bible
HNT	Handbuch zum Neuen Testament
HTKNT	Herders theologischer Kommentar zum Neuen Testament
HTR	*Harvard Theological Review*
HTS	Hamburger theologische Studien
HUT	Hermeneutische Untersuchungen zur Theologie
ibid.	*ibidem,* in the same place
ICC	International Critical Commentary
i.e.	*id est,* that is
Int	*Interpretation*
IRT	Issues in Religion and Theology
ITS	Innsbrucker theologische Studien
JAC	*Jahrbuch für Antike und Christentum*
JBL	*Journal of Biblical Literature*
JBTh	*Jahrbuch für biblische Theologie*
JSHRZ	Jüdische Schriften aus hellenistisch-römischer Zeit
JSNT	*Journal for the Study of the New Testament*
JSNTSup	Journal for the Study of the New Testament: Supplement Series
JTC	*Journal for Theology and the Church*
KBANT	Kommentare und Beiträge zum Alten und Neuen Testament
KD	*Kerygma und Dogma*
KEK	Kritisch-exegetischer Kommentar über das Neue Testament (Meyer-Kommentar)

KJV	King James Version
LCL	Loeb Classical Library
lit.	literally
LJS	Lives of Jesus Series
LMRT	Library of Modern Religious Thought
LNTS	Library of New Testament Studies
LSTR	Landauer Schriften zur Theologie und Religionspädagogik
LTB	Lüneburger theologische Beiträge
LW	Luther's Works
LXX	Septuagint (Greek Old Testament)
MBPAR	Münchener Beiträge zur Papyrusforschung und antiken Rechtsgeschichte
MdB	Le Monde de la Bible
MJS	Münsteraner judaistische Studien
MTA	Münsteraner theologische Abhandlungen
MThS	Münchener theologische Studien
MTS	Marburger theologische Studien
MTZ	*Münchener theologische Zeitschrift*
NAB	New American Bible
NASB	New American Standard Bible
NEchtB	Neue Echter Bibel
Neot	*Neotestamentica*
NETS	New English Translation of the Septuagint
NF	Neue Folge
NHC	Nag Hammadi Codices
NICNT	New International Commentary on the New Testament
NIGTC	New International Greek Testament Commentary
NovT	*Novum Testamentum*
NovTSup	Supplements to Novum Testamentum
NRSV	New Revised Standard Version
NTA	Neutestamentliche Abhandlungen
NTD	Das Neue Testament Deutsch
NTL	New Testament Library
NTOA	Novum Testamentum et orbis antiquus
NTS	New Testament Studies (Harnack series)
NTS	*New Testament Studies* (periodical)
NTTh	New Testament Theology
NTTS	New Testament Texts and Studies
NUSPEP	Northwestern University Studies in Phenomenology and Existential Philosophy
NW	*Neuer Wettstein: Texte zum Neuen Testament aus Griechentum und Hellenismus*. Edited by Georg Strecker and Udo Schnelle. Berlin: de Gruyter, 1996–

NZST	*Neue Zeitschrift für systematische Theologie*
OBO	Orbis biblicus et orientalis
OGIS	*Orientis Graeci Inscriptiones Selectae*. Edited by Wilhelm Dittenberger. 2 vols. Leipzig: Hirzel, 1903–5
ÖTK	Ökumenischer Taschenbuch-Kommentar
OTL	Old Testament Library
p(p).	page(s)
par.	parallel (to indicate textual parallels)
passim	here and there
PIBA	*Proceedings of the Irish Biblical Association*
PTh	*Pastoraltheologie*
PThSt	Paderborner theologische Studien
QD	Quaestiones disputatae
RAC	*Reallexikon für Antike und Christentum: Sachwörterbuch zur Auseinandersetzung des Christentums mit der antiken Welt*. Edited by T. Klauser et al. Stuttgart: Hiersemann, 1950–
rev.	revised (by)
RGG[4]	*Religion in Geschichte und Gegenwart Handwörterbuch für Theologie und Religionswissenschaft*. Edited by Hans Dieter Benz et al. 4th ed. Tübingen: Mohr, 1998–
RNT	Regensburger Neues Testament
RST	Regensburger Studien zur Theologie
RVV	Religionsgeschichtliche Versuche und Vorarbeiten
SAC	Studies in Antiquity and Christianity
SANT	Studien zum Alten und Neuen Testaments
SBAB	Stuttgarter biblische Aufsatzbände
SBB	Stuttgarter biblische Beiträge
SBLAB	Society of Biblical Literature Academia Biblica
SBLDS	Society of Biblical Literature Dissertation Series
SBLSBS	Society of Biblical Literature Sources for Biblical Study
SBS	Stuttgarter Bibelstudien
SBT	Studies in Biblical Theology
sc.	*scilicet*, namely
SCHNT	Studia ad Corpus Hellenisticum Novi Testamenti
SESJ	Suomen Eksegeettisen Seuran julkaisuja
SFEG	Schriften der Finnischen Exegetischen Gesellschaft
SGKA	Studien zur Geschichte und Kultur des Altertums
SHAW	Sitzungen der heidelberger Akademie der Wissenschaften
SIG	*Sylloge inscriptionum graecarum*. Edited by Wilhelm Dittenberger et al. 3rd ed. 4 vols. Leipzig: Hirzel, 1915–24
SIJD	Schriften des Institutum judaicum delitzschianum
SJLA	Studies in Judaism in Late Antiquity
SLA	Studien der Luther-Akademie

SMBen Série monographique de Benedictina
SNT Studien zum Neuen Testament
SNTI Studies in New Testament Interpretation
SNTSMS Society for New Testament Studies Monograph Series
StAltW Studienhefte zur Altertumswissenschaft
StAs Studia Anselmiana
StPB Studia post-biblica
SUNT Studien zur Umwelt des Neuen Testaments
SVF *Stoicorum veterum fragmenta*. Edited by Hans Friedrich August von Arnim. 4 vols. Leipzig: Teubner, 1903–24
SVR Studien zum Verstehen fremder Religionen
TAB Texte und Arbeiten zur Bibel
TANZ Texte und Arbeiten zum neutestamentlichen Zeitalter
TB Theologische Bücherei: Neudrucke und Berichte aus dem 20. Jahrhundert
TBLNT *Theologisches Begriffslexikon zum Neuen Testament*. Edited by L. Coenen and K. Haacker. Rev. ed. Wuppertal: Brockhaus, 1997–
TBT Theologische Bibliothek Töpelmann
TBü Theologische Bücherei
TDNT *Theological Dictionary of the New Testament*. Edited by G. Kittel and G. Friedrich. Translated by G. W. Bromiley. 10 vols. Grand Rapids: Eerdmans, 1964–76
TEH Theologische Existenz heute
TF Theorie und Forschung
TGl *Theologie und Glaube*
ThB *Theologische Beiträge*
THKNT Theologischer Handkommentar zum Neuen Testament
ThV *Theologische Versuche*
TLZ *Theologische Literaturzeitung*
TNIV Today's New International Version
TQ *Theologische Quartalschrift*
TRE *Theologische Realenzyklopädie*. Edited by G. Krause and G. Müller. Berlin: de Gruyter, 1977–
TRu *Theologische Rundschau*
TSAJ Texte und Studien zum antiken Judentum
TThZ *Trierer Theologische Zeitschrift*
TTS Trierer theologische Studien
TU Texte und Untersuchungen
TUGAL Texte und Untersuchungen zur Geschichte der altchristlichen Literatur
TZ *Theologische Zeitschrift*
UNT Untersuchungen zum Neuen Testament
USQR *Union Seminary Quarterly Review*
v(v). verse(s)

VS	*Fragmente der Vorsokratiker*. Edited by Hermann Diels. 8th ed. Hamburg: Rowohlt, 1957
VuF	*Verkündigung und Forschung*
WBC	Word Biblical Commentary
WD	*Wort und Dienst*
WdF	Weg der Forschung
WMANT	Wissenschaftliche Monographien zum Alten und Neuen Testament
WUNT	Wissenschaftliche Untersuchungen zum Neuen Testament
ZBA	Zaberns Bildbände zur Archäologie
ZBK	Zürcher Bibelkommentare
ZKG	*Zeitschrift for Kirchengeschichte*
ZNT	*Zeitschrift für Neues Testament*
ZNThG	*Zeitschrift für Neuere Theologiegeschichte*
ZNW	*Zeitschrift für die neutestamentliche Wissenschaft und die Kunde der älteren Kirche*
ZTK	*Zeitschrift für Theologie und Kirche*
ZWT	*Zeitschrift für wissenschaftliche Theologie*

Hebrew Bible

Gen.	Genesis
Exod.	Exodus
Lev.	Leviticus
Num.	Numbers
Deut.	Deuteronomy
Josh.	Joshua
Judg.	Judges
Ruth	Ruth
1 Sam.	1 Samuel
2 Sam.	2 Samuel
1 Kings	1 Kings
2 Kings	2 Kings
1 Chron.	1 Chronicles
2 Chron.	2 Chronicles
Ezra	Ezra
Neh.	Nehemiah
Esth.	Esther
Job	Job
Ps.	Psalms
Prov.	Proverbs
Eccles.	Ecclesiastes
Song	Song of Songs
Isa.	Isaiah
Jer.	Jeremiah
Lam.	Lamentations
Ezek.	Ezekiel
Dan.	Daniel
Hos.	Hosea
Joel	Joel
Amos	Amos
Obad.	Obadiah
Jon.	Jonah
Mic.	Micah
Nah.	Nahum
Hab.	Habakkuk
Zeph.	Zephaniah
Hag.	Haggai
Zech.	Zechariah
Mal.	Malachi

Greek Testament

Matt.	Matthew
Mark	Mark
Luke	Luke
John	John
Acts	Acts
Rom.	Romans
1 Cor.	1 Corinthians
2 Cor.	2 Corinthians
Gal.	Galatians
Eph.	Ephesians
Phil.	Philippians
Col.	Colossians
1 Thess.	1 Thessalonians
2 Thess.	2 Thessalonians
1 Tim.	1 Timothy
2 Tim.	2 Timothy
Titus	Titus
Philem.	Philemon
Heb.	Hebrews
James	James
1 Pet.	1 Peter
2 Pet.	2 Peter
1 John	1 John
2 John	2 John
3 John	3 John
Jude	Jude
Rev.	Revelation

Other Jewish and Christian Writings

Apoc. Abr.	*Apocalypse of Abraham*
As. Mos.	*Assumption of Moses*
Bar.	Baruch
2 Bar.	*2 Baruch (Syriac Apocalypse)*
1–2 Clem.	*1–2 Clement*
Did.	*Didache*
1 En.	*1 Enoch (Ethiopic Apocalypse)*
2 En.	*2 Enoch (Slavonic Apocalypse)*
4 Ezra	*4 Ezra*
Gos. Thom.	*Gospel of Thomas*
Hist. eccl.	Eusebius, *Historia ecclesiastica*
Ign. *Eph.*	Ignatius, *To the Ephesians*
Ign. *Magn.*	Ignatius, *To the Magnesians*
Ign. *Rom.*	Ignatius, *To the Romans*
Ign. *Smyrn.*	Ignatius, *To the Smyrnaeans*
Ign. *Trall.*	Ignatius, *To the Trallians*
Jub.	*Jubilees*
LAB	*Liber antiquitatum biblicarum* (Pseudo-Philo)
Let. Aris.	*Letter of Aristeas*
1–4 Macc.	1–4 Maccabees
Pol. *Phil.*	Polycarp, *To the Philippians*
Praep. ev.	Eusebius, *Praeparatio evangelica*
Pss. Sol.	*Psalms of Solomon*
Sib. Or.	*Sibylline Oracles*
Sir.	Sirach
T. Ash.	*Testament of Asher*
T. Benj.	*Testament of Benjamin*
T. Dan	*Testament of Dan*
T. Iss.	*Testament of Issachar*
T. Jos.	*Testament of Joseph*
T. Jud.	*Testament of Judah*
T. Levi	*Testament of Levi*
T. Naph.	*Testament of Naphtali*
T. Zeb.	*Testament of Zebulun*
Tob.	Tobit
Wis.	Wisdom of Solomon

Dead Sea Scrolls and Related Texts

CD	Cairo Genizah copy of the *Damascus Document*
1QH	*Hodayot* or *Thanksgiving Hymns*
1QM	*Milḥamah* or *War Scroll*

1QS	*Serek Hayaḥad* or *Rule of the Community*
1QSa	*Rule of the Congregation* (Appendix a to 1QS)
4Q175	*Testimonia*
4Q246	*Apocryphon of Daniel*
4Q401	*Sabbath Song*
4Q510	*Songs of the Sage*
4Q521	*Messianic Apocalypse*
4QFlor	*Florilegium*, also *Eschatological Midrash*
11QMelch	*Melchizedek*

Philo

Abraham	*On the Life of Abraham*
Agriculture	*On Agriculture*
Alleg. Interp.	*Allegorical Interpretation*
Confusion	*On the Confusion of Tongues*
Creation	*On the Creation of the World*
Decalogue	*On the Decalogue*
Dreams	*On Dreams*
Embassy	*On the Embassy to Gaius*
Flight	*On Flight and Finding*
Good Person	*That Every Good Person Is Free*
Heir	*Who Is the Heir?*
Migration	*On the Migration of Abraham*
Moses	*On the Life of Moses*
Planting	*On Planting*
Prelim. Studies	*On the Preliminary Studies*
QE	*Questions and Answers on Exodus*
Spec. Laws	*On the Special Laws*
Worse	*That the Worse Attacks the Better*

Josephus

Ag. Ap.	*Against Apion*
Ant.	*Jewish Antiquities*
JW	*Jewish War*
Life	*The Life*

Classical Authors

Aelius Theon

Prog.	*Progymnasmata*

Aeschylus

Eum.	*Eumenides*

Aesop

Fab.	*Fabulae*

Apuleius

Metam.	*Metamorphoses*

Aratus

Phaen.	*Phaenomena*

Aristotle

Eth. Nic.	*Nicomachean Ethics*
Pol.	*Politics*

Artemidorus

Onir.	*Onirocritica*

Cicero

Fin.	*De finibus*
Leg.	*De legibus*
Nat. d.	*De natura deorum*
Off.	*De officiis*
Or.	*De oratore*
Resp.	*De res publica*
Tusc.	*Tusculanae disputationes*

Claudius Aelianus

Var. hist.	*Variae Historiae*

Dio Cassius

Hist.	*Roman History*

Dio Chrysostom

Or. *Orationes*

Diodorus Siculus

Bibl. *Bibliotheca historica*

Diogenes Laertius

Vit. phil. *Vitae philosophorum*

Epictetus

Diatr. *Diatribae*
Ench. *Enchiridion*

Epicurus

Men. *Epistula ad Menoeceum*
Rat. sent. *Ratae sententiae*

Euripides

Alc. *Alcestis*
Bacch. *Bacchae*
Med. *Medea*

Grattius

Cyn. *Cynegetica*

Herodotus

Hist. *Historiae*

Hesiod

Op. *Opera et dies*
Theog. *Theogonia*

Homer

Il. *Ilias*
Od. *Odyssea*

Iamblichus

Vit. Pyth. *De vita pythagorica*

Isocrates

Or. *Orationes*

Lucian

Hist. conscr. *Quomodo historia conscribenda sit*

Martial

Epigr. *Epigrammata*
Spect. *Spectacula*

Musonius Rufus

Diss. *Dissertationes*

Ovid

Metam. *Metamorphoses*

Philostratus

Vit. Apoll. *Vita Apollonii*

Plato

Apol. *Apologia Socratis*
Gorg. *Gorgias*
Leg. *Leges*
Phaed. *Phaedo*
Phaedr. *Phaedrus*
Phileb. *Philebus*
Pol. *Politicus*
Prot. *Protagoras*
Resp. *Respublica*
Soph. *Sophista*
Symp. *Symposium*
Tim. *Timaeus*

Pliny the Elder

Nat. hist. *Naturalis historia*

Pliny the Younger

Ep. *Epistulae*

Plutarch

Alex. *Alexander*
Alex. fort. *De Alexandri magni fortuna aut virtute*
Caes. *Caesar*
E Delph. *De E apud Delphos*
Is. Os. *De Iside et Osiride*
Mor. *Moralia*
Num. *Numa*
Pel. *Pelopidas*
Pomp. *Pompeius*

Praec. ger.	*Praecepta gerendae reipublicae*
Princ. iner.	*Ad principem ineruditum*
Rom.	*Romulus*
Ser.	*De sera numinis vindicta*

Quintilian

Inst.	*Institutio oratoria*

Seneca

Apocol.	*Apocolocyntosis divi Claudii*
Clem.	*De clementia*
Ep.	*Epistulae morales*
Herc. fur.	*Hercules furens*
Ira	*De ira*
Marc.	*Ad Marciam de consolatione*
Nat.	*Naturales quaestiones*
Tranq.	*De tranquillitate animi*

Sophocles

Ant.	*Antigone*

Stobaeus

Anth.	*Anthologia*

Strabo

Geogr.	*Geographica*

Suetonius

Aug.	*Divus Augustus*
Cal.	*Gaius Caligula*
Dom.	*Domitianus*
Jul.	*Divus Julius*
Nero	*Nero*
Vesp.	*Vespasianus*

Tacitus

Ann.	*Annales*
Hist.	*Historiae*

Thucydides

Hist.	*Historia*

Virgil

Aen.	*Aeneas*

Xenophon

Mem.	*Memorabilia*

Anonymous texts

Hist. Alex.	*Historia Alexandri*
Hist. Aug.	*Historia Augusta*

1

Approach

Theology of the New Testament as Meaning-Formation

Since a theology of the New Testament must both (1) bring the thought world of the New Testament writings into clear focus and (2) articulate this thought world in the context of a contemporary understanding of reality, it has to work with different temporal planes. Its task is to envision the past in view of the present, to explicate it in such a way that its future relevance can be seen. New Testament theology is thus linked into the question of the lasting significance of past events. So it is always a historical discipline, and as such it must participate in theoretical debates on the nature and extent of historical knowledge. Thus the discipline of New Testament theology is involved from the start in the deliberations of the philosophy of history, how history as past reality is grasped, and which categories play a central role in this process.

People can understand reality only within the human capacity for interpretation, that is, for channeling past events into the worlds of human experience and ascribing significance to them in different ways. These processes are also events of "meaning-formation," for they always aim at establishing or maintaining a valid orientation to the world and to life. Meaning-formation can entail ascertaining the validity of one's present orientation, or expanding it, or initiating a new departure. It confers meaning on both past and present. *Such constructions provide the sense-making capacity that facilitates the individual's orientation within the complex framework of life.*[1] Meaning is an inherent

1. On meaning-formation as an aspect of historical theory, cf. Jörn Rüsen, "Historische Methode und religiöser Sinn," in *Geschichte im Kulturprozeß* (ed. Jörn Rüsen; Cologne: Böhlau,

aspect of human existence as such. It emerges from events, experiences, insights, thought processes, and hermeneutical accomplishments, and it comes together in concepts. These concepts then can provide perspective on the central issues of life, bridging temporal gaps. They can be presented in a narrative mode, and they can generate normative statements and cultural models.[2]

The category *meaning*[3] is particularly appropriate as a way of connecting the world of the New Testament and that of the present. In every age—including the Greco-Roman era—reality has been perceived through constant processes whereby religious meaning-formation happens in parallel with meaning-formation in other cultural domains: politics, philosophy, art, literature, economics, the natural sciences, and social structures. Human life is always a matter of the realization of meaning, so that the question is not whether human beings undertake meaning-formation but what resources, structure, quality, and argumentative force their efforts exhibit.

For a theology of the New Testament, the concept of meaning is key, for it enables divine and human to unite by encompassing the gift whereby God establishes meaning in Jesus Christ together with the testimony to that gift in the New Testament writings. The New Testament, as the basic documentary archive of Christianity, represents the formation of a meaning-formation or symbolic universe with an extraordinary history of effects. Early Christianity developed in a multicultural milieu with numerous, attractive, and competing religious and philosophical systems.[4] On the foundation of the Jesus-Christ-history, narrated in numerous ways in the New Testament, it succeeded in building, inhabiting, and constantly adding on to a "house of

---

2002), 11; on the multilayered term "meaning-formation," cf. E. List, "Sinn," in *Handbuch religionswissenschaftlicher Grundbegriffe* (ed. Günter Kehrer et al.; Stuttgart: Kohlhammer, 1988), 5:62–71. [For a good introduction in English to "meaning-formation" as an aspect of historical theory, see Frank R. Ankersmit, "Three Levels of 'Sinnbildung' in Historical Writing," in Jörg Rüsen, *Meaning and Representation in History* (Oxford: Berghahn Books, 2006), 108–22. I have usually rendered *Sinnbildung* by "meaning-formation," but note its relation to *Sinnwelt*, usually translated "universe of meaning" or "symbolic universe."—MEB]

2. Cf. Jörn Rüsen and K.-J. Hölkeskamp, "Einleitung," in *Sinn (in) der Antike* (ed. K.-J. Hölkeskamp et al.; Mainz: Von Zabern, 2003), 3: "The concept *meaning* may be defined as follows: It is a product of reflection on the connections within one's experienced world that proves to be plausible and dependable, serves to make sense of the world, to provide orientation within it, to form one's identity, and that leads to purposeful action."

3. The German word *Sinn* (meaning), like the English word *sense*, is derived from the Indo-Germanic root *sent-*, which basically means to take a particular direction, to go along a particular way. There is a connection with the Latin *sentio* (feel, perceive), *sensus* (sense, perception, understanding), *sententia* (meaning, purpose, thought); Old High German *sin* (Sinn), *sinnan* (strive for, desire); cf. Julius Pokorný, *Indogermanisches etymologisches Wörterbuch* (2 vols.; Bern: Francke, 1959), 1:908.

4. Cf. the collection of texts by Malte Hossenfelder, ed., *Antike Glückslehren: Kynismus und Kyrenaismus, Stoa, Epikureismus und Skepsis: Quellen in deutscher Übersetzung mit Einführungen* (Stuttgart: Kröner, 1996).

meaning" capable of grounding, establishing, and structuring human life as a whole. This meaning structure, or symbolic universe, obviously had tremendous hermeneutical potential at its disposal, and a theology of the New Testament must aim to ascertain and delineate the basic elements of its hermeneutical potential. The category *meaning* as the hermeneutical constant thus prevents a narrowing of the focus to issues of historical facts, for what is at stake is how we can appropriate the New Testament traditions historically and make them theologically accessible without violating their religious content and their formative power to generate meaning. The truth claim of these texts is not to be avoided, for *"truth" is meaning that makes a binding claim*. The goal is not a gutted Christian house, but an appreciation of this house that perceives its architecture, the load-bearing floors and walls, the doors and stairways that create connections between its components, and the windows that make it possible to look outside. At the same time, focusing on the category *meaning* opens to theology the possibility of entering into critical discourse with other academic disciplines devoted to meaning and truth, and doing so on the basis of its own normative tradition.

1.1 How History Is Made and Written

Jesus of Nazareth is a historical figure, and the New Testament is testimony to his impact on history. When a New Testament theology is written on this basis from a distance of two thousand years, the fundamental problems of historical inquiry and historical knowledge inevitably arise. How was history (*Geschichte*) made and how does research and writing about history (*Historie*) take place?[5] What happens when a document from the past that makes a claim on the future is interpreted in the present? How do historical reports

5. Regarding terminology: I use the German terms "Geschichte"/"geschichtlich" to refer to what happened, and "Historie"/"historisch" to indicate the ways in which historians attempt to determine what this was. "Historik" refers to the philosophical theory of history. Cf. H.-W. Hedinger, "Historik," in *Historisches Wörterbuch der Philosophie* (ed. Karlfried Gründer et al.; Darmstadt: Wissenschaftliche Buchgesellschaft, 1974). "Geschichte" is never directly available except as "Historie," but nonetheless the two concepts and terms must be distinguished, because the questions posed from the point of view of philosophical theories of history are not simply identical with "what happened" as that was understood by people in the past. [The German language has two words for "history," while English has but one. Many German authors, including some quoted by Schnelle, use the two words interchangeably. The nuances distinguished by Schnelle are sometimes difficult to preserve in English. Since the context usually makes clear which meaning is intended, I have generally rendered both words by *history* and its cognates, though sometimes using *event* or *story* for *Geschichte* to preserve the author's nuance, or rendering *geschichtlich* by *historic* in contrast to *historical*. See note 2 in §2.1 below. Here the original reads: "Wie entsteht Geschichte/Historie?"—MEB]

and their incorporation into the thought world of the historian/exegete relate to each other?[6]

Interest and Acquisition of Knowledge

From several points of view, the classical ideal of historicism—to present nothing more or less than "what actually happened"[7]—has proven to be an ideological postulate.[8] As the present passes into the past, it irrevocably loses its character as reality. For this reason alone it is not possible to recall the past, in intact form, into the present. The temporal interval signifies a fading away in every regard; it disallows historical knowledge in the sense of a comprehensive restoration of what once happened.[9] All that one can do is to declare in the present one's own interpretation of the past. The past is available to us exclusively in the mode of the present, and only in interpreted and selected form. What is relevant from the past is not that which is merely past, but that which influences world-formation and world-interpretation in the present.[10] The true temporal plane on which the historian/exegete works *is always the present*,[11] within which he or she is inextricably intertwined, so

6. Cf. Jörn Rüsen, *Historische Vernunft* (GH 1; Göttingen: Vandenhoeck & Ruprecht, 1983); Jörn Rüsen, *Rekonstruktion der Vergangenheit: Die Prinzipien der historischen Forschung* (GH 2; Göttingen: Vandenhoeck & Ruprecht, 1986); Jörn Rüsen, *Lebendige Geschichte: Formen und Funktionen des historischen Wissens* (GH 3; Göttingen: Vandenhoeck & Ruprecht, 1989); Hans-Jürgen Goertz, *Umgang mit Geschichte: Eine Einführung in die Geschichtstheorie* (Reinbek: Rowohlt, 1995); Christoph Conrad and Martina Kessel, *Geschichte Schreiben in der Postmoderne: Beiträge zur aktuellen Diskussion* (Stuttgart: Reclam, 1994). [Most of the works of Jörn Rüsen referred to here and in the following have not been translated into English, but his perspectives and major theses within the context of recent discussion are available in Jörn Rüsen, ed., *Western Historical Thinking: An Intercultural Debate* (New York: Berghahn Books, 2002), and Jörn Rüsen et al., eds., *Studies in Metahistory* (Pretoria: HSRC, 1993).—MEB]

7. Cf. Leopold von Ranke, "Geschichten der romanischen und germanischen Völker von 1494–1514," in *Leopold von Ranke's sämmtliche Werke* (ed. Alfred Wilhelm Dove and Theodor Wiedemann; 3rd ed.; Leipzig: Duncker & Humblot, 1875), vii: "People have conferred on history the responsibility of restoring the past, to make it useful for the instruction of years to come. The present work does not accept such a high office: it only wants to set forth what actually happened" (*wie es eigentlich gewesen [ist]*).

8. Cf. Goertz, *Umgang mit Geschichte*, 130–31.

9. Cf. Udo Schnelle, "Der historische Abstand und der Heilige Geist," in *Reformation und Neuzeit: 300 Jahre Theologie in Halle* (ed. Udo Schnelle; Berlin: de Gruyter, 1994), 87–103.

10. Cf. Johann Gustav Droysen, *Outline of the Principles of History* (trans. E. Benjamin Andrews; New York: Fertig, 1893), 11: "The data for historical investigation are not past things, for these have disappeared, but things which are still present here and now, whether recollections of what was done, or remnants of things that have existed and of events that have occurred."

11. Cf. Paul Ricœur, *Time and Narrative* (trans. Kathleen McLaughlin and David Pellauer; 3 vols.; Chicago: University of Chicago Press, 1984), 3:145: "The first way of thinking about the pastness of the past is to dull the sting of what is at issue, namely, temporal distance." Such thoughts are of course not new; cf. a comment by Aristippus (425–255 BCE), a student of Socrates, preserved in Claudius Aelianus, *Var. hist.* 14.6: "Only the present moment belongs to

that present understanding of past events is always decisively stamped by the historian's own cultural standards. The historian or exegete's social setting, traditions, and political and religious values necessarily affect what he or she says in the present about the past.[12] We are all committed to our various intellectual orthodoxies. Even the very preconditions of understanding, especially reason and the particular context in which it operates, are subject to a process of continuing transformation, inasmuch as historical knowledge is conditioned by the aims that direct the quest for knowledge in each period of intellectual history.

The writing of history is thus never an uncontaminated reproduction of "what happened." Rather, each act of history-writing includes something of its own history—the history, that is, of its writer! Insight into the historicalness of the knowing subject calls for reflection on his or her role in the act of understanding, for the knowing subject does not stand over history but is entirely interwoven within it. It is therefore altogether inappropriate to describe historical understanding in terms of a contrast between "objectivity" and "subjectivity."[13] The use of such terminology serves rather as a rhetorical strategy of declaring one's own position as positive and neutral in order to discredit other interpretations as subjective and ideological. The object known cannot be separated from the knowing subject, for the act of knowing also always effects a change in the object that is known. The awareness of reality attained in the act of knowing and the past reality itself do not relate as copy and original.[14] One should thus speak not of the "objectivity" of historical arguments but of their plausibility and fittingness.[15] After all, those reports introduced into historical arguments as "facts" are as a rule themselves already interpretations of past events. Already interpreted as meaningful, they necessarily undergo further meaning-formation in order to continue to be history. The past event itself is not available to us, but only the various understandings of past events mediated to us by various interpreters. Things do not become

---

us; neither what one has already done, nor what one expects of the future. The one is already gone, and the other may not happen" (trans. MEB).

12. Cf. J. Straub, "Über das Bilden von Vergangenheit," in *Geschichtsbewußtsein: Psychologische Grundlagen, Entwicklungskonzepte, empirische Befunde* (ed. Jörn Rüsen; Cologne: Böhlau, 2001), 45: "Representations of events and developments do not deliver mimetic models of events that once happened, but perceptions of events bound to particular capacities of understanding and interpretation. Such interpretations are formed from the perspective of a particular present by particular persons, and are thus directly dependent on the experiences, expectations, orientations and interests of these persons."

13. Cf. Goertz, *Umgang mit Geschichte*, 130–46.

14. Cf. Hans-Jürgen Goertz, *Unsichere Geschichte: Zur Theorie historischer Referentialität* (Stuttgart: Reclam, 2001), 29.

15. Cf. J. Kocka, "Angemessenheitskriterien historischer Argumente," in *Objektivität und Parteilichkeit* (ed. W. J. Mommsen and Jörn Rüsen; Munich: Deutscher Taschenbuch-Verlag, 1977), 469–75.

what they are for us until we ascribe meaning to them. History is not reconstructed, but unavoidably and necessarily *constructed*. The common perception that things need only be "reported" or "re-constructed" suggests a knowledge of the original events that does not exist in the manner presupposed by this terminology. Nor is history simply identical with the past; rather, it is always only a stance in the present from which one can view the past. Thus within the realm of historical constructions, there are no "facts" in the "objective" sense; interpretations are built on interpretations. Hence the truth of the statement: "Events are not [in themselves] history; they become history."[16]

Reality as Given

And yet we by no means give up on reference to actual events; rather, we reflect on the conditions under which their reality is perceived. To say that history is constructed does not imply anything arbitrary or self-derived; we proceed according to method and on the basis of data.* We must connect data from the sources in a meaningful framework, necessarily remaining within the academic discourse that makes it possible to receive and discuss the data.[17]

16. Cf. Johann Gustav Droysen, *Historik: Rekonstruktion der ersten vollständigen Fassung der Vorlesungen* (Stuttgart-Bad Cannstatt: Frommann-Holzboog, 1857), 69. On the same page Droysen judiciously comments regarding historical circumstances: "They are only historical because they are interpreted historically, not objective realities in and of themselves, but in and through our observation and appropriation. We must, so to speak, transpose them into a different key."

*[Schnelle is here opposing Radical Construction, a recent philosophical movement centered at the University of Vienna. The basic tenet of this view, popular among some postmodern authors, is that any kind of knowledge is constructed rather than perceived through senses. Among its leading proponents are Heinz von Foerster and Humberto R. Maturana. Maturana, as the founder of the epistemological theory of *autopoiesis*, focuses on the central role of the observer in the production of knowledge. For English introductions to the topic cf. Paul Watzlawick, *The Invented Reality: How Do We Know What We Believe We Know? Contributions to Constructivism* (New York: Norton, 1984), and Lynn Segal, *The Dream of Reality: Heinz von Foerster's Constructivism* (2nd ed.; Berlin: Springer, 2001).—MEB]

17. Despite the unavoidable constructive character of history writing, these considerations allow us to reject the frequently made charge that the historian's own will to power tends to dominate the objects of historical research. For a critique of the postmodern, radically constructivist theories of arbitrary historical construction, see Jörn Rüsen, "Narrativität und Objektivität," in *Geschichte im Kulturprozeß* (ed. Jörn Rüsen; Cologne: Böhlau, 2002), 99–124; and Jörn Rüsen, ed., *Kann gestern besser werden?* (Berlin: Kadmos, 2003), 11–12: "Even if, in the turbulent time of our own present, history is at our disposal, so we, the interpreters, are always already at its disposal. We, the ones who 'construct,' are as history's constructors always in the situation of already having been constructed by history itself." Günter Dux, *Historisch-genetische Theorie der Kultur: Instabile Welten: Zur prozessualen Logik im kulturellen Wandel* (Weilerswist: Velbrück Wissenschaft, 2000), 160: "The blind spot in logical absolutism, as we have known it in the postmodern understanding of Constructivism and the theoretical system associated with it, consists in the fact that Constructivism does not understand itself to be subject to any systemic complex of conditions."

Everything we say is always bound up in existing general understandings of time and reality;[18] without these preunderstandings, meaningful construction and communication would not be possible. Every human being is genetically preconstructed and is constantly being coconstructed by sociocultural dynamics. Reflection and construction are always later actions that refer to something already given. Thus self-consciousness is never based on itself but necessarily requires reference to something beyond itself that grounds it and makes it possible. The fact that the question of meaning is even possible, and that history can be seen as meaningful, points to an "unimaginable reality,"[19] preceding all being, that gives it reality. The fundamental principle is that history originates only after the event on which it is based has been discerned as relevant for the present, so that necessarily history cannot have the same claim to reality as the events themselves on which it is based.

Language and Reality

In addition to these epistemological insights we now come to *reflections on the philosophy of language*. History is always mediated to us in linguistic form; history exists only to the extent that it is expressed in language. Historical reports become history only through the semantically organized construction of the historian/exegete. In this process, language not only describes the object of thought accepted as reality but also determines and places its stamp on all perceptions that are organized as history. For human beings, there is no path from language to an independent, extralinguistic reality, for reality is present to us only in and through language. The past event is thus available only as memory, a reality that is mediated and formed by language. Language itself, however, is in turn culturally conditioned and subject to constant social

18. L. Hölscher, *Neue Annalistik: Umrisse einer Theorie der Geschichte* (Göttingen: Wallstein, 2003), 44, emphasizes this aspect: "Were it not for the relative stability of the categorical apparatus of basic models of reality, temporal though they are, historians could not even relate different portrayals of history to each other. It is the relative constancy of temporal categories that first makes possible the historical evaluation and balancing of different portrayals of [the same] history."

19. Cf. Jörn Rüsen, "Faktizität und Fiktionalität der Geschichte—Was ist Wirklichkeit im historischen Denken?" in *Konstruktion von Wirklichkeit: Beiträge aus geschichtstheoretischer, philosophischer und theologischer Perspektive* (ed. Jens Schröter and Antje Eddelbüttel; TBT 127; Berlin: de Gruyter, 2004), 31: "What makes meaning work? The fact that reality already impresses itself into historical thinking is a meaning-event, an event that generates historical meaning. Apart from this unimaginable reality it could not determine historical thinking so in the mental operations of historical consciousness, as is necessary for the fulfilling of its cultural orientation function. The awareness of this meaning as an element of unimaginable reality within one's life-world of human suffering and action is a procedural factor that binds secular and religious thinking together. Religion gives this unimaginable reality its own quality of meaning. Secular historical thinking hesitates to take this step but ultimately draws from similar wellsprings of meaning."

transformation. It is not surprising, then, that historical events are construed and evaluated differently in situations shaped by different cultures and values. Language is much more than a mere reflection of reality, for it regulates and places its own stamp on the appropriation of reality, and thereby also on our pictures of what is real. At the same time, language is not *the* reality itself, for language too first comes into being in the course of human history, and in the personal history of every human being within the framework of his or her biological and cultural development. This means that in this process it is decisively influenced by the varieties of human cultures and individual lives. This constant process of change to which language is subject can be explained only in relation to the different social contexts by which it is conditioned.[20] This means that the connection between the symbol that signifies and the reality signified must be maintained if one does not want to surrender reality itself.

Facts and Fiction

History is thus always a selective system by means of which interpreters order and interpret not merely the past but especially their own world.[21] The linguistic construction of past events always therefore takes place as a meaning-creating process that confers meaning on both past and present; such constructions provide the sense-making capacity that facilitates the individual's orientation within the complex framework of life. Historical interpretation means the creation of a coherent framework of meaning; facts become what they are for us only by the creation of such a historical narrative framework.[22] In this process, historical reports must be made accessible to the present and expressed in language, so that in the presentation or narration of historical events, "facts" and "fiction"[23]—data and

20. Goertz, *Unsichere Geschichte*, 50–51.

21. Ernst Cassirer, *An Essay on Man: An Introduction to a Philosophy of Human Culture* (New Haven: Yale University Press, 1992), 191: "History is not knowledge of external facts or events; it is a form of self-knowledge."

22. Cf. Chris Lorenz, *Konstruktion der Vergangenheit: Eine Einführung in die Geschichtstheorie* (trans. Annegret Böttner; Cologne: Böhlau, 1997), 17ff.

23. "Fiction" is not here used in the popular sense of "unreal" or "untrue," but is intended in the functional-communications sense, and thus approaches the original meaning of "fictio": "construction," "formation." [Cf. the use of "fabrication" in English.—MEB] Cf. Wolfgang Iser, *The Act of Reading: A Theory of Aesthetic Response* (Baltimore: Johns Hopkins University Press, 1978), 54: "If it [fiction] is not reality, this is not because it lacks the attributes of reality, but because it tells us something about reality, and the conveyer cannot be identical to what is conveyed. Furthermore, once the time-honored convention has been replaced by the concept of communication, attention must be paid to the hitherto neglected recipient of the message. Now if the reader and the literary text are partners in a process of communication, and if what is communicated is to be of any value, our prime concern will no longer be the *meaning* of the text (the hobbyhorse ridden by the critics of yore) but its *effect*. Herein lies the function of literature, and herein lies the justification for approaching literature from a functionalist standpoint."

the creative-fictive work of an author—are necessarily combined. In that historical reports are combined, historical gaps must be filled in, reports from the past and their interpretation in the present flow together to produce something new.[24] Interpretation inserts the past event into a new structure that it did not previously have.[25] There are only potential facts, for experience and interpretation are necessary to grasp the meaning-potential of an event.[26] "Bare" facts must have a meaning attached to them, and the structure of this process of interpretation constitutes the understanding of facts.[27] It is the fictional element that first opens up access to the past, for it makes possible the unavoidable rewriting of the presupposed events. The figurative, symbolic level is indispensable for historical work, for it develops the prefigured plan of interpretation that shapes the present's appropriation and interpretation of the past. This brings us to the second part of our reflections: the necessarily and inevitably constructive character of history is always part of meaning-formation.

1.2 History as Meaning-Formation

Human existence and action are characterized by their capacity for *meaning*.[28] No form of human life can be defined "without reference to meaning. It makes sense [*Sinn*] to understand meaning [*Sinn*] as the fundamental category of

24. Cicero, *Or.* 2.54: The historian Antipater is singled out for praise, because "he imparted to history a richer tone," while "the rest did not embellish their facts, but were merely chroniclers"; Luke 1:1–4; Plutarch, *Alex.* 1.1 (οὔτε γὰρ ἱστορίας γράφομεν ἀλλὰ βίους, "for I am not writing history but portraying lives"). These texts unmistakably illustrate that ancient authors too had a clear awareness of these connections (see further Thucydides, *Hist.* 1.22.1; Lucian, *Hist. conscr.* 51; Quintilian, *Inst.* 7.3.70).

25. Cf. the discussion in Goertz, *Unsichere Geschichte*, 16ff., oriented to how these issues have been dealt with in the history of scholarship. See further M. Moxter, "Erzählung und Ereignis," in *Der historische Jesus* (ed. J. Schröter and R. Bruckner; BZNW 114; Berlin: de Gruyter, 2002), 80: "One must say that the narration of the event already goes beyond the event itself on the basis of the temporal gap that separates them."

26. This constructive aspect of the knowledge process also applies to the natural sciences. Constructiveness and contextuality determine the fabrication of knowledge; the natural sciences are always an interpreted reality that increasingly reflects the invisible currents of political and economic interests that involve us both individually and globally. Cf. K. Knorr-Cetina, *Die Fabrikation von Erkenntnis: Zur Anthropologie der Naturwissenschaft* (Frankfurt: Suhrkamp, 1991).

27. Cf. Goertz, *Umgang mit Geschichte*, 87: "It is thus not pure facticity that constitutes a 'historical fact.' Rather, it is the significance of an event, which is only gradually perceived and adopted, and which otherwise would have sunk unnoticed into the past, that confers this special quality upon it. Not in its own time, but only after its time does a 'bare fact' become a historical fact."

28. Basic work: Alfred Schutz, *The Phenomenology of the Social World* (trans. George Walsh and Frederick Lehnert; London: Heinemann, 1972), 2:99–157.

human existence."[29] The insights of cultural anthropology have made it clear that meaning-formation is a necessary consequence of the ability of human beings to transcend both themselves and the life-world of their society and culture.[30] Meaning-formation is not an option that human beings may choose or decline, but something inevitable, necessary, and natural. Moreover, human beings are always born into a world of meaning.[31] The drive to make sense of things is an unavoidable part of human life, for the human life-world must be thought about, disclosed, and appropriated in some meaningful way—only so is human life and action possible in this world.[32] *Every religion—including early Christianity and the theologies that developed within it—is a form of meaning-formation and thus is such a process of disclosure and appropriation.* Concretely, this process of disclosure and appropriation takes place as historical meaning-formation. Historical meaning is constituted from the "three components of experience, interpretation, and orientation."[33] The meaningfulness of an event cannot be derived from its facticity alone; it still needs the experience of a particular person or persons before its meaning potential can be actualized.

Meaning and Identity

Meaning-formation is always bound to the projection of identity and succeeds only by projecting a convincing identity.[34] Human beings attain their identity above all by giving their lives an enduring orientation that connects all of their diverse desires and intentions into a stable, coherent, and intersubjectively defensible whole. Identity develops as a constant negotiation between the

29. Günter Dux, "Wie der Sinn in die Welt kam und was aus ihm wurde," in *Historische Sinnbildung: Problemstellungen, Zeitkonzepte, Wahrnehmungshorizonte, Darstellungsstrategien* (ed. Klaus E. Müller and Jörn Rüsen; Reinbek bei Hamburg: Rowohlt, 1997), 195.

30. Cf. Alfred Schutz and Thomas Luckmann, *The Structures of the Life-World* (trans. Richard M. Zaner and H. Tristram Engelhardt Jr.; 2 vols.; NUSPEP; Evanston: Northwestern University Press, 1973–83), 2:99–158. Their point of departure is the undeniable experience of everyday life that always necessarily transcends that of any individual, which means that existence is not livable without transcendence: we live in a world that was here before us and will be here after us. Reality almost always retreats from our efforts to grasp it, and the existence of other people, whose inner selves can never be truly known, provokes the question of our own selfhood.

31. Cf. Thomas Luckmann, "Religion—Gesellschaft—Transzendenz," in *Krise der Immanenz: Religion an den Grenzen der Moderne* (ed. Hans-Joachim Höhn and Karl Gabriel; Philosophie der Gegenwart; Frankfurt: Fischer, 1996), 114: "Meaning-traditions transcend the mere natural state of the newborn."

32. Jörn Rüsen, "Was heißt: Sinn der Geschichte?" in *Historische Sinnbildung: Problemstellungen, Zeitkonzepte, Wahrnehmungshorizonte, Darstellungsstrategien* (ed. Klaus E. Müller and Jörn Rüsen; Reinbek bei Hamburg: Rowohlt, 1997), 38.

33. Ibid., 36.

34. Cf. Thomas Luckmann, *Die unsichtbare Religion* (2nd ed.; Frankfurt: Suhrkamp, 1993), 93, who explains "worldview" as the matrix of meaning that forms the framework within which human organisms formulate their identity and thereby transcend their biological nature.

processes of positively defining oneself and coming to terms with experienced differences.[35] An identity is not formed in a vacuum; rather, an existing identity is taken up and transformed into a new one that is perceived as an improvement and strengthening of the previous self. This is why identity can never be grasped as a static entity, for it is part of an ongoing process of reformation, since "as unity and selfhood of the subject" identity is "conceivable only as a synthesis of different, heterogeneous elements that must be brought into relationship with each other."[36] The process of identity-formation is determined by three equal factors: (1) perceiving one's distinctness from the surrounding world; (2) bumping into boundaries, both self-imposed and externally determined; and (3) thus coming to an awareness that one actually exists as a discrete self. So also collective identities are formed by the processing of differentiating experiences and feelings of commonality. Symbols play a decisive role in this process, for only with their help can collective identities be created and maintained. Universes of meaning must be articulable in the world of secular reality and while keeping their content communicable. To a considerable extent this happens through symbols, which function in the life-world to build bridges "from one province of reality . . . to another."[37] Particularly in the processing of the "great transcendencies"[38] such as sickness, crises, and death, symbols play a fundamental role, for they belong to another level of reality and are themselves bearers of that reality, and thus can establish a relation with that level of reality. Symbols are a central category for the communication of religious meaning. Identity-formation is thus always integrated into a complex process of interaction between the individual or collective subject, its experience of differentiation and boundaries, its perception of self and nonself.

The respective determinations of identity are necessarily achieved through *universes of meaning* or *symbolic universes*, which as social constructions make interpretive models available for the meaningful experiencing of reality.[39] Symbolic universes are objectified as signs and symbols, and thus represent reality in

35. On the concept of identity cf. B. Estel, "Identität," in *Handbuch religionswissenschaftlicher Grundbegriffe* (ed. Günter Kehrer et al.; Stuttgart: Kohlhammer, 1988), 3:193–210; for an introduction to the current ways of posing the issues in the widespread debate over "identity," cf. Jürgen Straub, *Erzählung, Identität und historisches Bewußtsein: Die psychologische Konstruktion von Zeit und Geschichte* (2nd ed.; Frankfurt: Suhrkamp, 2000); Heidrun Friese, ed., *Identities: Time, Difference, and Boundaries* (Making Sense of History 2; New York: Berghahn Books, 2001).

36. J. Straub, "Temporale Orientierung und narrative Kompetenz," in *Geschichtsbewußtsein: Psychologische Grundlagen, Entwicklungskonzepte, empirische Befunde* (ed. Jörn Rüsen; Cologne: Böhlau, 2001), 39–40.

37. Schutz and Luckmann, *Structures*, 2:117.

38. Ibid., 99–134.

39. On the terms "universe of meaning" and "symbolic universe," cf. Peter L. Berger and Thomas Luckmann, *The Social Construction of Reality: A Treatise in the Sociology of Knowledge* (New York: Random House, 1966), 73ff.

a communicable form. Among other things, symbolic universes legitimize social structures, institutions, and roles; that is, they explain and provide the basis for things as they are.[40] In addition, symbolic universes integrate these roles into a meaningful whole within which individual persons or groups can act. They enable both synchronic coherence and the diachronic placement of individuals and groups in an overarching historical framework; that is, they provide a framework of meaning. *Religion* simply constitutes *the* symbolic universe as such.[41] Far and away more than law, philosophy, or political ideologies, religion claims to represent the one, all-encompassing reality that transcends all other realities: God, or The Holy. As the all-encompassing reality within which every human life is lived, religion presents a symbolic universe that, especially by means of symbols, integrates both individuals and groups into the wholeness of the universe, interprets the phenomena of life, offers guidelines for conduct, and ultimately opens up perspectives beyond death.[42] Understanding history in terms of meaning-formation and the formation of identity raises the question of mode: how does this understanding work in practice?

1.3 Understanding through Narration

A historical event is not meaningful in and of itself, nor does it play a role in the formation of identity, until its meaning potential has been inferred and established. This potential must be transferred from the realm of chaotic contingency into "an orderly, meaningful, intelligible contingency."[43] The fundamental construct that facilitates this transfer is *narration*,[44] for narrative sets up the meaning structure that makes it possible for human beings to come to terms with historical contingency.[45] *This is the form in which both*

40. Ibid., 42–43, 48–50, 86.

41. Cf. Luckmann, *Die unsichtbare Religion*, 108.

42. Cf. Peter L. Berger, *The Sacred Canopy: Elements of a Sociological Theory of Religion* (Garden City, NY: Doubleday, 1967), 32: "The tenuous realities of the social world are grounded [by religion] in the sacred *realissimum,* which by definition is beyond the contingencies of human meanings and human activity."

43. Paul Ricœur, *Zufall und Vernunft in der Geschichte* (Tübingen: Gehrke, 1986), 14.

44. Here we presuppose a broad understanding of narrative that is not bound to particular literary genres. Proceeding from the fundamental insight that experience of time must be processed in the narrative mode, to interpret "narrative as a meaning- or sense-laden linguistic form, or one that creates sense or meaning. That is to say: the narrative form of human thematizing makes sense of and confers meaning on the happenings and actions—independently of the particular content of the narrative presentation" (Straub, "Bilden von Vergangenheit," 51–52). For a broad concept of narrative, cf. also Roland Barthes, *The Semiotic Challenge* (trans. Richard Howard; New York: Hill and Wang, 1988), 95–135.

45. Cf. Straub, "Temporale Orientierung," 26–27; D. Fulda, "Sinn und Erzählung—Narrative Kohärenzansprüche der Kulturen," in *Handbuch der Kulturwissenschaften* (ed. Friedrich Jaeger; 3 vols.; Stuttgart: Metzler, 2004), 1:251–65.

the innermost human self and external events can be expressed. Narrative secures events in a temporal framework and gives permanence to the unique incident; only then are the formation, transmission, and reception of tradition possible. Narrative brings things into a factual, temporal, and spatial relationship; "it arranges things *ex post facto* in a plausible structure that shows they necessarily or probably happened that way."[46] A narrative establishes insight by creating new connections and allowing the meaning of the event to emerge. The processing of religious experiences occurs in a twofold manner, namely in/through narratives and ritual(s).[47] The religious experiences of groups or individuals trigger processes of meaning-formation that find expression in narratives and rituals[48] and thus lead also to the composition of texts, so that they can be further communicated. In the face of the cross and resurrection, meaning-formation was inevitable. All early Christian authors were faced with the task of fitting the chaotic contingency of the crucifixion and resurrection into a meaningful theological structure—and they did this through narrative.

Functions of Narrative

The first and fundamental function of narrative is *to constitute reality by setting it within a temporal framework.*[49] Narratives order reality in a particular way without which the communication of this reality would be utterly impossible.[50] A further function of narratives consists of the *formation and transmission of knowledge.* Narratives report, describe, and explain events, increase knowledge, and form a worldview within which human beings can orient themselves. Narratives establish relations and causal connections that make understanding possible.[51] Oppositions are broken down and new relationships are determined—the absolute and the finite, the temporal and the eternal, life and death.

A particularly important feature of narratives is the capacity to form, present, and stabilize *identity.* Narratives establish and authenticate a complex

46. Straub, "Temporale Orientierung," 30.

47. Cf. Luckmann, "Religion—Gesellschaft—Transcendenz," 120.

48. Cf. Aleida Assmann, *Zeit und Tradition: Kulturelle Strategien der Dauer* (Cologne: Böhlau, 1999), 15: "As actions intended to be repeated, rites secure continuity and duration by establishing the identical in the course of a changing world. They do not eliminate time, but constitute it by creating continuities."

49. Cf. ibid., 4: "Horizons of meaning are established through temporal constructions."

50. Cf. Jürgen Straub, "Geschichten erzählen, Geschichte bilden: Grundzüge einer narrativen Psychologie einer historischer Sinnbildung," in *Erzählung, Identität und historisches Bewußtsein: Die psychologische Konstruktion von Zeit und Geschichte* (ed. Jürgen Straub; 2nd ed.; Frankfurt: Suhrkamp, 2000), 124ff.

51. Cf. K. J. Gergen, "Erzählung, moralische Identität und historisches Bewußtsein," ibid., 170–202.

of meanings that leads through particular instances of identification to the formation of identity. Narratives evoke and convey memories, without which there can be no enduring identity. In particular, narratives function to sort out and process collective experiences, and evoke personal identification in members of the group, which then become orientations for life and action. This *orientation-formation* is one of the fundamental practical functions of narratives. Narratives open and close possible courses of action and provide structure for the free space in which decisions must be made. Narratives thus also always have a normative dimension; they function to orientate one's ethical perspective. An additional function of narratives is the *mediation of values and norms*, the provision or revision of standpoints. Since narratives mediate experiences and expectations, values and orientations, they contribute to the formation of an ethical and pedagogical consciousness. When the proposals presented in narratives are accepted and shared, they create the basis for common judgments and a common social world. Narratives bind people together in one sociocultural fabric and lay the foundation for joint action in the present and a common perspective on the future.

At the same time, narratives deliver the *basis for the formation of tradition*, of which they themselves are part, in that they generate and secure continuity, so that information, interpretations, values, and particular ways of life can be handed on through time.

Narration and Narratives in Early Christianity

The fundamentally constructive character of historical meaning-formation is clearly seen in the New Testament authors: especially with the help of narrative units, key terms, and symbols, they create symbolic universes that integrate individuals and groups into the wholeness of the cosmos, interpret the phenomena of life, offer guidelines for conduct, and ultimately open up perspectives that transcend death. Narratives are always concerned with memories, with interpreting experiences through time. Memory is the definitive reference to the experience of time. The New Testament narratives about Jesus Christ express a memory process, and they form a consciousness of history: they proclaim the meaningfulness of God's act in Jesus of Nazareth for past, present, and future. All the New Testament authors use narrative to establish an inner coherence between interpretation of the past, understanding of the present, and perspective on the future, so that those who receive the narrative receive the event that it preserves. Events are made present, given form in the process, resulting in meaning-formations as narratives. To connect times and topics into a coherent whole is to create a narrative.

All these functions of narrative make clear that the effort to make a clear distinction between fictional and nonfictional narration does not work. Because the memory-preserving narrative is always oriented to understanding and acting in the present, fictional and nonfictional elements flow together in every narrative. *Narrative theory thus a priori prohibits the alternative "historical Jesus"—"Christ of faith," for there cannot be any access to Jesus of Nazareth that excludes his significance for the present.* Narration is what opens up spaces for reception and interpretation in the first place, making possible the kind of transformations that lie before us in all New Testament writings.

The above considerations apply to oral as well as written narration, which in early Christianity should not be understood as mutually exclusive alternatives, since for a long time they existed alongside each other, with much cross-fertilization. Nonetheless, putting the narrative in writing gave it new accents, a process that demonstrably was already beginning in Paul's time and accelerated with the gospels. The written medium lessened the (emotional) immediacy of communication while creating some distance between the contents of the history and the way it was communicated. This distance created new potentialities for thought, interpretation, and transformation, and permitted the kind of dissociation, even alienation of effects that can occur in the theater; these are all inevitable when events are described, recorded, communicated, and received. Writing unburdened the memory, fixed the events in a particular form, abstracted them from the necessity of an immediate response, and thus created the room necessary for objectifications and interpretations of the narratives. As narrators became authors, hearers/readers could become critical in their reception; they could establish normative interpretations by arranging explanations, establishing terms and concepts, and making moral appeals.

After-as-Before

We have no records that come directly from Jesus or from his immediate associates but only testimony from a somewhat later time.[52] This is in no way a lack, for the posteriority[53] of memory signifies no epistemological loss, since the significance of an event is not really seen until viewed in retrospect. The past always exists only as present appropriation, and in the context of present identity it is repeatedly perceived and made accessible. Only within such an ongoing process can we recognize the relevant past, communicate it, and discern its significance. The distance of posteriority creates room for thinking things through in new and transformative ways. This allows the de-

52. In this regard Jesus of Nazareth finds himself in good company, for there are also no written traditions directly from Socrates. For Dio Chrysostom, *Orationes* 55.8–9, this is no deficiency but evidence of Socrates' powerful personality.

53. Eckart Reinmuth, "Neutestamentliche Historik," *TLZ* 8 (2003): 47–55, uses the term *Nachträglichkeit*, "supplementary-character" that memory adds to the event in the process of remembering. [Schnelle had used *Nachzeitigkeit*, translated *posteriority* above. In grammar, the term refers to the action of a subordinate clause that takes place later than the action of the main clause, e.g., "I know what you will do."—MEB]

velopment of the metaphorical potential inherent within the event itself and makes understanding possible. We will see how creative and multifaceted—how astute, incisive, and enduring—the later New Testament narratives of the Jesus-Christ-history proved to be.

Summary

We have reflected on fundamental issues concerning the origin of history, historical knowledge as the product of meaning-formation, and narrative as the primary form of perceiving, representing, and communicating historical events. What is the significance of these reflections for a theology of the New Testament?

1. Theology in general and New Testament theology in particular are no worse off epistemologically than any other domain of knowledge. All knowledge is a construction bound to particular standpoints and perspectives. Every academic discipline has its own appropriate object of study. For the discipline of theology as a whole, the object of study is God as the bearer and final ground of all being; for the theology of the New Testament, the object is the manifold witness of the New Testament.
2. Like all other academic disciplines, New Testament theology participates in the prior meaningfulness of all being, which is the basis upon which the posing of systematic questions and the formation of meaning are even possible in the first place.
3. Methodologically, the category of meaning is particularly important for grasping the work of New Testament authors, i.e., for interpreting it and presenting its contemporary significance.
4. Faced with the cross and resurrection, efforts at meaning-formation were unavoidable. New Testament authors responded in a variety of ways, as they all narrated the Jesus-Christ-history from their own perspective, in their own way, for their own community of faith.
5. The task of a theology of the New Testament is to apprehend these achievements of meaning-formation and to present them in their theological, literary, and history-of-religion dimensions. The aim is to facilitate authentic reception of the New Testament's meaning-formation in the present.

2

Structure

History and Meaning

Once we have decided what the task of New Testament theology is, we have to ask how to carry it out. What is the best starting point? How are theological perspectives to be related to the academic study of religion? Does it make sense to limit the scope of study to the canonical texts, and is it even possible to do so? How should we handle the issue of plurality and unity? Treating these necessary questions regarding the internal structure of a theology of the New Testament will lead us to our own methodological approach: *New Testament theology as meaning-formation.*

2.1 The Phenomenon of the Beginning

The approach chosen for access to a subject is always a heuristic move; every beginning point already promises to define the way forward for hearers and readers. This observation applies to the New Testament documents themselves as well as to New Testament theologies.

The Discontinuity Model

Rudolf Bultmann (1884–1976) begins his New Testament theology with a programmatic statement:

> The message of Jesus is a presupposition for the theology of New Testament rather than a part of that theology itself. For New Testament theology consists in the unfolding of those ideas by means of which Christian faith makes sure of its own object, basis, and consequences.[1]

Bultmann thus accepts the consequences of the nineteenth century's "quest of the historical Jesus," whose contradictory results *Martin Kähler* (1835–1912) had already attempted to overcome by his distinction between "the so-called historical Jesus and the historic biblical Christ." Kähler distinguishes on the one hand between "Jesus" and "Christ," and on the other between "historical" (*historisch*) and "historic" (*geschichtlich*; see note 5 in §1.1 above). By "Jesus" he means the man from Nazareth, by "Christ" the Savior proclaimed by the church. By "historical" he means the pure facts of the past, by "historic," that which has enduring meaning. His basic thesis: Jesus Christ can be apprehended only as he is portrayed in the gospels, not by means of academic historical reconstruction. Kähler considered it historically impossible and theologically illegitimate to make the historical Jesus the starting point for faith. "Certainly faith does not depend upon a christological dogma. But it is just as erroneous to make it depend on uncertain statements about an allegedly reliable picture of Jesus that has been tortuously extracted by the modern methods of historical research."[2] Bultmann was able to combine this position, which was in equal parts exegetical, theological, and epistemological, with the historical skepticism of form criticism, which he had himself definitively shaped. We have no reports that come from Jesus's own hand; rather, we know him only through the gospels, which are not biographies but testimonies of Christian faith. They contain much material that is secondary and reformulated, a considerable part of which originated in the post-Easter Christian communities. We know Jesus only as already clothed in the mythical trappings of early Christian faith; it is not really possible to penetrate behind the post-Easter kerygma. The consequences of these facts must be pursued radically. "I do indeed think that we can know almost nothing concerning the life and personality of Jesus, since the early Christian sources show no interest in either, are moreover fragmentary and often legendary; and other sources about Jesus do not exist."[3] Thus for a theology of the New Testament, the

1. Rudolf Bultmann, *Theology of the New Testament* (trans. Kendrick Grobel; 2 vols.; New York: Scribner, 1951), 1:3.

2. Martin Kähler, *The So-Called Historical Jesus and the Historic, Biblical Christ* (Seminar Editions; trans. Carl E. Braaten; Philadelphia: Fortress, 1964), 72–73.

3. Rudolf Bultmann, *Jesus and the Word* (trans. Louise Pettibone Smith and Erminie Huntress Lantero; New York: Scribner, 1958), 8. It may be surprising that Bultmann himself could nevertheless write a book about the historical Jesus. His point of departure: what we can know about the historical Jesus is not important, for this Jesus of Nazareth was a Jewish prophet—a prophet who, with all his challenges and perspectives, still stands within the framework of Judaism. Thus for Bultmann the history of Jesus stands within the history of Judaism, not that of Christianity.

preaching of Jesus is one presupposition alongside others. These other factors can be just as important, such as the Easter experiences of the disciples, Jewish Messianic expectations, and the myths of the surrounding Gentile world. Like Kähler, Bultmann sees in efforts to reconstruct the historical Jesus an insolvable problem and unfruitful enterprise. Like Kähler, Bultmann believes that faith must not be grounded on the uncertainties of historical research. Therefore, New Testament theology must take its signals from Paul and John, who had already accepted the distinction between the historical Jesus and the post-Easter proclamation of the Christ, the kerygma.[4]

The Continuity Model

While it is indeed impossible to write a biography of Jesus in the modern sense, there are nonetheless compelling grounds for beginning a theology of the New Testament with a delineation of the message of the pre-Easter Jesus of Nazareth.

1. The sources themselves prohibit a restriction to the post-Easter kerygma. Every verse of the gospels shows that their authors saw the origin of Christianity not in the kerygma but in the advent of Jesus of Nazareth. In comparison with other movements, the constant reference to the person of Jesus is striking. To a very considerable extent, the Jesus tradition has no other purpose than to present the person of Jesus himself. So also the post-Easter proclamation of the Christ points back at every turn to something prior to itself. It constantly refers to a historical event, and at its core lies the interpretation of something that actually happened (1 Cor. 15:3b, 4a: "died . . . and buried").
2. It is likewise impossible, from the point of view of narrative theory, to make a neat separation between the historical Jesus and the kerygma (see above, §1.3). Even Bultmann could not absolutely deny a connection between these two, but reduced the significance of Jesus of Nazareth for the kerygma to the "that" (das Dass) of his appearance in history.[5]

Cf. Rudolf Bultmann, *Primitive Christianity in its Contemporary Setting* (New York: Meridian Books, 1956), where the preaching of Jesus is dealt with under the rubric of "Judaism."

4. Both Hans Conzelmann and Georg Strecker regarded themselves as especially committed to the Bultmannian approach. Cf. Hans Conzelmann, *An Outline of the Theology of the New Testament* (trans. John Bowden; New York: Harper & Row, 1969), xiii–xviii, 1–8; and Georg Strecker, *Theology of the New Testament* (trans. M. Eugene Boring; New York: de Gruyter, 2000), 1–8.

5. Cf. Bultmann, *Theology of the New Testament*, 2:66, in reference to the Gospel of John: "John . . . presents only the fact [*das Dass*] of the Revelation without describing its content [*ihr Was*]." In fact, Bultmann thereby advocates a substitution theory: cf. Rudolf Bultmann, "The Primitive Christian Kerygma and the Historical Jesus," in *The Historical Jesus and the Kerygmatic Christ: Essays on the New Quest of the Historical Jesus* (ed. and trans. Carl E. Braaten and Roy A. Harrisville; Nashville: Abingdon, 1964), 41: "If it is true that the kerygma proclaims

Such a reduction to a completely abstract kernel makes its reception impossible.[6] The mere "That" of a person's appearance in history is so unclear that it can neither be communicated nor received; it cannot be narrated, at the most, can only be stated. The multiplicity of post-Easter narratives about Jesus Christ cannot be explained without a connection to the riches of the pre-Easter narrative world.

3. Finally, from the perspective of meaning theory it is clear that the alternative "historical Jesus—kerygma" is not possible and should be abandoned. The preaching of Jesus of Nazareth can be understood as a comprehensive example of meaning-formation. Jesus interpreted afresh the present activity of God as salvation and judgment, and placed them in a unique relation to his own person. Jesus's self-understanding cannot be made dependent on the use or nonuse of particular titles, but his advent and claim as a whole allow only one conclusion: he himself ascribed to his own person a unique role and office in the eschatological drama in which God was active. Jesus's own meaning-formation provides the foundation and point of departure for those formations of meaning that, though they probably had already begun before Easter, continued after Easter when changed conditions for understanding them prevailed.[7] A deep historical and theological chasm between a purportedly unmessianic self-understanding of Jesus and the christologically packed kerygma never existed.[8]

Among those who, with varying arguments, have committed themselves to the continuity model, we may mention especially J. Jeremias, L. Goppelt,

---

Jesus as the Christ, as the eschatological event, if it claims that Christ is present in it, then it has placed itself in the place of the historical Jesus; it represents him."

6. Cf. Hans Blumenberg, *Matthäuspassion* (4th ed.; Frankfurt: Suhrkamp, 1993), 221, who in reference to the kerygma formulates the issue as follows: "The reduction to this hard inarticulate kernel destroys the possibility of its reception."

7. This meaning-forming dynamic of the beginning speaks against the thesis of J. Schröter, that an outline of the ministry and message of Jesus could not provide the basis for a theology of the New Testament, since within a New Testament theology Jesus is only important from the perspective of the witnesses of faith, though New Testament theology cannot be independent of Jesus. See J. Schröter, "Die Bedeutung des Kanons für eine Theologie des Neuen Testaments," in *Aufgabe und Durchführung einer Theologie des Neuen Testaments* (ed. C. Breytenbach and J. Frey; WUNT 205; Tübingen: Mohr, 2007), 155.

8. That such a break existed is the real foundation of Bultmann's theses. Cf. Bultmann, *Theology of the New Testament*, 1:32: "It was soon no longer conceivable that Jesus's life was unmessianic—at least in the circles of Hellenistic Christianity in which the gospels took form." The decisive advocate of the unmessianic life of Jesus at the turn from the nineteenth to the twentieth century was William Wrede, *The Messianic Secret* (trans. James C. G. Greig; Library of Theological Translations; London: James Clarke, 1971), although he later revised his view, at least in part. In a letter to Adolf Harnack in 1905, he wrote: "I am now more inclined than previously to believe that Jesus chose to regard himself as the Messiah" (H. Rollmann and W. Zanger, "Unveröffentlichte Briefe William Wredes zur Problematisierung des messianischen Selbstverständnisses Jesu," *ZNThG* [2001], 317).

W. Thüsing, P. Stuhlmacher, U. Wilckens, and F. Hahn.* Jeremias works with the model "Call of Jesus—answer of the community"; Goppelt chooses the terminology of the New Testament "fulfillment event" as his hermeneutical starting point; Thüsing develops a highly complex system of "quest for Jesus" that sees Jesus's centeredness on God as the beginning point and inner kernel of all New Testament theology; Stuhlmacher works out a continuity of tradition and confession between the Old and New Testaments within the framework of a "biblical theology"; Wilckens sees the unity of (biblical) theology in the reality of the one God; and Hahn chooses the concept of revelation as the hallmark of continuity in the mighty acts of God (see below, §2.3).

Easter denotes neither the beginning nor an *absolutely* new quality of meaning-formation within God's new history instituted with the advent of Jesus of Nazareth, for Jesus's unique relation to God is the basis of all affirmations about him, both before and after Easter (see below, §2.4).[9] A distinction between pre- and post-Easter is certainly appropriate, if the differing time periods, the content of the respective calls to faith and obedience, and theological conceptions are to be rightly expressed. However, this does not justify the acceptance of a fundamental discontinuity, for the ministry of Jesus and its lasting effects stand at the beginning of the theology of the New Testament and are at the same time its continuum.

2.2 Theology and the Academic Study of Religion

In his programmatic essay of 1897, *William Wrede* (1859–1906) defined the task of historically oriented exegetes as follows: "The scholar must be guided by a purely objective interest in the discovery of new knowledge that accepts every result supported by compelling evidence."[10] The scholar must not be

*[Joachim Jeremias, *New Testament Theology: The Proclamation of Jesus* (New York: Scribner, 1971); Leonhard Goppelt and Jürgen Roloff, ed., *Theology of the New Testament* (trans. John E. Alsup; 2 vols.; Grand Rapids: Eerdmans, 1981); Wilhelm Thüsing, *Die Neutestamentlichen Theologien und Jesus Christus* (3 vols.; Düsseldorf: Patmos, 1981, 1988, 1999); Peter Stuhlmacher, *Biblische Theologie des Neuen Testaments* (2 vols.; Göttingen: Vandenhoeck & Ruprecht, 1992, 1999); Ulrich Wilckens, *Theologie des Neuen Testaments*, Band 1, *Geschichte der urchristlichen Theologie*, Teilband 1, *Geschichte des Wirkens Jesu in Galiläa* (2nd rev. ed.; 1a; 4 vols.; Neukirchen-Vluyn: Neukirchener Verlag, 2005); Ferdinand Hahn, *Theologie des Neuen Testaments* (2nd ed.; 2 vols.; Tübingen: Mohr, 2005).—MEB]

9. The statement of Hahn, *Theologie des Neuen Testaments*, 1:20, is to the point: "The beginning point for the discussion of the relation of the pre-Easter tradition and the post-Easter kerygma must be that with Jesus's life and ministry the kingdom of God is already breaking in. Thus already in the pre-Easter time it is a matter of the presence of salvation and its ultimate future."

10. William Wrede, "Über Aufgabe und Methode der sogenannten Neutestamentlichen Theologie," in *Das Problem der Theologie des Neuen Testaments* (ed. Georg Strecker; WdF 367; Darmstadt: Wissenschaftliche Buchgesellschaft, 1975), 84.

influenced by the concept of the canon or any other dogmatic construction. The object of his or her study must be the whole field of early Christian literature, which is to be read as testimony to a religion that was lived out in practice. Thus the appropriate designation for this field of study should be "The History of Early Christian Religion" or "History of Early Christian Religion and Theology."[11] In the present discussion, which tends to be critical of theology, and in which methodological pluralism and an attitude of "tolerance" prevail, Wrede's position has again become prominent.[12] H. Räisänen explicitly attaches himself to Wrede, renounces canonical boundaries, and postulates a history of early Christian theology on purely history-of-religion terms that proposes to deliver "matter-of-fact information on the character, background, and origin of the early history of Christianity."[13] He advocates strictly historical work, with philosophical-theological questions explicitly deferred to a second phase of the project. The highest goal of such a presentation is that it be fair to all concerned, both to the New Testament authors and to the competing religious systems in their context (Judaism, Stoicism, the cults of the Hellenistic world, the mystery religions). The perspective of the churchly insider is to be consciously avoided, and the material is to be regarded exclusively from the spectator standpoint of the outsider, so that the thought world and interests of early Christianity itself can be brought into clear focus. Exegetes must not adopt the religious standpoint of the material they are studying, for then they would be acting as preachers rather than scholars.[14] So also G. Theissen orients his work explicitly to the program of W. Wrede, which exhibits six distinctive qualities:[15] (1) distancing from the normative claims of religious texts; (2) ignoring canonical boundaries; (3) emancipation from the categories "orthodoxy" and "heresy"; (4) recognition of pluralism and contradictions in early Christian theological schemes; (5) the explanation of theological ideas from within the contexts of their own life-world; (6) an openness to the history-of-religions approach. Theissen specifically advocates an external perspective, wanting to keep access to the New Testament open for secularized contemporaries. He thus writes not a theology in the confessional sense but a theory of early Christian religion based on the generally accepted categories of the history of religion. He proceeds on the basis of the thesis: "Religion is a cultural sign language which promises a gain in life

11. Ibid., 153–54.

12. On this point, cf. the discussion of the works of Räisänen and Theissen by Andreas Lindemann, "Zur Religion des Urchristentums," *TRu* 67 (2002): 238–61.

13. Heikki Räisänen, *Neutestamentliche Theologie? Eine religionswissenschaftliche Alternative* (SBS 186; Stuttgart: Verlag Katholisches Bibelwerk, 2000), 75.

14. Ibid., 72ff.

15. Gerd Theissen, *The Religion of the Earliest Churches: Creating a Symbolic World* (trans. John Bowden; Minneapolis: Fortress, 1999), 323–24.

by corresponding to an ultimate reality."[16] This semiotic approach considers religion as a cultural system of signs expressed in myth, ritual, and ethos. Myths elucidate in narrative form the reality that fundamentally determines the world and life (see below, §4.6). Rituals are paradigmatic acts by means of which human beings break through their everyday behavior as a way of representing the Other Reality expressed in the myth. Every linguistic system of religious signs ultimately includes a corresponding ethos; in both Judaism and Christianity all conduct is organized with reference to the will of God. On this basis Theissen charts the transformation of early Christianity from an inner Jewish movement to an independent religious community, a transformation process that manifests both continuity and discontinuity with the Jewish system of signs.

Does the attempt to view the materials from the perspective of the academic study of religion in fact offer a neutral external perspective that can analyze the subject matter impartially and without ideological shackles? This question must receive a clear negative answer, for several reasons:

1. Considerations from the philosophy of history and identity theory have shown that it is not possible to assume a "neutral" position abstracted from one's own life history (see above, §1.1). The postulation of a neutral, value-free perspective, frequently made by historians of religion over against theologians, is itself an ideological instrument designed to bring other positions under suspicion. There is no no-man's-land in which one may take up a position. It is not possible to bracket out one's own history with all its values, in terms of either life history or methodology.
2. A central element of one's own life history is questing after and relating to God. The person who does not believe in God, no less than the person who does believe in God, necessarily brings this presupposition into his or her work. The insistence that the world be explained in terms of itself, without God, is by no means a "criterion of objectivity" but is essentially a decision of the will conditioned by one's life history, an act of volition, a supposition.[17] The nonexistence of God is no less an assumption than the existence of God! The will and suppositions of others do not provide sufficient grounds for theologians to bracket out their ideas of God from their theological and historical work. All historical

16. Ibid., 2.

17. Adolf Schlatter, "Atheistische Methoden in der Theologie," in *Die Bibel Verstehen: Aufsätze zur biblischen Hermeneutik* (ed. Adolf Schlatter and Werner Neuer; Giessen: Brunnen, 2002), 137, appropriately comments: "Every act of thought includes an act of will, so that what appears in our scholarship is what 'we will.' This does not mean that any of us ascribe to ourselves a sovereign ability to suppose anything we want, free from the necessity to give reasons and justification for our statements."

work unavoidably takes place within an overarching framework, so that desired objectivity and actual partiality must not be understood as mutually exclusive alternatives. "Partiality and objectivity are inseparably entwined . . . and suspended between the poles of theory construction and exegesis of sources. It is futile for research to attempt to have the one without the other."[18] In order to be able to write history at all, the theologian/historian of religion needs a theory of history that does not attempt to exclude the religious, cultural, and political values acquired in the experience of life—for indeed it cannot do so.

3. Religious movements and their texts can be adequately grasped only when one enters into some relation with them. Every interpreter stands in such a relation, which cannot be reduced to an ideologically conceived insider or outsider perspective. Rather, this relation is due to the life history of the interpreter and the methodological decisions and standpoints from which he or she approaches the text. It is not a matter of neutrality, which the one claims and the other allegedly cannot, but is entirely concerned with having a methodology and way of posing questions that is appropriate to the texts. When religious texts by their very subject matter pose the question of truth, sidestepping this claim as an indication of alleged neutrality is utterly impossible, because every interpreter always already stands in some relation to the texts and the positions they affirm.
4. The formation of the canon and the choices involved in this process are often regarded as demonstrating the ideological character of early Christianity. A canon, however, is not a matter of arbitrary decisions, either historically or theologically, but a natural factor within the process of identity-formation and self-definition of a religious movement. As a cultural phenomenon, it is by no means limited to early Christianity.[19] Since written documents are a presupposition for the survival of a movement, the formation of a canon cannot be understood as a repressive act, but represents an entirely natural development. It was not external (ecclesiastical) decisions but primarily internal impulses that led to canon formation.[20] Moreover, the demand for removal of canonical boundaries fails to recognize the function of a canon as the space where memory is cultivated in a way that generates meaning and provides norms, a space into which the members of the group may

18. R. Koselleck, "Standortbindung und Zeitlichkeit," in *Theorie der Geschichte* (ed. R. Koselleck et al.; Munich: Deutscher Taschenbuch-Verlag, 1977), 46.

19. Cf. the reflections of Jan Assmann, "Fünf Stufen auf dem Weg zum Kanon: Tradition und Schriftkultur im alten Israel und frühen Judentum," in *Religion und kulturelles Gedächtnis: Zehn Studien* (ed. Jan Assmann; Munich: Beck, 2000), 81–100.

20. Cf. Udo Schnelle, *The History and Theology of the New Testament Writings* (trans. M. Eugene Boring; Minneapolis: Fortress, 1998), 349–64.

> repeatedly enter to receive assurance, answers, and orientation. Commitment to a canon as a given historical reality and essential element of a religious movement in no way means that the concept of a canon becomes the key to New Testament theology or that extracanonical writings and questions posed by a history-of-religions approach are to be ignored. Materials and issues from these areas, however, do not constitute the primary reference points for interpretation, and neither do they determine its scope.[21]

Since, then, there is no outsider or insider perspective, and since abandoning the concept of God provides no enhancement of neutrality or scholarly discipline, but is itself nothing more than a supposition, or an accommodation to the ideologies of others, the theological standpoint must not, cannot, and need not be replaced by a history-of-religions approach. Neither theology nor the historical study of religions is better nor worse, more or less neutral or ideological; *they pose questions and work in different ways.* This difference is grounded in their object of study, for the historical study of religions deals with the forms of religious phenomena, while Christian theology deals with the God who has revealed himself in the history of Israel and in Jesus Christ.[22]

2.3 Diversity and Unity

One of the main problems in presenting a theology of the New Testament is the question of diversity and unity. No one denies the historical and theological diversity of the individual New Testament writings. The question is this: is there a unity that transcends these differences, and, if so, how can it be substantiated and presented? Bultmann responds in the negative; he casts his vote against a New Testament "dogmatics" and advocates for diversity in its development. "By this choice the opinion is expressed that there can be no normative Christian dogmatics, in other words, that it is not possible to accomplish the theological task once for all—the task which consists of unfolding

21. On practical grounds, some limitation on the extent of material dealt with must also be made by those who insist on the abrogation of the canonical limitation. The criteria for this are not easy to determine, for restricting the scope of study to literature from Christian circles cannot be done on the basis of history-of-religions or history-of-culture criteria, and the whole realm of Jewish and Greco-Roman materials would need to be included. Therefore, every author/reader/exegete must draw some sort of canonical grounds for himself or herself. Even for Philipp Vielhauer, *Geschichte der urchristlichen Literatur: Einleitung in das Neue Testament, die Apokryphen und die Apostolischen Väter* (Berlin: de Gruyter, 1975), 1–8, the attempt to make a selection on purely form-critical grounds includes some violence!

22. Ingolf U. Dalferth, "Theologie im Kontext der Religionswissenschaft," *TLZ* 126 (2001): 14: "Thus for theology, God is not one theme among others, but the horizon within which all phenomena of life are to be understood, if they are to be understood *theologically*."

that understanding of God, and hence of the world and man, which arises from faith—for this task permits only ever-repeated solutions, or attempts at solution, each in its particular historical situation."[23] The opposite position has multiple forms that follow two basic patterns:

1. The unity of the New Testament is found in its concentration on a person, a basic idea, or an especially clear thought pattern. Of special importance is the argumentation of Martin Luther, who understood Jesus Christ to be the "midpoint of Scripture": "All the genuine sacred books agree in this, that all of them preach and inculcate [treiben] Christ. And that is the true test by which to judge all books, when we see whether or not they inculcate Christ. For all the Scriptures show us Christ, Rom. 3[:21]; and St. Paul will know nothing but Christ, 1 Cor. 2[:2]. Whatever does not teach Christ is not yet apostolic, even though St. Peter or St. Paul does the teaching. Again, whatever preaches Christ would be apostolic, even if Judas, Annas, Pilate, and Herod were doing it."[24] With this as his reference point, Luther develops an immanent biblical criticism with a christological orientation that especially values the Gospel of John, the letters of Paul, and 1 Peter but casts a negative light not only on James, but also on Hebrews, Jude, and Revelation. Luther's approach, in varied forms, has continued to this very day.[25] E. Käsemann sees in the justification of the godless the midpoint of Scripture and of all Christian proclamation. "Because in it Jesus's message and work as message and work of the Crucified One, his glory and lordship, stand out unmistakably from all other religious affirmations, it must be considered the canon within the canon; it is quite simply the criterion for testing the spirits, including Christian preaching of the past and present."[26] Within the framework of a biblical theology, P. Stuhlmacher sees the concept of reconciliation as the central focus of Scripture: "As lived out by Jesus, modeled by the proclamation of Paul, and thought through by the Johannine school in the power of the

23. Bultmann, *Theology of the New Testament*, 2:237. To be sure, in practice Bultmann advocates a "canon within the canon," by the dominant place he gives Paul and John as the center of his *Theology*.

24. Martin Luther, *Preface to James and Jude* (LW 35; St. Louis: Concordia, 1956), 395.

25. A survey of research up to the 1970s is found in Wolfgang Schrage, "Die Frage nach der Mitte und dem Kanon im Kanon des Neuen Testaments, in der neueren Diskussion," in *Rechtfertigung: Festschrift für Ernst Käsemann zum 70. Geburtstag* (ed. Johannes Friedrich et al.; Göttingen: Vandenhoeck & Ruprecht, 1976), 415–42; for a review and documentation of the more recent discussion, see P. Balla, *Challenges to New Testament Theology* (WUNT 2.95; Tübingen: Mohr, 1997); Hahn, *Theologie*, 2:6–22; C. Rowland and C. M. Tuckett, eds., *The Nature of New Testament Theology* (Oxford: Oxford University Press, 2006).

26. Ernst Käsemann, *Das Neue Testament als Kanon* (Göttingen: Vandenhoeck & Ruprecht, 1970), 405.

Spirit, the one apostolic gospel of God's reconciliation with human beings through his only begotten Son Jesus Christ is quite simply the message of salvation for the world."[27]

2. The question of diversity and unity is not reduced to key concepts, but is understood as an independent and necessary element of the theology of the New Testament. According to H. Schlier, the task of theology is achieved only "when it also succeeds in making the unity of the different 'theologies' visible. Only then does it make sense to use this term and the contents it designates. Regarded theologically, this unity includes the different basic theological concepts and affirmations in a way that is not ultimately contradictory. It is a presupposition of the inspiration and canonicity of the New Testament, indeed for the whole Bible."[28] F. Hahn takes up these proposals and moves them to the center of his New Testament theology. Since a history of early Christian theology can only show the variety of New Testament thought patterns, there is need for a demonstration of the inner unity of the New Testament, carried out within the framework of a thematic development.[29] On the basis of the Old Testament and New Testament canon, only one comprehensive thematic category can fulfill this role: the concept of revelation. Hahn holds that making revelation the guiding concept means starting with the revelatory acts of God in the Old Testament, then following the revelatory event in the person of Jesus Christ, and from there moving on to soteriology, ecclesiology, and eschatology in light of God's revelatory acts in Christ. He deals with New Testament ethics in connection with ecclesiology.[30]

The objection to accepting a "midpoint" of the New Testament is that it becomes an unhistorical abstraction that does not do justice to the individual documents. One concept, such as the doctrine of justification found in Galatians and Romans or the concept of reconciliation, cannot even cover all of

27. Stuhlmacher, *Biblische Theologie des Neuen Testaments*, 2:320.

28. Heinrich Schlier, "Über Sinn und Aufgabe einer neutestamentlichen Theologie," in *Das Problem der Theologie des Neuen Testaments* (ed. Georg Strecker; WdF 367; Darmstadt: Wissenschaftliche Buchgesellschaft, 1975), 338–39. Schlier sees unity already in the old creedal formulations; they are to be developed by means of the great themes of God, God's kingdom, Jesus Christ, resurrection, Spirit, church, and faith.

29. Cf. also Wilckens, *Theologie des Neuen Testaments* 1:53, who divides his work into a historical and a systematic part, and states with regard to the second part: "There the task is to find the unifying basic motifs in the variety of the different traditional material. These motifs contain theological conceptions that partially stand in contradiction to each other. It was these conceptions that gave the early Christian movement, in its positively eruptive beginning period, its immense persuasive and expansive power."

30. Ferdinand Hahn, "Das Zeugnis des Neuen Testaments in seiner Vielfalt und Einheit," *KD* 48 (2002): 253.

Paul's theology, much less the New Testament as a whole! If Jesus Christ himself is seen as the "midpoint," then such a concentration on the highest level is less meaningful, since it fits everything and thus cancels itself out. A "biblical theology" is not possible, because (1) the Old Testament is *silent* about Jesus Christ, (2) the resurrection from the dead *of one who was crucified* cannot be integrated into any ancient system of meaning-formation (cf. 1 Cor. 1:23), and (3) while the Old Testament can well be thought of as the most important cultural and theological context for understanding the New Testament, it is by no means the only one.[31] If the unity of the New Testament is required by the concept of the canon, both theoretical and practical problems arise: how is the process of canon formation related to the understanding inherent in each of the individual writings, which are now subjected to a new, later, and foreign framework within which they must be understood? How is the relation between variety and unity to be represented: Is unity the overlapping of the two categories of material? Is variety completed and fulfilled in unity? Is unity the repetition of variety under changed conditions?[32]

Canonization as Certification of a Limited Variety

In answering these questions, we must note first that the variety point of view follows logically from the methodological approach taken in this book and from the historical evidence: because all New Testament authors, as narrators and interpreters, bring their own history and the current situation of their community into *their* Jesus-Christ-history, and thus each carries out his own process of meaning-formation, *variety clearly has the precedence*, and there can be no such thing as *the* New Testament theology in the singular.[33] Each New Testament writing is an independent linguistic and hermeneutical world, and thus an independent symbolic universe that is to be understood

31. See Christoph Dohmen and Thomas Söding, eds., *Eine Bibel, zwei Testamente: Positionen biblischer Theologie* (Paderborn: Ferdinand Schöningh, 1995) for a survey of the pros and cons of a biblical theology.

32. Here is where I see the problem of Hahn's delineation; he deals with variety and unity in equally extensive ways, which necessarily leads to considerable overlappings and repetitions under different contexts; cf. for example his treatment of "the law in Paul," Hahn, *Theologie*, 1:232–42; 2:348–55.

33. Differently ibid., 2:2: "The delineation of variety in the sense of a theological history of early Christianity is a necessary part of the project, but in and of itself is only a fragment. Only in connection with the effort to refer the different theological programs to each other and to inquire as to their unity can we speak of a 'theology of the New Testament' in the strict and authentic sense." Hahn uses the term *unity* to refer to an abstraction, which is *not* found in the texts in this way, and claims at the same time that this is the only possible way to achieve a theology of the New Testament in the singular. On the whole issue see James D. G. Dunn, *Unity and Diversity in the New Testament: An Inquiry into the Character of Earliest Christianity* (3rd ed.; London: SCM, 2006), and James D. G. Dunn, *New Testament Theology: An Introduction* (Nashville: Abingdon, 2009).

in its own terms. Variety is not the same as boundless plurality without any contours but is related strictly to the witness of the New Testament writings. There is variety in the New Testament, but only on a clear basis: the experience of God's eschatological act of salvation in the cross and resurrection of Jesus Christ. The individual New Testament authors necessarily work out the meanings of this basic experience, each in his own way, so that the predominant feature is not antithesis but polymorphy. Moreover, we may ask whether the term *unity* is appropriate after all as a response to the question that has been posed. Unity is a static concept dealing with a totality, with a tendency to unify by smoothing out differences. After all, the question of (theological) unity is alien to the New Testament authors themselves; it does not appear in the texts, and the history of early Christianity is anything but the history of a united movement!

The canon represents the final stage of a long process of canonization.[34] In turn, canonization is a natural and necessary element in identity-formation and clarification. Within every developing movement it is necessary to determine "the regulations for a particular segment of society that shares the same meaning-formation; this is done through the drawing of boundaries and the establishment of rules."[35] Canonization by no means speaks against an emphasis on variety; it expresses this variety. The process of canonization makes clear that the originating event both enables a variety of possible interpretations and limits their range. At the same time, it remains true that *for the process of canonization, the central issue regarding variety and its boundaries is not a question regarding individual New Testament writings*. A canon is always an end product; canonization is a continuing process that begins with the New Testament writings but is not identical to them. Moreover, the New Testament writings ground and represent their status from within themselves and need no later canonization to confer this status on them. For the most part, they came into the canon because they already possessed this status; they did not receive this status by being accepted into the canon.[36] Finally: a theology of the New Testament canon as a task that is necessarily related

34. On the origin and development of the canon, cf. Theodor Zahn, *Geschichte des Neutestamentlichen Kanons* (2 vols.; Leipzig/Erlangen: Deichert, 1888, 1892); Johannes Leipoldt, *Geschichte des Neutestamentlichen Kanons* (2 vols.; Leipzig: Heinrichs, 1907, 1908); Hans von Campenhausen, *The Formation of the Christian Bible* (trans. John Austin Baker; London: Adam & Charles Black, 1972); Bruce M. Metzger, *The Canon of the New Testament: Its Origin, Development, and Significance* (Oxford: Oxford University Press, 1987); Lee Martin McDonald and James A. Sanders, eds., *The Canon Debate* (Peabody, MA: Hendrickson, 2002), an important collection of essays.

35. Thomas Luckmann, "Kanon und Konversion," in *Kanon und Zensur* (ed. Aleida Assmann and Jan Assmann; BALK 2; Munich: Fink, 1987), 38.

36. In Paul's letters this is obvious, for example in 1 Thess. 2:13; 2 Cor. 10:10; Gal. 1:8–9; and the deutero-Paulines passim. So also the gospels (cf. Mark 1:1; Matt. 1:1–17; Luke 1:1–4; John 1:1–18), Acts, Revelation and all the longer letters legitimate themselves by their own claim;

both to exegesis *and* church history is not the same thing as a theology of the New Testament writings or theology of the New Testament. The number and order of the writings in the canon is not the work of the New Testament authors but represents the theological understanding of others.[37] Their view prevailed for good reasons but is not the view of the individual New Testament writings. As a collection that established the horizon of interpretation and facilitated group identity, we can speak of a canon only from the time in which its core contents existed as a collection: ca. 180 CE. Thus in relation to the individual writings, the canon is a secondary metalevel, which cannot really grasp either the particular historical perspective or the specific theological profile of a New Testament document taken in its own context. Neither does the canonical level illuminate the contribution of a particular author to the formation of early Christian identity.

Nonetheless, considered as a natural and historical development as well as from a theological point of view, the New Testament canon is the appropriate result of a centuries-long process of formation and selection, a historical reality that determines the scope of the materials with which New Testament theology must be concerned.

2.4 New Testament Theology as Meaning-Formation

The preceding considerations provide the methodological approach and the structure for this theology of the New Testament.

Methodological Approach

The writings of the New Testament are the result of a comprehensive and multilayered process of meaning-formation. Religious experiences of groups and individuals always generate such processes of meaning-formation, and these are then expressed in narratives, rituals, and the composition of texts to facilitate their communication. So in the face of the reality of the cross and resurrection such acts of meaning-formation were inevitable. *The resurrection of Jesus of Nazareth from the dead was a revelatory event that opened up the meaning of his life. Such an event called for acts of meaning-formation from those who believed it!* All early Christian authors were faced with the task of bringing the unique events of the cross and resurrection, which transcended

differently Schröter, "Bedeutung des Kanons," 137–38, who distinguishes strictly between the historical and canonical status, and considers the latter as definitive.

37. Entirely different is the judgment of J. Schröter, ibid., 154: "The historical and theological significance of the canon is first seen to be valid when the canon is validated as a document of the theological history and the writings it contains are interpreted *on the basis of their canonical context and relations.*"

the boundaries of everyday life, into a theological meaning structure. In so doing, they also achieved a *significant intellectual accomplishment.* By narrating and interpreting the history of Jesus Christ in a particular way, they ascribe particular roles and status to him; they write history and construct their own new religious world.[38] In so doing, all New Testament authors reject the split between a factual history of the earthly Jesus and an abstract kerygma-Christology separated from this history. To operate within the framework of such a split would have been inappropriate both to their own historical setting and to the christological content of the history they were writing. It is rather the case that with them the history of the earthly Jesus comes in view through the perspective of the present reality of salvation created by the Risen One.

The new religious world always also expresses the specific historical and cultural situation in which the New Testament authors lived and worked. They were woven into multiple cultural and political contexts that were determined by their origin, their current field of activity, their recipients, and religio-philosophical debates of the time. Cultures do not exist individually, on their own terms; much less do religions. Rather, they are always integrated into a network of relationships. That is even more the case for a new movement such as early Christianity, which for the sake of its capacity for appropriation and integration* had to make connections intentionally. This integrative capacity does not happen automatically, but must be consciously and purposely constructed. In this regard, the capacity for meaning-formation and the formation of new identities is decisive. The forming of an identity always occurs under the influence of one or more cultural contexts. Thus one's sense of identity in belonging to a particular ethnic group is essentially determined by objectifiable characteristics such as language, genealogy, religion, and the traditions that have developed within the group. Traditions, in turn, reflect cultural molding through texts, rituals, and symbols.[39] Although as a rule, identity-formation occurs within such a context, it always has a process character, is fluid, and is bound to changing situations.[40] Moreover, in a situation of overlapping cultures, identities can form successfully only by including and integrating differing influences. For authentic new cultural formations to develop, they

38. This is a fundamental insight, for "What is decisive is not to get out of the circle but to come into it in the right way," Martin Heidegger, *Being and Time* (trans. John Macquarrie and Edward Robinson [from the 7th German ed.]; Oxford: Blackwell, 1967), 194.

*[I have throughout translated *Anschlussfähigkeit* as "capacity for openness and integration" or "integrative capacity." Schnelle uses this term to indicate early Christianity's openness to ideas in its culture that had hermeneutical potential, and its capacity to integrate them into its developing theology without losing or compromising itself.—MEB]

39. Cf. Harald Welzer, "Das soziale Gedächtnis," in *Das soziale Gedächtnis: Geschichte, Erinnerung, Tradierung* (ed. Harald Welzer; 1st ed.; Hamburg: Hamburger Edition, 2001), 9–21.

40. Cf. K.-H. Kohle, "Ethnizität und Tradition aus ethnologischer Sicht," in *Identitäten* (ed. Aleida Assmann and Heidrun Friese; 2nd ed.; Frankfurt: Suhrkamp, 1999), 269–87. [This essay was not included in the English version of the volume: Heidrun Friese, ed., *Identities*.—MEB]

also need clarity (lack of ambiguity) and openness. Within the many-sided complexity of the Roman Empire, the early Christian mission was able to attain its capacity for appropriation and integration only because it was capable of incorporating different cultural traditions and developing them creatively: the Old Testament, Hellenistic Judaism, and Greco-Roman culture. Finally, meaning-formation always occurs in (changing) political contexts. The individual New Testament books deal with these political contexts in very different ways. In particular, the emperor cult as a political religion (see §9.1) could not be ignored. Approaches range from open confrontation and debate (Revelation, 1 Peter), through addressing it with symbolic or clearly allusive language (Paul, Mark, Luke, John, Colossians/Ephesians), to maintaining silent (Hebrews, James, Pastorals, 2 Peter, Jude).

The meaning-formations of the New Testament authors point to a high level of competency. Not only were they able to assert themselves within a truly pluralistic religious context; they have maintained their presence right up to the present in a reception history that is unique in world history. Since in antiquity religion and philosophy were never separated, in reading the New Testament writings we must take them seriously also as intellectual achievements. They deal with the central questions of what makes for a successful life, so we have to compare them with other contemporary religio-philosophical compositions on the same themes.

If the present study proceeds writing by writing (or author by author), should we not speak of a theology of the New Testament *writings* (plural) rather than of a theology of the New Testament? But we depart from the writing-by-writing approach at one decisive point: the message, ministry, and destiny of Jesus of Nazareth form the basis and beginning point for our presentation. Thus we will continue to speak of a *theology of the New Testament*,[41] by which we mean the theological conceptions that can be derived from the New Testament writings. These conceptions transcend a mere writing-by-writing treatment, so this study does not simply run down the list of New Testament books but has chapters on Jesus, on Paul, and on the theology of Q.

41. As a matter of fact, the term *theology of the New Testament* has always been a collective term under which very different types of compositions have been subsumed. Two examples, which could easily be multiplied: (1) R. Bultmann begins with the presuppositions of a theology of the New Testament (including the preaching of Jesus), to which he joins thematic surveys (kerygma of the earliest church, kerygma of the Hellenistic church prior to and alongside Paul), and then turns to two authors/groups of writings that for him, one might say, represent *the* theology of the New Testament: Paul and John. Finally, again in a survey fashion, the developments toward the early catholic church are presented. (2) F. Hahn distinguishes, under the main title *Theologie des Neuen Testaments*, between a history of the theology of early Christianity (vol. 1, *Die Vielfalt* [variety] *des Neuen Testaments*) and a thematic presentation (vol. 2, *Die Einheit* [unity] *des Neuen Testaments*). In vol. 1, the authors and groups of writings stand in the foreground, while vol. 2 is organized thematically—but still in such a manner that primarily it is the thought of the more prominent authors/writings that are expounded.

Structure

If the New Testament writings are understood as expressing early Christianity's inclusive capacity and processes of meaning-formation and identity-formation, then a theology of the New Testament is charged with the task of *comprehensively discerning and describing the construction of this world of meaning*. The beginning point must be Jesus of Nazareth, whose ministry and preaching constructed a symbolic universe that evoked other meaning-formations both before and after Easter. All New Testament authors used these meaning-formations as their fundamental reference point.[42] The first main focus must therefore be the delineation of Jesus's own thought world. This will be organized into thematic issues that result from sorting out and evaluating the tradition. Then follows a structured presentation of the symbolic universe of all the New Testament writings, from Paul through Revelation, organized primarily by chronology but partly in terms of subject matter.[43] The goal in each case is, so far as possible, to present the comprehensive thought world of each author. This is achieved through division into *thematic subdivisions*, which (1) are found in all the writings, and (2) can be grasped in terms of their fundamental assumptions, their variety, and their mutual interrelationships. The thematic sectors are:

1. Theology. What are the consequences of the revelatory event in Jesus Christ for the way God is portrayed? How should we think about the God who has made known his will in Jesus Christ, in both continuity and discontinuity with the first covenant?
2. Christology. In the context of his authoritative manner, his miracles, and his fate in Jerusalem, the unique God consciousness of Jesus of Nazareth calls for determining his relation to God, his essential nature, his functions, and his significance within the eschatological course of events that he himself inaugurated.
3. Pneumatology. The new and enduring experiences of the Spirit within early Christianity necessitated reflection on the reality and effects of the divine presence in the lives of believers.
4. Soteriology. From the very beginning, the Christ event was understood as a saving or redemptive event: as deliverance from judgment, hell (or the underworld), and ever-present death. Within the context of the

42. The basic decision in how best to structure a New Testament theology is (usually after an introductory chapter) whether to begin with Jesus of Nazareth (so L. Goppelt, W. Thüsing, P. Stuhlmacher, U. Wilckens, F. Hahn) or Paul (so R. Bultmann, H. Conzelmann, G. Strecker, H. Hübner, J. Gnilka).

43. It thus makes sense, for example, to treat the Pastoral Epistles with the other deutero-Paulines, and thus before the other ecclesial letters 1 Peter, James, and Hebrews, even though the Pastorals were written later.

numerous concepts of salvation in the ancient world, what truly saves and how salvation occurs were themes that had to be clarified.

5. Anthropology. Closely associated with soteriology is the question of the nature and purpose of human beings. In view of the Jesus-Christ-history, the question of the nature of humanity was posed afresh: the "new humanity" in Christ (2 Cor. 5:17; Eph. 2:15) moves to the center of reflection.
6. Ethics. Meaning-formations are always connected with the attaining of orientations that have to be translated into ethical concepts. Not only being, but action, had taken on a new shape for the early Christians. They were faced with the difficult task of developing an attractive ethical program in continuity with Jewish ethics and in the context of a highly sophisticated Greco-Roman ethic.
7. Ecclesiology. Among the formative experiences of the beginning epoch was the sense of a new community bound together by a common faith, which had to be thought through in ecclesial terms and translated into forms and structures. A balance was required between the immediate experience of the Spirit and the institutional structures that became necessary as time went on.
8. Eschatology. As an element of its meaning-formation, every religion and philosophy must develop an outline of how it understands the temporal order. This was especially true of early Christianity, for the present had to be brought into a new relationship with past and future, since the resurrection of Jesus Christ from the dead—a past event—determined the future, and thus also shaped the present. Early Christianity did not think of eschatology as merely the consummation of world history. The early Christians' reworked conceptions of time, built on an all-encompassing understanding of God, interpreted world history and the present from the point of view of the coming End.
9. Historical-theological standpoint. In this concluding thematic sector, we will attempt to locate the theology of each New Testament document within the process of early Christian meaning-formation and the history of early Christianity. The main aim is to delineate each writing's distinctive theological profile.

This basic nine-point schematic structure thus derives from the analysis of the writings and the historical development itself,[44] while at the same time it functions to provide structure and access to the subject matter. It organizes

44. It is not a matter of structuring the presentation according to a "dogmatic" outline following the rubrics of systematic theology, but of utilizing thematic topoi. It is a didactic-methodological decision oriented to the contents of the texts themselves. Such divisions are always heuristic decisions, to be evaluated on the basis of the extent to which they actually facilitate the understanding and communication of the material.

the material and the issues it raises and ensures that we not only present the common theological and christological themes of the individual writings (e.g., the "messianic secret" in Mark, law/righteousness in Matthew, the doctrine of justification in Paul, church offices in the Pastorals) but also grasp the whole breadth and wealth of the theology of each document. At the same time, this grid is flexible enough to enable exploration of the emphases and distinctive features of individual writings. This schema also lets us integrate appropriately the narrative structures of the writings, their decisions at crucial forks in the road, their stance in the context of other theological proposals and outlines, and the specific elements of each writing that contribute to identity-formation and the development of unity. We preserve the special character of each text without imposing its particular features on the whole New Testament, and we do not illegitimately impute insights from the wider collection to individual documents.

The lines of argument in the various New Testament documents are always *embedded in contexts that are conditioned* by historical, theological, history-of-religion, cultural, and political factors. Understanding the texts thus makes it absolutely necessary to present something of this context: the fundamental decisions made by the early church that shaped its future paths, the cultural and intellectual challenges, the political turning points, and the unavoidable conflicts. We will do this in four sections with the keyword *transformation* in their respective titles. Each section will precede the particular group of New Testament documents that represents central historical and theological turning points in regard to the situation that had prevailed previously.

3

Jesus of Nazareth

The Near God

Jesus of Nazareth is the basis and beginning point of all New Testament theology (see above, §2.1). But who was this wandering Galilean preacher and healer? What was his message, and what was his own self-understanding? To address these questions, we begin with prerequisite methodological and hermeneutical considerations.

3.1 The Quest for Jesus

The quest for the historical Jesus is a child of the Enlightenment.[1] For earlier periods it was taken for granted that the gospels provided reliable information

1. A summary and evaluation of older (pre-1906) research is presented in Albert Schweitzer, *The Quest of the Historical Jesus: A Critical Study of Its Progress from Reimarus to Wrede* (trans. W. Montgomery et al.; 3rd ["first complete"] ed.; Minneapolis: Fortress, 2000), which includes a helpful essay by James M. Robinson on Schweitzer's own work and some later developments. On the phase of research associated with R. Bultmann, cf. Heinz Zahrnt, *The Historical Jesus* (trans. J. S. Bowden; New York: Harper & Row, 1963); Werner Georg Kümmel and Helmut Merklein, *Vierzig Jahre Jesusforschung (1950–1990)* (2nd ed.; BBB 91; Weinheim: Beltz Athenäum, 1994); critical reviews of recent American research are found in N. T. Wright, *Jesus and the Victory of God* (COQG 2; Minneapolis: Fortress, 1996), 28–82; and M. Eugene Boring, "The 'Third Quest' and the Apostolic Faith," *Int* 50 (1996): 341–54; repr. in *Gospel Interpretation: Narrative-Critical and Social-Scientific Approaches* (ed. Jack D. Kingsbury; Harrisburg, PA: Trinity, 1998), 237–52. Relevant texts in the debate are found in Manfred Baumotte, *Die*

about Jesus. Prior to the Enlightenment, research on the gospels was essentially limited to efforts to harmonize them. In practice, New Testament exegesis functioned as an auxiliary discipline for systematic theology.

Phases of Research

Not until the end of the eighteenth century did scholars become aware that the pre-Easter Jesus and the Christ proclaimed by the four gospels (and the church) could not be the same figure. Of particular importance in this development was *Hermann Samuel Reimarus* (1694–1768). After his death, *Gotthold Ephraim Lessing* published seven fragments of his manuscript (1774–78) without divulging the author's identity. The seventh fragment, published in 1778, "On the Intentions of Jesus and His Disciples," had lasting effects.[2] In this essay, Reimarus distinguished between Jesus's own intention and that of his disciples: Jesus was a Jewish political Messiah who wanted to establish a this-worldly kingdom and liberate the Jews from foreign domination. After the crucifixion, the disciples, faced with the destruction of their dreams, stole Jesus's corpse and devised the message of his resurrection. Thus for Reimarus, the historical Jesus was not identical with the proclaimed Christ; history and dogma are two different things: "I find great cause to separate completely what the apostles say in their own writings from that which Jesus himself actually said and taught."[3]

In 1835/36 *David Friedrich Strauss* (1808–74) published his *Life of Jesus* that created quite a sensation, evoked a flood of attempts at refutation, and bestowed lifelong social ostracism on its author—though henceforth research could never ignore the book's fundamental thesis that the tradition about Jesus had been formulated in mythical terms.

> The exegesis of the ancient church set out from the double presupposition: first, that the Gospels contained a history, and secondly, that the history was a supernatural one. Rationalism rejected the latter of these presuppositions, but only to cling the more tenaciously to the former, maintaining that these books present unadulterated, though only natural, history. Science cannot remain satisfied with this half-measure: the other presupposition must also be relinquished, and the inquiry must first be made whether in fact, and to what extent, the ground on which we stand in the Gospels is historical.[4]

Frage nach dem historischen Jesus: Texte aus drei Jahrhunderten (Reader Theologie; Gütersloh: Güterloher Verlagshaus, 1984).

2. Charles H. Talbert, ed., *Reimarus: Fragments* (LJS 1; Philadelphia: Fortress, 1970). This edition combines this fragment with another, "On the Resurrection Narratives." The combination is titled "Concerning the Intention of Jesus and His Teaching."

3. Ibid., 64.

4. David Friedrich Strauss, *The Life of Jesus Critically Examined* (introduction by Peter C. Hodgson, ed.; trans. George Eliot; London: SCM, 1973), li.

Strauss consigns a considerable part of the historicity of the Jesus story to the realm of myth, so that a yawning chasm appeared between the reality of the historical event and the truth claim associated with it. Strauss hoped to resolve this problem by abstracting the essential element of the Christian faith from history and relocating it in the realm of ideas. This was a false hope, for over against the apparently positive gain stood a fundamental loss: in the long run, truth cannot be affirmed as something that transcends historical reality.

Albert Schweitzer's (1875–1965) history of Jesus research showed that nineteenth-century depictions of the life of Jesus tended to be projections. Schweitzer showed that each liberal picture embodied its author's own notion of the highest human ethical ideals. From this multiplicity of Jesus pictures, and from the exegetical difficulties involved in constructing a historically appropriate picture, M. Kähler and R. Bultmann infer, in different ways, that only the kerygmatic Christ or post-Easter kerygma is theologically relevant (see above, §2.1). M. Kähler emphasizes that Jesus Christ is only accessible to us as he is portrayed in the gospels, not as scholarly reconstructions represent him. In the view of R. Bultmann, we must accept the radical consequences of the fact that we know Jesus only as already clothed in a mythical garment, and that it is not possible to inquire behind this mythical kerygma. Bultmann follows Kähler in the view that faith cannot bind itself to apparently historical facts. Historical research is necessarily always in constant change, so that its results are never final. This would mean, so to speak, that faith must always be adjusted to the constantly changing results of the exegetes.

In 1954 *Ernst Käsemann* (1906–98) introduced a new round in the quest for the historical Jesus. He affirmed: "The question of the historical Jesus is, in its legitimate form, the question of the continuity of the gospel."[5] To be sure, this was a long way from claiming to be able to reconstruct the life of Jesus, but this new point of view recognized that the gap between the preaching of Jesus and that of the early church was not as wide and sharp as Bultmann had thought. Käsemann placed at the central point in the project the "criterion of dissimilarity," according to which we have relatively secure ground under our feet when something attributed to Jesus can be derived neither from Judaism nor from early Christianity. Influential Jesus books reflecting this phase of the discussion include the works of *Günther Bornkamm* (1905–90) and *Herbert Braun* (1903–91).

The recent *Jesus research in America* ("Third Quest")[6] does not represent a unified approach, but it clearly places the utilization of all sources

5. Ernst Käsemann, "The Problem of the Historical Jesus," in *Essays on New Testament Themes* (SBT 41; London: SCM, 1964), 46.

6. The term "Third Quest" is based on a tripartite division of the history of research: (1) The "Old Quest" of the nineteenth century with its reaction in the early twentieth century; (2) the "New Quest" from the middle of the twentieth century; (3) the "third" round beginning in the '80s of the twentieth century. It makes more sense to distinguish five epochs of Jesus research: (1) Enlighten-

(extracanonical tradition, archaeology, postulated "sources")[7] and a modified evaluation of sources (Qumran documents, Nag Hammadi discoveries, along with the *Gospel of Thomas*) at the center of the discussion.[8] Thus the Qumran discoveries are regarded as evidence for the complexity of Judaism in the first century CE;[9] this complexity makes it possible to interpret Jesus of Nazareth consistently within the framework of the Judaism of his time (e.g., G. Vermès, E. P. Sanders). The criterion of dissimilarity so highly valued by E. Käsemann is subjected to sharp criticism, and Jesus is regarded as an exceptional Jew within Judaism.[10] Some "Third Quest" scholars radically reevaluate the *Gospel of Thomas*, dating it not in the middle of the second century, but ca. 50 CE (J. D. Crossan), making it the oldest witness to the Jesus tradition. The result is a modified picture of Jesus in which futuristic eschatology is no longer central. Jesus is not the proclaimer of the coming kingdom of God, but a Spirit person, a social misfit, a charismatic wisdom teacher and reformer (M. J. Borg). However, the thoroughgoing decontextualization of Jesus's sayings, the secondary stylization of adopted forms, and the complete dissociation from the history of Israel all speak *clearly* for a later date for the *Gospel of Thomas*.[11]

---

ment (Reimarus/Strauss); (2) liberal Jesus research (H. J. Holtzmann); (3) deconstruction of the liberal picture of Jesus (J. Weiss, W. Wrede, A. Schweitzer, R. Bultmann); (4) the "New Quest" of the historical Jesus (E. Käsemann, E. Fuchs, G. Bornkamm, G. Ebeling, H. Braun); (5) the more recent (primarily) North American Jesus research ("Third Quest"); cf. also Gerd Theissen and Annette Merz, *The Historical Jesus: A Comprehensive Guide* (trans. John Bowden; Minneapolis: Fortress, 1998), 2–8; Boring, "Third Quest," 237–52, and the literature there given.

7. Here is to be noted especially the *Secret Gospel of Mark* (an alleged letter from Clement of Alexandria with two citations from an otherwise unknown *Gospel of Mark*), which the history-of-religions scholar M. Smith claims to have discovered. The letter is documented only by photographs, which are not compelling evidence. Stephen C. Carlson, *The Gospel Hoax: Morton Smith's Invention of Secret Mark* (Waco: Baylor University Press, 2005) argues that the alleged discovery is a forgery. Hans-Josef Klauck, *Apocryphal Gospels: An Introduction* (trans. Bryan McNeil; London; New York: T&T Clark International, 2003), and Eckhard Rau, *Das geheime Markusevangelium: Ein Schriftfund voller Rätsel* (Neukirchen: Neukirchener Verlag, 2003), finally come down on the side of authenticity, but regard the *Secret Gospel* as dependent on the Synoptics and date it in the second century.

8. Cf. the survey in A. B. du Toit, "Redefining Jesus: Current Trends in Jesus Research," in *Jesus, Mark and Q: The Teaching of Jesus and Its Earliest Records* (ed. Michael Labahn and Andreas Schmidt; JSNTSup 214; Sheffield: Sheffield Academic Press, 2001), 82–124.

9. Cf. here C. F. Evans, "The New Quest for Jesus and the New Research on the Dead Sea Scrolls," ibid., 163–83.

10. Cf. T. Holmén, "The Jewishness of Jesus in the 'Third Quest,'" ibid., 143–62.

11. Cf. J. Schröter and H.-G. Bethge, "Das Evangelium nach Thomas," in *Nag Hammadi Deutsch* (ed. Hans-Martin Schenke et al.; GCS NF 8; 2 vols.; Berlin: de Gruyter, 2001), 151–81. E. E. Popkes, "Die Umdeutung des Todes Jesu im koptischen Thomasevangelium," in *Deutungen des Todes Jesu im Neuen Testament* (ed. J. Frey and J. Schröter; WUNT 181; Tübingen: Mohr, 2005), 513–43, arguing from the central focus on soteriology, makes a persuasive case for a late date.

In some streams of North American Jesus research there was and is a clear tendency to promote real or postulated extracanonical tradition to a rank prior or parallel to the Jesus tradition of the Synoptics and the Johannine writings (H. Koester; J. M. Robinson;[12] J. D. Crossan; B. L. Mack[13]). The goal of such constructions is clearly to break the hold of the canonical gospels and to establish an alternative picture of Jesus based on other interpretations of the tradition. To do this, frequent use is made of the lust for sensationalism (Jesus and women; homosexual love; Jesus as prototype of alternative lifestyles; nontheological, undogmatic beginnings of Christianity). Mere supposition and unproven postulates are asserted as stimulants for a debate intended to have public effects.[14] Such constructions do not stand up to historical criticism, for neither the existence of a *Secret Gospel of Mark* nor a Signs Source[15] can be made probable, and the *Gospel of Thomas* belongs to the second century!

Finally, the recent "Third Quest" is characterized by a strong emphasis on issues in the realm of social history and the interpretation of culture,[16] as well as a withdrawal from genuine theological themes. Study is focused on the function of Jesus's radical ethic of love and reconciliation within the prevailing economic, political, and cultural situation, and attention is given to the particular form of Judaism in Galilee or agreements between the Jesus movement and the Cynic movement in Syria/Palestine.[17]

3.1.1 Jesus in His Interpretations

The new pictures of Jesus are also clearly a reflection of their own times. The Jesus of postmodernism fulfills all the political and cultural hopes of his interpreters: he overcomes all divisions based on gender, religion, culture, and politics and thus becomes a social reformer and universal reconciler. All

12. In this regard cf. the programmatic writing of James M. Robinson and Helmut Koester, *Trajectories through Early Christianity* (Philadelphia: Fortress, 1971). The current state of discussion is sketched by J. Schröter, "Jesus im frühen Christentum: Zur neueren Diskussion über kanonisch und apokryph gewordene Jesusüberlieferungen," *VuF* 51 (2006): 25–41.

13. Burton L. Mack, *Who Wrote the New Testament? The Making of the Christian Myth* (San Francisco: HarperSanFrancisco, 1996).

14. Cf. Roman Heiligenthal, *Der verfälschte Jesus: Eine Kritik moderner Jesusbilder* (Darmstadt: Primus, 1997), and Craig Evans, *Fabricating Jesus: How Modern Scholars Distort the Gospels* (Downers Grove, IL: InterVarsity, 2006).

15. Or "Semeia Source." Cf. Schnelle, *New Testament Writings*, 493–96.

16. As a survey of the contributions of selected German and Anglo-American authors, cf. Wolfgang Stegemann et al., eds., *The Social Setting of Jesus and the Gospels* (Minneapolis: Fortress, 2002). A combination of sociohistorical and archaeological approaches is found in John Dominic Crossan and Jonathan L. Reed, *Excavating Jesus: Beneath the Stones, behind the Texts* (San Francisco: HarperSanFrancisco, 2001).

17. Cf. Francis Gerald Downing, "The Jewish Cynic Jesus," in *Jesus, Mark and Q: The Teaching of Jesus and Its Earliest Records* (ed. Michael Labahn and Andreas Schmidt; JSNTSup 214; Sheffield: Sheffield Academic Press, 2001), 118–214.

aspects of Jesus's work that are not up-to-date recede into the background: his miracles, his pronouncements of judgment with their dark visions, and the reality that his mission ran aground on the sociopolitical conditions of the time. He is above all what we are and want to be: human, friend, and example. Seen against the background of the epistemological reflections on the writing of history discussed above (see chap. 1), there are no surprises here, for every portrait of Jesus is unavoidably a construction of the exegetes of its day.

One main feature of both the recent American Jesus research and European exegesis thus continues to be methodologically suspect: the effort to find the "historical," "real" Jesus *behind* the available sources.[18] Jesus research is thus widely understood as a reductionistic enterprise, with the goal of tracing out the actual events behind the multiplicity of interpretations. But even our increased knowledge of ancient Judaism, our deepened insights into the historical and social contexts of Galilee in the first century CE, and a more reflective methodology cannot overcome the relative and perspectival nature of all historical knowledge. An event attains historical quality only when narrated (see above, §1.3); facts or events of the past become a part of history only when they can be appropriated through processes of historical meaning-formation. Persons and events must be related to each other; the beginning and end of a historical course of events must be identified. The necessarily narrative presentation of an event by no means negates historiography's claims to rationality but is their presupposition. *The identity of Jesus of Nazareth can therefore be grasped in no other way than in his literary contexts.* We can still quest after authenticity and facts on the basis of a critical evaluation of the sources, but we will not find an answer that gets behind or goes beyond the narrative—and so always also fictional—character of the presentation of the Jesus-Christ-history in the gospels as we have them. The "historical Jesus" cannot be presented on the basis of a reproduction of sources or a reconstruction of given historical connections, nor as an attempt to get back to an uninterpreted Jesus, but only as a construction of the effects of Jesus in history, a construction that is aware of and respects the conditioned nature of understanding, the data of the tradition, a construction that is guided by a clear methodology.[19] Portrayals of Jesus can thus no longer be a quest

18. As one example, cf. James M. Robinson, "Der wahre Jesus? Der historische Jesus im Spruchevangelium Q," in *The Sayings Gospel Q: Collected Essays* (ed. Christoph Heil and Jozef Verheyden; BETL 189; Louvain: Leuven University Press, 2005), 17–26.

19. James D. G. Dunn, *Jesus Remembered* (Christianity in the Making 1; Grand Rapids: Eerdmans, 2003), 130, favors the category of "remembering": "The Synoptic tradition provides evidence not so much for what Jesus did or said in itself, but for what Jesus was remembered as doing or saying by his first disciples, or as we might say, for the impact of what he did and said on his first disciples." However, the bare concept of "remembering" is not adequate in itself, for memories are always already constructions of past events made under present conditions, and already filled with interpretations.

for the world behind the texts.[20] It is not possible to compose a historical and theologically responsible narrative of Jesus that bypasses the narrative representations of Jesus in the gospels, for they are already the earliest witnesses of a figuration of Jesus's effects in history.

Consequences

These reflections lead to several consequences:

1. If it is the narrative presentation itself that makes history possible in the first place—if there can be no memory of Jesus apart from this act of narratization—then we cannot continue to distinguish schematically between the narrative Jesus tradition and the tradition of his sayings. This distinction has sometimes been used in the past as though the sayings tradition had a higher claim to historical authenticity, and the narrative tradition was only a secondary development.[21] Both forms have the same claim to authenticity, for they both transmit what was narrated about Jesus as characteristic and thus worth remembering, and finally was written down. Not the genre but the analysis of individual elements in the tradition is essential for determining which event or saying can be claimed for Jesus. Portrayals of Jesus must take seriously the narrative setting of the tradition of Jesus's sayings and parables.
2. The quest for Jesus cannot be reduced to the "historical Jesus" or the "real Jesus,"[22] for if Jesus is accessible to us only in the narratives that present him, and therefore already interpret him, research cannot distinguish between a "purely historical" and a theological approach.[23] There is a historical quest for Jesus, but not a quest for the historical Jesus! Because

20. This is stressed by J. Schröter, "Die Frage nach dem historischen Jesus und der Charakter historischer Erkenntnis," in *The Sayings Source Q and the Historical Jesus* (ed. Andreas Lindemann; BETL 158; Louvain: Leuven University Press, 2001), 207–54.

21. So judges Rudolf Bultmann, *The History of the Synoptic Tradition* (trans. John Marsh; New York: Harper & Row, 1963), 47, concerning the didactic and controversy sayings: "this must be emphasized once more, the sayings have commonly generated the situation, not vice versa."

22. This is the way Gerhard Ebeling, for instance, defines the matter in the tradition of Bultmann: "'Historical,' then, means the appropriate method of perceiving historic reality. 'Historical Jesus' is therefore really an abbreviation for 'Jesus as he comes to be known by strictly historical methods, in contrast to any alteration and touching up to which he has been subjected in the traditional Jesus picture. Hence the 'historical Jesus' as good as means the true, the real Jesus." Gerhard Ebeling, "The Question of the Historical Jesus and the Problem of Christology," in *Word and Faith* (ed. Gerhard Ebeling; Philadelphia: Fortress, 1963), 290.

23. In contrast to the clear tendency in American Jesus research to play off a historical approach against a theological one; cf. E. P. Sanders, *Jesus and Judaism* (Philadelphia: Fortress, 1985), 333–34; John P. Meier, *A Marginal Jew: Rethinking the Historical Jesus*, vol. 1, *The Roots of the Problem and the Person* (ABRL 1; New York: Doubleday, 1991), 21–31. For an alternative tendency in American Jesus research, see, e.g., Leander Keck, *Who Is Jesus? History in the Perfect Tense* (Columbia: University of South Carolina Press, 2000).

Jesus of Nazareth has never been accessible apart from his significance for faith, research must also pose the pre-Easter questions of his consciousness of his own mission and the theological significance of his work.[24]

3. Every portrayal of Jesus must explain the different perceptions of his life and ministry that Jesus himself triggered both before and after Easter, and must offer a plausible account of the differing ways in which his post-Easter interpreters related their interpretations to the pre-Easter Jesus. The history of early Christianity was characterized from the very beginning by a high capacity for appropriation and integration, in regard to Hellenistic Judaism as well as Greco-Roman culture as such. A persistent integrative capacity is not simply identical with accommodation but gains its strength from the original event. That is to say, the origins of Christology and the different developments in the history of early Christianity up to and including the mission to the Gentiles without the precondition of circumcision, from the perspective of historical theory, also have points of contact in the ministry and message of Jesus of Nazareth. The unique claim of the pre-Easter Jesus, a differentiated Christology that had already developed very early, and the history of expansion of a new relation that is unique in world history can be convincingly explained only if the power of the beginnings was so strong and manifold that it could set forth such a multiplicity of interpretations.

3.1.2 Criteria for the Quest

Despite numerous differing opinions in matters of detail, exegesis is now united in the view that the quest of the historical Jesus is historically possible and theologically necessary. But how is this to be done? Which criteria can be used to filter out historically authentic sayings of Jesus from the broad stream of tradition, separating them from later interpretations and contemporizing accretions—without neglecting the basic considerations discussed above? The response to this question requires a discrimination between *fundamental criteria* and *material criteria*.

Fundamental Criteria

The decisive fundamental criterion is *comprehensive plausibility*, according to which it must be possible to reconstruct the message of Jesus in a way that is plausible both in the context of Judaism and in that of early Christianity.[25]

24. Cf. J. Frey, "Der historische Jesus und der Christ des Glaubens," in *Der historische Jesus* (ed. J. Schröter and R. Bruckner; BZNW 114; Berlin: de Gruyter, 2002), 297ff.

25. On the criteria of plausibility, see Gerd Theissen and Dagmar Winter, *The Quest for the Plausible Jesus: The Question of Criteria* (trans. M. Eugene Boring; Louisville: Westminster John Knox, 2002), 238–304.

The criterion of *contextual plausibility* proceeds on the basis that the alternative Jesus/Judaism is both historically and theologically false. Jesus cannot be abstracted from Judaism but must be understood within Judaism—more precisely, in the context of his Galilean world. Regarding Jesus as integrated within the models given in the linguistic and behavioral world of his historical context by no means excludes the possibility that Jesus assumed a critical stance within Judaism, for the Judaism of his time was no homogenized monolith but consisted of a variety of differing, even contradictory, streams.

At the same time, we have to explain how early Christianity could emerge in continuity with the preaching of Jesus. Alongside contextual plausibility is the second decisive criterion, the *plausibility of historical effects*, for to be considered historical, a portrayal of Jesus must facilitate an understanding not only of the message of Jesus within the Judaism of his time but also of the development from Jesus to early Christianity.[26] The fact that the message of Jesus originated in Galilee and is closely related to its Galilean context does not mean that it can be reduced to the social, cultural, and political realities already present in his situation. It has political dimensions but at its core is not a political message.[27] The reception history of Jesus's message makes this clear, for Jesus's proclamation of the kingdom of God—detached from its concrete historical and geographical location—was received within a very short time throughout the Mediterranean world. This was only possible because Jesus's message had, and has, *a quality that allows it to fit into the history of ideas as such*: the one God, who in new and surprising ways comes near to humanity in love, a God who intends to establish a new community of human beings, a community that does not depend on domination and violence. The two foundational criteria, contextual plausibility and the plausibility of historical effects, take up the insight from historical theory that enduring historical developments must have the capacity for appropriation and integration. This integrative capacity always functions within existing cultural contexts and sets new developments in motion.

Material Criteria

The following material criteria can be used for identifying authentic sayings of Jesus:

26. Cf. ibid., "What we know of Jesus as a whole must allow him to be recognized within his contemporary Jewish context and must be compatible with the Christian (canonical and noncanonical) history of his effects."

27. Methodologically, therefore, political and social history perspectives cannot provide the exclusive hermeneutical horizon (as tends to be the case in many American studies and those influenced by them), but they are nonetheless utilized when the texts themselves call for it. For Galilee as the specific context for Jesus's life, see below, §3.4.5 and §3.8.1; for the political dimensions of Jesus's message, see below, §3.4.1.

1. Criterion of multiple attestation. According to this criterion, tracing back a saying to Jesus himself is plausible when the saying is preserved in different streams of tradition (e.g., Jesus's stance toward divorce in Mark, Q, and Paul). This criterion also includes the mutual confirmation provided by the sayings tradition and the tradition of Jesus's deeds. When Jesus's words and his actions go in the same direction, complementing each other, this provides a strong argument for authenticity (e.g., Jesus's association with tax collectors and sinners).
2. Criterion of dissimilarity. R. Bultmann formulated this classical criterion as follows: "We can count on possessing a genuine similitude of Jesus where, on the one hand, expression is given to the contrast between Jewish morality and piety and the distinctive eschatological temper which characterized the preaching of Jesus; and where on the other hand we find no specifically Christian features."[28] The dissimilarity criterion stands in some tension with other criteria (e.g., contextual plausibility), and one can here speak of a certain overemphasis on "sayings," or note that the narrative tradition is given too little intrinsic historical value. Nonetheless, the basic idea involved in the criterion of dissimilarity is to be taken seriously: it can reveal such statements of Jesus that can be explained neither from the presuppositions and interests of Judaism nor from those of the early Christian community.
3. Criterion of coherence. This criterion depends on the postulate that the message of Jesus as a whole must manifest a certain coherence. Elements in the tradition that do not fit into this total picture must therefore be considered secondary. This criterion too contains a contradiction, for it always already presupposes a definite picture of the message of Jesus, which it then confirms. Nonetheless, here too the basic idea is valid. What agrees in substance with material that has already been identified by other criteria as belonging to Jesus can also be considered authentic.
4. Criterion of tendencies of the developing tradition. This criterion is based on the idea that as original Jesus material was transmitted, it was enriched by secondary elements that can be identified and removed by literary criticism. Literary-critical analysis here makes it possible to reconstruct the original saying of Jesus that generated the tradition (cf. Matt. 5:33–37).
5. Criterion of embarrassment. This criterion proceeds on the assumption that sayings or deeds of Jesus that would have been regarded as scandalous, embarrassing, or problematic in both Judaism and early

28. Bultmann, *History of the Synoptic Tradition*, 205. On the history of the dissimilarity criterion, see Theissen and Winter, *Quest*, 27–171.

Christianity must be regarded as authentic. Thus, for example, Jesus's baptism by John belongs to the bedrock of the tradition, for it was progressively minimized in early Christianity. Moreover, Jesus used immoral characters as principal figures in his parables, such as the shrewd but unethical manager of Luke 16:1–7. And finally, his association with tax collectors and sinners cast Jesus himself in a morally dubious role.

Every portrayal of Jesus is necessarily and unavoidably a *construction*, composed not arbitrarily but on the basis of tradition and by means of specific criteria.[29] Each criterion, taken by itself, pursues a particular line of questioning and is subject to contradiction. Taken together, however, the criteria complement each other and can be very effective. The picture as a whole is always constructed on the basis of individual analyses, while at the same time the total picture influences each individual analysis. This circular dynamic of the process is appropriate, for it provides a check on one-sidedness. The two dimensions of Jesus research proceed side by side and mutually interpret and supplement each other: analysis of the numerous individual sayings and stories, and the impression of Jesus's life as a whole that is both presupposed and constantly corrected.

In addition to the criteria named above, the *density of the tradition* is of fundamental importance, i.e., the points around which the tradition congeals. The more comprehensively the tradition is dominated by certain types of sayings (e.g., parables), perspectives (kingdom of God, judgment), deeds (e.g., healings) and events (e.g., conflicts with Pharisees, fellowship with the "unclean"), the more likely it is that they were central features in the life of Jesus. The density of the tradition at certain points lets the main outlines of Jesus's life and ministry emerge clearly[30] and shows how Jesus was perceived both before and after Easter. No historically plausible picture of Jesus can be drawn that bypasses the main lines of the narrative presentation of Jesus and thereby ignores these points around which the tradition congealed.

29. Albrecht Scriba, *Echtheitskriterien der Jesus-Forschung: Kritische Revision und konstruktiver Neuansatz* (Theos 74; Hamburg: Kovac, 2007), 107–14, in connection with the criteria of plausibility and history of effects, the criterion of "data evaluation." "This category includes especially the baptism of Jesus by John the Baptist, that Jesus did not continue to baptize during his own ministry, the date of Jesus's crucifixion, the modality and characteristics of the Easter visions, and the presuppositions for the reintroduction of baptism in early Christianity" (p. 240).

30. Ferdinand Hahn, "Methodologische Überlegungen zur Rückfrage nach Jesus," in *Rückfrage Nach Jesus* (ed. Karl Kertelge; Freiburg: Herder, 1974), 40–51, speaks of "components"; Thüsing, *Neutestamentlichen Theologien*, of "'structural components' of the ministry of Jesus, which include especially the conflicts, the preaching of the kingdom, and the call to discipleship."

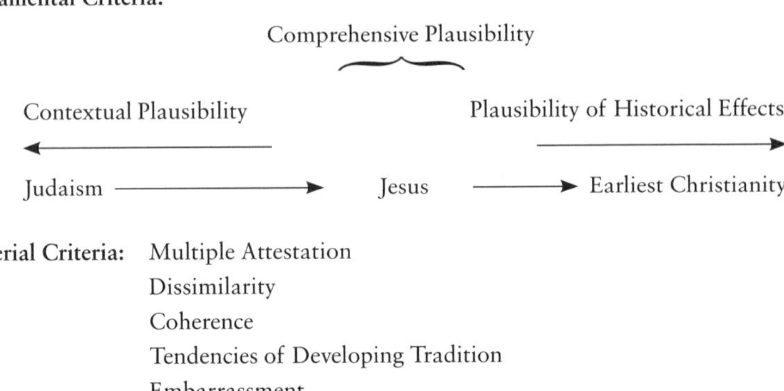

3.2 Beginning: John the Baptist

Jesus regarded himself as more closely associated with John the Baptist than with any other figure in Israel. Likewise, his contemporaries were already comparing the two (Matt. 11:18–19 par.; cf. Mark 2:18 par.; 6:14–16 par.), just as early Christian tradition recognized numerous connections between the two, and also between their respective groups of disciples (cf. Mark 2:18; Luke 1:5ff.; 11:2; John 1:35–51; 3:22ff.; 4:1–3; 10:40–42; Acts 19:1–7). *To understand Jesus of Nazareth, we must get acquainted with John the Baptist.*

3.2.1 John the Baptist as a Historical Figure

The New Testament and the writings of Josephus (37/38–ca. 100 CE) are the two most important sources for John the Baptist, pursuing their respective goals in the way the history is recounted. The New Testament accounts are influenced by the disputes with the Baptist movement and are clearly concerned to subordinate John to Jesus, to demote him to the eschatological forerunner and witness to the Messiah, Jesus (cf. Mark 1:7–8; Luke 3:16 par.; John 1:6–8, 15, 19ff.). Josephus (*Ant.* 18.116–119) represents John to his Greco-Roman readership as a teacher of virtue who was killed by Herod Antipas,

> though he was a good man and had exhorted the Jews to lead righteous lives, to practice justice towards their fellows and piety towards God, and so doing to join in baptism. In his view this was a necessary preliminary if baptism was to be acceptable to God. They must not employ it to gain pardon for whatever sins they committed, but as a consecration of the body implying that the soul was already thoroughly cleansed by right behavior. (*Ant.* 18.117)[31]

31. For analysis of the text, cf. K. Backhaus, *Die "Jüngerkreise" des Täufers Johannes* (PThSt 19; Paderborn: Schöningh, 1991), 266–74; S. Mason, *Josephus and the New Testament* (Peabody, MA: Hendrickson, 1992), 151–63.

Josephus does not mention any connection between John and Jesus, suppresses the Baptist's message of judgment, and represents his baptism as a mere ritual purification of the body with no relation to the forgiveness of sins. At the same time, Josephus's account shows that in ancient Judaism the Baptist was perceived as an independent figure in his own right.

Biographical and Geographical Data

The year of the Baptist's birth is unknown, but it was probably in the last years before the death of Herod the Great (4 BCE).[32] John probably came from an undistinguished priestly family (cf. Luke 1:5), and this priestly background was of great importance for his self-understanding and actions.[33] According to Luke 3:1, John began his ministry in the fifteenth year of Tiberius, i.e., in 28 CE; how long he was active we do not know. According to Mark 1:4–5, he appeared "in the wilderness" (cf. Q 7:24,[34] "And when they had left, he began to talk to the crowds about John: What did you go out into the wilderness to look at? A reed shaken by the wind?") and baptized in the Jordan. There are places in the lower Jordan that fit the biblical description, with accessibility, running water, and desert extending directly to the river. Probably the baptismal site was located *east* of the Jordan opposite Jericho,[35] for John associated a theological program with his choice of location: the events of

32. According to Luke 1:36, the Baptist was only six months older than Jesus. Historically, this is rather unlikely, for the tradition Luke uses intentionally wants to relate Jesus closely to the Baptist; cf. Ulrich B. Müller, *Johannes der Täufer* (Leipzig: Evangelische Verlagsanstalt, 2002), 17.

33. Hartmut Stegemann, *The Library of Qumran, on the Essenes, Qumran, John the Baptist, and Jesus* (Grand Rapids: Eerdmans, 1998), 220: "Especially in John the Baptist's case, it is historically beyond any doubt that he was of priestly birth, corresponding to what we read of his father Zechariah and his mother Elizabeth in Luke 1:5–25 and 1:39–79. John's quality as a mediator, stemming from his priestly origin, was certainly the decisive component of his active role in his baptisms, which made him, as ritual representative of God, the Baptist, and the baptisms performed by him an efficacious sacrament."

34. The siglum Q indicates the presumed text form for the sayings source, according to the Lukan chapter and verse numbers. The textual reconstruction usually follows James M. Robinson et al., eds., *The Critical Edition of Q: Synopsis Including the Gospels of Matthew and Luke, Mark and Thomas with English, German, and French Translations of Q and Thomas* (Hermeneia; Minneapolis: Fortress, 2000). [Schnelle generally cites the German translation of Q included in *The Critical Edition of Q*. I have cited the corresponding English translation of that volume, usually including the bracketed elements in the text, and rendering "Menschenson" as "Son of Man." When Schnelle departs from the text of *The Critical Edition of Q*, I have cited the NRSV or translated his German text.—MEB]

35. Cf. Stegemann, *Library of Qumran*, 212–18. According to John 1:28, John baptized "in Bethany across the Jordan," and in John 3:33 the location is specified as "Aenon near Salim." This location peculiar to John has not been convincingly identified. Cf. on this point Josef Ernst, "Wo Johannes taufte," in *Antikes Judentum und frühes Christentum: Festschrift für Hartmut Stegemann zum 65. Geburtstag* (ed. Bernd Kollmann et al.; BZNW 97; Berlin: de Gruyter, 1999), 350–63.

Israel's beginning are repeated in the eschatological time; Israel is again at the point of entrance into the Promised Land, which the Baptist now makes possible in a new and different way.[36] That the Baptist's ministry was east of the Jordan is also indicated by the tradition that he was executed by Herod Antipas, the tetrarch of Perea, probably in 29 CE (cf. Mark 6:17–29; Josephus, *Ant.* 18.118–119).[37] Finally, his appearance in the wilderness fits the account of his ministry and manner of life in Mark 1:6 (cf. Q 7:25).[38] His clothing was made of camel hair (cf. Elijah, according to 1 Kings 19:13, 19; 2 Kings 1:8 LXX; 2:8, 13–14), the same material the Bedouin used to make their clothes and tents. Likewise, the leather belt is a requisite of Bedouin life, a long strap made from the skin of the gazelle, which the Bedouin wore wrapped around the bare body as protection. The locusts and wild honey belong to the meager fare of the Bedouin, so that his contemporaries already interpreted his lifestyle as ascetic (cf. Mark 2:18; Q 7:33–34). Clothing, diet, and location all represent a distancing from culture and signal an existence outside the land Israel had taken over as its possession. Every aspect of John's life proclaimed the serious situation of judgment in which he sees his contemporaries living.

The substance of the *Baptist's message* can be identified with relative certainty; it is the proclamation of judgment and the call to repentance, entirely determined by an eschatological expectation that the end is near.

The Coming Wrath and Fiery Judgment

At the center of John's proclamation stands God's immediately imminent judgment (Q 3:7–9): "He said to the crowds coming to be baptized: Snakes' litter! Who warned you to run from the impending rage? So bear fruit worthy of repentance, and do not presume to tell yourselves, 'We have Abraham as father.' For I tell you, God can produce children for Abraham right out of these rocks!" John clearly lived in the certainty that all Israel was immediately

36. Cf. Stegemann, *Library of Qumran*, 214: "The actual background for John's peculiar choice of location is revealed by biblical tradition alone. John had chosen the place of his entry upon the public scene precisely at that location, opposite Jericho, where Joshua had once led the people of Israel across the Jordan into the Holy Land (Josh. 4:13, 19). His choice of the *east bank* of the Jordan as the place of his activity, then, corresponds to Israel's situation immediately *before* the crossing of the river."

37. While the anecdote in Mark 6:17–29 gives Herod's family relationships as the reason for John's execution, Josephus gives political reasons: John was so successful that the population streamed to him, and Herod Antipas had this successful competitor and critic taken out of the way. For a discussion of the problems, cf. Müller, *Johannes der Täufer*, 76–93.

38. All relevant models of interpretation are presented in E.-M. Becker, "Kamelhaare . . . und wilder Honig," in *Die bleibende Gegenwart des Evangeliums: Festschrift für Otto Merk* (ed. Roland Gebauer and Martin Meiser; MTS 76; Marburg: Elwert, 2003); H. Stegemann places the accent somewhat differently, taking the garment of camel hair to be a mark of elegance and nobility, and opines, "Grasshoppers fried in olive oil taste like French fried potatoes. Like wild honey, they are a delicacy" (Stegemann, *Library of Qumran*, 215).

threatened with the "impending rage." The metaphor of the "snakes' litter" functions as a threat of destruction, for snakes are trampled or struck dead. The appeal to Abraham is no longer possible; the threatening nearness of judgment is intensified with the announcement that it is "already" (ἤδη) present, and it is made concrete by the image of the ax and the tree. All this together makes it clear that there is no escape. Nowhere does the Baptist explain why God is angry; he confronts Israel in aggressive blatancy with his message of judgment. John here stands in the prophetic tradition (cf. Amos 5:18–20; 7:8; 8:2; Hos. 1:6, 9; Isa. 6:11; 22:14; Jer. 1:14),[39] which he intentionally takes up and sharpens, for the catastrophic judgment is not just going to come someday, but stands immediately before the hearers. If the ax is already in place, the one who will use it is on the way. The winnowing that separates wheat from chaff has already begun; then the chaff will be burned (Q 3:17). It is striking that in this small unit of tradition, the fire metaphor is used three times for God's judgment, each time with a different connotation (cf. Q 3:9, 16b, 17).[40] This imagery was apparently characteristic of the Baptist, even though it is not found in Josephus, Mark, or John.

The decisive theological marker that determines the future does not lie, however, in the sharpness and urgency of the annihilating judgment,[41] but in the *hopeless situation of those addressed*. Because God's act always involves both judgment and salvation,[42] God's saving act is always also an act of judgment. Here, however, the conventional separation involved in judgment (here the chosen righteous ones, there the apostates or the Gentiles) is radically rearranged. The Baptist does *not* share the understanding, widespread in ancient Judaism, that acknowledging one's guilt by confessing one's sins brings forgiveness from the God who holds firm to his covenant with the

39. On the prophetic traditions embodied in John's work cf. Michael Tilly, *Johannes der Täufer und die Biographie der Propheten: Die synoptische Täuferüberlieferung und das jüdische Prophetenbild zur Zeit des Täufers* (BWANT 17; Stuttgart: Kohlhammer, 1994).

40. Cf., e.g., Gen. 19:24; Exod. 9:24; Lev. 10:2; Num. 11:1; Joel 3:3; Mal. 3:9; Isa. 66:15–16. The Baptist's proclamation of the threatening judgment is a variation of the prophetic tradition of the "Day of the Lord" (cf., e.g., Amos 5:20; Isa. 5:20; 13:3, 6, 9, 13; Ezek. 7:3, 7, 8, 19; 30:3; Hab. 3:12; Joel 2:2; Zeph. 1:15, 18; Mal. 3:2). On the traditions of the Baptist's preaching, see F. Lang, "Erwägungen zur eschatologischen Verkündigung Johannes des Täufers," in *Jesus Christus in Historie und Theologie (FS Hans Conzelmann)* (ed. Georg Strecker; Tübingen: Mohr, 1975), 459–73.

41. On the types of judgment imagery cf. Egon Brandenburger, "Gerichtskonzeptionen im Urchristentum und ihre Voraussetzungen: Eine Problemstudie," in *Studien zur Geschichte und Theologie des Urchristentums* (ed. Egon Brandenburger; SBAB NT 15; Stuttgart: Verlag Katholisches Bibelwerk, 1993), 289–338; Michael Wolter, "'Gericht' und 'Heil' bei Jesus von Nazareth und Johannes dem Täufer," in *Der historische Jesus* (ed. J. Schröter and R. Bruckner; BZNW 114; Berlin: de Gruyter, 2002), 364–69.

42. This is rightly emphasized by Wolter, "'Gericht' und 'Heil,'" 367–68: "The judge acts as savior and vice versa; to judge and to save are 'correlative' dimensions of one and the same act of God."

ancestors despite Israel's repeated failure (cf., e.g., Neh. 9; Tob. 13:1–5; *Pss. Sol.* 17.5; *LAB* 9.4; *T. Levi* 15.4). The former possibility of repeated repentance on the basis of Israel's election is no longer available! Israel had lived in the confidence that, while God might well discipline the elect people, for the sake of the covenant, God would not completely reject them. John proclaims this to be a false confidence and destroys this false hope. A new and especially provocative aspect of his message is that it blocked the appeal to Abraham and the promises made to him. The repentance John calls for is not oriented to law and temple, but takes place in baptism.[43] This was not a matter of moral improvement; rather, the expression βάπτισμα μετανοίας εἰς ἄφεσιν ἁμαρτιῶν (Mark 1:4, "baptism of repentance for the forgiveness of sins") contains an anthropological premise: the whole of Israel is, in its present state, a community destined for disaster, subject to a disastrous judgment. The repentance proclaimed by John demands that Israel acknowledge that God's coming wrath is just. John understands this confession to be the only possibility that can save Israel from the coming disaster. In the near future, God will establish his universal rule, and the response to the Baptist's message will make the difference between salvation and catastrophe when the eschaton arrives. John's baptism is the eschatological sacrament of repentance; to accept it is to accept God's requirement as a kind of seal and voucher for the coming salvation. Thus John the Baptist is not merely a forerunner of the coming judge but is at the same time the mediator of salvation, for his baptism makes it possible to stand among the saved in the coming judgment. Who the coming judge will be is no longer clear in the texts as we have them.

The Coming Mightier One

A further central element in the message of the Baptist is that he points to a mightier one who is still to come (Q 3:16b–17): "I baptize you in water; but one who is to come after me is more powerful than I, whose sandals I am not fit to take off. He will baptize you in [holy Spirit and] fire.[44] His pitchfork is in his hand, and he will clear his threshing floor and gather the wheat into his granary; but the chaff he will burn with a fire that can never be put out." Who is this mightier one who will come immediately after the Baptist and carry out the fiery judgment? Research has wavered between a messianic figure and God himself.

43. On this point cf. Helmut Merklein, "Die Umkehrpredigt bei Johannes dem Täufer und Jesus von Nazareth," in *Studien zu Jesus und Paulus* (2 vols.; WUNT 43, 105; Tübingen: Mohr, 1987–98), 1:109–26.

44. The words πνεύματι ἁγίῳ καί are most probably a Christian interpretation. In favor of this view is the contrast between water baptism and Spirit baptism that was also used to distinguish between John's baptism and Christian baptism (cf. John 1:33; Acts 19:1–7); cf. Müller, *Johannes der Täufer*, 34.

The identification of the mightier one with God can be supported by the following arguments:

1. Only God can enact a new eschatological program that transcends all the Jewish expectations preserved in extant traditions, and only God can forgive sins.
2. In Q 3:17 the possessive pronouns ("his threshing floor," "his barn") refer to God; ὁ ἰσχυρός (the Mighty One) is a frequent name for God in the LXX, and what the mightier one is to do is the traditional work of God (cf. Isa. 27:12–13; Jer. 13:24; 15:7; Mal. 3:19).
3. In Luke 1:15–16 it is said that the son of Zechariah "will be great in the sight of the Lord" and that he "will turn many of the people of Israel to the Lord their God."[45]

Over against these arguments are others, however, that point to a mediating figure to be distinguished from God:

1. The Baptist's reference to another who is "mightier" and who will have an even more effective baptism is a way of relating the two that places them both in the same category, separated in degree but not in kind.
2. The anthropomorphism "whose sandals I am not fit to take off" (Q 3:16b) or "untie the thong of his sandals" (Mark 1:7b) is not appropriate as a reference to God.
3. John's question to Jesus, "Are you the one to come?" (Q 7:19), presupposes a mediating figure whose work is carried out on earth.
4. If John intends God as the Coming One, he would not have to distinguish himself so carefully from this figure, for God is obviously "mightier." An intermediate figure to be distinguished from God could be the Son of Man (cf. Dan. 7:13–14; *1 En.* 37–41),[46] the Davidic Messiah (cf. *Pss. Sol.* 17; the Eighteen Benedictions 14), or a mediating figure without a familiar title.[47]

It is difficult to decide between these two, but it seems that the claim made by the Baptist is ultimate, leaving no place for an additional mediating figure, but refers to God himself as the one who will act in the immedi-

45. Hahn, *Theologie*, 1:50.

46. Jürgen Becker, *Jesus of Nazareth* (trans. James E. Crouch; New York: de Gruyter, 1998), 46–47, argues for the Son of Man.

47. So Theissen and Merz, *Historical Jesus*, 211: "Since the salvation announced by Jesus is depicted as superior to John the Baptist and at the same time is bound up in time and substance with his person (cf. also Matt. 11:12/Luke 16:16; Matt. 11:16–19 par.), one can assume that Jesus identified himself with the mediating figure announced by John."

ate future.[48] The Baptist proclaims a redefinition of Israel transcending election, covenant, temple, and Torah, a definition of Israel that *only* God can ratify in the final judgment. In the context of Mal. 3, John understood himself as God's authorized eschatological agent, who was the first one to baptize other people.[49] He lived in the awareness that he was already making effective, in a sacramental way, the eschatological forgiveness that only God could grant.

3.2.2 *Jesus and John the Baptist*

The connections between Jesus and the Baptist are in the areas of their respective biographies, teachings, and their lasting effects on history.

Biographical Points of Contact

The fundamental element of biographical *continuity* is the historical fact that Jesus was baptized by John the Baptist (cf. Mark 1:9–11 par.). This in itself raises the question of whether this was a punctiliar event or whether Jesus continued for some time as a member of the Baptist's movement. To begin with, it is clear that by his baptism Jesus affirmed and adopted the Baptist's perspective: God will intervene in the world's history as its judge, and will do so in the immediate future. Israel can no longer appeal to its prerogative in salvation history and has totally fallen under God's judgment. Their common message of God's impending judgment almost certainly provided the greatest element of continuity between the Baptist and Jesus;[50] both stand outside the organized groups in Israel, and both belong to the prophetic tradition. At the same time, there are clear *differences* in how they presented themselves to the public and were perceived by outsiders: Josephus obviously knows nothing of a connection between the Baptist and Jesus, and Q 7:33–34 points to striking differences: "For John came neither eating nor drinking, and you say, 'He has a demon.' The Son of Man has come eating and drinking, and you say, 'Look, a person who is a glutton and a drunkard, a chum of tax collectors and sinners!'"[51] Even with his high praise for the Baptist (cf. Q 7:25, "But then what did you go out to see? A prophet?

48. See among others, Josef Ernst, *Johannes der Täufer: Interpretation, Geschichte, Wirkungsgeschichte* (BZNW 53; Berlin: de Gruyter, 1989), 305; Stegemann, *Library of Qumran*, 216; Müller, *Johannes der Täufer*, 34.

49. Cf. Stegemann, *Library of Qumran*, 218: "Indeed, until John's appearance, neither in Judaism nor in the world around had anyone baptized other persons. True, there was a plethora of ritual purifications, including the immersion of the entire body to that effect. But each person performed these rites of purification completely independently, without the cooperation of the baptizer."

50. Cf. Becker, *Jesus of Nazareth*, 47–49.

51. For analysis, cf. Backhaus, *Jüngerkreise*, 68–83.

Yes, I tell you, even more than a prophet."), Jesus makes a clear distinction between himself and John, for "the least in the kingdom of God is greater than John" (Q 7:28; cf. Q 16:16).

The tradition points to the group around John the Baptist as the place of Jesus's own spiritual roots. Both operated in a comparable socioreligious milieu, and Jesus was perceived as a parallel figure to John (cf. Mark 6:14–16 par.; 8:28). At the same time, there is no persuasive evidence that Jesus was a member of the Baptist's group for an extended period.[52] We must rather think of Jesus as a disciple of John for only a short time.[53]

Continuity and Discontinuity in Teaching

A *resolute theocentricity* connects Jesus's message to John's: they both proclaim the God who is now breaking into history in a new and decisive manner. The announcement of imminent judgment is thus the crucial connecting bridge. For Jesus, too, the whole people of Israel has come under the catastrophic judgment of God, and appeal to the saving plan in which Israel is God's elect people will be of no avail (cf. Luke 13:1–5). However, the Baptist and Jesus project God's imminent decisive act in different ways. For John, baptism is the eschatological sacrament of repentance and delivers from the coming catastrophe; thus John's message too must have been to some extent a message of salvation. Jesus places the accents differently; he does not baptize, and he separates the call to repentance from the act of baptism. He gives the Baptist's basic conviction a different importance, for in the message of Jesus the central focus is not judgment, but salvation. Jesus shares with John an acute expectation of the imminence of God's final saving act but sees the priority of God's saving act in relation to his own person, as the kingdom of God erupts in Jesus's own ministry. This means that for Jesus a present eschatology steps in alongside futuristic eschatology (see §3.4.2). The Baptist expected the "mightier one," i.e., God himself. In contrast, Jesus spoke of the future coming of the Son of Man, with whom he identified himself and whom he already represented on earth (see below, §3.9.2). While the Baptist graphically represented the ascetic life and performed his ministry in the wilderness, Jesus conducted an itinerant ministry in the populated areas of Galilee and also made his way to Jerusalem. It is also striking that Jesus turned to marginalized groups in a special way, and that he was especially remembered as a teller of parables and worker of miracles.

52. This is specifically emphasized by Backhaus, ibid., 110–12.

53. Cf. John P. Meier, *A Marginal Jew: Rethinking the Historical Jesus, Vol 2: Mentor, Message, and Miracles* (ABRL 2; New York: Doubleday, 1994), 129. I share the opinion of many others that the story of the Baptist's question in Q 7:18–19 is a post-Easter construction; for evidence and argument, see Backhaus, *Jüngerkreise*, 116–26.

Points of Contact in Their Historical Effects

During his lifetime John the Baptist had already gathered a group of disciples around himself, distinguished by particular practices of fasting and their own set prayer (cf. Mark 2:18 par., "The disciples of John and the disciples of the Pharisees were fasting"; Luke 5:33; 11:1). After Easter a competition emerged between John's disciples and the new Christian community that was in the process of formation, and there was some exchange of membership between the two groups (cf. John 1:35–51; 3:22; 4:1). There were some similarities between them, and their contemporaries regarded them as comparable movements. From the Christian perspective, the Baptist who had been a completely independent figure now became the "forerunner" who "prepared the way" for Jesus (cf. Mark 1:2 par.). The author of the Fourth Gospel finally completely annulled John's independence and made him into a mere witness to Jesus as God's Son (John 1:23, 27–34, 36; 3:27–30). Christians recognized in Jesus the crucified and risen Messiah, the Messiah promised by John, and took over his baptismal practice. At the same time, they distinguished their own baptism from that of John by their experience of the Spirit; while John baptized with only water, they baptized with water and Spirit (cf. Mark 1:8 par.; Acts 19:1–7). Even so, the Baptist's movement existed over an extended period and beyond the region of Palestine and Syria, as indicated by Acts 18:24–19:7.

Jesus's Independence

What was the basis of Jesus's independence over against his teacher? What happened to bring him to the conviction that God's ultimate intervention in history had already begun—not in the inbreaking of catastrophic judgment, but in a new and saving way? It was probably a visionary experience of Jesus that led to the insight that God is already present in acts of salvation (see below, §3.3.2 and §3.4). An echo of this vision is probably found in Luke 10:18: "I watched Satan fall from heaven like a flash of lightning."[54] The mythical power of evil has already been conquered; in the real world, Satan has already been removed from the center of things. Jesus thus appears on the scene as a charismatic miracle worker with a message of salvation for the poor and marginalized. The miracles that are already being performed by God and by Jesus himself convinced him that the time of salvation had already begun, that Satan had already been conquered, and that he himself had been chosen as the decisive figure in the eschatological drama.

54. The defeat of Satan is a sign that the final era of salvation is already breaking in; cf. *As. Mos.* 10.1. On the exegesis of Luke 10:18, see below, §3.6.2. The compositional series in Q, Mark, Matthew, and Luke (advent of the Baptist, baptism of Jesus, temptation) confirms a connection between Jesus's association with the Baptist, the recognition that the power of Satan had been broken, and the public appearance of Jesus.

3.3 Point of Departure: The Coming of the One God in His Kingly Power

For Jesus of Nazareth, all of life and the whole of reality is an act of God. *A fundamentally theocentric perspective permeates his view of the world as such.* In this worldview, God appears neither as the transcendent Other nor as the domesticated cultic deity but is new and surprising, powerfully and immediately present. *This experience of a new nearness of God and the formulation of a new image of God* are the elements that characterize Jesus's own symbolic universe.

3.3.1 The One God in the Preaching of Jesus

The uniqueness of the one God constitutes the foundation of Jesus's thinking and preaching. Israel's confession of Yahweh as the one and only God (cf. Deut. 6:4; Exod. 34:13; Hos. 13:4) became in Deutero-Isaiah the fundamental theological concept.[55] Yahweh, the "King of Israel," goes to court with the gods of the nations and proves they are nothing (cf., e.g., Isa. 41:21–29; 43:10). Positively, Yahweh shows his uniqueness in his total and exclusive responsibility for creation, history, and salvation. As the address to Cyrus summarizes:

> I am the LORD, and there is no other;
> besides me there is no god.
> I arm you, though you do not know me,
> so that they may know, from the rising of the sun
> and from the west, that there is no one besides me;
> I am the LORD, and there is no other.
> I form light and create darkness,
> I make weal and create woe;
> I the LORD do all these things. (Isa. 45:5–7)

Since Yahweh is the only God, it is his kingly power alone that is revealed in the deliverance of his people.

> I, I am the Lord, and besides me there is no savior . . .
> I alone am God, and so will I be in the future. (Isa. 43:11–13, author's translation)

Even in his own time, Deutero-Isaiah could announce the near advent of salvation with the cry, "Your God reigns" (Isa. 52:7). As the prophetic-apocalyptic tradition developed further, the motif of the oneness and uniqueness of God

55. Cf. Matthias Albani, *Der eine Gott und die himmlischen Heerscharen: Zur Begründung des Monotheismus bei Deuterojesaja im Horizont der Astralisierung des Gottesverständnisses im Alten Orient* (ABG 1; Leipzig: Evangelische Verlagsanstalt, 2000).

was always presupposed. The material connection between the kingdom of God and God's uniqueness is succinctly formulated in Zech. 14:9: "And the LORD will become king over all the earth; on that day the LORD will be one and his name one." God's uniqueness and his lordship over Israel belong directly together; God proves himself to be the only God by establishing his exclusive rule, and his name alone will be praised.

The One God in the Jesus Tradition

The uniqueness of God appears explicitly in the Jesus tradition in only four places: in the story of the healing of the lame man (Mark 2:1–12); in the question about the greatest commandment (Mark 12:28–34); in the pericope about the rich young man (Mark 10:17–27); and in Matt. 23:9, where Jesus says, "And call no one your father on earth, for you have one Father—the one in heaven."[56] In its present form, Mark 2:1–12 is a formation of the pre-Markan church, but in its substance it correctly preserves Jesus's claim to have the authority to forgive sins (Mark 2:5b). He takes the place reserved for God (cf. Mark 2:7, "Why does this fellow speak in this way? It is blasphemy! Who can forgive sins except the one God?" [author's trans.]), and acts on the basis of his unique God-consciousness.[57] So also, combining the love of God with the love of neighbor (taking up Deut. 6:5 and Lev. 19:18) goes back to Jesus (see below, §3.5.3). To be sure, there are already indications of this linkage in the Jewish tradition, but it does not explicitly occur. Jesus's whole message and ministry are permeated by this combination of love for God and neighbor. The fundamental significance of the uniqueness of God for Jesus's preaching is also manifest in contexts that do not speak explicitly of the "one God." In the Lord's Prayer, when Jesus prays "Hallowed be your name, your kingdom come" (Luke 11:2), it is clear that the hallowing of God's name aims ultimately at the acknowledgment of God as the only God, and thus that the coming of God's kingdom means the establishing of this God's will as all-pervasive. *With the promise and announcement of the coming rule of God, Jesus proclaims the eschatological revelation of God as the one and only God. In Jesus's preaching, the image of God's kingdom rests on the idea of God's uniqueness.* This relationship is probably the reason that Jesus made the concept of the kingdom of God the center of his message in a way that is without analogy elsewhere, and that all the other soteriological imagery is subsumed under this concept.[58]

56. In their parenetic orientation and arrangement, Mark 10:18 and Matt. 23:9 cannot be claimed directly for Jesus; for evidence and argument, see Helmut Merklein, "Die Einzigkeit Gottes als die sachliche Grundlage der Botschaft Jesu," in *Studien zu Jesus und Paulus* (2 vols.; WUNT 43, 105; Tübingen: Mohr, 1987–98), 2:155.

57. For analysis, cf. Otfried Hofius, "Jesu Zuspruch der Sündenvergebung," in *Neutestamentliche Studien* (ed. Otfried Hofius; WUNT 132; Tübingen: Mohr, 2000), 38–56.

58. Cf. Merklein, "Einzigkeit," 155–60.

Jesus's "Father/Abba" Language

Jesus's terminology for God is striking in that he addresses and describes God as "Father." This way of addressing God is not absolutely new, for it was already present both in Greco-Roman culture[59] and in Judaism.[60] To be sure, the frequency of the word πατήρ (father) in Jesus's mouth is noteworthy; it occurs about 170 times in the four gospels. Even though a large number of these cannot be attributed to the historical Jesus, this visible history of Jesus's historical impact shows that "Father" was Jesus's typical designation for God. The specific form of Jesus's address to God as Father, אַבָּא, was regarded in early Christian tradition as so characteristic that even in Greek texts the Aramaic word was not translated but transliterated as ἀββά (cf. Gal. 4:6, "And because you are children, God has sent the Spirit of his Son into our hearts, crying, 'Abba! Father!'"; Rom. 8:15, "For you did not receive a spirit of slavery to fall back into fear, but you have received a spirit of adoption. When we cry, 'Abba! Father!'"; and Mark 14:36, citing Jesus's prayer in Gethsemane, "Abba, Father, for you all things are possible; remove this cup from me; yet, not what I want, but what you want"). "Abba" is not without analogy as an address to God,[61] neither can the use of this word be made the basis for claiming a special consciousness of sonship for Jesus.[62] Jesus operated within the linguistic possibilities of the Judaism of his day, where it is precisely the simplicity of this address, not its exclusivity, that expressed Jesus's own nearness to God, a nearness in which he wanted to include his hearers. He does not reveal a new essence of God, or a new, previously hidden feature of God's character. Rather, the simplicity and openness of Jesus's way of addressing God presupposes a new, different way in which God deals with human beings. Jesus does not address Israel as a collective condemned *in toto* by God's judgment; his address tears Israel out of its past history of guilt and condemnation and speaks of God's eschatological salvation. Because this electing and regenerating act of God is already at work in the ministry of Jesus, those who place their trust in this act are already, in the here and now, in a direct relation to God that transcends temple, sacrifice, and central contents of the Torah, and of course such believers may speak

59. Zeus was frequently addressed as "Father"; cf., e.g., Homer, *Iliad* 34.308; Hesiod, *Theog.* 47–49; Dio Chrysostom, *Or.* 1.39–40; 2.75; 12.74–75 (Zeus as Father, King, Guardian and Savior of all people); 36.31, 35, 36.

60. Cf., e.g., Deut. 32:6; Isa. 63:16; 64:7; Jer. 3:4; Sir. 23:1, 4; 51:10; Wis. 14:3; 3 Macc. 5:7; 6:3, 8; 7:6.

61. On the linguistic analysis of אַבָּא, cf. G. Schelbert, "Abba, Vater!" *FZPT* 40 (1993); 41 (1994): אַבָּא is equivalent to the normal term "father," formed in analogy to אִמָּא, "mother." On the use of πατήρ in Jewish prayers, cf. Wis. 6:3, 8; 14:3; Sir. 23:1a, 4a LXX.

62. Contra Jeremias, *New Testament Theology,* 1:67: "The complete novelty and uniqueness of *'Abba* as an address to God in the prayers of Jesus shows that it expresses the heart of Jesus's relation to God. He spoke to God as a child to its father: confidently and securely, and yet at the same time reverently and obediently."

of and to God as "Abba" just as does Jesus himself. Jesus does not proclaim a new God, but rather the God of Israel reveals himself in a new way in the eschatological event of the kingdom of God proclaimed by Jesus.

In the *Lord's Prayer* the address to God as "Father/Abba" is directly linked with the petition for the sanctifying of the name and the coming of the Father's kingdom (Luke 11:2 par.). God's creative new work is to prevail and attain its goal, so that all confess the name of the one Father and thus acknowledge him as Lord and King. The we-petitions (Luke 11:3–4) are also expressed within this eschatological perspective, applying the divine action for which the first two petitions pray to the daily lives of those who pray. The prayer for the forgiveness of sins/debts (Luke 11:4a; cf. Matt. 6:14; Mark 11:25) underscores the human involvement in the present world, the electing act of God that takes away guilt, made real to those who are thus themselves ready to forgive others. The concluding petition (Luke 11:4b: "And do not bring us to the time of trial") expresses the awareness of those who pray this prayer that they cannot maintain this new relation to God out of their own resources, but only if God protects them through every trial and guards them in the time of testing. So also the petition for bread (Luke 11:3 par.) is thoroughly permeated with eschatology, for those who pray ask only for the bread necessary for today, i.e., they live in expectation of a future that extends beyond the provision of earthly supplies. The preceding petitions pray for the eschatological future. Worry about tomorrow is unnecessary, not only because the kingdom of God that may come tomorrow could show that today's worries were rash, but because the coming of the kingdom of God gives the certainty that the Father will provide what is necessary for every day until he has brought this coming to its fulfillment. Thus in Q the group of sayings leads from prayer (Q 11:9–13) and carefree trust (Luke 12:22b–31/Matt. 6:25–33) to the assurance that "your Father knows that you need [all] these things" (Luke 12:30 par.), and concludes with the admonition, "Rather, seek his [the Father's] kingdom, and [all] these things will be given to you as well" (Luke 12:31 par.). The recourse to motifs from the wisdom tradition that affirm the reality of this world as God's creation and illustrate the Father's care for this world shows that Jesus sees the everyday world in a new eschatological light (cf. "the birds of the air" and the "lilies [of the field]" in Luke 12:24, 27–28/Matt. 6:26, 28–30; also Luke 12:6–8/Matt. 10:29–31). The electing act of God gives Jesus the certainty that his Father knows what is necessary for life, and provides it (Luke 12:30b par.; cf. also Matt. 6:8). Jesus's eschatology is the proper framework within which to locate his Father-language for God, so that his theocentric message is structured eschatologically. The eschatological perspective shapes Jesus's picture of God, so that in Jesus's teaching one can speak of a coinciding of "upward look"(*Aufblick*) and "forward look" (*Ausblick*), of theology and eschatology,[63] of a mutual interpenetration of the upward look to the Father and the forward look to the coming of the kingdom. Jesus proclaims the one God as the Father who is acting eschatologically, whose lordship is already experienced in the present.

3.3.2 The New Image of God

Jesus introduced a new image of God, but it was by no means un-Jewish. To be sure, it stood in some tension with the prevalent images of God in Judaism, for Jesus (like the Baptist) disregarded central elements of the imagery for God in the Judaism of his time and gave a new evaluation to other traditions. In the first place, it is striking what Jesus does *not* appeal to:[64] he hardly uses the covenant concept, central for the Judaism of his time,[65] just as he makes only minimal appeal to the history of Israel, including the traditions of the exodus and conquest. It is striking that the patriarchal and Zion traditions appear in the context of the relation of Israel to the Gentiles and are decisively modified in the process (see below, §3.8.3). Although Jesus knows that he is sent to Israel, he does not adopt the common antithesis Israel/Gentiles and can point to Gentiles as models of faith (cf. Q 7:1–10). So also the religiously important distinction between "clean" and "unclean" is no longer valid for him (cf. Mark 7:15). His action in the temple (cf. Mark 11:15–18 par.) represents a sharp criticism of the prevailing temple cultus, which culminates in a fatal conflict with the Jewish and Roman authorities (see below, §3.10.1). For him, the temple belongs to the category of what will be destroyed (cf. Mark 14:58). So also the Torah, which had played such a dominant role in Jewish life since the middle of the second century BCE, is not at the center of Jesus's own message, but rather the kingdom of God, believed to be near and already experienced (see below, §3.4). Q 16:16 makes a clear distinction between the time of the law and prophets and the time of the kingdom of God, so that Jesus's new evaluation of the Torah is grounded in his eschatological perspective. The Torah is not abandoned or abolished but placed in a new theocentric-eschatological perspective:

> In the horizon of his proclamation of the kingdom, in which God's future is already becoming visible as life-giving, saving event (Matt. 11:5–6/Luke 7:22–23),

63. Heinz Schürmann, "Das 'eigentümlich Jesuanische' im Gebet Jesu: Jesu Beten als Schlüssel für das Verständnis seiner Verkündigung," in *Jesus, Gestalt und Geheimnis: Gesammelte Beiträge* (ed. Heinz Schürmann and Klaus Scholtissek; Paderborn: Bonifatius, 1994), 47.

64. Jürgen Becker, "Das Gottesbild Jesu," in *Jesus Christus in Historie und Theologie (FS Hans Conzelmann)* (ed. Georg Strecker; Tübingen: Mohr, 1975), 109–10.

65. Erich Grässer, "Jesus und das Heil Gottes," in *Der Alte Bund im Neuen: Exegetische Studien zur Israelfrage im Neuen Testament* (ed. Erich Grässer; WUNT 35; Tübingen: Mohr, 1985), 194–98.

> the instructions of the Torah and their exposition must be evaluated by the criterion: to what extent do they correspond to the kingdom of God as proclaimed and lived out by Jesus, i.e., to what extent do they correspond to the will of God expressed in the love command (Mark 12:28–34 par.; Matt. 5:43–48 par.; 9:13; 12:7; 23:23; cf. 7:12).[66]

It is no longer the past that dominates, but the experience of the present and the preview of God's future. This experience reveals a God who seeks the lost (Luke 15:1–10, 11–32) and turns toward humanity in mercy (cf. Matt. 18:23–27); a God whose will it is to save the sick and not the healthy, to grant forgiveness to sinners, and to bring the poor and oppressed to salvation. The image of the kind and forgiving God is also found in the Jewish tradition,[67] but Jesus places it at the center of his message in a new way, shaped by his eschatological perspective.

3.4 Center: The Proclamation of the Kingdom of God

Religious language always has a symbolic dimension, because God's reality is never directly accessible for human beings. Symbols point beyond themselves, open up new worlds of meaning,[68] mediate another reality within our own

66. Dieter Sänger, "Schriftauslegung im Horizont der Gottesherrschaft," in *Christlicher Glaube und religiöse Bildung: Frau Prof. Dr. Friedel Kriechbaum zum 60. Geburtstag am 13. August 1995* (ed. Hermann Deuser and Gerhard Schmalenberg; GSTR 11; Giessen: Selbstverlag des Fachbereichs Evangelische Theologie und Katholische Theologie und deren Didaktik, 1995), 107.

67. For the Greek tradition, cf. Plutarch, *Mor.* 1075E, which affirms the Stoics' critique of the Epicureans: "For they say that god is preconceived and conceived to be not only immortal and blessed but also humane and protective and beneficent [οὐ γὰρ ἀθάνατον καὶ μακάριον μόνον ἀλλὰ καὶ φιλάνθρωπον κηδεμονικὸν καὶ ὠφέλιμον]. This is true."

68. For comprehensive discussions of symbols, cf. Paul Ricoeur, *The Symbolism of Evil* (Boston: Beacon Press, 1967); Gerhard Kurz, *Metapher, Allegorie, Symbol* (4th ed.; Göttingen: Vandenhoeck & Ruprecht, 1997); Bernard Brandon Scott, *Jesus, Symbol-Maker for the Kingdom* (Philadelphia: Fortress, 1981); Michael Meyer-Blanck, *Vom Symbol zum Zeichen: Symboldidaktik und Semiotik* (2nd ed.; Rheinbach: CMZ-Verlag, 2002); Philip Ellis Wheelwright, *The Burning Fountain: A Study in the Language of Symbolism* (2nd ed.; Bloomington: Indiana University Press, 1968). Symbols (Greek σύμβολον: sign, pictorial meaning; συμβάλλω: throw together, connect, compare) always have a referential aspect and a bridge function, so they are always in need of interpretation and open to a metaphorical exposition. Metaphorical language (Greek μεταφορά, something carried over from one realm to another) is "a stylistic figure, in which, by means of a linguistic picture, i.e., in a transferred sense, reference is made to a subject or object" (so P. Löser, "Metapher," *RGG*[4] 5:1165), i.e., the intentional expression of similarity by means of dissimilarity. Metaphor, like symbol, accomplishes a transfer of meaning from one realm to another. Its pictorial nature makes it necessary to derive the meaning from the respective contexts in which it may be used. Metaphorical language always involves a creative element; something new is created or opened up, a new connection is made, a new order established. In the open-ended polyvalence of pictorial language, symbol and metaphor/metaphorical language are difficult

world of reality. They not only depict this new reality, but make it present in such a way that it can become an effective force within our world. They represent both the divine and human worlds and participate in both at the same time.[69] Symbols must be so chosen that, on the one hand, they are communicable to their hearers/readers, and, on the other hand, they represent what they symbolize in an appropriate way. *For Jesus of Nazareth, the central religious symbol is the kingdom/rule of God; he proclaims the coming of the one God in his royal power.*

3.4.1 History-of-Religions Presuppositions

As linguistic signs, symbols are always interwoven into the comprehensive network of elements that constitute a particular culture, especially its language. In the case of "kingdom/rule of God," this is the concept of God as king found in the Old Testament,[70] ancient Judaism,[71] and Hellenism.[72] Included in this broad semantic field (God as king and verbal expressions of ruling) are related associations (e.g., God as Lord and Judge), royal attributes and insignia (e.g., palace, throne, the royal court, glory and splendor), royal metaphors (e.g.,

---

to distinguish. Metaphor is above all else a linguistic form, while a symbol can take a concrete object and fill it with new meaning. "With metaphors, our attention is directed more to words, to the semantic compatibility and incompatibility of linguistic elements. With symbols, our attention is directed to empirical realities"(Kurz, *Metapher, Allegorie, Symbol*, 73). Metaphors must be spoken or read and are oriented to the present; symbols, in contrast, connect past and future, and have a consequential aspect.

69. Cf. Paul Tillich, *Systematic Theology*, vol. 1, *Reason and Revelation: Being and God* (Chicago: University of Chicago Press, 1951), 242: "We must speak of God as living in symbolic terms. Yet every true symbol participates in the reality which it symbolizes."

70. Cf. Werner H. Schmidt, *Königtum Gottes in Ugarit und Israel* (2nd rev. ed.; Berlin: Töpelmann, 1966); Jörg Jeremias, *Das Königtum Gottes in den Psalmen: Israels Begegnung mit dem kanaanäischen Mythos in den Jahwe-König-Psalmen* (FRLANT 141; Göttingen: Vandenhoeck & Ruprecht, 1987); Hermann Spieckermann, "Rechtfertigung," *TRE* 28:282–86; Stefan Schreiber, *Gesalbter und König: Titel und Konzeptionen der königlichen Gesalbtenerwartung in frühjüdischen und urchristlichen Schriften* (BZNW 105; Berlin: de Gruyter, 2000), 41–142 (God as king in the Old Testament and ancient Judaism).

71. Cf. here the volume of collected essays by Martin Hengel and Anna Maria Schwemer, eds., *Königsherrschaft Gottes und himmlischer Kult: Im Judentum, Urchristentum und in der hellenistischen Welt* (WUNT 55; Tübingen: Mohr, 1991).

72. Royal metaphors, combining the motifs in various ways, were widespread in the whole Hellenistic world. In his reflections of what constitutes true rulership, Dio Chrysostom, *Or.* 1.39–40, says: "For Zeus alone of the gods has the epithets of 'Father' and 'King' [πατὴρ καὶ βασιλεύς], 'Protector of Cities,' 'Lord of Friends and Comrades,' 'Guardian of the Race,' and also 'Protector of Suppliants,' 'God of Refuge,' and 'God of Hospitality,' these and his countless other titles signifying goodness and the fount of goodness. He is called 'King' because of his lordship and power [βασιλεὺς μὲν κατὰ τὴν ἀρχὴν καὶ τὴν δύναμιν ὠνομασμένος], 'Father' presumably because of his care and leniency [πατὴρ δὲ οἶμαι διά τε τὴν κηδεμονίαν καὶ τὸ πρᾷον]"; cf. further Dio Chrysostom, *Or.* 2.73–78; Epictetus, *Diatr.* 3.22.63. Basic to this whole complex of ideas is the view that the divine rulership of the cosmos is to be regarded as a model for rulership on earth.

the king as shepherd), and typical royal duties (preserve the peace, destroy the enemies). The point of departure for this imagery is the ancient world's direct experience of the unlimited authority and power of kings, whose enormous power made them readily available as symbols for God.

Religious Dimensions

Yahweh, enthroned in the temple or on Mt. Zion, is king over all the nations (cf. Isa. 6:1ff.; Ps. 47:9; 99:1–2, "The Lord is king; let the peoples tremble! He sits enthroned upon the cherubim; let the earth quake! The Lord is great in Zion; he is exalted over all the peoples"; Ps. 46–48, 84, 87, 96–99).[73] After the exile, the traditions associated with the reign of God were reinterpreted in an eschatological perspective, which clearly begins in Deutero-Isaiah. The King of Israel will turn to his people in a new way (cf. Isa. 41:21; 43:15; 44:6). He rules the nations and steers the course of history through their kings (cf. Isa. 41:2–3; 43:14–15; 44:6), reigning over history and creation (40:3–4, 41:4; 43:3). There thus emerges an unavoidable tension between the present and the hoped-for kingdom of God that also characterizes the preaching of Jesus. The futuristic element dominates in apocalyptic, where God will conquer his enemies in an eschatological battle. The idea of a final battle between two power blocs is found in numerous variations, in which especially Beliar/Belial emerges as God's ultimate enemy.

> He will make war against Beliar; he will grant the vengeance of victory as our goal. And he shall take from Beliar the captives, the souls of the saints; [11]and he shall turn the hearts of the disobedient ones to the Lord, and grant eternal peace to those who call upon him. [12]And the saints shall refresh themselves in Eden; the righteous shall rejoice in the New Jerusalem, which shall be eternally for the glorification of God. [13]And Jerusalem shall no longer undergo desolation, nor shall Israel be led into captivity, because the Lord will be in her midst [living among human beings]. The Holy One of Israel will rule over them in humility and poverty, and he who trusts in him shall reign in truth in the heavens. (*T. Dan* 5.10b–13; cf. Joel 3; Zeph. 3:15; Zech. 14:9; Isa. 24:21–23; Dan. 2:24–45; 2 Macc. 1:1–7; 1QM; *Sib. Or.* 1.65–86; 3.46–62, 716–723, 767–784)

Noteworthy is *Pss. Sol.* 17 (ca. 50 BCE), where the God of Israel is King forever (*Pss. Sol.* 17.1, 3, 46), while at the same time the expected Messiah appears as the representative of God's kingdom (*Pss. Sol.* 17.32, 34). As the ruler of Jerusalem and the land of Israel, he will purify the country of Gentiles (*Pss. Sol.* 17.21, 22, 28, 30), gather the scattered holy people (*Pss. Sol.* 17.26), and the Gentile nations will become forced labor for Israel and bring them tribute (*Pss. Sol.* 17.30–31). Here, as in numerous other texts (e.g., Dan. 2:44; 7:9–25; Obad. 15–21), God's rule over Israel is thought of in contrast to Gentile rule.

73. Becker, *Jesus of Nazareth*, 88–93, emphasizes the Zion motif.

According to the *Assumption of Moses*, which comes from around the beginning of the first century CE, at the eschaton God will inaugurate his kingship over the whole creation, "Then the devil will have an end" (*As. Mos.* 10.1), and "the Most High God will surge forth, the Eternal One alone. In full view will he come to work vengeance on the nations. Yea, all their idols he will destroy" (*As. Mos.* 10.7). In liturgical texts such as the Sabbath hymns from Qumran, a present perspective is predominant.[74] These hymns to God as the eternal heavenly king concentrate their descriptive praise on the heavenly, unlimited rule of God. The earthly cult participates in the heavenly worship by describing the heavenly liturgy in a way that is itself praise, and thus mostly leaves creation and history behind.[75] A further instructive example is the prayer of supplication in *1 En.* 84.2–6:

> Blessed are you, O Great King,
> you are mighty in all your greatness,
> O Lord of all the creation of heaven,
> King of kings and God of the whole world.
> Your authority and kingdom abide forever and ever; and your
>   dominion throughout all the generations of generations;
> all the heavens are your throne forever,
> and the whole earth is your footstool forever and ever and ever.
> For you have created (all), and all things you rule,
> And nothing is too hard for you.

Also, basic proto-rabbinic texts of Jewish faith show that the prayer for the coming and the presence of God's kingdom was a core element of Jewish hope at the time of Jesus. Thus the eleventh of the Eighteen Benedictions:

> Restore our judges as at the first,
> And our counselors as at the beginning;
> Remove from us grief and suffering;
> Reign thou over us, O Lord,
> Thou alone, in lovingkindness and tender mercy,
> And justify us in judgment.

74. Cf. Anna Maria Schwemer, "Gott als König und seine Königsherrschaft in den Sabbatliedern aus Qumran," in *Königsherrschaft Gottes und himmlischer Kult: Im Judentum, Urchristentum und in der hellenistischen Welt* (ed. Martin Hengel and Anna Maria Schwemer; WUNT 55; Tübingen: Mohr, 1991), 45–118.

75. Cf. 4Q401 14i: "wonderfully to praise Your glory [among the wise divine beings, extolling] Your kingdom among the utterly holy. They are honored in all the camps of the godlike beings and fe[ared by those who dir]ect human affairs, wondrous" (*Qumran Sectarian Manuscripts: A New English Translation* [Accordance Bible Software, 2008], CD-ROM, based on the book Michael O. Wise, Martin G. Abegg Jr., and Edward M. Cook, eds., *The Dead Sea Scrolls: A New English Translation* [New York: HarperCollins, 1996]).

> Blessed art thou, O Lord, the King who lovest righteousness
> and judgment.[76]

So also the traditional Qaddish Prayer:

> . . . and may He establish His kingdom . . . in your lifetime and your days and in the lifetimes of all the house of Israel, speedily and soon.[77]

Political Dimensions

Jesus made his proclamation of the kingdom of God in the context of *political kingdoms* that already existed. Jesus lived and conducted his ministry primarily in the minor kingdom of Herod Antipas (4 BCE–39 CE), who ruled over Galilee and Perea.[78] Like his father Herod the Great before him, Herod Antipas was a Hellenistic ruler, oriented to Rome, who at the same time emphasized his Jewish identity. He also followed his father's example in expressing his cultural convictions and claims to political power above all in great building projects in which urbanization was combined with Romanization and a commercialization of the rustic rural population.[79] He rebuilt Sepphoris and in 19 CE founded Tiberias as the new capital of Galilee (named after the emperor Tiberius), which was built entirely on the Hellenistic model.[80] The marriage of Herod Antipas to Herodias, who had previously been married to one of his half brothers, was denounced by John the Baptist (cf. Luke 3:19–20; Mark 6:14–29). This political-cultural criticism resulted in John's death (see above, §3.2.1). Apparently Herod Antipas was fearful of the kind of messianic movements led by both John and Jesus (cf. Luke 13:31–32). Such movements were not unusual in Palestine in the first part of the first century CE,[81] so that Herod Antipas possibly saw them as

76. The text given here is the presumed early text, based on the reconstruction of Gustaf Dalman, *The Words of Jesus: Considered in the Light of Post-biblical Jewish Writings and the Aramaic Language* (trans. David Miller Kay; Edinburgh: T&T Clark, 1909), 98.

77. Cited from *The Standard Prayer Book* (trans. Simeon Singer; New York: Bloch, 1915).

78. Cf. Peter Schäfer, *The History of the Jews in the Greco-Roman World* (New York: Routledge, 2003), 101–12.

79. Cf. Jonathan L. Reed, *Archaeology and the Galilean Jesus: A Re-examination of the Evidence* (Harrisburg, PA: Trinity, 2000); Crossan and Reed, *Excavating Jesus*.

80. For a survey, see S. Fortner, "Tiberias—Eine Stadt zu Ehren des Kaisers," in *Leben am See Gennesaret: Kulturgeschichtliche Entdeckungen in einer biblischen Region* (ed. Gabriele Fassbeck; ZBA; Munich: Von Zabern, 2002).

81. Still worthy of study is Rudolf Meyer, *Der Prophet aus Galiläa: Studie zum Jesusbild der drei ersten Evangelien* (Darmstadt: Wissenschaftliche Buchgesellschaft, 1970); cf. further Richard A. Horsley and John S. Hanson, *Bandits, Prophets, and Messiahs: Popular Movements in the Time of Jesus* (Minneapolis: Winston, 1985); Crossan and Reed, *Excavating Jesus*, 136–81 (forms of active and passive resistance against the Romans); a comprehensive study is available in Christoph Riedo-Emmenegger, *Prophetisch-messianische Provokateure der Pax Romana: Jesus von Nazaret und andere Störenfriede im Konflikt mit dem Römischen Reich* (NTOA 56;

endangering his own rule. Galilee as a whole was pervaded by deep structural tensions[82]—Jews and Gentiles, urban and rural, rich and poor, rulers and ruled.[83] When, in this context, Jesus announced the great turn of the ages, he addressed hearers who already had a deep longing for this new reign of God, a kingdom of God that had nothing to do with the attributes of imperial power and great building projects, and did not function by oppression and political and cultural corruption. The kingdom proclaimed by Jesus was still hidden in the present, but already made the claim to triumph over everything at the End. Jesus's claim to authority and his message of the present and coming kingdom of God could not long remain apolitical, even though it was not fundamentally conceived in political terms.[84]

Göttingen: Vandenhoeck & Ruprecht, 2005), 245–75. Josephus, *Ant.* 17.271–272, reports that in the period following the death of Herod the Great, "Then there was Judas, the son of the brigand chief Ezekias, who had been a man of great power and had been captured by Herod only with great difficulty. This Judas got together a large number of desperate men at Sepphoris in Galilee and there made an assault on the royal palace, and having seized all the arms that were stored there, he armed every single one of his men and made off with all the property that had been seized there. He became an object of terror to all men by plundering those he came across in his desire for great possessions and his ambition for royal rank [ζηλώσει βασιλείου], a prize that he expected to obtain not through the practice of virtue but through excessive ill-treatment of others." See additional texts below at §3.6.1.

82. Cf. here Gerd Theissen, *Die Jesusbewegung: Sozialgeschichte einer Revolution der Werte* (Gütersloh: Gütersloher Verlagshaus, 2004), 131–241; Richard A. Horsley, *Archaeology, History, and Society in Galilee: The Social Context of Jesus and the Rabbis* (Valley Forge, PA: Trinity, 1996).

83. A nice example is found in Josephus, *Life*, 374–384, which reports the conflicts between the rural population and the residents of Sepphoris and Tiberias, who favored good relations with Rome. The rural population wanted to destroy both cities and their inhabitants: "For they had the same detestation for the Tiberians as for the inhabitants of Sepphoris."

84. Differently Richard A. Horsley, *Jesus and Empire: The Kingdom of God and the New World Disorder* (Minneapolis: Fortress, 2003), 98, who speaks explicitly of "Jesus's prophetic condemnation of Roman imperial rule," appealing to such texts as Mark 12:17; 1:24; 3:22–27; 5:1–20. Horsley infers from the "political revolution" a "social revolution": "In the confidence that the Roman imperial order stood under the judgment of God's imminent kingdom, Jesus launched a mission of social renewal among the subject peoples" (p. 105). But the Jesus tradition as a whole provides no basis for the obviously wished-for thesis that Jesus carried on a battle against Roman (and thus also American) imperialism. Cf. the balanced reflections of Seán Freyne, *Jesus, a Jewish Galilean: A New Reading of the Jesus-Story* (London: T&T Clark, 2004), 136–49, who describes the social tensions in Galilee (especially those resulting from the economic conditions resulting from the newly founded cities), but without making them the key to his interpretation. Cf. also Riedo-Emmenegger, *Prophetisch-messianische Provokateure*, 305–6, who rightly points out that neither John the Baptist nor Jesus worked for a change in the external political situation, and that it is only this presupposition that can explain why the Romans left their respective disciples unmolested—differently than in the case of the other messianic prophets. The effects of Jesus's ministry were by no means apolitical, but the category of political activist, today much in demand, is not an appropriate means of grasping Jesus's intentions and his own claim to authority, i.e., it is neither historically nor hermeneutically adequate.

Dissociation

When Jesus chose "kingdom/reign of God" as the key term that summarized his message,[85] his choice was embedded in an extensive and varied cluster of motifs already present in the Judaism of his time. This observation is of great theological and hermeneutical significance. On the other hand, it is important to be clear that in no other theological structure did "kingdom/reign of God" play such a key role. Jesus takes up the widespread and encyclopedic concept of the kingdom of God, but at the same time adapts it to his own message by his singular concentration[86] on the abstraction מַלְכוּת/βασιλεία and by his addition of new elements to the image of God as king and ruler.[87] Moreover, Jesus *dissociates* his own message from the contemporary broad spectrum of associations in that he does not speak directly of God as king but concentrates on a very definite image expressed in a single key phrase. This distancing is the generative presupposition for a partial redefinition of God's essential nature expressed in Jesus's message.

3.4.2 Temporal Perspectives

Like all Jews, Jesus believed in a God who acts in history. Like John the Baptist in particular, he lived in an intensive expectation of the near advent of the kingdom of God, which he understood as a historical-cosmic reality and portrayed within space-time structure in a variety of ways. Jesus's relation to John the Baptist provides the initial pointers to Jesus's own temporal understanding of the kingdom of God.

John the Baptist and the Kingdom of God

Jesus himself made a direct connection between John the Baptist and the kingdom of God.[88] From Q 16:16 ("The law and the prophets were until John came. From then on the good news of the kingdom of God is violated, and the

85. Takashi Onuki, *Jesus: Geschichte und Gegenwart* (BTS 82; Neukirchen-Vluyn: Neukirchener Verlag, 2006), 44ff., places Jesus's talk of the kingdom of God in a comprehensive mythological network of imagery that formed the framework of Jesus's life and thought. Cf. also Keck, *Who Is Jesus*, 65–114.

86. Odo Camponovo, *Königtum, Königsherrschaft und Reich Gottes in den frühjudischen Schriften* (OBO 58; Göttingen: Vandenhoeck & Ruprecht, 1984), 444: "Nowhere in the literature of ancient Judaism does the kingdom of God stand in such a central place as in the message of Jesus. Accordingly, in Jesus's teaching there is a much more precise usage of the symbol."

87. One of the oldest occurrences of the abstraction "kingdom of God" is Obad. 21: "Those who have been saved shall go up to Mount Zion to rule Mount Esau; and the kingdom shall be the Lord's."

88. Helmut Merklein, *Jesu Botschaft von der Gottesherrschaft: Eine Skizze* (SBS 111; Stuttgart: Verlag Katholisches Bibelwerk, 1983), 27–36.

violent plunder it.")[89] it is not clear whether John is portrayed as belonging to the end of the period of the law and prophets, as belonging to the beginning of the time of the kingdom of God, or as the transitional figure between the two eras. The temporal expression μέχρι (until) corresponds to ἀπὸ τότε (from then on); both expressions indicate a sequence, for they are distinguished from each other in terms of content. All this speaks for an exclusive interpretation in which the Baptist is understood not to belong to the time of the kingdom.[90] If that were the case, then the Baptist would have anticipated Jesus's preaching in some form or another. "But precisely here is the deepest distinction between them."[91] For Jesus, the time after John exhibits a new quality, which means that John stands at the interface between the two ages. The saying in Q 7:28 points in the same direction, when Jesus says about John the Baptist: "I tell you, there has not arisen among women's offspring anyone who surpasses John. Yet the least significant in God's kingdom is more than he." Here, the Baptist does not belong within the kingdom of God, but is seen as marking the end of an epoch and the transition to the completely new epoch of the kingdom of God. Whether Q 7:28 goes back to Jesus or represents the interests of the post-Easter church, which wanted to keep Jesus and John separate, remains a disputed point. That at least the main content of the saying goes back to Jesus may be indicated by the continuity with Q 16:16 and the intense eschatological expectation found in both sayings. Moreover, three affirmations about the kingdom of God are found here that fit into the comprehensive portrayal of the kingdom of God in Jesus's teaching:

1. The comparison between the Baptist and the "least"[92] in the kingdom shows the otherness of God's rule and the newness of the kingdom of God, which is not to be compared with that of earthly rulers ("women's offspring").
2. The kingdom of God also has a spatial dimension.[93]

89. Indications that the saying goes back to Jesus are the provocative claim of Q 16:16 and the uncertain meaning of v. 16b; for evidence and argument, cf. Helmut Merklein, *Die Gottesherrschaft als Handlungsprinzip: Unters. zur Ethik Jesu* (FzB 34; Würzburg: Echter-Verlag, 1978), 90.

90. For supporting arguments, see ibid., 85ff.

91. Jürgen Becker, *Johannes der Täufer und Jesus von Nazareth* (BiS 63; Neukirchen-Vluyn: Neukirchener Verlag, 1972), 76.

92. The reference is to everyone who enters the kingdom of God; μικρότερος is a comparative with a superlative meaning; cf. Heinz Schürmann, *Das Lukasevangelium* (HTKNT 3; 2 vols.; Freiburg: Herder, 1969), 1:418; François Bovon, *Luke 1: A Commentary on the Gospel of Luke 1:1–9:50* (Hermeneia; 2 vols.; Minneapolis: Fortress, 2002), 1:284n50.

93. Ulrich Luz, *Matthew 8–20, A Commentary* (Hermeneia; trans. James E. Crouch; Minneapolis: Fortress, 2001), 139, considers ἐν τῇ βασιλείᾳ to indicate the saying is from the early church. But in the ancient world, kingdom/rulership was generally regarded as having a spatial aspect.

3. It already possesses a present dimension (ἐστίν), for only so is the comparison meaningful.

So also Q 7:18–19, 22–23 and Mark 2:18–19 show that Jesus contrasted the present time of eschatological salvation and the time of the Baptist and his disciples. It would be a misunderstanding, however, to demote the Baptist in Jesus's view to a mere forerunner or announcer. Jesus had an extremely high regard for the Baptist, giving him a unique place in God's redemptive plan (cf. Q 7:26). The advent of the Baptist is a turning point in God's history with Israel: *John stands on the threshold of the kingdom of God.*

The Future Kingdom of God

Sayings about the future kingdom of God, the coming reign of God, are found in almost every stream of early Christian tradition, and direct us to the center of Jesus's message:

1. The second petition of the Lord's Prayer, "Let your reign come" (Q 11:2, ἐλθέτω ἡ βασιλεία), looks forward to the revelation of God's holiness, glory, and reign.[94] On the one hand, there is a close parallel in the second petition of the Qaddish prayer ("Magnified and sanctified be his great name in the world which he hath created according to his will. May he establish his kingdom during your life and during your days, and during the life of all the house of Israel, even speedily and at a near time, and say ye, Amen."). On the other hand, the brevity and simplicity, as well as the language of the coming of the kingdom, point to characteristic features of Jesus's own speech.[95] The connection between a theocentric focus and an eschatological perspective is typical of Jesus's teaching; so also the way in which he leaves the petition nonspecific and undefined, which leaves it open for both future expansion and the experience of dissociation.
2. The expectation of the eschatological pilgrimage of the Gentiles to Jerusalem/Zion (cf., e.g., Isa. 2:2ff.; Mic. 4:1ff.; Isa. 43:1ff.; Bar. 4:36ff.) is taken up in Q 13:29, 28, "And many shall come from Sunrise and Sunset and recline with Abraham and Isaac and Jacob in the kingdom of God, but you will be thrown out into the outer darkness, where there will be wailing and grinding of teeth."[96] This prophetic threat pronouncement directs a sharp criticism against Israel's self-understanding as God's elect people.

94. For analysis, see Marc Philonenko, *Das Vaterunser: Vom Gebet Jesu zum Gebet der Jünger* (Tübingen: Mohr, 2002), 51–68; Ulrich Luz, *Matthew 1–7, A Commentary* (Hermeneia; trans. James E. Crouch; Minneapolis: Fortress, 2007), 318.

95. Cf. Luz, *Matthew 1–7*, 318.

96. For evidence and argument that the saying goes back to Jesus, see Merklein, *Handlungsprinzip*, 118; Luz, *Matthew 8–20*, 9.

They will be excluded from the eschatological banquet with the patriarchs, but Gentiles from the east and west will be included. Thus a universalistic tendency is present in Jesus's proclamation of the kingdom.

3. The eucharistic saying of Mark 14:25 is an unfulfilled prophecy: "Truly I tell you, I will never again drink of the fruit of the vine until that day when I drink it new in the kingdom of God." Jesus probably hoped that God's kingdom would break in so soon that he would be spared the way to death. A post-Easter origin of the saying is unlikely, for the focus is not on Jesus but on the kingdom of God. So also the parable of the Barren Fig Tree of Luke 13:6–9 clearly indicates Jesus's own eager expectation. The unfruitful fig tree is granted just one more year before it is cut down, i.e., before the coming judgment occurs.
4. Those sayings in which the future kingdom of God is proclaimed as an alternative world also have a claim to authenticity. In view of the marginalization of children in ancient society, Mark 10:15 must have had a provocative effect: "Truly I tell you, whoever does not receive the kingdom of God as a little child will never enter it." Jesus's saying about the rich in Mark 10:23 ("Then Jesus looked around and said to his disciples, 'How hard it will be for those who have wealth to enter the kingdom of God!'" cf. Mark 10:25) also looks forward to a new reality, as does the provocative statement in Matt. 21:31c, "Truly I tell you, the tax collectors and the prostitutes are going into the kingdom of God ahead of you." The coming new world is expressed in sayings such as "The first will be last" (Mark 10:31) and "For all who exalt themselves will be humbled, and those who humble themselves will be exalted" (Luke 14:11). The "last" are the poor, to whom the kingdom of God belongs, those who weep, who will be comforted, and the hungry, who will be filled (Luke 6:20–21). So also the blessing in the context of the parable of the Great Supper (Luke 14:15, "One of the dinner guests, on hearing this, said to him, 'Blessed is anyone who will eat bread in the kingdom of God!'"); and the rigorous challenges of Mark 9:42–48 portray the coming kingdom of God as a new world (cf. v. 47, "And if your eye causes you to stumble, tear it out; it is better for you to enter the kingdom of God with one eye than to have two eyes and to be thrown into hell").[97]

The Present Kingdom of God

A unique feature of Jesus's proclamation is that for him the coming kingdom of God is not only very near but already present.[98] He does not thereby

97. Sayings that set a deadline, such as Mark 9:1; 13:30; Matt. 10:30, are probably of post-Easter origin. They promise that the kingdom of God (or the Son of Man) will still come within the lifetime of the hearers, and offer encouragement in view of its delay.

98. David Flusser and R. Steven Notley, *Jesus* (3rd ed.; Jerusalem: Hebrew University Magnes Press, 2001), 110: Jesus "is the only Jew of ancient times known to us who preached not only

speak, however, of the presence of God as something generally available (as, e.g., in the temple), but of the proleptic presence of the future. The concrete identification of this present again shows the distancing, even alienating effect characteristic of Jesus's message:

1. In the original Beatitudes Jesus announces the presence of the kingdom of God to those who had been forced to regard themselves as outsiders: Q 6:20–21, "Blessed are you poor, for God's reign is for you. Blessed are you who hunger, for you will eat your fill. Blessed are you who mourn, for you will be consoled."[99] Those who are materially poor and oppressed have been deprived of their rights and the freedom to shape their own lives; they can only hope for mercy and help from beyond themselves. In this situation of absolute dependence, Jesus grants participation in the kingdom of God. He thereby reveals something about the essential nature of the kingdom of God: it is the riches of God's own sovereignty, God's goodness in gift-giving, God's acceptance of human beings. Where God's rulership takes place, there God alone is the giver and human beings are receivers. In the presence of God's kingdom, human beings can understand themselves only as those who are accepted, as those who have received a gift. The kingdom of God is not opened to any on the basis of what they have, their possessions, but by their sense of dependence on God's help. Like the poor, those who mourn and those who are hungry experience their distance from life. Those who mourn the death of a loved one know that part of their own life has been taken from them. Lamentation is the overt protest against this diminution of one's own life. Hunger is a direct threat to life. Hunger for life itself comes to expression in this fundamental need and longing for food.

---

that people stood at the threshold of the end of time, but that the new age of salvation had already begun."

99. The beatitudes to the poor (Matt. 5:3/Luke 6:20b), the hungry (Matt. 5:6/Luke 6:21), and the mourning (Matt. 5:4/Luke 6:21b) go back to Jesus (cf. M. Eugene Boring, "The Historical-Critical Method's 'Criteria of Authenticity': The Beatitudes in Q and Thomas as a Test Case," in *The Historical Jesus and the Rejected Gospels* [ed. Charles W. Hedrick; Semeia 44; Atlanta: Society of Biblical Literature, 1988], 9–44). This is indicated not only by the agreements between Matthew and Luke, but these three Beatitudes are distinguished from the others by alliteration—repetition of the Greek letter π. Cf. Georg Strecker, *The Sermon on the Mount: An Exegetical Commentary* (trans. O. C. Dean; Nashville: Abingdon, 1988), 28–47; Hans Weder, *Die "Rede der Reden": Eine Auslegung der Bergpredigt heute* (2nd ed.; Zürich: Theologischer Verlag, 1987), 40–41. Form-critical parallels to the Beatitudes are found in the Old Testament (e.g., Isa. 32:20; Deut. 33:29; Ps. 127:2) and ancient Judaism (Wis. 3:13; *As. Mos.* 10.8; *1 En.* 58.2; 99.10), as well as in pagan texts (e.g., Udo Schnelle and Georg Strecker, *Neuer Wettstein: Texte zum Neuen Testament aus Griechentum und Hellenismus* [Berlin: de Gruyter, 1996], I/1.2). One example: Hesiod, *Op.* 825, concludes his epochal work on the life of humanity with the sentence, "Happy and blessed is the one who knows all this, takes it to heart, remains guiltless in relation to the gods, attends to the flights of birds and avoids transgressions."

Jesus pronounces his blessing on both groups and grants them a share of life in the presence of the kingdom of God.

2. The presence of God's kingdom is manifest in the overthrowing of the power of the devil and the expulsion of evil. The exorcisms and healings, the petition in the Lord's prayer for deliverance from (the) evil (one) (Matt. 6:13b), the vision of Jesus in Luke 10:18, the charge that Jesus was in league with the evil spirits (cf. Q 11:14–15, 17–19), and the overthrow of Satan's power presupposed in Mark 3:27/Luke 11:21–22 make clear that the struggle against evil (or the evil one) is part of the central content of the teaching and work of Jesus.
3. In view of the breaking in of God's kingdom illustrated in the miraculous deeds of Jesus's ministry, people are freed from the powers of Satan to which they had been subjugated and restored to the kind of life for which they had been created. Jesus's healings testify to the presence of the dawning kingdom of God. This is programmatically formulated in Q 11:20, "But if it is by the finger of God that I cast out the demons, then God's reign has come upon you."[100] Also the eyewitnesses' praise in Q 7:22–23 and Q 10:23–34 point in the same direction (see below, §3.5.2); Jesus saw the present as the time of the turn of the ages, the dawning of the time of salvation.
4. The parables of growth testify to the hidden beginnings of the kingdom of God. Both the parable of the Seed Growing Secretly (Mark 4:26–29) and the double parable of the Mustard Seed and the Leaven (Q 13:18–19, 20–21) point to the reality that great things come from small beginnings. The decisive event, the sowing, has already taken place; the mustard bush is already growing, and the dough will soon be completely leavened.
5. So also in the saying about doing violence to the kingdom of God (Q 16:16). However the whole verse is interpreted, in any case the kingdom is understood to be a present reality. It has been present since the days of John the Baptist, and can "be violated" in the present.
6. The question about fasting in Mark 2:18–22 likewise points to the present as the time of fulfillment. Because the bridegroom is present, the disciples—in contrast to the followers of John the Baptist—cannot fast.
7. According to Luke 17:20–21, Jesus responds to the question of when the kingdom of God will come, "The kingdom of God is not coming with things that can be observed; nor will they say, 'Look, here it is!' or 'There it is!' For, in fact, the kingdom of God is among you [ἐντὸς ὑμῶν]." The translation, the meaning, and whether the saying can

100. The union of eschatology and miracles in Jesus's ministry in this way is unique in the history of religions; cf. Gerd Theissen, *The Miracle Stories of the Early Christian Tradition* (trans. Francis McDonagh; Philadelphia: Fortress, 1983), 278.

be traced back to Jesus are all disputed issues.[101] The saying can be understood in a spiritualizing sense, something like "The kingdom of God is a matter of one's inward being" (cf. *Gos. Thom.* 3, "The Kingdom is inside of you, and it is outside of you"). It is also possible to understand it in a spatial sense, "in your midst" (cf. *Gos. Thom.* 113, "The Kingdom of the Father is spread out upon the earth, and people do not see it"). Alongside the spiritual and local senses, there is also a dynamic interpretation, in the sense of "the kingdom of God is 'available to you,' or 'in your realm of experience,'" so that the saying would mean "the kingdom of God has emerged within your world of experience."[102] This interpretation relates the saying with others (esp. Q 11:20), for here the certainty of the presence of the kingdom of God is expressed in an exceptional way!

The Future Kingdom of God Already Present

What is the relationship between these statements about the future kingdom of God and those that declare that the kingdom is already present? Mark 1:15 provides a clue. There, at the beginning of his gospel, the evangelist summarizes Jesus's message: "The time is fulfilled, and the kingdom of God has come near; repent, and believe in the good news."[103] Because the kingdom of God is coming, the time is fulfilled, which means that the announcement of the present-eschatological kingdom and the promise of the future-eschatological kingdom cannot be regarded as alternatives. All the texts show that Jesus did not understand the kingdom/reign of God primarily in terms of a territory, but dynamically and functionally: God's future approaches the present in such a way that it can already be seen; God rules, and the powers of this world, including human beings, already stand under his lordship. The present is qualified as Jesus's own present, as the eschatological present, because God's ultimate saving act is already pressing into this world, inexorably and irresistibly, and will continue to do so until the rule of God, which will finally not tolerate any resistance from the powers of evil, becomes the sole reality that determines the universe and history. The futuristic sayings announce the inbreaking of the new world, and the sayings that portray the dawn of the kingdom in the present both offer the same assurance: God's new world begins now, is already hidden in the present. In prayer to God, and ultimately

101. Cf. the extensive discussion in Hans Weder, *Gegenwart und Gottesherrschaft: Überlegungen zum Zeitverständnis bei Jesus und im frühen Christentum* (BTS 20; Neukirchen-Vluyn: Neukirchener Verlag, 1993), 34–41.

102. So Weder, ibid., 39.

103. In its present form, the verse is primarily Markan. However, it can properly be regarded as an appropriate summary of the message of Jesus. Cf. Merklein, *Jesu Botschaft*, 56–58; Keck, *Who Is Jesus?* 79–85; 151ff.; M. Eugene Boring, *Mark: A Commentary* (NTL; Louisville: Westminster John Knox, 2006), 50–53.

in God's own reality, present and future are united: the Father's loving care in the present is one with the coming of God's kingdom in the future. In Jesus's understanding of time, the decisive boundary is between the past and the present, while the present and the future stand in unbroken continuity, *because the future as the dawning kingdom of God has already embraced the present.*[104] The kingdom of God has no past and has its own time: *the future already present.*

3.4.3 The Kingdom of God in Parables

The data of the tradition itself show the significance of the parables for understanding Jesus's proclamation of the kingdom of God. All the sources (Q, Mark, the materials peculiar to Luke and Matthew, the *Gospel of Thomas*) indicate that in his preaching of the kingdom, the linguistic form of the parable was utilized in an extraordinary way.[105]

Parables as Revelatory Texts

Jesus preferred the linguistic form of parable because of the particular way in which *it facilitated access to the essential nature of the kingdom of God.* Jesus was able to construct parables in such a manner that, by means of their internal structure, they themselves mediated the nearness of the dawning kingdom of God. By telling parables, he brought the reality of the kingdom of God within the reality of the human life-world. The *parables of contrast* function in this way. They are the only parables[106] in which the subject matter "kingdom of God" is transmitted in the same way by the different gospels

104. Weder (*Gegenwart*, 49) strongly emphasizes the present as the only temporal category appropriate for understanding Jesus's message of the kingdom, in order to distance him from apocalyptic conceptions: "The sayings of Jesus about the kingdom of God we have discussed show that *the understanding of the present* is the salient point in Jesus's eschatological proclamation. We insist on this over against all attempts to relegate Jesus to the category of contemporary apocalyptic, and then to make Jesus's understanding of the future the decisive element in his message."

105. On recent study of the parables, cf. Kurt Erlemann, *Gleichnisauslegung: Ein Lehr- und Arbeitsbuch* (Tübingen: Francke, 1999), 11–52.

106. On the parabolic form, cf. Udo Schnelle, *Einführung in die neutestamentliche Exegese* (6th ed.; Göttingen: Vandenhoeck & Ruprecht, 2005), 112–17. [German has two words for *parable,* usually not distinguished in English: *Gleichnis*, which might be rendered "analogy," and *Parabel.* Schnelle's footnote here indicates that he uses *Gleichnis* in the nontechnical, comprehensive sense as the term for parabolic speech in general, but in the treatment of individual texts distinguishes the terms as follows: *Gleichnis* is used for familiar, usual experiences, everyday scenes, for the world as perceived and experienced by everyone, the world that follows the conventional order of things. *Parabel* is used for the particular, individual case; it does not focus on the usual, but the extraordinary, the unique. These nuances are usually clear from the context, so I have not attempted to maintain them in translation, and have generally translated both by *parable/parabolic.*—MEB]

(cf. Mark 4:3–8, 26–29, 30–32; Q 13:18–19, 20–21).[107] In the parable of the *Sower* (Mark 4:3–8), the focus is on the effect of Jesus's message; it is not heard and acknowledged by all, but where it is accepted, it does not fail to produce dramatic results.[108] The parable of the *Seed Growing Secretly* (Mark 4:26–29) points to the certainty of the coming of God's kingdom, independently of human works. The seed grows by itself and produces fruit, and the harvest comes; human beings need not and cannot do anything to make it happen, but they are surprisingly granted time. In the same way the kingdom of God also comes by itself (Mark 4:28 αὐτομάτη, "automatically").[109] The time graciously given by God in the present must be used! In the parable of the *Mustard Seed*, Jesus portrays the present and future of the kingdom of God. In contrast to the inconspicuous beginnings, its reality still veiled in parables and miracles, the kingdom will come in the magnificent future with the glory of God. The parable of the *Leaven* illustrates the irresistible advance of the kingdom of God from this smallest of beginnings.

In the parables of contrast, the emphasis is on the conclusion, where the intention of the whole is finally obtained: the great tree, in which the birds nest, the permeation of the whole lump by the leaven, the separation of weeds from the grain, and the amazingly abundant harvest. From the point of view of the end, the beginning appears as an intended contrast, which now appears in a special light in its own right: *for the hearer, the truly surprising element is not the end, but the beginning.* Such an overwhelming subject as the kingdom of God is reflected in such a tiny item as a mustard seed,[110] in the muddled mixture of a grain field, in a little leaven. Here there is an intentional dissociation and alienation, for no one would have ever anticipated that the kingdom of God would be expressed in such an analogy. In particular, the association of leaven with the kingdom of God is alienating, for there are no previous instances in the whole tradition.[111] This dissociation is at once a *refusal and a revelation, a protest and the opening of a new world.* Jesus

107. In Mark 4:3–8 there is no explicit reference to the βασιλεία; it is suggested by the content and context.

108. For exegesis, cf. Hans Weder, *Die Gleichnisse Jesu als Metaphern: Traditions- und redaktionsgeschichtliche Analysen und Interpretationen* (Göttingen: Vandenhoeck & Ruprecht, 1978), 108–11.

109. The parable of the Tares (Matt. 13:24–30, 36–43), which replaces Mark 4:26–29, is possibly post-Easter; cf. Luz, *Matthew 8–20*, 253.

110. It is unclear whether mustard was a cultivated plant in Jesus's time, or whether it grew practically everywhere as a kind of weed; cf. the discussion in Christoph Kähler, *Jesu Gleichnisse als Poesie und Therapie: Versuch eines integrativen Zugangs zum kommunikativen Aspekt von Gleichnissen Jesu* (WUNT 78; Tübingen: Mohr, 1995), 85–88. If it was considered a weed, then an important dimension would be added to the parable's meaning: "The metaphor of faith-like-a-mustard-seed would obviously evoke the association of massive, incredible, and irresistible expansion" (p. 92).

111. Cf. ibid., 93.

does not speak "of" or "about" something but chooses an image. The image gives no information about what the kingdom of God is in the present and how long it will be before it is fully revealed. The image points rather to a surprise, to something entirely unexpected, and precisely in this way it opens up the newness of the kingdom of God. The parables of contrast refuse to provide a conceptual understanding of Jesus's ministry. They do not allow Jesus to be fitted in to an apocalyptic schedule, and they make it impossible to draw a direct, unbroken, visible, calculable, illuminating line of continuity between his ministry and the coming eschaton. Nonetheless, the parables reveal Jesus's mission, for they allow his hearers to share the unbounded hope and the ultimate certainty characteristic of Jesus himself. They allow the hopeless present to be understood in the perspective of a totally other future, and thus mediate hope in the kingdom of God without removing its mystery.

The eternal value of the kingdom of God comes to speech in the parables of the *Hidden Treasure* (Matt. 13:44) and the *Pearl* (Matt. 13:45–46), where the conduct of the finders takes center stage. In each case, the finder had different possibilities but chose the right one: with single-minded purpose, he devotes everything to obtaining the kingdom of heaven.[112] "Whoever finds the kingdom of God finds himself or herself as one who responds to this find with their whole being."[113] Jesus's parables facilitate the finding of the kingdom of God. Response to it is not compelled but results from its power of attraction, its value, and its promise. However, whoever rejects the new reality of the kingdom of God is warned by the parable of the *Net* (Matt. 13:47–50): at the last judgment there will be a separation between the evil and the good; this means the hearers of the parable presently have in their own hands the choice as to which group they will belong.

In the parables, Jesus not only brings God to speech but brings God so near to human beings that they can allow themselves to be grasped and changed by God's goodness. *The narrator himself vouches for the truth of what is narrated and the response demanded.* Several other parables of Jesus speak of what is surprising and new in the kingdom of God; in most of them the phrase "kingdom of God" itself is lacking—but they nevertheless have things to say about the kingdom of God, things that are absolutely unheard of.

3.4.4 The Kingdom of God and the Lost

Seen over against the case of John the Baptist, God's *saving* activity comes to speech in a new and comprehensive way with Jesus of Nazareth. Jesus's self-

112. Cf. Eta Linnemann, *Parables of Jesus: Introduction and Exposition* (3rd ed.; trans. John Sturdy; London: SPCK, 1966), 103; differently Weder, *Gleichnisse Jesu*, 140, who emphasizes the obviousness of the conduct.

113. Weder, *Gleichnisse Jesu*, 140.

understanding is expressed programmatically in Mark 2:17c, "I have come to call not the righteous but sinners."[114] The pair of categories δίκαιοι/ἁμαρτωλοί (righteous/sinners), also found elsewhere in Jesus's teaching (cf. Luke 15:7; 18:9–13), can precisely express the goal of his mission: his message of the dawning kingdom of God is directed to all Israel, and thus the reference to the "righteous" is by no means meant ironically. Above all, God's love and mercy must be communicated to sinners, for by God's goodness and forgiveness they can enter into a new relation with God; God accepts the sinner who is willing to repent. In memorable parables, Jesus tells of God's seeking the lost and their return to God.

In the parable of the *Lost Son* (Luke 15:11–32) Jesus interprets both God and humanity.[115] In the center stands the father, who loves his two sons impartially. To each of them he grants an inheritance that provides what they need for life. He does not respond to the extravagant and wasteful life of the younger son by withdrawing his love, but by accepting him unconditionally even before the son can own up to his guilt. To the older son too he declares his abiding love and enduring family ties, despite the son's protests (v. 31). The antithetically portrayed conduct of the two brothers reveals two possible human reactions to the experience and declaration of acceptance. Only through a life crisis does the younger brother obtain the insight that life far from the father is not possible. His acknowledgment of his own misconduct (vv. 18, 21: ἥμαρτον, "I have sinned") carries with it the expectation that punishment is warranted and will come. The height and breadth of the loving acceptance by the father is new and unexpected for the younger son. The older brother, in contrast, does not understand himself to be unconditionally accepted but sees his relation to the father as a matter of reward for good work. Only those who work and fulfill the requirements of the law are entitled to celebrate. The older son thereby entraps himself in a network of service-in-return-for-service-rendered that blocks his view of humanity's true situation of total dependence. In his eyes, there cannot be any such thing as radical forgiveness as the expression of abiding love. In the figure of the older brother it becomes clear: even those who reject the love of God still live from it.

In the parable of the *Lost Sheep*, the dominant idea is the joy over finding the lost.[116] Both the contrast between the one and the ninety-nine and the extraordinary behavior of the shepherd, who leaves the ninety-nine alone in the wilderness, express both the pain of loss and the joy of finding the lost

114. Mark 2:15–17 is an independent textual unit that preserves the oldest traditions; for reconstruction, cf. Merklein, *Handlungsprinzip*, 199–201.

115. For a comprehensive interpretation, cf. Wolfgang Pöhlmann, *Der Verlorene Sohn und das Haus: Studien zu Lukas 15,11–32 im Horizont der antiken Lehre von Haus, Erziehung and Ackerbau* (WUNT 68; Tübingen: Mohr, 1993).

116. Cf. Linnemann, *Parables*, 67; Joachim Jeremias, *The Parables of Jesus* (2nd rev. ed.; New York: Scribner, 1972), 135.

once again. The parable of the Lost Sheep seeks agreement from the hearer; everyone would act in the same way as the shepherd.[117] In the parable of the *Lost Coin*, the surprising element is the intensity with which the woman seeks. The hearer is involuntarily drawn into the dynamic of the story's action and shares in the joy over finding the lost money.

So also in the parable of the *Laborers in the Vineyard* (Matt. 20:1–16),[118] Jesus brings to speech the existence of human beings *coram Deo*. The narrative attains movement by the landlord's unusual arrangement of paying the workers by beginning with the one last hired (v. 8b). At first, those hired earlier handle the crisis generated by the landlord's untypical conduct by assuming that they too will be paid at a higher rate than their contract calls for. When this expectation goes unfulfilled, they charge the landlord with dealing unfairly (vv. 11–12). The landlord reacts to their—entirely understandable!—moral outrage (v. 12) by pointing out that he has fulfilled the terms of the contract and that he is free to do as he pleases with regard to the person who was hired last. The antithesis between the landlord and the workers hired first reveals two ways of being in the world: life lived according to the order of merit and life lived according to the order of grace. The thinking of the first workers is determined by the relation of work and payment—those who work more than others should receive more payment. On this basis, the first workers challenge the justice of the way the landlord has in fact paid his workers. The landlord can, of course, point out that he has kept the terms of their contract, so that the tables are abruptly turned, and the complainants become those who are complained against. Their thinking, which remains within the cause-and-effect framework that sees a firm connection between work and payment, gives them no ground for criticizing the landlord and those workers who were hired last. The landlord is free to act in his boundless grace, which demolishes all expectations—grace that does no one injustice, but at the same time grants much that is unexpected. This grace is not subject to any temporal limits, as is shown by the way in which the same offer is monotonously repeated throughout the day. In regard to accepting the offer, every time is the right time. Those who were hired first cannot grasp this openness, for they understand their employment not as the acceptance of an offer of grace, but as a contract obviously made on the basis of payment for services rendered. The landlord grants to all, at every time, the basis of their existence. His freedom is not limited, his grace is not a matter of calculation. In this parable Jesus thus brings God to speech, the God who accepts human beings and gives them what they need for their life. Human beings, in turn, learn to understand themselves as accepted by

117. Cf. Linnemann, *Parables*, 65.

118. On this point cf. Martin Petzoldt, *Gleichnisse Jesu und christliche Dogmatik* (Göttingen: Vandenhoeck & Ruprecht, 1984), 51–56.

their Lord, that their existence is not a matter of their own accomplishment, but defined by the grace of God.

In a way that is just as scandalous, Jesus illustrates God's unconditional forgiveness in the parable of the *Unforgiving Servant* (Matt. 18:23–35).[119] The narrative's point of departure is a situation of indebtedness, obviously expressed in hyperbolic terms. The amount of the debt (100 million denarii)[120] is unimaginably high, which places the conduct of both king and slave in a particular light. The king is characterized by the fact that he disregards the offer of his slave, has mercy on him, and forgives him all his debts. Against this background, the conduct of the slave in 18:28–30 simply cannot be imagined. Although he has himself just experienced limitless mercy, he deals unmercifully with the fellow slave who owes him a laughably trivial sum. In this parable, human beings appear before God as debtors, whose debts are so unimaginable that they cannot repay them even by giving up their whole lives. In their distress, people turn to God and ask for patience. God does not merely grant them more time to pay off the debt but forgives their whole immeasurable debt outright, without any conditions. In this unexpected—more than that, this inconceivable—act of acceptance of human beings, God shows his love and mercy. God does not merely give people more time, so they can attempt to free themselves from this precarious situation, which would in any case be a completely hopeless attempt. Instead, God gives people their lives back—a new life based on forgiveness. By conferring on them unearned pardon, God's own act preempts any human striving.

Jesus's parables point beyond themselves. They urge the hearer toward the insight that the parables are dealing with nothing less than his or her own life. The parables offer their hearers possibilities of (self-)identification, lead them to fundamental decisions so that they may seize their true life—which calls for changes in the way they see their present life. The parables aim to mediate the immediate saving nearness of the kingdom of God, so that the lost become the saved.

Word and Deed

Jesus's message of God's unconditional acceptance of human beings is made clear by *the turn to tax collectors and sinners* in his own ministry. This sort of conduct obviously soon gave him the reputation of being a friend of tax collectors and sinners, a glutton and drunkard (cf. Q 7:33–34). For Jesus, tax collectors and sinners are not irretrievably lost, for in Jesus's preaching and the conduct of his ministry, they are found again, which is the occasion

119. The parable as told by Jesus probably included only vv. 23b–30; see the extensive analyses and evidence in Alfons Weiser, *Die Knechtsgleichnisse der synoptischen Evangelien* (SANT 29; Munich: Kösel, 1971), 90ff.; and Norman Perrin, *Rediscovering the Teaching of Jesus* (New York: Harper & Row, 1967), 125–26.

120. Cf. Jeremias, *Parables*, 210.

for joy. The sins of the past have lost their power to separate and burden down, and this has happened without any advance requirements. Rather, the sinner lives from God's forgiveness, his unconditional acceptance.[121] Thus the arrival of God's kingdom is the presence of God's love. The hidden beginning of the kingdom of God happens in the form of the overpowering, unrestrained love of God for human beings, which they need, and this kingdom aims to bring about such love among human beings. These needy human beings are represented not only by the tax collectors and sinners, but by the poor, by women and children, by the sick, by Samaritans.

When Jesus not only preaches God's radical saving decision for humanity but also lives it out in the practice of his ministry, the question arises whether he also directly pronounced God's *forgiveness* to people. Both the encounter with the sinful woman (Luke 7:36–50) and the healing of the paralyzed man (Mark 2:1–12) indicate that Jesus forgave people their sins in a direct and personal way. To be sure, neither text goes back to Jesus in its present form, but they contain old traditions (Luke 7:37, 38, 47; Mark 2:5b, 10?) which show it is possible that Jesus pronounced God's forgiveness of sins or directly forgave sins himself. Such a practice would correspond to his message of God's unconditional affirmation of human beings. Jesus claims for himself what seems to have been reserved as God's own prerogative.[122]

Jesus manifests an obvious bias for *the poor*, and does so in the name of God,[123] a stance at once religious and social. In the first Beatitude, those who are blessed are those who have nothing, and can only stand along with the hungry and crying as those who are awarded the kingdom of God without any conditions whatever (Q 6:20). Wealth can separate from God, as is made clear in the threatening saying in Mark 10:25 and in the story of the rich man and poor Lazarus (Luke 16:19–31), a story in which characteristically only the poor person is named. It is not said that the rich man was unkind or that he had not given enough to charity; it is simply that riches in this world bring torment in the next world as a kind of balancing of accounts. The break with the world that is part of discipleship in the service of the proclamation of the kingdom of God includes also the giving up of one's property, as we see in the story of the rich young man (Mark 10:17–23). Jesus was especially sensitive to the plight of *women*, for they especially were placed at a disadvantage by the

121. Cf. Merklein, *Handlungsprinzip*, 191.

122. Cf. ibid., 201–3; Otfried Hofius, "Vergebungszuspruch und Vollmachtsfrage," in *Neutestamentliche Studien* (ed. Otfried Hofius: WUNT 132; Tübingen: Mohr, 2000), 57–69 (68: "The story in Mark 2:1–12 clearly presupposes a unity between Jesus's act and God's own action"). Ingo Broer, "Jesus und das Gesetz," in *Jesus und das jüdische Gesetz* (ed. Ingo Broer; Stuttgart: Kohlhammer, 1992), who evaluates Mark 2:1–12 exclusively within a Jewish conceptual framework, regards it as a post-Easter creation.

123. This aspect is emphasized by Luise Schottroff and Wolfgang Stegemann, *Jesus and the Hope of the Poor* (trans. Matthew J. O'Connell; Maryknoll, NY: Orbis Books, 1986), 17–37.

ritual law. Through menstruation and birth, women were frequently ritually impure, could not participate in the cult, were dispensed from the responsibility of reciting the Shema, were not allowed to study the Torah, and were without legal rights.[124] So also, Jesus had no scruples about associating with *Samaritans*, who did not possess the status of full Jews and were victims of religious discrimination. The same is true of his relation to *children*. Jesus even used both Samaritans and children as models of the right kind of life before God (cf. Mark 10:14–15; Luke 10:25–37). Jesus owned no ritual restrictions in his associations with other people. The boundless love of God has at least a preference for the religiously and socially disadvantaged. He crossed over the religious and legal lines that had been drawn in the name of God to keep the excluded in their place. His table fellowship with tax collectors, sinners, and women was an impressive demonstration of the new reality of the kingdom of God.

3.4.5 The Kingdom of God and Table Fellowship

Mealtimes always had a sacral character in ancient Judaism and were always accompanied by a prayer of gratitude and praise to God as the true host at every meal. Table fellowship therefore served both as a means of cultivating Jewish identity and as a public marker of separation from Gentiles or the irreligious. (Cf., e.g., *Jub.* 22.16, "And you also, my son, Jacob, remember my words, and keep the commandments of Abraham your father. Separate yourself from the Gentiles, and do not eat with them, and do not perform deeds like theirs, because their deeds are defiled, and all their ways are contaminated, and despicable, and abominable." Cf. also 3 Macc. 3:4; 4 Macc. 1:35; 5:16ff.; 1QS 6:20–21; Josephus, *JW* 2.137–139, 143–144.) In the first century CE, the food laws were at the very center of the Jewish understanding of the law;[125] the idea of ritual purity was the central focus of the thinking not only of the Pharisees, but of the Therapeutae and the Essenes as well.[126] Against this background, the kind of table fellowship practiced by Jesus constituted an attack on the very foundations of the biblical distinction between "clean" and "unclean" (cf. Lev. 10:10, "You are to distinguish between the holy and the common, and

124. On the legal situation of women in Judaism, cf. Günter Mayer, *Die jüdische Frau in der hellenistisch-römischen Antike* (Stuttgart: Kohlhammer, 1987).

125. Cf. the comprehensive evidence and argument for this in Christoph Heil, *Die Ablehnung der Speisegebote durch Paulus: Zur Frage nach der Stellung des Apostels zum Gesetz* (BBB 96; Weinheim: Beltz Athenäum, 1994), 23–123. So also, the conflicts in early Christianity about the food laws show that this was a decisive and controversial issue (e.g., Acts 11:3; Gal. 2:12–15).

126. Cf. Bernd Kollmann, *Ursprung und Gestalten der frühchristlichen Mahlfeier* (GTA 43; Göttingen: Vandenhoeck & Ruprecht, 1990), 234ff.; Dennis Edwin Smith, *From Symposium to Eucharist: The Banquet in the Early Christian World* (Minneapolis: Fortress, 2003).

between the unclean and the clean").[127] Jesus's participation in banquets has left numerous traces in the tradition (cf. Q 7:33–34; Q 10:7; Q 13:29, 28; Luke 14:15–24/Matt. 22:1–10; Mark 1:31; 2:15–17, 18–22; 3:20; 7:1–23; 14:3–9; Luke 8:1–3; 10:8, 38–42; 13:26; 14:1, 7–14; 15:1–2, 11–32; 19:1–10). They show that it must have been a special characteristic of Jesus to celebrate dinner parties, provide them with a particular interpretation, and thereby break cultural rules. The parable of the Great Supper (Luke 14:15–24/Matt. 22:1–10)[128] shows how Jesus took up contemporary ideas and distanced himself from them. In ancient Judaism, the idea was widespread that at the end of time God would hold a great banquet in immeasurable extravagance—for those who are righteous and saved (cf. Isa. 25:6; *Pss. Sol.* 5.8ff.). Jesus also speaks of God's eschatological banquet but has surprising news about it: the feast will take place, but the guests will not be those whom people had expected. Those who were invited first missed their opportunity, for they did not recognize the present *kairos* of the kingdom of God.[129] Instead of the invited guests, "street people" (Luke 14:23) are the ones who get to participate in the banquet, i.e., the poor and other people on the margins of society. Jesus hereby stands the ancient idea of honor and shame on its head, for God bestows honor precisely on those who have been excluded.[130] Similarly provocative is the perspective of the eschatological banquet in Q 13:29, 28: not the chosen people but the Gentiles will celebrate with Abraham, Isaac, and Jacob. A reversal of roles has happened, as declared in the blessings on the poor in Q 6:20 and Q 13:30: "The last will be first and the first last."

Jesus's practice of table fellowship could thus not go unnoticed. Thus, according to Mark 2:16, the scribes among the Pharisees raise the question of whether he eats with tax collectors and sinners, a question intended to discredit Jesus (cf. Q 7:34; Luke 15:1).[131] Jesus answers that he has been sent to sinners (Mark 2:17c); it is above all necessary that God's love and mercy be

127. In New Testament times, the Pharisees were attempting to apply this distinction to every area of life; cf. Jacob Neusner, "Die pharisäischen rechtlichen Überlieferungen," in *Das pharisäische und talmudische Judentum: Neue Wege zu seinem Verständnis* (ed. Jacob Neusner and Hermann Lichtenberger; TSAJ 4; Tübingen: Mohr, 1984), 51, who rightly identifies the "legalism" of the Pharisees as primarily "a matter of the food laws." Cf. Jacob Neusner, *From Politics to Piety: The Emergence of Pharisaic Judaism* (Englewood Cliffs, NJ: Prentice-Hall, 1973), 36, 73–85, 119–20.

128. The Q form can no longer be confidently reconstructed; cf. Ulrich Luz, *Matthew 21–28: A Commentary* (Hermeneia; trans. James E. Crouch; Minneapolis: Fortress, 2005), 232–38.

129. This aspect is emphasized by Weder, *Gleichnisse Jesu*, 187: "They should come *now*."

130. On this point cf. S. Scott Bartchy, "The Historical Jesus and Honor Reversal at Table," in *The Social Setting of Jesus and the Gospels* (ed. Wolfgang Stegemann et al.; Minneapolis: Fortress, 2002), 181: "In contrast to the prevailing assumption about life, honor was not in limited supply for the historical Jesus."

131. On the tax collectors, cf. F. Herrenbrück, "Wer waren die Zöllner?" *ZNW* 72 (1981): 194: "The New Testament tax collectors are very probably to be understood as Hellenistic minor leaseholders, and thus neither as the Roman major leaseholders responsible for taxes

made known to sinners, so they can return to God. Jesus thus intentionally and emphatically had table fellowship with those who were excluded by the official Judaism of his time. In these festive meals, God the creator himself provides for the eschatological care of his creatures and shows that his relation to sinners is that of the Merciful One. The creaturely aspect of these festive meals is not to be overlooked; God addresses human beings within the kingdom of God, which is already at work in their creatureliness, and grants them their prayer "Our day's bread give us today" (Q 11:3), freely giving them what is necessary for life (cf. Q 12:22b–31).

The festive meals illustrate how the dynamic of the kingdom of God makes itself effective and brings people within its realm. This table fellowship, like the parables and the miracles, marks the advent of the kingdom of God. In ancient Judaism, there was no parallel to these repeated festive meals with the ritually unclean as the expression and reality of the dawning kingdom of God. This open table fellowship practiced by Jesus, with its salvific character, belongs at the center of Jesus's ministry,[132] as is indicated not least by the continuing effects of the motif of table fellowship in the early church (cf. 1 Cor. 11:17–34; Mark 6:30–44; 8:1–10; 14:22–25; John 2:1–11; 21:1–14; Acts 2:42–47).

The Kingdom of God as God's New Reality

God's coming and acting in his kingdom is the basis, center, and horizon of Jesus's ministry. With his language of the kingdom/rule of God, Jesus not only diagnoses his own time but also constructs a comprehensive symbolic universe based on his experience and insight that God's saving act,which overcomes the world's evil, is already in motion.[133] The first striking feature of Jesus's language about the rule/kingdom of God is what is absent: national needs are not addressed, and the ritual separation of Gentiles and Jews no longer plays a role. Table fellowship in Galilean villages, not sacrificial ritual in the temple, signals the inbreaking of God's new reality. Jesus draws no boundaries within Israel: he sets the marginalized in the center—the poor, the women who have suffered discrimination, children, tax collectors, prostitutes; he integrates the sick, the ritually unclean, the lepers, those possessed by demons, and even Samaritans into the holy people of God. The beginning

(*publicani*) nor their employees (*portitores*). They were usually wealthy and belonged to the upper or upper-middle class."

132. Kollmann, *Ursprung*, 235ff.

133. All the statements cited about the reality of the kingdom of God manifest an exclusive connection to the person of Jesus, and speak against the thesis of Gerd Theissen, "Gruppenmessianismus: Überlegungen zum Ursprung der Kirche im Jüngerkreis Jesu," in *Jesus als historische Gestalt: Beiträge zur Jesusforschung: Zum 60. Geburtstag von Gerd Theissen* (ed. Gerd Theissen and Annette Merz; FRLANT 202; Göttingen: Vandenhoeck & Ruprecht, 2003), 255–81, who argues that not only Jesus but also the disciples were already pre-Easter representatives of the kingdom of God.

of the kingdom of God becomes visible in God's love to the disqualified. It means overwhelming freedom from guilt, fatherly love, invitation to the poor, the hearing of prayer, reward on the basis of grace, and joy. This is what Jesus narrates in his parables. Their characteristic feature is that they draw their hearers into their narrative world, so that hearers find themselves and their world confronted by the new world within the story. Thus they learn to understand themselves and their world in a new way. The parables mediate the nearness of the strange new world of Jesus's message, so hearers can experience the unexpected dawning and already present kingdom of God in the midst of their everyday world.

The kingdom of God is for Jesus by no means only an idea, a concept, but a very concrete, world-toppling reality. He understood himself to be the beginning of this new reality.[134] It is presupposed throughout that the coming of the kingdom of God is a reality, expressed in Jesus's statements in ways that are sometimes alienating in their concreteness. The messengers are instructed to greet no one along the way (Q 10:4). Only those aware of the significance of greeting rituals in eastern culture can understand how drastically alienating this command is. Those who would follow cannot even say good-bye to their families, cannot even linger to bury their own fathers (cf. Q 9:59–60). Such statements would be inconceivable if the kingdom of God were not thought of as something entirely concrete, the end of all things; God is actually bringing it to pass here and now, thus canceling every human obligation. In Galilee, the extended family was the location of one's social identity,[135] which means that here too Jesus and his followers abandon the conventional structures of thought and society.

Not only so—the kingdom of God develops its own dynamic. Jesus speaks of the kingdom as an acting subject: "it has come near" (Mark 1:15), "it is present" (Luke 11:20), "it is coming" (Luke 11:2), "it is in your midst" (Luke 17:21). For Jesus, the kingdom of God is obviously an event in its own right, an event which, to be sure, takes human beings into itself, but is not determined or triggered by human action. It functions by its own power (cf. Mark 4:26–29).[136]

Scholarly interpretation of the kingdom of God has suffered from an antagonism between an ethical, individualistic understanding of the king-

134. Cf. Merklein, *Jesu Botschaft*, 145–64.

135. Cf. Halvor Moxnes, *Putting Jesus in His Place: A Radical Vision of Household and Kingdom* (Louisville: Westminster John Knox, 2003).

136. The textual data as a whole points to the fact that "kingdom/rule of God" in Jesus's message must be understood in an eschatological context, so that an "uneschatological," primarily ethical-political interpretation of Jesus, as advocated in some recent American exegesis (cf., e.g., Marcus J. Borg, *Jesus: A New Vision; Spirit, Culture, and the Life of Discipleship* [San Francisco: Harper & Row, 1987], 14–21; Mack, *Who Wrote the New Testament?* 40–50) is simply shattered by the textual data itself.

dom as a present reality and an apocalyptic, cosmic understanding of the kingdom as a future reality. The classical advocates of the ethical interpretation are Albrecht Ritschl (1822–89) and Adolf von Harnack (1851–1930). In his 1875 *Instruction in the Christian Religion*, §5, Ritschl states: "The kingdom of God is the divinely ordained highest good of the community founded through God's revelation in Christ; but it is the highest good only in the sense that it forms at the same time the ethical ideal for whose attainment the members of the community bind themselves to each other through a definite type of reciprocal action."[137] Harnack based his understanding of the kingdom of God primarily on the parables; this is where the nature of the kingdom becomes visible: "The kingdom of God comes by coming to the individual."[138] Johannes Weiss (1863–1914) published his contrasting interpretation in 1892, *Jesus's Proclamation of the Kingdom of God*. For him, Jesus's "kingdom of God" meant neither a moral ideal nor an inner religious assurance but God's bringing an end to this world and creating a new one, entirely at the divine initiative and without human action. The inbreaking of the kingdom of God is a cosmic catastrophe that will happen very soon. "Jesus's activity is determined by the strong and unwavering feeling that the messianic time is imminent."[139] Albert Schweitzer intensified this position: the kingdom of God "lies beyond the borders of good and evil; it will be brought about as a cosmic catastrophe through which evil is to be completely overcome . . . *the kingdom of God is super-moral*."[140]

Each interpretative model sees something that is correct about Jesus's message: there can be no doubt that Jesus's perspective was directed toward the coming kingdom of God that was to appear in the immediate future, in which God himself will bring the new reality into being. The coming of the kingdom of God does mean the coming of a new, real world. At the same time, the kingdom of God reveals and makes available a new ethical energy hitherto undreamed of, which opens humanity to a new way of life. Because the kingdom of God stands for *God's lordship in the present and the future—God's nearness, God's love, God's taking the side of the poor and oppressed, God's justice, God's will, God's victory over evil, and God's own goodness*—it determines all aspects of the proclamation and activity of Jesus and his followers.

137. Albrecht Ritschl, "Instruction in the Christian Religion," in *Three Essays* (trans. Phil Hefner; Philadelphia: Fortress, 1972), 222.

138. Adolf von Harnack, *What Is Christianity?* (trans. Thomas Bailey Saunders; New York: Harper & Row, 1957), 56.

139. Johannes Weiss, *Jesus's Proclamation of the Kingdom of God* (trans. Richard H. Hiers and David Larrimore Holland; Lives of Jesus Series; Philadelphia: Fortress, 1971), 129.

140. Albert Schweitzer, *The Mystery of the Kingdom of God: The Secret of Jesus's Messiahship and Passion* (trans. Walter Lowrie; New York: Schocken Books, 1964), 101–2.

3.5 Ethics in the Horizon of the Kingdom of God

Scholars dispute whether one can speak of an "ethic" of Jesus. If by "ethics" one refers to a level of discourse determined by reflection and theory, then one must speak of "morality"—of Jesus's moral statements and his stance on particular moral issues—but not of his "ethics."[141] On the other hand, there are several indications that Jesus was far more than the proponent of a contextual ethos:[142]

1. Many of his ethical statements are grounded in principles and cannot be reduced to ad hoc responses.
2. Jesus's ethical statements manifest a clear structure and an internal weighting according to which the love commandment plays the central role.
3. Finally, Jesus's (sometimes radical) statements on ethical issues can be integrated into his ministry as a whole. So it makes sense to continue to speak of Jesus's ethic.

3.5.1 Creation, Eschatology, and Ethics

Jesus's ethic is oriented to the will of God. In view of the coming kingdom of God, which involves the overcoming of evil, God's will is to be actualized in the original meaning that it had at creation. Protology and eschatology thus form a unity in Jesus's thought, held together by Jesus's understanding of God. Within the horizon of the kingdom of *God*, it is a matter of proclaiming and implementing the original will of *God*.[143] For Jesus, a theology of creation in the wisdom tradition and radical ethics in view of the present-and-coming kingdom of God are not mutually exclusive alternatives but supplement each other in his theocentric perspective.

The Will of the Creator

Jesus can offer effusive praise to God the creator, who in his goodness lets the sun shine on good people and bad (Matt. 5:45) and without whose will not

141. Cf. in this sense Wayne A. Meeks, *The Origins of Christian Morality: The First Two Centuries* (New Haven: Yale University Press, 1993), 4; Wolfgang Stegemann, "The Contextual Ethics of Jesus," in *The Social Setting of Jesus and the Gospels* (ed. Wolfgang Stegemann et al.; Minneapolis: Fortress, 2002), 167: "In my opinion, Jesus formulated no ethic and was also no teacher of virtues. When he expressed himself in regard to particular values and convictions of his society and culture, it was rather a matter of taking a stand contingent on the particular problems he faced. His statements do not give the impression of systematic reflection, nor do they represent a theory of the good life or appropriate conduct."

142. On the possible differences between ethics and ethos, see below, §6.6.

143. Cf. Hartmut Stegemann, "Der lehrende Jesus," *NZST* 24 (1982): 12.

a hair falls from our heads (Matt. 10:29–31). God cares for the birds and the lilies, so how much more will he take care of human beings (Matt. 6:25–33)![144] In Jesus's teaching, however, these ideas from the wisdom tradition (cf. Sir. 30:23b–31:2) do commend a carefree life as a generalized ethical maxim, but in Matt. 6:33 are placed in a specific framework: "But strive first for the kingdom of God and his righteousness, and all these things will be given to you as well."[145] This orientation to the kingdom of God brings fulfillment to the lives of the disciples. This wisdom thinking with an eschatological stamp is a distinctive characteristic of Jesus's own preaching.[146] Human activity is given a new goal: it is not oriented to one's own existence, but to God's rule. This turn toward God's kingdom, and thus toward God the creator, defines human life by what it was originally created to be.

This creatureliness of human being is manifest above all by adhering to the original will of the creator God. In Mark 10:2–9, Jesus grounds the indissolubility of marriage on the original will of God in creation. It corresponds to the will of God and thus at the same time to the creatureliness of human life, that man and wife remain together their whole life (Mark 10:9, "Therefore what God has joined together, let no one separate"). In contrast, the possibility of divorce was given through Moses as a concession to human σκληροκαρδία (hardness of heart), as something that is ultimately contrary to human life as God the creator intended it. In Jesus's rejection of divorce, he not only enhances the status of women in Jewish society but places himself over the authority of Moses, claiming for himself the authority to reaffirm the original will of God directed to human welfare. At the same time, he nullifies the divorce arrangements represented by Deut. 2:1–4!

In its present literary form, Mark 10:2–9 does not derive from Jesus, but it probably represents his position.[147] This is confirmed in 1 Cor. 7:10–11

144. The nucleus of this text that goes back to Jesus comprises (apart from redactional supplements) vv. 25–26, 28–33. For evidence and argument, see Luz, *Matthew 1–7*, 338–48 (without 25d, e; 32a); Joachim Gnilka, *Das Matthäusevangelium* (2 vols.; HTKNT 1; Freiburg: Herder, 1986), 252. Merklein, *Handlungsprinzip*, 174–83, provides a penetrating analysis and interpretation.

145. In Matt. 6:33 καὶ τὴν δικαιοσύνην αὐτοῦ (and his righteousness) is a Matthean addition; cf. Walter Bauer et al., eds., *Orthodoxy and Heresy in Earliest Christianity* (2nd ed.; Philadelphia: Fortress, 1971), 152; M. Eugene Boring, "Rhetoric, Righteousness, and the Sermon on the Mount," in *Listening to the Word: Studies in Honor of Fred B. Craddock* (ed. Gail R. O'Day and Thomas G. Long; Nashville: Abingdon, 1993), 53ff.

146. On the issue of wisdom tradition in Jesus's message, cf. Ben Witherington, *Jesus the Sage: The Pilgrimage of Wisdom* (Minneapolis: Fortress, 1994); Martin Ebner, *Jesus, ein Weisheitslehrer? Synoptische Weisheitslogien im Traditionsprozess* (HBS 15; Freiburg i.B.: Herder, 1998); Dieter Zeller, "Jesu weisheitliche Ethik," in *Jesus von Nazaret—Spuren und Konturen* (ed. Ludger Schenke; Stuttgart: Kohlhammer, 2004), 193–215. As examples of wisdom ethics in Jesus's teaching, Zeller lists Mark 5:42; 6:25b; 8:35, 36–37; 10:21; Matt. 5:33–37, 39b–40, 44–45; 6:7a, 8b, 19–21, 24, 26, 28b–30, 31–32b; 7:7, 9–11; 10:29, 31b; Luke 6:24, 31, 36–37; 16:25; 17:3–4b; 18:2–5.

147. For analysis, see Jürgen Sauer, *Rückkehr und Vollendung des Heils: Eine Untersuchung zu den ethischen Radikalismen Jesu* (TF 133; Regensburg: Roderer, 1991), 96–148.

(without the parenthesis introduced by Paul in v. 11a), where Paul bases the indissolubility of marriage on the word of the Lord. The exceptions in Matt. 5:32 (παρεκτὸς λόγου πορνείας) and Matt. 19:9 (μὴ ἐπὶ πορνείᾳ) are Matthean.[148]

The sayings of Jesus in Mark 2:27 and 3:4 are directed toward reestablishing the order of creation: the Sabbath, as the work of the Creator, should serve to enhance life, and the acts of human beings should be oriented to this maxim. Like the healings (see below, §3.6.3) and the sayings critical of the Torah (see below, §3.8.2), Jesus's ethical statements include a dimension of creation theology. Because creation means life as willed by God the creator, who is at once the giver and preserver of life, human beings must constantly be aware that their life comes from God and must at the same time follow the will of God, which is intended to enhance and preserve life.

Jesus likewise sees the political order as grounded in the divine will, so long as the state is fulfilling its responsibilities given by God and does not presume to overreach them. This theme is dealt with in exemplary fashion in Mark 12:13–17,[149] where Jesus's own position is marked by v. 17, "Give to the emperor the things that are the emperor's, and to God the things that are God's." Those who posed the question obviously wanted to provoke Jesus to state his own position regarding a central issue of the *political ethics* of the time. The question was so stated that either answer Jesus gave would be to his disadvantage. If he gave a clear yes to the question of paying taxes to Rome, he could be charged with being a friend of Rome and an enemy of his own people. A clear no would mean that he could be denounced to the authorities as an agitator. If one keeps in mind the ways in which political and religious life were thoroughly interwoven in the ancient world, the critical component of v. 17b will not be missed. To be sure, Jesus does not challenge the right and power of the state, but he reduces the significance of the state to a purely functional level. Taxes are to be paid to the emperor, but nothing more! With this determination of the issue, Jesus makes every ideological or religious exaltation of the state impossible. Finally, v. 17b presents an additional relativizing of the emperor. Here lies the point of Jesus's answer: obedience to God has priority over everything else. It is obedience to God, nothing more or less, that determines what Caesar gets and does not get. Taxes are owed to the Caesar, for he needs them in order to fulfill his political responsibility, but no religious honor is due him. *The coins belong to Caesar, but human beings belong to God*. In view of God's claim on human life, the rights of Caesar and state are necessarily limited. Jesus's answer thus takes a middle path: he is no

148. Cf. Strecker, *Sermon on the Mount*, 77.

149. Markan redaction is evident only in v. 13, so that it is quite possible that the setting of the whole apophthegm has a setting in the life of Jesus; for analysis, cf. most recently Stefan Schreiber, "Caesar oder Gott (Mk 12,17)?" *BZ* 48 (2004): 65–85.

anti-Roman revolutionary[150] who fundamentally calls into question the rights and existence of the state. He grants the state its rights, on a purely functional level, at the same time making it clear that the state has a right, but a clearly limited right, within God's right to the whole of human life.

3.5.2 The Ethical Radicalism of Jesus

The will of God proclaimed by Jesus intends to enable human beings to live a truly human life together, and to overcome disruptions through a new, unanticipated way of living. In the *antitheses of the Sermon on the Mount* he sets forth God's unconditional will in a way that cannot be ignored.

The evangelist Matthew found the first, second, and fourth antitheses in his special material and on this basis created a series of six antitheses.[151] The "again" (πάλιν) of Matt. 5:33a sets off the first series of three from the second series. While the first three antitheses deal with conduct among fellow Christians (anger against one's brother or sister, adultery, divorce), the second series speaks to relations with non-Christians (oaths, revenge, love of enemies). The oldest layer of the tradition of antitheses 1, 2, and 4 comprises Matt. 5:21–22a (ἠκούσατε . . . ἔσται τῇ κρίσει), Matt. 5:27–28b (ἠκούσατε . . . ἐμοίχευσεν αὐτήν), and Matt. 5:33–34a (ἠκούσατε . . . μὴ ὀμόσαι ὅλως) and probably belongs to Jesus's own preaching. In the course of the tradition process, this oldest sayings material was expanded by examples and explanations. The antitheses formulated by the evangelist also contain old tradition, though only the demand to renounce revenge (Matt. 5:39b–40/Luke 6:29), the absolute ἀγαπᾶτε τοὺς ἐχθροὺς ὑμῶν in Matt. 5:44a/Luke 6:27a, and the grounding of Matt. 5:45/Luke 6:35 in creation theology can with some probability be traced back to Jesus himself.

In the *first antithesis* Jesus contrasts his own rule to the Old Testament prohibition of killing (Exod. 20:15; Deut. 5:18): "You have heard that it was said to those of ancient times, 'You shall not murder'; and 'whoever murders shall be liable to judgment.' But I say to you that if you are angry with a brother or sister, you will be liable to judgment" (Matt. 5:21–22a). Anger against a brother or sister already brings the person under judgment. Jesus does not give an interpretation of the Old Testament law, but goes beyond it. What is called for is a radical new orientation toward one's fellow human being. Otherwise, one inevitably comes under judgment. The content of the command against

150. Just as Mark 12:17 already suggests a certain distancing from the Zealots, so Matt. 26:52 is probably to be understood as critical of the Zealots ("Put your sword back into its place; for all who take the sword will perish by the sword"). Jesus's instructions in the Sermon on the Mount are, after all, incompatible with the violence of the Zealots. Cf. Martin Hengel, *War Jesus Revolutionär?* (Stuttgart: Calwer, 1970); and Martin Hengel, *Victory over Violence: Jesus and the Revolutionists* (trans. David E. Green; Philadelphia: Fortress, 1973).

151. Strecker, *Sermon on the Mount*, 62–64.

anger is not new (cf. 1QS 6:25–27).[152] The surprising aspect is that Jesus's rejection of anger goes beyond the Torah and affirms it only in a qualified sense, as inadequate. Jesus interprets the will of God in such a way that it persistently applies to the whole of human life, including spontaneous impulses. Even to ask whether anger might not be justified in some cases would be an attempt to portion off a part of one's life to which God's will does not apply.

In the *second antithesis* Jesus answers the Old Testament command against adultery (Exod. 20:14; Deut. 5:17) with his own thesis that the lustful look is already counted as adultery: "You have heard that it was said, 'You shall not commit adultery.' But I say to you that everyone who looks at a woman with lust has already committed adultery with her in his heart" (Matt. 5:27–28). The problem is not the look itself but the lustful intention that stands behind it. By ἐπιθυμία (lust), Jesus refers to the human craving to get something that is not one's own.[153] The person expects from such striving to attain a deeper and fuller enjoyment of life. Jesus prohibits such striving, because it includes a destructive power. The sanctity of marriage is broken, and human beings are separated from the true existence as God's creatures that is to determine their lives.

So also the prohibition of oaths in the *fourth antithesis* brings human life as a whole under its purview (Matt. 5:33–34a, "Again, you have heard that it was said to those of ancient times, 'You shall not swear falsely, but carry out the vows you have made to the Lord.' But I say to you, 'Do not swear at all.'"). By the oath that certifies the truth of sworn statements, other statements are exempted from responsibility to the truth. In practice, therefore, the oath serves to license lies. One part of life, in which the will of God—truthfulness—applies, is separated from the rest of life, in which this demand does not apply. Jesus's command is intended to abolish this distinction. The will of God applies in every aspect of life.

Jesus demands the *renunciation of revenge* (Matt. 5:39b, 40/Luke 6:29).[154] This is by no means simply a matter of purely passive conduct that leads to suffering. Jesus's provocative command to turn the other cheek and to give the undergarment along with the cloak is the precise opposite of passivity in that it calls for extreme action on the part of the disciple, who is called to put into practice the fundamental command of love even in apparently hopeless situations. Jesus himself lives by an unusual code of conduct that is not based on calculation of benefits, is free from his own personal agenda, and is effective precisely in this renunciation—and this is the life to which he calls others.

In its unqualified form, the *command to love one's enemies* is without analogy (Matt. 6:27a, ἀγαπᾶτε τοὺς ἐχθροὺς ὑμῶν [love your enemies]). To be

152. Cf. Merklein, *Handlungsprinzip*, 261n306; Luz, *Matthew 1–7*, 234–35.

153. Weder, *Rede*, 114.

154. For analysis, cf. Luz, *Matthew 1–7*, 270–80; Strecker, *Sermon on the Mount*, 81–85. In v. 39b, Matthew adds τὴν δεξιάν (the right).

sure, there are close parallels both in Judaism and elsewhere in the Hellenistic world, but they always include various motives as their basis and are thus not really the same as Jesus's unqualified demand.[155] The love for which Jesus calls knows no bounds; limitation is no longer possible, which means such love cannot be restricted to the "neighbor." In the extreme example of the enemy, Jesus shows how far love must go. There are no limits; love is to be extended to all human beings. God's own radical, unconditional love erupts into the everydayness of human life, encouraging people to love their enemies and thus participate in God's own love for them. There is no way to provide a basis for such love from within the empirical world, for such extraordinary conduct can receive its meaning and binding force only by being based on God's own loving actions. Because the creator himself demolishes the friend-foe schema by his loving-kindness toward good and evil people alike (Matt. 5:45), human beings too can violate the conventional boundaries between friend and enemy, and the category "enemy" becomes meaningless.[156]

Directly connected with this conception, Jesus presents a *new understanding of leadership*, formulated to the disciples in Mark 10:42b–44,[157] "You know that among the Gentiles those whom they recognize as their rulers lord it over them, and their great ones are tyrants over them. But it is not so among you; but whoever wishes to become great among you must be your servant, and whoever wishes to be first among you must be slave of all." The ancient understanding of rulership is here subjected to a radical critique, in which the true ruler is characterized not by oppression and exploitation but by service and care for others.[158]

155. Parallels are found in the literature of Hellenistic Judaism, but especially in the realm of Greco-Roman philosophy. Pythagoras was already credited with the following saying that people should treat each other in such a way "as not to make friends into enemies, but to turn enemies into friends" (Diogenes Laertius, *Vit. phil.* 8.23). Cf. further Plato, *Resp.* 1.334b–336a; *Crito* 49b–c; Seneca, *Ira* 2.32.1–33.1; 3.42.3–43.2; *Ep.* 120.9–10; Musonius, *Diss.* 10; Epictetus, *Diatr.* 1.25.28–31; 2.10.13–14, 22–24; 3.20.9–12; 22.54–56; 4.5.24; *Ench.* 42; Plutarch, *Mor.* 143f–144a; 218a; 462c–d; 799c; additional texts in *NW* 1.1 at Matt. 5:24.

156. The comment of François Bovon (*Luke*, 1:239) is on target: "In the act of loving their enemies, Christians act *on behalf of* the future of their enemies. . . . In the behavior of the Christians, the enemies will discover someone facing them in love, where they expected an opponent." [The German edition followed by Schnelle continues: "When one recognizes this new situation, one may anticipate a new attitude towards oneself, one's fellow human beings, and to God."—MEB]

157. The text does not go back to Jesus in its present form, but Mark 10:42–44 had probably already had an extensive history in the pre-Markan tradition as a fixed unit; cf. Joachim Gnilka, *Das Evangelium nach Markus* (EKKNT 2; Zürich: Benziger, 1979), 2:99–100. But when debates about leadership arose in the Jesus movement, a stimulus from the sayings of Jesus probably stood at the very beginning of the development of this tradition, especially since the aspect of service fits well within the tendencies of the message of Jesus as a whole.

158. In terms of subject matter, this position corresponds to Dio Chrysostom's vision of the ideal ruler; cf. *Or.* 1–3.

A further aspect of Jesus's ethical radicalism is represented by Jesus's *prohibition of judging* in Matt. 7:1, "Do not judge, so that you may not be judged."[159] Jesus forbids all judging, because in every human judgment there is the potential for condemnation. With the divine passive κριθῆτε in Matt. 7:1b, Jesus bases his prohibition on what will happen at the last judgment. Because this divine judgment will happen in the immediate future, human beings should orient their own lives to this coming judgment and renounce any judging of others; to set oneself up as judge of others in the present will necessarily result in one's own condemnation in the final judgment.

Jesus's *critique of wealth* is also an expression of his ethical radicalism, as expressed in the blessing of the poor (Q 6:20), in the challenge to live without anxiety (Matt. 6:25–33), or in Mark 10:25,[160] "It is easier for a camel to go through the eye of a needle than for someone who is rich to enter the kingdom of God." While the rich *are already excluded* from the kingdom of God, the poor are promised entrance to it; a more paradoxical and sharper critique of wealth as an obstruction in the road that leads to the kingdom of God is difficult to imagine![161] The sharp contrast between the kingdom of God and this world is also visible in Q 9:59–60,[162] "But another said to him: Master, permit me first to go and bury my father. But he said to him: Follow me, and leave the dead to bury their own dead." The burial of parents was considered a sacred duty in all of antiquity, so that here Jesus makes a frontal attack on the law, customary duty, and piety,[163] which is related to the ethos of the new *familia dei* (cf. Q 14:26; Mark 10:29) and the homelessness of the Son of Man (Q 9:57–58). The prohibition of divorce (see above, §3.5.1), the prohibition of fasting in Mark 2:18–20, and the criticism of the temple in Mark 11:15–19 (see below, §3.10.1) can also be seen as dimensions of Jesus's ethical radicalism.

The transgression of conventional boundaries inherent in Jesus's ethical radicalism challenges his hearers, in an extreme way, to overcome the divisions that separate human beings and to reestablish the original will of God. These challenges are essentially unqualified and only understandable within the horizon of the dawning kingdom of God;[164] they call for a way of

159. That Matt. 7:1 comes from Jesus himself is undisputed; cf. Strecker, *Sermon on the Mount*, 143–44; Luz, *Matthew 1–7*, 349–50.

160. For analysis of the relevant texts, cf. Sauer, *Vollendung*, 277–343.

161. Criticism of wealth is found everywhere in antiquity; cf., e.g., Dio Chrysostom, *Or.* 4.91. Nonetheless, the radicality of Jesus's sayings remains, for he avoids any sublimation, as practiced for example by the Roman millionaire Seneca: "The shortest way to wealth is the disdain of wealth" (*Ep.* 62.3).

162. On this point cf. Martin Hengel, *The Charismatic Leader and His Followers* (trans. James Greig; New York: Crossroad, 1981), 8–15.

163. According to Sanders, *Jesus and Judaism*, 267, this is the only instance in which Jesus calls for a violation of the written Torah.

164. Schweitzer, *Mystery*, 97, emphasizes that, in view of the expected near advent of the kingdom of God, the ethical radicality of Jesus's ethical demands was conditioned by tempo-

life that knows itself to be determined by God alone.[165] The proclamation that the kingdom of God is presently breaking into human life presents the will of God as something new, radical, and ultimate. *Jesus formulates this proclamation on the basis of his own authority*; he does not derive it from the Old Testament, which, in the light of the dawning kingdom of God, is seen as now surpassed but at the same time also deepened and extended. Only life in accord with the will of God brings human beings to the life they were intended to live at the creation. They are to hold fast to this ultimate word of the creator God as the norm for their life and work. By orienting themselves entirely to God and thus being freed from themselves, they can allow their lives to be determined by love that seeks the welfare of others. So also, in failing to live by the will of God and falling under the threatening judgment to come, human beings are entirely dependent on God, for only by repentance can they escape God's righteous judgment. The radicality of Jesus's demand thus corresponds to the way in which human beings are totally dependent on God.[166] Jesus himself does not raise the question of whether these demands can be fulfilled, a question that might lead to a negation of human freedom of decision and thus to a legalism and functionalism. These radical demands are *intentionally distancing*; as *exemplary sayings* they function as challenges to depend entirely on God in view of the dawning kingdom of God, and thereby to facilitate a truly human existence.

3.5.3 The Love Command as the Center of Jesus's Ethic

As God's creatures, human beings are obligated to do God's will. They must therefore submit themselves not to some other despot but to the will of God, which comprises God's love and takes concrete form in God's creative acts. The love commandment has a threefold form, as the central focus of Jesus's ethic is expressed as love for the *neighbor* (cf. Matt. 5:43), as love for the *enemy* (Matt. 5:44), and as the *double commandment of love* (Mark 12:28–34).

---

ral and material restrictions: "As repentance unto the Kingdom of God the ethics also of the Sermon on the Mount is interim ethics." This means, "Every ethical form of Jesus, be it ever so perfect, leads therefore only up to the frontier of the Kingdom of God, while every trace of a path disappears so soon as one advances upon the new territory. There one needs it no more" (p. 102). For Schweitzer, however, this by no means signifies that the content of Jesus's ethic must be abandoned as a guide for the way people should live in the world (until the advent of the kingdom of God), for it is only the element of near expectation as the basis for this ethic that cannot be taken over. The "interim" in "interim ethics" thus applies only to the grounding, not to the substance, of Jesus's ethics!

165. Cf. Weder, *Rede*, 154.

166. Cf. Jost Eckert, "Wesen und Funktion der Radikalismen in der Botschaft Jesu," *MTZ* 24 (1973): 319.

The Double Commandment of Love

In Mark 12:28–34, Jesus responds to the scribe's question, "Which commandment is the first of all?" with the words, "'You shall love the Lord your God with all your heart, and with all your soul, and with all your mind, and with all your strength.' The second is this, 'You shall love your neighbor as yourself.' There is no other commandment greater than these." In its present literary form, the double commandment of love does not go back directly to Jesus, for the elaboration of the aspect of reason (cf. the addition of διάνοια [mind], present in the LXX but not in the MT), the emphasis on the spectrum of anthropological terms, the specific priority of the love commandment to the sacrificial laws in v. 33, and the stress on monotheism all indicate that, in literary-historical terms, the traditional unit comes from Hellenistic Judaism. Thus the double commandment of love is often seen as not particularly distinctive of the preaching of Jesus.[167] However, there are also indications that the substance of the double commandment of love does indeed go back to Jesus himself:[168]

1. The combination of Deut. 6:5 and Lev. 19:18 is in fact documented in the Jewish tradition,[169] but very rarely, just as the numbering of the two commandments is seldom attested.[170]
2. The text contains no Christology of any sort; it is excluded by the strong emphasis on monotheism.[171]

167. Cf. Günther Bornkamm, "Das Doppelgebot der Liebe," in *Geschichte und Glaube* (ed. Günther Bornkamm; BEvT 53; Munich: Kaiser, 1968), 37–45; Christoph Burchard, "Das doppelte Liebesgebot in der frühchristlichen Überlieferung," in *Studien zur Theologie, Sprache und Umwelt des Neuen Testaments* (ed. Christoph Burchard and Dieter Sänger; WUNT 107; Tübingen: Mohr, 1998), 3–26; M. Ebersohn, *Das Nächstenliebegebot in der synoptischen Tradition* (MTS 37; Marburg: Elwert, 1993).

168. See especially Gerd Theissen, "Das Doppelgebot der Liebe: Jüdische Ethik bei Jesus," in *Jesus als historische Gestalt: Beiträge zur Jesusforschung: Zum 60. Geburtstag von Gerd Theissen* (ed. Gerd Theissen and Annette Merz; FRLANT 202; Göttingen: Vandenhoeck & Ruprecht, 2003), 57–72. On the whole issue, cf. Victor Paul Furnish, *The Love Command in the New Testament* (Nashville: Abingdon, 1972); Luise Schottroff et al., *Essays on the Love Commandment* (Philadelphia: Fortress, 1978).

169. Only a few of many examples: *Let. Aris.* 131; Philo, *Spec. Laws* 2.63, 95; 4.147; *T. Iss.* 5.2; 7.6; *T. Zeb.* 5.3; *T. Jos.* 11.1. Numerous other examples are found in Klaus Berger, *Die Gesetzesauslegung Jesu: Ihr historischer Hintergrund im Judentum und im Alten Testament* (WMANT 40; Neukirchen-Vluyn: Neukirchener Verlag, 1972), 1:99–136; Andreas Nissen, *Gott und der Nächste im antiken Judentum: Untersuchungen zum Doppelgebot der Liebe* (WUNT 15; Tübingen: Mohr, 1974), 224–46; 389–416; Hermann Strack and Paul Billerbeck, eds., *Kommentar zum Neuen Testament aus Talmud und Midrasch* (6 vols.; Munich: Beck, 1924), 1:357–59; 3:306; O. Wischmeyer, "Das Gebot der Nächstenliebe bei Paulus," *BZ* 30 (1986): 162ff.

170. Cf. Martin Hengel, "Jesus und die Tora," *ThB* (1978): 170.

171. Cf. Theissen, "Doppelgebot," 69: "The Markan double commandment of love cannot be a Christian creation, since its monotheism excludes the honoring of Jesus as Lord alongside God, and the positive portrayal of the scribe points to a time prior to the time of the fundamental

3. Both contextual plausibility and the plausibility of historical effects speak for tracing the substance of the double commandment back to Jesus. On the one hand, it is interwoven into the traditions of Judaism and can therefore be related to the Jew Jesus of Nazareth, while on the other hand, a distinctive profile can be discerned. The double commandment of love could thus very well have been a characteristic of Jesus's own preaching that documents his claim.[172] In particular, the command to love one's enemies illustrates how Jesus extended the command to love the neighbor beyond the national perspective of Lev. 19:18. Strong effects in the history of reception (cf. Mark 12:28–34 par.; Gal. 5:14; Rom. 13:8–10; John 13:34–35) likewise favor the view that an impulse from Jesus himself stood at the beginning of this tradition.
4. The substance of the double command is found not only in the sayings tradition but also in the narrative tradition. The example story of the Good Samaritan illustrates love for the foreigner (Luke 10:30–37),[173] which is Jesus's response to the question "Who is my neighbor?" The story is concerned with the scope and boundaries of the obligation to fulfill the love command. Jesus tells the story from the perspective of the man who fell among thieves. By taking as his example the Samaritan, a person victimized by religious and political discrimination, Jesus illustrates the limitless obligation of love, which does not attain its goal in the merely reasonable and usual. The two Jews who do not manifest love are intentionally contrasted with the compassionate Samaritan. Here again is an alienating, distancing effect, intended to make it clear that love for neighbor does not maintain the conventions and prejudices of the culture but dares to set them aside and in sovereign freedom to transcend any hindrance that might otherwise block interpersonal access. So also the story of the sinful woman in Luke 7:36–50 illustrates love for the sinner.[174] The fellowship with God vouched for by Jesus is

---

parting of the ways between Christians and Jews." Theissen supposes that Jesus took over the double commandment from John the Baptist.

172. Martin Hengel, "Jesus der Messias Israels," in *Der messianische Anspruch Jesu und die Anfänge der Christologie: Vier Studien* (ed. Martin Hengel and Anna Maria Schwemer; WUNT 138; Tübingen: Mohr Siebeck, 2001), 75, sees in the formulation of the double commandment "in a way that transcends Moses and all the prophets" a reference to Jesus's messianic claim.

173. For exegesis cf. Wolfgang Harnisch, *Die Gleichniserzählungen Jesu: Eine hermeneutische Einführung* (Göttingen: Vandenhoeck & Ruprecht, 1985), 275–96; Philip Francis Esler, "Jesus and the Reduction of Intergroup Conflict," in *The Social Setting of Jesus and the Gospels* (ed. Wolfgang Stegemann et al.; Minneapolis: Fortress, 2002), 197–211.

174. The story in its present form does not go back to Jesus, but a basic form with a stable narrative scheme may be claimed to represent an event in the life of Jesus: "(1) Jesus is invited to a meal; (2) a woman comes in and anoints Jesus; (3) this gesture evokes a negative reaction; (4) Jesus defends the accused woman; and (5) he recognizes her action as worthy of praise" (Bovon, *Luke*, 1:387–88).

oriented not to religious barriers but to the needs of people who sincerely seek forgiveness.

The Love Ethic

With regard to content, the love commandment is the very center of Jesus's ethic. It no longer tolerates any restriction and thus corresponds to the unrestricted goodness of the Creator. Jesus's love command is *concrete*, as shown in the concrete examples that dominate the texts: blessing, doing good, being reconciled to one's neighbor, forgiveness, not calling one's brother or sister a "fool," paying the poor their due, giving away one's fortune, not judging, not seeing the splinter in the brother's or sister's eye. Jesus is by no means concerned only with a new attitude and perspective on things, for both the concreteness of the commands and their radical, extreme character should remove any doubt that his commands are in fact given with absolute seriousness. Jesus's love command is *exemplary* precisely in its radicality. His sayings are exemplary statements, his narratives are exemplary stories, and his acts are exemplary deeds that release their power in different situations and in various ways. They cannot be translated into other situations on a one-to-one basis, for it belongs to the essential nature of love to be spontaneous, to embrace the whole of life, to realize itself in ever new ways in new situations. In this sense, Jesus's commands are much more than prescriptions: they are exemplary pointers; they pick out paradigmatic examples that are easily remembered because of their vivid imagery; and they show what the life Jesus calls for could look like in various situations. The scope in which Jesus's commands are valid extends far beyond what is actually addressed in the particular texts. At the same time, obedience to his commands always includes a dimension of freedom that allows one to find out what love means concretely in a new situation. The removal of boundaries postulated by Jesus by no means leads to an arbitrary, anything-goes mentality but calls for a positive orientation to love, which cannot be expressed in just *any* way.

3.6 Jesus as Healer: God's Miraculous Power

Jesus of Nazareth was perceived first of all to be a healer, and *it was as a charismatic healer that he achieved widespread influence*. Both the Synoptics and the Gospel of John place the central focus of their narratives on Jesus's influential ministry as exorcist and healer.[175] All the criteria used in establishing

175. Also to be mentioned is the testimony of Josephus, *Ant.* 18.63–64, which probably has a historical nucleus (cf. Theissen and Merz, *Historical Jesus*, 64–74), and who also mentions Jesus as a miracle worker: "For he was one who did surprising deeds and was a teacher of such people as accept the truth gladly." In addition, note that "the historical effect of Jesus within Judaism was closely bound up with his miracles—more closely, indeed, than with any statement

a historical picture of Jesus (see above, §3.1.2) permit only one conclusion, that in the villages around the Sea of Gennesaret Jesus appeared above all as an influential healer and was revered as such by the mostly impoverished inhabitants who crowded around him.

3.6.1 *Cultural Context*

In antiquity (but not only then), miracle-working healers are a standard cultural phenomenon. Jesus's ministry was conducted in a context in which Jewish and Hellenistic miracle workers were a common sight.[176] The *Qumran texts*, in the context of a pronounced doctrine about the spirits, make clear reference to magical-pharmacological practices and incantation rituals to ward off demons.[177] "Since the findings from Qumran that point to the exorcism of demons are primarily of non-Essene origin, the healing practices implied there point beyond the Qumran community itself, as representative of broad streams of contemporary Judaism."[178] In the *early rabbinic* tradition, Honi the Circle Drawer and Rabbi Hanina ben Dosa are of particular significance. Honi (first century BCE), who worked rain-making miracles by drawing a magic circle, is mentioned both in the rabbinic traditions and by Josephus (*Ant.* 14.22–24).[179] Hanina ben Dosa emerged in Galilee about the same time as Jesus, and obviously was known primarily as a miracle worker (especially as one who healed by prayer), but numerous other miraculous acts were also ascribed to him (healings at a distance, power over demons).[180] Moreover, the Mishnah tractate *Aboth* transmits three sayings of Hanina ben Dosa that present him "as a warm-hearted lover of men, a true Chasid."[181] It is probably no accident that the two most significant Jewish miracle workers of the first century appeared in Galilee. The distinctive

in Jesus's preaching!" (Michael Becker, *Wunder und Wundertäter im frührabbinischen Judentum: Studien zum Phänomen und seiner Überlieferung im Horizont von Magie und Dämonismus* [Tübingen: Mohr, 2002], 424).

176. On this point see the description in Bernd Kollmann, *Jesus und die Christen als Wundertäter: Studien zu Magie, Medizin und Schamanismus in Antike und Christentum* (FRLANT 170; Göttingen: Vandenhoeck & Ruprecht, 1996), 61–118 (Hellenism); 118–73 (ancient Judaism).

177. To be mentioned here is especially 4Q510 4–5: "And I, the Instructor, proclaim His glorious splendor so as to frighten and to te[rrify] all the spirits of the destroying angels, spirits of the bastards, demons, Lilith, howlers and [desert dwellers]." Cited according to Michael O. Wise et al., eds., *The Dead Sea Scrolls: A New English Translation* (New York: HarperCollins, 1996).

178. Kollmann, *Wundertäter*, 137.

179. On this point cf. Becker, *Wunder*, 290–337.

180. Extensive presentation and analysis of all important texts in ibid., 337–78. Becker regards the texts in which Hanina is called "son of God" as a reflection of Christian traditions (p. 377).

181. Géza Vermès, "Hanina ben Dosa," in *Post-biblical Jewish Studies* (ed. Géza Vermès; SJLA 8; Leiden: Brill, 1975), 197.

climatic and cultural conditions of this land obviously helped facilitate the extraordinary events that happened within its borders. Independently of the other types of charismatics, the first century also saw the emergence of *Jewish sign prophets*.[182] In the decades before the eruption of the Jewish war, Josephus reports the repeated appearance in Palestine of such sign prophets, who wanted to legitimize their (political) claims through eschatological miracles. About 35 CE, a prophet from Samaria promised his followers that he would rediscover the missing temple vessels on Mount Gerizim (Josephus, *Ant.* 18.85–87). As a result, the Samaritans armed themselves and marched on the holy mountain. Shortly after 44 CE, a certain Theudas proclaimed that the Jordan would dry up to permit his followers to cross over on dry land (*Ant.* 20.97–99), which would have been a repetition of the miracles at the Jordan performed by Joshua and Elijah (cf. Josh. 3; 2 Kings 2:8). The procurator Fadus had Theudas beheaded and killed many of his followers. Under the procurator Felix (52–60 CE), an anonymous prophet appeared who did signs and wonders in the wilderness, announcing a new exodus (*Ant.* 20.167–168; *JW* 2.259). A prophet from Egypt led his followers to the Mount of Olives and promised that the walls of Jerusalem would fall down at his command (*Ant.* 20.168–172; *JW* 2.261–263; cf. Acts 21:38). Again, the Romans intervened and killed many of his followers. It is characteristic of the sign prophets that they worked from a combination of eschatological and sociopolitical motivations: the miracles of the beginnings of Israel's history would be repeated in the end time as confirming signs that the promised eschatological salvation is already beginning—including the liberation of the House of Israel from the Romans. According to Acts 5:36, Jesus's opponents understood him to be such a sign prophet, and his trial before Roman authorities shows that they placed Jesus of Nazareth in this category (see below, §3.10.1).

From the broad field of *Hellenistic miracle workers*, the Neopythagorean wandering philosopher Apollonius of Tyana (d. 96/97 CE), whose biography was written by Philostratus at the beginning of the third century, is of particular importance.[183] Behind numerous legendary elaborations, one can still detect a historical figure who with enlightened philosophical sovereignty demonstrated competence in numerous intellectual and scientific disciplines of the time. He also manifested a variety of miraculous powers, including healing; rescued people from various dangers; and repeatedly came into conflict with the rulers of the time. It is striking that not only do almost all of Jesus's healing miracles have parallels in Apollonius,[184] but there are also parallels

182. Cf. P. W. Barnett, "The Jewish Sign Prophets—A.D. 40–47: Their Intentions and Origin," *NTS* 27 (1981): 679–97.

183. Cf. Erkki Koskenniemi, *Apollonios von Tyana in der neutestamentlichen Exegese: Forschungsbericht und Weiterführung der Diskussion* (WUNT 2.61; Tübingen: Mohr [Siebeck], 1994).

184. A catalog of comparable texts is found in Gerd Petzke, *Die Traditionen über Apollonius von Tyana und das Neue Testament* (SCHNT 1; Leiden: Brill, 1970), 124–34; cf. also the extensive

to their respective beginnings (miraculous birth) and endings (resurrection and appearances); Jesus of Nazareth and Apollonius of Tyana can be seen as thoroughly parallel figures.[185]

3.6.2 The Varied Character of Jesus's Healing Work

Exorcisms constitute the center of Jesus's healing work.[186] They are found in all strata of the tradition, are present in both the sayings and narrative traditions, for the most part have no trace of post-Easter interests, and can be integrated into the ministry of Jesus as a whole.[187] Moreover, the Beelzebul controversy[188] shows that probably already during Jesus's lifetime a dispute broke out as to the power behind his healing abilities: "He has Beelzebul, and by the ruler of the demons he casts out demons" (Mark 3:22b). Jesus responds to this charge with a saying from the wisdom tradition, according to which the kingdom of Satan cannot endure if it is divided against itself. However, his own success as an exorcist points in a completely different direction: "No one can enter a strong man's house and plunder his property without first tying up the strong man; then indeed the house can be plundered" (Mark 3:27; cf. Matt. 9:34). *The fundamental overthrow of the power of Satan and the re-establishment of life as intended by the creator that his overthrow brings about were obviously at the center of Jesus's own experience of reality—an experience both evoked and confirmed by the exorcisms.* Alongside Mark 3:27, this observation is indicated above all by Jesus's vision recounted in Luke 10:18 ("I watched Satan fall from heaven like a flash of lightning"),[189] by the connection

---

collection of materials in Georg Luck, ed., *Magie und andere Geheimlehren in der Antike: Mit 112 neu übersetzten und einzeln kommentierten Quellentexten* (Stuttgart: Kröner, 1990).

185. At one point, Christian influence on the Apollonius tradition seems to be clear, for the story of Apollonius's resuscitation of a young woman in Rome (Philostratus, *Vit. Apoll.* 4.45) is probably indebted to Luke 7:11–17.

186. This is the consensus of contemporary scholarship; I cite only two illustrative examples: Dieter Trunk, *Der messianische Heiler: Eine redaktions- und religionsgeschichtliche Studie zu den Exorzismen im Matthäusevangelium* (HBS 3; Freiburg: Herder, 1994); Kollmann, *Wundertäter*.

187. An analysis of all texts is found in Kollmann, *Wundertäter*, 174–215.

188. For a comprehensive analysis see Trunk, *Der messianische Heiler*, 40–93.

189. The meaning of Luke 10:18 is disputed in current research; see especially S. Vollenweider, "'Ich sah den Satan wie einen Blitz vom Himmel fallen' (Lk 10,18)," *ZNW* 79 (1988): 187–203 and Weder, *Gegenwart*, 43: "Jesus does not bring the kingdom, but the coming of the kingdom brings Jesus with it. Therefore, Jesus is not a factor in the struggle at the eschatological turn of the ages; it is rather the case that his life represents the celebration of this turn." Vollenweider and Weder dispute that combat imagery was typical of Jesus's message and ministry. This line of argument is based on an underlying general principle, but particular texts speak against it. Thus, for example, the petition for deliverance from evil/the Evil One in Matt. 6:13b only makes sense if evil is still exercising its power. Above all, however, is the dynamic concept of the kingdom of God itself, which presupposes the ultimate destruction of Satan still to come, not that this has

between exorcisms and the inbreaking of the kingdom of God in Q 11:20, and by the petition in the Lord's Prayer for deliverance from the Evil One (Matt. 6:13b). The struggle against evil/the Evil One was the central content of the teaching and acts of Jesus.[190] He thus shared the convictions of ancient Judaism, in which the overthrow of Satan and his demons signals the inbreaking of the end time. (Cf. *As. Mos.* 10.1, "Then his [i.e., God's] kingdom will appear throughout his whole creation, then will the devil have an end, yea, sorrow will be led away with him." Cf. further e.g., *T. Dan* 5.10–13; *T. Levi* 18.12; Isa. 24:21–22; *Jub.* 10.1, 5; 1QS 3:24–25; 4:20–22; 1QM 1:10.) *For Jesus, the real opposition to the coming of the kingdom of God is the rule of Satan.* In view of the breaking in of the kingdom of God, already making its presence felt in Jesus's miracles,[191] people are being freed from subjection to powers of Satan and restored to the kind of life intended for them at creation (cf. Q 7:22–23). The exorcisms, in particular, point to the restoration of the status at creation; they are signs of and protests against the subjection of human beings to the powers of evil (cf. Luke 13:16, "And ought not this woman, a daughter of Abraham whom Satan bound for eighteen long years, be set free from this bondage on the sabbath day?").[192] The story of the return of the evil spirit (Q 11:24–26) shows the extent to which Jesus lived within the world of contemporary views of exorcism. An exorcism was a battle. Jesus conquered the demons with the usual techniques (threatening of the demon, interrogation of the demon to learn its name, formula of expulsion, prohibition of return), freeing people from all spirits that cause sickness, including epilepsy (Mark 1:23–28; 9:14–29) and mental illness (Mark 5:1–20).[193]

Luke 13:32b points to the close connection between exorcisms and *healings*: "Listen, I am casting out demons and performing cures." No struggle was involved in the healings, but the central focus was on the transmission of healing

---

already been accomplished. On the significance of Luke 10:18, cf., e.g., Merklein, *Jesu Botschaft*, 68–72; Becker, *Jesus of Nazareth*, 169–86; Kollmann, *Wundertäter*, 191–95; Michael Theobald, "'Ich sah den Satan aus dem Himmel stürzen': Überlieferungskritische Beobachtungen zu Lk 10,18–20," *BZ* 49 (2005): 174–90; Onuki, *Jesus*, 48–49.

190. Stegemann, "Der lehrende Jesus," 15.

191. Theissen, *Miracle Stories*, 280: "Jesus sees his own miracles as events leading to something unprecedented. They anticipate a new world."

192. Luke 13:11–13 is an exorcism story (v. 11, "And just then there appeared a woman with a spirit that had crippled her for eighteen years"), which has been secondarily amplified into a Sabbath healing (cf. v. 14).

193. Christian Strecker, "Jesus and the Demoniacs," in *The Social Setting of Jesus and the Gospels* (ed. Wolfgang Stegemann et al.; Minneapolis: Fortress, 2002), 119–24, argues against the psychological model of explaining New Testament portrayals of sickness, which tend "to rationalize them in a functional manner and to pathologize the phenomena of possession described in the New Testament" in order to fit them into our understanding of reality (ibid., 119). He regards Jesus's exorcisms as ritual acts in which "the identity of the possessed person is constituted anew, their ranks and positions in the social order revised, and the cosmic order reestablished" (ibid., 125).

power to the afflicted person.[194] Sickness here appears as a deficiency in vital energy, as a weakness that can bring one to the very doors of death, but which is overcome by transmitting the positive life-giving power. The transmission of this power can take place in a variety of ways: In Mark 5:25–34 (healing of the woman with a hemorrhage), the healing power is activated without Jesus's knowledge. In Mark 1:29–31 (the healing of Peter's mother-in-law), a touch accomplishes the miracle, and in the case of the leprous person (Mark 1:40–45) the healing takes place by means of touch and miracle-working word. Healing techniques (use of saliva, miracle-working word) are illustrated in Mark 7:31–37 (healing of a person with speech and hearing impediments) and Mark 8:22–26 (healing of a blind person). In the healing of blind Bartimaeus (Mark 10:46–52), the motif of faith is the central focus. Healings at a distance are narrated in Mark 7:24–30 (the Syrophoenician woman) and in Matt. 8:5–10, 13 (the centurion of Capernaum); both traditions may have a primitive nucleus that preserved the memory of Jesus's healing of a Gentile child. Not only the narrative tradition, but the tradition of Jesus's sayings also testifies to Jesus's healing ministry. The praise of the eyewitnesses in Q 7:22–23 presupposes this: "The blind regain their sight and the lame walk, the skin-diseased are cleansed and the deaf hear, and the dead are raised, the poor are evangelized. And blessed is whoever is not offended by me." This text has a noteworthy parallel in 4Q521, where likewise the divine deeds of the anointed one that establish eschatological salvation are enumerated:[195] liberation of prisoners, removal of blindness, and deliverance of the oppressed (cf. Isa. 42:7). The text goes further: "God will heal the sick, raise the dead, and preach good news to the suffering." So also Q 10:23–24 shows that the presence of Jesus was seen as the time of eschatological salvation: "Blessed are the eyes that see what you see! For I tell you: Many prophets and kings wanted to see what you see, but never saw it, and to hear what you hear, but never heard it."

Validating miracles, found in the Jesus tradition in connection with the problems of sin and Sabbath observance, have the function of establishing a new practice.[196] In Mark 2:23–28 and 3:1–6, Jesus adopts the basic Jewish principle that the Sabbath rules can be suspended in cases of emergency, but at the same time extends it. In Mark 2:1–12 he claims the authority to forgive sins, which belongs to God alone. In their present form, all three texts bear markers of post-Easter redaction, but the sayings in each that provide the nucleus of the story go back to Jesus (Mark 2:10–11, 27; 3:4–5), and the location of the stories in conflicts with the Pharisees and scribes may also be historical.

194. For analysis of the texts cf. Kollmann, *Wundertäter*, 215ff.

195. Cf. Johannes Zimmermann, *Messianische Texte aus Qumran: Königliche, priesterliche und prophetische Messiasvorstellungen in den Schriftfunden von Qumran* (WUNT 2.104; Tübingen: Mohr, 1998), 343–89.

196. On the distinction between healing miracles and validating ("rule") miracles, cf. Theissen, *Miracle Stories*, 106–14.

While the exorcisms, healings, and validating miracles are anchored in the ministry of the historical Jesus with great probability, the *nature miracles* pose numerous questions in regard to their tradition history (gift miracles, Mark 6:30–44 par.; 8:1–10 par.; deliverance miracle: Mark 4:35–41; epiphanies: Mark 6:45–52 par.).[197] In the case of the feeding stories, there are clear indications of a post-Easter origin: the connections with 2 Kings 2:42–44, the echoes of eucharistic language, the doubling of the tradition, and the enhancement of the miraculous elements. So also there is evidence that the stories of calming the storm and walking on the water originated in the post-Easter Christian community: the numerous parallels in the history of religions, the echoes of Old Testament texts, and the strong christological motifs. The stories of Jesus's raising people from the dead (cf. Mark 5:22–24, 35–43; Luke 7:11–17) are presupposed in the early tradition (cf. Q 7:22–23), but the observation that they are variations of the story of Jesus's own resurrection points to a post-Easter origin.

3.6.3 *Jesus of Nazareth as Healer*

That Jesus carried on a ministry of miraculous healings and exorcisms is historically indisputable.[198] Their theological interpretation must attend to three distinctive features:

1. In Jesus's message and ministry, the connection between miracle and eschatology (cf. Q 11:20) is unparalleled in the history of religions. His exorcisms and healings are embedded in an eschatological-theocentric view of reality as a whole. With the fundamental overthrow of Satan's power (cf. Mark 3:27; Luke 10:18), the kingdom of God is making space for itself.
2. So also the emphasis on faith in the New Testament's tradition of miracle stories is singular, appearing in both the sayings tradition (Mark 11:22–23) and the narrative tradition (Mark 9:23–24; 10:52a). The sick person's absolute trust in Jesus and confidence in the power of faith itself belong together and generate undreamed of powers.
3. Not only the eschatological perspective but also the dimension of creation theology make it clear that Jesus's miracles belong within the comprehensive framework of his whole ministry. The kingdom of God makes itself present in parables, in table fellowship with tax collectors and sinners, in Jesus's ethic and interpretation of the law, and in his

197. Cf. the line of argument pursued by Kollmann, *Wundertäter*, 271–80, who also provides an analysis of texts not cited here.

198. Cf. Theissen, *Miracle Stories*, 277; Hans Weder, "Wunder Jesu und Wundergeschichten," *VuF* 29 (1984): 28; Kollmann, *Wundertäter*, 306–7.

> exorcisms and healings. It is precisely the exorcisms and healings that have a dimension of creation theology: they aim at restoring the state of the world as God created it; they are signs and protests against the subjection of human life to the powers of evil.

Jesus's healing activity manifests a comprehensive image of humanity, for human beings are seen as at once intellectual, emotional, bodily, and social beings. In the ancient world, sickness usually resulted in some kind of social exclusion,[199] so that Jesus's healings also functioned to reintegrate the person into society. All these aspects distinguish Jesus of Nazareth from magicians, for his healings presuppose a personal relationship, operate with a minimum of technique, and lead to social stability and trust/faith.[200] In contrast to others, Jesus accepted no pay for his healings (cf. Mark 5:26) and made no distinction between poor and rich (cf. Q 7:3, 8). Moreover, he rejected miracles that merely demonstrated his amazing powers (cf. Mark 8:11 par.), and he performed no punitive miracles.[201]

Insight into the fact that modern worldviews are constructed, not simply given, and thus that they are relative and in constant flux, broadens our perspective anew to perceive the work of God the creator in all its dimensions. For a long time, the reductionistic fixation on the issue of the facticity of "miracles" has been a barrier to perceiving the multidimensional aspects of Jesus's healing activity. This activity is an integral part of his ministry in word and deed and makes God's healing presence and coming in his kingdom visible, a reality that can be experienced in body and soul.

3.7 The Imminent Judgment: Nothing Is without Its Consequences

According to the testimony of the Old Testament, God's eschatological judgment will establish justice, with salvation for the righteous and damnation for the wicked.[202] This concept of God's righteous judgment is a fundamental

199. Thus demon possession and leprosy resulted in exclusion from society; blindness and other physical handicaps usually resulted in unemployment, and thus inevitably in poverty and begging.

200. Contra John Dominic Crossan, *The Historical Jesus: The Life of a Mediterranean Jewish Peasant* (San Francisco: HarperSanFrancisco, 1991), 168–224, who represents Jesus as a social revolutionary. Morton Smith, *Jesus the Magician* (San Francisco: Harper & Row, 1978), 81–139, thinks that Jesus not only used magical rites and techniques, but also propagated magical doctrines and understood himself as a magician. In response, cf. J.-A. Bühner, "Jesus und die antike Magie: Bemerkungen zu M. Smith, Jesus der Magier," *EvT* 43 (1983): 156–75; Becker, *Wunder*, 425–30; Walter Wink, "Jesus as Magician," *USQR* 30 (1974): 3–14 (response to Smith's earlier work).

201. Mark 11:12–14, 20–21 (cursing the fig tree) is probably post-Easter; cf. Kollmann, *Wundertäter*, 275–76.

202. Cf. Bernd Janowski, "Gericht," *RGG*[4] 733: "God 'saves' in that he 'judges,' i.e., in that he does not ignore evil but punishes injustice . . . Within the horizon of interrelated justice, 'judg-

element of the worldview found in the Old Testament and the writings of ancient Judaism;[203] John the Baptist had placed God's condemnation of the wicked at the final judgment at the very center of his message. It is thus not surprising that the Jesus traditions also include the idea that God condemns the wicked.

Theologically, this idea of judgment, with a strong emphasis on damnation, is ambivalent. It frequently arises from the fantasies of omnipotence harbored by those groups that see damnation of their foes as the just recompense for the group's own present lack of success, incapacity, or oppression: God's future pronouncement of damnation will reestablish justice. Such a wish may be understandable but provides no basis for the desired destruction of life on God's part. Anyway, the image of God's judgment cannot be reduced to such a negative dimension (see below, §6.8.3). The image contains a positive affirmation as well: God is not indifferent to what happens in the life of an individual human being and in history as a whole. If the idea that God will act as eschatological judge both to save and to condemn is simply eliminated, then what human beings do with their lives has no final evaluation, and human life itself remains ambiguous. Injustice would finally triumph over justice, and evil and negation would have the last word. It is precisely as creator that God demonstrates in the final judgment that God himself is ultimately responsible for his creation.

3.7.1 *Jesus as Representative of God's Judgment*

Like John the Baptist, Jesus sees all Israel as threatened by God's condemning verdict and makes no use of the conventional contrasting pair "Israel/Gentiles."

Judgment against Israel

Jesus's message of salvation is directed to an Israel that has misused its covenant relation with God, so that its election is not a matter of blessing but has become an item on the prosecutor's agenda. This is affirmed by the double saying about the Galileans who had been killed by Pilate and those killed in Jerusalem by a tower that collapsed: "Do you think that because these Galileans suffered in this way they were worse sinners than all other Galileans? No, I tell you; but unless you repent, you will all perish as they did. Or those eighteen

---

ing' and 'saving' are correlative acts, and the judgment of God is the theological response to the question of the ultimate foundation of right living and just action." Cf. the relevant background discussions in Calvin J. Roetzel, *Judgement in the Community: A Study of the Relationship between Eschatology and Ecclesiology in Paul* (Leiden: Brill, 1972).

203. Cf., e.g., *1 En.* 50–66; an analysis of relevant texts is found in Marius Reiser, *Jesus and Judgment: The Eschatological Proclamation in Its Jewish Context* (trans. Linda M. Maloney; Minneapolis: Fortress, 1997), 19–166.

who were killed when the tower of Siloam fell on them—do you think that they were worse offenders than all the others living in Jerusalem? No, I tell you; but unless you repent, you will all perish just as they did" (Luke 13:1–5). Jesus intentionally lifts two individual events from an isolated cause-effect nexus and places them in a theological horizon. These events become something of a warning sign for all Israel, on whom God's judgment will fall with unexpected terror, unless they repent. For Jesus, "repentance" means the acceptance of his message; the turn involved in repentance is turning to him.

This exceptional claim is also visible in Q 11:31–32,[204] "The queen of the South will be raised at the judgment with this generation and condemn it, for she came from the ends of the earth to listen to the wisdom of Solomon. . . . Ninevite men will arise at the judgment with this generation and condemn it." Jesus declares that "this generation," i.e., all Israel addressed as a single entity, will be condemned in the last judgment unless they repent and accept his message. The woes pronounced on the Galilean cities[205] in Q 10:13–15 are clearly related to the saying about the queen of the South and the Ninevites and are no less provocative: "Woe to you, Chorazin! Woe to you, Bethsaida! For if the wonders performed in you had taken place in Tyre and Sidon, they would have repented long ago, in sackcloth and ashes. Yet for Tyre and Sidon it shall be more bearable at the judgment than for you. And you, Capernaum, up to heaven will you be exalted? Into Hades shall you come down!" Numerous woe oracles are pronounced against the Gentile cities of Sidon and Tyre (cf. Isa. 23:1–4, 12; Jer. 25:22; 47:4; Ezek. 27:8; 28:21–22; Joel 4:4). Jesus takes up this tradition, but in a way that distances him from conventional ideas: the catastrophe of divine judgment will fall not on the Gentiles but on Israel itself. The criterion is the response to Jesus's miracles, which communicate the inbreaking of the kingdom of God and thus also validate Jesus's own claim. Capernaum, the primary location of this aspect of Jesus's ministry, has already received the pronouncement of judgment. The saying about the pilgrimage of the Gentiles to Zion in Q 13:28–29 and the parable of the Great Supper in Luke 14:15–24/Matt. 22:1–10 have a similar threatening character (see above, §3.4.5). In them too, current ideas of Israel's favored status are rejected. Finally, the function of eschatological judgment that will be exercised by the Twelve in Q 22:28, 30 makes it clear that one's response to Jesus will be the decisive factor in the coming judgment.

Judgment against Individuals

The second grand category of Jesus's pronouncements of God's judgment is directed to individuals. This category stands in the background of Matt.

204. Analysis in ibid., 206–21; Christian Riniker, *Die Gerichtsverkündigung Jesu* (EHS 23.653; Bern: Lang, 1999), 287–300.

205. On this point cf. Riniker, *Gerichtsverkündigung*, 301–33.

7:1–2 ("Do not judge, so that you may not be judged. For with the judgment you make you will be judged."), for God's coming judgment is the motivation for the conduct here called for. The judgment motif is extremely sharp in Q 17:34–35, "I tell you, on that night there will be two in one bed; one will be taken and the other left. There will be two women grinding meal together; one will be taken and the other left." Jesus's statements are apodictic and provocative. The time of the coming judgment cannot be calculated. It can strike anyone. Jesus makes the announcement of the twofold judgment without any supporting reasons: it is simply the case that one will be saved and the other lost. The unexpected danger of the coming judgment is also the theme of the parable of the *Rich Fool* (Luke 12:16–20).[206] From his perspective, the farmer is acting on the basis of sound common sense ("I will do this: I will pull down my barns and build larger ones, and there I will store all my grain and my goods. And I will say to my soul, 'Soul, you have ample goods laid up for many years; relax, eat, drink, be merry.'"), but in his own self-absorption he has forgotten God! God has the last word ("You fool! This very night your life is being demanded of you. And the things you have prepared, whose will they be?"), a word that demands an answer on precisely this relation—resulting in the man's condemnation. To forget God is to lose one's own life.

In a completely different way the threat of the coming judgment appears as the theme in the parable of the *Unjust Steward* (Luke 16:1–8a).[207] The story has elements of a criminal case combined with comedy or farce, as the narrator entices the hearer to follow the plight of the manager and his resolute action aimed at saving his own skin. In a life-threatening situation, the manager does everything possible to secure his own future. There is no comment on his illegal and immoral conduct as such. Rather, the story communicates how important it is to be aware of Jesus's message of coming judgment and its results, a message that calls the hearers to resolute, immediate, and wise response in order to save their own lives from the coming catastrophe, just as the manager had done.

How much is staked on human decision in view of the approaching judgment is illustrated in the double parable of the *House Built on the Rock* in Q 6:47–49.[208] Just as the house builder avoided the catastrophe by making present decisions with an eye on the future, so people can avoid the catastrophic judgment to come by acting wisely, namely by obedience to the message of Jesus. Recognizing the signs of the times is also the challenge of Q 17:26–28. Jesus reminds his contemporaries that Noah's generation and the people of Sodom

206. See the extensive analysis in Bernhard Heininger, *Metaphorik, Erzählstruktur und szenisch-dramatische Gestaltung in den Sondergutgleichnissen bei Lukas* (NTA NF 24; Münster: Druckhaus Aschendorff, 1991), 107–21.

207. Cf. the discussion of the extent of the original parable and the interpretation in Merklein, *Handlungsprinzip*, 135–36.

208. On whether the parable derives from Jesus, cf. Luz, *Matthew 1–7*, 385–86.

and Gomorrah in Lot's time were suddenly punished by God's judgment. The inevitable, inescapable catastrophe here commands central attention, for Noah's and Lot's salvation is not described. It is also striking that the immoral conduct of the generation of the flood and of the inhabitants of Sodom and Gomorrah is not described. Israel's lostness is not calibrated in terms of its immoral deeds but in terms of its response to Jesus. This is also the focus of the parable of the *Playing Children* in Q 7:31–34.[209] With an illustration from everyday life,[210] Israel's rejection of John and Jesus is presented with exquisite sharpness. The point of the imagery (v. 32b, "We fluted for you, but you would not dance; we wailed, but you would not cry") consists of the fact that those addressed made no move to respond to the challenges and invitations presented by John and Jesus and the new situation they represented (vv. 33–34, "For John came, neither eating nor drinking, and you say: He has a demon! The Son of Man came, eating and drinking, and you say: Look! A person who is a glutton and drunkard, a chum of tax collectors and sinners!"). The rejection of the Son of Man leads inevitably to condemnation in the coming judgment.

Jesus as Representative of God's Judgment

All the preceding texts clearly indicate that Jesus made response to him and his message the criterion of acceptance or rejection in the coming judgment: those who accept his message will be saved, those who reject it will be condemned.[211] This claim is emphatically articulated in Q 12:8–9: "Anyone who speaks out for me in public, the Son of Man will also speak out for him before the angels. . . . But whoever may deny me in public will be denied before the angels."[212] At the last judgment the Son of Man himself will exercise the final decision; unlike other texts, where he functions only as witness, here he is the judge (see below, §3.9.2). *In Jesus's message of the coming judgment there is a pointed emphasis on his personal claim; condemnation is the result of rejecting Jesus.* Jesus claims not only to announce and execute God's judgment, but he is himself that judgment: salvation and condemnation is decided with reference to Jesus's person.[213] Jesus ignores the special status of Israel among the nations, launches a sharp attack on Israel's claim to election and

209. On this point cf. Riniker, *Gerichtsverkündigung*, 361–91.

210. Aesop's fable of the fish who did not dance to the fisher's flute playing (*Fab.* 11) may stand in the (more distant) background.

211. Cf. Wolter, "'Gericht' und 'Heil,'" 387.

212. Analysis in Riniker, *Gerichtsverkündigung*, 333–51; differently Werner Zager, *Gottesherrschaft und Endgericht in der Verkündigung Jesu: Eine Untersuchung zur markinischen Jesusüberlieferung einschliesslich der Q-Parallelen* (BZNW 82; Berlin: de Gruyter, 1996), 457ff. Cf. also M. Eugene Boring, "The Unforgivable Sin Logion Mark 3:28–29/Matt. 12:31–32/Luke 12:10: Formal Analysis and History of the Tradition," *NovT* 17 (1976): 258–79; Christoph Heil et al., eds., *Q 12:8–12: Confessing or Denying—Speaking against the Holy Spirit—Hearings before Synagogues* (Documenta Q; Louvain: Peeters, 1997).

213. Cf. Reiser, *Jesus and Judgment*, 310–11; Riniker, *Gerichtsverkündigung*, 457ff.

salvation, and connects the presupposed guilt to their response to his person; to repent is to turn to Jesus. This message of condemnation in the coming judgment thus shows itself to be a *fundamental element in the message and ministry of Jesus as a whole*.[214] This element may not be eliminated as a matter of worldview,[215] for the function of these declarations of condemnation is to call people to recognize the signs of the time, to shake them up and force them to a decision: the coming of God in his kingdom, already represented by Jesus, cannot remain without consequences, so the announcement of judgment is the necessary negative side of his announcement of salvation. Whoever emphasizes the salvific character of Jesus's message of the kingdom may not ignore its judgmental character for those who reject it.

3.8 Jesus and the Law: To Will the Good

It is no accident that the relation of Jesus to the Torah is one of the most disputed themes of New Testament theology. Here exegetical judgments are interwoven with political, cultural, and religious concerns (one's personal relation to Judaism, the history of Judaism in the twentieth century, Christian-Jewish dialogue) and lead to positions that are defended with emotion and passion. While the older exegesis labored under the need to contrast Jesus with Judaism, or at least to make him an outstanding figure in his Jewish context,[216] in recent exegesis the dominant wish has been to place Jesus seamlessly within the multifaceted Judaism of his time.[217] Each strategy is tendentious, for they

214. Cf. Zager, *Gottesherschaft*, 311–16: "For the historical Jesus, *the kingdom of God and the last judgment were inseparable*" (316).

215. Classically Harnack, *What Is Christianity*, 54–55, who believes Jesus probably had similar ideas about the devil and the last judgment with his contemporaries. But this, he argues, was only the external, dispensable husk; the kernel was Jesus's own view of the kingdom of God.

216. Cf. Bultmann, *Jesus and the Word*, 83: "The obedience for which Jesus asks is easy, because it frees a man from dependence on a formal authority, and therefore frees him also from the judgment of the men whose profession it is to explain this authority"; Käsemann, "Problem of the Historical Jesus," 37: "Certainly he was a Jew and made the assumptions of Jewish piety, but at the same time he shatters this framework with his claim"; Günther Bornkamm, *Jesus von Nazareth* (9th ed.; Stuttgart: Kohlhammer, 1971), 71: "But it is no less clear that through Jesus's word and conduct the delusion of the inalienable, quasi-enforceable privileges of Israel and its ancestors are attacked and shaken to their very roots" [MEB trans. from 1971 German edition]; Leonhard Goppelt, *Theologie des Neuen Testaments* (3rd ed.; Göttingen: Vandenhoeck & Ruprecht, 1976), 148, ". . . that the newness of Jesus's message in fact shook Judaism to the very roots" [trans. MEB; the standard English translation here uses the language of supersessionism, not in the German text]; Leonhard Goppelt and Jürgen Roloff, eds., *Theology of the New Testament* (trans. John E. Alsup; 2 vols.; Grand Rapids: Eerdmans, 1981), 97: "Jesus actually superseded Judaism at its very roots through a new dimension."

217. Cf., e.g., Sanders, *Jesus and Judaism*, 319: "In fact, we cannot say that a single one of the things known about Jesus is unique: neither his miracles, nonviolence, eschatological hope or promise to outcasts." This position is of course not new; already at the beginning of the

do not maintain the tension of interpreting Jesus as a figure *within* Judaism while *at the same time* showing how it was that he came into conflict with Jewish groups and authorities and illuminating the resulting history in which early Christianity emerged.

3.8.1 Theologies of the Law in Ancient Judaism

There is no dispute about the exalted place occupied by the Torah within ancient Judaism.[218] To be sure, there were always different interpretations of the Torah and thus different theologies of the law.[219] Especially important in this connection was the formation of the *Pharisees*, *Sadducees*, and *Essenes* within the broad context of the Maccabean revolt (cf. 1 Macc. 2:15–28).[220] Josephus sees the distinctive character of the *Pharisees* in their understanding of tradition,[221] which was also what set them apart from the Sadducees:

> For the present I wish merely to explain that the Pharisees had passed on to the people certain regulations (νόμιμα) handed down by former generations (ἐκ πατέρων διαδοχῆς) and not recorded in the law of Moses, for which reason they are rejected by the Sadducean group, who hold that only those regulations should be considered valid which were written down (in Scripture), and that those which were handed down by former generations need not be observed. (*Ant.* 13.297)

In New Testament times, the content of this tradition probably included purity rules (cf. Mark 7:1–8, 14–23; Rom. 14:14), regulations about tithing (cf. Matt. 23:23), and particular forms of vows (cf. Mark 7:9–13). According to

---

historical-critical method H. S. Reimarus declared that Jesus had not come in order to bring some new teaching in contrast to Judaism: "Moreover, he was a born Jew and intended to remain one; he testifies that he has not come to abolish the law, but to fulfill it" (Talbert, ed., *Fragments*, 71–72). Cf. further Albert Schweitzer, *Paul and His Interpreters: A Critical History* (New York: Schocken Books, 1964), p. ix: "If the view developed at the close of my *Quest of the Historical Jesus* is sound, the teaching of Jesus does not in any of its aspects go outside the Jewish world of thought and project itself into a non-Jewish world, but represents a deeply ethical and perfected version of the contemporary Apocalyptic."

218. On the history of the origin and historical effects of the Torah, cf. Frank Crüsemann, *Die Tora: Theologie und Sozialgeschichte des alttestamentlichen Gesetzes* (Munich: Kaiser, 1992); on the Judaism of Jesus's time, cf. the survey in Dunn, *Jesus Remembered*, 255–311.

219. A survey is found in Hermann Lichtenberger, "Das Tora-Verständnis im Judentum zur Zeit des Paulus," in *Paul and the Mosaic Law* (ed. James D. G. Dunn; Grand Rapids: Eerdmans, 2001), 7–23.

220. Cf. here the critical inventory in Günter Stemberger, *Jewish Contemporaries of Jesus: Pharisees, Sadducees, Essenes* (trans. Allan W. Mahnke; Minneapolis: Fortress, 1995); still worth reading is G. Baumbach, *Jesus von Nazareth im Lichte der jüdischen Gruppenbildung* (Berlin: Evangelische Verlagsanstalt, 1971).

221. On the history and basic theological view of the Pharisees, cf. Roland Deines, "Pharisäer," *TBLNT* 2:1455–68.

Josephus, *Life* 191, the Pharisees "set themselves apart from others by their precise knowledge" (τῶν ἄλλων ἀκριβείᾳ διαφέρειν). They were more pious than the others, "and observed the law more conscientiously" (καὶ τοὺς νόμους ἀκριβέστερον ἀφηγεῖσθαι).[222] The aim of the Pharisaic movement was the sanctification of everyday life through comprehensive observance of the law; they saw special importance in keeping the ritual prescriptions even beyond the confines of the temple. Thus the Torah was to some extent updated in order to accommodate it to the multifaceted situations of everyday life (cf., e.g., *Let. Aris.* 139–169; Josephus, *Ant.* 4.198; Mark 2:23–24; 7:4). Of particular importance was the separation of a radical wing within the Pharisees, who saw themselves as followers of Phinehas (Num. 25) and Elijah (1 Kings 19:9–10) and thus called themselves *Zealots* (οἱ ζηλωταί, "the zealous ones"). This group was formed in 6 CE under the leadership of Judas the Galilean from Gamala and a Pharisee called Saddok (cf. Josephus, *Ant.* 18.3–10). The Zealots were characterized by an intensification of the first commandment, by strictness in their observance of the Sabbath regulations, and by rigorous practice of the laws of ritual purity.[223] They strove for the establishment of a radical theocracy and rejected the Roman domination of the Jewish people on religious grounds.

Only vague statements about the *Sadducees'* understanding of the Torah can be made. They rejected the particular traditions of the Pharisees, including the concept of the resurrection of the dead and belief in angels (cf. Mark 12:18–27; Acts 23:6–8). Their concentration on the written Torah included a stricter attitude on legal questions than was the case with the Pharisees (cf. Josephus, *Ant.* 18.294; 20.199).[224]

According to the evidence in the Qumran documents, the *Essenes* also advocated a very strict understanding of the Torah[225] and claimed for themselves a special insight into the true interpretation and significance of the Torah: "But when those of them who were left held firm to the commandments of God He instituted His covenant with Israel for ever, revealing to them things hidden, in which all Israel had gone wrong: His holy Sabbaths, His glorious festivals, His righteous laws, His reliable ways. The desires of His will, which Man should carry out and so have life in them [Lev. 18:5; Neh. 9:29], He opened up to them" (CD 3:12–16; cf. 6:3–11). These special insights concerned especially questions of the religious calendar and the Sabbath, with

222. Josephus, *JW* 1.110; cf. further *JW* 2.162; *Ant.* 17.41.

223. On the Zealots' understanding of the law, cf. Martin Hengel, *The Zealots: Investigations into the Jewish Freedom Movement in the Period from Herod I until 70 A.D.* (trans. David Smith; Edinburgh: T&T Clark, 1989), 149–228.

224. On the whole issue, cf. Otto Schwankl, *Die Sadduzäerfrage (Mk 12,18–27 parr): Eine exegetisch-theologische Studie zur Auferstehungserwartung* (BBB 66; Frankfurt: Athenäum, 1987).

225. Cf. Stegemann, *Library of Qumran*, 201–2.

numerous additional prescriptions regarding the life of the community. It is precisely these texts discovered at Qumran that let us perceive that the Torah and its interpretation were not settled issues in first-century Judaism.[226] Thus, for example, the *Temple Scroll* gives texts from the Pentateuch not only in linguistically stylized form and a different order, but also contains new commandments without any basis in the Pentateuch.

While the Essenes bound salvation strictly to living in the Holy Land, *Hellenistic Judaism of the Diaspora* represented a completely different situation. In the context of the omnipresent Hellenistic culture, Judaism had to open itself up to some of the prevailing influences in order to maintain its identity at all. In the process of this development, the Torah was both universalized and ethicized, understood as the wisdom embodied in creation and intended to regulate life as such.[227] Human beings were adapted to follow the Torah, understood as universal moral law, because following it led to a life of reason, harmony, and peace with God, other human beings, and oneself. Thus the Torah, concentrated into a few commandments, becomes a kind of instruction in virtue that could be expressed in Hellenistic vocabulary and thought patterns. In this regard, *Philo's* understanding of the law is important; he combines the Torah of Sinai, the law of creation, and the law of nature as one unified revelation from God.[228] According to Philo, the creator God of the Old Testament is responsible both for φύσις (nature) as the principle on which the world is based and for the Torah, so that they must be thought of in tandem. Since the creation of the world and the giving of the law were related "in the beginning," natural law is just as much of divine origin as the Torah: "His exordium [Moses' first words of Genesis, 'in the beginning'], as I have said, is one that excites our admiration in the highest degree. It consists of an account of the creation of the world, implying that the world is in harmony with the law, and the law with the world, and that the man who observes the law is constituted thereby a loyal citizen of the world, regulating his doings by the purpose and will of Nature, in accordance with which the entire world itself also is administered" (*Creation* 3). The written Torah from Sinai is essentially much older, for both Moses as the "living law"[229] and the concept of

226. Cf. K. Müller, "Beobachtungen zum Verhältnis von Tora und Halacha in frühjüdischen Quellen," in *Jesus und das jüdische Gesetz* (ed. Ingo Broer; Stuttgart: Kohlhammer, 1992), 105–34.

227. Extensive discussion in Nissen, *Gott und der Nächste*, 219ff.; Reinhard Weber, *Das Gesetz im hellenistischen Judentum: Studien zum Verständnis und zur Funktion der Thora von Demetrios bis Pseudo-Phokylides* (ARGU 10; Frankfurt: Lang, 2000).

228. On this point cf. Reinhard Weber, *Das "Gesetz" bei Philon von Alexandrien und Flavius Josephus: Studien zum Verständnis und zur Funktion der Thora bei den beiden Hauptzeugen des hellenistischen Judentums* (ARGU 11; Frankfurt: Lang, 2001).

229. Cf. Philo, *Moses* 1.162: "Perhaps, too, since he was destined to be a legislator, the providence of God which afterwards appointed him without his knowledge to that work, caused him long before that day to be the reasonable and living impersonation of the law."

the νόμος ἄγραφος (unwritten law; cf. *Abraham* 3–6) permit Philo to think in terms of a protological creation-Torah that emphasizes both the temporal and the material continuity of God's acts. Philo constantly interprets the individual laws as elaborations of the Decalogue, which is in turn correlated to the law of nature. By means of this ethicizing of both the natural law and the particular laws of the Torah, Philo is able to construct a grand synthesis of Jewish and Greek-Hellenistic thought.

A further example of the multifaceted Jewish understanding of the law is provided by the *allegorizers* mentioned by Philo (*Migration* 89–93). They give the law a symbolic sense and neglect literal obedience. In the context of his critique of this position, Philo discusses the law of circumcision, which was obviously understood by the allegorists as referring only to a symbolic act: "It is true that receiving circumcision does indeed portray the excision of pleasure and all passions, and the putting away of impious conceit, under which the mind supposed that it was capable of begetting by its own power: but let us not on this account repeal the law laid down for circumcising" (*Migration* 92).[230]

In *Jewish apocalypticism* the law functioned above all as the norm for God's final judgment. A radical obedience to the law was combined with the hope of God's future salvation, which would replace the distress of the present.[231]

Finally, it is important to note the geographical and climatic setting of Jesus's ministry, since reality-construction always takes place in, and is inevitably conditioned by, particular geographical and social contexts.[232] Jesus worked almost exclusively around the Lake of Gennesaret,[233] characterized by a Mediterranean climate that made possible a way of life that, especially in contrast to the mountainous areas of Israel, can be described as easygoing and pleasant. In the time of Jesus, Galilee was by no means un-Jewish but doubtless had its own cultural and religious profile.[234] It is difficult to imagine

230. Although Philo himself does not share the position of the allegorists, his content is not all that different from theirs, as is seen, for example in *QE* 2.2: "the sojourner is one who circumcises not his uncircumcision but his desires and sensual pleasures and the other passions of the soul. For in Egypt the Hebrew nation was not circumcised [οὐ περιτέθητο] but being mistreated with all kinds of mistreatment by the inhabitants in their hatred of strangers, it lived with them in self-restraint and endurance."

231. On this point cf. Heinrich Hoffmann, *Das Gesetz in der frühjüdischen Apokalyptik* (SUNT 23; Göttingen: Vandenhoeck & Ruprecht, 1999).

232. Cf. Halvor Moxnes, "The Construction of Galilee as a Place for the Historical Jesus," *BTB* 31 (2001): 26–37, 64–77.

233. Cf. Gabriele Fassbeck, ed., *Leben am See Gennesaret: Kulturgeschichtliche Entdeckungen in einer biblischen Region* (ZBA; Munich: Von Zabern, 2002).

234. Introductions and surveys are found in Willibald Bösen, *Galiläa als Lebensraum und Wirkungsfeld Jesu* (Freiburg: Herder, 1985); Eric Meyers, "Jesus and His Galilean Context," in *Archaeology and the Galilee* (ed. Douglas R. Edwards and C. Thomas McCollough; Atlanta: Scholars Press, 1997), 57–66; Freyne, *Jewish Galilean*; Rudolf Hoppe, "Galiläa—Geschichte, Kultur, Religion," in *Jesus von Nazaret—Spuren und Konturen* (ed. Ludger Schenke; Stuttgart:

that Jesus was unacquainted with the Hellenistic cities of Sepphoris[235] and Tiberias, even though the New Testament does not mention them, especially since an urban milieu is presupposed in Q 12:58–59 (cf. also Matt. 6:2, 5, 16; Mark 7:6; Luke 13:15; 19:11ff.).[236] It was certainly the case that in Galilee Jews encountered and lived with Gentiles on a daily basis, and that the problems of ritual purity were dealt with more often and more openly than was probably the case in Jerusalem. In addition, with a smaller proportion of Pharisees, life in Galilee was subject to less control in such matters. When Jesus holds up the centurion of Capernaum as a model of faith for Israel (Matt. 8:10b/Luke 7:9b), he thereby illustrates a positive evaluation of individual Gentiles that goes beyond merely being in contact with them. Jesus's openness to non-Jews and his distance from a discriminating observance of the Torah probably has some connection with the Galilean context of his ministry.

3.8.2 Jesus's Stance vis-à-vis the Torah

Where does Jesus fit in to this multifaceted Jewish theology of the law? A key text for answering this question is found in the *Sermon on the Mount*, especially the *antitheses* (see above, §3.5.2). These antithetical formulations are something new in ancient Judaism; there are no exact parallels to this form.[237] The decisive theological problem is, whom or what does this form of speech interpret or criticize, and in what sense? The passive form ἐρρέθη (it was said) could refer to the speech of God in the Scripture, so that "the antithesis formulas pit Jesus's word against that of the Bible itself."[238] Thus Jesus would be located within the broad spectrum of Jewish interpretations of the Torah, so that even the antitheses, with the exception of the unqualified command to love one's enemies, formulate nothing that was not already (more or less) paralleled in Judaism.[239] The decisive element, however, is the claim expressed

Kohlhammer, 2004), 42–58; Jens Schröter, *Jesus von Nazareth: Jude aus Galiläa—Retter der Welt* (BG 15; Leipzig: Evangelische Verlagsanstalt, 2006), 77–102. One must suppose that Jesus could make some use of the Greek language, at least passively; cf. Stanley E. Porter, "Jesus and the Use of Greek in Galilee," in *Studying the Historical Jesus: Evaluations of the State of Current Research* (ed. Bruce Chilton and Craig A. Evans; NTTS 19; Leiden: Brill, 1994), 123–54.

235. A personal note: anyone who has once walked the 3.5 miles from Nazareth to Sepphoris can hardly imagine, with the best will in the world, that Jesus was never there.

236. Cf. Meyers, "Galilean Context," 60–61: "It seems reasonable therefore to conclude that Jesus's Galilean ministry could hardly have avoided the two Herodian cities, Sepphoris and Tiberias."

237. Cf. Luz, *Matthew 1–7*, 228.

238. Ibid., 1:230.

239. D. Sänger emphases that the antitheses are embedded within the thought world of Judaism ("Schriftauslegung," 79–102) as does Karl-Wilhelm Niebuhr, "Die Antithesen des Matthäus: Jesus als Toralehrer und die frühjüdische weisheitliche Torarezeption," in *Gedenkt an das Wort: Festschrift für Werner Vogler zum 65. Geburtstag* (ed. Christoph Kähler et al.; Leipzig: Evangelische Verlagsanstalt, 1999), 175–200.

in the emphatic "But I say to you." Jesus does not derive his authority from the Scripture; his authority is inherent in what he himself says. "The antitheses do not interpret the Bible; they extend and surpass it."[240] This claim can be understood only against the background of Jesus's proclamation of the kingdom of God: with the dawn of God's kingdom, a new reality becomes operative. With the dawn of God's kingdom, the will of God is proclaimed anew, in its ultimate and radical form.[241] Jesus formulates this will on his own authority; he does not derive it from the Old Testament but proclaims God's will, in the light of God's dawning kingdom, as the final authority. Jesus does not thereby abolish the Torah, but neither does he think and argue on the basis of the Torah—which in practice means a *relativizing* of the Torah.

Clean and Unclean

Something similar can be said about Jesus's stance on *issues of ritual purity*. Jesus saying, "I have come to call not the righteous but sinners" (Mark 2:17) already shows that, while Jesus does not question the doing of righteousness, and thus the claim of the law, he does not ascribe to the law the power to determine access to God in the present. Righteousness remains righteousness, but God does not love only the righteous. God's love, which Jesus proclaims in the advent of the kingdom of God, surpasses the love previously given to Israel in the gift of the Torah. Contact with a leprous person, which is mentioned in Mark 1:41 only in passing, is ritually defiling in the highest degree. The same is true for the healing of the woman with the issue of blood (Mark 5:25–34) or the encounter with the Syrophoenician woman (Mark 7:24–30). Jesus paid no attention to ritual laws of any sort in his contacts with people. The unbounded love of God for all people, including especially those who have been religiously excluded, at least points in the direction of declaring such laws, which in Israel were upheld in the name of God, to be obsolete.

So also Mark 7:15 is to be understood in this sense. Here Jesus combines his characteristic theology of creation with his basic eschatological perspective. The fundamental distinction "pure-impure" has not been in force from the time of the creation on; it does not occur until Gen. 7:2 distinguishes clean and unclean animals. The purity laws as the legitimatization for drawing religious boundaries that separate and exclude people have lost their significance, because for Jesus impurity comes from another source: "There is nothing outside a person that by going in can defile, but the things that come out are what

240. Luz, *Matthew 1–7*, 1:230.

241. Hengel, "Jesus und die Tora," 171, describes Jesus as bringing a completely new Torah, "which, on the one hand, expounds the traditional Torah, but at the same time stands in a certain contrast to it and even more to the way it was interpreted in his time. Jesus brings the new Torah as the one who fulfills the law and the prophets, and brings the true, original will of God for the dawning kingdom of God."

defile" (Mark 7:15). In favor of the authenticity[242] of Mark 7:15 are the form of antithetic parallelism, the ease of retranslation into Aramaic, the location in a context where it does not comfortably fit, the variations in Mark 7:18b and 20, the reception of the saying as a word of the Lord in Rom. 14:14, and, finally, its unprecedented newness.[243] Just as the precise direction of the impact of the original saying is no longer clear, so its meaning and significance are also vigorously disputed. The original meaning, in contrast to its meaning in its present Markan context, can hardly be limited to the ritual domain, for τὰ ἐκ τοῦ ἀνθρώπου ἐκπορευόμενα (what comes out of a person) hardly permits such a narrow application. Thus the meaning cannot refer only to different sorts of food that make one ritually unclean, for with these words Jesus includes all that comes from people—their thoughts and deeds, which can make them unclean before God.[244] Jesus does not merely let the formal idea of being unclean before God fall away, but he denies that such an uncleanness, in any form whatsoever, can come to the person from outside. This in fact means a relativizing of the purity laws of Lev. 11–15. Jesus thereby sets himself off from Pharisees, Sadducees, and the Essenes of Qumran, for despite their different interpretations and practices, the cultic-ritual norms were of fundamental importance for all these groups. They functioned not only as visible markers separating them from the Gentiles and the religiously lax of their own people but also as an expression of their obedience to the Torah and the word of God given through Moses and still in force.[245] Mark 7:15 is thus to be understood in an exclusive sense[246] and has a meaning that in fact relativizes

242. Exemplary analyses with discriminating lines of argument, but with a final decision for authenticity, are found in Werner Georg Kümmel, "Äussere und innere Reinheit des Menschen bei Jesus," in *Heilsgeschehen und Geschichte* (ed. Erich Grässer et al.; 2 vols.; MTS 1; Marburg: Elwert, 1965), 1:117–29; J. Taeger distinguishes between what is a matter of fundamental principle and what is not, in Ingo Broer and Jens-W. Taeger, eds., *Jesus und das jüdische Gesetz* (Stuttgart: Kohlhammer, 1992), 23–34; G. Theissen, "Das Reinheitslogion Mk 7,15 und die Trennung von Juden und Christen," in *Jesus als historische Gestalt: Beiträge zur Jesusforschung: Zum 60. Geburtstag von Gerd Theissen* (ed. Gerd Theissen and Annette Merz; FRLANT 202; Göttingen: Vandenhoeck & Ruprecht, 2003), 73–89.

243. In my opinion, there is no true parallel to Mark 7:15; Philo, *Creation* 119, comes close.

244. Cf. Kümmel, "Reinheit," 122.

245. For the Pharisees, cf. Neusner, "Pharisäische und talmudische Judentum," 43–51; Neusner, *Politics to Piety*, passim. For the position of the Sadducees, cf. Emil Schürer, *The History of the Jewish People in the Age of Jesus Christ (175 B.C.–A.D. 135)* (2nd English ed.; 3 vols.; Edinburgh: T&T Clark, 1973), 2:407–14; for Qumran, cf. H.-W. Kuhn, "Jesus vor dem Hintergrund der Qumrangemeinde," in *Grenzgänge: Menschen und Schicksale zwischen jüdischer, christlicher und deutscher Identität: Festschrift für Diethard Aschoff* (ed. Folker Siegert and Diethard Aschoff; MJS 11; Münster: Lit, 2002), 53: "There is no mistaking the contrast between the rigorous understanding of the Torah as found in the Qumran texts and Jesus's own conduct with regard to the Torah, especially concerning the Sabbath and issues of purity."

246. Cf. Hengel, "Jesus und die Tora," 164, on Mark 7:15: "Here we meet a fundamental break between Jesus and the Palestinian Judaism of his time, which then has further effects in the early church and led to bitter disputes."

the Torah; it does not merely rank the love command above the purity laws.[247] Paul already understands this saying of Jesus as a critique of the Torah (Rom. 14:14),[248] and there are also parallels elsewhere in Jesus's own teaching. Along with his fellowship with the ritually unclean, his critique of the Pharisees (cf. Luke 11:39–41; Matt. 23:25), and his healings on the Sabbath, note above all Q 10:7, where Jesus sends his disciples forth with the instruction to eat and drink whatever is set before them. Just as, in view of the dawning kingdom of God, the present is no time for fasting (cf. Mark 2:18b, 19a; Matt. 11:18–19/ Luke 7:33–34), so also the food laws have lost their significance for the relation of people to each other and to God. The kind of purity God desires cannot be institutionalized; it is a matter of a person's whole life. The creatureliness of human life is not expressed in religious or social separation, but in the genuine acceptance of life as given by the Creator.

The Sabbath

The *Sabbath healings* point in this same direction, which likewise aim at reestablishing the original order of creation. Thus the saying of Jesus in Mark 2:27 declares that the Sabbath was created for human beings, not human beings for the Sabbath.[249] In this text, the key verb ἐγένετο (it is created) refers to the original will of God expressed in creation. The Sabbath healings are in the service of human beings, in that they free them from the business of everyday life and concern with themselves, giving them time to cultivate the all-important relation to God. In the priestly story of creation, the seventh

247. So, e.g., Ulrich Luz, "Jesus und die Pharisäer," *Judaica* 38 (1982): 242–43; Merklein, *Jesu Botschaft*, 96; Christoph Burchard, "Jesus von Nazareth," in *Die Anfänge des Christentums: Alte Welt und neue Hoffnung* (ed. Jürgen Becker; Stuttgart: Kohlhammer, 1987), 47.

248. Heikki Räisänen, "Jesus and the Food Laws," *JSNT* 16 (1982): 89ff., sees behind Mark 7:15 not the earthly Jesus but "an 'emancipated' Jewish Christian group engaged in Gentile mission" (90); a similar line of argument is found in Sanders, *Jesus and Judaism*, 266–67. Each can, in fact, present a few arguments against the authenticity of Mark 7:15, but cannot refute the main arguments for authenticity.

249. For the analysis of Mark 2:23–28, cf. Lutz Doering, *Schabbat: Sabbathalacha und -praxis im antiken Judentum und Urchristentum* (TSAJ 78; Tübingen: Mohr, 1999), 409–32. Among those who trace Mark 2:27 back to Jesus: Eduard Lohse, "Jesu Worte über den Sabbat," in *Die Einheit des Neuen Testaments: Exegetische Studien zur Theologie des Neuen Testaments* (ed. Eduard Lohse; 2nd ed.; Göttingen: Vandenhoeck & Ruprecht, 1973), 68; Jürgen Roloff, *Das Kerygma und der irdische Jesus* (Göttingen: Vandenhoeck & Ruprecht, 1970), 52ff.; Heinz-Wolfgang Kuhn, *Ältere Sammlungen in Markusevangelium* (SUNT 8; Göttingen: Vandenhoeck und Ruprecht, 1971), 75; Gnilka, *Markus*, 1:123; Dieter Lührmann, *Das Markusevangelium* (HNT 3; Tübingen: Mohr, 1987), 64–65; Hans Hübner, *Das Gesetz in der synoptischen Tradition: Studien zur These einer progressiven Qumranisierung und Judaisierung innerhalb der synoptischen Tradition* (2nd ed.; Göttingen: Vandenhoeck & Ruprecht, 1973), 121; Volker Hampel, *Menschensohn und historischer Jesus: Ein Rätselwort als Schlüssel zum messianischen Selbstverständnis Jesu* (Neukirchen-Vluyn: Neukirchener Verlag, 1988), 199ff.; Doering, *Schabbat*, 423–24; Boring, *Mark*, 87–92.

day already appears as a time set apart by God that helps human beings to orient themselves in time and history (Gen. 2:2–3). This service for which the Sabbath was created was partially lost in the history of postexilic Judaism.[250] While the Sabbath did become the central focus of understanding the Torah, at the same time its service of providing a particular quality to time tended to be understood as a static contrast between Sabbath and human beings. In some parts of the Sabbath halakha, human beings were subordinated to the Sabbath and its requirements. Thus in the context of Sabbath regulations, CD 11:16–17 states that "Any living human who falls into a body of water or a cistern shall not be helped out with ladder, rope, or instrument" (cf. further *Jub.* 2.25–33; 50.6ff.; CD 10:14–12, 22; Philo, *Moses* 2.22). Jesus breaks through these inversions of the initial purpose of the Sabbath and through his Sabbath healings demonstrates the original meaning of this day: he facilitates the recovery of life (cf. Luke 13:10–17) and makes it possible for human beings to return to the life for which they were created: to live one's life in the presence of the Creator. So also in Mark 3:4, it is a matter of the original will of God in regard to the Sabbath ("Is it lawful to do good or to do harm on the sabbath, to save life or to kill?").[251] The Sabbath is there to serve the good, and this consists in saving and maintaining life. God's will is human salvation in the comprehensive sense, and the Sabbath is to be subordinated to this radical turn toward the enhancement of human life. To neglect this good is for Jesus not a neutral passivity, but is actually the doing of evil; it means killing instead of giving life. God's "yes" to human life—the God who cares about and for human life—stands over all the commandments. An interpretation of the divine commandments that does not take this fact into consideration misses the meaning of the revelation of God's will. Doing good cannot desecrate the Sabbath.

Jesus's minimizing the importance of the *tithing* regulations (cf. Lev. 27:30) in Matt. 23:23a–c points in this same direction. The tithe was a difficult financial burden for the lower and middle classes of Galilee, so Jesus here adopts a position clearly different from that of the Pharisees (cf. Luke 18:12).[252]

Decentering the Torah

Three observations are crucial in evaluating Jesus's stance to the Torah:

250. On this point, cf. Eduard Lohse, "σάββατον, σαββατισμός, παρασκευή," *TDNT* 7:1–34; Doering, *Schabbat*, 23–536 emphasizes the multilayered aspect of the Jewish Sabbath halakha (Elephantine, *Jubilees*, Qumran, Diaspora, Josephus, Pharisees, Sadducees, early Tannaites).

251. For the analysis of Mark 3:1–6, cf. Doering, *Schabbat*, 441–57. Mark 3:4 is considered an authentic saying of Jesus by, e.g., Hübner, *Gesetz in der synoptischen Tradition*, 129; Roloff, *Kerygma*, 63–64; Gnilka, *Markus*, 1:126; Lohse, "σάββατον," 67; Doering, *Schabbat*, 423ff.

252. Tithing belongs to the central core of proto-rabbinic tradition; cf. Jacob Neusner, "Introduction," in *Understanding Rabbinic Judaism* (ed. Jacob Neusner; New York: Ktav, 1974), 13.

1. The Torah and its disputed interpretations are not the center of Jesus's ministry and teaching.[253] The new reality of God's coming in his kingly power determines Jesus's stance to the Torah, as it determines his ministry as a whole (cf. Q 16:16). The advent of Jesus means the arrival of the truly new. (Mark 2:21–22, "No one sews a piece of unshrunk cloth on an old cloak; otherwise, the patch pulls away from it, the new from the old, and a worse tear is made. And no one puts new wine into old wineskins; otherwise, the wine will burst the skins, and the wine is lost, and so are the skins; but one puts new wine into fresh wineskins.")
2. Within Jesus's stance to the Torah and its interpretation, it is important to distinguish his sharpening of the demands of the Torah in the ethical realm and his relaxing the demands of the Torah on matters of ritual law.[254]
3. There is no indication that Jesus intended to abolish the Torah or subject it to a fundamental critique. At the same time, it must be underscored that his thinking is not oriented to the Torah, but to the kingdom of God. Because God's original will in the creation corresponds to God's eschatological will,[255] Jesus combines eschatology and protology, which leads to a decentering of the Torah. This decentering is not to be equated with rejection or abolition, but for Jesus it was not the gift of the Torah but the love of God in his kingdom that was the open door through which every person could come to God.

Such an interpretation of the law remains within Judaism, explains the conflicts with other Jewish groups (cf. Mark 2:1–3:6; 12:13–17; Luke 7:36–50; 8:9–14; Matt. 23:23), and lets us understand why it was that, probably very early, the new Christian group that was forming appealed to Jesus in its critique of the law.

3.8.3 Jesus, Israel, and the Gentiles

Like other New Testament traditions, those that deal with Jesus's relation to Israel and the Gentiles are multilayered. Jesus understood that his fundamental mission was to Israel, commissioned by God to proclaim the kingdom of God to his own people.

The Twelve

A visible expression of this understanding of his mission is the institution of the Twelve. In favor of the historicity of this group is above all the fact that

253. Cf. Becker, *Jesus of Nazareth*, 284; Sänger, "Schriftauslegung," 105.
254. Cf. Theissen and Merz, *Historical Jesus*, 359–71.
255. Cf. Stegemann, "Der lehrende Jesus," 11ff.

the post-Easter community would hardly have formulated the statement that Judas, as a member of the narrow circle of disciples, betrayed Jesus (Mark 14:10, 43 par.), if this had not been the historical fact.[256] The group of the Twelve is already mentioned in the pre-Pauline tradition of 1 Cor. 15:5, that Christ "appeared to Cephas, then to the Twelve." The "Twelve" is here a firm institution, even though Judas no longer belongs to it and only Peter is mentioned. Moreover, after Easter the Twelve no longer played any identifiable historical role; much more important are the apostles who are called through an appearance of the risen Lord. Only later, in Mark, Matthew, Luke, and in the Revelation of John are the Twelve identified with the apostles. The group of the Twelve thus probably goes back to the pre-Easter time, and its importance can be seen especially in Q 22:28, 30, "You who have followed me will sit on thrones judging the twelve tribes of Israel." The Twelve obviously represented Israel, constituted as a unity of twelve tribes. Again Jesus combines protology and eschatology, for Israel in his day was not composed of twelve tribes; i.e., the Twelve represented the whole people of Israel in its original form, which is also its eschatological form. The group of the Twelve is to be understood as an anticipation of the eschatological wholeness of Israel, as an analogy, so to speak, of the kingdom of God that was already dawning in Jesus's ministry, hidden but proleptically present. The group of the Twelve thus corresponds to the present aspect of the kingdom of God, already signaling the beginning of the reunification of the whole Israel that is being brought about by God. In this sense one can say Jesus's perspective was that of eschatological Israel, and he understood his mission as the prelude to Israel's new creation by God.

Israel and the Gentiles

The content of Jesus's interpretation of the beginning of the kingdom of God as the boundless love of God, particularly focused on the disadvantaged and marginalized, includes the tendency to *extend the boundaries of Israel*. People who from the Jewish perspective were marginal figures are reintegrated within Israel. Thus the tax collector Zacchaeus is declared to be also a son of Abraham (Luke 19:9), and Samaritans are put on the same level as Jews (cf. Luke 10:30ff.).[257] Another sign of Jesus's openness is his incidental positive contacts with Gentiles: the traditions of the centurion of Capernaum and the Syrophoenician woman (Matt. 8:5–10, 13; Mark 7:24–30) have an

256. On this point cf. B. Rigaux, "Die 'Zwölf' in Geschichte und Kerygma," in *Der Historische und der kerygmatische Christus: Beiträge zum Christusverständnis in Forschung und Verkündigung* (ed. Helmut Ristow and Karl Matthiae; Berlin: Evangelische Verlagsanstalt, 1960), 468–86.

257. This is in tension with Matt. 10:5b, "Go nowhere among the Gentiles, and enter no town of the Samaritans." Jesus's openness to Samaritans (cf. Luke 9:51–56; 10:30–35; 17:11–19; John 4) speaks in favor of the view that this saying does not go back to Jesus, but to Q^{Mt}; cf. Luz, *Matthew 8–20*, 71–74.

authentic historical core[258] and give evidence of a *nonprogrammatic but real openness* to Gentiles. This is seen also in the parable of the Great Supper (Luke 14:16–24) and in the prophetic threat oracle Q 13:29, 28. The parable of the Great Supper illustrates that God can carry out his saving plan in unexpected ways, for those originally invited will not participate in the grand banquet. In a similar way, Jesus takes up the motif of the eschatological pilgrimage of the nations to Zion[259] in such a way that it does not serve to confirm the promises to Israel; the order of priority is reversed. The motif of the eschatological people of God was thematized in ancient Israel in two different ways: the expansion of the people of God could be expected at the eschaton, when the nations stream to Jerusalem/Zion in order to worship the true God (cf. *1 En.* 90; *Testaments of the Twelve Patriarchs*). On the other side, there were powerful streams of Jewish tradition that called for strict separation from the Gentiles, to the point of fighting against them (Qumran, *Pss. Sol.*).[260] It is striking that Jesus reverses the first motif and does not even mention the second. In Jewish tradition, the idea of Israel's opposition to the Gentiles is firmly connected to that of the kingdom of God, so that Jesus must have been aware of this view. But unlike, for example, the Zealots, Jesus did not make this opposition part of his understanding of the kingdom of God, for he saw in the political and economic distress of his people, which the Beatitudes indicate he by no means overlooked, only the external surface of a problem that in reality goes much deeper. Like John the Baptist, Jesus probably began with the premise that Israel, in its present state, was threatened by the coming judgment of God, and on its own terms no longer had any right to claim God's earlier promises of salvation for itself (cf. Matt. 3:7–10; Luke 13:3, 5). Jesus clearly took these ideas so seriously that he utilized the traditional contrast between Israel and the Gentiles to avoid ascribing any claim to salvation on Israel's part and could not portray eschatological salvation merely as liberation from Gentile oppression. He interpreted the presence of salvation as victory over Satan, who appears as accuser of both Israel and the Gentiles. The oneness and uniqueness of God manifests itself as the victory over Satan, who has taken captive both Israel and the Gentiles (cf. Mark 3:27; Luke 11:20). On the basis of these premises, it would have been meaningless to speak of the Gentiles as the opponents of God's kingdom in the conventional way. If Jesus was completely uninterested in the restoration of Israel's political independence, it was not out of any lack of interest

258. Gerd Theissen, *The Gospels in Context: Social and Political History in the Synoptic Tradition* (trans. Linda M. Maloney; Minneapolis: Fortress, 1991), 61–81, 226–27, provides evidence.

259. Cf. here Joachim Jeremias, *Jesus's Promise to the Nations* (SBT 24; Naperville, IL: Allenson, 1958), 40–52.

260. Wolfgang Kraus, *Das Volk Gottes: Zur Grundlegung der Ekklesiologie bei Paulus* (WUNT 85; Tübingen: Mohr, 1996), 45–95, provides an analysis of the relevant texts.

in political issues as such, but rather out of a particular understanding of Israel. The restoration of political sovereignty to the people and the Davidic kingdom as a political issue, and especially as a religious issue, did not fit his idea of the eschatological action of God. This corresponds to the fact that Jesus expresses only minimal interest in his people's legal system.

In this context it is also helpful to notice the other themes of Jewish self-understanding that Jesus does *not adopt*. He does not speak of the election of Israel, never appeals to the merits of the patriarchs, and does not make the tradition of exodus and the land one of his own themes. At least in regard to the current temple cultus in Jerusalem, if not the temple cultus as such, Jesus took a very critical stance (see below, §3.10.1). One can say that even though Jesus knew that he had been sent to the people of Israel, he shows little theological interest in the historical basis of Israel's election and its realization in the politics and law of the present. The openness Jesus manifests now and again to Gentiles, the reversal of eschatological expectations, and his distancing himself from the basic convictions of ancient Judaism does not at all change the fact that Jesus knew himself to be charged with a mission essentially restricted to Israel. *There can be no doubt, however, that he was an extraordinary Jew with an extraordinary claim, a surprising openness and a new vision of the present and future act of God for humanity.*[261] Jesus was not striving for a renewal of the Jewish religion, but for a new orientation for the Jewish faith. To be sure, the later Gentile mission of early Christianity cannot appeal directly to Jesus, but it corresponds to Jesus's idea of the boundless love of God, extends and deepens this idea in a way that takes up a strong impulse from Jesus while at the same time going far beyond him.

3.9 Jesus's Self-Understanding: More Than a Prophet

His connecting the kingdom of God to his person, his practice of forgiveness of sins, his miracles, the claim represented in his antitheses, his announcement of God's judgment—all these clarify Jesus's claim in a way that goes beyond exegetical judgments on particular passages. If here is "more than Solomon, more than Jonah" (cf. Q 10:23–24), the question is posed of Jesus's own self-understanding. This question can be answered only by comparing the Jesus tradition with the three primary types of messianic expectation in ancient

261. On the variety of ways the Jewishness of Jesus is understood in recent scholarship, cf. T. Holmén, "The Jewishness of Jesus in the 'Third Quest,'" in *Jesus, Mark and Q: The Teaching of Jesus and Its Earliest Records* (ed. Michael Labahn and Andreas Schmidt; JSNTSup 214; Sheffield: Sheffield Academic Press, 2001), 143–62, who states: "'Jewishness' has become a fluid concept. Fluidity of concepts inevitably leads to confusion. Confusion, again, is a favorable soil for conclusions not based on coherent thinking, but rather on preconceptions lurking in the mind of every scholar" (156).

Judaism:[262] the expectation of an eschatological prophet, the expectation of a heavenly Son of Man, and the expectation of a religious-political Messiah.[263]

3.9.1 Jesus as Eschatological Prophet

Like John the Baptist (cf. Mark 11:32; Matt. 14:4; Luke 1:76), Jesus of Nazareth was identified as a prophet (cf. Luke 7:16, "Fear seized all of them; and they glorified God, saying, 'A great prophet has risen among us!' and 'God has looked favorably on his people!'"). The influence of the Elijah tradition (cf. Mal. 3:23) is especially clear in Mark 6:15 ("But others said, 'It is Elijah.' And others said, 'It is a prophet, like one of the prophets of old.'") and Mark 8:27–28 ("'Who do people say that I am?' And they answered him, 'John the Baptist; and others, Elijah; and still others, one of the prophets.'"). A common proverb[264] is placed in Jesus's mouth in Mark 6:4, "Prophets are not without honor, except in their hometown, and among their own kin, and in their own house." Jesus's host in Luke 7:39 says, "If this man were a prophet, he would have known who and what kind of woman this is who is touching him—that she is a sinner." People asked Jesus to perform signs of prophetic legitimization (cf. Mark 8:11; Matt. 12:38–39; Luke 11:16, 30), and in Mark 14:65 he is mocked by covering his head, striking him, and challenging him to "prophesy" who it was who hit him.

It is no longer clear whether Jesus understood himself to be the eschatological prophet in terms of Isa. 61:1 (cf. Q 7:22). In any case, he used prophetic forms of speech (cf. the threat oracles of Q 10:13–15; 11:31–32), he had visions (Luke 10:18), and he performed symbolic acts like those of the Old Testament prophets (call of the disciples, table fellowship with the ritually unclean, the expulsion of merchants and money changers from the temple, and the Last

262. A survey is found in Hermann Lichtenberger, "Messianische Erwartungen und messianische Gestalten in der Zeit des Zweiten Tempels," in *Messias-Vorstellungen bei Juden und Christen* (ed. Ekkehard Stegemann and Albert H. Friedlander; Stuttgart: Kohlhammer, 1993), 9–20; cf. the important collection of essays in James H. Charlesworth, ed., *The Messiah: Developments in Earliest Judaism and Christianity* (Minneapolis: Fortress, 1992).

263. That Jesus was directly aware of being "Son of God" cannot be demonstrated. Central texts such as Mark 1:11; 9:7; 15:39 (see below, §8.2.2), or passages in which Jesus refers to himself absolutely as "the Son" (Luke 10:22 par.; Mark 13:32) can hardly represent pre-Easter tradition. The linguistic usage "your father" is to be explained from the address character of the relevant sayings (Luke 12:30 par.; 6:36 par.; 12:32; Mark 11:25 par.; Matt. 6:8; 18:35; 23:9). The addressing of God as "Abba" cannot be the basis for inferring an explicit consciousness of being God's Son (see above, §3.3.1). For analysis, cf. Ferdinand Hahn, *The Titles of Jesus in Christology: Their History in Early Christianity* (trans. Harold Knight and George Ogg; New York: World, 1969), 279–333. On the "son of David" concept, cf. Martin Karrer, "Von David zu Christus," in *König David—biblische Schlüsselfigur und europäische Leitgestalt: 19. Kolloquium (2000) der Schweizerischen Akademie der Geistes- und Sozialwissenschaften* (ed. W. Dietrich and H. Herkommer; Freiburg, Schweiz: Universitätsverlag; Stuttgart: Kohlhammer, 2003), 327–65.

264. Cf., e.g., Plutarch, *Mor.* 604D; Dio Chrysostom, *Or.* 47.6.

Supper with the disciples; in another sense, the miracles may also be included in this category). As is the case with several Old Testament prophets, one may discern a deep identity of life and message: the life of the prophet stands entirely in the service of his message and becomes an expression of it. So also, parallels from the history of religions, such as the Jewish sign prophets (see above, §3.6.1), and the expectation of an eschatological prophet like Moses (Deut. 18:15–18) at Qumran (cf. 1QS 9:9–11; 4Q175)[265] suggest that Jesus may have understood himself as the eschatological prophet.

However, in two different sayings Jesus rejects the prophetic category as inadequate to identify him (Q 11:32, "more than Jonah is here"; Luke 16:16 "the law and the prophets were in effect until John," and after that comes something new). Moreover, there is no (relatively undisputed) authentic saying in which Jesus explicitly identifies himself as a prophet, and the Old Testament messenger category by no means does justice to his claim. So also the echoes of Deut. 18:15 in Mark 9:7 cannot be attributed to Jesus but represent Markan Christology (see below, §8.2.2). In sum: *Jesus's self-understanding, message, and actions cannot be contained within the dimensions of the prophetic category.*[266]

3.9.2 Jesus as Son of Man

Jesus's most frequent self-description is ὁ υἱὸς τοῦ ἀνθρώπου (the Son of Man).[267] The fixed expression (with the doubled article in Greek) is found 82 times in the New Testament (Mark, 14 times; Matthew, 30 times; Luke, 25 times; John, 13 times),[268] with the exception of John 12:34 always in the mouth of Jesus.[269] For Greek ears, this is a very strange translation of the Aramaic

265. On the prophetic-messianic traditions at Qumran, cf. Zimmermann, *Messianische Texte aus Qumran*, 312–417; John J. Collins, *The Scepter and the Star: The Messiahs of the Dead Sea Scrolls and Other Ancient Literature* (New York: Doubleday, 1995).

266. Cf. Hengel, *Charismatic Leader*, 67; Dunn, *Jesus Remembered*, 664–66. Differently Géza Vermès, *Jesus the Jew: A Historian's Reading of the Gospels* (Philadelphia: Fortress, 1973), 99, according to whom "prophet" "appears to be the description Jesus himself preferred"; E. P. Sanders, *The Historical Figure of Jesus* (New York: Penguin Books, 1993), 261: "He was a prophet, and an eschatological prophet"; Wright, *Jesus and the Victory of God*, 163: "Rather, I suggest that Jesus was seen as, and saw himself as, a prophet; not a particular one necessarily, as though there were an individual set of shoes ready-made into which he was consciously stepping, but a prophet like the prophets of old, coming to Israel with a word from her covenant god, warning her of the imminent and fearful consequences of the direction she was traveling, urging and summoning her to a new and different way"; Freyne, *Jewish Galilean*, 168 and elsewhere, who sees Isaiah and Daniel as the background for Jesus's understanding of his own identity.

267. On the controversial history of research, cf. Kümmel and Merklein, *Jesusforschung*, 340–74.

268. Cf. further *Gos. Thom.* 86; Acts 7:56; Rev. 1:13; only the indeterminate form υἱὸς ἀνθρώπου is found in the LXX.

269. Cf. Mogens Müller, "Menschensohn im Neuen Testament," *RGG*[4] 1098–1100.

בר (א)נשׁא or the Hebrew בן אדם, which have a primarily generic sense:[270] the individual as a member or representative of the human race. The meaning of the phrase derives from its complex prehistory in the Old Testament and Judaism.

The point of departure for this development is the statement from the apocalyptic vision of Dan. 7:13–14, "As I watched in the night visions, I saw one like a human being coming with the clouds of heaven. And he came to the Ancient One and was presented before him. To him was given dominion and glory and kingship, that all peoples, nations, and languages should serve him. His dominion is an everlasting dominion that shall not pass away, and his kingship is one that shall never be destroyed." In this context, the Son of Man is probably an exalted angelic figure who proclaims God's eschatological judgment.[271] The expression "Son of Man" did not become a central title within Jewish messianology. There are only two passages where it appears with messianic overtones in extant texts of later Jewish tradition, *1 En.* 37–71 (the "Similitudes") and *4 Ezra* 13. Neither of these texts is a unified literary composition, so one can speak of a "Son of Man tradition" only in a very nonhomogeneous sense.[272] The Similitudes of *1 Enoch* were edited in the middle of the first century BCE; Son of Man sayings occur at various layers of the traditions they incorporate. The Son of Man, as a figure like an angel, is portrayed especially as the universal judge (*1 En.* 46.4ff.) who gathers the righteous as the eschatological congregation (e.g., 45.3–4; 47.4; 48.1–7). Like himself, so also the righteous are the elect. He "will become a staff for the righteous ones in order that they may lean on him and not fall." *Fourth Ezra* 13, which comes from the end of the first century CE, portrays the advent and eschatological functions of this figure in the context of a storm vision: "As I kept looking the wind made something like the figure of a man come up out of the heart of the sea. And I saw that this man flew with the clouds of heaven; and wherever he turned his face to look, everything under his gaze trembled" (13.3). He will judge the nations that stream to Mount Zion and will gather the people of Israel. He thus carries out the responsibilities assigned to the Davidic Messiah, according to *Pss. Sol.* 17.26–28. The differences between Dan. 7 and *1 Enoch*/*4 Ezra* indicate that, at the time of Jesus, there were probably different forms of the Son of Man tradition; these described eschatological

270. On this point cf. Carsten Colpe, "ὁ υἱὸς τοῦ ἀνθρώπου," *TDNT* 8:405–6.

271. On the meaning of בר (א)נשׁא see especially Klaus Koch and Martin Rösel, "Das Reich der Heiligen und des Menschensohns: Ein Kapitel politischer Theologie," in *Die Reiche der Welt und der kommende Menschensohn: Studien zum Danielbuch* (Neukirchen-Vluyn: Neukirchener Verlag, 1995), 157–60.

272. For analysis, cf. Karlheinz Müller, "Menschensohn und Messias," in *Studien zur frühjüdischen Apokalyptik* (ed. Karlheinz Müller; SBAB 11; Stuttgart: Verlag Katholisches Bibelwerk, 1991), 279–322.

functions rather than conveyed a fixed image of an eschatological person.[273] In any case, it is clear that the traditions deal with *a heavenly figure in human form who functions as judge, ruler, and savior.*

It is very unlikely that the central Son of Man sayings in the New Testament were first formulated in the later post-Easter period, for they are not appropriate for the later church's mission, and their absence in Paul is probably intentional. Why would the later church have given a primary place in its christological reflections to a phrase hardly understandable in Greek and focused on the word ἄνθρωπος (human being)?[274] The Aramaic בר (א)נשא, probably replaced by the Greek ὁ υἱὸς τοῦ ἀνθρώπου early on, likely takes up a key feature of Jesus's own language. Alongside this plausible understanding of the effect of Jesus himself on the way the tradition developed and the numerous instances of the term in all streams of the tradition, the lack of the Son of Man terminology in the church's own confessional statements about Jesus make it likely that Jesus himself used the "Son of Man" terminology.

Jesus's Son of Man sayings can be grouped in three categories, which partially overlap and supplement one another.

The Present Work of the Son of Man

The sayings about the present work of the Son of Man contain very different connotations. There are sayings in which the Son of Man title appears in conjunction with Jesus's authority (Mark 2:10 par., "'But so that you may know that the Son of Man has authority on earth to forgive sins'—he said to the paralytic"; Mark 2:28 par., "So the Son of Man is lord even of the sabbath"). In other sayings, it is the sending of Jesus, his mission as a whole, that is the subject (Mark 10:45, "For the Son of Man came not to be served but to serve, and to give his life a ransom for many"; Luke 19:10, "For the

273. On this point cf. Collins, *The Scepter and the Star*, 173–94, who argues that texts from apocalyptic circles prior to and alongside the New Testament indicate that ideas about the Son of Man were not firmly fixed. Such texts portray him as a messianic figure involved in the eschatological destruction of God's enemies.

274. This question cannot be answered by any of those who see all the Son of Man sayings as church formulations, e.g., Philipp Vielhauer, "Gottesreich und Menschensohn in der Verkündigung Jesu," in *Aufsätze zum Neuen Testament* (ed. Philipp Vielhauer; TB 31; Munich: Kaiser, 1965), 90–91; Conzelmann, *Theology of the New Testament*, 131–37; Anton Vögtle, *Die "Gretchenfrage" des Menschensohnproblems: Bilanz und Perspektive* (QD 152; Freiburg i.B.: Herder, 1994), 175. [To ask the "Gretchen question" is to ask about someone's deepest religious or political convictions; from Goethe, *Faust*, I.—MEB] That Jesus used Son of Man with reference to himself is argued by H. E. Tödt, *The Son of Man in the Synoptic Tradition* (trans. Dorothea M. Barton; NTL; Philadelphia: Westminster, 1965), 329–47; Jürgen Roloff, *Jesus* (Munich: Beck, 2000), 118–19; Merklein, *Jesu Botschaft*, 154–64; Theissen and Merz, *Historical Jesus*, 548–52; Schröter, *Jesus von Nazareth*, 252–53. On the history of research, cf. Vögtle, *Gretchenfrage*, 22–81 (hypotheses re. authenticity), 82–144 (post-Easter formulations).

Son of Man came to seek out and to save the lost"). The saying in Q 7:34 is formulated retrospectively, but in a way appropriate to the actual facts of Jesus's association with victims of social and religious discrimination: "The Son of Man has come eating and drinking, and you say, 'Look, a glutton and a drunkard, a friend of tax collectors and sinners!'" Finally, the Son of Man title seems to evoke the ideas of lowliness, hiddenness, and vulnerability (Q 9:58, "And Jesus said to him: 'Foxes have holes, and birds of the sky have nests; but the Son of Man does not have anywhere he can lay his head'"). The saying in Q 11:30 points to a judgment context ("For as Jonah became to the Ninevites a sign, so also will the Son of Man be to this generation"), as does Q 12:8–9 ("Anyone who may speak out for me in public, the Son of Man will also speak out for him before the angels. . . . But whoever may deny me in public will be denied before the angels"; cf. Mark 8:38). This last text poses special issues:[275] does Jesus here refer to the Son of Man as a figure different from himself? In and of itself, the possibility of such an understanding does not automatically point to a post-Easter origin. Jesus could just as well have spoken these words in the context of the Passion. If one takes the saying in isolation, then it *can* refer to the future Son of Man as a different person than Jesus.[276] But if one takes into consideration the claim of Jesus as a whole, it is more than improbable that he understood himself to be the forerunner or messenger of another eschatological figure.[277] While Q 12:10 (speaking against the Holy Spirit) certainly, and Mark 2:10; 10:45a; Luke 19:10 (as variants of Mark 2:17; Luke 5:32) are possibly of post-Easter origin, the other authentic sayings indicate that Jesus interpreted his own activities in terms of the Son of Man figure, used in its everyday sense ("my own person").

275. According to Vögtle, *Gretchenfrage*, 9, the saying in Q 12:8 plays a "key role" in the issue of whether the earthly Jesus used the term "Son of Man." The Matt. 10:32 parallel to Luke 12:8 does not contain the Son of Man terminology (Πᾶς οὖν ὅστις ὁμολογήσει ἐν ἐμοὶ ἔμπροσθεν τῶν ἀνθρώπων, ὁμολογήσω κἀγὼ ἐν αὐτῷ ἔμπροσθεν τοῦ πατρός μου τοῦ ἐν [τοῖς] οὐρανοῖς [everyone who acknowledges me before others, I also will acknowledge before the angels of God]). So also the parallel Q 12:10 speaks only in the passive of forgiveness at the last judgment (ἀφεθήσεται), probably to be understood as a divine passive pointing to God himself as the one who grants sanctions. Thus especially P. Hoffmann has argued for Son of Man in Luke as Lukan redaction (Paul Hoffmann, "Der Menschensohn in Lukas 12:8," *NTS* 44 [1998]: 357–79). However, the Matthean editing of the saying is clearly discernible, and the Matthean context did not make it easy to take over the Son of Man terminology (cf. Vögtle, *Gretchenfrage*, 17–18), so that it is best to continue to regard the saying in Q 12:8 as originally referring to the Son of Man (so, e.g., Jens Schröter, *Erinnerung an Jesu Worte: Studien zur Rezeption der Logienüberlieferung in Markus, Q und Thomas* [WMANT 76; Neukirchen-Vluyn: Neukirchener Verlag, 1997], 362–65; and C. M. Tuckett, "Q 12,8 Once Again—'Son of Man' or 'I'?" in *From Quest to Q: Festschrift James M. Robinson* [ed. Jon Ma Asgeirsson et al.; BETL 146; Louvain: Leuven University Press, 2000], 171–88).

276. So, e.g., Bultmann, *Theology of the New Testament*, 1:30.

277. Cf. Riniker, *Gerichtsverkündigung*, 348; Schröter, *Jesus von Nazareth*, 253.

The Suffering Son of Man

The sayings about the suffering Son of Man are the three Passion predictions (Mark 8:31 par.; 9:31 par.; 10:33–34) and the sayings about the handing over/betrayal of the Son of Man (Mark 14:21 par., "For the Son of Man goes as it is written of him, but woe to that one by whom the Son of Man is betrayed! It would have been better for that one not to have been born"; Mark 14:41, "He came a third time and said to them, 'Are you still sleeping and taking your rest? Enough! The hour has come; the Son of Man is betrayed into the hands of sinners'"; cf. also Luke 17:25; 24:7). It is very probable that the sayings about the suffering and rising Son of Man are post-Easter formulations, for they are missing from the sayings source Q and are clearly influenced by post-Easter christological reflections.[278]

The Coming Son of Man

While the sayings about the present actions of the Son of Man are related to the tradition of everyday language, the sayings about the coming Son of Man are associated with the traditions of visionary language. Thus in Mark 14:62 Jesus announces his future activity as judge: "Jesus said, 'I am; and "you will see the Son of Man seated at the right hand of the Power," and "coming with the clouds of heaven."'" Other such sayings also belong to a context of judgment and parousia: Q 12:40, "You also must be ready, for the Son of Man is coming at an hour you do not expect"; Q 17:24, "For as the lightning streaks from Sunrise and flashes as far as Sunset, so will the Son of Man be on his day"; Q 17:26, 30, "As it took place in the days of Noah, so will it be in the day of the Son of Man"; Matt. 10:23b, "Truly I tell you, you will not have gone through all the towns of Israel before the Son of Man comes"; Matt. 19:28, "Jesus said to them, 'Truly I tell you, at the renewal of all things, when the Son of Man is seated on the throne of his glory, you who have followed me will also sit on twelve thrones, judging the twelve tribes of Israel'"; and the traditions about confessing and denying already discussed (Q 12:8–9/Mark 8:38).

The sayings about the coming Son of Man are difficult to evaluate historically. On the one hand, Jesus appears to have connected his present and future activity as judge with the concept of the Son of Man (Q 12:8–9); on the other hand, the Son of Man who will return as judge plays a central role in the christological conception of the sayings source Q (see below, §8.1.2)—indicating a post-Easter (re-)formulation of the sayings. While Luke 18:8b and Matt. 24:30 are post-Easter formulations, and the Q sayings they introduce received their literary form in the post-Easter community, it is still probably the case that

278. Cf. Theissen and Merz, *Historical Jesus*, 552. Differently Stuhlmacher, *Biblische Theologie*, 120–21, who regards an earlier form of Mark 9:31 and Mark 10:45 as authentic sayings of Jesus about the suffering Son of Man.

Jesus himself made a fundamental connection between his present and future destiny and the figure of the Son of Man.[279]

Jesus adopted the expression "Son of Man" because it was not a central concept in Jewish apocalypticism, but *as an open-ended expression that was not already firmly defined* it was an appropriate term to characterize his own work. Traits of the pre-Easter ministry of Jesus are manifest especially in the sayings about the present activity of the Son of Man, emphatically so in Q 7:33–34 and Q 9:58. The expression "Son of Man" must probably here be understood not in the generic sense but as a title. A striking aspect of both sayings is that the authority of the Son of Man is not publicly obvious but concealed. This paralleling of veiled and revelatory speech has a structural parallel in Jesus's language for the kingdom of God: *just as the kingdom of God is a reality that is at once openly revealed and hidden, so also the present work of the Son of Man is effective not by its obvious power but in its hiddenness.*

3.9.3 *Jesus as Messiah*

Of the 531 instances of Χριστός (Christ) or Ἰησοῦς Χριστός (Jesus Christ), more than half (270) are found in Paul. It is significant that Χριστός is already an integral part of the oldest Christian confessions (cf. 1 Cor. 15:3b–5; 2 Cor. 5:15) and that they bind together affirmations of the death and resurrection of Jesus, which represents the whole drama of God's saving act in Christ. For Paul, Ἰησοῦς Χριστός has become a titular name. The apostle is aware that Χριστός was originally an appellative, and that Ἰησοῦς is a proper name, for he never speaks of a κύριος Χριστός (Lord Christ). When connected with Ἰησοῦς in one phrase, Χριστός is thus for Paul a cognomen that can have titular overtones. At the same time, the title was so fused with the person of Jesus himself and his specific destiny that it soon became simply an epithet for Jesus, or even a part of his name, from which the name "Christian" was later derived (Acts 11:26).

The point of departure and presupposition for the development of messianic ideas is the royal anointing and dynasty pronouncements in the Old Testament (cf. 1 Sam. 2:4a; 5:3; 1 Kings 1:32–40; 11; 2 Sam. 7; Ps. 89; 132).[280] From these, the multilayered traditions of ancient Judaism developed; in particular, at the turn of the first century CE there was a wide variety of these messianic hopes.[281] The idea of a political-*royal* Messiah (cf. *Pss. Sol.* 17; 18;

279. Cf. also Dunn, *Jesus Remembered*, 759–61.

280. Cf. Ernst-Joachim Waschke, *Der Gesalbte: Studien zur alttestamentlichen Theologie* (BZAW 306; Berlin: de Gruyter, 2001).

281. Cf. the recent treatments of Gerbern S. Oegema, *Der Gesalbte und sein Volk: Untersuchungen zum Konzeptualisierungsprozess der messianischen Erwartungen von dem Makkabäern bis Bar Koziba* (SIJD 2; Göttingen: Vandenhoeck & Ruprecht, 1994); Schreiber, *Gesalbter und König: Titel und Konzeptionen der königlichen Gesalbtenerwartung in frühjüdischen und urchristlichen*

2 Bar. 72.2) who will drive the Gentiles out of the land and restore justice is found alongside hopes with *prophetic* (cf. CD 2:12; 11QMelch) and *priestly*-royal traits (cf. 1QS 9:9–11; 1QSa 2:11–12; CD 12:23; 14:19; 19:10–11; 20:1). The broad spectrum of Jewish eschatological views and their potential for combining with one another is evidenced by the connections between Son of Man and messianic ideas (cf. *1 En.* 48.10; 52.4; *4 Ezra* 12.32; 13), and by messianic figures who appeared without the Messiah-terminology (messianic prophets).[282]

Χριστός is an essential element in the oldest New Testament traditions, but whether Jesus himself claimed the Χριστός title for himself must be clarified by an analysis of the Synoptic tradition. The findings are surprisingly meager and ambiguous. There are seven instances of the title in Mark, the eighteen references in Matthew are essentially dependent on Mark, and Luke's two volumes connect the Christ-title with an emphatic Spirit-Christology, especially by the author's interpretation of Isa. 61:1–2. The key texts are Mark 8:29 ("Peter answered him, 'You are the Messiah'") and Mark 14:61–62 ("Again the high priest asked him, 'Are you the Messiah, the Son of the Blessed One?' Jesus said, 'I am'"). Both texts are integral parts of Mark's own Christology and hardly provide a precise account of actual historical events.

Nonetheless, there is much evidence that Jesus triggered messianic expectations by his words and deeds. Mark 8:27–30 could indicate that some saw Jesus as the fulfillment of political-messianic expectations. The messianic ovation at his entry into Jerusalem (cf. Mark 11:8–10), the cleansing of the temple, and especially the inscription on the cross (see below, §3.10.1) suggest that Jesus intentionally fanned the flames of messianic hopes. The inscription on the cross, ὁ βασιλεὺς τῶν Ἰουδαίων (The King of the Jews), can hardly have originated from either Jews or Christians, and strongly supports the view that the Romans executed Jesus as a messianic pretender.[283] This means that the question of Jesus's kingship/messiahship *must* have played a decisive role in his trial,[284] apart from our ability to determine whether or not Jesus actively claimed the title for himself. So also, the rapid and extensive spread of the title Χριστός in the oldest post-Easter traditions is best understood if there was a connection between his ministry and his fate.

Schriften, 145–534; William Horbury, *Jewish Messianism and the Cult of Christ* (London: SCM, 1998); Charlesworth, ed., *Messiah*. On the complex messianic ideas of Qumran, cf. Zimmermann, *Messianische Texte aus Qumran*, 23ff.

282. A listing of the most inflammatory of these figures is found in Crossan, *Historical Jesus*, 451–52.

283. Hengel, "Messiah Israels," 50.

284. J. Frey, "Der historische Jesus und der Christus der Evangelien," in *Der historische Jesus* (ed. J. Schröter and R. Bruckner; BZNW 114; Berlin: de Gruyter, 2002), 262ff.; Schröter, *Jesus von Nazareth*, 262ff.

However isolated texts may be evaluated, the evidence as a whole permits only one *historical* conclusion: *the life of Jesus was not unmessianic!*[285] Jesus's claim to represent the present-and-coming kingdom of God, his freedom with reference to the Torah, his sovereign call to discipleship, his conviction that he was the decisive figure in God's coming judgment, that he was Son of Man who would be enthroned by God at the parousia and was already working with his authority—all this permits only the one conclusion that Jesus made an enormous claim for his own person, a claim made by no Jew before or after him.

At the same time, it is evident that this claim was made in a remarkably veiled manner, which shows that Jesus did not present himself in the given categories of clear theological doctrines, but from situation to situation in almost paradoxical stories and sayings. Jesus communicated experiences of the kingdom of God but rejected every demand for a legitimating sign and every direct proof of his authority. He demanded commitment to his message as the highest priority and bound salvation and condemnation to his own person, all the while both distancing himself from and surpassing all the known varieties of messianic authority. It was not knowledge about Jesus that was decisive but the encounter with him and his message, getting oneself involved in God's new reality.

3.10 Jesus's Destiny in Jerusalem: End and Beginning

In 30 CE, at the conclusion of his public ministry, Jesus went with his disciples and wider circle of followers to the Passover festival in Jerusalem.[286] He did this in continuity with his previous proclamation of the kingdom of God, and doubtless did so intentionally, for both his prior spectacular ministry in Galilee and his entrance into Jerusalem (Mark 1:1–11 par.) generate the expectation of a climax of these events.

3.10.1 Arrest, Trial, and Crucifixion

Jesus did not withdraw from the ovations at his entry into Jerusalem, i.e., he accepted the messianic expectations with which they were bound up (Mark 11:9–10). Since the entry also contains ceremonial elements associated with rulers, it could be interpreted in a political sense. Closely connected in both time and substantive meaning is the cleansing of the temple (Mark 11:15–18 par.).[287]

285. Contra Bultmann, *Theology of the New Testament*, 1:27: "Moreover the synoptic tradition leaves no doubt about it that *Jesus's life and work* measured by traditional messianic ideas was *not messianic*."

286. For the chronological framework of Jesus's appearance, cf. Theissen and Merz, *Historical Jesus*, 151–60.

287. Cf. Maurits Sabbe, "The Cleaning of the Temple and the Temple Logion," in *Studia Neotestamentica: Collected Essays* (ed. Maurits Sabbe; BETL 98; Louvain: Leuven University

Cleansing of the Temple

Jesus found in the temple courts money changers and those who sold sacrificial animals, which originally served to facilitate the orderly operation of the sacrificial system. The priests could not personally examine every animal brought for sacrifice. The money changers too provided a helpful service, for according to Exod. 30:11–16 every male Jew aged twenty and older had to pay a double drachma as temple tax. The details and extent of the temple cleansing can no longer be reconstructed, but it appears that Jesus used violence against (some of) the money changers and animal merchants. Connected with this action is a prophetic threat oracle against the temple, the kernel of which is preserved in Mark 13:2, "Not one stone will be left here upon another; all will be thrown down."[288] The cleansing of the temple and the threatening oracle against it were not aimed at a restoration of a temple cultus that would be pleasing to God, as had been called for repeatedly in the history of Judaism.[289] Instead, in Jesus's view the presence and coming of the kingdom of God meant that the temple had lost its function as the place where atonement for sins was made. Because the dominion of evil was coming to an end, there was no longer any need for temple sacrifices.[290]

Arrest and Preliminary Hearing

What role did the Jewish authorities play in the proceedings against Jesus? They probably interpreted Jesus's action against the temple as a challenge to the economic and political order, which the Sadducees especially would take as a valid reason to bring charges against him.[291] *Not "the Jews," but the Sadducees appear as the driving force that led to Jesus's arrest* (cf. Mark 14:1, 43, 53, 60; 15:11; Josephus, *Ant.* 18.64, "When Pilate, upon hearing him accused by men of the highest standing among us, had condemned him to be

---

Press, 1991), 331–54; Thomas Söding, "Die Tempelaktion Jesu," *TThZ* 101 (1992): 36–64; Ekkehard Stegemann, "Zur Tempelreinigung im Johannesevangelium," in *Die Hebräische Bibel und ihre zweifache Nachgeschichte: Festschrift für Rolf Rendtorff zum 65. Geburtstag* (ed. Erhard Blum; Neukirchen-Vluyn: Neukirchener Verlag, 1990), 503–16; Sauer, *Vollendung*, 426–59; Kurt Paesler, *Das Tempelwort Jesu: Die Tradition von Tempelzerstörung und Tempelerneuerung im Neuen Testament* (FRLANT 184; Göttingen: Vandenhoeck & Ruprecht, 1999), 233–49; Jostein Ådna, *Jesu Stellung zum Tempel: Die Tempelaktion und das Tempelwort als Ausdruck seiner messianischen Sendung* (WUNT 2.119; Tübingen: Mohr Siebeck, 2000), 300–333; Wolfgang Reinbold, *Der Prozess Jesu* (BTS 28; Göttingen: Vandenhoeck & Ruprecht, 2006), 130–37.

288. For evidence and argument, cf. Paesler, *Tempelwort*, 76–92 (Mark 14:58 is a post-Easter variant of Mark 13:2).

289. Cf. ibid., 244: "symbolic disabling and abolition of the Jerusalem cult system."

290. Sauer, *Vollendung*, 455–59.

291. Cf. Sanders, *Historical Figure of Jesus*, 260: "I conclude that Jesus's symbolic action of overthrowing tables in the Temple was understood in connection with a saying about destruction, and that the action and the saying, in the view of the authorities, constituted a prophetic threat." Differently Becker, *Jesus of Nazareth*, 332–36, who considers the story of the cleansing of the temple to be unhistorical.

crucified").[292] In this connection, there is an informative tradition in Josephus that shows that prophecy against the temple and the city of Jerusalem called for Jewish officials responsible for jurisdiction in the capital city to participate in a legal action for which the Romans were basically responsible.[293] The text confirms the existence of an established process of appeal. An official procedure against the prophet Jesus ben Ananias was begun. He was first brought before members of the Sanhedrin for a hearing and then turned over to the procurator. He was scourged, which as a rule was preliminary to carrying out a death sentence, i.e., the Jewish authorities could initiate charges leading to the death penalty, but the ultimate decision was in the hands of the Romans—and in this case resulted in acquittal. A similar course of events is to be supposed for the proceedings against Jesus of Nazareth. The cleansing of the temple obviously made Jesus subject to the charge of attacking the public economic and political order.[294] From the point of view of the Sadducees, his action against the temple was a challenge to the operation of the temple cult. Crime against the temple was one of the "extremely rare cases that induced the Roman legal authority in the province Judea to participate on their own 'cognitio' in the Jewish jurisdiction of the capital city, by way of an exception clause."[295] It was most likely the Sadducees who initiated the legal proceedings against Jesus that led to his arrest and hearing before the High Council. Jesus was then handed over to the governor, who conducted his own investigation and was responsible for the death sentence.

292. H. Ritt, "Wer war schuld am Tod Jesu," *BZ* 31 (1987): 165–75.

293. Josephus, *JW* 6.300–305: "But a further portent was even more alarming. Four years before the war, when the city was enjoying profound peace and prosperity, there came to the feast at which it is the custom of all Jews to erect tabernacles to God, one Jesus, son of Ananias, a rude peasant, who, standing in the temple, suddenly began to cry out, 'A voice from the east, a voice from the west, a voice from the four winds, a voice against Jerusalem and the sanctuary, a voice against the bridegroom and the bride, a voice against all the people.' Day and night he went about all the alleys with this cry on his lips. Some of the leading citizens, incensed at these ill-omened words, arrested the fellow and severely chastised him. But he, without a word on his own behalf or for the private ear of those who smote him, only continued his cries as before. Thereupon, the magistrates, supposing, as was indeed the case, that the man was under some supernatural impulse, brought him before the Roman governor; there, although flayed to the bone with scourges, he neither sued for mercy nor shed a tear, but merely introducing the most mournful of variations into his ejaculation, responded to each stroke with 'Woe to Jerusalem!' When Albinus, the governor, asked him who and whence he was and why he uttered these cries, he answered him never a word, but unceasingly reiterated his dirge over the city, until Albinus pronounced him a maniac and let him go."

294. On the temple, cf. Johann Maier, "Beobachtungen zum Konfliktpotential in neutestamentlichen Aussagen über den Tempel," in *Jesus und das jüdische Gesetz* (ed. Ingo Broer and Jens-W. Taeger; Stuttgart: Kohlhammer, 1992), 173–213.

295. Klaus E. Müller, "Möglichkeit und Vollzug jüdischer Kapitalgerichtsbarkeit," in *Der Prozess gegen Jesus: Historische Rückfrage und theologische Deutung* (ed. Karl Kertelge and Josef Blank; QD 112; Freiburg i.B.: Herder, 1988), 82–83.

Trial and Crucifixion

The Jewish capital jurisdiction received its authority from the Roman procurator and was entirely subject to him.[296] Josephus specifically notes with regard to the first procurator, Coponius (6–9 CE), that he ruled with unlimited authority and had also received from the emperor the authority to pronounce and execute capital punishment.[297] After the hearing before the High Council, Jesus was taken to the Praetorium, Pilate's office and official residence.[298] Why was Jesus condemned after such a short trial? The Romans certainly did not let themselves be pressured by Jewish authorities without any grounds, and pointing to internal doctrinal disputes among the Jews is not sufficient to explain Roman intervention. The triumphal procession into Jerusalem, the action in the temple, Jesus's statement in Mark 15:2–3 par. ("'Are you the King of the Jews?' He answered him, 'You say so'"), and the inscription on the cross (Mark 15:26 par., ὁ βασιλεὺς τῶν Ἰουδαίων, "The King of the Jews") indicate that the Romans obviously took Jesus to be a (religious-political) agitator who could exploit the tense situation at a Passover festival for his own purposes.

Josephus illustrates the explosiveness of this charge. In the turmoil after the death of Herod the Great, two men attempted to become king: a certain Judas[299] and a servant of Herod the Great named Simon.[300] With their troops, they plundered and burned, but then they were wiped out by the Romans. Afterward, a certain Athronges[301] attempted to gain the throne. He claimed to be the king and fought both against the Romans and the family of Herod the Great. He too was defeated by the Romans and their supporters.[302] Josephus characterizes these turbulent times in a summary statement: "And so Judea was filled with brigandage. Anyone might make himself king as the head of a band of rebels whom he fell in with, and then would press on to the destruction of the community, causing trouble to few Romans and then only to a small degree, but bringing the greatest slaughter upon their own people."[303] Josephus then reports that the Roman governor Varus brutally suppressed other rebellions, and once had two thousand Jews crucified.[304] Behind Josephus's description of

296. On this point cf. especially ibid., 44–58, who also debates other theses.

297. Cf. Josephus, *JW* 2.117; *Ant.* 18.2.

298. On Pilate, cf. the recent study of K. St. Krieger, "Pontius Pilatus—ein Judenfeind? Zur Problematik einer Pilatus-biographie," *BN* 78 (1995): 63–83. He emphasizes that all our sources for Pilate are tendentious and are to be evaluated with care in regard to their portrayal of him as an especially unprincipled person.

299. Cf. Josephus, *Ant.* 17.272.

300. Cf. Josephus, *Ant.* 17.273ff.

301. Cf. Josephus, *Ant.* 17.278ff.

302. For an analysis of the most important texts, cf. Hengel, *Zealots*, 256–71; 318–24; P. Egger, "*Crucifixus sub Pontio Pilato*" (NTA 32; Münster: Aschendorff, 1997), 72ff.

303. Josephus, *Ant.* 17.285.

304. Cf. Josephus *Ant.* 17.295; cf. also *Ant.* 20.102, which reports the ca. 46 CE crucifixion of Simon and James, the two sons of Judas, the founder of the Zealot movement, by the Procurator Tiberius Alexander.

the groups as "bandits" we can perceive messianic and social hopes directed to freeing the country from Roman domination and establishing a more just order. According to *Pss. Sol.* 17.21ff., the king chosen and sent by God will not only drive out the Gentiles but also rule over his people with justice.

Pilate had Jesus scourged and delivered to crucifixion. Crucifixion was the preferred Roman means of capital punishment for slaves and rebels, an especially gruesome and disgraceful punishment.[305] It was probably on Friday the 14th of Nisan (April 7) of the year 30 that Jesus of Nazareth was crucified by the Romans as an agitator.[306]

3.10.2 Jesus's Understanding of His Death

It is remarkable that, despite the obvious danger, Jesus did not leave Jerusalem. According to the Synoptic Passion stories, he had plenty of opportunity to do so. The possibility of being arrested could not have caught Jesus by surprise, for he knew the tense political situation in Jerusalem, had the death of John the Baptist ever before him, and had been warned to flee from Herod Antipas, the ruler of his own country (Luke 13:31).[307] When he remained in Jerusalem despite this clear danger, and even acted in provocative ways, then everything speaks for the view that Jesus saw his coming death as a real possibility and did nothing to avoid it. If one asks what such conduct must mean, then, alongside a few sayings in the Synoptic tradition, one must reflect above all on the tradition of the Last Supper.[308]

Different sayings *could* presuppose Jesus's knowledge of his death, for example: Luke 12:49–50 ("I came to bring fire to the earth, and how I wish it were already kindled! I have a baptism with which to be baptized, and what stress I am under until it is completed!"); Luke 13:31–32 ("At that very hour some Pharisees came and said to him, 'Get away from here, for Herod wants to kill you.' He said to them, 'Go and tell that fox for me, "Listen, I am casting out demons and performing cures today and tomorrow, and on the third day I finish my work."'");

305. Here the basic study is Martin Hengel, *Crucifixion* (trans. John Bowden; Philadelphia: Fortress, 1977). Cf. also H.-W. Kuhn, "Die Kreuzesstrafe während der frühen Kaiserzeit," *ANRW* 2.25.1 (Berlin: de Gruyter, 1982), 648–793.

306. A consensus on this dating is becoming increasingly prevalent; cf. most recently Rainer Riesner, *Paul's Early Period: Chronology, Mission Strategy, Theology* (trans. Douglas W. Stott; Grand Rapids: Eerdmans, 1998), 35–58; Géza Vermès, *Die Passion: Die wahre Geschichte der letzten Tage im Leben Jesu* (Darmstadt: Primus, 2005), 138.

307. Cf. Freyne, *Jewish Galilean*, 165: "Jesus cannot have been unaware of the consequences of his symbolic action for his own future."

308. Wright, *Jesus and the Victory of God*, 651–52, sees in Jesus's proclamation of the return of Yahweh to Mount Zion the center of Jesus's self-understanding and the reason for his procession to Jerusalem, including his action in the temple. Against this view is the obvious fact that Σιών (Zion) does not appear at all in Jesus's preaching (Σιών is found in the gospels only in Matt. 21:5 and John 12:15).

Mark 14:7 (Jesus in the story of the anointing at Bethany: "For you always have the poor with you, and you can show kindness to them whenever you wish; but you will not always have me"; cf. Mark 2:19). All these texts are ambiguous, for in each case it is not clear whether they originated before or after Easter, nor is their reference to Jesus unambiguous. More important in this regard is the eucharistic tradition and the individual sayings related to it.

The Last Supper

Jesus's last meal with his disciples must be seen in the context of his prior practice of table fellowship, and thus also in relation to his proclamation of the kingdom of God (see above, §3.4.5). The nearness of the kingdom of God attains concrete expression in Jesus's practice of eating with social and religious outsiders, "For the Son of Man came to seek out and to save the lost" (Luke 19:10). Jesus's last meal, though shared only with his disciples, anticipates and guarantees the coming table fellowship in the kingdom of God, just as his previous eating with tax collectors and sinners had done. In this context the eschatological perspective of Mark 14:25 is of fundamental importance: "Amen I tell you, I will never again drink of the fruit of the vine until that day when I drink it new in the kingdom of God."[309] The eschatological perspective points ahead to the table fellowship of the coming kingdom of God. In Jewish texts, a grand meal is a widespread picture for the eschatological fellowship in God's new world (cf. Isa. 25:6–12). The eschatological perspective sets the Last Supper as a preliminary sign of this grand banquet in the coming kingdom. The content of Mark 14:25 clarifies two points:

1. At least directly before his arrest, Jesus reckoned with his coming death and intentionally said farewell to his disciples.
2. The conviction that he was about to die by no means caused Jesus to give up hope for the coming kingdom of God. To be sure, the time of its coming was indefinite, expressed by the vague "until that day," but the sure hope of the coming of the kingdom remained unbroken.

Moreover, Mark 14:25 can be understood as a prophecy of his own death: Jesus drinks for the last time before he participates in the banquet of the kingdom of God. It is also possible that he hoped that the kingdom would break in so soon that he would be spared the way to death.

That Jesus held a last meal with his disciples immediately prior to his arrest is historically very probable (cf. 1 Cor. 11:23c). As was the case with his table

309. The pre-Easter origin of Mark 14:25 is supported above all by the fact that the focus is not on Jesus and his destiny, but on the kingdom of God. Cf. Helmut Merklein, "Erwägungen zur überlieferungsgeschichte der neutestamentlichen Abendmahlstraditionen," in *Studien zu Jesus und Paulus* (2 vols.; WUNT 43, 105; Tübingen: Mohr, 1987), 1:170–74, who rightly understands Mark 14:25 as the hermeneutical key to the problem of the eucharistic tradition.

fellowship of his prior meals, Jesus did this in the awareness of the presence of God and in the expectation of the coming of God's kingdom. It is no longer clear whether this was a *Passover* meal.[310] The following points weigh against it:

1. Paul, or his tradition—our oldest written documentation—knows nothing of the Last Supper as a Passover meal (cf. the Passover motif in 1 Cor. 5:7);
2. Mark 14:12 is clearly secondary (so also Luke 22:15).
3. Jesus was probably executed on the 14th of Nisan (cf. John 18:28; 19:14; so also 1 Cor. 5:7); but the Passover festival begins on the 15th of Nisan.

In favor of a Passover setting for the Last Supper is the fact that the course of the meal *can* be understood within the framework of a Passover meal (especially in Luke). It is in fact likely that Jesus celebrated the Last Supper in connection with the Passover festival; at the same time, the theological importance of this historically unsolvable problem is slight.

The Last Supper receives its special character through Jesus's consciousness of his approaching death. Jesus connected his imminent death with the expectation that the ultimate manifestation of the kingdom of God would then break in (Mark 14:25). Jesus could not have thought of his death apart from his consciousness of his unique relation to God and his bold awareness of God's presence manifest especially in his proclamation of the kingdom of God and in his miracles. *Jesus's consciousness of his exalted status means that he must have had an interpretation of his coming death!* This interpretation could not be simply in continuity with the table fellowship of the earthly Jesus, for his impending death raised the question of the meaning of his mission as a whole. Thus his person received a central significance, since the presence of the kingdom of God and the miracles were already causally dependent on his personal identity (cf. Luke 11:20). This also meant that the imminent event of Jesus's death called for an interpretation of Jesus's person that only he could give.[311] Jesus probably understood his death in dependence on Isa. 53 as the giving of himself for the "many" (cf. Mark 10:45).[312] Jesus's death thus stands in continuity with the life of the earthly Jesus, who lived "for others." In the course of the Last Supper, Jesus expressed this self-giving metaphorically in the *words of institution* (cf. Mark 14:22,

310. Joachim Jeremias, *The Eucharistic Words of Jesus* (trans. Norman Perrin; New York: Scribner, 1966), 26–35, argues for this view. The opposite position is argued, on good grounds, by Kollmann, *Ursprung*, 158–61.

311. Cf. Heinz Schürmann, ed., *Gottes Reich—Jesu Geschick: Jesu ureigener Tod im Licht seiner Basileia-Verkündigung* (Freiburg: Herder, 1983), 185–245.

312. On Mark 10:45b, cf. Jürgen Roloff, "Anfänge der soteriologischen Deutung des Todes Jesu (Mk. X. 45 und Lk. XXII. 27)," in *Exegetische Verantwortung in der Kirche: Aufsätze* (ed. Jürgen Roloff and Martin Karrer; Göttingen: Vandenhoeck & Ruprecht, 1990), 117–43.

24): τοῦτό ἐστιν τὸ σῶμά μου (this is my body) . . . τοῦτό ἐστιν τὸ αἷμά μου . . . ὑπὲρ πολλῶν (this is my blood . . . for many).[313]

The significance of these words of institution is not guided specifically by the Passover meal that provided their immediate setting; Jesus's *gestures* give them a broader meaning. The common drinking from one cup could mean that as Jesus faced death he wanted to be assured that the fellowship he had established among them would continue beyond his death. Jesus thus celebrated the Last Supper with the awareness that with his death, the kingdom of God would break in, and with it the final judgment. He gives his life in order that "the many" may be saved in this eschatological event. His expectation that with his death the final coming of the kingdom of God would be revealed was not fulfilled (Mark 15:34). God acted for him in an unexpected way, by the resurrection from the dead, but at the same time in continuity with his hope: *Jesus's death is and remains the saving event for "the many."* After Easter, the Last Supper became the sign of remembrance of the Coming One who has already come and the sign of the fulfillment of his mission. Through this sign, in the power of the Holy Spirit, he makes himself known as the living, present, and active subject of his own memorial, as the founder of a new covenant, and as the coming Lord of humanity and the world. This fundamental structure has impressed itself on all the eucharistic traditions, despite the variety of their forms.

When Jesus deliberately went to Jerusalem without attempting to avoid the consequences of his intentionally provocative actions, and at the Last Supper gave the interpretation of his approaching death, the conclusion is unavoidable: Jesus hoped and expected that with his appearance in Jerusalem the ultimate form of the kingdom of God would break into history. *Thus the end of his life stands in direct continuity with his previous works. Jesus's servant pro-existence*[314] *for God, God's kingdom, and for humanity embraces and characterizes his life and death in the same way.*

313. A convincing reconstruction of the exact words and gestures at the Last Supper is hardly possible; a subtle and astute analysis of the eucharistic traditions is found in Merklein, "Abendmahlstraditionen," 158–74; cf. further, with various emphases, Jeremias, *Eucharistic Words*, 138–203; Heinz Schürmann, *Der Einsetzungsbericht: Lk 22,19–20* (NTA 4; Münster: Aschendorff, 1955); Hermann Patsch, *Abendmahl und historischer Jesus* (Stuttgart: Calwer, 1972); Kollmann, *Ursprung*, 153–89; Jens Schröter, *Das Abendmahl in der frühchristlichen Literatur: Frühchristliche Deutungen und Impulse für die Gegenwart* (SBS 210; Stuttgart: Katholisches Bibelwerk, 2006), 25–134.

314. Cf. Heinz Schürmann, "'Pro-Existenz' als christologischer Grundbegriff," in *Jesus, Gestalt und Geheimnis: Gesammelte Beiträge* (ed. Heinz Schürmann and Klaus Scholtissek; Paderborn: Bonifatius, 1994), 286–315; and John A. T. Robinson, "The Man for Others," in *The Human Face of God* (Philadelphia: Westminster, 1973), 212–44. [*Pro-Existenz* is a German theological term designating a life lived for others. Cf. Dietrich Bonhoeffer's portrayal of Jesus as the Man for Others.—MEB]

4

The First Transformation

The Emergence of Christology

The proclamation, life, and destiny of Jesus of Nazareth provide the foundation for the first Christians' new world of experience and thought. This first transformation generates a Christology as the conceptual and narrative development of the salvific meaning of the Christ event, in which Jesus is seen as Messiah, Kyrios, and Son of God. It is no longer Jesus who is the proclaimer; now he is the one who is proclaimed. What Jesus himself once said and how Jesus was experienced and rethought now flow into each other and form something new: Jesus himself becomes the object of faith and the content of the confession.

How is this transition from Jesus's own preaching to preaching about Jesus to be described? Two basic conceptual models are possible:

1. The model of discontinuity: Adolf von Harnack made a sharp distinction between the simple gospel of Jesus, which was concerned with the Father alone, and the later christological development, which Paul influenced decisively. "In those leading features of it which we described in the earlier lectures the whole of the Gospel is contained, and we must keep it free from the intrusion of any alien element: God and the soul, the soul and its God."[1] Rudolf Bultmann also votes for the discontinuity

1. Harnack, *What Is Christianity*, 142. The French church historian appropriately formulated the matter: "Jesus foretold the kingdom, and it was the church that came" (Alfred Loisy, *The Gospel and the Church* [Lives of Jesus Series; Philadelphia: Fortress, 1976], 166). Loisy did

model, but he chooses a psychological explanation: "Jesus had counted on the breaking in of the kingdom; this did not happen. The earliest Christian community had counted on the appearance of the Son of Man; this did not happen either. The embarrassment thus created was the sole driving force for the development of Christology and the relapse into an apocalyptic understanding of time."[2]

2. The continuity model is advocated by Joachim Jeremias: "The post-Easter message of the church and the pre-Easter message of Jesus belong inseparably together. Neither may be isolated from the other, nor may their differences be ironed out. More precisely: they are related to each other as call and response."[3] According to Leon Goppelt, "Jesus represented a Christology as veiled witness to himself; the apostles developed this Christology as an open confession, and from there as teaching that gave clarity to this confession."[4] W. Thüsing attempts to ground New Testament theology as a whole in a single unifying perspective, "because Jesus was also 'the Son' during his earthly life (even though he could be recognized as such in the full sense only after Easter), because the basic theological structure of the 'gospel' did not emerge only after Easter, because the material structures of the eschatological-theological message of Christianity are deeply influenced by Jesus's own message. The 'post-Easter transformation' as a whole had, in its essential character, already been stamped by the character of the life and ministry of Jesus as a whole (the 'structural components' of Jesus's own life)."[5] For F. Hahn, the identity of the earthly Jesus with the risen Lord is "the foundation of all Christian affirmation. Every isolated theological evaluation of the pre-Easter Jesus story contradicts the witness of the whole New Testament."[6] Both developments are possible in a partially combined form: the post-Easter Christology could be a really new element that had only a minimal point of contact in the life of the pre-Easter Jesus, or none at all, but it could also be a

---

not intend this statement to be ironic or disdainful, but was arguing that the original form of the gospel could not be maintained; continuity with the beginnings could only be maintained through the discontinuity of the church. For nuance and context of Loisy's most famous and often misunderstood comment, cf. B. B. Scott's introduction to the English republication of Loisy's work, xxxvii–xlii, and William R. Baird, *History of New Testament Research*, vol. 2, *From Jonathan Edwards to Rudolf Bultmann* (Minneapolis: Fortress, 2002), 165–72.

2. *Protokoll der Tagung "Alter Marburger,"* October 25, 1957, p. 7.

3. Joachim Jeremias, *Neutestamentliche Theologie* (3rd ed.; Gütersloh: Gütersloher Verlagshaus G. Mohn, 1979), 279 [trans. MEB from German 3rd ed.; English translation of German 1st ed. Jeremias, *New Testament Theology*, does not include this statement].

4. Goppelt and Roloff, *Theology of the New Testament*, 2:18.

5. Thüsing, *Neutestamentlichen Theologien*, 1:247; on the "structural components" of Jesus's life, cf. 70–71.

6. Hahn, *Theologie*, 1:125.

consistent updating of the pre-Easter claims of Jesus under the changed perspectives of the Easter events.

The clarification of this question requires that we consider the decisive factors for the formation of early Christology.

4.1 Jesus's Pre-Easter Claim

The preceding analyses (see chap. 3 above) have shown that Jesus's appearance in history, with its charismatic, prophetic, sapiential, and messianic dimensions, is to be considered unique even when regarded only from the perspective of the history of religions. *There is no other figure of antiquity who made a comparable claim, with a comparable effect, as did Jesus of Nazareth.*[7] When Jesus bound the establishment of the kingdom of God exclusively to his own person, so that his actions represented the inbreaking of the kingdom of God, then he must necessarily have thought of himself as standing in some nearness to God, such that to think of God was also to think of Jesus. When he made his own person the criterion of eschatological judgment (Q 12:8–9), emerged on the stage of history as a miracle worker, and forgave sins just as God did—when he placed his own station above that of Moses, and with the call of the Twelve aspired to the restitution of Israel in a new form—then the eschatological quality of the pre-Easter Jesus is the basis for the explicit Christology developed after Easter. Already in his pre-Easter life, Jesus had made a unique claim that was changed by the resurrection, but at the same time made even stronger.

The origin of the early Christology is grounded, however, not only in the personal claim of Jesus, but also in the content of his teaching. One can speak of a *plausibility of historical effects with regard to both the person and the actions of Jesus.* Witness the lines of continuity that can be drawn between early Christianity and the life and teachings of Jesus:[8]

1. Jesus did not bind the will of God to the performance of ritual acts but emphasized the ethic of love for God and neighbor. From this point,

7. From the history of religions point of view, the only possible comparable figures are Pythagoras (ca. 570–480 BCE) and Apollonius of Tyana (d. 98 CE). Pythagoras was obviously a charismatic figure who was at home in all areas of the philosophy and science of his time, a figure who captivated everyone who knew him. On the historical Pythagoras, cf. Christoph Riedweg, *Pythagoras: Leben, Lehre, Nachwirkung; Eine Einführung* (Munich: Beck, 2002). Apollonius appeared in history as a wandering philosopher in the tradition of Pythagoras, and as a miracle worker with political influence. In about 200 CE, Philostratus composed the standard work on the life of Apollonius. Cf. Koskenniemi, *Apollonius*.

8. On this point cf. Ulrich Luz, "Das 'Auseinandergehen der Wege': Über die Trennung des Christentums vom Judentum," in *Antijudaismus—christliche Erblast* (ed. Walter Dietrich et al.; Stuttgart: Kohlhammer, 1999), 56–73.

early Christianity could develop an ethic of love not directly bound to the Torah. Jesus's actions as a whole were perceived and interpreted as the healing restoration of the disturbed relationship of human beings with God and with one another.

2. God's boundless love opens perspectives that extend beyond the election of Israel. Although Jesus knew that in principle he was sent only to Israel, his symbolic actions in behalf of Gentiles facilitated the early Christians' carrying of their message beyond Israel.
3. Jesus attributed only a minimal significance to the temple, so early Christians were not particularly inclined to localize the worship of God at a specific place. Jesus obviously interpreted the fundamental pillars of the Judaism of his time in a way that was open to transformation toward universalism.

4.2 The Resurrection Appearances

The appearances of the Risen One as a central element of the Easter phenomenon were obviously the initiating events for the fundamental realization of early Christianity: the Jesus of Nazareth who had died shamefully on the cross is no lawbreaker but has been raised from the dead and has taken his place forever by the side of God. *The exceptional attributes of the pre-Easter Jesus are transformed into the unsurpassable superiority of the post-Easter Lord.* A comparison of the Easter narratives of the gospels with 1 Cor. 15:3b–5 shows that the basic framework of all the Easter narratives comprises three elements: (1) a burial narrative (1 Cor. 15:4, "and he was buried"); (2) an appearance report (1 Cor. 15:5a, "and that he appeared to Peter"); (3) an appearance to the disciples as a group (1 Cor. 15:5b–7).[9]

Like the evangelists (Mark 16:1–8 par.; John 20:1–10, 11–15), Paul also presupposes the *empty tomb*.[10] He does not explicitly mention it, but the logic of the references to burial and resurrection in 1 Cor. 15:4 points to the empty tomb, as does the "being buried with him" of Rom. 6:4, for Jewish anthropology would presuppose a bodily resurrection.[11] In addition, this argument is axiomatic: *the resurrection message could not have been preached in Jerusalem with such success if the body of Jesus had remained in a mass grave or an*

9. For bibliography on the Easter event, see the notes in §6.2.2.

10. Differently Bultmann, *Theology of the New Testament*, "The accounts of the empty grave, of which Paul knows nothing, are legends."

11. Cf. the recent argument of Martin Hengel, "Das Begräbnis Jesu bei Paulus und die leibliche Auferstehung aus dem Grabe," in *Auferstehung = Resurrection: The Fourth Durham-Tübingen Research Symposium: Resurrection, Transfiguration and Exaltation in Old Testament, Ancient Judaism and Early Christianity* (ed. Friedrich Avemarie and Hermann Lichtenberger; WUNT 135; Tübingen: Mohr, 2001), 139ff.

unopened private tomb.[12] Neither Jesus's enemies nor his disciples would have been unaware of the place of Jesus's burial.[13] In terms of historical thinking, the success of the Easter message in Jerusalem is not conceivable without an empty tomb. The recent discovery in the northeast section of Jerusalem of the remains of a victim who was crucified in the time of Jesus shows[14] that the remains of an executed prisoner could be delivered to relatives or friends for burial. To be sure, the empty tomb by itself remains ambiguous, and only the appearances of the Risen One reveal its significance.[15]

The point of departure for the *appearance traditions*[16] is the primary epiphany of Jesus to Peter (cf. 1 Cor. 15:5a; Luke 24:34), for it is the basis for the distinctive position of Peter in early Christianity.[17] In the Gospel of John, the appearance tradition begins with the appearance to Mary Magdalene (John 20:11–18), and only after this does Jesus appear to his male disciples (John 20:19–23). Mark announces that Jesus will meet his disciples in Galilee (Mark 16:7), but he does not narrate this event. In Matthew, Jesus appears first to Mary Magdalene and the other Mary (cf. Matt. 28:9–10), and in Luke, to the disciples on the road to Emmaus (Luke 24:13ff.). The accounts still suggest that Jesus probably appeared first to Peter and Mary Magdalene or several women. The appearance accounts manifest no particular apologetic tendencies,[18] for, although according to Jewish law women were not fully qualified to be witnesses, they play an important role in almost all the reports of appearances found in the gospels. After appearing to individuals, Jesus

12. Paul Althaus, *Die Wahrheit des christlichen Osterglaubens* (BFCT 42; Gütersloh: Bertelsmann, 1940), 25: "In Jerusalem, at the place of the execution and burial of Jesus, not long after his death, it was proclaimed that he had been raised. This fact requires that in the circles of the earliest Christian community there was reliable evidence that the grave had been found empty."

13. Differently Gerd Lüdemann, *What Really Happened to Jesus: A Historical Approach to the Resurrection* (Louisville: Westminster John Knox, 1996), 23, who asserts, without mentioning any evidence, "As neither the disciples nor Jesus's next of kin bothered about Jesus's body, it is hardly conceivable that they were informed about its resting place" so that later they could at least retrieve and bury his bones.

14. H.-W. Kuhn, "Der Gekreuzigte von Giv'at ha-Mivtar: Bilanz einer Entdeckung," in *Theologia crucis, signum crucis: Festschrift für Erich Dinkler zum 70. Geburtstag* (ed. Carl Andresen and Günter Klein; Tübingen: Mohr, 1979), 303–34; Raymond E. Brown, *The Death of the Messiah: From Gethsemane to the Grave; A Commentary on the Passion Narratives in the Four Gospels* (2 vols.; ABRL; New York: Doubleday, 1994), 949–51, and the bibliography he gives.

15. Ingolf U. Dalferth, "Volles Grab, leerer Glaube?" *ZTK* 95 (1998): 394–95. Against Dalferth it must be said, however, that also from the theological point of view it is not irrelevant whether the tomb was empty.

16. For analysis of the texts cf. Ulrich Wilckens, *Resurrection: Biblical Testimony to the Resurrection: An Historical Examination and Explanation* (trans. A. M. Stewart; Atlanta: John Knox, 1978), 6–73.

17. Cf. Hans Campenhausen, *Der Ablauf der Osterereignisse und das leere Grab* (4th ed.; SHAW; Heidelberg: Winter, 1977), 15.

18. Ibid., 41.

appeared before different groups of disciples, to the Twelve or to the group of more than five hundred (1 Cor. 15:6). These group appearances were followed by other individual appearances, like that to James and finally to Paul (cf. 1 Cor. 15:7–8).

On the basis of these reflections, we can summarize *the discernible historical data* quickly: After Jesus's arrest, the disciples fled, probably back to Galilee. Only a few women dared to witness the crucifixion (from a distance) and later to seek out the grave. Jesus was buried by Joseph of Arimathea, a sympathizer from a prominent Jerusalem family (cf. Mark 15:43; John 19:38). Jesus's first appearances took place in Galilee (cf. Mark 16:7; 1 Cor. 15:6[?]), and there were also possibly appearances in Jerusalem (cf. Luke 24:34; John 20). Peter probably regathered the members of the Twelve and other disciples, both men and women, to whom Jesus then appeared. Further individual appearances followed, like that to James and to Paul, which concluded this epoch of special appearances. The appearance tradition was connected very early to the tradition of the empty tomb; in the light of the Easter appearances, this grave, located near the place of execution, became itself a witness of the resurrection.

What was the nature of the appearances? It is theologically important that they are an element of the proclamation of Jesus's resurrection, i.e., they cannot be separated from the one fundamental affirmation: God raised Jesus from the dead. From the history-of-religions and history-of-traditions points of view, they are understood as visions in the context of apocalyptic imagery, according to which in the end times God will give a few chosen individuals insight into his acts.[19] Due to the paucity of available materials, the reality content of the appearances cannot be understood in psychological terms, nor is an interpretation of the appearances as faith experiences adequate,[20] for this would minimize the special status of the appearances as forming the *basis* of faith. "On the other hand, the visions must have been of such a nature it was possible—even necessary—to interpret them in the sense of affirmations of the resurrection."[21] Like the resurrection itself, the appearances too are to be understood as a transcendent *event* deriving from God, an event that generated the disciples' transcendent *experiences* (see below, §6.2.2.I). Such experiences of transcendence can be worked through and reconstructed in a

19. Cf. Ulrich Wilckens, "Der Ursprung der Überlieferung der Erscheinungen des Auferstandenen," in *Zur neutestamentlichen Überlieferung von der Auferstehung Jesu* (ed. Paul Hoffmann; Darmstadt: Wissenschaftliche Buchgesellschaft, 1988), 139–93.

20. In this sense cf., e.g., Ingo Broer, "'Der Herr ist wahrhaft auferstanden' (Lk 24,34): Auferstehung Jesu und historisch-kritische Methode; Erwägungen zur Entstehung des Osterglaubens," in *Auferstehung Jesu, Auferstehung der Christen: Deutungen des Osterglaubens* (ed. Ingo Broer and Lorenz Oberlinner; QD 105; Freiburg i.B.: Herder, 1986), 39–62.

21. Helmut Merklein, *Der erste Brief an die Korinther* (ÖTK 7; Gütersloh: Gütersloher Verlagshaus, 1992), 282.

twofold manner: "narratives, in which the experiences of transcendence are made communicable and prepared for retelling, and rituals, whereby such experiences are commemorated and the transcendent reality is evoked."[22] Both the formula traditions and the narrative traditions do this; in each case they are *necessarily* consolidated in a variety of forms conditioned by their own times and made available for the intersubjective discourse of the churches. Baptism, the Lord's Supper, and worship were ritual locations in which the experiences were renewed and confirmed.

Easter thus became the *foundational story* of the new movement.[23] The texts disclose to us what the events set in motion and the significance ascribed to them. Historically and theologically, it is most important to note that Paul is very reserved about depicting his transcendental experience as an authentic witness of appearances and points to the decisive theological realization: the crucified one is risen! The appearances of the Risen One as transcendent experiences of a particular kind become the basis for the sure conviction that God, through his creative Spirit (cf. Rom. 1:3b–4a), has acted in Jesus Christ and has made him to be the decisive eschatological figure.

4.3 Experiences of the Spirit

Alongside the appearances of the Risen One, the effective work of the Spirit is the second *experiential dimension* that affected the formation of early Christology. While the appearances were strictly limited, the Spirit worked at large, without restraints. From the history-of-religions point of view, God and the Spirit always belong together. In the realm of Greco-Roman culture, it was especially in the teaching of the Stoics that the deity worked in the sphere of the spirit.[24] In the Judaism of antiquity, the idea that the Spirit of God would be poured out in the eschatological times was of great importance (cf., e.g., Ezek. 36:25–29; Isa. 32:15–18; Joel 3:1–5 LXX; 1QS 4:18–23). The Messiah was portrayed as a figure endowed with the power of the Spirit, and the metaphors of temple and divine indwelling were expressed in terms of the Spirit.[25]

The beginning of this development was probably signaled in early Christianity by spontaneous experiences of the Spirit: "God has given us his Spirit" (cf. 1 Thess. 4:8; 1 Cor. 1:12, 14; 2 Cor. 1:22; 5:5; 11:18). The reception of the

22. Luckmann, "Religion—Gesellschaft—Transcendenz," 120–21.

23. Cf. R. von Bendemann, "Die Auferstehung von den Toten als 'basic story,'" *GuL* 15 (2000): 148–62.

24. Cf. the illustrative texts in *NW* 1.2:226–34; M. Eugene Boring et al., eds., *Hellenistic Commentary to the New Testament* (Nashville: Abingdon, 1995), §§402, 455, 628, 631.

25. Cf. the foundational work of Friedrich Wilhelm Horn, *Das Angeld des Geistes: Studien zur paulinischen Pneumatologie* (FRLANT 154; Göttingen: Vandenhoeck & Ruprecht, 1992), 61ff.

Spirit is also recognizable by observable phenomena (cf. Gal. 3:2; Acts 8:18), especially in miraculous healings (1 Cor. 12:9, 28, 30), ecstatic glossolalia (e.g., Acts 2:4, 11; 4:31), and in prophetic speech (cf. 1 Cor. 12; 14; Acts 10; 19). With legendary embellishment, but with a core of reliable historical tradition, the book of Acts describes the workings of the Spirit in the earliest Christian communities. The Holy Spirit appears as the "power from on high" promised by Jesus (Luke 24:49; Acts 1:5, 8) that came to the disciples on Pentecost (Acts 2:4). The Spirit is given to all who accept the preaching of the apostles and are baptized (cf. Acts 2:38). According to the earliest tradition, Jesus's own ministry from his baptism on had been characterized by the power of the Holy Spirit (cf. Mark 1:9–22; Acts 10:37). Jesus was raised from the dead by the Spirit of God (Rom. 1:3b–4a; 6:4; 8:11; 1 Pet. 3:18; 1 Tim. 3:16), and it is the Spirit that now determines the new mode of being and work of the Risen One (2 Cor. 3:17, "Now the Lord is the Spirit"; cf. 1 Cor. 15:45). In the baptismal event, the work of the Spirit delivers believers from the power of sin and determines their new being from that point on (cf. 1 Cor. 12:13; 6:19; Rom. 5:5). Paul, our oldest literary witness, shares the understanding that there are observable signs of the eschatological reception of the Spirit (cf., e.g., 1 Thess. 1:5; Gal. 3:2–5; 1 Cor. 12:12), and admonishes the churches not to quench the Spirit (1 Thess. 5:19).

The Jewish hope was that the Spirit who inspires and gives life would return in the eschatological age. The oldest Christian affirmations about the work of the Spirit express the conviction that this hope is now being fulfilled. From the power of the Spirit of God in their midst, the earliest Christians recognized the reality of the resurrection of Jesus Christ from the dead.

4.4 The Christological Reading of Scripture

The historical appearance of Jesus in Israel pointed the early Christians to the Scriptures of Israel. *It is from the Scriptures that Christology derives its language*, as declared in 1 Cor. 15:3–4; the postulate "according to the Scriptures" (κατὰ τὰς γραφάς) is a fundamental theological signal. The early Christians live in and from the Scriptures of Israel. To be sure, their reading takes place under changed conditions that affect how these texts are understood, for now Jewish Christians read their Scriptures anew (primarily in the LXX translation)[26]

26. As introduction to this area of study, cf. Ernst Würthwein, *The Text of the Old Testament: An Introduction to the Biblia Hebraica* (trans. Erroll F. Rhodes; Grand Rapids: Eerdmans, 1979), 49–74; Robert Hanhart, "Die Bedeutung der Septuaginta in neutestamentlicher Zeit," *ZTK* 81 (1984): 395–416; Martin Hengel, *The Septuagint as Christian Scripture: Its Prehistory and the Problem of Its Canon* (Old Testament Studies; trans. Mark E. Biddle; Edinburgh: T&T Clark, 2002); Martin Hengel and Anna Maria Schwemer, *Die Septuaginta zwischen Judentum und Christentum* (WUNT 72; Tübingen: Mohr, 1994); Michael Tilly, *Einfuhrung in die Sep-*

from the perspective of the Christ event. This rereading of the Scriptures occurs within a twofold dynamic: the Scriptures become the frame of reference for Christology, and Christology gives the Scriptures a new orientation point.[27]

The christological rereading of Scripture in early Christianity leads to different models of affirming the continuity of God's acts in history with God's own promises. Through God's saving act in the cross and resurrection of Jesus of Nazareth it became clear to the first Christians that there must be a fundamental connection between this event and God's saving acts in the history of Israel. This fundamental conviction is expressed in a variety of models: *typology* (prototype), *promise and fulfillment*, as well as in the exegetical methods of *allegory* and *midrash*, by the *combination of citations*, by *quotation variations*, and by *allusions*.

In the *undisputed letters of Paul* we find eighty-nine citations from the Old Testament,[28] in which the distribution within the individual letters is to be noted: quotations are lacking in the oldest (1 Thessalonians) and the two latest (Philippians and Philemon), while the most citations are found in the writings in which the apostle must work through current problems or conflicts (the letters to the Corinthians, Galatians, and especially Romans). Theologically, for Paul the Scripture is *witness to the gospel*, for the promises of God (cf. ἐπαγγελία in Gal. 3 and Rom. 4) find their confirmation in the gospel of Jesus Christ (cf. 2 Cor. 1:20; Rom. 15:8).

Five quotations with specific introductions are found in the *sayings source Q*, notably in the story of Jesus's temptation (cf. Q 4:4, 8, 10–11, 12; see also Q 7:27).[29]

Mark locates citations at the central places in his gospel (cf. Mark 1:2–3; 4:12; 11:9; 12:10, 36; 14:27); they confirm the story as God's saving history, without becoming a central element in Mark's Christology.[30] Remarkably, in Mark the expression "but let the Scriptures be fulfilled" first appears late in the gospel, in a subordinate clause (Mark 14:49).

In *Matthew*, the *fulfillment quotations* are a constituent element of the evangelist's Christology (cf. Matt. 1:23; 2:6, 15, 18, 23; 4:15–16; 8:17; 12:18–21;

---

tuaginta (2004); Karen H. Jobes and Moisés Silva, *Invitation to the Septuagint* (Grand Rapids: Baker Academic, 2000).

27. A survey is provided by Steve Moyise, *The Old Testament in the New* (Continuum Biblical Studies Series; New York: Continuum, 2001).

28. Cf. Dietrich-Alex Koch, *Die Schrift als Zeuge des Evangeliums: Untersuchungen zur Verwendung und zum Verständnis der Schrift bei Paulus* (BHT 69; Tübingen: Mohr, 1986), 21–23. For the individual citations, in addition to Koch cf. especially Hans Hübner et al., *Vetus Testamentum in Novo*, vol. 2, *Corpus Paulinum* (Göttingen: Vandenhoeck & Ruprecht, 1995).

29. Cf. Dale C. Allison, *The Intertextual Jesus: Scripture in Q* (Harrisburg, PA: Trinity, 2000).

30. For Mark, cf. Moyise, *Old Testament in the New*, 21–33; Joel Marcus, *The Way of the Lord: Christological Exegesis of the Old Testament in the Gospel of Mark* (Louisville: Westminster John Knox, 1992).

[13:14–15;] 13:35; 21:5; 27:9–10, each with redactional introduction; cf. also 26:54, 56).[31] In accord with the hermeneutical model "promise-fulfillment," they present comprehensively the manner in which individual items from the life of Jesus, his deeds as well as his words and even the Passion story, correspond to the Scriptures, confirm and fulfill them. The introductory formulae have certain points in common; following the statement about fulfillment there is a reference to the Scripture text, which can include the name of the prophet (Isaiah, Jeremiah). The key verb πληρόω is usually in the passive, pointing to the act of God. Thereby the main lines of Matthew's Christology come to expression: the story of Jesus is God's own story.

In *Luke*, the central idea is that the *prophetic promises* are fulfilled in the advent of Jesus (cf. Luke 1:70; 4:21; 18:31; 24:44; Acts 3:21).[32] Following the time of the law and the prophets comes the present time of the preaching of the kingdom of God (Luke 16:16). The time of salvation that appeared in the ministry of Jesus continues in the church's universal preaching of the gospel (cf. Acts 10:34–35).

John goes one step further; for him, Jesus is the hidden subject of Scripture (John 5:46, "If you believed Moses, you would believe me, for he wrote about me"). Identifiable citations that are distinguishable from their Johannine context[33] are found in John 1:23, 51; 2:17; 6:31, 45; 10:34; 12:13, 15, 27, 38, 40; 13:18; 15:25; 16:22; 19:24, 28, 36, 37; 20:28; cf. also 3:13; 6:45; 7:18, 38, 42; 17:12. It is noticeable that the two main sections of the gospel use different introductory formulae. While in the first part of the gospel the participle γεγραμμένον with ἐστίν is found five times (cf. 2:17; 6:31, 45; 10:34; 12:14),

31. Cf. especially the analyses of Georg Strecker, *Der Weg der Gerechtigkeit: Untersuchung zur Theologie des Matthäus* (3rd ed.; FRLANT 82; Göttingen: Vandenhoeck & Ruprecht, 1971), 48–84 (cf. below, §8.3); Wilhelm Rothfuchs, *Die Erfüllungszitate des Matthaüs-Evangeliums: Eine biblisch-theologische Untersuchung* (BWANT 88; Stuttgart: Kohlhammer, 1969), 189–99; Luz, *Matthew 1–7*, 125–31. On Matthew's interpretation of Scripture as a whole, cf. M. J. J. Menken, *Matthew's Bible: The Old Testament Text of the Evangelist* (BETL 173; Louvain: Leuven University Press, 2004); M. Eugene Boring, "Matthew: Introduction, Commentary, and Reflections," in *The New Interpreter's Bible* (ed. Leander Keck; Nashville: Abingdon, 1995), 8:151–54, "Matthew as Interpreter of Scripture."

32. Cf. here Moyise, *Old Testament in the New*, 45–62.

33. Günter Reim, *Studien zum alttestamentlichen Hintergrund des Johannesevangeliums* (SNTSMS 22; Cambridge: Cambridge University Press, 1974); Bruce G. Schuchard, *Scripture within Scripture: The Interrelationship of Form and Function in the Explicit Old Testament Citations in the Gospel of John* (SBLDS 133; Atlanta: Scholars Press, 1992); Andreas Obermann, *Die christologische Erfüllung der Schrift im Johannesevangelium: Eine Untersuchung zur johanneischen Hermeneutik anhand der Schriftzitate* (WUNT 2.83; Tübingen: Mohr, 1996); Wolfgang Kraus, "Johannes und das Alte Testament," *ZNW* 88 (1997): 1–23; Hans Hübner et al., *Vetus Testamentum in Novo*, vol. 1/2, *Evangelium Johannis* (Göttingen: Vandenhoeck & Ruprecht, 2003); Michael Labahn, "Jesus und die Autorität der Schrift," in *Israel und seine Heilstraditionen im Johannessevangelium: Festgabe für Johannes Beutler SJ zum 70. Geburtstag* (ed. Michael Labahn et al.; Paderborn: Schöningh, 2004), 185–206.

the new introductory formulae in the second main part of the gospel (from 12:38 on) speak specifically of the fulfillment of God's will in the Passion of Christ. Here not only do the Scriptures point to Jesus, but Christ bears witness to himself in them. Thereby a fundamental change of perspective occurs; Christology not only receives its impulse from the Scripture, but the [preexistent] Christ has already placed his stamp on the content of Scripture. Within this framework of the temporal and material priority of the Christ event, John attributes an extraordinarily high rank to Scripture: as a witness to Christ, Scripture comments on and deepens the true knowledge of the Son of God.

A few *individual texts* play a special role in early Christianity's reception of the Old Testament.

With Gen. 15:6 and Hab. 2:4b, Paul virtually puts all other Old Testament texts out of commission. By interpreting Hab. 2:4b LXX in Gal. 3:11 and Rom. 1:17 in a particular way, the apostle binds the faithfulness of God not to those righteous ones who live from the Torah, but to those who believe in Jesus Christ as the justifying event. The chronological distance between Gen. 15:6 and Gen. 17 has for Paul a *theological* quality. While, from the Jewish point of view, circumcision is the comprehensive demonstration of Abraham's obedience to God's commands, Paul separates circumcision from the righteousness that comes by faith. This righteousness by faith preceded circumcision, so that circumcision can be understood as merely a subsequent acknowledgment and confirmation of righteousness by faith.

In the formation of early Christology, Ps. 110:1 LXX assumed a key position:[34] "The Lord said to my lord, 'Sit on my right until I make your enemies a footstool for your feet.'" Here the early Christians found the normative scriptural documentation for Jesus's heavenly dignity and function: he has been exalted to God's right hand, participates in the power and glory of God, and from there puts his lordship into effect (cf. 1 Cor. 15:25; Rom. 8:34; Mark 12:36; 14:62; Matt. 22:44; 26:64; Luke 20:42; 22:69; Acts 2:34; Col. 3:1; Eph. 1:20; Heb. 1:3, 13; 8:1; 10:12). In this context, the first Christians very early applied the title "Lord," with which God was frequently addressed, to Jesus (cf. the use of Joel 3:5 LXX in Rom. 10:12–13, and 1 Cor. 1:31; 2:16; 10:26; 2 Cor. 10:17), thereby expressing the unique authority of Jesus in distinction from all other claims to authority.[35] In the formation of the Son of God Christology (cf. 1 Thess. 1:9–10; Rom. 1:3b–4a; Mark 1:11; 9:7), Ps. 2:7 most likely took

34. Cf. Martin Hengel, "Psalm 110 und die Erhöhung des Auferstandenen zur Rechten Gottes," in *Anfänge der Christologie: Festschrift für Ferdinand Hahn zum 65. Geburtstag* (ed. Cilliers Breytenbach et al.; Göttingen: Vandenhoeck & Ruprecht, 1991), 43–74. On the reception of the Psalms in early Christianity in general, cf. Steve Moyise and M. J. J. Menken, eds., *The Psalms in the New Testament* (London: T&T Clark International, 2004).

35. Marinus de Jonge, *Christology in Context: The Earliest Christian Response to Jesus* (Philadelphia: Westminster, 1988), 203–5.

on central significance ("The Lord said to me, 'My son you are; today I have begotten you'" NETS; cf. also 2 Sam. 7:11–12, 14).

As an intertextual phenomenon, this christological rereading of Scripture accomplished two things: it placed the Old Testament texts referred to in a new horizon of meaning, while at the same time legitimizing the theological position of the New Testament authors. In this process, the substantial center of their thought was provided not by the weight of Scripture but by God's eschatological saving act in Jesus Christ. Central contents of Jewish theology (Torah, election) are thought through anew, and the text of Scripture is incorporated in a productive intertextual process of interpretation.

4.5 History-of-Religions Context

The development of early Christology took place *in continuity with the basic affirmations of the Jewish faith*, which provided important conceptual categories: God is one, God is the creator, Lord, and preserver of the world. The traditions of ancient Judaism[36] also made it possible to hold fast to a monotheistic faith, while at the same time confessing Jesus of Nazareth as Χριστός, κύριος, and υἱὸς τοῦ θεοῦ. For early Christianity, it was obvious and natural to transfer to Jesus exalted titles that were primarily anchored in Judaism (see §3.9 and §4.6). *In the Jewish view there is and can be only one God, but he is not alone.* Numerous heavenly mediating figures such as Wisdom (cf. Prov. 2:1–6; 8:22–31; Wis. 6:12–11:1), the Logos, and the Name of God reside in immediate nearness to God.[37] Biblical patriarchs such as Enoch (cf. Gen. 5:18–24)[38] or Moses and the archangel Michael[39] are in God's presence and

36. Larry W. Hurtado, *One God, One Lord: Early Christian Devotion and Ancient Jewish Monotheism* (Philadelphia: Fortress, 1988), 17–92; William Horbury, "Jewish Messianism and Early Christology," in *Contours of Christology in the New Testament* (ed. Richard N. Longenecker; Grand Rapids: Eerdmans, 2005), 23, states "that early Christian conceptions of a crucified but spiritual and glorious Messiah are best interpreted by Jewish representations of the Messiah as a glorious king embodying a superhuman spirit."

37. As examples, cf. Wis. 9:9–11; Philo, *Confusion* 146–147. For analysis of the early wisdom traditions in the New Testament, cf. Hermann von Lips, *Weisheitliche Traditionen im Neuen Testament* (WMANT 64; Neukirchen-Vluyn: Neukirchener Verlag, 1990), 267–80 (he appropriately emphasizes that we cannot speak of an explicit "Wisdom Christology"). On the Wisdom features in the Christology of the sayings source Q, see below, §8.1.2.

38. For sample texts, cf. *1 En.* 61.

39. Cf., e.g., Dan. 10:13–21; *1 En.* 20.5; 71.3; 90.21. On the possible significance of ideas about angels for the formation of early Christology, cf. C. Rowland, *The Open Heaven* (New York: Crossroad, 1982); J. E. Fossum, *The Name of God and the Angel of the Lord* (WUNT 36; Tübingen: Mohr, 1985); Loren T. Stuckenbruck, *Angel Veneration and Christology: A Study in Early Judaism and in the Christology of the Apocalypse of John* (WUNT 2.70; Tübingen: Mohr, 1995). S. Vollenweider, "Zwischen Monotheismus und Engelchristologie," *ZTK* 99 (2002): 3–27, clearly sees, to be sure, the limits of an angelological interpretation (isolated texts form

now work as God's commissioned agents. Though participants in the heavenly world, they are not in the same category as God and in no way endanger faith in the one God. As created and subordinate beings, they are not in competition with God; their divine attributes are described in the language of human hierarchies, representing God's presence and activity in the world and for the world. At the same time, there are obvious *fundamental differences*[40] between such beings and the one God: (1) The personified divine attributes were not persons in their own right with independent fields of operation. (2) They were not cultically worshiped. (3) Within this broad spectrum of Jewish ideas, it was nonetheless inconceivable that one who had died such a shameful death could be given divine honors.

By developing its hope and conceptuality of the *resurrection of the dead* within the context of the apocalyptic thought of the third and second centuries BCE, Judaism also formed the history-of-religions framework and background for the formation of Christology.[41] The only undisputed text in the Old Testament that expresses this resurrection hope is Dan. 12:2–3, "Multitudes who sleep in the dust of the earth will awake: some to everlasting life, others to shame and everlasting contempt. Those who are wise will shine like the brightness of the heavens, and those who lead many to righteousness, like the stars for ever and ever." One can also name as a second central text Isa. 26:19, "But your dead will live; their bodies will rise. You who dwell in the dust, wake up and shout for joy. Your dew is like the dew of the morning; the earth will give birth to her dead." The resurrection hope presupposed in both texts has a prehistory in the Old Testament; one may point to Isa. 26 and Ezek. 37:1–14. The resurrection hope is then documented in numerous texts from the second and first centuries BCE: Wis. 3:1–8; *1 En.* 46.6; 48.9–10; 51.1; 91.10; 93.3–4; 104.2; *Pss. Sol.* 3.10–12; *LAB* 19.12–13; 2 Macc. 7:9; *T. Benj.* 10.6–10. It is particularly important that the resurrection faith is also found among the Essenes. In 4Q521 2.2:12, God is praised with the words "For He shall heal the critically wounded, He shall revive the dead, He shall send good news to the afflicted." In the same manuscript the following text is found in 4Q521 7.2:6, "The Reviver [rai]ses the dead of His people."[42]

---

the point of departure for comprehensive constructions, adventurous lines of development in the history of the tradition are postulated, the fading out of Sophia and Logos ideas, angel conceptuality is only partially and minimally taken up by New Testament authors). Nonetheless, he would like to regard angelology as a *praeparatio christologica*. He names five areas in which attributes of God are applied to Jesus: names and titles, creation, rulership of the world, salvation, worship.

40. Hurtado, *One God, One Lord*, 93–124.

41. On this point cf. Schwankl, *Sadduzäerfrage*, 173–274.

42. Cited according to *Qumran Sectarian Manuscripts: A New English Translation* based on Michael O. Wise, Martin G. Abegg Jr., and Edward M. Cook, eds., *The Dead Sea Scrolls: A New English Translation* (New York: HarperCollins, 1996).

Genuine Greek-Hellenistic ideas very likely also played a role in the formation of early Christology and facilitated its reception. The idea that a god could become human and a human being become a god is not Jewish but Greek. The incarnation of gods or godlike beings (and the divinization of human beings) as a genuinely Greek view points to presuppositions in the cultural history of the times that must have played important roles in the formation[43] and reception[44] of early Christology. An anthropomorphic polytheism is the trademark of Greek religion[45] (classically expressed in Euripides, *Alc.* 1159, "The divine takes on many forms," πολλαὶ μορφαὶ τῶν δαιμονίων). Divine beings in human form were already central in Greek thought of the classical period; Homer reports: "We know that gods go about disguised in all sorts of ways, as people from foreign countries, and travel about the world to see who does amiss and who righteously."[46] The origins of culture itself are traced back to the intervention of the gods. Thus Zeus sent Hermes to teach humanity justice and shame;[47] Hermes, Hercules, and Apollo, as messengers of the gods, assumed human form and carried out their mission as gods among human beings.[48] Gods in human form can be thought of as originating from

43. This is rightly emphasized by Dieter Zeller, "Die Menschwerdung des Sohnes Gottes im Neuen Testament und die antike Religionsgeschichte," in *Menschwerdung Gottes—Vergöttlichung von Menschen* (ed. Dieter Zeller; NTOA 7; Göttingen: Vandenhoeck & Ruprecht, 1988), 141–76. Martin Hengel, *The Son of God: The Origin of Christology and the History of Jewish-Hellenistic Religion* (trans. John Bowden; Philadelphia: Fortress, 1976), 40, in his debate with the history of religions school and R. Bultmann, poses false alternatives when he states concerning the Greek ideas of the gods: "All this gets us no nearer to the mystery of the origin of Christology." It is a matter of the cultural context in which the early christological affirmations originated and could be adopted; the Greek-Hellenistic *also* belongs here.

44. The classical approach of tradition history must be extended to include the aspects of reception history; cf. Dieter Zeller, "New Testament Christology in Its Hellenistic Reception," *NTS* 46 (2001): 332–33.

45. Walter Burkert, "Griechische Religion," *TRE* 14:238ff. The foundational legends of Greek religion are handed on in Herodotus, *Hist.* 2.53.2: "For Homer and Hesiod were the first to compose Theogonies, and give the gods their epithets, to allot them their several offices and occupations, and describe their forms" (Rawlinson). It is also true, however, that critique of the anthropomorphism of the Homeric world of the gods was found quite early in Greek thought, insisting that among the gods there could really be only "one" God; cf. Xenophanes (ca. 570–475 BCE, frg. B 23: "Among gods and human beings, only one God is the Greatest" [εἷς θεὸς ἔν τε θεοῖσι καὶ ἀνθρώποισι μέγιστος]).

46. Homer, *Od.* 17.485–486 (*NW* 2.2:1232). Cf. Homer, *Il.* 2.167–172; 5.121–132; 15.236–238; *Od.* 7.199–210 (*NW* 1.2:55); Euripides, *Bacch.* 1–4, 43–54 (*NW* 2.1:672–73); Plato, *Soph.* 216A–B (*NW* 2.2:1232); Diodorus Siculus, *Bibl.* 1.12.9–10 (*NW* 2.2:1232–33); Dio Chrysostom, *Or.* 30.27: "Now, as long as life was but newly established, the gods both visited us in person and sent harmosts [governors], as it were, from their own number at first to look after us, such as Heracles, for example, Dionysus, Perseus, and the others, who, we are told, were the children of the gods, and that the descendants of these were born among us."

47. Cf. Plato, *Prot.* 322C–D (*NW* 1.2:56).

48. One only need note Acts 14:11–12, after Paul's miracle in Lystra: "When the crowds saw what Paul had done, they shouted in the Lycaonian language, 'The gods have come down

this world or as coming from the eternal world. Plutarch can report on the origin of Apollo: "For my native tradition removes this god from among those deities who were changed from mortals into immortals, like Heracles and Dionysus, whose virtues enabled them to cast off mortality and suffering; but he [sc. Apollo] is one of those deities who are unbegotten and eternal" (LCL).[49] Hercules, as a son of God in obedience to Zeus, destroys injustice and lawlessness on the earth; Zeus rewards him with immortality for virtue (ἀρετή).[50] Mythical figures of the primeval period such as Pythagoras and famous miracle workers such as Apollonius of Tyana[51] appear as gods in human form who use their divine powers in the service of humanity. Empedocles travels around as an immortal god, healing people and doing good.[52] The hero cult continued in the ruler cult, which finally merged into the Roman emperor cult.[53] In the great accomplishments and victories of historical progress, deities are revealed in human form.[54]

Plutarch's reflections on the nature of the numerous real or ostensible gods are informative:

> Better, therefore, is the judgment of those who hold that the stories about Typhon, Osiris, and Isis are records of experiences of neither gods nor men but of demigods (δαιμόνων μεγάλων), whom Plato and Pythagoras and Xenocrates and Chrysippus, following the lead of early writers on sacred subjects, allege to have been stronger than men and, in their might, greatly surpassing our nature,

---

to us in human form!' Barnabas they called Zeus, and Paul they called Hermes, because he was the chief speaker."

49. Plutarch, *Pel.* 16 (*NW* 1.2:57–58 [see above, §4.3]).

50. Cf. Isocrates, *Or.* 1.50; Epictetus, *Diatr.* 2.16.44, "he [Hercules] was believed to be a son of God, and was"; *Ench.* 15 (Because of their exemplary character, Diogenes and Hercules are made co-regents with the gods, "and are thus rightly called divine beings."); Diodorus Siculus, *Bibl.* 4.15.1; Dio Chrysostom, *Or.* 1.84, where it is reported of Hercules, son of Zeus, that he brought tyranny to an end and protected every just kingship: "And therefore he is the savior of the world and of humanity" (καὶ διὰ τοῦτο τῆς γῆς καὶ τῶν ἀνθρώπων σωτῆρα εἶναι). From among the innumerable Hercules traditions, worthy of note is also Dio Chrysostom, *Or.* 8.28, which reports about Hercules and his agonizing struggles: "But now, after his death, they honor him more than all the others, consider him to be a god, and say that he dwells with Hebe. They all pray to him to deliver them from their troubles—to him, who bore the greatest troubles of all."

51. Cf. the texts in *NW* 1.2:59 and in Boring, *Hellenistic Commentary,* §§7, 31, 55, 61, 88, 119, 132, 198, 228, 229, 230, 290.

52. Cf. Diogenes Laertius, *Vit. phil.* 8.62: "I go about among you an immortal god, no more a mortal, so honored by all, as is meet, crowned with fillets and flowery garlands. Straightway as soon as I enter with these, men and women, into flourishing towns, I am reverenced and tens of thousands follow, to learn where is the path which leads to welfare, some desirous of oracles, others suffering from all kinds of diseases, desiring to hear a message of healing."

53. On this cf. H. Funke, "Götterbild," *RAC* 11:659–828. The ideal ruler believes "not only in the gods, but the good spirits [δαίμονας] and demi-gods [ἥρωας, heroes], which are the souls of good men that have cast off this mortal nature" (Dio Chrysostom, *Or.* 3.54).

54. Cf. Burkert, "Griechische Religion," 247–48.

> yet not possessing the divine quality unmixed and uncontaminated, but with a share also in the nature of the soul and in the perceptive faculties of the body, and with a susceptibility to pleasure and pain and to whatsoever other experience is incident to these mutations. . . . Plato calls this class of beings an interpretative and ministering class, midway between gods and men (ὅτε Πλάτων ἑρμηνευτικὸν τοιοῦτον ὀνομάζει γένος διακονικὸν ἐν μέσῳ θεῶν καὶ ἀνθρώπων), in that they convey thither the prayers and petitions of men, and thence they bring hither the oracles and the gifts of good things. (*Is. Os.* 360–361)

In the context of a growing (pagan) monotheism, Plutarch postulates a group of intermediate beings who maintain contact with the true deities and have an indispensable function for human beings.[55]

The concept of intermediate beings that were both divine and human[56] was thus acceptable to non-Jews on the basis of their own cultural background.[57] For Jews, however, the idea was intolerable that human beings like the Roman Caesar would presume to consider themselves divine and would actually be worshiped.[58] Here the Christology of the early Christians is distinct from both Jewish and Greco-Roman thinking, for the divine sonship of one who had been crucified continued to be regarded in both realms as an alien and scandalous idea (cf. 1 Cor. 1:23).

The formation of early Christology did not occur in discernible spatial or temporal stages; on the contrary, within a very compressed period of time, the different christological views emerged alongside each other and partially

55. Cf. further Plutarch, *Is. Os.* 361: "She herself [sc. Isis] and Osiris, translated for their virtues from good demigods into gods [ἐκ δαιμόνων ἀγαθῶν δι᾽ ἀρετῆς εἰς θεοὺς μεταλαβόντες], as were Heracles and Dionysus later, not incongruously enjoy double honors, both those of gods and demigods [ἅμα καὶ θεῶν καὶ δαιμόνων], and their powers extend everywhere, but are greatest in the regions above the earth and beneath the earth." On Plutarch's concept of God/gods cf. Rainer Hirsch-Luipold, ed., *Gott und die Götter bei Plutarch: Götterbilder—Gottesbilder—Weltbilder* (RVV 54; Berlin: de Gruyter, 2005).

56. Seneca, *Herc. fur.* 447–450, on the disputed origin of Hercules: "*Lycus*: Why blaspheme Jove? The race of mortals cannot mate with heaven. *Amphityron*: That is the common origin of many gods." Hercules is called υἱὸς τοῦ Διός ("Son of Zeus"), for example, in Dio Chrysostom, *Or.* 2.78; 66.23; as ἡμίθεος (semi-god) in *Or.* 31.16; 69.1; as ἥρως (hero) in *Or.* 33.1, and is reckoned among the gods in *Or.* 33.45. Cf. further *Or.* 33.47 (Hercules as the first ancestor of Tarsus). In Dio Chrysostom, Hercules is regarded as the prototype of the Cynics and of just rulers. The numerous Hercules traditions in his works show how obvious and widespread was the veneration of this figure in the first century CE.

57. It is not a matter of causes or dependence, but of the horizons of understanding and reception of common ideas from the culture! It is thus all the more difficult to understand that Larry W. Hurtado, *Lord Jesus Christ: Devotion to Jesus in Earliest Christianity* (Grand Rapids: Eerdmans, 2003), virtually ignores the whole Greco-Roman realm. So also, advocates of the "new perspective" such as James D. G. Dunn, *The Theology of Paul the Apostle* (Grand Rapids: Eerdmans, 1998), or N. T. Wright, *Paul in Fresh Perspective* (Minneapolis: Fortress, 2005) simply bypass this area of research so important for understanding Paul.

58. Cf. Philo, *Embassy* 118 (*NW* 1.2:54–55).

interrelated with each other. A thorough process of theological and linguistic interpenetration that began early on attempted to determine more closely, in the relationship of Jesus to God, his identity as the earthly human being who is also the Risen One. Very quickly the central categories of ancient thought were transferred to Jesus by means of a variety of honorific titles, in order to define him as the place and means of God's self-revelation. There was no development from a "low" Jewish Christian Christology to a "high" Hellenistic syncretistic Christology.[59] Rather, from the very beginning Hellenistic Judaism provided central concepts that were important for early Christianity's new deployment of intermediate beings and titles. Moreover, the central christological titles and the concept of a mediator between God and humanity were open to independent Hellenistic reception. All essential christological statements about Jesus associated with titles of majesty had already been formed some time before Paul, who adopted them from Christian tradition: the resurrected Jesus is the Son of God (1 Thess. 1:10; Gal. 1:16; Rom. 1:4); the name of God had been conferred on him (Phil. 2:9–10). He is identified with God or is the image of God (Phil. 2:6; 2 Cor. 4:4) and the bearer of God's glory (2 Cor. 4:6; Phil. 3:21). As preexistent, he had participated in the divine act of creation (Phil. 2:6; 1 Cor. 8:6); expressions and citations that properly refer to God are applied to him (cf. 1 Cor. 1:31; 2:16; Rom. 10:13). His place is in heaven (1 Thess. 1:10; 4:16; Phil. 3:20) at the right hand of God (Rom. 8:24), and from there he exercises universal dominion (1 Cor. 15:27; Phil. 3:21), which includes the heavenly powers (Phil. 2:10). Sent from God, he is presently at work in the church (Gal. 4:4–5; Rom. 8:3); he is God's authorized representative at the last judgment, which will take place at his parousia (1 Thess. 1:10; 1 Cor. 16:22; 2 Cor. 5:10).

These views can neither be systematized nor traced back to a uniform, cohesive milieu. On the contrary, we should realize that early Christian communities in different places were originators and transmitters of these ideas, for the Jesus event was understood and appropriated in earliest Christianity in a variety of ways. The inclusion of Jesus in the worship of God originated from the overwhelming religious experiences of the earliest Christians, especially the resurrection appearances and the present working of the Spirit. The worship practice of the earliest churches must also be counted among the essential factors within this process. First Corinthians 16:22 ("*Marana tha*" [Our Lord, come!]) shows that the unique status and significance of the exalted Christ characterized congregational worship from the very beginning (cf. also 1 Cor. 12:3; 2 Cor. 12:8).[60] He made possible the new access to God,

59. Werner R. Kramer, *Christ, Lord, Son of God* (SBT 50; trans. Brian Hardy; London: SCM, 1966) and Hahn, *Titles of Jesus*, are somewhat slanted in favor of this distinction; cf. the careful self-correction in Hahn, *Titles of Jesus*, 347–51.

60. On the significance of worship practice for the formation of early Christology, cf. Wolfgang Schrage, *Unterwegs zur Einzigkeit und Einheit Gottes: zum "Monotheismus" des Paulus*

which was acknowledged in worship by the Spirit-inspired address to God, ἀββά ("Abba," "Father," Gal. 4:6; Rom. 8:15; Mark 14:36). Liturgical practice included instruction to "glorify the God and Father of our Lord Jesus Christ" (Rom. 15:6). Baptism, eucharist, and acclamation stand in an exclusive relation to the name of Jesus; this multiplicity of perspectives points to the new and revolutionary religious experience on which they are based. Alongside theological reflection, the liturgical invocation and ritual worship of Jesus were further anchor points for the construction, development, and expansion of christological ideas.

4.6 Language and Shape of Early Christology: Myth, Titles, Formulae, and Traditions

The life, ministry, destiny, and continuing life and work of Jesus Christ led believers in Christ to the insight that in him God himself had acted and continued to be present.

Myth

This could only be expressed in the form of myth (μῦθος: language, narrative about God or gods), for here it must be true that history had been opened up for something that could not be represented in purely historical terms: in Jesus of Nazareth, God became a human being. This interweaving of the divine world with human history can be formulated, communicated, and received only in mythical form. Myth is a hermeneutical system, within a given culture, that aims to interpret world, history, and human life in a meaningful way, leads to identity-formation, and provides a guide for living.[61] Myths are primarily presented as narrative; they elucidate in narrative form the powers that fundamentally determine the way things are. Myths thereby make available the indispensable symbols for meaningful appropriation of the world and life. Myth opens the understanding to perceive the being of the

---

und seiner alttestamentlich-frühjüdischen Tradition (BTS 48; Neukirchen-Vluyn: Neukirchener Verlag, 2002), 158–67; Martin Hengel, "Abba, Maranatha, Hosanna und die Anfänge der Christologie," in *Denkwürdiges Geheimnis: Beiträge zur Gotteslehre, Festschrift für Eberhard Jüngel zum 70. Geburtstag* (ed. Ingolf Ulrich Dalferth et al.; Tübingen: Mohr, 2004), 154: "In the earliest Aramaic-speaking church, the acclamations *Abba* and *Maranatha* already express fundamental convictions."

61. On the concept of myth, cf. Roland Barthes and Helmut Scheffel, *Mythen des Alltags* (Frankfurt: Suhrkamp, 2006 [1957]); Leszek Kolakowski, *Die Gegenwärtigkeit des Mythos* (Munich: Piper, 1984); Kurt Hübner, *Die Wahrheit des Mythos* (Munich: Beck, 1985); Gerhard Sellin, "Mythos," *RGG*[4] 1697–99; Mircea Eliade, *Myth and Reality* (New York: Harper & Row, 1963).

world in terms of divine activity and formulates the obligatory implications for a group's understanding of itself and its world.

Myth possesses its own rationality, which is not qualitatively different from modern scientific rationality but uses different categories. The worldview of the natural sciences also rests on axiomatic basic affirmations that define the general way in which reality may be perceived. These axioms set forth the framework within which all scientific thinking and affirmation can take place; they are the referential system in which everything is interpreted and processed; they determine the questions that can be addressed to reality, and thus the answers that can be given. "Reality as grasped by science is accordingly not reality as such, but reality that is only and always already interpreted in a particular way. The answers it gives us depend on our questions."[62] Myth also provides an interpretation of the world, but in a different way from that which occurs in the thinking of the modern natural sciences. Myth is an experiential system, a means of explaining and ordering experience. "To be sure, myth does not explain with the help of natural laws and historical rules, but through *archai*, whether these refer to the realm of nature or to human life."[63] Myth is thus not some sort of deficit or lack of reason that must be overcome through "demythologization."[64] On the contrary, myth is an indispensable element of any interpretation of the world—and thus also of faith, which makes human history transparent to divine activity. Myth permits the bringing of different realities into relation with one another and thus allows them to be understood. Thus myth that understands its own purpose is anything but an objectification of God, for myth is aware of the essential inexpressibility of God and renounces any attempts that make God available for human disposition or make human beings into mere instruments for alleged divine purposes.

Myths portray the acts of God through narratives; in early Christianity, this means narrating the act of God in and through Jesus of Nazareth. At the center of the New Testament's mythical language stands the divinization of Jesus of Nazareth, which began very early in all realms of the emerging Christian faith. This mythologizing did not take place by way of adoption of ready-made concepts. Rather, on the basis of Jewish (monotheism) and Greco-Roman ways of thinking (incarnation of a god/divinization of a human being), Jesus's pre-

62. Hübner, *Wahrheit*, 252.

63. Ibid., 257.

64. Rudolf Bultmann's program of "demythologizing" proceeded on the basis not only of a historical sense of superiority, but also from a conviction that the kind of thinking inherent in the world of modern natural science was superior; cf. Rudolf Bultmann, "New Testament and Mythology," in *Kerygma and Myth* (ed. Hans Werner Bartsch; New York: Harper, 1961); and idem, *Jesus Christ and Mythology* (London: SCM, 1958). For discussion of Bultmann's approach, cf. Karl Jaspers and Rudolf Bultmann, *Myth and Christianity. An Inquiry into the Possibility of Religion without Myth* (New York: Noonday Press, 1958); and Bernd Jaspert, *Sackgassen im Streit mit Rudolf Bultmann: Hermeneutische Probleme der Bultmannrezeption in Theologie und Kirche* (St. Ottilien: EOS Verlag Erzabtei St. Ottilien, 1985).

Easter claim was combined with the resurrection event in such a way that a new, independent myth came into being. *This does not mean that history is replaced by myth, but that history is integrated into a comprehensive, transcendent reality.* This fundamental understanding is already clear in 1 Cor. 15:3–5 (see below, *Traditional Formulae*), for the key historical data introduced by Paul ("Christ died . . . was buried . . . was raised . . . appeared to Cephas") are first placed in a meaningful framework by the declarations "for our sins" and "according to the Scriptures."[65] The divine and human reality is then presented in a particular way in the new literary genre, the gospel. In terms of the history of literature, this new form is oriented to the genre of ancient biography but at the same time is permeated with elements that transcend history: what was from the "beginning" (cf. Gen. 1:1; Mark 1:1; John 1:1) could be narrated only in mythical terms. The christological titles, especially, express the view that the Jesus Christ who acts in history belongs to the heavenly world. The gospels thus become the fundamental documents of a new religion, at the center of which stands the Christ myth: the story of the Son of God, Jesus of Nazareth, who made his advent on the stage of history for the sake of humanity and who "died for our sins" so that we might live (2 Cor. 8:9).

Early Christology

As the decisive early witness, Paul confirms that the early Christology soon developed a firm language and form in titles, formulae, and traditions. According to 1 Cor. 15:1–3a,[66] Paul had handed on to the church what he himself had previously received (cf. 1 Cor. 15:3b–5). In 1 Cor. 11:2 Paul praises the church "because you remember me in everything and maintain the traditions, just as I passed them on to you." According to 11:23a Paul received the eucharist tradition from the Lord, and he hands it on to the church (11:23b–26). We are no longer able to say when and where Paul had been instructed in his prior and special knowledge of the Christian faith. According to Acts 9:17–18 he received the Spirit and was baptized in Damascus; perhaps instruction in the Christian faith was included in this event. There is no doubt that Paul had received such a catechesis very early in his Christian life, for he began his independent mission work soon after his call to be an apostle (cf. Gal. 1:17).

In terms of form criticism and tradition history, the early christological affirmations can be divided into different categories, even if there is some variation in the wording and combination of motifs within the formulae.

65. Sellin, "Mythos," 1698.

66. The terms παραλαμβάνω and παραδίδωμι in 1 Cor. 11:23a and 15:3a reflect the technical terminology of the Jewish transmission of tradition; cf. Hans Conzelmann, *1 Corinthians: A Commentary on the First Epistle to the Corinthians* (Hermeneia; trans. James W. Leitch; Philadelphia: Fortress, 1975), 195–96, 251.

They cannot always be precisely located in the life of the early church, and they do not always exactly fit form-critical classifications.[67]

Christological Titles

The christological titles are abbreviations of the saving event as a whole. Each title actualizes the saving event within its particular perspective; they affirm who and what Jesus of Nazareth is for the community of faith.[68] The central title Χριστός or Ἰησοῦς Χριστός (see above, §3.9.3), which is already firmly set in the oldest creedal tradition (cf. 1 Cor. 15:3b–5; 2 Cor. 5:15), takes *the saving event as a whole* as its theme. Already in Paul, statements about the crucifixion (1 Cor. 1:21; Gal. 3:1, 13), death (Rom. 5:6, 8; 14:15; 15:3; 1 Cor. 8:11; Gal. 2:19, 21), resurrection (Rom. 6:9; 8:11; 10:7; 1 Cor. 15:12–17, 20, 23), preexistence (1 Cor. 10:4; 11:3a–b) and earthly life of Jesus (Rom. 9:5; 2 Cor. 5:16) are combined with the Χριστός title. From such foundational statements that refer to the Christ event as a whole, Χριστός affirmations then branch off into different areas. Thus Paul speaks of πιστεύειν εἰς Χριστόν (Gal. 2:16, to believe in Christ; cf. Gal. 3:22; Phil. 1:29), of the εὐαγγέλιον τοῦ Χριστοῦ (the gospel of Christ, cf. 1 Thess. 3:2; 1 Cor. 9:12; 2 Cor. 2:12; 9:13; 10:14; Gal. 1:7; Rom. 15:19; Phil. 1:27), and understands himself as an apostle of Christ (cf. ἀπόστολος Χριστοῦ, 1 Thess. 2:7; 2 Cor. 11:13). So also in the gospels, the title Ἰησοῦς Χριστός assumes a central position, as clearly seen, for example, in Mark 1:1; 8:29; 14:61; Matt. 16:16 and the Lukan Spirit-Christology (see below, §8.4.3). It is no surprise that Χριστός can be used as a self-explanatory title even in letters to predominantly Gentile churches, for the addressees could appropriate Χριστός from its usage in their cultural background in the context of ancient anointing rituals. The anointing rituals widespread in the whole Mediterranean area point to a linguistic usage common to antiquity in general, according to which "when someone or something is anointed, that person or thing becomes holy, near to God, given over to God."[69] Thus both Jewish Christians and Gentile Christians[70] could understand the word Χριστός as affirming Jesus's unique holiness and nearness to God, so that precisely in its capacity as a *titular name* Χριστός (or Ἰησοῦς Χριστός) became for Paul the ideal missionary term.

67. Ralph Brucker, *"Christushymnen" oder 'epideiktische Passagen'?* (FRLANT 176; Göttingen: Vandenhoeck & Ruprecht, 1997), 1–22.

68. Comprehensively presented in Hurtado, *Lord Jesus Christ*, 98–118.

69. Martin Karrer, *Der Gesalbte: Die Grundlagen des Christustitels* (FRLANT 151; Göttingen: Vandenhoeck & Ruprecht, 1991), 211.

70. The term *Gentile Christians* (German: *Heidenchristen*, which could be translated "heathen" or "pagan" Christians) can be misunderstood if it suggests that persons from the world of Greco-Roman religions, prior to their joining the new movement of believers in Christ, had no religious experience that can be taken seriously.

The title κύριος (Lord; cf. Ps. 110:1), found 719 times in the New Testament, projects a different perspective.[71] By speaking of Jesus as "Lord," believers place themselves under the authority of the exalted Lord who is *present* in the life of the church. Κύριος expresses Jesus's unique dignity and function: he had been exalted to God's right hand, participates in the power and glory of God, and from there exercises his lordship. The Kyrios title suggests the presence of the exalted Lord in the life of the church, as is seen most clearly in two anchor points of the tradition: the church's acclamation of Jesus as Lord, and the eucharistic tradition. By its acclamation of Jesus as Lord, the church acknowledges the status of Jesus as Lord and confesses its own faith in him and obedience to him (cf. 1 Cor. 12:3; Phil. 2:6–11). The God of the Christians works through his Spirit, so that they cry out in the worship services κύριος Ἰησοῦς (Jesus is Lord), and not ἀνάθεμα Ἰησοῦς (Jesus be cursed). The title κύριος appears with particular frequency in the eucharistic tradition (cf. 1 Cor. 11:20–23, 26ff., 32; 16:22). The church assembles in the powerful presence of the Lord, whose salvific but also punitive powers are effective in the celebration of the Lord's Supper (cf. 1 Cor. 11:30). Alongside the liturgical dimension of the Kyrios title, Paul also includes an ethical component. The Kyrios is the ultimate authority, the reference point for deciding all the issues of daily life (Rom. 14:8, "If we live, we live to the Lord, and if we die, we die to the Lord; so then, whether we live or whether we die, we are the Lord's."). In Mark and Matthew, the κύριος title plays only a subordinate role, while Luke not only refers to the earthly Jesus (e.g., Luke 7:13, 19; 10:1, 39, 41) and the Risen One (Luke 24:3, 4) as "Lord" but can even use this title of Jesus in the Nativity story (Luke 1:43; 2:11). Finally, the κύριος title also has political associations—it expresses the unique authority of the exalted Lord, marking it off from other claims.[72] The increasing religious reverence for the Roman emperor was combined with the Kyrios title (especially in the eastern part of the empire; cf. Acts 25:26; Suetonius, *Dom.* 13.2), and κύριος (or the feminine κυρία) acclamations are also found in the mystery cults.[73] In the expanding mission of early Christianity, the κύριος Ἰησοῦς Χριστός crossed paths with many other Lords; precisely for this reason it was necessary to make clear that this predicate did not place Jesus in a category with numerous others.

71. Cf. Kramer, *Christ, Lord, Son of God*, 65–107; 151–82; Hahn, *Titles of Jesus*, 68–135; 349–51; Joseph A. Fitzmyer, S.J., "Κύριος," *EDNT* 2:239–331; Vermès, *Jesus the Jew*, 103–28; David B. Capes, *Old Testament Yahweh Texts in Paul's Christology* (WUNT 2.47; Tübingen: Mohr, 1992).

72. Cf. de Jonge, *Christology*, 184–85.

73. On this point cf. Plutarch, *Is. Os.* 367, where Isis is named ἡ κυρία τῆς γῆς, "ruler of the earth" ["ruler," κυρία is here the fem. form of "Lord," κύριος—MEB]; for further examples, cf. *NW* 2.1:313–16; Dieter Zeller, "Kyrios," *DDD*, 492–97.

The title υἱὸς (τοῦ) θεοῦ (Son of God) is found about eighty times in the New Testament. From the point of view of tradition history, it stands in close continuity with Ps. 2:7 and is connected with a variety of christological concepts.[74] Paul (fifteen examples) took it over from the tradition (cf. 1 Thess. 1:9–10; Rom. 1:3b–4a); the careful location of υἱός within the structure of Paul's arguments shows that he attributed great theological importance to this title. *The Son title expresses both the close relationship of Jesus Christ with the Father and his function as the one who mediates God's salvation to human beings* (cf. 2 Cor. 1:19; Gal. 1:16; 4:4, 6; Rom. 8:3). In Mark, υἱὸς (τοῦ) θεοῦ becomes the central christological title, comprehending both Jesus's heavenly glory and his earthly role (see below, §8.2.2). So also Matthew develops a distinctive Son of God Christology (see below, §8.3.2). The title is not central in Luke-Acts.

Of particular importance is the *text-pragmatic function* of the christological titles. They are especially dense in the letter prescripts and opening paragraphs of the gospels, where they belong to the *metacommunicative* signals by which communication is initiated and symbolic universes are defined. A precondition for successful written communication is the establishment of a *common understanding of reality* between author and addressees. This reality, with its past, present, and future dimensions, is named by the christological titles and at the same time is made present and validated as the common knowledge granted by faith.[75]

Traditional Formulae

Some early texts that formulate in terse, pregnant form the past saving event in christological terms are called *belief formulae* (*pistis formulae*).[76] The central text is the pre-Pauline tradition 1 Cor. 15:3b–5, which has a basic structure that is clearly apparent in the Greek text, characterized by naming the event and its interpretation.[77]

74. The relevant material is discussed in Hengel, *Son of God*, 7–16; 57–84; Larry W. Hurtado, "Son of God," in *Dictionary of Paul and His Letters* (ed. Gerald F. Hawthorne et al.; Downers Grove, IL: InterVarsity, 1993), 900–906; Antje Labahn and Michael Labahn, "Jesus als Sohn Gottes bei Paulus," in *Paulinische Christologie: Exegetische Beiträge; Hans Hübner zum 70. Geburtstag* (ed. Udo Schnelle et al.; Göttingen: Vandenhoeck & Ruprecht, 2000), 97–120. On Qumran (in addition to 4QFlor 1:11–13 and 1QSa 2:11, see especially 4Q246) cf. Joseph A. Fitzmyer, SJ, "The 'Son of God' Document from Qumran," *Bib* 74 (1993): 153–74; Zimmermann, *Messianische Texte aus Qumran*, 128–70.

75. Cf. Udo Schnelle, "Heilsgegenwart: Christologische Hoheitstitel bei Paulus," in *Paulinische Christologie: Exegetische Beiträge; Hans Hübner zum 70. Geburtstag* (ed. Udo Schnelle et al.; Göttingen: Vandenhoeck & Ruprecht, 2000), 178–93.

76. Kramer, *Christ, Lord, Son of God*, 15–40.

77. On the interpretation of this text cf. Hans Conzelmann, "On the Analysis of the Confessional Formula 1 Corinthians 15:3–5," *Int* 20 (1966): 15–25; Christian Wolff, *Der erste Brief*

ὅτι Χριστὸς (that Christ)
ἀπέθανεν (died)
ὑπὲρ τῶν ἁμαρτιῶν ἡμῶν (for our sins)
κατὰ τὰς γραφὰς (according to the Scriptures)
καὶ ὅτι ἐτάφη (and that he was buried)
καὶ ὅτι ἐγήγερται (and that he was raised)
τῇ ἡμέρᾳ τῇ τρίτῃ (on the third day)
κατὰ τὰς γραφὰς (according to the Scriptures)
καὶ ὅτι ὤφθη Κηφᾷ εἶτα τοῖς δώδεκα (and that he appeared to Cephas, then to the Twelve)

The grammatical subject is Χριστός (Christ); the sentence deals with the destiny of the decisive figure of all humanity; individual personal history and universal history are united in one story. This unity is possible because God is to be thought of as the actual subject throughout, as indicated by the passive forms of the verbs θάπτω and ἐγείρω (bury, raise) and the twofold interpretative κατὰ τὰς γραφάς (according to the Scriptures). The series "dead—buried" and "raised—appeared" names the events in their chronological and objective order. The tenses of the verbs are significant, for the aorist forms of ἀποθνήσκω and θάπτω designate an event completed in the past, while the perfect passive ἐγήγερται[78] stresses the continuing effect of the event.[79] Christ has been raised from the dead, and the resurrection means the continuing impact of Christ as the Crucified One. The passive ὤφθη in v. 5, in connection with the Old Testament theophanies, emphasizes that the appearances of the Risen One are according to God's will. That the first epiphany was to Cephas is firmly anchored in the tradition (cf. 1 Cor. 15:5; Luke 24:34), as are the appearances to the group of disciples (cf. Mark 16:7; Matt. 28:16–20; Luke 24:36–53; John 20:19–29). The interpretation is based on the testimony of Scripture; the ὑπέρ-expression (for . . .) could be an allusion to Isa. 53:10–12; Ps. 56:14; 116:8, while the "third day" has several hermeneutical possibilities (historical memory; reference to Hos. 6:2; the

des Paulus an die Korinther (THKNT 7; Leipzig: Evangelische Verlagsanstalt, 1996), 354–70; Gerhard Sellin, *Der Streit um die Auferstehung der Toten: Eine religionsgeschichtliche und exegetische Untersuchung von 1. Korinther 15* (FRLANT 138; Göttingen: Vandenhoeck & Ruprecht, 1986), 231–55; Andreas Lindemann, *Der Erste Korintherbrief* (HNT 9.1; Tübingen: Mohr, 2000), 325–33; Wolfgang Schrage, *Der erste Brief an die Korinther* (EKKNT 7; 4 vols.; Zürich: Benziger, 1991), 4:31–53; Helmut Merklein and Marlis Gielen, *Der erste Brief an die Korinther* (ÖTK 7; Gütersloh: Gütersloher Verlagshaus, 2005), 247–83.

78. On ἐγείρω cf. 1 Thess. 1:10; 2 Cor. 4:14; Rom. 4:24b; 6:4; 7:4; 8:11b.

79. Cf. Friedrich Blass and A. Debrunner, *A Greek Grammar of the New Testament and Other Early Christian Literature* (trans. Robert W. Funk; Chicago: University of Chicago Press, 1961), §342.

significance of the third day in ancient cultures' views of death).[80] Views comparable to 1 Cor. 15:3b–5 are found in Luke 24:34, where the passive forms of the verbs once again reveal that God alone is the acting subject in the event: "It is true! The Lord has risen and has appeared to Simon" (ὄντως ἠγέρθη ὁ κύριος καὶ ὤφθη Σίμωνι).

Paul used additional formulations of the death and resurrection of Jesus that had already been shaped in the traditions he received: 1 Thess. 4:14 ("We believe that Jesus died and rose again" [ὅτι Ἰησοῦς ἀπέθανεν καὶ ἀνέστη]); 1 Cor. 15:12, 15; 2 Cor. 4:14; Gal. 1:1; Rom. 4:24; 8:34; 10:9b ("if you . . . believe in your heart that God raised him from the dead" [ἐὰν . . . πιστεύσῃς ἐν τῇ καρδίᾳ σου ὅτι ὁ θεὸς αὐτὸν ἤγειρεν ἐκ νεκρῶν]); 14:9; Col. 2:12; 1 Pet. 1:21; Acts 3:15; 4:10. The *death formulae* emphasize the soteriological dimension of the Christ event as "dying for us," as found in 1 Thess. 5:9–10; 1 Cor. 1:13; 8:11; 2 Cor. 5:14; Rom. 5:6, 8; 14:15; 1 Pet. 2:21; 3:18; 1 John 3:16.[81] The *self-giving formulae* formulate God's act in the Son as happening "for us" (Gal. 1:4; 2:20; Rom. 4:25; 8:32; 1 Tim. 2:5–6; Titus 2:14).[82] To be noted is also the pre-Pauline tradition in Rom. 1:3b–4a, which can also be designated a *Son formula*.[83] Here Christ is regarded in his fleshly existence as Son of David, in his spiritual existence as Son of God. He is Son of God by virtue of his resurrection, which is effected according to Rom. 1:4a by the πνεῦμα ἁγιωσύνης (Spirit of holiness), i.e., the Spirit of God. Jesus first becomes Son of God when he is enthroned at the resurrection, a perspective that does not presuppose Jesus to have been Son of God in a preexistent state or during his earthly life. The work of the Son is also central in the pre-Pauline *mission kerygma* of 1 Thess. 1:9–10.[84] The Gentiles turn from idols to the Son who saves them from the judgment of God, the God "who raised him from the dead" (ὃν ἤγειρεν ἐκ τῶν νεκρῶν). The sending of the Son is also portrayed in formulae already shaped by the tradition; in Gal. 4:4 and Rom. 8:3, these are united with the concept of preexistence (Gal. 4:4, "But when the fullness of time had come, God sent his Son, born of a woman, born under the law").

80. All possibilities are discussed by Wolff, *1. Korintherbrief*, 364–67; and Martin Karrer, *Jesus Christus im Neuen Testament* (GNT 11; Göttingen: Vandenhoeck & Ruprecht, 1998), 42–43.

81. On this topic cf. Klaus Wengst, *Christologische Formeln und Lieder des Urchristentums* (Gütersloh: Gütersloher Verlagshaus, 1972), 78–86.

82. Here cf. Wiard Popkes, *Christus Traditus: Eine Untersuchung zum Begriff der Dahingabe im Neuen Testament* (ATANT 49; Zürich, Stuttgart: Zwingli Verlag, 1967), 131ff.

83. For analysis, cf. Eduard Schweizer, "Röm 1,3f und der Gegensatz von Fleisch und Geist bei Paulus," in *Neotestamentica: Deutsche und Englische Aufsätze, 1951–1963; German and English Essays, 1951–1963* (ed. Eduard Schweizer; Zürich: Zwingli Verlag, 1963), 180–89.

84. Cf. the analysis of Claus Bussmann, *Themen der paulinischen Missionspredigt auf dem Hintergrund der spätjüdisch-hellenistischen Missionsliteratur* (EHS 23.3; Bern: Lang, 1971), 38–56.

Hymnic Texts

Hymns are songs of praise to God or the gods (cf. Epictetus, *Diatr.* 1.16.20–21), which can be composed in different lengths and metrical styles.[85] The oldest hymn in the New Testament is probably Phil. 2:6–11, a key witness to early Christology. Speaking of Jesus Christ, it declares:

[6]ὃς ἐν μορφῇ θεοῦ ὑπάρχων	[6]who, though he was in the form of God,
οὐχ ἁρπαγμὸν ἡγήσατο τὸ εἶναι ἴσα θεῷ,	did not regard equality with God as something to be exploited,
[7]ἀλλὰ ἑαυτὸν ἐκένωσεν	[7]but emptied himself,
μορφὴν δούλου λαβών,	taking the form of a slave,
ἐν ὁμοιώματι ἀνθρώπων γενόμενος·	being born in human likeness.
καὶ σχήματι εὑρεθεὶς ὡς ἄνθρωπος	And being found in human form,
[8]ἐταπείνωσεν ἑαυτὸν	[8]he humbled himself
γενόμενος ὑπήκοος μέχρι θανάτου,	and became obedient to the point of death—
θανάτου δὲ σταυροῦ.	even death on a cross.
[9]διὸ καὶ ὁ θεὸς αὐτὸν ὑπερύψωσεν	[9]Therefore God also highly exalted him
καὶ ἐχαρίσατο αὐτῷ τὸ ὄνομα	and gave him the name
τὸ ὑπὲρ πᾶν ὄνομα,	that is above every name,
[10]ἵνα ἐν τῷ ὀνόματι Ἰησοῦ	[10]so that at the name of Jesus
πᾶν γόνυ κάμψῃ	every knee should bend,
ἐπουρανίων καὶ ἐπιγείων καὶ καταχθονίων	in heaven and on earth and under the earth,
[11]καὶ πᾶσα γλῶσσα ἐξομολογήσηται	[11]and every tongue should confess
ὅτι κύριος Ἰησοῦς Χριστὸς	that Jesus Christ is Lord,
εἰς δόξαν θεοῦ πατρός.	to the glory of God the Father.

Since the analyses of E. Lohmeyer[86] these verses have been regarded as a pre-Pauline text that Paul has incorporated into this context. Evidence for a traditional unit is provided by the occurrence of vocabulary not found elsewhere in the New Testament (ὑπερυψόω [to exalt highly], καταχθόνιος [under the earth]), or found only here in Paul (μορφή [form] and ἁρπαγμός [something to be exploited]), by the heaping up of participles and relative clauses, by the strophic construction of the text, by the interruption of the letter's train of

85. As pagan hymns, cf. for example Anton Weiher, ed., *Homerische Hymnen: Griechisch und deutsch* (6th ed.; Munich: Artemis, 1989), a collection of hymns of varying length to Greek gods.

86. Cf. Ernst Lohmeyer, *Kyrios Jesus: Eine Untersuchung zur Phil. 2,5–11* (2nd ed.; SHAW 4; Heidelberg: C. Winter, 1961); for a survey of recent research, cf. Jürgen Habermann, *Präexistenzaussagen im Neuen Testament* (EHS 23.362; Frankfurt: Lang, 1990), 91–157; Brucker, *Christushymnus*, 304, 319.

thought, and by the contextual transitions in Phil. 2:1–5, 12–13. Most scholars regard v. 8c (θανάτου δὲ σταυροῦ [death on a cross]) as Pauline redaction, for in the hymn itself only the fact of Jesus's death, not its manner, is important. The structure of the pre-Pauline unit is disputed. E. Lohmeyer arranges the traditional unit into six strophes of three lines each, which are divided into two equal stanzas by the new beginning made by διό (therefore) in v. 9. In contrast, J. Jeremias[87] proceeds on the formal principle of *parallelismus membrorum* and advocates a structure of three sections of four lines each (*a*: vv. 6–7a; *b*: vv. 7b–8; *c*: vv. 9–11). All other reconstructions are simply variations of these two pioneering suggestions. The metric-strophic structure of Phil. 2:6–11 will continue to be disputed, but what remains clear is the bipartite structure of the text with v. 9 as the hinge: vv. 6–8, 9–11. From the point of view of form criticism, the text is mostly called a "hymn," but other classifications have also emerged: "encomium,"[88] "epainos,"[89] or "didactic poem."[90] From the history-of-religions point of view, the hymn is not a unity; the second section (vv. 9–11), with its Old Testament allusions and formal liturgical elements, points to the thought world of Judaism, while the first section (vv. 6–7) manifests strong terminological and conceptual parallels to Hellenistic religio-philosophical writings.[91] The *Sitz im Leben* of the hymn is the church's liturgy (cf. Col. 3:16).

Already prior to Paul, christological reflection had seen Christ's *change of status* as involving not only postexistence but preexistence. This scenario is based on an idea that has influenced several New Testament writings: *one can only become what one already essentially is.* The hymn explicitly emphasizes the juxtaposition of μορφὴ θεοῦ (form of God, v. 6) and μορφὴ δούλου (form of a slave, v. 7). Jesus Christ leaves his divine status and places himself in the crassest, most opposite situation imaginable. The hymn portrays and reflects further on the stages of this fundamental event. Jesus Christ divests himself of his divine power and assumes the helpless status of a slave; not lordship but weakness and humiliation are now his lot.[92] Verse 9 marks the

87. Cf. Joachim Jeremias, "Zur Gedankenführung in den paulinischen Briefen (4. Der Christushymnus Phil 2,6–11)," in *Abba: Studien zur neutestamentlichen Theologie und Zeitgeschichte* (Göttingen: Vandenhoeck & Ruprecht, 1966), 274–76; Joachim Jeremias, "Zu Philipper 2,7: ἑαυτὸν ἐκένωσεν," in *Abba*, 56–62.

88. Klaus Berger, *Formgeschichte des Neuen Testaments* (Heidelberg: Quelle & Meyer, 1984), 345.

89. Brucker, *Christushymnus*, 319–20; 330–31.

90. Nikolaus Walter et al., eds., *Die Briefe an die Philipper, Thessalonicher und an Philemon* (NTD 8.2; Göttingen: Vandenhoeck & Ruprecht, 1998), 56–62.

91. On this cf. S. Vollenweider, "Der 'Raub' der Gottgleichheit: Ein religions-geschichtlicher Vorschlag zu Phil 2,6(–11)," *NTS* 45 (1999): 413–33; S. Vollenweider, "Die Metamorphose des Gottessohnes," in *Das Urchristentum in seiner literarischen Geschichte: Festschrift für Jürgen Becker zum 65. Geburtstag* (ed. Ulrich Mell and Ulrich B. Müller; BZNW 100; Berlin: de Gruyter, 1999), 285–306.

92. On Paul's own interpretation of the hymn in Phil. 2:6–11, see below, §6.2.1.

turning point in this event, linguistically indicated by the new subject ὁ θεός (God). Jesus Christ's exaltation to a new status occurs in the conferral of the new name (vv. 9b–10), followed by his installation and acknowledgment as Cosmocrator (vv. 10–11b). Acclamation as Lord and worship by the whole universe correspond to the will of God and redound to God's glory (v. 11c). The new status of Jesus Christ is more than a mere restoration of his preexistent equality with God.[93] Only his willingness to enter into the humiliation that leads to the cross makes possible his exaltation to be ruler of the world, which means that even the Preexistent One has undergone a transformation in order to attain his true identity.

Another early *Christ-hymn* is found in Col. 1:15–20 (see below, §10.1.2). The traditional hymn begins with a sudden change of style in v. 15 and is composed of two strophes, as indicated by both formal signals and by its content. The first strophe (vv. 15–18a) speaks of the cosmic significance of the Christ event, and the second strophe (vv. 18b–20) focuses on its soteriological dimension. Interpretative additions of the author are found in v. 18a (τῆς ἐκκλησίας, "[of] the church") and in v. 20 (διὰ τοῦ αἵματος τοῦ σταυροῦ αὐτοῦ, "through the blood of his cross"). The reference to the crucifixion binds the cosmic dimensions of the Christ event to the cross and thus to history. Clear parallels to the Philippians hymn are present; in both texts the hymn is integrated into their respective contexts by interpretative additions. From a history-of-religions perspective, the hymn has points of contact with the conceptuality of Hellenistic Judaism, where Wisdom receives attributes here applied to Christ (preexistence, mediator of creation, universal lordship).[94]

Additional Traditions

Acclamations belong to the context of early Christian liturgy, where they function as the congregation's testimony to the lordship of Jesus Christ (cf. 1 Cor. 12:3; 16:22). Extremely important is the pre-Pauline εἷς-tradition of 1 Cor. 8:6,[95] a unity tradition constructed on the Greek word εἷς (one). It boldly unites the story of God with that of Jesus Christ: "Yet for us there is [only] one God, the Father, from whom all things came and for whom we live; and

93. Cf. Günther Bornkamm, "Zum Verständnis des Christus-Hymnus Phil 2,6–11," in *Studien zu Antike und Urchristentum* (ed. Günther Bornkamm; 3rd ed.; BEvT 28; Munich: Kaiser, 1970), 171–72.

94. See the documentation in Eduard Lohse, *Colossians and Philemon: A Commentary on the Epistles to the Colossians and to Philemon* (trans. William R. Poehlmann and Robert J. Karris; Hermeneia; Philadelphia: Fortress, 1971), 41–61.

95. For documentation of the pre-Pauline character of this tradition and for specification of the numerous contacts with the history of religions, cf. Schrage, *Korinther*, 2:216–25, and Dieter Zeller, "Der eine Gott und der eine Herr Jesus Christus," in *Der lebendige Gott: Studien zur Theologie des Neuen Testaments; Festschrift für Wilhelm Thüsing zum 75. Geburtstag* (ed. Thomas Söding; NTA NF 31; Münster: Aschendorff, 1996), 34–49.

there is but one Lord, Jesus Christ, through whom all things came and through whom we live." This text reflects the relation of *the*ology and *Christ*ology within the horizon of monotheism; the εἷς-predication applies to the Father, but at the same time to the one Lord Jesus Christ. The result is not a splitting of the one God into two gods; rather, the one Lord is included in the linguistic and conceptual domain of the one God. In regard to his origin and essence, Christ belongs entirely on God's side of reality. At the same time, the one Lord remains subordinate to the one God, and that not only in the sequence of the text,[96] for the creator God is the Father of the Lord Jesus Christ. The precise arrangement of prepositional phrases in v. 6b and 6d develops the idea of subordinate parallelism. At first, creation and salvation are referred to God and the Lord in identical terms (τὰ πάντα . . . ἡμεῖς), but then a fundamental differentiation is expressed by the following prepositions ἐκ and διά. The world owes its existence to the one God alone; only this God is the origin of all that is. The Kyrios is the preexistent mediator of creation, in that the one God causes "everything" to come into being through the one Lord.

The tradition that came to Paul also included "sayings of the Lord."[97] He quotes them (in 1 Thess. 4:15ff.; 1 Cor. 7:10–11; 9:14; 11:23ff.) but does not always present them as sayings known to us from the Synoptic tradition of Jesus's sayings. Pre-Pauline *baptismal traditions* are found in 1 Cor. 1:30; 6:11; 2 Cor. 1:21–22; Gal. 3:26–28; Rom. 3:25; 4:25; 6:3–4.[98] *Eucharistic traditions* are found in 1 Cor. 11:23b–25; 16:22. An obvious *confessional formula* is found in Rom. 10:9a; traditional topoi of *parenesis* are present in 1 Cor. 5:10–11; 6:9–10; 2 Cor. 12:20–21; Gal. 5:19–23; Rom. 1:29–31; 13:13.[99]

The Origin of Christology

All historical, theological, and history-of-religions observations support the thesis that the origin of Christology is *a natural result* of the pre-Easter

96. On target is the comment of Thüsing, *Neutestamentlichen Theologien*, 3:371: "Despite the unimaginable close unity with himself, by which God has established with the crucified Jesus by raising him from the dead, the specific relationship between the two is preserved; even more: it is only through these mutual relations that the unity is fundamentally structured and thereby (re-)constituted. Only a mediator who lives in unity with God can be 'mediator of God's immediacy.'"

97. A critical analysis of the history of research, with an extensive bibliography, is provided by Frans Neirynck, "Paul and the Sayings of Jesus," in *Evangelica II: 1982–1991; Collected Essays* (ed. Frans van Segbroeck; BETL 99; Louvain: University Press, 1991), 511–68.

98. Cf. the analysis in Udo Schnelle, *Gerechtigkeit und Christusgegenwart: Vorpaulinische und paulinische Tauftheologie* (GTA 24; Göttingen: Vandenhoeck & Ruprecht, 1983), 33–88; 175–215.

99. For elaboration, cf. Georg Strecker, *History of New Testament Literature* (trans. Calvin Katter and Hans-Joachim Mollenhauer; Harrisburg, PA: Trinity, 1997), 68–80; Wiard Popkes, *Paränese und Neues Testament* (SBS 168; Stuttgart: Verlag Katholisches Bibelwerk, 1995).

claim of Jesus and the foundational encounters of the first Christians with the Risen One and the Holy Spirit. The question of Jesus's identity as the one who came from God already emerged in the days of Jesus's earthly life and was intensified in view of his readiness to die for his mission and message. Above all, the appearances of the Risen One were understood by the earliest Christians as God's confirmation of Jesus's message. These appearances called for a deepened reflection on the essential being of Jesus Christ and his relation to God, which led to an application of divine predicates to Jesus. *Because Jesus himself embodied the image of God that he proclaimed, he himself was taken up into this image.* The continuity model best explains the development from Jesus's pre-Easter claim to his post-Easter veneration as Lord: his significance is changed and strengthened since Easter. Very early, an amazing spectrum of confessional statements developed affirming the preexistence, mediating role in creation, and universal lordship of the Lord Jesus Christ. Within the Scriptures of Israel and the theological models of ancient Judaism, as well as within the thought world of Greco-Roman religions, the early Christians found decisive means for understanding and interpreting the Christ event—means that helped them formulate their early Christology. The adoption of christological titles always included, however, their *recoding*, filling them with new content. What Jesus of Nazareth once said, and how Jesus Christ was experienced after the cross and resurrection, now flow into each other and form something new: Jesus Christ himself becomes the object of faith and the content of the Christian confession. In the time after Jesus, it was appropriate that what he had said and done continued to be recounted, because his person is not separable from his proclamation and his deeds. Jesus Christ was not venerated as a "second" god, but was included in the worship of the "one God" (Rom. 3:30, εἷς θεός). What prevailed was *an exclusive monotheism in binitarian form*. In Jesus, one encountered God, *the God who is defined christologically*. The relation of Jesus to God was not thought through in ontological categories; rather, the experience of God's act in and through Jesus was the beginning of such reflections.

The origin of Christology from the preaching and claim of Jesus is *a natural historical and theological process*. Proceeding from the preaching and deeds of Jesus, and newly inspired by the Easter events, the early Christians developed *a comprehensive process of developing and nurturing meanings, traditions, and texts*. The purpose of this process was to preserve the stock of traditions and continue to reform them through strenuous hermeneutical efforts to mediate their past meaning to the present. This process generated the New Testament documents, which to this day remain the foundational documents for Christian faith.

5

The Second Transformation

The Early Christian Mission without the Precondition of Circumcision

The gospel of the crucified and risen Jesus Christ, which was first proclaimed in and around Jerusalem, was one variation of Jewish identity alongside others. This situation changed when conflicts within the earliest church generated an independent mission outside Jerusalem conducted by leading members of the Greek-speaking segment of the church.

5.1 The Hellenists

Luke pictures the time of the first church's beginnings as the epoch of unity in prayer, the eucharist, doctrine, and in life and work (cf. Acts 2:34, 44). So too, his portrayals of the social and economic relationships within the earliest church stand under the rubric of unity, as the summaries in Acts 2:42–46; 4:32–35 specifically point out.[1] The initial picture of unity displays fissures,[2]

1. Cf. Hans-Josef Klauck, "Gütergemeinschaft in der klassischen Antike, in Qumran und im Neuen Testament," in *Gemeinde—Amt—Sakrament: Neutestamentliche Perspektiven* (ed. Hans-Josef Klauck; Würzburg: Echter, 1989), 69–100; Gerd Theissen, "Urchristlicher Liebeskommunismus," in *Text and Contexts: Biblical Texts in Their Textual and Situational Contexts: Essays in Honor of Lars Hartman* (ed. Tord Fornberg et al.; Oslo: Scandinavian University Press, 1995), 689–712; Freidrich Wilhelm Horn, "Die Gütergemeinschaft der Urgemeinde," *EvT* 58 (1998): 370–83.

2. Martin Hengel, "Zwischen Jesus und Paulus: Die 'Hellenisten,' die 'Sieben,' und Stephanus," *ZTK* 72 (1975): 151–206; Gerd Theissen, "Hellenisten und Hebräer (Apg 6,1–6): Gab es

when, without any transition or explanation, in Acts 6:1–6 Luke suddenly mentions two different groups of leaders: the Twelve and the group of Seven. The Twelve probably represents a group established by Jesus himself, which symbolically represented the wholeness of the twelve tribes of Israel (see above, §3.8.3). The group of Seven was also a fixed term in early Christianity, since in Acts 21:8 Philip is designated as "one of the Seven."[3] Luke connects the formation of the group of Seven with a conflict within the Jerusalem community: the widows of the Hellenists felt overlooked or neglected in the internal welfare program, which led to a conflict between the "Hellenists" and the "Hebrews." The terminology of Ἑβραῖοι (Hebrews) and Ἑλληνισταί (Hellenists/Greeks) indicates that the conflict had primarily linguistic and cultural causes. The Ἑβραῖοι speak Aramaic; the Ἑλληνισταί are followers of Jesus who stem from the Jewish Diaspora and speak Greek.[4] The language difference probably led to the formation of separate worship services, and this liturgical-cultic distancing then resulted in a separation of the benevolent work, as depicted in Acts 6:1–6. It is striking that the group of Seven is composed exclusively of men with Greek names, that the group is not reported to have done anything to carry out its diaconal responsibilities, and that Stephen, the outstanding figure in this group, is anything but an administrator of a welfare program. In Acts 6:8–15 he is presented as a Spirit-filled person with charismatic gifts, and above all as the exponent of a faction within the earliest church that was critical of the law and the temple (Acts 6:13–14). Stephen's successful missionary activity within the Hellenistic synagogues of Jerusalem and especially his criticism of the existing temple cult were probably felt as a provocation; hence his lynching (by stoning, Acts 7:54–60).[5] In the conflict between Hebrews and Hellenists, their differing theological concepts also obviously played a role, which, again, can be explained by the origins and cultural background of each group. The Greek-speaking Diaspora Jews, unlike the Aramaic-speaking members of the community, did not regard themselves as bound to temple observance and strict Torah interpretation. For this reason, perhaps, only the Hellenistic Jewish followers of Jesus were persecuted after the stoning of Stephen, not the apostles (cf. Acts 8:1–3). We should probably suppose that the Hellenists carried out their mission program mainly in Samaria and in the Hellenistic cities of Galilee, the borderlands of Syria and Palestine, and along the Mediterranean coast (cf. Acts 8:4–40). Hellenistic Christians also came to

eine Spaltung in der Urgemeinde?" in *Geschichte—Tradition—Reflexion: Festschrift für Martin Hengel zum 70. Geburtstag* (ed. Hubert Cancik et al.; 3 vols.; Tübingen: Mohr, 1996), 323–43; Dietrich-Alex Koch, "Crossing the Border: The 'Hellenists' and Their Way to the Gentiles," *Neot* 39 (2005): 289–312.

3. The origin of the number seven could be related to the interpretation of Deut. 16:18, which gives the instruction that seven men should rule in each city; cf. Josephus, *Ant.* 4.214, 287.

4. For documentation, see Hengel, "Zwischen Jesus und Paulus," 161ff.

5. Cf. Theissen, "Hellenisten und Hebräer," 322–36.

Damascus, where Paul was later received into the church after his conversion (cf. Acts 9:10ff.). The Hellenists probably also worked in Alexandria, for the Alexandrian missionary Apollos emerged in Corinth at the beginning of the 50s (cf. 1 Cor. 3:4ff.; Acts 18:24–28). Possibly, even the church in Rome was founded by the Hellenists.

The Hellenists developed basic approaches to theological and christological issues that opened up emerging Christianity for mission in the broader world of Greco-Roman religion. They were probably the first to think through in a theological way the meaning of the spontaneous gifts of the Holy Spirit that also appeared among non-Jews (cf. Acts 2:9–11). Early on, they translated traditions from and about Jesus into Greek, thus opening the message of Jesus to the Greek-speaking world. They could thereby unite with the universalistic tendencies and the infrastructure of Hellenistic Judaism as well as with Jesus traditions that manifested an openness to non-Jews. Within ancient Judaism around the beginning of the first century CE, there existed a remarkable range of ideas regarding the expected eschatological turning of the nations to Yahweh (cf., e.g., *T. Levi* 18.9; *T. Jud.* 24.5–6; 25.3–5; *T. Benj.* 9.2; 10.6–11; *T. Ash.* 7.2–3; *T. Naph.* 8.3–4; *1 En.* 90.33–38; Sir. 44:19–23; *Pss. Sol.* 17.31; *2 Bar.* 68.1–8; 70.7–8; *4 Ezra* 13.33–50; *Jub.* 22.20–22).[6] To be sure, there is no evidence that Jewish groups carried on an organized Gentile mission, but especially in Diaspora Judaism, the universal dimensions of the Yahweh faith were strongly emphasized, and there was an openness to non-Jewish culture. The tradition still contains clear traces of Jesus's own openness to non-Jews, in that he did not avoid encounters with Gentiles (cf. Mark 7:24–30, 31–34; Matt. 8:5–10, 13), and a few sayings raise questions against the priority of Israel in salvation history (cf. Q 13:29, 28; 14:23).

5.2 Antioch

Acts 11:19–20 describes the flight of the persecuted Hellenists to other locations:

> Now those who had been scattered by the persecution in connection with Stephen traveled as far as Phoenicia, Cyprus, and Antioch, telling the message only to Jews. Some of them, however, men from Cyprus and Cyrene, went to Antioch and began to speak to Greeks also, telling them the good news about the Lord Jesus.

Antioch of Syria on the Orontes, the third largest city in the Roman Empire, offered optimal conditions for the early Christian mission, for its popula-

6. On this point cf. the analyses of Kraus, *Das Volk Gottes*, 12–110.

tion included numerous Greeks who were disposed positively toward the Jewish religion.[7] The proselyte Nicholas, a member of the group associated with Stephen, also came from Antioch (Acts 6:5), and it was in Antioch that Hellenistic Jewish Christians made the transition to a successful preaching mission among the Greek population (Acts 11:20).[8] As the story is told in Acts, Barnabas and Paul did not belong to the Antioch church from the very beginning but began their work there only after the Gentile mission without the precondition of circumcision had already begun (Acts 11:22–25). Clearly Antioch was the location of Paul's first contact with the Jerusalem Hellenists.[9] The mission of the Antioch church among Jews, and especially among Gentiles, must have been successful, for according to Acts 11:26 it was in Antioch that the term Χριστιανοί (Christians) was first applied to the followers of the new teaching, now predominantly Gentile. Early in the 40s Christians were thus perceived for the first time to be a distinct group alongside Jews and Gentiles. From the Gentile perspective they were a non-Jewish movement, and must have attained a recognizable theological profile and their own organizational structure.[10]

The Significance of Antioch

The outstanding place held by Antioch in the history of early Christian theology has always been the occasion for inferring far-reaching historical and theological conclusions. For the history-of-religions school, Antioch not only provided the missing link between the earliest Jerusalem church and Paul but also was the birthplace of Christianity as a syncretistic religion. Here the radical development took place that was so important for the history of early Christianity: "Jesus goes from being the expected Messiah to being the cult-hero

7. Cf. Josephus, *JW* 7.45: The Jews in Antioch "were constantly attracting to their religious ceremonies multitudes of Greeks, and these they had in some measure incorporated with themselves." On Antioch, see Martin Hengel and Anna Maria Schwemer, *Paul between Damascus and Antioch: The Unknown Years* (trans. John Bowden; Louisville: Westminster John Knox, 1997), 178–204.

8. That these reports represent a different perspective than Luke's own speaks for their historicity. In his view, missionary work on Cyprus was first initiated by Paul and Barnabas (cf. Acts 13:4; 15:39). It was not Peter, but unknown Christian missionaries, who initiated the decisive epoch in the history of earliest Christianity (Acts 10:1–11:18). On the analysis of Acts 11:19–30 cf. Alfons Weiser, *Die Apostelgeschichte* (ÖTK 5; Würzburg: Echter Verlag, 1981), 273–80. This cannot mean, of course, that prior to Antioch there was no preaching to the non-Jewish Greek-speaking population! The mission in Samaria, Damascus, Arabia, and Cilicia certainly also included this group; cf. Hengel and Schwemer, *Between Damascus and Antioch*, 201–4.

9. Julius Wellhausen, *Kritische Analyse der Apostelgeschichte* (Berlin: Weidmann, 1914), 21.

10. Adolf von Harnack, *The Mission and Expansion of Christianity in the First Three Centuries* (2nd ed.; trans. James Moffatt; New York: Putnam, 1908), 411–12.

who is present as lord of his community."[11] So also in current research, Antioch is regarded as the soil from which early Christian theology sprang—especially Paul's theology. Not only was Paul taught the fundamentals of Christian faith here; all his important distinctive theological views had already been developed in his Antioch period. "Thus on the whole we can say that what Paul used later from the old tradition essentially came from the knowledge of the Antiochene community."[12] But the New Testament texts provide no verification for these far-ranging historical and theological conclusions.[13]

1. According to Acts 11:26, Barnabas and Paul worked together only one year in Antioch itself,[14] and they are portrayed by Luke as teachers of the Antioch church. Luke minimizes the direct residence of Paul in Antioch, which, in comparison with the residence of the apostle in Corinth (Acts 18:4, a year and a half) and Ephesus (Acts 19:10, more than two years), must be regarded as entirely normal. To be sure, Paul returned to Antioch at the conclusion of his first missionary tour (cf. Acts 14:28), but again, in comparison with the stations of his later missionary journeys, this is his usual procedure.
2. Paul mentions Antioch only in Gal. 2:11, in connection with the time between his first and second visits to Jerusalem, so that in fact he is entirely silent about the period of his initial work at Antioch.

There can be no doubt about the special place of the Antioch church in the history of early Christian theology, just as its influence on Paul is likewise unquestioned. Antioch was a significant station in the course of Paul's life. *Here the early Christian missionaries achieved the transition to a mission to adherents of Greco-Roman religions, a mission programmatically free from the precondition of circumcision.* At the same time, we must guard against "allowing [Antioch] to become a 'holding tank' for our ignorance about early Christian connections."[15] Pauline theology does present itself as oriented to

11. Wilhelm Bousset, *Kyrios Christos: Geschichte des Christusglaubens von den Anfängen des Christentums bis Irenaeus* (Göttingen: Vandenhoeck & Ruprecht, 1967), 90; cf. *Kyrios Christos: A History of the Belief in Christ from the Beginnings of Christianity to Irenaeus* (trans. John E. Steely; Nashville: Abingdon, 1970), 136.

12. Jürgen Becker, *Paul: Apostle to the Gentiles* (trans. O. C. Dean; Louisville: Westminster John Knox, 1993), 104.

13. For a critique of the widespread "pan-Antiochism" in scholarly literature, see also Hengel and Schwemer, *Between Damascus and Antioch*, 286–91.

14. Cf. Johannes Weiss, *Earliest Christianity: A History of the Period A.D. 30–150* (trans. Frederick C. Grant; 2 vols.; New York: Harper, 1937, 1959), 136; Gerd Lüdemann, *Early Christianity according to the Traditions in Acts: A Commentary* (trans. John Bowden; Minneapolis: Fortress, 1989), 134–35.

15. Andreas Wechsler, *Geschichtsbild und Apostelstreit: Eine forschungsgeschichtliche und exegetische Studie über den antiochenischen Zwischenfall (Gal 2,11–14)* (BZNW 62; Berlin: de Gruyter, 1991), 266.

tradition, but may never be reduced and simplified to the mere repetition of materials provided to him by others.

5.3 The Stance of Paul

After his call Paul neither consulted with other people nor went to Jerusalem to those who were apostles before him, "but I went immediately into Arabia and later returned to Damascus" (Gal. 1:17b).[16] We have no information regarding Paul's stay in *Arabia*, but it probably refers to the rocky desert area southeast of Damascus, which formed the northern part of the Arab kingdom of Nabatea. At that time the economic influence of Nabatea also embraced *Damascus* (2 Cor. 11:32), where Paul returned and for the first time worked within an established Christian community. Paul did not visit *the original church in Jerusalem* until the third year after his call to be an apostle (35 CE; cf. Gal. 1:18–20). Following his brief visit to Jerusalem, Paul went in about 36/37 into the areas of *Syria and Cilicia* (Gal. 1:21). "Syria" most likely refers to the area around Antioch-on-the-Orontes, and "Cilicia" the environs of Tarsus. Paul probably worked at first in the area of Tarsus and Cilicia. We cannot determine the character of this mission either from Paul's own later letters or from Acts. This missionary work of about six years[17] had probably not been too successful, for about 42 CE Paul teamed up with Barnabas as the "junior partner" in the Antioch mission. The personal legend of Acts 4:36–37 and the list in Acts 13:1 indicate the special importance of Barnabas (also in relation to Paul); in Gal. 2:1, 9 he appears as a spokesperson in the discussion at the Apostolic Council with a status equal to Paul's. Paul fully acknowledged and accepted Barnabas (cf. 1 Cor. 9:6) but withstood him at the incident in Antioch (Gal. 2:11–14). We can perceive Barnabas's theological views only indirectly, but along with Paul he was certainly an open advocate of the mission to non-Jews that did not make circumcision a precondition for entering the Christian community.[18]

16. On the problems of Pauline chronology cf. Udo Schnelle, *Apostle Paul: His Life and Thought* (trans. M. Eugene Boring; Grand Rapids: Baker Academic, 2005), 47–56.

17. The length of this mission is difficult to calculate; as arguments for the duration mentioned above we may mention: (1) With the expression "About that time" in Acts 12:1a, Luke makes a temporal connection between the beginning of the work of Barnabas and Paul in Antioch and the persecution in Jerusalem by Agrippa I (cf. Acts 12:1b–17). This persecution probably occurred in 42 CE (Cf. Riesner, *Paul's Early Period*, 117–23). (2) The famine mentioned in Acts 11:28 and the support given by the Antioch Christians to Jerusalem (Acts 11:29) fall in the period between 42 and 44 CE (cf. Riesner, *Paul's Early Period*, 125–36). Somewhat differently Hengel and Schwemer, *Between Damascus and Antioch*, 171–78, who calculate Paul's stay in Cilicia as lasting three or four years (36/37–39/40 CE), during which time he had an independent and successful mission before joining the Antioch project (ca. 39/40–48/49 CE).

18. On Barnabas cf. especially Bernd Kollmann, *Joseph Barnabas: Leben und Wirkungsgeschichte* (SBS 175; Stuttgart: Verlag Katholisches Bibelwerk, 1998); Hengel and Schwemer,

After completing their mission in Syria and parts of Asia Minor, Barnabas and Paul returned to Antioch, only to be sent to the Apostolic Council (cf. Acts 15:1–2). Paul himself gives a somewhat different picture of the concrete occasion of the Jerusalem trip in Gal. 2:2a, "I went up in response to a revelation." He thus no longer represents his presence at the Apostolic Council within the framework of the mission program of the Antioch church. One can suppose that the Lukan view of history causes Luke to place the connection of Barnabas and Paul to the Antioch church in the foreground at the Apostolic Council. However, Paul himself also formulates his own portrayal tendentiously, for he wants to emphasize his independence from Jerusalem and the other churches. Furthermore, he discloses his own understanding of why he participated in the Apostolic Council: μή πως εἰς κενὸν τρέχω ἢ ἔδραμον ("in order to make sure that I was not running, or had not run, in vain," Gal. 2:2c). Torah-observant Jewish Christians had intervened in the congregations founded by the apostle, taken note of their freedom (from the Torah), and come to the Apostolic Council to insist that Christian converts from the Greco-Roman religious world be circumcised (Gal. 2:4–5). Paul had been carrying out his mission without requiring Gentile converts to be circumcised, which from the strict Jewish and Jewish-Christian point of view meant that it advocated complete freedom from the Torah.[19] Paul was obviously afraid that the agitation of these opponents would influence the Jerusalem leaders to reject and nullify his mission, so that his apostolic commission to found churches could not be carried out (cf. 1 Thess. 2:19; 1 Cor. 9:15–18, 23; 2 Cor. 1:14). Even more drastic: the apostle saw that if he were to fail in the task to which he alone had been commissioned, his glory on the Day of Christ, his eschatological salvation, was in danger (cf. Phil. 2:16).

The Apostolic Council is also indirectly a result of significant *changes in the history of the early Jerusalem church*. Under the persecution of Agrippa I in 42 CE, not only was James the son of Zebedee killed (Acts 12:2), but Peter gave up the leadership of the Jerusalem church and left the city (Acts 12:17). James the Lord's brother (cf. Mark 6:3) took over his position, as is clearly indicated by a comparison of Gal. 1:18–19 with Gal. 2:9 and 1 Cor. 15:5 with 1 Cor. 15:7, as well as by the last words of Peter in Acts 12:17b ("Tell this to James and to the [Jerusalem] believers") and the picture of the church in Acts 15:13; 21:18.[20] While Peter himself was probably open to accepting uncircumcised Gentiles into the new movement (cf. Acts 10:34–48; Gal. 2:11–12) and later was

---

Between Damascus and Antioch, 211–20; Markus Öhler, *Barnabas: Der Mann in der Mitte* (BG 12; Leipzig: Evangelische Verlagsanstalt, 2005).

19. Paul never engaged in or advocated a Gentile mission that was in principle "free from the law," for the central ethical content of the Torah (e.g., the Decalogue) was also valid for Christians converted from the world of Greco-Roman religion (see below, §6.5.3).

20. Cf. Gerd Lüdemann, *Opposition to Paul in Jewish Christianity* (trans. M. Eugene Boring; Minneapolis: Fortress, 1989), 44–52.

a sympathetic participant in the Gentile mission (cf. 1 Cor. 1:12; 9:5), we must see James and his group as representatives of a strict Jewish Christianity (cf. Gal. 2:12a) that consciously understood itself within Judaism and considered Torah-observance a requirement for acceptance into the new movement.[21] He rejected table fellowship between Jewish Christians and Gentile Christians (Gal. 2:12a) and was obviously highly respected by the Pharisees. Josephus reports that after the martyrdom of James in 62 CE, the Pharisees bitterly demanded the deposition of Ananus, the high priest who was responsible for James's death.[22] Very likely those who advocated the circumcision of Gentile Christians felt that their demand was strongly supported by the theological position of James.

The problem that occupied the Apostolic Council in 48 CE became an issue of increasing concern for Paul after he began his independent mission, as is reflected in his letters composed between 50 and 56 CE. What criteria must those fulfill who would belong to the elect people of God in continuity with the first covenant? Should circumcision as the sign of God's covenant (cf. Gen. 17:11), and thus of membership in the elect people of God,[23] also be a general requirement for Christians of the Greco-Roman tradition? Must a Gentile who wants to become a Christian first become a Jew? Since from the Jewish perspective a person became a proselyte and thus a member of the elect people of God only by circumcision and ritual immersion, from the strict Jewish Christian point of view it seemed clear that the new status among the redeemed people of God came only by baptism in the name of Jesus Christ *and* by circumcision.[24] The problem that occupied the Apostolic Council (and the conflict at Antioch) thus emerged at a time when the ritual and social requirements of Christianity had not been fully defined. Neither the Christian "identity markers" nor the "lifestyle" that these implied had yet been clarified. Could Christian churches from the Greco-Roman tradition be recognized as belonging to the same church as Jewish Christians, who for the most part still participated in the life of the synagogue? Previous Jewish self-understanding had considered it fundamental that one's national-cultural community and one's religious community were one and the same—must this now be given up? Does maintaining the codes of holiness and ritual purity matter? How do believers in Jesus come to participate in the people of God, and how do the promises of God's covenant with Israel come to apply to them? To what extent should markers of Jewish identity such as circumcision, table fellowship only

21. Cf. also Wolfgang Kraus, *Zwischen Jerusalem und Antiochia: Die "Hellenisten," Paulus und die Aufnahme der Heiden in das endzeitliche Gottesvolk* (SBS 179; Stuttgart: Katholisches Bibelwerk, 1999), 134–39.

22. Cf. Josephus, *Ant*. 20.199–203.

23. Cf. Otto Betz, "Beschneidung," *TRE* 5:716–22.

24. The possibility of becoming a full member of the Jewish community without circumcision probably never existed; cf. the analysis of the texts in Kraus, *Das Volk Gottes*, 96–107.

with one's own people, and Sabbath observance also apply to the emerging Gentile churches? Does the fundamental change of status that has already occurred when one professes Christian faith involve additional changes in one's status that must be worked out? Are baptism *and* circumcision obligatory initiation rites for all believers in Christ, or does baptism alone make possible full acceptance into the people of God?

The Apostolic Council provided no generally accepted answers to these questions,[25] so further disputes were unavoidable. Pauline theology is bound up with early Christianity's process of self-definition, which was so full of conflict, and is to be understood essentially against this background. At the same time, it sets forth the decisive solution to these problems.

25. Cf. Schnelle, *Apostle Paul*, 121–37.

6

Paul

Missionary and Thinker

Paul was undoubtedly the outstanding missionary and theological thinker of earliest Christianity. As we approach this multisided personality and look carefully at the history of what he accomplished, we must take into consideration his particular historical situation and the theological challenges it involved (see above, §5.3). While the Gentile mission without the precondition of circumcision had begun prior to Paul, through its success he became a practitioner and then inevitably the theologian of this movement. The great achievements of his Gentile mission generated enormous problems for him, for it fell to his lot *as the first Christian theologian* to take into account those unavoidable aporias that increasingly confronted developing Christianity. He had to think through disparate issues and bring into some kind of conceptual consistency what could not really be harmonized: God's first covenant remains valid, but only the new covenant saves. The elect people of God must be converted to Christ so that, along with Gentile believers, they could become the one true people of God. As *homo religiosus*, Paul was also a significant intellectual; the same holds true of Paul as of other great thinkers of his time: all the intellectual giants of the New Testament period were theologians, and vice versa (e.g., Cicero, Philo, Seneca, Epictetus, Plutarch, Dio Chrysostom). This is in no way surprising, for every significant system of Greco-Roman philosophy culminates in a theology.[1] Philosophy and theology belonged together in the

1. A survey is provided by Wilhelm Weischedel, *Der Gott der Philosophen: Grundlegung einer philosophischen Theologie im Zeitalter des Nihilismus* (3rd ed.; Darmstadt: Wissenschaftliche Buchgesellschaft, 1994), 39–69.

ancient world; their themes were interwoven, and unlike moderns, the ancients did not regard them as mutually antagonistic. To be sure, Paul was not a philosopher in terms of ancient categories; but his theology manifests an *intellectual potency*.[2] His translation of religious experiences and convictions into a conceptual mode gave them the systematic quality needed for generating the kind of impact his thought has had.

In order to displace established systems of interpretation, new convictions and models of thinking must be able to hold their own in the context of competing systems and discursive models that shape the cultural and religious thought world. They must also manifest a capacity for appropriation and integration, plausibility, and the ability to deal with unanticipated developments. All this can be said of Paul, and for this reason his theology is also to be reckoned as one of the significant intellectual accomplishments of antiquity.[3] The enduring success of Christianity in general and of Pauline theology in particular is essentially related to the fact that they were attractive both to people's deep feelings and to their intellect. They gave plausible answers to the pressing questions of human life.

The Presence of Salvation as the Center of Pauline Theology

In view of the great intellectual challenges and turbulent history of early Christianity, Paul could survive only because he made the basis, beginning point, and center of his thought and life *an unshakable theological conviction: the eschatological presence of salvation from God in Jesus Christ*. The zealous Pharisee was overwhelmed by the experience and insight that in the crucified and risen Jesus Christ, who was soon to return from heaven, God had put into effect his ultimate purpose for the salvation of the whole world. God himself brought about the turn of the ages; God brought a new reality into being, in which the world, and the situation of human beings in the world, appeared in a different light. A completely unexpected, singular event fundamentally changed Paul's thinking and his life. Paul was set the

2. On Paul's education, cf. Tor Vegge, *Paulus und das antike Schulwesen: Schule und Bildung des Paulus* (BZNW 134; Berlin: de Gruyter, 2006), 194: "In regard to Paul's background and education, in this investigation it is regarded as probable that Paul, as son of a Roman citizen, in his hometown received a literary education of the general Greek-Hellenistic type. With a speech teacher, he would have worked through the *Progymnasmata* and would have become familiar with philosophical teaching and ethos."

3. It is no accident that in the most recent times it is precisely the philosophers who have rediscovered Paul; cf. Jacob Taubes and Aleida Assmann, *The Political Theology of Paul* (Cultural Memory in the Present; Stanford, CA: Stanford University Press, 2004); Alain Badiou, *Saint Paul: The Foundation of Universalism* (Cultural Memory in the Present; trans. Ray Brassier; Stanford, CA: Stanford University Press, 2003); Giorgio Agamben, *Die Zeit, die bleibt: Ein Kommentar zum Römerbrief* (Frankfurt: Suhrkamp, 2006).

task of interpreting afresh, from the perspective of the Christ event, the history of the world and God's saving activity within it—God's acts in the past, present, and future, and his own role in God's plan. Pauline theology is thus equally an appropriation of the new and an interpretation of the past. Paul drafted an eschatological scenario: its foundation is God's saving will, its decisive act is the resurrection and parousia of Jesus Christ, its determining power is the Holy Spirit, its present goal is the participation of believers in the new being, and its final goal is transformation into spiritual existence with God. Since the resurrection of Jesus Christ, the Spirit of God is again at work in the world, and baptized Christians are delivered from sin and live in a qualitatively new relationship with God and the Lord Jesus Christ. The election of Christians and their call to be participants in the gospel, which are manifest in their baptism and reception of the Spirit, are effective until the end, so that the present experience of salvation and future hope modulate into each other as one reality.[4] It is not merely a new understanding of reality; the new reality itself has, in a full sense, already begun! Believers thus already participate in a universal process of transformation that began with the resurrection of Jesus Christ from the dead, continues in the present power and saving work of the Spirit, and will end with the transformation of the whole creation into the glory of God.[5] Pauline theology as a whole is stamped with the idea of the presence of salvation.

6.1 Theology

Jewish monotheism is the basis of Pauline thought, for the only real God is the one, true God of Israel who acts in history.[6] Paul's theology per se is in direct continuity with the fundamental Jewish affirmation: God is one, the creator, the Lord who will bring his creative purpose to completion. At the same time, Christology effects a basic change in Paul's theology, for Paul proclaims a christological monotheism.

4. Daniel G. Powers, *Salvation through Participation: An Examination of the Notion of the Believers' Corporate Unity with Christ in Early Christian Soteriology* (CBET 29; Louvain: Peeters, 2001), 234: "Paul even describes the believers' eschatological resurrection as a participation in Jesus's resurrection."

5. Cf. Albert Schweitzer, *The Mysticism of Paul the Apostle* (trans. William Montgomery; London: Adam & Charles Black, 1931), 117: "The peculiarity of the Pauline mysticism is precisely that being-in-Christ is not a subjective experience brought about by a special effort of faith on the part of the believer, but something which happens, in him as in others, at baptism."

6. The linguistic data already signals the importance of the theme, for in the undisputed Pauline letters ὁ θεός appears 430 times; 1 Thess., 36 times; 1 Cor., 106 times; 2 Cor., 79 times; Gal., 31 times; Rom., 153 times; Phil., 23 times; Philem., 2 times.

6.1.1 The One True God, the Creator

The unity and uniqueness of God are fundamental convictions of Jewish faith;[7] there is only one God, beside whom there is no other (Deut. 6:4b LXX, "Hear, O Israel: The Lord is our God, the Lord alone!"; cf., e.g., Isa. 44:6; Jer. 10:10; 2 Kings 5:15; 19:19). In *Let. Aris.* 132, a didactic section about the nature of God begins with the statement "that God is one, that his power is shown in everything, every place being filled with his sovereignty." In sharp contrast to the polytheism of antiquity, Philo emphasizes, "Let us, then, engrave this deep in our hearts as the first and most sacred of commandments, to acknowledge and honor one God who is above all, and let the idea that gods are many never even reach the ears of the man whose rule of life is to seek truth in purity and guilelessness."[8] For Paul, the unity of God is the intellectual and practical foundation of all his thinking. Granted, numerous so-called gods exist in heaven and on earth (cf. 1 Cor. 8:5; 10:20), but "for us there is one God, the Father, from whom are all things and for whom we exist" (1 Cor. 8:6a). The Christians in Thessalonica converted from idols to serve the one true God (1 Thess. 1:9–10), and Paul writes programmatically to the Roman church, "God is one; and he will justify the circumcised on the ground of faith and the uncircumcised through that same faith" (Rom. 3:30). The fundamental criterion for distinguishing God, the law, Moses, and the angels in Gal. 3:19–20 is the creedal statement "God is one" (ὁ δὲ θεὸς εἷς ἐστιν). The knowledge of God's unity also has ethical dimensions for Paul, for in the dispute about eating meat sacrificed to idols, the fundamental principle is "we know that 'no idol in the world really exists,' and that 'there is no God but one'" (1 Cor. 8:4).

God's deity is manifest first of all in his *acting as creator*. For Paul, the whole world is God's creation (1 Cor. 8:6; 10:26),[9] and the creator God of Genesis is none other than the one who acts in Jesus Christ and in Christian believers (2 Cor. 4:6). God "calls into existence things that do not exist,"[10] "gives life to

7. On the development of monotheism in the history of Israelite religion, cf. Albani, *Der eine Gott*; Schrage, *Unterwegs zur Einzigkeit*, 4–35; Walther Eichrodt, *Theology of the Old Testament* (OTL; Philadelphia: Westminster, 1967), 1:220–27. Outsiders too regard monotheism as the distinctive aspect of Judaism; thus Tacitus emphasizes, "The Jews have purely mental conceptions of Deity, as one in essence" (*Hist.* 5.5.4).

8. Philo, *Decalogue* 65; cf. also Josephus, *Ant.* 3.91. To be sure, pagan philosophers also ridiculed the many gods of antiquity; cf. Cicero, *Nat. d.* 1.81–84.

9. On creation and cosmos in Pauline thought, cf. G. Baumbach, "Die Schöpfung in der Theologie des Paulus," *Kairos* 21 (1979): 196–205; Heinrich Schlier, *Grundzüge einer paulinischen Theologie* (Freiburg: Herder, 1978), 55–63; Jörg Baumgarten, *Paulus und die Apokalyptik: Die Auslegung apokalyptischer Überlieferungen in den echten Paulusbriefen* (WMANT 44; Neukirchen-Vluyn: Neukirchener Verlag, 1975), 159–79; Dunn, *Theology of Paul*, 38–43.

10. Of course, the idea that God is the father and creator of the world/universe is also found in the Greco-Roman tradition; cf. Plato, *Tim.* 28c; Cicero, *Nat. d.* 1.30.

the dead" (Rom. 4:17), and is the "Father" of the world (1 Cor. 8:6; Phil. 2:11). Only about this God can it be said, "For from him and through him and to him are all things" (Rom. 11:36a). Prior to the world and history stands God, "who is over all" (Rom. 9:5) and of whom it is said that at the end he will be "all in all" (1 Cor. 15:28). All things are God's creation, and they remain so even when human beings, by worshiping idols, flee the destiny for which they were created.[11] God allows himself to be perceived in his created works (Rom. 1:20, 25), but even though human beings knew about God, "they did not honor him as God or give thanks to him, but they became futile in their thinking, and their senseless minds were darkened" (Rom. 1:21). Again and again human beings are drawn away to worship the powers who by their very nature are not gods (Gal. 4:8). Despite this compulsion to create gods for themselves or to set themselves in God's place, human beings (and the world) remain God's creation. God the creator still orders human life by providing political (Rom. 13:1–7) and social (1 Cor. 7) structures. Believers are called to discern and follow the will of God (1 Thess. 4:3; Rom. 12:1). As Lord of history, God guides its events and determines the time of salvation (Gal. 4:4), and as Judge, God has the last word on human destiny (Rom. 2:5ff.; 3:5, 19).

Believers need have no fear of the last judgment, for the apostle is sure "that neither death, nor life, nor angels, nor rulers, nor things present, nor things to come, nor powers, nor height, nor depth, nor anything else in all creation, will be able to separate us from the love of God in Christ Jesus our Lord" (Rom. 8:38–39). Not only do creation and humanity have the same origin; their future destiny is also bound together. For Paul, protology and eschatology, universal history and individual history correspond to each other because God is the source and goal of all that is (cf. Rom. 8:18ff.). Everything comes from God, everything is sustained in existence by God, and everything is on its way to God. The creator God shows his life-giving power in the resurrection of Jesus Christ, in which he will also grant believers participation: "If the Spirit of him who raised Jesus from the dead dwells in you, he who raised Christ from the dead will give life to your mortal bodies also through his Spirit that dwells in you" (Rom. 8:11).

6.1.2 The Father of Jesus Christ

In Paul's thought, theology is not replaced by Christology; rather, the question of Jesus's identity and status is answered in terms of God's act.[12] God's act in and through Jesus Christ is the foundation of Christology. God sent Jesus Christ (Gal. 4:4–5; Rom. 8:3–4), God delivered him over to death, and God

11. Becker, *Paul*, 381.

12. Cf. Schrage, *Unterwegs zur Einzigkeit*, 200: "Jesus Christ can only be understood from the dual perspective 'from God and to God.'"

raised him from the dead (Rom. 4:25; 8:32). Through Christ, God reconciled the world (2 Cor. 5:18–19) and justifies those who believe (Rom. 5:1–11).[13] The church is challenged to orient its life to God in Christ Jesus (Rom. 6:11). Jesus Christ demonstrated his own obedience to God (Phil. 2:8; Rom. 5:19). *The* distinguishing characteristic of the God proclaimed by Paul is that God raised Jesus Christ from the dead (cf. 1 Thess. 1:10; 4:14; 1 Cor. 15:12–19). God is the source of all χάρις (grace; Rom. 1:7; 3:24; 1 Cor. 15:10) and the goal of redemptive history (1 Cor. 15:20–28). Behind the Christ event stands the saving will of God, and God alone, with effective power. At the same time, however, the act of God is the expression of the unique dignity and office of Jesus Christ. Paul does not reflect on the relation of God to Jesus Christ in the conceptual-ontological categories of later doctrinal developments, but two lines of thought are nonetheless obvious. On the one hand, there is a clear tendency toward *subordination* in Pauline Christology. Thus in 1 Cor. 11:3 Paul presupposes a graduated scale:[14] "Christ is the head of every man, and the husband is the head of his wife, and God is the head of Christ." A subordination on the part of Christ is also indicated in 1 Cor. 3:23 (you belong to Christ, and Christ belongs to God)[15] and 15:28 (the Son himself will also be subjected to the one who put all things in subjection under him, so that God may be all in all). Especially 1 Cor. 15:23–28 speaks of a temporal limitation to the rule of Christ and thus clearly signals the subordination of the Son to the Father. In Phil. 2:8–9 the obedience of the Son to the Father is the presupposition for his exaltation as Lord. At the same time, the Pauline formulations can be seen as the beginnings of thinking of God and Christ as *equals*. In Phil. 2:6 the preexistent one is termed ἴσα θεῷ (equal with God), and in Rom. 9:5 Paul apparently identifies the Christ descended from Israel (Χριστὸς κατὰ σάρκα) with God ("from them is traced the human ancestry of the Messiah, who is God over all; may he be praised forever!").[16]

The Mediator

Paul can obviously portray without any sense of inconsistency the relation of Jesus Christ to God in terms of subordination, coordination, or belonging to the same category. These lines converge and meet in the role of mediator.

13. On διὰ Χριστοῦ in Paul, cf. Wilhelm Thüsing, *Gott und Christus in der paulinischen Soteriologie* (3rd ed.; Münster: Aschendorff, 1986), 164–237.

14. For analysis, see ibid., 20–29.

15. Cf. ibid., 10–20.

16. The translation given above [my rendering of Schnelle's German—MEB] is what both corresponds most closely to the Greek syntax and is the most difficult option in terms of content; cf. H.-C. Kammler, "Die Prädikation Jesu Christi als 'Gott' und die paulinische Christologie," *ZNW* 94 (2003): 164–80. On the pro and con of this translation, cf. Ulrich Wilckens, *Der Brief an die Römer* (Neukirchener-Vluyn: Neukirchener Verlag, 1978), 2:189. For the issue in general, cf. Raymond E. Brown, *Jesus: God and Man* (Modern Biblical Reflections; New York: Macmillan, 1967).

Just as Jesus Christ is the *mediator of creation*, so he is the *mediator of salvation*. The pre-Pauline tradition of 1 Cor. 8:6[17] develops this line of thought by boldly interrelating God's history with the history of Jesus Christ: "Yet for us there is one God, the Father, from whom are all things and for whom we exist, and one Lord, Jesus Christ, through whom are all things and through whom we exist." This text reflects the relation of theology proper and Christology within a monotheistic framework; the predication that God is εἷς (one) applies not only to the Father but at the same time to the Lord Jesus Christ. This does not mean splitting the one God into two gods; rather, the uniqueness of God reveals itself only in the unique saving work of Jesus Christ.[18] Regarding origin and essential being, Christ belongs entirely on the side of God; there is no competition between the one God and the one Lord. Nevertheless, the one Lord remains subordinate to the one God, for the creator God is the Father of the Lord Jesus Christ. The universe owes its existence to the one God alone; only God is the origin of all that is. The Kyrios is the preexistent mediator of creation; the one God creates "all things" through the one Lord. The whole creation is ineradicably bound to Jesus by the will of God: "Therefore God also highly exalted him and gave him the name that is above every name, so that at the name of Jesus every knee should bend, in heaven and on earth and under the earth, and every tongue should confess that Jesus Christ is Lord, to the glory of God the Father" (Phil. 2:9–11). It corresponds to the saving will of God for his creation that powers, authorities, and human beings acknowledge Jesus Christ as mediator of both creation and salvation. The preexistent Christ stands at the beginning of creation and, as the Resurrected One, is the prototype of the new creation. As the "image of God" (2 Cor. 4:4, εἰκὼν τοῦ θεοῦ), Jesus Christ participates in the very being of God; the Son is the revelation of the true being of the Father. Christ takes up the believers into a historical process, at the end of which stands their own transformation; their destiny is to "be conformed to the image of his Son, in order that he might be the firstborn within a large family" (Rom. 8:29). The statements about the role of Jesus Christ as mediator of creation are indebted to the experience of him as mediator of salvation; that is, protology points to soteriology from

17. In addition to the standard commentaries, for interpretation see Thüsing, *Paulinischen Soteriologie*, 225–32; Otfried Hofius, "Christus als Schöpfungsmittler und Erlösungsmittler: Das Bekenntnis 1Kor 8,6 im Kontext der paulinischen Theologie," in *Paulinische Christologie: Exegetische Beiträge; Hans Hübner zum 70. Geburtstag* (ed. Udo Schnelle et al.; Göttingen: Vandenhoeck & Ruprecht, 2000), 47–58.

18. Cf. Thüsing, *Neutestamentlichen Theologien*, 3:374: "The uniqueness of the Kyrios is specifically different than the uniqueness of God—but, nevertheless, it is the uniqueness of the Kyrios that constitutes the uniqueness of God (thus theologically, by incorporating the Crucified One into the heart of the divine mystery). Through the uniqueness of the Lord Jesus Christ his Son, God wills to realize his own uniqueness as the One who acts in creation and new creation."

the very beginning. Redemption is no chance event but was built into creation from the foundation of the universe.[19]

Paul's understanding of the relation of Jesus Christ to God can best be expressed by saying that *they belong to the same category*.[20] Jesus Christ is at the same time subordinate to the Father and fully incorporated into his essence and status. This dynamic may be shifted neither in the direction of preserving a presumed "pure" monotheism nor toward using the New Testament to establish the ontological doctrinal categories of the later church. Rather, this dynamic is the appropriate way to understand the actual situation, namely, that the post-Easter process of meaning-formation could express the reality of the Christ event only as a paradox that permits no unilinear solutions: *the one God has fully revealed himself once and for all in the one human being Jesus of Nazareth; "revealed" here refers to an event that cannot be "thought up," but can only be "opened up" from the other side.*

How are the continuity and discontinuity of Pauline theology (i.e., theology proper) and Christology with Judaism to be determined? In the first place, we can speak of continuity regarding several points:

1. Paul chooses as the beginning point of his theology not the life and ministry of Jesus of Nazareth, but God's act through him in the cross and resurrection, and so this initial principle already points to the primacy of theology.
2. Paul affirms continuity in God's own acts. The concept of preexistence (cf. 1 Cor. 8:6; 10:4; Gal. 4:4; Rom. 8:3; Phil. 2:6),[21] like the reflections on the history of God's promise in Gal. 3:15–18 and Rom. 4 and 9–11, shows that from the beginning Paul thinks of the history of God's mighty acts as the history of Jesus Christ. Paul interprets the history of Israel consistently from the perspective of faith in Jesus Christ and as finding its goal in him—and theologically he must do so.[22] Only so can he show the selfhood of God present in his acts; only in this way can

19. Cf. Hofius, "Christus als Schöpfungsmittler und Erlösungsmittler," 56.

20. Cf. Thüsing, *Paulinischen Soteriologie*, 258: "The Pauline Christocentrism is inherently oriented to God because Paul's Christology is already theocentric; and from this perspective, the orientation of his Christocentrism to God is just as thoroughly consistent as is Christ's κυριότης ['lordship'] and his work in the Spirit."

21. On Paul's concept of preexistence, cf. Habermann, *Präexistenzaussagen*, 91–223; Lips, *Weisheitliche Traditionen*, 290–317; Martin Hengel, "Präexistenz bei Paulus?" in *Jesus Christus als die Mitte der Schrift: Studien zur Hermeneutik des Evangeliums* (ed. Christof Landmesser et al.; BZNW 86; Berlin: de Gruyter, 1997), 479–517; Thomas Söding, "Gottes Sohn von Anfang an: Zur Präexistenzchristologie bei Paulus und den Deuteropaulinen," in *Gottes ewiger Sohn: Die Präexistenz Christi* (ed. Rudolf Laufen; Paderborn: Schöningh, 1997), 57–93.

22. Contra Paul-Gerhard Klumbies, *Die Rede von Gott bei Paulus in ihrem zeitgeschichtlichen Kontext* (Göttingen: Vandenhoeck & Ruprecht, 1992), 213: "For Paul, God is not to be defined in a way that transcends his acts in the history of Israel."

he avoid splitting the unified concept of God and history. Paul would not and could not question the identity of the God of Israel with the Father of Jesus Christ. It was impossible for him to separate the saving act of God in Jesus Christ from the history of Israel. There is only one divine history, which is determined from the beginning by the role of Jesus Christ as mediator of both creation and salvation.

3. In terms of the history of tradition, Paul takes up ideas from ancient Judaism into his understanding of the relation of God and Jesus Christ, in the process wrenching the framework of the traditional concepts to accommodate the new meaning—since in the Jewish frame of reference it was utterly impossible to think of one who had died on a cross to be revered as divine.

While the concept of God vouches for the continuity to Judaism, Christology warps and breaks open every category of unity and provides the basis for the theological and thus also the historical discontinuity between developing early Christianity and Judaism.[23] Paul's christological monotheism changes and goes beyond fundamental Jewish concepts. Since, from the very beginning, the history of the crucified Jesus Christ was understood as the authentic history of God, a new image and understanding of God were formed: God is God in the way he has revealed himself in Jesus Christ.[24] The crucified God of Paul is incompatible with the God of the Old Testament. The Old Testament remains silent about Jesus Christ, even if by daring exegesis Paul attempts to break this silence and have the Old Testament speak as a Christian book. If God has made the ultimate revelation of himself in the contingent event of the cross and resurrection, then the idea of a continuity in the history of salvation and election that is oriented to belonging to the elect people of God, to the land, to the Torah or the covenant, is no longer sustainable. Paul does not want to draw this conclusion, indeed he cannot do so; so he attempts to avoid doing so by redefining the people of God (see below, §6.7.1). For Jews and strict Jewish Christians, such a redefinition was unacceptable because it would mean a thoroughgoing reinterpretation of their own salvation history. In terms of God's saving act, Jewish particularism and early Christian universalism could not both be true at the same time—the two symbolic universes were incompatible.[25] Thus, already for Paul, despite all

23. One can hardly claim, however, as does Klumbies, ibid., 252, that Paul "incidentally develops a fundamentally new formulation of theo-logical thought."

24. The comment of Hofius, "Christus als Schöpfungsmittler und Erlösungsmittler," 58, is on target: "For it is *one thing* to speak of God's 'Wisdom' or 'Logos' as the highest powers of God, whether as hypostatizations or personifications, and to ascribe a cosmological or soteriological function to them but *an entirely different thing* to make these statements about a historical human being, and one who had been crucified at that!"

25. Differently N. Elliott, "Paul and the Politics of Empire," in *Paul and Politics: Ekklesia, Israel, Imperium, Interpretation: Essays in Honor of Krister Stendahl* (ed. Richard A. Horsley; Harrisburg, PA: Trinity, 2000), 19ff., who disputes the contrast between Christian universalism

reassurances to the contrary, Christology is the explosive charge that demolished the initial unity between Christian believers and Judaism.

6.1.3 The God Who Acts in Election and Rejection

With sovereign, ineluctable freedom, God encounters human beings as the one who calls and elects but also as the one who rejects.[26] Paul interprets his own history in these categories when he says that it pleased God "who had set me apart before I was born and called me through his grace . . . to reveal his Son to me" (Gal. 1:15–16). The apostle knows that he, like his churches, has been included in the divine history of election, a history that began with Abraham, reached its goal in the Christ event, and will find its fulfillment in the transformation of believers into the heavenly reality at the parousia. Paul already has this awareness when he develops his theology of election in his first letter: the Thessalonian Christians should understand their call as God's gracious choice in the eschatological era (1 Thess. 1:4; 2:12; 5:24), because they have turned from idols to the one true God (1:9). The Thessalonians can be confident: "For God has destined us not for wrath but for obtaining salvation through our Lord Jesus Christ" (5:9). God is not bound by human standards but chooses those who by human standards are foolish, weak, lowly, and despised (1 Cor. 1:27–28). According to God's will, salvation comes through the foolishness of the message of the cross, not through human wisdom (1 Cor. 1:18ff.), and humanity is divided into the two categories of those who are being saved and those who are lost (2 Cor. 2:15–16).

It is no accident that Paul's thinking on election and rejection find their culmination in Rom. 9–11. They are located here as the consistent development of the Pauline idea of freedom, the problem of Israel's role, and the doctrine of justification as these are elaborated in the Letter to the Romans. The apostle's reflections on God's eschatological determination of believers and the cosmos in Rom. 8:18ff. are already going in the direction of the complex of problems involving predestination: "And those whom he predestined he also called; and those whom he called he also justified; and those whom he justified he also

---

and Jewish particularism with the argument that Paul's universalism derives from his Jewish heritage.

26. For an analysis of Paul's statements about predestination, see Ulrich Luz, *Das Geschichtsverständnis des Paulus* (BEvT 49; Munich: Kaiser, 1968), 227–64; Gerhard Maier, *Mensch und freier Wille: Nach der jüdischen Religionsparteien zwischen Ben Sira und Paulus* (WUNT 12; Tübingen: Mohr, 1971), 351–400; Bernhard Mayer, *Unter Gottes Heilsratschluss; Prädestinationsaussagen bei Paulus* (FzB 15; Würzburg: Echter Verlag, 1974); Günter Röhser, *Prädestination und Verstockung: Untersuchungen zur frühjüdischen, paulinischen und johanneischen Theologie* (Tübingen: Francke, 1994), 113–75.

glorified" (Rom. 8:30). In Rom. 9–11 Paul advocates a double predestination.[27] God calls whom he wills and rejects whom he wills (cf. Rom. 9:16, 18; 2 Cor. 2:15). God's chosen people Israel suffers defeat and is again reestablished; the Gentiles come to share in salvation, but God can also remove this new branch from the olive tree (Rom. 11:17–24). The predestinarian statements "express the fact that the decision of faith does not, like other decisions, go back to this-worldly motives of any sort whatever—that, on the contrary, such motives lose all power of motivation in the presence of the encountered proclamation. . . . At the same time, this means that faith cannot appeal to itself to establish its own decision."[28] The Pauline statements about predestination are by no means exhausted, however, by this interpretation centered on the believing life of individuals. They are primarily theological affirmations that communicate a reality revealed by God in Scripture. God the creator owns the ineluctable freedom to choose and reject. Free will is thus for Paul predicated exclusively of God. The infinite distinction between creator and creature is the basis for the specific perspective from which Paul thinks of human beings. God meets human beings as the one who calls; "to be human is to be called and addressed by God."[29] Christian existence is grounded in the call of God. It is thus something not at the individual human being's own disposal but rather can be appropriated only by hearing. Ὁ καλέσας ἡμᾶς (the one who called us) becomes in Paul a central predicate of God (cf. 1 Thess. 2:12; 5:24; Gal. 1:6; 5:8). God encounters the individual human being as the calling "I," whose will is made known in the Scripture.[30] Regarding salvation, individual human beings can understand themselves only as ones who receive, who are given a gift. As creatures, they are fundamentally incapable of devising and executing salvation and meaning. If human beings want to understand and assess their own situation appropriately and realistically, they must acknowledge and take seriously their creatureliness, which means knowing their limits. It is not the creature, but only the Creator, who makes decisions about salvation and damnation.

What function do the statements about predestination have in the structure of Paul's thought as a whole? They were givens within the apostle's worldview, but he activated them with differing degrees of intensity. On the one hand, Paul always thinks within a broad framework that presupposes salvation, rejection, and judgment; on the other hand, only in Rom. 9–11 does he plumb the argumentative depths of this thematic complex. The particular conversa-

27. Emphatically Maier, *Mensch und freier Wille*, 356–57; differently Röhser, *Prädestination*, 171 et passim, arguing that for Paul, God's will and human decision are not mutually exclusive alternatives.

28. Bultmann, *Theology of the New Testament*, 1:330. [The second statement, though in the German text, was not included in the standard English translation.—MEB]

29. Hans Hübner, *Gottes Ich und Israel: Zum Schriftgebrauch des Paulus in Römer 9–11* (Göttingen: Vandenhoeck & Ruprecht, 1984), 31–32.

30. Ibid., 31–35.

tional situation of Romans requires that he provide an extensive discussion of predestination. Paul's aim is to preserve the freedom of God; this is why he specifically emphasizes a fundamental theological insight: God's act is independent of human deeds or presuppositions, and God's will always precedes our own decision. God's electing grace is the same as God's justifying grace. Both the exclusive doctrine of justification and the statements about predestination are in the service of preserving God's freedom and the character of salvation as a gift not at human disposal.[31] This goal of Paul's argument, together with the observation that the statements about predestination in Rom. 9–11 emerge as a function of the exclusive doctrine of justification and the Israel thematic, should be a warning against forcing them into a firmly structured, static doctrine of predestination. At the same time, against tendencies toward relativizing and leveling out Paul's theology, it is nonetheless true that Paul advocates a double predestination. This understanding, which understands free will regarding salvation as a predicate of God, not something belonging to human beings, is organically integrated into Paul's theology as a whole and necessarily arises from it. Salvation and damnation are equally grounded in the ineluctable decision of God (differently James 1:13–15). They do not, however, stand alongside each other having the same rank, for God's universal saving will has been revealed in the gospel of Jesus Christ,[32] whereas God's no is a mystery withdrawn from human knowledge.

6.1.4 God's Revelation in the Gospel

God's revelation is fulfilled in the εὐαγγέλιον (gospel),[33] which with regard to its origin and authority is the εὐαγγέλιον τοῦ θεοῦ (the gospel of God, 1 Thess. 2:2, 8–9; 2 Cor. 11:7; Rom. 1:1; 15:1). Ἐυαγγέλιον thus means much more than "good news"; it is an effective means by which salvation is communicated, a faith-generating event and a faith-effecting power, proceeding from God in the power of the Spirit, its goal being the salvation of human beings (cf. 1 Thess. 1:5; 1 Cor. 4:20; Rom. 1:16–17). The gospel was not transmitted to Paul by human agents but was revealed to him directly by God through the appearance of Jesus Christ (cf. Gal. 1:11ff.; 2 Cor. 4:1–6; Rom. 1:1–5). Paul

31. Luz, *Geschichtsverständnis*, 249: "Paul's statements about predestination are intended to be statements about God alone, not statements about human decisions and history."

32. God's yes is specifically emphasized by Michael Theobald, *Der Römerbrief* (Darmstadt: Wissenschaftliche Buchgesellschaft, 2000), 276: "The dialectic of election and rejection, call and hardening in Rom. 9–11 are eschatologically overruled by the confession of 11:32 to the God who 'has imprisoned *all* in disobedience so that he may be merciful to *all*.'"

33. Cf. Georg Strecker, "Das Evangelium Jesu Christi," in *Eschaton und Historie: Aufsätze* (ed. Georg Strecker; Göttingen: Vandenhoeck & Ruprecht, 1979), 183–228; Stuhlmacher, *Biblische Theologie*, 1:311–48; Helmut Merklein, "Zum Verständnis des paulinischen Begriffs 'Evangelium,'" in *Studien zu Jesus und Paulus* (2 vols.; WUNT 43, 105; Tübingen: Mohr, 1987–98), 1:279–95; Dunn, *Theology of Paul*, 163–81; Koch, *Schrift als Zeuge*, 322–53.

is permitted to serve the gospel and must do so, for the decision is not at his own disposal (cf. Rom. 15:16). Granted, the gospel is mediated through the human word of the apostle, but it cannot be reduced to that; it is the word of God that encounters his hearers in his own preaching (cf. 1 Thess. 2:13; 2 Cor. 4:4–6; 5:20). Paul stands under the compulsion of the gospel itself, for "an obligation is laid on me, and woe to me if I do not proclaim the gospel" (1 Cor. 9:16). For Paul, God's initiating the proclamation of the gospel is itself part of God's saving work, which precedes the faith and salvation experience of the church of Jesus Christ.[34] As an eschatological event, the gospel must be proclaimed to the whole world (cf. 2 Cor. 10:16 and Rom. 10:15–16, which take up Isa. 52:7 LXX), for it aims for the salvation of humanity and thus has a soteriological quality (cf. 2 Cor. 4:3–4). The church in Corinth was begotten by the gospel (1 Cor. 4:15); the service of the gospel unites Paul and his churches (2 Cor. 8:18; Philem. 13); Paul struggles for the gospel (cf. Gal. 1:6ff.; Phil. 1:7; 2:22; 4:3) and endures everything rather than place an obstacle in the way of the gospel of Christ (1 Cor. 9:12). His sole concern is to be a participant in the saving power of the gospel: "I do it all for the sake of the gospel, so that I may share in its blessings" (1 Cor. 9:23).

Regarding its content, the gospel is the εὐαγγέλιον τοῦ Χριστοῦ (cf. 1 Thess. 3:2; 1 Cor. 9:12; 2 Cor. 2:12; 9:13; 10:14; Gal. 1:7; Rom. 15:19; Phil. 1:27). This gospel has a very definite shape and a clearly determined content; Paul therefore fights mightily against anyone who preaches a different gospel. According to Paul, the content of the gospel (cf. 1 Thess. 1:9–10; 1 Cor. 15:3–5; 2 Cor. 4:4; Rom. 1:3b–4a) can be described as follows: From the very beginning, God intended to save the world through Christ (cf. 1 Cor. 2:7; Rom. 16:25); God announced this saving will through the prophets (cf. Rom. 1:2; 16:26) and had it witnessed through the Scripture (cf. 1 Cor. 15:3–4; Gal. 3:8).[35] When the time was fulfilled, God sent his Son, who achieved the salvation of the world and humanity by his death on the cross and his resurrection (cf. Gal. 4:4–5; Rom. 1:3–4; 15:8; 2 Cor. 1:20). Until the sending of the Son, both Jews and Gentiles lived unaware of the true will of God, which is now proclaimed in the gospel by Paul, called by God to be apostle to the Gentiles. Thus, for Paul the ultimate saving will of God in Jesus Christ is summarized in the gospel, the message of the crucified Son of God (cf. 1 Cor. 1:17).[36] In the suffering and resurrection of his Son, God has made known his saving will, and he has entrusted the proclamation of this saving event to his apostles. The gospel definitively controls the preaching of the apostle and reveals itself as the eschatological saving power of God. Directly addressed to humanity (2 Cor. 5:20, "Be reconciled to God!"), the gospel is the active and effective communication of salvation from God;

34. Stuhlmacher, *Biblische Theologie*, 1:315.

35. On this point cf. Dunn, *Theology of Paul*, 169–73.

36. Merklein, "Verständnis des paulinischen 'Evangelium,'" 291–93.

it is equally valid for Jews and Gentiles when they acknowledge Jesus Christ as Savior. The gospel is "the power of God for salvation to everyone who has faith" (Rom. 1:16). For Paul, the proclamation of the gospel is inseparably related to the judgment: "According to my gospel, God, through Jesus Christ, will judge the secret thoughts of all" (Rom. 2:16). Salvation and judgment cannot be separated in Paul's thought. Because the gospel is the message of salvation, to reject it cannot be without consequences, just as the acceptance of it has consequences. Therefore in the gospel Jesus Christ appears not only as Savior but also as judge. At the same time, it is also clear that for Paul the gospel is above all a δύναμις θεοῦ that saves those who accept in faith the saving message of the crucified and risen Jesus Christ.

The Pauline churches appropriated the term εὐαγγέλιον in a particular cultural setting. The verb εὐαγγελίζομαι derives from a predominantly Old Testament and Jewish background.[37] It appears in the Septuagint as well as the writings of ancient Judaism, where it must be translated "to announce eschatological salvation." Εὐαγγελίζομαι in the religious sense is also documented in Hellenistic literature (cf. Philostratus, *Vit. Apoll.* 1.28; Philo, *Embassy* 18, 231). The substantive εὐαγγέλια is used in the Septuagint without any recognizable theological content,[38] in contrast to the central role the word plays in the *ruler cult*. Thus, in the Priene calendar inscription (9 BCE), the birthday of Augustus is celebrated in the following words: "The birthday of the god Augustus was the beginning for the world of the good tidings [εὐαγγελίων]."[39] Josephus relates how the εὐαγγέλια of Vespasian's promotion to the emperor's office was celebrated with sacrifices: "Quicker than thought, rumor spread the news of the new emperor in the east. Every city kept festival for the good news and offered sacrifices on his behalf."[40] The ascension of Drusilla and Claudius to heaven, the prelude to their deification, is ironically described by Seneca as "good news."[41] In first-century linguistic usage, the terms εὐαγγέλιον/εὐαγγελίζομαι were closely related to emperor worship[42] and thus had politico-religious overtones. The early churches were quite aware of these ideas when they adopted the gospel terminology from their cultural environs, but at the same time, by using the singular εὐαγγέλιον they fundamentally distinguished

37. The prehistory of the terms εὐαγγέλιον and εὐαγγελίζομαι in the Old Testament and Judaism is comprehensively presented by Peter Stuhlmacher, *Das paulinische Evangelium* (FRLANT 95; Göttingen: Vandenhoeck & Ruprecht, 1968), 109ff.

38. The singular εὐαγγέλιον is not found in the Septuagint, and the plural εὐαγγέλια only in 2 Sam. 4:10; cf. also ἡ εὐαγγελία in 2 Sam. 18:20, 22, 25, 27; 2 Kings 7:9. Gerhard Friedrich, "εὐαγγέλιον," *TDNT* 2:725, appropriately comments: "The NT use of εὐαγγέλιον does not derive from the LXX."

39. Cf. *NW* 2.1:6–9 and Boring, *Hellenistic Commentary* §§225–26.

40. Cf. Josephus, *JW* 4.618; cf. also 4.656 (*NW* 2.1:9–10).

41. Cf. Seneca, *Apocol.* 1.3. Seneca satirizes the *apotheosis* of Claudius as his *apocolocyntosis* (pumpkinification).

42. Cf. Strecker, "Evangelium Jesu Christi," 188–92.

their usage from the plural εὐαγγέλια used in their environment. Paul's usage too can be seen within the framework of this early Christian strategy, in which the culture's vocabulary was adopted only to be turned against it: the true and exclusive good news is the message of the cross and resurrection. It is not the advent of the emperor that saves but the Son of God who comes from heaven (cf. 1 Thess. 1:9–10).

The variety inherent in Paul's proclamation of the gospel and the very limited function of εὐαγγέλιον in Galatians, Romans, and Philippians in a critique of the law show that the Pauline gospel can by no means be understood as fundamentally a "gospel of freedom from the law" from the very beginning.[43] The issue of the law is a secondary theme within the gospel concept. The gospel that proceeds from God, at its core, is filled with christological-soteriological and eschatological content:[44] the event of Jesus's death and resurrection is, as such, the saving event (cf. 1 Cor. 15:3b–5) that determines the present and future of all humanity. The gospel is the power of God calling to salvation, a power that wants to liberate and save a world enslaved under the power of sin. God speaks in the gospel and defines himself through the gospel as the one who loves and saves. The gospel is the presence of the powerful God, the God who wants to lead human beings to faith.

6.1.5 The New Image of God

God is not directly accessible but can be thought of only in images. The ancient world was filled with different sorts of imagery for the divine (cf. Acts 17:16). Why, in a truly multireligious society, did both Jews and Gentiles turn to the image of God presented by early Christianity? An essential reason was its monotheism, which was already the basis for antiquity's fascination with Judaism. The multiplicity of gods and the ways they were portrayed in the Greco-Roman world[45] obviously suffered a loss of plausibility, reflected in Cicero's comment: "The gods have as many names as mankind has languages."[46] Because the throng of gods could hardly be numbered, the question naturally arose as to which gods should be worshiped and in what ways.[47] The philosopher thus asks, "Then, if the traditional gods whom we worship are really divine, what reason can you give why we should not include Isis and Osiris in

43. Contra Ferdinand Hahn, "Gibt es eine Entwicklung in den Aussagen über die Rechtfertigung bei Paulus?" *EvT* 53 (1993): 344, who states: "The essence of the gospel, in terms of content and effect, is established with the help of the theme of justification."

44. Cf. Strecker, "Evangelium Jesu Christi," 225; Merklein, "Verständnis des paulinischen 'Evangelium,'" 286.

45. On the early period of Greek religion, cf. Werner Wilhelm Jaeger, *Die Theologie der frühen griechischen Denker* (Darmstadt: Wissenschaftliche Buchgesellschaft, 1964).

46. Cicero, *Nat. d.* 1.84.

47. Cf. Cicero, *Nat. d.* 3.40–60.

the same category? And if we do so, why should we repudiate the gods of the barbarians? We shall therefore have to admit to the list of the gods oxen and horses, ibises, hawks, asps, crocodiles, fishes, dogs, wolves, cats, and many beasts besides."[48] The absurdity to which this line of argument leads is obvious: the conventional religions and cults neutralize one another and can no longer satisfy the needs of those who are upwardly mobile economically and intellectually.[49] The middle-Platonist Plutarch attempted to avoid this danger by pointing out that the deity is named differently among different peoples yet is in fact the same for all human beings:

> So for that one rationality [λόγος] which keeps all things in order and the one Providence which watches over them and the ancillary powers that are set over all, there have arisen among different peoples, in accordance with their customs, different honors and appellations. Thus men make use of consecrated symbols, some employing symbols that are obscure, but others those that are clearer, in guiding the intelligence toward things divine. . . . Wherefore in the study of these matters it is especially necessary that we adopt, as our guide in these mysteries, the reasoning [λόγος] that comes from philosophy, and consider reverently each one of the things that are said and done, so that . . . we may not thus err by accepting in a different spirit the things that the laws have dictated admirably concerning the sacrifices and festivals.[50]

> Because God is unmoved and timeless, in whom there is neither "earlier nor later, no future nor past, no older nor younger; but He, being One [ἀλλ' εἷς ὤν] has with only one 'Now' completely filled 'Forever'; and only when Being is after His pattern is it in reality Being, not having been or about to be, nor has it had a beginning nor is it destined to come to an end. Under these conditions, therefore, we ought, as we pay him reverence, to greet him and to address him with these words, 'Thou art'; or even, I vow, as did some of the men of old, 'Thou art One.'"[51]

There were two sources of the knowledge of God:[52] (1) the idea of deity implanted in the human consciousness in view of the majesty of the cosmos, and (2) the traditional images of God conveyed in the old myths and customs.

48. Cicero, *Nat. d.* 3.47.

49. Rodney Stark, *The Rise of Christianity: A Sociologist Reconsiders History* (Princeton: Princeton University Press, 1996), 37–45.

50. Plutarch, *Is. Os.*, 67–68.

51. Plutarch, *E Delph.* 20.

52. Cf. Dio Chrysostom, *Or.* 12. Dio's "Olympian Address" is an impressive example of the attempts to breathe new life into Greek religion and its cultic apparatus. Zeus is praised as the universal, peaceful, and merciful God who protects humanity as their Father and King, and who provides them all they need for a successful life. See text and commentary in Hans-Josef Klauck and Balbina Bäbler, *Olympische Rede, oder, Über die erste Erkenntnis Gottes* (Texte zur Forschung; Darmstadt: Wissenschaftliche Buchgesellschaft, 2000).

In the Hellenistic world, the plausibility of each of these had declined for many people. The more the anthropomorphic imagery of the Greek myths of the gods was subjected to skeptical critique, the more the concept of one God necessarily gained in persuasive power, as henotheism and the exclusive monotheism associated with it.[53]

Paul stands firmly in the tradition of Old Testament monotheism and can use the tendencies of Greco-Roman religion for his own purposes;[54] *nonetheless, he encourages and expects his hearers to accept a new view of the world, to accept a new God.* This God is one but not alone; this God has *a name, a history, and a face: Jesus Christ.* The image of God has become visible, for Jesus Christ is the image of God (2 Cor. 4:4). The God proclaimed by Paul is a personal God who acts in history and cares about human beings. This God is neither withdrawn from the world nor immanent in it but in Jesus Christ has turned to the world (cf. Gal. 4:4–5; Rom. 8:3). It is not a universal myth but a concrete act that determines the early Christian picture of God. The open or concealed anthropomorphic language for the gods/God had already been overcome in Christianity prior to Paul by the real and abiding incarnation of God in Jesus Christ. Here is the decisive difference between the ideas of God advocated by Paul and those of the three leading philosophical schools at the time of Paul: middle Platonism, Stoicism, and Epicureanism (cf. Acts 17:18). Middle Platonism's view of the divine was characterized by a strong emphasis on the absolute transcendence and otherness of God, his categorical otherness from all that is human, and thus his disappearance into an unapproachable distance. Plutarch formulates it thus:

> What, then, really is Being? It is that which is eternal, without beginning and without end, to which no length of time brings change. For time is something that is in motion, appearing in connection with moving matter, ever flowing, retaining nothing, a receptacle, as it were, of birth and decay, whose familiar "afterwards" and "before," "shall be" and "has been," when they are uttered, are of themselves a confession of Not Being. . . . But God is (if there be need to say so), and He exists for no fixed time, but for the everlasting ages which are immovable, timeless, and undeviating. (Plutarch, *E Delph.* 19–20)[55]

53. Of course, it is to be noted that from the earliest days of Greek theology of which we are aware, the canonization of anthropomorphic polytheism of a Homer and Hesiod in Herodotus (*Hist.* 2.49–58) and the skepticism/atheism of a Protagoras (born ca. 490 BCE) stood unreconciled alongside each other. Cf. Protagoras's famous first sentence of *On the Gods*: "Concerning the gods I am unable to know that they exist, or that they do not exist, or what they are like in appearance" (*VS* 80 B 4). In Diogenes Laertius, *Vit. phil.* 9.51, this dictum is given a nice basis: "Much stands in the way of knowledge: the ambiguity of the matter itself, and the brevity of human life."

54. On pagan monotheism, cf. Schrage, *Unterwegs zur Einzigkeit*, 35–43.

55. The principle of God's immutability already dominates the thinking of the pre-Socratics (Xenophanes, Parmenides, Heraclites); cf. Wilhelm Maas, *Unveränderlichkeit Gottes:*

Stoicism advocated a monistic pantheism, according to which the deity is present and active in all forms of existence. It is immanent within the world and omnipresent and precisely for this reason is not tangibly comprehensible. Chrysippus (282–209 BCE) teaches, "The divine power is located in the reason, in the soul and spirit of all nature, and that the world itself and the world-soul that permeates it all is God."[56] Nothing exists beyond the material elements of all being; there is neither a transcendent creator God nor a metaphysical grounding of the world. An opposing concept of deity is found in Epicurus. For him, the gods live a carefree life beyond this world of time without being concerned with human beings. "For a god does nothing, is not involved in any business, not burdened with any work, but enjoys his own wisdom and virtue and abandons himself to living in eternal bliss."[57] As immortals, the gods can neither suffer nor turn toward the world in loving compassion.[58] They have withdrawn from the seamy side of life and have nothing in common with human beings. Obviously, at the beginning of the Christian era, the traditional ancient teaching about the gods had lost its persuasive power, so that even their existence was questioned.[59]

The philosophical critique of polytheism and the withdrawal of the gods/God into an inapproachable distance, or their disappearance into direct experience of the present, prepared the way for Christian monotheism. While polytheism offered no personal relation to God, the God proclaimed by Paul combined two attractive basic principles: *this God is both the Lord of history and Lord of one's personal life*. In the early Christian churches, both realms coalesced not only in their thinking but also in their religious practice. Christians lived in the awareness of belonging to the group of human beings whom God had chosen to reveal to the world both his saving will and his judgment. They were convinced that God through Jesus Christ had conferred meaning and purpose on history as a whole and on each individual life. This meaning embraced both daily life and a living hope for what lies beyond this life. The early Christian proclamation was directed both to the everyday life of the

---

Zum Verhältnis von griechisch-philosophischer und christlicher Gotteslehre (PThSt 1; Munich: Schöningh, 1974).

56. Cicero, *Nat. d.* 1.39; cf. further Diogenes Laertius, *Vit. phil.* 7.135–136, 142. Aetios says of God, "He is also that stream of breath that blows through the whole world, and takes on different descriptions according to the matter through which he comes"(*SVF* 2.1027).

57. Cicero, *Nat. d.* l.51; cf. further Epicurus, *Men.* 123: "The gods do in fact exist: knowledge of them is directly available and illuminating. But they do not exist in the forms as thought of by the masses." All the essential texts on the theology of Epicurus are found in Rainer Nickel, *Wege zum Glück* (Sammlung Tusculum; Düsseldorf: Artemis & Winkler, 2003).

58. Cf. Cicero, *Nat. d.* 1.95, 121; Diogenes Laertius, *Vit. phil.* 10.76–77.

59. Cf. Cicero, *Nat. d.* 1.94: "But if none of these [the philosophers] discerned the truth about the divine nature, it is to be feared that the divine nature is entirely nonexistent." Cf. further 1.63: "And did not Diagoras, called 'the atheist,' and later Theodorus openly deny the divine existence?"

believer and to the ultimate issues of life, such as the meaning of death. Here developing Christianity was considerably different from the ideas prevalent in its environment. *The God of Christians was a God of life who demanded commitment but also granted freedom, a God already experienced in the present who also guaranteed the ultimate future.* The central role was played not, as in Greek thought, by an unpredictable fate,[60] but by the God who had revealed himself in Jesus Christ, the one God who determines life's present and future. Early Christianity offered a comprehensive and reasonable framework for living one's life, one that took up the hopes of antiquity for eternal life beyond this world, at the same time giving the individual a convincing perspective on life within this world.

6.2 Christology

In contrast to the gospels, Paul narrates no Jesus-Christ-history. Instead he chooses a variety of christological leitmotifs, and takes up from a number of semantic fields metaphors used in Christian preaching and their related imagery, in order to elaborate the meaning of the Christ event in all its dimensions. He has a clear point of departure: the conviction that Jesus Christ and his fate represent and model the love of God as God's saving will for humanity. He liberates from the slavery to sin and death and grants authentic life in the here and now.

6.2.1 Transformation and Participation

One fundamental idea characterizes Paul's Christology:[61] God has transformed the Jesus who was crucified and dead into a new mode of being. A *change of status* occurs here: Jesus of Nazareth did not remain in the status of those who are dead and distant from God's presence, but God conferred on him the status of equality with God. This overwhelming experience and insight were granted to Paul at Damascus, and his letters reflect the various ways Paul had pondered the significance of this transfer of Jesus from the realm of death to life with God. The point of departure for Paul's theology,

60. Cf. the remark of Kleanthes transmitted by Epictetus, *Ench*. 53: "O Zeus, and you, almighty Fate, lead me to that goal that was once determined by you. I will follow without complaining. If I did complain, I would be a blasphemer and a coward, and would have to follow anyway!" The importance of this belief in fate is seen in an especially impressive manner in tomb inscriptions; cf. Imre Peres, *Griechische Grabinschriften und neutestamentliche Eschatologie* (WUNT 157; Tübingen: Mohr Siebeck, 2003), 34–41. On the theory and practice of Greco-Roman belief in fate, cf. Cicero's compositions *De fato* and *De divinatione*.

61. Udo Schnelle, "Transformation und Partizipation als Grundgedanken paulinischer Theologie," *NTS* 47 (1986): 58ff.

as for that of prior early Christian tradition, was the conviction that God had raised Jesus from the dead (e.g., 1 Thess. 1:10; 2 Cor. 4:14; Rom. 8:11). God and Jesus Christ were resolutely thought of together; the Son participates fully in the deity of the Father. Thus, already before Paul, christological reflection had extended the change in Jesus's status from the resurrection to his preexistence. It was only Jesus's own willingness to descend to the way of the cross that gained him his exalted status as Lord of the universe; that is, even the Preexistent One underwent a transformation in order to become what he was to be (cf. Phil. 2:6–11).

The goal of the transformation of Jesus Christ is the participation of believers in this fundamental event:[62] "For you know the generous act of our Lord Jesus Christ, that though he was rich, yet for your sakes he became poor, so that by his poverty you might become rich" (2 Cor. 8:9); "For our sake he made him to be sin who knew no sin, so that in him we might become the righteousness of God" (2 Cor. 5:21). Easter is an act of God involving not only Jesus but disciples and apostles, for God has revealed that the Crucified One is now the Living One. The resurrection of Jesus Christ from the dead is thus for Paul a once-for-all act, but its continuing effects have brought about a fundamental change in the world. The God of the resurrection is the one who "gives life to the dead and calls into existence the things that do not exist" (Rom. 4:17b). God so identifies himself with the crucified Jesus of Nazareth that the lifegiving power revealed in the resurrection continues to be effective: "For to this end Christ died and lived again, so that he might be Lord of both the dead and the living" (Rom. 14:9). The power of the resurrection of Jesus Christ is at work in the present and generates its own assurance: "But if we have died with Christ, we believe that we will also live with him" (Rom. 6:8; cf. 2 Cor. 1:9; 5:15). Christ was "handed over to death for our trespasses and was raised for our justification" (Rom. 4:25). When Paul himself was near death, his participation in the power of the resurrection was the ground of his hope of attaining the resurrection from the dead (Phil. 3:10–11). With the resurrection of Jesus Christ from the dead, a universal dynamic was set in motion that affects not only the destiny of the individual believer but the whole cosmos (cf. Phil. 3:20–21). As the way of salvation, the way of Christ is aimed at the believers' participation; as the prototype, the way of Jesus Christ from death to life opens up the way for humans to follow the same way and makes it possible for them to do so. According to Paul's conviction, this way introduces a new epoch, at the end of which stands the universal transformation. Then God will be "all in all" (1 Cor. 15:28).

62. Cf. Schweitzer, *Mysticism*, 115: "The original and central idea of the Pauline Mysticism is therefore that the Elect will share with one another and with Christ a corporeity which is in a special way susceptible to the action of the powers of death and resurrection, and in consequence capable of acquiring the resurrection state of existence before the general resurrection of the dead takes place."

The Philippians 2:6–11 Hymn as Paradigmatic History

The basic concepts of Paul's Christology are already present in compressed form in the pre-Pauline paradigmatic history of Phil. 2:6–11 (see above, §4.6). The hymn shows that already prior to Paul, christological reflection had extended the *change of status* from postexistence to preexistence. Paul takes up the Christology of the traditional piece and embeds it in a *parenetic line of argument*, as seen in Phil. 2:1–5. There are both compositional and terminological points of contact between this section and the hymn itself. Thus the humility of Christ expressed by ταπεινόω (to humble) in 2:8 illustrates the humility (ταπεινοφροσύνη) to which the church is called in 2:3. The obedience of the humiliated Christ appears as the foil to the self-interest and quarreling that the church must overcome (2:3). Finally, the summarizing formulation of the preexistent one's abasement (ἑαυτὸν ἐκένωσεν [he emptied himself], 2:7) points to the fundamental affirmation of 2:4, according to which a Christian should not seek his or her own interests but the interests of others. The hymn also has a connection to the following 2:12; there Paul takes up the idea of Christ's obedience as the basis for the ethical stance the church is called to adopt. The church is challenged to take what the Lord has done in the incarnation, crucifixion, and enthronement as a pattern to be imitated in its own ethics. Christ thus appears in Phil. 2 as both prototype and example. Believers can and should follow Christ in the awareness that, just as is the case with the apostle himself, they do not yet stand in the state of fulfilled salvation but are on the way to the day of Christ's return, the judgment, and the resurrection (Phil. 3:12ff.). God is the one who provides this possibility, for it is God who is at work among the believers, enabling both their will and their deeds (Phil. 2:13). Just as Christ did not look after his own interests but gave himself over to death on the cross, so Christians too should not live in self-seeking competition but in humility and unity. The transformation of the Son grounds and makes possible the participation of believers in this same transformation.

With the addition in 2:8c ("death on the cross") Paul inserts his own theology of the cross into the traditional hymn.[63] Jesus Christ not only renounces his equality with God and his life but dies in the most extreme shame conceivable.[64] A sharp theo-political point is built into this idea: now acclamation and worship are rightly directed to the Crucified One. Over against a church that was too inclined to take pride in its location in a city that was a Roman colony, Paul,[65] from his Roman prison, cites the hymn of Phil. 2:5–11[66] to

63. For evidence and argument, see Ulrich B. Müller, *Der Brief des Paulus an die Philipper* (THKNT 11.1; Leipzig: Evangelische Verlagsanstalt, 1993), 105.

64. Cf. Otfried Hofius, *Der Christushymnus Philipper 2,6–11: Untersuchungen zu Gestalt und Aussage eines urchristlichen Psalms* (WUNT 17; Tübingen: Mohr, 1976), 63.

65. In my opinion, Philippians was written in Rome ca. 60 CE; for evidence and argument, see Schnelle, *New Testament Writings*, 130–33.

66. Peter Pilhofer, *Philippi* (WUNT 87, 119; 2 vols.; Tübingen: Mohr, 1995).

emphasize the *political* dimension of the Christ event. One who was crucified by the Romans receives, by God's direct intervention, an unsurpassable status, so that worship and confession belong to him alone. Three aspects of Paul's emphasis are of particular importance:

1. Whereas kings and rulers have gained power by violence and predatory aggressiveness, Jesus Christ humbled himself and thereby became the true sovereign. He thus embodies the exact opposite of the ruler who exalts himself.[67]
2. Total homage and honor were reserved for the emperor alone. Dio Cassius[68] reports the 66 CE visit of King Tiridates of Parthia, who made a triumphal procession from the Euphrates to Rome in order to pay homage to Nero: "He knelt on the ground, crossed his arms, named Nero his Lord and worshiped him. He said, 'I have come to you who are my god, to worship you as Mithras. I shall be whatever you would order me to be, because you are my destiny and fortune.' To which Nero replied: 'You have done well by coming here to enjoy my presence in person.'"
3. Also, the Kyrios title in Phil. 2:11 and the Savior title in 3:20 each have anti-imperial connotations. A Greek inscription from the time of Nero has the formula "Nero, Lord of the Whole World,"[69] and the Roman emperors were praised as "saviors," especially in the eastern part of the empire.[70]

Over against this politico-religious claim, the hymn places a new reality that surpasses every earthly power and points to a better alternative. The Philippian Christians receive their citizenship not from the Roman authorities but from heaven (3:20–21). Paul is consistent with this distinction when he describes their life with the term πολιτεύομαι (conduct one's life as a citizen) in 1:27, the only place he uses this verb. Paul, a prisoner in Rome, presents his church with an alternative model: weakness and rulership are in truth assigned in a completely different way than appears at first glance.

67. Cf. Vollenweider, "Gottgleichheit," 431. Reference is often made in this context to Plutarch, *Alex. fort.* 1.8.330D, where Plutarch defends Alexander the Great as the model world robber: "For he did not overrun Asia like a robber nor was he minded to tear and rend it, as if it were booty and plunder bestowed by unexpected good fortune."

68. Dio Cassius, *Hist.*, Epitome to Book 63.

69. Cf. *NW* 1.2:249.

70. Cf. the documentation at John 4:42 in *NW* 1.2:239–56; cf. also Michael Labahn, "'Heiland der Welt': Der gesandte Gottessohn und der römische Kaiser—ein Thema johanneischer Christologie," in *Zwischen den Reichen: Neues Testament und römische Herrschaft: Vorträge auf der Ersten Konferenz der European Association for Biblical Studies* (ed. Michael Labahn and Jürgen Zangenberg; TANZ 36; Tübingen: Francke, 2002), 149ff.

Pauline theology is political to the extent that the new symbolic universe it mediates directly concerns people's lives as citizens, their way of life.[71] With the proclamation of Jesus Christ, Paul introduces a new and unsurpassable eschatological authority; he gives a new definition to the message of peace and prosperity, rulership, salvation, peace, grace, and righteousness/justice—formerly defined by the empire and its rulers—and postulates an irresistible transformation of the world. This comprehensive redefinition has political consequences, but Paul adopts no intentional political stance in the modern sense.[72] Individual Pauline texts or concepts do in fact have an anti-imperial impact (e.g., Phil. 2:6–11; the titles "Lord" and "Savior"), but this circumstance does not amount to an "anti-imperial theology."[73] There is no direct anti-Roman or even Rome-critical statement in Paul. On the contrary, Rom. 13:1–7, the only direct statement from Paul with regard to the Roman Empire, specifically calls for its authority to be acknowledged.[74] In addition, the imminent advent of the exalted Christ already casts a transitory light on all earthly institutions (1 Cor. 7:29–31).

6.2.2 Cross and Resurrection

Paul himself is the last direct witness of the transformation of Jesus of Nazareth from death to life. At Damascus he was granted an Easter appear-

71. Among the meanings of ἡ πολιτεία is "the life one lives as a citizen, the citizen's way of life"; cf. Franz Passow et al., *Handwörterbuch der griechischen Sprache* (5th ed.; 4 vols.; Leipzig: Vogel, 1841), 990.

72. This is a different perspective from that current in some streams of Anglo-American "anti-imperial" Pauline interpretation, where Pauline theology as a whole is seen as permeated by a Rome-critical, "anti-imperial" orientation. Cf. the wide range of essays in Richard A. Horsley, *Paul and Empire: Religion and Power in Roman Imperial Society* (Harrisburg, PA: Trinity, 1997); Richard A. Horsley, *Paul and Politics: Ekklesia, Israel, Imperium, Interpretation: Essays in Honor of Krister Stendahl* (Harrisburg, PA: Trinity, 2000); John Dominic Crossan and Jonathan L. Reed, *In Search of Paul: How Jesus's Apostle Opposed Rome's Empire with God's Kingdom: A New Vision of Paul's Words and World* (New York: HarperSanFrancisco, 2004); N. T. Wright, "Paul's Gospel and Caesar's Empire," in *Paul and Politics: Ekklesia, Israel, Imperium, Interpretation: Essays in Honor of Krister Stendahl* (ed. Richard A. Horsley; Harrisburg, PA: Trinity, 2000), 59–79.

73. Cf. the on-target comment on methodology by S. Vollenweider, "Politische Theologie im Philipperbrief?" in *Paulus und Johannes: Exegetische Studien zur paulinischen und johanneischen Theologie und Literatur* (ed. Dieter Sänger and Ulrich Mell; WUNT 198; Tübingen: Mohr Siebeck, 2006), 468: "Interpretation would do well to protect itself by secretly formulating a virtual antithesis for every potentially political motto."

74. The relativizing of Rom. 13:1–7 is found especially in North American exegesis. Cf. N. Elliott, "Romans 13:1–7 in the Context of Imperial Propaganda," in *Paul and Empire: Religion and Power in Roman Imperial Society* (ed. Richard A. Horsley; Harrisburg, PA: Trinity, 1997), 184–204 (Rom. 13 as tactical accommodation); Robert Jewett, *Romans: A Commentary* (Hermeneia; Minneapolis: Fortress, 2007), 789–90 (it is not the Roman or Greek gods, but the Father of Jesus Christ who grants political authority).

ance: "Last of all, as to one untimely born, he appeared also to me" (1 Cor. 15:8). God's grace was revealed to him, the small one (Latin *paulus* [small]), the least among the apostles (1 Cor. 15:9, ἐλάχιστος, superlative of μικρός [small]). The appearance of the Risen One made Paul certain that Jesus had not remained in death as a crucified transgressor of the law but that he has taken his rightful place at God's side (cf., e.g., 1 Thess. 4:14; 2 Cor. 4:14; Rom. 6:9; Phil. 2:6–11). The resurrection[75] of Jesus Christ from the dead is therefore the objectively real presupposition for the theological relevance of the cross, which means that *the person of the Crucified One is first revealed in the light of the resurrection.* We must therefore first deal with the Pauline understanding of the resurrection before the cross can come into view as historical locus and thematic theological symbol of God's act.

Resurrection

The resurrection of Jesus Christ from the dead is the central content of Paul's symbolic universe.[76] It has always been regarded as patently incredible. Luke had already presented the Epicureans and Stoics as ridiculing Paul's preaching of the resurrection in Athens (Acts 17:32). Texts from antiquity show that people then were by no means so "naive" that they all simply believed in a life after death, as the immortality of the soul or as bodily resurrection.[77] To be sure,

75. Regarding terminology: Because in the New Testament God is consistently the subject of the act and Jesus of Nazareth is the object, we will sometimes speak of the raising (*Auferweckung*) of Jesus Christ in order to emphasize this passive element. However, the term "resurrection" (*Auferstehung*, rising) has pervasively established itself in the general discussion as a term describing the whole event. It is also used here without suggesting that Jesus played an active role in his own resurrection.

76. A selection from the enormous literature on the topic: Campenhausen, *Osterereignisse*; Hans Grass, *Ostergeschehen und Osterberichte* (2nd ed.; Göttingen: Vandenhoeck & Ruprecht, 1961); F. Viering, *Die Bedeutung der Auferstehungsbotschaft für den Glauben an Jesus Christus* (Berlin: Evangelische Verlagsanstalt, 1967); Willi Marxsen, *The Resurrection of Jesus of Nazareth* (Philadelphia: Fortress, 1970); Karl Martin Fischer, *Das Ostergeschehen* (2nd ed.; Göttingen: Vandenhoeck & Ruprecht, 1980); Paul Hoffmann, ed., *Zur neutestamentlichen Überlieferung von der Auferstehung Jesu* (Darmstadt: Wissenschaftliche Buchgesellschaft, 1988); Paul Hoffmann, "Die historisch-kritische Osterdiskussion von H. S. Reimarus bis zu Beginn des 20. Jahrhunderts," in *Zur neutestamentlichen Überlieferung von der Auferstehung Jesu* (ed. Paul Hoffmann; Darmstadt: Wissenschaftliche Buchgesellschaft, 1988), Hoffmann, "Osterdiskussion," 15–67; Ingolf U. Dalferth, *Der auferweckte Gekreuzigte: Zur Grammatik der Christologie* (Tübingen: Mohr, 1994); Gerd Lüdemann, *The Resurrection of Jesus: History, Experience, Theology* (Minneapolis: Fortress, 1994); Dalferth, "Grab," 379–409; Theissen and Merz, *Historical Jesus*, 474–511 (a survey or research on the resurrection and how it has been interpreted).

77. Pliny, *Nat. hist.* 2.26–27, indicates that some things are impossible even for the gods, "who cannot bestow eternity on mortals or recall the deceased"; 7.188: "for the same [human] vanity prolongs itself into the future and fabricates for itself a life lasting even into the period of death, sometimes bestowing on the soul immortality, sometimes transfiguration, sometimes giving sensation to those below, and worshiping ghosts and making a god of one who has already ceased to be even a man."

gods and demigods such as Hercules could come back from the dead,[78] but the resurrection of one who had been crucified was regarded as "foolishness" (1 Cor. 1:23). When it comes to integrating the idea of resurrection from the dead into human thought, the deficiency in the world of human experience requires that we proceed in an exploratory manner in three progressive stages: We will first ask what reality content Paul ascribes to the resurrection of Jesus Christ from the dead, then present relevant explanatory models. Finally, we will discuss our own model for understanding the resurrection.

I. The Reality of the Resurrection for Paul

Paul leaves no doubt about the significance of the resurrection as the foundation of Christian faith: "If Christ has not been raised, then our proclamation has been in vain and your faith has been in vain" (1 Cor. 15:14); "If Christ has not been raised, your faith is futile and you are still in your sins. . . . If for this life only we have hoped in Christ, we are of all people most to be pitied" (15:17, 19). For Paul, resurrection, appearance, kerygma, and faith constitute an irreversible series. In 1 Cor. 15 Paul gives a literary elaboration of this chronological series of events. Although he is himself an authentic witness of the resurrection, here too he anchors his Christology in church tradition (cf. 15:1–3a) in order to make clear that the resurrection of Jesus Christ from the dead is the foundation of faith for all Christians. The gospel has a definite form, and only in this form does it manifest itself for the Corinthians as a gospel that saves. Believers must therefore hold fast to the confession "that Christ died for our sins in accordance with the scriptures, and that he was buried, and that he was raised on the third day in accordance with the scriptures, and that he appeared to Cephas, then to the twelve" (15:3b–5). Neither Paul nor the Corinthians can simply have their own version of the gospel; both are directed to the one gospel already given (see above, §6.1.4). The content of the gospel is the tradition of the death and resurrection of Christ. Jesus Christ died for our sins according to the will of God; the statement about his burial functions to confirm the reality of his death. The event of Jesus's death as a whole has its counterpart in the event of Jesus's resurrection as a whole. This resurrection overcomes death, understood both as God's last enemy and as the end of every individual life. Both the idea of Jesus's burial and the idea of the visible appearances of the Resurrected One point to the fact that both Paul and the tradition understand the death and resurrection of Jesus as bodily events in space and time.[79] Likewise Paul's extension of the list of witnesses (15:6–9) functions to demonstrate the bodily, and thus verifiable, resurrection of Jesus Christ from the dead,[80] since many of the five hundred brothers and

78. Cf. Seneca, *Herc. fur.* 612–613.

79. Here Paul stands in the tradition of Jewish anthropology and eschatology; cf. Hengel, "Begräbnis," 139–72.

80. Cf. Wolff, *1. Korintherbrief*, 375.

sisters are still alive and can be interrogated. Bultmann rightly understands the intention of this text when he emphasizes, "I can understand this text only as an attempt to make the resurrection of Christ credible as an objective historical fact."[81] But he then continues, "And I see that Paul is betrayed by his apologetic into contradicting himself. For what Paul says in 15:20–22 of the death and resurrection of Christ cannot be said of an objective historical fact."[82] What Paul understood as historical event Bultmann wants to relegate to the realm of myth in order to maintain the credibility of the gospel in the modern world. Paul, however—and he is the only witness to the resurrection from whom we have written reports—obviously understood the resurrection of Jesus Christ from the dead as an event within history, an event that had completely changed his own life. By citing the tradition in 15:3b–5 and by filling out the list of witnesses, Paul is also defending his own authority as an apostle.[83] He brings the accepted tradition up to the time when the risen Christ appeared personally to him, and thus makes clear to the Corinthians that he saw the Risen One in the same way as the other witnesses, including Cephas. Paul thereby touches on three problem areas: (1) the bodily resurrection of Jesus, (2) his own testimony to this event, and (3) an understanding, derived from the foregoing, of the bodily resurrection from the dead. For Paul, this understanding of the resurrection is not a question of interpretation but a constituent element of the gospel itself. Only if Jesus Christ was raised from the dead bodily, and therefore in reality, can Christians place their hope in God's eschatological act of salvation.

The Corinthian conception of resurrection in contrast to Paul's. Some members of the Corinthian church denied a future resurrection because they had a different anthropology from Paul's.[84] They probably thought of the human person as a dichotomy, distinguishing between the self, as the invisible I-soul, and the visible body.[85] In contrast to later Gnostic views, for the Corinthians, the body was not as such regarded negatively; rather, in their view, it was merely an earthly-temporary entity excluded from the eschatological redemption.[86] Only

81. Rudolf Bultmann, "Karl Barth, 'The Resurrection of the Dead,'" in *Faith and Understanding* (ed. Robert W. Funk; trans. Louise Pettibone Smith; London: SCM, 1969), 83.

82. Ibid., 83–84.

83. This aspect is specifically emphasized by Peter von der Osten-Sacken, "Die Apologie des paulinischen Apostolats in 1Kor 15,1–11," in *Evangelium und Tora: Aufsätze zu Paulus* (ed. Peter von der Osten-Sacken; TB 77; Munich: Kaiser, 1987), 131–49.

84. For reasons that exegetes have given for their denial of the resurrection, cf. the survey of research in Sellin, *Auferstehung*, 17–37.

85. Cf. ibid., 30: "The Corinthians denied the resurrection from the dead as such because they could not accept the ideas of bodily existence in eternal salvation that were bound up with it."

86. Cf. Plutarch, *Mor.* 1096: "Human existence is composed of two elements, of body and soul, and of these two the soul has the priority." From the realm of popular piety, cf., e.g., Plutarch's account of the goal of the redeemed souls in *Is. Os.* 78: "But when these souls are

the higher part of the person, the spiritual I-soul, has hope for a life beyond this one.[87] Since the body is the earthly house for the soul, it has no bearing on the matter of salvation, and the Corinthians could regard it as irrelevant; this way of thinking could find expression both in unbridled sexual license and in sexual asceticism (cf. 1 Cor. 6:12–7:40). Because the body is transitory and doomed to die but the soul was thought of as immortal, the Corinthians rejected the idea of an eschatological bodily resurrection. Evidently, for the Corinthians, life is not finally attained when death is overcome at the Lord's parousia but when the Spirit is conferred at baptism;[88] this is the place where the essential transformation of the self occurs. For them, the irrevocable gift of the Spirit was already the absolute assurance of salvation because it not only granted entrance into the new being but was itself already the new being. The apostle shares the view of the objective reality of the Spirit expressed in such ideas (cf. 5:5; 3:15–16); in contrast to the Corinthian theology, however, Paul cannot think of the human self as a disembodied "I." Human existence is constituted in bodily terms; the body is not excluded from God's saving acts in the present and future. This was already true in God's saving act in Jesus of Nazareth, for not only did the crucified one have a body, but the Risen One has a body as well (cf. 10:16; 11:27; Phil. 3:21). Baptism grants incorporation into the whole destiny of Jesus, both with the bodily crucified one and with the bodily Risen One. Thus Paul intentionally defers until 1 Cor. 15:29 the strange practice of vicarious baptism[89] because, against the intention of the Corinthians, it shows that a purely spiritual understanding of the resurrection does not square with the essence of baptism.

For Paul, *there is no human existence apart from bodily existence*, and so reflection on life after death must include the question of bodily life after death. For him, the question of the "how" of the resurrection can thus be only the question of what sort of body the resurrection body will be (cf. 1 Cor.

---

set free and migrate into the realm of the invisible and the unseen, the dispassionate and the pure, then this god becomes their leader and king, since it is on him that they are bound to be dependent in their insatiate contemplation and yearning for that beauty which is for men unutterable and indescribable."

87. Cf. Hans-Heinrich Schade, *Apokalyptische Christologie bei Paulus: Studien zum Zusammenhang von Christologie und Eschatologie in den Paulusbriefen* (GTA 18; Göttingen: Vandenhoeck & Ruprecht, 1981), 192–93.

88. Traditions from Hellenistic Judaism illuminate this idea; cf. Wolff, *1. Korintherbrief*, 214.

89. For older interpretations, see Mathias Rissi, *Die Taufe für die Toten: Ein Beitrag zur paulinischen Tauflehre* (ATANT 42; Zürich: Zwingli Verlag, 1962). Selections from more recent literature can be found in Schnelle, *Gerechtigkeit und Christusgegenwart*, 150–52; Sellin, *Auferstehung*, 277–84; Wolff, *1. Korintherbrief*, 392–97; Horn, *Angeld des Geistes*, 165–67; Gordon D. Fee, *The First Epistle to the Corinthians* (NICNT; Grand Rapids: Eerdmans, 1987), 762–67; Joel R. White, "Baptized on account of the Dead," *JBL* 116 (1997): 487–99; Dieter Zeller, "Gibt es religionsgeschichtliche Parallelen zur Taufe für die Toten (1Kor 15,29)?" *ZNW* 98 (2007): 68–76.

15:35b). Paul opens this discussion in 1 Cor. 15:35ff.,[90] but only after he had previously described Christ as "the firstfruits of those who have died" (ἀπαρχὴ τῶν κεκοιμημένων) in 1 Cor. 15:20 and given an outline of the final events in 15:23–28. He thereby constructs an irreversible timeline, which can begin only with the resurrection of Jesus Christ. In 15:42–44 Paul exploits hermeneutically what he has just said by interpreting the resurrection of what has been sown: just as the perishable is sown and the imperishable rises, so the σῶμα ψυχικόν (physical body) is sown and the σῶμα πνευματικόν (spiritual body) is raised. Paul answers the question of the "how" of the resurrection with this antithesis:[91] on the one hand, bodily life is the basic presupposition of the resurrection; on the other hand, the resurrection body is defined as a spiritual body and thus sharply distinguished from the present perishable world. In 15:45–49 Paul provides the basis for his thinking of the resurrection body as a spiritual body. As a πνεῦμα ζῳοποιοῦν (life-giving spirit), Christ creates the spiritual resurrection body (15:45), and as the prototype of the new being, he is at the same time its prime example and model. Just as the earthly state of the πρῶτος ἄνθρωπος (first human being), Adam, caused and determined the perishable nature of humans, so the heavenly state of the δεύτερος ἄνθρωπος (second human being) will cause and determine the future imperishable being.

Their cultural background causes the Corinthians to exclude bodily existence from the realm of immortality and to regard the Spirit as the true realm of God's activity. In contrast, Paul adopts Greek models of argument to include the body within the realm of God's act and reverses the Corinthians' order of things: "But it is not the spiritual that is first, but the physical, and then the spiritual" (1 Cor. 15:46). The miraculous creative power of God raised Jesus from the dead, and it is God who will also act in the resurrection of the dead and the transformation of the Corinthians who are still alive at the parousia.

Paul understands the bodily resurrection of Jesus Christ from the dead as an act of God on the Crucified One, an act that introduces the eschatological times and thus becomes the basis for a new view of the world and history. The resurrection becomes a predicate of God, who is the God "who gives life to the dead and calls things that are not as though they were" (Rom. 4:17b; cf. 8:11). God identifies himself so closely with the crucified Jesus of Nazareth that his life-giving power revealed in the resurrection has continuing effects:

90. For interpretation, cf. Schade, *Apokalyptische Christologie*, 204ff.; Wolff, *1. Korintherbrief*, 402ff.; Jeffrey R. Asher, *Polarity and Change in 1 Corinthians 15: A Study of Metaphysics, Rhetoric, and Resurrection* (HUT 42; Tübingen: Mohr, 2000), 91–145.

91. The antithesis πνευματικός/ψυχικός (spiritual/physical) is found for the first time in Paul; in terms of the history of religions, it probably derives from Jewish wisdom theology (cf. Philo, *Creation* 134–147; *Alleg. Interp.* 1.31–42, 88–95; 2.4–5); cf. Richard A. Horsley, "Pneumatikos vs. Psychikos," *HTR* 69 (1976): 269–88; Sellin, *Auferstehung*, 90–175; Horn, *Angeld des Geistes*, 194–98.

"For this very reason, Christ died and returned to life so that he might be the Lord of both the dead and the living" (Rom. 14:9). The powers of the resurrection of Jesus Christ continue to work in the present, and they evoke their own assurance: "Now if we died with Christ, we believe that we will also live with him" (Rom. 6:8; cf. 2 Cor. 1:9; 5:15). Moreover, the resurrection of Jesus Christ also visibly changes Paul's own life, so that for him its substantive reality is not only a new judgment about what God has done in Jesus of Nazareth but brings into being a new and palpable reality.[92]

II. On Understanding the Resurrection

The experiences of Paul near Damascus are not our own; his worldview does not belong to everyone.[93] How can one speak of the resurrection of Jesus Christ from the dead within the terms of the modern world? How is it possible to affirm the truth of the good news of the resurrection of Jesus Christ from the dead in a time when truth claims are exclusively bound to the rationalistic methods of (natural) science? What plausibility do the arguments of the disputers and the advocates of the reality of the resurrection possess? Three interpretative models are significant in the current discussion.

a. Projections of the disciples as the cause of the resurrection faith (subjective-visions hypothesis). David Friedrich Strauss (1808–74) presented arguments against the Easter faith that have set the agenda for the discussion up to the present day.[94] He strictly distinguished between the appearance tradition and the tradition of the empty tomb. In his opinion, the historical origin of the Easter faith lies in the visions of the disciples in Galilee, far removed from Jesus's burial place; the empty tomb stories appeared only in secondary legends. The appearance stories point to visions of the disciples that were evoked by their pious charismatic experiences and their stressful situation. Strauss is thus an advocate of the subjective-vision hypothesis, according to which the disciples' visionary experiences can be rationally explained on the basis of their specific historical situation.[95] To a considerable degree, Strauss makes Jesus's historicity evaporate into the realm of myth, with the result that a cavernous gap

92. In the 1960s discussion that lingers today, this aspect is intentionally minimized or played down; cf., e.g., Marxsen, *Resurrection*, 111, who denies that 1 Cor. 15 intends to prove anything, and states, "Consequently one cannot appeal to Paul in any attempt to hold fast to the historical nature [as it is sometimes expressed] of Jesus's resurrection." [The bracketed phrase was left untranslated in the standard English translation.—MEB]

93. Cf. G. E. Lessing, "On the Proof of the Spirit and Power," in *Lessing's Theological Writings* (ed. Henry Chadwick; LMRT 2; trans. Henry Chadwick; London: Adam & Charles Black, 1956), 51: "Fulfilled prophecies, which I myself experience, are one thing; fulfilled prophecies, of which I know only from history that others say they have experienced them, are another."

94. Cf. Lüdemann, *Resurrection of Jesus*, 198 and elsewhere. Lüdemann follows Strauss in all essential points. For a critique of the historiographical and theological deficiencies in Lüdemann's constructions, cf. Dalferth, "Grab," 381ff.

95. David Friedrich Strauss, *The Old Faith and the New* (trans. Mathilde Blind; New York: H. Holt, 1873), 81–82.

appears between the reality of the historical event and the truth claim of the resurrection faith. Strauss hoped to resolve the tension he had thereby created by transferring the core of the Christian faith from the realm of history to the realm of ideas.[96] This is a deceptive hope, for the apparently positive results stood before a fundamental deficit: If the disciples are the cause and subject of the resurrection faith, then this event can be integrated into our understanding of reality. But it thereby loses its claim to be the truth, for in the long run truth cannot be maintained when unrelated to historical reality.

Various levels of objections are to be raised against this derivation of resurrection faith from internal psychological processes:

1. The historical argument: G. Lüdemann follows Strauss in regarding the traditions of the empty tomb as late apologetic legends. Lüdemann supposes that even the earliest Christian community did not know the location of Jesus's grave.[97] This is a thoroughly questionable historical argument, for Jesus's crucifixion clearly attracted much attention in Jerusalem. Thus neither Jesus's opponents nor his disciples and sympathizers would have been unaware[98] of the place where Joseph of Arimathea buried Jesus (Mark 15:42–47; see above, §4.2). Given that Jesus's disciples emerged in Jerusalem shortly afterward with the message that Jesus had been raised from the dead, the issue of Jesus's tomb must have been centrally important from the very beginning. It would have been easy to refute the disciples' preaching by pointing to a tomb that still contained Jesus's body.
2. The history-of-religions argument: There are no parallels from the history of contemporary religion to the concept of a person who after dying appeared to his or her associates.[99] If the appearances are understood exclusively on the basis of internal psychological phenomena, then there would have been other models for conceiving the event in order to express Jesus's special position. From the history-of-religions perspective, the eschatological affirmations of the early Christians are a unique combination.
3. The methodological argument: Strauss and Lüdemann necessarily present not an "objective" and historically cogent representation of

96. Cf. David Friedrich Strauss, *The Life of Jesus Critically Examined* (introduction by Peter C. Hodgson ed.; trans. George Eliot; London: SCM, 1973), 780: "This is the key to the whole of Christology, that, as subject of the predicate which the church assigns to Christ, we place, instead of an individual, an idea, but an idea which has an existence in reality, not in the mind only, like that of Kant."

97. Cf. Lüdemann, *Resurrection of Jesus*, 117: "The tomb was evidently unknown."

98. The redactional comment about the flight of the disciples in Mark 14:50 (cf. the πάντες-motif in Mark 14:27, 31, 50) by no means indicates that all Jesus's followers left Jerusalem.

99. Karrer, *Jesus Christus*, 35–36.

the resurrection event but their own history with Jesus of Nazareth. Their argument is determined by their epistemologically unfounded assumption that their analysis of the literary process by which the event was communicated is completely authoritative in deciding its reality. Such an analysis, however, can produce no assured results, for it does not apply to the event itself but only to its literary interpretations as found in particular texts, and the way these are interpreted is in turn dependent on the exegete's understanding of reality and history, which inevitably determines the actual results. The decision about the reality and truth content of the resurrection event thus always occurs within the premises of the worldview and the life history of the interpreters; these premises set forth the normative worldview and guiding interests of the interpretation and spring from within the interpreters themselves. In the subjective-vision hypothesis, the argument is based especially on psychological assumptions and historical postulates derived from them, without their advocates' having thought through the hermeneutical deficits involved in this approach.[100]

b. Resurrection dissolved into the kerygma. Following the (negative) results of the nineteenth century's quest for the historical Jesus, Bultmann intentionally abandoned the attempt to illuminate the Easter faith by historical methods: "The church had to surmount the scandal of the cross and did it in the Easter faith. How this act of decision took place in detail, how the Easter faith arose in individual disciples, has been obscured in the tradition by legend and is not of basic importance."[101] Bultmann understands Easter as an eschatological event, that is, an event that puts an end to all previous history, an event whose source is God, who brings in a new world and a new time. Since the resurrection is an eschatological event, Easter is misunderstood when one attempts to understand it by this-worldly criteria, for the resurrection is not a miracle that can be certified by evidence. This basic hermeneutical decision Bultmann finds in the New Testament itself, for there the Crucified One is not proclaimed in such a way "that the meaning of the cross is . . . disclosed from the life of Jesus as a figure of past history, a life that needs to be reproduced by historical research. On the contrary, Jesus is not proclaimed merely as the crucified; he is also risen from the dead. The cross and the resurrection form an inseparable unity."[102] But how exactly are the cross and resurrection related

100. For critique of Strauss and the subjective-vision hypothesis, cf. Grass, *Ostergeschehen*, 233ff.; for critique of Lüdemann, cf. Reinhard Slenczka, "'Nonsense' (Lk 24,11)," *KD* 40 (1994): 170–81; Ulrich Wilckens, "Die Auferstehung Jesu: Historisches Zeugnis—Theologie—Glaubenserfahrung," *PTh* 85 (1996): 102–20; Wolfhart Pannenberg, "Die Auferstehung Jesu—Historie und Theologie," *ZTK* 91 (1994): 318–28.

101. Bultmann, *Theology of the New Testament*, 1:45.

102. Bultmann, "New Testament and Mythology," 38.

to each other? The resurrection is nothing else than "an attempt to convey the meaning of the cross."[103] This eschatological event, once set in motion by God, continues to happen as the word is proclaimed and faith is generated. Thus it is correct to say that Jesus "has risen into the kerygma,"[104] inasmuch as the proclamation of the word is the continuation of God's eschatological act effective for believers. One may participate in an eschatological event in only one way, when one is inducted into the new world, that is, eschatological existence, and confesses in faith "that the cross really has the cosmic and eschatological significance ascribed to it."[105]

This procedural concept, specifically indebted to modern thought, raises two necessary questions:

1. In this coordination of cross and resurrection, what reality content is attributed to the resurrection? If the resurrection is "an expression of the meaning of the cross," then it is not a matter of making a judgment about its objective reality but a reflective judgment of a subject,[106] a judgment that marks the subject's own hermeneutical standpoint. Just how Bultmann thinks of Jesus's having risen into the kerygma remains unclear. The reality of the resurrection and one's confession of it are intentionally no longer distinguished and are thus effectively identified as the same thing. We have here an elegant but vague formulation that consciously veils the reality affirmed.[107] Precisely at the spot where the fundamental relation between history and truth needs to be clarified, "the meaning of each delimiting statement remains stuck in unresolved ambiguity."[108]
2. It is not possible to renounce the analysis of the historical dimensions of the resurrection event, because both the oldest tradition and Paul himself understand the resurrection event as an event bound to space and time. Moreover, if the powers of the resurrection continue at work in Christian faith, they must have a historical beginning point. To fail to pose the question of the historical dimensions of the resurrection of Jesus Christ is to lag behind the New Testament.[109]

103. Ibid., 39.

104. Bultmann, "Primitive Christian Kerygma," 42.

105. Bultmann, "New Testament and Mythology," 39.

106. Cf. the astute reflections of H.-G. Geyer, "Die Auferstehung Jesu Christi: Ein Überblick über die Diskussion in der evangelischen Theologie," in *Die Bedeutung der Auferstehungsbotschaft für den Glauben an Jesus Christus* (ed. F. Viering; Berlin: Evangelische Verlagsanstalt, 1967), 93–94.

107. For critique, cf. Karl Barth, *Church Dogmatics*, vol. 3.2, *The Doctrine of Creation* (trans. Geoffrey W. Bromiley et al.; Edinburgh: T&T Clark, 1960), 443–47.

108. Geyer, "Auferstehung Jesu Christi," 96.

109. The lively dispute about the cross and resurrection since 1945 is documented in Bertold Klappert, ed., *Diskussion um Kreuz und Auferstehung: Zur gegenwärtigen Auseinandersetzung in Theologie und Gemeinde* (9th ed.; Wuppertal: Aussaat Verlag, 1985).

c. Resurrection as real event in space and time. W. Pannenberg understands the Easter appearances as the objective expression of the manifestations of the Risen One.[110] He opposes the reductionistic worldview of modern times, which dogmatically excludes God from the world of reality. "'Historicity' does not necessarily mean that what is said to have taken place historically must be like other known events. The claim to historicity that is inseparable from the assertion of the facticity of an event simply involves the fact that it happened at a specific time. The question whether it is like other events may play a role in critical evaluation of the truth of the claim but is not itself a condition of the actual truth claim the assertion makes."[111] If the possibility of God's acting in time and history is held open, then there are also weighty historical arguments for the credibility of the Easter narratives. For Pannenberg, the tomb tradition, regarded historically, is just as original as the appearance tradition but is independent of it regarding the facts reported. It was only in the light of the appearances that the empty tomb became a witness of the resurrection; apart from the appearances, it remains ambiguous. Thus two mutually confirming witnesses for the Easter event vouch for its objectivity. "And in fact, not the report of the discovery of the empty tomb, taken by itself, but rather the convergence of the independent appearance tradition originating in Galilee with the Jerusalem tomb tradition has considerable weight in forming a historical judgment. In making historical judgments—to speak in general—the convergence of different findings has great importance."[112] Pannenberg does not avoid historical inquiry and argument and thus necessarily moves into the realm of judgment calls influenced by life history and worldview. The conclusiveness of *two* witnesses[113] that he presupposes may not, however, be able to bear the burden of proof, for Pannenberg himself thereby remains within the thought patterns of modern historical positivism.[114]

III. Resurrection as Transcendent Event

In modern times, thought has been historicized and the concept of truth subsumed under the rational methods of the prevailing science, resulting in a fundamental change in the way biblical texts and their claims are perceived. "Historicization has removed the Bible into the far distant temporal context

110. Wolfhart Pannenberg, *Jesus, God and Man* (2nd ed.; trans. Lewis L. Wilkins and Duane A. Priebe; Philadelphia: Westminster, 1977), 93–98.

111. Wolfhart Pannenberg, *Systematic Theology* (trans. Geoffrey W. Bromiley; 3 vols.; Grand Rapids: Eerdmans, 1991), 2:360–61.

112. Pannenberg, "Auferstehung Jesu," 327–28.

113. The coordination of appearances and empty tomb but also the proleptic element in the pre-Easter Jesus's claim to authority and God's raising him from the dead are mutually confirmatory; cf. Pannenberg, *Jesus, God and Man*, 53–73.

114. For critique of Pannenberg, see esp. Eckart Reinmuth, "Historik und Exegese—zum Streit um die Auferstehung Jesu nach der Moderne," in *Exegese und Methodendiskussion* (ed. Stefan Alkier and Ralph Brucker; TANZ 23; Tübingen: Francke, 1998), 1–8.

of its origin, opening a temporal gap between its past origins and its present meaning that—and this is the decisive point—the same methodological means cannot close."[115] The spotlights of the history of research have revealed decisive strategies for avoiding this dilemma or for constructing a bridge across the chasm. Resulting methodological insights include:

1. The problems cannot be resolved by declaring that inquiry about the resurrection from the dead is historically impossible or theologically illegitimate.[116] In each case, one simply avoids the question of whether the accounts of the resurrection event refer to something real; faith and reality are torn apart. The resurrection is left in the rubble of bygone history,[117] and when the connection to an original event is severed, faith becomes merely an ideological assertion.
2. Hermeneutical and historiographical reflections must precede the necessary historical inquiry, for they determine the respective constructions of reality and the concept of truth associated with each. With these methodological presuppositions, the following discussion attempts to understand the resurrection as a transcendent event.

Hermeneutical and historiographical considerations. When dealing with the topic of the resurrection, one must think in a special way about the question of the range and capability of historical knowledge (see above, §1.1), for it is beyond our experience of reality. Historical knowledge always takes place in view of a temporal gap from the event itself, which is always fading into the past beyond our grasp. This temporal gap is an absolute barrier to historical knowledge in the sense of comprehensively establishing "what actually happened." Moreover, historical events must always be interpreted, a state of affairs that results in the relativity of all historical knowledge. History is constructed only in the interpretation of the knowing subject; history is always a constructed model of what really happened, a mock-up of the event itself. In this process the worldview of the historian necessarily serves as the lens through which the data are viewed; that is, the understanding of reality accepted by the historian—his or her religious or religionless disposition—necessarily determines what can and what cannot be counted as historical.[118]

115. Rüsen, "Historische Methode," 358.

116. So, e.g., Conzelmann, *Theology of the New Testament*, 204, in the diction of the '50s and '60s: "The question of the historicity of the resurrection must be excluded from theology as being a misleading one. We have other concerns, 'that the cross shall not be made void of meaning'" (1 Cor. 1:17).

117. So, e.g., Dalferth, "Grab," 385: "It is the cross, not the resurrection, that anchors the faith in history. One can ask historical questions about the cross but not about the resurrection."

118. Appropriately, Pannenberg, *Systematic Theology*, 2:362: "Our judgment regarding the historicity of the resurrection of Jesus depends not only on examining the individual data (and

The prevailing worldviews are themselves subject to a constant process of change. No worldview can claim for itself a special place in history, for every worldview undergoes unavoidable changes, can never be an absolute, but itself always participates in the relativities of history. So simply pointing out that the New Testament worldview differs from the contemporary worldview does not show that it is deficient, because each generation must speak clearly within its own worldview—without later generations' being able to derive any absolute cognitive advance from their later worldview.

History is never simply there for all to see but is always constructed only through the retrospective view of the knowing subject. In modern times, this process of construction is oriented to particular methods as markers of scientific rationality, so that the prevailing truism is, "No meaning without method."[119] Methodology demystifies the meaning potential inherent in historical memory and levels everything out to a uniform mass. In the case of the resurrection, this demystification of history goes under the name of "analogy." Historical events can be properly evaluated only when they have analogies, when they can be understood within the nexus of cause and effect.[120] This is not the case with the resurrection of Jesus Christ from the dead, for—regarded historically—it deals with a singular phenomenon. So immediately the question arises whether such a unique event is historically credible. Can something be considered a historical event if it is absolutely unique over against all preceding history? The answer to this question depends on the theory of history accepted by each exegete.[121] Adherents of nomological conceptions will declare everything unhistorical that lies outside the realm of law as defined by themselves. In contrast, if one sees the constitutive element of history in temporal experiences, the horizon of one's perceptions change. "For the sake of its function in orientation, historical thinking has recourse to further experiences that are disregarded within the schema of nomological explanation, namely, experiences that do not fit the rule that change is always self-caused within a closed system. Such further experiences, in contrast to what is perceptible from the nomological approach, have the status of contingency."[122] For our question, this means that the appearances of the risen Jesus and the resurrection events that lie behind them may not be proved by historical method, but neither can

---

the related reconstruction of the event) but also on our understanding of reality, of what we regard as possible or impossible prior to any evaluation of the details."

119. Rüsen, "Historische Methode," 345.

120. Extremely influential, even to the present day, on this point is the work of Ernst Troeltsch, "Historical and Dogmatic Method in Theology," in *Religion in History* (ed. James Luther Adams and Ernst Troeltsch; trans. James Luther Adams and Walter E. Bense; Minneapolis: Fortress, 1991), 11–32, who expounds historical criticism, analogy, and correlation as the fundamental concepts of the historical, and thus of the real.

121. On this point, cf. Rüsen, *Rekonstruktion der Vergangenheit*, 22–86.

122. Ibid., 41.

they be excluded, if one includes the experiential category of contingency in one's construction of history.

Resurrection as transcendent event. If one's theory of history allows the possibility of the resurrection of Jesus Christ from the dead, and admits that the appearances of the Risen One that followed must be granted the same possible reality content as other events of the past, then the question arises as to the event's actual relation to reality. Although it cannot be subsumed [*einordnen*] under the categories of human reality, it can be coordinated [*zuordnen*] with them. It cannot be subsumed under human categories because for Paul, as for the New Testament as a whole, the resurrection is always understood strictly as the exclusive act of God (cf. 1 Thess. 4:14; 1 Cor. 6:14a, 15; Gal. 1:1; Rom. 4:24–25; 6:9; 8:11; 10:9). Properly speaking, the acting subject in the resurrection is God, which means that discourse regarding the resurrection of Jesus Christ is above all else a declaration concerning God himself and therefore is not available for current empirical verification.[123] The reality of the resurrection—since it is the creative act of God that raises the crucified and dead Jesus of Nazareth—must be distinguished from human experiences, appropriations, and expressions of this reality. If one combined and identified these two (divine act and its human experience and expression), then the question of the reality of this event could no longer be answered, and the possibility of divine act would be dependent on human confession. *When human beings equate God's possibilities with their own, they are no longer talking about God!*

To be sure, regarding the resurrection as God's act on Jesus of Nazareth does not do away with the question of the relation of this event to reality. Claiming that God himself speaks in the resurrection event and that God's act as such is not described but can only be confessed[124] must again be considered only an elegant avoiding of the problems. How is something supposed to be the foundation of my faith and thus of my understanding of reality if it cannot be brought into some relation to my reality? In my opinion, this necessary coordination is achieved with the concept of transcendence. The resurrection is first of all and essentially an event that goes beyond (*transcendere*) normal experience, an event that originates in God. It does not emerge, however, as the transcendence of the absolutely Holy One, or as the distancing monotheism of God the wholly Other, but rather as the act of the God who transcends his own eternity and, without giving up his freedom, enters into the realm of the creaturely world, of which is created by and belongs to God.[125] Within

123. Cf. C. Schwöbel, "Auferstehung," *RGG*[4] 1:926: "The act of God is the common reference point in speaking of the resurrection of the dead Jesus, in the faith of the earliest church that Jesus thereby comes to participate in the life of God and that he was certified as living by God himself, and in the commission to spread this message further."

124. So Dalferth, *Der auferweckte Gekreuzigte*, 56.

125. Cf. Tillich, *Systematic Theology*, 1:263: "God is immanent in the world as its permanent creative ground and is transcendent to the world through freedom. Both infinite freedom

the created world, human beings are the creatures whose being is permeated by experiences of transcendence. Human beings live in a world that is ultimately out of their reach, a world that was there before them and will be there after they are gone.[126] They can experience the world but not simply fuse themselves with it. The differences between experiences of one's own "I" and experiences that transcend one's self result not only in experiences of difference but in experiences of transcendence. Every experience at its core points to something absent and foreign to oneself, which evokes an experience of transcendence along with the experience of "ordinary" things.[127] To the transcendental dimensions of our experiences, alongside sleep and crises, belongs above all death,[128] whose reality cannot be doubted but nevertheless cannot be experienced. As the boundary situation of life, death is the location where resurrection, the transcendent event that proceeds from God, encounters the experiences of transcendence of the first witnesses of Jesus's resurrection. God's creative act on the crucified and dead Jesus of Nazareth calls forth in the first witnesses, including Paul, experiences of transcendence that open into meaning. The decisive experience and insight is that *in the resurrection of Jesus Christ from the dead, God has made death the locus of his love for human beings.*

These special experiences of transcendence cannot be subsumed under the categories of our reality, but they can be coordinated with them, for our reality is permeated throughout with different sorts of experience of transcendence. If one does not restrict the concept of experience to the natural sciences,[129] the experiences of the early witnesses of the resurrection are by no means so categorically different from "normal" experience as is commonly supposed. In particular, the early Christians processed their special experiences of transcendence in the way that experiences of transcendence fundamentally must be constructively processed: through meaning-formation.

The Appearance to Paul on the Damascus Road

The appearance of the Risen One to Paul (see above, §4.2) is also to be understood as a transcendent event that comes from God. At Damascus, God granted Paul a new evaluation of the Christ event (cf. 1 Cor. 9:1; 15:8; 2 Cor.

---

and finite human freedom make the world transcendent to God and God transcendent to the world."

126. Here I am following the reflections of Schutz and Luckmann, *Structures*, 2:102–30.

127. Luckmann, *Die unsichtbare Religion*, 167, distinguishes between "little" transcendent experiences (everyday events) and "great" transcendencies (above all, sleep and death).

128. Cf. Schutz and Luckmann, *Structures*, 2:125–29.

129. Cf. Hübner, *Wahrheit*, 340: "Whoever claims that science has proven the absolute and universally accepted validity of the laws of nature is advocating not science but a dogmatic metaphysic of science."

4:6; Gal. 1:12–16; Phil. 3:4b–11; Acts 9:3–19a; 22:1–16; 26:12–18), which gave him new knowledge on four fundamental points:[130]

1. Theological knowledge: God again speaks and acts; at the end of the age God reveals his saving act in a new way. Through God's intervention, completely new perspectives are opened up in and for history.
2. Christological knowledge: The crucified and risen Jesus of Nazareth now belongs forever at God's side; he is God's representative who takes his place in heaven as the "second power." As "Lord" (1 Cor. 1:9, κύριος), "the Anointed One" (1 Cor. 15:3, Χριστός [Christ, Messiah]), "Son" (Gal. 1:16, υἱός) and "image of God" (2 Cor. 4:4, εἰκὼν τοῦ θεοῦ), Jesus Christ is the permanent mediator of God's power and revelation. His exaltation and proximity to God reveal the honor of his unique office.
3. Soteriological knowledge: In the present, the exalted Christ already grants believers participation in his reign. They are already incorporated within a process of universal transformation that began with Christ's resurrection, continues in the power of the Spirit, and will soon move to its climactic conclusion at the parousia and judgment.
4. The biographical dimension: God has elected Paul and called him to announce this unheard-of good news to the nations. Paul himself thus becomes an integral element in God's plan of salvation, for he is the one through whom the gospel must be delivered to the world in order to save those who believe.

The texts have only a minimum to say about how this new knowledge came to Paul. The Damascus experience no doubt had both external (cf. 1 Cor. 9:1; 15:8) and internal (Gal. 1:16; 2 Cor. 4:6) dimensions, possibly including hearing a voice (cf. καλέω [call] in Gal. 1:15). But Paul provides no further interpretation of the content or of the psychology involved, so we should draw no conclusions beyond what these texts themselves say.[131]

The overwhelming experience of the risen Jesus Christ determined the life of the apostle from that point forward. God acts to open new horizons for Paul: human judgment on the crucified Jesus was invalidated; Jesus had not died on the cross as one under God's curse, but he belongs at God's side, where he

130. For analysis of the texts and a more comprehensive interpretation of the Damascus event, cf. Udo Schnelle, "Vom Verfolger zum Verkündiger: Inhalt und Tragweite des Damaskusgeschehens," in *Forschungen zum Neuen Testament und seiner Umwelt* (ed. Christoph Niemand; Frankfurt: Lang, 2002), 299–323.

131. Cf. Werner Georg Kümmel, *Römer 7 und das Bild des Menschen im Neuen Testament: Zwei Studien* (TBü 53; Munich: Kaiser, 1974), 160, who warns with regard to elaborate interpretations of the Damascus event: "All psychological hypotheses and all claims that go beyond what can be extracted from the sources only pass by the facts and forget the appropriate respect for historical reality."

continues as God's representative, the bearer of God's glory. Damascus is the fundamental point of departure for Pauline meaning-formation. Whereas he could formerly understand the proclamation of the crucified Messiah only as provocation, the Damascus experience led him to the insight that the cross was filled with the inherent potential for unexpected meaning. Paul now combines biographical thinking with universal perspectives, for he stands before the task of taking his experience and interpretation of a past event that happened to one individual and erecting a meaning structure that provides orientation in the present and hope for the future. From the religious certainty of the Damascus event, Paul sets in motion a process of universalistic meaning-formation that will have unparalleled effects, making it possible for all people to understand their own existence within the whole scheme of things.

The Cross

For Paul, the Risen One is and remains the Crucified One (2 Cor. 13:4, "For he was crucified in weakness, but lives by the power of God"). The salvific significance of the resurrection casts the death of Jesus in a new light. For Paul, there is an interaction between death and resurrection. The resurrection is the objective grounding for the saving significance of Jesus's death, while at the same time the resurrection kerygma, in Paul's hermeneutic, presents the ultimate meaning of the cross. Even after the resurrection, Jesus remains the crucified one (the perfect passive participle ἐσταυρωμένος, 1 Cor. 1:23; 2:2; Gal. 3:1).[132] "The Risen One still bears the nail prints of the cross."[133] In Paul, a biographical experience attains theological quality. He persecutes Jesus's followers because of their claim that the Messiah is one who has been crucified. In the context of Deut. 21:22–23, this message must be resisted as blasphemy. Paul was convinced that the curse pronounced by the Torah applied to one who had been crucified (Gal. 3:13). The revelation at Damascus reversed the coordinates of this theological system. Paul recognized that the accursed one on the cross is the Son of God; that is, in the light of the resurrection, the cross was transformed from the place of the curse to the place of salvation. Thus Paul can call out to the Corinthians, "We proclaim Christ crucified, a stumbling block to Jews and foolishness to Gentiles" (1 Cor. 1:23).

The cross appears in Paul's letters (1) as historical location, (2) as argumentative and theological theme, and (3) as theological symbol.

1. Paul's talk of the cross is always permeated by theology. This does not mean, however, that Paul detaches it from history but that his beginning point is the cross as the *place where Jesus of Nazareth died*. By using the expression

132. Cf. Blass and Debrunner, *Grammar*, §340: the perfect tense "denotes the continuance of the completed action."

133. Gerhard Friedrich, *Die Verkündigung des Todes Jesu im Neuen Testament* (BTS 6; Neukirchen-Vluyn: Neukirchener Verlag, 1982), 137.

σκάνδαλον τοῦ σταυροῦ (scandal/stumbling block of the cross, 1 Cor. 1:23; Gal. 5:11), Paul refers to the concrete, degrading manner of the crucifixion, a death that identifies the victim not as Son of God, but as a criminal. To revere a victim of crucifixion as Son of God appeared to the Jews as theologically scandalous[134] and to the Greco-Roman world as lunacy.[135] The central place of the crucified one in the Pauline symbolic universe meant that every current cultural plausibility was stood on its head, for now the cross is the *signum* of divine wisdom.[136]

Paul holds fast to the cross as the historical location of the love of God. He resists a complete kerygmatizing of the unique historical event. God's time-transcending act identifies itself as salvific because it has a real place and a real time, a name and a history.[137] Pauline theology's concentration on the exalted and present Kyrios Jesus Christ is based on his identity with the crucified and dead Jesus of Nazareth. Faith cannot flee into the mythical realm because it is rooted in this world by the cross, as the Pauline addition in Phil. 2:8c (θανάτου δὲ σταυροῦ) makes clear. The concrete, once-for-all uniqueness of the saving event and its unmistakable character (cf. Rom. 6:10) are indispensable for the identity of Christian faith. Thus Paul asks the Corinthians, "Was Paul crucified for you?" (1 Cor. 1:13a). If Pilate had known who Jesus of Nazareth truly is, he would not have crucified the "Lord of glory" (1 Cor. 2:8).[138] The offense of the cross has continuing effects; Paul is persecuted because he proclaims the cross (Gal. 5:11), while his opponents avoid persecution and thus abolish the scandal of the cross (Gal. 6:12; Phil. 3:18). Only as the unique event of the past does the cross become the eschatological event, that is, the event that transcends time. The presence of the cross in preaching presupposes that only the crucified one is the Risen One, and so the significance of the cross is always bound to its historical location.

2. The cross appears in several Pauline contexts as an *argumentative and theological theme*, especially in 1 Corinthians. In Corinth it has to do with rightly determining the identity of God's wisdom. Paul attempts to make clear to this church, which is striving for present fulfillment, that wisdom is revealed at the place where human beings suppose only foolishness is to be

134. On the translation of σκάνδαλον as "offense" [*Anstoß*], cf. Hans Wolfgang Kuhn, "Jesus als Gekreuzigter in der frühchristlichen Verkündigung bis zur Mitte des 2. Jahrhunderts," *ZNW* 72 (1975): 36–37.

135. Cf. Pliny the Younger, *Ep.* 10.96.8: "muddled wild superstition."

136. There are, however, possible cultural points of contact; thus in Plato the just man appears as dishonored: "They will tell you that the just man who is thought unjust will be scourged, racked, bound—will have his eyes burnt out; and at last, after suffering every kind of evil, he will be impaled [ἀνασχινδυλεύω, skewer, nail to]: Then he will understand that he ought to seem only, and not to be, just" (*Resp.* 2.361c).

137. Hans Weder, *Das Kreuz Jesu bei Paulus: Ein Versuch, über den Geschichtsbezug des christlichen Glaubens nachzudenken* (Göttingen: Vandenhoeck & Ruprecht, 1981), 228ff.

138. For interpretation, cf. Wolff, *1. Korintherbrief*, 55–57.

found (1 Cor. 1:18ff.). God's way of working can be read off the cross, as the God who has chosen the weak and despised (1 Cor. 1:26–29) and who has led the apostle to a way of life and thought determined by the Lord (1 Cor. 2:2). If some in the church suppose that they are already in the state of fulfillment that is to occur only at the end of history (1 Cor. 4:8), then they have exchanged God's wisdom for their own or for the wisdom of the world. There is no wisdom or glory that can bypass the Crucified One (1 Cor. 2:6ff.); the resurrection can be declared only as the resurrection of the one who was crucified. The truth of the matter is thus: "For the message of the cross is foolishness to those who are perishing, but to us who are being saved it is the power of God" (1 Cor. 1:18).

The Corinthians do not simply eliminate the cross;[139] they neutralize it by interpreting it merely as Jesus's passageway to true spiritual existence, as the Preexistent One returns to the place from which he came. In contrast to Paul, the Corinthians understand the gift of the Spirit primarily as the overcoming of the limitations of their previous creaturely existence, as an increasing of their vital forces and life expectancy.[140] In the context of their present and individualistic beginnings in this new life, both suffering and sin are minimized. The central idea is the intensification of life's possibilities through a deity whose destiny has already overcome the limitations of death and who now guarantees the reality of the transcendent world in the present life. The Corinthians wanted to escape the limitations of creaturely existence; not humility, but exaltation and lordship seem to them to be the appropriate expression of their redeemed state. In contrast, the apostles are "fools for Christ's sake" (1 Cor. 4:10). They provide a different model of the saved life in that, for the sake of the church, they conduct their ministry in weakness, danger, and poverty (cf. 4:11–13). They thus represent the category of the truly wise, who know themselves to be independent of all external evaluation, obligated only to their commission and their message. Accordingly, the form of apostolic existence bears the stamp of the Crucified One.

The essential nature of apostleship is concisely expressed in the *peristasis (hardship) catalogs*; it is hardly an accident that of the four such catalogs, three are found in 2 Corinthians (1 Cor. 4:11–13; 2 Cor. 4:7–12; 6:4–10; 11:23–29).[141]

139. Cf. Thomas Söding, "Das Geheimnis Gottes im Kreuz Jesu (1Kor)," *BZ* 38 (1994): 71–92.

140. Cf. Horn, *Angeld des Geistes*, 248, who rightly argues that the Corinthian enthusiasm was the product of their baptismal theology.

141. For analysis, see Erhardt Güttgemanns, *Der leidende Apostel und sein Herr: Studien zur paulinischen Christologie* (Göttingen: Vandenhoeck & Ruprecht, 1966), 94ff. Martin Ebner, *Leidenslisten und Apostelbrief: Untersuchungen zu Form, Motivik und Funktion der Peristasenkataloge bei Paulus* (FzB 66; Würzburg: Echter Verlag, 1991), 196ff.; Markus Schiefer-Ferrari, *Die Sprache des Leids in den paulinischen Peristasenkatalogen* (SBB 23; Stuttgart: Katholisches Bibelwerk, 1991), 201ff.; Gerhard Hotze, *Paradoxien bei Paulus: Untersuchungen zu einer elementaren Denkform in seiner Theologie* (NTA NF 33; Münster: Aschendorff, 1997), 252–87.

The peristasis catalogs compactly express the motif that the whole life of the apostle is determined by the Christ event as God's saving act for humanity in both sovereignty and lowliness. The apostle always bears the death of Jesus in his own body "so that the life of Jesus may also be made visible in our bodies. For while we live, we are always being given up to death for Jesus's sake, so that the life of Jesus may be made visible in our mortal flesh. So death is at work in us, but life in you" (2 Cor. 4:10b–12). Apostolic existence entails participation in the event of Jesus's cross, and that participation cannot be reduced to mere verbal preaching; it is a reality that involves the apostle's whole existence. The life of the apostle is the *existential illustration of the kerygma*, so that the apostle can follow no other path than his Lord.

For Paul, the cross of Christ is the decisive theological criterion; he gives no argument for the cross but speaks from the fact of the cross as the axiomatic foundation of what he has to say. Even more, the cross of Christ is a present reality in the message of the cross (1 Cor. 1:17–18). The Scripture has already testified that the content of God's wisdom can never be filled in from the wisdom of the world (1:19); both must be strictly distinguished from each other, for they are not derived from comparable sources of knowledge. Not in the heights of human wisdom and knowledge but in the depths of suffering and death has the father of Jesus Christ shown himself to be the God hospitable to humanity. God's act in Jesus Christ is thus manifest as a paradoxical event that both anticipates and contradicts human doing and human wisdom.[142]

3. In every place where the cross is introduced into Paul's argumentative contexts, it is also a *symbol*. Because it first of all continues to be a historical location, the cross is able to be both fact and symbol at the same time.[143] It has a referential character, pointing to an actual event of the past, but through the power of the Spirit, this past event is also made real in the present. As the place of the once-for-all transfer of Jesus Christ into the new realm of being, the present existence of the believer is also stamped with the reality of the cross. In each case it designates the crossing over from death to life and attains its present dimension in a twofold ritual context:

1. In baptism, the believer is incorporated into the event of Christ's crucifixion and resurrection in that here the power of sin and death is overcome and the status of the new being is conferred. The perfect

142. How radically Paul's theology of the cross contradicts the contemporary Greek-Hellenistic picture of God is seen, e.g., in Diogenes Laertius, *Vit. phil.* 10.123, where Epicurus challenges his students to construct an appropriate idea of God: "First, think of God as an immortal and happy being, corresponding to the idea of God usually held, and do not impute anything to him that clashes with his immortality or his eternal bliss."

143. Cf. Christian Strecker, *Die liminale Theologie des Paulus: Zugänge zur paulinischen Theologie aus kulturanthropologischer Perspektive* (Göttingen: Vandenhoeck & Ruprecht, 1999), 262–63.

passive verb συνεσταύρωμαι (I have been crucified with) in Gal. 2:19, like σύμφυτοι γεγόναμεν (united with him in a death like his) in Rom. 6:5, underscores the reality and power of the baptismal event in which the believer is crucified with Christ, a power at work in the present and determining it anew.

2. In Galatians Paul develops a critique of the Judaists' demand for circumcision, a critique based on his theological understanding of the cross. Circumcision was made a competitor with baptism as the initiation ritual into the people of God and thereby became a competitor with the cross. Circumcision maintained the ethnic differences between Jews and other peoples, whereas the cross symbolized the transvaluation of all previous values, and baptism specifically abolished all previous privileges (Gal. 3:26–28). The cross symbolizes God's surprising act, which puts all human standards out of commission. The wisdom of the cross is incompatible with the wisdom of the world. The cross radically calls into question every human self-assertion and individualistic striving after salvation because it leads to weakness rather than power, to mourning rather than celebration, to shame rather than to glory, to the lostness of death rather than the glory of salvation already fulfilled in the present. This foolishness of the cross cannot be identified with any ideology or philosophy and refuses to be made the instrument of any program because it is grounded solely in the love of God.

This language of the cross is a distinctive element of Pauline theology. The apostle does not develop it from church tradition but from his own biography: at Damascus God revealed to him the truth about the crucified one, who did not remain in the realm of death. The word of the cross designates the foundational transformation process in the Christ event and in the lives of baptized believers, and so it leads directly to the center of Pauline thinking.[144] *The theology of the cross appears as a fundamental interpretation of God, the world, and life; it is the midpoint of the Pauline symbolic universe.* It instructs one to interpret reality by beginning with the God who reveals himself in the crucifixion of Jesus and to orient one's thinking and acting by this revealed reality. Human values, norms, and categories receive a new interpretation in the light of the cross of Christ, for God's values are the revaluing of all human values. The gospel of the crucified Jesus Christ grants salvation through faith because this is where God reveals himself, the God who wants to be the savior of human beings precisely in their lostness and nothingness. In the cross, God reveals his love, which is able to suffer and therefore able to renew.

144. Contra Kuhn, "Jesus als Gekreuzigter," 40, who locates the Pauline statements about the cross exclusively in a polemical context; 1 Cor. 1:23; 2:2; Gal. 3:1 show clearly that the language of the cross was a constituent element of Paul's proclamation from the very beginning.

6.2.3 Salvation and Liberation through Jesus Christ

For Paul, Jesus Christ the Crucified and Risen One is the central figure of the end time. He completely determines the apostle's understanding of reality: "For his sake I have suffered the loss of all things, and I regard them as rubbish, in order that I may gain Christ" (Phil. 3:8). Paul sees the world, life and death, present and future, all from the perspective of the Christ event, and it is already true that "all things are yours, whether Paul or Apollos or Cephas or the world or life or death or the present or the future—all belong to you, and you belong to Christ, and Christ belongs to God" (1 Cor. 3:21–23). Paul's symbolic universe is definitively shaped by the conception that in the end time Jesus Christ acts first of all as savior and liberator; *savior* from the coming *wrath of God* and *liberator* from the *power of death*.[145]

Only the Son of God, Jesus Christ, saves believers from the wrath of God in the coming judgment (cf. 1 Thess. 1:10). It is not God's will that believers be subject to wrath; they will receive salvation through the Lord Jesus Christ (1 Thess. 5:9; Rom. 5:9).[146] The gospel is the power of God for the salvation of believers (Rom. 1:16). Paul prays for the people of Israel, that they too will be saved (Rom. 10:1). He himself lives in the awareness that salvation is now nearer than the time when he and the Roman Christians became believers (Rom. 13:11). Because God has raised Jesus Christ from the dead, those who have been called to faith hope confidently for salvation at the imminent parousia (cf. 1 Thess. 4:14; 5:10).

Especially in the thanksgiving section at the beginning of his letters, Paul emphasizes the salvation of the churches as the content of his prayer of gratitude. The initial section of the communication is especially important, for it sets up the new common understanding of reality and essentially determines the mutual understanding between apostle and church for which he strives.[147] In his letter to the Thessalonians, Paul reminds them of their election as the presupposition of their salvation (1 Thess. 1:4, 10). He assures the Corinthians that Jesus Christ will "strengthen you to the end, so that you may be blameless on the day of our Lord Jesus Christ. God is faithful; by him you were called into the fellowship of his Son, Jesus Christ our Lord" (1 Cor. 1:8–9). On the "day of the Lord" the Corinthian Christians will be Paul's boast (2 Cor. 1:14), and this confidence alone comforts him in his present troubles (2 Cor. 1:5).

145. Cf. the foundational work of William Wrede, *Paul* (trans. Edward Lummis; Boston: American Unitarian Association, 1908), 85–121; Schweitzer, *Mysticism*, 65–74; E. P. Sanders, *Paul and Palestinian Judaism: A Comparison of Patterns of Religion* (Philadelphia: Fortress, 1977), 421–27; Strecker, *Theology of the New Testament*, 116–38.

146. Thüsing, *Paulinischen Soteriologie*, 203–6.

147. Stefan Alkier, *Wunder und Wirklichkeit in den Briefen des Apostels Paulus: Ein Beitrag zu einem Wunderverständnis jenseits von Entmythologisierung und Rehistorisierung* (WUNT 134; Tübingen: Mohr, 2001), 91ff.

Paul thanks God, "who in Christ always leads us in triumphal procession, and through us spreads in every place the fragrance that comes from knowing him" (2 Cor. 2:14). Only through faith in the Son of God, Jesus Christ, do human beings have access to God and thus to salvation. Apart from this faith, rulership is exercised by "the god of this world" (2 Cor. 4:4) and by unbelief, which leads to ruin. Although the thanksgiving section is missing from the Letter to the Galatians, Paul nonetheless extends the greeting formula in his characteristic manner: "Grace to you and peace from God our Father and the Lord Jesus Christ, who gave himself for our sins to set us free from the present evil age, according to the will of our God and Father" (Gal. 1:3–4). Paul is effusive in his praise of the salvific status of the Roman church (Rom. 1:5–12; 15:14–15), for the whole world speaks of its faith (Rom. 1:18). So also, in Phil. 1:5–6 the apostle explicitly portrays the temporal framework of God's act in the past and present up to the future judgment: "because of your sharing in the gospel from the first day until now. I am confident of this, that the one who began a good work among you will bring it to completion by the day of Jesus Christ." The apostle and his churches are convinced that their election, visibly manifest in baptism, and their call as participants in the gospel maintain their validity into the eschaton.

The Christ event strips the power from death, personified as God's eschatological antagonist (cf. 1 Cor. 15:55), and Jesus Christ is manifest as the liberator from the power of death and the powers associated with it, σάρξ (flesh) and ἁμαρτία (sin). As the last enemy, death will be subjugated to Christ at the end of time (1 Cor. 15:26), then the creation itself will be set free from its "bondage to decay" (Rom. 8:21). Paul develops these ideas extensively in his Adam/Christ typology (Rom. 5:12–21), which is stamped with the conception of two figures that determine humanity as a whole: Adam and Christ. As death entered the world through the transgression of the first central figure, so the power of death is reversed and destroyed by God's gracious act in Christ. Of course, death continues to exist as a biological reality, but it has lost its eschatological dimension as a power that separates from God. Although, as individual figures, Adam and Christ each determine the destiny of humanity as a whole, at the same time Jesus surpasses Adam, for the disaster Adam brought about is more than abolished through God's eschatological gift of grace. So also the idea of ransom/redemption (ἀπολύτρωσις, 1 Cor. 1:30; Rom. 3:24; 8:23; ἐξαγοράζω, Gal. 3:13; 4:5; ἀγοράζω, 1 Cor. 6:20; 7:23) concisely expresses the liberating act of Jesus Christ: Jesus Christ took upon himself what held human beings in bondage; he paid "for us" the price of our liberation[148] from the powers of sin and death (see below, §6.5.2).

148. On the possible background of the redemption metaphor (purchasing freedom for a slave) in the history of religions, cf. Friedrich, *Verkündigung des Todes Jesu*, 82–86; Gerhard Barth, *Der Tod Jesu Christi im Verständnis des Neuen Testaments* (Neukirchen-Vluyn: Neukirchener

The consequence of the freedom obtained by Christ is σωτηρία (salvation, deliverance). In worship, the congregation invokes Jesus Christ as "Savior," who as Cosmocrator will transform the earthly and transient body (Phil. 3:20–21). Salvation will occur at the imminent parousia of the Lord (Rom. 13:11); it is the consequence of repentance (2 Cor. 7:10) and the content of the Christian hope (1 Thess. 5:8–9). Salvation is already present in the proclamation of the apostle (2 Cor. 6:2) and takes place in the call of believers (cf. 1 Thess. 2:16; 1 Cor. 1:18; 15:2; 2 Cor. 2:15). The church can live in the confidence that its faith and its confession will save it (Rom. 10:9–10). The present experience of salvation and the confidence of future salvation collapse into each other: "For in hope were we saved" (Rom. 8:24, τῇ γὰρ ἐλπίδι ἐσώθημεν).

6.2.4 The Substitutionary Death of Jesus Christ "for Us"

Paul makes use of differing interpretative models in order to portray the salvific meaning of the death of Jesus. The dominant basic model is the concept of *substitution*,[149] which is concisely expressed in the concept of Jesus's pro-existence. Semantically, however, the term "substitution" itself is not univocal but points to a whole range of meanings that includes christological, soteriological, and ethical motifs. The concept combines phenomena that may be distinguished but cannot always be separated. In particular, the relation atonement/substitution is a problem in Pauline thought,[150] for Paul's terminology does not correspond precisely to the German word *Sühne* or the English word *atonement*.[151] At the same time, "substitution" is associated with such motifs as forgiveness of sins, sacrifice, and suffering for others, which could be among the images of atonement included in the interpretative horizon of the word. Also, the death of Jesus "for" (ἀποθνήσκω ὑπέρ) can be accentuated

Verlag, 1992), 71–75; D. F. Tolmie, "Salvation as Redemption," in *Salvation in the New Testament* (ed. J. G. Van der Watt; NovTSup 121; Leiden: Brill, 2005), 247–69.

149. Cf., e.g., Gerhard Delling, "Der Tod Jesu in der Verkündigung des Paulus," in *Studien zum Neuen Testament und zum hellenistischen Judentum: Gesammelte Aufsätze 1950–1968* (ed. Ferdinand Hahn et al.; Göttingen: Vandenhoeck & Ruprecht, 1970), 336–46; Cilliers Breytenbach, "Versöhnung, Stellvertretung und Sühne," *NTS* 39 (1993): 77–78; Jens Schröter, *Der versöhnte Versöhner: Paulus als unentbehrlicher Mittler im Heilsvorgang zwischen Gott und Gemeinde nach 2 Kor 2,14–7,4* (TANZ 10; Tübingen: Francke, 1993), 316.

150. For the history of research, cf. F. Bieringer, "Traditionsgeschichtlicher Ursprung und theologische Bedeutung der ὑπέρ–Aussagen im Neuen Testament," in *The Four Gospels, 1992: Festschrift Frans Neirynck* (ed. Frans van Segbroeck et al.; 3 vols.; BETL 100; Louvain: Leuven University Press, 1992), 1:219–48. For the history of the problem in recent discussion, see J. Frey, "Probleme der Deutung des Todes Jesu," in *Deutungen des Todes Jesu im Neuen Testament* (WUNT 181; Tübingen: Mohr, 2005), 3–50. Cf. also J. Christine Janowski et al., eds., *Stellvertretung: Theologische, philosophische und kulturelle Aspekte* (Neukirchen-Vluyn: Neukirchener Verlag, 2006).

151. Cf. Breytenbach, "Versöhnung, Stellvertretung und Sühne," 60ff.

differently, linguistically speaking, for the preposition ὑπέρ with the genitive[152] can have the derived meaning "for the benefit of," "in the interest of," "for the sake of," or "in place of, instead of."[153] In order to avoid prejudicing the content, we must analyze the relevant texts individually, beginning with the pre-Pauline tradition. We will therefore presuppose the following understanding of "substitution": "*to do something for others, and thus also do it in their stead, in order to produce a salvific effect.*"

In the pre-Pauline tradition of 1 Cor. 15:3b, the substitutionary formulation refers to the removal of the sins of the confessing community (Χριστὸς ἀπέθανεν ὑπὲρ τῶν ἁμαρτιῶν ἡμῶν [Christ died for our sins]).[154] Because Christ is named as the specific subject of the event and there is no mention of sacrificial categories, we should not here speak of atonement. Jesus's giving of himself ([διδόναι] ὑπὲρ τῶν ἁμαρτιῶν) in Gal. 1:4 is for the liberation of human beings from the power of the present evil age.[155] The apocalyptic background again speaks for an interpretation that is not influenced by the concept of atonement in the priestly document of the Pentateuch ("P"): the vicarious self-giving of Jesus Christ effected our deliverance from the bondage of the old aeon, a bondage that came to expression in "our" sins. The "handing over" formula in Rom. 4:25 is probably influenced by Isa. 53:12 LXX,[156] without bringing in the atonement theology of the Priestly document:[157] Jesus Christ's substitutionary self-giving removes the negative effects of "our" transgressions, just as his resurrection makes possible "our" justification.

Coming from the pre-Pauline to the Pauline level, 1 Thess. 5:10 already shows the apostle's fundamental concept: Jesus's death "for" makes possible the new creation and salvation of human beings. Jesus Christ died "for us [ὑπὲρ ἡμῶν], so that whether we are awake or asleep we may live with him." The substitutionary concept can also have ecclesiological dimensions (1 Cor. 1:13, "Was Paul crucified for you?") and ethical aspects (Jesus died for the weak brother or sister; 1 Cor. 8:11, δι' ὃ Χριστὸς ἀπέθανεν [for whose sake Christ died]; ὑπὲρ οὗ), and that without making use of the sin/atonement language and imagery. The substitutionary concept in the strict sense (instead of, in the place of) is found in 2 Cor. 5:14b–15: "We are convinced that one has died for

152. Paul's statements on substitution are constructed primarily using ὑπέρ with the genitive (cf. 1 Thess. 5:10; 1 Cor. 1:13; 15:3; 2 Cor. 5:14, 15, 21; Gal. 1:4; 2:20; 3:13; Rom. 5:6, 8; 8:32; 14:15); with διά in 1 Cor. 8:11; Rom. 4:25.

153. The original meaning of ὑπέρ was "over" in the local sense; cf. Passow et al., *Handwörterbuch*, 2.2:2066–67.

154. For analysis, cf. most recently Thomas Knöppler, *Sühne im Neuen Testament: Studien zum urchristlichen Verständnis der Heilsbedeutung des Todes Jesu* (Neukirchen-Vluyn: Neukirchener Verlag, 2001), 127–29, who sees Isa. 53:4–55 LXX and 1 Kings 16:18–19 in the background.

155. For analysis, cf. ibid., 129–31.

156. So, e.g., ibid. 132; differently Koch, *Schrift als Zeuge*, 237–38.

157. Cf. Breytenbach, "Versöhnung, Stellvertretung und Sühne," 70.

all; therefore all have died. And he died for all, so that those who live might live no longer for themselves, but for him who died and was raised for them." Christ "loved me and gave himself for me [ὑπὲρ ἐμοῦ]" (Gal. 2:20), and so the present reality is this: "He who did not withhold his own Son, but gave him up for all of us [ὑπὲρ ἡμῶν πάντων], will he not with him also give us everything else?" (Rom. 8:32). In Gal. 3:13 Paul combines the imagery of substitution with that of redeeming someone from slavery: "Christ redeemed us from the curse of the law by becoming a curse for us [ὑπὲρ ἡμῶν]."[158] Those who once were slaves have now become sons and daughters (Gal. 3:26–28; 4:4–6). Christ died in the place of the sinner in that "For our sake [ὑπὲρ ἡμῶν] he [God] made him to be sin who knew no sin, so that in him [Christ] we might become the righteousness of God" (2 Cor. 5:21).[159] Jesus's death is not some sort of heroic achievement (cf. Rom. 5:7, "Indeed, rarely will anyone die for a righteous person—though perhaps for a good person someone might actually dare to die")[160] but a dying for the godless (Rom. 5:6), "for us," for sinners (Rom. 5:8). God sent his Son to take away sin (περὶ ἁμαρτίας, Rom. 8:3), who entered into sin's own territory in order to overcome its power. The tradition of the sending-Christology here stands in the background (cf. Gal. 4:4–5; 1 John 4:9; John 3:16–17), so that a general concept of reconciliation, not the specific sacrificial offerings of the Old Testament atonement theology, is the conceptual matrix.[161] So also the idea that Christ's death is for our benefit (in the interest of, for the advantage of), in that it sets aside our sins, allows room for introducing the idea of atonement as a heuristic category. "Often the two aspects can be separated only with difficulty. The substitutionary death is a dying for the benefit of those who are spared, and the Christ who dies for the benefit of human beings takes upon himself what should apply to them, so that his atoning death is also a substitutionary death."[162]

We should strictly distinguish the background of the "for us" statements in the history of the tradition from the preceding imagery, for such statements have nothing to do with the cultic offering of a sacrifice.[163] The idea of cultic atonement by no means forms the tradition-historical background of the Pau-

158. For a comprehensive analysis of Gal. 3:10–14 cf. Christoph Schluep, *Der Ort des Christus: Soteriologische Metaphern bei Paulus als Lebensregeln* (Zürich: TVZ, Theologischer Verlag Zürich, 2005), 227–307.

159. The ἁμαρτία of 2 Cor. 5:21 is by no means to be understood as a sin offering; cf. Karrer, *Jesus Christus*, 122: "While a sin offering atones for sins that have already happened, here the sinless one takes the place of sin as such and removes this power from its place."

160. In Rom. 5:7 there is clearly present the Hellenistic idea of one person dying to protect another person, the fatherland, or a virtue; cf. the texts in *NW* 1.2:592–97, 715–25; 2.1:117–19.

161. With Breytenbach, "Versöhnung, Stellvertretung und Sühne," 71–72, contra Stuhlmacher, *Biblische Theologie*, 1:291.

162. Friedrich, *Verkündigung des Todes Jesu*, 74.

163. Cf. ibid., 75; Barth, *Der Tod Jesu*, 59; further in Breytenbach, "Versöhnung, Stellvertretung und Sühne," 66, who appropriately notes regarding Rom. 3:25, "Prior to composing

line ὑπὲρ statements,[164] since it is precisely the characteristic LXX expression of Leviticus, ἐξιλάσκεσθαι περί (to make atonement for/on behalf of), that Paul does *not* employ as his term for atonement for sin (cf. Lev. 5:6–10 LXX).[165] Instead it is much more likely that the Greek idea of the substitutionary death of the righteous, whose death effects the expiation/taking away of sin, is the starting point for the formation of this tradition.[166] This idea especially had already deeply influenced Jewish martyr theology, as we find, for example, in 2 Macc. 7:37–38; 4 Macc. 6:27–29; 17:21–22. In pre-Pauline Hellenistic Jewish Christianity,[167] the eucharistic tradition (1 Cor. 11:24b, τοῦτό μού ἐστιν τὸ σῶμα τὸ ὑπὲρ ὑμῶν, lit. "this is my body for you") had also influenced, with a limited adoption of the language of Isa. 53:11–12 LXX,[168] the development of the idea of the death of the righteous as a substitute for all. This breaks the irresolvable connection between sin and death and thereby makes possible a new and authentic life. This idea is particularly concentrated in the formulae of death (cf. 1 Thess. 5:10; 1 Cor. 1:13; 8:11; 15:3b; 2 Cor. 5:14–15; Gal. 2:21; Rom. 5:6–8, 14–15) and self-giving (cf. Gal. 1:4; 2:20; Rom. 4:25; 8:32).[169] Paul adopts it and emphasizes the universal dimensions of the event: the crucified one suffers the violence of death for humanity in order to deliver humanity from the ruinous powers of sin and death.

6.2.5 Atonement

The concept of atonement as understood in its context of temple and sacrifice is *not* a central element of Pauline theology.[170] Paul takes it up only once, though it is in a central theological passage;[171] in Rom. 3:25–26 he speaks of Jesus Christ, "whom God put forward as a sacrifice of atonement [ἱλαστήριον,

---

this one passage, Paul had managed without the language of 'atonement' and 'atone' when he is explaining to his churches the gospel he proclaims."

164. Contra Wilckens, *Römer*, 1:240, according to whom "throughout the New Testament the cultic idea of atonement is the horizon within which the saving significance of Jesus's death is thought through."

165. Cf. Breytenbach, "Versöhnung, Stellvertretung und Sühne," 69.

166. Cf., e.g., Seneca, *Ep.* 76.27: "If the situation calls for you to die for your country, and the price of saving them is that you give your own life"; cf. also *Ep.* 67.9; Cicero, *Fin.* 22.61; *Tusc.* 1.89; Josephus, *JW* 5.419. Further data in *NW* 1.2:592–97, 715–25. For a substantive discussion of the issue, cf. Barth, *Der Tod Jesu*, 59–64.

167. Cf. Breytenbach, "Versöhnung, Stellvertretung und Sühne," 205–15.

168. Cf. Barth, *Der Tod Jesu*, 56–59.

169. For analysis, cf. Wengst, *Christologische Formeln*, 55–86.

170. Differently, e.g., Martin Gaukesbrink, *Die Sühnetradition bei Paulus: Rezeption und theologischer Stellenwert* (FzB 32; Würzburg: Echter Verlag, 1999), 283: "Paul formulates and develops his Christology, which biographically goes back to the Damascus event, theologically in terms of the atonement tradition."

171. For evidence of the pre-Pauline character of Rom. 3:25–26, cf. Schnelle, *Gerechtigkeit und Christusgegenwart*, 68–69.

'place or means of atonement'] by his blood, effective through faith. He did this to show his righteousness, because in his divine forbearance he had passed over the sins previously committed." The breadth of the meaning of the word ἱλαστήριον and the problems of deriving its meaning from a unilinear understanding of its tradition history[172] show that it is appropriate to understand ἱλαστήριον in Rom. 3:25 in the broad sense of "means of atonement."[173] It is God who created the possibility of atonement by setting forth Jesus Christ as the means of atonement. Both the tradition and Paul himself emphasize the theocentricity of the event: the point from which salvation proceeds is the act of God. This emphasis reveals continuity with the Old Testament's basic perspectives regarding atonement. It by no means suggests a sadistic deity who demands sacrifice as satisfaction for the sins of humanity. On the contrary, atonement is the initiative of God himself: "For the life of the flesh is in the blood; and I have given it to you for making atonement for your lives on the altar; for, as life, it is the blood that makes atonement" (Lev. 17:11). God alone is the acting subject in the event of atonement; God provides the sacrifice through which humanity is ritually set free from sin and breaks the ruinous connection between the sinful act and its consequences.[174] In a similar way, the pre-Pauline tradition of Rom. 3:25–26a had already broken through the Old Testament framework in multiple ways: whereas in the Old Testament cultus the atoning effect of the sacrifice was restricted to Israel, the Christ event brings universal forgiveness of sins. The sacrificial ritual of the Old Testament required yearly repetition, but Jesus's death on the cross is the eschatological, once-for-all event. What happened on the cross within salvation history is made real for the individual in baptism: forgiveness of

172. One explanatory model derives ἱλαστήριον from the cultic ritual on the great Day of Atonement (cf. Lev. 16; Ezek. 43). This is done, with variations, by Wilckens, *Römer*, 1:193; Stuhlmacher, *Biblische Theologie*, 1:193–94; Wolfgang Kraus, "Der Tod Jesu als Sühnetod bei Paulus," *ZNW* 3 (1999): 150–57; Gaukesbrink, *Sühnetradition*, 229–45; Knöppler, *Sühne im Neuen Testament*, 113–17; C. Breytenbach, "Sühne," *TBLNT* 2:1691. Another model sees Rom. 3:25 against the background of 4 Macc. 17:21–22, where atoning power is attributed to the sacrificial death of the martyrs. See Eduard Lohse, *Märtyer und Gottesknecht: Untersuchungen zur urchristlichen Verkündigung vom Sühntod Jesu Christi* (FRLANT 46; Göttingen: Vandenhoeck & Ruprecht, 1955), 151–52. J. W. van Henten, "The Tradition-Historical Background of Romans 3,25: A Search for Pagan and Jewish Parallels," in *From Jesus to John: Essays on Jesus and New Testament Christology in Honour of Marinus de Jonge* (ed. Martinus C. de Boer; JSNTSup 84; Sheffield: JSOT Press, 1993), 101–28, provides an analysis of all relevant texts, with the result "that the traditional background of the formula probably consists of ideas concerning martyrdom" (126); Klaus Haacker, *Der Brief des Paulus an die Römer* (THKNT 6; Leipzig: Evangelische Verlagsanstalt, 1999), 99–100.

173. Cf. Hans Lietzmann, *An die Römer* (5th ed.; HNT 8; Tübingen: Mohr, 1971), 49–50; Schnelle, *Gerechtigkeit und Christusgegenwart*, 70–71; Barth, *Der Tod Jesu*, 38–41.

174. Cf. the foundational work of Bernd Janowski, *Sühne als Heilsgeschehen: Studien zur Sühnetheologie der Priesterschrift und zur Wurzel* כפר *im Alten Orient und im Alten Testament* (WMANT 55; Neukirchen-Vluyn: Neukirchener Verlag, 1982).

previous sins. This is where the tradition attains its soteriological high point, for here it is a matter not only of proclaiming the Christ event but of seeing its soteriological dimension made real in the believer's own experience: the forgiveness of sins that occurs in baptism.[175] The universality of God's saving act in Christ can be believed only when it is experienced in the particularity of one's own existence. Paul takes up the fundamental ideas from the tradition and extends them with the interpretative addition διὰ τῆς πίστεως (through faith). Faith, as a human stance and outlook made possible by God, grants participation in the saving event. In faith the person experiences a new purpose and orientation; in the forgiveness of sins received in baptism, the person is justified. The resulting righteousness, the being-right with God, was already understood in the pre-Pauline tradition not as a *habitus*, a static mode of life, but rather as an assignment to be fulfilled, corresponding to the act of God that had already occurred for the person.

Is the atonement model capable of adequately expressing the theological intentions of the tradition and the apostle? In particular, is the image of sacrifice an appropriate way of grasping the saving effect of the death of Jesus? These questions have arisen not only within the modern horizon but above all from the fundamental differences between Old Testament atonement theology and Rom. 3:25–26a.[176] For the atonement ritual, the laying on of hands (performed by the one making the offering) and the blood ritual (enacted by the priest) are constitutive (Lev. 16:21–22). Moreover, a ritual transfer of identity follows, in which the animal is identified with the one offering the sacrifice, and only so does the killing of the animal become a sacrifice. Nothing in the crucifixion of Jesus really corresponds to these fundamental elements of the sacrificial ritual. The cross has God as its exclusive acting subject throughout; God acts on his own initiative at the cross and incorporates humanity into this event without any activity or previous achievement from the human side. It is not necessary for human beings to make contact with the holy; in Jesus Christ, God comes to human beings. Sacrifice stands for something different, pointing to something that mediates between two parties, whereas at the cross only God himself is involved. The Philippians hymn (Phil. 2:6–11) shows that—in the categories of sacrificial offering—we must speak of God's offering himself. But Paul does not speak of the cross in these terms because the cross has abolished the soteriological relevance of every sacrificial cult. The concept of sacrificial offering is thus structurally inappropriate for the Pauline thought world, and it can hardly be an accident that only in the tradition found in Rom. 3:25–26 does Paul take up a text that thinks in the categories of atonement and sacrifice.

175. Cf. Schnelle, *Gerechtigkeit und Christusgegenwart*, 71.

176. On this point cf. Ingolf U. Dalferth, "Die soteriologische Relevanz der Kategorie des Opfers," *JBTh* 6 (1991): 173–94.

6.2.6 Reconciliation

The concept of reconciliation is a very powerful christological model. The noun καταλλαγή (reconciliation, 2 Cor. 5:18, 19; Rom. 5:11; 11:15) and the verb καταλλάσσω (reconcile, 1 Cor. 7:11; 2 Cor. 5:18; Rom. 5:10) are found in the New Testament only in Paul's letters. In terms of the history of traditions, this term most probably came into New Testament theology from the language and conceptual world of Hellenistic diplomacy.[177] In classical and Hellenistic texts, both διαλλάσσω and καταλλάσσω designate an act of reconciliation in political, social, and personal relations, without any religious or cultic components.[178] It is important to distinguish semantically between καταλλάσσω (reconcile) and ἱλάσκομαι (atone), since the two terms derive from different worlds of thought.[179] Whereas καταλλάσσω describes the event of reconciliation on the human plane, ἱλάσκομαι points to an event in the sacred realm. To be sure, there is a fundamental difference in content between the postulated background in Hellenistic tradition and the Pauline concept of reconciliation: for Paul, God himself grants reconciliation as the creative acting subject. This is, in every way, more than a mere offer of reconciliation or appeal for reconciliation.

The point of departure for the affirmations in 2 Cor. 5:18–21 is the new reality of baptized believers as καινὴ κτίσις ἐν Χριστῷ (new creation/existence in Christ, 5:17a). Paul points to God, whose reconciling act has made possible a change in God's relationship to humanity. Paul develops the structure of this new relationship with the concept of reconciliation, which is thought of in strictly theocentric terms (5:18a, τὰ δὲ πάντα ἐκ τοῦ θεοῦ [all this is from God]) and is established christologically (διὰ Χριστοῦ [through Christ]). The overcoming of sin as the power that separates God and humanity requires God's initiative, for only God can put an end to sin (5:19). Within this reconciling event, the Pauline apostolate is given a special role. In 5:20, Paul designates it with the verb πρεσβεύω (to be an envoy, ambassador),[180]

177. Cf. the illuminating texts in *NW* 2.1:450–55.

178. Cf. Cilliers Breytenbach, *Versöhnung: Eine Studie zur paulinischen Soteriologie* (WMANT 60; Neukirchen-Vluyn: Neukirchener Verlag, 1989), 221: "The Pauline concept of καταλλάσσειν and the Old Testament כפר tradition have no points of contact in the history of tradition that could provide a basis for biblical theology"; cf. C. Breytenbach, "Versöhnung," *TBLNT* 2:1777: "It is a matter of reconciliation terminology, not religious terminology." Differently Otfried Hofius, "Erwägungen zur Gestalt und Herkunft des paulinischen Versöhnungsgedankens," in *Paulusstudien* (ed. Otfried Hofius; 2 vols.; WUNT 51; Tübingen: Mohr, 1989), 14: "The Pauline idea of reconciliation is . . . decisively influenced by the message of Deutero-Isaiah." Of English works, cf. especially Ralph P. Martin, *Reconciliation: A Study of Paul's Theology* (New Foundations Theological Library; Atlanta: John Knox, 1981).

179. Cf. Friedrich, *Verkündigung des Todes Jesu*, 98–99; Breytenbach, "Versöhnung, Stellvertretung und Sühne," 60ff.; Stuhlmacher, *Biblische Theologie*, 320, now acknowledges at least a semantic distinction.

180. Hapax legomenon in the undisputed Pauline letters; elsewhere in the New Testament only in Eph. 6:20.

which comes from Hellenistic ambassadorial terminology.[181] Just as the ambassador plays a decisive role in the signing of a treaty of reconciliation, the message and office of the apostle are part of God's own reconciling work.[182] As a called apostle, Paul can proclaim to the world that God has acted in Jesus Christ to reconcile the world to himself (2 Cor. 5:19). God himself has thus created the presupposition for Paul's office, not only to announce to the world that reconciliation is possible but to make his appeal in Christ's stead: "Be reconciled to God" (5:20b). In 5:21 Paul brings in the soteriological relevance of the Christ event as the basis that makes this surprising entreaty possible. God brings sin and righteousness into a new relationship in that Christ has taken our place: he becomes sin, and in him we become God's righteousness. The parallelism of these two clauses speaks in favor of understanding ἁμαρτία as "sin," not in the sense of "sin offering."[183] Because Christ is in no way affected by the realm where sin is dominant, he can represent us in becoming sin, in order thereby to effect our incorporation into the realm where he is Lord.

Whereas Paul does not in 2 Cor. 5 directly connect reconciliation and sin, Rom. 5:1–11 extends the line of argument, already made in Rom. 3:21ff., about God's justifying act through the atoning death of Jesus and places justification, atonement, and reconciliation in relation to each other.[184] Justification by faith is seen in Rom. 5:1 as a definitive reality that determines the present life of Christians. It grants the peace of God that becomes reality in the gift of the Spirit (cf. 14:17). As those who have been baptized, believers stand in the grace of God and now have access to God (5:2). This presence of salvation gives the church the power not only to bear the troubles of the present but to attain a living hope stamped by faith and patient endurance. The existence of those who are justified and reconciled is thus simultaneously an existence in θλίψις (trouble, suffering) and an existence in hope that is shaped by its view of the eschatological act of God. Believers are not saved from the contradictions of life, the temptations and challenges to their own existence and to their faith, the threats of hopelessness and doubt; rather, the essence of faith reveals itself in the fact that believers can bear up under these threats and come through them. The power to do this comes from the Holy Spirit, received by believers at baptism, the Spirit that thenceforth effectively and powerfully determines the life of Christians (5:5). The death of Jesus "for us" reveals God's love, which makes possible the

181. Cf. Breytenbach, *Versöhnung: Eine Studie zur paulinische Soteriology*, 65–66.

182. Dio Chrysostom, *Ad Nicomedienses* (*Or. 38*) 17–18 (*NW* 2.1:455).

183. Cf. Breytenbach, *Versöhnung: Eine Studie zur paulinische Soteriology*, 136–41; Schröter, *Der versöhnte Versöhner*, 314ff.; differently, Stuhlmacher, *Biblische Theologie*, 1:195; Kraus, "Tod Jesu," 26, who see the background here as atonement theology.

184. For this interpretation, cf. Michael Wolter, *Rechtfertigung und zukünftiges Heil: Untersuchungen zu Röm 5,1–11* (BZNW 43; Berlin: de Gruyter, 1978).

justification of the sinner and reconciliation with God (Rom. 5:6–8). In 5:9 Paul explicitly refers back to 3:25 by using the expression ἐν τῷ αἵματι αὐτοῦ (through his blood). The atoning death of the Son effects both justification and reconciliation (5:9–10). Both justification and reconciliation are thus ways of designating the new relation of human beings to God, which God makes possible by destroying the power of sin in the atoning death of Jesus Christ. The godless thus become those who are justified, and God's enemies become those who are reconciled.

Both 2 Cor. 5 and Rom. 5 show that Christ's death "for us" makes possible the new relationship to God that Paul designates as reconciliation.

1. Reconciliation, for Paul, is the act of God alone;[185] God alone is subject and object of reconciliation. It is not human beings who propitiate God, encourage God to adopt a new attitude to us, or reconcile God to us through any of our own acts;[186] instead the new relationship to God and the resulting new being of those who are baptized, justified, and reconciled are due only to the once-for-all and continually present act of God in Jesus Christ.
2. God's reconciliation with the world is an act of universal peace (2 Cor. 5:19; Rom. 11:15). It is limited neither to Israel nor to believers but is intended to apply to all human beings and the whole creation.[187]
3. Reconciliation occurs concretely in the acceptance of the message of reconciliation, the gospel.
4. This acceptance effects a transformation in the whole person. Those who were previously alienated from God now have access to God and are granted the privilege of life in the power of the Spirit.[188]

6.2.7 *Justification*

Just as one cannot imagine a high culture without philosophy, law, and religion, so the concept of God in such cultures is inconceivable apart from the concept of justice. These fundamental connections determine not only central sections of the Old Testament but also classical Greece and Hellenism.

185. The comment of Breytenbach, "Versöhnung," 2:1779, is on target: "The acting subject of reconciliation is God (2 Cor. 5:18–19). This is the theologically new element in relation to the minimal 'religious' use in the few passages in Hellenistic Jewish texts, which know the deity only as the object of the reconciling act of human beings."

186. Cf., in this sense, 2 Macc. 1:5; 7:33; 8:29; Josephus, *Ant.* 6.151; 7.153; *JW* 5.415.

187. This aspect is emphasized by Ernst Käsemann, "Erwägungen zum Stichwort Versöhnungslehre im Neuen Testament," in *Zeit und Geschichte: Dankesgabe an Rudolf Bultmann zum 80. Geburtstag* (ed. Erich Dinkler and Hartwig Thyen; Tübingen: Mohr, 1964), 47–59.

188. Cf. Friedrich, *Verkündigung des Todes Jesu*, 116–17.

Cultural and Historical Milieu

In the Old Testament, central theological themes cluster around the term צדקה/δικαιοσύνη.[189] The connection between "righteousness" and "right" (or justice and just [*Gerechtigkeit* and *Recht*]) is obvious, for one cannot think of God's righteousness apart from God's acting on behalf of what is right. "The Lord works vindication and justice for all who are oppressed" (Ps. 103:6; cf. Ps. 11:7). In the assembly of divine beings, Yahweh holds court, judging the other gods, and demands: "Give justice to the weak and the orphan; maintain the right of the lowly and the destitute" (Ps. 82:3). The basic instructions of the Torah include: "You shall not render an unjust judgment; you shall not be partial to the poor or defer to the great: with justice you shall judge your neighbor" (Lev. 19:15). The obligation to create justice for his people and to protect them from oppression rests especially on the king (cf. Jer. 22:3; Ps. 72:4; Prov. 31:8–9). The effective realm of God's justice extends over the righteous life: "Those who have clean hands and pure hearts, who do not lift up their souls to what is false, and do not swear deceitfully . . . will receive blessing from the Lord and vindication from the God of their salvation" (Ps. 24:4–5). The idea of righteousness as the beneficial *gift* of God is directly connected with *universal* images, and so justice and righteousness become elements of the divine epiphany (Ps. 97:1–2, 6). Also, God's creative power and his continuing intervention for the good of creation are expressions of his righteousness (cf. Ps. 33:4–6; 85:10–14), so that the cosmic order is described as righteousness, which "unites cosmic, political, religious, social, and ethical aspects."[190] Salvation and righteousness/justice become synonymous with the universal acts of God, which include the nations (cf. Ps. 98:2; Isa. 45:8, 21; 51:5–8). Monotheism and universalism combine to form a view of history in which God's righteousness appears as kingship, gift, claim, power, and salvation.

The profound transformations following the Babylonian exile decisively stamped the character of *ancient Judaism*. The consciousness of being the elect people of God, the hope in God's continuing faithfulness, the Torah as the saving gift of God, and the associated attempt of the Jewish people

189. A survey of this theme is given in J. Scharbert, "Gerechtigkeit," *TRE* 12:404–11; and Spieckermann, "Rechtfertigung," 28:282–86. [In German as in Greek (but not in English), the same word is used for "justice" and "righteousness," and their adjectival and verbal cognates are from the same root. English-speaking readers will note the connection between "justice" and "justification," but modern English has no verb for "make righteous." In his translation of Bultmann's *Theology of the New Testament,* Kendrick Grobel revived the Old English verb "rightwise" (i.e., "justify," "make right"). Cf. Grobel's explanatory footnote in Bultmann, *Theology of the New Testament*, 1:253, and the adoption of this terminology by Schubert M. Ogden, ed., *Existence and Faith: Shorter Writings of Rudolf Bultmann* (New York: Meridian Books, 1960).—MEB]

190. Hans Heinrich Schmid, *Gerechtigkeit als Weltordnung. Hintergrund und Geschichte der alttestamentlichen Gerechtigkeitsbegriffes* (BHT 40; Tübingen: Mohr [Siebeck], 1968), 166. Among those critical of this conception is Crüsemann, *Tora*, 430–31.

to redefine themselves by ritual demarcation from all other peoples became central elements of the Jewish religion.[191] God's binding himself to his people is expressed by the gift of the *Torah*,[192] which Judaism understood as a gracious gift of God and as the document validating God's covenant (cf., e.g., Sir. 24; *Jub.* 1.16–18). The Torah is far more than rules for life or social order; by observing it, one enters into God's kingdom, acknowledging the rule of God and enlisting in its service. Loyalty to the Torah, as observing and respecting the will of God, is thus the response expected from Israel to God's election. Within this comprehensive conception of things, righteousness is not the result of human achievement but God's promise to humanity (cf. *Jub.* 22.15, "And may he renew his covenant with you, so that you might be a people for him, belonging to his inheritance forever. And he will be God for you and for your seed in truth and righteousness throughout all the days of the earth"; cf. *1 En.* 39.4–7; 48.1; 58.4). Particularly at Qumran a deepened understanding of sin (cf. 1QH 4:30; 1QS 11:9–10) was combined with an elitist consciousness of election and a radicalized Torah obedience (cf. CD 20:19–21).[193] The community's repentance for ritual and ethical offenses responds to the gracious working of the righteousness of God in the end time through the revelation of his will among those God has chosen. Nevertheless, those who are faithful to their religious duties still need God's mercy; the righteousness of God is God's faithfulness to his covenant and his people, from which human righteousness springs up in response (1QH 1:26–27; 3:21; 12:35–37; 1QS 10:25; 11:11ff.).

Psalms of Solomon[194] mediates the basic insight that those who trust in God receive righteousness through God's mercy (*Pss. Sol.* 2.33–34).[195] God is

191. On the historical process involved, cf. Johann Maier, *Zwischen den Testamenten: Geschichte und Religion in der Zeit des zweiten Tempels* (NEchtB 3, Supplementary Series; Würzburg: Echter Verlag, 1990), 191–247; on the basic theological presuppositions, cf. Nissen, *Gott und der Nächste*, 99–329; on the understanding of the law and righteousness, cf. Meinrad Limbeck, *Die Ordnung des Heils: Untersuchungen zum Gesetzesverständnis des Frühjudentums* (Düsseldorf: Patmos, 1971), passim, and Holger Sonntag, ΝΟΜΟΣ ΣΩΤΗΡ: *Zur politischen Theologie des Gesetzes bei Paulus und im antiken Kontext* (TANZ 34; Tübingen: Francke, 2000), 109–65.

192. On the Torah, cf. Maier, *Zwischen den Testamenten*, 212ff.; and Nissen, *Gott und der Nächste*, 330ff.

193. Cf. Otto Betz, "Rechtfertigung in Qumran," in *Rechtfertigung: Festschrift für Ernst Käsemann zum 70. Geburtstag* (ed. Johannes Friedrich et al.; Göttingen: Vandenhoeck & Ruprecht, 1976), 17–36; Mark A. Seifrid, *Justification by Faith: The Origin and Development of a Central Pauline Theme* (NovTSup 68; Leiden: Brill, 1992), 81–108.

194. Written ca. the middle of the first century BCE in Palestine; cf. Joachim Schüpphaus, *Die Psalmen Salomos: Ein Zeugnis Jerusalemer Theologie und Frömmigkeit in der Mitte des vorchristlichen Jahrhunderts* (Leiden: Brill, 1977), 137; S. Holm-Nielsen, *Die Psalmen Salomos* (JSHRZ 4.2; Gütersloh: Gütersloher Verlagshaus, 1977), 59; Mikael Winninge, *Sinners and the Righteous: A Comparative Study of the Psalms of Solomon and Paul's Letters* (ConBNT 26; Stockholm: Almqvist & Wiksell International, 1995), 12–16.

195. Cf. Udo Schnelle, "Gerechtigkeit in den Psalmen Salomos und bei Paulus," in *Jüdische Schriften in ihrem antik-jüdischen und urchristlichen Kontext* (ed. Hermann Lichtenberger and Gerbern S. Oegema; JSHRZ Studien 1; Gütersloh: Gütersloher Verlagshaus, 2002), 365–75.

just and takes pity on those who submit themselves to his just judgment (*Pss. Sol.* 8.7). The plumb line for God's mercy is the law, which provides the criteria for God's righteous judgment and in which his righteousness is revealed. "The Lord is faithful to those who truly love him, to those who endure his discipline, to those who live in the righteousness of his commandments, in the law, which he has commanded for our life. The Lord's devout shall live by it forever; the Lord's paradise, the trees of life, are his devout ones" (14.1–3). Thus the righteous are those who are willing to live according to the law and to trust in God's mercy. What really makes righteousness possible, however, is that the devout belong to the elect people of God. The mercy of God to the devout and the gift of life that comes through the law are the expression and result of Israel's election (cf. *Pss. Sol.* 9.6, 10; 10.4). The basis for the theological thinking of the *Psalms of Solomon* is a contrasting pair: Israel as the righteous and Gentiles or unfaithful Jews as sinners (cf. 13.7–12).[196] The righteousness of the devout is a status concept that fundamentally separates them from the Gentiles. Admittedly, the devout also sin, but God's faithfulness and mercy are by no means abolished by unintentional sins. Instead God cleanses from sin and thus brings the repentant sinner to a righteous life oriented to the law (cf. 3.6–8; 9.6, 12; 10.3).

Classical Greece and the world of *Hellenism* are also profoundly stamped by reflection on the meaning of righteousness and justice.[197] In Plato's thought, the relation of law and justice occupies a central place, for *justice* is the *norm of the law*. In his myth of the origin of culture, justice and law are the presupposition for the participation of all human beings in justice and righteousness.[198] The lawgiver instructed by Zeus will be a person who "will always and above all things in making laws have regard to the greatest virtue, which, according to Theognis, is loyalty in the hour of danger, and may be truly called perfect justice" (Plato, *Leg.* 1.630c). Justice stands in first place among the cardinal virtues (*Resp.* 4.433d–e), for it has a key role as both a social and a universal category and is thus supremely important for ordering both the individual soul and the state. Aristotle does not distinguish between law and ethics; righteousness/justice as the general ordering principle comprehends both (*Eth. Nic.* 5.1130a, "Justice in this sense, then, is not part of virtue but virtue entire").[199] In terms of content, *the laws define what is right*,

196. On the determination of "sinners" and "righteous" in the *Psalms of Solomon*, cf. Winninge, *Sinners and the Righteous*, 125–36.

197. A survey is provided in Albrecht Dihle, "Gerechtigkeit," *RAC* 10:233–360; cf. further Sonntag, ΝΟΜΟΣ ΣΩΤΗΡ, 7–1008, 202.

198. Cf. Plato, *Prot.* 322c–d, which portrays how Zeus commissioned Hermes to bring justice and law to humanity.

199. The distinction between natural law and positive law in Aristotle, *Eth. Nic.* 5.1134b–1135a, had a great impact on later history: "Of political justice part is natural and part legal: natural, that which everywhere has the same force and does not exist by people's thinking

for, "since the lawless man was seen to be unjust and the law-abiding man just, evidently all lawful acts are in a sense just acts" (*Eth. Nic.* 5.1129B).[200] Because what is lawful is identified with what is just, it follows that violation of the law is an offense against justice (cf. *Eth. Nic.* 5.1130B). Justice thus grows from the laws and is their effect, for just actions are oriented to the law and create justice.

In Hellenistic philosophy, in a culture that was taking on worldwide dimensions and thus focusing less on the polis and more on the individual, one of the effects was a shift in the understanding of justice itself. In this process, justice/righteousness and piety became in part synonyms without abolishing the connection with the law. The fundamental continuity between *right*, *justice/righteousness*, *law*, and a *successful life* also determined ethical thinking at the beginning of the first century CE. For Cicero, this was an unchangeable relationship: "Therefore law is the distinction between things just and unjust, it is formulated in view of that original nature that is the basis of all things, to which human laws are oriented, in that they punish the evil and defend and protect the good" (*Leg.* 2.13). Righteousness/justice, is *the* virtue and comes from insight into the nature of things. "Thus all things honorable are to be sought for their own sake" (*Leg.* 1.48). For Dio Chrysostom (Dio of Prusa), the ideal king receives his rulership from Zeus. "Whoever looks to him for his law and rule, and rules his people well will receive a good reward and a happy ending" (*Or.* 1.45; cf. 75.1). The law grants to both the society and the individual the justice and protection to which they are entitled (*Or.* 75.6). The divine unity of law and justice includes person and institution; as the ordering principle, justice always has an importance that is both individual/moral and universal/principial. These connections make it possible for Hellenistic Jewish thinkers such as Philo of Alexandria and Josephus to form a synthesis that combines Greek thinking about law and justice/righteousness with Jewish traditions. Philo combines the Greek doctrine of virtue with the Decalogue: "For each of the ten pronouncements separately and all in common incite and exhort us to wisdom and justice and godliness and the rest of the company of virtues" (*Spec. Laws* 4.134). Philo can reduce the innumerable individual Jewish laws to two basic principles: "one of duty to God as shown by piety and holiness, one of duty to men as shown by humanity and justice" (*Spec. Laws* 2.63; cf. 2.13–14). The Torah is subject to a strong ethical impulse that corresponds to the Greek and Hellenistic concentration on the concept of justice/righteousness but without giving up its universal aspect.[201]

---

this or that; legal, that which is originally indifferent, but when it has been laid down is not indifferent."

200. Cf. also Plato, *Symp.* 196B–C; *Resp.* 1.338D–339A; *Gorg.* 489A–B; *Pol.* 294D–295A; *Leg.* 10.889E–890A.

201. Cf. Weber, *Das "Gesetz" bei Philon*, 337ff.

The Genesis of the Pauline Doctrine of Justification

The combination of law, righteousness/justification, and life, and thus the *theme* of righteousness and justification, was a given in Paul's cultural situation. At the same time, he had to make new classifications and combinations, for his Christ hermeneutic demanded that the three key concepts—law, righteousness, life—be brought together in a new system of coordinates. Do the letters allow us to recognize a general and consistent *doctrine* of justification, or must we introduce terminological and conceptual differentiations into their content in order to do justice to a complex set of relationships?

The textual data shows that righteousness/justification in Paul is obviously a multilayered phenomenon that calls for an explanatory model on the *diachronic plane*.[202]

Within Pauline theology, righteousness is primarily bound to the *baptismal traditions* (1 Cor. 1:30; 6:11; 2 Cor. 1:21–22; Rom. 3:25–26a; 6:3–4; 4:25).[203] The ritual anchoring of the righteousness thematic is no accident,[204] for baptism is the place where the fundamental change of status for the Christian occurs, the place where one is transferred from the realm of sin into the realm of righteousness. The baptismal tradition not only deals with the theme of righteousness but develops a self-consistent sacramental-ontological *doctrine* of justification: in baptism, as the place of participation in the Christ event, the Spirit effectively separates believers from the power of sin and grants them the status of righteousness so that, looking forward to the parousia of Jesus Christ, they can live a life corresponding to the will of God. This doctrine of justification can be described as inclusive because, without any criteria of exclusion, it aims at making the individual righteous and incorporating him or her into the church. Faith, the gift of the Spirit, and baptism constitute one holistic event: in baptism the believer enters the realm of the spiritual

202. Cf. Schnelle, *Gerechtigkeit und Christusgegenwart*, 100–103; Thomas Söding, "Kriterium der Wahrheit? Zum theologischen Stellenwert der paulinischen Rechtfertigungslehre," in *Worum geht es in der Rechtfertigungslehre? Das biblische Fundament der "Gemeinsamen Erklärung" von katholischer Kirche und Lutherischem Weltbund* (ed. Thomas Söding and Frank-Lothar Hossfeld; QD 180; Freiburg: Herder, 1999), 211–13; Wilckens, *Theologie des Neuen Testaments,* 3:131–36.

203. Cf. Gerhard Delling, *Die Taufe im Neuen Testament* (Berlin: Evangelische Verlagsanstalt, 1963), 132; Karl Kertelge, *Rechtfertigung bei Paulus: Studien zur Struktur und zum Bedeutungsgehalt des paulinischen Rechtfertigungsbegriffs* (Münster: Aschendorff, 1967), 228–49; Eduard Lohse, "Taufe und Rechtfertigung bei Paulus," in *Die Einheit des Neuen Testaments* (Göttingen: Vandenhoeck & Ruprecht, 1973), 228–44; Ferdinand Hahn, "Taufe und Rechtfertigung," in *Rechtfertigung: Festschrift für Ernst Käsemann zum 70. Geburtstag* (ed. Johannes Friedrich et al.; Göttingen: Vandenhoeck & Ruprecht, 1976), 104–17; Ulrich Luz, "Gerechtigkeit," *EKL*, 2:91: "The presupposition for the Pauline doctrine of justification was that the early Christian congregations understood baptism as an anticipation of God's final judgment and thus as a real making-righteous (1 Cor. 6:11). . . . The Pauline doctrine of justification is thus no innovation but is rooted in the church's interpretation of baptism"; Wilckens, *Theologie*, 3:132–33.

204. Strecker, *Die liminale Theologie des Paulus*, 210.

Christ, personal communion with Christ is established, and redemption has really begun, which then continues in righteousness in a life determined by the Spirit.[205] *It is clear that this doctrine of justification in the context of baptism is organically connected with the constitutive foundational views of Pauline Christology: transformation and participation.*[206] Through his resurrection from the dead, Jesus Christ has entered the realm of God's life and power, and in baptism he grants to believers, through the gift of the Spirit, participation in the new being already in the here and now. Baptized believers live as those who have been delivered from the power of sin in Christ's realm of salvation, where the Spirit holds sway, and their new being ἐν Χριστῷ (in Christ) is comprehensively determined by the life-giving powers of the Risen One. As a ritual of status transformation, baptism brings into being not only a new perception of reality; those who are baptized are truly changed, as is reality itself.[207] Within this conception, the law/Torah has neither a negative nor a positive function; the basic structure of the *inclusive doctrine of justification* does not involve the law/Torah.

In contrast, it is *nomology*, a doctrinal understanding of the law, that determines the argumentation of the letters to the Galatians, the Romans, and the Philippians.[208] This shift results from the current situation in each of the churches, not from a deficiency in the inner logic of the inclusive doctrine of justification.[209]

205. Schnelle, *Gerechtigkeit und Christusgegenwart*, 100–103; Helmut Umbach, *In Christus getauft, von der Sünde befreit: Die Gemeinde als sündenfreier Raum bei Paulus* (Göttingen: Vandenhoeck & Ruprecht, 1999), 230–32.

206. Powers, *Salvation through Participation*, 122: "Justification is the result of the believer's participation in Jesus's resurrection life."

207. From the perspective of cultural anthropology, cf. Clifford Geertz, "Thick Description: Toward an Interpretative Theory of Culture," in *The Interpretation of Cultures: Selected Essays* (ed. Clifford Geertz; New York: Basic Books, 1973), 122: "Having ritually 'lept' [*sic*] . . . into the framework of meaning which religious conceptions define, and the ritual ended, returned again to the common-sense world, a man is—unless, as sometimes happens, the experience fails to register—changed. And as he is changed, so also is the common-sense world, for it is now seen as but the partial form of a wider reality which corrects and completes it."

208. There is a clear semantic connection here, for Paul speaks at length about righteousness/justification only in those contexts where he is also reflecting on the law; cf. δικαιόω/δικαιοσύνη 12 times in Galatians, 49 times in Romans, 4 times in Philippians; νόμος 32 times in Galatians, 74 times in Romans, 3 times in Philippians.

209. Historically speaking, the exclusive justification doctrine of Galatians represents a new response to a new situation. To this extent the statement of W. Wrede about the Pauline doctrine of justification holds true: "It is the polemical doctrine of Paul, is only made intelligible by the struggle of his life, his controversy with Judaism and Jewish Christianity, and is only intended for this. So far, indeed, it is of high historical importance, and characteristic of the man." Wrede, *Paul*, 123. So also the famous dictum of Albert Schweitzer sees the matter rightly: "The doctrine of righteousness by faith is therefore a subsidiary crater, which was formed within the rim of the main crater—the mystical doctrine of redemption through the being-in-Christ" (Schweitzer, *Mysticism*, 225).

The demand of the Galatian Judaists that Gentile Christians also be circumcised not only represented a breaking of the agreements made at the Apostolic Council and placed in question the success of the Pauline mission but was directed against *the* fundamental principle of all Pauline theology: the locus of life and righteousness is Jesus Christ alone. If the law/Torah could give life, as understood for example in Sir. 17:11 LXX ("He bestowed knowledge upon them, and allotted to them the law of life"), then Christ would have died in vain. For Paul, there can be only one eschatological figure who is relevant for salvation: Jesus Christ. When the law is no longer regarded as an adiaphoron, as had been the case previously (as, e.g., in 1 Cor. 9:20–22), but receives a status that matters for salvation, then the issue of whether the law is in fact able to provide salvation must be moved to the center of the argument. Paul decides this question in the negative, for "the scripture has imprisoned all things under the power of sin, so that what was promised through faith in Jesus Christ might be given to those who believe" (Gal. 3:22; cf. Rom. 3:9, 20). In accord with God's will, the power of sin is stronger than the ability of the law/Torah to deliver from it. The law/Torah may no longer be thought of as the foundation of the special position of Israel in the history of election, so the hamartiological differentiation between Jews and Gentiles is also invalidated "because no one will be justified by the works of the law" (Gal. 2:16; cf. Rom. 3:21, 28). In Galatians, Romans, and Philippians, Paul extends the basic views of the inclusive doctrine of justification connected with baptism to an *exclusive doctrine of justification* characterized by universalism and antinomism.[210] On the sociological plane, it was directed at establishing the equality of Gentile Christians; in response to the Judaistic challenge, it guaranteed Gentile Christians, as baptized believers, unqualified membership in the elect people of God. Moreover, the fundamental culture of mutuality that provided the basis for Roman society (mutuality between human beings as well as between human beings and the gods) is fundamentally changed when Paul radically rejects any human claims on God's favor. No human being is righteous before God (Rom. 3:23), and God alone is good (Rom. 5:7). Furthermore, the undeserved gift of divine righteousness does not come through a benefactor endowed with honor, but through one who has been crucified as a criminal. Because no one has any claim to God's benefits on the basis of race, gender, or social status, Paul brings about a democratizing of the understanding of grace. Theologically, the exclusive doctrine of justification not only negated every sociological function of the law/Torah and summarized its ethical relevance in the love command; it also removed every particularistic or national element from the consciousness of election and

210. Cf. Söding, "Kriterium der Wahrheit," 203: "It is doubtful that the apostle advocated the theology of justification from the very beginning in the form found in Galatians and Romans." Cf. further Luz, "Gerechtigkeit," 2:91; Wilckens, *Theologie*, 3:131.

formulated a universal image of God:[211] entirely apart from considerations of race, sex, and nationality, God gives his sin-conquering righteousness to every human being through faith in Jesus Christ. Thus the stance expressed in Gal. 2:19; 3:26–28; Rom. 3:25; 4:25; 6:3–4 shows that Paul intentionally plays off the inclusive and exclusive doctrines of justification against each other. He thus guards his exclusive doctrine of justification, based on a radicalized anthropology and a universalized understanding of God, from becoming an otherworldly abstraction by declaring baptism to be the place where God's universal saving act in Jesus Christ can be experienced in the particularity of one's own existence.

The Righteousness of God

These fundamental insights are concentrated in the key theological term of Paul's Letter to the Romans: δικαιοσύνη θεοῦ (righteousness/justification of [or from] God).

The meaning of δικαιοσύνη θεοῦ is a disputed point in recent research.[212] Whereas R. Bultmann and H. Conzelmann understand δικαιοσύνη θεοῦ in the anthropological context as gift, that is, as righteousness/justification imputed through faith (cf. Phil. 3:9),[213] E. Käsemann and P. Stuhlmacher interpret δικαιοσύνη θεοῦ as a *terminus technicus* already present in Jewish apocalyptic that Paul takes into his own theology.[214] As a key term in the Pauline doctrine of justification, it is crucial for how this doctrine is to be understood, and is thus decisive for Pauline theology as a whole. They rightly object, against Bultmann and Conzelmann, that an interpretation of δικαιοσύνη θεοῦ oriented primarily to the individual neglects the universal aspects of a theology of creation and history. But there are also significant objections to be raised against the approach of Käsemann and Stuhlmacher. The question of God's righteousness was indeed already raised for Paul from the Old Testament and the literature of ancient Judaism, but δικαιοσύνη θεοῦ was not a *terminus technicus* of traditional Jewish apocalyptic. The phrase "righteousness of God" is found in Jewish texts (cf. Deut. 33:21; *T. Dan* 6.10; 1QS 10:25; 11:12; 1QM 4:6), but not as a fixed formula.[215] The statements in the Qumran literature

211. Cf. Badiou, *Paul*, 76: "The One is only One insofar as it is for all: such is the maxim of universality when it has its root in the event. Monotheism can only be understood by taking into consideration the whole of humanity. Unless addressed to all, the One crumbles and disappears."

212. For the history of research, cf., most recently, Seifrid, *Justification by Faith*, 1–75.

213. Cf. Bultmann, *Theology of the New Testament*, 1:271, 285; Conzelmann, *Theology of the New Testament*, 220.

214. Cf. Ernst Käsemann, "'The Righteousness of God' in Paul," in *New Testament Questions of Today* (ed. Ernst Käsemann; NTL; London: SCM, 1969); Peter Stuhlmacher, *Gerechtigkeit Gottes bei Paulus* (Göttingen: Vandenhoeck & Ruprecht, 1965), 73.

215. For evidence and argument, see Schnelle, *Gerechtigkeit und Christusgegenwart*, 93–96, 217–19; Becker, *Paul*, 367; Seifrid, *Justification by Faith*, 99–107.

about the righteousness of God do present a parallel to Paul's but cannot be considered a presupposition of the apostle's own doctrine of justification. There was intensive reflection on the subject of righteousness at Qumran, on the basis of a radicalized image of humanity and God, but this reflection did make "righteousness of God" the predominant *terminus technicus* for God's act in establishing righteousness. What is striking, rather, is that at Qumran divine and human righteousness was described in several different ways.

The data in the Pauline texts shows that δικαιοσύνη θεοῦ is a *multidimensional concept*. In 2 Cor. 5:21 the gift character of δικαιοσύνη θεοῦ predominates; the "of" represents a *genitivus auctoris* (genitive of source).[216] Believers participate in the substitutionary death of Jesus Christ and are transferred by baptism and the gift of the Spirit into a new realm of existence. The character of δικαιοσύνη θεοῦ as power is clear in Rom. 1:17,[217] indicated linguistically by ἀποκαλύπτεται (is revealed).[218] Now Jesus discloses God's eschatological saving will, which makes itself known powerfully in the gospel of the righteousness of God in Jesus Christ for those who believe. In Rom. 3:5 human righteousness and the righteousness of God (subjective genitive) stand opposed to each other in a legal dispute. Here it is not a matter of the revelation of the righteousness of God in the gospel[219] but a quality of the nature of the God who establishes his righteousness/justice in the judgment and proves the unrighteousness of humanity. In Rom. 3:21–22 δικαιοσύνη θεοῦ appears twice, but each instance has a different connotation. Δικαιοσύνη θεοῦ in 3:21 is to be read as a revelatory concept, meaning that in the Christ event God has made himself known as the one who makes (others) righteous and establishes justice. Here the term "righteousness of God" does not communicate something about God, but in it God's revelation takes place as an event. It is to this epoch-making event that the law and the prophets bear witness, so that the law itself confirms its own end as the source of righteousness. In 3:22 Paul is thinking of δικαιοσύνη θεοῦ in its anthropological aspect. Faith in Jesus Christ is the form in which the righteousness of God (i.e., the righteousness that comes from God) is appropriated. By faith, Jesus is the righteousness of God for all who believe. Whereas the righteousness of God appears in 3:21 as the universal power of God, in 3:22 the character of God's righteousness as gift is the predominant meaning. In Rom. 3:25 Paul takes up ideas already fixed in the tradition (see above, §6.2.5) in order to connect the ritual experiences of the Roman church with his exclusive doctrine of justification. The subjective

216. Cf., e.g., Hans Windisch, *Der zweite Korintherbrief* (9th ed.; KEK 6; Göttingen: Vandenhoeck & Ruprecht, 1924), 78–84.

217. For exegesis, cf. Stuhlmacher, *Gerechtigkeit Gottes*, 78–84.

218. Dieter Zeller, *Der Brief an die Römer* (RNT; Regensburg: Pustet, 1985), 43, is on target with his comment: "The righteousness of God is made eschatologically available already in the present (verb in present tense!)."

219. Cf. ibid., 78–79.

genitive in δικαιοσύνη θεοῦ does not merely designate a quality of God but means the righteousness appropriate to the God who reveals himself universally in the event of the cross, the righteousness realized in the remission of prior sins that takes place in baptism. The universal dimension of δικαιοσύνη θεοῦ is also seen in Rom. 10:3. Here Israel is reproached for seeking its own righteousness, not the righteousness that comes from God. The chosen people closes itself off from the will of God as revealed in Jesus Christ and does not submit to the δικαιοσύνη θεοῦ (subjective genitive).[220] Instead Israel undertakes the hopeless task of establishing its own righteousness by works of the law. God's action here concerns peoples, so that an interpretation of δικαιοσύνη θεοῦ focusing exclusively on the individual and neglecting its cosmological dimension would not square with the textual data.[221] At the same time, Phil. 3:9 lets us see clearly that a choice between the individual and cosmic dimensions of δικαιοσύνη θεοῦ would be just as wrong. There Paul refers the justifying act of God entirely to the individual existence of the believer (Phil. 3:9a, καὶ εὑρεθῶ ἐν αὐτῷ [and be found in him], i.e., Christ). The righteousness of God (genitive of source: righteousness from God) does not result from the law/Torah but is given to human beings through faith in Jesus Christ.

Depending on the context, δικαιοσύνη θεοῦ is thus to be interpreted as a *universal-forensic concept* (Rom. 1:17; 3:5, 21, 25; 10:3) and as a *concept expressing transfer and participation* (2 Cor. 5:21; Rom. 3:22; Phil. 3:9). The "righteousness of God" concisely designates both the revelatory act and the act of the believer's incorporation and participation in God's justifying/rightwising act in Jesus Christ. The limited use and application of the expression,[222] its restrictive function in the predominantly negative formulations,[223] its concentration in the Letter to the Romans, and the variety of its context-dependent meanings show clearly that δικαιοσύνη θεοῦ is *not* the *key concept* of Pauline theology *as a whole*.[224] Paul can fully set forth his theology without having to fall back on the expression δικαιοσύνη θεοῦ. In the Letter to the Romans, "righteousness of God" does function as a major theological concept because, in the wake of the Galatian crisis and in view of the delivery of the collection in Jerusalem, Paul must give his Christology a theocentric profile and provide a solution to the problematic of the law: the Christ event manifests the righ-

220. Cf. Wilckens, *Römer*, 2:220.

221. Cf. Stuhlmacher, *Gerechtigkeit Gottes*, 93.

222. The seven explicit instances of the term δικαιοσύνη θεοῦ (2 Cor. 5:21; Rom. 1:17; 3:5, 21, 22; 10:3; Phil. 3:9) stand in contrast to other terms dealing with the realm of salvation: πνεῦμα 120 times; ἐν Χριστῷ 37 times; πίστις 91 times; πιστεύω 42 times; δικαιοσύνη 38 times; δικαιόω 25 times; ζωή 27 times; ἐλπίς 25 times.

223. Cf. Sanders, *Paul and Palestinian Judaism*, 492.

224. Hans Hübner, *Biblische Theologie des Neuen Testaments* (3 vols.; Göttingen: Vandenhoeck & Ruprecht, 1990), 1:177: "To be sure, this term does not occur elsewhere in the whole Pauline corpus in the sense in which Paul uses it in Romans. The 'righteousness of God' is thus for Paul a concept that developed out of the late phase of his theology."

teousness that comes from God and is appropriated by faith, the righteousness that alone allows human beings to stand justified before God and that thus removes any soteriological significance from the law/Torah (cf. Rom. 6:14b).

The Theological Content of the Doctrine of Justification

If one keeps in mind the Pauline statements on righteousness and justification *as a whole*, then one sees a way of thinking that, with all its historical and theological distinctions, still has a systematic quality. The point of departure for such a line of thought is the insight, revolutionary in the ancient world, that righteousness is not essentially a matter of doing but a matter of *being*.

For Aristotle, actions define righteousness/justice: "It is well said, then, that it is by doing just acts that the just man is produced, and by doing temperate acts the temperate man; without doing these no one would have even a prospect of becoming good."[225] Righteousness/justice appears as the highest human virtue, a virtue attained by one's own actions. In ancient Judaism there was undoubtedly the basic conviction that sinful human beings are dependent on God's mercy and goodness. The covenant idea, as the central form of expression of Israel's relation to God, is based on God's prior election of Israel. Nevertheless, the question of salvation remained connected to human actions inasmuch as God was expected to act as the righteous judge, merciful to the righteous but punishing the lawless and the lawbreakers (*Psalms of Solomon*, Qumran writings). To be sure, Paul too knows the fundamental difference between Israel as the righteous and the Gentiles as sinners (cf. Rom. 9:30), but he does not make it the foundation of his system of thought. Instead he completely redefines the relation between righteous and sinners: no one belongs to the group of the righteous, and everyone, Gentiles and Jews, belongs to the group of sinners (cf. Rom. 1:16–3:20). But by faith in Jesus Christ, both Jews and Gentiles can attain righteousness. The Pauline status-schema is marked by a universal beginning point: all human beings are hopelessly subject to the power of sin (cf. Gal. 3:22; Rom. 3:9–10); that is, all human beings have the status of sinners even if they belong to a privileged group and practice justice. Righteousness can come only through the transfer from the realm where sin rules into the realm of Christ. In Jewish thought, deep insight into the power of sin, consciousness of dependence on God's mercy, belonging to the elect people of God, and Torah observance all necessarily form a unity in which each element supplements the other. Righteousness is radically understood from the Godward perspective, but at the same time, religious privileges in contrast to other peoples remain in place. In contrast, Paul negates every special religious status, for his Christ-hermeneutic allows no distinctions at all regarding either sin or righteousness. Righteousness is the result of the new life constituted by Christ in baptism. God grants participation in his life-giving

225. Aristotle, *Eth. Nic.* 2.1105B.

power in that he annihilates sin by the gift of the Spirit and establishes the existence of baptized believers anew. Paul advocates a universalism in which the believer's relation to God is not defined by nation, land, temple, or law. He thus distances himself from Jewish thinking that can be described as national and particular. *For Paul, righteousness/justification in the strict sense is not a matter of doing but of being. God's act is prior to any human activity; the new being has the character not of a deed but of a gift.*[226] Before God, the person is not the sum of his or her deeds; as a person, one can be distinguished from one's works. No one can be adequately understood and evaluated on the basis of their own actions and projects. It is not one's doing that defines oneself, but solely one's relation to God. *The person standing before God is a different person than the one regarding himself or herself!* The doctrine of justification is related to the fundamental insights regarding human nature, ecclesiology, and ethics, but originally and above all to the core insight of the Christian understanding of identity: the subject knows itself as immediately and directly grounded in God's prior act; it is constituted in its relation to God and understands itself as accepted by God, held in being and preserved by God. Thus the doctrine of justification is also the Christian symbolization of the inviolable human dignity of every individual.[227]

The Pauline doctrine of justification is not only a matter of religious knowledge but also an intellectual achievement that, in terms of its lasting quality, simply cannot be assigned a high enough value: righteousness/justice as the key concept to all religious, philosophical and political systems can as a whole only be something human beings receive, not something they can produce. Every human attempt to bring justice, in the comprehensive sense, into being ends up, inevitably and necessarily, in a totalitarian system. The Pauline insight of the gift character of righteousness/justice wards off that attempt from the very beginning, and therefore describes a fundamental condition of human freedom.

6.3 Pneumatology

For Paul, the foundational insight and experience of the *resurrection of Jesus Christ and the powerful, effective presence of the Holy Spirit* are foundational.

226. Hans Weder, "Gesetz und Sünde: Gedanken zu einem qualitativen Sprung im Denken des Paulus," in *Einblicke ins Evangelium: Exegetische Beiträge zur neutestamentlichen Hermeneutik; gesammelte Aufsätze aus den Jahren 1980–1991* (ed. Hans Weder; Göttingen: Vandenhoeck & Ruprecht, 1992), 340, appropriately comments: "The question is whether 'my truth' is something to hear, accept, and believe, or something that first comes into being as I make something of myself."

227. It is thus no accident that the concept of human rights has Christian roots; cf. Georg Nolte and Hans-Ludwig Schreiber, eds., *Der Mensch und seine Rechte: Grundlagen und Brennpunkte der Menschenrechte zu Beginn des 21. Jahrhunderts* (Göttingen: Wallstein, 2004).

The presence of salvation is manifest through participation in the work of the Spirit.[228] The Pneuma functions in Paul as the quintessence of the new status of the believer as life determined by the Spirit.

6.3.1 *The Spirit and the Structure of Pauline Thought*

The structure of Paul's thought can be understood as the internal networking of pneumatology with theology proper (the doctrine of God), Christology, soteriology, anthropology, ethics, and eschatology.[229] The integrative power of pneumatology is what enables Paul to impart a systematic quality to his interpretation of the Jesus-Christ-history.

For *theology proper*, this means that the reality of God in the world is the reality of the Spirit. By the πνεῦμα (spirit, breath), which is always primarily the Spirit that proceeds from God (cf. 1 Thess. 4:8; 1 Cor. 1:12–14; 2 Cor. 1:22; 5:5; Gal. 4:6; Rom. 5:5), the life-giving power of the Creator is manifest.[230] The Spirit of God not only effected the resurrection of Jesus (cf. Rom. 1:3b–4a) but is at the same time the new mode of being and working of the Risen One himself, his dynamic and effective presence (cf. 2 Cor. 3:17; 1 Cor. 15:45). The working of the Spirit of God sets believers free from the powers of sin and death (Rom. 8:9–11). The Spirit that Christians have received has its origin in God (cf. 1 Cor. 2:12; 6:19) and Christ (Rom. 8:9), so that *the Spirit, as subject of a higher order, is now the power that determines Christian existence.* The new universal working of the Spirit of God is for Paul the foundation of his whole theology, for the act of God's Spirit in Jesus Christ and in believers is *the* sign of the present time of salvation. Nonetheless, the Spirit, as the powerful gift of God, in all its manifestations is no independent force but remains united with its origin.[231]

In the realm of *Christology*, the point of departure is the resurrection event: Jesus Christ was raised from the dead through the Spirit of God (cf. Rom. 1:3b–4a; Rom. 6:4; 2 Cor. 13:4), and the work of God's Spirit is the basis for his unique eschatological status. The Spirit's unique relation to God nourishes

228. Cf. Panim Kim, "Heilsgegenwart bei Paulus: Eine religionsgeschichtlich-theologische Untersuchung zu Sündenvergebung und Geistgabe in den Qumrantexten sowie bei Johannes dem Täufer, Jesus und Paulus" (diss., Georg August Universität, Göttingen, 1996), 180: "After the cessation of prophecy in Israel, for Paul the Spirit of God begins to work anew in the world with the death and resurrection of Jesus Christ."

229. On the integrating and organizing function of pneumatology, cf. also Schlier, *Grundzüge*, 179–94; Friedrich Wilhelm Horn, "Kyrios und Pneuma bei Paulus," in *Paulinische Christologie: Exegetische Beiträge; Hans Hübner zum 70. Geburtstag* (ed. Udo Schnelle et al.; Göttingen: Vandenhoeck & Ruprecht, 2000), 385–431; Dunn, *Theology of Paul*, 413–41.

230. Cf. Horn, "Kurios und Pneuma," 59.

231. Cf. the foundational work of Wilhelm Thüsing, *Per Christum in Deum: Studien zum Verhältnis von Christozentrik und Theozentrik in den paulinischen hauptbriefen* (2nd ed.; NTA NF 1; Münster: Aschendorff, 1969), 152–63.

the being and ministry of the risen Lord as Pneuma (2 Cor. 3:18). The Spirit is also a decisively formative christological power, for Christ and the Spirit are in a sense equivalents (2 Cor. 3:17, ὁ δὲ κύριος τὸ πνεῦμά ἐστιν [now the Lord is the Spirit]).[232] This programmatic declaration is explained in 3:16, where the identification[233] of κύριος and πνεῦμα is not a static equation of the two, but is understood as describing the dynamic presence of the exalted Lord. The attribute of the Spirit applies even to the preexistent Christ (1 Cor. 10:4). The relation between the Spirit and Christ is so close that for Paul it is impossible to have one without the other (cf. Rom. 8:9b, "Anyone who does not have the Spirit of Christ does not belong to him"). Since the resurrection, Jesus Christ stands united with his own, as Pneuma and in the Pneuma. The exalted Christ works as πνεῦμα ζῳοποιοῦν (life-giving Spirit, 1 Cor. 15:45)[234] and confers a σῶμα πνευματικόν (spiritual body) on his own at the resurrection (1 Cor. 15:44).[235] The Spirit of the Lord is the dynamic that shapes believers' lives (cf. Phil. 1:19). They become part of his body; communion with the exalted Lord is a communion in the Spirit (1 Cor. 6:17, "Anyone united to the Lord becomes one spirit with him").

The work of the Spirit has *soteriological* and *anthropological* dimensions. By receiving the Spirit of God (cf. 1 Thess. 4:8; 1 Cor. 2:12; 2 Cor. 1:22; 11:4; Gal. 3:2, 14; Rom. 5:5; 8:15), baptized believers are already in the living present placed within the realm of communion with Christ and thus within the realm of salvation. Because Christ and his own belong on the side of the Spirit, they are not subject to the domination of the world of flesh, sin, and death. They can move forward toward the future judgment in the confidence that the gift of the Spirit is the first installment of what is yet to come (cf. 2 Cor. 1:22; 5:5), and future and present modulate into one reality in the saving work of the Spirit. The relation of the Spirit to anthropology means that baptized believers, through the gift of the Spirit of God/Christ, experience a new orientation and determination, for the Spirit is the creator and preserver of the new being. As the beginning of communion with Christ, reception of the Spirit in baptism (cf. 1 Cor. 6:11; 10:4; 12:13; 2 Cor. 1:21–22; Gal. 4:6; Rom. 8:14) marks the beginning of the believer's participation in the saving event.

232. Differently, Horn, "Kurios und Pneuma," 66–67.

233. Cf. Ingo Hermann, *Kyrios und Pneuma: Studien zur Christologie der paulinischen Hauptbriefe* (SANT 2; Munich: Kösel-Verlag, 1961), 48ff., whose comments are on target.

234. The term πνεῦμα ζῳοποιοῦν is found only here in the New Testament; cf. Horn, *Angeld des Geistes*, 197–98; Dunn, *Theology of Paul*, 261. First Corinthians 15:46 shows that Paul is arguing against Spirit enthusiasm and intentionally relates the concept of the Spirit to that of the exalted Lord.

235. Johannes Sijko Vos, *Traditionsgeschichtliche Untersuchungen zur Paulinischen Pneumatologie* (Assen: Van Gorcum, 1973), 81, appropriately formulates the matter: "As the eschatological Adam, Christ is Pneuma in his substance just as he is in his function. As Pneuma, Christ creates his own in his own image, and this means that he transforms them into his own spiritual mode of being."

Baptism places the Christian in the realm of the spiritual Christ, while at the same time the exalted Lord (cf. Gal. 2:20; 4:19; 2 Cor. 11:10; 13:5; Rom. 8:10) and the Spirit (cf. 1 Cor. 3:16; 6:19; Rom. 8:9, 11) are at work in the believer. The statements in which Christ and Spirit are paralleled or identified designate for Paul a fundamental reality:[236] just as the believer is incorporated in the Spirit of Christ, so Christ dwells in the believer as πνεῦμα. Life in the Spirit appears as the consequence and effect of the baptismal event, which, as a saving event, is in turn an event in the power of the Spirit. Paul thereby points out a fundamental anthropological transformation, for the life of the Christian has taken a decisive turn: as those determined by the Spirit, Christians live in the sphere of the Spirit and orient their lives to the working of the Spirit (cf. Rom. 8:5–11).[237] Life can be lived according to the flesh (κατὰ σάρκα) or according to the Spirit (κατὰ πνεῦμα)—there is no third option. The Spirit also has a noetic function,[238] for only the Spirit of God grants insight into God's plan of salvation: "Now we have received not the spirit of the world, but the Spirit that is from God, so that we may understand the gifts bestowed on us by God" (1 Cor. 2:12).

The *ethics* of the Christian life are also based on the Spirit, for the new being takes place in harmony with the Spirit, which appears as ground and norm of the new way of life (cf. Gal. 5:25; 1 Cor. 5:7; Rom. 6:2, 12; Phil. 2:12–13). Christians have entered into a life determined by the Spirit. The Spirit is the power and principle of the new life, and so Paul asks the Galatians in bewilderment, "The only thing I want to learn from you is this: Did you receive the Spirit by doing the works of the law or by believing what you heard?" (Gal. 3:2). At the same time, it becomes clear: there is no change without a new way of living. The Spirit conferred as a gift must be accepted. Precisely because the Spirit incorporates baptized believers into the sphere of God and the realm of the church, they are not in the vacuum of a world free of any ruling powers, but instead stand under the call to new obedience made possible by the Spirit.[239] The "newness of life" (Rom. 6:4) takes place in the "new life of the Spirit" (Rom. 7:6).

Finally, as the ἀρραβών (deposit, down payment, cf. 2 Cor. 1:22; 5:5) and the ἀπαρχή ("firstfruits," cf. Rom. 8:23), the Spirit is the guarantor of God's

236. Cf. Schnelle, *Gerechtigkeit und Christusgegenwart*, 120–22; and S. Vollenweider, "Der Geist Gottes als Selbst der Glaubenden," *ZTK* 93 (1996): 169–72.

237. Cf. Bultmann, *Theology of the New Testament*, 1:227–28.

238. As a pagan parallel, cf. Cicero, *Tusc.* 5.70, where, after listing the joys of the wise, it is said, "To the soul occupied day and night in these meditations there comes the knowledge enjoined by the god at Delphi [γνῶθι σεαυτόν, know thyself], that the mind should know its own self and feel its union with the divine mind, the source of the fullness of joy unquenchable."

239. Käsemann consistently emphasizes this aspect (cf., e.g., Ernst Käsemann, *Commentary on Romans* [trans. Geoffrey W. Bromiley; Grand Rapids: Eerdmans, 1980], 28: "For the apostle knows of no gift which does not also challenge us to responsibility, thereby showing itself as a power over us and creating a place of service for us").

eschatological faithfulness. The Spirit grants the transition into the post-mortal pneumatic mode of existence of the believers (cf. 1 Cor. 15:44–45) and bestows eternal life (Gal. 6:8, "but if you sow to the Spirit, you will reap eternal life from the Spirit"). Within this event, the Spirit even stands beside the creature and intercedes for the saints before God (cf. Rom. 8:26–27).[240] After all, it is not only individual personal existence, but the whole creation that God will bring into the new being. Creation and humanity not only have the same origin; their future destiny is also bound together. In Paul's thought, protology and eschatology, universal history and individual history are correlated, because God is the beginning and goal of all that is (cf. Rom. 8:18ff.).[241] Everything comes from God, everything continues to exist by God's power, and everything goes to and finds its goal in God.

The Spirit, conferred in baptism and living in the Christian, appears as *the continuing reality of the divine life-giving power*. Through the Spirit, God will grant believers participation in what God has already done for Christ (cf. Rom. 8:11).

6.3.2 The Gifts of the Spirit

The Spirit confers gifts and effectively operates in the life of the churches. All baptized believers are given the *essential, foundational* gifts of the Spirit. An essential distinctive mark of the Spirit is that it bestows and creates *freedom* (2 Cor. 3:17b, "where the Spirit of the Lord is, there is freedom"; see below, §6.5.5). The life principle of the Spirit itself frees baptized believers from the enslaving powers of the law, sin, and death (Rom. 8:2). As those who have been "born according to the Spirit," baptized believers belong no longer to the realm of slavery but to that of freedom (cf. Gal. 4:21–31). The new relation to God and Jesus Christ through the gift of the Spirit establishes believers in the status of *adopted children* (Rom. 8:15, "For you did not receive a spirit of slavery back into fear, but you have received a spirit of adoption, through which we cry, 'Abba! Father!'"). As children of God, believers are joint heirs with Christ both in suffering and in glory (cf. Rom. 8:17; Gal. 4:6–7). The power of *love* now shapes the lives of Christians "because God's love has been poured into our hearts through the Holy Spirit that has been given to us" (Rom. 5:5b). Love is first on the list of the fruit of the Spirit (cf. Gal. 5:22); love has its origin in God, attains concrete form in Christ, and gives hope to human beings (cf. Rom. 5:5a). Love is the ground of hope because the destiny of Jesus Christ is the embodiment of love. Participation in this destiny assures Christians that the effective power of life that comes from God continues beyond death, for their hope is in the "God

240. For exposition, cf. Horn, *Angeld des Geistes*, 294–97.

241. Peter von der Osten-Sacken, *Römer 8 als Beispiel paulinischer Soteriologie* (Göttingen: Vandenhoeck & Ruprecht, 1975), 319–20.

who raises the dead" (2 Cor. 1:9). Apart from love, all human manifestations of life are nothing, for they lag behind the new reality God has brought into being.[242] Love is the very opposite of individualism and egoism; love does not seek its own but reveals its essential nature precisely by enduring evil and doing good. It is no accident that 1 Cor. 13 stands between the two chapters that deal with the dangers of misusing charismatic gifts (1 Cor. 12 and 14).[243] Paul makes it clear that even the most extraordinary charismatic gifts are of no use unless they are permeated through and through with love. When the charismatic gifts someday pass away, as they will, and the present forms of knowledge cease, love will remain, which is superior even to faith and hope—for it is the most complete expression of the nature of God.

As the first and greatest gift, love is the criterion for identifying the *current* work of the Spirit.[244] Because Jesus Christ is the embodiment of the love of God,[245] Paul binds the question of the validity of various spiritual works to an appropriate understanding of Christ (cf. 1 Cor. 12:1–3).[246] When in worship the community confesses its faith in the crucified and Risen One with the acclamation Κύριος Ἰησοῦς (Jesus is Lord), it orients its own life to the way of love lived out by Jesus of Nazareth. Paul calls on the Corinthians, in particular, to remember this fundamental fact when he points out to the congregation that the Spirit at work within it originates in and from God. God is the final cause of all activities and the giver of all spiritual gifts in their various workings (cf. 1 Cor. 12:6b, "it is the same God who activates all of them in everyone"; cf. also 1 Cor. 1:4; 7:7; 12:28–30), so that an anthropological monopolization of the Spirit does not increase the power of its works but rather silences them. The insight into the unity and indivisibility of the Spirit produces the kind

242. Appropriately, Hans Weder, "Die Energie des Evangeliums: Hermeneutische Überlegungen zur Wirklichkeit des Wortes," *ZTK* 9 (1995): 94–119, who argues that love has a reality "that is not created by those who love but who are themselves supported and carried along by love" (95).

243. On context and analysis, cf. Oda Wischmeyer, *Der höchste Weg: Das 13. Kapitel des 1. Korintherbriefes* (SNT 13; Gütersloh: Gütersloher Verlagshaus, 1981); Thomas Söding, *Das Liebesgebot bei Paulus: Die Mahnung zur Agape im Rahmen der paulinischen Ethik* (NTA 26; Münster: Aschendorff, 1995), 127–46; Florian Voss, *Das Wort vom Kreuz und die menschliche Vernunft: Eine Untersuchung zur Soteriologie des 1. Korintherbriefes* (FRLANT 199; Göttingen: Vandenhoeck & Ruprecht, 2002), 239–71.

244. On the line of argument in 1 Cor. 12–14 cf. the extensive treatment in Ulrich Brockhaus, *Charisma und Amt: Die paulinische Charismenlehre auf dem Hintergrund der frühchristlichen Gemeindefunktionen* (Wuppertal: Brockhaus, 1972), 156–92; Wischmeyer, *Der höchste Weg*, 27–38; Wolff, *1. Korintherbrief*, 282–348; Schrage, *Korinther*, 108ff.; Lindemann, *Der Erste Korintherbrief*, 261–316.

245. Cf. Günther Bornkamm, "Der köstlichere Weg," in *Das Ende des Gesetzes: Paulusstudien* (ed. Günther Bornkamm; BEvT 16; Munich: Kaiser, 1961), 110: "Ἀγάπη is related to the variety of χαρίσματα as Christ is related to the members of the body."

246. On 1 Cor. 12:1–3, cf. Matthias Pfeiffer, *Einweisung in das neue Sein: Neutestamentliche Erwägungen zur Grundlegung der Ethik* (Gütersloh: Gütersloher Verlagshaus, 2001), 211–15.

of life that knows it is in harmony with the creative work of the Spirit. Paul emphasizes the gift character of the Spirit, and the fact that its works are not at human disposal by using the terms πνευματικά (lit. spiritual phenomena) and χαρίσματα (gifts) as synonyms (1 Cor. 12:1; 12:4); the Spirit is the power of grace, and χαρίσματα grow out of χάρις (cf. Rom. 12:6). Paul underscores the indissoluble connection between the work of the Spirit and love by defining the church as σῶμα Χριστοῦ (body of Christ). The body, as the life space created by Christ, obligates the individual members to live and act in a way that is responsible only to love (see below, §6.7.1 and §6.7.2).[247] Therefore the diversity of the Spirit's activities must correspond to the unity of the one church, for both have the same origin: *God's love through the Son in the power of the Spirit*. The Spirit produces what is useful to the church and leads to its edification, so that not the individualistic self-realization of the individual member but only the edification (οἰκοδομή) of the congregation as a whole corresponds to the work of the Spirit (cf. 1 Cor. 14:3, 5, 26). All charismatic gifts must be measured by the principle πάντα πρὸς οἰκοδομὴν γινέσθω (1 Cor. 14:26, "Let all things be done for building up").

6.3.3 Father, Son, and Spirit

Paul does not advocate a trinitarian *doctrine* as later fixed in ontological categories and expressed in the concept of persons.[248] Nonetheless, there are expressions and images that show beginning reflection on how Father, Son, and Holy Spirit are related. The point of departure is the basic *theocentric* characteristic of all Pauline theology; everything comes from God and goes to God. Also, Paul clearly distinguishes Christ and the Spirit and places them in a graduated series. Of these three, it is said only of Christ that he is the Son of God (cf. Gal. 4:4; Rom. 1:3) who died for our sins in order to gain salvation for us (cf. 1 Cor. 15:3ff.; 2 Cor. 5:15; Rom. 5:8).[249] On the foundation of this primary ordering of theology proper and Christology, we can describe the internal unitive role of pneumatology: the Spirit certifies and represents the salvation willed by God and effected in the Christ event (Rom. 8:9); it names, makes present, and powerfully determines the new being. The Spirit comes from God and is closely related to Jesus Christ in its works. As the power of God, it leads people to faith in Jesus Christ (cf. 1 Cor. 2:4–5), enables confession to the Kyrios (cf. 1 Cor. 12:3), and sanctifies the believers (cf. 1 Cor.

247. Cf. ibid., 221ff.

248. Cf. Gordon D. Fee, *God's Empowering Presence: The Holy Spirit in the Letters of Paul* (Peabody, MA: Hendrickson, 1994), 829–42; Horn, *Angeld des Geistes*, 415–17.

249. Appropriately, Heinrich Schlier, *Der Brief an die Galater* (10th ed.; KEK 7; Göttingen: Vandenhoeck & Ruprecht, 1949), 249: "The Spirit is, of course, not a power given with existence itself but the power of Christ himself that overcomes existence along with Christ. The Spirit is Christ in the power of his emerging presence with us."

6:11; Rom. 15:16). The Spirit certifies the new status of adopted children of God (Gal. 4:4ff.), pours the love of God into the hearts of believers (Rom. 5:5), and finally effects the transformation into eschatological glory (cf. 1 Cor. 15:44–45; Rom. 8:18ff.).

This fundamental relatedness to God and Jesus Christ does not, however, exclude the Spirit from having a certain independent status. The relation of the Spirit to God and Jesus Christ cannot be satisfactorily described in the categories of subordination, coordination, or identity, for the Spirit also has its own personal reality (1 Cor. 12:11, "All these are activated by one and the same Spirit, who allots to each one individually just as the Spirit chooses"). The Spirit does not appear in Paul as an independent person but is still thought of in personal terms. The Spirit leads to the Father, for it teaches believers to say "Abba" (cf. Rom. 8:15, 27),[250] makes intercession for the saints before God, and even searches out the depths of God (cf. 1 Cor. 2:10). Although the Spirit works only as a power from God and acts only on behalf of God and the Kyrios, it still has a personal aspect. For the believing community, the Spirit opens up dimensions of reality that rational thought cannot deal with, an enlightenment of reason that does not disparage rational thought but ennobles it.

The internal interconnectedness of theology proper, Christology, and pneumatology constitutes the field of activity of Pauline thought and can be described as follows: *the Spirit is classified with God and Christ in that through God's Spirit, Christ becomes a life-giving Pneuma.* The Pneuma comes from God and binds baptized believers to God through Christ. Thus the concept of the salvific, divine, life-giving power links the three fundamental realms of Pauline thought.

6.4 Soteriology

God's saving and redeeming act in Jesus Christ is the beginning and orientation point of all Paul's thought, so that it bears a soteriological stamp throughout. Salvation/redemption of believers happens by virtue of their participation in God's saving/redeeming act. Salvation takes place "in hope" (Rom. 8:24) and is grounded in the *pro nobis* (for us) of God's love for humanity (Rom. 8:31–39). The reality that the fullness of salvation is yet to come in no way minimizes, however, the conviction that the transfer into the new reality has

250. Cf. Horn, *Angeld des Geistes*, 418–22. [In German, as in Greek, the pronoun referring to the Spirit is determined by the grammatical gender of the word for "Spirit" (neuter in Greek; masculine in German). English is not so structured, and so the choice of pronoun seems to communicate whether the Spirit is thought of in personal terms (he, she) or not (it) and thus cannot communicate the way the term is used in either Greek or German. English translations of the Bible and of theological works in German (and other languages) must make choices not necessary or meaningful in Greek or German.—MEB]

already effectively begun, for *what has already happened*, not what is still to come, is the definitive content of the Pauline gospel. For Paul, the presence of salvation was real: "See, now [νῦν] is the acceptable time; see, now [νῦν] is the day of salvation!" (2 Cor. 6:2b). A new time has broken into the present, which Paul describes with a variety of metaphors: the present is the time of grace and salvation; participation in Christ changes being and time.

6.4.1 The New Being "with Christ"/"in Christ"

Just as Jesus Christ defines the beginning and end points of the saving event by his resurrection and parousia, so he also determines the whole life of believers during the intervening time. Paul communicates the idea of participation in salvation above all with the imagery of being σὺν Χριστῷ (with Christ) and ἐν Χριστῷ (in Christ).

With Christ

The phrase σὺν Χριστῷ and other such expressions using the preposition σύν[251] primarily describe entrance into the realm of salvation and the transition into ultimate communion with Christ. In Rom. 6 the basic participatory character of Pauline theology is expressed semantically by the unusual frequency of σύν (6:8) or its compounds (6:4, 5, 6, 8). The transformation to a new life in the power of the Spirit has already begun, not only as a changed perception of the world but in a real sense, for in baptism the believer is incorporated in the somatic destiny of Jesus Christ. In baptism, Jesus's death and the powers of his resurrection are present, so that what happens in baptism must be understood as a sacramental re-experiencing of the death of Jesus, which in baptism becomes present reality, and as incorporation into the reality of the resurrection. The powers of the resurrection are also at work in the Lord's Supper; Paul warns the Corinthians, "For all who eat and drink without discerning the body eat and drink judgment against themselves. For this reason many of you are weak and ill, and some have died" (1 Cor. 11:29–30). The powers at work in the sacrament can bring God's judgment on those who participate in it in an unworthy manner.

The reality of the resurrection permeates the believers' whole existence, determining their new being in the present and the future. Jesus Christ died for those who have been called, so that they may "live with him" (cf. 1 Thess. 4:17, σὺν κυρίῳ ἐσόμεθα [we will be with the Lord]; 5:10, σὺν αὐτῷ ζήσωμεν [that . . . we may live with him]). God will act for the members of the eschatological community just as he acted for Jesus Christ (2 Cor. 4:14). Paul regards Christians as already having the status of sonship (cf. Gal. 3:26; 4:6–7; Rom. 8:16);

251. For analysis, cf. Peter Siber, *Mit Christus leben: Eine Studie zur paulinischen Auferstehungshoffnung* (Zürich: Theologischer Verlag, 1971).

they have put on Christ (Gal. 3:27; Rom. 13:14), so that Christ is formed in them (Gal. 4:19). As heirs of the promise (cf. κληρονομία, Gal. 3:18; κληρονόμος, Gal. 3:29; 4:1, 7; Rom. 4:13–14; cf. further 1 Cor. 6:9–10; 15:50), they already participate in God's saving work; they have been granted the status of God's children and the freedom that goes with it (Gal. 5:21). Regarding both suffering and glory, believers are "joint heirs with Christ" (Rom. 8:17, συγκληρονόμοι Χριστοῦ); they are destined to be conformed to the image of the Son of God (Rom. 8:29). The reality of the resurrection penetrates the existence of Christians, even into their bodily sufferings (cf. 2 Cor. 4:10–11; 6:9–10). Near the end of his life, Paul longs for unbroken, constant communion with Christ (Phil. 1:23, σὺν Χριστῷ εἶναι). He wants to participate in the power of both Christ's resurrection and his sufferings "by becoming like him in his death, if somehow I may attain the resurrection from the dead" (Phil. 3:10–11). Jesus Christ will transform "the body of our humiliation" to conform to "the body of his glory," for he has the power (ἐνέργεια) "that also enables him to make all things subject to himself" (Phil. 3:21). In the here and now, Christians have already been placed in a tension-filled field of activity that powerfully affects their lives both now and beyond death.

In Christ

The sphere within which the new life is lived, between the beginning of salvation and its consummation, Paul describes with the phrase εἶναι ἐν Χριστῷ (being in Christ). This expression is much more than a "formula"; it must be regarded as *the* essential theme that runs uninterrupted through his theology.[252] The external data are already significant: forms of ἐν Χριστῷ ('Ιησοῦ) (in Christ [Jesus]) occur sixty-four times in Paul's letters, and the derived expression ἐν κυρίῳ (in the Lord) thirty-seven times.[253] Paul is not the creator of the expression ἐν Χριστῷ, as shown by the pre-Pauline baptismal traditions in 1 Cor. 1:30; 2 Cor. 5:17; and Gal. 3:26–28.[254] Nonetheless, he can still be regarded as the real champion of this image, which not only was made by him into a concise

252. On ἐν Χριστῷ, cf. Adolf Deissmann, *Die neutestamentliche Formel "in Christo Jesu"* (Marburg: Elwert, 1892); and idem, *St. Paul, A Study in Social and Religious History*, trans. by Lionel R. M. Strachan (New York: Hodder & Stoughton, 1912), 138–42; Friedrich Büchsel, "'In Christus' bei Paulus," *ZNW* (1949): 141–58; Fritz Neugebauer, *In Christus =* Ἐν Χριστῷ*: Eine Untersuchung zum Paulinischen Glaubensverständnis* (Göttingen: Vandenhoeck & Ruprecht, 1961); Schnelle, *Gerechtigkeit und Christusgegenwart*, 106–23, 225–35; Mark A. Seifrid, "In Christ," in *Dictionary of Paul and His Letters* (ed. Gerald F. Hawthorne et al.; Downers Grove, IL: InterVarsity, 1993), 433–36; Jürgen Roloff, *Die Kirche im Neuen Testament* (GNT 10; Göttingen: Vandenhoeck & Ruprecht, 1993), 86–99; L. Klehn, "Die Verwendung von ἐν Χριστῷ bei Paulus," *BZ* 74 (1994): 117–23; Strecker, *Theology of the New Testament*, 117–22; Joachim Gnilka, *Paulus von Tarsus, Apostel und Zeuge* (HTKNT 6; Freiburg: Herder, 1996), 255–60; Strecker, *Die liminale Theologie des Paulus*, 189–211.

253. Klehn, "ἐν Χριστῷ bei Paulus," 68.

254. Cf. further 2 Cor. 5:21b; Gal. 2:17; 5:6; Rom. 3:24; 6:11, 23; 8:1; 12:5.

definition of what it means to be Christian but must also be understood as his "core ecclesiological definition."[255] The primary meaning of ἐν Χριστῷ is to be understood in a local sense, indicating a sphere of being:[256] by baptism the believer is incorporated into the sphere of the pneumatic Christ, and the new life is constituted by the conferral of the Spirit as the down payment on salvation, which begins in the present and is fulfilled in the eschatological future redemption. Human beings are torn out of their self-oriented lives and find their true selves in their relation to Christ. This local/sphere-of-being sense of ἐν Χριστῷ dominates in 1 Thess. 4:16; 1 Cor. 1:30; 15:18, 22; 2 Cor. 5:17; Gal. 2:17; 3:26–28; 5:6; Rom. 3:24; 6:11, 23; 8:1; 12:5. The variety and complexity of the ἐν Χριστῷ statements and the fact that such statements with different levels of meaning are found alongside one another can all be derived from this basic local/sphere-of-being sense.[257] With the expression ἐν Χριστῷ, Paul unites the vertical and horizontal realms:[258] from communion with Christ (cf. Gal. 3:27) grows a new *communitas* of baptized believers that now transcends fundamental gender, ethnic, and social alternatives (Gal. 3:28; 1 Cor. 12:13). Thus ἐν Χριστῷ appears as the sphere in which changes affecting reality take place and are lived out. The baptized are determined by Christ in every aspect of life, and in their community the new being assumes visible form. The world not only is declared to be different but has really been changed because the powers of the resurrection already are at work in the present through the gift of the Spirit.

6.4.2 Grace and Salvation

The transformation of the Son and the participation of believers in this saving event change the way they perceive and understand time. Time is likewise subject to a transformative process, for "the ends of the ages have come" (1 Cor. 10:11c). The Pauline νυνὶ δέ (but now) impressively marks out the eschatological turning point from the old age to the new:[259] "But in fact Christ has been raised from the dead, the first fruits of those who have died" (1 Cor. 15:20; cf. 2 Cor. 6:2; 13:13; Rom. 3:21; 6:22; 7:6). Baptized believers are now

255. Hans Hübner, "Die paulinische Rechtfertigungstheologie als ökumenisch-hermeneutisches Problem," in *Worum geht es in der Rechtfertigungslehre? Das biblische Fundament der "Gemeinsamen Erklärung" von katholischer Kirche und Lutherischem Weltbund* (ed. Thomas Söding and Frank-Lothar Hossfeld; QD 180; Freiburg: Herder, 1999), 91.

256. Cf. Schnelle, *Gerechtigkeit und Christusgegenwart*, 109–17; Seifrid, "In Christ," 433–34; Umbach, *In Christus getauft*, 220–21; Strecker, *Die liminale Theologie des Paulus*, 191–92.

257. Albrecht Oepke, "ἐν," *TDNT* 2:538: "This underlying spatial concept gives us the clue to the true significance of the formula ἐν Χριστῷ Ἰησοῦ and its parallels." Schnelle, *Gerechtigkeit und Christusgegenwart*, 117–22; Klehn, "ἐν Χριστῷ bei Paulus," 77.

258. Strecker, *Die liminale Theologie des Paulus*, 193ff., speaks of a vertical and horizontal communion with Christ.

259. Cf. Luz, *Geschichtsverständnis*, 168–69.

(νῦν) justified through the blood of Christ (Rom. 5:9) and have now (νῦν) received reconciliation (Rom. 5:11). Paul is certain that "salvation is nearer to us now than when we became believers" (Rom. 13:11). The present and future are the time of grace (χάρις) and salvation (σωτηρία).

Grace

Paul consistently uses χάρις (grace) in the singular; this linguistic usage already signals the fundamental idea of his doctrine of grace: *grace proceeds from God, is concentrated in the Christ event, and is effective for baptized believers.* Because Jesus Christ personifies the grace of God, Paul can use the χάρις of God and the χάρις of Christ as parallel expressions (Rom. 5:15). Christ appears as the one who bestows grace on the apostle and the churches (cf. 2 Cor. 8:9; 12:9; Gal. l:16). Believers already stand in a state of grace (cf. 1 Cor. 1:4; Rom. 5:21), for through the Christ event they have been lifted out of their entanglement in the past history of condemnation (Rom. 5:15–16); grace triumphs over the powers of sin and death.[260] The present truth is that "just as sin exercised dominion in death, so grace might also exercise dominion through justification leading to eternal life through Jesus Christ our Lord" (Rom. 5:21). All this happens "for your sake, so that grace, as it extends to more and more people, may increase thanksgiving, to the glory of God" (2 Cor. 4:15). The Spirit is given to those who believe and are baptized (1 Cor. 2:12, aorist passive participle χαρισθέντα), so that now through God's grace they recognize the new time in which they live. They participate in God's saving work through the faith they have received as a gift (cf. Rom. 4:16; Phil. 1:29). God's reconciliation with human beings through Jesus Christ is concretely realized in the gifts of righteousness and grace (cf. 2 Cor. 5:18–6:2; Rom. 5:1–11). Paul understands *the collection for Jerusalem* to be a work of grace because it confers a concrete form on God's saving work (cf. 1 Cor. 16:3; 2 Cor. 8:1, 4, 6–7, 19; 9:8, 14–15). The prototype for this χάρις is the grace of Christ, for through his poverty he confers riches on the community of faith (cf. 2 Cor. 8:9). Especially the reflections on the procedures for carrying out the collection found in 2 Cor. 8–9 and Rom. 15:25–28 show that Paul argues his doctrine of grace against the background of the contemporary principle of mutuality.[261] Reciprocity was a fundamental principle of Hellenistic society, according to which the benefactions of patrons (e.g., the Roman emperor) and the gratitude/obedience of the recipients obviously belong together. The exchange of goods and services between people of different social status who

260. On the Pauline understanding of χάρις cf. Bultmann, *Theology of the New Testament*, 1:288–92; Hans Conzelmann, "Χαίρω, χάρις, κτλ.," *TDNT* 9:393–96; Dieter Zeller, *Charis bei Philon und Paulus* (SBS 142; Stuttgart: Verlag Katholisches Bibelwerk, 1990), 138–96; Dunn, *Theology of Paul*, 319–23; James R. Harrison, *Paul's Language of Grace in Its Graeco-Roman Context* (WUNT 2.172; Tübingen: Mohr Siebeck, 2003), 211ff.

261. Cf. Harrison, *Language of Grace*, 294–332.

are thereby bound together into a network of patrons and clients permeated both public and private life. Paul specifically designates the collection as χάρις (cf. 1 Cor. 16:3; 2 Cor. 8:4, 7, 19) and says in regard to Macedonia and Achaia: "They were pleased to do it, and indeed they owe it to them. For if the Gentiles have shared in the Jews' spiritual blessings, they owe it to the Jews to share with them their material blessings" (Rom. 15:27). At the same time, he says in Rom. 3:24: ". . . and are justified freely by his grace through the redemption that came by Christ Jesus." *Here Paul's word δωρεάν (freely) represents a breakthrough in Hellenistic society's principle of mutual benefactions and obligations.* God's gracious act is without presuppositions, but not without intention; it is not oriented to the various ways of thinking in terms of status, but is universal and independent of either social or cultural characteristics.[262]

Even the apostle's time in prison can be described as χάρις because it furthers the preaching of the gospel (cf. Phil. 1:7). The grace of God thus becomes the real bearer of the apostle's work (cf. 2 Cor. 1:12) and of the churches, for the "spiritual gifts" (χαρίσματα, lit. "the effects of grace") also owe their existence to the one grace (Rom. 12:6). When, at the beginning and conclusion of his letters, Paul emphasizes the grace in which his churches stand (cf. 1 Thess. 1:1; 5:28; 1 Cor. 1:3; 16:23; 2 Cor. 1:2; 13:13; Gal. 1:3; 6:18; Rom. 1:5; 16:20; Phil. 1:2; 4:23; Philem. 3), he is not only following a liturgical convention but naming an existing reality: both apostle (cf. 1 Cor. 3:10; Gal. 1:15; 2:9; Rom. 1:5; 12:3; 15:15) and church owe their existence and continuance to the grace of God alone. Paul contrasts his earlier life with his call to be an apostle: "But by the grace of God I am what I am, and his grace toward me has not been in vain. On the contrary, I worked harder than any of them—though it was not I, but the grace of God that is with me" (1 Cor. 15:10). It is grace that carries him through difficult situations, for grace shows its strength precisely in enduring severe tests and challenges (cf. 2 Cor. 12:9). It is not the goodwill of Caesar[263] that graces and changes the life of human beings but the gracious turning of God toward humanity in Jesus Christ. Grace is not a feeling, emotion, or quality of God but his unexpected, free, and powerful act. Grace is the expression of God's love, for "God proves his love for us in that while we still were sinners Christ died

262. The beginnings of a comparable universal perspective from a philosophical perspective are found in Epictetus, *Diatr.* 4.1.102–110 (103–104: "And so, when you have received everything, and your very self, from Another, do you yet complain and blame the Giver, if He take something away from you? Who are you, and for what purpose have you come? Did not He bring you into the world? Did not He show you the light?").

263. Cf. the catalog of materials in Gillis Petersson Wetter, *Charis: Ein Beitrag zur Geschichte des ältesten Christentums* (UNT 5; Leipzig: Brandstetter, 1913), 6–19; Conzelmann, "χάρις," 9:366–67; Zeller, *Charis*, 14–32; Harrison, *Language of Grace*, 61–62, 87–90, 226ff. The classic statement is Nero's declaration of freedom to the Greeks in Corinth, 67 CE (cf. *NW* 1.2:249–50).

for us" (Rom. 5:8).[264] Therefore Paul constantly hopes that Israel, too, will share in the grace of God (Rom. 11:1ff.).

In his letters to the Galatians and the Romans, Paul relates χάρις statements to his exclusive doctrine of justification, which is determined by nomology. He expresses surprise at how quickly the Galatians had turned aside from grace (Gal. 1:6) and says, "You who want to be justified by the law have cut yourselves off from Christ; you have fallen away from grace" (Gal. 5:4). Overflowing grace appears as a power by which the actual, unavoidable condemnation of humanity is averted (Rom. 5:16). Christians have been delivered from sin and death and find themselves in the objective status of saving grace. Because the Christ event and not the law/Torah saves them, the apostle can specify that the new status of Christians means that "sin will have no dominion over you, since you are not under law but under grace" (Rom. 6:14). Romans 6 makes it clear that the antinomian distortion of the Pauline concept of grace can also be based on the fundamental idea that believers participate in the grace of God through baptism (cf. Rom. 6:1, "Should we continue in sin in order that grace may abound?"). But Paul emphatically rejects opponents' logic and points to the basic salvific datum of Christian existence, namely, baptism. The fundamental conception of Pauline soteriology is not bound to a negative understanding of the law or a particular conception of justification[265] but derives positively from the logic of transformation and participation. Through the Son's change of status, baptized believers are placed in a new status, namely, grace.[266] With his extensive use of the term χάρις (63 times in Paul, of 155 times in the New Testament), Paul signals that he understands the new time as the time of grace.

Deliverance

With the term σωτηρία (salvation, deliverance), Paul takes up a second central metaphor of the religious world of antiquity, as a means of interpreting the new time in which Christians know themselves to live. In New Testament times, the semantic field σωτήρ/σωτηρία/σῴζω (savior/salvation/save) has both political and religious connotations: the Roman Caesar is the savior of the world who not only guarantees the political unity of the empire but grants its citizens prosperity, well-being, and meaning and purpose for their lives.[267] The idea of deliverance

264. For the internal connection between the concepts of love and grace, cf. Bultmann, *Theology of the New Testament*, 1:291–92.

265. Differently Bultmann, ibid., 1:284, who practically identifies χάρις and δικαιοσύνη (θεοῦ) (the righteousness [of/from God]): "'Righteousness,' then, has its origin in God's grace." Similarly, Conzelmann, *Theology of the New Testament*, 213–20, and Dunn, *Theology of Paul*, 319–23, argue that the exclusive doctrine of justification as found in Romans is *the* complete statement of Paul's doctrine of grace.

266. Cf. Powers, *Salvation through Participation*, 235: "The exegesis of the various passages in early Christian literature in this study has demonstrated that Paul's essential conception of salvation is that of participation."

267. Cf. §10.4.1, §10.4.2, §10.4.4.

played a central role in the competing religious views that offered a meaningful framework for one's life, such as those of the mystery cults.[268] In the face of blind, raging destiny and the inevitability of suffering and death, the initiates hope to participate in the dramatized destiny of a god who has experienced death as the passageway to new life. After fulfilling the rites of the cult, the initiate is "reborn" to a happy and successful new life that already begins in the present (cf. Apuleius, *Metam.* 11.16.2–4; 21.7). Around the turn of the first century CE, the theme of ancient philosophy in general (Cicero, Seneca, Epictetus, Plutarch) was the overcoming of fate and the emotions in order to live a life governed by reason. Philosophy and religion strove for the possibilities and means for the illumination of being and for forms of cultivating self-realization.

It is against this complex background that the early Christian message of the salvation of believers in Jesus Christ must be read. Paul outbids all competing promises, for the gospel he proclaims comprehends all realms of time and being and saves from the justified wrath of God (cf. Rom. 1:16ff.). Those who trust in this message are no longer anxious as they face the unpredictable powers of the future. God has destined them not for wrath but for salvation (1 Thess. 5:9; Rom. 5:9). The foolishness of the preaching of the cross saves; on the cross God has shown the wisdom of the world to be foolishness (1 Cor. 1:18, 21). Paul proclaims the gospel in a variety of ways in order to save at least some (cf. 1 Cor. 9:22; 10:33). He prays for Israel, that it will be saved (cf. Rom. 10:1; 11:14), and finally attains the prophetic insight that at the Lord's return "all Israel" will be saved (Rom. 11:26). The saving gospel has a particular form (cf. 1 Cor. 15:2); it is the power of God (Rom. 1:16), and every one who confesses it with the mouth (i.e., publicly) will be saved (Rom. 10:9, 13). How much Paul thought of σωτηρία as a real, tangible event is shown by 1 Cor. 3:15; 5:5; 7:16: the self of the baptized will be saved in the fire of judgment even if their works or bodies are lost; the sanctification of the unbelieving partner makes possible his or her salvation. Because the powers of the resurrection are already at work in the present and continue into the future, salvation is much more than a new kind of consciousness of those who consider themselves saved; σωτηρία is a concretely real event and, at the same time, a universal event that transforms being and time.

6.5 Anthropology

Paul intensively pursues the question of human identity: what constitutes, supports, and limits authentic human existence? His answers to these ques-

268. Cf. Thomas Söding, "Das Geheimnis Gottes im Kreuz Jesu," in *Das Wort vom Kreuz: Studien zur paulinischen Theologie* (ed. Thomas Söding; WUNT 93; Tübingen: Mohr, 1997), 79–80.

tions stand within the tradition of Old Testament faith in God the creator but also incorporate traditions from Hellenistic anthropology, which he combines into his own interpretation of what it means to be authentically human. Human beings cannot live out of themselves, from their own resources, for they always find themselves thrown into a contested arena, caught up in the conflicting influences of preexisting powers. As creatures, human beings are not autonomous simply because they possess reason[269] but are exposed to the powers that prevail in creation: God, and evil in the form of sin.

6.5.1 Body and Flesh

For Paul, the creatureliness of human beings is manifest in corporeality.[270] The reality of sin means that this bodily character of human life is always an endangered corporeality; thus Paul distinguishes σῶμα (body) and σάρξ (flesh).

Body/Corporeality

The key term σῶμα (body, corporeality) appears in Paul first as a *neutral* designation of the human physical constitution. Abraham had a body that was already practically dead (Rom. 4:19). When Paul issues his condemnation of the immoral person in Corinth, he is absent in body (1 Cor. 5:3, ἀπὼν τῷ σώματι; cf. also 2 Cor. 10:10) but present in spirit (Spirit?). Paul bears the marks of Jesus on his body (Gal. 6:17), such as from wounds that he had received in beatings during his mission work (cf. 2 Cor. 11:24–25). In a marriage each partner has a claim on the body of the other (1 Cor. 7:4, "For the wife does not have authority over her own body, but the husband does; likewise the husband does not have authority over his own body, but the wife does"). Virgins must be concerned for the holiness of their bodies (1 Cor. 7:34). As the place of human desires and weaknesses, the body must be tamed (1 Cor. 9:27).

Paul also uses σῶμα in a *negative* sense in Rom. 6:6 (σῶμα τῆς ἁμαρτίας, body of sin) and Rom. 7:24 (σῶμα τοῦ θανάτου, body of death). Those who have been baptized have really died to sin (cf. Rom. 6:1ff.), but sin itself is not dead. It lives on in the world and continues to tempt and test the body. This is why Paul challenges his readers not to let sin reign in their mortal bodies (σῶμα θνητόν, Rom. 6:12; cf. 8:10–13). In Rom. 8:9 the apostle explicitly emphasizes the change of existence that transpires in baptism from the realm of σάρξ into the realm of the πνεῦμα (Spirit). Thus Rom. 8:10–11, 13 can speak

269. Differently Dio Chrysostom, *Or.* 36.19, who formulated the understanding of human being that is still predominant today: "What is a human being? A mortal being endowed with reason."

270. For the history of research, cf. Karl-Adolf Bauer, *Leiblichkeit, das Ende aller Werke Gottes* (Gütersloh: Gütersloher Verlagshaus, 1971), 13–64. Robert Jewett, *Paul's Anthropological Terms: A Study of Their Use in Conflict Settings* (AGJU 10; Leiden: Brill, 1971), 201–50.

of being no longer determined by σάρξ but only of being confronted by σάρξ. The σῶμα as such has not become a slave to the alien powers of σάρξ and ἁμαρτία,[271] yet it finds itself in constant danger of being taken over by them again. Σῶμα *refers to the self, the person, while* σάρξ *is an alien power that attempts to take it over as its own domain.*

Paul uses the term σῶμα in a *positive* sense as his comprehensive expression for the human self.[272] The body is essentially much more than food and drink (1 Cor. 6:13a); it is not defined by biological functions but, rather, belongs to the Lord (1 Cor. 6:13b). On earth Christians must place their bodies at the disposal of their Lord as "a living sacrifice, holy and acceptable to God, which is your spiritual worship" (Rom. 12:1b). It is precisely in bodily existence that faith acquires visible form. As the dwelling place of the Holy Spirit, the body is no longer available for one's own arbitrary disposition (1 Cor. 6:19). The autonomous "I" is no longer in control of the body of the believer because God himself has established the body as the place where he will be glorified: "glorify God in your body" (1 Cor. 6:20; cf. Phil. 1:20). To withhold the body from the Lord's service is to withhold oneself completely. For Paul, there is no human identity apart from bodily existence, and so he also thinks of the resurrection reality and thus postmortal existence in bodily terms. Just as believers on earth are connected bodily to Christ, so the Resurrected One effects the transition and transformation of human beings from mortal to postmortal existence. God's life-giving power, present in the Spirit, overcomes even death and creates a spiritual body (σῶμα πνευματικόν), into which the mortal human self and thus one's personal identity are taken up into a qualitatively new mode of existence (cf. 1 Cor. 15:42ff.). The present "body of our humiliation" (Phil. 3:21, τὸ σῶμα τῆς ταπεινώσεως ἡμῶν) will be conformed "to the body of his glory" (τῷ σώματι τῆς δόξης). What happened to Christ as "the first fruits of those who have died" (1 Cor. 15:20) will also happen to believers.

The σῶμα is the interface between the givenness of human existence in the world and the act of God for human beings.[273] Precisely because a human

271. Contra Bultmann, *Theology of the New Testament*, 1:197, who comments regarding Rom. 8:13 that here the σῶμα has fallen under the sway of an alien power and that the πράξεις τοῦ σώματος (passions of the body) are nothing else than ζῆν κατὰ σάρκα (to live according to the flesh). For critique, cf. Bauer, *Leiblichkeit*, 168–69.

272. Bultmann, *Theology of the New Testament*, 1:194, formulates it concisely: "Man does not *have* a *soma*; he *is* a *soma*."

273. Paul thereby makes a fundamental break with the (Platonizing) body-soul dualism that was advocated at the beginning of the first century CE in many variations. As examples, cf. Plutarch, *Mor.* 1001B–C: "There are two constituent parts of the universe, body and soul. The former god did not beget; but, matter having submitted itself to him, he formed and fitted it together by binding and bounding the unlimited with suitable limits and shapes. The soul, however, when it has partaken of intelligence and reason and concord, is not merely a work but also a part of god and has come to be not by his agency but both from him as source and out of his substance."

being both is a body and has a body,[274] God's saving act in Jesus Christ embraces and determines the body and thereby the person's concrete existence and history.

Flesh, Materiality

Just as with σῶμα, Paul can use σάρξ (flesh, materiality) first in a *neutral* sense, to designate the physical aspect of the human condition. Sicknesses are described as "weakness of the flesh" (NRSV "physical infirmity," Gal. 4:13) or "thorn in the flesh" (2 Cor. 12:7). Circumcision takes place "in the flesh," there is a "distress in this life" (NRSV; lit. "distress in the flesh," 1 Cor. 7:28), and there are different kinds of flesh (1 Cor. 15:39, humans, fish, cattle, birds). In the genealogical sense, σάρξ stands for membership in the people of Israel (Gal. 4:23, 29; Rom. 4:1; 9:3; 11:14).

The term σάρξ receives an explicitly *negative* connotation in the places where Paul assigns to the realm of the flesh those who live out of their own resources and trust in themselves.[275] He calls the Corinthians "fleshly" (σάρκινος), immature children in Christ (1 Cor. 3:1), who live by purely human standards and thus live "fleshly" (1 Cor. 3:3). Paul designates the transient reality excluded from the kingdom of God as "flesh and blood" (σάρξ καὶ αἷμα, 1 Cor. 15:50; Gal. 1:16; cf. also 1 Cor. 5:5; 2 Cor. 4:11; Rom. 6:19).[276] The apostle speaks several times in negative form of a "life in the flesh" (cf. 2 Cor. 10:3; Gal. 2:20; Phil. 1:22, 24; Philem. 16), by which he expresses a negative judgment on normal human existence. In contrast, while Paul of course lives ἐν σαρκί (in the flesh), he does not live κατὰ σάρκα (according to the flesh; cf. 2 Cor. 10:3). Fleshly people are characterized by self-centeredness and self-satisfaction, relying on their own abilities, making their own knowledge the standard of what is reasonable and real. A life κατὰ σάρκα means life without access to God, a life imprisoned in what is earthly and transient (cf. Rom. 7:14b). Here σάρξ is the summary expression for a life separated from, and opposed to, God. The real acting subject of life is sin, which results in death (Rom. 7:5, "While we were living in the flesh [ἐν τῇ σαρκί], our sinful passions, aroused by the law, were at work in our members to bear fruit for death").

Only God can liberate from this fateful interplay of flesh, sin, and death. This liberation took place fundamentally in the sending of the Son ἐν ὁμοιώματι σαρκὸς ἁμαρτίας ("in the likeness of sinful flesh," Rom. 8:3). Jesus assumed the very mode of existence in which sin exercises its power over human beings. The death and resurrection of Jesus Christ disarmed sin of its power in the very place where it is effective: in the flesh. In Paul the σάρξ/πνεῦμα contrast is not

274. So Bauer, *Leiblichkeit*, 185, in a critical extension of Bultmann's definition cited above; Paul uses σῶμα to designate both the personal self and the corporality of human existence.

275. The important foundational work is still Bultmann, *Theology of the New Testament*, 1:192–203.

276. Wolff, *1. Korintherbrief*, 205.

a metaphysical but a historical dualism. Because there is no human existence outside the flesh and the act of God occurs for human beings in the realm of the flesh, the flesh appears as the location where human beings either stubbornly persist in their self-centeredness or through the Spirit let themselves be placed in the service of God. For Paul, it is precisely *not* the case that in their earthly existence believers are removed from the flesh; rather, the Spirit overcomes the natural self-assertion inherent in the flesh.

6.5.2 Sin and Death

The distinctive features of the Pauline understanding of sin are already manifest in the apostle's *linguistic usage*.[277] Paul characteristically uses the term ἁμαρτία in the singular (cf., e.g., 1 Cor. 15:56; 2 Cor. 5:21; Gal. 3:22; Rom. 5:21; 6:12; 7:11). Plural forms are found in pre-Pauline traditional formulations outside the Letter to the Romans (cf. 1 Thess. 2:16; Gal. 1:4; 1 Cor. 15:3, 17). In Romans, a document in which Paul reflects intensively on the nature of sin, the singular ἁμαρτία clearly dominates, with only three instances of the plural (the citations from the Septuagint in Rom. 4:7 and 11:27; and Rom. 7:5, τὰ παθήματα τῶν ἁμαρτιῶν). The distribution of the word is striking: of the 173 occurrences of ἁμαρτία in the New Testament, 59 are in the undisputed Pauline letters; of these, 48 are found in Romans (the rest: 1 Thessalonians, 1 time; 1 Corinthians, 4 times; 2 Corinthians, 3 times; Galatians, 3 times; the word is missing from Philippians and Philemon). In 1 Thessalonians Israel is considered to be rejected because of its transgressions/misdeeds (1 Thess. 2:16),[278] but the basic idea of the Pauline doctrine of sin first clearly emerges in 1 Corinthians: Christ "died for our sins" (1 Cor. 15:3b; cf. 15:17); that is, he overcame the power of sin through the cross and resurrection. In passing and without systematic reflection, 1 Cor. 15:56 states that sin is the sting of death and gains its power through the law.[279] According to 2 Cor. 5:21, God made the nonsinner Jesus Christ to be sin for us "so that in him we might become the righteousness of God." The anarthrous ἁμαρτία in 2 Cor. 11:7 is to be understood in the sense of "mistake, error" (NRSV "Did I commit a sin?"; it means, "Did I do something wrong?").[280] The logic that becomes characteristic of Romans appears already in Galatians: according to the will of the Scripture (and thus of God), the Jews too stand under the power of

277. On Paul's linguistic usage, cf. Günter Röhser, *Metaphorik und Personifikation der Sünde: Antike Sündenvorstellungen und paulinische Hamartia* (Tübingen: Mohr, 1987), 7ff.

278. For analysis, cf. Umbach, *In Christus getauft*, 68–70.

279. For exegesis of 1 Cor. 15:56, cf. Friedrich Wilhelm Horn, "1Korinther 15,56—ein exegetischer Stachel," *ZNW* 82 (1991): 88–105; Thomas Söding, "'Die Kraft der Sünde ist das Gesetz' (1Kor 15,56): Anmerkungen zum Hintergrund und zur Pointe einer gesetzeskritischen Sentenz des Apostels Paulus," *ZNW* 83 (1992): 74–84.

280. Cf. Windisch, *Korintherbrief*, 334.

sin, to which everything is subject, in order that the promises may be given to those who believe (Gal. 3:22). If the Galatians want to have themselves circumcised, they fall short of the liberating power of the death of Jesus "for our sins" (Gal. 1:4). Christ cannot be a servant of the power of sin (Gal. 2:17),[281] for through him it becomes clear that the law/Torah cannot set people free from sin. In Romans the connection between the extensive treatment of the righteousness/law theme and the doctrine of sin is obvious. When Paul gives a comprehensive statement of his nomology and declares the hamartiological equality of Jews and Gentiles (Rom. 1:18–3:20), he must also reflect on the nature and function of sin.

The universality and fateful character of sin is shown by its temporal priority to every human life. From the time of Adam's sin, the world is characterized by the givenness of the connection of sin and death (cf. Rom. 5:12; further: *4 Ezra* 3.7, 21; 7.1, 118; *2 Bar.* 23.4). Sin was in the world before the law (Rom. 5:13; cf. 7:8b); "the law came in [later, with only temporary status]," (νόμος δὲ παρεισῆλθεν, Rom. 5:20). So also the factual judgment that Jews and Greeks are equally "under sin" (Rom. 3:9; cf. Gal. 3:22, ὑπὸ ἁμαρτίαν) presupposes the antecedent character of sin. *Sin is a fateful power that precedes and determines the existence of every human being.* Ultimately, it is the reality of sin and of sinful actions that provides the point of departure for Paul's line of argument. Human beings always find that they are already in the realm of sin and death, already stuck in a woeful situation for which they are not responsible.[282] The power of sin has them in its grasp just because they belong to the human race. Still and all, this does not mean that Paul absolves individual human beings of their own responsibility. The character of sin as an act is especially clear in Rom. 3:23, where Paul summarizes the preceding comprehensive argument: "All have sinned [πάντες γὰρ ἥμαρτον] and fall short of the glory of God." Both the vices of the pagans (cf. Rom. 1:24–32) and the fundamental contrast of orthodoxy and orthopraxy of the Jews (cf. Rom. 2:17–29) result in their respective doing or not-doing, so that it can be said: "All who have sinned apart from the law will also perish apart from the law, and all who have sinned under the law will be judged by the law" (Rom. 2:12). Paul grounds his factual judgment "all are under sin" in Rom. 3:9 with a comprehensive series of proofs from Scripture, with quotations that point clearly to the nature of sin as an act. Here, one's guilty status before God (Rom. 3:19b) is not the result of a fate, but the result of one's own actions. Sin as acts for which human beings themselves are responsible is declared programmatically in Rom. 14:23: "Whatever does not proceed from faith is sin" (πᾶν δὲ ὅ οὐκ ἐκ πίστεως ἁμαρτία ἐστίν). The universal dominion of sin is thus the

281. Cf. Umbach, *In Christus getauft*, 88–90.
282. Cf. Weder, "Gesetz und Sünde," 362.

result of both its fateful character and its character as human action.[283] When sinful actions occur, they have already been preceded by and are the result of the antecedent power of sin (cf. Rom. 5:12, "Therefore, just as sin came into the world through one man, and death came through sin, and so death spread to all because all have sinned").[284]

In *Rom.* 7 Paul develops the relation of sin and law that is central for his thought. Here he explicitly emphasizes that sin is much more than some sort of defect in the way one lives one's life. It has the character of an inescapable power to which every person apart from faith is enslaved. Sin, in the form of (evil) desire, is even able to commandeer the law/Torah and to pervert its intended function as implementing the life-giving will of God into its opposite (Rom. 7:7–13). This fundamental insight provides the basis for the apostle's anthropological argument in 7:14–25a,[285] which elaborates on the inescapable involvement of the "I" under the power of sin. This allows him to absolve the law/Torah of any guilt for its involvement in the way it actually functions in opposition to God in the world. In 7:14, Paul designates a general state of affairs still at work in the present: human beings as creatures of flesh are subject to the power of sin. The universality of this statement is underscored by Paul's use of ἐγώ (I). The first-person singular pronoun is a literary device that has parallels in the psalms of lamentation (cf. Ps. 22:7–8) and in the Qumran literature (cf. 1QH 1:21; 3:23–34; 1QS 11:9ff.).[286] Both the stylistic form of the first person singular and the generalizing character of Rom. 7:14, along with the reference to Rom. 8:1ff., suggest that the ἐγώ is an exemplary, general "I" that represents the situation of human beings outside the sphere of faith from the perspective of the believing insider.[287]

283. Cf. Röhser, *Metaphorik*, 118.

284. Cf. Umbach, *In Christus getauft*, 201, on Rom. 5:12: "By the sinning, or disobedience, of the one (Adam) ἡ ἁμαρτία [sin] came into the world, that is, to all human beings (12d) and since then has determined the general human condition in both action (ἥμαρτον [they sinned]) and its result (θάνατος [death])."

285. In addition to the standard commentaries, for analysis cf. R. Weber, "Die Geschichte des Gesetzes und des Ich in Römer 7,7–8,4," *NZST* 29 (1987): 147–79; Otfried Hofius, "Der Mensch im Schatten Adams," in *Paulusstudien II* (ed. Otfried Hofius; WUNT 143; Tübingen: Mohr, 2002), 104–54; Hermann Lichtenberger, *Das Ich Adams und das Ich der Menschheit: Studien zum Menschenbild in Römer 7* (WUNT 164; Tübingen: Mohr Siebeck, 2004); Volker Stolle, *Luther und Paulus: Die exegetischen und hermeneutischen Grundlagen der lutherischen Rechtfertigungslehre im Paulinismus Luthers* (ABG 10; Leipzig: Evangelische Verlagsanstalt, 2002), 210–32.

286. On this point cf. Kümmel, *Römer 7*, 127–31; Gerd Theissen, *Psychological Aspects of Pauline Theology* (trans. John P. Galvin; Philadelphia: Fortress, 1987), 216–26.

287. Kümmel, *Römer 7*, 74ff., thoroughly discusses this insight in a programmatic way. Theissen, *Psychological Aspects*, 201, is among those who see in Rom. 7 an echo of personal, individual experiences. Differently, Sanders, *Paul and Palestinian Judaism*, 98: "Romans 7, in other words, does not actually describe anyone, except possibly the neurotic. Why, then, is it there? The cry of anguish is probably a cry of theological difficulty."

In Rom. 7:15 Paul explains that human beings simply find themselves to be already sold under the power of sin: the "I" finds itself in a fundamental conflict with itself, not doing what it wants to do but what it hates. In the next verse, Paul infers from this conflict that the law/Torah is good in itself, for it is sin that generates the conflict between willing and doing. The apostle underscores the nature of sin as a power in Rom. 7:17–20 with the metaphor of the indwelling of sin within human beings. Here, too, the reference to Rom. 8 is unmistakable, for in 8:9–10 Paul says that the Spirit of God, the Spirit of Christ, or Christ dwells in the believers (all three expressions are equated). Sin and Christ appear as two competing powers, and the human being seems to function only passively as the place where powers dwell that may bring either life or death.[288] If sin prevails in human life, one comes to ruin, whereas Christ/the Spirit grants the person life (cf. 8:11). In Rom. 7:18–20 Paul emphasizes the absolute hopelessness of the situation of humanity apart from faith, once again developing the contradiction between willing and doing. Although human beings can in fact will the good, they are not able to accomplish it because of the sin that dwells within them. In Rom. 7:21 the "I" itself draws up a summary account and confirms that an inherent rule is in effect: the good will manifests itself concretely in an evil act. Here νόμος does not mean the Old Testament Torah but describes an inherent law[289] that will be explained in Rom. 7:22–23. Human beings are not able by their own power simply to choose the good and reject the evil because the sin dwelling and battling within completely dominates them. Thus Rom. 7:23 portrays a fundamental anthropological state of affairs: human beings are torn in two and of themselves are not in the situation to restore their own integrity. According to the internal logic of Rom. 7, no one can save them from this situation. But for Paul, this is not the last word, as 7:25a indicates.[290] The deliverance of humanity from this hopeless situation has appeared in Jesus Christ; *therefore Paul thanks God for deliverance from the realm of sin's rulership, a deliverance accomplished in Jesus Christ and made available through the Spirit.* Romans 8 appears as the appropriate continuation of the Pauline argument in 7:7ff., clearly indicated linguistically by the second person singular pronoun of Rom. 8:2 that continues the first person singular of Rom. 7. Moreover, Rom. 8 is indeed the

288. According to Röhser, *Metaphorik*, 119ff., Rom. 7 does not portray a conflict within human beings but a transpersonal event; contra Paul Althaus, *Paulus und Luther über den Menschen: Ein Vergleich* (3rd ed.; SLA 14; Gütersloh: Bertelsmann, 1958), 41–49, who wants to understand Rom. 7 as a conflict within the individual human being; similarly Timo Laato, *Paulus und das Judentum: Anthropologische Erwägungen* (Åbo: Åbo Akademis Förlag, 1991): "Romans 7 includes nothing that does not fit the Christian, or—formulated more sharply—everything included in Rom. 7 fits only the Christian."

289. Cf. Weber, "Geschichte des Gesetzes," 159; Hofius, "Der Mensch im Schatten Adams," 142.

290. Rom. 7:25b is a gloss; cf., e.g., Käsemann, *Romans*, 211–12.

presupposition of Rom. 7, *for the perspectives elaborated by Paul in Rom. 8 have already been the basis for all he says in Rom. 7.*

What caused Paul to develop such a hypostatization of sin? The point of departure for his reflections can hardly be found in his anthropology,[291] for his view of the human condition pictured above is not available for objective observation but can be seen only by faith. On the contrary, here too the logic is shaped by the fundamental idea of the Pauline Christ hermeneutic: only faith in Jesus Christ saves, and so alongside him no other authority can have a salvific function. Not anthropology but Christology and soteriology provide the foundation for the Pauline doctrine of sin.

The Origin of Evil in the Discourse of Antiquity

Paul's understanding of the nature of sin functions not only within his own system of thought, however, but also makes an original contribution to a debate that was carried on both in Judaism and in the Gentile Hellenistic world: *the question of the origin of evil and the cause of defective human conduct.* According to Paul, sin is the real cause for the fact that the good intentions of human beings are perverted into their opposite, which can finally result only in death. Epictetus (ca. 50–130 CE) also reflects on this typical difference between what one really wants to do and what one actually does (*Diatr.* 2.26.1).[292] But there is a fundamental difference between Paul and Epictetus when they explain the reason for this contradiction. In Epictetus we have an optimistic view of life, in which wrong conduct can be overcome by right knowledge. Paul does not share this confidence, since for him the acting subject is really sin, not the knowledgeable human being. In a way different from that of Epictetus, Cicero (106–43 BCE) reflects on the question of whether the evil in the world is the work of the gods. "For if the gods gave man reason, they gave him malice" (*Nat. d.* 3.75). Human beings use the divine gift of reason not for the good but in order to betray each other. It would thus have been better if the gods had withheld reason from humans (cf. *Nat. d.* 3.78). But now, when good people have troubles and things go well for bad people, stupidity prevails, and we find that "we, for whose welfare you say that the gods have cared most fully, are really in the depth of misfortune" (*Nat. d.* 3.79). The gods must therefore be subject to this charge: "They should have made everyone good, if they were really concerned for humanity" (*Nat. d.* 3.79).

291. Bultmann, *Theology of the New Testament*, 1:191, seems close to sharing this misunderstanding when he emphasizes, "Therefore, Paul's theology can best be treated as his doctrine of man: first, of man prior to the revelation of faith, and second, of man under faith."

292. For the Greco-Roman traditions in the background of Rom. 7:14ff. (e.g., Euripides, *Med.* 1076–1080), cf. Hildebrecht Hommel, "Das 7. Kapitel des Römerbriefes," in *Sebasmata: Studien zur antiken Religionsgeschichte und zum frühen Christentum* (ed. Hildebrecht Hommel; 2 vols.; Tübingen: Mohr, 1983), 141–73; R. von Bendemann, "Die kritische Diastase von Wissen, Wollen und Handeln," *ZNW* 95 (2000): 35–63.

Seneca (4–65 CE), as an immediate contemporary of Paul, has a predominantly pessimistic evaluation of the human situation. Both humanity as a whole (*Ep.* 97.1, "No epoch is free from guilt") and individual human beings (*Ira* 2.28.1, "Not one of us is without guilt") fail to attain true insight and moral goodness. Experience teaches that even the most circumspect transgress (cf. *Ira* 3.25.2), so that this insight is unavoidable: "We have all sinned [*peccavimus omnes*]—some in serious, some in trivial things; some by deliberate intention, some by chance impulse, or because we were led away by the wickedness of others; some of us have not stood strongly enough by good resolutions, and have lost our innocence against our will and though still clinging to it" (*Clem.* 1.6.3). No one can pronounce his or her own acquittal; all are guilty when they examine their own conscience (cf. *Ira* 1.14.3). The unerring judgment of Seneca the philosopher and the experiences of Seneca the psychologist force the conclusion on him that human beings never live up to their potential. The reflections of Dio Chrysostom on the origin of good and evil are also worthy of note. While the good must always be ascribed to God (*Or.* 32.14), it must be said of evil, "but evils come from quite a different source, as it were from some other fount close beside us. . . . [Good, fresh water is the gift of the gods] whereas the filthy, evil-smelling canals are our own creation, and it is our fault such things exist" (*Or.* 32.15).

In a completely different cultural context, namely, in *4 Ezra* (after 70 CE), we also find a pessimistic argument about the state of the world and the human situation. Although God has given the law/Torah, sin and ignorance still prevail. "For this reason, therefore, those who live on earth shall be tormented [in the coming judgment], because though they had understanding, they committed iniquity; and though they received the commandments, they did not keep them; and though they obtained the law, they dealt unfaithfully with what they received" (*4 Ezra* 7.72). There are only a few righteous (*4 Ezra* 7.17–18, 51) because the rule of sin is so pervasive, and so the question forces itself on the author, "For who among the living is there that has not sinned, or who is there among mortals that has not transgressed your covenant?" (*4 Ezra* 7.46). The author obviously has no confidence that the law can change this situation: "For all who have been born are entangled in iniquities, and are full of sins and burdened with transgressions" (*4 Ezra* 7.68). The Qumran texts also manifest great similarities to Paul.[293] Here, too, the human creature is flesh and thus separated from God and delivered inescapably into the power of sin; the "flesh" belongs to the dominion of sin (cf. 1QS 4:20–21).[294] Not only blatant sinners but even the devout author of the Qumran community belongs "to wicked mankind, to the company of unjust flesh" (1QS 11:9) and has in his flesh the perverse spirit (1QS 4:20–21),

293. Cf. here Karl G. Kuhn, "Πειρασμός–ἁμαρτία–σάρξ im Neuen Testament und die damit zusammenhängenden Vorstellungen," *ZTK* 49 (1952): 209ff.; Kim, "Heilsgegenwart," 35–40.

294. On the understanding of sin in the Qumran texts, cf. Hermann Lichtenberger, *Studien zum Menschenbild in Texten der Qumrangemeinde* (SUNT 15; Göttingen: Vandenhoeck & Ruprecht, 1980), 79–89, 209–12.

for the flesh is sin (1QH 4:29–30). Human beings are not able on their own to choose the good and reject the evil, but sin that dwells and struggles within them dominates them fully (cf. 1QS 4:20–21). Rather, everything depends on God, who "shapes the [human] spirit" (1QH 15:22) and, through the Holy Spirit (1QS 4:21), wipes out the spirit of wickedness that resides in human flesh. Unreserved observance of the Torah (cf., e.g., 1QS 2:2–4; 5:8–11),[295] along with complete dependence on the grace of God, makes it possible for the devout to follow God's will and to practice righteousness (1QS 11:12).

Paul's position within the religious and philosophical debates about the origin of evil and its conquest exhibits originality not in its analysis but in its resolution. Like many of his contemporaries, the apostle sketched a gloomy picture of the human condition. He derived this evaluation, however, not by observing the given situation or by insight into the inner nature of human beings but from God's liberating act in Jesus Christ. The hopeless situation of those who were to be saved corresponds to the magnitude of the saving act. The Pauline solution is distinguished by two components:

1. It takes up the contemporary religious-philosophical discourse and shows itself to be an attractive and competent conversation partner.
2. It opens up to human beings an insightful and practicable possibility of being freed from their situation.

Paul differs from all other systems by the thesis that, for Christians, sin has already been overcome in baptism,[296] so that those who are baptized are essentially already liberated from the enslaving power of sin. Paul's mythological language about sin has this conviction at its core: *human beings cannot extricate themselves from the essentially destructive reality of human life.* Rather, they are delivered from the deficiency and self-centeredness of their own thinking only when they anchor their existence in God; this means that the new life cannot be a mere extension of the old, for a change of lordship brings about a changed life. This possibility is opened up by the Christ event, which becomes concretely present in baptism, frees one from the power of sin, and places one in the freedom given by the Spirit.

6.5.3 Law

Paul lived in a cultural context already familiar with numerous models of the positive function of the law or laws, not only in his Jewish mother religion but also in the originally Greco-Roman realm.[297]

295. On the understanding of law in the Qumran texts, cf. ibid., 200–212.

296. Kim, "Heilsgegenwart," 108–11.

297. The importance of this area of research for Paul's understanding of the law has only been gradually recognized; cf. O. Behrends and W. Sellert, eds., *Nomos und Gesetz: Ursprünge*

Guidelines Provided by Cultural History

Within the political communities of antiquity, the law (νόμος)[298] is the norm that fosters respect for the gods[299] and justice between human beings, thus making life possible.[300] According to Aristotle, justice receives its internal purpose and determination from the laws, so that he can state, "Whoever disdains the laws is unjust, and as we have seen those who respect them are just. This means therefore: everything lawful is in the broadest sense of the word just" (*Eth. Nic.* 5.1138a). Human justice results from living in accordance with a norm; a righteous life is a life that corresponds to the law. Since the laws have the power to establish and nurture culture, they preserve the life of the individual, save the polis as a whole from destruction, and thus have a life-giving and salvific function.[301] The laws also regulate the relation of human beings to the gods. Piety results from relating to the gods according to the laws (cf. Plato, *Leg.* 10.885b). According to Chrysippus, a life lived according to nature means not to do anything "forbidden by the common law [ὁ νόμος ὁ κοινός], the law that is right reason [ὀρθὸς λόγος] which permeates the whole world, which is identical with Zeus the ruler of the universe" (Diogenes Laertius, *Vit. phil.* 7.88). Human beings are part of a reality structured and guided by law as an element in the divine order of the world.

In the first century there was also a widespread awareness that in addition to the countless individual laws, there is *one* law: "For Justice is one; it binds all human society, and is based on one law, which is right reason applied to command and prohibition" (Cicero, *Leg.* 1.42). The law includes much more than rules, for it is the presupposition established by the gods for a successful life (Cicero, *Leg.* 1.58, "But it is certainly true that, since law ought to be a reformer of vice and an incentive to virtue, the guiding principles of life may be derived from it"). The true law already existed before the fixing of particular laws in writing, for it proceeds from reason, which originated at the same time

---

und Wirkungen des griechischen Gesetzesdenkens, Göttingen 1995 (AAWGPH 3.209; Göttingen: Vandenhoeck & Ruprecht, 1995); for the realm of New Testament exegesis, cf. Hans Hübner, "Das ganze und das eine Gesetz: Zum Problemkreis Paulus und die Stoa," in *Biblische Theologie als Hermeneutik: Gesammelte Aufsätze/Hans Hübner zum 65. Geburtstag* (ed. Antje Labahn and Michael Labahn; Göttingen: Vandenhoeck & Ruprecht, 1995), 9–26; Sonntag, ΝΟΜΟΣ ΣΩΤΗΡ; Klaus Haacker, "Der 'Antinomismus' des Paulus im Kontext antiker Gesetzestheorie," in *Geschichte—Tradition—Reflexion: Festschrift für Martin Hengel zum 70. Geburtstag* (ed. Hubert Cancik et al.; Tübingen: Mohr, 1996), 387–404; Francis Gerald Downing, *Cynics, Paul, and the Pauline Churches: Cynics and Christian Origins II* (London: Routledge, 1998), 55–84.

298. The Greek word νόμος is derived from νέμω (distribute, divide), and has as its basic meaning "distribution, giving someone their due portion; arrangement, regulation; order;" cf. Pokorný, *Wörterbuch*, 763.

299. Cf. Plato, *Leg.* 10.885b: "No one who in obedience to the laws believed that there were gods, ever intentionally did any unholy act, or uttered any unlawful word." Cf. further *Leg.* 12.996b–e.

300. Cf. the textual examples and analyses provided in Sonntag, ΝΟΜΟΣ ΣΩΤΗΡ, 18–46.

301. Cf. the analyses of texts in ibid., 47–105.

as the divine spirit. “Wherefore the true and primal law, applied to command and prohibition, is the right reason of supreme Jupiter” (Cicero, *Leg.* 2.10). For both individual and society, life can be attained only when insight is attained into the divinely willed order. Thus Dio Chrysostom can launch into a song in praise of the law: “The law is a guide to life . . . , a good rule for how to live” (*Or.* 75.1; cf. 80.5). The gods themselves serve the law, for it guarantees order in the cosmos. It goes without saying that law and justice/righteousness belong together, for both are the guarantors of life.[302] Plutarch (*Mor.* 780E) counsels kings to avail themselves of the gifts conferred by the gods, which include above all the law and justice: “Now justice is the aim and end of the law, but law is the work of the ruler, and the ruler is the image of God who orders all things” (δίκη μὲν οὖν νόμου τέλος ἐστί, νόμος δ’ ἄρχοντος ἔργον, ἄρχων δ’ εἰκὼν θεοῦ τοῦ πάντα κοσμοῦντος). In Greek-Hellenistic thinking, the true law is seen as a power and ordering principle in being itself that facilitates and sustains life.

There is, of course, no question about the outstanding position held by the Torah within ancient Judaism (see above, §3.8.1). Still, ancient Judaism had a spectrum of theologies of the law (e.g., cultural [Diaspora Judaism influenced by its Hellenistic environment];[303] apocalyptic;[304] political-theological [the differing views of Pharisees, Sadducees, Essenes, and Zealots]), and isolated individual voices that may have challenged the law’s ability to deliver what it promised.[305]

In the cultural contexts of both the Greco-Roman world and Judaism, it was absolutely inconceivable that Paul and his churches, according to their self-understanding, would live “lawlessly,” that is, *without life-giving and salvific norms*. As with righteousness/justice, so also the *theme* of the law was already a given in his cultural milieu. The course of Paul’s life from zealous Pharisee to battle-scarred apostle to the Gentiles is broken by numerous fault lines, which have also influenced his statements about the law/Torah. It is thus necessary to distinguish between a diachronic and a synchronic approach to this thematic complex.

Diachronic Analysis

The autobiographical statements in Gal. 1:13–14 and Phil. 3:5–9 permit three conclusions:

1. Paul was a zealot for the Torah who perceived himself as blameless regarding Torah observance and surpassed all his contemporaries in his dedication to the traditions of the fathers.

302. Cf. Dio Chrysostom, *Or.* 75.6, 8.

303. Comprehensive analyses (without Philo and Josephus) are found in Weber, *Das Gesetz im hellenistischen Judentum*, 37–322.

304. Cf. on this topic Hoffmann, *Gesetz*, 71ff.

305. Cf. Philo, *Migration* 89–90; *4 Ezra* 7.72; 8.20–36, 47–49; Josephus, *Ant.* 4.141–155; Strabo, *Geogr.* 16.2.35–38.

2. If, as a ζηλωτής (zealot) Paul tended toward the radical wing of Pharisaism, then he was thoroughly at home in the world of the Torah and its interpretation. He knew the whole spectrum of Jewish exegesis of the law,[306] so the thesis that Paul misunderstood or misrepresented the Jewish understanding of the law must be considered mistaken.
3. His rootedness in Pharisaic tradition would lead us to expect that the problem of the law continued to be an important and sensitive theme for the apostle to the Gentiles.

Paul's own accounts of his call at Damascus to be apostle to the Gentiles give no indications, however, of any direct law-critical content (see above, §6.2.2). What we have instead is that God revealed to Paul the persecutor that the crucified Jesus of Nazareth is now exalted as Son of God at the Father's side, where he belongs, where he continues to reign, and whence he exercises his saving power. If the core of the Damascus event is interpreted in christological-soteriological terms, the question naturally arises: what consequences must such a revolutionary event have for the former Pharisee's understanding of the law? For the earliest period of the apostle's work, we can only speculate: Paul joined the Antiochene Gentile mission, which was already expanding (cf. Acts 11:25–26), and thus adopted the theory and practice of evangelism already in practice there. To begin with, the position of the Antiochene believers in Christ who had come from Hellenistic Judaism (cf. Acts 11:20–21) was critical of the temple, not critical of the law.[307] They made the overwhelming discovery that God also gives the Holy Spirit to the Gentiles (cf. Acts 10:44–48; 11:15). On this basis they saw the inevitability of reevaluating the place in salvation history for believers who came to Christ from paganism. They then abandoned the requirement of circumcision, a decision that removed the Torah from a direct relation to the question of salvation. The fact that believers in Christ who had come from Judaism and paganism made the same confession, κύριος Ἰησοῦς (Jesus is Lord; cf. Acts 11:20), overruled previous criteria of precedence and subordination. What role did the Torah play in this context of the Gentile mission, which no longer required circumcision? Probably only a minor role, for relaxing the precondition of circumcision was tantamount to abandoning the ritual law as such (cf. Acts 10:14–15, 28; 11:3); and even the ethical core of the Torah, the Decalogue, which posed no problems for Christians from a non-Jewish background, is cited only in Rom. 7:7 and 13:9. The Apostolic Council with its "apostolic decree" (Acts 15:29)[308] and traditions embedded in

306. Cf. Hoffmann, *Gesetz*, 337.

307. This point is specifically emphasized by Eckhard Rau, *Von Jesus zu Paulus: Entwicklung und Rezeption der antiochenischen Theologie im Urchristentum* (Stuttgart: Kohlhammer, 1994), 79.

308. On the interpretation of the Apostolic Council and "apostolic decree," cf. Schnelle, *Apostle Paul*, 117–35.

the Pauline letters tend to confirm this picture. Those at the Apostolic Council who insisted on circumcision for Gentile Christians were unsuccessful, and the apostolic decree represents the attempt of some Jewish Christian circles to at least maintain a minimum of the ritual law as still in force for Gentile Christians, which in turn means they had not previously been observed by Gentile Christians. Traditions such as 1 Cor. 7:19; Gal. 3:26–28; 5:6; 6:15 emphasize the new status of all baptized believers before God, quite apart from circumcision or uncircumcision. Paul's stance toward the Torah in the early period of his missionary work thus seems to be that Gentile Christians are included in the people of God through faith and baptism, not by circumcision and the ritual Torah observance that would follow. Faith and the Spirit serve as new norms regulating the relation of God to human beings, while baptism, not circumcision, functions as the decisive initiation rite. *According to their own understanding, Paul and his churches were never "lawless," even though this is the way they were seen from the perspective of militant Jewish Christians and Jews.*

Paul's understanding was that the Apostolic Council confirmed this arrangement, but at the same time Paul accepted the older, strict Jewish Christian way practiced by the Jerusalem church and its sympathizers. The distinction between the Pauline "gospel for the uncircumcised" and the Petrine "gospel for the circumcised" (Gal. 2:7)[309] is not a new arrangement that first came into force in 48 CE but the continuation of different concepts of mission that had already been practiced for some time. What conclusion do we draw with regard to Paul's understanding of the law? As the real newcomer, Paul acknowledged the full scope of the coexistence of different initiation rites, and thus of different conceptions of the law, that had been in place for some time and were already a part of Christian history when he came on the scene. Acts 11:3 and the conflict at Antioch indicate that the difference between these two conceptions concerned primarily the evaluation of the food laws and their consequences (e.g., regarding the eucharistic celebrations). Moreover, the Jerusalem church increasingly found itself in a completely different cultural and political situation than Paul's. Its goal was to find a way to remain within Judaism; it thus wanted and needed to attach a different importance to the Torah than was the case for Paul.

The compromise at the Apostolic Council, then, turned out to be only a pseudo-solution, for it was either interpreted differently by opposite sides of the issue or accepted only temporarily. Moreover, the agreement did not resolve the problems of mixed congregations (cf. the Antioch conflict); and the Jerusalem church came under increasing political pressure to drop its acceptance of the Gentile mission that did not require circumcision and to renounce its connection to the (in Jewish eyes) apostate Paul. With at least the

309. Cf. ibid., 122–25.

approval of the Jerusalem church, a countermission began with the goal of accepting Gentile Christians into proselyte status on the condition that they be circumcised, thus leaving the whole new movement of believers in Christ in Judaism or, as the case may be, integrating them into it. The unresolved or repressed problems surfaced with full force in the Galatian crisis, and Paul saw that he was challenged to think through and resolve the problematic of the law under changed presuppositions.

Thus a *differentiation* is unavoidable: until the Galatian crisis, Paul acknowledged two streams of early Christianity, with the Jerusalem church (and its sympathizers) on the one side and the younger, predominantly Gentile Christian churches on the other side, each with its own way of relating to others and with its own evaluation of the Torah. Paul and his churches were free from the precondition of circumcision, and the Torah played only a subordinate role or none at all. The data of the letters themselves confirms this assessment, for in 1 Thessalonians and the Corinthian letters, the law/Torah is either not mentioned at all (1 Thessalonians, 2 Corinthians) or referred to only in passing. Except for the allusion in 1 Cor. 15:56, Paul makes no reference to the function of the law/Torah; that is, Paul felt no need for a doctrine of the law because the law/Torah was not an urgent topic. Ethical instruction was not based primarily on the Torah,[310] and the new concept of righteousness was connected not with the Torah but with baptism. *The Galatian crisis changed the situation abruptly and dramatically*[311] *because now the problem of the law was massively forced upon them from outside, in the form of the demand for circumcision.*[312] In the predominantly Gentile churches also, the issue of the Torah shifted from the periphery to the center, and Paul saw himself compelled to do what the Jerusalem Christians had already done: abandon the concept that there were different ways to deal with the issue of the law and to provide a fundamental clarification of the significance of the Torah for Jews and Gentiles. This meant that rethinking missions strategy and theology acquired fundamental importance:

1. Requiring circumcision of Gentile converts would have deeply affected the expansion of the movement.

310. Cf. Andreas Lindemann, "Die biblischen Toragebote und die paulinische Ethik," in *Paulus, Apostel und Lehrer der Kirche: Studien zu Paulus und zum frühen Paulusverständnis* (ed. Andreas Lindemann; Tübingen: Mohr, 1999), 91–114.

311. Cf. Wrede, *Paul*, 122ff. Among others who vote for the Galatian crisis as the point of departure for the doctrine of justification in Galatians an Romans we may mention Strecker, *Theology of the New Testament*, 139–40; Wilckens, *Theologie*, 3:136ff.; Philip Francis Esler, *Galatians* (London: Routledge, 1998), 153–59; F. E. Udoh, "Paul's View on the Law," *NovT* 42 (2000): 237.

312. Completely different is the view of Mark D. Nanos, *The Irony of Galatians: Paul's Letter in First-century Context* (Minneapolis: Fortress, 2002), 6, who argues the Galatian "influencers" did not enter the Galatian churches from outside (e.g., from Jerusalem).

2. The question of circumcision was obviously and unavoidably related to the question of obtaining life through the Torah,[313] i.e., the soteriological quality of the Christ event would have been vitiated.

The downright breathless, highly emotional, and tense argumentation of Galatians, like the corrections to it provided in Romans, shows that in the Letter to the Galatians Paul for the first time advocates *this* form of a doctrine of justification and the law.[314] Paul demotes the Torah in that he evaluates it as secondary both chronologically (Gal. 3:17) and materially (3:19–20). Its role in history was only to be a custodian and disciplinarian (cf. 3:24). This time of bondage has now come to an end in Christ, who liberated human beings into the freedom of faith (Gal. 5:1). Believers from both Judaism and paganism are legitimate heirs of the promises to Abraham on another basis than circumcision and the Torah (3:29). In Galatians Paul abolishes the privileged hamartiological status of Jews and Jewish Christians (2:16) and places them in the same category as humanity as a whole—in a history determined by sin (cf. 3:22). Circumcision and the Torah do not figure in the soteriological self-definition of Christianity,[315] because God directly reveals himself in Jesus

313. The term "works righteousness," found in the older discussions and attacked by Anglo-American scholars, is obviously not adequate to grasp the different levels of Jewish soteriology. At the same time, it becomes ever more clear that the "covenantal nomism" postulated by Sanders, *Paul and Palestinian Judaism*, 511–14 and passim, is nothing more than the application of an ideal type of Pauline and Reformation categories to Judaism (grace always stands at the beginning!). For a critique of this conception cf. Simon J. Gathercole, *Where Is Boasting? Early Jewish Soteriology and Paul's Response in Romans 1–5* (Grand Rapids: Eerdmans, 2002), who shows that in numerous Jewish texts (e.g., Sir. 51:30; Bar. 4:1; 2 Macc. 7:35–38; *Jub.* 30.17–23; *Pss. Sol.* 14.2–3; *LAB* 64.7; *T. Zeb.* 10.2–3) following the Torah and the attaining of life belong inseparably together. Cf. further Friedrich Avemarie, *Tora und Leben: Untersuchungen zur Heilsbedeutung der Tora in der frühen rabbinischen Literatur* (TSAJ 55; Tübingen: Mohr, 1996), who concludes: "The principle of retribution remains unbroken; no doubt remains that fulfilling the commands is rewarded and transgression of them is punished," even if it is frequently emphasized "that the better kind of obedience is not motivated by hope of reward, but is done for God's sake or for the sake of the command itself" (578).

314. On this point cf. Schnelle, *Apostle Paul*, 277–94.

315. There can therefore be no talk whatever of a Paul who does not criticize the Torah itself, but only its relevance for Gentile Christians, as is often claimed by the "new perspective." On this influential stream of interpretation in the Anglo-Saxon realm cf., in addition to the numerous publications of E. P. Sanders and J. D. G. Dunn, especially N. T. Wright, *What Saint Paul Really Said: Was Paul of Tarsus the Real Founder of Christianity?* (Grand Rapids: Eerdmans, 1997). A current survey of the research is presented by Michael B. Thompson, *The New Perspective on Paul* (GBS 26; Cambridge: Grove Books, 2002); Stephen Westerholm, *Perspectives Old and New on Paul: The "Lutheran" Paul and His Critics* (Grand Rapids: Eerdmans, 2004). For a critical view of the "new perspective," cf. A. J. M. Wedderburn, "Eine neuere Paulusperspektive?" in *Biographie und Persönlichkeit des Paulus* (ed. E.-M. Becker and Peter Pilhofer; WUNT 187; Tübingen: Mohr Siebeck, 2005), 46–64; J. Frey, "Das Judentum des Paulus," in *Paulus: Leben—Umwelt—Werk—Briefe* (ed. Oda Wischmeyer; Tübingen: Francke, 2006), 35–43. On the one hand, the "new perspective" does correct erroneous images of ancient Judaism and clarifies

Christ, and baptized believers participate in this saving event by the gift of the Spirit.

The expression ἔργα νόμου (works of the law/Torah) plays a key role in Pauline nomology (cf. Gal. 2:16; 3:2, 5, 10; Rom. 3:20, 28; in addition, cf. Phil. 3:9).[316] What does Paul mean by ἔργα νόμου, and what theological conception does he associate with it? R. Bultmann sees in the "works of the law" a misguided zeal for the law and understands Paul to have rejected such works "because *man's effort to achieve his salvation by keeping the Law* only leads him into sin, indeed this effort itself in the end *is already sin.*"[317] Thus, for Bultmann, Paul does not merely consider the result of failing to keep the law to be sin; the intention to be righteous before God by keeping the law is already sinful. For J. D. G. Dunn, ἔργα νόμου are not the prescriptions of the Torah, the keeping of which earns one credit in God's eyes, but Jewish "identity markers" such as circumcision, the food laws, and the Sabbath, which distinguish Jews from Gentiles. Paul evaluates these identity markers negatively only when they are claimed as the basis for Jewish prerogatives and restrict the grace of God. "In sum, then, the 'works' which Paul consistently warns against were, in his view, Israel's misunderstanding of what her covenant law required."[318] Paul does not oppose the law as such, does not disparage works of the law, but votes against the law as a marker of national identification, directing his critique against an understanding of the Torah oriented to special privileges for those who observe it. Paul's doctrine of justification thus is not primarily concerned with the relation of the individual to God but is a matter of assuring the rights of Gentile Christians. The critique of Bultmann's view is correct in that for Paul the possibility of attaining life by keeping the Torah is not merely a rhetorical concession. The Scripture explicitly affirms this way (cf. Lev. 18:5 in Gal. 3:12b; also Rom. 2:13; 10:5). Paul relegates neither the Torah itself nor fulfilling the commands of the Torah to the realm of sin, but the fact is that from the perspective of the curse of the law against those who fail to keep it, the ἔργα νόμου always bring one into the realm of sin because no one really lives by what is written in the Torah (Gal. 3:10b). It must therefore be objected against the "new perspective" that with his language of the ἔργα νόμου Paul *introduces fundamentally new theological affirmations.*[319] The

---

elements of the Jewish background of Paul's theology, but at the same time, it is itself subject to criticism. In addition to the numerous points made by J. Frey, the "new perspective" almost completely ignores the Greco-Roman context of Paul's thought.

316. Summary of the discussion and further literature in Schnelle, *Apostle Paul*, 280–84. The current controversy is taken up and continued in Michael Bachmann and Johannes Woyke, eds., *Lutherische und neue Paulusperspektive: Beiträge zu einem Schlüsselproblem der gegenwärtigen exegetischen Diskussion* (WUNT 182; Tübingen: Mohr Siebeck, 2005).

317. Bultmann, *Theology of the New Testament*, 1:262–63, italics original.

318. Dunn, *Theology of Paul*, 366.

319. Cf. here Otfried Hofius, "'Werke des Gesetzes': Untersuchungen zu der paulinischen Rede von den ἔργα νόμου," in *Paulus und Johannes: Exegetische Studien zur paulinischen und*

uniformly negative use of this phrase by Paul makes clear that the ἔργα νόμου are the results of the regulations of the Torah, regulations intended actually to be done. The realm of human deeds is constitutive for Paul's argument (cf. the use of ποιέω [do], in Gal. 3:10–12), for it is only this realm that makes possible sin's assault. The "works of law" cannot lead to righteousness/justification, because the power of sin thwarts the Torah's promise of life. In the course of this argument Paul also is saying something about the Torah itself: in contrast to the πνεῦμα, the Torah does not have the power to withstand the hostile intrusion of sin (cf. 5:18). Regarding its promise of life, the Torah falls short of its own promises; the power of sin reveals the weakness of the Torah. Paul virtually makes the *insufficiency of the Torah* his point of departure.

Compared with Galatians, Paul's Letter to the Romans manifests substantial changes on three levels:[320]

1. Paul introduces δικαιοσύνη θεοῦ (righteousness/justification of/from God) as a major theological term in order to underpin the theological substructure of the argument in Galatians (cf. Rom. 3:21, δικαιοσύνη θεοῦ χωρὶς νόμου [the righteousness of God apart from law]; cf. also Rom. 6:14b; 10:1–4).
2. This new term makes it possible for him to have a partially new evaluation of the law/Torah (cf. Rom. 3:31; 7:7, 12; 13:8–10); the law/Torah is no longer criticized as such but has itself now become primarily the victim of the power of sin.
3. Paul fundamentally rethinks the relation of God's righteousness to the election of Israel.

These changes derive from the apostle's particular historical situation in relation to the Jerusalem and Roman churches (delivery of the collection; mission to Spain) but also from the polemically one-sided argument of the Letter to the Galatians. The Letter to the Philippians takes up the results of the doctrine of justification as set forth in Romans (cf. Phil. 3:5, 6, 9), and its understanding of the law also stands in continuity with this preceding letter to Rome.

This historical sketch shows how closely each stage of Paul's understanding of the law is connected with the course of his life and ministry. We cannot, therefore, speak of *the* understanding of the law held by the apostle, for Paul necessarily and appropriately worked out the application of the theme of

johanneischen Theologie und Literatur (ed. Dieter Sänger and Ulrich Mell; WUNT 198; Tübingen: Mohr Siebeck, 2006), 271–310.

320. By no means is it merely a matter of "deeper discussions" found in Romans, as supposed by Becker, *Paul*, 395. Nor is the objection persuasive that the brief temporal interval between Galatians and Romans speaks against changes in the meantime (so Dunn, *Theology of Paul*, 131), for both the textual data of each letter and the apostle's changed historical situation point to the fact that Paul had developed his position further.

the law in different ways corresponding to his historical situation. The letters to the Galatians and to Rome document a late phase of this process, which represents a final stage of development both chronologically and materially. They provide the point of departure for the synchronic analysis of Paul's understanding of the law.

Synchronic Analysis

Paul speaks in very different ways about the law/Torah. Paul makes *positive* statements about the character of the law (Rom. 7:12, "So the law is holy, and the commandment is holy and just and good"; cf. also Rom. 7:16b, 22) and the possibility of obeying it (Gal. 3:12, "Whoever does the works of the law will live by them"; Rom. 2:13, "the doers of the law . . . will be justified"; cf. also Gal. 5:3, 23; Rom. 2:14–15). Galatians 5:14 and Rom. 13:8–10 explicitly emphasize the positive connection between the love commandment and fulfilling the law. He also makes *negative* statements regarding the character and function of the law/Torah. The law/Torah is deficient in both its substance (cf. Gal. 3:19, 23, 24; 4:5; 5:4; Rom. 6:14b, "You are not under law but under grace") and its chronological status (cf. Gal. 3:17, 430 years after the promise; Gal. 3:24, a "custodian/disciplinarian" until Christ came; Rom. 5:20a, "But law came in [later]"; Rom. 7:1–3), in contrast to the promise fulfilled in Jesus Christ. The law/Torah is contrasted with the Spirit (Gal. 3:1–4; 5:18), faith (Gal. 3:12, 23), the promise (Gal. 3:16–18; Rom. 4:13), and righteousness (Gal. 2:16; 3:11, 21; 5:4; Rom. 3:28; 4:16). It has the function of revealing sin[321] (Rom. 3:20–21a, "For 'no human being will be justified in his sight' by deeds prescribed by the law, for through the law comes the knowledge of sin. But now, apart from law, the righteousness of God has been disclosed"; Rom. 4:15b, "where there is no law, neither is there violation"; cf. 1 Cor. 15:56; Rom. 5:13, 20; 7:13). There are other negative functional descriptions of the law/Torah: "For the law brings wrath" (Rom. 4:15a); the law/Torah evokes sinful passions (7:5); the law/Torah imprisons (7:6a). The law/Torah is incapable of breaking through the power of sin. What was once given to provide life (cf. Deut. 30:15–16) now shows itself to be the accomplice of death. According to Gal. 3:22, this situation corresponds to the Scripture and thus to the will of God; in contrast, Rom. 7:14ff.; 8:3, 7 only affirms the weakness of the law/Torah over against the power of sin. In Rom. 7:7 Paul emphatically rejects the objection that immediately comes to mind, that the law/Torah is itself sin. All the same, Rom. 4:15; 5:13; 7:5, 8, 9 does evoke this inference, for here Paul attributes an active role to the law, which activates sin and thus sets the fateful process in motion that ends in eschatological death.

Finally, we note that Paul also makes *paradoxical* statements about the law, in which a law/rule/norm is described that does not refer to the Torah (Gal.

321. Cf. Ps. 19:13; 32; 51; 119.

6:2, "the law of Christ"; Rom. 3:27, "the law of faith"; Rom. 8:2, "The law of the Spirit of life in Christ Jesus has set you free from the law of sin and of death"; Rom. 10:4, Christ as τέλος of the law/Torah[322]).

Can these different series of statements be brought together conceptually without harmonization, or must we simply say that Paul has differing doctrines of the law?[323] Are Paul's positions on the law/Torah perhaps even in such conflict with each other that a comprehensive view is impossible?[324] The attempt to resolve this problematic complex should proceed in two steps: (1) First, one must have in view the conceptual problems Paul faced. (2) One must then ask how the individual lines of Paul's understanding of the law are related to one another and whether they can be brought together into a consistent overall understanding.

1. The objective beginning point for Paul's understanding of the law is the knowledge that God's ultimate will is the salvation of humanity in Jesus Christ. But then how is God's initial revelation in the Torah related to the Christ event? Paul could not affirm a direct or even a gradual contrast between the two revelations unless he also wanted to accept irreconcilable contradictions in his image of God. Was the first revelation inadequate to grant life to humanity? Why did God first concern himself with the people of Israel, and only later with the whole world? What value is there in the Torah if Gentiles can completely fulfill the will of God even without circumcision? Paul wanted to hold firmly to both: on the validity of the first revelation and the belief that salvation comes only through the second. Paul stood before two opposing fundamental principles, neither of which he could give up: a valid divine institution had already been established, and only faith in Jesus Christ can save. Paul thus stood before an unsolvable problem; he both wanted and needed to prove a continuity that did not exist: the continuity of the saving act of God in the first covenant with that of the second covenant. For "if God's own people must be converted in order to remain the people of God, then the previously established covenant cannot be satisfactory as such."[325] The conceptual problems were intensified by open questions in praxis, as Jewish Christians and Gentile Christians attempted to establish a common life. This situation, which the Torah did not foresee and for which it provided no regulations, allowed for different interpretations and thus meant that conflicts were

322. In Rom. 10:4 τέλος is to be understood in the temporal sense as "end." Cf. Schnelle, *Apostle Paul*, 346–47.

323. Cf. Sanders, *Paul and Palestinian Judaism*, 84: "He did not have, however, one single theology of the law. It was not the starting point of his thought, and it is impossible to give one central statement about the law which explains all his other statements."

324. Cf. Heikki Räisänen, *Paul and the Law* (2nd ed.; WUNT 29; Tübingen: Mohr, 1987), 199–202, 256–63.

325. Heikki Räisänen, "Der Bruch des Paulus mit Israels Bund," in *The Law in the Bible and in Its Environment* (ed. Timo Veijola; Göttingen: Vandenhoeck & Ruprecht, 1990), 167.

preprogrammed. Moreover, the problem of the law played a central role in the separation of early Christian congregations from Judaism. Thus the law problematic also brought pressure on Paul and his churches from outside, for both militant Jews and Jewish Christians stood in opposition to Paul.

2. Paul had to maintain the freedom of the Gentile Christians from the requirement of circumcision, allege the ritual and soteriological inadequacy of the Torah for both Jewish and Gentile Christians, and at the same time postulate that the law/Torah is also fulfilled by Christians. Only so was it possible to affirm the continuing validity of the first covenant and the exclusive salvific character of the new covenant. Moreover, it was necessary for him to refute the charge of "lawlessness" that had certainly been raised by the line of argument pursued in Galatians.

The Pauline solution consisted in *redefining the essential nature of the law*. A first step in this direction is represented by Gal. 5:14: "For the whole law is summed up in a single commandment, 'You shall love your neighbor as yourself.'" This idea first attains a systematic quality in the Letter to the Romans, in which Paul has gained some distance from the polemical agitation of Galatians and can also describe the positive importance of the law/Torah for Christian believers. Romans 13:8–10 is a key text in this regard; the thesis that love is the fulfilling of the law/Torah (Rom. 13:10, πλήρωμα οὖν νόμου ἡ ἀγάπη) secures the Pauline argument in a fourfold perspective:

1. It permits the claim of bringing the law to full validity in its innermost essence and fulfilling it, without attributing any sort of soteriological function to it.
2. At the same time, this idea facilitates the necessary reduction of the law/Torah into this one principle in view of the Gentile mission that did not require circumcision.
3. Both by concentrating the law/Torah into one command or a few basic ethical principles[326] and by defining the essence of the law as love, Paul stands within the tradition of Hellenistic Judaism. There the tendency prevailed to identify the commands of the Torah with a doctrine of virtue oriented to human reason,[327] an approach that allowed Hellenistic Judaism both to preserve the Torah and to open it up to a more universal application. Εὐσέβεια (piety, religious devotion), as the highest form of virtue, included the virtue of love.[328]

326. Cf. *Let. Aris.* 131, 168; *T. Dan* 5.1–3; *T. Iss.* 5.2; Philo, *Spec. Laws* 1.260; 2.61–63; *Decalogue* 154ff.; Josephus, *Ag. Ap.* 2.154; *Ant.* 18.117. Differently than in Paul, however, the exaltation of particular commands did not repeal the authority of the other commandments; on this point, cf. the recent work of Weber, *Das Gesetz im hellenistischen Judentum*, 236–39.

327. Cf. ibid., 320: "Thus the Nomos is basically a form of the doctrine of virtue, for the purpose of virtue is the formation of character."

328. Cf., e.g., Philo, *Decalogue* 108–110.

Their cultural background thus made it easier for Jewish Christians and proselytes to appropriate the Pauline solution to the problem posed by the law.[329]

4. But also in the Greco-Roman cultural context, the conviction was prevalent that kindness and love represent the true form of righteousness/justice and the fulfilling of the laws: "And further, if nature ordains the desire to promote the interests of a fellow man, whatever he may be, just because he is a fellow man, then it follows, in accordance with the same nature, that there are interests that all men have in common. And if this is true, we are all subject to one and the same law of nature; and if this also is true, we are certainly forbidden by nature's law to wrong our neighbor" (Cicero, *Off.* 3.5.27). The law that is identical with reason and in harmony with nature can be no different in Rome from that in Athens, for "one eternal and unchangeable law will be valid for all nations and all times, and there will be one master and ruler, that is, God, over us all, for he is the author of this law, its promulgator, and its enforcing judge. Whoever is disobedient is fleeing from himself and denying his human nature, and by reason of this very fact he will suffer the worst penalties, even if he escapes what is commonly considered punishment" (Cicero, *Resp.* 3.22). Those who attend to the law of reason can do no harm to their fellow human beings; they are in harmony with God, nature, and themselves. It is therefore important to turn to philosophy, for "Zeus, the common father of all humans and gods, commands it and goads you on to do it. For his law and command is: Be just, do right, practice charity, be considerate, noble-minded, master of troubles and desires, free from all envy and every evil intention. In a word, the law of Zeus commands human beings to be good [ἀγαθὸν εἶναι κελεύει τὸν ἄνθρωπον ὁ νόμος τοῦ Διός]."[330]

The agreement with Gal. 6:2; Rom. 3:27; 8:2; 13:8–10 is obvious: the rule, the command, the will of God is one thing: love!

The Solution

The different lines along which Paul develops his statements about the law/Torah cannot simply be harmonized or explained entirely in terms of the different church situations he addresses. Paul wrestled with the themes imposed upon him and achieved *a solution that was in the process of solidification*,

329. Although in Jewish ethical instruction the love commandment was not of outstanding importance, it did have a significant position; cf. Karl-Wilhelm Niebuhr, *Gesetz und Paränese: Katechismusartige Weisungsreihen in der frühjüdischen Literatur* (WUNT 2.28; Tübingen: Mohr, 1987), 122ff. and passim.

330. Musonius, *Diss.* 16.

which he presented in Romans. Concentrating on the concept of love made it possible for Paul to continue to advocate in Romans the theological position he had developed in Galatians, but without being branded as "lawless." In Gal. 6:2 ("Bear one another's burdens, and in this way you will fulfill the law of Christ"), Rom. 3:27 ("the law of faith"), and in Rom. 8:2 ("the law of the spirit of life in Christ Jesus") Paul plays with the term νόμος and understands it in the sense of "rule/norm/order."[331] Faith and love in the power of the Spirit appear as the new norms to which Christians are bound, each of which excludes independent boasting before God. This is confirmed by Rom. 13:8–10, where love is defined as *the* fulfillment of the law. Because Christians already live on the basis of these norms, Paul can also affirm that they by no means do away with the law/Torah, but establish it (Rom. 3:31). The modulation into love removes the law/Torah's destructive power of religious zeal and thus strengthens its functions as servant.

Paul sets out a *new definition* in that he formulates his interpretation of the Torah (partially from his own strict Jewish perspective) as "the law." This new formulation of the Torah (love as the center and goal, which is at the same time the denial of any soteriological function and the abrogation of the ritual prescriptions) *integrates it into an overriding concept of law* that was equally accessible to Jewish and Gentile Christians on the basis of their respective cultural backgrounds.[332] By means of the concept of love, the apostle *synthesizes* Jewish and Greco-Roman understandings of law and thus attains a consistent, well-rounded integration of the law thematic within his project of meaning-formation. By this rewriting of the basic terminology, *Paul manages to combine what cannot be combined, in order to provide the necessary means for communicating his message within his cultural situation.* Neither the Jewish nor the Greco-Roman cultural context permits "freedom from the law"; in all Paul's statements about the law, Paul is not concerned with "freedom from the law," but with the issue of how the soteriological exclusiveness of the Christ event, the fulfillment of the law by love, and the freedom of Gentile believers from the precondition of circumcision could all be brought together into one line of thought.

331. For evidence and argument, cf. Udo Schnelle, "Das Gesetz bei Paulus," in *Biographie und Persönlichkeit des Paulus* (ed. Eve-Marie Becker and Peter Pilhofer; WUNT 187; Tübingen: Mohr Siebeck, 2005), 265–69. Heikki Räisänen, "Sprachliches zum Spiel des Paulus mit Nomos," in *Glaube und Gerechtigkeit: In memoriam Rafael Gyllenberg (18.6.1893–29.7.1982)* (ed. Rafael Gyllenberg et al.; SFEG 38; Helsinki: Suomen Eksegeettisen Seuran, 1983), 134–49, presents linguistic parallels to the use of νόμος as "rule/order/norm."

332. It is helpful to note that Paul also follows this path when dealing with other central theological questions. In Rom. 2:28–29 he redefines what it means to be a Jew and what circumcision is. In Rom. 4:12 he takes up this new definition of circumcision and in Rom. 9:6–7 Paul issues a new definition of Israel. Redefinition, which means rewriting the basic vocabulary with new content, is always necessary when symbolic universes are incompatible as previously formulated but must be brought together on a higher plane.

6.5.4 Faith

Faith for Paul is a new qualification of the self, for by faith the person enters the realm of God's love for the world. The foundation and possibility of faith are given in God's saving initiative in Jesus Christ. Faith does not rest on human decision but is a gift of God's grace.[333] This was already true for Abraham: "For this reason it depends on faith, in order that the promise may rest on grace [Διὰ τοῦτο ἐκ πίστεως, ἵνα κατὰ χάρις], and be guaranteed to all his descendants, not only to the adherents of the law but also to those who share the faith of Abraham, for he is the father of all of us" (Rom. 4:16). The basic structure of the Pauline concept of faith is clearly revealed in Phil. 1:29: "For he has graciously granted you the privilege [ὅτι ὑμῖν ἐχαρίσθη] not only of believing in Christ [οὐ μόνον τὸ εἰς αὐτὸν πιστεύειν], but of suffering for him as well." Faith is a work of the Spirit, for "no one can say 'Jesus is Lord' except by the Holy Spirit" (1 Cor. 12:3b).[334] Faith is numbered among the fruits of the Spirit (cf. 1 Cor. 12:9; Gal. 5:22). Faith opens up a new relationship to God, a relationship human beings can only gratefully receive. The gift character of πίστις/πιστεύω (faith/believe) also determines the close relationship between faith and preaching in Paul's thought. Faith is ignited by the gospel, the power of God (Rom. 1:16). It pleased God, "through the foolishness of our proclamation, to save those who believe" (1 Cor. 1:21). Early on, the word was spread about the apostle: "The one who formerly was persecuting us is now proclaiming the faith he once tried to destroy" (Gal. 1:23). According to Rom. 10:8, Paul preaches the "word of faith" (τὸ ῥῆμα τῆς πίστεως). Faith grows out of preaching, which in turn goes back to the word from/about Christ (Rom. 10:17, "So faith comes from what is heard, and what is heard comes through the word of Christ"). Thus Christ himself is active in the word of preaching. In 1 Cor. 15:11b Paul concludes his basic instruction with the words "so we proclaim and so you have come to believe." It is not the rhetorical art of the preacher or the enthusiastic human yes in response that leads to faith but the Spirit and power of God (cf. 1 Cor. 2:4–5). The Spirit mediates the gift of faith and at the same time gives its content a characteristic stamp, thus giving unity to the church. Spirit and faith are related in Paul's thought as cause and effect inasmuch as the Spirit opens the door to faith and the believer then leads his or her life in the power of the Spirit. Thus Paul testifies, "For through the Spirit, by faith, we eagerly wait for the hope of righteousness" (Gal. 5:5). Finally, Gal. 3:23, 25 indicates that for Paul "faith" has dimensions that go far beyond the

333. Cf. the foundational reflections of Gerhard Friedrich, "Glaube und Verkündigung bei Paulus," in *Glaube im Neuen Testament: Studien zu Ehren von Hermann Binder anlässlich seines 70. Geburtstags* (ed. Ferdinand Hahn and Hans Klein; BTS 7; Neukirchen-Vluyn: Neukirchener Verlag, 1982), 100ff.

334. Contra Bultmann, *Theology of the New Testament*, 1:330, who states "that Paul does not describe faith as inspired, attributable to the Spirit."

individualistic coming-to-believe: "coming" to faith possesses a quality related to salvation history, for faith replaces the Torah as a soteriological entity and opens up for humanity a new access to God.

The basic structure of the Pauline concept of faith as a saving and thus life-giving power and gift of God shows that it is inappropriate to speak of faith as a "free deed of obedience . . . this sort of decision,"[335] or as "reception and preservation of the message of salvation."[336] Such language does in part name important aspects of the Pauline concept of faith, but at the same time it reverses cause and effect, for it is God's act that first makes faith possible.[337] Faith is not the presupposition or condition of the saving event, but a part of it! It is God who "is at work in you, enabling you both to will and to work for his good pleasure" (Phil. 2:13). Thus faith originates from God's saving initiative; it is God who calls human beings into the service of preaching the gospel (cf. Rom. 10:13–14, "For, 'Everyone who calls on the name of the Lord shall be saved.' But how are they to call on one in whom they have not believed? And how are they to believe in one of whom they have never heard? And how are they to hear without someone to proclaim him?"). God alone is the giver, and human beings are receivers, so that Paul can consistently contrast life that comes from faith and life that comes from the law/Torah (cf. Gal. 2:16; 3:12; Rom. 3:21–22, 28; 9:32).

Faith attains its form in the act of *confession*, as programmatically formulated by Paul in Rom. 10:9–10: "If you confess with your lips that Jesus is Lord and believe in your heart that God raised him from the dead, you will be saved. For one believes with the heart and so is justified, and one confesses with the mouth and so is saved." No one may adopt a neutral stance toward the content of the faith—it can only be confessed or denied. Precisely in the act of confession, the believer turns away from himself or herself and turns toward God's saving act, so that the believer begins to participate in the ultimate salvation of the future. Believers do not remain private individuals but communicate their faith, stepping over boundaries. Thus the believer cannot keep silent; rather, "'I believed, and so I spoke'—we also believe, and so we speak [καὶ ἡμεῖς πιστεύομεν, διὸ καὶ λαλοῦμεν]" (2 Cor. 4:13b, quoting Ps. 115:1 LXX [Ps. 116:10]). For Paul, the content of faith is not to be separated from the act of faith, which brings one into relationship with God and others (cf. 1 Thess. 4:13; 1 Cor. 15:14); Paul presupposes this content as the knowledge shared by the community of faith (cf. 1 Thess. 4:13; 1 Cor. 3:16; 6:1–11, 15–16, 19; 10:1; 12:1; 2 Cor. 5:1; Gal. 2:16; Rom. 1:13; 11:25; and passim).

As a gift of God, faith always at the same time includes the individual factor of each particular person's life of faith and activates human freedom to

335. Ibid., 1:316.

336. Käsemann, *Romans*, 107.

337. Friedrich, "Glaube und Verkündigung," 109: "Faith is a decision made by God."

act.[338] Paul frequently speaks of "your faith" (1 Thess. 1:8; 3:2, 5–7, 10; 1 Cor. 2:5; 2 Cor. 1:24; 10:15; Rom. 1:8, 12; Phil. 2:17; and passim), by which he emphasizes especially the missionary dimension of the faith of the churches of Thessalonica and Rome. For the apostle, there was a "growing in faith" (2 Cor. 10:15); new insights and knowledge increase, purify, and change faith. Faith is subject to changes but does not abandon its fundamental convictions. In Rom. 12:3 Paul admonishes the charismatics not to go beyond the boundaries to which they too are subject, but to think with sober judgment according to the measure of faith (μέτρον πίστεως) that God has assigned. Believers must discern and assess which gifts they have been given, and each must find his or her appropriate place in the life of the church.

Faith is grounded in the love of God made known in Jesus Christ (cf. Rom. 5:8), so that *love appears as the active and visible side of faith* (Gal. 5:6, "the faith that is active through love"). Paul insists that the lives of believers manifest a harmony of thinking and acting, of conviction and deed. At the same time, he is aware that believers sometimes fail (Gal. 6:1), speaks of those who are "weak in faith" (Rom. 14:1), promises the Philippians progress in faith (Phil. 1:25), and challenges his readers to stand fast in the faith (1 Cor. 16:13; 2 Cor. 1:24; Rom. 11:20). Faith does not confer on people any visibly new quality but sets them into a historical movement and situation where they can demonstrate it, resulting in obedience (Rom. 1:5, "We have received grace and apostleship to bring about the obedience of faith among all the Gentiles for the sake of his name").

On the one hand, Paul takes up the linguistic usage of Hellenistic Judaism[339] and pagan Hellenism,[340] but on the other hand he goes beyond this

338. Concisely stated by Adolf von Schlatter, *Der Glaube im Neuen Testament* (5th ed.; Stuttgart: Calwer, 1963), 371: "The will grounded in faith is love."

339. Cf. the comprehensive treatment in Dieter Lührmann, "Pistis im Judentum," *ZNW* 64 (1973): 19–38.

340. The main examples are cited and interpreted in Gerhard Barth, "Pistis in hellenistischer Religiosität," in *Neutestamentliche Versuche und Beobachtungen* (ed. Gerhard Barth; Waltrop: Spenner, 1996), 173–76; G. Schunack, "Glaube in griechischer Religiosität," in *Antikes Judentum und frühes Christentum: Festschrift für Hartmut Stegemann zum 65. Geburtstag* (ed. Bernd Kollmann et al.; BZNW 97; Berlin: de Gruyter, 1999), 299–317. In the Greek world, the words "faith" and "believe" are first of all associated with more than fifty oracle shrines. The reality of oracles had been a widespread cultural phenomenon from around the seventh or sixth century BCE and continued to have an influence on all realms of public and private life into late antiquity. In this context, "faith" meant "to believe in revelations from the gods" that served to interpret the future destiny of a person, especially in crisis and times of upheaval. Worthy of note is the testimony of Plutarch, who assumed the office of one of the two high priests in the oracle center at Delphi about 95 CE. For Plutarch, faith is self-evident, for the gods are the guarantors of social and individual stability; he refers to "the reverence and faith implanted in nearly all mankind at birth" (*Mor.* 359E–360A). The content of faith is the foreknowledge of the gods and their help for human beings, especially in times of distress or in the border situations of life, such as sickness and death.

by making πίστις/πιστεύω the *central and exclusive designation* for one's relation to God and thus also the *distinguishing mark* of one's identity.[341] A second distinguishing feature is the orientation of faith to Jesus Christ. For Paul, faith is always faith in the God who raised Jesus Christ from the dead (cf. Rom. 4:17, 24; 8:11). Jesus Christ is at one and the same time the one who generates faith and the content of this faith.[342] The center of faith is thus not the believer but the one believed in. Because faith grows out of the preaching of the gospel, it is ultimately the act of God, grounded only in the Christ event. Rather, God places human beings in faith and sets them on a new way, the ground and goal of which is Jesus Christ. Doubtless, faith also includes biographical and psychological elements and the factor of human decision, but it is preceded by God's fundamental decision. Paul sees faith not as an isolated phenomenon of human experience, but as a new determination of existence by God. In the same way, faith is a new orientation for one's life, a new way of living. The person shifts from a self-centered to a God-centered life. Faith localizes persons in their relation to God and becomes real in their love for other people.

6.5.5 Freedom

In its very essence, the Christian life is a life of freedom: "For freedom Christ has set us free" (Gal. 5:1). Freedom for Paul is "a basic principle of the gospel."[343] Christian freedom is the result of the liberation from sin effected by Jesus Christ and appropriated in baptism. Freedom is thus not a possibility of human existence as such; human beings cannot attain or realize it on the basis of their own powers. The universal power of sin excludes freedom as a goal of human striving. To be sure, people can have a feeling of individual freedom and deny the power of sin, but this changes nothing with regard to the actual enslaving domination of sin in the lives of such people. Only the saving act of God in Jesus Christ can be realized as the liberating event in a comprehensive sense, because only here are the oppressive powers of sin and death overcome.

Especially in his debate with the Corinthians, Paul makes clear the *paradox at the base of his concept of freedom*: freedom as love in commitment to Christ. Freedom is not the realization of individual potential but can be expressed only in love for others. Paul takes up the motto of the "strong," πάντα μοι ἔξεστιν (all things are lawful for me), only in order to immediately relativize it and make it more precise (1 Cor. 6:12; 10:23). The goal of Christian freedom

341. Cf. Gerhard Barth, "Πίστις," *EDNT* 3:95.

342. Cf. Friedrich, "Glaube und Verkündigung," 102–6.

343. As appropriately stated by Thomas Söding, "Die Freiheit des Glaubens," in *Frühjudentum und Neues Testament im Horizont Biblischer Theologie* (ed. Wolfgang Kraus et al.; WUNT 162; Tübingen: Mohr Siebeck, 2003), 133.

is not indifference, for it is essentially a term of participation and relationship: baptized believers participate in the freedom attained through Christ, a freedom that becomes authentic only in relation to other Christians and the Christian community. The model for this concept of freedom is given by Jesus Christ as the crucified one, the one who died for his brothers and sisters (cf. 1 Cor. 8:11; Rom. 14:15). Christian freedom is for Paul the freedom given by Jesus Christ as a gift, so that a misuse of this freedom, as a sin against one's fellow Christians, is at the same time a sin against Christ. In 1 Cor. 9, Paul presents himself as a model for the kind of freedom that is willing to give up its own rights for the sake of others. The apostle forgoes his legitimate right to support by the churches in order to further the preaching of the gospel (cf. 9:12, 15–16). Whereas in antiquity freedom and servitude were mutually exclusive alternatives, for Paul they mutually condition and complement each other. The apostle's freedom is realized precisely in the service of the gospel, which means active love for others (cf. 9:19; Gal. 5:13).

Because, through the Christ event, the present is already proleptically qualified by the future (1 Cor. 7:29–31), Paul challenges Christians to bring their self-understanding and ethical conduct into line with the eschatological turn of the ages. The Pauline ὡς μή (as if not) aims at participation in this world but with a certain distancing of oneself from it, participation in the life of the world without falling victim to it—a kind of *freedom from the world while living in the world*.[344] Because what is to come already shapes the present, the present loses its determinative character. We still have to acknowledge the historical reality of the ordering structures of this world, but at the same time this world is passing away, and Paul calls for an inner freedom and independence. Baptized believers should thus remain in their present social status but without ascribing it any power to really determine things. The institution of marriage, like the institution of slavery, is a structure of the old age; those who remain overly involved in them have not understood the signs of the times (cf. 1 Cor. 7:1, 8). Nevertheless, those already married should remain so (cf. 1 Cor. 7:2–7); slaves, too, should remain in their present status (1 Cor. 7:21b),[345] for in the church the fundamental social alternatives have long since been removed (cf. 1 Cor. 12:13; 2 Cor. 5:17; Gal. 3:26–28; 5:6; 6:15). The Letter to Philemon shows, however, that Paul's recommendations are not bound to any ideology, for this letter by no means excludes the option of freedom for a Christian slave. But when Christian slaves do gain their freedom, they still know that they have long since been set free in Christ.

344. On this point cf. Herbert Braun, "Die Indifferenz gegenüber der Welt bei Paulus und bei Epiktet," in *Gesammelte Studien zum Neuen Testament und seiner Umwelt* (ed. Herbert Braun; 3rd ed.; Tübingen: Mohr, 1971), 159–67.

345. On the problem of Paul's view of slavery, cf. James Albert Harrill, *Slaves in the New Testament: Literary, Social, and Moral Dimensions* (Minneapolis: Fortress, 2006), 17–57.

While the Corinthian letters contain no text in which freedom is understood as "*freedom from the law, sin, and death*," this meaning comes to the fore in Galatians and Romans (see above, §6.5.2). Freedom from sin as liberation by God in Jesus Christ includes for Paul freedom from the law/Torah in its enslaving function.

The universal dimensions of the Pauline concept of freedom are revealed in Rom. 8:18ff.[346] The freedom of the believer and the *liberty of creation* converge here and are embedded in a comprehensive perspective on the future. Through Adam's transgression, the creation was involuntarily subjected to futility, but still with hope (Rom. 8:20; cf. *4 Ezra* 7.11–12). Creation itself participates in the hope of believers: "The creation itself will be set free from its bondage to decay and will obtain the freedom of the glory of the children of God" (Rom. 8:21). The assurance of this future event is given by the Spirit, which, as the initial gift, is not only the pledge and guarantee that the Christian hope is authentic but also comes to the help of believers who struggle to hold on to their hope in difficult situations (8:26–27). The Spirit intercedes for the saints before God in a language commensurate with the situation. The confidence of faith makes it possible for Paul in 8:28–30 to give a comprehensive portrayal of the "glorious liberty of the children of God." God himself will call for the freedom of the children of God, which will attain its goal in the believers' participation in the glory of God that has appeared in God's own Son.

Freedom was a central theme in the Greco-Roman world in every phase of its intellectual history.[347] At the very same time early Christianity was developing, theories about the nature of freedom were having powerful effects. Epictetus composed an entire book titled Περὶ Ἐλευθερίας (freedom; in *Diatr.* 4.1), and three of Dio Chrysostom's speeches were on slavery and freedom (*De servitute et libertate* 1, 2 [*Or.* 14, 15]; *De libertate* [*Or.* 80]). Both Epictetus and Dio began with a popular understanding of freedom: freedom as freedom to act without any constraints. They chose this point of departure for their reflections in order to destroy an externally oriented concept of freedom. Epictetus put forward arguments based on experience

346. Cf. F. Stanley Jones, *"Freiheit" in den Briefen des Apostels Paulus: Eine historische, exegetische und religionsgeschichtliche Studie* (GTA 34; Göttingen: Vandenhoeck & Ruprecht, 1987), 129–35; Samuel Vollenweider, *Freiheit als neue Schöpfung: Eine Untersuchung zur Eleutheria bei Paulus und in seiner Umwelt* (FRLANT 147; Göttingen: Vandenhoeck & Ruprecht, 1989), 375–96.

347. See the descriptions and interpretations in Dieter Nestle, *Eleutheria: Studien zum Wesen der Freiheit bei den Griechen und im Neuen Testament* (HUT 6; Tübingen: Mohr, 1967); Dieter Nestle, "Freiheit," *RAC* 8:269–306; Vollenweider, *Freiheit als neue Schöpfung*, 23–204; Hans Dieter Betz, *Paul's Concept of Freedom in the Context of Hellenistic Discussions about the Possibilities of Human Freedom: Protocol of the Twenty-sixth Colloquy, 9 January 1977* (Berkeley: The Center, 1977); Gerhard Dautzenberg, "Freiheit im hellenistischen Kontext," in *Der neue Mensch in Christus: Hellenistische Anthropologie und Ethik im Neuen Testament* (ed. Hans Dieter Betz and Johannes Beutler; QD 190; Freiburg: Herder, 2001), 57–81.

and insight: a rich senator is still the slave of the emperor (*Diatr.* 4.1.13), and any free man who falls in love with a beautiful young slave becomes her slave (*Diatr.* 4.1.17). Who can be free when even the kings and their friends are not free? Because freedom understood as an external circumstance is not an adequate understanding of true freedom, what matters is to distinguish between the things we can control and the things over which we have no power (*Diatr.* 4.1.81). The given circumstances of life are not really at our disposition, but we can have control over our attitude to them. "Purify your judgments, lest something not your own may fasten itself to them or grow together with them, and may give you pain when it is torn loose. And every day while you are training yourself, as you do in the gymnasium, do not say that you are 'pursuing philosophy' (indeed an arrogant phrase!) but that you are a slave presenting your emancipator in court; for this is the true freedom. This is the way in which Diogenes was set free by Antisthenes, and afterwards said that he could never be enslaved again by any man" (*Diatr.* 4.1.112–115). Dio Chrysostom argued similarly when he refused to define freedom and slavery as objective states concerning one's birth or external, clearly perceivable circumstances, for both freedom and slavery are ambiguous terms whose true meaning is realized only in one's experience. "And so when a man is well-born in respect to virtue, it is right to call him 'noble,' even if no one knows his parents or his ancestors either. . . . We should make no distinction between the two classes. Nor is it reasonable to say that some are of ignoble birth and mean, and that others are slaves" (*Or.* 15.31). Epictetus and Dio Chrysostom represent a broad stream of tradition in the history of ancient philosophy that flows through the Stoics and Epicureans all the way to the Skeptics: true freedom is the inner independence of the wise, those who have made peace with their own feelings (ἀταραξία), who have placed themselves under the will of God (and thus the law of nature) by a knowledge of their own emotions and by refusing to be dominated by them.

Paul removes freedom from the sphere of human activity; for him *it has the character of a gift*, not an act. From this point of departure, the apostle advocates an independent position in the ancient debate about freedom. He takes up the concept of inner freedom, but modifies it decisively in its basic structure by giving it a new foundation, in that he describes freedom as the discovery of a supporting external reality: God. Paradoxically, it is only in becoming God's slave that one becomes truly free, for freedom in the full sense of the word belongs to God alone. Freedom is grounded outside of human existence; it is not located in human life itself. Human freedom is dependent on something not at human disposal. Freedom does not come as the result of one's own resolute decision but is a gift that can be received only from God and is realized in love. The norm for freedom is love. Love recognizes other human beings as God's children and orients itself to what they and the world need. Freedom is more than being able to do what I choose; it is revealed in acts of loving concern for others.[348]

6.5.6 *Additional Anthropological Terms*

Paul designates and characterizes the innermost self of human beings in different ways. In the process, he can make connections with both Old Testament and Greco-Roman ideas.

At the center of human self-awareness is the *conscience*. The term συνείδησις (conscience) appears thirty times in the New Testament, fourteen of them in Paul. The most intensive concentration (eight times) is found in the dispute about food sacrificed to idols in 1 Cor. 8 and 10. The συνείδησις appears here as the self's *internal court of judgment*. The subject about which conscience makes judgments is human conduct, which is tested regarding its agreement with traditional norms.[349] When the "strong" make use of the freedom available to them by continuing to eat meat that has been sacrificed to idols, they mislead the "weak" into doing the same, which brings the weak into an internal conflict of conscience. The "strong" thus sin against Christ (1 Cor. 8:13), who also died for the weak members of the community (8:12). The freedom of the individual is clearly limited by the conscience of the other person, who must not be placed in such a stressful circumstance. Συνείδησις thus describes an authoritative court that judges the person's conduct by given norms.[350]

In Rom. 2:14–16 συνείδησις appears as a universal human phenomenon: "When Gentiles, who do not possess the law, do instinctively what the law requires, these, though not having the law, are a law to themselves. They show that what the law requires is written on their hearts, to which their own conscience also bears witness; and their conflicting thoughts will accuse or perhaps excuse them." Here conscience, as an awareness of norms, includes the capacity to make moral judgments about oneself; it means knowledge about oneself and one's conduct. As a phenomenon inherent in human beings, conscience confirms for Paul the existence of the law among the Gentiles. In Rom. 9:1 the conscience steps forth as an independent, personified witness for the truth and examines the agreement between convictions and conduct (cf. also 2 Cor. 1:23; 2:17; 11:38; 12:19). According to Rom. 13:5,[351] insight into the meaning of political power and order should lead Christians to subject

348. Cf. here Hans Weder, "Die Normativität der Freiheit," in *Paulus, Apostel Jesu Christi: Festschrift für Günter Klein zum 70. Geburtstag* (ed. Michael Trowitzsch; Tübingen: Mohr, 1998), 129–45.

349. Cf. Hans-Joachim Eckstein, *Der Begriff Syneidesis bei Paulus: Eine neutestamentlich-exegetische Untersuchung zum "Gewissensbegriff"* (WUNT 2.10; Tübingen: Mohr, 1983), 242–43.

350. On the unity of the Pauline line of argument, cf. ibid., 271.

351. For exegesis, cf. ibid., 276–300.

themselves to institutionalized authority: "Therefore one must be subject, not only because of wrath but also because of conscience." Inasmuch as it resists evil and promotes good, political authority originates in the will of God. As in Rom. 2:15, Paul is here thinking about the conscience resident in every human being, not about a specifically Christian conscience.

The Old Testament and ancient Judaism had no equivalent for the Greek συνείδησις.[352] Paul probably adopted the term συνείδησις from Hellenistic popular philosophy. Here συνείδησις mostly meant the awareness that regarded one's own acts as morally bad or good.[353] Because the gods have given them wisdom, human beings are capable of self-awareness. "For he who knows himself will realize, in the first place, that he has a divine element within him, and will think of his own inner nature as a kind of consecrated image of God; and so he will always act and think in a way worthy of so great a gift of the gods" (Cicero, *Leg.* 1.59). Since God has equipped human beings with their own inherent capabilities, they are able to distinguish between good and evil, for God has "placed a monitor at the side of each one of us, namely the guardian angel [δαίμων] of each person, a monitor who never slumbers, and who cannot be gotten around" (Epictetus, *Diatr.* 1.14.12; cf. *Diatr.* 2.8.11–12; Seneca, *Ep.* 41.1–2; 73.76). So also the phenomenon of a bad conscience (cf., e.g., Seneca, *Ep.* 43.4–5; 81.20; 105.8) points to an authority resident in each person, intertwined with virtue and reason, that insists on conduct that accords with the law of nature: "We should, therefore, have a guardian, as it were, to pluck us continually by the ear and dispel rumors and protest against popular enthusiasms" (Seneca, *Ep.* 94.55).

Paul understands συνείδησις as a neutral authority for evaluating actions already done (both one's own acts and those of others) on the basis of values and norms that have been internalized. For Paul, conscience does not itself contain the basic knowledge of good and evil but rather a *co*-knowledge, a knowledge-with, of norms that serve as the basis for making judgments that can be either positive or negative.[354] As a relational concept, the conscience does not itself set norms but makes judgments as to whether given norms are in fact observed. Neither can conscience be seen as distinctive of Christians,

352. Cf. ibid., 105ff.

353. On the concept of conscience in Roman and Greek authors, cf. Hans-Josef Klauck, "'Der Gott in dir' (Ep 41,1): Autonomie des Gewissens bei Seneca und Paulus," in *Alte Welt und neuer Glaube: Beiträge zur Religionsgeschichte, Forschungsgeschichte und Theologie des Neuen Testaments* (ed. Hans-Josef Klauck; NTOA 29; Göttingen: Vandenhoeck & Ruprecht, 1994), passim; Hans-Josef Klauck, "Ein Richter im eigenen Innern: Das Gewissen bei Philo von Alexandrien," in *Alte Welt und neuer Glaube: Beiträge zur Religionsgeschichte, Forschungsgeschichte und Theologie des Neuen Testaments* (ed. Hans-Josef Klauck; NTOA 29; Göttingen: Vandenhoeck & Ruprecht, 1994), 33–58; H. Cancik-Lindemaier, "Gewissen," in *Handbuch religionswissenschaftlicher Grundbegriffe* (ed. Günter Kehrer et al.; Stuttgart: Kohlhammer, 1988), 3:17–31.

354. Eckstein, *Syneidesis*, 311ff.

pagans, or Jews; it is *a general human phenomenon*. Its function is the same for all human beings, but the norms that are presupposed in making judgments can be very different. Love, and reason renewed by the Spirit—these are the relevant and decisive norms for Christians, on the basis of which they make judgments about their own conduct and that of others.

Paul expresses the special *dignity* of human beings with the εἰκών motif (image, reflection, prototype).[355] The εἰκών concept receives fundamental theological significance by being used in speaking of Christ as the image of God. In 2 Cor. 4:4 the apostle explains[356] how it came about that the gospel is veiled to unbelievers; the god of this age has blinded their minds "to keep them from seeing the light of the gospel of the glory of Christ, who is the image of God [ὅς ἐστιν εἰκὼν τοῦ θεοῦ]." Here εἰκών appears as a category of participation: the Son participates in the δόξα of the Father; in him the true nature of God becomes visible because he is the image of the God who is compassionately concerned for humanity.

All the statements about the relation of believers to the image of Christ are based on the concept of Christ as the image of God. In 1 Cor. 15:49 Paul emphasizes, in contrast to the Corinthians' understanding of salvation oriented to the present, that they will not bear the image of the heavenly man Jesus Christ until the eschatological event, for the earthly man Adam still determines the present. According to Rom. 8:29, the goal of God's election is that believers "be conformed to the image of his Son, in order that he might be the firstborn within a large family." Although this event first takes place at the future resurrection of believers, it has a present dimension as well, for in baptism believers already participate in the reality of Christ as the image of God (Rom. 6:3–5). According to 2 Cor. 3:18, the divine glory rests on the Risen One in all its fullness, so that he is at once both the prototype and the goal of the Christian's transformation. In 1 Cor. 11:7–8 Paul refers explicitly to Gen. 1:26–27: "For a man ought not to have his head veiled, since he is the image and reflection of God; but woman is the reflection of man. Indeed, man was not made from woman, but woman from man." Paul directs this statement against the custom, evidently widespread in Corinth, whereby women participated in worship without the customary head covering. He is probably dealing with a new practice, unknown in other congregations (cf. 1 Cor. 11:16), which may have originated in efforts toward women's emancipation by segments of the Corinthian church, efforts they saw as directly inspired by the Spirit.[357] On the basis of his creation theology, Paul argues against this

355. Cf. the comprehensive discussion of history-of-religion connections in Friedrich Wilhelm Eltester, *Eikon im Neuen Testament* (BZNW 23; Berlin: Töpelmann, 1958), 15–170.

356. On this point cf. Jacob Jervell, *Imago Dei: Gen 1,26f. im Spätjudentum, in der Gnosis und in den paulinischen Briefen* (FRLANT 76; Göttingen: Vandenhoeck & Ruprecht, 1960), 214–18.

357. Cf. Wolff, *1. Korintherbrief*, 70–71.

abolition of previous conventions, basing the distinction between men and women and its practical consequences on the fact that the man was created in the image of God (cf. Gen. 2:22).

In Pauline thought, the καρδία (heart) is another center of the human self.[358] The love of God is poured out into human hearts through the Holy Spirit (Rom. 5:5). The Holy Spirit works in the heart. God sent the Spirit of his Son "into our hearts" (Gal. 4:6), and in baptism gave us the Spirit "in our hearts" as the ἀρραβών (first installment, 2 Cor. 1:22). Baptism leads to an obedience from the heart (Rom. 6:17), and human beings stand in a new relationship of dependence that brings salvation: they now serve God, which means righteousness and justice. There is a circumcision of the heart, a circumcision that is spiritual and not literal (Rom. 2:29), an inner change from which a new relationship with God grows. Hearts are strengthened by God (1 Thess. 3:13), and the peace of God, "which surpasses all understanding, will guard your hearts and your minds in Christ Jesus" (Phil. 4:7). The heart can open itself to the saving message of Jesus Christ or close itself off from it (2 Cor. 3:14–16). Repentance and confession begin in the heart (Rom. 10:9–10). Here mouth relates to heart as the act of confession relates to the act of faith; that is, the saving act of God in Christ grasps the whole person. Precisely as the innermost organ, the heart determines the whole person. In both the positive and the negative sense, the heart is the center of one's being where crucial decisions are made (1 Cor. 4:5). The heart knows the will of God (Rom. 2:15); it stands fast in resisting the passions (1 Cor. 7:37) and is eager to help the needy (2 Cor. 9:7). All the same, the heart can also be darkened and without understanding (Rom. 1:21; 2:5), and it can be hardened (2 Cor. 3:14–15). God searches and tests the heart (1 Thess. 2:4; Rom. 8:27), and reveals its intentions (2 Cor. 4:5).

In contrast to his opponents, Paul makes no use of letters of recommendation. The Corinthian church itself is his letter of recommendation, "written on our hearts, to be known and read by all" (2 Cor. 3:2). Paul struggles for his church, and pleads with them, "Make room in your hearts for us" (2 Cor. 7:2). He opens his heart to the church (2 Cor. 6:11) and assures them, "You are in our hearts, to die together and to live together" (2 Cor. 7:3). When Paul uses the word καρδία, he designates the deepest inner core of the person, the seat of the understanding, feelings, and will, the place where the ultimate decisions of life are made and where God's act through the Spirit begins.

The Hebrew language has no equivalent for νοῦς (*thinking, reason, mind, understanding*), a central term in Hellenistic anthropology.[359] Paul uses νοῦς

358. Paul's use of καρδία stands in the tradition of Old Testament anthropology. Cf. Hans Walter Wolff, *Anthropology of the Old Testament* (Philadelphia: Fortress, 1974), 40–58.

359. Classically, Plato, *Phaedr.* 247c–e, presents the mind as the highest and best part of the soul, making the moral life possible by its ability to discern what virtue is; cf. further Aristotle, *Eth. Nic.* 10.1177a (the mind as the epitome of the divine, the most valuable part of the inner

in 1 Cor. 14:14–15, his discussion of glossolalia, as the authority of critical reason in contrast to the uncontrolled and unintelligible speaking in tongues. Prayer and praise take place both in the divine Spirit and in the human mind (14:15). In 14:19 νοῦς means a clearly understood communication by which the church is instructed: "In church I would rather speak five words with my mind, in order to instruct others also, than ten thousand words in a tongue." So also, in Phil. 4:7 νοῦς designates the rational mind, the human capacity for understanding, which is surpassed by the peace of God. In 1 Cor. 1:10 Paul appeals for the unity of the Corinthian church, that they have one mind and one purpose. Paul speaks in 1 Cor. 2:16 of the νοῦς Χριστοῦ (mind of Christ) and in Rom. 11:34 of the νοῦς κυρίου (mind of the Lord), in each case referring to the Holy Spirit, which transcends human judgment.[360] In the context of the dispute between the "strong" and "weak" in Rome, Paul challenges each group "to be fully convinced in their own minds" (Rom. 14:5). According to Rom. 7:23, the law in one's members fights against the law of the mind. In terms of content, the expression νόμος τοῦ νοός (law of my mind) corresponds to the νόμος τοῦ θεοῦ (law of God) in Rom. 7:22 and refers to the person who is oriented to God. In the mind, this person wants to serve God, but the sin dwelling within shatters these good intentions. In Rom. 12:2 Paul warns the church not to accommodate itself to this sinful and transient world but to let God work a transformation in its whole existence, which takes place as a renewing of the νοῦς. By νοῦς Paul here means *reasonable knowing and thinking* that maintain a *new orientation* through the work of the Spirit. Christians receive a new power and capacity for making judgments that enable them to discern the will of God. The mind cannot renew itself out of its own resources but is dependent on the initiative of God, who places the mind in his service, for which it was originally intended.[361]

With the distinction between the ἔσω ἄνθρωπος (inner person) and the ἔξω ἄνθρωπος (external person),[362] Paul makes use of an image from Hellenistic philosophy. It enables him to take up a philosophical ideal of his time and at the same time recoins it in terms of his theology of the cross.

It is not possible to delineate a clear tradition-historical derivation of the ἔσω/ἔξω ἄνθρωπος imagery.[363] The beginning point is probably Plato, *Resp.*

life); Diogenes Laertius, *Vit. phil.* 7.54 (according to Zeno, reason is the primary criterion of truth); Epictetus, *Diatr.* 2.8.1–2 (the essence of divine being is νοῦς); further documentation in *NW* 1.2:230ff.

360. Cf. Friedrich Lang, *Die Briefe an die Korinther* (17th ed.; NTD 7; Göttingen: Vandenhoeck & Ruprecht, 1994), 47.

361. Cf. Günther Bornkamm, "Faith and Reason in Paul's Epistles," *NTS* 4 (1958): 93–100.

362. For the history of research, cf. Jewett, *Paul's Anthropological Terms*, 391–95; Theo K. Heckel, *Der innere Mensch: Die paulinische Verarbeitung eines platonischen Motivs* (WUNT 2.53; Tübingen: Mohr, 1993), 4–9; Hans Dieter Betz, "The Concept of the 'Inner Human Being' (ὁ ἔσω ἄνθρωπος) in the Anthropology of Paul," *NTS* 46 (2000): 317–24.

363. A comprehensive discussion of additional examples is found in Heckel, *Der innere Mensch*, 11–88; Christoph Markschies, "Innerer Mensch," *RAC* 18:266ff.

9.588A–589B, where he states in 589A: "To him the supporter of justice makes answer that he should ever so speak and act as to give the man within him [τοῦ ἀνθρώπου ὁ ἐντὸς ἄνθρωπος] the most complete mastery over the entire human creature" (trans. Jowett). In Hellenistic philosophy around the beginning of the first century CE, the idea was prevalent that the authentic, thinking person, who can distinguish the essential from the unessential, lives a disciplined life free from the passions and makes himself or herself inwardly independent of external circumstances. In contrast, the "external" person is imprisoned by the senses of the external world, with the result that he or she is dominated by passions and anxiety (cf. Philo, *Worse* 23; *Prelim. Studies* 97; *Planting* 42). Seneca makes repeated reference to the internal divine power, which preserves and builds up the fragile body (soul, spirit, reason): "If you see a man who is unterrified in the midst of dangers, untouched by desires, happy in adversity, peaceful amid the storm, who looks down upon men from a higher plane, and views the gods on a footing of equality, will not a feeling of reverence for him steal over you? Will you not say: 'This quality is too lofty to be regarded as resembling this petty body in which it dwells? A Divine power has descended upon that man.'"[364]

In contrast to Hellenistic anthropology, Paul does not understand the distinction between the ἔσω ἄνθρωπος and the ἔξω ἄνθρωπος as an anthropological dualism. Instead the apostle regards the life of the believer from different perspectives.[365] In the context of a peristasis catalog (2 Cor. 4:8–9), Paul says in 2 Cor. 4:16, "So we do not lose heart. Even though our outer nature [ἔξω ἄνθρωπος] is wasting away, our inner nature [ἔσω ἄνθρωπος] is being renewed day by day." Externally the apostle is being worn away by the many sufferings entailed in his mission work. But at the same time the δόξα θεοῦ (glory of God, 4:15, 17) works in the ἔσω ἄνθρωπος, so that believers in their inner selves know that their lives are determined by the Lord who is present with them, who strengthens and renews them. They can thus bear external suffering and hardship because they participate in the life-giving power of the Risen One and so overcome the troubles and decline of the body. In Rom. 7:22 the ἔσω ἄνθρωπος agrees joyfully with the will of God and thus lives in peace with himself or herself. The power of sin, however, perverts the actual existence of believers, who in their striving after the good are subject to the "law of sin" in their members. With the term ἔσω ἄνθρωπος Paul designates the "I" within the human self that is open for the will of God and the work of the Spirit.

Autonomous and Heteronomous Anthropology

Both the Jewish-Hellenistic (cf. 4 Maccabees) and Greco-Roman anthropology can include positive portrayals of the possibilities of human existence.

364. Seneca, *Ep.* 41.4–5 (*NW* 2.1:439–40).

365. Cf. Walter Gutbrod, *Die paulinische Anthropologie* (BWANT 67; Stuttgart-Berlin: Kohlhammer, 1934), 85–92.

Plutarch certainly sees clearly that, while human beings are made vulnerable by their bodily passions, "in his most vital and important parts he stands secure . . . Therefore we should not altogether debase and depreciate [human] Nature in the belief that she has nothing strong, stable, and beyond the reach of Fortune, but, on the contrary, since we know that the corrupt and perishable part of man wherein he lies open to Fortune is small, and that we ourselves are masters of the better part, in which the greatest of our blessings are situated—right opinions and knowledge and the exercise of reason terminating in the acquisition of virtue, all of which have their being inalienable and indestructible—knowing this, we should face the future undaunted and confident" (*Mor.* 475C–D). Fate (ἡ τύχη) can strike human beings with misfortune and sickness, but if they use insights from philosophy and virtue (ἡ ἀρετή), they will not be overcome by them. Paul, however, does not share this view that people have such inherent capacities at their disposal, as though they had resources within themselves by which they could autonomously deal with their own tendencies and emotions, and direct their own conduct. He attributes this power neither to reason nor to virtue. On the contrary, human beings have an internal separation between willing and doing and cannot unify their existence on their own. For Paul, the ground of human possibilities for a successful life lies beyond human beings themselves. It is not the model of autonomy, but that of heteronomy, that determines Pauline anthropology: it is God himself, who gives human beings a new life through Jesus Christ in the Holy Spirit, a life that is realized in baptism, faith, life in the power of the Spirit. The "new creation" (2 Cor. 5:17) does not have to be constructed and manipulated by human beings but is God's own creation.

This concept is both a religious experience and an intellectual achievement. It would be a total misunderstanding to subsume Paul's anthropology under a pessimistic view of humanity; *his view of human beings is not merely pessimistic, but realistic!* This is also where its intellectual strength is to be found: Paul by no means denies the destructiveness of human being and acting, but does not consider it the last word. With his affirmations of love, faith, and hope, he places the positive dynamics of human being at the center of his understanding of humanity.

6.6 Ethics

Paul does not outline his ethic on the basis of knowing and acting, as though it were a subject who acts autonomously as a reasonable and moral being,[366]

366. So, for example, the Stoic concept, in which human beings participate in the divine reason that permeates all things, so that to live a moral life is to live in accord with this divine reason. Cf. Musonius, *Diss.* 2: "the disposition to morality resides in the soul of man . . . the seed of virtue [σπέρμα ἀρετῆς] implanted." It is especially by practice that this positive disposition

but, in accord with his theology as a whole, chooses as his point of departure the image of participation in the new being, an existence delivered from the power of sin. This image takes concrete form in new actions. Paul constantly reminds the churches of the bases and results of such a life.[367]

6.6.1 Participation and Correspondence

Interpreters often express the basic idea of Paul's ethic on the model of indicative and imperative.[368] "The indicative is the foundation for the imperative."[369] However, the indicative-imperative schema cannot really bear the weight of the Pauline ethic,[370] for it is static in nature and fails to grasp the dynamic structures of the Pauline ethic as a whole; it makes an artificial division in what Paul presents as a more sweeping continuity embracing being and life.[371] The Pauline ethic does not fall apart into particular aspects but must be seen within the framework of the fundamental unity of being and acting in the power of the Spirit.

The point of departure for Paul's understanding of ethics is the new being, since incorporation into the death and resurrection of Jesus Christ is not limited to the act of baptism but, through the gift of the Spirit, determines the present and future life of those who are baptized (cf. Gal. 3:2, 3; 5:18;

---

is built up. On the Stoic ethical system cf. Maximilian Forschner, *Die stoische Ethik: Über den Zusammenhang von Natur-, Sprach- und Moralphilosophie im altstoischen System* (Stuttgart: Klett-Cotta, 1981).

367. This raises the question of the relation of ethics and ethos. The two are usually distinguished as follows: Ethics indicates a theoretical approach to the philosophical/theological understanding of moral values, norms, and actions. In contrast, ethos refers to the practical, typical way of life of a person or group that does not always require to be grounded and thought through. Cf. Michael Wolter, "Christliches Ethos nach der Offenbarung des Johannes," in *Studien zur Johannesoffenbarung und ihrer Auslegung: Festschrift für Otto Böcher zum 70. Geburtstag* (ed. Friedrich Wilhelm Horn and Michael Wolter; Neukirchen-Vluyn: Neukirchener Verlag, 2005), 191.

368. Survey of research in Folker Blischke, *Die Begründung und die Durchsetzung der Ethik bei Paulus* (Leipzig: Evangelische Verlagsanstalt, 2007), 21–38.

369. Bultmann, *Theology of the New Testament*, 1:332.

370. The problems of the indicative-imperative schema are seen most clearly by Hans Windisch, "Das Problem des paulinischen Imperativs," *ZNW* 23 (1924): 265–81. Of the recent research, cf. especially K. Backhaus, "Evangelium als Lebensraum: Christologie und Ethik bei Paulus," in *Paulinische Christologie: Exegetische Beiträge; Hans Hübner zum 70. Geburtstag* (ed. Udo Schnelle et al.; Göttingen: Vandenhoeck & Ruprecht, 2000), 9–14; Blischke, *Ethik bei Paulus*, passim; R. Zimmermann, "Jenseits von Indikativ und Imperativ," *TLZ* 132 (2007): 259–84.

371. The most important issue: how can the gift of salvation become a task to be completed? Cf. Klaus Wengst, "Gesetz und Gnade," in *Ja und Nein: Christliche Theologie im Angesicht Israels; Festschrift zum 70. Geburtstag von Wolfgang Schrage* (ed. Klaus Wengst et al.; Neukirchen-Vluyn: Neukirchener Verlag, 1998), 172. Additional problematic areas: Must the newness of the new being first be realized? Are baptized believers set free only "on probation"? In what does the actual soteriological quality of the imperative consist?

Rom. 6:4). Those whose lives are now located within the sphere of Christ are new creations (cf. 2 Cor. 5:7); where Paul speaks of newness of life, he builds on a christological foundation, not an ethical one (cf. 2 Cor. 4:16; 5:17; Gal. 6:15; Rom. 6:4; 7:6). Those who have been baptized have put on Christ (Gal. 3:27) and are entirely determined by him, for Christ lives in them and wants to be formed in them (cf. Gal. 4:19). Jesus Christ is both prototype and model [*Urbild und Vorbild*], as the ethical interpretation of the Christ hymn in Phil. 2:6–11 makes clear. For Paul, Christ himself appears as the content and constant theme of ethics.[372] *The theme of ethics is what the new being (the new life in the sphere of Christ) looks like as expressed in what one does and the way one lives.* What has happened to baptized believers has placed its stamp on their whole life. Just as Christ died to sin once and for all, so those who have been baptized are no longer under the power of sin (Rom. 6:9–11). Just as Jesus obediently walked the way of the cross and overcame sin and death (Rom. 5:19; Phil. 2:8), so Paul challenges the Roman Christians to be obedient servants of righteousness (Rom. 6:16; cf. 1 Cor. 9:19). Christ gave himself up for our sins; he was not concerned for his own advantage (Gal. 1:4; Rom. 3:25; 8:32). Because Christ died out of love for humanity and this love now controls and sustains the church (2 Cor. 5:14; Rom. 8:35, 37), it determines the Christian life as a whole (1 Cor. 8:1; 13; Gal. 5:6, 22; Rom. 12:9–10; 13:9–10; 14:15). Just as Christ became the servant of humanity by going to the cross (Rom. 15:8; Phil. 2:6ff.), so Christians are to serve one another (Gal. 2:6). What began in baptism continues in the lives of those baptized: they have been placed on the way of Jesus, they imitate Christ, so that the apostle can even say, "Be imitators of me, as I am of Christ" (1 Cor. 11:1; cf. 1 Thess. 1:6; 1 Cor. 4:16). The Christian life is founded on Jesus's way to the cross, which is at the same time the essential criterion of this life. The ethical *proprium christianum* is thus Christ himself,[373] so that for Paul, ethics means the active dimension of participation in Christ.

Against this background, the texts in which the apostle speaks explicitly of the relation between Christology (or soteriology) and ethics become clear. In 1 Cor. 5:7a Paul at first formulates in the imperative ("Clean out the old yeast so that you may be a new batch") and only then adds the first basis for this action: "as [καθώς] you really are unleavened." The content of the admonition to the Corinthians is identical with the affirmation of what they already are; that is, it is a matter of two aspects of a single reality, which Paul then names

372. Cf. on this point Heinz Schürmann, "'Das Gesetz des Christus' Gal 6,2: Jesu Verhalten und Wort als letztgültige sittliche Norm nach Paulus," in *Studien zur neutestamentlichen Ethik* (ed. Heinz Schürmann and Thomas Söding; SBAB 7; Stuttgart: Verlag Katholisches Bibelwerk, 1990), 53–77.

373. On the problem of the *proprium* (that which is characteristically Christian) of the Pauline and New Testament ethic, cf. Georg Strecker, "Strukturen einer neutestamentlichen Ethik," *ZTK* 75 (1978): 136ff.

as the second basis for this action: "For [καὶ γάρ] our paschal lamb, Christ, has been sacrificed" (1 Cor. 5:7b). The new being gained through Christ does not permit the purity and holiness of the church to be violated; baptized believers are to live out what they are already. Galatians 5:25 also points in this direction: "If we live in the Spirit, let us also be in harmony with the Spirit" (Εἰ ζῶμεν πνεύματι, πνεύματι καὶ στοιχῶμεν).[374] By no means is the verb στοιχέω to be taken merely as a synonym for περιπατέω (walk); it means "agree with," "be in harmony with." The accent is thus not placed on the demand; rather, it is a matter of a relationship, which is expressed with the dative πνεύματι (in/by the Spirit): live in harmony with the Spirit. It is the Spirit of God, who is responsible for both the willing and the doing (Phil. 1:6; cf. 2:13). What they have already attained should now be lived out (Phil. 3:16). It is thus not a matter of realizing a gift but of abiding and living in the realm of grace, and that means in the sphere of Christ. "To be a Christian is mimesis of Christ,"[375] and the form of the new life that corresponds to Christ is love (cf. Gal. 5:13). In the Pauline ethic, love is the critical principle of interpretation by which everything is to be oriented; it is the goal of every action.[376] Whoever does not act out of love is out of step with the new being (cf. 1 Cor. 3:17; 6:9–10; 8:9–13; 10:1ff.; 2 Cor. 6:1; 11:13–15; Gal. 5:2–4, 21; Rom. 6:12ff.; 11:20–22; 14:13ff.). This always happens when believers do not recognize the new orientation for their life,[377] when they fall back into old ways of thinking and living, or when they suppose that they are already in the state of perfection.

The beginning point and foundation of Paul's ethic are the unity of life and action of the new being as participation in the Christ event. Jesus Christ provides both the foundation and the character for the Christian life, and Christians are those who live in the sphere of Christ by the power of the Spirit and whose actions correspond to this new being.

6.6.2 The New Way of Life in Practice

The instructions Paul gives for the Christian life, and the reasons for following his instructions, vary from letter to letter. In 1 Thessalonians the near parousia of the Lord and the related understanding of judgment function as the motivation for a blameless life in holiness (cf. 1 Thess. 3:13; 4:3, 4, 7; 5:23).[378] Paul explicitly acknowledges the ethical status of the church but at

374. The translation reflects Gerhard Delling, "στοιχέω κτλ.," *TDNT* 7:667–69.

375. Backhaus, "Evangelium als Lebensraum," 24.

376. Cf. Weder, "Normativität," 136ff.

377. Paul designates this new existence with the verb φρονέω, found twenty-two times in Paul. Cf. Backhaus, "Evangelium als Lebensraum," 28–30.

378. Cf. Udo Schnelle, "Die Ethik des 1. Thessalonikerbriefes," in *The Thessalonian Correspondence* (ed. Raymond F. Collins and Norbert Baumert; BETL 87; Louvain: University Press, 1990), 295–305; Blischke, *Ethik bei Paulus*, 39–99.

the same time encourages it to make further progress (cf. 1 Thess. 4:1–2). In 4:3–8, the contents of Paul's admonitions to live a moral and honorable life remain within the framework of the ethic of Hellenistic Judaism. In accordance with the conventional ethics prevalent in the whole letter, the church is instructed to live quietly and unobtrusively (1 Thess. 4:11) so that outsiders are not offended (4:12). The ethical competence of non-Christian Gentiles that Paul here presupposes shows that he is not striving for some sort of ethical superiority in the church. He does not base his instructions on the Old Testament; he makes his point of departure the ethos already valued by both Christians and the surrounding pagan world.

The two Corinthian letters present a differentiated picture.[379] The Corinthians are exhorted, like all the other churches, to adopt Paul's teaching and way of life as the pattern of their own lives (1 Cor. 4:16–17). That Paul again takes up the word ὁδός (way) in 12:31 shows that he intends the way of love. He lives and teaches the love of Christ that has been received; this is why the churches should adopt him as their model. The instructions Paul adds in 1 Cor. 5–7, dealing with various conflicts, reveal the very different sorts of argument Paul might use to support his ethics. Although in 5:13b Paul can support his case for excluding the immoral person from the church by citing Deut. 17:7b LXX, what really bothers him is that such things do not occur even among non-Christian Gentiles (cf. 1 Cor. 5:1b). Paul's prohibition in 1 Cor. 6:1–11 of settling legal disputes among Christians by going to pagan courts has no parallel in Jewish tradition.[380] Paul does not support the warning against immorality in 1 Cor. 6:12–20 with biblical texts that deal with the same subject matter, such as Prov. 5:3; 6:20–7:27; Sir. 9:6; 19:2; instead, he cites Gen. 2:24, a text that originally had nothing to do with the theme of immorality. So also in 1 Cor. 7, biblical texts play no role as bases for his ethical instructions and recommendations. There are, in fact, no Old Testament texts that support the apostle's tendentious critique of marriage. There are, however, parallels with Cynic instruction: marriage and children hinder the Cynic from his real mission of being the gods' scout and herald among human beings (cf. Epictetus, *Diatr.* 3.22.67–82). The prohibition of divorce given by the Lord (1 Cor. 7:10–11) contradicts explicit regulations of the Torah (one need only see Deut. 24:1). In 1 Cor. 7:17–24 Paul develops the ethical maxim of remaining in the status in which one was called, which is likewise to be understood against a Cynic-Stoic background.[381] One's actions must always be oriented to existing circumstances, for a false understanding of things produces suffering (cf. Teles, frg. 2). So also, 1 Cor. 7:19 reflects Hellenistic influence, for "obeying the

379. For analysis, cf. Lindemann, "Toragebote," 95–110; Michael Wolter, "Ethos und Identität in paulinischen Gemeinden," *NTS* 43 (1997): 435ff.; Blischke, *Ethik bei Paulus*, 100–239.

380. Cf. the parallel in Plato, *Gorg.* 509c (*NW* 2.1:278).

381. Extensive evidence is given in Will Deming, *Paul on Marriage and Celibacy: The Hellenistic Background of 1 Corinthians 7* (2nd ed.; Grand Rapids: Eerdmans, 2003), 159–65.

commandments of God" (τήρησις ἐντολῶν θεοῦ) cannot refer to the Torah, for the Torah commands circumcision; it is not an indifferent matter, as in 1 Cor. 7:19a. Paul again proceeds on the basis of a general understanding of what is considered ethical; there is direct access to the commands of God, into which human beings as such can have insight.[382] Scriptural quotations (cf. 1 Cor. 10:7, 26) and allusions (cf. 11:3, 8, 9) do have some weight in the argumentation of 10:1–11:1. Even here, however, Paul does not derive his instructions directly from Scripture.[383]

Second Corinthians confirms this judgment, for the only two relevant citations of Scripture in 2 Cor. 8:15 and 9:9 merely provide the basis for the promise that those who contribute to the collection will receive surpassing grace from God. In Gal. 5:14 Paul cites Lev. 19:18b, where it is clearly a matter of the love that has appeared in Jesus Christ (cf. Gal. 5:6). The norm of the new being is exclusively the Spirit, who explicitly appears in 5:18 as *the* contrast to the Torah.[384] The Christian (and Hellenistic) virtues of love, joy, peace, patience, kindness, generosity, faithfulness, gentleness, and self-control (5:22–23a) are traced back exclusively to the Spirit. It is only as an addendum that Paul notes, "There is no law against such things" (5:23b). In particular, the catalogs of virtues and vices (cf. 1 Cor. 5:10–11; 6:9–10; 2 Cor. 12:20–21; Gal. 5:19–23; Rom. 1:29–31) develop an ethical model that is interested in accommodation to the conventions of the time. They originated in Hellenistic philosophy, found acceptance in Hellenistic Jewish literature, and were very popular, especially in New Testament times.[385]

The assumption that there is a common moral standard among Jews, pagans, and Christians is Paul's point of departure for his argument in Rom. 2:14–15 (cf. also 13:13).[386] He adopts the Hellenistic idea that ethical instruction comes through nature, the reason/logos, apart from external, that is, written laws.[387] So also in 12:1–2, Paul does not derive the will of God from the Torah. These

382. Epictetus argues similarly: "What directions shall I give you? Has not Zeus given you directions? Has he not given you that which is your own, unhindered and unrestrained, while that which is not your own is subject to hindrance and restraint?" (*Diatr*. 1.25.3).

383. Cf. Lindemann, "Toragebote," 110: "Paul's concrete instructions in 1 Corinthians show that Paul is not oriented to the Torah when he is giving ethical norms or making decisions in conflict situations."

384. For analysis, cf. Blischke, *Ethik bei Paulus*, 240–306.

385. Cf. the materials edited in Siegfried Wibbing, *Die Tugend- und Lasterkataloge im Neuen Testament und ihre Traditionsgeschichte unter besonderer Berücksichtigung der Qumran-Texte* (BZNW 25; Berlin: Töpelmann, 1959); Ehrhard Kamlah, *Die Form der katalogischen Paränese im Neuen Testament* (WUNT 7; Tübingen: Mohr, 1964). Sample texts are given in *NW* 2.1:54–66; 575–76.

386. For Romans, cf. Blischke, *Ethik bei Paulus*, 307–69.

387. Cf. the documentation in *NW* 2.1:71–85. The oldest extant example of the concept of a reasonable ethic is probably Heraclitus, frg. 112: "To think reasonably is the greatest virtue [σωφρονεῖν ἀρετὴ μεγίστη], and wisdom consists in speaking the truth and living in harmony with nature, harkening to it."

first two verses constitute a kind of title for this major division of the letter devoted to ethics and serve to guide the reader; they define the framework of reference within which the following statements are to be understood. The Roman Christians should themselves determine what the will of God is, on the basis of their own investigation and reflection (12:2, δοκιμάζειν ὑμᾶς τί τὸ θέλημα τοῦ θεοῦ [discern what is the will of God]), and they thereby undertake a task also given to philosophers when they inquire what is good, evil, or indifferent. "Therefore, the first and greatest task of the philosopher is to test the impressions [δοκιμάζειν τὰς φαντασίας] and discriminate [διακρίνειν] between them, and to apply none that has not been tested" (Epictetus, *Diatr.* 1.20.6–7). Paul labels the will of God with the standard categories of popular philosophy: the good, the acceptable, the perfect. The correspondence between Rom. 12:1–2 and 12:9ff. clarifies this: "Love is the Christian definition of the good."[388] In the tradition of philosophical critique of the cult,[389] Christians are challenged to present their bodies as acceptable sacrifices to God, for this is their "reasonable worship" (λογικὴ λατρεία; NRSV "spiritual worship"). The new understanding of God has a corresponding reasonable worship, oriented to the reason that is itself the gift of God.

In Rom. 13:1–7 Paul deals with the relation of the Christian to the state. The section is intentionally permeated with secular terms and concepts,[390] which make a direct christological interpretation impossible. The Roman church should fit itself into the created structures of the world. The general admonition calling for obedience is concretized with the example of 13:6: the Romans pay taxes and thereby acknowledge the authorities established by God. The imperial officials in charge of taxes and customs carry out their work as nothing less than λειτουργοὶ θεοῦ (God's servants). In 13:7 Paul concludes his instruction with a generalization: "Pay to all what is due them—taxes to whom taxes are due, revenue to whom revenue is due, respect to whom respect is due, honor to whom honor is due." The interpretation of this disputed passage must attend carefully to its location within the structure of Romans: it is parenesis, not dogmatics![391] Since the state accepts the tasks of administering

388. Wilckens, *Römer*, 3:20.

389. Philo states: "What is precious in the sight of God is not the number of victims immolated but the true purity of a rational spirit [πνεῦμα λογικόν] in him who makes the sacrifice" (*Spec. Laws* 1.277). So also, Dio Chrysostom says of the just ruler: "being firmly resolved in his own heart never to receive a gift from wicked men, he believes that the gods also do not delight in the offerings or sacrifices of the unjust, but accept the gifts made by the good alone" (*Or.* 3.52–53; cf. also 13.35; 31.15; 43.11). More examples in H. Wenschkewitz, "Die Spiritualisierung der Kultusbegriffe," *Angelos* 4 (1932): 74–151; *NW* 1.2:220–34.

390. Basic proof given in A. Strobel, "Zum Verständnis von Röm 13," *ZNW* 47 (1956): 67–93; cf. also Haacker, *Die Brief des Paulus an die Römer*, 293–303; texts are cited in *NW* 2.1:199–206.

391. Cf. Käsemann, *Romans*, 359. Extensive reflections on the pragmatics of the text are found in Helmut Merklein, "Sinn und Zweck von Röm 13,1–7: Zur semantischen und pragmatischen

and putting into effect the power assigned it by God, Christians are responsible to support it in these tasks. Moreover, 13:1–7 manifests *a political connotation currently relevant to Paul's readers*, for his instruction to acknowledge the political authorities, and thus the *Pax Romana*,[392] is probably to be understood against the background of the increasing tensions between the Roman authorities and the independent movement that was developing into a recognizably Christian community.[393] The Romans are beginning to perceive the Christians as a group that worships an executed criminal as a god and that proclaims the imminent end of the world. The Neronian persecution of 64 CE, only eight years after Romans was written, shows that there must have been increasing tensions between the Christians on the one hand and the Roman authorities and people on the other.

Paul most clearly takes up the terminology of popular philosophy in Phil. 4:8: "Finally, beloved, whatever is true, whatever is honorable, whatever is just, whatever is pure, whatever is pleasing, whatever is commendable, if there is any excellence and if there is anything worthy of praise, think about these things." In Paul's list, especially εὔφημος (commendable) and ἔπαινος ([worthy of] praise) are noteworthy as political-social terms; they are aimed at social acceptance, which Paul expects from the church in Philippi. When he uses ἀρετή (virtue), he is adopting the key concept in Greek educational theory and integrating the life of the Philippians thoroughly into the contemporary ethos. It is, after all, the task of the philosopher who is active in the political and social scene to make clear "what justice is, what a sense of duty is, what the capacity to suffer is, what bravery, disdain for death, knowledge of God is, and what a precious good a good conscience is."[394] As a lifestyle and technique for happiness, as the "science of life,"[395] it becomes the task of philosophy to enliven the capacity for virtue already present in humanity or to cultivate

Struktur eines umstrittenen Textes," in *Studien zu Jesus und Paulus* (2 vols.; WUNT 43, 105; Tübingen: Mohr, 1987–98), 2:405–37.

392. On this point cf. Klaus Wengst, *Pax Romana: And the Peace of Jesus Christ* (Philadelphia: Fortress, 1987), 19–71; Riedo-Emmenegger, *Prophetisch-messianische Provokateure*, 5–196. From the time of Augustus, at the center of this concept stood the emperor himself, who, as the Pontifex Maximus, guaranteed the continuation and cohesion of the Imperium Romanum, holding together the commonwealth and assuring peace and prosperity by his clever politics. As a sample text, cf. Valerius Maximus, book 1; Plutarch, *Num.* 9: "The chief of the Pontifices, the Pontifex Maximus, had the duty of expounding and interpreting the divine will, or rather of directing sacred rites, not only being in charge of public ceremonies, but also watching over private sacrifices and preventing any departure from established custom, as well as teaching whatever was requisite for the worship or propiation of the gods."

393. Johannes Friedrich et al. ("Zur historischen Situation und Intention von Röm 13,1–7," *ZTK* 73 [1976]: 131–66), with reference to Tacitus, *Ann.* 13.50–51 (restrained protest against the tax pressure in 58 CE), see the historical background of Rom. 13:1–7 in the increased burden of Roman taxes on the citizenry that occurred in 58 CE.

394. Seneca, *Tranq.* 3.4.

395. Cicero, *Fin.* 3.4: "Philosophy is the science of life."

insight in human beings so that they may orient their lives to these virtues. Because a moral life is synonymous with philosophy and because philosophy teaches how to live,[396] it can be thoroughly compared with the paraclesis of the apostle.

The material content of the paraclesis[397] of the Pauline letters is not basically different from the ethical standards of the surrounding world. Paul uses the Old Testament as a normative ethical authority only in a very reserved manner; the Torah is concentrated into the love command (cf. Rom. 13:8–10) and thus integrated into the contemporary ethos (see above, §6.5.3). *Nonetheless, the love commandment is given a more exclusive place than in any contemporary ethical system.*[398] Love was appropriate in a particular way as the fundamental ethical principle, because it could equally comprehend the new relation to God that was received as a gift, the new self-understanding, and the changed relationship to the neighbor.[399] When Paul begins to speak of the aspects of the new being that call for ethical action, he activates the memory of his hearers and readers and strives for solutions to their problems. Paul does not emphasize that the material content of his ethical instruction is new, but that it has a new *basis*. He evaluates the human capacity for action and its development in the light of the Christ event and proceeds from there to a new interpretation of life and history, which is fundamentally different from the Hellenistic ethic of reason:[400] only participation in the Christ event frees from the power of sin and enables, by the power of the Holy Spirit, a life lived in love that conforms to Christ's own life, a life that will endure beyond death and the judgment.

396. Cf. Seneca, *Ep.* 20.2: "Philosophy teaches to act, not to speak."

397. The term *paraclēsis* better expresses the basic Pauline approach than *parenesis*: *Paraclēsis* is used by Paul himself (παρακαλέω, thirty-nine times; παράκλησις, eighteen times), but not *parenesis* (παραινέω in the New Testament only Acts 27:9, 22); cf. Anton Grabner-Haider, *Paraklese und Eschatologie bei Paulus: Mensch und Welt im Anspruch der Zukunft Gottes* (NTA NF 4; Münster: Aschendorff, 1968).

398. Cf. Michael Wolter, "Die ethische Identität christlicher Gemeinden in neutestamentlicher Zeit," in *Marburger Jahrbuch Theologie*, vol. 13, *Woran orientiert sich Ethik?* (MTS 67; Marburg: Elwert, 2001), 80–84.

399. Cf. Söding, *Liebesgebot*, 272: "The love commandment is the core statement of Pauline ethics."

400. The decisive difference between Paul and the (Stoic) ethic of reason, which was also entirely oriented to a theological understanding of life (cf., e.g., Cicero, *Leg.* 1.33–34 or Epictetus, *Diatr.* 1.1.7), is their contrasting evaluations of the reality of evil and the capability of human beings to extract themselves from this reality. Stoic ethics are characterized by the idea of moral development. "They reach their peak in the knowledge that happiness consists in complete harmony of the person with himself or herself, and that this can only be attained by reason, by harmony with the divine world-reason" (Maximilian Forschner, "Das Gute und die Güter: Zur stoischen Begründung des Wertvollen," in *Über das Handeln im Einklang mit der Natur: Grundlagen ethischer Verständigung* [ed. Maximilian Forschner; Darmstadt: Primus, 1998], 46). The obviously widespread deviation from this ideal is mostly explained with a lack of insight into these relationships and the "evil" of humanity.

At the same time, early Christianity participates in a highly reflective Jewish-Hellenistic and Greco-Roman ethical tradition. What is essentially human must not be newly created and thought through, but it does appear in a new perspective—the perspective of faith, manifest in the way one lives. Pauline paraclesis aims at a life lived in accord with the Christ event and points to an inner concord between the gospel that is believed and the gospel as lived. It is a matter of knowing and living out the innate unity of faith and life in the power of the Spirit. The Pauline ethic is equally an ethic of command and an ethic of insight.

6.7 Ecclesiology

For Paul, participation in the salvation Christians have in common can happen only in the fellowship of believers. For him, being a Christian is identical with being in the church; his mission is a church-founding mission, and his letters are church letters.

6.7.1 Basic Ecclesiological Terms

Of the 114 instances of ἐκκλησία (church, congregation) in the New Testament, 44 are found in Paul, and of these, 31 are found in the two Corinthian letters. In adopting the term ἐκκλησία to designate the essential nature of the local assemblies of the new community, Paul takes up a word with political overtones. In the Greek-Hellenistic realm, ἐκκλησία refers to the assembly of free men with the right to vote, a usage also found in Acts 19:32, 39.[401] First Thessalonians 2:14, 1 Cor. 15:9, Gal. 1:13, and Phil. 3:6 (Paul a persecutor of the church) show that the designation ἐκκλησία τοῦ θεοῦ (assembly of God) had already been used in Jerusalem for the new movement of believers in Christ. On the one hand, ἐκκλησία is taken from the Septuagint as the translation of קהל,[402] relating the Christian community to Israel as the people of God, and on the other hand the fact that συναγωγή (synagogue) was *not* taken over shows that the self-understanding of the earliest church distinguished itself from Judaism.

With the semantic neologism ἐκκλησία τοῦ θεοῦ, the new movement identified itself as an independent reality.[403] Paul intentionally orients his own

401. On the whole subject, cf. Andrew D. Clarke, *Serve the Community of the Church: Christians as Leaders and Ministers* (Grand Rapids: Eerdmans, 2000), 11–33.

402. Cf. Deut. 23:2–4; Num. 16:3; 20:4; Mic. 2:5; 1 Chron. 28:8; קהל can also be translated as συναγωγή; cf., e.g., Isa. 56:8; Jer. 38:4; Ezek. 37:10. On the various derivation theories, cf. Jürgen Roloff, "Ἐκκλησία," *EDNT* 1:411–12.

403. The Greek construction ἐκκλησία τοῦ θεοῦ is found only in Paul (1 Thess. 2:14; 1 Cor. 1:2; 10:32; 11:16, 22; 15:9; 2 Cor. 1:1; Gal. 1:13) and in literature dependent on him (Acts 20:28; 2 Thess. 1:1, 4; 1 Tim. 3:5, 15).

understanding to the basic secular meaning of ἐκκλησία, for he considers the local assembly of believers to be of primary importance, as indicated by the local designations in 1 Thess. 1:1; 1 Cor. 1:2; 2 Cor. 1:1; Gal. 1:2.[404] At the same time, it is the one church of God that is represented in each local manifestation, so that the designation ἐκκλησία τοῦ θεοῦ can be applied to the local congregation (1 Thess. 1:1; 1 Cor. 1:2), to the group of congregations in the same area (2 Cor. 1:1; Gal. 1:2), and to Christianity as a whole (1 Thess. 2:14; 1 Cor. 10:32; 11:16, 22; 12:28; 15:9; Gal. 1:13; Phil. 3:6). For Paul, the local congregation represents the whole church in a particular location;[405] he knows *no hierarchical structure that connects local congregations and the whole church*, but each part or manifestation of the church can in turn stand for the whole. The whole church is present in the local congregation, and the local congregation is a part of the whole church. Thus, terminologically, ἐκκλησία as the assembly of Christians in one location should be translated "congregation" (*Gemeinde*), and when it means the worldwide group of Christians as a whole, it should be translated "church" (*Kirche*).[406]

Paul also uses ecclesiological terminology adopted from the tradition history of Old Testament–Jewish imagery and from the pre-Pauline tradition, such as "the saints" (οἱ ἅγιοι) and "the elect" (οἱ ἐκλεκτοί). Very often the prescript of the letters includes a designation of the congregation as ἅγιοι (1 Cor. 1:2; 2 Cor. 1:1; Rom. 1:7; Phil. 1:1), which, like ἐκκλησία τοῦ θεοῦ, can be used alternatively for individual congregations (1 Cor. 16:1; 2 Cor. 8:4; Rom. 15:26) and for the whole church (1 Cor. 14:33, ταῖς ἐκκλησίαις τῶν ἁγίων [the churches of the saints]). For Paul, Christians are not "saints" on the basis of a special ethical quality but as those who have been incorporated by baptism into God's saving act in Jesus Christ. They belong to God, the Spirit of God dwells in them (1 Cor. 3:16; 6:19), and their body is holy because it is the temple of God (1 Cor. 3:17b). In direct connection with ἐκκλησία and in close proximity to ἅγιος stands the word group κλητός (called), κλῆσις (calling), ἐκλογή (election), and ἐκλεκτός (elect);[407] this word group is of great significance for Pauline ecclesiology. In 1 Thess. 1:4 Paul gives thanks for the election (ἐκλογή) of the Thessalonian Christians, who had been converted from paganism. In 1 Cor. 1:26ff. Paul interprets the calling (κλῆσις) of the weak, foolish, and disdained of this world as the confirmation of the paradoxical act of God on the cross. Election is entirely a matter of grace (Gal. 1:6; Rom. 1:6), so that

404. Cf. Roloff, *Kirche im Neuen Testament*, 98–99.

405. Cf. Käsemann, *Romans*, 336.

406. Cf. Roloff, "Ἐκκλησία," 1:413. [This distinction is more important in Europe, where there is a long tradition of an established church, than in North America and other English-speaking areas, where "church" has always been used for the local congregation, for groups of congregations, for the denomination, and for the church as a whole. I have therefore not attempted to maintain this distinction consistently in the English translation.—MEB]

407. Cf. Conzelmann, *1 Corinthians*, 25–29.

Paul can speak of a predestination of believers that will be eschatologically validated (Rom. 8:29–39; cf. 1 Cor. 2:7). One can see how closely calling and sanctification belong together for Paul by noting 1 Cor. 1:2 and Rom. 1:7, where he speaks of "called saints." Those whom God has called, separated (cf. Gal. 1:15; Rom. 1:1), and laid hold of are indeed holy.

Foundational Metaphors

Alongside the primary ecclesiological vocabulary, Paul's statements about the church are characterized by *three foundational metaphors*: "in Christ" (ἐν Χριστῷ), "body of Christ" (σῶμα Χριστοῦ), and "people of God" (λαὸς θεοῦ). Their space and time aspects provide a comprehensive portrayal of the location and nature of Christian existence in the community of believers.

1. The phrase ἐν Χριστῷ designates the location of the Christian life as that close, saving relation of every individual Christian, and all of them together, with Jesus Christ (see above, §6.4.1). By baptism believers are incorporated into the sphere of the spiritual Christ and are ἐν Χριστῷ a new creation (2 Cor. 5:17). The baptized have "in Christ" a participation in the κοινωνία (fellowship, communion) of the one Spirit (2 Cor. 13:13; Phil. 2:1), which now determines their life in the church. Incorporation into the sphere of lordship of Christ has concrete effects both in the life of the individual believer and in shaping the life of the church. It is the basis not only for communion with Christ, but also makes possible a new fellowship of believers with one another (cf. Gal. 3:26–28). While in Roman society one's family background and social class were determinative for one's status, in the Christian community the fundamental distinctions hallowed by antiquity, based on family, gender, and race, no longer counted (cf. 1 Cor. 12:13; Gal. 3:26–28; Rom. 1:14). All are "children of God," all are "one in Christ Jesus" (Gal. 3:26, 28)—hence arises a completely new openness in how people are perceived and how one relates to them. This was an important reason for the success of the early Christian mission.[408]

2. The christological foundation of Paul's ecclesiology is also seen in the σῶμα Χριστοῦ imagery, for the idea of incorporation into the body of Christ emphasizes the priority of Christology to ecclesiology. The point of departure for the ecclesiological use of σῶμα in Paul is the way σῶμα Χριστοῦ is spoken of in Rom. 7:4 and in the eucharistic tradition (1 Cor. 10:16; 11:27). Whereas σῶμα Χριστοῦ in 1 Cor. 10:16; 11:27; and Rom. 7:4 means the body of Christ

408. Cf. Eva Ebel, *Die Attraktivität früher christlicher Gemeinden: Die Gemeinde von Korinth im Spiegel griechisch-römischer Vereine* (WUNT 2.178; Tübingen: Mohr Siebeck, 2004), who sees the key to the success of the early Christian congregations in their openness to people of every social status, all vocations, and both sexes. This openness was their greatest contrast to pagan associations. The conversion of "whole houses" (cf. 1 Cor. 1:16; Acts 16:15; 18:8) shows that those who belonged to every status and layer of society could belong to the new community. Because there were no entrance requirements that excluded them, especially women and members of the lower social classes (particularly slaves) joined the new communities in great numbers.

given on the cross for the church, in 1 Cor. 10:17 the ecclesiological inference is drawn from ἕν σῶμα οἱ πολλοί ἐσμεν (we who are many are one body). The fundamental identification of the church with the body of Christ is explicitly found only in 1 Cor. 12:27: Ὑμεῖς δέ ἐστε σῶμα Χριστοῦ (now you are the body of Christ). Paul also makes use of this image in 1 Cor. 1:13; 6:15–16; 10:17; Rom. 12:5; and 1 Cor. 12:12–27.[409] In 1 Cor. 12:13 ("For in the one Spirit we were all baptized into one body"), Paul develops the idea of the σῶμα Χριστοῦ in a characteristic manner: (a) In regard to its members, the body of Christ is preexistent. It does not come into being by human decisions and mergers but is a pre-given reality that makes these possible in the first place. (b) By baptism the individual Christian is integrated into the body of Christ that already existed. Baptism does not constitute the body of Christ but is the historical location of reception into this body and the concrete expression of the unity of the church grounded in Christ. The exalted Christ does not exist without his body, the church. So also, participation in the σῶμα Χριστοῦ manifests itself precisely in the corporeality of the believer: "Do you not know that your bodies are members of Christ?" (1 Cor. 6:15). Because believers, including their bodies, belong totally to their Lord, they are at the same time members of the body of Christ.

Just as the body is one even though it has many members, so in the church there are many callings and gifts but only one church (1 Cor. 1:10–17; 12:12ff.; Rom. 12:5). The multiplicity of charisms and the unity of the church are complementary ideas. Likewise the relation of individual members to each other may illustrate the concept of the body: they are not all the same, but all are interconnected and need each other, and thus they are all of equal value. The church does not form the body of Christ by its own actions, but its conduct corresponds to this body.

3. The programmatic proclamation of the gospel to Gentiles without the precondition of circumcision presented Paul with the challenge of understanding the continuity and discontinuity of the church with Israel.[410] In this context, the linguistic usage of the apostle is noteworthy, for Paul refers to the "people [of God]" (λαὸς [θεοῦ]) only five times, all in citations from the Old Testament, and it is not accidental that four of these are found in his Letter to the Romans (1 Cor. 10:7/Exod. 32:6; Rom. 9:25–26/Hos. 2:25; Rom. 10:21/Isa. 65:2; Rom. 11:1–2/Ps. 93:14 LXX [Ps. 94:14]; Rom. 15:10/Deut. 32:43). Moreover, the apostle explicitly avoids speaking of the *one* people of God

409. On this point cf. Eduard Schweizer and Friedrich Baumgärtel, "σῶμα," *TDNT* 7:1063–66.

410. In the Old Testament and the literature of ancient Judaism, numerous texts testify to reflection on the integration of the Gentiles into the people of God (for an analysis, cf. Kraus, *Das Volk Gottes*, 16–110). However, the Gentile mission with no requirement of circumcision represented a completely new phenomenon that is illuminated by these texts but cannot be reduced to what is already found in them.

composed of Jews and Gentiles, or of the "old" and "new" people of God. Nonetheless, showing the unity of God's acts in history and the continuity of the people of God in salvation history is a central theme of Pauline ecclesiology. The apostle wrestled with this theme his whole life, as shown by the different positions he assumes in his letters and by his organizing the collection for the Jerusalem church (see below, §6.8.4).

Paul speaks of the election of the Thessalonians (cf. 1 Thess. 1:4; 2:12; 4:7; 5:24) but says nothing about Israel and does not cite the Old Testament.[411] Instead, he emphasizes in 1 Thess. 2:16 that God's wrath has already come upon the Jews. In 1 Cor. 10:1–13, on the one hand, the rootedness of the church in Israel is expressed; on the other hand, Paul transcends this image and leaves it behind, for the events of the exodus can only now be rightly understood—they were written down as warnings for the ἐκκλησία (1 Cor. 10:11). The statement in 1 Cor. 10:4 presupposing the preexistence of Christ again combines continuity and discontinuity: the ancestors of the wilderness generation are at the same time the ancestors of the Christians, but God was not pleased with them and punished them. Paul's understanding of Scripture consistently applies God's dealing with Israel to the current situation of the church because he proceeds on the assumption that these prior acts for Israel were always done with the future church in view and that they are now fulfilled in the life of the church.[412] In 2 Cor. 3:1–18 Paul sets forth these ideas explicitly:[413] the covenant promises are disclosed only by a christological rereading because until the present day a barrier to understanding lies over the Scripture (2 Cor. 3:16–18). Moses is the representative of a glory that has faded away, whereas Christ represents the liberating new covenant in the power of the Spirit (cf. 2 Cor. 3:6; 1 Cor. 11:25).

The idea of the superiority of the new covenant is also dominant in the Letter to the Galatians, for although Paul does emphasize the continuing validity of God's covenant with Abraham (cf. Gal. 3:15–18), he regards it as only truly fulfilled in Christ. Therefore only those who believe the Christian message are legitimate descendants of Abraham and heirs of God's promises. In contrast, Jews oriented to the law/Torah are illegitimate children of Abraham, descendants of Ishmael, who was rejected by God, and their status is that of slaves

411. For an analysis of the text from the perspective of the people-of-God imagery, cf. ibid., 120–55, who, however, minimizes the aspect of discontinuity.

412. Cf. Roloff, *Kirche im Neuen Testament*, 120–21.

413. For exegesis of 2 Cor. 3:1–18, cf. Erich Grässer, "Der Alte Bund im Neuen," in *Der Alte Bund im Neuen: Exegetische Studien zur Israelfrage im Neuen Testament* (ed. Erich Grässer; WUNT 35; Tübingen: Mohr, 1985), 1–134; Scott J. Hafemann, *Paul, Moses, and the History of Israel: The Letter/Spirit Contrast and the Argument from Scripture in 2 Corinthians 3* (WUNT 81; Tübingen: Mohr, 1995); Manuel Vogel, *Das Heil des Bundes: Bundestheologie im Frühjudentum und im frühen Christentum* (TANZ 18; Tübingen: Francke, 1996); Sini Hulmi, *Paulus und Mose: Argumentation und Polemik in 2 Kor 3* (SESJ 77; Göttingen: Vandenhoeck & Ruprecht, 1999).

(cf. Gal. 4:21–31). Here Paul advocates a *consistent theory of disinheritance*;[414] the true Israel, the "Israel of God" (Gal. 6:16; cf. 4:26; Phil. 3:3), are those who believe, for only they have the legitimate status of descendants of Abraham. In the Letter to the Romans, Paul abandons this rigorous standpoint and, by means of a complex argument, attains a new vision. Christ was born of the seed of David according to the flesh (Rom. 1:3), so that God's saving act for believers is accomplished through Israel. The gospel is for the Jews first, the covenant with Abraham retains its validity (Rom. 4), and the law/Torah is "holy and just and good" (Rom. 7:12). But Jews can no longer appeal to the privileges of circumcision and the law/Torah (Rom. 2:17ff.), for according to the will of God only one's stance toward the gospel decides who belongs to the true Israel. With the intentional use of Old Testament and Jewish traditions, in Rom. 9–11 Israel is no longer confined to the empirical national group (cf. 9:6ff.), and the reception of the Gentiles appears as the natural consequence of God's will after the Jews rejected the gospel (Rom. 2:17ff.; 11:25, 31–32). Paul has hope for his people, however, that at the end of time they will still be converted to Christ (Rom. 11:25–36).

These three foundational metaphors,[415] like the primary vocabulary, express the basic approach of Paul's ecclesiology: *participation in the Christ event takes shape in the life of the church*. Christology and ecclesiology do not merely coincide or collapse into each other, but Christology determines ecclesiology because "no one can lay any foundation other than the one that has been laid; that foundation is Jesus Christ [ὅς ἐστιν Ἰησοῦς Χριστός]" (1 Cor. 3:11).

6.7.2 Structures and Tasks

Paul constantly reminds the churches of God's loving act in Jesus Christ that provided salvation and delivered them from the coming wrath (1 Thess. 5:9), reconciled the world to himself (2 Cor. 5:18–21), and gives it peace, righteousness, and life (cf. Rom. 5). *Jesus's own conduct became for Paul a structuring principle of his ecclesiology*.[416] Through his pro-existence (see above, §3.10.2), Jesus overcame the kind of thinking that operates with the categories of domination and violence, replacing them with the principle of a life of service for others (cf. Phil. 2:1–11). The church knows itself to

414. Cf. Roloff, *Kirche im Neuen Testament*, 125–26.

415. Roloff, ibid., 130–31 and Kraus, *Das Volk Gottes*, 350–61, both emphasize the inner connection between the concepts "people of God" and "body of Christ." While the body metaphor focuses on the present growth of the church, the idea of the people of God is anchored "in the depths of the story of God" (Kraus, *Das Volk Gottes*, 351). Moreover, the series Gal. 3:26–28, 3:29 clearly illustrates that Paul can think of the spatial and historical dimensions of ecclesiology at the same time.

416. Cf. Roloff, *Kirche im Neuen Testament*, 133.

be called to a life determined by love for others, which finds its visible expression in the unity and fellowship of baptized believers. Its members are to be like-minded in both their thinking and their pursuits (2 Cor. 13:11; Rom. 12:16; Phil. 2:2), to admonish and encourage one another (1 Thess. 5:14; Gal. 6:1–2; Rom. 15:14), and always attempt to discern the will of God (Rom. 12:2; Phil. 1:9–10; 4:8). Christians should attempt to do good always and for everyone but especially for their brothers and sisters of the Christian community (Gal. 6:10; cf. 1 Thess. 3:12). The love of brothers and sisters within the family of God is *the* mark of Christian existence (1 Thess. 4:9; Rom. 12:10). In humility, Christians should regard others as better than themselves (Rom. 12:10; cf. Phil. 2:3). None should look out for their own advantage and live only for themselves (1 Thess. 4:6; 1 Cor. 10:24, 33–11:1; 13:5; 2 Cor. 5:15; Rom. 15:2ff.; Phil. 2:4), but each should bear the burden of the other (Gal. 6:2). Christian love, as the determining power in the life of the church, is essentially unlimited (1 Cor. 13) and applies to everyone. It knows no egotistic selfishness, no quarreling, and no divisive party spirit, for love builds up the church (1 Cor. 8:1). This love changes even the social structures of the church because believers have all things in common (Gal. 6:6) and because they help those in need (cf. Gal. 4:10ff.) and practice hospitality (Rom. 12:13). The abundance of one supplies for the lack of another (2 Cor. 8:13–14).

Discipleship as Imitation

When Paul calls on his churches to imitate him as he himself imitates Christ (1 Thess. 1:6; 1 Cor. 4:16; 11:1), he sees himself holding a middle position in the chain, linking the model to be imitated (Christ) and the followers who imitate. In this sense Paul also commends himself *as model* in two respects: (1) Paul's engagement for the gospel and the welfare of the churches surpasses that of all other apostles (cf. 1 Cor. 15:10, "I worked harder than any of them—though it was not I, but the grace of God that is with me"; cf. 2 Cor. 11:23; 6:4–5). He struggles tirelessly for the preservation and well-being of the churches (cf. 1 Thess. 2:2; 1 Cor. 9:25; Phil. 1:30)[417] and works day and night in order not to be a burden to them (cf. 1 Thess. 2:9; 1 Cor. 4:12). He runs the race and strives for the victor's crown (cf. 1 Thess. 2:19; 1 Cor. 9:24–26; Phil. 2:19; 3:14); his greatest worry is that he will have worked in vain and that on the day of the Lord he will have nothing to show for his labors (cf. 1 Thess. 3:5; Gal. 4:11; Phil. 2:16). (2) Paul presents himself

417. On the ἀγών (struggle) motif, cf. Victor C. Pfitzner, *Paul and the Agon Motif. Traditional Athletic Imagery in the Pauline Literature* (NovTSup 16; Leiden: Brill, 1967); Rainer Metzner, "Paulus und der Wettkampf: Die Rolle des Sports in Leben und Verkündigung des Apostels (1Kor 9:24–27; Phil 3:12–16)," *NTS* 46 (2000): 565–83; Uta Poplutz, *Athlet des Evangeliums: Eine motivgeschichtliche Studie zur Wettkampfmetaphorik bei Paulus* (HBS 43; Freiburg i.B.: Herder, 2004).

as a model to the churches also regarding his sufferings.[418] He always carries about in his body the death of Jesus (2 Cor. 4:10; cf. Gal. 4:17), sees himself constantly exposed to death διὰ Ἰησοῦ (for Jesus's sake) or for the sake of the gospel (2 Cor. 4:11; cf. 1 Cor. 4:10; 9:23; Philem. 13), and wants to become like Jesus in his death (cf. Phil. 3:10; 1:20). Paul understands his sufferings to be a constituent element in his apostolic mission and sees them in close relationship to Christ's own sufferings (cf. 1 Thess. 2:2; 2 Cor. 4:11; Phil. 1:7, 13; 2:17; Philem. 9, 13). All this happens "for your sake" (2 Cor. 4:15); Paul's sufferings are a sacrifice on behalf of the churches (cf. 2 Cor. 12:15). But the church too is exposed to experiences of suffering, for it is constantly threatened from outside and from within (cf. 1 Thess. 1:6; 2:14; 2 Cor. 1:7; Phil. 1:29–30). *Participation in the suffering of Jesus corresponds to Christian existence* (cf. Rom. 6:3–4), *just as does participation in the powers of his resurrection* (cf. Rom. 6:5), and so both shape the self-understanding of the church. Although apostle and church both participate in the sufferings of Christ, here also Paul embodies the model of Christian existence: he was called as apostle by the suffering Lord and demonstrates to his churches that not only the resurrection but suffering determines the life of the individual Christian and the shape of the church's life.

Charism and Office

The dynamism of the basic structure of Paul's ecclesiology is also revealed in the relation between prescribed, orderly leadership tasks and charismatic gifts. Paul classifies the life of the congregation clearly within the *realm of the Spirit*. The vocabulary he chooses clearly reveals the apostle's own emphasis: the terms πνευματικός/πνευματικά (spiritual person/things) and χάρισμα/χαρίσματα (gift[s] of grace) are found exclusively in the authentic letters of Paul and the literature dependent on them.[419] They appear to be words newly coined within early Christianity and are used exclusively to describe the spiritual gifts in their various dimensions. Whereas πνευματικός and πνευματικά portray the powerful, effective presence of the divine, χάρισμα and χαρίσματα point to the gift character and source of the extraordinary phenomena that break out in the church's life. Paul himself probably introduced the term

418. This point is elaborated, with different accents, by Michael Wolter, "Der Apostel und seine Gemeinden als Teilhaber am Leidensgeschick Jesu Christi," *NTS* 36 (1990): 535–57; Hermann von Lips, "Die 'Leiden des Apostels' als Thema paulinischer Theologie," in "*. . . Was ihr auf dem Weg verhandelt habt": Beiträge zur Exegese und Theologie des Neuen Testaments; Festschrift für Ferdinand Hahn zum 75. Geburtstag* (ed. Peter Müller et al.; Neukirchen-Vluyn: Neukirchener Verlag, 2001), 117–28.

419. Πνευματικός or πνευματικά is found 26 times in the New Testament: in the undisputed letters of Paul, 19 times, of which 15 are found in 1 Corinthians (7 times in Colossians, Ephesians, 1 Peter). Χάρισμα or χαρίσματα is found 17 times in the New Testament: 14 in the undisputed letters of Paul, of which 7 are in 1 Corinthians and 6 in Romans (once in 2 Corinthians; and once each in 1 Timothy, 2 Timothy, and 1 Peter).

χάρισμα into the debate[420] in order to clarify the true nature of the charismatic phenomena for the Corinthians, who were especially endowed with such gifts. The Corinthians spoke of πνευματικά (cf. 1 Cor. 12:1), emphasizing thereby their individual capabilities as the media of the divine power, whereas Paul points to the external origin of the work of the Spirit and derives from this the priority of the Spirit's work for the "edification" (οἰκοδομή) of the whole congregation (cf. 1 Cor. 14:12). Because the Spirit is one and indivisible, it is the nature of the Spirit's gifts to further the unity of the church. The multiple and diverse charisms (cf. 1 Cor. 12:28) document, each in its own way, the richness of the Spirit's work, and charisms are misused when they lead to showmanship and disputes about rank. Moreover, the more extraordinary charisms such as glossolalia, prophecy, and the gift of healing represent only a fragment of the spectrum of the work of the Spirit in the life of the church. Love, as the purest and highest form of the presence of the divine, rejects domination and places itself in the service of others (cf. 1 Cor. 13), so that everything that serves the οἰκοδομή of the church demonstrates that it is an authentic gift of the Spirit.

If the Spirit effects, furthers, and orders the building up of the church, then for Paul there can be no conflict between individual-pneumatic capabilities and the tasks of administration and teaching, for all have their source in the same Spirit. The image of the organism (cf. 1 Cor. 12:12–31) makes clear that the individual gifts, capabilities, and tasks can carry out their ministry only as part of the whole. The alternative frequently posed between charism and office[421] *does not exist for Paul* because the work of the Spirit is indivisible. In 1 Cor. 12:28 the functions assigned to particular persons and the extraordinary capabilities given to others are equally considered the activity of God. The verb ἔθετο (install [someone], make [someone] to be something), and the enumeration and juxtaposition of gifts that grow from a call spontaneously and extraordinarily, over against those that are mediated by being assigned a particular task in the church's life, show that, for Paul, Spirit and law are not opposed to each other.[422] So also the list of charismatic gifts in Rom. 12:6–8 documents the basic tendency of Paul's approach: the charisms concretize God's gracious turning to the world, so that abilities to organize, administer, and encourage are naturally considered the workings of God's Spirit. In 1 Cor. 12:28 Paul formulates the first three charisms in terms of persons, which thus signals that a definite group exercises particular

420. Cf. Brockhaus, *Charisma und Amt*, 189–90; Roloff, *Kirche im Neuen Testament*, 137.

421. Cf. Rudolf Sohm, "Begriff und Organisation der Ekklesia," in *Das Kirchliche Amt im Neuen Testament* (ed. Karl Kertelge; WdF 439; Darmstadt: Wissenschaftliche Buchgesellschaft, 1977), 53: "The ἐκκλησία is Christianity as a whole, the body of Christ, the Lord's bride—a spiritual reality withdrawn from earthly norms, including that of law."

422. The comment of Roloff, *Kirche im Neuen Testament*, 139, is on target: "The Spirit itself sets law by establishing particular functions as obligatory."

responsibilities for a set period. In this sense, one can speak of offices playing a role in Paul's ecclesiology.[423]

Offices

The *apostolic office* emphasizes in a particular way the calling, ability to establish churches, and the leadership abilities of early Christian missionaries. In the earliest period, this office was concentrated in Jerusalem (cf. 1 Cor. 15:3–11; Gal. 1:17, 19), but by no means can it be restricted to the Twelve or the Jerusalem church. The expression "then to all the apostles" in the list of witnesses to the resurrection appearances (1 Cor. 15:7), the reference to Andronicus and Junia[s], who were already apostles before Paul (Rom. 16:7), the call of Paul to be "apostle to the Gentiles" (cf. Gal. 1:1; Rom. 15:15ff.), the concept and terminology of apostleship associated with Antioch (cf. Acts 13:1–3; 14:4, 14), the dispute in 2 Cor. 11:5, 13; 12:11 regarding how apostleship is to be defined, and the image of apostles in the sayings source Q (cf. Luke 10:4; Matt. 10:8)—all these show that the circle of apostles had expanded within the early Christian mission.[424] An appearance by, or legitimization from, the risen Christ by no means was authorization for apostleship; otherwise the "more than five hundred brothers and sisters" of 1 Cor. 15:6 would all have been apostles. Moreover, the only early Christian missionary that Paul really accepted is not called an apostle, namely, Apollos (cf. 1 Cor. 3:5ff.; 4:6; 16:12). In the long run, it is not calling and sending that legitimize the apostolic office but the capacity of the apostle to establish churches and to represent the gospel convincingly as the norm of God's grace among the churches, through which the apostle himself assumes a normative role (cf. 1 Thess. 1:6; 1 Cor. 4:16; 11:1; Phil. 3:17). The apostle embodies, in his person and his work, the servant form of the gospel (cf. 2 Cor. 4:7–18); he is himself the exemplar of the new being, and the churches are the seal of his apostleship and his glory in the last judgment (cf. 1 Thess. 2:19; 1 Cor. 2:9; 2 Cor. 3:2). Paul too manifests this apostolic competence to found, lead, and guide the churches, but in his case, after the initial preaching and basic instruction that had founded the churches, he continued to be present among them through his coworkers and his letters.

Prophetic speech is a normal ingredient of early Christian church life. Already in 1 Thess. 5:20 Paul exhorts, "Do not despise prophetic speech."

423. Cf. ibid., 139ff. Clarke, *Serve the Community*, passim, has a comprehensive treatment of the influence of Greco-Roman social structures (esp. the patron-client system) on the constitution and leadership structures of early Christianity, in order then to argue that in principle the *diakonia* established by Jesus as the norm represents the *proprium* (characteristic nature) of the structures of the new movement.

424. For the most part, scholars tend to see a historical line of development from the Jerusalem apostolate, based on resurrection appearances, to the charismatic itinerant apostolate as seen in the traditions of the sayings source Q and the Antiochene traditions (cf. Jürgen Roloff, "Apostel I," *TRE* 3:433ff.).

Early Christian prophets appear as distinctive groups in various strands of early Christian tradition: Acts 13:1; 15:32; 20:23; 21:4, 10 presupposes early Christian prophets in Greece and Asia Minor; Eph. 3:5; 4:11; and 1 Tim. 1:18; 4:14 look back on the beginnings of the church, when prophets were obviously at work; and Rev. 11:18; 16:6; 18:24; 22:9 regards the prophets as the central independent group within the worldwide church.[425] The prophetic office probably originated in the early Palestinian church (cf., e.g., Acts 11:28, Agabus); in Jerusalem the experience of the church convinced it that the time of the cessation of prophecy was over and that the Spirit of God was now at work again (cf. Acts 2:17–18). Likewise, in the original Greco-Roman cultural realm, prophecy was a familiar form of religious communication.[426] What functions were exercised by the early Christian prophets? First of all, they interpreted God's past and future saving acts in Jesus Christ (cf. Acts 20:23; 21:4; Eph. 3:5), revealed the will of the risen Jesus for the church, and gave their testimony for Jesus (cf. Rev. 19:10). Thus the early Christian prophets also participated in the process of handing on and interpreting the tradition, for they transmitted sayings of Jesus and gave them new interpretations in the awareness that the Spirit was present with them.[427] Their testimony for Jesus was evidently presented in different forms, so that ecstatic speech, visions, the contemporizing of sayings of Jesus as the word of the present Lord, and new instructions of the exalted Lord for the church were all expressions of their prophetic abilities. Paul listed prophecy among the forms of intelligible speech and distinguished it from glossolalia (cf. 1 Cor. 14:5). When several prophets were present in the same worship service, their messages should be critically evaluated by the other members of the church (cf. 14:29). Here too the edification of the church served as the critical norm (14:26), for prophetic speech could not be permitted to disrupt the order and unity of the worship service (cf. 14:31).

Whereas the prophets are the vehicle of the exalted Lord, present in the Spirit, who speaks his revelatory word for the present, the task of the early Christian teachers was concerned with interpreting the (oral or written) kerygma and with the exposition of traditional texts (e.g., the Septuagint).[428]

425. See the comprehensive treatment of M. Eugene Boring, *The Continuing Voice of Jesus: Christian Prophecy and the Gospel Tradition* (Louisville: Westminster John Knox, 1991); see also Gerhard Dautzenberg, *Urchristliche Prophetie: Ihre Erforschung, ihre Voraussetzungen im Judentum und ihre Struktur im ersten Korintherbrief* (BWANT; Stuttgart: Kohlhammer, 1975), and David E. Aune, *Prophecy in Early Christianity and the Ancient Mediterranean World* (Grand Rapids: Eerdmans, 1983).

426. Cf. Kai Brodersen, ed., *Prognosis: Studien zur Funktion von Zukunftsvorhersagen in Literatur und Geschichte seit der Antike* (AKG 2; Münster: LIT, 2001), 2001.

427. On early Christian prophets as transmitters and creators of elements of the Jesus traditions, cf. Boring, *Continuing Voice of Jesus*, 189–265.

428. Cf. Alfred Zimmermann, *Die urchristlichen Lehrer: Studien zum Tradentenkreis der Didaskaloi im frühen Urchristentum* (WUNT 2.12; Tübingen: Mohr, 1984).

In 1 Cor. 12:28, Gal. 6:6, and Rom. 12:7b, Paul presupposes the existence of teachers in the congregation (cf. also Eph. 4:11; Acts 13:1; James 3:1; *Did.* 11–15). They had to be able to read and write and needed to be familiar with the Jesus traditions and the Septuagint as well as the conventional rules of interpretation in order to be able to interpret the new eschatological times for the church. The tasks of a teacher presuppose a high degree of personal presence and continuity, related to a particular time, subject matter, and place, and so here too we may speak of a particular office in the early church.

In Phil. 1:1 Paul mentions, without further explanation, ἐπίσκοποι and διάκονοι (overseers/supervisors and helpers/servants). He obviously refers to several persons who carry out generally recognized tasks in the life of the community and whose special position is underscored by being mentioned in the letter's greeting. This linguistic usage suggests that the ἐπίσκοποι had a position of leadership within the congregation. The term probably refers to leaders of house churches (cf. 1 Cor. 1:14; 16:15–16, 19; Rom. 16:5, 23; Acts 18:8)[429] who made their homes available for the church meetings and who supported the congregations in various ways as their patrons. Their normal authority predisposed them for this office as the church in Philippi grew and divided into several house churches.[430] The διάκονοι functioned as helpers of the ἐπίσκοποι; especially in the celebration of the eucharistic meals, they may have assumed responsibility for the preparations, and their duties included the collection and administration of the offerings.[431]

6.7.3 *The Church as the Realm of Freedom from Sin*

A central question for Pauline ecclesiology (and ethics) was whether and in what sense sin (see above, §6.5.2) continues to be present in the sphere of the church. Can sin still exercise its power within the church? What is the meaning of the ethical shortcomings that doubtless continue within the life of the church?

Paul's linguistic usage gives some pointers for answering these questions. As a rule, Paul does not use the singular ἁμαρτία to describe human misconduct. In 1 Thess. 4:3–8 he warns the Thessalonian Christians against πορνεία (fornication), ἐπιθυμία (lustful passion), and πλεονεξία (greed), but without speaking of sin. The life of holiness Paul calls for has as its opposite not "sin" but "impurity" (1 Thess. 4:7, ἀκαθαρσία).[432] Paul deals with the flagrant case

429. On this point, cf. the comprehensive analyses of Roger W. Gehring, *Hausgemeinde und Mission: Die Bedeutung antiker Häuser und Hausgemeinschaften-von Jesus bis Paulus* (BWM 9; Giessen: Brunnen, 2000), 320–84; idem, *House Church and Mission: The Importance of Household Structures in Early Christianity* (Peabody, MA: Hendrickson, 2004), 185–228.

430. Cf. ibid., 352–59.

431. Cf. Roloff, *Kirche im Neuen Testament*, 143.

432. For analysis, cf. Umbach, *In Christus getauft*, 67–81; the plural ἁμαρτίαι in 1 Thess. 2:16 reflects the tradition incorporated and interpreted in this text.

of immorality in 1 Cor. 5 under the aspect of the purity of the church. Because this holiness is endangered, the evildoer must be excluded for the sake of the community and for his own sake.[433] The legal disputes in court before pagan judges are not in accord with the purity of the church (1 Cor. 6:1–11). Only at the end of his argument in 1 Cor. 5–6 (at 6:18), does Paul use the terms ἁμαρτάνω (to sin) and ἁμάρτημα (offense; NRSV, "sin")—once each—but he still avoids using the noun "sin" (ἁμαρτία) in this context. Because believers are united most closely with Christ precisely in their bodily existence, sexual misconduct endangers this union and is not compatible with the purity of the church. Thus Paul can recommend marriage as a means of avoiding sexual misconduct (ἁμαρτάνω, 1 Cor. 7:28, 36). In 1 Cor. 8:12 Paul makes a direct connection between the way one conducts oneself with fellow Christians and one's relation to Christ. Whoever sins against a brother or sister (ἁμαρτάνοντες εἰς τοὺς ἀδελφούς) sins against Christ (εἰς Χριστὸν ἁμαρτάνετε). Because the church is a sphere of sanctification and holiness, offenses have not only ethical dimensions but also soteriological aspects. This is an idea that Paul elaborates in 1 Cor. 10:1–13, touches on in 15:34, and formulates in 15:17 as follows: "If Christ has not been raised, your faith is futile and you are still in your sins."[434] In 1 Cor. 11:27ff. Paul sharply attacks the abuses at the eucharistic meal, but without speaking of "sin." In 2 Cor. 12:19–13:10 Paul specifically warns the Corinthian Christians that when he comes to them the third time, he will not spare those "who previously sinned and have not repented of the impurity, sexual immorality, and licentiousness that they have practiced" (2 Cor. 12:21). Paul uses the verb προαμαρτάνω (to sin previously) only in 12:21 and 13:2; in each case it is a perfect participle that describes the misconduct of church members that had not yet been set aside.[435] Likewise Paul does not relate the conflict with the ἀδικήσας (wrongdoer) in 2 Cor. 2:5–11 to the concept and terminology of sin. The culprit had been excluded by the congregation (2:6) and may now be readmitted to their fellowship. Forgiveness is necessary, for Satan is just waiting for the discord to continue so that he can again infiltrate the church (cf. 2 Cor. 2:11).[436]

The Letter to the Galatians confirms that *Paul does not use* ἁμαρτία *as a designation of human failures*. The apostle here carries on an extremely sharp debate with his Judaistic opponents who have invaded the church, but without using the word "sin" to describe their actions. Likewise the false conduct

433. On the topic of church discipline in Paul, cf. Ingrid Goldhahn-Müller, *Die Grenze der Gemeinde: Studien zum Problem der Zweiten Busse in Neuen Testament unter Berücksichtigung der Entwicklung im 2. Jh. bis Tertullian* (GTA 39; Göttingen: Vandenhoeck & Ruprecht, 1989), 115–56.

434. In 1 Cor. 15:17, the plural ἁμαρτίαι reflects the traditional usage in 1 Cor. 15:3; cf. Conzelmann, *1 Corinthians*, 266.

435. Cf. Umbach, *In Christus getauft*, 141.

436. For analysis, cf. ibid., 170–82.

of Peter is not described as ἁμαρτία (cf. Gal. 2:14), and in the context of the admonitions in the parenetic section of the letter in 6:1, Paul merely uses the term παράπτωμα (transgression). The plural ἁμαρτίαι is the term for human deeds in the traditional formula incorporated in 1:4. But this is in contrast to the specific Pauline use of the singular ἁμαρτία in Gal. 2:17. In Paul's usage, "sin" denotes a sphere of power, a field of activity, opposed to the sphere in which Christ exercises lordship.

The distinctive profile of the Pauline concept of sin also shapes the line of argument in the Letter to the Romans (see above, §6.5.2), for Paul's references to sin concern strictly the past. He reminds the church members of their baptism, the place where they experienced a fundamental transformation of their lives; there believers died to sin, there they were placed in the sphere of Christ and righteousness (Rom. 6:3ff.). Paul uses antithetical terms to portray dramatically the new reality in which the baptized live: "So you also must consider yourselves dead to sin and alive to God in Christ Jesus" (Rom. 6:11). For the church, sin is a reality that belongs to the past, and 6:14a states expressly, "For sin will have no dominion over you." Accordingly, Paul never associates the Lord's Supper with the forgiveness of sins. Because Christians have been freed from sin, they have now become servants of righteousness (Rom. 6:18). The power of grace surpasses the effectiveness of sin (cf. Rom. 5:12–21), which has now been conquered and now perceived by the baptized as a destructive power of the past (cf. Rom. 7:7–8, 14). The Letter to the Philippians also confirms the Pauline conception of the church as a realm free from sin, for ἁμαρτία and related terms in the singular are not found in the letter, although misbehavior and problems in the church are addressed (cf. Phil. 1:17; 3:2ff.).

Because the new being in Christ in the power of the Spirit has begun not merely in name but in reality,[437] the baptized are no longer in the realm of sin's power but in the church as a realm that is free from sin. The sanctification of the church includes drawing a sharp boundary between itself and the world. It also shapes the empirical form of the church, for Paul does not know the ecclesiological concept of the church as a *corpus mixtum*.[438] The church belongs on the side of light and has cast off the works of darkness (1 Thess. 5:1ff.; Rom. 13:11–14). It does not conform to the world (Rom. 12:2), no longer practices the works of the flesh (Gal. 5:19ff.), and shines with a heavenly light in a perverse world (Phil. 2:14–15).

Within this framework of thought, what function does the Pauline paraclesis exercise? The Pauline admonitions and imperatives (e.g., 1 Cor. 6:18; 7:23; 8:12) testify that Christians can again fall under the power of sin. Paul knows

437. Cf. Hans Windisch, *Taufe und Sünde im ältesten Christentum bis auf Origenes: Ein Beitrag zur altchristlichen Dogmengeschichte* (Tübingen: Mohr, 1908), 104.

438. Cf. Wolf-Henning Ollrog, *Paulus und seine Mitarbeiter: Untersuchung zu Theorie und Praxis der paulinischen Mission* (WMANT 50; Neukirchen-Vluyn: Neukirchener Verlag, 1979), 137.

the temptations to which Christians are exposed (cf. 1 Cor. 7:5; 10:9, 13; Gal. 6:1). Satan appears as an angel of light and attempts to deceive the church (cf. 2 Cor. 11:13–15). The church in Galatia falls from grace if it places itself back under the servitude of the law, which in turn is only an instrument of sin. The defeat of the old reality does not mean for baptized believers that they are taken out of the world as such, for they continue to live ἐν σαρκί and still must confront the temptations of sin. Especially in the form of evil desire (ἐπιθυμία), sin emerges from the past of the baptized as a reality to be reckoned with (Rom. 7:7ff.). Paul saw in evil desire the real mainspring of evil, for behind all the commandments of the second table of the Decalogue stands evil desire (murder, adultery, covetousness). The power of the Spirit enables the baptized to withstand these temptations, however, if they attune their thinking and acting to the new being. The imperative demands that life be brought into harmony with the new being, and only so does the power of sin remain a past reality and the church a realm free from sin.

6.8 Eschatology

With the resurrection of Jesus Christ from the dead, a past event definitively determines the future and thus places its stamp on the present as well. Paul lived with an intense expectation: the impending advent of the crucified and risen Jesus Christ was a factor that shaped his symbolic universe until his life's end (cf. Phil. 4:5, "The Lord is near").[439] All creation is moving to that consummation, and Paul saw himself as riding the crest of this movement. To be sure, the death of others makes the living ask about their own destiny, so eschatology must always also provide a persuasive answer to the questions of life and death. Every theory about death is a theory about life, and vice versa. Paul is certain that the finitude of the world cannot abolish the reality of Christian life, for the Spirit of God/Christ continues beyond death as the believers' true selfhood.

6.8.1 Participation in the Life of the Risen One

In 1 Thess. 4:13–18 the death of members of the congregation posed a threat to the church's symbolic universe, which was countered by the apostle with the fundamental confession of faith: "Since we believe that Jesus died and rose again" (4:14a; cf. 1:10). He derives a *soteriological logic* from this confession, which is *determined by the concept of participation*. Baptized believers participate in the destiny of the decisive figure of the end time,

439. On the structure of Pauline eschatology cf. also Becker, *Paul*, 440–49; Dunn, *Theology of Paul*, 461–98.

Jesus Christ. Just as God raised him from the dead, death is not the last word for church members who have died; like the living, they will be received into eternal communion with the risen Jesus (4:17, πάντοτε σὺν Κυρίῳ ἐσόμεθα [we shall be with the Lord forever]). Baptized believers are already "children of light and children of the day" (5:5) and thus eschatological persons; in 5:10 the cross is explicitly pointed out as the basis that makes this new being possible.[440] Likewise in 1 Cor. 15:20–22 Paul bases what he says on the fundamental Christian confession (cf. ἐγήγερται [he was raised], 1 Cor. 15:4a, 20a), and he infers from this the turn of the ages. Christ was raised as the "first fruits [ἀπαρχή] of those who have died"; that is, he not only is the first of all the resurrected in chronological terms but *is himself the resurrection paradigm*.[441] The temporal and material aspects are complementary; Jesus is the *first* one to whom God's eschatological act of salvation applies. For Paul there are two bearers of human destiny, each of which is a prototype who determines the being of those who belong within his category (1 Cor. 15:21). Adam preceded Christ both chronologically and functionally, for by his transgression he brought about the hopeless situation that has now been taken away in Christ. Paul formulates the antithetical superiority of Christ's act in universal terms: "For as all die in Adam, so all will be made alive in Christ" (1 Cor. 15:22).[442] The repeated πάντες (all) of 1 Cor. 15:22 raises the question of not only whether all human beings must die because of Adam's transgression but whether all human beings will also be made alive in/through Christ; it potentially applies to all human beings, but they must appropriate it for themselves through faith. The consistent orientation of the eschatological event to Christ is obvious: it was for Christ as the "first fruits" that God acted to initiate the new being, it was through Christ that humanity's unavoidable subjection to death was abolished, and it is those belonging to Christ who participate in present and future salvation (cf. also 2 Cor. 1:9; 4:14; Gal. 1:1; Rom. 4:17, 24; 10:9; 14:9). At his parousia Christ will manifest his lordship to all, when all enemies, including death, will be finally overcome, and then will hand over lordship, and himself, to God (1 Cor. 15:23–28).

The *fundamentally participatory character* of Pauline eschatology and the related qualification of the present as the time of salvation determined by the future are also evident in Rom. 6:4–5 and 8:11. In Rom. 6:4–5 Paul infers from participation in Jesus's death in baptism a participation in the reality of his resurrection, which is already manifest in the present as transformation into

440. On this point cf. Wolfgang Harnisch, *Eschatologische Existenz: Ein exegetischer Beitrag zum Sachanliegen von 1. Thessalonicher 4,13–5,11* (FRLANT 110; Göttingen: Vandenhoeck & Ruprecht, 1973), 150.

441. Cf. Lindemann, *Der Erste Korintherbrief*, 343.

442. According to 1 Cor. 15:23, only those who belong to Christ are saved, so that the πάντες of v. 22 includes only believers; cf. Powers, *Salvation through Participation*, 153. Differently Lindemann, *Der Erste Korintherbrief*, 344.

a new existence. The apostle intentionally avoids speaking of a present resurrection of baptized believers, a view that was probably advocated in Corinth (cf. 1 Cor. 4:8; 10:1ff.; 15:12) and is found in various forms in later literature of the Pauline school (Col. 2:12; 3:1–4; Eph. 2:6; 2 Tim. 2:18). The *reservation* regarding the future thereby expressed (cf. 1 Cor. 13:12; 2 Cor. 4:7; 5:7; Rom. 8:24) imposes no limitation on the full participation of Christians in the new being[443] but expresses the temporal structure of Christian existence:[444] Christians live their lives between the world-changing acts of the resurrection of Christ and his parousia, so that we may speak of the presence and assurance of salvation but not yet of the full reality of salvation. Although believers live in the end time, the end has not yet come!

Romans 8:11 makes clear that the distinctive structure of Christian existence is based exclusively in God's eschatological act: God gives the Spirit to baptized believers; God is the one who through the Spirit raised Jesus from the dead and who will also give life to the mortal bodies of those who are bound to Christ by this same Spirit. By his gift of the Spirit, God in a way is giving himself, when he grounds the new life in baptism and renews it after death. *Baptized believers will be taken by and into God's Spirit, which means into God's own self.*

Eschatological Existence

The relation of Christians *to the world* and their actions *in the world* are likewise defined by their specific location in time. They know that they have already been delivered from the enslaving powers of the world and that they can use the things of the world without lapsing back into their power (cf. 1 Cor. 7:29–31). The manner in which they live their lives is oriented to their new being ἐν Χριστῷ (cf. Gal. 3:26–28), and they know that all they do must be done in love (Gal. 5:22). Also, the exemplary destiny of the apostle illustrates how powerfully the events of the eschatological future already shine into the present as a source of strength, how the reality of the future already fully determines the present.[445] Present sufferings can be endured in the confidence that the God who raised Jesus from the dead will also raise

443. Differently Strecker, *Die liminale Theologie des Paulus*, 452, who regards "the aspect of threshold existence as fundamental" for all levels of Pauline theology.

444. It is thus inappropriate to speak of an "already and not yet of salvation," as done, e.g., by Günter Klein, "Eschatologie," *TRE* 10:283; Dunn, *Theology of Paul*, 466–72. It is also subject to misunderstanding to speak of an "eschatological reservation" (so, e.g., Andreas Lindemann, "Eschatologie," *RGG*[4] 2:1556), for regarding the eschaton Paul has no "reservation" but, rather, a temporal qualification because the final consummation has not yet arrived. The way forward on this point is found in the suggestion of Sören Agersnap, *Baptism and the New Life: A Study of Romans 6:1–14* (Aarhus: Aarhus University Press, 1999), 401, that "already"/"not yet" be replaced with "already"/"even more."

445. Cf. Rudolf Bultmann and Erich Dinkler, ed., *The Second Letter to the Corinthians* (trans. Roy A. Harrisville; Minneapolis: Augsburg, 1985), 124.

up the believers (cf. 2 Cor. 4:14). Paul thinks of Jesus's resurrection, which has already happened, and the resurrection of baptized believers, which is yet to come, as a functional unity; the past is synchronous with the future, which in turn shapes the present.[446] The characteristic interlocking of present and future also appears in Phil. 3:10–11. It is not the case that present participation in the suffering of Jesus provides access to the future; to the contrary, rather, the reality of the future, which is grounded in God's past act, makes it possible to persevere through the sufferings of the present. Christian expectation of the future is therefore a *well-grounded* hope (cf. 1 Thess. 1:3; 2 Cor. 3:12; Gal. 5:5; Rom. 5:2, 4; 8:24),[447] for it is not subject to the ambiguities of what is to come. Whereas in Greek thought the future and thus hope were perceived as both attractive and threatening,[448] believers live in the unqualified confidence that the future has lost its threatening character. Hope, like faith and love, is a fundamental component of Christian existence (1 Cor. 13:12).

The new being of baptized believers can be described in both functional and temporal aspects as *eschatological existence*: they participate fully in the ultimate turn of the ages brought about by God's act in Jesus Christ, and they know that they live in a present already determined by the future.

6.8.2 The Final Events

Paul's letters reveal clearly to what a great extent the differing church situations affected the shape of his eschatological thinking. The movement was new, so questions and answers had not yet been fully clarified; this central area of early Christian meaning-formation was still under construction. Especially for Paul himself, the resurrection of Jesus Christ from the dead and the parousia, expected in the near future, were the firm chronological and material cornerstones of his understanding of the final events, yet he obviously continued to think through how these events should be described,

446. Because past and future both shape the present, Paul can take up the doctrine of the two ages only partially and in a broken form, as he does when speaking of the "wisdom of this age" (cf. 1 Cor. 1:20; 2:6; 3:18) or of the "ruler" of this world (cf. 1 Cor. 2:8; 2 Cor. 4:4; Gal. 1:4; Rom. 12:2). The dominant role of Christology for Paul makes it impossible for him to take over whole eschatological schemes from Judaism, and so he consistently avoids speaking of the "new" or the "coming" age; on Paul's appropriation of the doctrine of the two ages, cf. Baumgarten, *Paulus und die Apokalyptik*, 181–89.

447. Cf. on this point Gottfried Nebe, *"Hoffnung" bei Paulus: Elpis und ihre Synonyme im Zusammenhang der Eschatologie* (SUNT 16; Göttingen: Vandenhoeck & Ruprecht, 1983).

448. Classically, Sophocles, *Ant.* 615–619: "Hope flits about on never-wearying wings [ἡ γὰρ δὴ πολύπλαγκτος ἐλπίς]; / Profit to some, to some light love she brings; / But no man knoweth how her gifts may turn, / Till 'neath his feet the treacherous ashes burn." Cf. further Plato, *Phileb.* 33c–34c, 39a–41b. The masterly survey of Rudolf Bultmann, "ἐλπίς κτλ.," *TDNT* 2:517–23, is still very valuable.

and ventured to make midcourse corrections in order to maintain a consistent view.[449]

Transformations

The first extant expression of this theme was already forced upon Paul by the unexpected fact that some members of the church in Thessalonica had died before the Lord's parousia (1 Thess. 4:13–18). Paul responds with an explanation that for the first time combines the parousia with the resurrection of dead Christians. After an introduction to the problem (4:13) and a preliminary answer falling back on the kerygma of the death and resurrection of Jesus (4:14), in 4:15–17 Paul provides a second answer that summarizes (4:15) and quotes (4:16–17) a traditional saying of the Lord. The instruction then concludes with the exhortation to encourage and comfort one another with the answer he has given to their question about the premature deaths (4:18). The goal of the whole event is "being with the Lord," which directly presupposes that all will be *taken up to be with him*, which in turn indirectly presupposes the resurrection of those who have died in Christ. The problematic of the delay of the parousia and the historicity of Christian faith is what compels Paul to introduce the concept of a resurrection of dead believers in the first place.[450] But in 4:13–18 he also holds on to his original eschatological conception that at the parousia all believers will be taken up to be with the Lord. Here the resurrection of believers who have died before the parousia functions only to make it possible for them to be taken up at the parousia. In 1 Thessalonians the death of Christians before the parousia is clearly the exception. Paul thinks of himself and most of the church as among those who will be alive when the Lord returns (4:15, 17), doubtless in the conviction that the parousia was very near. There is no discussion of the question of how the resurrection of dead church members will take place or how the residence of all the faithful in the heavenly world with Jesus Christ should be imagined.[451]

449. Scholars have always noted changes within Pauline eschatology. In addition to the works of Hunzinger, Wiefel, and Schnelle (*Wandlungen*, 37–48) mentioned in the bibliography, cf., e.g., Walter Grundmann, "Überlieferung und Eigenaussage im eschatologischen Denken des Paulus," *NTS* 8 (1961): 17ff.; Jürgen Becker, *Auferstehung der Toten im Urchristentum* (SBS 82; Stuttgart: KBW Verlag, 1976), 66ff.; Schade, *Apokalyptische Christologie*, 210–11; Strecker, *Theology of the New Testament*, 209–16. Among those who are skeptical about theories that Paul's eschatology underwent changes are Paul Hoffmann, *Die Toten in Christus: Eine religionsgeschichtliche und exegetische Untersuchung zur paulinischen Eschatologie* (NTA NF 2; Münster: Aschendorff, 1966), 323–29; Luz, *Geschichtsverständnis*, 356–57; Siber, *Mit Christus leben*, 91ff.; Baumgarten, *Paulus und die Apokalyptik*, 236–38; Lindemann, "Eschatologie," 2:1556.

450. Cf. Udo Schnelle, "Der erste Thessalonicherbrief und die Entstehung der paulinischen Anthropologie," *NTS* 32 (1986): 207–24.

451. Cf. Nikolaus Walter, "Leibliche Auferstehung? Zur Frage der Hellenisierung der Auferweckungshoffnung bei Paulus," in *Paulus, Apostel Jesu Christi: Festschrift für Günter Klein zum 70. Geburtstag* (ed. Günter Klein and Michael Trowitzsch; Tübingen: Mohr, 1998), 110–11.

In the Corinthian letters, we see this theme in a different light, with changes brought about by the passing of time, by the independent theological developments among the Corinthian Christians, and by Paul's reflections that take the changed situation into account. Paul continues to hold fast to his unbroken acute expectation of the near parousia (cf. 1 Cor. 7:29; 10:11; 16:22), but instances of Christians who die before the Lord's return are no longer considered unusual (cf. 1 Cor. 7:39; 11:30; 15:6, 18, 29, 51). For the Corinthians in their cultural context, the σῶμα (body) theme was apparently of decisive importance. Paul responded to this situation and made the issue of corporeality a central aspect of his eschatology. In comparison with 1 Thess. 4:13–18 and the preceding argumentation of 1 Cor. 15, Paul introduces a new category in 15:50–54: the metaphor of transformation.[452] Both those who have already died and those who are still alive at the parousia will receive imperishable bodies. Although the σῶμα concept no longer appears, and the categorical difference between two kinds of bodies no longer fits the metaphorical framework in 1 Cor. 15:52–54,[453] the argument as a whole indicates that the imperishable, immortal postmortal existence is probably identical with the σῶμα πνευματικόν (spiritual body) of 15:44.

Whereas in 1 Thess. 4:13–18 and 1 Cor. 15:51ff. Paul's use of the pronoun ἡμεῖς had made very clear that he expected to be among the living at the Lord's return (1 Thess. 4:17; 1 Cor. 15:52), in 2 Cor. 5:1–10 for the first time he reckons with the possibility of his own death before the parousia (5:1–2, 8). This decisive adjustment in the apostle's situation is reflected in the decline of apocalyptic elements in the portrayal of the final events and the increased appropriation of Hellenistic conceptuality with its dualistic and individualistic tendencies. Now the σῶμα terminology is used exclusively for the earthly body (5:6, 8) and is seen in a negative light.[454] The idea of departure from the present body has its closest parallel in the Greek view that the true homeland of the soul is in the transcendent world[455] and that existence in the body is living in a foreign country.[456] Paul intentionally avoids using the term "soul" but at the same time no longer defines resurrection existence explicitly as "bodily" existence, thus coming closer to the Corinthians' own thinking. In terms of his worldview, Paul uses the metaphor of "seeing" (5:7) in order to maintain an intentional vagueness. It is the divine Spirit alone that guarantees continuity

452. Cf. ibid., 114–15.

453. This is rightly emphasized by ibid., 115.

454. Cf. W. Wiefel, "Die Hauptrichtung des Wandels im eschatologischen Denken des Paulus," *TZ* 30 (1974): 77; Walter, "Leibliche Auferstehung," 116: "'Body' is now no longer a concept that can describe both the earthly *and* the heavenly mode of being, and thus Paul also develops the auxiliary concept of 'transformation' (of one corporeality into another, new corporeality)."

455. Seneca, *Ep.* 102.24, on the future life: "Another realm awaits us, another situation. Still, we can tolerate heaven only from a distance. Therefore, every time of decision waits without fear: it is not the last hour for the soul, but for the body" (*NW* 2.1:944–45).

456. Cf., e.g., Plato, *Phaedr.* 67c–d.

(5:5), which, in the imagery of 5:2–4, makes possible being "further clothed" with the "heavenly dwelling."

So also, in the Letter to the Romans, death before the parousia is no longer the exception but already the rule (cf. Rom. 14:8b, "So then, whether we live or whether we die, we are the Lord's").[457] The parousia of the Lord, it is true, is still thought of as imminent (cf. 13:11–12; 16:20), but the comparative in the expression "For salvation is nearer to us now than when we became believers" (13:11c) suggests an awareness of its delay. As an affirmation of eschatological hope, the phrase ζωὴ αἰώνιος (eternal life, the life of the age to come) gains increasing significance in Romans, which contains four of the five Pauline instances (cf. Gal. 6:8; Rom. 2:7; 5:21; 6:22, 23). This expression designates the future mode of being of those who are saved, which no longer is subject to any temporal limitation. In Romans Paul gives no programmatic presentation on the course of the final events, but Rom. 8:11 and 8:23 clearly indicate that once again the concept of a transformation of the body stands in the foreground.[458]

In Philippians we see the consolidation of two tendencies already visible in Paul's previous writings: Paul now reflects openly on the possibility of his death before the parousia, and he concentrates his eschatological imagery on the destiny of the individual.[459] In Phil. 1:20 the apostle speaks of his earthly body, in which Christ will be glorified "whether by life or by death." In 1:21–24 Paul wavers between the expectation of further life in this world and his own imminent death, together with his confidence that immediately after death he will be with Christ (1:23, σὺν Χριστῷ εἶναι). Philippians 1:23 looks forward to being in the presence of Christ immediately after death, without reference to the parousia and the resurrection. The singular formulation "if somehow I may attain the resurrection from the dead" (3:11, εἴ πως καταντήσω εἰς τὴν ἐξανάστασιν τὴν ἐκ νεκρῶν), with its double use of ἐκ (out of, from), likewise points to an early resurrection immediately after death.[460] To be sure, here, as in all of Paul's letters, the parousia is the horizon of all the apostle's eschatological statements (cf. 4:5b; 1:6, 10; 2:16; 3:20b), but as Paul nears the end of his life, he reconsiders his own destiny. Because he now thinks that he may die before the parousia, the parousia and the resurrection of the dead that will then take place can no longer be the one and only point of orientation.

457. On the eschatology of Romans, cf. G. Storck, "Eschatologie bei Paulus" (Göttingen: Georg August Universität, 1979), 117–59.

458. The comment of Walter, "Leibliche Auferstehung," 120, is on target: "Thus not redemption *from* the body or out of the body but the salvific *transformation* of the body."

459. Cf. Wiefel, "Eschatologischen Denken," 79–81.

460. Cf. C. H. Hunzinger, "Die Hoffnung angesichts des Todes im Wandel der paulinischen Aussagen," in *Leben angesichts des Todes: Beiträge zum theologischen Problem des Todes. Helmut Thielicke zum 60. Geburtstag* (ed. Bernhardt Lohse; Tübingen: Mohr, 1968), 87.

In central aspects of Paul's eschatology we can speak of *transformations*, that is, of *progressive steps in the apostle's thought* that correspond to the changing historical situations with which he was dealing.[461] For all that, the acute expectation of the near end remained the horizon of his thought, as the present and future Christ event continued to be the foundation of Pauline eschatology, but the status of the individual and the course of the final events themselves were adjusted as it became apparent that time was continuing. Paul obviously continued to hold fast to his conviction of the soon coming of the Lord, while simultaneously making appropriate adjustments in his eschatological affirmations.[462] As long as he firmly believed he would still be alive to experience the Lord's parousia, he portrayed the final events in terms of a broadly conceived apocalyptic scenario (cf. 1 Thess. 4:13–18; 1 Cor. 15:51ff.). But the realization that he might die before the parousia led to eschatological statements oriented to his own individual destiny. This change in his thought is appropriate, for eschatological statements are always held as a matter of anticipation, and the apostle could not ignore the fact that time was continuing. At the same time, "being with the Lord"/"being with Christ" (σὺν Χριστῷ εἶναι, 1 Thess. 4:17/Phil. 1:23) continued to be the foundational constant element of Pauline eschatology.

Corporeality and Life after Death

Paul also attained new and transformed insights on the question of the "how" of postmortal existence, insights that to no small degree were influenced by the way bodily existence was evaluated in Greek thought. Such thought was largely under the influence of the Platonic idea that immediately after death the immortal soul separated from the perishable body, so the body could have no significance for postmortal existence.[463] Thus Cicero states regarding the death of Hercules and Romulus and their going to the heavenly world, "Their bodies were not taken up to heaven, for Nature would not allow that which comes from the earth to be removed from the earth" (*Resp.* 3.28). Seneca emphasizes that the body is laid aside at death: "Why love such a thing as though it were your own possession? It was merely your covering. The day will come which will tear you forth and lead you away from the company of the foul and noisome womb" (*Ep.* 102.27). It is clear for Epictetus, too, that the body hinders freedom, so that the cry of the philosophy student is

461. Cf. Udo Schnelle, *Wandlungen im paulinischen Denken* (SBS 137; Stuttgart: Verlag Katholisches Bibelwerk, 1989), 37–48.

462. Lindemann, "Eschatologie," 1556, regards the changes as entirely occasioned by the differing situations to which Paul's letters were addressed.

463. Classically, Plato, *Phaed.* 80A: "And which does the soul resemble? The soul resembles the divine, and the body the mortal—there can be no doubt of that, Socrates" (ἡ μὲν ψυχὴ τῷ θείῳ, τὸ δὲ σῶμα τῷ θνητῷ); on the large number of doctrines of the soul current at the beginning of the first century, cf. Cicero, *Tusc.* 1.17–25, 26–81.

understandable: "Epictetus, we can no longer endure to be imprisoned with this paltry body, giving it food and drink, and resting and cleansing it, and, to crown all, being on its account brought into contact with these people and those. Are not these things indifferent—indeed, nothing—to us? And is not death no evil? Are we not in a manner akin to God, and have we not come from him?" (*Diatr.* 1.9.12–13). According to Plutarch, the only thing that survives is the image originally derived from the gods: "Yes, it comes from them, and to them it returns, not with its body, but only when it is most completely separated and set free from the body, and becomes altogether pure, fleshless, and undefiled."[464] Likewise in Hellenistic Judaism, the view was widespread that at death the perishable body is left behind and only the soul survives (cf., e.g., Wis. 9:15; Philo, *Migration* 9, 192). Against the cultural background of this historical situation Paul had to answer the question of the nature of life after death. His answer avoided the idea of the immortality of the soul but could not entirely do away with the negative evaluation of bodily existence. Whereas 1 Thess. 4:13–18 does not touch on the question at all, and 1 Cor. 15 presents Paul's initial answer, 2 Corinthians especially shows how Paul partly came to terms with the (Hellenistic) argumentation of the churches.[465] At the same time, the Roman and Philippian letters show that the line taken in 1 Cor. 15 continued to dominate: the body transformed by the divine Spirit preserves the identity of the self and as σῶμα πνευματικόν belongs to the divine world.

6.8.3 The Judgment

The idea of judgment was deeply rooted in both Jewish and Greek ideas of the transcendent world.[466] In Paul, the concept of judgment is found in various rhetorical contexts:[467]

464. Plutarch, *Rom.* 28; cf. also *Mor.* 382E.

465. Nikolaus Walter, "Hellenistische Eschatologie bei Paulus," *TQ* 176 (1996): 63: "All in all, we must conclude that the development of eschatological ideas in Paul took a clear step in the direction of Hellenization. And so we should probably also say regarding 2 Cor. 5:1–10 that a development of Paul's ideas of eschatological matters can in no way be denied."

466. On this point, cf. Peres, *Grabinschriften*, 60–69. Classically Plato, *Gorg.* 524A: "And these, when they are dead, shall give judgment in the meadow at the parting of the ways, whence the two roads lead, one to the Islands of the Blessed, and the other to Tartarus."

467. On this point cf. Ernst Synofzik, *Die Gerichts- und Vergeltungsaussagen bei Paulus: Eine traditionsgeschichtliche Untersuchung* (GTA 8; Göttingen: Vandenhoeck & Ruprecht, 1977); Matthias Klinghardt, "Sünde und Gericht von Christen bei Paulus," *ZNW* 88 (1997): 56–80; Matthias Konradt, *Gericht und Gemeinde: Eine Studie zur Bedeutung und Funktion von Gerichtsaussagen im Rahmen der paulinischen Ekklesiologie und Ethik im 1 Thess und 1 Kor* (BZNW 117; Berlin: de Gruyter, 2003), who formulates the matter appropriately: "That God judges the world (Rom. 3:6) is a firmly rooted element in Paul's thought. But just *how* God does this can be expressed in different ways by Paul, according to what the rhetorical situation calls for."

1. Within the eschatological passages of letter introductions (1 Thess. 2:19; 3:13; 1 Cor. 1:7b–9; 2 Cor. 1:13–14; Phil. 1:6, 10–11) and conclusions (1 Thess. 5:23–24; Rom. 16:20; Phil. 4:19–20).
2. In polemical statements against opponents (1 Thess. 2:16c; 1 Cor. 3:17; 2 Cor. 11:14, 15; Gal. 1:6–9; 5:10; Rom. 3:8; Phil. 1:28; 3:19).
3. In ethical admonitions (1 Cor. 3:12–15; 4:4–5; 5:5, 12–13; 6:2–3; 8:8; 10:12–13; 11:29–32; Rom. 12:19–20), in which the motif of sanctification receives particular significance (1 Cor. 1:8; 7:34; 2 Cor. 7:1; Phil. 1:9–11; 2:15–18). Especially in 1 Corinthians, the numerous references to judgment make it clear that the apostle understands the believer's relation to Christ to be a dynamic event[468] that can even include the loss of salvation (cf. 1 Cor. 5:1–13; 6:18; 8:11–12). For Paul, the Christian life is not a status attained once for all but a dynamic formation and continual realization of the effective call of God within everyday life.
4. References to judgment in the context of God's wrath on Jews and Gentiles alike (Rom. 1:18–3:20). Here the idea of a judgment according to works plays a particular role.

Judgment according to Works

The concept of a judgment according to one's works is also firmly anchored in both the Greco-Roman and Jewish worlds.[469] In Paul's writings, it emphatically appears in 2 Cor. 5:10 ("For all of us must appear before the judgment seat of Christ, so that each may receive recompense for what has been done in the body, whether good or evil"), and in Rom. 2:5c–8, which says about the Day of Wrath that God will "repay according to each one's deeds" (2:6). How is the idea of judgment according to works related to Paul's doctrine of justification as spelled out in Romans? We can see the problem clearly by comparing Rom. 2:6 with 3:28, where Paul says: "For we hold that a person is justified by faith apart from works prescribed by the law." For Paul, justification occurs as one stands before God through faith in the saving event accomplished by God in Jesus Christ. This justification remains valid even in the court of eschatological judgment. There, where God's judgment is rendered according to works, every human being would be lost, because no one can produce works that will stand the test before God. Therefore, all that counts is the saving work of Jesus Christ, which is presented to humankind in the form of the Pauline gospel, as a matter of faith (cf. Rom. 2:16, "on the day when, according to

468. For analysis, cf. Konradt, *Gericht und Gemeinde*, 197–471.

469. From the Jewish realm cf., e.g., Ps. 61:13 LXX; *Pss. Sol.* 2.16–17; a comprehensive presentation of the material is found in Wilckens, *Römer*, 1:127–31. For the Greco-Roman realm, cf. as a classic text Plato, *Phaed.* 113D–114C; for the New Testament period cf., e.g., Seneca, *Herc. fur.* 727–738, which reports of the underworld: "Is the report true that in the underworld justice, though tardy, is meted out, and that guilty souls who have forgot their crimes suffer due punishment? Who is that lord of truth, that arbiter of justice?"

my gospel, God, through Jesus Christ, will judge the secret thoughts of all"). *Precisely because there is a judgment according to works, human beings are directed to the grace of God alone!* For Paul, justification by grace through faith and judgment according to works form a unity. God alone accomplishes justification for human beings by his grace, because they are and remain sinful creatures in need of the Judge's pronouncement of acquittal.[470]

Theologically, the concept of judgment expresses that God is not indifferent to the life of the individual and to history as a whole. If judgment were not pronounced, then a person's actual deeds would remain unevaluated and dubious. The murderer would triumph over his victim, and the oppressor would get away with his evil. If there were no judgment, then world history and the life of the individual would themselves be the judgment. But because no deed, and no failure to act, is without consequences, and because they must be evaluated and judged for the sake of humanity, the concept of judgment is to be evaluated positively. It preserves human dignity and value to know that God has not turned away from his creation. In Jesus Christ, human beings may hope that God's grace has the last word (1 Thess. 5:9; Rom. 5:9–10).[471]

6.8.4 Israel

For Paul, the relation to Israel is simultaneously a biographical, a theological, and—at the end of his life—an eminently eschatological problem. The transition of salvation from the Jews to the Christians forcefully posed the question of God's relation to the people of Israel and the validity of his promises.

The earliest extant statement of the apostle regarding Israel, in 1 Thess. 2:14–16, already makes clear the interrelationship of biography and theology. Paul charges the Jews with what he himself had previously done: putting obstacles in the way of the saving proclamation of the gospel. For Paul, God had already pronounced judgment on the Jews; God's wrath had *already* descended on them.[472] In 1 Corinthians Paul has no extensive discussion of the relation of the young Christian movement to Israel, only referring in 1 Cor. 10:1ff. to the wilderness generation as a negative example warning the Corinthian enthusiasts.[473] In contrast, 2 Cor. 3 offers an insight into Paul's self-understanding as

470. On this point cf. Wilckens, *Römer*, 1:142–46.

471. Cf. Synofzik, *Vergeltungsaussagen*, 108–9: "In the judgment, human beings themselves cannot pronounce their own acquittal, but can only have it spoken to them through the gospel and believe on the saving act of God in Christ."

472. Cf. Günter Haufe, *Der erste Brief des Paulus an die Thessalonicher* (THKNT 12.1; Leipzig: Evangelische Verlagsanstalt, 1999), 48: "Because of their resistance to the divine plan of salvation, the Jews have already fallen under the wrath of God, even if this situation is not yet externally observable and is still hidden from them as well."

473. On this point cf. Schnelle, *Gerechtigkeit und Christusgegenwart*, 155–56.

an apostle and his christological interpretation of the Old Testament. By means of the antithesis "letter"/"Spirit" (2 Cor. 3:6), Paul designates the fundamental difference between the old covenant and the new. The glory of the office of proclamation of the gospel far surpasses the glory on the face of Moses, which he had to conceal from the people by veiling his face (cf. Exod. 34:29–35). In 2 Cor. 3:14 Paul explains the blindness of Israel as it encounters the glory of the revelation in Christ: "But their minds were hardened." This explanation directly spotlights the present guilt of Israel: not Moses but Israel itself is responsible for its unbelief.[474] Since it refuses to accept the revelation in Christ, the Old Testament also remains a closed book to it, for the veil that lies over the Old Testament to this very day can be removed only in Christ (2 Cor. 3:14b–15). For Paul, the Old Testament promises point to Christ, and only from the perspective of faith in him is an authentic understanding of the Old Testament possible. God remains faithful, Israel is hardened, but the apostle reckons with the possibility of its turning to Christ, and so two important changes may be observed in the view expressed in 1 Thess. 2:14–16: (1) God's final judgment on Israel has not been pronounced, for Israel can still convert, and (2) the Old Testament is fulfilled in Christ because God stands by his promises.

For the stance of the apostle to Israel, the expression Ἰσραὴλ τοῦ θεοῦ (Israel of God) in Gal. 6:16 is revealing: "As for those who will follow this rule, peace be upon them, and mercy, and upon the Israel of God." The meaning is revealed by the immediate context. Paul once again speaks polemically against his opponents (6:12–14), and then in Gal. 6:15 adds his credo on which his polemic is based, that neither circumcision nor uncircumcision counts for anything, for all that matters is the new existence in Jesus Christ (cf. 3:26–28; 1 Cor. 7:19; 2 Cor. 5:17). Those who agree with this rule are those to whom the conditional blessing (καὶ ὅσοι) in Gal. 6:16 applies. When one notes the function of 6:15 as the interpretative key to 6:16, the correspondence of granting the blessing with the conditional curse in 1:8,[475] the textual agreements with Jewish prayers,[476] and the copulative meaning of καί (and) before ἐπὶ τὸν Ἰσραὴλ τοῦ θεοῦ (on the Israel of God), then Ἰσραὴλ τοῦ θεοῦ can only refer to the Galatian church in the inclusive sense: the whole church of Jews and Gentiles, to the extent that they understand themselves to be committed to the new existence described in 6:15.[477] The "Israel of God" is this inclusive

474. Cf. Victor Paul Furnish, *II Corinthians* (AB 32A; Garden City, NY: Doubleday, 1984), 233.

475. Cf. Hans Dieter Betz, *Galatians: A Commentary on Paul's Letter to the Churches in Galatia* (Hermeneia; Philadelphia: Fortress, 1979), 544–45.

476. Cf. the nineteenth benediction of the Shemoneh Esreh (Babylonian recension): "Let peace, happiness and blessing, grace, love and mercy come on your people Israel"; cf. Strack and Billerbeck, *Kommentar*, 4:214.

477. Cf. Betz, *Galatians*, 544–45; Gerd Lüdemann, *Paulus und das Judentum* (TEH 215; Munich: Kaiser, 1983), 29.

church, not empirical Israel (cf. 1 Cor. 10:18, lit. "Israel according to the flesh"). This interpretation fits into the flow of thought in the Letter to the Galatians as a whole, for the debate with the Judaists also includes a sharp separation from unbelieving Judaism. In Gal. 4:25 the earthly Jerusalem represents the people of Israel, which not only belongs to the realm of slavery but is traced back by the apostle to Hagar and Ishmael, so that Abraham and Sarah have no connection to empirical Israel. A more radical demarcation can hardly be imagined! In 4:30–31 Paul concludes, formulating the result of his allegory of Sarah and Hagar by stating his view of God's saving acts: God has rejected the Jews, and only the Christians are heirs of the promise.

In Romans the theological and biographical problems involved in the Paul-Israel relation become more intense and then modulate into a new eschatological dimension. The question of the validity of the promises made to Israel, in view of the revelation of the righteousness of God apart from the law, is already broached in Rom. 1:16 and 2:9–10 (Ἰουδαίῳ τε πρῶτον [to the Jew first]), is thematized in 3:1–8, and then is taken up in Rom. 9–11 as a specific issue requiring thorough discussion.[478] God's righteousness is at stake, if the election of Israel, the promises to the patriarchs, and the covenants are no longer valid (Rom. 9:5). The word of God would then have failed (9:6). But Paul argues the converse: the election of Israel is still in effect, the promises are still valid, but God's revelation in Jesus Christ has brought Israel to a crisis point. In Rom. 9–11 Paul wants to demonstrate the faithfulness of God in contrast to the unfaithfulness of Israel that has so far prevailed. He sets forth his ideas in a train of thought that is filled with tensions, repeatedly adopting new viewpoints and ways of considering the issue. He begins by distinguishing empirical Israel (Israel according to the flesh) and the Israel defined by the promise, which alone is the true Israel (9:6–8). Then he affirms that only a remnant of Israel is elect while the rest remain hardened (11:5ff.). Finally, through the idea that the election of the Gentiles will ultimately bring salvation to Israel, he comes to his crowning thesis in 11:26a: πᾶς Ἰσραὴλ σωθήσεται (all Israel will be saved).[479] This *crowning thesis* of Pauline *eschatology* and *soteriology* poses numerous problems. In the first place, the point in time to

478. In addition to the analyses of Rom. 9–11 in the standard commentaries, cf. Luz, *Geschichtsverständnis*, 64–108; Hübner, *Gottes Ich*; Hans-Martin Lübking, *Paulus und Israel im Römerbrief: Eine Untersuchung zu Römer 9–11* (EHS 23.260; Frankfurt: Lang, 1986); Heikki Räisänen, "Römer 9–11: Analyse eines geistigen Ringens," *ANRW* 2.25.4 (Berlin: de Gruyter, 1987), 2891–2939; Dieter Sänger, *Die Verkündigung des Gekreuzigten und Israel: Studien zum Verhältnis von Kirche und Israel bei Paulus und im frühen Christentum* (WUNT 75; Tübingen: Mohr, 1994); Theobald, *Römerbrief*, 258–85; Angelika Reichert, *Der Römerbrief als Gratwanderung: Eine Untersuchung zur Abfassungsproblematik* (FRLANT 194; Göttingen: Vandenhoeck & Ruprecht, 2001), 147–221.

479. On the structure of Rom. 11:25–27, cf. Ferdinand Hahn, "Zum Verständnis von Röm 11,26a," in *Paul and Paulinism: Essays in Honour of C. K. Barrett* (ed. Morna Dorothy Hooker and S. G. Wilson; London: SPCK, 1982), 227.

which this announced event refers is hardly disputed, since v. 26b refers to the advent of Christ at the parousia (cf. 1 Thess. 1:10). In the interpretation of πᾶς Ἰσραήλ, the immediate context and the corresponding expression πλήρωμα τῶν ἐθνῶν (fullness of the Gentiles) are decisive. In v. 20, unbelief is named as the basis for Israel's exclusion from salvation, which must be overcome (v. 23) as the condition for Israel's inclusion. Verse 23 especially diminishes the likelihood of an interpretation of v. 26a that does not include faith in Christ.[480] In v. 25b πλήρωμα does not refer to the full number of Christians from among the Gentiles, for only then do the apostle's concept of faith and his preaching of judgment retain their validity. Even so, πᾶς Ἰσραήλ does not mean simply ethnic Israel, but rather only that part of Israel that has come to faith in God's eschatological act whereby Israel will turn toward salvation.[481] In addition to v. 23, this interpretation is supported by the distinction between the Israel of promise and the Israel "according to the flesh" of 9:6, as well as the apostle's comment in Rom. 11:14b that he hopes to save *some* of his "own people."[482]

Finally, the apostle's use of σῴζω/σωτηρία (save/salvation) makes it clear that for him there is no salvation apart from faith.[483] In Rom. 1:16 salvation is granted only to those who believe, to the Jews first and then to the Greeks. The qualification of σωτηρία by δικαιοσύνη θεοῦ and πίστις in the foundational theological statement of Rom. 1:16–17 remains determinative for any broader understanding. In Rom. 5:9, 10 righteousness by faith is paralleled by the blood of Christ, which makes salvation from the coming wrath possible. The form σωθήσεται in the Isaiah quotation in Rom. 9:27 is revealing, since it refers specifically to only a remnant of Israel and thus prejudices the understanding of σωθήσεται in 11:26a. Moreover, Rom. 10:9–13 expressly emphasizes that only faith in Jesus Christ grants salvation. According to Rom. 10:12, there is no difference between Jews and Gentiles, but Christ is the Lord of Jews and Gentiles. Why should the Jews be provoked to jealousy by the Gentile Christians, if Israel already possesses everything the Gentiles have anyway? Why is Paul so deeply troubled (Rom. 9:2–3; 10:1) if Israel could come to salvation while bypassing Christ?

According to Rom. 11:25–27, Paul expected an act of God in the end times that would lead to the conversion and thus the salvation of Israel when Christ appears at the parousia.[484] He obviously speaks in vv. 25b and 26a as a *prophet*

480. On the meaning of Rom. 11:23, cf. also ibid., 228–29. Verse 23 speaks decisively against the thesis of F. Mussner, "'Ganz Israel wird gerettet werden' (Röm 11,26)," *Kairos* 18 (1976): 241–55, that in Rom. 11:26a Paul indicates that Israel has a "special way" to salvation.

481. According to Rom. 9:27, only a remnant of Israel will be saved.

482. Cf. Hahn, "Röm 11,26a," 229.

483. Cf. Hübner, *Gottes Ich*, 117.

484. Cf. Käsemann, *Romans*, 305: "Its [Israel's] full conversion is expected, but it is bound up with the fact that salvation has come first to the Gentiles."

who gives information about an event that *cannot be derived from the kerygma on the basis of arguments*.[485] Here prophecy serves Paul as a means of obtaining theological knowledge that fills in a lacuna in theological reflection. He thus sees the faithfulness and identity of God preserved, the God who will not reject Israel forever, but who has subjected both Jews and Gentiles to disobedience, so that in Jesus Christ he could have mercy on both (cf. Rom. 11:32). Precisely the plurality of solutions shows how rigorously Paul has struggled with this theme and how deeply he was personally involved in it.[486] If God does not hold fast to the continuity of his promises, then how can the gospel be credibly proclaimed? Thus in Rom. 9–11 the ultimate issue is the deity of God, God's righteousness and faithfulness in the face of human unfaithfulness, but it also concerns Paul's own credibility and the meaning of his own life and personal destiny. Paul is certain that God remains true to himself and that in the final days will by his miraculous power bring Israel to conversion and thus to salvation. Paul thus at the same time admits that this problem cannot be solved by human beings in the present but calls for an extraordinary act of God in the future.

The position of the apostle regarding Israel has undergone *radical changes*. It is not possible to reconcile 1 Thess. 2:14–16 with Rom. 11:25–26, and so we must speak of a revision of Paul's stance on the issue.[487] Whereas in the former passage God has already rejected his people, in the latter he will save them. Why did Paul revise his judgment about Israel? The way in which each situation conditioned his thinking called for new reflections on Israel, which then led to new judgments about the facts of the matter. The polemic in 1 Thess. 2:14–16 is solely conditioned by the Jewish opposition to the Gentile mission. But 2 Cor. 3 already shows that for Paul a new situation again evokes different statements. The Letter to the Galatians, where the confrontation with the Judaists must necessarily influence the theological evaluation of Israel, provides confirmation. Finally, the Letter to the Romans itself speaks for the way the situation

485. Cf. Helmut Merklein, "Der Theologe als Prophet," in *Studien zu Jesus und Paulus* (2 vols.; WUNT 43, 105; Tübingen: Mohr, 1987–98), 2:402–3; M. Eugene Boring, *Sayings of the Risen Jesus: Christian Prophecy in the Synoptic Tradition* (SNTSMS 46; Cambridge: Cambridge University Press, 1982), 103–10; Thomas W. Gillespie, *The First Theologians: A Study in Early Christian Prophecy* (Grand Rapids: Eerdmans, 1994); Wayne A. Meeks, introduction to *The Writings of St. Paul* (ed. Wayne A. Meeks and John T. Fitzgerald; 2nd ed.; New York: Norton, 2007), xxii–xxiv.

486. Cf. Gerd Theissen, "Röm 9–11—Eine Auseinandersetzung des Paulus mit Israel und sich selbst: Versuch einer psychologischen Auslegung," in *Fair Play: Diversity and Conflicts in Early Christianity; Essays in Honour of Heikki Räisänen* (ed. Heikki Räisänen et al.; NovTSup 103; Leiden: Brill, 2002), 326: "When Paul engages in such intellectual struggles concerning the salvation of all Israel, he is wrestling with the issue of his own salvation."

487. Among those who understand the matter in this sense are Räisänen, "Römer 9–11," 25.4:2925. Wilckens, *Römer*, 2:209, rightly emphasizes that "the result of the first move in Paul's thought in Rom. 9 (and then also the result of his second step in Rom. 10) is superseded and neutralized when he finally reaches the goal of his thought in chapter 11."

conditions Paul's stance on the issue, for here Paul is dealing with a church, unknown to him personally, in which there were obvious disputes between Jewish Christians and Gentile Christians (cf. Rom. 14:1–15:13), a church in which he must assume that his Jewish Christian opponents had already exercised some influence. In addition, there is the personal situation of the apostle: he sees his mission in the east as complete (Rom. 15:23) and wants to deliver the collection to Jerusalem so that he can then continue his work in the west (Rom. 15:24ff.). Both the collection, as a visible bond of unity between Jewish Christians and Gentile Christians, and the actual numerical predominance of Gentile Christians in the churches established in Paul's previous missionary work made it necessary for him to reflect afresh on the destiny of Israel. Inseparably bound up with the existence of the original church in Jerusalem as the holy remnant of Israel was the theological question of the destiny of that part of Israel that had so far failed to accept the revelation in Christ. Paul's decision, despite his statement in 1 Cor. 16:3, to go to Jerusalem himself in order to make good on his promised service to the church there—a decision that he knew involved some danger—also posed the theological problem of the faithfulness and righteousness of God toward Israel. In addition, Paul had gained a different view of his Gentile mission. Whereas in 1 Thess. 2:14–16 hindrance to this mission still occasioned vigorous polemic, Paul saw a different function for the Gentile mission as he finished his work in the east: its purpose is to provoke the Jews so that they too will come to faith and be saved (Rom. 11:13–15).

6.8.5 Death and New Life

Paul's eschatology involved a restructure of time itself,[488] for with the resurrection of Jesus Christ an irreversible turn of the ages had taken place. A past event determines the present and anticipates the future as the paradigm of what is to come. From this standpoint it was possible for Paul to resolve the problem posed by the death of members of the community. In this process he could incorporate some motifs from Jewish apocalyptic, but by no means could he take over self-contained systems for structuring meaning and time, for the uniquely new aspects of the event required an independent solution. It called for an outline of an eschatological scenario whose functional and temporal anchor points would be formed by the resurrection of Jesus Christ from the dead and his imminent return from God, whose confidence would be nourished by the present experience of the Spirit, and whose outlook for the future would lie in the hope of an analogous act of God: Jesus of Nazareth

488. On the New Testament understanding of time, cf. Gerhard Delling, *Das Zeitverständnis des Neuen Testaments* (Gütersloh: Bertelsmann, 1940); Gerhard Delling, *Zeit und Endzeit: Zwei Vorlesungen zur Theologie des Neuen Testaments* (Neukirchen-Vluyn: Neukirchener Verlag, 1970); Kurt Erlemann, *Endzeiterwartungen im frühen Christentum* (Tübingen: Francke, 1996).

serves as prototype for God's creative, life-giving power. Within this model, the Spirit, as the mode of the continuing presence of God and Jesus Christ in the church, guarantees the necessary functional and temporal continuity or duration between the two anchor points, so that baptized believers live in the consciousness of contemporaneity with these events, which factually are past and still to come.

Theories of Death in Antiquity

The theme of death played an important role not only for Paul but also for competing systems of meaning and construals of time, for every statement about death is a statement about life, and vice versa. Especially in the Greco-Roman world, there existed a multiplicity of ideas about death and the possibility of life after death. We find not only faith that the immortal soul continues to live but also numerous skeptical variations on this theme.[489] Epicurus developed an independent and still fascinating theory of death as the absence of time: "Death is nothing to us; for the body, when it has been resolved into its elements, has no feeling, and that which has no feeling is nothing to us" (*Rat. sent.* 2 [in Diogenes Laertius, *Vit. phil.* 10.139]). This awareness is in itself adequate to overcome the fear of death, which otherwise hinders living a fulfilled life; the fact of the matter is that "the practice of a fulfilled life and a fulfilled death are one and the same" (Epicurus, *Men.* 126). Cicero repeats a mixture of Platonic and Epicurean ideas: "In what sense then, or for what reason do you say that you consider death an evil, when it will either render us happy if our souls survive, or free from wretchedness if we are without sensation?" (*Tusc.* 1.25). Nor does Seneca express any fear of death: "And what is death? It is either the end, or a process of change [*Mors quid est? Aut finis aut transitus*]. I have no fear of ceasing to exist; it is the same as never having begun. Nor do I shrink from changing into another state, because I shall, under no conditions, be as cramped as I am now" (*Ep.* 65.24).[490] According to Epictetus, death is neither an evil nor the state of nonbeing but only the transition from one state of being to another (*Diatr.* 3.24.93–95). Dio Chrysostom sees the matter as follows: "God, therefore, looking upon these things and observing all the banqueters, as if he were in his own house,

489. Cf., e.g., *SVF* 2.790: "Chrysippus says, however, that death is the separation of the soul from the body"; Eusebius, *Praep. ev.* 20.20.6: "'The soul,' say the Stoics, 'comes into being and passes out of existence.'" Comprehensive overviews are provided by Erwin Rohde, *Psyche: The Cult of Souls and Belief in Immortality among the Greeks* (trans. W. B. Hillis; Freeport, NY: Books for Libraries Press, 1972); Martin P. Nilsson, *A History of Greek Religion* (trans. F. J. Fielden; Westport, CT: Greenwood Press, 1980), 498–535; Walter Burkert, *Greek Religion* (trans. John Raffan; Cambridge, MA: Harvard University Press, 1985); Manuel Vogel, *Commentatio Mortis: 2Kor 5,1–10 auf dem Hintergrund antiker Ars Moriendi* (FRLANT 124; Göttingen: Vandenhoeck & Ruprecht, 2006), 45–209.

490. Cf. Seneca, *Ep.* 54.3–5; 99.29–30; *Marc.* 19.4–5.

how each person has comported himself at the banquet, ever calls the best to himself; and, if he happens to be especially pleased with any one, he bids him remain there and makes him his boon and companion" (*Or.* 30.44).

In view of the number of quite attractive answers to the problem of death, there arises the question of the Pauline model's ability to hold its own. In Judaism prior to the destruction of the temple, the concept of resurrection was the dominant but by no means the only model.[491] Among the Greeks, skepticism prevailed concerning any sort of continuing bodily existence after death, however it was conceived. Already in Aeschylus, *Eum.* 545, one can read this about the finality of death: "For once the dust soaks up a man's blood, there is no resurrection for him [οὔτις ἔστ' ἀνάστασις]." Especially among the Cynics is there great hesitation regarding theories of life after death.[492] A tradition about Diogenes reports, "But some say that when dying he left instructions that they should throw him out unburied, that every wild beast might feed on him, or thrust him into a ditch and sprinkle a little dust over him"(Diogenes Laertius, *Vit. phil.* 6.79). Here too Paul transcended intellectual and cultural boundaries by *combining* the Jewish concept of resurrection with the Greek view of the spirit as the present and enduring divine power of life and thus facilitated the reception of his views in the Hellenistic world. Rituals are also essential factors in the construal of a culture's time and identity. Especially baptism, as the place where the Spirit is conferred and the new life begins, stamps Christian existence with an unmistakable character of the "I" that endures even beyond death through the life-giving power of God. *In death, my relationship to myself and to other human beings comes to an end, but not God's relation to me.* Thus narratives too confer lasting meaning on a unique event and so facilitate a particular construal of time. By presenting the Jesus-Christ-history as the model for God's love and creative power, which overcome even death, Paul opens up to people from all ethnic and national groups and from all social levels the possibility of breaking out of traditional preconceptions and trusting the continuity of God's love. Time is not abolished but entrusted to God's righteousness, goodness, and mercy. Neither Hellenism's cultural-imperial construal of time nor Jewish apocalypticism's destruction of time in the eschatological catastrophe were able to arouse a comparable assurance.

6.9 Setting in the History of Early Christian Theology

Paul was not the founder of early Christianity but *was the one who gave it definitive shape.* While ancient Judaism sought to preserve its religious and

491. Cf. Günter Stemberger, "Auferstehung 3: Antikes Judentum," *RGG*[4] 1:916–17.

492. On this point cf. Downing, *Pauline Churches*, 242–49.

ethnic identity, formative Christianity programmatically transgressed ethnic, cultural, and religious boundaries, especially in the form of the Pauline mission, which had abandoned the precondition of circumcision. He propagated a *universal plan of messianic redemption* that embraced people of all nations and cultures. It was not the drawing of boundaries but acculturation (cf. 1 Cor. 9:20–22) and enculturation, as well as transethnic conceptions (cf. Gal. 3:26–28), that set the definitive tone for the Pauline mission. The intentionally transnational, transcultural mission transcended class distinctions and attracted a broad spectrum of members. Its magnitude, speed, and results have no analogy in antiquity. Pauline Christianity created a new cognitive identity that in part took up previous cultural identities and at the same time fundamentally reformed them. Paul thereby created the basis for Christianity as a world religion.

Paul's achievement, and also his tragedy, consisted in the fact that he created something new without wanting to break off the continuity with the old—but he did not really achieve this aim. It was not possible for him either to convert the majority of Israel to maintain a firm connection with the earliest church in Jerusalem. In order to continue affirming the unity of what in fact had separated, Paul was compelled to work out retrospective rationalizations, especially on the question of the law and the problematical issue of how Israel continues as the people of God. His understanding of God did not permit him to declare the abrogation of the first covenant. He could not accept, and did not want to accept, that God made or had to make a second attempt in order to bring deliverance and salvation for the world.[493] Therefore Paul *had to* accept lines of argument that were in part contradictory, vague, and artificial.[494] All this did not derive from his arbitrariness or lack of theological competence but was already objectively present in the issues he faced, questions that essentially are still with us. They cannot be answered, because God alone knows the answers!

To think of Paul exclusively as the successful missionary does not do him justice. His work could only have been so successful because he propagated an attractive understanding of God, the world, and human life, an understanding that *appealed to the intellect in form and content*. As the philosopher "explains and proclaims the essence of the divine perhaps most truly and completely

493. Cf. Sanders, *Paul and Palestinian Judaism* 127–28, who rightly emphasizes that Paul's thought was guided by unshakable axioms that could not be brought into logical consistency.

494. This aspect is not noticed by Räisänen, 266–67, when he states, "It is a fundamental mistake of much Pauline exegesis in this century to have portrayed Paul as 'the prince of thinkers' and the Christian 'theologian par excellence.'" Paul was more than an original thinker, for despite the problems mentioned above, his work possesses a systematic quality that Räisänen's statement does not take into account. On the problem of the logic of Pauline thought, cf. Moisés Mayordomo-Marín, *Argumentiert Paulus logisch? Eine Analyse vor dem Hintergrund antiker Logik* (WUNT 188; Tübingen: Mohr Siebeck, 2005); M. Eugene Boring, "The Language of Universal Salvation in Paul," *JBL* 105 (1986): 269–92.

with his mind,"[495] so the missionary and God-thinker Paul proclaims the ultimate saving plan of God in Jesus Christ. The ancient Greeks (like modern people) proceeded on the conviction that they could attain the right direction for their lives through their own thinking and acting.[496] Paul outlines a new and different picture: all the attributes that human beings generally ascribe to their own subjectivity are ascribed by Paul to God: love, freedom, justice, and meaning. Only God as the ground of humanity's being in the external world is able to ground and preserve the freedom and dignity of the human subject. For Paul, the "for us" of the salvation obtained in Jesus Christ becomes the fundamental formula of theological grammar. Here Paul is fundamentally different from all thinkers of antiquity. The philosopher propagates the autonomy to be realized by the self; over against this, the apostle offers autonomy as the gift of God.

495. Dio Chrysostom, *Or.* 12.47.

496. Cf. Musonius, *Diss.* 2: "Human beings can by nature live free from sin" (trans. MEB). Cf. on this perspective M. Pohlenz, *Der hellenische Mensch* (Göttingen: Vandenhoeck & Ruprecht, 1947), 304, 345, and passim.

7

The Third Transformation

Composition of Gospels as Innovative Response to Crises

A watershed in the history of early Christian theology occurred in the decade 60–70 CE. Problems generated by external influences and by the internal logic of the community's own faith created a situation in which a new orientation had to be developed that involved both theological integration and literary genres.

7.1 Death of the Founders

Three of the most important figures in early Christianity died as martyrs at almost the same time, shortly before the outbreak of the Jewish war: James the brother of Jesus was killed in 62 CE in Jerusalem; Peter and Paul were probably killed in 64 CE in Rome. Their deaths generated a distinct turning point in the self-understanding of the early Christian community, a critical moment that generated significant literary by-products. The place of the eyewitnesses (cf. 1 Cor. 15:3–5) is now taken by writings of a new literary genre—gospels—and by pseudepigraphical letters (theological documents pseudonymously claiming apostolic authority: the deutero-Paulines and letters in the names of Peter, James, and Jude). These are yoked to a particular historical consciousness: the period of the eyewitnesses is definitely past, so the Jesus-Christ-history must be presented in a new and lasting form for the sake of future recipients.

The testimony of the first witnesses, who had mediated the original events and provided the community's authentic identification, would continue in the form of pseudepigraphical writings, and the ways they had understood the faith would continue to shape early Christianity.

Peter and Paul

Simon (Peter) belonged to the first group of disciples, along with his brother Andrew (cf. Mark 1:16–20; John 1:41–42), and became an acknowledged leader both in the circle of Jesus's original disciples and in the earliest Christian community.[1] His confession of Jesus as Messiah (Mark 8:27–30), the symbolic name "Peter" ([noble] stone; cf. Mark 3:13–16), and the eschatological promise in Matt. 16:18–19 clearly reveal his special status, which was not abrogated by the fact that during the trial of Jesus, Peter had denied his master (Mark 14:54, 66–72). Peter was numbered among the definitive witnesses of the resurrection (cf. 1 Cor. 15:5; Mark 16:7; Luke 24:34) and became the first leader of the earliest Jerusalem church (cf. Gal. 1:18; Acts 1:15; 2:14–42; 3:1–26, and through chap. 12). He left Jerusalem at the time of the persecution under Herod Agrippa I (cf. Acts 12:17) and gradually became an advocate of the mission to Gentiles that did not require circumcision (cf. Gal. 2:11–12; Acts 10:1–11, 18). He later did mission work in the area of the Pauline churches (cf. 1 Cor. 1:12; 9:5),[2] and in that context evidently also came to Rome, where he was killed.[3]

Paul wanted to travel from Corinth to Jerusalem to deliver the collection (Rom. 15:22–33), and then to Rome, where he hoped to receive support from the church for his projected mission to Spain.[4] Luke gives an extensive report of Paul's stay in Jerusalem, his imprisonment, and his trip to Rome as a prisoner (cf. Acts 21:15–28:31), although we are still in the dark about many events of this period. The open-ended conclusion of Acts is significant

1. For recent study of Peter, cf. especially C. Böttrich, *Petrus: Fischer, Fels, und Funktionär* (BG 2; Leipzig: Evangelische Verlagsanstalt, 2001); and Martin Hengel, *Der unterschätzte Petrus: Zwei Studien* (Tübingen: Mohr Siebeck, 2006); cf. also Raymond E. Brown et al., eds., *Peter in the New Testament* (Minneapolis: Augsburg, 1973); Pheme Perkins, *Peter: Apostle for the Whole Church* (Columbia, SC: University of South Carolina Press, 1994).

2. Martin Karrer, "Petrus im paulinischen Gemeindekreis," *ZNW* 80 (1989).

3. *1 Clem.* 5.2–4 reports: "Because of jealousy and envy the greatest and most righteous pillars were persecuted and fought to the death. Let us set before our eyes the good Apostles. There was Peter, who, because of unrighteous jealousy [ζῆλον ἄδικον], endured not one or two but many trials, and thus having given his testimony went to his appointed place of glory."

4. On the final period of Paul's life, cf. Friedrich Wilhelm Horn, ed., *Das Ende des Paulus: Historische, theologische und literaturgeschichtliche Aspekte* (BZNW 106; New York: de Gruyter, 2001); Heike Omerzu, *Der Prozess des Paulus: Eine exegetische und rechtshistorische Untersuchung der Apostelgeschichte* (BZNW 115; Berlin: de Gruyter, 2002); Schnelle, *Apostle Paul*, 381–86.

both historically and theologically. Although Paul is the book's hero, at first covertly and then from chapter 15 on openly, Acts does not disclose how his story ends. The author himself knows the real purpose of Paul's last visit to Jerusalem (cf. Acts 24:17), and in Acts 20:24–25 already looks back on his death, but he neither makes the purpose explicit nor narrates Paul's death. It is clear from Rom. 16 that Paul is personally acquainted with numerous Roman Christians. Yet in Acts there is no clear encounter between Paul and the Roman church (cf. Acts 28:16). Instead, as is typical for his procedure in Acts, Paul first establishes contact with the local synagogue (cf. Acts 28:17ff.). In Rome, as elsewhere, the rejection of his message by Jews is what first causes Paul to turn to the Gentiles. This way of telling the story gives the impression that Paul was the first to establish a church in Rome, though Acts 28:15 presupposes a non-Pauline origin for the Roman church. What impels Luke to tell the story this way? We must suppose that he had available only a few reliable historical traditions for this period of Paul's life.[5] Here we should note the tendency throughout Luke's two volumes to absolve the Romans of any guilt for the death of Jesus or for hindering the Christian mission (see below, §8.4). It is thus likely that Luke would have remained silent about Paul's conviction and execution in Rome, although he knew about the apostle's death (cf. Acts 19:21; 20:23–25; 21:11). Only so much can be said with historical confidence: Paul reached Rome as part of a prisoner transport, and was able to continue his mission there despite his imprisonment. Paul appears as a lonesome man, in no way supported by the Roman church, a man whose mission among the Roman Jews achieved only minimal success. This situation fits the personal tradition in 2 Tim. 4:10–16, which agrees with Acts 28:16–31 in a decisive point: Paul has been left in the lurch by his fellow workers; only Luke is with him! Even though the strands of tradition in Acts and 2 Timothy argue quite differently in terms of details, they agree that Paul received no support from his fellow workers, and probably none from the Roman church. The emphasis on zeal/jealousy and strife in *1 Clem.* 5.4–5 confirms this picture;[6] the disputes that had raged around the person of Paul between Christians of Jewish background and those from the Greco-Roman world—or between Jews and Christians, or both—continued

5. Cf. Heike Omerzu, "Das Schweigen des Lukas: Überlegungen zum offenen Ende der Apostelgeschichte," in *Das Ende des Paulus: Historische, theologische und literaturgeschichtliche Aspekte* (ed. Friedrich Wilhelm Horn; BZNW 106; New York: de Gruyter, 2001), 151–56, who regards Acts 28:16, 23, 30–31 as a traditional core.

6. Cf. *1 Clem.* 5.5–7: "Because of jealousy and strife [διὰ ζῆλον καὶ ἔριν] Paul showed the way to the prize for patient endurance. After he had been seven times in chains, had been driven into exile, had been stoned, and had preached in the east and in the west, he won the genuine glory for his faith, having taught righteousness to the whole world and having reached the farthest limits of the west. Finally, when he had given his testimony before the rulers, he thus departed from the world and went to the holy place, having become an outstanding example of patient endurance."

in Rome. Paul was left to die alone, probably in the Neronian persecution (cf. Tacitus, *Ann.* 15.44.2–5; Suetonius, *Nero* 16.2).

James

James, the brother of Jesus, along with Peter, Mary Magdalene, and Paul, was acknowledged to have received a special revelation of the risen Lord (1 Cor. 15:7, "He appeared to James, then to the Twelve"). In the earliest period of the Jerusalem church he had not yet come to the fore; it was only after the expulsion of the Hellenists from Jerusalem (cf. Acts 8:1ff.) that James, as biological brother of the Lord and advocate of a Torah-true line, became one of the leading figures in the early Christian movement. At Paul's first visit to Jerusalem in 35 CE, Peter was the apparent leader of the earliest church (cf. Gal. 1:18). The Apostolic Council in 48 CE reveals a changed situation in which the "pillars" in Jerusalem are listed as James, Peter, and John (Gal. 2:9), i.e., James is now the decisive figure. Peter's departure from Jerusalem was probably also a contributing factor, since according to Acts 12:17–18 Peter had fled before the aggressive actions of Herod Antipas. Moreover, we may assume that James and Peter espoused differing theological positions. Very early, Peter manifested an openness to the Gentile mission, while James obviously advocated a strict Jewish Christian position, which after the Apostolic Council was also directed against the Pauline mission, which did not require circumcision. James's loyalty to the law is emphasized not only in the New Testament literature[7] but also in Josephus's report of his martyrdom (*Ant.* 20.197–203). Josephus transmits the story that, during the power vacuum between the death of Festus and the inauguration of his successor, the Sadducean high priest Ananus, son of the Annas of the Synoptic Gospels, moved against James and other members of the Jerusalem church. In 62 CE, Ananus the Younger presumably called together the Sanhedrin and had James and other Jewish Christians stoned to death on the charge that they violated the Torah.[8] This decision, made by the Sadducean majority, evoked the firm resistance of the Pharisees, who ultimately intervened successfully with the new Roman governor Albinos. Although James the Lord's brother had divorced himself from the Pauline concept of mission,

7. In *Gospel of Thomas* 12 he appears as "James the Just" (cf. further Eusebius, *Hist. eccl.* 1.3 and elsewhere); for an analysis of the James tradition, cf. Martin Hengel, "Jakobus, der Herrenbruder—der erste Papst?" in *Paulus und Jakobus: Kleine Schriften III* (ed. Martin Hengel; WUNT 141; Tübingen: Mohr, 2002), 549–82; Wilhelm Pratscher, *Der Herrenbruder Jakobus und die Jakobustradition* (FRLANT 139; Göttingen: Vandenhoeck & Ruprecht, 1987).

8. Cf. Josephus, *Ant.* 20.200: "And so he convened the judges of the Sanhedrin and brought before them a man named James, the brother of Jesus who is called the Christ [τὸν ἀδελφὸν Ἰησοῦ τοῦ λεγομένου Χριστοῦ], and certain others. He accused them of having transgressed the law and delivered them to be stoned."

he was no longer able to save the early church during this phase in which nationalism was intensifying within broad streams of Judaism.

7.2 Delay of the Parousia

The death of the founders required the community to rethink how to remain connected to the events and persons that called it into being. A second problem was directly connected with this, a problem that likewise contained a temporal and material dimension: the delay of the expected parousia of Jesus Christ.[9] Within early Christianity there developed very quickly a basically unified eschatological perspective: the resurrection of Jesus Christ from the dead and the experiences of the Spirit assured the believers that Jesus would come back soon as the "Son" (cf. 1 Thess. 1:9–10), "Lord" (cf. Phil. 4:5; Rev. 22:20), or "Son of Man" (cf., e.g., Mark 8:38; 13:24–27; 14:62; Matt. 10:23; Luke 18:8). The risen Lord would soon reappear as judge (1 Cor. 16:22, μαράνα θά [our Lord, come]). His reappearance was expected in the near future (cf. 1 Thess. 5:23; 1 Cor. 1:7; 15:23), and determined both the thinking and acting of the earliest Christians. As time passed, they faced a considerable task of rethinking and reinterpretation, for if the early Christians were to maintain their faith in the Lord's return, they needed an explanation for both their continued confidence and the fact of its delay.

In the case of *Paul*, the direct expectation of the near parousia is the consistent horizon of his eschatology (see above, §6.8); until the end of his life, the imminent advent of the crucified and risen Jesus Christ was a formative element of his symbolic universe (cf. Phil. 4:5, "the Lord is near"). The whole creation is moving in this direction, and Paul saw himself on the leading edge of this movement. Nonetheless, even in Paul there were already hints of an awareness that the parousia was being delayed:

1. The unexpected death of members of the church compelled Paul to extend the eschatological schedule (1 Thess. 4:13–18).
2. The prolongation of time meant that Paul had to relocate his own place in the eschatological events. While in 1 Thess. 4:17 and 1 Cor. 15:51 he expected to be transformed and taken up to the heavenly world before he died, it is clear that by the time he wrote 2 Cor. 5:1–10, and especially Phil. 1:21–23, he reckoned with the possibility of his own death before the parousia.

9. On the delay of the parousia in early Christianity, cf. Werner Georg Kümmel, *Promise and Fulfillment: The Eschatological Message of Jesus* (SBT 23; London: SCM, 1961); Erich Grässer, *Das Problem der Parusieverzögerung in den synoptischen Evangelien und in der Apostelgeschichte* (BZNW 22; Berlin: Töpelmann, 1957); Strecker, *Theology of the New Testament*, 327–42; Kurt Erlemann, *Naherwartung und Parusieverzögerung im Neuen Testament: Ein Beitrag zur Frage religiöser Zeiterfahrung* (TANZ 17; Tübingen: Francke, 1995).

3. The comparative ἐγγύτερον (nearer) in Rom. 13:11 indicates the growing awareness that the Lord's parousia is being delayed: "Salvation is nearer to us now than when we became believers."

On the one hand, the *sayings source Q* manifests an eager expectation that the kingdom of God will come soon (cf. Q 11:2–4), but it also contains thematic statements reflecting the delay of the parousia (see below, §8.1.8). In the parable of the Faithful and Unfaithful Slaves (Q 12:42–46), v. 45 states, "But if that slave says in his heart, 'My master is delayed [χρονίζει],' and if he begins to beat his fellow slaves." The motif of uncertainty about the time of the parousia also dominates the parable of the Pounds: "A nobleman went to a distant country to get royal power for himself and then return. When [after a long time] he returned, having received royal power, he ordered these slaves, to whom he had given the money, to be summoned so that he might find out what they had gained by trading" (Q 19:12, 15). Q 17:23 warns against false prophecy that the Son of Man will return soon, and commands the believers, "Do not follow them!" This is related to the Q motifs of alertness in view of the uncertainty of when the end will come: "For as the lightning flashes and lights up the sky from one side to the other, so will the Son of Man be in his day."

Mark integrates the expectation of the parousia into an eschatological schedule (see below, §8.2.8), thus holding fast both to the assurance of the imminent advent of the Son of Man and the indefiniteness of the exact time (Mark 13:24–27). He connects the eschatological expectation to the historical event of the destruction of the temple (Mark 13:2ff.) while at the same time disconnecting it from a particular historical schedule, because only God knows the date when the Coming One will appear (cf. Mark 13:27). Mark exemplifies a view that is aware of the delay of the parousia but does not necessarily lead to a de-eschatologized understanding of the faith. In Mark this awareness leads to an even more intensive expectation (cf. Mark 13:14, 17, 18, 30, "Truly I tell you, this generation will not pass away until all these things have taken place"), combined with a clear awareness of delay (cf. Mark 13:10, "And the good news must first be proclaimed to all nations," 21, 33–36). The intensification of the imminent expectation generated the possibility of rethinking the prolongation of the expected time and of strengthening the awareness of the community's election (cf. Mark 13:20). In other words, in Mark's time around 70 CE, imminent expectation and awareness of the delay of the parousia were not alternatives between which the community had to choose.[10]

Theological thinking in eschatological concepts required that expectations and reality be brought into a meaningful relation, so that the nearness of the end and the distance from the new beginning did not represent an antithesis—and that despite the fact that history continued.

10. On the eschatological concepts of Matthew and Luke, see below, §8.3.8 and §8.4.8.

7.3 Destruction of Jerusalem and the Earliest Christian Congregation

In the ancient world, the loss of a central temple as the place of religious and political identity was always a major turning point in the history of a people.[11] The almost complete destruction of the temple by the Romans in 70 CE brought ancient Judaism into a deep crisis[12] and was also of great significance for early Christianity. Not only the earliest church in Jerusalem and Judea but also the new movement as a whole lost a central connecting link to its origins. Jesus of Nazareth had taken action against the commercialization of the temple (cf. Mark 11:15–19) but did not oppose the existence of the temple as such. For the earliest church, Christians regarded the temple as their obvious point of contact to Judaism as well as the center of their spiritual lives and their proclamation (cf., e.g., Acts 2:46; 3:1, 8; 5:20, 25; 21:26). This loss had to be worked through especially on two levels:

1. The integration of the destruction of the temple into the pattern of eschatological events (cf. Mark 13:2ff.) related the event both to the will of God and the community's own eschatological hopes.
2. Jesus Christ himself was understood to be the new temple, which would be rebuilt in three days (cf. Mark 14:58). Early Christianity thereby attached itself to a broad stream within the Hellenistic world that no longer related the true worship of God or the gods to a particular religious center.[13]

With the fall of the temple in the tumult of the Jewish war and the conquest of Jerusalem, the earliest church in Jerusalem also probably went under. We have no primary sources, only the report in Eusebius, *Hist. eccl.* 3.5.3:[14] "The people of the church in Jerusalem were commanded by an oracle given by revelation before the war to those in the city who were worthy of it to depart and dwell in one of the cities of Perea which they called Pella." According to this report, the Jerusalem church would have survived the fall of Jerusalem

11. For the Greek realm, cf. Frank Teichmann, *Der Mensch und sein Tempel: Griechenland* (Stuttgart: Urachhaus, 1980); for the Jewish temple theology with its concepts of holiness and purity, cf. 55ff. Cf. also Beate Ego et al., eds., *Gemeinde ohne Tempel = Community without Temple: Zur Substituierung und Transformation des Jerusalemer Tempels und seines Kults im Alten Testament, antiken Judentum und frühen Christentum* (WUNT 118; Tübingen: Mohr Siebeck, 1999).

12. For the sequence of events in the Jewish war, cf. Helmut Schwier, *Tempel und Tempelzerstörung: Untersuchungen zu den theologischen und ideologischen Faktoren im ersten jüdisch-römischen Krieg (66–74 n. Chr.)* (NTOA 11; Göttingen: Vandenhoeck & Ruprecht, 1989), 4–54.

13. Texts in *NW* 1.2:226–34.

14. On the relation of comparable reports and competing traditions in other historians in comparison with Eusebius, see Lüdemann, *Opposition to Paul*, 200–213.

in relative security. There are, however, significant reasons to question the historicity of this Pella tradition:[15]

1. It is attested only late, and only in one source. The fate of the earliest Jerusalem church was of general interest in early Christianity; if there had been reliable information, it would likely have been documented earlier and by several authors.
2. Pella was a Gentile city; moreover, Josephus indicates that it was destroyed at the beginning of the Jewish war.[16] Would the strict Jewish Christians of Jerusalem have fled to a Gentile city?
3. The virtual disappearance of the earliest local church (not of Jewish Christianity!) from the historical record after 70 CE speaks against the supposition that it survived the destruction of Jerusalem.
4. The Pella tradition can be explained as the local tradition of a Jewish Christian community in Pella that—probably in the second century CE—traced its origin back to the original church.

The death of James the Lord's brother shows that the earliest Jerusalem church found itself in the crosshairs of the nationalistic groups. If one also takes into consideration the radical aggression of these circles, at the beginning of the war, against those who possibly or actually were deviating from the militarist party line,[17] then the conclusion is unavoidable: the earliest Jerusalem church perished in the tumults of the war, and thereafter had no influence on the development of early Christianity. To be sure, some Jewish Christian groups continued to exist,[18] but they had lost their natural point of reference with the earliest church, so that the urban congregations of Asia Minor, Greece, and Italy attained more and more importance.

7.4 The Rise of the Flavians

With the suicide of Nero in 68 CE, the last male member of the Julio-Claudian family who could trace his lineage directly back to Caesar perished. At first Galba became emperor, but he was already very old and had no member of his own family to succeed him. At the beginning of 69, the first revolts among the unhappy legions in Germany took place; they acclaimed Vitellius

15. Cf. the extensive discussion of Lüdemann, ibid., 200–213. On the other hand, J. Wehnert argues for the historicity of the Pella tradition: Jürgen Wehnert, "Die Auswanderung der Jerusalemer Christen nach Pella—historisches Faktum oder theologische Konstruktion?" *ZKG* 102 (1991): 231–55 (the Jerusalem Christians left Jerusalem just prior to the beginning of the Jewish war).

16. Josephus, *JW* 2.458.

17. Cf., e.g., Josephus, *JW* 2.562.

18. Cf. Georg Strecker, "Judenchristentum," *TRE* 17:310–25.

as emperor. One of Galba's erstwhile followers, Otho, also rose up against the emperor, and Galba lost his life in this putsch. Otho died in the ensuing battle against Vitellius, who then became the sole ruler. The continuing unrest in the individual armies, along with the indecisive leadership of Vitellius, led to the acclamation of Vespasian as emperor by the armies of the east, with the support of the Egyptian prefect Julius Alexander and the Syrian governor Mucianus. After a brief period of chaos and civil war in which Vitellius was killed, Vespasian's troops finally placed him on the throne at Rome.

Vespasian did not come from an old family of the Roman nobility[19] and had to legitimize his claim to authority. He thus embellished his rule with religious dimensions, presenting himself as the long-expected ruler who was to arise from the Orient. Both Tacitus[20] and Suetonius[21] document this tradition, according to which the victorious conquerors of Judea, Vespasian and Titus, fulfilled prophecies that the Jews understood to refer to their own history. Flavius Josephus played a special role in this understanding, emerging as propagandist for the role Providence had determined for Vespasian. He claimed that, while still a prisoner, he had prophesied that Vespasian would receive worldwide dominion (cf. Josephus, *JW* 3.399–408; 4.622–629; Suetonius, *Vesp.* 5.6; Dio Cassius, *Hist.* 65.1.4) and placed the inauguration of Vespasian's

19. Cf. Suetonius, *Vesp.* 1: "The empire, which for a long time had been unsettled and, as it were, drifting, through the usurpation and violent death of three emperors, was at last taken in hand and given stability by the Flavian family. This house was, it is true, obscure and without family portraits, yet it was one of which our family had no reason whatever to be ashamed, even though it is the general opinion that the penalty which Domitian paid for his avarice and cruelty was fully merited." On the Flavians, cf. Heinz Bellen and Hans Volkmann, *Grundzüge der römischen Geschichte* (8th ed.; Grundzüge 4; Darmstadt: Wissenschaftliche Buchgesellschaft, 1982), 81–115.

20. Tacitus, *Hist.* 5.13.1–2, in the context of reporting the conquest of the Jerusalem temple: "Prodigies had occurred, which this nation, prone to superstition, but hating all religious rites, did not deem it lawful to expiate by offering and sacrifice. There had been seen hosts joining battle in the skies, the fiery gleam of arms, the temple illuminated by a sudden radiance from the clouds. The doors of the inner shrine were suddenly thrown open, and a voice of more than mortal tone was heard to cry that the Gods were departing. At the same instant there was a mighty stir as of departure. Some few put a fearful meaning on these events, but in most there was a firm persuasion that in the ancient records of their priests was contained a prediction of how at this very time the East was to grow powerful, and rulers, coming from Judea, were to acquire universal empire. These mysterious prophecies had pointed to Vespasian and Titus, but the common people, with the usual blindness of ambition, had interpreted these mighty destinies of themselves, and could not be brought even by disasters to believe the truth."

21. Suetonius, *Vesp.* 4.5: "There had spread over all the Orient an old and established belief, that it was fated at that time for men coming from Judea to rule the world. This prediction, referring to the emperor of Rome, as afterwards appeared from the event, the people of Judea applied to themselves; accordingly they revolted." Dio Cassius, *Hist.* 64.9, says of Vespasian: "Portents and dreams had also come to him, pointing to his sovereignty long beforehand."

rule in a religious context, associating it with the term εὐαγγέλια (good news of victory).[22] The stylizing of Vespasian as bringer of peace to the world (cf. Tacitus, *Hist.* 4.3) and the Arch of Titus show that the Flavians intentionally included the conquest of the Jews in their propaganda even at Rome.[23] And finally, the miracles attributed to Vespasian[24] are to be regarded as politico-religious propaganda. In Alexandria, shortly after he became emperor, he is supposed to have healed a blind man, or both a blind man and a man with a withered hand (cf. Mark 3:1–6; 8:22–26; 10:46–52). He presented himself in the style of a living Serapis and was venerated as Son of Ammon, the Egyptian Zeus.[25] So also the relation of the philosophers to Vespasian (distancing to complete rejection), indicates that he intentionally fostered the emperor cult as a way of assuring his claim to office.[26]

The Gospel of Mark and the new literary genre it represents thus originated in a time when other versions of the "good news" were being proclaimed, a time when the emperor was presented as a miracle worker and as the savior figure who was to arise from the east. In the context of these claims, the Gospel of Mark (as well as the later gospels) narrates a different saving history, in which one who was crucified by the Romans emerged from the east as Son of God, miracle worker, and Messiah. The propaganda of the Flavians was certainly not the factor that triggered the creation of the gospel genre,[27] but it was an element that provided some stimulus, a factor to which Mark intentionally alludes several times (cf. Mark 1:1, 11; 9:7; 10:42–45; 15:39).[28]

22. Cf. Josephus, *JW* 4.618, 656 (*NW* 2.1:9–10). To be noted is the connection between εὐαγγέλια, the elevation of Vespasian to emperor, and the offering of sacrifices. On Josephus, cf. Mason, *Josephus*.

23. On this point cf. S. Panzram, "Der Jerusalemer Tempel und das Rom der Flavier," in *Zerstörungen des Jerusalemer Tempels: Geschehen, Wahrnehmung, Bewältigung* (ed. Johannes Hahn and Christian Ronning; WUNT 142; Tübingen: Mohr Siebeck, 2002), 166–82.

24. Cf. Tacitus, *Hist.* 4.81.1–3; Suetonius, *Vesp.* 7.2–3; Dio Cassius, *Hist.* 46.8.1 (*NW* 1.2). Cf. also Josephus, *Ant.* 8.46–48. On the emperor as healer and miracle worker, cf. Manfred Clauss, *Kaiser und Gott: Herrscherkult im römischen Reich* (Stuttgart: Teubner, 1999), 346–52.

25. Cf. Papyrus Fouad 8; and Clauss, *Kaiser und Gott*, 113–17.

26. Cf. Suetonius, *Vesp.* 13, 15; Tacitus, *Hist.* 4.5.1, 2.

27. Differently Gerd Theissen, "Evangelienschreibung und Gemeindeleitung: Pragmatische Motive bei der Abfassung des Markusevangeliums," in *Antikes Judentum und frühes Christentum: Festschrift für Hartmut Stegemann zum 65. Geburtstag* (ed. Bernd Kollmann et al.; BZNW 97; Berlin: de Gruyter, 1999), 389–414, who explicitly designates Mark as an "anti-gospel": "In this situation the evangelist Mark composes an anti-gospel to the εὐαγγέλια of the rise of the Flavian dynasty" (397). The statement of Bellen and Volkmann, *Römische Geschichte*, 95, is more reserved: "Christianity emerged on the literary scene for the first time with its own literary genre: the gospels."

28. Cf. the comprehensive discussion of Eve-Marie Becker, "Der jüdisch-römische Krieg (66–70 n. Chr.) und das Markus-Evangelium," in *Die antike Historiographie und die Anfänge der christlichen Geschichtsschreibung* (ed. Eve-Marie Becker; BZNW 129; Berlin: de Gruyter, 2005).

7.5 The Writing of Gospels as Innovative Response to Crises

It is no accident that the new literary genre gospel originated in about 70 CE. In the first place, the composition of gospels is the result of a natural process within the framework of a particular combination of historical conditions.[29] The pre-Markan collections (Mark 2:1–3:6; chaps. 4, 10, 13) and the Passion narrative point to the inherent tendency of such materials to coalesce into larger complexes of texts, and the sayings source Q, as well as Luke 1:1, explicitly confirms that there were preliminary stages of gospel composition. As creator of the gospel genre, Mark thus stands within a process that had begun before him. In addition, the fading expectation of the imminent parousia, the multiplicity of theological streams in first-century Christianity, and the concrete questions of Christian ethics called for a new orientation in time and history. The evangelists overcame these problems especially by adopting and adapting traditions of salvation history, the working out of practical ethical norms, and the introduction of offices that ordered and instructed the churches. These historicizing, ethicizing, and institutional tendencies at work on the earlier traditions are plain to see in Matthew and Luke, but they are also clearly discernible already in Mark.[30] Thus the literary character of the gospels corresponds to their functions in the internal life of the church, where they provided the foundation for preaching, worship, catechesis, and direction for the church's life.[31]

When history did not come to an end, this natural and unavoidable development was strengthened by the death of the founding generation, the persecution of Christians in Rome, the loss of the temple and the earliest Jerusalem church, as well as the politico-religious propaganda of the Flavians. Early Christianity had to both maintain continuity with the beginnings and rework its traditions in the light of current issues. The new literary genre gospel presented, in the first place, a Jesus-Christ-history oriented to biography, thus preserving the Jesus traditions, as the memory of earliest Christianity, from disappearing into the dark abyss of history. But more than that, the gospels have from the pragmatic perspective an *integrative and innovative* function. The evangelists wrote as members of churches, putting together pictures of Jesus from the extant tradi-

29. This insight was already present in the earlier studies of the form critics; cf. Martin Dibelius, *From Tradition to Gospel* (New York: Scribner, 1935); Bultmann, *History of the Synoptic Tradition*; Karl Ludwig Schmidt, *The Place of the Gospels in the General History of Literature* (trans. Byron R. McCane; Columbia: University of South Carolina Press, 2002).

30. These insights from the perspective of redaction criticism are combined in Georg Strecker, "Redaktionsgeschichte als Aufgabe der Synoptikerexegese," in *Eschaton und Historie: Aufsätze* (ed. Georg Strecker; Göttingen: Vandenhoeck & Ruprecht, 1979), 9–32.

31. The pragmatic aspects of gospel composition are emphasized in Gerd Theissen, *Lokalkolorit und Zeitgeschichte in den Evangelien: Ein Beitrag zur Geschichte der synoptischen Tradition* (Freiburg: Universitätsverlag; Göttingen: Vandenhoeck & Ruprecht, 1989).

tions of their congregations that corresponded to the churches' convictions.[32] In this process, their particular integrative achievement consisted in their bringing together contradictory or tensive church traditions about Jesus (e.g., theology of glory and theology of the cross, particularism and universalism). An essential function of gospel composition consisted in the building of consensus, a necessary presupposition for the survival of a community in such a crisis situation. Above all, the innovative potential of the gospels is seen at the levels of reinterpretation of both thought and action that must be developed for *both the church's view of itself and the ways it was regarded by outsiders*. Each gospel outlines a picture of its community's position in its historical context that leads to the community's self-definition and orientation. In this process, demarcation of the community from its parent religion is of fundamental importance. Since early Christianity originated as a renewal movement within Judaism, it was necessary to present plausible grounds for the separation. By composing gospels, the new movement provided a new founding narrative for itself and definitively separated from the communal narrative world of Judaism. From the internal perspective, it was necessary to develop models for the common life of the community in which the different streams of early Christianity could come together and stay together. This included not only the relationship of Christians from Jewish and Greco-Roman traditions, but also the relationship of rich and poor, male and female, and believers endowed with extraordinary gifts of the Spirit and "ordinary" Christians. All the gospels provide narratives intended to promote and facilitate the unity and common life of different groups in the church. Furthermore, with the emergence of the genre of written gospels, the influence of wandering charismatics, closely related to the oral tradition, declined. So norms for new structures of authority and official leadership had to be established.

32. A completely different view is advocated by Richard Bauckham, "For Whom Were Gospels Written?" in *The Gospels for All Christians: Rethinking the Gospel Audiences* (ed. Richard Bauckham; Grand Rapids: Eerdmans, 1998), 9–48. In contrast to classical redaction criticism, he regards the evangelists not as exponents of their church or churches, but, "The evangelists, I have argued, did not write for specific churches they knew or knew about, not even for a large number of such churches. Rather, drawing on their experience and knowledge of several or many specific churches, they wrote *for any and every church* to which their Gospels might circulate" (ibid., 46). As evidence for his view, Bauckham points especially to the high degree of mobility of early Christian missionary/evangelists, and to the difficulties involved in reconstructing the particular churches purportedly presupposed by the individual gospels. Bauckham's suppositions, framed very generally, are not confirmed by the gospel texts. Against his view we may note in particular (1) the distinct narrative and theological profile of the individual gospels, which clearly reveal that (2) each evangelist uses his own language, perception of the world, theological outline, and strategies for overcoming problems that are specifically not directed toward giving answers to all problems, and are also not thought of as providing help for whatever questions one wants to address to them. (3) The gospels aim at strengthening the emerging early Christian identity; a *general* identity-formation never existed in either antiquity or later epochs. The gospels attain their intended goals only when one knows the specific issues and problems of potential reader-hearers and engages them as such.

The *origination and dissemination* of the gospels was abetted by two factors:

1. Early Christianity was predominantly a bilingual movement, so that the gospels could be received and read throughout the Roman Empire and in a wide spectrum of educational levels.[33]
2. In the first century CE the codex became much more widely used, which, especially for longer documents, had great advantages over the scroll.[34] Rome appears to have been a center for this development,[35] and we may suppose that from the beginning of the period of gospel composition Christians made good use of this new method of publication.

The gospels are equally the result of a natural historical process and the intentional adaptation to a crisis situation. As authentic, developed tradition, they have the inherent power to reinterpret what was of lasting value in the tradition and to preserve it for the future in constantly renewed and continually renewable forms. Their reception to the present day shows how successful they were in this effort, and what innovative potential lies within the gospel texts.

33. For the pagan literature, cf. Elaine Fantham, *Literarisches Leben im antiken Rom: Sozialgeschichte der römischen Literatur von Cicero bis Apuleius* (Stuttgart: Metzler, 1998). In my opinion, early Christian literature must be newly evaluated within the framework of the history of ancient literature as a whole, for it by no means belongs to the category of popular, nonliterary works (*Kleinliteratur*), as the older form criticism supposed.

34. Cf. Theodor Birt, *Das antike Buchwesen in seinem Verhältniss zur Litteratur* (Berlin: Hertz, 1882), 371ff.; David Trobisch, *The First Edition of the New Testament* (Oxford: Oxford University Press, 2000), 69–77.

35. Martial, *Epigr.* 1.2: "You who want my little books to keep you company wherever you may be and desire their companionship on a long journey, buy these, that parchment compresses in small pages"; 14.192: "This mass that has been built up for you with many a leaf contains the fifteen plays of Naso."

8

The Sayings Source, the Synoptic Gospels, and Acts

Meaning through Narration

Early Christians, in order to preserve the meaning of what had happened, found it necessary to appropriate past events in narrative form (see above, §1.3 and §7.5). This they did in a particular way in the sayings source (Q), the Synoptic Gospels, and the Acts of the Apostles.

Narrative Structures

To carry out this function, narratives had to be able to utilize numerous structural types. The first task of every narrative is to bring together a number of related events into a coherent sequence.[1] If we regard a narrative as consisting basically of beginning, middle, and end, then the beginning and end, as boundary markers, are especially important. The beginning brings the hearers/readers into the narrative world and makes them a part of it. Thus the beginning of a narrative shapes the way it is intended to be understood and so has a basic hermeneutical function. The end of a narrative is just as important, for a decent narrative must establish a goal that it intends to reach

1. For elaboration, cf. Gérard Genette, *Narrative Discourse: An Essay in Method* (trans. Jane E. Lewin; Ithaca, NY: Cornell University Press, 1980), 25–32. Cf. also M. Eugene Boring, "Narrative Dynamics in 1 Peter: The Function of Narrative World," in *Reading 1 Peter with New Eyes: Methodological Reassessments of the Letter of First Peter* (ed. Robert L. Webb and Betsy Bauman-Martin; LNTS 364; Edinburgh: T&T Clark, 2007), 8–12.

or explain. Events that are particularly relevant for the conclusion are especially important, for they play a role within the course of the narrative that establishes the character of the whole. Of fundamental importance for any narrative are the causal connections that bind events together and constitute the logical order of the narrative (not necessarily its chronological order). The story is normally constituted through narration in chronological order, but the sequence of events in real-world time (diegetic order; referential sequence) and their arrangement in the narrative (narrative order; poetic sequence) do not always agree (anachronism). A film, for example, can begin with the end of the hero's life and then tell the story as a series of flashbacks. There are basically two forms of narrative anachronism: analepsis and prolepsis.[2] In analepsis, an event belonging to an earlier point in "real-world time" is narrated later; in prolepsis, an event belonging to a later point in "real-world time" is narrated earlier. A prolepsis is found, for example, in the narration of the cleansing of the temple in the Gospel of John. In all probability, this event occurred at the end of Jesus's ministry, but for theological reasons John placed it at the beginning. An important factor in the temporal structure of a narrative is *duration*. As a rule, narratives represent events as having a temporal duration in the framework of their chronological order (cf., e.g., the data indicating time and place in Mark 1). The third element of the temporal structure of a narrative is that of *frequency*: how often is a particular event narrated? Repetition typically points to the importance of a specific event (cf. the threefold narration of Paul's call in Acts). Another important issue is how the story is presented and the mode of the *narrator*'s presence in the story. Generally speaking, the narrator is omnipresent within the work, inasmuch as it is the narrator who arranges the material, determines the order of its events, and gives the narrative its general character. The way in which the narrative structure is put together indicates what narrators want to reveal of themselves and their worlds. Because narratives also always relate the narrator to the narrative in some way, they provide information and insight into the particular narrator's view of the world.

To the "how" of the narrative there is a corresponding "what"—what happens in the narrative? First, we must distinguish between the elements of the act–event–story continuum (*Ereignis, Geschehen, Geschichte*).* The act is the smallest unit of the plot (*Handlung*). When a subject does something that involves several acts in succession, these acts form an event. When the events are placed in a series according to certain rules of both chronology and content, then the events result in a connected story. Every story has a plot.[3] The plot, with its

2. Cf. Genette, *Narrative Discourse*, 47–79.

*[Schnelle makes a distinction between two German words that are both usually translated in English as *event*. I have used *act* for the smaller elements of which an *event* is composed.—MEB]

3. For an introduction to a narrative approach to the gospels, cf. Mark Allen Powell, *What Is Narrative Criticism?* (Minneapolis: Fortress, 1990).

related dramatic dimensions, point of view, and characterization, constitutes the meaningful lines that determine the text. Every narrative contains guiding elements such as persons, objects, statements of norms, events, quotations, traditions, and other elements that essentially determine how the reader appropriates the story.

The structural elements incorporate contingent acts into meaningful narratives. Both the art of narrative and the beginning and ending of a narrative lift the act from the realm of mere contingency and give it a meaning. The facticity of an act alone is not sufficient basis for meaning. It requires the interpretative narrative to bring out its meaning potential, to make it understandable and significant. Successful narratives are formations of historical-narrative meaning; they create, develop, and make plausible meaningful connections. It is the narrative that first opens up room for reception and interpretation, that makes possible hermeneutical transformations as especially represented in the gospels. The gospels are narrative syntheses of experiences with Jesus of Nazareth that generate meaning. They concur in the basic data of their Jesus-Christ-history, but arrange the material in differing ways, in each case emphasizing those aspects that are important for the identity-formation of their respective communities.

The gospels are characterized by those factors that generate meaning, those guidelines embedded in the narrative that determine the course of the story. These guidelines determine the orientation and meaning of the individual stories and each gospel as a whole. In this process, there is a close relationship between the particular theological conceptions of each gospel and the kind of identity-formation and confirmation for which it strives, for the young churches first need the clarification of numerous problems and education in their new view of the world and of themselves. This clarification is precisely what is accomplished by the new literary genre gospel[4] (alongside the letters), for in them the experiences with Jesus of Nazareth become present as remembering-through-narration.

The gospels are thus engaged in the cultivation of texts, traditions, and meanings. They attempt to preserve the stock of traditions and to develop it further, and by vigorous reinterpretation to mediate meaning from the past to the present.

4. On the new literary genre gospel, cf. the recent work of Richard A. Burridge, *What Are the Gospels? A Comparison with Graeco-Roman Biography* (SNTSMS 70; Cambridge: Cambridge University Press, 1992); Dirk Frickenschmidt, *Evangelium als Biographie: Die vier Evangelien im Rahmen antiker Erzählkunst* (TANZ 22; Tübingen: Francke, 1997); Detlev Dormeyer, *Das Markusevangelium als Idealbiographie von Jesus Christus, dem Nazarener* (SBB 43; Stuttgart: Katholisches Bibelwerk, 1999); Dirk Wördemann, *Das Charakterbild im bios nach Plutarch und das Christusbild im Evangelium nach Markus* (SGKA 1.19; Paderborn: Schöningh, 2002).

8.1 The Sayings Source as Proto-Gospel

The sayings source Q is the first (perceptible) outline of the life and teaching of Jesus of Nazareth.[5] The beginnings of the Q group possibly reach back to pre-Easter times,[6] but the shaping of the traditions and the formation of the group's itinerant mission work and its internal structure did not emerge in full swing until after Easter. The sayings source underwent a process of formation that came to an end between 50 and 60 CE.[7] Whether one can speak of a "theology" of the sayings source at all was previously disputed, but more recent research has shown that the sayings source, in its (reconstructed) final form is a work that was intentionally composed with both literary and theological aspects,[8] presenting its own independent portrayal of Jesus.

8.1.1 Theology

In the sayings source Q, the God of Israel comes in view primarily as "Father" (πατήρ, fifteen times).[9] God is the compassionate, caring Father,

5. On terminology: Within the framework of the two-source theory the siglum Q (*Quelle*, source) was introduced, probably by Johannes Weiss. Cf. Frans Neirynck, "The Symbol Q (Quelle)," in *Evangelica: Gospel Studies = Evangelica: études d'Évangile: Collected Essays* (ed. Frans van Segbroeck; BETL 60; Louvain: Leuven University Press, 1982), 683–89; Frans Neirynck, "Recent Developments in the Study of Q," in *Logia: Les paroles de Jésus: The Sayings of Jesus: Mémorial Joseph Coppens* (ed. Joël Delobel and Tjitze Baarda; BETL 59; Louvain: Uitgeverij Peeters, 1982), 29–75; John S. Kloppenborg Verbin, *Excavating Q: The Historical Setting of the Sayings Gospel* (Minneapolis: Fortress, 2000), passim; in James M. Robinson, "History of Q Research," in *The Critical Edition of Q: Synopsis including the Gospels of Matthew and Luke, Mark and Thomas with English, German, and French Translations of Q and Thomas* (ed. James M. Robinson et al.; Hermeneia; Minneapolis: Fortress, 2000), xix–lxxi; Harry T. Fleddermann, *Q: A Reconstruction and Commentary* (BiTS 1; Louvain: Peeters, 2005), 3–39.

6. Cf. the sketch in Migaku Sato, *Q und Prophetie* (Tübingen: Mohr, 1988), 375–79.

7. On theories of origin and redaction, cf. Schnelle, *New Testament Writings*, 179–96. I proceed on the basis that, while we must take into consideration that the Q materials had an extensive and written history prior to being incorporated into Q, we are unable to distinguish consistent layers on the basis of literary criteria. The following discussion is based on the presumed final form of the sayings source, as presented by Paul Hoffmann and Christoph Heil, *Die Spruchquelle Q: Studienausgabe Griechisch und Deutsch* (Darmstadt: Wissenschaftliche Buchgesellschaft, 2002). [I have mostly adopted and adapted the English translation provided in Robinson et al., eds., *Critical Edition of Q*, though sometimes preserving the NRSV of Luke or Matthew as reflecting the nuance of Schnelle's interpretation.—MEB]

8. Q is treated in a variety of ways in theologies of the New Testament. While it goes virtually unmentioned in the theologies of Rudolf Bultmann and Ferdinand Hahn, and is not evaluated as an independent theological construction by Peter Stuhlmacher, Georg Strecker and Ulrich Wilckens present a summary treatment.

9. On this point, cf. Athanasius Polag, *Die Christologie der Logienquelle* (1st ed.; Neukirchen-Vluyn: Neukirchener-Verlag, 1977), 59–67; Christoph Heil, *Lukas und Q: Studien zur lukanischen Redaktion des Spruchevangeliums Q* (BZNW 111; Berlin: de Gruyter, 2003), 282–86.

who "raises his sun on bad and good" (Q 6:35c), so that it can be said, "Be merciful, just as your Father . . . is merciful." The confidence in prayer and trust in God's care are inimitably expressed in the vocative πατήρ-address of the Lord's Prayer (Q 11:2b–4) and the adjoining section about God's hearing and answering prayer 11:9–13 (v. 13, "So if you, though evil, know how to give good gifts to your children, by how much more will the Father from heaven give good things to those who ask him?"; cf. also Q 12:6–7). The boundless trust in God's good purposes removes the oppressive burden from the cares of life and transforms them into boundless assurance (Q 12:22b, 24–30), for "your Father knows that you need them [all]" (12:30). God is the one who seeks the lost and rejoices when those who have strayed return home (Q 15:4–5a, 7, 8–10).[10] The unique relationship between the Father-God and the Son is thematically expressed in the double logion Q 10:21–22 (see below, §8.1.2). Here God appears not as the creator, but primarily as the revealer God, who makes known his will exclusively to his Son: the inauguration and final victory of his kingdom (βασιλεία τοῦ θεοῦ in Q 6:20; 7:28; 10:9; 11:2, 20, 52; 12:31; 13:18, 20, 29, 28; 16:16). As in the preaching of Jesus, so also in Q, the kingdom of God appears as a field of activity and a dominion that is already exercising its power in the present while still to come in the future. The self-understanding and the activities of the Q group were deeply influenced by this conviction (see below, §8.1.7). As in the preaching of Jesus, God is the acting subject of the kingdom, whose lordship is already being exercised and irresistibly presses toward its final realization, with or without human compliance (Q 13:18–21).[11] The stance that human beings take toward this new reality determines their destiny, for in Q God is the God who also commands and judges. One cannot serve both God and Mammon (Q 16:13). God is the Lord of the harvest (Q 10:2), who commands and acts in ways that cannot be calculated (Q 19:12–26). The place of Israel in salvation history no longer grants them favored status, for "God can produce children for Abraham right out of these rocks!" (Q 3:8), and at the eschatological banquet in the kingdom of God, it is foreigners who take their place with Abraham, Isaac, and Jacob, not those who supposed that they had a permanent reserved place (Q 13:29, 28). God's salvation comes to those who were not promised it in advance, but now accept his invitation (Q 14:16–21, 23).

The dominant picture in Q as a whole is that of the merciful, universal God, who lets his sun rise on all, good and bad, and through his royal power is on the way to creating a new reality. It is not the covenantal election of Israel,

10. Christoph Heil, "Beobachtungen zur theologischen Dimension der Gleichnisrede Jesu in Q," in *The Sayings Source Q and the Historical Jesus* (ed. Andreas Lindemann; BETL 158; Louvain: Leuven University Press, 2001), 649–59.

11. Cf. Heinz Schürmann, "Das Zeugnis der Redequelle für die Basileia-Verkündigung Jesu," in *Gottes Reich—Jesu Geschick: Jesu ureigener Tod im Licht seiner Basileia-Verkündigung* (ed. Heinz Schürmann; Freiburg: Herder, 1983), 65–152; Fleddermann, *Commentary*, 143–51.

nor the omnipotence of God that stand in the central place, but God's care for those who are on the "roads": "Go out on the roads, and whomever you find, invite, so that my house may be filled" (Q 14:23).

8.1.2 Christology

Whether the sayings source Q even has a Christology is disputed, since the title Χριστός (anointed, Messiah) is missing, there is no Passion narrative, and the resurrection of Jesus from the dead is not really a theme.[12] But if "Christology" means the conceptual, narrative, and functional explanations of the significance of Jesus, taken as a whole, without making the explanations dependent on particular concepts or themes, then we can indeed speak of a Q Christology.[13]

Titles

In the contemporary perspective, the decisive peculiarity of the sayings source Q is that Christology is not developed on the basis of the Passion and resurrection (see below, §8.1.4) but rather on the basis that the "words of the appearing Son of Man open up the future directly from Jesus's earthly works."[14] The *Son of Man* title dominates Q's christological conception.[15] Understanding the significance and function of this designation for Jesus requires analysis not only of the individual Son of Man sayings but especially of their location within the composition and their interplay with other christological images and concepts. Q's christological perspective becomes clear in the statement of the Baptist in Q 3:16b: "I baptize in water, but the one to come after me is more powerful than I." For the Q community, this Coming One is doubtless Jesus of Nazareth, as indicated by the resumptive reference

12. Classically Adolf von Harnack, *The Sayings of Jesus: The Second Source of St. Matthew and St. Luke* (trans. J. L. Wilkinson; NTS 2; London: Williams and Norgate, 1908), 234, according to whom "Q has no interest in Christological apologetics such as would explain the choice, the arrangement, and the coloring of the discourses and sayings it contains."

13. A survey is provided by Christopher M. Tuckett, *Q and the History of Early Christianity* (Edinburgh: T&T Clark, 1996), 209–37.

14. Karrer, *Jesus Christus*, 306.

15. For bibliography, see the notes in §3.9.2; cf. in addition Paul Hoffmann, "QR und der Menschensohn," in *Tradition und Situation: Studien zur Jesusüberlieferung in der Logienquelle und den synoptischen Evangelien* (ed. Paul Hoffmann; NTA NF 28; Münster: Aschendorff, 1995), 243–78; Tuckett, *Q and the History of Early Christianity*, 239–82; Jens Schröter, "Jesus der Menschensohn: Zum Ansatz der Christologie in Markus und Q," in *Jesus und die Anfänge der Christologie: Methodologische und exegetische Studien zu den Ursprüngen des christlichen Glaubens* (ed. Jens Schröter; BTS 47; Neukirchen-Vluyn: Neukirchener Verlag, 2001), 140–79; A. Järvinen, "The Son of Man and His Followers: A Q Portrait of Jesus," in *Characterization in the Gospels: Reconceiving Narrative Criticism* (ed. David M. Rhoads and Kari Syreeni; JSNTSup 184; London: T&T Clark, 2004), 180–222; Heil, *Lukas und Q*, 289–97.

in Q 7:19: "Are you the one to come, or are we to expect someone else?" The whole document intends to show that the Jesus who has come is the Coming One expected by the Q community. Within this revelatory process the Son of Man title plays a central role. The first Son of Man saying is directed to the troubled present of the Q community (Q 6:22, "Blessed are you when they insult you and persecute you, and say every kind of evil against you, because of the Son of Man"). Their confession of the Son of Man will be rewarded in heaven (Q 6:23), while resistant Israel (Q 7:31, "this generation") rejects the message of the Son of Man, placing him in absolutely the wrong categories (Q 7:34, "The Son of Man came, eating and drinking, and you say: Look! A person who is a glutton and drunkard, a friend of tax collectors and sinners"). The present fate of the earthly Son of Man as an outsider is also expressed in Q 9:58, "Foxes have holes, and the birds of the sky have nests, but the Son of Man does not have anywhere he can lay his head." While the preceding sayings focus on the present and earthly Son of Man and his relation to the Baptist, the perspective changes in Q 11:30 ("For as Jonah became to the Ninevites a sign, so also will the Son of Man be to this generation"), for now the spotlight is on the Son of Man who will come in the future to judge Israel. Confession of him in the present decides one's fate in the coming judgment (Q 12:8), so that the challenge is to remain alert: "You also must be ready, for the Son of Man is coming at an hour you do not expect" (Q 12:40). This motif of the Son of Man who will come suddenly and unexpectedly for judgment is massively reinforced in the concluding words of the saying source Q (17:24, 26, 30): "For as the lightning streaks from Sunrise and flashes as far as Sunset, so will be the Son of Man on his day" (17:24). *The compositional goal of the Son of Man sayings is doubtless to identify the earthly Son of Man who already acts with authority with the Son of Man who will return in judgment*. By means of the Son of Man conceptuality, the sayings source Q is able to "establish the claim of the earthly Jesus within the horizon of his return for eschatological judgment,"[16] and thereby to legitimate the claim of the Son of Man himself and his followers with great drama and force.[17]

While the *Son of God* title appears only in Q 4:3, 9, it still receives a central role by virtue of its compositional location in the temptation narrative. After the opening scenes featuring the Baptist in Q 3, the temptation narrative presents the testing of Jesus's readiness as Son of God to suffer and die (Q 4:3, 4), the acceptance of his destiny in Jerusalem (Q 4:9–12), and his renunciation of earthly power (Q 4:5–8). Jesus's endowment with the Spirit, along with the voice of God (Q 3:21–22) and the citations from Scripture, underscore the

16. Schröter, "Jesus der Menschensohn," 175.

17. It is obvious that the figure of the Son of Man was the central orientation point for the Q group and its self-understanding, so that Hoffmann's thesis that it was the post–70 CE redaction that first gave the Son of Man concept this exclusive position must be considered unlikely. (Cf. Hoffmann, "QR und der Menschensohn," 272–78.)

legitimization of the Son through his obedience to the Father in the face of the severest forms of temptation. Q 4:1–13 is the narrative and christological control center of the sayings source Q, for the testing of Jesus in suffering and temptation is demonstrated in Q not in a Passion story but in the temptation story. Thus the whole theological conception of the sayings source Q is held together by the temptation narrative, which may not be assigned to a late redactional layer.[18] Before Jesus enters the stage of history as one who teaches and acts with authority, the temptation narrative characterizes his essential nature as Son of God, who lives in full accord with the Father. This central aspect of Q's portrait of Jesus is also dominant in Q 10:21–22, where the absolute υἱός (Son) appears: "At that time he said, 'I thank you, Father, Lord of heaven and earth, for you hid these things from sages and the learned, and disclosed them to children. Yes, Father, for that is what it has pleased you to do. Everything has been entrusted to me by my Father, and no one knows the Son except the Father, nor does anyone know the Father except the Son, and to whomever the Son chooses to reveal him." This saying has striking parallels in John 3:35; 5:22, 26–27; 10:15; 13:3; 17:2, and formulates the unique relation between Father and Son: in his free sovereignty the Father turns to the Son and reveals to him, and thus to the Q community as the dependent children (Q 10:21 νήπιοι), the mystery of his will. The transmission of revelatory authority to the Son by the Father affirms the Son's (and the Q community's) exclusive insight into God's plans for his eschatological acts in the coming of

18. For analysis, cf. Paul Hoffmann, "Die Versuchungsgeschichte in der Logienquelle: Zur Auseinandersetzung der Judenchristen mit dem politischen Messianismus," in *Tradition und Situation: Studien zur Jesusüberlieferung in der Logienquelle und den synoptischen Evangelien* (ed. Paul Hoffmann; NTA NF 28; Münster: Aschendorff, 1995), 193–207; M. Hüneburg, *Jesus als Wundertäter in der Logienquelle* (ABG 4; Leipzig: Evangelische Verlagsanstalt, 2001), 91–125; Michael Labahn, "Der Gottessohn, die Versuchung und das Kreuz: Überlegungen zum Jesusporträt der Versuchungsgeschichte in Q 4,1–13," *ETL* 80 (2004): 402–22. In the older theories of the origin of Q and related models of stratification, Q 4:1–13 was excluded (so Dieter Lührmann, *Die Redaktion der Logienquelle: Anhang; Zur weiteren Überlieferung der Logienquelle* [WMANT 33; Neukirchen-Vluyn: Neukirchener Verlag, 1969], 56, or at most assigned to the latest redactional stage, as e.g., John S. Kloppenborg, *The Formation of Q: Trajectories in Ancient Wisdom Collections* [SAC; Philadelphia: Fortress, 1987], 247–48). More recent research, in contrast, predominantly regards the temptation narrative as belonging to the original composition of the document. Thus Schröter, *Erinnerung*, 448, comments regarding the temptation story "that here we by no means have a foreign unit later attached to the real corpus." Fleddermann, *Commentary*, 253, emphasizes that the temptations "form an integral part of Q from its beginning"; cf. C. M. Tuckett, "The Temptation Narrative in Q," in *The Four Gospels, 1992: Festschrift Frans Neirynck* (ed. Frans van Segbroeck et al.; 3 vols.; BETL 100; Louvain: Leuven University Press, 1992), 1:479–507; Hüneburg, *Wundertäter*, 123; Labahn, "Versuchungsgeschichte," 405–6. In addition to numerous connections between the motifs of the temptation story and the Q corpus as a whole, the importance of the theological function discussed above for the conception of Q argues that the story was an original part of Q.

the kingdom of God.[19] *Within the Q community, Jesus unquestionably had the status of the Son of God, so that this in itself would be enough to speak of a Christology of the sayings source Q.*[20]

Closely related to the double saying Q 10:21–22 are the statements about *Wisdom*. The Q community considers itself to be among the "children of Wisdom" (Q 7:35), who, in contrast to "this generation" (unresponsive Israel) hear and follow the message of the Son of Man (Q 7:31–34). In Q 11:49–51 Jesus refers to a speech of Wisdom, who sends sages and prophets, some of whom will be persecuted and killed—just as happened in the previous history of Israel. Again the conclusion is drawn, "Yes, I tell you, 'an accounting' will be required of this generation" (Q 11:51b). This historical perspective also prevails in Q 11:31, which declares, "The queen of the South will be raised at the judgment with this generation and condemn it, for she came from the ends of the earth to listen to the wisdom of Solomon, and look, something more than Solomon is here!" This superiority, like the antithesis of Q 10:21 and the differentiation between Jesus and Wisdom in Q 7:35 and Q 11:49, shows that the Jesus of Q is not identified with Wisdom, and that σοφία cannot be considered a christological title.[21] But the sayings source Q[22] is probably part of a broad stream of early Christian theology that adapted motifs from the wisdom stream and utilized them fruitfully for Christology.

The *Kyrios* title (Lord) is used in addressing Jesus in Q 7:6 and 9:59, and in 6:46 this title is declared to be inadequate when not accompanied by corresponding deeds ("Why do you call me Master, Master, and do not do what I say?"). In the parables, κύριος does not point to Jesus, but to God (Q 12:42–43, 45–46; 13:25).[23]

Narrative and Functional Christology

The profile of a Christology is also indicated by the narrative mode by which the author/final redactor presents Jesus of Nazareth, and by the func-

19. The matter is rightly formulated by Fleddermann, *Commentary*, 454: "Q's Christology climaxes in this pericope. Jesus—the Coming One, the Son of Man—as the Son of God reveals God fully as Father to those with privileged eyes and ears who receive the revelation."

20. The brief comment of James D. G. Dunn, *Christology in the Making. A New Testament Inquiry into the Origins of the Doctrine of the Incarnation* (Philadelphia: Westminster, 1980), 36, is not adequate: "The divine sonship of Jesus has apparently no particular significance for Q."

21. Cf., e.g., Lührmann, *Redaktion der Logienquelle*, 99; Ronald A. Piper, *Wisdom in the Q-Tradition* (Cambridge: Cambridge University Press, 1989), 175; Heil, *Lukas und Q*, 302; differently James M. Robinson, "Basic Shifts in German Theology," *Int* 16 (1962): 83–84.

22. The whole wisdom tradition in Q is cataloged and analyzed in Lips, *Weisheitliche Traditionen*, 197–227.

23. Marco Frenschkowski ascribes a greater significance to the κύριος title in Q. Cf. Marco Frenschkowski, "Kyrios in Context," in *Zwischen den Reichen: Neues Testament und römische Herrschaft: Vorträge auf der Ersten Konferenz der European Association for Biblical Studies* (ed. Michael Labahn and Jürgen Zangenberg; TANZ 36; Tübingen: Francke, 2002), 95–118.

tions attributed to Jesus.[24] We have already pointed out the fundamental importance of the *temptation narrative* of Q 4:1–13 for Q's Christology: at the very beginning of his ministry, Jesus validates himself as the Son of God and proves his unique nature in the disputes with the devil. From that point on, Jesus's speeches, sayings, and deeds stand under the sign of Jesus's exalted status, who does not serve the "kingdoms of the world" (Q 4:5), but proclaims the kingdom of God.[25] In the narrative structure of the sayings source Q, the significance of Jesus is essentially determined by his *relation to the Baptist*.[26] The announcement of the "more powerful one who is to come after me" in Q 3:16–17 is taken up in Q 7:18–19, 22–28, so that the first section of Q is framed by the complex of materials dealing with John the Baptist. This arrangement communicates John's identity in relation to Jesus in a twofold way:

1. The Baptist is more than a prophet (Q 7:26), underscored by the exclusive significance he is given in Q 16:16:[27] the Baptist is not numbered among the prophets of the past epoch of "the law and the prophets," but he is oriented to the history of the kingdom of God.
2. Q 11:32 explicitly states, in view of the appearance of the Ninevites at the last judgment: "and look, more than Jonah is here."

The category "prophet" is thus not adequate to comprehend the nature and function of Jesus. The Baptist is already "more than a prophet," and thus points to the "more" of Jesus as that of Son of God and Son of Man.[28] A basic part of the narrative structure of the sayings source Q is the movement from presenting Jesus as the teacher to Jesus as the coming judge. This portrait is motivated and expedited by the disputes with "this generation" in Q 7:31; 11:29, 30, 31, 32, 50–51 and the emphasis on the crisis situation for Israel generated by the advent of Jesus and the ministry of the Q community (cf. Q 13:24–27; 13:29, 28, 30, 34–35; 14:16–18, 21–22; 22:28, 30). The lack of a Passion story strengthens the perspective of the intensifying debate and the brevity of the time before the judgment comes, whose inbreaking force is already felt.

Of greater importance for Christology are the *functions* ascribed to Jesus in the sayings source Q. First of all, Jesus is the *proclaimer of the word*, who announces the kingdom of God, pronounces blessing on the poor (Q 6:20–22), authoritatively teaches nonviolence and love for enemies as the will of God (Q 6:32, 34), and presents the evil of judging others with imagery

24. Cf. also Hurtado, *Lord Jesus Christ*, 246–48.

25. Cf. Fleddermann, *Commentary*, 152.

26. On the portrayal of the Baptist in the sayings source Q, cf. Heil, *Lukas und Q*, 118–44.

27. Cf. ibid., 126.

28. This does not, of course, exclude prophetic traditions and forms of speech; cf. Boring, *Continuing Voice of Jesus*, 189–234.

(Q 6:37–38) that reduces it to absurdity. Living by his will is a matter of salvation (Q 6:46–49), and even the rejection of his followers is not without consequences, for "Whoever takes you in takes me in, and whoever takes me in takes in the one who sent me" (Q 10:16). In parables, Jesus brings God's new world near to his hearers (see above, §8.1.1), and sends forth his followers on a mission to Israel (Q 10:2–12). As preacher of the word, Jesus takes on the functions of the *proclaimer and mediator of salvation*, for "Blessed are the eyes that see what you see" (Q 10:23–24). Confession of Jesus determines salvation or rejection. The whole sayings source Q is permeated by the challenge of call and decision (cf. Q 11:23, 33; 12:8–9); the acceptance or rejection of Jesus's message is a matter of salvation or being lost (Q 14:16–23).[29] Jesus has come to bring fire on the earth (Q 12:49); his person and his message are polarizing (Q 12:51, 53). It is a matter of rightly judging the present time (12:54–56), because Jesus functions *as judge*. The woes against the Galilean cities (Q 10:13–15), the judgments pronounced against "this generation" (11:31–32, 49–51), the woes against the Pharisees (Q 11:42–44) and scribes/teachers of the law (Q 11:46b–48) and the announcement that Israel stands before a crisis in 13:24–35 make clear that Jesus comes on the scene as eschatological judge. Because the judgment is imminent, according to Q 12:58–59 Jesus urgently commands that people be reconciled to their enemies. The appearance of the Son of Man for judgment will be universally visible (Q 17:24), and those addressed should do everything in their power to be sure that it does not happen to them as it did to the people in the days of Noah (Q 17:26–27).

Finally, Jesus also appears in the sayings source Q as a *miracle worker.* The series "Programmatic Speech" (Q 6:20–49) followed by Healing the Centurion's Slave (Q 7:1–10)[30] already makes clear that the sayings source Q orients its portrayal of Jesus to both speaking *and* acting (concretely: healing).[31] The centurion receives the salvation Jesus brings and, in contrast to Israel, demonstrates the appropriate response to Jesus, namely faith. Q 7:22 intensifies this idea; by enumerating Jesus's saving acts, this text defines one's response to Jesus as decisive for salvation: "And blessed is he who is not offended by me" (7:23). The Qumran parallel 4Q521 also suggests a messianic context for Q 7:22, for there comparable miraculous saving acts are regarded as the phenomena enacted by God that accompany the advent of the Messiah. The eschatological character of Jesus's deeds also becomes visible in the missions discourse in which the disciples are explicitly charged to heal the sick (Q 10:9). In the woes pronounced on Chorazin and Bethsaida, Jesus's mighty deeds even become a criterion in the last judgment (Q 10:13–15). The miracle motif

29. Cf. Heil, *Lukas und Q*, 344.

30. Extensive analysis in Hüneburg, *Wundertäter*, 125–41.

31. Cf. M. Hüneburg, "Jesus als Wundertäter," in *The Sayings Source Q and the Historical Jesus* (ed. Andreas Lindemann; BETL 158; Louvain: Leuven University Press, 2001), 639–40.

determines the narrative sequence of Q 11:14–36,[32] where exorcisms appear as the visible demonstration of the end of the evil one and Jesus's victory over the kingdom of the strong one. The determining aspect here is the unique relation of Jesus to God expressed in Q 11:20: "But if it is by the finger of God that I cast out demons, then there has come upon you God's reign."[33] In this context, Q 11:23 must be read as a clear and pointed christological emphasis, where one's stance to Jesus determines salvation or catastrophe: "Whoever is not for me is against me, and whoever does not gather with me scatters."

It has become clear that we need have no hesitation in claiming that the sayings source Q has a Christology. The unique manner in which Jesus's acts are portrayed as God's acts is seen not only in the miracle stories, but also in the temptation story, in Jesus's preaching of the kingdom of God, in the authority with which he teaches, and in the Son of Man and Son of God titles. The wisdom and prophetic categories are transcended, and functions are ascribed to Jesus that qualify him as the eschatological savior figure. His followers see themselves legitimized by Jesus as participants in God's reign who announce the lordship of the Son of Man. It is thus not sufficient to speak only of an "implicit" or "low" Christology of the sayings source Q,[34] or to play off Christology and theology proper against each other.[35] Finally, the narrative presentation of the person of Jesus in the sayings source Q as a whole shows that it is not possible to assign differing Christologies to different literary strata.[36] It is rather the case that Jesus of Nazareth, with his proclamation of the kingdom of God, his unity with God (Q 10:22), and his identity as the earthly, exalted, and Coming One stands at the center of the sayings source Q as a whole.[37]

32. On this point cf. Hüneburg, *Wundertäter*, 181–225.

33. Cf. Michael Labahn, "Jesus Exorzismen (Q 11,19–20)," in *The Sayings Source Q and the Historical Jesus* (ed. Andreas Lindemann; BETL 158; Louvain: Leuven University Press, 2001), 617–33.

34. So Jens Schröter, "Entscheidung für die Worte Jesu," *BK* 54 (1999): 73, who argues "One can speak only with limitations of a Christo-logy [in Q]." Similarly J. Schröter, "Q et la christologie implicite," in *The Sayings Source Q and the Historical Jesus* (ed. Andreas Lindemann; BETL 158; Louvain: Leuven University Press, 2001), 289–316.

35. Cf. Kloppenborg Verbin, *Excavating Q*, 391: "The center of Q's theology is not Christology but the reign of God."

36. When this is done, it is usually presupposed that there was a development from a "lower" to "higher" Christology; while in the earlier layers one finds only hints of Christology or none at all, in later redaction Christology comes more and more into the foreground. So, e.g., Polag, *Die Christologie der Logienquelle*, 171–87; Kloppenborg Verbin, *Excavating Q*, 392: "Even at the main redactional phase (Q^2), where christological statements are more in evidence." For a critique of these reductionistic conceptions on the methodological level, cf. Schröter, *Erinnerung*, 436ff.; on the christological level, cf. Hurtado, *Lord Jesus Christ*, 217–57, who explicitly rejects the thesis of a "low" Christology in the sayings source Q.

37. Cf. the sketch of the Christology and theology of the sayings source Q in Fleddermann, *Commentary*, 129–54.

8.1.3 Pneumatology

In the sayings source Q the work of the Holy Spirit plays a significant role, although the word πνεῦμα is found in this sense only five times.[38] John the Baptist says in Q 3:16 that the "coming one" (Jesus) will baptize with the Holy Spirit and fire. The legitimization of Jesus by the Spirit of God is also affirmed by the baptismal Spirit in Q 3:21–22, although the text of Q cannot be reconstructed here with any confidence.[39] The Spirit is personified in Q 4:1 and Q 12:12: the Spirit leads Jesus into the wilderness and stands by his persecuted followers when they are on trial in the synagogues. A forensic situation is also presupposed in the enigmatic logion Q 12:10, "And whoever says a word against the Son of Man, it will be forgiven him: but whoever speaks against the Holy Spirit, it will not be forgiven him." This saying most likely belongs in the disputes of the Q missioners with their opponents and has both a pre- and post-Easter perspective.[40] The pre-Easter rejection of the Son of Man can be forgiven, but not the post-Easter rejection of the message of the Q missioners, which would be a denial of Jesus's divine sonship and thus a blasphemy against the Holy Spirit. Here we see the rudiments of the extravagant claims of the Q missioners actually to represent God's eschatological acts in salvation and judgment.

8.1.4 Soteriology

We have already referred to the fact that the sayings source Q presupposes the death and resurrection of Jesus, but does not evaluate it in christological terms (see above, §8.1.2). We find neither formulaic traditions (as in Paul) nor a Passion narrative (as in the Synoptic Gospels). Should we infer from this that the death and resurrection of Jesus had no salvific significance for the sayings source Q, that we should attribute no soteriological quality to them?

Only one unambiguous reference to Jesus's death on the cross is found in Q: "The one who does not take one's cross and follow after me cannot be my disciple" (Q 14:27). The (violent) death of the prophets serves to interpret the death of Jesus in Q 11:49–51 and Q 13:34–35 ("Jerusalem, Jerusalem, who kills the prophets and stones those sent to her!"), and the reference to Jerusalem in

38. Positive examples are Q 3:16; 4:1; 12:10; uncertain are Q 3:22; 12:12. The references to πνεῦμα in Q 11:24, 26 are about the return of the "unclean spirit."

39. With James M. Robinson and Paul Hoffmann, *Critical Edition of Q*, 18–20, I consider Q 3:1–22 to be original, since Q 4:1–11 presupposes the concepts of both the Holy Spirit and divine sonship, making a firm connection between the stories of baptism and temptation (cf. Mark 1:9–11, 12–13).

40. Wolfgang Wiefel, *Das Evangelium nach Matthäus* (THKNT 1; Berlin: Evangelische Verlagsanstalt, 1998), 238; Boring, "Matthew: Introduction, Commentary, and Reflections," 8:286–87 and the literature there given.

Q 4:9–12 had already evoked a negative connotation. Finally, the sayings in Q 6:22–23 (28); 12:4; 17:33 presuppose a situation of persecution for Jesus (and the community). So also there is only minimal use of resurrection ideas and imagery; Jesus's resurrection from the dead is not mentioned explicitly at all, and allusions can be found at the most in Q 7:22; 11:31. To be sure, individual logia such as Q 12:10; 13:35a ("I tell you, you will not see me until 'the time' comes when you say: Blessed is the one who comes in the name of the Lord"), and entire complexes of motifs, such as the idea of Jesus's future coming to act as judge, can be understood only in the context of Jesus's resurrection as the real basis for Q's theology as a whole. So also the consistent claim of Q to proclaim Jesus's words with an unsurpassable authority[41] points to the resurrection as the basis for Q's theological conception.

Any explanation of this tensive combination of data must fit the basic theological conception of the sayings source Q as a whole.[42] The fact that Q is entirely oriented to Jesus as teacher could plausibly explain the fact that Passion, death, and resurrection are spoken of only allusively. Q concentrates on the identification of the earthly Jesus with the exalted Lord; only this identity confers authority on the words of Jesus and grounds the Q community's faith that Jesus's message has ultimate relevance for present and future. In the testimony of the sayings source Q, the significance of Jesus is not mediated indirectly by kerygmatic formulae or by repeating the Passion story, but is experienced directly by hearing and acting on the words of Jesus. Within this model, it is only consistent that the legitimacy and testing of Jesus is dem-

41. Cf. James M. Robinson, "Der wahre Jesus? Der historische Jesus im Spruchevangelium Q," *ZNT* 1 (1998): 21–22; James M. Robinson, *The Gospel of Jesus: In Search of the Original Good News* (San Francisco: HarperSanFrancisco, 2005), 141–54.

42. The literature provides numerous explanatory attempts: Paul Hoffmann, *Studien zur Theologie der Logienquelle* (NTA NF 8; Münster: Aschendorff, 1972), 142, sees in the revelatory logion Q 10:22 a reflection of the Easter experience of the group: "Through the Easter experience of the group it became clear to Jesus's followers that Jesus's claim and thus his message did not come to an end with his death, but were validated in a way they could never have imagined." Sato, *Q und Prophetie*, 383, gives the following answer to the question of why Q contains no Passion narrative: "No prophetic book of the Old Testament reports the death of the prophet." According to Kloppenborg Verbin, *Excavating Q*, 379, Q is interested throughout in Jesus's death and vindication by being exalted by God, "but that Q's approach to these issues is significantly different from those of Paul . . . and Mark and post-Markan gospels." Lips, *Weisheitliche Traditionen*, 278, argues Q understood Jesus as the rejected messenger of Wisdom, the death of Jesus pointed to the nearness of the coming kingdom, "without attributing saving significance to Jesus's death itself." For D. Seeley, "Jesus's Death in Q," *NTS* 38 (1992): 222–34, the "noble death" of the Stoic-Cynic philosophers was the model followed by Q. Robinson, "Der wahre Jesus?" 21, states: "To say it in exaggerated style, the Sayings Gospel is itself the Easter miracle!" According to Fleddermann, *Commentary*, 106, "Q contains no passion narrative because Q ends when Jesus stops talking, but Jesus does refer to his death." Labahn, "Versuchungsgeschichte," 404, emphasizes "that the exceptional obedience of Jesus in the suffering and death on the cross represents a key for decoding the difficult story of Jesus's temptations." A survey of research on the issue is given by Kloppenborg Verbin, *Excavating Q*, 363–79.

onstrated not by his perseverance in the Passion but by the temptation story. In this conception, however, Easter is no foreign body, for it is precisely through the resurrection of Jesus that his words have lost none of their relevance in the post-Easter period. Easter requires that the sayings of the earthly and exalted Jesus be transmitted and proclaimed, without making Easter itself a separate theme.[43] In addition, it must be kept in mind that both the tradents and the recipients of the traditions found in the sayings source Q have extratextual information at their disposal that can include Jesus's death and resurrection. It is to be remembered that the sayings source Q understands the meaning of Jesus's sending as a whole as an act of salvation and deliverance, in a way that extends beyond the Passion thematic. Jesus seeks the lost and rejoices over their finding and those who have been found (Q 15:4–5a, 7, [8–10]). Whoever does the will of God and remains faithful in confessing the Son of Man may be certain of heavenly reward (Q 6:23a; 10:7; 12:33). The kingdom of God is already being realized in the midst of his followers (Q 17:20), and promises a magnificent conclusion, rulership over Israel (Q 22:28, 30).

8.1.5 Anthropology

Although the sayings source Q has no reflective systematic anthropology, there are individual sayings with anthropological force. The challenge to lay up treasures in heaven that will not pass away is grounded in the statement, "For where your treasure is, there will also be your heart" (Q 12:34). The heart is the seat of both good and evil in human beings: "The good person from the good treasure casts up good things, and the evil person from the evil treasure casts up evil things. For from exuberance of heart the mouth speaks" (Q 6:45). There is a direct connection between the inner composition of a human being and his or her outward deeds, for "from the fruit the tree is known" (Q 6:44a). Like the heart, so also the eye expresses human nature: "The lamp of the body is the eye. If your eye is generous, your whole body is radiant; but if your eye is jaundiced, your whole body is dark" (Q 11:34). An influence of Hellenistic dualistic anthropology is present in the distinction between body and soul in Q 12:4–5:[44] "And do not be afraid of those who kill the body, but cannot kill the soul. But fear the one who is able to destroy both the soul and body in Gehenna." To be sure, the idea of the immortality of the soul is not taken over, for God's omnipotence is seen precisely in the fact that he can also destroy the soul. The human capacity for sin, and dependence on God's goodness, are the themes of the prayer for forgiveness of guilt (Q 11:4)

43. The judgment of H. E. Tödt, that "the ideas of the passion kerygma remain excluded," is too undifferentiated; the issue is more nuanced. See Tödt, *Son of Man*, 244.

44. This influence was mediated via Hellenistic Judaism; parallels are given in Dieter Zeller, *Die weisheitlichen Mahnsprüche bei den Synoptiker* (Würzburg: Echter Verlag, 1977), 96–100.

and of Q 11:13: "So if you, though evil, know how to give good gifts to your children, by how much more will the Father from heaven give good things to those who ask him!" Faith in Jesus as an unconditional trust in his power is demonstrated in the example of the Roman centurion (Q 7:9b: "I tell you, not even in Israel have I found such faith") and in Q 17:6 there is no limit to such power ("If you have faith like a mustard seed, you might say to this mulberry tree: Be uprooted and planted in the sea! And it would obey you.").

The term νόμος (law) occurs only twice in the sayings source Q (Q 16:16–17, "The law and the prophets were until John . . . it is easier for heaven and earth to pass away than for one iota or one serif of the law to fall"). While, on the one hand, the Baptist represents a turning point in the significance of the law (v. 16), according to v. 17 its validity continues undiminished. On the other hand, neither individual Mosaic laws nor Moses himself appear in Q.[45] Individual texts such as Q 9:59–60 and 14:26 place Torah commands in question, and the woes against the Pharisees (Q 11:42, 39b, 41, 43) and the scribes (Q 11:46b, 52, 47–48) present a clear criticism against those Jewish groups that wanted to extend the influence of the Torah in daily life. This does not mean that the Torah is rejected, but rather that the ritual prescriptions are clearly relativized in favor of the ethical requirements: "Woe to you, Pharisees, for you tithe the mint and dill and cumin, and give up justice and mercy and faithfulness. But these one must do, without giving up those" (Q 11:42). In any case, it is clear that in the sayings source Q the central guidelines and soteriological principles are provided not by the Torah, but by "the message and person of Jesus, Lord and Son of Man."[46]

8.1.6 Ethics

In the sayings source Q, ethics is a matter of a lifestyle nourished by the community's conviction that they are the authorized followers of the Son of Man who has come—and who will come again—to announce to Israel the kingdom of God in salvation and judgment. Q's *ethical radicalism* reveals that the followers of Jesus who compiled and transmitted this collection understood themselves to be in direct continuity with Jesus and the power of his words. In particular, the *programmatic speech* of Q 6:20–49 has the compositional function of presenting the ethic of Q.[47] The promise of the kingdom of God

45. Cf. Heil, *Lukas und Q*, 318–20.

46. D. Kosch, *Die eschatologische Tora des Menschensohnes. Untersuchungen zur Rezeption der Stellung Jesu zur Tora in Q* (NTOA 12; Göttingen: Vandenhoeck & Ruprecht, 1989), 450.

47. For analysis, cf. Elisabeth Sevenich-Bax, *Israels Konfrontation mit den letzten Boten der Weisheit: Form, Funktion und Interdependenz der Weisheitselemente in der Logienquelle* (MTA 21; Altenberge: Orlos, 1993), 371–437; Paul Hoffmann, "Tradition und Situation: Zur 'verbindlichkeit' des Gebots der Feindesliebe in der synoptischen Tradition und in der gegenwärtigen Friedensdiskusion," in *Tradition und Situation: Studien zur Jesusüberlieferung in der*

in the Beatitudes (6:20–23) constitutes the foundation of Q's ethical teaching, while the command to love one's enemies (Q 6:27) represents its basic norm. The absolute command of love for enemies is both expanded and given a sharper focus in the prayer for the persecutor in Q 6:28 and the twin sayings of 6:29–30: they redefine the relation of law and justice by their renunciation of counterattack and revenge and the unlimited willingness to provide for the needs of others. The sayings source Q thereby broadens Jesus's own conception by extending the command to love the enemy beyond personal enemies to those hostile groups that oppose one's own. Despite danger and hostility, the social situation is to be changed for the better by the power of love that transcends social boundaries. God the creator is the model for this, and the promise of becoming "children [lit. sons] of God" functions as the motivation (Q 6:35–36). It is now a matter of abandoning the principal of reciprocity (Q 6:32a, "If you love those loving you, what reward do you have?") and of doing the unconventional: to cease judging others and to attend first to one's own blindness and narrowness (Q 6:37–42). The Golden Rule is presented in its positive form, and, since it extends to the circle of addressees to all people, constitutes one of the universal dimensions of the programmatic speech: "And the way you want people to treat you, that is how you treat them" (Q 6:31).[48] There was a common negative form of the Golden Rule that refers to all social relationships. Thales, for example, says (according to Diogenes Laertius, *Vit. phil.* 1.37), "How can we best live a good and just life? By not doing ourselves what we disapprove in others." Almost all instances of the positive form manifest a particular limited perspective, in that they belong within the ethos of rulership, friendship, and family.[49] In the sayings source Q this exclusiveness is removed, so that both the acting subject and those for whom the action is performed are all universalized. The explicit emphasis on doing the will of Jesus (Q 6:46–49), in connection with the metaphor of fruit-bearing and the concept of reward (Q 6:43–45), clearly displays the ethical conceptuality of the sayings source Q: it is a matter of unconditional obedience and undivided commitment to doing the will of God/Jesus. The eschatological promises of the Beatitudes are related to eschatological judgment: the promise applies only to those who put the words of Jesus into practice; salvation is a matter of doing, not merely hearing, the words of Jesus.

Ethical radicalism is also found outside the programmatic speech, for example, in the call to renounce worry and concern about one's own plans

---

Logienquelle und den synoptischen Evangelien (ed. Paul Hoffmann; NTA NF 28; Münster: Aschendorff, 1995), 15–30; Fleddermann, *Commentary*, 266–335.

48. On the traditional background of the saying and its setting in the history of religions cf. Albrecht Dihle, *Die goldene Regel: Eine Einführung in die Geschichte der antiken und frühchristlichen Vulgärethik* (StAltW 7; Göttingen: Vandenhoeck & Ruprecht, 1962); all relevant texts are found in *NW* 1.1.2 at Matt. 7:12.

49. Cf. Theissen, *Jesusbewegung*, 264–68.

("Do not be anxious about your life," Q 12:22b–31), the prohibition of divorce in Q 16:18, and the command about unlimited forgiveness to the repentant brother or sister in Q 17:3–4. The sayings source Q connects renunciation of violence and retaliation with a radical ethos of abandonment of home and property. The situation of the Son of Man who has no place to lay his head (Q 9:58) becomes a model for his followers, who must hate father and mother as the presupposition for belonging to the family of God (Q 14:26).[50] The conventional relationships so basic for ancient life and thought lose their significance (Q 12:51, 53, "Do you think that I have come to hurl peace on the earth? I did not come to hurl peace, but a sword! For I have come to divide son against father, and daughter against her mother, and daughter-in-law against her mother-in-law."). Social conventions such as the duty to bury one's parents (Q 9:59–60) or social greetings (Q 10:4e) are annulled, and even minimal equipment for the dangers of travel must be left behind (Q 10:4).

The ethic of the sayings source Q is integral to its whole concept: the radical, undivided way of life it calls for is oriented to the life and words of the Son of Man Jesus of Nazareth, who removed the boundaries of God's love and promised his followers God's own care in his kingdom.

8.1.7 Ecclesiology

The sayings source Q has no thought-out ecclesiology, but it is not only its radical ethic that allows us to draw inferences regarding the structure and mission activity of the Q community. Perhaps the distinctive character of the Q missioners and their community is best characterized by the catchword "itinerant radicalism."[51] Especially the missions discourse in Q 10:2–12 can be read as the model for this mission. Despite great external dangers (Q 10:2, "Be on your way! Look, I send you like sheep in the midst of wolves."), the missioners are instructed not only to do without money, but to take not even the minimal equipment necessary for traveling (Q 10:4). The appearance of the missioners in houses and towns, their tremendous claims and demands, their severe lifestyle and rejection as portrayed in Q 10:5–12 bear the marks of ideal

50. Cf. here P. Kristen, *Familie, Kreuz und Leben: Nachfolge Jesu nach Q und dem Markusevangelium* (MTS 42; Marburg: Elwert, 1995), 55–155.

51. On this point, cf. Gerd Theissen, "Wanderradikalismus," in *Studien zur Soziologie des Urchristentums* (ed. Gerd Theissen; WUNT 19; Tübingen: Mohr, 1992), 79–105. Critical questions against this position (based on ideal types) are raised by Thomas Schmeller, *Brechungen: Urchristliche Wandercharismatiker im Prisma soziologisch orientierter Exegese* (SBS 136; Stuttgart: Verlag Katholisches Bibelwerk, 1989), 50ff., who rightly relativizes the usual sociological and psychological explanatory models. M. Tiwald, "Der Wanderradikalismus als Brücke zum historischen Jesus," in *The Sayings Source Q and the Historical Jesus* (ed. Andreas Lindemann; BETL 158; Louvain: Leuven University Press, 2001), 523–34, presents a sketch of the itinerant radicalism of the Q community.

types.[52] The Q missioners, in direct continuity with Jesus, bound salvation and judgment to the response to their message. If one adds to this their ethos of homelessness (Q 9:58; 10:4e), abandonment of family (Q 14:26), and their commitment to nonviolence (Q 6:29–30), one sees a radical understanding that relies completely on God's care (Q 12:22–32) and God's kingdom/rule (Q 10:9b). It is no accident that the block of teaching in Q 10 concludes with the Lord's Prayer and wisdom instruction about prayer (Q 11:2b–4, 9–13).

We need not think the Q missioners were numerous (Q 10:2, "The harvest is plentiful, but the laborers are few"). The tradents of the sayings source Q had a twofold organizational structure: alongside the itinerant missioners (cf. Q 9:57–62; 10:1–12, 16; 12:22–31, 33–34) were widespread settled communities of Jesus's followers (cf. Q 13:18–21; 16:18; 13:39–40).[53] Such a way of life was really not so exceptional in the history of early Christianity, for Paul and his closest circle of coworkers had already been practicing a comparable radical style of life and mission (cf. 1 Cor. 9:5, 14–15), and the *Didache* still presupposes this phenomenon in the Syro-Palestinian area at the beginning of the second century CE (cf. *Did.* 11, 13).[54] The settled sympathizers in the local communities[55] presented the wandering missioners a material basis for their work by providing shelter (Q 9:58) and provisions (Q 10:5–7). Numerous Q sayings presupposed settled community life, such as the parables of the Mustard Seed and Leaven (Q 13:18–21), the prohibition of divorce (Q 16:18), or the saying about the householder and the thief (Q 12:39–40).[56] So also a twofold social stratification of the Q community can be detected. Numerous logia presuppose material poverty (Q 6:20–21; 7:22; 11:3), while the challenge to decide between God and Mammon (Q 16:13) or heavenly and earthly treasures (Q 12:33–34), as well as the call to give freely in Q 6:30, points to some material wealth in the community (cf. also the parable of the Great Supper of Q 14:15–24). The relation between the itinerant missioners and the settled members of the group need not be thought of in static terms; there was surely a lively exchange of membership between the two groups, as each was partly recruited from the other.[57]

52. For analysis, cf. Tiwald, "Wanderradikalismus," 98–211.

53. Cf. Sato, *Q und Prophetie*, 375ff.

54. There is no reason to suppose the Q community carried on a programmatic mission outside Jewish territory or Jewish populations. The positive reference to the centurion of Capernaum (Q 7:1–10) and to the Gentile cities of Tyre and Sidon (Q 10:13–15; cf. 11:30–32) serve mainly as negative foils for Israel's rejection; cf. Tuckett, *Q and the History of Early Christianity*, 393–404. This does not exclude the possibility, however, that after the failure of the mission to Israel the Q missioners later sought to win Jewish people in the cities of Phoenicia and/or Syria (Q 10:13–14). The reception of Q and the Q missioners by Matthew and his community then could have occurred in southern Syria (cf. Matt. 4:24).

55. On this point cf. Theissen, *Jesusbewegung*, 55–90.

56. Cf. further Q 6:43, 47–49; 7:32; 11:11–13; 14:42–46; 12:58; 13:25.

57. Differently Schmeller, *Brechungen*, who regards the itinerant missioners as commissioned by the Q community, formulating his analysis as follows: "1. Q is a community document.

The Q communities and their missioners saw themselves as subject to massive threats and persecutions (Q 6:22–23; 12:4–7, 11–12), to which they responded with demonstrative trust in God, fearless confession (Q 12:8–9), and the faithfulness of loyal slaves (Q 12:42–46).

8.1.8 Eschatology

The eschatology of the sayings source Q is directly related to the conflicts of the Q community.[58] The determining factor is the debate with Israel and the rejection of the Q community's message by large segments of Israel, as we see above all in the sayings about "this generation" (Q 7:31; 11:29–32, 50–51).[59] "This generation" rejects the message of the Q missioners (Q 7:31), it is "evil" (Q 11:29), and the Son of Man will be for it a sign of judgment (Q 11:30–32, 50–51). The crisis for Israel is manifest above all in the loss of its priority in salvation history (Q 13:24–30; 14:16–18, 21–22), which results in judgment (Q 13:34–35). *At the center of Q's eschatology stands the image of threateningly imminent judgment* (Q 3:7–9, 16–17; 10:12–15; 17:23–37). Jesus's own message of judgment (see above, §3.7) is taken up by Q and strengthened by the composition of Son of Man sayings, for in the latter part of Q the Son of Man steps forth ever more clearly as the coming judge (Q 12:40; 17:24, 26, 30). The operative criterion in the judgment will be the acceptance or rejection of Jesus's message of the kingdom of God. Whoever rejects this message will not only be subject to the judgment (Q 10:13–15; 11:31–32), but according to Q 12:10 such rejection is unforgivable. Therefore, one should fear the one who can destroy not only the body but the soul (Q 12:5). Because God's judgment is imminent, Q 12:58–59 commands speedy reconciliation with one's enemy. According to Q 17:24, when the judgment comes it will then be obvious to everyone, but only those who recognize the signs of the times can hope for salvation (Q 17:26, 28, 30). Finally, the announcement of judgment against Israel in Q 22:28, 30 marks the conclusion of the sayings source Q, and also the end point of Israel.[60] We cannot say

---

2. The Q community sent out missioners who lived as itinerant charismatics. 3. We cannot determine which of the Q sayings, if any, are to be attributed exclusively to the itinerant charismatics. 4. The missions discourse is community tradition, and can be evaluated as something like a constructive testimony to the lifestyle of the itinerant charismatics" (96).

58. Dieter Zeller, "Der Zusammenhang der Eschatologie in der Logienquelle," in *Gegenwart und kommendes Reich: Schülergabe Anton Vögtle zum 65. Geburtstag* (ed. Peter Fiedler and Dieter Zeller; SBB 6; Stuttgart: Verlag Katholisches Bibelwerk, 1975), 67–77, presents a good survey.

59. Cf. Lührmann, *Redaktion der Logienquelle*, 47.

60. For exposition, cf. Paul Hoffmann, "Herrscher in oder Richter über Israel? Mt 19,28/Lk 22,28–30 in der synoptischen Tradition," in *Ja und Nein: Christliche Theologie im Angesicht Israels; Festschrift zum 70. Geburtstag von Wolfgang Schrage* (ed. Klaus Wengst et al.; Neukirchen-Vluyn: Neukirchener Verlag, 1998), 253–64.

for sure whether for Q Israel is thereby ultimately rejected; the intensity of the debate can be taken as evidence that the Q community and Israel were still close to each other, but it could also point to increasing alienation and ultimate separation.[61]

In the coming grand assize, judgment will be according to works, and "because all will be raised at the same time, each one will hear the judgment of the other, and in some cases even influence the outcome (Q 11:31–32)."[62] In the judgment, one may hope for reward for missionary work and for remaining true to the confession under duress (Q 6:22–23; 10:7; 12:33), but it is also possible that some will be surprised when they are rejected (Q 13:24–27). Despite the intensity of the expectation of the end, in a few places an awareness of delay of the parousia can already be perceived. The suddenness of the coming of the Son of Man at a time that cannot be calculated (Q 12:39–40), and especially Q 12:45, point in this direction: "But if that slave says in his heart: My master is delayed, and begins to beat his fellow slaves. . . ." So also, an awareness of the delay of the parousia can be clearly perceived in Q 19:12–24, which is to be repressed by a massive threat of judgment.

8.1.9 Setting in the History of Early Christian Theology

As the first story of Jesus's life and teaching, the sayings source Q has great importance within the history of early Christianity in its earliest formative period, for in it for the first time Jesus of Nazareth steps forth comprehensively as a defining phenomenon within the memory of his followers. The sayings source Q is an independent, distinctive portrayal of Jesus that is not adequately represented by the common designation "sayings source" or "sayings gospel." On the contrary, it presents an independent theological and also narrative profile. The sayings source Q is the first (reconstructable) document that develops Jesus's life and work conceived as a connected narrative and in a reflective theological framework,[63] in which the significance of Jesus is seen in

61. There is a corresponding variation of opinions among exegetes. Among those who vote for a continuing near expectation are Sevenich-Bax, *Konfrontation*, 186–90; and Martin Karrer, "Christliche Gemeinde und Israel: Beobachtungen zur Logienquelle," in *Gottes Recht als Lebensraum: Festschrift für Hans Jochen Boecker* (ed. Peter Mommer; Neukirchen-Vluyn: Neukirchener Verlag, 1993), 145–63; on the other side are, for example, Freidrich Wilhelm Horn, "Christentum und Judentum in der Logienquelle," *EvT* 51 (1991): 344–64, who argues that in the successive redactions of Q there was an increasing distance from Israel. So also Dieter Zeller, "Jesus, Q, und die Zukunft Israels," in *The Sayings Source Q and the Historical Jesus* (ed. Andreas Lindemann; BETL 158; Louvain: Leuven University Press, 2001), 351–69, emphasizes that the continuing sharpness of the pronouncements of judgment against Israel should not be minimized.

62. Robinson, "Sayings Gospel Q," 22.

63. The literary (and theological) unity of Q is argued by Fleddermann, *Commentary*, 124–28.

the extension and proclamation of his words. For the first time, an emphatic biographical interest characterizes the portrayal of Jesus and (differently from Paul), the central focus is not only on the meaning of his life as a whole. The internal logic of Jesus's life and the basic data of his message are suspended between the poles of the past and future comings of the Son of Man. Because Q attributes such great importance to the individual traditions of Jesus's life and work, the sayings source Q can be described as a "proto-gospel."[64] The incorporation of Q in Matthew and Luke shows that Q was understood and valued in this sense.

The theology of the sayings source Q derives from the basic conviction that one's stance to Jesus and his message has salvific significance.[65] A theological presupposition holds Q together, namely, "the conviction of the tradents that Jesus opens the possibility for human beings who encounter him to decide for God and his kingdom, and to live by this decision within history; Jesus's own word in this whole process continues to be an effective power."[66] Neither the promise of salvation nor the threat of judgment can be separated from the speaker. Also in Q, Jesus's proclamation begins with the announcement of salvation; the Beatitudes of Q 6:20–21 concisely formulate the promise of salvation, which is not bound to any other conditions. Jesus pronounces blessed those who have seen with their own eyes and heard with their own ears (Q 10:23–24). The time of salvation has broken in, for "the blind regain their sight and the lame walk around, the skin-diseased are cleansed and the deaf hear, and the dead are raised and the poor are evangelized" (Q 7:22). The disciples are sent out to proclaim peace (Q 10:5–6) and to announce the nearness of the kingdom of God (Q 10:9, 11). The stance one takes with regard to Jesus and his message is not without consequences, for rejection of Jesus's announcement of salvation results in the threat of judgment. The Q missioners see themselves bound together in a fateful association with their Lord: they live as he lived, do what he did, and anticipate sharing with him in the eschatological lordship (Q 22:28, 30). Thus the sayings source Q created a fundamental theological concept that facilitated the understanding of Jesus's ultimate significance without a Passion kerygma. To be sure, the reception of Q by Matthew and Luke changed the way in which Q's message was structured, but at the same time the sayings source Q, with its radical picture of Jesus as it was incorporated in the canonical gospels, shaped their message, and later Christian thought, in a way that still endures.

64. On the different judgments as to the form of Q and its designation, cf. Schnelle, *New Testament Writings*, 191–93.

65. Cf. D. Kosch, "Q und Jesus," *BZ* 36 (1992): 44ff.

66. Athanasius Polag, "Die theologische Mitte der Logienquelle," in *Das Evangelium und die Evangelien: Vorträge vom Tübinger Symposium 1982* (ed. Peter Stuhlmacher; WUNT 28; Tübingen: Mohr, 1983), 110.

8.2 Mark: The Way of Jesus

Mark probably wrote his gospel in Rome around 70 CE for a predominantly Gentile Christian church.[67] By creating the new literary genre gospel, he provided the first extensive Jesus-Christ-history. Thus Mark's presentation of the events and characters, geographical and chronological framework, arrangement of the course of events, choice of narrative perspective,[68] and theological insights essentially determined the early Christian portrayal of Jesus Christ.

8.2.1 Theology

The Gospel of Mark has a theocentric orientation; this is indicated already by the *linguistic data* (θεός [God], 48 times in Mark versus only 51 times in the much-longer Matthew). In the semantic field θεός the dominant expression is βασιλεία τοῦ θεοῦ (kingdom/rule of God, 14 times). Other significant expressions: υἱὸς τοῦ θεοῦ (Son of God, 4 times), κύριος (Lord, 8 times in reference to God) and πατήρ (Father, 4 times in reference to God).[69] Mark makes clear to his hearers/readers that only the Son of God, Jesus Christ, is authorized to proclaim that the time is fulfilled and the kingdom of God has come near.

The Prologue Lays the Theocentric Foundation

The prologue, Mark 1:1–15, functions as a programmatic opening text for the gospel as a whole.[70] The way the gospel is presented in 1:1 already signals

67. Cf. Schnelle, *New Testament Writings*, 197–216. I argue the gospel originated shortly after 70 CE because the juxtaposition of the temple that still exists on the narrative level and the temple to be *completely* destroyed in the future presupposes that the destruction had already occurred. The Roman conquest of Jerusalem and the temple could have been foreseen, but not the complete destruction of the temple.

68. In addition to the essays in F. Hahn (ed., *Der Erzähler des Evangeliums: Methodische Neuansätze in der Markusforschung* [SBS 118/119; Stuttgart: Katholisches Bibelwerk, 1985]) and T. Söding (ed., *Der Evangelist als Theologe: Studien zum Markusevangelium* [SBS 163; Stuttgart: Katholisches Bibelwerk, 1995]), for the narrative analysis of Mark, see David Rhoads et al., *Mark as Story: An Introduction to the Narrative of a Gospel* (2nd ed.; Minneapolis: Fortress, 1999); Norman R. Petersen, "'Literarkritik,' The New Literary Criticism and the Gospel according to Mark," in *The Four Gospels, 1992: Festschrift Frans Neirynck* (ed. Frans van Segbroeck et al.; 3 vols.; BETL 100; Louvain: Leuven University Press, 1992), 2:935–48; C. Breytenbach, "Der Erzähler des Evangeliums: Das Markusevangelium als traditionsgebundene Erzählung?" in *The Synoptic Gospels: Source Criticism and the New Literary Criticism* (ed. F. Neirynck and Camille Focant; BETL 110; Louvain: Leuven University Press, 1993), 77–110.

69. Cf. also δύναμις (power, 4 times); ἀββά (Father, once); εὐλογητός (blessed, once); οὐρανός (heaven, once).

70. Hans-Josef Klauck, *Vorspiel im Himmel? Erzähltechnik und Theologie im Markusprolog* (BTS 32; Neukirchen: Neukirchener Verlag, 1997); M. Eugene Boring, "Mark 1:1–15 and the Beginning of the Gospel," in *How Gospels Began* (ed. Dennis E. Smith; Semeia 52;

the relation of message and messenger that is characteristic for Mark.[71] The genitive construction Ἰησοῦ Χριστοῦ υἱοῦ θεοῦ[72] (Jesus Christ the Son of God) not only reveals the narrative's main character as both preacher of the gospel and its content,[73] but sets up a characterization that could hardly be heightened as the horizon within which readers will understand the following narrative: Jesus is the Messiah and the Son of God. These christological predicates, however, continue to be theological affirmations (in the sense of "theology proper"), for it is as Son of *God* that Jesus Christ proclaims the gospel of *God* of the nearness of the kingdom of *God* (Mark 1:14–15). Mark 1:1 obviously corresponds to 1:14–15,[74] for only here is the term εὐαγγέλιον (gospel) made more precise by the genitive construction "of God." For Mark, there is no conflict between the theological proclamation of Jesus and the christological proclamation of the church.[75] God's dawning kingdom is the content of the gospel, just as the words and deeds of Jesus are the content of the gospel, for this Jesus is not only a figure within history, but the crucified and risen Son of God, and thus is the subject of the gospel, of which God is the initiator and author.

God himself speaks in the words of the Scripture citation Mark 1:2 (Exod. 23:20/Mal. 3:1 LXX) in such a way that they point both to the advent of John the Baptist and to Jesus's proclamation of the will of God. The portrayal of John the Baptist as the forerunner who announces the coming of Jesus (Mark 1:4–8) emphasizes the extraordinary importance of the story to follow, for the reader has every right to expect that the one who baptizes with the Spirit (1:8) will do truly great things. The story of Jesus's baptism in 1:9–11 under-

Atlanta: Society of Biblical Literature, 1990), 43–82; J. Dechow, *Gottessohn und Herrschaft Gottes: Der Theozentrismus des Markusevangeliums* (WMANT 86; Neukirchen: Neukirchener Verlag, 2000), 22–44; G. Guttenberger, *Die Gottesvorstellung im Markusevangelium* (BZNW 123; Berlin: de Gruyter, 2004), 56–74.

71. G. Arnold, "Mk 1,1 und Eröffnungswendungen in lateinischen Schriften," *ZNW* 68 (1977): 123–27.

72. On the originality of υἱὸς θεοῦ (Son of God) in Mark 1:1, cf. the recent study of Dechow, *Gottessohn*, 24–26.

73. Cf. M. Feneberg, *Der Markusprolog: Studien zur Formbestimmung des Evangeliums* (SANT 36; Munich: Kösel, 1974), 118, who argues the genitive construction has a multiple meaning: "The beginning of the gospel, which is brought through Jesus Christ, the Son of God, is also the originator of the gospel (subjective genitive) which is also the gospel about him (objective genitive), and which he himself is (epexegetical genitive)." Contra Hans Weder, "'Evangelium Jesu Christi' (Mk 1,1) und 'Evangelium Gottes' (Mk 1,14)," in *Die Mitte des Neuen Testaments: Einheit und Vielfalt neutestamentlicher Theologie; Festschrift für Eduard Schweizer zum siebzigsten Geburtstag* (ed. Ulrich Luz and Hans Weder; Göttingen: Vandenhoeck & Ruprecht, 1983), 402, who argues Mark 1:1 should be understood only as an objective genitive.

74. On the programmatic function of Mark 1:14–15, see Lührmann, *Markusevangelium*, 32.

75. In view of the theological *and* christological content of Mark 1:1–15, the alternative as formulated in Dechow, *Gottessohn*, 42, seems inadequate: "For Mark, the primary thing is to confront the reader with the eschatological message of Jesus; in contrast to this message, the transcendent identity of the messenger himself plays only a subordinate role."

scores Jesus's special relationship with God and functions as the narrative development of Mark 1:1. The author makes the Son of God title more precise for the hearer/reader in two ways: (1) The Spirit of *God* qualifies the Son of *God*, who (2) is loved by God in a unique way. The temptation narrative in 1:12–13 functions as a prolepsis of the conflicts that will dominate the later story. Jesus resists Satan, for he belongs on God's side, so that angels serve him and the wild animals do not bother him. Mark 1:14–15 brings the story to the point where the Baptist's announcement is fulfilled, so that thereafter he need not appear as an active character in the narrative. These two verses function to set the tone for the whole gospel, as they compactly formulate the theological-eschatological preaching of Jesus Christ: the saving nearness of the kingdom of God is a challenge to repent and to believe. *In Mark, the gospel of God, which is proclaimed by the Son of God, and the kingdom of God all belong inseparably together.*

Jesus's Authorization by the One God of Israel

In the Gospel of Mark, God himself declares his unique relation to Jesus. The voice from heaven in Mark 1:11 ("You are my Son, the Beloved; with you I am well pleased") and 9:7 ("This is my Son, the Beloved; listen to him") qualifies, legitimizes, and authorizes Jesus in the presence of the hearers/readers of the gospel and before all the world. From the Hellenistic point of view, the transfiguration story as a whole presents Jesus as a divine being striding across the earth, who here takes the opportunity to reveal his divine glory.[76] Throughout antiquity, heavenly voices served as part of a courtroom-like setting in which revelatory and authorization scenes transpired,[77] a setting that made it possible for God to speak directly, without anthropomorphic elements. The heavenly messenger at the empty tomb had a comparable function (16:6–7), for the message that Jesus has been raised and will appear to his disciples in Galilee is the word of God; it vouches for the truth and reality of the events not plotted in the gospel.

The citations from the Old Testament[78] are another authorizing authority, in which, for the most part, God himself speaks through Jesus. The introductory citations of Mark 1:2–3 already make this claim (Exod. 23:20; Mal. 3:1; Isa. 40:3), for it is God, the Lord of history, who begins to fulfill his promises to Israel by the advent of Jesus. In the debates with his opponents, the citations

76. Cf. *NW* 1.1 on Mark 9:2–8 par.

77. Cf. Peter Kuhn, *Offenbarungsstimmen im antiken Judentum: Untersuchungen zur Bat Qol und verwandten Phänomenen* (TSAJ 20; Tübingen: Mohr, 1989), and the examples in *NW* 1.2:622–23.

78. Cf. here Alfred Suhl, *Die Funktion der alttestamentlichen Zitate und Anspielungen im Markusevangelium* (Gütersloh: Gütersloher Verlagshaus Gerd Mohn, 1965); Marcus, *Way of the Lord*; Thomas R. Hatina, *In Search of a Context: The Function of Scripture in Mark's Narrative* (JSNTSup 232; London: Sheffield Academic Press, 2002).

from Scripture show that Jesus, in both his life and teaching, is in explicit agreement with the will of God (cf. Mark 10:19). The conduct of his opponents, who have no real knowledge of Scripture (cf. 2:25; 12:10–11, 26, 35ff.), is guided by merely human norms (7:6–7). In contrast, Jesus's own sovereign knowledge of Scripture is seen not only in his enlightening of the unbelief and misunderstanding of the masses and his disciples, but above all in his compliance with the Scripture (cf. 10:19) and his powerful interpretation (cf. 12:26) of the Word of God. The Scripture, and the will of God firmly established in it, confirm and legitimize Jesus (cf. 12:36).

One noteworthy text underscores the theocentric conception of the oldest gospel: in the didactic discussion about the greatest commandment in Mark 12:28–34, the fundamental monotheistic confession of Israel's faith is explicitly cited in v. 29, "Hear, O Israel: The Lord is our God, the Lord is one" (Deut. 6:4 LXX), and then a variation in v. 32 in dependence on Deut. 4:35; Exod. 8:6; and Isa. 45:2 LXX: "He is one, and beside him there is no other." Neither the citation nor the variation is taken over by Matthew or Luke, so that Mark is alone among the gospels in emphasizing the *monotheistic confession of faith* of early Christianity, the more so as he directly alludes to it in Mark 2:7 and 10:18[79] and speaks in 12:26 of the God of Abraham, Isaac, and Jacob. It is the one God of Israel who acts in continuity with himself in Jesus of Nazareth and brings his promises to fulfillment.

God's Kingdom and Glory

So also the central content of Jesus's message is theocentric in its orientation, focused in the phrase ἡ βασιλεία τοῦ θεοῦ (the kingdom/rule of God in Mark 1:15; 4:11, 26, 30; 9:1, 47; 10:14–15, 23–25; 12:34; 14:25; 15:43). The βασιλεία is a new reality opened up by God that, in the texts Mark has adopted,[80] has a particular temporal and spatial dimension. In 1:15; 9:1; 10:23–25; 14:25; 15:43, the kingdom appears as a near, but still future reality. In 4:11; 10:13–15; and 12:34, the kingdom has primarily a present significance. Spatial dimensions are found in 9:1 ("to see the kingdom of God"); 9:47; 10:23–25 ("to enter the kingdom of God"); in 10:15 ("to receive the kingdom of God"); 12:34 ("not far from the kingdom of God"); and 14:25 ("to drink of the fruit of the vine anew in the kingdom of God").

Mark understands the kingdom of God to be primarily a future reality that, despite its nondescript beginnings (cf. 4:26–29, 30–32), is in the present already developing its saving dynamic. The kingdom to arrive at the turn of the ages, when God's rule and saving power will be manifest to all, has already drawn

79. On this point cf. Joachim Gnilka, "Zum Gottesgedanken in der Jesusüberlieferung," in *Monotheismus und Christologie: Zur Gottesfrage im hellenistischen Judentum und im Urchristentum* (ed. Hans-Josef Klauck; QD 138; Freiburg i.B.: Herder, 1992), 151–52.

80. According to ibid., 187, Mark 10:24 is the only redactional kingdom-saying in Mark.

near (1:15, καιρός). This message is making its claim upon people, opening up the possibility of attaining true life. The readiness to repent and live a changed life corresponds to the announcement that the time is fulfilled (1:15), for radical decisions are unavoidable in view of the approaching kingdom of God (9:42–48). Mark regards wealth as a great danger that can prevent entrance into the kingdom of God (10:17–27). In contrast to the person of wealth and power stands the child, dependent and without legal rights, embodying the attitude God wants in view of the new reality of the kingdom of God (10:13–16).[81] True, authentic life, and forgiveness and eschatological salvation, are made present in Jesus's proclamation of the kingdom/rule of God. The "secret of the kingdom of God" (4:11, μυστήριον . . . τῆς βασιλείας τοῦ θεοῦ) is nothing other than the person of Jesus Christ, the Son of God (1:1). In Mark, kingdom theology and Christology are not antitheses or alternatives, but Christology has a theocentric foundation: God's kingdom/rule constitute the framework and content of Jesus's own preaching.[82]

The Good News of God

The good news of Jesus Christ (Mark 1:1) is as such the good news of *God* (1:14).[83] All seven instances of the term εὐαγγέλιον (1:1, 14–15; 8:35; 10:29; 13:10; 14:9) derive from the evangelist himself.[84] While in the tradition prior to Mark the term εὐαγγέλιον was always understood as the message about Jesus Christ, so that an objective genitive Ἰησοῦ Χριστοῦ was always to be supplied, a fundamental change takes place in Mark's own usage. In 1:1, Jesus is both proclaimer and content of the good news, the genitive Ἰησοῦ Χριστοῦ indicating both subject and object of the gospel.[85] The correspondence between 1:1 and 1:14–15 shows that for Mark the Jesus Christ proclaimed in the gospel is at the same time the preacher of the gospel, without making any contrast between the theological (in the sense of "theology proper") message of Jesus and the christological testimony of the church. The good news of God comprises God's saving will and power, just as it includes Jesus's preaching, life, death, and resurrection as these continue to be proclaimed by the Markan community after Easter. The good news of God always has and always will have the good news of Jesus Christ as its content, just as the good news of Jesus Christ is always the message from and about God.

81. For a comprehensive analysis, cf. Peter Müller, *In der Mitte der Gemeinde: Kinder im Neuen Testament* (Neukirchen-Vluyn: Neukirchener Verlag, 1992), 56–78.

82. Cf. Thomas Söding, *Glaube bei Markus* (SBB 12; Stuttgart: Katholisches Bibelwerk, 1987), 191–96.

83. This aspect is explicitly emphasized by Dechow, *Gottessohn*, 274–80.

84. Documentation in Georg Strecker, "Literarkritische Überlegungen zum εὐαγγέλιον-Begriff im Markusevangelium," in *Eschaton und Historie* (ed. Georg Strecker; Göttingen: Vandenhoeck & Ruprecht, 1979), 76–89.

85. Cf. Gnilka, *Markus*, 1:43.

The words and deeds of Jesus Christ are the content of the gospel, but this does not mean that for Mark Jesus was only a figure of past history; rather, the crucified and risen Son of God is not only the object of the gospel but its acting subject as well.[86] Mark underscores his conviction that Jesus represents the gospel and the gospel represents Jesus by the addition of "for the sake of the gospel" to "for my sake" in 8:35 and 10:29 (cf. also the universal preaching of the gospel in 13:10; 14:9). The evangelist thereby makes an inseparable connection between the Jesus of the historical past, who is also the risen Jesus Christ at work in the life of the church, and the gospel about Jesus proclaimed by the church and represented in the new literary genre gospel. At the same time, the plotted narrative internal to the text and the narrative world external to the text modulate into each other, a constituent dynamic of the gospel genre. The call to decision spoken at the level of the plotted narrative transcends the narrative framework and is addressed to the Markan church, which experiences the Jesus Christ represented in the gospel as accessible and present. The manner in which Mark presents the earthly way of the Son of God, Jesus Christ, takes up a tendency already perceptible in the early Christian creed of 1 Cor. 15:3b–5: confession of the crucified and risen Jesus Christ is not possible unless it is fundamentally related to the way of the earthly Jesus.[87] God himself makes Jesus his Son (Mark 1:9–11) and authorizes him as proclaimer of the good news, so that the historiographical presentation of the way of Jesus, the christological implications, and theological foundation always condition each other in such a way that Easter is no break in the one ongoing story. The good news as presented by Mark deals with the manifestation of the saving power of God in the life, death, and resurrection of Jesus Christ, a reality of the past, present, and future.

The Will of God

In the Gospel of Mark, Jesus's way from the very beginning corresponds to the will of God (Mark 1:2–3).[88] It is doing the will of God, not biological family ties, that decides who belongs to the family of God (3:31–35; 8:34–38). It is God's will that the original meaning of the Sabbath be respected, which means saving life rather than destroying it (2:23–28; 3:1–6), for "You abandon the commandment of God and hold to human tradition" (7:8; cf. 7:13). Jesus knows the will of God and will not allow it to be perverted by human tradition. He knows that only by following the will of God can life—authentic, eternal life—be attained, and thus points the rich young man away from himself to God: "Why do you call me good? No one is good but God alone" (10:18). The

86. Cf. the comprehensive treatment in Söding, *Glaube*, 198–251.

87. Cf. Hengel, "Begräbnis," 127: "From the very beginning, the gospel as narrative of the saving event stood as a necessary parallel to the gospel as kerygma."

88. Cf. Guttenberger, *Gottesvorstellung*, 117–82.

appended quotation from the Decalogue (10:19) underscores Jesus's whole-hearted devotion to the will of God. Even his opponents recognize that Jesus is committed to the truth without showing favoritism to anyone, for "you teach the way of God in accordance with truth" (12:14). Jesus knows what belongs to God and what belongs to Caesar (12:13–17). The parable of 12:1–12 emphatically expresses God's past and present activity.[89] The choice of Israel (12:1) represents God's will, as do the sending of the servants (12:2–5) and the ultimate coming of the son (12:6). With the killing of the beloved only son (12:6; cf. 1:11), an irreversible turn occurs in the relation between God and the tenants. God's goodness and patience are revealed despite all opposition in the new beginning made in the "cornerstone" Jesus Christ, already announced in the Scriptures (Ps. 118:22 LXX in Mark 12:10–11), and by the new tenants (Mark 12:9) who bring forth the fruits expected of them. Jesus knows himself to be embraced by the will of God even in his own death, as in prayer he confesses his trust and obedience: "Abba, Father, for you all things are possible; remove this cup from me; yet, not what I want, but what you want" (14:36).

Jesus's own *theocentricity* is the foundation of the Markan gospel; the evangelist portrays Jesus as the authorized Son of God and Messiah, the one who puts teeth into phrases about doing the will of God in the crisis present to the Markan church. He calls for faith in God (Mark 11:22, "Have faith in God"), who is the one God of the living and not of the dead (12:27), whose omnipotence means that all things are possible (10:27).[90]

8.2.2 Christology

As theology proper is the foundation of Markan thought, so Christology is its center.[91] The distinctive achievement of the evangelist consists precisely in the fact that he presents the earthly life of the Son of God, Jesus Christ; that is to say, God's legitimization of Jesus of Nazareth and his subsequent exalted status are transformed into a narrative of the way of the pre-Easter Jesus. All these aspects must be seen as a unity, for neither the theology proper

89. On the interpretation of Mark 12:1–12, see the recent works of Rainer Kampling, *Israel unter dem Anspruch des Messiah: Studien zur Israelthematik im Markusevangelium* (SBB 25; Stuttgart: Katholisches Bibelwerk, 1992), 153–95; Thomas Schmeller, "Der Erbe des Weinbergs," *MTZ* 46 (1995): 183–201; Ulrich Mell, *Die "anderen" Winzer: Eine exegetische Studie zur Vollmacht Jesu Christi nach Markus 11,27–12,34* (WUNT 77; Tübingen: Mohr, 1994), 29–188.

90. On the motifs of God's power and omnipotence, cf. the extensive treatment in Guttenberger, *Gottesvorstellung*, 183–217.

91. Differently François Vouga, "Habt Glauben an Gott," in *Text and Contexts: Biblical Texts in Their Textual and Situational Contexts: Essays in Honor of Lars Hartman* (ed. Tord Fornberg et al.; Oslo: Scandinavian University Press, 1995), 107: "The real theme and center of the Gospel of Mark is not Christology, but τὸ μυστήριον τῆς βασιλείας τοῦ θεοῦ and the beginning of its proclamation and its history in this world."

nor the Christology can be abstracted from the narrative, for everything is woven together in such an interdependent way that every element depends on every other.[92]

Christological Titles

A first direct expression of the evangelist's narrative-christological conception is the intentional location of christological titles within the narrative.

The title υἱὸς θεοῦ (*Son of God*) receives an entirely distinctive meaning within the arrangement of the gospel, for this title not only provides a structuring principle for the narrative (cf. Mark 1:1, 11; 3:11; 9:7; 12:6; 14:61; 15:39) but presents a compact response to the leading question of Markan Christology, "Who is this?" (cf. 1:27; 4:41; 6:2–3, 14–16; 8:27ff.; 9:7; 10:47–48; 14:61–62; 15:39). This preferential use of υἱὸς θεοῦ is no accident, for this title could be heard in a meaningful way both by Jews and by people of Greco-Roman religious background.[93] Already 1:1 makes clear that the earthly way of Jesus is at the same time the way of the Son of God. Jesus Christ is equally related to heaven and earth; therefore his story is both heavenly and earthly. He is already Son of God at the very beginning of the narrative, yet he *becomes* Son of God within the narrative.[94] Mark clarifies this fundamental coherence on several levels. He uses the expression ὁ υἱός μου ὁ ἀγαπητός (1:11; 9:7, "my Son, the Beloved") or υἱὸς ἀγαπητός (beloved son) to link the stories of baptism (1:9–11), transfiguration (9:2–9) and the allegorical parable of the Wicked Tenants and to make them into key texts for the gospel as a whole. They form a connected line of christological recognition in that here the heavenly and earthly worlds are brought together by the voice of God, with each scene using the term υἱός for Jesus to indicate that he belongs to God. While the baptism and transfiguration scenes manifest and present the divine status of Jesus in formulaic terms, the allegorized parable of the Wicked Tenants is the prelude to the Passion, so that all three texts lead to the confession

92. Cf. Frank J. Matera, *New Testament Christology* (Louisville: Westminster John Knox, 1999), 26, who argues that none of the christological titles "can be understood adequately apart from Mark's narrative; for the Christology is in the story, and through the story we learn to interpret the titles."

93. Cf. Adela Yarbro Collins, "Mark and His Readers: The Son of God among Jews," *HTR* 92 (1999): 393–408; Adela Yarbro Collins, "The Son of God among Greeks and Romans," *HTR* 92 (2000): 85–100; see now Adela Yarbro Collins, *Mark: A Commentary* (Hermeneia; Minneapolis: Fortress, 2007), ad loc.

94. This twofold structure is to be explained in terms of Mark's situation, which of course already presupposed a Christology but within the new gospel genre wants to clarify how Jesus became what he already was. This does not mean that Mark advocates a preexistence Christology (contra Ludger Schenke, "Gibt es im Markusevangelium eine Präexistenzchristologie?" *ZNW* 91 [2000]: 53ff.), for the logical train of thought of contemporary exegesis cannot eliminate the simple fact that Mark does not translate a preexistence Christology into literary form, and thus that he was not a proponent of such a Christology.

of the centurion under the cross: "Truly this man was God's Son!"[95] In the compositional framework of the gospel, baptism, transfiguration, rejection, and confession beneath the cross are the foundation pillars around which Mark arranges his traditions in the form of a life of Jesus. The title υἱός thus marks the substantial center, for it facilitates the embracing of Jesus's divine being and his way of suffering and death as a united whole. Jesus's being and character are firmly established at the beginning; he is God's Son, and his essential being does not change. But for human beings he *becomes* God's Son, for they need a process of perception and recognition.[96] This process is the life of Jesus, as presented by Mark in the new literary genre, the gospel. This process of perception and recognition does not attain its goal until the end of the gospel, at the cross. Only here, it is a human being, not God, who acknowledges Jesus as υἱὸς θεοῦ (15:39). In the internal narrative logic of the gospel, this was previously known only by God (1:11; 9:7), the demons (3:11; 5:7), and the Son himself (1:11; 12:6; 14:61–62). Human beings must go with Jesus the whole way from baptism to the cross in order to attain an appropriate and authentic knowledge of Jesus's Sonship. At the end of this way, the acclamation of the Roman centurion beneath the cross involuntarily evokes a comparison with the imperial cult, for the greatest power on earth does not belong to the Caesar honored as a god or son of a god,[97] but to the Son of God Jesus Christ. The central christological title of the oldest gospel would certainly have been heard with the overtones of the contemporary emperor cult.[98] As a positive christological affirmation, this title is at the same time a massive question mark placed against the emperor cult as a political religion, for it is not the emperor, but one crucified by the Romans who is the Son of God! The exorcism story in 5:1–20 must also be read as a polemic against the all-encompassing claim of the Roman Caesar. The demons are called "Legion" (5:9, λεγιών; a legion was a division of the Roman army, from 4,200 to 6,000 men), they take refuge in an unclean herd of swine and finally drown (5:9–11). Not only the Gerasene but the land itself is now free (from the Romans)! The story about the dispute over their respective rank in the coming kingdom (10:35–45), with its rejection of conventional principles of rulership, is most likely also directed against the powers claimed by the imperial cult.

95. Cf. D. S. du Toit, "'Gesalbter Gottessohn'—Jesus als letzter Bote Gottes: Zur Christologie des Markusevangeliums," in ". . . *Was ihr auf dem Weg verhandelt habt": Beiträge zur Exegese und Theologie des Neuen Testaments; Festschrift für Ferdinand Hahn zum 75. Geburtstag* (ed. Peter Müller et al.; Neukirchen-Vluyn: Neukirchener Verlag, 2001), 39.

96. R. Weber, "Christologie und 'Messiasgeheimnis': Ihr Zusammenhang und Stellenwert in den Darstellungsintentionen des Markus," *EvT* 43 (1983): 115–16.

97. On the emperor as "Son of God," cf. the texts in *NW* 1.1 at Mark 15:39. On the emperor as divine, cf. Clauss, *Kaiser und Gott*, 217–419.

98. This aspect receives particular emphasis in Martin Ebner, "Kreuzestheologie im Markusevangelium," in *Kreuzestheologie im Neuen Testament* (ed. Andreas Dettwiler and Jean Zumstein; WUNT 151; Tübingen: Mohr, 2002).

While the Son of God title designates Jesus as to his essential being, the *Son of Man title* (ὁ υἱὸς τοῦ ἀνθρώπου) points more to his work and function.[99] The present Son of Man who acts in power is the focus of Mark 2:10; 2:28, where Jesus enters into debate with Jewish exegetical traditions and gives them a new determination. In 8:38, the function of the Son of Man as judge stands in the foreground. The confession or rejection of Jesus's present proclamation of the kingdom of God (cf. 9:1) results in either salvation or condemnation. For Mark, these are two sides of the same coin, because each is unconditionally joined to the person of Jesus. Mark 13:26 and 14:62 deal with the future coming of the Son of Man. The heaping up of christological titles is striking in 14:61–62: υἱὸς θεοῦ, υἱὸς τοῦ εὐλογητοῦ (Son of the Blessed), and υἱὸς τοῦ ἀνθρώπου. Mark 14:61–62 marks a christological culmination point and high point of the gospel: the Jesus who has no perceivable power, who is being handed over to violence, is spoken of by Mark in the highest terms imaginable. Even if the emphasis here lies on the Son of Man title, it is still clear that for Mark the titles are mutually supplementary and interpret each other. An orientation to Passion theology is dominant in the sayings about the suffering Son of Man in 8:31; 9:9, 12, 31; 10:33, 45; 14:21, 41. Here we have a specifically Markan form of speech, not previously documented in early Christianity. All examples are found after 8:27, and it is especially the three Passion predictions in 8:31; 9:31; and 10:33 that open up the way from Galilee to Jerusalem,[100] the place of his suffering and death in lowliness and mockery. Since 8:27 it has been clear without reservation that Jesus is on his way to the cross, and that Mark thinks backward from the event of the cross, i.e., that his language about the suffering Son of Man is a form of Markan theology of the cross.

The Χριστός title (*anointed/Messiah*) appears in the gospel at two hermeneutical and theological key locations: Mark 1:1 and 8:29 (cf. also 9:41; 12:35; 13:21; 14:61; 15:32). Mark 1:1 characterizes the Markan proclamation not only as the gospel about Jesus Christ; as the Χριστός, Jesus is both content and proclaimer of the gospel (see above, §8.2.1). What is true of the Son title applies also to the Christ title: Jesus is already what he *becomes* in the course of the narrative. The scene in 8:29 illuminates this aspect of Mark's Christology, where the gospel's only explicit predication of Jesus as the Christ is expressed by Peter: "You are the Messiah" (σὺ εἶ ὁ Χριστός). By placing this confession under the command to silence (8:30), adding the first Passion prediction (8:31), and sharply rejecting Peter's inappropriate request that Jesus should avoid such suffering (8:32–33), the evangelist gives literary and theological expression to his own Christology. In principle, Peter has rightly recognized *that* Jesus is

99. On this point cf. U. Kmiecik, *Der Menschensohn im Markusevangelium* (FzB 81; Würzburg: Echter Verlag, 1997).

100. Cf. Weber, "Christologie und 'Messiasgeheimnis,'" 116–17.

the Messiah, but it is equally important to keep hold of *how* Jesus will be the Messiah—and this Peter does not (yet) see. The suffering Son of Man and the exalted Christ are one and the same; there is no exaltation without humiliation, and conversely, the suffering and death of the Messiah is not the last word. Here Mark by no means places the Χριστός title under an eschatological reservation;[101] rather, he preserves the paradoxical mystery of the person of Jesus Christ, which cannot be derived merely from scribal reflection. Mark 12:35–37 rejects the view that the Christ is the Son of David.[102] The true rank of the Christ is rather expressed in Ps. 110:1 LXX, which places the κύριος (Lord)[103] in direct relation to God. God acts in a way that cannot be calculated in advance and cannot be derived from historical observation.[104]

The Mystery of Jesus's Person

The Markan secrecy theory also serves to facilitate the recognition of Jesus Christ as Son of God. Mark uses a variety of literary means to indicate that God's saving act in Christ occurs in a way that is hidden from ordinary perception. Each of these literary means should be understood within the framework of a comprehensive christological theory of secrecy and mystery—the messianic secret.

1. The demons recognize Jesus's messiahship, but Jesus commands them to be silent. In Mark 1:25, 34; 3:12, Jesus commands silence to demons who have identified him with messianic designations (1:24: ὁ ἅγιος τοῦ θεοῦ [the Holy One of God]; 3:11: σὺ εἶ ὁ υἱος τοῦ θεοῦ [you are the Son of God]).[105] While the command to silence in 1:25 can be seen as an exorcistic technique of overcoming the demon that was an element of the pre-Markan traditional story, the two commands for the demons to be silent in the summaries of Jesus's mighty deeds in 1:32–34 and 3:7–12 must clearly be seen as redactional.[106] Mark wants to make clear that

101. Differently Hahn, *Theologie*, 1:501: "The Christ title is used of the earthly Jesus proleptically, like 'Son of David,' and is to be understood in the sense of Messiah *designatus*."

102. On the Son of David imagery, cf. also Mark 10:47–48; 11:10.

103. Κύριος serves in the LXX citations primarily as a designation of God (cf. Mark 11:9; 12:11, 29–30, 36; cf. also 12:9; 13:20), but also as a title for Jesus (Mark 1:3; 5:19; 11:3; 12:36–37; 13:35), as an address to Jesus, and as a description of his acting with authority (Mark 2:28).

104. Cf. James M. Robinson, *The Problem of History in Mark* (SBT 11; London: SCM, 1962), 32, 46–49, 59–60.

105. In Mark 5:8, as Jesus's reaction to the demon's recognition of him (5:7), the evangelist places a command for the demon to come out in place of a command to silence. A command to silence would not fit this story, which in the pre-Markan tradition had already included an exchange between Jesus and the demons.

106. For analysis, cf. Gnilka, *Markus*, 1:76–77, 85–86, 133. B. Kollmann, "Jesu Schweigegebote an die Dämonen," *ZNW* 82 (1991): 267–73, also considers the command to silence in Mark 1:25 to be redactional.

one can perceive Jesus's identity based on miracles without adequately understanding his divine sonship. Jesus's mighty deeds do not yet make him the Son of God.[107]

2. The secretive performance of miracles. Jesus forbids spreading the news of his miraculous deeds, but this order is disobeyed. In Mark 5:43a and 7:36a, in the context of a miracle story, Jesus commands those present, or the one who has been healed, not to make the healing public. This command is disobeyed in 7:36b, just as the specific prohibition in the traditional story of 1:44 is broken in 1:45.[108] Such prohibitions of publicizing Jesus's miracles are intended to prevent Jesus's being defined by his miraculous deeds alone, which would usurp his true identity. In the miracle stories, the mystery of Jesus's person is not yet adequately revealed, while at the same time the violation of his commands to silence shows that, nevertheless, Jesus's epiphany in miraculous deeds cannot be repressed (cf. also 7:24!).[109] Mark by no means has a negative view of this state of affairs; he only wants to reject the claim that the person of Jesus is absolutely identified with the miracle stories. Most of the commands to silence and prohibitions of publicizing his miracles cannot be explained at the level of narrative logic within the story line itself, but rather point to a christological meta-theory.
3. The disciples' lack of understanding. Prior to 8:27, the disciples' failure to understand has to do with Jesus's teaching (4:13; 7:18) and his person (4:40–41; 6:52). After 8:27, the picture changes: both the private instruction of the disciples and their misunderstanding intensify. While in 8:17, 21 the disciples are represented as still obdurate and hard-hearted, a turn in the story occurs with Peter's confession at 8:29. A transformation in the disciples' level of understanding has taken place, for they are now aware that Jesus is the Messiah. However, the command to silence in 8:30, and Peter's reaction to the first Passion prediction, show that in 8:27–33 the disciples fail to understand the mystery of Jesus's suffering and death as the key to his identity, which continues to be the case in

107. Guttenberger, *Gottesvorstellung*, 288–332, interprets the messianic secret within the horizon of its relation to monotheism and Christology, with the following understanding of the function of the command to silence to the demons: "With the command to silence to the demons, Mark introduces an additional precautionary measure into the framework of the secrecy motif, by means of which he guards Jesus from violating the first commandment and the charge that he leads others to do so" (p. 331).

108. On the redactional character of Mark 1:45; 5:43a; 7:36, cf. Gnilka, *Markus*, 1:91, 211, 296.

109. Cf. Marco Frenschkowski, *Offenbarung und Epiphanie* (WUNT 2.79–80; 2 vols.; Tübingen: Mohr, 1995), 211: "The numinous betrays its presence; its true essence always shimmers through its hiddenness." Frenschkowski understands Mark's presentation of Jesus as a whole in terms of the model of "hidden epiphanies" that was widespread in antiquity. Cf. Frenschkowski, *Offenbarung und Epiphanie*, 2:148–224.

9:5–6, 30–32; 10:32–34. One might say that Mark uses the disciples' lack of understanding to illustrate how the person of Jesus must not be understood. A holistic understanding of Jesus's person cannot be limited to his majesty and glory and exclude his suffering. A full recognition of Jesus's identity requires both.

4. The command for the disciples to remain silent. The two commands to the disciples to remain silent in 8:30 and 9:9 are of great significance for the Markan secrecy theory. With the command in 8:30, Mark makes it clear[110] that Peter's confession, taken by itself, is not a complete and final recognition of the person of Jesus. This is confirmed by the following first Passion prediction and Peter's reaction to it. William Wrede[111] had already recognized the fundamental importance of 9:9 for the secrecy theory ("As they were coming down the mountain, he ordered them to tell no one about what they had seen, until after the Son of Man had risen from the dead"). For Mark, the command to silence is in force only until the resurrection; from then on the secret of Jesus's person can be proclaimed.[112] Moreover, neither the resurrection theme nor the termination of the command to silence can be explained from the internal logic of the narrative of 9:2–8. And finally, we must note that the Markan motif of the disciples' lack of understanding in v. 10 and the temporal limit assigned to the command to silence in v. 9 are very closely related. In each case, the point is[113] that a full knowledge of the identity of Jesus Christ cannot be attained prior to and apart from the cross and resurrection.

Directly related to the Markan secrecy theory are: the instances where Jesus heals people nonpublicly, apart from the crowds (cf. 5:37, 40; 7:33; 8:23); the reduction of the circle of disciples who are interior to what Jesus says and does (cf. 5:37; 13:3); Jesus's withdrawal in search of privacy (cf. 1:35, 45; 3:7, 9; 6:31–32, 46; 7:24); and topological motifs such as οἶκος, οἰκία ("house," cf. 7:17, 24; 9:28, 33; 10:10), πλοῖον, πλοιάριον ("boat," cf. 3:9; 6:32, 54; 8:13–14), ὄρος ("mountain," cf. 3:13; 6:46; 9:2, 9; 13:3), and ἔρημος τόπος ("lonely place," cf. 1:35, 45; 6:31–32).

110. Contra Rudolf Pesch, *Das Markusevangelium*, vol. 1, *Kommentar zu Kap. 1,1–8,26;* vol. 2, *Kommentar zu Kap. 8,27–16,20* (4th ed.; 2 vols.; HTKNT; Freiburg i.B.: Herder, 1984), 2:33, 39, Mark 8:30 should be regarded as redactional; cf. among others, Gnilka, *Markus*, 2:10; Weber, "Christologie und 'Messiasgeheimnis,'" 118.

111. Cf. Wrede, *Messianic Secret*, 67–70.

112. Heikki Räisänen, *The "Messianic Secret" in Mark* (Edinburgh: T&T Clark, 1990), 184–93, 255; Pesch, *Markusevangelium*, 2:39, 77, regard Mark 9:9 as pre-Markan tradition. The agreements in form and content with the clearly redactional commands to silence in Mark 5:43 and 7:36 speak against this.

113. Both are redactional; cf. Eduard Schweizer, *The Good News according to Mark* (trans. Donald H. Madvig; Richmond: John Knox, 1970), 184–86; Gnilka, *Markus*, 2:40; Lührmann, *Markusevangelium*, 157.

The parable theory of Mark 4:10–12, the nucleus of which is pre-Markan, is not a direct component of the Markan secrecy theory.[114] The secrecy concept in Mark is not an apologetic theory intended to explain Jewish unbelief, nor does it imply an intentional hardening of Israel. On the contrary, it is intended to facilitate the right understanding of the person of Jesus. Thus the evangelist corrects the parable theory in 4:13b in no small way, and by his use of the motif of the disciples' lack of understanding creates a direct connection to the secrecy theory.

The individual elements of the Markan secrecy theory do not originate from a historical interest but are aimed at the readers, with the intent of leading them to a full understanding of Jesus's identity as the Christ. At the same time, the secrecy theory makes it possible for the evangelist Mark to combine the pre-Markan miracle stories and the Passion traditions within the framework of the new literary genre gospel, and thus to fuse them into a new unity.[115] Moreover, 9:9 makes it clear that the secrecy theory must be understood as a form of Mark's theology of the cross.[116] The Son of God, Jesus Christ, remains the same in his suffering and his deeds of power.

Jesus's Authority

Authority (ἐξουσία occurs 10 times in Mark, 10 times in Matthew, 16 times in Luke, 8 times in John) is a key concept and term of Mark's Christology. Mark's exceptional interest in this concept (redactional in 1:22, 27; 3:15; 6:7; 11:28, 29, 33; 13:34; traditional only in 2:10)[117] is manifest at the levels of both

114. On the relation of Mark 4:33, 34 to the parable theory, cf. Gnilka, *Markus*, 190–91.

115. G. Theissen assigns a pragmatic function to the secrecy motif: from the parallelism between the narrative world of the text and the real world of the hearer/reader we can infer that the successive stages of revealing the secret and the increasing threat to Jesus has a counterpart in the social world of the Markan church; cf. Theissen, "Evangelienschreibung," 405.

116. W. Wrede did not trace the messianic secret back to the evangelist Mark but saw it as the work of the church after Easter but prior to Mark. It originated from the necessity of reconciling the unmessianic life of Jesus and the faith of the post-Easter church. In the history of research, neither the idea of non-messianic Jesus traditions nor that of a pre-Markan origin of the messianic secret has found support. In particular, the works of Eduard Schweizer have shown that Mark himself is to be seen as the originator of the secrecy theory (cf. Eduard Schweizer, "The Question of the Messianic Secret in Mark [1965]," in *The Messianic Secret* [ed. C. M. Tuckett; IRT 1; London: SPCK, 1983], 65–74; and Eduard Schweizer, "Mark's Theological Achievement [1964]," in *The Interpretation of Mark* [ed. William R. Telford; 2nd ed.; SNTI; Edinburgh: T&T Clark, 1995], 63–88). H. Räisänen makes a complete separation between the "parable theory" and the messianic secret, giving a negative answer to the question of the unity of Mark's secrecy theory (or theories); cf. Räisänen, *Messianic Secret*, 76–143. A similar argument is mounted by Pesch, *Markusevangelium*, 40–41, who regards Mark as a conservative redactor with no independent christological conceptions.

117. Klaus Scholtissek, *Die Vollmacht Jesu: Traditions- und redaktionsgeschichtliche Analysen zu einem Leitmotiv markinischer Christologie* (NTA 25; Münster: Aschendorff, 1992), 281.

content and composition. The story in Mark 1:21–28 introduces the whole ministry of Jesus under the key term ἐξουσία: "They were all amazed, and they kept on asking one another, 'What is this? A new teaching—with authority'" (1:27). Jesus's authority, revealed in word and deed, qualifies him in a special way, for he participates uniquely in God's authority by forgiving sins (2:10), makes authoritative judgments about the Sabbath (2:27–28; 3:4), heals the sick (e.g., 1:40–45), criticizes the way his contemporaries interpret the law (2:1–3:6), and with commanding authority calls people to be his followers (e.g., 1:16–20; 3:13–19; 6:6b–13). Such claims could not continue without protests, resulting in the fundamental christological question, "By what authority are you doing these things? Who gave you this authority to do them?" (11:28). In the context of 11:27–33; 12:1–12, Jesus appears as the one authorized by the eschatological power of God, thus expressing the ἐξουσία concept in a way that unites Jesus's person and work. The ἐξουσία of the earthly Jesus is the "expression of the messianic commission of the Son of God to proclaim and mediate the nearness of the kingdom of God."[118] Mark 2:1–3:6 as prelude to the Passion, along with 11:27 and 12:1–12, makes clear that Mark understands the Passion as the consequence of the sending of the Messiah and Son of God Jesus of Nazareth with the full authority of God. In the obedient acceptance of the will of God (14:36, "Remove this cup from me; yet, not what I want, but what you want") the reader sees not only the dignity and exalted nature of Jesus's person, but the consistent agreement of his mission with the will of God. As the visible expression of Jesus's participation in God's own authority, the ἐξουσία concept unfurls Jesus's exalted messianic status as Son of God and highlights the relation of teaching, deed, and personal status.

Miracles and Christology

Miracle stories are almost completely lacking in the sayings source Q and are found only sporadically in the sources peculiar to Matthew and Luke; Mark and his sources are the primary bearers of the miracle tradition. The breadth and variety of such narrative forms is impressive: (1) exorcisms: Mark 1:21–28; 5:1–20; 9:14–27; (2) healing miracles: 1:29–31, 40–45; 5:21–43; 7:31–37; 8:22–26; 10:46–52; (3) miracles of deliverance: 4:35–41; (4) epiphany miracles: 6:45–52; (5) gift miracles: 6:30–44; 8:1–9; (6) mixed forms: 2:1–12; 3:1–6; 7:24–30; (7) summaries of Jesus's miracle working activities: 1:32–34; 3:7–12; 6:53–56.

At the center of the pre-Markan miracle tradition[119] stands the miracle worker himself, so that these narratives can be regarded as *miracle worker*

118. Ibid., 293.

119. On the pre-Markan miracle tradition, cf. Dietrich-Alex Koch, *Die Bedeutung der Wundererzählungen für die Christologie des Markusevangeliums* (BZNW 42; Berlin: de Gruyter, 1975), 8–41.

stories that elaborate a healing Christology. From the point of view of the history of tradition, such miracle stories are attached to the Elijah-tradition (compare Mark 5:7 with 1 Kings 17–18). Parallels to these motifs are also found in the Hellenistic tradition of the "divine man" (θεῖος ἀνήρ) (miraculous knowledge and foreknowledge: Mark 2:8; 3:2; 4:39–40; 6:37; 8:4–5; fear and astonishment: 4:41; 5:15, 17, 33, 42; 6:49–50; faith as recognition of the miracle worker: 4:40; 5:34, 36; worship/reverence: 5:6; visible manifestation of divine power: 5:30; power over nature: 4:41; 6:48–50; avoidance of publicity: 5:40; use of miraculous words or techniques: 7:33–34).

Like the Hellenistic miracle stories, so also the pre-Markan miracles tradition emphasizes the abilities of the miracle worker, who establishes his credentials by performing amazing feats. To be sure, there is an important difference in that in the pre-Markan miracle traditions faith extends beyond the miracle itself to the miracle worker. It is saving faith, with a soteriological meaning that goes far beyond mere belief that the miracle happened. This is manifest in the terminology, with a much higher frequency of words related to πιστεύω in the pre-Markan tradition than in comparable Hellenistic miracle stories (cf. Mark 2:5; 4:40; 5:34, 36; 9:23–24; 10:52). The Markan miracle stories express the faith experiences of individuals and the community,[120] making visible Jesus's life-giving participation in God's creative power as healing, deliverance from danger, and overcoming threats to authentic life. In the pre-Markan church, as in the evangelist's own composition, Jesus's miracles are a central element of Christian proclamation. In many of their acclamations, one can overhear the reactions of those who responded to the Christian mission. Because Jesus had authorized his disciples, and through them the post-Easter Christians of Mark's own time, to continue his own miraculous ministry (cf. Mark 7:6, 13; 9:28, 38ff.), the mighty acts of Jesus continue in the present of the Markan church, and continue to call forth faith. Thus the Markan faith community sees its own reality grounded in the miracles of the earthly Jesus and continues to tell about them.

For Mark, the miracle stories are of central importance, for they are testimonies of the history of Jesus's own self-revelation as the Christ. The miracle stories portray Jesus's power to embody and mediate the presence of God's kingdom. In them the divine epiphany is manifest in Jesus's own person. The healings fulfill the promised rule of God as liberation from the power of demons and evil. In particular, the summaries of Jesus's miracle-working ministry show that Mark understands Jesus's advent as a *continuing, enduring* miraculous ministry. The eucharistic echoes in both feeding miracles (cf. 6:41; 8:6) allow the present life of the Markan church to be seen in the light of Jesus's miraculous deeds; the hunger of both Jews (6:30–44) and Gentiles

120. Cf. here Detlev Dormeyer, *Das Markusevangelium* (Darmstadt: Wissenschaftliche Buchgesellschaft, 2005), 222–28.

(8:1–9) is satisfied, as they are now fed in the common eucharist. So also, a critical reference to the Caesar cult is present in these stories in a way that cannot be overlooked. Jesus of Nazareth appears as *the* miracle worker, whose saving acts surpass the miracles claimed by the Caesar;[121] Jesus's power can send the demons named Legion (λεγιών) into unclean swine and so drown them in the sea (5:1–20).

The evangelist does not relativize the miracles, but *integrates* them into his theological conception as a whole.[122] In this way he is able to cope with the knowledge that the Jesus Christ who expresses his authority in mighty deeds is and remains the same sovereign Christ who truly suffers and dies. In the Passion story Jesus likewise remains the determining agent whose sovereignty lies in the background, the one who can either speak or remain silent. He does not seek death, but it comes to him and he willingly accepts it, and thus remains true to his divine legitimation even in death. Jesus's miracles and his suffering constitute a unity; it is precisely through the commands to silence to the demons and the disciples that Mark orients the whole of Jesus's ministry to the cross and resurrection,[123] without thereby relativizing the divine revelation that occurs in the miracles. Faith in the crucified and risen Son of God and faith in the Jesus who performs miraculous deeds are for Mark one and the same.[124]

Christology as Narrative

By means of the gospel as a new literary genre, Mark created for early Christianity the normative memory of Jesus Christ. The gospel form brings together historical memory of Jesus, his proclamation as the messianic Son of God, and God's act in the Passion and resurrection. It is the narrative form of the gospel[125] that makes it possible for Mark to exhibit how Jesus's mighty

121. On this point cf. Clauss, *Kaiser und Gott*, 346–52. Especially to be noted are Calpurnius Siculus, *Eclogues* 4.97–101; Plutarch, *Caes.* 37.7; 38:4–6; Dio Cassius, *Hist.* 40.46.3–4 (Caesar calms a storm); Suetonius, *Vesp.* 7; Tacitus, *Hist.* 4.81.1 (*NW* 1.2:480–81; Vespasian heals a blind person); *Hist. Aug. Hadrian* 25.1–4 (Hadrian heals a blind person); Martial, *Epigr.* 1.6; 4.2, 30 (emphasis on the Caesar's miraculous powers).

122. Cf. Koch, *Wundererzählungen*, 188–93.

123. Cf. Dormeyer, *Das Markusevangelium*, 212.

124. Boring, *Mark,* 258, who likewise does not regard the different Markan perspectives as mutually exclusive alternatives: "His narrative includes each perspective on Jesus without adjusting it to the other."

125. Scholars in the United States and in South Africa have consistently pressed on with this approach. The narrator of the gospel and the narrative world created by the author are kept in view; attention is given to the narrative point of view, i.e., the way in which the narrator presents the story. The third-person form of the narrative, the omniscient author, the various levels of time and space, the way in which characters are brought on the narrative stage, the scenes and the events that comprise them, structural connections within the narrative, psychological elements in the presentation and comprehensive narrative structures—all these are carefully investigated. Cf. Willem S. Vorster, "Markus—Sammler, Redaktor, Autor oder Erzähler?" in *Der Erzähler*

deeds and his suffering have an inherent unity that requires that they be seen together. Together they illustrate that Jesus's destiny was not an accident or tragic fate, but the result of his loyalty to his mission. Mark intends to affirm the validity of both: Jesus's power manifest in his deeds, *and* his weakness revealed in suffering even to death on Golgotha; the earthly mission *and* the resurrection and the coming parousia. For Mark, Jesus is not only a figure of the past, but a figure of the present and the future. For him, everything depends on the fact that one can understand and believe in Jesus, the powerful miracle worker and teacher, only from the point of view of his death and resurrection. By presenting the way of the Son of God from baptism to the announcement of the appearances of the Risen One, with the intention of leading to a right understanding of his person, the literary genre gospel becomes the literary expression of the theological realization that the crucified Jesus of Nazareth proceeded on his way from the very beginning as Son of God.[126] The literary genre gospel is thus a form *sui generis*, the result of the theological insight that God himself acts in the unique and irreplaceable history of Jesus of Nazareth. There is thus for Mark no real tension between pre- and post-Easter, history and kerygma, or internal versus external narrative levels of the text, for his theological achievement consists precisely in the fact that in each case he has resolutely understood and presented both aspects as a unity.[127] By firmly binding historiographical-biographical narrative to kerygmatic address and presenting Jesus's way to the cross as dramatic event, he maintains and preserves what is in his eyes the historical and theological identity of Christian faith. Confession of the crucified and risen Jesus Christ is not possible without this fundamental bond with the way of the earthly Jesus.

Mark constructed his gospel according to the laws of drama and visual demonstration; it must be read and understood *as a whole*. The action is marked by *two conflict dynamics*. The *first* is Jesus's conflict with the religious authorities of his time, a conflict that begins in Galilee and comes to its bitter end in Jerusalem. In contrast to the readers and hearers of the gospel, Jesus's opponents in the narrative do not know Jesus's identity. They are unaware that the promises of Scripture are being fulfilled (1:2–3), they do not hear the heavenly voice at Jesus's baptism (1:9–11), neither are they privy to the instruction given to the disciples (cf. 4:11–12, 34; 9:31). In 2:1–3:6, this

---

des Evangeliums: Methodische Neuansätze in der Markusforschung (ed. Ferdinand Hahn; SBS 118/119; Stuttgart: Verlag Katholisches Bibelwerk, 1985), 35–36: "Was Mark a collector, editor, or narrator? . . . In my opinion, there is adequate evidence to show that Mark presents the story of Jesus to us as he saw it, and for this reason I would call him a narrating author. He is certainly not merely a collector."

126. The judgment of Hans Conzelmann, "Present and Future in the Synoptic Tradition," *JTC* 5 (1968): 43, is still fundamental: "The secrecy theory is the hermeneutical presupposition of the genre 'gospel.'"

127. On this point cf. Hans Friedrich Weiss, *Kerygma und Geschichte* (Berlin: Akademie Verlag, 1983).

conflict is structured and dramatized in five conflict dialogues.[128] In these conflict dialogues, all the important groups opposing Jesus appear: the scribes (2:6), scribes and Pharisees (2:16), Pharisees (2:18), and finally the Pharisees together with the Herodians (3:6). The opposition intensifies from one story to the next, until finally the decision to put Jesus to death is made in 3:6. The conflict attains a high point in 11:15–18, where by cleansing the temple Jesus makes a frontal attack against the religious authorities in Jerusalem. Finally, Jesus comes into conflict with the Roman institutions (15:1–40), which seals his immediate fate.

The *second conflict dynamic* allows it to become increasingly clear *who* Jesus is. Heavenly voices (Mark 1:11; 9:7), demons (1:24; 5:7), Jesus himself (14:61–62), and a Roman (15:39) reveal and testify to the secret of Jesus's identity, the person of Jesus Christ—he is the suffering Son of God. In the central part of the gospel "on the way" to Jerusalem (8:27–10:52), the knowledge of this identity is compressed into the narrative: the confession of Jesus's messiahship (8:27–30) is followed by a threefold parallel composition: (1) Passion prediction 8:31; 9:31; 10:32–34; (2) misunderstanding by the disciples 8:32b, 33; 9:32–34; 10:35–40; (3) renewed instruction of the disciples 8:34–9:1; 9:35–37; 10:41–45. The framing of this section by two stories of healing blindness has a metaphorical character. The eyes of the disciples, and with them the eyes of the Markan church, are to be opened to see who this Jesus of Nazareth is: the suffering Son of God who calls people to a discipleship that involves suffering.

These two dynamics converge at Mark 14:28 and 16:7 and lead to a surprising resolution: the Crucified One will reveal himself in Galilee to the disciples as the Risen One. At the end of his narrative, Mark directs the readers' view back to the beginning, where the story of Jesus began, i.e., the whole gospel is intended to be (re-)read from the perspective of the announcement of the appearances of the risen Christ in Galilee, the founding experiences of the Markan church.[129]

Whether Mark intentionally decided not to *narrate* the appearances of the Risen One, or whether the original conclusion of Mark has been lost, is an issue that cannot be easily resolved. It could be that Mark intentionally omitted stories of Jesus's appearances in order to avoid a *theologia gloriae* that would understand Jesus's death on the cross only as a transition to glory.[130]

128. Cf. on this point the extensive discussions in Martin Albertz, *Die synoptischen Streitgespräche: Ein Beitrag zur Formengeschichte des Urchristentums* (Berlin: Trowitzsch, 1921); Kuhn, *Sammlungen*; Joanna Dewey, *Markan Public Debate: Literary Technique, Concentric Structure and Theology in Mark 2:1–3:6* (SBLDS 48; Chico, CA: Scholars Press, 1980); J. Killunen, *Die Vollmacht im Widerstreit* (AASFDHL 40; Helsinki: Soumalainen Tiedeakatemia, 1985); W. Weiss, *"Eine neue Lehre in Vollmacht"* (BZNW 52; Berlin: de Gruyter, 1989).

129. Cf. K. Backhaus, "'Dort werdet ihr ihn sehen' (Mk 16,7): Die redaktionelle Schlussnotiz des zweiten Evangeliums als dessen christologische Summe," *TGl* 76 (1986): 277–94.

130. So, e.g., Andreas Lindemann, "Die Osterbotschaft des Markus," *NTS* 26 (1979/80): 298–317.

The silence of the women and the omission of the appearance stories would then parallel the commands to silence within the framework of the Markan messianic secret. This would also bring Mark's theology of the cross into sharper profile: renouncing any narrative presentation of the resurrection reality allows the cross to stand out all the more as the place of salvation. An intentional narrative strategy may also be at work: "Mark's narrative ends as it began (cf. 1:4–8): the voice of a messenger from God points to Jesus, who as the victor is now on his way to Galilee. As in 1:9 Jesus himself steps onto the narrative stage, so now the disciples, and with them the readers, are challenged to see themselves as placed in a new narrative made possible by the encounter with the Risen One in Galilee—the story of discipleship."[131] Entirely different circumstances are evoked by the supposition that Mark 16:1–8 points to the apotheosis of Jesus, "whereby the apocalyptic idea of resurrection is translated into the Roman world of ideas. Jesus's remains cannot be found: 'He is not here' (Mark 16:6)—in accord with the mythical model of the death of Hercules, whose bones could not be found after his self-immolation, which was the decisive signal that the dead one had been received in the world of the gods."[132] Finally, the "absence" of Jesus could be related to a theological program oriented primarily to the earthly Jesus rather than the resurrected Lord.[133]

However, the reality of the resurrection is presupposed theologically as the basis of Markan Christology and soteriology in the narrative of the empty tomb (Mark 16:1–8), the conflict dialogue with the Sadducees concerning the resurrection of the dead (12:18–27), the concept of the Son of Man who will come in glory (13:24–27), and the redactional verses 14:28 and 16:7,[134] but it is not set out in narrative form in the present form of the gospel. Could Mark on this point be a follower of Paul, for whom the reported appearances of the Risen One functioned for the grounding of theology (cf. 1 Cor. 15:5–8)? Did the evangelist and his hearers/readers think in the categories of modern narrative theorists? Both views are improbable; more likely, the original conclusion of the gospel has been lost,[135] for Mark 9:2–8 as prolepsis of the appearance stories and ἠγέρθη (aorist passive, "he was raised") in 16:6 clearly indicate

131. Ludger Schenke, *Das Markus-Evangelium* (Stuttgart: Kohlhammer, 1988), 350.

132. Ebner, "Kreuzestheologie," 166; as parallel, cf. Plutarch, *Num.* 22.

133. So D. S. du Toit, *Der abwesende Herr: Strategien im Markusevangelium zur Bewältigung der Abwesenheit des Auferstandenen* (WMANT 111; Neukirchen: Neukirchener Verlag, 2006), who argues that Mark gives a radical response to the question of Jesus's absence by referring to the earthly Jesus: "He thus developed the concept of the gospel as the substitute for Jesus. The gospel compensates for Jesus's absence, since after Easter the gospel itself represents the presence of the earthly Jesus in the world with his own, and continues to make his message present" (444–45).

134. The redactional character of Mark 14:28 and 16:7 can hardly be disputed; cf., e.g., Gnilka, *Markus*, 2:252, 338; Lührmann, *Markusevangelium*, 242, 270.

135. On this point cf. Schnelle, *New Testament Writings*, 206–7.

that Mark understood the resurrection to be God's act on Jesus, originally combined with the narration of appearance stories.

8.2.3 Pneumatology

Mark does not elaborate a comprehensive pneumatology but integrates central affirmations about the work of the Holy Spirit into his narrative about Jesus Christ. The expression πνεῦμα ἅγιον appears for the first time when the Baptist's announcement in Mark 1:8 ("I have baptized you with water; but he will baptize you with the Holy Spirit") sets up a parallel between John and Jesus in which the latter is superior, an announcement fulfilled in the baptismal event of 1:9–11. God equips Jesus with the Spirit and thereby qualifies him in a special way, enabling him henceforth to function in the power of the divine Spirit. The brief temptation story of 1:12–13 already illuminates these circumstances, for it is the Spirit of God that leads Jesus into the wilderness, at the same time enabling him to withstand the temptations of Satan. After this prelude, Jesus can prevail in the disputes with the "unclean spirits" as reported in the miracle stories (cf. 1:23, 26, 27; 3:11, 29, 30; 5:2, 8, 13; 6:7; 7:25; 9:17, 20, 25). The demons know of Jesus's special status as Son of God (cf. 1:27; 3:11; 5:7) and must submit to the Spirit of God.

The ecclesiological dimension of pneumatology is seen in the disciples' participation in Jesus's deeds done in the power of the Spirit; in Mark 6:7 they exercise power over "unclean spirits," a power they were promised at their call in 3:15: "And he appointed twelve, whom he also named apostles, to be with him, and to be sent out to proclaim the message, and to have authority to cast out demons." With the disciples as the connecting link, the Markan church's own practice of exorcism participates in Jesus's powerful authority over "unclean spirits." The puzzling saying concerning blasphemy against the Holy Spirit (3:29, "Whoever blasphemes against the Holy Spirit can never have forgiveness, but is guilty of an eternal sin"; cf. Q 12:10) could be related to this practice, for failed attempts at exorcism, invoking the power of the Holy Spirit, might have evoked insult and ridicule. Clearly the post-Easter situation with its local pressures stands in the background of Mark 13:11, where the community is promised that the Holy Spirit will intervene and defend it. The Markan church understands itself to be bound to the Son of God Jesus Christ by its own deeds performed in the power of the Spirit, for it knows that it is grounded in the baptism of the Holy Spirit promised in Mark 1:8 and owes its present existence to the working of this Spirit.[136]

136. It is striking that Mark narrates no baptismal activity of Jesus and thus does not immediately explain the meaning of Mark 1:8. He probably understands the mission of the Markan church as the continuing result of the baptizing activity of Jesus, which has not yet been ultimately concluded.

8.2.4 Soteriology

Mark reflects on the salvific meaning of the ministry, death, and resurrection of the Son of God Jesus Christ in a multilayered line of thought.[137] The point of departure for the *theological dimension* of his soteriology is the saving will of God that includes the destiny of Jesus as a whole and is pointedly focused in the δεῖ (it is necessary) of the Passion predictions (cf. Mark 8:31): Jesus follows the saving plan of God of his own free will, renounces any attempt to save himself (15:29–32), and unites his own will with the will of God. Mark 12:1–12 makes clear that Jesus's death was not the end of tragic history (*Unheilsgeschichte*), but a new beginning of salvation history (*Heilsgeschichte*). As the suffering Righteous One[138] (cf. Ps. 22 in Mark 15:24, 29, 34), the innocent one takes persecution and insult upon himself and renounces any attempt at self-justification. He drinks the cup of suffering (10:38–39; 14:36) and accepts the judgment of God against sinners as their substitute. The pitying comment in 15:31 ("He saved others; he cannot save himself") fundamentally misjudges the salvific power of the cross. The community of faith is to learn to understand the life and death of the Son of God/Son of Man (cf. 14:61–62), along with the reality of the resurrection, as the decisive event of the kingdom of God.[139] Thus the resurrection of individuals from the dead is obviously presupposed as the new creation and proof of the power of the living God (12:18–27).

Mark 10:45 explicitly expresses the *christological dimension* of soteriology: "For the Son of Man came not to be served but to serve, and to give his life a ransom for many."[140] This verse leads into the very center of Markan soteriology: Jesus's ministry in going to his death fulfills and completes the ministry of his life: his *proexistence* comprises service, self-giving, and substitution. Jesus verifies his ministry by his redemptive death, whose uniqueness and exclusivity is interpreted by the motif of universal atonement achieved by Jesus's giving his own life. Jesus atones for the guilt of the many, pours out his blood "for many" (Mark 14:24, ὑπὲρ πολλῶν), and thus makes possible the acceptance of the kingdom of God (the *basileia*) in faith and action. The action

137. Cf. the concise presentation by K. Backhaus, "'Lösepreis für viele' (Mk 10,45)," in *Der Evangelist als Theologe* (ed. Thomas Söding; SBS 163; Stuttgart: Katholisches Bibelwerk, 1995), 91–118; cf. also H. J. B. Combrink, "Salvation in Mark," in *Salvation in the New Testament* (ed. J. G. Van der Watt; NovTSup 121; Leiden: Brill, 2005), 33–66.

138. On this motif, cf. Dieter Lührmann, "Biographie des Gerechten als Evangelium: Vorstellungen zu einem Markus-Kommentar," *WD* 14 (1976): 25–50; M. L. Gubler, *Die frühesten Deutungen des Todes Jesu* (OBO 15; Göttingen: Vandenhoeck & Ruprecht, 1977), 95–205.

139. On the Markan Passion narrative, cf. Reinhard Feldmeier, *Die Krisis des Gottessohnes* (WUNT 21; Tübingen: Mohr, 1987); Brown, *Death of the Messiah*, and the extensive bibliography he gives.

140. On this key text, cf. Karl Kertelge, "Der dienende Menschensohn," in *Jesus und der Menschensohn: Für Anton Vögtle* (ed. Rudolf Pesch et al.; Freiburg i.B.: Herder, 1975), 225–39.

at the Last Supper symbolically illuminates the Markan new interpretation of the traditional motif of atonement and substitution in the light of Jesus's kingdom-ministry:[141] "Truly I tell you, I will never again drink of the fruit of the vine until that day when I drink it new in the kingdom of God" (14:25). The blood of the new covenant and the present-and-future kingdom establish a new relationship between God and human beings, for in the eating of the bread and drinking of the wine, believers participate in Jesus's saving work. In this way, the eschatological salvation of the kingdom of God is present in the Markan church. It reads the gospel "as a whole as narrative soteriology,"[142] for Jesus's authority to forgive sins[143] and grant authentic life (2:5–6; 3:4; 5:23, 28, 34; 6:56) and saving faith in the gospel are not relics of a past history, but present in their saving effects. Faith as discipleship to Jesus Christ is the answer to the anguished question of the masses, "Then who can be saved?" (10:26): "for God all things are possible" (10:27).

The Gospel of Mark narrates how the kingdom of God comes to human beings, who suffer under the domination of Satan (1:13; 4:15), demons, and sickness, as God's gift of salvation. Jesus acts for "the many" both in his life and his death, so that Jesus's *proexistence* can be rightly viewed as the *primary soteriological category* of the oldest gospel.

8.2.5 Anthropology

The two dominant categories of Mark's anthropology are καρδία (heart) and ψυχή (life, soul). Jesus came in order to save life (Mark 3:4) by giving his own life (10:45). So also, his disciples attain true life only by following him in the path of suffering (8:35–36). Love for God is a matter of one's innermost being, the heart and soul (12:30). The heart is one's personal center, where one can decide for faith in the gospel (11:23) or harden one's heart and keep one's distance (8:17). Evil thoughts come forth from the heart (7:15, 19, 21), so that distinctions between "clean" and "unclean" as the criterion for one's relation to God and as the norm for how to live one's life are no longer valid. The value of a person is not determined by observing ritual prescriptions, for "The sabbath was made for humankind, and not humankind for the sabbath" (2:27).

The Law

The lack of the word νόμος (law) in the gospel is related to a theological and anthropological concept that Mark expresses in narrative form:[144] the Markan

141. Cf. Söding, *Glaube*, 180ff.

142. Backhaus, "Lösepreis," 107.

143. On this point, cf. Hofius, "Sündenvergebung," 38–56.

144. On Mark's understanding of the law, cf., with different emphases, the studies of Heikki Sariola, *Markus und das Gesetz: Eine redaktionskritische Untersuchung* (AASFDHL 56; Helsinki: Suomalainen Tiedeakatemia, 1990) and Rainer Kampling, "Das Gesetz im Markusevangelium,"

church is oriented to the person of Jesus rather than the law, and knows that God himself legitimates its living in this way, for in the presence of Moses, God says "Listen to *him* [i.e., Jesus]" (9:7; cf. Deut. 18:15 LXX). In the collection of conflict dialogues in Mark 2:1–3:6, the *value of the individual person* against external religious claims is established by Jesus himself. His table fellowship with publicans and sinners is not oriented to ritual prescriptions, for "Those who are well have no need of a physician, but those who are sick" (2:17a). The evangelist's view is expressed programmatically in 7:1–23, for Jesus's work among Gentiles begins by declaring that the Jewish ritual laws are no longer in force.[145] The healing of a Gentile woman (7:24–30), a person with hearing and speech impediment (7:31–37), and the feeding of the four thousand (8:1–10) must be understood as illustrations of the abolition of the fundamental distinction "clean/unclean." The acclamation in 7:37, "He has done everything well," in its Markan context refers to Jesus's ministry among Gentiles. As the feeding of the five thousand (6:30–44) constitutes the conclusion of Jesus's ministry among the Jews, so the feeding of the four thousand forms the conclusion of his work among the Gentiles. The eucharistic overtones in 8:6 make it clear that, from Mark's perspective, Jesus had table fellowship with Gentiles, and this fellowship is now continued in the life of the Markan church. In Mark's judgment, the *authority of Jesus* makes it possible for people from a Jewish religious background to live together in one religious community with those from a Greco-Roman religious background. Table fellowship in the Christian community includes both groups (2:15–16; 7:24ff.), for human beings, not ritual laws, stand at the center of God's will (2:23–28; 3:1–6). Therefore the double command of love (12:28–34) has a universal application, takes up the Decalogue into itself (10:18–19), sets new priorities, and points to faith as the basis for human beings' relation to God.

Faith

In Mark, the words πίστις/πιστεύω ("faith/believe") occur almost exclusively in the mouth of Jesus,[146] which means that all the aspects of faith are consistently focused on the person of Jesus Christ. The programmatic call for faith in Mark 1:15 ("Repent, and believe in the good news") makes clear

in *Der Evangelist als Theologe* (ed. Thomas Söding; SBS 163; Stuttgart: Katholisches Bibelwerk, 1995), 119–50.

145. The declaration in Mark 7:19c must be noted: καθαρίζων πάντα τὰ βρώματα ("Thus he declared all foods clean"). In 7:17–18, Mark binds the theme of the law to his theory of the messianic secret in a threefold way: (1) the motif of withdrawal; (2) the disciples' lack of understanding; (3) his parable theory. Jesus's stance to the law evokes from his opponents the decision to kill him (cf. Mark 3:6; 7:1), but it also evokes lack of understanding on the part of his own disciples!

146. Cf. Mark 1:15; 4:40; 5:34, 40; 9:19, 23, 42; 10:52; 11:22–25; 13:21; exceptions: Mark 9:24; 15:32.

that it is both the earthly and the risen Son of God who calls for faith, evokes it, and makes it possible.[147] Faith is the *trust* that God's rule has come near and will be fulfilled in his Son. In the healing stories, Mark illustrates what faith means and how human beings come to faith, as the power that faith gives to step across boundaries becomes visible, and people have experiences with Jesus that generate faith.[148] Faith overcomes barriers (2:1–12), will not allow itself to be pushed away (5:21–43), and seeks closeness to Jesus despite barriers (10:46–52). People such as Bartimaeus, the Syrophoenician woman (7:24–30), the nameless person with hearing and speech impediments (7:31–37), or the desperate father in 9:14–29 learn through their own experience that Jesus is the Son of God who brings God's kingdom near in body and soul, and thereby overcomes anxiety, despair, and unbelief.[149] They thus become figures that represent the meaning of faith, whose trust in Jesus encourages and challenges the church to grasp saving faith and to act on it: "Immediately he regained his sight and followed him on the way" (10:52). The way of faith is also illustrated in his portrayal of the disciples, who respond to Jesus in wholehearted commitment (1:16–20; 6:6b–13), confess faith in him (8:27–30), deny and abandon him (14:50, 66–72), but nevertheless are accepted by Jesus (14:28; 16:7). What it means to believe is also illustrated by the numerous nameless persons who help the sick, the children who are models of the purity of faith (10:17–22), the insightful scribe (12:28–34), the poor widow with her readiness to give (12:41–44), the woman who anoints Jesus (14:3–9), Joseph of Arimathea (15:43), and the women at the crucifixion, burial, and empty tomb (15:40–16:8). Faith in God's nearness in Jesus comes to expression in prayer (11:22–25), faith that has unbounded hope, knowing that in following Jesus's own way of suffering it finds its true life (8:34–38).

8.2.6 Ethics

The way of faith is for Mark the way of discipleship, in which Jesus's teaching is the norm for living and acting.[150] Because repentance, faith, and discipleship belong inseparably together, the evangelist points his community to the will of God that is reestablished in the teaching of Jesus the Teacher

147. Cf. Söding, *Glaube*, 522ff.

148. For an extensive analysis, cf. ibid., 385–511.

149. The hardening of the opponents (Mark 3:1–6) or of the outsiders is traced back to God's decision and act in 4:11–12.

150. On Mark's ethic, cf. Wolfgang Schrage, *The Ethics of the New Testament* (trans. David E. Green; Philadelphia: Fortress, 1988), 138–43; Rudolf Schnackenburg, *Die Sittliche Botschaft des Neuen Testaments* (2nd ed.; 2 vols.; HTKNT Suppl. 2; Freiburg: Herder, 1986, 1988), 2:110–21 [the 1973 English translation of an earlier edition does not contain this section—MEB]; Thomas Söding, "Leben nach dem Evangelium," in *Der Evangelist als Theologe* (ed. Thomas Söding; SBS 163; Stuttgart: Katholisches Bibelwerk, 1995), 167–95; Russell Pregeant, *Knowing Truth, Doing Good: Engaging New Testament Ethics* (Minneapolis: Fortress, 2008), 145–63.

(3:35).[151] The creative center of God's will is the *double commandment of love for God and neighbor* (12:28–34).[152] Mark intentionally places this paragraph at the end of the series of Jerusalem conflict dialogues, at the same time signaling continuity with the basic convictions of Jewish and Hellenistic ethics by his positive portrayal of the scribe's response. Love for God and neighbor appears as the decisive foundation and fundamental orientation for the life of the believer. It is an all-embracing principle, for it comes from the heart and calls for the use of one's reason and all one's faculties. The criteriological function of this command is revealed in a twofold way: (1) love for God, as the *first* commandment, is the foundation for and facilitating power of love for the neighbor; (2) the double command ranks ahead of all other instructions and provides the normative content by which they are to be judged. Mark sees the double commandment as realized above all in mutual service (9:33–37; 10:35–45). Serving others as the basic principle of Christian existence is brought into sharp profile in contrast to the reality of Roman rule: "You know that among the Gentiles those whom they recognize as their rulers lord it over them, and their great ones are tyrants over them. But it is not so among you; but whoever wishes to become great among you must be your servant, and whoever wishes to be first among you must be slave of all" (10:42–43). Jesus's response to the question of paying tribute to Rome in the conflict dialogue of 12:13–17—"Give to the emperor the things that are the emperor's, and to God the things that are God's" (v. 17)—also relativizes the power of the state, rejects the religio-political claim of the emperor, and assigns his power only a functional importance that cannot include any religious reverence. So also 13:9–13 presupposes persecutions in which Mark wants to encourage his community to fearless confession in a hostile context.

Within the community, such topics as divorce (Mark 10:1–12) and one's relation to children (10:13–16) and to wealth (10:17–31) stand in the foreground. The attention to children is particularly noticeable (cf. also 9:35–37), for it plays no role in comparable Jewish and Greco-Roman instruction.[153] The honor due to parents called for in 7:10–13, however, is in line with the common expectations of antiquity. The story of the young man in 10:17–34 is a

151. Jesus is presented in Mark as "teacher" of the disciples and thus of the Markan church in a way different from any other gospel (διδάσκω, 17 times; διδάσκαλος, 12 times; διδαχή, 5 times); cf. Ludger Schenke, "Jesus als Weisheitlehrer im Markusevangelium," in *Die Weisheit—Ursprünge und Rezeption: Festschrift für Karl Löning zum 65. Geburtstag* (ed. Martin Fassnacht; NTA 44; Münster: Aschendorff, 2003), 125–38; Boring, *Mark*, 205–6, 253–54; Paul J. Achtemeier, "'He Taught Them Many Things': Reflections on Marcan Christology," *CBQ* 42 (1980): 465–81; Vernon K. Robbins, *Jesus the Teacher: A Socio-Rhetorical Interpretation of Mark* (Philadelphia: Fortress, 1984); Edwin Keith Broadhead, *Teaching with Authority: Miracles and Christology in the Gospel of Mark* (JSNTSup 74; Sheffield: JSOT Press, 1992).

152. Cf. the extensive analysis by Karl Kertelge, "Das Doppelgebot der Liebe im Markusevangelium," *TThZ* 103 (1994): 38–55.

153. Cf. Müller, *Mitte*, 81–164.

narrative elaboration of the theme of the danger of riches: he leads a model life, and Jesus "looking at him, loved him" (10:21), so that this story of a call to discipleship that misfired is heard by the church as a warning. At the same time, the story by no means excludes rich people (cf. 10:27), and the disciples may rejoice in their heavenly reward. In the present, however, they must be ready to deny themselves and take up their cross, for following Jesus is the way of the cross. Mark 8:34–9:1 makes clear that Jesus himself has already followed this way and opened it up for believers to follow. By collecting sayings that originally circulated as individual units of tradition and arranging them into a small sayings collection, the evangelist makes clear that ethics are also to be understood in the light of the cross.[154] So also, confession of the Lord is part of the ethic of discipleship, for those who deny the Son of Man now will not be accepted by the Son of Man in the judgment. The Gospel of Mark, as a narrative of the "way" of Jesus from baptism to the cross, is a call to suffering discipleship to Jesus Christ. Mark wants to direct his church both to an authentic confession of the person and work of Jesus Christ and to practical following of the "way" of Jesus; confession of one's faith and living it out in practice belong inseparably together.[155]

The integration of the cross into the center of ethical thinking shows emphatically that we should speak of Mark's *christological ethic*. He binds his instructions to the foundational event of the sending, ministry, and suffering of Jesus Christ, in whom God's nearness and presence are manifest in his kingdom.

8.2.7 *Ecclesiology*

Mark does not develop a conceptual ecclesiology with specific emphases comparable to that of Paul or Matthew; so, for example, the term ἐκκλησία (church) is entirely missing.[156] Nonetheless, we can speak of a Markan ecclesiology, especially because the conduct of the disciples is depicted in a way that models the life of the later church. They are not only the historical connecting links between Jesus and the Markan church but also serve as examples that bind together these pre-Easter and post-Easter times.[157] It is no accident that

154. On this point, cf. Kristen, *Kreuz*, 156–228.

155. Cf. Schenke, "Weisheitslehrer," 136: "The narrated life of Jesus has paradigmatic character: the disciples and the readers are called to follow behind Jesus and to imitate his life."

156. Roloff, *Kirche im Neuen Testament*, 144ff., is, in my opinion, mistaken in that he does not deal with Mark at all. Contrast Karl Kertelge, "Jüngerschaft und Kirche: Grundlegung der Kirche nach Marcus," in *Der Evangelist als Theologe* (ed. Thomas Söding; SBS 163; Stuttgart: Katholisches Bibelwerk, 1995), 151–65.

157. On Mark's understanding of discipleship, cf. Ernest Best, *Following Jesus: Discipleship in the Gospel of Mark* (JSNTSup 4; Sheffield: University of Sheffield, 1981); R. Busemann, *Die Jüngergemeinde nach Markus* (BBB 57; Bonn: Hannstein, 1983); C. Clifton Black, *The Disciples according to Mark: Markan Redaction in Current Debate* (JSNTSup 27; Sheffield: JSOT Press,

the summary of Jesus's message in Mark 1:15 is directly followed by the call of the first disciples (1:16–20), for the secret of the kingdom of God is given to the disciples (4:11). Within the narrated world of the gospel, the disciples, both male and female (cf. 15:47; 16:1–8), are models transparent to the church that hears and reads Mark's gospel.[158] They are called by Jesus himself (1:16–20; 3:13–18) and are authorized already during his lifetime to continue his mission (6:6–13).[159] In the story of Jesus's sending out the disciples, the Markan church recognizes in their teaching and actions the origin of its own mission, which thus has the character of an authentic continuation of Jesus's own mission.

Within this conceptual framework, the Twelve have a distinctive function, for Mark understands the Twelve as uniquely certified bearers of the continuity between Jesus's time and the later church.[160] The Twelve are exceptionally authorized and sent out to extend the gospel of Jesus Christ the Son of God, and thereby to continue the ministry of Jesus himself (cf. 3:13–19; 6:6b–13:30). The Twelve are the representatives of the salvific promise of God, the post-Easter churches owe their existence to their work (6:7ff.), and they signify the launching of the early church's mission (13:10). Mark interprets the circle of the Twelve as the prototype for understanding how particular responsibilities are to be perceived in the later church, both within (cf. 9:33–50; 10:35–45) the church and outside it (cf. 3:14–15; 6:6b–13:30). The Twelve carry out the basic functions of the post-Easter community of disciples: they preach the gospel of Jesus Christ, authorized in word and deed, and their own readiness to serve stands in for the salvation achieved in Jesus's giving of himself. Among those who follow Jesus, authority is not exercised in a relation characterized by domination and power over those to whom the good news is addressed, or over those lower on the ecclesiastical totem pole, but in the binding promise of the gospel of Jesus Christ and devotion to it. The authority granted to the Twelve is based exclusively on its origin: the nearness of the kingdom of God mediated by the Christ event. The authorized witnesses, messengers, and mediators of the gospel stand in a strict relationship of service to this message. Their authority is located in their service; their exceptional service is the badge of their authority. Mark's portrayal of the disciples as the connecting link between the time of Jesus and his own present illustrates who Jesus

1989); Suzanne Watts Henderson, *Christology and Discipleship in the Gospel of Mark* (SNTSMS 135; Cambridge: Cambridge University Press, 2006).

158. Cf. Hans-Josef Klauck, "Die erzählerische Rolle der Jünger im Markusevangelium: Eine narrative Analyse," *NovT* 24 (1982): 1–26; Robert C. Tannehill, "The Disciples in Mark: The Function of a Narrative Role (1977)," in *The Interpretation of Mark* (ed. William R. Telford; 2nd ed.; SNTI; Edinburgh: T&T Clark, 1995), 134–57.

159. For an analysis of the ecclesiological dimension of Mark's understanding of ἐξουσία, cf. Scholtissek, *Vollmacht*, 254–79.

160. Within the circle of the Twelve, we also find smaller groups of three (Mark 5:37; 9:2–8; 14:33), four (1:16–20; 13:3), and two (cf. 9:35–45). Peter is also mentioned separately (cf. 8:29; 16:7), and cf. Joseph of Arimathea (15:42–46).

Christ is and what discipleship means as participation in Jesus's own way to the cross, so that for him, ethics and ecclesiology are bound most closely together. *For Mark, the church is an ideal community that follows Jesus in service, preaching, and suffering.*

8.2.8 Eschatology

Eschatology is one of the central themes of the Gospel of Mark.[161] Its christological foundation is clearly revealed in Jesus's preaching of the kingdom in word and deed (see above, §8.2.2). It has become irreversible through Jesus's death "for the many" (Mark 10:45; 14:24), for God's kingdom is dawning not only in the event of Jesus's life, death, and resurrection, but also in the post-Easter preaching of the Markan church.[162] The resurrection kerygma (16:6) opens up the "secret of the kingdom of God" (4:11), which has already begun inconspicuously in the present (4:30–32), is subject to many dangers (4:13–20), but will certainly come to completion and fulfillment (4:26–29). Despite all dangers, faith in Jesus will strengthen and save, just as Jesus came to the aid of the disciples in the story of calming the storm (4:35–41). The kingdom of God is for Mark a future reality (cf. 4:29, 32; 9:47; 10:23; 14:25; 15:43), while also at work in the present and drawing near its consummation (9:1, "Truly I tell you, there are some standing here who will not taste death until they see that the kingdom of God has come with power"). This consummation will occur at the parousia of the Son of Man, who stands at the center of the eschatological expectation of the Markan church.

Jesus Christ is the earthly representative of the kingdom of God and at the same time its heavenly representative as the Son of Man who is still to come. His parousia coincides with the ultimate establishment of the kingdom of God (cf. Mark 8:38; 9:1; 14:25). Mark believes that the parousia is to happen in his immediate future (13:30, "Truly I tell you, this generation will not pass away until all these things have taken place"), while at the same time the admonitions to remain constantly alert (13:33–37) and the program of a worldwide evangelism that must take place before the end (13:10) clearly

161. On Mark's eschatology, cf. Cilliers Breytenbach, *Nachfolge und Zukunftserwartung nach Markus: Eine methodenkritische Studie* (ATANT 71; Zürich: Theologischer Verlag, 1984), 279: "The Markan Christology and theology of the cross are imbedded in the eschatological framework of the gospel as a whole. Just as the kingdom of God breaks in according to God's plan for history as a whole, so the death and resurrection of the Son of Man is subject to the divine 'must'"; Klaus Scholtissek, "Der Sohn Gottes für das Reich Gottes," in *Der Evangelist als Theologe* (ed. Thomas Söding; SBS 163; Stuttgart: Katholisches Bibelwerk, 1995); J. M. Nützel, "Hoffnung und Treue: Zur Eschatologie des Markusevangeliums," in *Gegenwart und kommendes Reich: Schülergabe Anton Vögtle zum 65. Geburtstag* (ed. Peter Fiedler and Dieter Zeller; SBB 6; Stuttgart: Verlag Katholisches Bibelwerk, 1975), 79–90.

162. Cf. here Söding, *Glaube*, 150–97.

reveal a certain consciousness that the parousia is delayed.[163] In the context of the Jewish war, the church longs for a clear answer to the question of when the Son of Man will come (13:4). In contrast, Mark separates the announcement of apocalyptic phenomena from those of this-worldly historical events and declares that only God knows the day when the Son of Man will return (13:32). The church must take seriously what the one whom they now await as the coming Son of Man said to his disciples on the way to Jerusalem, and what he suffered in Jerusalem; they must integrate the actual fact of the suffering and dying of the Son of Man into their understanding of the kingdom of God as its decisive event, and in their own following of this way must make service to the neighbor the standard of their own life. For the present, that means a bold, worldwide proclamation of the gospel (13:10), which will be aware of false prophets (13:6, 21–23) and will not withdraw from suffering in behalf of the gospel (cf. 13:14–20). God alone is Lord of history and in his almighty power has shortened the days of tribulation that must occur before the End (13:19–20).

The close connection between eschatology and discipleship is also manifest in the combination of discipleship sayings with eschatological views (cf. Mark 8:34–9:1; 10:23–31, 35–40; 13:5–13, 24–27).[164] The returning Son of Man will gather his own (13:27), who will then receive eternal salvation as their just reward (cf. 4:24–25; 8:35; 9:41; 10:29–30, 40; 13:13), while the unfaithful and obdurate will be excluded from salvation (cf. 3:28–29; 4:11–12, 25b).

For Mark, it is clear that the proclamation of the kingdom of God finds its beginning, content, and goal in Jesus Christ, is being put to the test and validated in the church's present preaching of the gospel, and will be consummated in the coming of the Son of Man.

8.2.9 Setting in the History of Early Christian Theology

It would be difficult to overestimate the importance of the Gospel of Mark in the development of early Christian theology.

1. With the new literary genre gospel, Mark composed the first extensive Jesus-Christ-history and through his narrative presentation and theological insights formed the basis of the early Christian portrayal of

163. On the analysis of Mark 13, cf. Egon Brandenburger, *Markus 13 und die Apokalyptik* (FRLANT 134; Göttingen: Vandenhoeck & Ruprecht, 1984); Kmiecik, *Menschensohn*, 26–83; George R. Beasley-Murray, *Jesus and the Last Days: The Interpretation of the Olivet Discourse* (Peabody, MA: Hendrickson, 1993).

164. Cf. Breytenbach, *Nachfolge*, 338: "The Markan understanding of discipleship is altogether oriented to the eschatological future. The christological perspective on the past event is constantly supplemented by the look toward the future. The Crucified One himself is expected as the coming Son of Man."

Jesus Christ, as we see especially in the reception of the Gospel of Mark by Matthew, Luke, and John. By firmly binding together historical-biographical narrative text and kerygmatic address and portraying the event of Jesus's way to the cross in dramatic terms, he maintained and safeguarded the historical and theological identity of Christian faith.

2. The sayings source Q and Luke 1:1 suggest the existence of forerunners of the gospel form and probably also gospels no longer extant, so that Mark represents a decisive achievement in early Christianity: he saves a wide variety of Jesus-traditions from being forgotten, binds them together in one narrative, and presents Jesus of Nazareth as both proclaimer and proclaimed. Mark is the first author in early Christianity who makes a comprehensive presentation of the historical dimension of the advent of Jesus Christ his central focus, and thus prevents a dehistoricizing of the Jesus-Christ-history, as occurs later, for example, in the *Gospel of Thomas*. With his gospel, Mark thus creates a central building block in the cultural memory of early Christianity.
3. Mark presupposes the messiahship of Jesus (1:1), develops this confession of faith along narrative lines, and sets forth in his gospel in what sense Jesus Christ was already the Son of God, and yet becomes God's Son in the course of the narrative. The secrecy theory as a central christological narrative strategy preserves the fundamental unity of exalted status and humility in the person of Jesus Christ. Mark shows how Jesus wants to gather his people in the sign of the kingdom of God through his powerful, authoritative word, his acts of healing, and his willingness to give himself over to death for the sake of others. The evangelist thus takes up the central ideas of Pauline theology and makes them the central focus of a dramatic narrative: the crucified Jesus of Nazareth is the Son of God. At the same time, the first evangelist goes beyond Paul at one decisive point. He not only proclaims the eschatological identity of Jesus Christ as Son of God and Messiah but transforms this affirmation into a plausible narrative.

8.3 Matthew: The New and Better Righteousness

The Gospel of Matthew, written in Syria in about 90 CE (cf. Matt. 4:24), gives evidence of a Christian community that has gone through a painful process of self-identification that was both in continuity and discontinuity with Judaism. Matthew represents a stream of early Hellenistic Judaism and Hellenistic Jewish Christianity that used the Septuagint as its Bible and that realized it had obligations to both particularistic and universalistic aspects of its faith. The evangelist is in the process of working through the failure of the mission to Israel, the separation from the mainstream of Judaism, and the new orientation of the Christian community to the Gentiles. The Jesus-Christ-history he composes is always transparent to the history and present experience of his own church.

8.3.1 Theology

Matthew's own θεός nomenclature does not advance essentially beyond that of Mark (θεός occurs forty-eight times in Mark, fifty-one times in Matthew). God appears in his composition as the creator (Matt. 19:4) and preserver of nature, who shares his goodness with all human beings, and the animal world as well (5:45; 6:26–27; 10:29–31). Continuity with Israel plays a central role in his concept of God. Expressions such as "the God of Israel" (15:31), "the God of Abraham, Isaac, and Jacob" (22:32), and "the living God" (16:16; 26:63) clearly reveal the roots of his God-language in Jewish tradition. Such language is concerned with *God's acts in history*: the God who plants the vineyard and repeatedly sends his prophets to it, finally sending his own Son (21:33–46); the God who repeatedly sends invitations to the great banquet for his Son (22:1–14), and who at the end of the age will judge the nations through his Son (25:31–46). This God is a God who makes demands (6:24), who expresses his ultimate will through the Son (5–7), and who at the same time is the merciful and generous God who promises a reversal of relationships in the way things are (5:8–9, "Blessed are the pure in heart, for they will see God. Blessed are the peacemakers, for they will be called children of God").

God as Father

The image of God as Father, common throughout the ancient world as an image for God and a common mode of addressing the deity,[165] receives a particular character in Matthew's imagery for God (πατήρ occurs 63 times in Matthew, 19 times in Mark, 56 times in Luke). The Father makes the sun come up and provides rain (Matt. 5:45), sees what goes in secret (6:4, 6, 18), knows the needs of the disciples before they ask (6:8, 32), provides food (6:26), connects his own willingness to forgive to human conduct (6:14–15), and comes to the aid of those who ask for help (7:11). At the center of the image of God as father, however, stands the special relation to God in which Jesus stands and in which the disciples also share, with the differentiation expressed in the "your Father" for the disciples (5:16, 45, 48; 6:1, 4, 6, 8, 15, 26, 32; 7:11; 10:20, 29; 18:14) and the "my Father" Jesus uses for himself (7:21; 8:21; 10:20, 29, 32–33; 11:27; 12:50; 15:4; 16:17; 18:10, 19, 35; 20:23).[166] When Jesus speaks in terms of his own Father, the

165. On Matt. 6:9 see the examples of parallels in *NW* 1.1.2.
166. Cf. Gnilka, "Gottesgedanken," 154–58.

mediation of the gift of salvation stands in the foreground, as illustrated by 11:25–27, "I thank you, Father, Lord of heaven and earth, because you have hidden these things from the wise and the intelligent and have revealed them to infants; yes, Father, for such was your gracious will. All things have been handed over to me by my Father; and no one knows the Son except the Father, and no one knows the Father except the Son and anyone to whom the Son chooses to reveal him." Jesus knows the revealed will of the Father and makes it known with authority (cf. 7:21; 12:50; 18:14), he announces how God will act in eschatological judgment (18:35; 20:23), and he is expected at table in the kingdom of his Father (26:29). So also the disciples, in the person of Peter, participate in the revelation of the Father (16:17, "And Jesus answered him, 'Blessed are you, Simon son of Jonah! For flesh and blood has not revealed this to you, but my Father in heaven'"). The predominance of the expression "your Father" in the Sermon on the Mount makes clear that the disciples are directed to the Father's will, which they are to fulfill in their own conduct. Imitation of the heavenly Father has as its goal that the disciples should be perfect (5:48). Both lines of the address to God as Father, that of the disciples and that of Jesus himself, converge in the Lord's Prayer in 6:9.[167] This model presents prayer as above all else the place where God is glorified, where it is not a matter of human wishes; the first three petitions of the Lord's Prayer are for God's holiness, kingdom, and lordship (6:9–10), a prayer shared by the Son and the disciples alike. Because the Father is the ground of all being and at the same time the One who transcends all, the prayer concerned with God and God's acts always includes a corresponding act on the part of human beings. God's holiness, kingdom, and lordship are grounded in God's own being, are demonstrated in his acts, and call for human response. Here we see a basic aspect of Matthew's way of thinking: the integration of theology, Christology, and ethics as the indissoluble unity of gift and assignment (*Gabe* and *Aufgabe*), prayer and action. "Prayer makes it possible for Jesus's disciples to understand his demands as the Father's will and to draw strength from that understanding. Prayer is not made superfluous by action; instead, action is constantly dependent on prayer."[168]

The Gospel of Matthew can be understood at every level as an effort to open a new access to God for its hearers/readers, validated by Jesus the teacher who stands at the center of the narrative (see below, §8.3.2). The presupposition for this is the indissoluble unity between God and Jesus, a unity that is not first created by the resurrection, but is foundational from the very beginning, as shown above all by the Emmanuel affirmations.

167. For interpretation of the address to God as "Father" in the Lord's Prayer, cf. Luz, *Matthew 1–7*, 314–16.

168. Ibid., 326.

8.3.2 Christology

The point of departure for Matthew's Christology is the fundamental conviction that Jesus of Nazareth is the Messiah and Son of God promised in the Scriptures of Israel. He portrays Jesus as the shepherd of Israel, concerned for his people, who establishes his universal kingdom for all peoples. In this we already see that the Emmanuel-Christology provides the framework for the narrative character of Matthean Christology.

Christology in the Narrative

The first citation of Scripture in 1:23 ("Look, the virgin shall conceive and bear a son, and they shall name him Emmanuel"), with its Matthean interpretation ("which means, '*God with us*'"), and the eschatological promise in Matt. 28:20 ("And remember, I am with you always, to the end of the age") form an inclusio decisive for understanding the whole Gospel of Matthew.[169] With μεθ' ἡμῶν (1:23, "with us") or μεθ' ὑμῶν (28:20, "with you") Matthew signals the fundamental motif of his composition: *God's presence and faithfulness with his people in Jesus Christ*. Matthew expresses in narrative form how God is "with us" in the way followed by the church, in its obedience, suffering, and confession of Jesus. At the same time, this motif binds together the motifs of the earthly Jesus and the exalted Christ. Matthew 1:23 opens the story of Jesus to the presence of God in it, and 28:20 establishes the presence of the exalted Lord in the earthly Jesus, *so that the universal perspective of the end is already present at the beginning*. The Emmanuel affirmation interprets the Jesus-Christ-history as the abiding presence of God with his church. Matthew is thus to be understood as an advocate of a Christology oriented to the status of Jesus as exalted Lord, for *God himself acts in Jesus Christ*.

With the *prologue* (Matt. 1:2–4:22), Matthew begins his new history of origins[170] with the expression βίβλος γενέσεως ("Book of 'Genesis,'" 1:1), a titular introductory phrase that shows he wants his story to be understood against the background of biblical stories. He establishes the internal relationship between the first covenant and the Christ event through the five reflection citations (see below, §8.3.8) in 1:22–23; 2:15, 17–18, 23; 4:14–15. The prologue begins like an ancient biography, with the hero's ancestry, but at the same time abducts the reader into different worlds. In chapters 1–2, Matthew develops the meaning of the two christological titles in the superscription of

169. Hubert Frankemölle, *Jahwebund und Kirche Christi* (Münster: Aschendorff, 1974), 7–83.

170. The main argument for this division is the repetition of the summary of Matt. 4:23 in 9:23; cf. Ulrich Luz, *The Theology of the Gospel of Matthew* (trans. J. Bradford Robinson; Cambridge: Cambridge University Press, 1993), 22.

his gospel: Son of David and Son of Abraham.[171] Jesus is presented as Son of David in the sense of Jewish messianic theology, one who really comes from the House of David, because the righteous descendant of David adopts him into the Davidic line in obedience to God's will (1:18–25). The (un-Jewish) concept of a virgin birth is taken up in 1:18–25.[172] However, the birth itself is not narrated, but only presupposed by the story in 1:25 and 2:1. The prologue already prefigures the movement of the gospel as a whole: in the persecution by the authorities in Jerusalem (2:1–12), the flight to Egypt (2:13–15), Herod's murder of the children (2:16–18), and the return to Galilee (2:19–23) a movement takes place against the background of the Moses story that is repeated in the gospel as a whole: the Nazorean Jesus (2:23) proclaims the will of God in Galilee, is then again persecuted by the authorities in Jerusalem, and opens the way of salvation to the Gentiles.[173]

Thus in the prologue Jesus's way already appears as the *way of God* to the *Gentiles*. The initial mission focusing on Jewish synagogues was unsuccessful (cf. Matt. 23:34; 10:17) and for Matthew was already long in the past; now the whole world is the mission field of the Matthean church (28:16–20). When Jesus Christ appears in 1:1 as son of Abraham, and the genealogy begins in 1:2 with Abraham, a universal perspective is already suggested at the very beginning, for God can raise up children of Abraham from stones (cf. 3:9). The women mentioned in the genealogy (Tamar, Ruth, Rahab, and the wife of Uriah, Matt. 1:3–6) are all non-Jewish, which again expresses a universal aspect.[174] The four Gentile women at the beginning correspond to "all nations" at the end. In Matt. 2:1–2, the Magi, as representatives of the Gentile world, offer homage to Jesus, while the Jewish king attempts to kill the child. The dominant motifs of chapters 1–2 (genealogy, divine origin and protection of the hero, Magi, astronomical signs) all have numerous parallels in Greco-Roman tradition[175] and thus make contact with the hopes and aspirations of people of Greco-Roman religious background. In Matthew's conception of things, God's saving activity for the Gentile world did not begin only after Israel's rejection of Jesus but was there from the very beginning.

In Matt. 3–4, both John the Baptist and Jesus appear as representatives of the righteousness that the following Sermon on the Mount calls for (3:15), in that they follow the will of God, and Jesus remains faithful despite every

171. On this point, cf. Moisés Mayordomo-Marín, *Den Anfang hören: Leserorientierte Evangelienexegese am Beispiel von Matthäus 1–2* (FRLANT 180; Göttingen: Vandenhoeck & Ruprecht, 1998).

172. Gen. 6:1–4 shows that Judaism rejected sexual contact between the divine and human worlds.

173. Cf. Luz, *Theology of the Gospel of Matthew*, 26–30.

174. Cf. Hartmut Stegemann, "Die des Uria," in *Tradition und Glaube: Das frühe Christentum in seiner Umwelt; Festgabe für Karl Georg Kuhn zum 65. Geburtstag* (ed. Gert Jeremias et al.; Göttingen: Vandenhoeck & Ruprecht, 1971), 266ff.

175. Cf. the examples in *NW* 1.1.2 ad loc.

temptation. While Matthew emphasizes that John and Jesus stand in different locations in salvation history, he also portrays the message of John as already anticipating that of Jesus: the kingdom of God has come near (3:2; 4:17). Thus the Baptist, with his preaching of judgment, is not only the forerunner of the Messiah, but is himself a representative of the kingdom of heaven.[176]

In the *Sermon on the Mount*, Jesus appears as the teacher of the "better righteousness." Matthew takes up the strong ethical impulse of the sayings source Q, with its emphasis on doing the will of God (cf., e.g., Matt. 7:21, 24–27), while at the same time relativizing orthopraxy (cf. 7:22–23), and with Q emphasizes the indicative of salvation (cf. 5:3–15). The Sermon on the Mount of Matt. 5–7 and the cycle of miracle stories in Matt. 8–9 are framed and bound together through the repetition of almost the same words in 4:23 and 9:35, presenting Jesus as *Messiah of word* and *Messiah of deed*.[177] The major rearrangement of Markan material in Matt. 8–9 is the result of the evangelist's theological purpose: here Matthew narrates the founding legend of the church of Jews and Gentiles and the concomitant break with Israel.[178] The *attempt to preach to Israel* (9:35–11:16) and the *failure of this mission* to Israel and its leaders (11:7ff.) determine the following narrative line. In 12:1–16:20 the clash between Jesus and the leaders of Israel intensifies, the depth of the conflict surfacing especially in 12:14 (decision to put Jesus to death) and the polemical extremes of 12:22–45; 15:1–20; and 16:1–12. This line is further developed in 16:21; 19:1–12; and 20:17–19, while the narrative spotlight is focused on the founding of the community of disciples in and outside Israel (16:21–20:34), of which the discourse on community life in 18 is the center. The grand confrontation with the leaders of the Jewish people comes in 21:1–24:2, in which especially the Pharisees receive sharp criticism in chapter 23 (cf. also the conflict texts in 21:12–17, 23–46; 22:1–14, 15–22, 23–33, 34–40). Also in 26:3–5, 14–26, 47–58, 59–68 and 27:11–26, 38–44, the narrative focuses on the conflict between Jesus and all the leading groups within Judaism. There is a noteworthy distinction drawn between the people as a whole (ὄχλος) and the political/religious leaders, for the people are open to Jesus's message (4:23–25; 7:28–29; 23:1) and actions (e.g., 9:8, 33–34; 12:23; 19:2; 21:8–9). Only because they are misled by their leaders do the crowds demand the release of Barabbas rather than Jesus (27:20). Matthew makes a

176. On Matthew's understanding of the Baptist, cf. G. Häfner, *Der verheißene Vorläufer* (SBB 27; Stuttgart: Katholisches Bibelwerk, 1994).

177. Cf. J. Schniewind, *Das Evangelium nach Matthäus* (5th ed.; NTD 1; Göttingen: Vandenhoeck & Ruprecht, 1950), 36: "The Messiah of word the proclaimer, is portrayed in chaps. 5–7; the Messiah of deed, the healer, is portrayed in chaps. 8–9."

178. On this point, cf. Christoph Burger, "Jesu Taten nach Matthäus 8 und 9," *ZTK* 70 (1973): 272–87; Ulrich Luz, "Die Wundergeschichten von Mt 8–9," in *Tradition and Interpretation in the New Testament: Essays in Honor of E. Earle Ellis for His 60th Birthday* (ed. Gerald F. Hawthorne and Otto Betz; Grand Rapids: Eerdmans, 1987), 149–65.

different use of the term λαός ("people," in the sense of "people of God").[179] The citations of Scripture in 2:6; 4:16; 13:15, and 15:8 make clear that the evangelist adopts the linguistic usage of the LXX, using λαός primarily in its sense of the chosen people of God. The people of Jesus (1:21) and God (2:6; 4:16), together with their representatives (21:23; 26:3, 47; 27:1), harden themselves against the new claim made by Jesus. The climax of this plotline occurs in the exclamation of the whole people (πᾶς ὁ λαός): "His blood be on us and on our children!" (27:25). Matthew's intention is clear: inasmuch as Israel and its leaders refuse the claim of Jesus Christ, he denies them the status of "people of God." Because Jesus frees his people from their sins (1:21) by his ministry (9:1–8) and his death (20:28; 26:28), Matthew links the concept "people of God" to discipleship to Jesus and his saving work. The new people of God who believe in Jesus and are instructed by him come from the nations (28:19).

The escalating conflict of Jesus with Israel and its leaders is the narrative line that determines the content and composition of the Matthean Jesus-Christ-history.[180] *The mission of the Matthean church to Israel has failed, and the evangelist has no more hopes for it* (cf. Matt. 22:8–10; 23:37–24:2; 28:15b). The reality in which he lives is that the way of salvation has already been opened to the nations (24:14, "This good news of the kingdom will be proclaimed throughout the world, as a testimony to all the nations; and then the end will come"), which he grounds programmatically in 28:16–20.

From Israel to the Nations

The appearance of the Risen One, his enthronement as Lord of all, and the mission charge in Matt. 28:16–20 not only form the narrative conclusion of the Gospel of Matthew; this scene is the point toward which all lines in the gospel converge, and it is the point of departure from which the gospel is meant to be read.[181] Matthew 28:16–20 is thus the *theological* and *hermeneutical key* for the right understanding of the composition read as a whole.[182]

179. Cf. here Frankemölle, *Jahwebund*, 199–220.

180. Cf. Luz, *Theology of the Gospel of Matthew*, 64: "Matthew arranged his story of Jesus according to an 'internal principle.' He told it as the story of Jesus's conflict with Israel."

181. The comment of O. Michel is on target: "The whole gospel was written under this theological presupposition of Matt. 28:18–20 (cf. Matt. 28:19 with 10:5ff.; 15:24; Matt. 28:20 with 1:23; the return to the baptismal scene of Matt. 3:1ff.). Yes, we can even say that the conclusion returns in a certain way to the beginning, and teaches us that the whole gospel, the story of Jesus, is to be understood 'from the end.' *Matthew 28:18–20* is the key to understanding the whole book" (Otto Michel, "Der Abschluß des Matthäus-Evangeliums," in *Das Matthäus-Evangelium* [ed. Joachim Lange; WdF 525; Darmstadt: Wissenschaftliche Buchgesellschaft, 1980], 125).

182. For the pioneering analysis that is still foundational, cf. Günther Bornkamm, "Der Auferstandene und der Irdische: Mt 28,16–20," in *Zeit und Geschichte: Dankesgabe an Rudolf Bultmann zum 80. Geburtstag* (ed. Erich Dinkler and Hartwig Thyen; Tübingen: Mohr, 1964), 289–310.

The present form of Matt. 28:16–20 is due to the redactional work of the evangelist, who is partly dependent on church tradition (cf. 2 Chron. 36:23 as an initiating text). Thus vv. 16 and 17 are to be regarded as Matthean composition, in terms of both language and content.[183] Verse 18a is also redactional (προσέρχομαι [approach, come to], fifty-two times in Matthew; on ἐλάλησεν αὐτοῖς λέγων [he spoke to them, saying], cf. 13:3; 14:27; 23:1), while pre-Matthean motifs echo in v. 18b (e.g., the juxtaposition of οὐρανός and γῆ, heaven and earth). Verse 19a in turn points clearly to the evangelist (πορεύεσθαι [go, proceed], in, for example, 9:13; 10:7; 18:12; 21:6; μαθητεύω redactionally in 13:52; 27:57), while the baptismal formula in v. 19b reflects the baptismal practice of the church. Verse 20 contains several linguistic usages characteristic of Matthew (e.g., τηρέω [keep, observe], διδάσκω [teach]; on συντέλεια τοῦ αἰῶνος [end of the age], cf. 13:39, 49; 24:3). The promise of v. 20b takes up 18:20 and thus probably comes from the evangelist.

At the center of Matt. 28:16–20 stands the concept of the universal lordship of Jesus, as expressed in the enthronement of v. 18b, the fourfold πᾶς [all] of vv. 18b, 19a, 20a, 20b, in the mission charge of vv. 19–20a, and in the promise of the risen Christ's enduring presence in v. 20b. This confession of faith of the Matthean church is the goal to which the presentation of Jesus throughout the gospel proceeds. Although Jesus is granted universal authority (ἐξουσία) through the resurrection, texts that express such authority are nonetheless found in the story of the earthly Jesus (cf. 11:27): in each case it is God who confers such ἐξουσία on the Son. It is not the ἐξουσία as such, but the realm in which this authority is exercised, that is given without limitations in 28:18b. For Matthew, the claim and command of the Risen One corresponds to the claim and command of the earthly Jesus. The Emmanuel motif (cf. 1:23; 28:20) opens up the story of Jesus as pointing to God, while at the same time binding the abiding presence of the Risen One to the life of the earthly Jesus. Jesus appears as the only authentic teacher, whose commands are valid not only for his disciples, but also for the whole world. The authority of the Risen One authorizes the disciples, and thereby the present Matthean church, to carry out his mission among the nations,[184] obligates them to extend Jesus's teaching throughout the world, and thereby to be the church of Jesus Christ. The concluding Great Commission thus packs together central themes of Matthean theology that permeate and determine the gospel throughout.

The perspective of Matt. 28:16–20 thus not only represents the final chord of the composition but is present from the beginning on: Jesus's way in *the gospel represents the way of God to the nations*. The signals indicating this perspective in Matt. 1–2 have already been mentioned, but further observations may be added: After John the Baptist's proclamation of judgment on

183. Cf. Strecker, *Weg der Gerechtigkeit*, 208ff.

184. On the understanding of ἔθνη, see below, §8.3.7.

Israel (3:1–12), and with the reconstitution of the people of Abraham and the reference to Galilee of the Gentiles (4:12, 15), in connection with his Sermon on the Mount Jesus programmatically performs healings for those outside social boundaries (8:1–4, a leprous person; 8:5–13, a Gentile; 8:14–15, a woman). Matthew 8–9, as founding legend of the Matthean church, signals the evangelist's own location: he lives in a church of Jewish and Gentile Christians, for whom the first paradigmatic example of faith is a Gentile (cf. 8:10). In the narrative of the centurion of Capernaum, the Matthean community recognizes its own story. The centurion acknowledges and accepts the priority of Israel in salvation history (8:8), at the same time becoming the firstling among Gentile Christians, while Israel becomes subject to judgment (8:11–12).[185] Matthew 10:17–18 presupposes that the disciples proclaim the gospel among both Jews and Gentiles.[186] Likewise, 12:21 and 13:38a point to the universal mission among the nations, while the unlimited world mission is grounded in 12:18–21 with the longest reflection citation in the gospel (Isa. 42:1–4).[187] It is only consistent with this proclamation of the gospel to all nations that they appear before the throne of the Son of Man at the last judgment (cf. Matt. 25:31–46).

Jesus as Teacher

The image that dominates Matt. 28:16–20 permeates the whole Gospel of Matthew: *Jesus as authorized and commanding teacher of the disciples and the people.*[188] It is to be noted first of all that in the *five great speeches* composed by the evangelist from traditional elements, the Matthean Jesus presents himself to the hearers/readers as teacher—the Sermon on the Mount (chaps. 5–7), the discipleship discourse (chap. 10), the parables discourse (chap. 13), the community instruction (chap. 18), and the eschatological discourse (chaps. 24–25)—are all concluded and interrelated with the expression "Now when Jesus had finished saying these things" (7:28; 11:1; 13:53; 19:1; 26:1). The variation in the concluding formula at 26:1 (πάντας τοὺς λόγους τούτους) emphasizes that the speeches are connected in both content and composition. A pattern can also be recognized in the order and arrangement of the five speeches: the two most extensive speeches are at the beginning and the end,

185. Ulrich Luz's exegesis minimizes the importance of this text when he says the centurion of Capernaum was for Matthew "a marginal figure with a future perspective" (Luz, *Matthew 8–20*, 12).

186. Cf. Gnilka, *Mattäusevangelium*, 1:376–77.

187. Cf. R. Walker, *Die Heilsgeschichte im ersten Evangelium* (FRLANT 91; Göttingen: Vandenhoeck & Ruprecht, 1967), 78–79.

188. According to Yueh-Han Yieh, *One Teacher: Jesus's Teaching Role in Matthew's Report* (WUNT 2.124; Tübingen: Mohr, 204), 321, Jesus appears as the *one teacher* "in four major roles—polemic, apologetic, didactic and pastoral—to defend, define, shape, and sustain Matthew's church as it strived to survive the devastating crises of Jewish hostility, self identity, community formation, and church maintenance."

directed to the people and the disciples, chapters 10 and 18 only to the disciples, while chapter 13 is again addressed to both people and disciples (13:2, 10). As chapter 13 is the center of the whole complex in regard to form, so *the reality of the kingdom of God is the center in terms of content.*[189] The fivefold form, like the initial speech on the mountain, evokes the image of Moses, so that the speeches formulate the binding instruction from God for his people in a distinctive way.

Smaller speech complexes are found in Matt. 11:7–19 (John the Baptist), 11:20–30 (woes on Galilean cities, thanksgiving to the Father, call to the weary and burdened), 12:22–37 (the Beelzebul speech), and 15:1–20 (speech about clean and unclean). Matthew loves to group materials by significant numbers: in addition to the five speech complexes, there are three pre-Matthean antitheses (5:21–22, 27–28, 33–37) and three Matthean antitheses (5:31–32, 38ff., 43ff.), the triad alms, prayer, and fasting in 6:1–8, seven Beatitudes (5:3–9, pre-Matthean composition), seven petitions in the Lord's Prayer (6:9–13), seven parables (13:1–52), seven woes (23:1–36), and ten miracles by Jesus (8:1–9:34).

As the first and most extensive speech, the Sermon on the Mount of Matt. 5–7 is certainly placed in a key position in the gospel's structure,[190] all the more so as the concluding 28:20 (also on the [same?] mountain) explicitly alludes to it. The Sermon on the Mount is the nucleus and summary of what the disciples are to teach to all nations. In the process of composition, Matthew interweaves central aspects of his Christology: the framework of 5:1–2 and 7:28–29 portrays it as spoken both to the disciples and the people, i.e., the Sermon on the Mount is not special instruction for a particular subgroup but applies to all believers. The initial Beatitudes (5:3–12) not only provide a powerful rhetorical introduction but above all signal something about the speech as a whole: it begins with Jesus's pronouncement of salvation [*Heilszuspruch*], so that in Matthew, too, command [*Anspruch*] is based on promise [*Zuspruch*]. The double parable of Salt and Light (5:13–16) strengthens the declaration [*Zuspruch*] of 5:13–14 ("You are the salt of the earth . . . You are the light of the world"), while at the same time in 5:13b–16 the command [*Anspruch*] comes to the fore, which is then programmatically formulated in 5:17–20 (see below, §8.3.5). The text is concerned with the better, i.e., greater and deeper righteousness/justice as

189. The comment of Hubert Frankemölle, *Matthäus: Kommentar* (Düsseldorf: Patmos, 1994), 101, is on target: It is the speeches that "first make the Gospel of Matthew what it is; otherwise, it would only be a new edition of Mark expanded by the introduction in the first two chapters."

190. For the Sermon on the Mount, in addition to the standard commentaries on Matthew, see especially the works of Strecker, *Sermon on the Mount*; Hans Dieter Betz, *The Sermon on the Mount: A Commentary on the Sermon on the Mount, including the Sermon on the Plain (Matthew 5:3–7:27 and Luke 6:20–49)* (Hermeneia; Minneapolis: Fortress, 1995); idem, *Essays on the Sermon on the Mount* (trans. L. L. Welborn; Philadelphia: Fortress, 1985); and Weder, *Rede.*

expressed in the antitheses of 5:20–48. The theme of righteousness/justice (see below, §8.3.6) is elaborated in 6:1–7:12 in a threefold way, as righteousness in reference to God (6:1–18), as righteousness for the kingdom of heaven (6:19–34), and with love as the foundational principle of the greater righteousness (7:1–12). The concluding section (7:13–27) sets forth action, what one does, as the criterion of righteousness and justice, joined with clear warnings. Hearing or making the proper confession of faith does not guarantee entrance into the kingdom of heaven, but only *doing* the will of God.

As is the case with the Sermon on the Mount, so also the other speeches do not expedite the action in the course of the narrative, but make the hearer/reader pause in order to experience being taught fundamental instructions directly from the mouth of Jesus;[191] the external pause in the narrative corresponds to the internal progress of the hearer/reader. The *discipleship discourse* (Matt. 9:36–11:1) incorporates the disciples into Jesus's own mission proclamation (cf. 4:17/10:7). The ministry of Jesus to Israel now finds its counterpart in the sending of the disciples to Israel. The *parables discourse* (13:1–53) provides a commentary on both the history of Jesus and the church's own history. Parenetic and salvation-history traits are included (especially in the metaphors of sowing and harvest) that demand to be taken seriously by virtue of their being told against the background of the coming judgment (13:40–43). Ecclesiological themes dominate the *community discourse* (18:1–35); the discourse deals with the humility and lowliness of the disciples, seeking the "little ones" and those who have gone astray, and the brotherly admonition to prayer, exclusion from the community, and limitless forgiveness. At the center of the speech, however, stands a christological promise: "For where two or three are gathered in my name, I am there among them" (18:20). While the location of the *eschatological discourse* (24:3–25:46) is, after all, already designated by its source in Mark 13, in Matthew the speech is not so much concerned with speculations about the last days but the life of faith, for the line of argument leads to the parenesis in Matt. 24:32–25:30.

The five speeches, like the gospel as a whole, impress the readers—and command them—that Jesus's teaching is to be understood as the binding interpretation of the *will of God*. By proclaiming the binding validity of the words of the earthly Jesus (Matt. 28:20a), the Risen One ascribes ultimate authority to them.

Christological Titles

The christological titles also express this authority. While the Gospel of Mark presents them all in the context of the messianic secret, in Matthew

191. Luz, *Matthew 1–7*, 12, formulates this matter as follows: "*The five major discourses are spoken, as it were, 'beyond the window' of the Matthean story of Jesus.* That is, they are spoken directly to the readers and are Jesus's direct commandment to them."

they primarily emphasize the exalted status of Jesus. Matthew introduces the title υἱὸς Δαυίδ (*Son of David*) already in 1:1 and uses it 17 times in his gospel (Mark, 7 times; Luke, 13 times). In the tradition and imagery of Jewish national-political messianism (*Pss. Sol.* 17.21), and inspired by Mark 10:46–52, Matthew gives this title a characteristic stamp. In the first place, Matthew presents Jesus as a divinely legitimated descendant of the Davidic dynasty and thus as the Messiah expected in Jewish tradition (Matt. 1:1–17). The Emmanuel motif (Matt. 1:23) then leads into the image of the merciful and healing Son of David. The title appears with striking frequency in connection with healings, especially healings of blind persons (9:27; 12:23; 20:30–31; 21:14–16). Jesus is the healing Son of David who carries out his ministry in Israel, and yet is not recognized by the blind leaders of Israel. Matthew 22:41–46 gives the title a universal perspective, taking up Ps. 110:1 LXX, and with Matt. 28:18–20 in view, presents the Messiah of Israel as κύριος (Lord) of the world.[192] Matthew's use of the Χριστός (*Anointed, Messiah*) title (sixteen times) is strongly influenced by his Markan source. The messianic status of Jesus is already explicitly indicated in the birth story by the titular use of ὁ Χριστός (Matt. 1:17; 2:4; cf. also 1:1, 16, 18). Of central significance is Matt. 16:16, where Matthew expands the title of Mark 8:29 through the predication ὁ υἱὸς τοῦ θεοῦ τοῦ ζῶντος (the Son of the living God), explicitly repeating the title ὁ Χριστός in the command to silence in Matt. 16:20. Matthew applies messianic traditions from the Old Testament to Jesus, at the same time redefining them, for example, when he describes Jesus's miracles in Matt. 11:2 as the "deeds/works of the Christ."[193]

The Son of Man title (ὁ υἱὸς τοῦ ἀνθρώπου) has a central place in Matthew's Christology (twenty-nine times).[194] The arrangement and placing of the title already signals how Matthew wants it to be understood: Son of Man sayings, directed not to the public but to the disciples (and thus to the church), provide an interpretation of the story of Jesus as a whole. Thus there are no

192. Ulrich Luz, "Eine thetische Skizze der matthäischen Christologie," in *Anfänge der Christologie: Festschrift für Ferdinand Hahn zum 65. Geburtstag* (ed. Cilliers Breytenbach et al.; Göttingen: Vandenhoeck & Ruprecht, 1991), 226, emphasizes the limited range of the title "Son of David," "namely to characterize the advent of Jesus as the fulfillment and transformation of the messianic hopes of Israel, and thereby to help the community work through the shock it has experienced in the separation of the Christian community and the synagogue."

193. This aspect is emphasized by Gerd Theissen, "Vom Davidssohn zum Weltherrscher: Pagane und jüdische Endzeiterwartungen im Spiegel des Matthäusevangeliums," in *Das Ende der Tage und die Gegenwart des Heils* (ed. E.-M. Becker and W. Fenske; AGJU 44; Leiden: Brill, 1999), 145–64. Theissen argues Matthew takes up the messianic expectations of his Jewish context and transforms them. Jesus Christ "is the fulfillment of both Jewish and Gentile hopes. His lordship is an alternative to every political form of world rulership."

194. On this point, cf. Jack Dean Kingsbury, *Matthew as Story* (2nd rev. and enl. ed.; Philadelphia: Fortress, 1988), 95–103; Heinz Geist, *Menschensohn und Gemeinde: Eine redaktionskritische Untersuchung zur Menschensohnprädikation im Matthäusevangelium* (FzB 57; Würzburg: Echter, 1986).

Son of Man sayings in the Sermon on the Mount (the first example is 8:20), and they are concentrated in chapters 16–17 (Passion predictions) and 24–26 (the coming of the Son of Man in judgment). The Son of Man sayings that Matthew adds to his Markan source are primarily about the coming Son of Man (Matt. 13:41; 16:28; 19:28; 24:30a; 25:31). In its use of Son of Man sayings, the Matthean community is reflecting on the works (Matt. 8:20; 9:6; 11:19; 12:8; 13:37), suffering (17:12, 22; 20:18, 28; 26:2, 24, 44), death and resurrection (12:40; 17:9), and return of the Son of Man in judgment (10:23; 16:27–28; 19:28; 24:27, 30, 39, 44; 25:31; 26:64). There is obviously an emphasis on the *majestic coming of the Son of Man in judgment*. In the final and decisive Son of Man saying, Jesus says publicly: "From now on you will see the Son of Man seated at the right hand of Power and coming on the clouds of heaven" (26:64). The Matthean church, living in the assurance of the universal lordship and confident trust in the coming of the Son of Man, knows that it has been sent to the nations with this message.

Matthew also places his own accent on the titles Son and Son of God (ὁ υἱὸς τοῦ θεοῦ, fifteen times). The title appears with particular frequency in the prologue, where God or an angel directly reveals Jesus as Son (1:22–23, 25; 3:17). Thus 3:15–17 and the antithetical placement of 4:8–10 and 28:16–18 clearly reveal the Matthean conception: it is the Son, obedient to the will of God, who enters his reign as ruler of the world as the Suffering Righteous One (cf. Ps. 22; Wis. 2:18). A key christological text is Matt. 11:25–30: "All things have been handed over to me by my Father; and no one knows the Son except the Father, and no one knows the Father except the Son and anyone to whom the Son chooses to reveal him" (11:27). Matthew interprets this exclusive revelatory communion between Jesus and God in 11:28–30 by referring to Jesus's paradigmatic life and work, and thus binds together the vertical and horizontal elements of his Christology, in which Jesus is at once example and prototype (*Vorbild, Urbild*). The central motifs of love, trust, and obedience are also dominant in 16:13–28; 17:5; 26:59–66; 27:40, 43. As an example to others, the Son obedient to God walks the path of suffering, from which the disciples will also not be spared.

The title κύριος (Lord) is not exceptionally important for Matthew, for whom it mostly has only an honorific and confessional character (cf., e.g., 7:21; 8:2, 6, 8; 9:28; 10:24; 15:22, 27; 17:4).

Matthean Christology is characterized by its bringing together the portrayals of Christ as the one who teaches, heals, obeys his heavenly Father, and lives a life that is to be the paradigm for his followers with the imagery of the exalted Lord of all, the one of whom it can be said "God is with us," and through whom God's gracious eschatological will is made known to all nations.[195]

195. Kingsbury, *Matthew as Story*, 2nd ed., 42.

8.3.3 Pneumatology

Unlike Luke and John, Matthew has no pronounced pneumatology. Jesus's conception through the Spirit of God in Matt. 1:20–21 is significant, receiving its confirmation when the Spirit descends on Jesus at his baptism (3:13–17). Jesus appears in 8:16 and 12:18ff. as the bearer of the Spirit who drives out unclean spirits. The command in 28:19 adds to the Matthean profile of the Spirit, "Go therefore and make disciples of all nations, baptizing them in the name of the Father and of the Son and of the Holy Spirit." The connection of baptism and the triadic formula is not coincidental, for baptism is the place where the Spirit is conferred (cf. 1 Cor. 6:11, and further 1 Cor. 12:4–6, 13; 2 Cor. 13:13; 1 Pet. 1:2; *Did.* 7.1, 3; 9.5), and *baptism in the name* is the place of invocation, affirmation, and confession of the triune God.[196] Despite the omission of εἰς ἄφεσιν ἁμαρτιῶν (for forgiveness of sins) in the Baptist's message (cf. Matt. 3:2 with Mark 1:4), it is to be supposed that in the Matthean church, too, both baptism and the eucharist (Matt. 26:28) were regarded as the places where sin is forgiven. At the conclusion of the gospel, hearers/readers are reminded of Jesus's paradigmatic conduct at his baptism, and are encouraged, in the name of the triune God and in his presence, to proclaim the good news to all peoples.

8.3.4 Soteriology

Foundational for Matthean soteriology is the conception that in Jesus Christ God is with his people. Jesus has come to save his people from their sins, although this message turns out to be fiercely rejected from the Jewish side. Matthew sets this *fundamental promise* into his narrative by framing it with Matt. 1:21–22/28:16–20, which declares Jesus's salvation of the lost and his gracious concern for sinners (8:1–9:34). Matthew 9:9–13 portrays Jesus's call to discipleship and his table fellowship with tax collectors and sinners. Thus Jesus appears as the Son of God who acts with authority to change the situation of human beings before God: "For I have come to call not the righteous but sinners" (9:13b). The forgiveness of sins, according to 1:21 an essential element of Jesus's commission, is directly spoken to the paralyzed man in 9:5 and bound to Jesus's death and resurrection in 26:28, which are present in the eucharist in their power to wipe away sins.

In Matt. 9:9, Jesus's compassionate commitment to others is related to the call of the tax collector Matthew to be a disciple, a call that places baptized believers in the realm of salvation, so that they are now commanded to proclaim this same obligatory call to discipleship to all nations. The disciples (of all times)

196. On this point cf. L. Hartmann, *Auf den Namen des Herrn Jesus* (SBS 148; Stuttgart: Katholisches Bibelwerk, 192).

are to be perfect as God is perfect (5:48). The compassionate commitment of God/Jesus corresponds to the demand to fulfill the will of God: "Not everyone who says to me, 'Lord, Lord,' will enter the kingdom of heaven, but only the one who does the will of my Father in heaven" (7:21). The unmerciful servant (18:23–35) had experienced God's compassionate goodness, but turned away from his fellow servant and thus from God, so that he is subject to judgment. In the parable of the Workers in the Vineyard (20:1–15), those who are not willing to let God's own goodness be effective exclude themselves from salvation (20:15, "Are you envious because I am generous?"). In Matthew, God's gracious act in the call to discipleship carries with it the inescapable expectation of doing the will of God. Does Matthew thus advocate a dual soteriological conception in which human activity steps in alongside God's act as the condition of salvation?[197] There is no doubt that the evangelist places the accents differently than does Paul, by ascribing to the Torah a fundamental significance in one's relation to God and defining the believer's relation to Judaism differently than does Paul.[198] Nonetheless, we cannot speak here of irreducible contradictions, but of noticeably different setting of the accents:

1. Matthew, too, gives a clear priority to God's act, the fundamental promise of God's being with us in Christ (1:21–22; 28:16–20), which means that God's omnipotence and grace are the foundation for all the calls to obey God's commands (see below, §8.3.5 and §8.3.6).
2. It is not by accident that the antitheses (Matt. 5:21–48) are framed by the basic promises and affirmations of the Beatitudes and sayings about salt and light, on the one hand, and the declaration that the person is not constituted by his or her works (6:4b, "and your Father who sees in secret will reward you"), on the other hand. The mercy of God and the promised blessing stand at the beginning!
3. The Lord's Prayer (6:9–13) also shows that Matthew clearly places the priority on God's grace.
4. In Matt. 28:19–20, baptism as the basis for the saving relation to God precedes teaching and response to it.[199]
5. Also in Paul, putting faith into practice is decisively important; Paul's ethical and ecclesiological views are, in his own way, no less categorical than Matthew's (see above, §6.7 and §6.8).

197. This is explicitly affirmed by Christof Landmesser, *Jüngerberufung und Zuwendung zu Gott* (WUNT 133; Tübingen: Mohr, 2001), 145: "According to the Gospel of Matthew, however, eschatological salvation is secondarily conditioned by the fact that the comprehensive fulfillment of the will of God interpreted by Jesus as binding, alongside his calling disciples to follow him, is an additional necessary presupposition for entrance into the kingdom of heaven."

198. Cf. the sketch in Luz, *Theology of the Gospel of Matthew*, 146–53.

199. Cf. Gerhard Friedrich, "Die formale Struktur von Mt 28,18–20," *ZTK* 80 (1983): 182–83; P. Nepper-Christensen, "Die Taufe im Matthäusevangelium," *NTS* 31 (1985): 189–207.

To set Paul up as the standard of a proper soteriology[200] is to underestimate the fact that all New Testament authors had to express their understanding within the specific conditions of their own symbolic universe, and that they therefore *cannot* be simply contrasted with each other.

8.3.5 Anthropology

While the Gospel of Matthew contains no anthropological concepts arranged in terms of topics, it certainly does relate the question of the essential nature of human beings inseparably to the will of God and to the law as the plumb line and norm of this will (Matt. 5:48, "Be perfect, therefore, as your heavenly Father is perfect"). Anthropology and ethics (see below, §8.3.6) are interwoven in Matthew, because for him the essential nature of human beings is inseparable from human action, so that human beings are constituted by an inseparable unity of being and act.

The Law in Matthew

The evangelist understands Jesus's appearance in history to signify the fulfillment of the law, not its destruction. However tradition and redaction are sorted out in Matt. 5:17–20,[201] Matthew has taken over the text as a whole, so that it is valid for him without reservation. The Torah is not annulled, not even its smallest part of a letter, for Jesus has come to fulfill it all.[202] This statement, however, is only the first step in the hermeneutical task with which Matthew challenges his fellow interpreters. Here too the fundamental presupposition for understanding Matthew's approach is the priority of God's mercy and unconditional trust in God's goodness as set forth in the Beatitudes and elsewhere (cf. 5:45; 6:25–34; 7:7–11). At the same time, there remains a tension between the basic declaration of 5:17–20 and the antitheses of 5:21–48, a

200. As obviously the case in Martin Hengel, "Zur matthäischen Bergpredigt und ihrem jüdischen Hintergrund," in *Judaica et Hellenistica: Kleine Schriften I* (ed. Roland Deines; WUNT 90; Tübingen: Mohr, 1996), 254: "If Matthew had the first (or last) word in Christian theology, then Paul would be a heretic"; cf. Landmesser, *Jüngerberufung*, 157: "The decisive question for the disciples, the answer to which first made possible a responsible life in the world, remains an open question in Matthew's theology." The matter is harmonized as follows by Roland Deines, *Die Gerechtigkeit der Tora im Reich des Messias* (WUNT 177; Tübingen: Mohr, 204), 651: "The difference between Jesus and Paul is not to be sought in their soteriological understanding of the law in the presence of the kingdom of God, but in the historical interpretation of the law."

201. For analysis, cf. Strecker, *Sermon on the Mount*, 52–60; Luz, *Matthew 1–7*, 210–25; Deines, *Gerechtigkeit*, 257–428. It is in any case clear that Matt. 5:17 is primarily redactional, and v. 20 entirely so. Verse 18 is a tangle of traditions that cannot be unraveled; v. 19c–d is also perhaps to be attributed to Matthew.

202. It is thus not possible to distinguish between the moral law affirmed by Matthew and the ceremonial law he rejects, as done, e.g., by Strecker, *Weg der Gerechtigkeit*, 30–33. Matthew 23:23, 26; 24:20 show that Matthew also holds fast to ritual laws.

tension that cannot be discussed away or eliminated by hermeneutical tricks. The antitheses represent an intensification of God's demand that cannot be adequately explained either by the cited Old Testament texts or by the later history of interpretation.

The question thus remains, in what sense does Matthew understand Jesus to have fulfilled the law? By no means merely as a repetition of the will of God as formulated in the Old Testament, but by his reinterpretation of the law with authority. The correspondence between Matt. 5:20 and 5:48 shows that the antitheses are concrete examples of the better righteousness for which the evangelist calls, examples that express the meaning of the "more" for which this righteousness calls. The law remains thereby as an essential element of God's righteous will, while at the same time it is the authority of the one who speaks that determines its content.[203] In the first antithesis (5:21–26) Jesus radicalizes the Torah's prohibition of murder. So also the second antithesis, on adultery (5:27–30), as a radicalization of a command of the Torah, remains within the framework of the possibilities of contemporary Torah interpretation. In contrast, the third antithesis on divorce (5:31–32) represents an annulment of a command of the Torah (cf. Deut. 24:1, 3). So also the absolute prohibition of oaths in Matt. 5:33–37 springs the framework of Old Testament–Jewish thinking, and is grounded in the authority of Jesus alone. As he had already done with the preceding commandment on divorce, so also here, Matthew adjusts this command to the realities of everyday life, without thereby eliminating the original intention of Jesus. With the rejection of the Old Testament principle of retaliation in Matt. 5:38–42 and the absolute command of love for enemies in 5:43–48, the preacher of the Sermon on the Mount departs from the world of Jewish thought[204] and emphasizes that the true will of God is found only in the absolute love of God that knows no boundaries. The antitheses reveal how Matthew understands Jesus's fulfilling of the law: the validity and authority of God's law does not lie in the text of the Old Testament tradition, but exclusively in the authority of Jesus. The ἐξουσία of Jesus makes it possible to annul a valid command of the Torah and, at the same time, to put the true will of God in force. Thus for Matthew, making the commands of the Torah more precise and intense, and annulling a command of the Torah altogether, are not alternatives or contradictions, because both are grounded and held together by the authority of Jesus.[205] It is not the Old Testament law

203. Cf. Deines, *Gerechtigkeit*, 649: "The Torah cannot contribute anything to this eschatological righteousness by its previous functions. It remains, however, as a present expression of the will of God to the extent that it leads to the ἐντολαί [commands] of Jesus. Nonetheless, in the First Gospel the way into the universal kingdom is made possible by Jesus alone."

204. For history-of-religions parallels cf. *NW* 1.1.2 on Matt. 5:44.

205. Eckart Reinmuth, *Anthropologie im Neuen Testament* (Tübingen: Mohr, 2006), 68, formulates the anthropological dimensions of the Sermon on the Mount as follows: "Their internal logic is not aimed at the excessive demands, but on the possibilities for truly human life that are

as such but Jesus's authoritative interpretation of the Old Testament that is obligatory for the Matthean church.[206] In this process, Jesus's authority does not merely set aside a mistaken interpretation of the Torah but rather sets his own claim over against that of what the Torah actually says, in order to restore its original intention. This intention is expressed in the principle of love for God and others, as the first and final antitheses show by placing all the others within their framework.[207]

The love command is the center of Matthew's understanding of the law; the better righteousness (Matt. 5:20) and perfection (5:48) for which Jesus calls are identical with the Golden Rule in 7:12. They attain concrete form in acts of mercy (cf. Hos. 6:6 in Matt. 9:13; 12:7; and further in 23:23c), and in the unlimited love of God and neighbor (cf. 19:19; 22:34–40), which once again find their highest expression in love for enemies. For Matthew, loyalty to the law is not found in the observance of many individual prescriptions, commands, and rules, but only in deeds of love and justice, so that we can speak of a "transformation of the Torah through the gospel."[208] Matthew makes relative evaluations: "Woe to you, scribes and Pharisees, hypocrites! For you tithe mint, dill, and cummin, and have neglected the weightier matters of the law: justice and mercy and faith. It is these you ought to have practiced without neglecting the others" (23:23). As the summary of Matthew's understanding of the law, its compelling validity is made real only by the one whose authority lets God's true will be heard again. The Matthean understanding of the law must therefore be grasped primarily in relation to his Christology.

8.3.6 Ethics

The previous discussions have already indicated that Matthew is rightly designated as *the* gospel of the New Testament centrally concerned with ethics. Above all, his portrayal of Jesus as teacher (see above, §8.3.2), and the thematic of the law woven into the gospel throughout, focus the spotlight of Matthew's thought on the issue of ethics. *The foundation of the Matthean*

---

opened up where human beings allow themselves to be addressed and freed by God's gracious act. The antitheses make it clear that this liberation can be realized as a paradigm change from exchange to gift. To be human is more than the exchanges of items of equal value that occur among equals . . . for the Sermon on the Mount, to be human is primarily a matter of receiving a gift, and it is only in this perspective that its commands can be understood."

206. Deines, *Gerechtigkeit*, 648: "The Torah no longer has an independent function alongside Jesus's command, not even for Jewish Christians. Instead, the disciples (and their successors in the churches), are instructed to promulgate the commands of the 'one Teacher' (S. Byrskog). The Torah never appears as a binding norm independently of Jesus's teaching and interpretation, i.e., the διδάσκειν of the Christian teachers is exclusively determined by Christology, including its instruction about righteousness."

207. Cf. Luz, *Matthew 1–7*, 226, 232.

208. So Deines, *Gerechtigkeit*, 645.

ethic is its firm bond to the person, teaching, and work of Jesus Christ. To believe in Jesus means at the same time to do his will, which is the same as doing the will of God.

Righteousness/Justice

Just as Jesus himself understands his work as the fulfilling of all righteousness (Matt. 3:15; cf. 21:32 on the Baptist), δικαιοσύνη (righteousness/justice) is the central content of the Matthean ethic (3:15; 5:6, 10, 20; 6:1, 33; 21:32), made particularly clear by the fact that all the instances of δικαιοσύνη are from Matthew's editorial hand.[209] Jesus has fulfilled God's righteousness requirement (3:15); this is the basis of righteousness in Matthew. Righteousness as the requirement of human conduct appears in 5:6, 10; 6:1, 33,[210] i.e., the conduct willed by God and corresponding to his kingdom. The "better" righteousness of 5:20 is Jesus's teaching and its requirement of the community to live in a particular way in order to enter into the kingdom of heaven.[211] This "better" righteousness manifests itself in an ethical conduct set forth as obligatory examples in the antitheses; its goal and norm is perfection (5:48).[212] Matthew thereby advocates a different concept of righteousness from that of Paul, a necessary result of his affirmation of the Torah and his emphasis on human deeds.[213] For both Paul and Matthew, righteousness is a relational concept that, to be sure, may be presented with different emphases: when Matthew speaks of "your" righteousness (5:20; 6:1), he gives relatively greater importance to human actions than does Paul, who calls for a life that corresponds to God's gift of righteousness (see above, §6.2.7 and §6.6). Sharply formulated: for Paul, God's act comes first; for Matthew, human actions.

209. Cf. Strecker, *Weg der Gerechtigkeit*, 153.

210. Cf. Luz, *Matthew 1–7*, 195, 199, 299.

211. Schrage, *Ethics*, 147, 152.

212. According to Strecker, *Weg der Gerechtigkeit*, 149–58, Matthew consistently means by δικαιοσύνη the ethical stance of the disciples, their doing what is right. Differently, e.g., M. Fiedler, "'Gerechtigkeit' im Matthäusevangelium," *ThV* 8 (1977): 63–75; Heinz Giesen, *Christliches Handeln: Eine redaktionskritische Untersuchung zum* δικαιοσύνη *Begriff im Matthäus-Evangelium* (EHS 23.181; Frankfurt: Lang, 1982), 259: "According to our interpretation, 'righteousness' in Matthew refers to the gift of God, even though Matthew does draw the ethical dimension emphatically into the foreground." Deines, *Gerechtigkeit*, 647, speaks of a "Jesus-righteousness": "By this I mean that righteousness is not possible apart from Jesus. Those who are obedient to the call to discipleship thereby come to share in this righteousness, and this is why it can be spoken of as *their* righteousness. The disciples' righteousness, however, continues to be oriented to the Jesus-righteousness in its origin and consequences." For a different point of view, cf. Pregeant, *Knowing Truth, Doing Good*, 123–44.

213. Deines, *Gerechtigkeit*, 647, harmonizes too much: "As Jesus fulfilled all righteousness, so the disciples are to do likewise. As Jesus did not perform his mighty deeds of healing the sick, feeding the hungry, driving out demons, and proclaiming the kingdom of God in order to become righteous, but as the Righteous One did these things and thus fulfilled all righteousness, so it is to be with his disciples (6:1)."

The *Sermon on the Mount* is the compositional and material center of Matthew's ethical conception. What is its theme? While Georg Strecker regards Matt. 5:20 ("Unless your righteousness exceeds that of the scribes and Pharisees . . .") as the theme and center of the Sermon on the Mount, U. Luz understands the Lord's Prayer as the true center of Jesus's first great speech in Matthew.[214] For Matthew, these probably were not seen as alternatives, since for him the demand for righteousness and the dependence on grace belong together. To whom does the Sermon on the Mount apply? Is it addressed to everyone, is it intended only for the Christian church, or can only an exclusive group or the individual fulfill the radical demands of the Sermon on the Mount?[215] That disciples and crowds stand side by side in 5:1 and 7:28–29 excludes a two-level ethic, for *the Sermon on the Mount is the universal ethic for all who follow Jesus*. The issue of whether anyone can actually fulfill the commands of the Sermon remains disputed. The ethical radicalism of the Sermon raises the question of to what extent, if at all, Matthew himself thought of its demands as practical. Can the demands of the Sermon on the Mount be fulfilled as timeless imperatives? We should accept the view that for Matthew himself, the issue of practicality was not even raised. "For Matthew, as for the entire church until well after the Reformation, it was clear the Sermon on the Mount is practicable. It not only must be done; it can be done."[216] It is a matter of committing oneself completely to the will of God in view of the near approach of the kingdom of God. The disciples are charged to orient their ethic to Jesus's teaching and his acting with authority. Just as Jesus himself in Gethsemane (cf. 26:42) fulfilled the third petition of the Lord's Prayer, (cf. 6:10), the church should commit itself to doing the will of God. The lasting validity of old and new commandments are no contradiction for Matthew, for they both attain their validity by the authority of Jesus Christ. This conception of things transcends the idea of "works righteousness," since for Matthew it is precisely the indissoluble unity of command and promise that characterizes his understanding of righteousness (see above, §8.3.5).[217] The words of the Sermon on the Mount and all other ethical instructions are all spoken by Jesus Christ as Lord of all, *and for this reason alone they are words of grace!*[218]

214. Cf. Strecker, *Sermon on the Mount*, 27; Luz, *Matthew 1–7*, 172–74, 309.

215. On this issue, cf. Gerhard Lohfink, "Wem gilt die Bergpredigt?" *TQ* 163 (1983): 264–84.

216. Luz, *Matthew 1–7*, 391.

217. Cf. Strecker, *Weg der Gerechtigkeit*, 171: "Corresponding to the content of the message of Jesus, it is identical with the imperative, the 'gift' of the kingdom consists of its 'demand.'" Strecker thus speaks of an "indicatival imperative" (cf. Matt. 11:28–30).

218. Cf. Strecker, *Sermon on the Mount*, 33–35; Luz, *Matthew 1–7*, 391–92.

Reward and Punishment

This grace, however, does not occur in a way that transcends the demand for doing the will of God, so that the concepts of *reward* (cf. Matt. 5:12, 19; 6:1, 19–21; 10:41–42; 18:1–5; 19:17, 28–29; 20:16, 23; 25:14ff.) and *punishment* (cf. 5:22; 7:1, 21; 13:49–50; 22:13; 24:51; 25:11–13, 30) remain central elements of ethical motivation in Matthew, as does the related image of *judgment* (see below, §8.3.8). Jesus will return as the Son of Man who is the judge (7:22–23; 13:30, 41; 16:27; 24:29–31; 25:31), and the separation between those who are elect and called will not take place until the future judgment (cf. 24:42–51). Then the criterion of doing the will of God will make clear who can be called "righteous" and who will be thrown into the "furnace of fire" (13:36–43, 47–50). Faith *in practice* will be the decisive criterion for the individual who stands before God's judgment (16:27, "For the Son of Man is to come with his angels in the glory of his Father, and then he will repay everyone for what has been done"). Thus Matthew's ethic is not so much dependent on the nearness of the coming judgment as on its reality—it will actually happen.[219] According to the parable of the Wedding Banquet (22:1–14), many are called, good and bad alike, but only those who show they have the "wedding robe," i.e., good works, are counted among the elect and are not thrown out by the king (cf. also 7:21). By means of the image of the final judgment, Matthew speaks to his church about its absolute responsibility. At the same time, his story of the last judgment in 25:31–46 shatters all schemes meant to calculate in advance what is to happen in the final assize, for what counts as good and evil deeds are not recognized until then, and the decisions of the judge himself are entirely unexpected. The reality of rejection and grace is represented by the judge of the world, Jesus Christ himself, for no other can do it. Eschatological reward is promised to those who do not calculate in advance on receiving it, who act in good will out of the public eye rather than on the basis of reward (6:1–4), who really allow themselves to be led by love, for love does not calculate.

Matthew's understanding of the law also applies to his understanding of ethics: *the demand to do the will of God is fulfilled by following the law of love.* This is revealed by the sharpening of the command to love the neighbor (Matt. 5:21–26), the command to love the enemy (5:44), the Golden Rule as conclusion and goal of the Sermon on the Mount (7:12), and the double command of love for God and neighbor in 22:34–40. The love commandment unlocks all the commandments from within, gives them new meaning, and orients them toward the new reality of the kingdom of heaven.

219. Cf. Siegfried Schulz, *Neutestamentliche Ethik* (Zürich: Theologischer Verlag, 1987), 455.

8.3.7 Ecclesiology

Matthew displays a deeper interest in the church than any of the other evangelists. He is the only gospel writer to explicitly use the word ἐκκλησία (Matt. 16:18; 18:17, "assembly," "congregation," "church").[220]

The Disciples

The primary concept of Matthean ecclesiology is discipleship (μαθητής occurs 72 times in Matthew, 46 times in Mark, 37 times in Luke).[221] The disciples as a group not only constitute the historical connection to Jesus but represent models of faith in practice for all times. When at his baptism Jesus declares that *we* must fulfill all righteousness (Matt. 3:15), the disciples are already included. Discipleship is a form of existence in which the disciple is unconditionally bound to the person and teaching of Jesus. For Matthew, to be a Christian means to be a disciple, a way of life that becomes real only in actually following Jesus (cf. 4:18–22; 8:23; 9:19, 37–38; 12:49–50; 19:16–28). The earthly Jesus's call to discipleship corresponds to the present of the Matthean church's response to the gospel, as it commits itself to the will of the risen Jesus Christ (28:19). Discipleship is lived out in the midst of troubles (cf. 8:23ff.); it calls for a willingness to suffer (cf. 10:17–25), strength to humble oneself (cf. 18:1ff.) to serve others with deeds of compassion and love (cf. 20:20ff.; 25:31–46). As the church commits itself to this way of life, it knows that it is sustained by the promise of the Risen One to be with his church (cf. 18:20; 28:20). Like the disciples in the experience of stilling the storm (8:23–27), the Matthean church knows that in all the hostility and danger it faces, it is secure in the presence of Jesus Christ. The post-Easter disciples are sent forth on a universal mission and call others to discipleship. In the Gospel of Matthew, they always represent the church, they are presented in such a way that they are transparent to the church of Matthew's own day (18:1–35). Differently from the usage of ἀπόστολος (apostle), the noun μαθητής (disciple) and verb ἀκολουθέω (follow) facilitate the community's identification with the action of the pre-Easter story. The disciples appear as those who learn and understand (13:13–23, 51; 16:12; 17:13), at the same time as they are those "of little faith" (8:26; 14:31; 16:8), even doubting the reality of the resurrection (28:17b "but some doubted"). They are the salt of the earth and the light of the world (5:13, 14–16), ready and able to confess their faith to carry out the mission on which they are sent (Matt. 10), but at the same time fearful and capable of denying their Lord (14:30–31; 26:21–22, 31, 34). In the gospel's picture of the

220. Luke only uses ἐκκλησία in Acts.

221. On Matthew's understanding of discipleship, cf. Ulrich Luz, "The Disciples in the Gospel according to Matthew," in *The Interpretation of Matthew* (ed. Graham Stanton; IRT 3; London: SPCK, 1983), 98–128; Richard Alan Edwards, *Matthew's Narrative Portrait of Disciples: How the Text-connoted Reader Is Informed* (Harrisburg, PA: Trinity, 1997).

disciples, the members of the Matthean church recognize patterns of faith as it is lived out, in all its aspects.

Peter

Peter has a special position within the circle of disciples and in the church.[222] He appears as the "first" apostle (Matt. 10:2), as spokesperson for the circle of disciples (15:15; 18:21), and in 14:28–31 his conduct is held up as a didactic example of the right relation of faith and doubt. The saying to Peter (16:17–19), which the evangelist inserts in the Markan series between the confession of Jesus as the Christ and the command to silence, is foundational for Matthew's understanding of Peter's role.[223] The saying exhibits a complex structure:

1. The macarism of v. 17 ("Blessed are you, Simon son of Jonah! For flesh and blood has not revealed this to you, but my Father in heaven") refers directly to the preceding confession.
2. The introductory formula v. 18a is followed by three logia, of similar structure, that deal respectively with the building of the church (v. 18b, "You are Peter, and on this rock I will build my church, and the gates of Hades will not prevail against it"), the giving to Peter of the keys to the kingdom of heaven (v. 19a, "I will give you the keys of the kingdom of heaven"), and the authority to bind and loose (v. 19b, "and whatever you bind on earth will be bound in heaven, and whatever you loose on earth will be loosed in heaven").

Verse 18b probably preserves very old tradition, based on a wordplay with Πέτρος (Peter) and πέτρα (rock cliff),[224] drawing a connection between the conferring of the name and the interpretation of its meaning, so that the name also expresses a function. The saying likely originated early in the tradition, but hardly goes back to Jesus, for the expression μου τὴν ἐκκλησίαν (my congregation/church) presupposes a post-Easter situation. This key saying, along with the logion about binding and loosing (cf. John 20:23) presents Peter as the guarantor of the Matthean tradition and as prototype of the confessing disciple and Christian teacher. In contrast to the scribes and Pharisees, Peter's interpretation of the tradition opens up the kingdom of heaven to people

222. On this point cf. Luz, *Matthew 8–20*, 366–77; Roloff, *Kirche im Neuen Testament*, 162–65.

223. In addition to the standard commentaries, cf. the analyses of Ferdinand Hahn, "Die Petrusverheißung Mt 16,18f.," in *Exegetische Beiträge zum ökumenischen Gespräch* (ed. Ferdinand Hahn; Göttingen: Vandenhoeck & Ruprecht, 1986), 185–200; Paul Hoffmann, "Der Petrus-Primat im Matthäusevangelium," in *Neues Testament und Kirche: für Rudolf Schnackenburg* (ed. Joachim Gnilka; Freiburg i.B.: Herder, 1974), 94–114.

224. On this point, cf. Peter Lampe, "Das Spiel mit dem Petrusnamen—Matt. XVI.18," *NTS* 25 (1979): 227–45.

(Matt. 23:13, "But woe to you, scribes and Pharisees, hypocrites! For you lock people out of the kingdom of heaven. For you do not go in yourselves, and when others are going in, you stop them."). The Matthean church is thus firmly grounded on the rock (cf. 7:24–27).

The authority to bind and loose is also given to the church as a whole, according to Matt. 18:18, so that Peter is the example and representative of all disciples: the knowledge, authority, and strength of faith given to him, but also his doubt and weakness, are also shared by the church as such. As the present form of the Gospel of Matthew reflects the way of the church from its Jewish Christian beginnings to its present praxis of universal mission to the nations, so also the course of Peter's own life, which as the primary witness of the Easter event (cf. 1 Cor. 15:5) opens to a liberal Judaism (Gal. 2:11ff.), and finally carries on a mission to the Gentiles (cf. 1 Cor. 1:12; 9:5). It is quite possible that these striking agreements ground the extraordinary role of Peter in the Matthean church.

Structures

The exceptional position of Peter and the parallels between Matt. 16:19 and 18:18 raise the question of how the Matthean church was structured. We should first note that the church has no institutionalized offices (cf. 23:8–12), understands itself as a *community of brothers and sisters* (cf. 23:8) constituted by baptism and the call to radical discipleship. At the same time, prophets are active in its midst (cf. 10:41; 23:34; also 5:12; 10:20), as are scribes (cf. 13:52; 23:34; also 8:19) and charismatic miracle workers (cf. 10:8). It is clear that mutual care as fellow members of the family of God plays a central role in the life of the church, the love of God that does not abandon sinners but seeks them out and restores them to the church. Jesus himself is again the model for this kind of love, "So it is not the will of your Father in heaven that one of these little ones should be lost" (18:14). The question of *forgiveness of sins* is thus of central importance, for Jesus is the one who saves his people from their sins (1:21), and the authority to forgive sins is conferred on the church (9:8; 26:28). This authority is reflected in the *disciplinary rule* of 18:15–17, which is to be understood as an institutionalized procedure for church discipline.[225] Old Testament traditions are adapted and set forth as a three-stage procedure: (1) A private conversation with the church member (v. 15); (2) if no resolution is forthcoming, a further conversation in which one or two other witnesses is involved (v. 16), and if all else fails, (3) the case is to be dealt with by the whole assembly of the church. If the offending party does not respond to this final hearing, excommunication follows (v. 17b, "Let such a one be to you as

225. For exegesis, cf. most recently Goldhahn-Müller, *Die Grenze der Gemeinde*, 164–95; Stefan Koch, *Rechtliche Regelung von Konflikten im frühen Christentum* (WUNT 174; Tübingen: Mohr, 2004), 66–83.

a Gentile and a tax collector"). The goal of this procedure is to restore the member of the community who is about to fall away from the path of discipleship. Matthew's goal is thus not to preserve a pure community of saints, but to maintain an ordered community, aware of its origin and its assignment. On the whole, the data reveal a community that is already characterized by considerable institutionalization.[226]

Internal Dangers

We can no longer say with certainty what the problems were that generated these reactions by the evangelist. It is clear, however, that two acute problems threatened the church:

1. The repeated call to do the will of God (Matt. 7:21; 12:50; 21:31) signals that a fundamental problem was abiding in the realm of God's grace without allowing faith and love to languish. Matthew addresses his comprehensive parenesis to "little faith" (cf. 6:30; 14:31; also 8:26; 16:8; 17:20) by placing emphasis on doing the whole Torah (5:17–19) or righteousness (3:15; 5:6, 10, 20; 6:1, 33; 21:32), on perfection (5:48; 19:21), and on the fruits of faith (3:10; 7:16–20; 12:33; 13:8; 21:18–22, 33–46). With the call to courageous practice of faith and remaining steadfast in faith, the evangelist includes references to the last judgment (e.g., 3:10; 5:29; 7:16ff.; 10:15; 18:21–35; 19:30; 23:33, 35–36; 24:42). It is hardly an accident that only in Matthew are pictures of the last judgment brought in as motivation for parenesis (cf. 7:21ff.; 13:36ff.; 25:31ff.). The community has an assignment in and for the world, and thus it includes "bad and good" as does the world itself (5:45). It exists as corpus permixtum, in which righteous and unrighteous live together (13:24–30, 47–50; 22:10; 25:31–46), and for precisely this reason the evangelist calls for staying awake and alert (24:42; 25:13), for "many are called, but few are chosen" (22:14). At the same time, the promise applies, "the one who endures to the end will be saved" (24:13).
2. The evangelist warns the church in Matt. 7:15 and 24:11 against ψευδοπροφῆται (false prophets). The theological profile of these opponents remains unclear, mainly because they are lumped together with Hellenistic antinomians (5:17–20; 7:13–27; 11:12–13; 24:10–13).[227] Matthew charges them with ἀνομία ("lawlessness"; cf. 7:23; 24:12); they produce

226. Cf. Luz, *Matthew 1–7*, 49.

227. Here the basic work is still Gerhard Barth, "Matthew's Understanding of the Law," in *Tradition and Interpretation in Matthew* (ed. Günther Bornkamm et al.; NTL 30; trans. Percy Scott; Philadelphia: Westminster John Knox, 1963), 58–164. Cf. also Eduard Schweizer, "Gesetz und Enthusiasmus bei Matthäus," in *Das Matthäus-Evangelium* (ed. Joachim Lange; WdF 525; Darmstadt: Wissenschaftliche Buchgesellschaft, 1980), 350–76; Eduard Schweizer, "Observance of the Law and Charismatic Activity in Matthew," *NTS* 16 (1970): 213–30. A catalog of the

bad fruit (cf. 7:16–20), and they do not do the will of God (cf. 7:21). The opponents obviously subvert Matthew's comprehensive ethical conception (cf. 24:12), and thereby endanger the unity of the church.

Church and Israel

The relation of the church and Israel is not only the central issue in Ma - thew's ecclesiology, but in his theology as a whole. Bound up with the way one answers this question are the very different judgments about the historical location of the evangelist and his theological conception. The gospel contains *data representing various tensions*: On the one hand, there are reflections of a *particular Jewish Christian stance*, for the gospel's language, structure, reception of the Scripture, argumentation, and the history of its effects point to this milieu. On the other hand, numerous references speak in favor of a *universal standpoint* that has long since gone beyond the borders of Judaism.[228]

The problem can be compactly illustrated in relation to Matt. 10:5b–6 ("Go nowhere among the Gentiles, and enter no town of the Samaritans, but go rather to the lost sheep of the house of Israel"; cf. 15:24) and 28:16–20. How are the specific limitations of the mission and its programmatic universalism to be related?[229] Different explanatory models are possible:

1. Historical succession, according to which Matt. 10:5b–6 documents the older version of the Matthean community's understanding of its mission charge, and 28:16–20 the later understanding.[230] The exclusive mission to Israel is no longer in force.
2. This model can be combined with an interpretation of salvation history that understands Israel has now given up its place in salvation history to the universal church (supersession model),[231] or at least that the particular limitation to Israel has now been nullified by an expansion model.[232]
3. The complementary model, according to which the mission to Israel and the universal mission are both valid and represent no inconsistency, because they are not of the same character. The Jewish self-understanding

range of proposed solutions (Zealots, Pharisees, Essenes, strict Jewish Christians, Paulinists) is found in Luz, *Matthew 1–7*, 376–77.

228. On this point, cf. the survey by Deines, *Gerechtigkeit*, 19–27.

229. A survey of research is provided by Axel von Dobbeler, "Die Restitution Israels und die Bekehrung der Heiden," 91 (2000): 21–27.

230. Cf., e.g., Luz, *Matthew 8–20*, 72–75.

231. Cf. Wolfgang Trilling, *Das wahre Israel: Studien zur Theologie des Matthäus Evangeliums* (3rd ed.; SANT 10; Munich: Kösel, 1964), 215: "Matthew as the final redactor thinks decisively in Gentile Christian, universal terms." Strecker, *Weg der Gerechtigkeit*, 34: "The non-Jewish, Hellenistic elements of the redaction suggest that the author is to be located in Gentile Christianity."

232. Gnilka, *Mattäusevangelium*, 362–63.

of Matthew and the coming of the nations in the context of prophetic traditions are mutually supplementary.[233]

In view of the complex variety of textual data and divergent interpretations thereof, the decisive factual issue remains: is the mission to Israel still a current issue that determines the theological conception of the evangelist in his own time and the historical situation of the church for which he writes? There can be no doubt that the history of Matthew's church has been shaped by the mission to Israel, which is still present in the world of the text represented by the gospel, but there are clear evidences that it is no longer the decisive issue for the evangelist's own thought. The mission to Israel turned out to be a failure (11:20–24; 23:37–39; 28:15), and the break with Israel already lies in the distant past. This failure had led to repression and persecution from the Jewish side against members of the church (10:17–18; 23:34).[234] Distance from and disputes[235] with Israel groups appear at the linguistic level in, for example,

233. Cf. Dobbeler, "Restitution," 27–44. Similarly Matthias Konradt, "Die Sendung zu Israel und zu den Völkern im Matthäusevangelium im Lichte seiner narrativen Christologie," *ZTK* (2004): 424, argues that Matthew's position is characterized by the fact that "on the one hand, the special position of Israel is adopted in a positive sense, while on the other hand he is an advocate of the mission to the Gentile world, and wants to combine the two. If one combines this with the recent attempts to locate the gospel in the context of the process of Jewish formation after 70 CE as discussed in the introduction to this work, then Matthew's story of Jesus in my opinion appears as an effort at legitimization, and/or an attempt to enlist recruits for a variation of Jewish faith programmatically open to the Gentile world in a new way, in contrast and conflict with the Pharisees' tactics, which appear to be exercising a dominant influence on the synagogues."

234. Thereby the addition καὶ τοῖς ἔθνεσιν in Matt. 10:18 shows clearly that for the evangelist the dispute lies some time in the past, and that he has integrated it in his universal conception of history. Cf. Strecker, *Weg der Gerechtigkeit*, 30.

235. Differently Günther Bornkamm, "End-Expectation and Church in Matthew," in *Tradition and Interpretation in Matthew* (ed. Günther Bornkamm et al.; NTL; trans. Percy Scott; Philadelphia: Westminster John Knox, 1963), 22: "That here the picture of the Jewish-Christian congregation arises, which holds fast to the law and has not yet broken away from union with Judaism but rather stands in sharp contrast to a doctrine and mission free from the law (which Matthew would regard as lawlessness) is crystal clear." Cf. Reinhart Hummel, *Die Auseinandersetzung zwischen Kirche und Judentum im Matthäusevangelium* (BEvT 33; Munich: Kaiser, 1963), 29, 31, 159–60, who argues Matthew's church still belongs within Judaism in an external sense, but has become inwardly independent. Cf. further in this sense J. Andrew Overman, *Matthew's Gospel and Formative Judaism: The Social World of the Matthean Community* (Minneapolis: Fortress, 1990); Anthony J. Saldarini, *Matthew's Christian-Jewish Community* (Chicago: University of Chicago Press, 1994); David C. Sim, *The Gospel of Matthew and Christian Judaism: The History and Social Setting of the Matthean Community* (Edinburgh: T&T Clark, 1998); M. Vahrenhorst, *"Ihr sollt überhaupt nicht schwören": Matthäus im halachischen Diskurs* (WMANT 95; Neukirchen: Neukirchener Verlag, 2002), all of whom argue that Matthew and the Pharisees represent competitive claims to leadership *within* Israel. Cf. also Marlis Gielen, *Der Konflikt Jesu mit den religiösen und politischen Autoritäten seines Volkes im Spiegel der matthäischen Jesusgeschichte* (BBB 115; Bodenheim: Philo, 1998), 473: "The self-understanding

the stereotyped references to "their synagogues" or "your synagogues" (4:23; 9:35; 10:17; 12:9; 13:54; 23:34; cf. also 6:2, 5; 23:6) and the "scribes and Pharisees" (cf. 5:20; 12:38; 15:1; 23:2, 13, 15, 23, 25, 27, 29). Matthew exposes the "hypocritical" deeds of the Pharisees and scribes (cf., e.g., 6:1–18; 23:1–36) and calls instead for the "better" righteousness that surpasses theirs (5:20), the complete fulfilling of the original will of God (5:21–48; 6:9, 10b; 12:50; 15:4; 18:4; 19:3–9; 21:31), presented as the presupposition for entrance into the kingdom of heaven (23:13). The standpoint of Matthew himself becomes visible in 24:14 ("And this good news of the kingdom will be proclaimed throughout the world, as a testimony to all the nations; and then the end will come"). *The universal mission to all nations is the theological matrix in which Matthew and his church live.*[236] Numerous indications within the gospel point in this universalistic direction (see above, §8.3.2), such as the exposed location of the mission command as the hermeneutical and theological key to the gospel. The expression πάντα τὰ ἔθνη in 24:9, 14; 25:32; 28:19 is not simply identical with τὰ ἔθνη, but is meant universally and is to be translated with "all nations,"[237] which obviously includes Israel.[238] The Matthean church is no longer within Judaism, for it does not practice circumcision, but in the commission of the Risen Lord practices baptism and proclaims a proto-trinitarian understanding of God (28:19).[239] Neither is the Matthean church on the way to beginning a mission to all peoples, but has long since been carrying out such

---

of Matthew and his church is Jewish, the separation from those that do not confess faith in Jesus Christ has probably not yet taken place," and Konradt, "Sendung," 424, who points out that "the evangelist is concerned to position his church as the legitimate trustee of the theological inheritance of Israel." For critical analysis and discussion of the different positions, cf. also Luz, *Matthew 1–7*, 54, who summarizes, "In my opinion the Matthean community, whose mission in the land of Israel has come to an end, no longer belongs to the Jewish synagogue."

236. Cf. Luz, *Matthew 1–7*, 51–52; Luz, *Matthew 21–28*, 626–36, who has changed his mind on this decisive point from that expressed in earlier editions of his commentary, and now accepts it as true that for the Matthean church "the Gentile mission is already under way even in its midst" (3:631). Cf. further Roloff, *Kirche im Neuen Testament*, 146–54; P. Foster, *Community, Law and Mission in Matthew's Gospel* (WUNT 177; Tübingen: Mohr, 2004), 253: "At the time of the writing of the Gospel the group had broken away from its former religious setting and was operating as an independent entity."

237. On this point cf. Luz, *Matthew 21–28*, 628–31. Luz states, "The mission command is not 'in addition to Israel go to the other nations'" (630).

238. Ibid., 631, advocates a mediating position: "The mission command of the Lord of heaven and earth—that is, of the whole world—is, in my judgment, *fundamentally* universal and is for all nations. While it does not exclude a continuing mission to Israel, Matthew probably has no great hopes for it."

239. A completely different view is represented by Peter Fiedler, *Das Matthäusevangelium* (THKNT 1; Stuttgart: 2006), 21–22, whose point of departure is that Gentile males who become members of the Matthean church (and thus to Judaism) must be circumcised, and that for Matthew baptism is associated with Jewish proselyte baptism. When Matthew says *nothing* about the circumcision of "his teacher" Jesus of Nazareth, and *never* mentions circumcision, how can one then argue that his church nonetheless practiced it?

a mission (cf., alongside 28:18–20, especially 12:21; 13:38a; 24:9–14; 26:13). This interpretation can very easily take account of both 10:5b–6 and 28:16–20, for if one takes seriously the narrative form of Matthew's presentation, then *the earthly Jesus speaks in Matt. 10:5b–6 and the Risen Lord in 28:16–20.* The expansion of the church's mission being carried out by the church and theologically grounded by the gospel corresponds to the ultimate will of the cosmic Lord Jesus Christ.[240]

An additional consideration is that, for the Matthean community, the rejection of Israel has long since been a reality (cf. Matt. 8:11–12; 21:39ff., 43; 22:9; 27:25; 28:15), indicated above all by the Matthean editing of Mark 12:1–12. Matthew elaborates the allegorical traits already present in Mark into a representation of the whole history of salvation in which God's address to Israel through the prophets was constantly rejected until it finally comes to its climax in the killing of the Son. According to this revised version of the parable, the vineyard, explicitly identified in v. 43 with the kingdom of God, is taken from Israel and given to a people who will produce the fruits of the kingdom (21:43). Matthew sees the punishment of Israel not only in the killing of the tenants, the leaders of Israel, but above all in the transfer of salvation to the church. The kingdom of God is taken from Israel and given to the church, because in the past, Israel did not produce the required fruit. The Matthean composition of the immediate context in 21:33–46 confirms this. In connection with the question of authority found in his Markan source, the evangelist chooses an item from his special tradition, the parable of the Two Sons (Matt. 21:28–32), and then follows the parable of the Wicked Tenants with that of the Wedding Banquet from the sayings source Q (Matt. 22:1–14). The common element in all three stories is that they all are aimed at the abolition of Israel's priority in salvation history. The connection between the parable of the Two Sons and that of the Wicked Tenants is made by the key word ἀμπελών (vineyard) in 21:28 and 21:33, in the unexpected entrance of others into the kingdom of God and in the role of John the Baptist within salvation history as the forerunner, who was rejected by Israel just as the Son was later.

All three pericopes reveal Matthew's historical standpoint: Israel's disobedience in the past, visible in their persecution and killing of the prophets, has reached its high point in the killing of God's Son. God has thus punished the previously chosen people and transferred the gift of salvation, the βασιλεία τοῦ θεοῦ, to a people who will produce fruit according to his will. This dissolution of Israel's favored status in salvation history through the church has, in Matthew's understanding, already taken place, and he describes it retrospectively from the perspective of a community of Christians from both Judaism

240. Thus, differently from Luz, *Matthew 1–7*, 51.

and the nations.[241] The Matthean church does not legitimize itself within the framework of Judaism,[242] but proclaims a new identity under the lordship of its teacher of all nations, the Son of God and Messiah Jesus of Nazareth.

8.3.8 Eschatology

The eschatology of the Gospel of Matthew is one key to understanding its historical and theological location. Statements about God's future acts reveal something about the present situation of the evangelist.

Fulfilling the Will of God

For Matthew, the will of God revealed in the Old Testament arrives at its goal in Jesus Christ, as is especially clear in the reflection citations. These *reflection citations* (fulfillment quotations),[243] each with redactional introduction, are found in Matt. 1:23; 2:6, 15, 18, 23; (3:3); 4:15–16; 8:17; 12:18–21; (13:14–15); 13:35; 21:5; 27:9–10 (cf. further 26:54, 56).[244] In them the Matthean understanding of salvation history comes to expression in a particular way, according to the hermeneutical model "promise and fulfillment": the Christ event is the exclusive fulfillment of the Old Testament promises. The introductory formulae have common elements, in that the idea of fulfillment (πληρόω occurs 16 times in Matthew; 3 times in Mark; 9 times in Luke) is followed by the reference to the Scripture passage, which can also give the name of the prophet (Isaiah, Jeremiah). Several citations manifest a mixed text in which all known textual forms of the Old Testament are found.[245] The citations contain basic themes of Matthean theology (Matt. 1:23, Emmanuel; 2:15, Son of God; 21:5, the nonviolent king), in part being stylized in a biographical direction (cf. 2:6, 15, 18, 23; 4:15–16; 21:5; 27:9).[246] The concentration of such citations in the prologue has a programmatic character, for Matthew wants thereby to point his hearers/readers in a particular direction for understanding the story as a

241. Differently, e.g., Konradt, "Sendung," 415: "The universal Gentile mission is not the response to the rejection of Jesus by Israel and/or to Israel's rejection."

242. Deines, *Gerechtigkeit*, 24ff., rightly points to the (surprising) history of Matthew's acceptance and effects, which does not understand its original context to be Judaism, but Jewish Christianity.

243. The category "*reflection* citations" includes all citations with introductions indicating a relation between the Christ event and the Old Testament, while "*fulfillment* citations" in the strict sense refers only to citations whose introduction includes the word πληρόω ("fulfill").

244. For analyses, cf. especially Strecker, *Weg der Gerechtigkeit*, 49–84; Rothfuchs, *Erfüllungszitate*; Luz, *Matthew 1–7*, 125–31; Boring, "Matthew," 151–54, "Matthew as Interpreter of Scripture."

245. For details, see especially Krister Stendahl, *The School of St. Matthew and Its Use of the Old Testament* (Philadelphia: Fortress, 1968), 39–142.

246. Strecker, *Weg der Gerechtigkeit*, 72, 85, emphasizes the historical-biographical aspect.

whole. This prologue already places the spotlight on Jesus as the Savior who comes from Israel, but is for all nations (cf. 2:15, 18, 23; 4:15). Here we meet a motif that is also a determining factor in later citations (cf. 8:17; 12:18–21 [v. 21, "And in his name the Gentiles will hope"]; 13:14–15; 21:16). After the parting of the ways between Judaism and Matthew's own community, which has turned to a universal mission to all nations, Matthew emphasizes for his own sake, and for the sake of his church's past and present, *that Jesus's way that proceeds out of Israel to all the nations is the fulfillment of the whole Scripture.*

The Kingdom of Heaven

Matthew also integrates Jesus's language of the rule of God into his own theological conception. Differently from Mark, Matthew speaks predominantly of the "kingdom of Heaven" (βασιλεία τῶν οὐρανῶν, thirty-two times), which corresponds to synagogal usage. As in Jewish tradition generally, so also in Matthew a strong ethical accent is connected with the "kingdom of Heaven":[247] "But strive first for the kingdom of God and his righteousness, and all these things will be given to you as well" (Matt. 6:33; cf. 3:2; 4:17; 7:21; 13:24, 31, 33, 34, 44, 45, 47; 16:19). The coming kingdom (6:10) also determines how one must act in the present. It is a matter of conducting one's life in the present in such a way that one will be able to enter the kingdom at the last judgment. At the same time, however, the evangelist knows that the community is dependent on the boundless mercy of God (cf. 18:1ff., 20:1ff.). The kingdom appears in 25:34 as the very essence of salvation; it is preexistent and will be granted to the elect at the final judgment. Matthew likewise relates his understanding of the kingdom of God/heaven to the relation to Judaism. The parting of the ways with Judaism is the theme of 8:11; 21:43; 22:1–10; 24:14; Matthew's redactional addition to the Markan text at 24:14 concisely indicates his historical standpoint: the "gospel of the kingdom," i.e., the preaching of Jesus as presented in the Gospel of Matthew, is being proclaimed to the nations in Matthew's own present, "and then will the end come." Matthew and his church lived in an expectation of the imminent parousia, indicated for example by the use of Mark 13:28–32 in Matt. 24:32–36 (cf. further Matt. 3:2; 4:17; 10:7, 23; 16:28; 24:22). The singular formulation "kingdom of the Son of Man" (Matt. 13:41; 16:28) or the "kingdom of Jesus" (20:21) suggests that Matthew

247. Theissen, "Ende der Tage," 164, sees in the Gospel of Matthew a concept of rulership intentionally contrasted with contemporary understanding: "A completely new way of world rulership is here announced, a rulership through ethical commands. It is located on another plane than that of Roman and Herodian rule, a different level than the expectations of rulership conventional in the eastern Mediterranean. It is different from contemporary Jewish messianic expectations. What we can observe in the Gospel of Matthew is not only the fulfilling of these expectations. The gospel is a witness for the transformation of political power into ethics."

distinguishes between the "kingdom of Heaven" and the "kingdom of the Son of Man," which has broken in with the resurrection and will extend until the parousia.[248] At the same time, the reader cannot fail to note an awareness of the delay of the parousia, for the call to remain alert in the parable of the Ten Virgins explicitly warns, "As the bridegroom was delayed, all of them became drowsy and slept" (25:5).

The Last Judgment

The central place of eschatology in Matthew's theology is seen in the fact that he makes the last judgment a dominant theme in the composition of his gospel.[249] This theme extends through the whole gospel, beginning with the preaching of the Baptist (Matt. 3:7–12), goes through the Sermon on the Mount (7:13–27), the missionary discourse (10:32–33, 39–42), the parables discourse (13:37–43, 47–50), the church discourse (18:23–35), and into the eschatological discourse (Matt. 24–25). In addition, numerous text complexes include the judgment metaphor (cf., e.g., 8:11–12; 11:6, 20–24; 12:33–37; 16:25–27; 18:8–9; 19:27–30; 20:11–16; 21:18–20; 22:11–14; 23:34–24:2). Matthew takes over a large number of judgment texts from the sayings source Q, strengthens the judgment theme and makes it more specific by a literary technique: by editing each of the five speech complexes so that they conclude with a judgment saying, *all five of the great speeches of the gospel become judgment speeches addressed to the church*. At the center of the event of the coming judgment stands the exalted appearance of the Son of Man, who is to appear in the near future (16:27–28; 24:30–31; 25:31). It is not God who acts as judge, but the Son of Man, so that Jesus-as-exclusive-Teacher corresponds to Jesus-as-exclusive-Judge. Judgment is according to works (16:27, "Then he will repay everyone for what has been done"), for it is not the attitude of faith, but its fruits that make the difference (3:8–10; 7:15–20; 13:8, 22–23, 26; 24:45, 49; 25:20–33). *Doing the will of God as obedience to the teaching of Jesus is the one criterion in the last judgment,* so that eschatology, too, stands in the service of ethics, as specifically indicated by the parenetic insertion 24:32–25:30 in the eschatological discourse. The emphasis on what one has done indeed explicitly excludes any human calculation. Matthew 25:31–46 illustrates this: those who are righteous are unaware of their deeds and have not calculated on any reward. Matthew thus places his church and all human beings under the judgment of the Son of Man, and no human being can know the outcome of this judgment.

248. Cf. Jürgen Roloff, "Das Reich des Menschensohnes: Ein Beitrag zur Eschatologie des Mattäus," in *Eschatologie und Schöpfung* (ed. M. Evang et al.; BZNW 89; Berlin: de Gruyter, 1997), 275–92.

249. Cf. on this point Daniel Marguerat, *Le jugement dans l'Évangile de Matthieu* (MdB; Geneva: Labor et Fides, 1981); Luz, *Matthew 21–28*, 285–96.

8.3.9 Setting in the History of Early Christian Theology

The dispute with Judaism has no doubt influenced Matthew's thinking, but this factor alone by no means is adequate to explain the theological thought of the evangelist. Matthew is a creative author who in several respects places new accents on the developing early Christian tradition and inscribes himself deeply in the memory of the developing church:

1. The Gospel of Matthew takes over the Gospel of Mark as its basic narrative, but at the same time is so structured that it cannot be defined merely in terms of this relationship. It is intentionally composed as a book (1:1) conceived for reading aloud in the church's worship. The five great speeches, in particular, reveal the didactic competence of the evangelist. He was probably himself a teacher in the church (cf. 13:52)[250] and presents Jesus as primarily the Teacher of the church and the nations. It is no accident that in the history of the church Matthew became its primary gospel,[251] for its presentation of Jesus as authoritative teacher and world ruler, as well as the catechetical arrangement of the gospel as a whole, has impressed for all time humanity's picture from and about Jesus Christ.[252] Alongside James, Matthew is the New Testament author who insists that faith is a matter of action in a way that cannot be misunderstood.
2. Like no other gospel, Matthew preserves Jewish Christian traditions, combining them with the opening of the universal mission to the nations in a way that produces something new: his gospel. Like Paul, Matthew legitimizes the Gentile mission, but without minimizing the significance of the Torah. Matthew maintains the claim of the whole Torah but within a new hermeneutical framework. The Matthean understanding "did not regard the Torah as an independent reality alongside Jesus. Instead, Jesus was the only teacher even in reference to the law and was the key to its understanding."[253] The Matthean church grew out of Judaism, but no longer belonged to the synagogue; it had its own founding history, its own officers, and its own theological profile.[254] The

250. Cf. on this point Stendahl, *School*, 20 (Matthew as a "handbook issued by a school"); Strecker, *Weg der Gerechtigkeit*, 39 (a Christian scribe); Luz, *Matthew 1–7*, 43–44 (Matthew as creative exponent of his community); Hengel, "Zur matthäischen Bergpredigt," 234–35 ("sort of the head of a Christian school").

251. Wolf-Dietrich Köhler, *Die Rezeption des Matthäusevangeliums in der Zeit vor Irenäus* (WUNT 2.24; Tübingen: Mohr, 1987).

252. The comment of John Nolland, *The Gospel of Matthew: A Commentary on the Greek Text* (NIGTC; Grand Rapids: Eerdmans, 2005), 38, is on target: "Matthew does not write to have people engage with his theology, but rather to engage with Jesus."

253. Luz, *Matthew 1–7*, 51.

254. On the history of the anti-Jewish effects of Matthean texts (cf. Matt. 27:25, "Then the people as a whole answered, 'His blood be on us and on our children'"), cf. the traditions in Ulrich

somewhat inconsistent data preserved in the gospel are best explained by supposing that the evangelist Matthew was the advocate of a liberal Hellenistic Diaspora Jewish Christianity.[255] The bracketing out of the circumcision problem in the Gospel of Matthew points in the same direction, for in Palestinian Judaism, which was more conservative, it was considered disdain for the Torah, while such praxis was widespread in Diaspora Judaism.[256] For all believers of all time, baptism is now the entrance into the church of God (28:19). So also the gospel's history of effects in the ancient church suggests its origin in the context of a Jewish Christianity open to a universal mission. Moreover, rigid historical categories such as "Jewish Christianity" and "Gentile Christianity" have for some time been inadequate to fit the reality represented by the Matthean church and the evangelist's self-understanding.[257] Matthew does not think in particularistic Jewish-Christian or Gentile-Christian terms, but in universal terms! Only so could he preserve the Jewish heritage and the claims associated with it within the developing church. The Gospel of Matthew thus manifests a fundamentally inclusive structure; it unites disparate streams within itself that are constituted into a new reality by the dominant position of Christology.[258] The comprehensive reception of the "first" gospel in the early church shows that from the very beginning it was understood in ways that transcend the alternatives that scholarship has attempted to force upon it.

3. Matthew's compositional and theological independence indicates an advanced stage in the history of early Christian theology, characterized primarily by an ethicizing of the Christian message (see §8.3.6).[259]

Luz, "Der Antijudaismus im Matthäusevangelium als historisches und theologisches Problem," *EvT* 53 (1993): 310–27. In the context dominated by North American exegetical perspectives, wherever Matthew is understood *within* Judaism, there is a side effect that is no doubt intended, namely, that the possibly anti-Jewish statements in Matthew can be seen as legitimate forms of inner-Jewish polemic. Cf. Anthony J. Saldarini, "Reading Matthew without Anti-Semitism," in *The Gospel of Matthew in Current Study: Studies in Memory of William G. Thompson, SJ* (ed. David Edward Aune; Grand Rapids: Eerdmans, 2001), 166–84.

255. Cf. in this sense Stegemann, "'Die des Uria,'" 271, who states "that the Judaistic components of Matthean theology are at the very outset those of Hellenistic Judaism."

256. Cf. ibid., 273.

257. Cf. K. C. Wong, *Interkulturelle Theologie und multikulturelle Gemeinde im Matthäusevangelium* (NTOA 22; Göttingen: Vandenhoeck & Ruprecht, 1992), 125–54, who wants to explain the "Gentile- and Jewish-Christian" texts in terms of the equal status of Gentile and Jewish Christians, who got along quite well within the Matthean church.

258. Cf. K. Backhaus, "Entgrenzte Himmelsherrschaft: Zur Endeckung der paganen Welt im Matthäusevangelium," in *"Dies ist das Buch . . .": Das Matthäusevangelium (FS H. Frankemölle)* (ed. Rainer Kampling; Paderborn: Schöningh, 2004), 75–103.

259. Cf. Christian Strecker, "Das Geschichtsverständnis des Matthäus," in *Das Matthäus-Evangelium* (ed. Joachim Lange; WdF 525; Darmstadt: Wissenschaftliche Buchgesellschaft, 1980), 326–49.

There is also a historicizing of the traditional material, as expressed, for example, in the references to the particular stations in the course of Jesus's life (especially in Matt. 1–2), or the fulfillment of Scripture that takes place in the life of Jesus (see above, §8.3.8). Finally, we can perceive the institutionalization of the traditional material, which attains an institutionalized authority and importance beyond what we see in Mark (and Paul) (cf. Matt. 13:52; 16:17–18; 18:15–16; 23:34; 28:19).

8.4 Luke: Salvation and History

Luke introduces something completely new into early Christianity: *he writes a two-volume history of the origins of Christianity.* In doing so, he explicitly reflects on and justifies this new step (Luke 1:1–4), gives an extensive retrospective survey of the unique beginning (1:5–2:52), and in the Acts of the Apostles writes a sequel to the gospel. This *expansion of the framework within which the story is told* corresponds to a changed perspective: the spread of the gospel in the world, and hence the necessity of telling the story within that world's religious, economic, and political conditions, is the theme of Luke-Acts. The existence of numerous Christian congregations in the eastern Mediterranean, as far west as Rome, provides the historical framework for the evangelist's composition of both works between 90 and 100 CE. He obviously addresses primarily the propertied, educated urban class with an interest in religious and philosophical matters (cf., e.g., Luke 1:1–4; Acts 17:22–31; 19:23–40; 25:13–26:32), with the intent of persuading them of the trustworthiness of Christian teaching. Luke understands the gospel and Acts as a narrative unity, to be read and understood as a whole, a unified historical composition, so that any adequate interpretation must be based on both writings.[260] Luke 1:1, by referring to events that had been fulfilled "among us," already has in view the scenes portrayed in Acts. Luke 1:2 mentions not only those "who were eyewitnesses from the beginning," but also the "ministers of the word" like those represented in Acts. In turn, Acts 1:1 looks back on the "first writing" (πρῶτον λόγον). Luke does not begin with the term εὐαγγέλιον ("gospel," as in Mark 1:1), or βίβλος ("book," as in Matt. 1:1), but speaks of a διήγησις

260. Here the foundational work is Robert C. Tannehill, *The Narrative Unity of Luke-Acts: A Literary Interpretation* (2 vols.; Philadelphia: Fortress, 1986, 1990). Cf. also G. Wasserberg, *Aus Israels Mitte—Heil für die Welt* (BZNW 82; Berlin: de Gruyter, 1998), 31: "Luke-Acts is a self-contained narrative whole." J. Schröter, "Lukas als Historiograph," in *Die antike Historiographie und die Anfänge der christlichen Geschichtsschreibung* (ed. Eve-Marie Becker; BZNW 129; Berlin: de Gruyter, 2005), 237–62, works out the ways in which the gospel and Acts belong fundamentally together, but also points out differences that must not be overlooked: "The Gospel of Luke stands, so to speak, between the Gospel of Mark and the Acts of the Apostles, in that it takes up the Markan story of Jesus and so reworks it that it becomes one element in a more comprehensive historical work" (243).

(narrative/report);[261] he wants his work to be understood as a historical account. Above all, the prologue (Luke 1:1–4) clearly reveals Luke's literary ambitions as a writer and his theological intentions;[262] his work is the *expression of a changed historical consciousness and a different view of history*! Luke's modus operandi as an author is characterized by a historicizing of the traditions he has received, presenting them in a more biographical manner, as well as the use of rhetorical-dramatic formation of the composition.[263] As both historian and theologian, Luke is interested in the beginnings of Christian history and the continuity that derives from them. He is concerned to be complete, precise, and solid, thereby joining the tradition of ancient historiography, as indicated by the synchronisms and concern for precise dates in Luke 1:5; 2:1, 2; 3:1, 2; Acts 11:28; 18:12. Moreover, Luke's distinctive interest in dividing salvation history into separate but interrelated epochs is not without parallels among his contemporaries, since the historical monographs of Sallust in particular manifest a comparable structure.[264] The two volumes of Luke's twofold composition can thus be described as *historical monographs*, which does not alter the fact that Luke's portrayal of the life of Jesus in volume 1 is a gospel.[265] The widespread genre of the historical monograph made it possible for Luke to present the whole history of Jesus and his later effects by representing it as divided into individual *epochs*, in which "epochs" are not clearly separated temporal units but connected and overlapping periods characterized by specific perspectives. At the same time, Luke places his own stamp on this genre, for the "trustworthiness" (ἀσφάλεια, Luke 1:4) of what has happened does not rest on the events themselves, but on God as the Lord of history.[266] Speaking in literary terms, with his historical work Luke creates a piece of world literature! It is precisely as historian that he intends also to be a *narrator* or *storyteller*, addressing the emotions of his hearers/readers

261. According to Aelius Theon, *Prog.* 78.16–17, "The narrative/report [διήγημα] is a developed presentation of things that happened or as though they had happened."

262. For Luke's theological program cf. the foundational work of Günter Klein, "Lukas 1,1–4 als theologisches Programm," in *Das Lukas-Evangelium* (ed. G. Braumann; WdF 280; Darmstadt: Wissenschaftliche Buchgesellschaft, 1974). Cf. also Loveday Alexander, *The Preface to Luke's Gospel: Literary Convention and Social Context in Luke 1.1–4 and Acts 1.1* (Cambridge: Cambridge University Press, 1993).

263. Cf. here Manfred Diefenbach, *Die Komposition des Lukasevangeliums unter Berücksichtigung antiker Rhetorikelemente* (FTS 43; Frankfurt a.M.: Knecht, 1993). Illustrations of Luke's narrative technique are provided by his refinement of the episodic style of the traditions he received and his composition of longer textual units interpreted by framing them with introductions and conclusions. Additional characteristics of Luke's compositional technique are the additions, supplements, and narrative variations of the same story; cf. Anton Dauer, *Beobachtungen zur literarischen Arbeitstechnik des Lukas* (AMT 79; Frankfurt a.M.: A. Hain, 1990).

264. Cf. Eckhard Plümacher, "Neues Testament und hellenistische Form: Zur literarischen Gattung der lukanischen Schriften," *ThV* 14 (1979): 109–23.

265. Cf. ibid., 116–17.

266. Cf. also the use of καθεξῆς ("rightly ordered in a series").

and recounting the new "way of salvation" (Acts 16:17) found in faith in and discipleship to Jesus Christ.

8.4.1 Theology

The fact that the word θεός (God) is found 118 times in Luke and 168 times in Acts[267] is the expression of a considered theology within the framework of Luke's conception of salvation history.

God as the Lord of History

One basic idea permeates Luke's two volumes: God's promises have come to fulfillment in Jesus Christ, for in his story, and in the story of the spread of the gospel from Jerusalem to Rome, God demonstrates that he is the sole Lord of history. *This idea of fulfillment, in the form of dividing salvation history into distinct periods, determines the theological line along which the story is developed, in both the macrostructure and microstructure of Luke-Acts.* The macrostructure manifests an unmistakable correspondence between Luke 1:1 ("the events that have been fulfilled among us"), Luke 24:44–47 (the resurrected Jesus speaks: "These are my words that I spoke to you while I was still with you—that everything written about me in the law of Moses, the prophets, and the psalms must be fulfilled . . . that repentance and forgiveness of sins is to be proclaimed in his name to all nations, beginning from Jerusalem"), and Acts 28:28 (the last words of Paul: "Let it be known to you then that this salvation of God [τὸ σωτήριον τοῦ θεοῦ] has been sent to the Gentiles; they will listen"). The course of the gospel from Israel to the nations fulfills God's will for history, conceived before history began and now being eschatologically fulfilled. The microstructure of the distinct stages of salvation history is also characterized by this confidence that God's plan is being fulfilled. After the programmatic introduction of the concept of fulfillment in Luke 1:1; 2:40 emphasizes the wisdom of the boy Jesus ("The child grew and became strong, filled with wisdom; and the favor of God was upon him"); the next stage is Jesus's inaugural sermon in Nazareth as the beginning of his public ministry (Luke 4:21, "Then he began to say to them, 'Today this scripture has been fulfilled in your hearing'"). With the use of the verb συμπληρόω (completely fulfill), Luke connects the concept of fulfillment with the fundamental content

267. Cf. the survey in François Bovon, "Gott bei Lukas," in *Lukas in Neuer Sicht: Gesammelte Aufsätze* (ed. François Bovon; trans. Elizabeth Hartmann et al.; BTS 8; Neukirchen-Vluyn: Neukirchener Verlag, 1985), 98–119; Gnilka, "Gottesgedanken," 159–62; Karl Löning, "Das Gottesbild der Apostelgeschichte im Spannungsfeld von Frühjudentum und Fremdreligionen," in *Monotheismus und Christologie: Zur Gottesfrage im hellenistischen Judentum und im Urchristentum* (ed. Hans-Josef Klauck; QD 138; Freiburg i.B.: Herder, 1992), 88–117; Daniel Marguerat, "The God of Acts," in *The First Christian Historian: Writing the "Acts of the Apostles"* (ed. Daniel Marguerat; SNTSMS 121; Cambridge: Cambridge University Press, 2002), 85–108.

of God's saving acts in the Passion of Jesus and his ascension ("When the days drew near [συμπληροῦσθαι] for him to be taken up, he set his face to go to Jerusalem") and the gift of the Spirit to the nations (Acts 2:1, "When the day of Pentecost had come" [συμπληροῦσθαι]). The incorporation of the nations into God's saving acts in history and the fulfillment of God's promises to Israel are central in Luke 21:24 and 24:44; this theme is further developed in Acts 1:16; 3:18 in view of the gift of the Spirit, and then in Acts 19:21 is connected with Paul as *the* protagonist of the worldwide mission to the Gentiles. With the conclusion of his mission and turning toward Jerusalem, Rome already comes in view for the hearers/readers, and thus the present time of the Lukan church. Acts 3:18–21 illustrates Luke's fundamental concept of God and history: "In this way God fulfilled what he had foretold through all the prophets, that his Messiah would suffer. Repent therefore, and turn to God so that your sins may be wiped out, so that times of refreshing may come from the presence of the Lord, and that he may send the Messiah appointed for you, that is, Jesus, who must remain in heaven until the time of universal restoration [ἀποκαταστάσεως πάντων] that God announced long ago through his holy prophets." Luke thinks in terms of distinct periods of history, but each does not begin afresh without presuppositions. What has preceded always continues to be present and is developed further. His structuring of history begins with creation,[268] extends through the time of the law and the prophets, the time of Jesus, and the time of the church to the time of parousia/ultimate fulfillment, within which *the time of Jesus and the time of the church are clearly the center.*

Luke describes the time before Jesus's appearance in history as the epoch of promise (cf. Acts 7:2–53), while the advent of Jesus brings the time of fulfillment. So also, Luke 16:16 suggests such a periodization of history: "The law and the prophets were in effect until John came; since then the good news of the kingdom of God is proclaimed, and everyone tries to enter it by force." The mark of the new time is the preaching of the kingdom of God, which not only characterizes the ministry of Jesus but includes the time of the church (Acts 28:31). While the center of the Lukan conception of history is clearly recognizable, the transitions between the individual epochs are not so clearly marked. In Luke 16:16 it is not obvious whether John the Baptist still belongs within the epoch of the "law and the prophets" or already stands within the new time.

Hans Conzelmann argues for an *exclusive* meaning of ἀπὸ τότε (since then), and can consider the μέχρι Ἰωάννου (until John came) of Luke 16:16a as supporting his case.[269] The epoch of the law and the prophets extends through

268. One need only note Acts 4:24, "Sovereign Lord, who made the heaven and the earth, the sea, and everything in them," or 14:15, or 17:24.

269. Cf. Hans Conzelmann, *The Theology of St. Luke* (trans. Geoffrey Buswell; New York: Harper & Row, 1961), 16, and often elsewhere. Throughout this discussion it is important to note that the German title of Conzelmann's work is *Die Mitte der Zeit*, "The Middle of Time."

the time of John the Baptist, and the new time begins with the appearance of Jesus, *the middle of time*. Two additional arguments can be presented for this exclusive interpretation:

1. According to Luke 1:76, John is "prophet of the Most High," in contrast to Jesus, who is "Son of the Most High" (Luke 1:32).
2. Luke waits until after he has narrated the arrest and imprisonment of John to report Jesus's baptism (cf. Luke 3:19, 20 with 3:21–22), so that God is to be thought of as the One who baptizes Jesus.

On the other hand, there are arguments for an *inclusive* interpretation of Luke 16:16:

1. The synchronism of Luke 3:1–2 presents the Baptist as the beginning of the decisive time of salvation.[270]
2. Luke 3:18 designates the preaching of the Baptist as proclamation of the gospel; the Baptist preaches the coming Messiah (Luke 3:16–17).
3. According to Acts 1:21–22, the decisive epoch of salvation history begins with the appearance of John the Baptist.
4. The paralleling of the birth stories and their allocation in Acts 13:23–25 show that in Luke's understanding John and Jesus do not belong to different epochs of salvation history; the Baptist belongs within the exposition of the story of Jesus.

This pro and con shows that Luke 16:16 cannot be used as evidence for a precise Lukan division of salvation history into individual epochs.

While Jesus's ministry in Jerusalem, his death on the cross, and the resurrection form the conclusion of the time of Jesus, determining the beginning of the adjoining epoch in the history of salvation in Luke-Acts, *the time of the church*, is not so clear. For Hans Conzelmann, Luke portrays the time of the church as beginning with the outpouring of the Holy Spirit on Pentecost.[271] The problematic element in this arrangement is Jesus's ascension. Already in Luke 24:47 the risen Jesus has referred to the extension of the mission throughout the world (cf. Acts 1:8), and Luke 24:49 looks ahead to the giving of the Spirit (cf. Acts 1:4–5, 8). When the ascension takes place before the eyes of the disciples (Luke 24:51; Acts 1:9–11), they are legitimized as eyewitnesses; in view of the portrayal of the ministry of the apostles that is to follow, this was a decisive event. Moreover, the "forty days" (Acts 1:3) in which the Risen One instructs the apostles signal that the ascension is a decisive transition that brings the Easter event to an end. *The*

270. Thus the preaching of the kingdom of God begins with the Baptist. Cf. Werner Georg Kümmel, "Das Gesetz und die Propheten gehen bis Johannes," in *Das Lukas-Evangelium* (ed. G. Braumann; WdF 280; Darmstadt: Wissenschaftliche Buchgesellschaft, 1974), 398–415.

271. Conzelmann, *Theology of St. Luke*, 186, 206, and elsewhere.

ascension thus maintains the continuity between the time of Jesus and the time of the church, with the apostles as the bearers of this continuity. A rigid separation between the time of Jesus and the time of the church is thus not possible; rather, the ascension of Jesus makes possible the existence of the church in the world. The time of Jesus is for Luke the central time of salvation, from which the church derives its existence and which must constantly be its reference point.[272]

The discussion of the theological structure of Luke-Acts was determined for a long time by the theses of Hans Conzelmann, according to which Luke overcame the problem of the delay of the parousia by formulating an outline of salvation history. "Luke has understood that the expectation of an imminent end cannot be continued. That he works deliberately is clear from the fact that not only does the expectation of an imminent end simply disappear, but it is also replaced by a picture of salvation history."[273] Luke's outline of salvation is divided into three successive epochs,[274] in which God's plan for humanity from creation to the parousia of Christ is realized: (1) the time of Israel as the time of the law and the prophets (Luke 16:16); (2) the time of Jesus as the *middle of time*, a Satan-free period (Luke 4:14–22:2); (3) the time of the church as the time of the Spirit (Acts 2:1ff.). So also the ministry of Jesus can, in Conzelmann's view, be subdivided into three stages of Jesus's self-understanding: his "Messianic consciousness" (cf. Luke 3:21–9:17), his "Passion consciousness" (cf. Luke 9:18–19:27), and his "kingship consciousness" (cf. Luke 19:28–23:56). To be sure, there is an unmistakable periodization in the structure of Luke-Acts, and Luke resolutely thinks through the meaning of God's salvation within a historical framework. But more recent exegesis has found Conzelmann's precise division between these epochs of salvation history to be problematic, for Luke 16:16 is not to be understood in an exclusive sense, and Jesus's ascension forms the link between the time of Jesus and the time of the church that not only separates them but binds them together.

In contrast to Conzelmann, G. Schneider emphasizes that a bipartite structure is constitutive for Luke's understanding of salvation history, namely "that Luke joins the time of Jesus most closely to that of the church (within the perspective of the proclamation of the kingdom of God in both periods), and

272. Cf. Roloff, *Kirche im Neuen Testament*, 191: "The church, as it emerged through the witness of Jesus's messengers, stands in a continuity with the story of Jesus determined by God's own act."

273. Conzelmann, *Theology of the New Testament*, 149–50.

274. The essential points of Conzelmann's interpretation were anticipated in the work of Heinrich von Baer, *Der Heilige Geist in den Lukasschriften* (BWANT 39; Stuttgart: Kohlhammer, 1926), 108: "We have established that the concept of salvation history is the leading motif in Luke's composition." Cf. further the foundational work of Martin Dibelius and Eduard Lohse, "Lukas als Theologe der Heilsgeschichte," in *Das Lukas-Evangelium* (WdF 280; Darmstadt: Wissenschaftliche Buchgesellschaft, 1974), 64–90.

places both over against the time of the law and the prophets (Luke 16:16)."[275] Furthermore, Schneider does not evaluate the Lukan understanding of salvation history as a substitute for the imminent expectation of the parousia. "Instead, the orientation to salvation history serves to demonstrate the continuity of the proclamation from the prophets to Jesus, and from Jesus through his apostolic witnesses up to the real missionary to the Gentiles, Paul."[276] K. Löning disputes that Luke thought in terms of epochs of salvation history at all: "Instead, all the events reported by Luke belong within the history of Israel, so that some of them cannot be separated off and assigned to other epochs of history distinct from the time of Israel; it is impossible to assign the Israel thematic to a particular time within the Lukan narrative nexus that precedes the advent of Jesus, a time that is to be considered past from the perspective of Jesus's ministry."[277] M. Wolter speaks of only one epoch: "Luke narrates the history of the Christian-Jewish parting of the ways as in fact a section excised from the history of the people of God, that is, as *an epoch of the history of Israel*."[278]

Even if the precise determination of the particular divisions and transitions remains uncertain, the basic conception can still be discerned: God's acts in history are directed toward a goal that expresses in every epoch his *saving purpose*.[279] Events throughout salvation history bear the stamp of God's foreknowledge, advance planning, and providence (cf. Acts 1:16; 2:25, 31; 3:18, 20; 4:28; 7:52; 10:41; 13:24; 22:14; 26:16). God's sovereign will appoints and determines (Acts 2:23; 4:28; 5:38; 7:30; 10:42; 13:22, 36; 21:14), and the divine δεῖ (it must, it is necessary) determines the course of history: Jesus "must" be in the temple (Luke 2:49), he "must" preach (Luke 4:43), and he "must" go the way to Jerusalem and the Passion. So also, the step-by-step expansion of the gospel in the world stands under the divine plan. The first words of Peter are, "The scripture had to [δεῖ] be fulfilled" (Acts 1:16); despite all threats

275. Gerhard Schneider, *Die Apostelgeschichte* (HTKNT 5; Freiburg: Herder, 1980), 136–37; cf. also Jürgen Roloff, "Die Paulusdarstellung des Lukas," *EvT* 39 (1979): 528 note 53; Weiser, *Apostelgeschichte*, 31–32. For M. Korn, *Die Geschichte Jesu in veränderter Zeit* (WUNT 2.51; Tübingen: Mohr, 1993), 272: "The history of Jesus is the 'middle of time' in the factual sense. It divides history into the time of expectation and the time of fulfillment. Jesus's ministry, together with the works of the church in his name, constitute the eschatological time of salvation characterized by the preaching of the gospel (Luke 16:16)."

276. Schneider, *Apostelgeschichte*, 137.

277. Karl Löning, "Das Evangelium und die Kulturen: Heilsgeschichtliche und kulturelle Aspekte kirchlicher Realität in der Apostelgeschichte," *ANRW* 2.25.1 (Berlin: de Gruyter, 1982), 2608. Löning is correct that the Israel thematic is present throughout Luke-Acts; nonetheless, this does not mean that the two central epochs, the time of Jesus and the time of the church, are abolished.

278. Michael Wolter, "Das lukanische Doppelwerk als Epochengeschichte," in *Die Apostelgeschichte und die hellenistische Geschichtsschreibung* (ed. Cilliers Breytenbach and Jens Schröter; AJEC 57; Leiden: Brill, 2004), 272.

279. Cf. Siegfried Schulz, "Gottes Vorsehung bei Lukas," *ZNW* 54 (1963): 104–16.

and resistance, one "must" [δεῖ] obey God rather than any human authority (Acts 5:29); Peter comes unwillingly to realize that God has already determined that the Gentiles shall also hear the gospel (Acts 10:14–16), that God shows no partiality (Acts 10:34). And finally, Luke three times emphasizes that Paul "must" see Rome (Acts 19:21; 23:11; 27:24, an angel speaks to Paul: "Do not be afraid, Paul; you must [δεῖ] stand before the emperor").[280] Even the emperor serves the will of God, for it is at his order that Mary and Joseph go to Bethlehem (Luke 2:1–21), and the appeal to Caesar is what brings Paul to Rome (Acts 25:11). The speeches in Acts are for Luke particularly appropriate places to communicate to the hearers/readers "insight into the meaning of the historical moment concerned, but one which goes beyond the facts of history"[281] (cf. especially Acts 5:29–32; 10:34–43; 13:16–41; 17:22–31; 20:18–35).

God also demonstrates his lordship over history by his repeated interventions in the course of events. God guides history according to his purpose through the resurrection of Jesus Christ from the dead (see below, §8.4.2), through the Holy Spirit (see below, §8.4.3), through angels (see the subsection below, "God's Messengers: The Angels"), through prophecies (Luke 1:41–45, 76–79; 2:29–32, 36–38; Acts 11:27–30; 21:10–11), and especially through the call of Paul (Acts 9:3–19a; 22:6–16; 26:12–18) and his endowment with the ability to work miracles (cf. Acts 19:11, "God did extraordinary miracles through Paul"; cf. also Acts 13:6–12; 14:8–10; 16:16–40; 20:7–12; 28:3–9).

God, Israel, and the Nations

According to Luke, God's acts in history are fulfilled as the gift of the gospel of the kingdom of God to Israel (cf. Luke 4:43; 8:1; 16:16; Acts 8:12; 28:28, 31) and the nations (cf. Luke 2:32; 24:47; Acts 9:15; 11:1, 18; 28:28). Jesus's mission to Israel as presented in the gospel, and Acts as the history of the universal mission, are for Luke a unity, a single story whose plot line is nonetheless multilayered and not without tensions: (1) At the beginning of his two-volume work, Luke already draws the picture of the saving event of Jesus Christ as *in Israel and for Israel* (Luke 1:16, "He will turn many of the people of Israel to the Lord their God"). Luke 1:5–2:52 formulates God's salvific intention and thereby the theological foundation of his historical composition: Jesus Christ is the fulfillment of the hopes long cherished by the Jewish faithful (Luke 1:68, "Blessed be the Lord God of Israel, for he has looked favorably on his people and redeemed them"). In

280. Cf. C. Burfeind, "Paulus *muß* nach Rom," *NTS* 46 (2000): 83: "With his three missionary journeys of Paul, Luke has structured the story line of Acts from a theological point of view: first the Gentile mission is legitimized, then the independence of this mission from the synagogue, and finally the political relevance of this universalizing of Christianity becomes ever more clear."

281. Martin Dibelius, "The Speeches in Acts and Ancient Historiography," in *Studies in the Acts of the Apostles* (ed. Martin Dibelius and Heinrich Greeven; London: SCM, 1956), 140.

the figures of Zechariah, Elizabeth, Mary, and Joseph, the hearers/readers get acquainted with the contemporary world of Jewish hopes, hopes that begin to be fulfilled with the birth of John the Baptist[282] and Jesus of Nazareth. All this happens in and around the temple, the center of Jewish piety.[283] So also, Acts 1–5 communicates the image of a sincerely religious Israel that is being converted, as thousands of Jews are baptized—again, in the temple precincts (cf. Acts 2:41; 4:4; 5:12–16). Israel repents, so one can speak of the church's beginning "as a kind of Jerusalem springtime."[284] (2) With this laying of the foundation for Luke's story, *from the very beginning* there is a second central motif: out of Israel there grows *the people of God composed of Jews and Gentiles who believe in Christ as the bearer of the promises to Israel*. Simeon's prophecy in Luke 2:29–35 prominently demonstrates that the universality of salvation, which is constitutive for both Luke and Acts, is already anchored in the very beginning of the narrative. This anchoring is expressed emphatically by the combinations in the citation of Luke 2:29–32: "Master, now you are dismissing your servant in peace, according to your word; for my eyes have seen your salvation [τὸ σωτήριον], which you have prepared in the presence of all peoples [τῶν λαῶν], a light for revelation to the Gentiles [ἐθνῶν] and for glory to your people Israel ['Ισραήλ]." At the same time, the negative reaction of parts of Israel already come into view: "This child is destined for the falling and the rising of many in Israel, and to be a sign that will be opposed" (Luke 2:34; cf. 1:16). *The mission to the Gentiles did not begin only after parts of Israel rejected the gospel, for God's saving will was directed from the very beginning to both Israel and the nations.*[285] In addition to Simeon's prophecy, numerous other texts

282. On this point cf. C. G. Müller, *Mehr als ein Prophet: Die Charakterzeichnung Johannes des Täufers im lukanischen Erzählwerk* (HBS 31; Freiburg: Herder, 2001), 296: "Except for Jesus, John is the only main character in Luke-Acts whose whole life is narrated, from the special circumstances of his birth to his death and his continuing influence after his death. This in itself makes clear that for the narrator Luke, John the Baptist is not a minor character but a protagonist in the story he narrates."

283. On Luke's understanding of the temple, cf. Michael Bachmann, *Jerusalem und der Tempel* (BWANT 109; Stuttgart: Kohlhammer, 1980) and Heiner Ganser-Kerperin, *Das Zeugnis des Tempels: Studien zur Bedeutung des Tempelmotivs im lukanischen Doppelwerk* (NTA, Münster: Aschendorff, 2000).

284. Gerhard Lohfink, *Die Sammlung Israels* (SANT 39; Munich: Kösel, 1975), 55.

285. Cf. Michael Wolter, "'Reich Gottes' bei Lukas," *NTS* 41 (1995): 560, according to whom the Gentile mission "was for Luke always a part of God's salvific plan for history. Precisely this state of affairs, that with the inbreaking of the kingdom salvation is being sent to the ἔθνη (nations) in the same way as to Israel, is what Israel fails to understand—a lack of understanding documented by the hardening of their hearts"; Wasserberg, *Israels Mitte*, 134–37 and elsewhere; C.-P. März, "The theologische Interpretation der Jesus-Gestalt bei Lukas," in *Gedenkt an das Wort: Festschrift für Werner Vogler zum 65. Geburtstag* (ed. Christoph Kähler et al.; Leipzig: Evangelische Verlagsanstalt, 1999), 149: "The beginning of Jesus's ministry directed to Israel thus seems to be already determined by those impulses that will eventuate in his exaltation

also point in this direction. Only in Luke 3:6 is the text from Isaiah, already present in Luke's source, extended to include Isa. 40:5, so that the content of John's message is universalized: καὶ ὄψεται πᾶσα σὰρξ τὸ σωτήριον τοῦ θεοῦ (and all flesh shall see the salvation of God). The genealogy of Jesus in Luke 3:23–38 not only emphasizes that Jesus is directly the Son of God (cf. Luke 1:35), but by referring to Adam indicates that all human beings are called to salvation. Jesus's inaugural sermon in Nazareth (Luke 4:16–30) ends up in a hostile rejection by his own people. The parable of the Great Supper in Luke 14:16–24, unlike the Matthean version, reports two invitations from the Lord, giving as the reason for the second invitation: "Compel people to come in, so that my house may be filled" (Luke 14:23b). God's great banquet hall will be filled with guests other than those expected (Luke 24:24, "For I tell you, none of those who were invited will taste my dinner"). Especially important is Luke 24, a transitional chapter in which both lines continue and lead into the story in Acts.[286] The resurrection of Jesus as the hope of Israel stands at the center of the Emmaus story of 24:13–35, while 24:47–48 formulates universally, "that repentance and forgiveness of sins is to be proclaimed in his name to all nations [πάντα τὰ ἔθνη], beginning from Jerusalem. You are witnesses of these things." This verse not only requires that the story be continued but already anticipates Acts 1:8. Does the expression πάντα τὰ ἔθνη here include or exclude Israel from "all the nations"? With only two exceptions, Luke always uses λαός to designate the Jewish people (eighty-two times in Luke-Acts),[287] while ἔθνη as a rule refers to non-Jews (exceptions: Acts 24:17; 28:19). To be sure, the reference to Jerusalem and the further course of the narrative in Acts speak for an inclusive interpretation of this reference, i.e., Israel is included here in the proclamation of the Christian message.[288]

In Acts 1:6–7, the question about the time of the restoration of the kingdom to Israel remains unanswered. Instead, the disciples are commissioned to be witnesses "in Jerusalem, in all Judea and Samaria, and to the ends of the earth" (Acts 1:8b). *Within the narrative, the Risen One himself twice legitimizes the universal preaching of the gospel* (Luke 24:47; Acts 1:8)! In the course of the

and the sending of his messengers into the worldwide mission. His way turns out to generate a separation within Israel as a differentiation phase that brings the offer of salvation before the people, an offer that though often refused was not thereby destroyed, but now seeks its way to the Gentiles without thereby losing its reference to Israel. The open ending of Acts 28:30–31 shows that this process has not yet come to an end."

286. On the transitional passages in Luke-Acts, cf. Héctor Sánchez, *Das lukanische Geschichtswerk im Spiegel heilsgeschichtlicher Übergänge* (PThSt 29; Paderborn: Schöningh, 2001).

287. Within the narrative the Jewish people in its historical reality as λαός is a flexible reality, mostly identical with the ὄχλος (crowd) that at first joyfully welcomes the message of Christ; only afterward do the majority reject it. On the complex details, cf. Daniel Marguerat, "Juden und Christen im lukanischen Doppelwerk," *EvT* 54 (1994): 241–64.

288. Cf. Wasserberg, *Israels Mitte*, 200–203.

narrative, this program and its goal are transformed into practice; after the successful preaching to Israel in Acts 1–5[289] and the crisis resulting in the death of Stephen (Acts 6:8–7:60), the preaching mission proceeds to the area around Israel (Acts 8), then reaches its decisive transition in the Cornelius narrative of Acts 10:1–11:18: God himself turns to the Gentile world (cf. Acts 10:4, 13ff., 28b, "God has shown me that I should not call anyone profane or unclean"; 10:35, "In every nation [ἐν παντὶ ἔθνει] anyone who fears him and does what is right is acceptable to him"; 11:9, 17–18). Peter's experience of gradually learning the will of God illustrates to the Lukan church the far-ranging implications of the event, which cannot be reversed by later opposing forces (cf. Acts 15:1–2) but leads to the table fellowship between believers in Christ from both Jewish and Gentile backgrounds (cf. Acts 15:22–29).

In this process the *person of Paul* plays a decisive role, for the story line of Acts really revolves around the figure of Paul (see below, §8.4.7). For Luke, the converted Jew Paul is the primary witness for the continuity of salvation history in the turning point of early Christian mission history from the Jews[290] to the Gentiles. He appears almost unnoticed as an "extra" in the scene at Acts 7:58, only to later become the real hero of the book.[291] For Luke, he is not, like the apostles, one of the original witnesses who laid the foundations for the faith, but *the* representative of the second Christian generation. According to Luke, Paul embodied the Jewish way of life (cf. Acts 16:3, the circumcision of Timothy; Acts 18:18b; 21:23ff., Nazirite vow and sacrifice in the temple), at the same time becoming an exponent of the universal preaching of the gospel. Using this development in early Christianity as a model, Luke's portrayal of Paul is both a description and an apology for his life. The theological aim of Luke's portrayal of Paul intensifies in the final third of Acts (19:21–28:31), which describes Paul's way from Jerusalem to Rome. In the course of telling this story, Luke portrays the developing antithetical relation between Jerusalem and Rome, which is of fundamental importance for his narrative. Jerusalem appears at first in Luke's story as the place of Israel's salvation. Here the earliest Christian community lives in exemplary fellowship (Acts 2:42–47; 4:32–35), so that Jerusalem represents the continuity

289. Lohfink, *Die Sammlung Israels*, 55, formulates the program of Acts 1–5 as follows: "In the time of the earliest apostolic preaching, the true Israel is gathered from among the Jewish people. And this Israel that hardened itself by its rejection of Jesus lost its claim to be the true people of God—and became Judaism instead."

290. Luke's language is here particularly striking, for Ἰουδαῖοι appears only 5 times in the gospel (Luke 7:3; 23:3, 37–38, 51), but 79 times in Acts. Here the Ἰουδαῖοι become increasingly the opponents of the spread of the gospel (clear from 9:22–23 on; cf. 12:3; 13:5, 43, 45; 14:1, 4; 16:3; 17:1, 5, 10, 17; 18:5, 12, 14, 19, 28; 19:13, 33; and elsewhere).

291. For an analysis of the biographical Pauline passages in Acts, see especially Christoph Burchard, *Der dreizehnte Zeuge: Traditions- und kompositionsgeschichtliche Untersuchungen zu Lukas' Darstellung der Frühzeit des Paulus* (FRLANT 103; Göttingen: Vandenhoeck & Ruprecht, 1970).

between Israel and the church.[292] At the same time, however, Jerusalem is the place where the leaders of Israel and, at their instigation, the Jews/the people increasingly harden themselves against the Christian message. Just as the apostles and the earliest church are constantly exposed to threats and persecution (cf. Acts 4:1–22; 6:8–15; 7:54–60; 8:1), so also Paul becomes a suffering witness (cf. Acts 21:27–22:21; 23:1–11, 12–22). By rejecting the testimony of the Twelve, the earliest church, and Paul, Jerusalem is transformed from the place of salvation to the place of disaster—the place where God's salvation is rejected. Luke makes it clear, however, that God has not bound the church, as the bearer of the promises to Israel, to Jerusalem. By the mission to all nations, God has opened up a new scope of operations represented by the world capital, the city of Rome (cf. Acts 9:15, "He is an instrument whom I have chosen to bring my name before Gentiles and kings and before the people of Israel"). The turning point in salvation history from the Jews to all nations corresponds, in Luke's perspective, to the turn from Jerusalem to Rome.[293] Luke thus tells the story of Paul on the model of the historical development at the end of which stands the Gentile Christian church at the close of the first century, and also his own church. In view of the final parting of the ways with Judaism, the story of Paul legitimizes the one church composed of Gentile Christians and Jewish Christians. "Paul has become for Luke's church a figure with whom it can identify; in his story it gains insight into the great turn that has taken place in its own history."[294] The concluding scene of Acts makes Paul's centrality programmatically clear (Acts 28:17–31), while also raising numerous historical, legal, and theological questions. Historically, it is clear from Rom. 16 that Paul knew many members of the Roman church. Yet there is no real meeting between Paul and the Roman church in Acts (cf. Acts 28:16). Instead, Paul—as always in Acts—first makes contact with the local synagogue (cf. Acts 28:17–28). In Rome too it is only after his message has been rejected by the Jews that Paul turns to the Gentiles. This takes up the line of Acts 13:46 ("Then both Paul and Barnabas spoke out boldly, saying, 'It was necessary that the word of God should be spoken first to you. Since you reject it and judge yourselves to be unworthy of eternal life, we are now turning to the Gentiles'"; cf. Acts 18:6), at the same time striking the final chord of the two-volume work:[295] "Let it be known to you then that this

292. Lohfink, *Die Sammlung Israels*, 93–99.

293. Cf. Eckhard Plümacher, "Rom in der Apostelgeschichte," in *Geschichte und Geschichten: Aufsätze zur Apostelgeschichte und zu den Johannesakten* (ed. Eckhard Plümacher et al.; WUNT 170; Tübingen: Mohr Siebeck, 2004), 135–69.

294. Cf. Jürgen Roloff, "Die Paulus-Darstellung des Lukas," in *Exegetische Verantwortung in der Kirche: Aufsätze* (ed. Martin Karrer; Göttingen: Vandenhoeck & Ruprecht, 1990), 520.

295. Cf. Plümacher, "Geschichte und Geschichten," 135: "The weight of Paul's last words in Acts can hardly be overestimated, since they proclaim nothing less than the end of the whole epoch and, at the same time, the breaking in of a new one."

salvation of God has been sent to the Gentiles; they will listen" (Acts 28:28). With the expression τὸ σωτήριον τοῦ θεοῦ (the salvation of God), Luke intentionally takes up the prophecy of Simeon of Luke 2:30 and the testimony of John the Baptist in 3:6 (τὸ σωτήριον is found only in Luke 2:30; 3:6; Acts 28:28) in order to emphasize both the continuity and the discontinuity of the event: from Israel sprang God's salvation, which had been promised to Israel and has not gone over to all nations without breaking the continuity of God's promises to Israel (cf. Acts 13:23; 15:14–17; 28:20).[296] While in Luke 2:30 and 3:6 salvation is for all peoples, Jews and Gentiles alike, in Acts 28:28 only the Gentiles are the addressees of God's message of salvation, and it is explicitly said that "they will hear." Paul is the witness and protagonist of this development, a development that has proceeded according to God's will and will henceforth determine the Christian mission.

Does this mean that Luke hereby formulates a fundamental principle of turning away from unbelieving Israel/the Jews, a principle that can never be revised? This is a difficult question to answer, for Luke's language is not clear.[297] On the one hand, Israel is not an acting subject in the narrative (in contrast to λαός, ὄχλος, and the Ἰουδαῖοι), but a category of salvation history. Israel is and remains *the* bearer of God's promise (Luke 1:16, 54, 68, 80; 2:25, 32, 34; Acts 1:6; 2:36; 4:10; 5:31; 7:23, 37; 10:36; 13:17, 23–24; 23:6; 26:6–7; 28:20) and therefore cannot be rejected or replaced.[298] On the other hand, Acts 13:46–48; 15:14; 28:25–28 suggest just such a replacement; according to Luke

296. Differently Jacob Jervell, *Die Apostelgeschichte* (17th ed.; KEK 3; Göttingen: Vandenhoeck & Ruprecht, 1998), 92–93: "The history of Israel does not come to an end, but proceeds straight ahead into the church, namely as the history of the one people of God." But one can hardly say "straight ahead" as a description of what happens in the book of Acts!

297. It is thus no surprise that there is a broad range of opinions in the secondary literature. Among those who speak of a lasting exclusion of unbelieving Israel are Ernst Haenchen, *Die Apostelgeschichte* (15th ed.; Meyer-Kommentar; Göttingen: Vandenhoeck & Ruprecht, 1977), 112: "Luke no longer hopes, as did Paul, for the conversion of Israel" [These words do not appear in the 14th German edition from which the English translation was made, but cf. Ernst Haenchen, *The Acts of the Apostles: A Commentary* (Philadelphia: Westminster, 1971), 126, 128–29.—MEB]; Heikki Räisänen, "The Redemption of Israel," in *Luke-Acts: Scandinavian Perspectives* (ed. P. Luomanen; Göttingen: Vandenhoeck & Ruprecht, 1991), 94–114. Among those who understand Luke to affirm a future salvation for Jews who do not believe in Christ are: Helmut Merkel, "Israel in lukanischen Werk," *NTS* 40 (1994): 371–98; Robert C. Tannehill, "Israel in Luke-Acts," *JBL* 104 (1985): 69–85; Klaus Haacker, "Das Bekenntnis des Paulus zur Hoffnung Israels nach der Apostelgeschichte des Lukas," *NTS* 31 (1985): 437–51. This interpretation is also supported by Luke 13:35 and the apokatastasis concept in Acts 3:21. Daniel Marguerat, "The Enigma of the End of Acts," in *The First Christian Historian: Writing the "Acts of the Apostles"* (ed. Daniel Marguerat; SNTSMS 121; Cambridge: Cambridge University Press, 2002), 205–30, argues that Luke intentionally leaves the conclusion of Acts open-ended, so that readers themselves can and must continue to develop the story of Paul and the relation between church and synagogue in their own times.

298. R. von Bendemann, "Paulus und Israel in der Apostelgeschichte des Lukas," in *Ja und Nein: Christliche Theologie im Angesicht Israels; Festschrift zum 70. Geburtstag von Wolfgang*

2:34 Israel is divided by the revelation in Christ,[299] and in Acts 9:15 and 28:28 the Gentiles as independent receivers of salvation are clearly placed before Israel. These conflicting statements are inherent in the matter itself, for Luke wants to show his Gentile Christian churches from the very beginning[300] how God's salvation promised to Israel has found its way to the Gentiles and yet has remained true to itself. By so doing he wanted to avoid the idea that the Israel concept was itself divided, but on the other hand needed to portray the historical development from empirical Israel/the Jews to the Gentiles. How he himself imagined the solution to this problem is possibly set forth in Acts 28:20b: "It is for the sake of the hope of Israel that I am bound with this chain." The proclamation of the gospel is understood, including its connection with Paul and despite the continuing opposition of the Jews, as the abiding hope for Israel. *Luke connects opposition to the gospel primarily with the Jews (and the people that partly act at their initiative), but binds the promise and hope exclusively to Israel, while at the same time making it clear that this hope finds its fulfillment in the church (comprised of Gentiles, God-fearers, and Jews who believe in Christ).*

God as Father and Advocate of the Poor

In Luke too God appears in the first place as the Father of Jesus Christ. Thus the twelve-year-old Jesus says to Mary and Joseph, "Did you not know that I must be in my Father's house?" Jesus speaks of God as his Father in numerous other places (e.g., Luke 9:26; 10:22; 22:29; 24:49) or is portrayed as Son of God (Luke 3:22; 9:35; 10:21; 22:42; 23:46). The disciples are allowed to share in this special relationship with God; they too may call God their Father and imitate God's character in their own lives (Luke 6:36; 11:2, 13; 12:30, 32).

As the Father of Jesus Christ, God reveals himself as the merciful and gracious one, who intervenes for the weak, the lost, and those without rights, changing the circumstances in unexpected ways.[301] The Magnificat formulates this agenda programmatically: "His mercy is for those who fear him from generation to generation. He has shown strength with his arm; he has scattered the proud in the thoughts of their hearts. He has brought down the powerful from their thrones, and lifted up the lowly; he has filled the hungry with good things, and sent the rich away empty. He has helped his servant Israel, in remembrance of his mercy" (Luke 1:50–54). In the Gospel of Luke, this is the God whom Jesus proclaims and the model he adopts for his own life. Thus

Schrage (ed. Klaus Wengst et al.; Neukirchen-Vluyn: Neukirchener Verlag, 1998), 301–2, rightly emphasizes this.

299. Cf. Lohfink, *Die Sammlung Israels*, 30.

300. On the relation of Luke 1:1–4 as prologue and Acts 28:17–31 as epilogue to Luke-Acts, cf. Loveday Alexander, "Reading Luke-Acts from Back to Front," in *The Unity of Luke-Acts* (ed. J. Verheyden; BETL 142; Louvain: Leuven University Press, 1999), 419–46.

301. On this point cf. Schottroff and Stegemann, *Jesus and the Hope of the Poor*, 67–120.

Jesus rejects worldly power and splendor, as offered by the devil in Luke 4:6. God is near to the poor (2:7, 24; 16:9–31), and distant from the rich (6:20–26; 16:9–31). God stands beside those who have no rights (18:1–8), the despised and disdained (18:9–14), and those who cannot appeal to their genealogy and social class (7:1–10; 10:25–37; 17:11–19). God breaks through and reverses earthly standards (14:15–24); God alone looks within, into people's hearts: "God knows your hearts; for what is prized by human beings is an abomination in the sight of God" (16:15). God thereby demonstrates in a new way that he is the God of the ancestors (Acts 3:13), as the God of Abraham, Isaac, and Jacob (Luke 13:16, 28; 19:9; 20:37; Acts 13:26), who shows his faithfulness in new ways. He is the seeking God, as underscored by the parables of the Lost Sheep, the Lost Coin, and the Lost Son in Luke 15. He is the God who hears the prayers of his children (Luke 11:5–13; 18:1–8). He accepts and forgives (Luke 7:36–50; 18:13; 19:3–4), and he turns toward those who know they are dependent on him for everything. And finally: he removes the barriers that separate people (Acts 10, 15) and creates for himself one new people.

God and the Gods

Paul's speech on the Areopagus in Acts 17:19–34 is of extraordinary importance for the Lukan understanding of God.[302] In the Acts speeches delivered by the apostle, God is the one who raised Jesus Christ from the dead (Acts 2:24, 36; 3:13, 15; 4:10; 5:31; 10:40; 13:30) and therefore the one human beings should confess as the living God (cf. Acts 14:15–17). Paul's speech in Athens opens up a new cultural horizon. In the center of ancient intellectual history, the apostle does not simply reject Greco-Roman polytheism but turns it into an argument for the truth of his own message (Acts 17:22–23).[303] In identifying the "unknown god" with the one true God, Paul has made an explicit point of contact with the prevailing culture, with the goal of integrating Greco-Roman concepts of God within the understanding of God that he proclaims. He explicitly affirms the omnipresence of God (vv. 27–28), at the same time rejecting all attempts to objectify this divine presence. The decisive intellectual argument that stands in the background is: *a god in the plural is no God at all.* People of Greco-Roman religious background could turn to the one true God without completely throwing overboard the ideas of their own

302. The basic study is still Martin Dibelius, "Paul on the Areopagus," in *Studies in the Acts of the Apostles* (ed. Martin Dibelius and Heinrich Greeven; London: SCM, 1956), 26–77, who is entirely right in calling this passage "a climax of the book" (26). Jervell, *Apostelgeschichte*, 454, is entirely wrong in regarding this passage as secondary.

303. J. Jervell has an entirely different understanding of the Lukan Paul: "What we find here is thus pure paganism. Precisely this is what Athens means for him" (Jervell, *Apostelgeschichte*, 453). In contrast to this view, see the argument developed in M. Lang, "Leben in der Zeit: Pragmatische Studien aus der römischen Sicht zur 'christlichen Lebenskunst' anhand des lukanischen Paulusbildes" (ThD diss., Martin-Luther-Universität, Halle-Wittenberg, 2007), 179–232.

culture.[304] At the same time, Luke marks out with great precision the point where theology and philosophy must part company: the resurrection of Jesus Christ from the dead (v. 32).

Acts 17:19–34 is not only soaked with local color[305] and full of religious and philosophical allusions (see below, §8.4.5), but is a basic text for the Lukan understanding of God. *The God of Israel revealed in Jesus Christ is the one true God, the one who stands behind all sincere worship of God, the one who can be found by all.* Luke is clearly appealing to the more educated people of his time, for he deliberately enriches the Areopagus speech with material from the world of ancient philosophy: Paul is paralleled to Socrates, who was also accused of introducing "foreign gods/demons" (cf. Acts 17:18 with Xenophon, *Mem.* 1.1; Plato, *Apol.* 29D). In Acts 17:28 ("For 'In him we live and move and have our being'; as even some of your own poets have said, 'For we too are his offspring'"), Paul makes a positive use of a fundamental idea of Greek theology and philosophy (one need only note Xenophon, *Mem.* 1.4.18; 4.3.14; Plato, *Leg.* 10.899D; Aratus, *Phaen.* 1–5). As in other passages of his two-volume work (cf. Luke 1:1–4, literary proem; Luke 1:5–2:52, birth and childhood stories in the biographical tradition of Hellenism; Luke 24:50–53/ Acts 1:1–8, apotheosis; Acts 2:42–47; 4:32–37, the Hellenistic ideal of community; Acts 5:19; 20:35; 26:14, key sayings and adages of the hero), Luke shows that he knows his way around in the intellectual world of antiquity and so is an author whom people of that world can trust.

God's Messengers: The Angels

Luke has a conspicuous interest in angels (ἄγγελος occurs 24 times in the gospel, 21 times in Acts); they appear with particular frequency at the beginning and end of the gospel. An angel "of the Lord" (Luke 1:11) announces the birth of the Baptist and of Jesus (Luke 1:8–20, 26–38; 2:8–12). So also angels announce the message of Jesus's resurrection, ascension, and coming again (Luke 24:4–7:23; Acts 1:10–11). Angels take care of the righteous dead (Luke 16:22) and accompany the return of the Son of Man. As spiritual beings in the service of God, they belong entirely to the divine world and cannot die (Luke 20:36). In the stories of Acts, angels are active in miracles of deliverance from prison (Acts 5:19; 12:7–11);[306] their saving intervention advances the mission (cf. Acts 12:4–11), as does the announcement of the divine will through angels in Acts 8:26; 10:3, 7, 22; 11:13; and in 27:23–24,

304. This is also seen in the accommodation to Hellenistic predicates for God, as in Luke's inclusion of Q 6:35c–d (sons/children of the Most High; God's kindness); cf. Heil, *Lukas und Q*, 272.

305. Winfried Elliger, *Paulus in Griechenland: Philippi, Thessaloniki, Athen, Korinth* (Stuttgart: Verlag Katholisches Bibelwerk, 1987), 193ff.

306. On the miracles of liberation, cf. J. Hintermaier, *Die Befreiungswunder der Apostelgeschichte* (BBB 143; Berlin: Philo, 2003).

where an angel comes to Paul and reveals that he will stand before Caesar in accordance with God's will.

The angels function as spokespersons for God, mediating God's gracious and caring presence and carrying out God's saving or punishing (Acts 12:23) intervention. Where angels appear, something new is revealed, and the history of salvation is led forward or even turned in a new direction.

God's Word: The Scripture

Within the salvation-historical frame that constitutes the plot of Luke's historical composition, he gives a central importance to the Scripture.[307] The gospel and Acts include about fifty citations from the Old Testament (LXX)[308] but, noticeably, only from particular sections. With only one exception (Luke 2:23–24), the only citations from the Pentateuch were already contained in his sources; Luke's own emphasis lies almost exclusively on the Psalms and especially the Prophets. Luke's theological program is thereby correlated to his appropriation of the Scripture: *in Jesus Christ God's promises are being fulfilled*. This basic idea is exemplified at the end of the Gospel of Luke, formulated as a saying of the risen Jesus: "These are my words that I spoke to you while I was still with you—that everything written about me in the law of Moses, the prophets, and the psalms must be fulfilled (δεῖ πληρωθῆναι πάντα)" (Luke 24:44; cf. 24:7, 25–27, 44–46). In Acts 3:18, this aspect is taken up and bound exclusively to the prophetic writings ("In this way God fulfilled what he had foretold through all the prophets, that his Messiah would suffer"). The idea of the suffering, death, and resurrection of the Messiah is already found in the Scripture and now has been fulfilled in the Christ event. For Luke, the Scripture refers to the resurrection and offers proof of its reality.

Luke's preference for the prophets (especially Deutero-Isaiah)[309] is already seen in the opening chapters. The substance of the quotation from Isa.

307. On Luke's use and understanding of Scripture, cf. Traugott Holtz, *Untersuchungen über die alttestamentlichen Zitate bei Lukas* (TU 104; Berlin: Akadamie Verlag, 1968); Martin Rese, *Alttestamentliche Motive in der Christologie des Lukas* (SNT 1; Gütersloh: Güterloher Verlagshaus, 1969); J. Jervell, "Die Mitte der Schrift: Zum lukanischen Verständnis des Alten Testaments," in *Die Mitte des Neuen Testaments: Einheit und Vielfalt neutestamentlicher Theologie; Festschrift für Eduard Schweizer zum siebzigsten Geburtstag* (ed. Ulrich Luz and Hans Weder; Göttingen: Vandenhoeck & Ruprecht, 1983), 79–96; Craig A. Evans and James A. Sanders, eds., *Luke and Scripture* (Minneapolis: Fortress, 1993); D. Rusam, *Das Alte Testament bei Lukas* (BZNW 112; Berlin: de Gruyter, 2003).

308. Cf. the catalog in Schneider, *Apostelgeschichte*, 234–35.

309. R. von Bendemann, "'Trefflich hat der Heilige Geist durch Jesaja, den Propheten, gesprochen . . .' (Apg 28,25): Zur Bedeutung von Jesaja 6,9f für die Geschichtskonzeption des lukanischen Doppelwerkes," in *Das Echo des Propheten Jesaja: Beiträge zu seiner vielfältigen Rezeption* (ed. N. C. Baumgart et al.; LTB 1; Münster: Lit, 2004), 72, rightly emphasizes: "The particular significance of Isaiah for Luke-Acts is not the result of an unbroken faithfulness to the Bible per se. It is rather the result of a decidedly new reading with a very different symbolic system, and already presupposes a decidedly Christian appropriation of the great prophet."

40:3–5 in Luke 3:4–6 is taken up in Acts 28:28 (Isa. 40:5 LXX, τὸ σωτήριον τοῦ θεοῦ), forming an inclusio that expresses Luke's universal perspective: by their acceptance of the gospel, all can participate in God's saving act. Luke places another hermeneutical key in the hands of the hearers/readers with his quotation of Isa. 61:6–7/58:6 LXX in Jesus's inaugural sermon in Nazareth (Luke 4:18–19). God's liberating good news for the poor is put into effect now, in the appearance of Jesus (Luke 4:21, "Today this scripture has been fulfilled in your hearing"). The citations in the Passion story also constitute a Lukan emphasis, again elaborating the event and interpreting its meaning. The citation of Isa. 53:12 LXX in Luke 22:37 is also explicitly bound to the concept of fulfillment, and the summary reminders of the Scripture in Luke 18:31; 24:25–27, 44–47 serve to prove that the suffering, death, and resurrection of Jesus Christ fulfill the plan of God formulated in the Scripture. Then in Luke 24:45–49 the theme of the hermeneutical horizon of reception of the Scripture is made explicit: the Passion and resurrection of the Christ to which the Scripture attests have as their goal the forgiveness of the sins of all nations. This means that the universal perspective of the proclamation of the gospel to all nations is according to the Scripture and was taught and practiced by Jesus himself. The selection of Matthias to take Judas's place in Acts 1:16, 20 is likewise understood in terms of the divine "must," which now comes to fulfillment. The majority of citations in Acts are seen from the perspective of the divine promise (cf. Acts 2:16–21, 25–28, 30–31, 34–35; 3:22–23, 25; 4:11, 25–26; 7:42–43; 8:32–33; 13:33–35, 40–41; 15:15–17; 28:26–27),[310] according to which the actual course of mission history, with its turn to the Gentiles, corresponds to the eschatological will of God written in Scripture. In accord with his theological program in Luke 1:1–4 (1:1, "the events that have been fulfilled among us"), by his reception of Scripture the evangelist emphasizes *the reliability of the promises*, i.e., *the faithfulness of God*. The horizon of promise is the theological center of the Old Testament citations in Luke-Acts. In the Christ event God keeps faith with his own promise, in that he creates the church from within Israel.[311]

In summary: The *literary continuity of Luke-Acts* is the direct expression of its *theological continuity*, namely the continuity of God's acts in history. Luke's concern is to make clear to the third Christian generation its location in salvation history; thereby also to assure it that the Christian witness it has received is in continuity with the prophets, with Jesus, and with the eyewitnesses of his ministry; and thus ultimately to emphasize God's faithfulness to the divine promises.

310. On the citation of Isa. 6:9–10 LXX in Acts 28:26–27, cf. Rusam, *Das Alte Testament bei Lukas*, 437ff., who states: "The question is not whether or not there is any hope for the Jews. The quotation has nothing to say about this."

311. Cf. Lohfink, *Die Sammlung Israels*, 96.

8.4.2 Christology

As with the other gospels, so also with Luke: we can infer the evangelist's Christology primarily from the way he describes Jesus's relation to God, from the variety of christological themes and titles he uses, and—especially so in the case of Luke—from the way he deals with Jesus within the narrative structure of the composition as a whole. The Christology of the Third Gospel is embedded in the way in which the evangelist thinks of history as divided into specific epochs, which facilitates his use of new narrative perspectives. Thus Jesus's life and ministry appears as a special segment of God's saving action in history, the *middle of time*. At the same time, this segment remains a part of the narrative composition as a whole. It begins with the story of Jesus's origins.

Jesus's Origins

In literary terms, Luke 1:5–2:52 is a prologue, since the synchronism of 3:1–2 clearly begins a new section. All the same, such descriptions as "prologue" or "birth and childhood stories" are misleading, if they are understood to refer to Luke 1–2 as only a preliminary or introductory section with no essential function in the larger work.[312] What we actually have here is the narrative presentation of Jesus's origins, portraying his special relation to God and thus the *foundation* of the saving event as a whole. In the manner of Hellenistic literature, and in clear competition with the stylized stories about Augustus that were widespread under the Pax Romana,[313] Luke underscores the extraordinary origins of his hero, and with an artistry[314] that also uses Jewish traditions[315] to compose this prelude to his two-volume work.[316] At first, Jesus's relation to John the Baptist is presented by placing them in parallel: much more than any of the other evangelists, the Baptist is a parallel figure to Jesus (cf. Luke

312. As in the work of Conzelmann, *Theology of St. Luke*, 16, 18ff., who does not really deal with Luke 1–2, and begins with John the Baptist at 3:1 under the heading "Prologue."

313. This becomes clear when one compares Luke 2:1, 14: "Glory to God in the highest heaven, and on earth peace among those whom he favors!" Ovid, *Metamorphoses* 15.830, praises the son of the Caesar, who has just been murdered, with the words, "Whatsoever habitable land the earth contains shall be his, and the sea also shall come beneath his sway. When peace has been bestowed on all lands he shall turn his mind to the rights of citizens, and as a most righteous jurist promote the laws."

314. For evidence and argument that Luke himself is the composer of this section, cf. Walter Radl, *Der Ursprung Jesu: Traditionsgeschichtliche Untersuchungen zu Lukas 1–2* (HBS 7; Freiburg: Herder, 1996), 56–65. He shows that both the literary techniques of the composition and the thematic range of the contents have numerous parallels throughout Luke-Acts.

315. The analyses vary widely in their results; on the issue as a whole, cf. ibid., 66ff. On the Benedictus (Luke 1:68–79) and Magnificat (Luke 1:46–55), cf. Ulrike Mittmann-Richert, *Magnifikat und Benediktus: Die ältesten Zeugnisse der judenchristlichen Tradition von der Geburt des Messias* (WUNT 2.90; Tübingen: Mohr, 1996).

316. So Schürmann, *Lukas*, 18.

1:15–17, 67–79) while at the same time remaining the forerunner (cf. 1:76; 3:1–18). At the center of Luke's foundation for his christological thought as a whole stands the relation between God and Jesus. His conception by the Holy Spirit (1:35) goes beyond any concept of election or adoption, for *Jesus is in a direct sense the Son of God* (1:32, 35; 2:49; cf. 3:38) and Lord (1:17, 43, 76; 2:11).[317] At the same time, Luke clearly emphasizes the human traits of the man Jesus (2:40, 52: Jesus increases in wisdom; cf. 3:21; 9:18, 28–29; 22:37). Luke explicitly declares that the birth of John, and especially the birth of Jesus, must be understood as fulfilling the hopes of Israel (1:14–17, 32–33, 46–55, 68–79; 2:10–11, 25–26, 29–32, 38). The motif of promise and fulfillment also determines Luke 1–2; those who live "in expectation" such as Simeon and Anna (2:25, 38) provide the hearers/readers of Luke-Acts with the assurance that the promises are being fulfilled. So also the activity of the Spirit of God (see below, §8.4.3) in Luke 1–2 serves the fulfillment motif; Elizabeth (1:41), Zechariah (1:67), and Simeon (2:25–27) are filled with the Spirit, the Baptist will be filled with the Holy Spirit (1:15), and Jesus owes his existence to the power of the Spirit through Mary (1:35). Finally, the Nunc Dimittis (2:29–32) and Simeon's prophecy (2:34–35) thematize the reception of the gospel among the Gentiles portrayed in Acts, as proclaimed by Paul in Acts 28:26–28 (each time with citations from Isaiah!). The visit of the twelve-year-old Jesus to the temple, in which his extraordinary wisdom is demonstrated, is pictured in the style of the Hellenistic biographical convention, where such stories were obligatory,[318] but it is unique within the whole gospel tradition.

What is to happen in the gospel and Acts is already proclaimed in Luke 1–2 and at the same time is set in motion by the Spirit of God.

The Middle of Time

Luke characterizes the time of Jesus as *a time free of the activity of Satan*, and thus as the middle of time.[319] Satan disappears at the end of the temptation story (4:13, "When the devil had finished every test, he departed from him until an opportune time"), and does not reappear until 22:3, when he enters Judas and begins his activity again. The vision in 10:18 underscores the unique quality in the appearance of Jesus on the stage of history. Through this perspective, Luke highlights the ministry of Jesus in Israel as the time of salvation in a special way, without, however, separating it from the other epochs. After being

317. The idea, associated with the virginal conception, that extraordinary human beings such as the Greek heroes were begotten by a divine being, has numerous parallels in Greek and Roman tradition. One need only mention: Hector (Homer, *Il.* 24.258–259); Hercules (Hesiod, *Theog.* 940–44); Pythagoras (Iamblichus, *Vit. Pyth.* 5–8); Plato (Diogenes Laertius, *Vit. phil.* 3.1–2); Alexander the Great (*Hist. Alex.* 13.1–2); Augustus (Suetonius, *Aug.* 94.4).

318. On this point, cf. Nils Krückemeier, "Der zwölfjahrige Jesus im Tempel (Luke 2:40–52) und die biographische Literatur der hellenistischen Antike," *NTS* 50 (2004): 307–19.

319. Cf. Conzelmann, *Theology of St. Luke*, 170 and elsewhere.

portrayed in parallel with Jesus in the birth stories, John the Baptist continues to be present in the narrated world of the two-volume work (Luke 7:18–35; 16:16; Acts 1:22; 10:37; 11:16; 13:24–25; 18:24–28; 19:1–7), and the time of Jesus is placed firmly in continuity with the time of the church by the idea of fulfillment, by the ascension, the work of the Spirit, and the proclamation of the kingdom of God.[320] In regard to content, the *immediate Jesus-time* is marked by the concentration of Jesus's ministry on Israel.

Jesus's inaugural sermon in Nazareth thus has programmatic importance (Luke 4:16–30). Luke omits Mark 1:14–15 and signifies the beginning of Jesus's public ministry with a prophetic self-proclamation.[321] By applying Isa. 61:1 LXX to himself, Jesus appears as *the* bearer of the Spirit, *the* Anointed One (Luke 4:18a), who now fulfills God's eschatological will: "He has anointed me to bring good news to the poor. He has sent me to proclaim release to the captives and recovery of sight to the blind, to let the oppressed go free, to proclaim the year of the Lord's favor" (Luke 4:18b–19). By utilizing the idea of fulfillment in 4:21 ("Today this scripture has been fulfilled in your hearing") and the terms εὐαγγελίζεσθαι and κηρύσσειν for the proclamation of the good news of salvation, this scene not only describes the program of Jesus's ministry in the Gospel of Luke, but clearly incorporates the missionary proclamation of the whole of Luke-Acts (cf. Acts 8:4–40; 10:36, 38). Just as Jesus at the *beginning* of his ministry emphasizes that he must proclaim the kingdom of God in the cities of Israel (Luke 4:43), so Paul at the *end* of the two-volume work proclaims the kingdom of God in Rome (Acts 28:31). Finally, the rejection of Jesus in his hometown (Luke 4:23–30) is an anticipation of the fate of many missionaries, including Paul.[322]

This inaugural sermon in Nazareth begins Jesus's ministry in Galilee in word and deed in such a way that the double perspective of preaching and miracles formulated in Luke 4:18 stands in the foreground. Miracles and healings are found in 4:31–37, 38–39, 40–41, 42–44; 5:1–11, 12–16, 17–26; 7:1–10, 11–17, 21; 8:22–25, 26–39, 40–56; 9:10–12, 37–43. Teachings are predominant in 5:33–39; 6:17–49; 8:4–15, 16–18, 19–21. Teaching and miracles interpret each other and are epiphanies of the authority of the Messiah. Both illustrate Jesus's concern for the poor, the sinners, the social outsiders (cf. Luke 6:17–49, Sermon on

320. Cf. Gerhard Schneider, *Das Evangelium nach Lukas: Kapitel 1–10* (ÖTK 3.1; Gütersloh: Gütersloher Verlagshaus Gerd Mohn, 1977), 98. Contra Conzelmann, *Theology of St. Luke*, who wants to see the "clear manifestation of salvation" as only the immediate time of Jesus delimited by 4:13 and 22:3.

321. For analysis, cf. Ulrich Busse, *Das Nazaret-Manifest Jesu* (SBS 91; Stuttgart: 1978); Korn, *Geschichte Jesu*, 56–85.

322. On the paralleling of Jesus and Paul, cf. Walter Radl, *Paulus und Jesus im Lukanischen Doppelwerk: Untersuchungen zu Parallelmotiven im Lukasevangelium und in der Apostelgeschichte* (EHS 23.49; Frankfurt: Lang, 1975).

the Plain; 5:27–32, the tax collector Levi; 7:36–50, the sinful woman; 8:1–3, the women who accompany Jesus).

The perspective is changed at the story of the transfiguration (Luke 9:28–36), framed by the Passion predictions in 9:18–22, 43–45, for here Jerusalem and Jesus's Passion and resurrection come into view. In the *travel narrative* (9:51–19:27),[323] Luke orients his narrative all the more strongly in this direction by extending Mark's third Passion prediction (cf. Luke 18:31–34) with three additional references to the Passion (12:49–50; 13:31–33; 17:25). Jesus's way to Jerusalem, which begins in Luke 9:51, is the way to suffering and glory, the way that according to 22:42 he *must* walk. So also the reference to the ascension in 9:51 ("When the days drew near for him to be taken up . . .") underscores the interweaving of suffering and glory characteristic of Luke. The travel narrative is oriented to parenesis, for by means of its connections to his Passion theology Luke teaches that Jesus's way to the cross is to be understood as his continuing concern for the lost (15), the poor (16:16–31), the Samaritans (10:25–37),[324] and as the continuing offer of the kingdom of God to Israel, a concern that will continue in the life of his followers (see below, §8.4.8).

Passion, Cross, Resurrection, and Ascension

As presented by Luke, the goal of the life of Jesus is Jerusalem (cf. within the travel narrative esp. Luke 13:22; 17:11), where he will make the temple his distinctive place of teaching (Luke 19:29–21:38). The Passion and Easter constitute for Luke an inseparable unity; the Easter events all occur on a single day and reach their end and climax with the ascension (Luke 24:1–53). The Lukan Easter narratives feature four dominant aspects:

1. Luke understands the way to Jerusalem and the time of the Passion (22:1–23:56) as the will of God that leads to glory (22:37; 24:26, "Was it not necessary that the Messiah should suffer these things and then enter into his glory?"; 24:46, "Thus it is written, that the Messiah is to suffer and to rise from the dead on the third day"). Jesus is the suffering righteous prophet (cf. Luke 23:47; Acts 3:14) whose way to the cross stands under the divine "must" (cf. also Luke 17:25; 24:7; Acts 1:16; 2:23a; 3:18; 7:52; 8:32–35; 9:16; 14:22; 17:3; 19:21; 25:10).

323. R. von Bendemann, *Zwischen* ΔΟΞΑ *und* ΣΤΑΥΡΟΣ*: Eine exegetische Untersuchung der Texte des sogenannten Reiseberichts im Lukasevangelium* (BZNW 101; Berlin: de Gruyter, 2001), passim, disputes the existence of a Lukan travel narrative. Cf. Karl Löning, *Das Geschichtswerk des Lukas* (2 vols.; Stuttgart: Kohlhammer, 2006), who appropriately describes the travel narrative as Luke's central "literary structural concept."

324. On this point cf. Martina Böhm, *Samarien und die Samaritai bei Lukas: Eine Studie zum religionshistorischen und traditionsgeschichtlichen Hintergrund der lukanischen Samarientexte und zu deren topographischer Verhaftung* (WUNT 2.111; Tübingen: Mohr, 1999).

2. Luke explicitly relates Jesus's death on the cross to the fundamental orientation of his mission: to seek and save the lost (cf. 19:10; 22:27).[325] On the cross, the dying Jesus turns explicitly to one of the criminals crucified with him, the one who acknowledges his guilt and expresses repentance (23:42–43, "Then he said, 'Jesus, remember me when you come into your kingdom.' He replied, 'Truly I tell you, today you will be with me in Paradise'").
3. The resurrection of Jesus Christ from the dead is the hermeneutical key to understanding the whole Jesus-Christ-history and the Scripture (Luke 24:45, "Then he opened their minds to understand the Scriptures"; cf. Acts 3:18; 17:3; 26:23).[326]
4. In the Emmaus pericope and the story of the ascension, Luke emphasizes the tangible corporeality of the resurrected body of Jesus, and repeatedly notes that his body did not experience corruption (Acts 2:31; 10:41; 13:34, 37), since for him resurrection and exaltation are closely related (cf. Luke 22:69; 24:26; Acts 1:22; 2:33–36: the ascension as enthronement at God's right hand; 5:31; 7:55; 13:32–33).[327]

All the narrative lines in the gospel converge in chapter 24, which is also a transitional chapter, since both v. 47 ("that repentance and forgiveness of sins is to be proclaimed in his name to all nations, beginning from Jerusalem") and the ascension lead into the story line of Acts. Luke has composed this transition intentionally and with great care, for the first story of the ascension in 24:50–53 has also been designed as the conclusion of the gospel.[328] The "great joy" of the disciples points directly back to the Christmas story (χαρὰ μεγάλη is found only in Luke 2:10 and 24:52). The miraculous act of God at the beginning corresponds to God's act at the resurrection, as the disciples fall down and worship the exalted and glorified Lord.[329] Luke places the accents differently in Acts 1:1–11, for the real theme of his second story of the ascension is the parousia (cf. vv. 6–8) of the Jesus who is presently departing to heaven (see below, §8.4.8). Luke illustrates the meaning of this event for his readers by utilizing the familiar Greco-Roman literary form of apotheosis:[330] God's

325. It is probably due to Luke 19:10 that Luke omits Mark 10:45.

326. Cf. here especially Joachim Wanke, *Die Emmauserzahlüng: Eine redaktionsgeschichtliche Untersuchung* (ETS 31; Leipzig: Sankt-Benno-Verlag, 1973).

327. Cf. Rudolf Schnackenburg, *Jesus in the Gospels: A Biblical Christology* (Louisville: Westminster John Knox, 1995), 157–62, who points out that for Luke, resurrection and ascension must be understood as a single act of participation in the lifegiving power of God.

328. Cf. Gerhard Lohfink, *Die Himmelfahrt Jesu: Untersuchungen zu den Himmelfahrts- und Erhöhungstexten bei Lukas* (SANT 26; Munich: Kösel, 1971).

329. Lohfink, ibid., 254, describes the disciples adoration as the "christological high point of the gospel."

330. Cf. here Peter Pilhofer, "Livius, Lukas, und Lukian: Drei Himmelfahrten," in *Die frühen Christen und ihre Welt: Greifswalder Aufsätze 1996–2001* (ed. Peter Pilhofer et al.; WUNT 145;

faithfulness, manifest in the story from conception to ascension, continues in the universal preaching of the gospel and will come to its ultimate fulfillment at the parousia, for the one who is ascending to heaven will come again!

Christological Titles

Jesus is described or addressed as κύριος (Lord) very often in Luke-Acts. The title κύριος can be used of the unborn child (Luke 1:43), the newborn (2:11), the one who carries out his ministry on earth (7:13, 19; 10:1, 39, 41; 11:39; 12:42; 13:15; 17:5, 6; 18:6; 19:8, 31, 34; Acts 1:21; 20:35), and the Risen One (24:3, 34; Acts 1:6; 2:36; 4:33; 7:59, 60; 9:27). The κύριος title was probably connected very early with the appearances of the Risen One (24:34, "The Lord has risen indeed, and he has appeared to Simon!"), and then its usage developed and expanded so that it almost became a proper name for Jesus (cf. 19:31, 34). Typical Lukan expressions are telling, in that they show to what a great extent the κύριος title had already become normal linguistic usage: Christians are "added to the Lord" (cf. Acts 5:14; 9:35, 42; 11:17, 21, 24; 14:23; 16:31; 20:21), the disciples "proclaim the Lord Jesus" (Acts 11:20; 14:3; 28:31), or act, preach, and baptize in his name (Acts 8:16; 9:28; 19:5, 13, 17; 21:3). Luke can speak of the "fear of the Lord" (Acts 9:31), the "grace of the Lord" (Acts 15:11), or the "way of the Lord" (Acts 18:25; cf. 16:17, "the way of salvation"; 19:23, "the new way"). An ironic political use of κύριος is found in Acts 25:26, where Festus, in reference to Caesar (v. 25), says about Paul, "I have nothing definite to write to our sovereign [κύριος] about him."

The Χριστός title (Christ, Messiah, Anointed) appears less often in Luke-Acts (12 times in the gospel; 25 times in Acts). Its predicative character emerges clearly when it refers to the "Lord's Anointed" (Luke 2:26), the promised Messiah (cf. Luke 2:11, 26; 3:15; 4:41; 9:20; 22:67). Jesus is the one uniquely appointed as Messiah before time began (Acts 3:20). Luke rejects a political understanding of Χριστός, explicitly correcting the idea that a Messiah from the house of David (Luke 20:41) must not suffer (cf. Luke 23:5, 39; 24:26, 46; Acts 3:18; 17:3). The authentic Messiah is the suffering and risen Messiah (cf. Acts 2:22–36).

The υἱὸς θεοῦ title (Son of God) in the Gospel of Luke expresses Jesus's unique status,[331] for it never appears in the mouth of a human being but is used only by God or angels (Luke 1:35; 3:22; 9:35), by the devil or demons (4:3, 9, 41; 8:28), and in Jesus's own words (Luke 2:49; 10:22; 20:13; 22:29, 42, 70; 23:34, 46; 24:49). This title already plays a significant role at the presentation of Jesus (Luke 1:32, 35; 2:49; 3:22, 23b, 38; 4:3, 9). Jesus's status as Son of God

---

Tübingen: Mohr Siebeck, 2002), 166–82; the relevant history-of-religions material is presented by E. Bickermann, "Die römische Kaiserapotheose," *ARW* 27 (1929): 1–34.

331. Cf. J. Kremer, "'Dieser ist der Sohn Gottes,'" in *Der Treue Gottes trauen: Beiträge zum Werk des Lukas; für Gerhard Schneider* (ed. Claus Bussmann and Walter Radl; Freiburg i.B.: Herder, 1991), 137–57.

does not begin at the resurrection (Rom. 1:3–4) or before all time (John 1:1–5; 3:16), but with his human existence (Luke 1:35). Psalm 2:7 may stand in the background ("You are my Son; today I have begotten you"), as indicated by Luke 1:32 and Acts 13:33. Unlike Mark (see above, §8.2.2), Luke associates no underlying secrecy theme with the Son title. The exemplary character of Jesus, which is central for Luke, is manifest in the Son's obedience to God (Luke 2:49; 4:3, 9), which comes to its final goal on the cross (cf. Luke 23:46, "Father, into your hands I commend my spirit"). Luke intentionally stretches a taut inclusio between his first use (Luke 1:35) and last use of the term (cf. Luke 22:70, "All of them asked, 'Are you, then, the Son of God?' He said to them, 'You say that I am'"): Jesus's Sonship is the result of his conception by the Holy Spirit and finds its fulfillment in the Passion and Easter. Along the way, the Son title appears at key turning points of the plot (Luke 3:22, baptism; 4:4, 9: temptation; 9:35, journey to Jerusalem).

The title Son of Man (ὁ υἱὸς τοῦ ἀνθρώπου) appears often in Luke (twenty-five times), and is thoroughly embedded in his Christology of Jesus's pathway to the lost, his Passion, and resurrection/ascension.[332] The evangelist adds seven new sayings to the tradition (cf. 17:22, 25; 18:8; 19:10; 21:36; 22:48; 24:7) that represent all three groups of the Son of Man sayings. Luke 19:10 is characteristic ("For the Son of Man came to seek out and to save the lost"); by adding ζητῆσαι (to seek), Luke clearly expresses his own soteriological concern. He also reinforces the "must" of the suffering of the Son of Man (Luke 24:7, "The Son of Man must be handed over to sinners, and be crucified, and on the third day rise again"). The evangelist also introduces a new eschatological accent, for he is the first to associate the Son of Man with Jesus's post-resurrection exalted status (Luke 22:69, "From now on the Son of Man will be seated at the right hand of the power of God"; cf. Acts 7:56). In the parables calling for alertness, the dominant idea is that of the sudden, unexpected coming of the Son of Man (Luke 18:8; 21:36).

Luke has a conspicuous interest in Jesus as a prophet.[333] In his inaugural sermon in Nazareth, when he steps onto the public stage as a prophetic figure (4:16–30), the people regard him as a "great prophet" (7:16); for the disciples on the road to Emmaus he was "a prophet, mighty in deed and word before God and all the people" (24:19); and in Acts 3:22 he appears as the promised "prophet like Moses" to whom previous prophets had pointed (Acts 3:24–25).

332. Cf. Gerhard Schneider, "'Der Menschensohn' in der lukanischen Christologie," in *Lukas, Theologe der Heilsgeschichte* (ed. Gerhard Schneider; BBB 59; Bonn: Hannstein, 1985), 98–113.

333. On this point cf. Gottfried Nebe, *Prophetische Züge im Bilde Jesu bei Lukas* (BWANT 127; Stuttgart: Kohlhammer, 1989). The term *prophet* provided Luke with "a spacious and complex semantic field, rich with motifs and historical substance, that obviously allowed him to present Jesus within the wide context of titular Christology, along with his sayings, deeds, and fate" (207).

Thus Jesus's teaching, and especially his miracles, are placed in a prophetic context. Traditional motifs of prophetic understanding and prophetic polemic appear in Luke 7:39; 9:7–8, 19; 13:33. Jesus also appears as one who can see into the future (Luke 9:22, 44) and as one who with prophetic insight knows peoples' hearts (5:22; 6:8; 7:39–47; 22:21). The traditions about the sufferings of the prophets are important for Luke, as found in the perspective of the Deuteronomic historians in Acts 7:52 and in the wake of the suffering servant tradition in Luke 22:37; Acts 8:32–35 (cf. Luke 2:32; 4:18–19; 18:14).

It is hardly accidental that in Luke 2:11 Luke designates the newborn Jesus as σωτήρ ("Savior"; cf. Acts 5:31; 13:23; also Luke 1:32; 22:45; Acts 10:38). The Roman emperors claimed this title in particular for themselves;[334] in Luke's narrative it becomes the ironic attribute of an anti-history: *a defenseless child with no rights is the true "Savior," and his message will extend across the world until it reaches Rome and the emperor.*

Distinctive Features of Luke's Portrayal of Jesus

Luke places conspicuous accents in his portrait of Jesus. One we have already mentioned several times: *Jesus's compassionate concern for the poor*, a particular theme of Lukan ethics (see below, §8.4.6). Like no other evangelist, Luke emphasizes *Jesus's own humanity and his concern for other human beings*. The boy Jesus increases in wisdom and grace (cf. Luke 1:39–40), and at twelve in the temple he already has surpassing wisdom, yet remains subject to his parents (2:51–52). In the miracle stories too Jesus's humanity is linked with the wisdom and grace he has received from God: witness the stories of healing of the woman suffering from a physical handicap (13:10–17) and the man with dropsy (14:1–6), as well as the stories of the Good Samaritan and the Prodigal Son, where the motif of compassion appears explicitly (10:33; 15:20). Numerous characters and scenes in Jesus's parables manifest common human features (11:5–8, the Importunate Friend at Midnight; 16:1–8, the Unjust Steward; 17:7–10, the Unprofitable Servants; 18:1–6, the Unjust Judge; 18:9–14, the Pharisee and the Publican).[335] Jesus does not hesitate to touch a leprous person (5:13), or to let himself be touched by sick people (8:44–48). In no other gospel are words in the semantic field associated with healing so widely used. Jesus restores people physically, so that the amazed crowds break out in rejoicing (5:26, "We have seen incredible things today"; cf. 13:17). Jesus does not turn down invitations (cf. 7:34, 36; 14:1), and Zacchaeus is converted by Jesus's compassionate concern (19:1–10). Jesus pays attention to ordinary people, people who have maintained their dignity, people whose love for God and other human beings makes them ready to sacrifice, people like the poor widow of 21:1–4. Thus the Lukan Jesus is presented as the true benefactor,

334. On σωτήρ ("Savior"), see below, §10.4.1, §10.4.2, and §12.2.4.
335. Cf. here Heininger, *Metaphorik*.

who "went about doing good and healing all who were oppressed by the devil, for God was with him" (Acts 10:38).

As in no other gospel, *women* are included in the story of Jesus.[336] In the stories of Jesus's birth and childhood, Elizabeth, Mary, and Anna (cf. Luke 1:5ff.) appear as bearers of the whole christological kerygma and prototypes of Christian existence. An anonymous woman praises Mary, saying to Jesus, "Blessed is the womb that bore you and the breasts that nursed you!" (11:27; cf. 1:42). Jesus's response illustrates the Lukan intention: "Blessed rather are those who hear the word of God and obey it!" (11:28). *The women are witnesses and bearers of the Christian message.* Hearing the word and reflecting on it are among the exceptional qualities of Mary (2:19), and thus of all believers. The story of Mary and Martha (10:38–42) underscores this idea with the model of reflective listening on the one hand and restless activity on the other: hearing the word stands in the foreground, and right actions proceed only on this basis. The story of the sinful woman (7:36–50) presents the transition of a woman from the margins of society to a place among Jesus's followers. In contrast to the Pharisees, her sins are forgiven (7:50), and Luke understands her to be one of the "many others" who follow Jesus (8:3).[337] Not only does the note about women who followed Jesus (8:1–3) contain a valuable historical report, but the women are presented as ideal disciples by their following Jesus, by their readiness to give material goods (cf. Luke 18:22; 19:8; Acts 2:44–45; 4:32–47), and by the negative foil in Acts 5:1–11. After Easter, Lydia (Acts 16:14–15) represents the type of propertied women disciples from synagogue circles that we should perhaps presuppose in Luke's own church, or that of Theophilus (Luke 1:3; Acts 1:1). They probably provided material support for the congregation and were hosts to traveling missionaries.

Jesus at prayer is another distinctive feature of the Gospel of Luke. Surrounded by praise and prayer in the birth stories (Luke 1:46–55, 68–79; 2:14, 29–32) and the disciples' prayer and praise in the concluding verse of the gospel (Luke 24:53, "They were continually in the temple blessing God"), the intervening narrative repeatedly portrays Jesus at prayer. In Luke 5:16, after healing many people Jesus withdrew to a deserted place in order to pray alone; he goes up on a mountain and spends the whole night in prayer to God (6:12); he is transfigured while praying with his disciples (9:18, 28–29); the anxiety in Gethsemane about his coming death becomes an intensive struggle in prayer

336. On this point cf. Luise Schottroff, "Frauen in der Nachfolge Jesu in neutestamentlicher Zeit," in *Traditionen der Befreiung* (ed. Willy Schottroff and Wolfgang Stegemann; 2 vols.; Munich: Kaiser, 1980), 165–85; Helga Melzer-Keller, *Jesus und die Frauen: Eine Verhältnisbestimmung nach den synoptischen Überlieferungen* (HBS 14; Freiburg i.B.: Herder, 1997); Sabine Bieberstein, *Verschwiegene Jüngerinnen, vergessene Zeuginnen: Gebrochene Konzepte im Lukasevangelium* (NTOA 38; Göttingen: Vandenhoeck & Ruprecht, 1998).

337. Cf. Hans Klein, *Das Lukasevangelium* (KEK 1.3; Göttingen: Vandenhoeck & Ruprecht, 2006), 299.

(22:41, 44). Jesus thereby becomes a model for believers, for remaining alert and at prayer (cf. 21:36) is the right stance before both God and human beings. In the story of the persistent widow (18:1–8), the later church recognizes that God hears persistent prayer: "Ask, and it will be given you; search, and you will find; knock, and the door will be opened for you" (11:9). Those who pray rightly bow before God in humility and do not boast of their own accomplishments (18:9–14). Instead, they pray for the Holy Spirit (11:13), from whose inspiration true prayer is addressed to the Father in humility. The earliest church implements this counsel in exemplary fashion. Acts presents it as a community engaged in prayer (Acts 1:14; 3:1; 6:4; 8:15; 9:11, 40; 10:9; 11:5; 12:5, 12; 14:23; 16:16, 25; 21:5), a church whose prayer opens itself to guidance by the power of God at decisive moments in its own history: in the choice of Matthias (Acts 1:24); in the communal sharing of goods (Acts 2:42); in the commissioning of Barnabas and Paul (Acts 13:3); and in the farewell speech at Miletus (Acts 20:36). Compared to the other gospels, the author of the Gospel of Luke places prayer in a central place in his narrative; one could call him the prayer-evangelist.

The Christology of Acts

The narrative perspective of Acts, which differs from that of the gospel, requires a different way of presenting the presence of Jesus.[338] With the expression "what Jesus did and taught from the beginning" in the first verse of Acts, Luke takes up the story of what Jesus has done and is doing, and continues it with new accents: *Jesus Christ, in the light of the Passion and Easter kerygma, is present as the one raised from the dead whose effects and significance continue.* This is seen first of all in the miracles performed by the apostles (Peter, Acts 3:1–10; 5:12–16; 9:32–43; Paul, Acts 13:4–11; 14:8–14; 19:11–12; 20:7–12; 28:1–10; summaries, Acts 2:43; 4:30, 33; 5:12; 14:3);[339] in these miracles the Crucified and Risen One reveals his continuing power as the Living One. The active subject in the performance of these miracles is Jesus himself (cf. Acts 4:10), so that they become confirming signs of his resurrection and of the saving nearness of God. The miracles are also signs of the end time that has broken in with the resurrection of Jesus and the gift of the Holy Spirit. Stephen's speech (Acts 7:2–53)[340] as the

338. On the Christology of Acts, cf. Matera, *Christology*, 64–82.

339. On the miracles in Acts, cf. Frans Neirynck, "The Miracle Stories in the Acts of the Apostles," in *Les Actes des Apôtres* (ed. J. Kremer; BETL 48; Louvain: Leuven University Press, 1979), 13–158.

340. In addition to the standard commentaries, for analyses of Stephen's speech see Ulrich Wilckens, *Die Missionsreden der Apostelgeschichte* (WMANT 5; Neukirchen: Neukirchener Verlag, 1974), 208–24; Holtz, *Zitate*, 85–127; John J. Kilgallen, *The Stephen Speech: A Literary and Redactional Study of Acts 7,2–53* (AB 67; Rome: Biblical Institute Press, 1976), Francis Gerald Downing, "Ethical Pagan Theism," *NTS* 27 (1981): 544–63.

conclusion of Luke's portrayal of the earliest church and the transition to the church's mission beyond Jerusalem clearly reveals Luke's own perspective: the break in God's history with Israel leads to an accusation against the Sanhedrin (Acts 7:51–53) and a vision of the glory of God with the exalted Jesus as the Son of Man at the right hand of God (Acts 7:55–56). Thereby the prophecy of Luke 22:69 is fulfilled, and Stephen becomes the first martyr and witness to the fact that God's saving plan for history will be accomplished even against the will of his own people.

The mission speeches in Acts[341] speak very often of the suffering, death, and resurrection of Jesus (cf. Acts 2:22–23, 36; 3:13–15, 17ff.; 5:30; 10:39; 13:27–28; outside the speeches, cf. Acts 4:8, 10–11, 25–28; 8:32–35; 17:3; 20:28c; 26:23). Peter's Pentecost sermon formulates the basic statement of the Christology of Acts: salvation comes from calling on the name of Jesus, who was given over to the cross through God's plan and foreknowledge. God raised him from the dead, exalted him to his right hand, and now gives the Spirit (cf. Acts 2:21–35). Summary: "Therefore let the entire house of Israel know with certainty that God has made him both Lord and Messiah, this Jesus whom you crucified" (Acts 2:36). It is noticeable that there is no emphasis on Jesus's death "for us," but that Jesus's death is understood primarily as the result of the disobedience of the Jews (cf. Acts 2:22–23; 3:13b–15a; 4:10; 5:30b; 10:38–39; 13:27–29). God's saving act is contrasted with their disobedience (cf. Acts 2:24, 36; 3:13a, 15b; 4:10; 5:31a; 10:40; 13:30–31), which becomes the basis of the call to repentance (Acts 2:37–38; 3:19; 4:11; 5:30–31; 10:42–43; 13:38–41). This schema could be the continuation of an older tradition.[342] In any case, it is clear that *God's act in raising Jesus from the dead stands at the center of the Christology of Acts* (cf. also Acts 3:15, 26; 4:2, 33; 17:18, 32; 23:6–9; 24:15, 21; 26:8, 23).[343] The resurrection is the presupposition and basis of the Christian mission, as Luke makes clear above all by the threefold account of the call of Paul by the risen Lord (cf. Acts 9:3–19; 22:6–16; 26:12–18).

341. The mission speeches are found in Acts 2:14–39; 3:12–26; 4:8b–12; 5:29–32; 10:34–43; 13:16–41. They essentially present Luke's own perspective. Cf. Wilckens, *Missionsreden*, 200ff.

342. So, for example, Jürgen Roloff, *Die Apostelgeschichte* (NTD 5; Göttingen: Vandenhoeck & Ruprecht, 1981), 49–51. Cf. also Ferdinand Hahn, "Das Problem alter christologischer Überlieferungen in der Apostelgeschichte unter besonderer Berücksichtigung von Acts 3, 19–21," in Kremer, *Les Actes des Apôtres*, 129–54; de Jonge, *Christology*, 108–11; Martin Rese, "Die Aussagen über Jesu Tod und Auferstehung in der Apostelgeschichte—ältestes Kerygma oder lukanische Theologumena?" *NTS* (1984): 335–53, argues for Lukan composition. The lack of unambiguous criteria for identifying older tradition in Acts makes it difficult to determine pre-Lukan elements, yet it is likely that, in varying degrees, Luke incorporated some traditional material in the speeches.

343. On this point cf. Thomas Knöppler, "Beobachtungen zur lukanischen theologia resurrectionis," in "*. . . Was ihr auf dem Weg verhandelt habt": Beiträge zur Exegese und Theologie des Neuen Testaments; Festschrift für Ferdinand Hahn zum 75. Geburtstag* (ed. Peter Müller et al.; Neukirchen-Vluyn: Neukirchener Verlag, 2001), 51–62.

What significance is attributed to the cross in Luke-Acts (the issue concerns both volumes, but here we focus on Acts)? While previous research tended to claim that "nothing is said of the saving significance of the cross of Christ,"[344] more recent study is no longer oriented to measuring Luke's theology by that of Paul, and its results are more differentiated.[345] In Luke 22:19–20 ("This is my body, which is given for you"), and especially in Acts 20:28, the soteriological significance of the cross is explicitly emphasized: "Keep watch over yourselves and over all the flock, of which the Holy Spirit has made you overseers, to shepherd the church of God that he obtained with the blood of his own Son." The citation of Isa. 53:7–8 LXX in Acts 8:32–33 likewise points to Jesus's substitutionary suffering (cf. further Acts 3:13–15; 4:27), so that one cannot simply deny that this perspective is also included in Acts.

As a whole, the Christology of Acts is characterized by quite a large number of titles, traditions, and perspectives.[346] Jesus appears as a man from Nazareth (Acts 2:22; 3:6; 4:10; 6:14; 22:8; 26:9) who is the Messiah from David's line (Acts 2:25–28), whose name saves (Acts 2:12; 3:6; 4:10), the Servant whom God raised from the dead (Acts 3:26) and who as the Messiah (Acts 10:36–40) appeared to chosen witnesses, who now proclaim the message of the one who is Savior of both Israel and the Gentiles (Acts 13:25–41).

8.4.3 Pneumatology

Alongside Paul and John, it is especially Luke among New Testament authors who develops a pneumatology with distinctive contours. The work of the Holy Spirit is a central means by which Luke presents his theology of differentiated historical epochs, as indicated by the concentration of references to the Spirit at the beginning of both the gospel and Acts. The Spirit represents the saving power of God at work in the stories of Elizabeth, John the Baptist, and Simeon (Luke 1:15, 41, 67, 80; 2:25–26). As this creative divine power, the Spirit is the basis of the relation between God and Jesus, for Jesus's earthly existence is grounded in the work of the Spirit (Luke 1:35). The Spirit is visibly present at Jesus's baptism (cf. Luke 3:22), who will now himself baptize with the Spirit and fire (cf. 3:16; Acts 1:5; 11:16). The Spirit leads Jesus into the desert (Luke 4:1), then directs him to Nazareth (cf. 4:14), where Jesus makes the central declaration, "The Spirit of the Lord is upon me, because he has anointed me . . ."

344. Philipp Vielhauer, "On the 'Paulinism' of Acts," in *Studies in Luke-Acts* (ed. Leander Keck and J. Louis Martyn; Nashville: Abingdon, 1966), 45.

345. Cf. Frieder Schütz, *Der leidende Christus: Die angefochtene Gemeinde und der Christuskerygma der lukanischen Schriften* (BWANT 89; Stuttgart: Kohlhammer, 1969); Anton Büchele, *Der Tod Jesu im Lukasevangelium: Eine redaktionsgeschichtliche Untersuchung zu Lk 23* (1st ed.; FTS 26; Frankfurt a.M.: Knecht, 1978); Korn, *Geschichte Jesu*, 173–259.

346. Thomas Söding, *Der Gottessohn aus Nazareth: Das Menschsein Jesu im Neuen Testament* (Freiburg i.B.: Herder, 2006), 223–44.

(4:18). The whole ministry of Jesus now appears as the fulfillment of God's promise by the bearer of the Spirit, Jesus of Nazareth. After Luke 1–4, statements about the Spirit clearly recede, until Luke 24:49, when Jesus himself, prior to his ascension, promises to send the Spirit to his disciples (cf. Acts 1:8). Then, according to Acts 1:6–8, the gift of the Holy Spirit appears as the crucial equipment of Christ's witnesses during the time of the Lord's absence. The manifestations of the Spirit serve to demonstrate that Jesus has been exalted to heaven: "Being therefore exalted at the right hand of God, and having received from the Father the promise of the Holy Spirit, he has poured out this that you both see and hear" (Acts 2:33). The gift of the Spirit by the risen and exalted Christ is thus the basis for the worldwide mission of the church and the gathering of the saved community. For Luke, Pentecost is the fulfillment of the Baptist's announcement that Jesus would baptize with the Holy Spirit (cf. Luke 3:16; Acts 1:5; 2:4). The existence of Jesus and the existence of the church are both the work of the Spirit; *in each case, the Spirit not only introduces the new epoch, but leads it forward in power*!

Especially in Acts, the work of the Spirit is the motor that drives the history of salvation forward.[347] In Jerusalem, the Spirit enables the disciples and all the hearers in Jerusalem to proclaim the message, so that Pentecost becomes a prototype of what is to happen later: the proclamation of the risen Jesus Christ, through the power of the Spirit, is understood and accepted by people of very different cultural backgrounds. In baptism, the Spirit is given to Christians (Acts 2:38), and leads the mission forward according to God's eternal plan and foreknowledge (Acts 2:23, πρόγνωσις; cf. 4:28; 15:7; 20:27), even against manifold opposition and obstacles. The great success in Jerusalem (Acts 2:41, 47; 4:4; 5:14; 6:1, 7)[348] is followed by the mission to Samaria, which is validated by the Samaritans' reception of the Spirit (Acts 8:15). So also the evangelization of the Ethiopian occurs through the Spirit's active intervention, for it brings Philip in contact with the Ethiopian (Acts 8:29) and then carries him away after he has been baptized (Acts 8:39). The key passages in the further developments of the Acts story are the Cornelius pericope and the Apostolic Council. After God granted Peter the insight that "God shows no partiality, but in every nation anyone who fears him and does what is right is acceptable to him" (Acts 10:34–35), the Holy Spirit also falls on Gentiles, and thus palpably confirms this new dimension of God's plan of salvation (Acts 10:45). The Spirit selects Barnabas and Paul for the first missionary journey (Acts 13:2), and thus puts into effect the program of evangelistic mission without the prerequisite of circumcision. The Spirit is active also in bringing about unanimity at the Apostolic Council (cf. Acts 15:28) and in the transi-

347. Cf. J. Kremer, "Weltweites Zeugnis für Christus in der Kraft des Geistes," in *Mission im Neuen Testament* (ed. Karl Kertelge; QD 93; Freiburg i.B.: Herder, 1982), 145–63.

348. According to Lohfink, *Die Sammlung Israels*, 47–55, what happens here exemplifies the intended regathering of Israel.

tion of the mission to Europe (Acts 16:6–7). Paul's whole mission in Greece stands under the sign of the Spirit's work. A further epochal event is the installation of congregational elders in their office; in Paul's speech at Miletus (Acts 20:13–38), Luke legitimizes the structure of offices and congregations of his own time (cf. Acts 20:28). Finally, at the end of his two-volume work, Luke qualifies the saying about the hardening of Israel in Isa. 6:9–10 cited in Acts 28:26–27 as the word of the Holy Spirit. It is in accord with God's will that the majority of his chosen people close themselves off from the gospel and fail to repent.[349]

Included in the post-Easter work of the Spirit is that of *maintaining the memory* of Jesus's saving work and the present *witness* to Jesus. The Spirit already speaks in the words of Scripture through David (Acts 1:16; 4:25–26) and Isaiah (Acts 28:25), prophesying the suffering of Jesus and the hardening of Israel. The apostles on Pentecost (Acts 2:4, 17–18); Peter before the rulers, elders, and scribes (Acts 4:8); Stephen (Acts 6:8, 10; 7:55); Philip (Acts 8:29); Paul at the time of his call (Acts 9:17); and Barnabas in Antioch (Acts 11:23–24) are all "filled with the Holy Spirit," so that in word and deed they bear witness to Jesus. As Peter and the apostles stood before the council and the whole body of the elders of Israel, they asserted, "We are witnesses to these things, and so is the Holy Spirit whom God has given to those who obey him" (Acts 5:32). Already in the gospel, the Spirit appears as equipping the disciples for threatening situations and persecution (Luke 12:11–12, "When they bring you before the synagogues, the rulers, and the authorities, do not worry about how you are to defend yourselves or what you are to say; for the Holy Spirit will teach you at that very hour what you ought to say"). This

349. The interpretation of Acts 28:26–27 as a key passage for Luke's pneumatology and soteriology is a disputed point among scholars. For example, Wasserberg, *Israels Mitte*, 115, understands the text to refer to those "Jews who do not believe in Jesus, and do not believe because their hearts are divinely hardened," and is thus Luke's explanation for the reality that Jews had in fact rejected the Christian message. He thus regards speculations about Luke's views on the future of Israel to be groundless. A different point of view is represented by, for example, Martin Karrer, "'Und ich werde sie heilen': Das Verstockungsmotiv aus Jes 6,9f in Apg 28,26f," in *Kirche und Volk Gottes: Festschrift für Jürgen Roloff zum 70. Geburtstag* (ed. Martin Karrer et al.; Neukirchen-Vluyn: Neukirchener Verlag, 2000), 255–71; and V. A. Lehnert, "Die 'Verstockung Israels' und biblische Hermeneutik," *ZNT* 16 (1998): 13–19, who understand this text precisely as evidence for Luke's consistently positive perspective on Israel. The pros and cons of these arguments are weighed by Bendemann, "Echo des Propheten Jesaja," 69, who concludes: "For Luke, differently than for Paul (due to temporal distance and different sociocultural worlds), Isaiah is the guarantor of continuity. The establishment of such *continuity* is also finally served by the citation of Isa. 6:9–10. By placing the past negative resonance of the Jews under the sign of the divine hardening, it can by no means be interpreted as their final response. That the Jewish people, treated in such a highly symbolic manner using Isaiah's soteriological categories from the very beginning of Luke's narrative in the birth stories, has not accepted this salvation, remains a riddle at the end of the narrative, a mystery that can only be worked through *theologically*."

promise is fulfilled in many scenes in the Acts story of the early Christian mission. Peter and John (Acts 4:19, "Whether it is right in God's sight to listen to you rather than to God, you must judge"), Peter and the apostles (Acts 5:29), Stephen, and especially Paul (cf. Acts 13:50; 14:5–6, 19; 16:25–40; 17:13; 18:12; 19:23–41; 21:27–40) all bear witness to the gospel of Jesus Christ in the face of numerous difficulties.

The central role of the Holy Spirit in Luke's composition as a whole is obvious: the Spirit as the Spirit of *God* is the real acting subject in the history of Jesus Christ and the history of the universal Gentile mission. After Easter, the risen and exalted Lord confers the Holy Spirit on the apostles; the Spirit extends the work of Jesus into the church and thus preserves the continuity of God's saving acts in history. The Spirit not only repeatedly intervenes in the course of salvation history, but also is active in fundamental historical decisions as the church sets its directions for its future mission. The Spirit is the medium of the gospel message and of the power of God, equipping the church for courageous witness.

8.4.4 Soteriology

Lukan soteriology manifests a number of distinctive features.[350] It is apparent that the concept of atonement/expiation and that Jesus died "for us" recede and that the salvific function of the cross of Christ does not have such a central place as in Paul or Mark. Luke does not take over Mark's reference to the "ransom for many" (Mark 10:45), and the atoning death of the Servant of God is omitted from the quotation of Isa. 53:7–8 in Luke 22:37 and Acts 8:32–33. However, these ideas are by no means altogether absent (cf. Acts 3:26a, "For you first, God raised up His Servant . . ." [NASB]; cf. also Acts 20:28; Luke 23:42–43), and such texts have a considerable christological-soteriological weight. It is characteristic for Luke, however, that *Jesus's whole existence—his life, death, and resurrection, i.e., the Christ event as a whole—brings salvation to humanity.* Thus salvation is already grounded in the birth of Jesus. In the birth story, the angel of 2:11 proclaims the fundamental statement of Lukan soteriology: "To you is born this day in the city of David a Savior [σωτήρ], who is the Messiah, the Lord." It can already be said of the unborn child that it gives "knowledge of salvation to his people by the forgiveness of their sins" (Luke 1:77). The birth of Jesus in a stable is related to the fundamental orientation of his ministry, "to seek and save the lost" (19:10). His life as a whole is a service to others (22:27), with the

350. The deficient character of Luke's soteriology (and theology) is emphasized by, e.g., Haenchen, *Acts*, 92; Käsemann, "Problem of the Historical Jesus," 28–29; Conzelmann, *Theology of St. Luke*, 201, "There is no trace of any Passion mysticism, nor is any direct soteriological significance drawn from Jesus's suffering or death. There is no suggestion of a connection with the forgiveness of sins"; Wilckens, *Missionsreden*, 126 ("While the death of Jesus is foreseen as part of God's plan, no soteriological significance is attributed to it").

goal of bringing those who are lost, excluded, and disdained back to God. This happens in the miracles, and especially in the acceptance of penitent sinners, as shown for example in the parables of the lost sheep, coin, and son (15), the story of the sinful woman (7:35–50), and the Zacchaeus pericope (19:1–10). Jesus's compassionate reaching out to him changes Zacchaeus's life, and Jesus announces to him, "Today salvation has come to this house, because he too is a son of Abraham" (19:9). In the life of Jesus, God again draws near to humanity, so that salvation is possible. However, people must accept this nearness; for Luke, God does not save people apart from their own decision, i.e., without repentance and living a renewed life, as shown in the discussions of Luke's understanding of sin and ethics (see below, §8.4.5 and §8.4.6).

Jesus's compassionate turning toward the lost is also seen in his way to the cross, which Luke pictures as an example for his followers, and which even has an effect on the spectators at the crucifixion: "And when all the crowds who had gathered there for this spectacle saw what had taken place, they returned home, beating their breasts" (Luke 23:48). Luke emphasizes that Jesus was condemned and executed as an innocent man; Pilate three times confirms his innocence (23:4, 14, 22), and Herod also corroborates that finding (23:15). Jesus suffers and dies explicitly as a good man who has been unjustly condemned (23:47, "When the centurion saw what had taken place, he praised God and said, 'Certainly this man was innocent'"),[351] a man who at the cross was considered a criminal (22:37). It is precisely while he is on the cross that he explicitly turns to the lost (22:51; 23:28–31, 39–43) and forgives them their sins (23:34, "Father, forgive them; for they do not know what they are doing"), i.e., Jesus subjects himself to humiliation on the cross, in order that here too he can be near those who are humiliated. Because of his obedience to God (22:42–44), the one who has been brought low by human beings is raised up by God (18:14b; 24:26), and thereby opens the way of salvation to all who are with him.[352] Since he has been exalted to his place in the heavenly world, he can now act for the salvation of human beings, above all by his gift of the Spirit. Here the fundamental conception of Luke's soteriology becomes clear: *Jesus is the "Author of life"* (Acts 3:15, ἀρχηγὸς τῆς ζωῆς; cf. 5:31), *he ascends to heaven and thereby opens the way of salvation (Acts 16:17). The individual stages of this way are significant as part of the whole Christ event, and may neither be isolated nor negated.*[353] Thus in his entire existence he is at one and

351. A comparison with Mark 15:39 is informative here, revealing how independently each evangelist has worked with their traditions and sources.

352. Cf. Walter Grundmann, *Das Evangelium nach Lukas* (THKNT 3; Berlin: Evangelische Verlagsanstalt, 1971), 455: "The mighty act of God that takes place in the cross and resurrection of Jesus Christ consists in the fact that his way leads through suffering and death to glory, through humiliation to exaltation."

353. Thus the thesis of Barth, *Der Tod Jesu*, 134, is off the mark: "The significance of Jesus's death is thus [for Luke] very restricted: it is only a transitional stage on the way to glory." On

the same time the ground, author, and prototype of salvation. The strong ethical components within Luke's soteriology are to be explained within the context of the Lukan church: the exemplary character of the life and death of a hero is widespread in Greco-Roman thinking.

Acts proclaims the soteriological dimension of Jesus's way of salvation, for "there is salvation in no one else, for there is no other name under heaven given among mortals by which we must be saved" (Acts 4:12). Within the perspective of the coming judgment, it is Jesus's exaltation to God's right hand that makes possible the forgiveness of sins (Luke 24:47; Acts 2:38; 3:19ff.; 5:31; 17:30–31) and the salvation of the Gentiles (Acts 13:47); this is the message of salvation, this is the way of salvation (Acts 13:26; 16:17).

Salvation is appropriated by receiving the word, i.e., by faith (Acts 2:21, "Everyone who calls on the name of the Lord shall be saved"). By receiving the proclaimed message and confirming this acceptance by baptism, one receives salvation (cf. Acts 2:40; 11:14; 14:9; 16:30–31, 33). Faith is the only appropriate response to the missionaries' preaching of salvation. Thus Acts 15:11 shows Luke's essential proximity to Paul, in that Luke also understands salvation as a matter of grace: "We believe that we will be saved through the grace of the Lord Jesus, just as they will" (ἀλλὰ διὰ τῆς χάριτος τοῦ κυρίου Ἰησοῦ πιστεύομεν σωθῆναι καθ' ὃν τρόπον κἀκεῖνοι). Moreover, for Luke there is an organic relationship between pneumatology and soteriology, since according to Acts 5:31 and 13:38–39 the gift of the Spirit from the exalted Lord is the presupposition for repentance and the forgiveness of sins. The time of "ignorance" (ἄγνοια in Acts 3:17; 13:27; 17:23, 30) is now past, for salvation is now proclaimed throughout the world by the witnesses of the gospel.[354]

At the center of Luke's soteriology stands the idea of the saving significance of the way of Jesus that leads to God. His life as a whole is understood as service, as seeking and saving the lost; thus his way from God and to God becomes the way of salvation for all who believe.

8.4.5 Anthropology

As is the case with the Lukan soteriology, so also Luke's anthropology has a distinctive character. On the one hand, Luke's views are close to the perspectives of Hellenistic anthropology, for example, when he makes "the good" (τὸ ἀγαθόν) a basic anthropological-ethical category (Luke 6:45a, "The good person out of the good treasure of the heart produces good"), and when he has

---

the other hand, Peter Doble, *The Paradox of Salvation: Luke's Theology of the Cross* (SNTSMS Cambridge: Cambridge University Press, 1996) argues for an independent *theologia crucis* in Luke.

354. On this point cf. Sylvia Hagene, *Zeiten der Wiederherstellung: Studien zur lukanischen Geschichtstheologie als Soteriologie* (NTA NF 42; Münster: Aschendorff, 2003), 324ff., who places the concept of "saving knowledge" at the center of Luke's soteriology.

Paul speak in Acts 17:27–29 of the kinship between God and human beings. On the other hand, he explicitly avoids dualistic anthropological statements (cf. Luke 12:4–5 and the omission of Mark 14:38b) and in his anthropological conceptuality remains in the Old Testament tradition.

Anthropological Terms

With the term καρδία (heart) Luke describes the personal center, the seat of feelings and awareness, where decisions are made about one's whole orientation to life, either in a positive or negative sense (cf., e.g., Luke 1:17, 66; 2:19, 35; 3:15; 5:22; 6:45; 8:12; 12:34; Acts 2:46; 4:32; 8:21; 11:23; 28:27). God knows the heart and detests what human beings consider right and just: "You are those who justify yourselves in the sight of others; but God knows your hearts; for what is prized by human beings is an abomination in the sight of God" (Luke 16:15). So also for Luke the term ψυχή (soul) stands for the vital principle, "life" in its natural sense (cf. Luke 1:46; 6:9; 9:24; 10:27; Acts 4:32; 14:22; 20:10, 24). Likewise, the parable of the Rich Fool (Luke 12:16–21) shows that ψυχή can also refer to the fundamental orientation of one's life (cf. Acts 15:24). Luke powerfully illustrates by the character of the rich farmer that human striving to secure one's own life does not in fact lead to true life (Luke 12:15, "Be on your guard against all kinds of greed; for one's life does not consist in the abundance of possessions"; cf. 12:21, 25).[355] Luke uses the term σάρξ (flesh) in a way that sets him apart from other New Testament authors by using it to describe the resurrected body of Jesus (Luke 24:39; Acts 2:31).

A central term of Luke's anthropology is πίστις/πιστεύω ("faith/believe").[356] At the macro level, Luke 1:45 ("Blessed is she who believed that there would be a fulfillment of what was spoken to her by the Lord") and Luke 24:25 (the Emmaus disciples) make clear the basic structure of Luke's concept of faith: *faith originates and is effective in acknowledging the trustworthiness of the divine word of promise.* Faith is a living thing, and must therefore be strengthened (Luke 17:5–6; 22:32–33); it is confirmed and made strong by events that can be seen as the fulfillment of promises (cf., e.g., Acts 9:31; 11:18; 15:30–35). As insight into God's saving plan for history, faith for Luke has a strong noetic function, for it recognizes the way of salvation manifest in Jesus as the realization of the saving will of God (cf. Acts 2:22–24). Thus πίστις/πιστεύω vocabulary appears frequently in the context of conversion stories (Acts 2:44; 4:4; 5:14; 8:12; 9:42; 11:21, 24; 13:48; 14:1; 17:12, 34; 18:8, 27; 19:2–6, 18), in which the progression "preaching—faith as acceptance of the word—baptism—forgiveness of sins—reception of the Holy Spirit" represents

355. The comment of Reinmuth, *Anthropologie*, 104, is on target: "What makes people unsalvageable is their effort to secure their own life."

356. Cf. Jens-W. Taeger, *Der Mensch und sein Heil: Studien zum Bild des Menschen und zur Sicht der Bekehrung bei Lukas* (SNT 14; Gütersloh: G. Mohn, 1982), 106–23; Reinmuth, *Anthropologie*, 113–20.

the ideal case (cf. Acts 8:12–13; 10:42–48; 14:1; 17:12, 34; 18:8; 19:2–6). Faith is by no means an abstraction without concrete results, but *a saving event*; whether through Jesus's miracles (Luke 8:48; 17:19; cf. also 7:9; 8:12, 25; 9:50; Acts 13:12; 14:9, Paul's miracles) or the preaching of missionaries (Acts 16:31). The typical phrase is ἡ πίστις σου σέσωκέν σε (Luke 8:48; 17:19, "Your faith has saved you"; Acts 16:31, "Believe on the Lord Jesus, and you will be saved, you and your household"). Faith is considered salvific not least because it is linked to the forgiveness of sins. In Acts 10:43, forgiveness of sins is directly joined to faith in Jesus Christ as judge over life and death, "All the prophets testify about him that everyone who believes in him receives forgiveness of sins through his name" (cf. Acts 26:18; Luke 5:20).

Sin and the Forgiveness of Sins

Luke's perspective on sin corresponds to his anthropology as a whole. With only one exception (Acts 7:60), the evangelist uses the plural ἁμαρτίαι, thereby signaling his understanding: *sins are concrete failures in one's conduct in the realm of ethics and morality*.[357] Thus the "prodigal son" twice confesses his unacceptable lifestyle with the words "Father, I have sinned against heaven and before you" (Luke 15:18, 21). Likewise, in the story of the "sinful woman" in Luke 7:36–49, "sins" refers to immoral acts, in the Lord's Prayer "sins" means one's individual failures (Luke 11:4), and in Acts 25:7–8, Paul defends himself with the claim that he has not "sinned" against the emperor, i.e., has done nothing that violates the empire's law and order. Thus Luke can also speak of the "just/righteous" as those whose conduct distinguishes them from other people (cf. Luke 1:6; 2:25; 23:50–51; Acts 10:2, 4, 22, 31, 35; 11:24; 22:12). Jesus has come to call not the righteous but sinners (Luke 5:32), and in heaven there is more joy over one "sinner" who repents than over ninety-nine "righteous" (Luke 15:7).

The forgiveness of sins is grounded in the Christ event (Acts 5:31) and becomes effective in changed conduct,[358] as a reorientation of one's whole perspective that results in a new way of life. This becomes clear already with John the Baptist (cf. Luke 1:77–78; 3:3), for in response to his preaching of repentance the people ask, "What then should we do?" (3:10b), and concrete instructions follow (3:11–14). Zacchaeus gives half his property to the poor and restores fourfold what he had obtained by oppression, which results in the promise of salvation. The parables of the lost sheep, coin, and son (15:1–32) portray God as the one who seeks, who goes after sinners and accepts them when they repent. So also Jesus goes into the house of Zacchaeus (19:1–10), enjoys table fellowship with him, and accepts him as a sinner.

357. Cf. Taeger, *Mensch*, 31ff.

358. Appropriately Bovon, *Luke*, 1:182: "Without the salvation-historical work of Jesus Christ, forgiveness is impossible, but without the human μετάνοια [repentance] it cannot be realized."

The risen Lord himself reveals to the disciples on the road to Emmaus that in his name "repentance and forgiveness of sins is to be proclaimed in his name to all nations" (κηρυχθῆναι ἐπὶ τῷ ὀνόματι αὐτοῦ μετάνοιαν εἰς ἄφεσιν ἁμαρτιῶν εἰς πάντα τὰ ἔθνη, Luke 24:47). Acts narrates how this commission is carried out; the ideal type of conversion story combines calling on the name, baptism, forgiveness of sins, and gift of the Holy Spirit (Acts 2:38; cf. also 3:19; 5:31; 10:43; 13:38; 22:16; 26:18). This event is located in the act of conversion, where recognition and correction come together: turning away from one's previous conduct and the new orientation involved in turning to the true God (cf Luke 7:36–50; 19:1–10; 23:39–43; Acts 8:26–39; 13:7–12; 16:13–15). Luke understands conversion primarily as an act of human insight and decision—primarily but not exclusively, for everything finally stands under the "year of the Lord's favor/acceptance" (Luke 4:19; cf. 1:77; 3:3), and is embedded in his eschatological perspective (cf. further Acts 3:16; 16:14 [it is said of Lydia, "The Lord opened her heart to listen eagerly to what was said by Paul"]; 26:29).[359]

The Law

Luke's statements about the law are multilayered. In Luke 1–2, all the characters are represented as keeping the Jewish law faithfully (cf. 2:22–24:27, 39), and Jesus's burial takes place in accord with the law (23:56). So also the harmonious picture of the earliest Jerusalem church in the temple precincts (Acts 1–5) points in this direction. Luke's portrayals of Stephen and Paul fit into this picture; the charge that Stephen had spoken against the law is explicitly designated as false (Acts 6:13–14), and the Jewish people have lost their claim to the law because they have rejected Moses and the prophets (Acts 7:53, "You are the ones that received the law as ordained by angels, and yet you have not kept it"). Paul takes second place to no one in his observance of the law; he circumcises Timothy (Acts 16:3) and undertakes the Nazirite vow in order to disarm all the objections against himself personally (cf. Acts 21:20ff.). Paul defends his faithfulness to the laws of both the Jewish people (Acts 22:3, 12) and the Roman authorities (Acts 24:14). The Lukan Paul makes the generalization, "I have in no way committed an offense against the law of the Jews, or against the temple, or against the emperor" (Acts 25:8). So also, the omission of Mark 7 underscores the Lukan idea of continuity between Judaism and the church.[360] One can obtain life by keeping the com-

359. Taeger, *Mensch*, 221, emphasizes human initiative very strongly: "The decision made in response to the proclamation of the gospel—Luke considers this important—is not removed from human responsibility; the promise of salvation is bound to this prior decision."

360. This aspect is emphasized by Matthias Klinghardt, *Gesetz und Volk Gottes* (WUNT 2.32; Tübingen: Mohr, 1988), passim; on the Lukan understanding of the law, cf. further Helmut Merkel, "Das Gesetz im lukanischen Doppelwerk," in *Schrift und Tradition: Festschrift für Josef Ernst zum 70. Geburtstag* (ed. Knut Backhaus and Franz Georg Untergassmair; Paderborn: Schö-

mandments (Luke 10:28), if one adds to this giving up one's possessions and discipleship to Jesus.

On the other hand, faith remains the condition of salvation (Luke 7:50; 8:48; Acts 16:31); except for the love command, the law receives no independent significance in Luke's ethics (see below, §8.4.6); God himself annuls the law's fundamental contrast between "clean" and "unclean" (Acts 10:28; 11:9); and in Acts 13:38–39, under the distinct influence of traditional Pauline theology, the law is portrayed as inadequate to save: "Let it be known to you therefore, my brothers, that through this man forgiveness of sins is proclaimed to you; by this Jesus everyone who believes is set free from all those sins from which you could not be freed by the law of Moses." In Acts 15:10, in response to the demand that Gentiles who want to become Christians must be circumcised, Peter makes a (remarkable!) argument: "Now therefore why are you putting God to the test by placing on the neck of the disciples a yoke that neither our ancestors nor we have been able to bear?" Here, circumcision is tacitly separated from the law and regarded as generally no longer in force. This is followed with a brief formula with Pauline overtones: "We believe that we will be saved through the grace of the Lord Jesus, just as they will" (Acts 15:11).[361]

How are these two series of statements to be related to each other? Luke 24:44 presents a possible explanatory model when the risen Lord says to the disciples on the way to Emmaus: "Everything written about me in the law of Moses, the prophets, and the psalms must be fulfilled." *Because the law was fulfilled in the life, death, and resurrection of Jesus, Luke can adjudicate a continuing significance to the law as newly interpreted within the framework of his concept of continuity between Israel and the church.* The "apostolic decree" (Acts 15:20, 29; 21:25) is located precisely within this line of thought: it formulates for Jewish Christians, God-fearers, and people from Greco-Roman religious backgrounds an acceptable compromise that does not include the precondition of circumcision.[362] It is thus no accident that at the end of Luke-Acts Paul is still attempting to bring the Jews in Rome to Jesus and the kingdom of God "from the law of Moses and from the prophets" (Acts 28:23).

---

ningh, 1996), 119–33; Hans Klein, "Rechtfertigung aus Glauben als Ergänzung der Gerechtigkeit aus dem Gesetz," in *Ja und Nein: Christliche Theologie im Angesicht Israels; Festschrift zum 70. Geburtstag von Wolfgang Schrage* (ed. Klaus Wengst et al.; Neukirchen-Vluyn: Neukirchener Verlag, 1998), 155–64.

361. Following H. Klein, Hahn (*Theologie*, 1:573) appropriately comments: "In this respect justification by faith supplements and overlaps justification by the law."

362. On the apostolic decree, cf. Jürgen Wehnert, *Die Reinheit des christlichen Gottesvolkes aus Juden und Heiden: Studien zum historischen und theologischen Hintergrund des sogenannten Aposteldekrets* (FRLANT 173; Göttingen: Vandenhoeck & Ruprecht, 1997).

Human Kinship with God

In the Areopagus speech (see above, §8.4.1), the Lukan Paul advocates an anthropology that consciously adopts basic assumptions of Stoic thought[363] in order to highlight the cultural standard of the "new way" (Acts 19:23) and establish the new group's capacity for making contact with and taking over ideas from its social and religious milieu. The concept of "seeking God" in Acts 17:27 (". . . so that they would search for God and perhaps grope for him and find him—though indeed he is not far from each one of us") has parallels in the Greek tradition (cf. Plato, *Apol.* 19B; *Gorg.* 457D; Xenophon, *Mem.* 1.1.15). Luke concludes the discourse with a poetic touch that incorporates the idea of human kinship with the divine in a positive sense, "For 'In him we live and move and have our being'; as even some of your own poets have said, 'For we too are his offspring'" (Acts 17:28). In the Greek (and later Roman) philosophy and theology, the ideas that God can be known from the world of nature, and that a kinship relation between God and humanity can be inferred from that knowability, are basic assumptions underlying the understanding of reality. It was already attributed to a saying of Pythagoras that "human beings are kin to God" (Diogenes Laertius, *Vit. phil.* 8.27; cf. further Plato, *Leg.* 10.899D; Cicero, *Nat. d.* 2.33–34; *Tusc.* 1.28.68–69; Seneca, *Ep.* 41.1; Epictetus, *Diatr.* 1.6.19; 2.8.11; 4.1.104). So also Dio Chrysostom, at practically the same time as Luke (ca. 40–120 CE), indicates that the idea that gods and human beings share a common essence was widespread. "An idea regarding him and a conception of him common to the whole human race . . . a conception that is inevitable and innate in every creature endowed with reason, arising in the course of nature [κατὰ φύσιν] without any human teacher . . . rendered manifest God's kinship with man and furnished many evidences of this truth" (*Or.* 12.27). Dio emphasizes, "For inasmuch as these earlier men were not living dispersed far away from the divine being or beyond his borders apart by themselves, but had grown up in the very center of things. . . . How, then, could they have remained ignorant and conceived no inkling of him who had sowed and planted and was now preserving and nourishing them, when on every side they were filled with the divine nature . . . They dwelt on earth, but beheld the light of heaven" (*Or.* 28–29). It fits Luke's optimistic view of human nature (in contrast to that of Paul), that he reckons with the possibility of a natural, reasonable knowledge of God. This does not at all mean that he denies his Christian standpoint, for his perspective is framed by faith in the acts of God at creation and resurrection.[364] Within

363. It needs to be remembered that such ideas had already found an entrée in Hellenistic Judaism; cf. W. Nauck, "Die Tradition und Komposition der Areopagrede," *ZTK* 53 (1956): 11–52.

364. One does not do justice to the Areopagus speech if the historical Paul as the norm of truth stands in the background, as even J. Roloff, in an otherwise exemplary analysis tends to do: "there is no reference at all to the cross" (Roloff, *Apostelgeschichte*, 267). The same is true

this framework, however, Luke has no hesitation about affirming the basic idea of the Areopagus speech: *every human being is related to God and can attain a knowledge of God.*

8.4.6 Ethics

A concern for ethics is embedded in Luke's concepts of Christian origins and his concern for continuity between Israel and the church, as signaled by the recurring question "What should we/I do?" in Luke 3:10; 10:25; 16:3; 18:18; Acts 2:37; 16:30. The prevalence of ethical motifs in the gospel, which recedes somewhat in Acts, shows that Luke understands the ethical requirement to be anchored in the time of beginnings, i.e., concretely in the life of Jesus and the earliest church.[365] This concern is primarily oriented to three problem areas that resulted from the successful mission to the Gentiles in Asia Minor and Europe without the precondition of circumcision.

Wealth and Poverty in the Christian Community

By the turn of the first century CE, the church included some members with property and high social status (cf. Acts 17:4; 18:8), so that the right use of money and property became a central problem of Lukan ethics (cf. Luke 3:11; Acts 2:45; 4:34–37). Wealthy people in the church were self-righteous and greedy (cf. Luke 12:13–15; 16:14–15); they disdained the poor (Luke 18:9) and were in danger of letting their striving after wealth cause them to fall away from the faith (cf. Luke 8:14; 9:25). Luke addresses these negative aspects of his church with a multilayered line of argument. John the Baptist already stands in the service of an ethical conception, as shown in his responses to questions from various social groups (Luke 3:10–14).[366] Luke modulates the demand for μετάνοια (repentance) into the realm of ethics and calls for "fruits worthy of repentance" (3:8). Acceptance of the baptism of repentance is realized in a new way of life that proceeds from the threefold question "What should we do?" (3:10, 12, 14); vv. 10–11 suggest a willingness to give generously, while vv. 12–14 forbid tax collectors and soldiers to misuse their privilege and power. In the *Sermon on the Plain* (6:20–49) Luke interprets the command to love one's neighbor in the sense of his ethic of benevolence. He rejects the ethic of mutuality structured according to how others respond (6:32–34) and presents a different model: "But love your enemies, do good, and lend, expecting nothing in return. Your reward will

---

when Luke is seen only within the framework of a resolute Jewish-Christian line of argument that is supposed to keep its distance from everything "pagan"; so Löning, "Das Evangelium und die Kulturen," 2632–36, and Jervell, *Apostelgeschichte*, 452ff.

365. Cf. Friedrich Wilhelm Horn, *Glaube und Handeln in der Theologie des Lukas* (GTA 26; Göttingen: Vandenhoeck & Ruprecht, 1983), 35.

366. For analysis, cf. ibid., 91–97.

be great, and you will be children of the Most High; for he is kind to the ungrateful and the wicked" (6:35). In the *thematic blocks* Luke 12:13–34 and 16:1–31, the evangelist deals comprehensively with wealth regarded as a problem, for the meaning of life is not found in what one possesses (cf. 12:15), and the lust for more money is against the will of God (cf. 12:15; 16:14). So also the stories of the disciples' dispute about rank in the kingdom of God (9:46–48; 22:24–27) and the great banquet (14:7–24) critique the attitude of wealthy Christians. The call to discipleship and the abandonment of one's possessions condition each other (cf. 5:11, 28; 8:3; 9:3; 10:4; 18:28) in such a way that Luke 14:33 is downright programmatic: "So therefore, none of you can become my disciple if you do not give up all your possessions." The call to distance oneself from one's possessions is coupled with the readiness *to give alms* (cf. 11:41; 12:21, 33–34; 16:9, 27–31). The programmatic command of Luke 12:33a comes from the evangelist: "Sell your possessions, and give alms." Thus the call to discipleship extended to the wealthy ruler (18:18–23) is associated with the challenge to sell all (πάντα only in Luke 18:22, not in the parallels) and to give to the poor. "Indeed, it is easier for a camel to go through the eye of a needle than for someone who is rich to enter the kingdom of God" (Luke 18:25). Luke still maintains that such giving is a voluntary choice (cf. Acts 5:4) conditioned by individual possibilities (cf. Acts 11:29). The Ebionite traditions (Luke 1:46–55; 6:20–26; 16:19–26), which originally proclaimed a reversal of relationships in the next world, become for Luke a call to human beings to change their ways in this world.

In contrast to the tensions in his own church, the evangelist portrays the *earliest Jerusalem church as a loving community that voluntarily shared its goods.*[367] Its members renounced claims to their own property for the sake of those in need (Acts 2:45; 4:34), so that private property was used in common (Acts 4:32). Acts 2:45 portrays the role of the apostles in the sale and distribution of goods: "They would sell their possessions and goods and distribute the proceeds to all, as any had need." Further nuances are reported in the second summary; as previously in Acts 2:44, so in 4:32 the ancient ideal of friendship is put into practice (ἅπαντα κοινά, "to have everything in common"),[368] and for the first time the hearers/readers learn that members of the church had houses and land (cf. Acts 4:34). In Acts 4:36–37 an isolated tradition about Barnabas's sale of property is mentioned, the proceeds of which he turned

367. On this point cf. Klauck, "Gütergemeinschaft," 69–100; Theissen, "Liebeskommunismus," 689–712; Horn, "Gütergemeinschaft," 370–83.

368. As parallels from antiquity, cf., e.g., Diogenes Laertius, *Vit. phil.* 8.10; Iamblichus, *Vit. Pyth.* 168–169 (Pythagoras as the originator of this concept); Diogenes Laertius, *Vit. phil.* 6.72 (the Cynic Diogenes); Plato, *Resp.* 5.462A; Aristotle, *Eth. Nic.* 8.1159A; 9.1168B; Cicero, *Off.* 1.51; Philo, *Good Person* 75–91; Josephus, *JW* 2.119–161. For discussion and interpretation, cf. B. H. Mönning, "Die Darstellung des urchristlichen Kommunismus nach der Apostelgeschichte des Lukas" (ThD diss., Georg August Universität, Göttingen, 1978).

over to the apostles for distribution. The considerable aporias of these summaries are obvious:

1. The conduct of the earliest church makes no sense economically, since by the sale of their property they lost their economic and social livelihood.
2. Luke's portrayal of the earliest church is contradictory, for the story of Ananias and Sapphira in Acts 5:1–11 presupposes it was not the case that "everyone had everything in common," and that this was not expected.
3. The juxtaposition of general statements about the sale of all property and the individual case of Barnabas indicates that Luke has generalized individual cases.
4. Paul presupposes private property in his churches as self-evident. If the community of goods in Jerusalem ever existed in the way Luke describes, it was not followed in any other and later churches.

These observations lead to the conclusion that Luke has generalized cases of individuals who sold their property and applied the model to the early Jerusalem church as a whole. In particular, the reference to Barnabas in Acts 4:36–37 points in this direction, for there would be no point in relating what Barnabas did if everyone else in the Jerusalem church was doing the same. It was probably the case that the apostles received the proceeds from the sale of individual houses and property and apportioned them according to the needs of individual members of the church.

Luke has a broad spectrum of statements that deal with issues with and criticisms of the wealthy (Luke 1:53; 6:24–25; 8:14; 12:13–21; 14:15–24; 16:14–15, 19–31), promises to the poor (1:53; 4:18–19; 6:20–21; 7:22), calls to abandon one's property (5:11, 28; 12:33–34; 14:33; 18:18–30), and generous deeds of charity and care for others (3:10–11; 6:33–38; 8:1–3; 16:9; 19:1–10; 21:1–4). How are all these types of statements to be related to one another? Luke's parenesis is addressed primarily to the rich people in his church, challenging them to distance themselves from their wealth, since it could lead to their falling away from the faith. He can be labeled neither as an "evangelist of the rich" nor as an "evangelist of the poor," but is "evangelist of the whole church."[369] His goal is not an uncompromising critique of the wealthy but the actualization of a community of love that embraces both rich and poor in one church—an aim that presupposes the wealthy are willing to give alms.[370] To this extent,

369. Cf. Horn, *Glaube und Handeln*, 243.

370. Ibid., 231 and elsewhere, sees Luke's own concept of social ethics reflected in the exhortation to the wealthy to give alms. In contrast, Schottroff and Stegemann, *Jesus and the Hope of the Poor*, 116, speak of an equality of possessions within the church as Luke's social goal. Kiyoshi Mineshige, *Besitzverzicht und Almosen bei Lukas: Wesen und Forderung des lu-*

Luke does write *a gospel directed to the wealthy on behalf of the poor*. "The evangelist directs his message primarily to the propertied Christians of his church, to their lack of charity and sense of superiority, criticizes their insistence on an ethic of mutuality, and points to the right way of unreserved generosity and doing good."[371] Christian existence is not oriented to wealth and affluence but to loving service to one's neighbor. Luke thus uses as models both the sharing of property by Jesus's disciples in the earliest Jerusalem church and the generosity of the Roman sympathizer Cornelius, whose "prayers and alms before God" are explicitly mentioned twice (Acts 10:4, 31). Luke intends that these pictures of unreserved commitment to discipleship, and the ideal of life together in a loving community that is actually put into practice, should also have a formative influence on his own church. By presenting the church as a loving, sharing community of faith, he takes up the teaching of Jesus that he has Paul summarize in his farewell speech as his legacy to the church in Acts 20:35: "It is more blessed to give than to receive."

The Relation of the Christian to the State

As he portrays the encounters between Jesus (and Paul) with representatives of the state, Luke already has in view the situation of the church in the Roman Empire.[372] Thereby to be noted at the compositional level is the remarkable

kanischen Vermögensethos (WUNT 2.163; Tübingen: Mohr Siebeck, 2003), 263–64, regards this theme as part of Luke's thinking in terms of historical epochs: "Luke thinks of three different periods of history: the time of Jesus, the time of the church's beginnings, and his own time. Renunciation of possessions applies [only] to the time of Jesus. Thus the first disciples left all their possessions when they decided to follow Jesus. This type of renunciation was no longer required in the time of the church. In its place, the community of goods was the norm for the earliest days of the church. . . . Differently from either of the preceding two periods, in Luke's own time neither renunciation of property nor community of goods was required. Instead, the Christians of his own time, including his readers, are challenged to support needy members of the church through freewill offerings." Vincenzo Petracca, *Gott oder das Geld: Die Besitzethik des Lukas* (TANZ 39; Tübingen: Francke, 2003), 354, regards Luke's central theme of saving the lost to be concretized in two ways by the theme of possessions: "On the one hand, seeking the lost leads to salvation for the poor and the outsider. On the other hand, salvation for the rich and respected facilitates their help for the poor and outsider, the expression of their unreserved devotion to God instead of striving for property and social prestige."

371. Horn, *Glaube und Handeln*, 107.

372. The literature on this theme is very extensive; cf., e.g., Gerhard Schneider, *Verleugnung, Verspottung und Verhör Jesu nach Lukas 22,54–71: Studien zur lukanischen Darstellung der Passion* (SANT 22; Munich: Kösel, 1969); Radl, *Paulus und Jesus*; W. Walaskay, *"And So We Came to Rome": The Political Perspective of St. Luke* (SNTSMS 49; Cambridge: Cambridge University Press, 1983); Philip Francis Esler, *Community and Society in Luke-Acts* (SNTSMS 57; Cambridge: Cambridge University Press, 1987); Wolfgang Stegemann, *Zwischen Synagoge und Obrigkeit: Zur historischen Situation der lukanischen Christen* (FRLANT 152; Göttingen: Vandenhoeck & Ruprecht, 1991); Michael Wolter, "Die Juden und die Obrigkeit bei Lukas," in *Ja und Nein: Christliche Theologie im Angesicht Israels; Festschrift zum 70. Geburtstag von Wolfgang Schrage* (ed. Klaus Wengst et al.; Neukirchen-Vluyn: Neukirchener Verlag, 1998),

parallelism between Jesus's hearing before the authorities (Luke 22:1–23:56) and the prolonged procedure of Paul's trial from his arrest in Jerusalem to his arrival in Rome (Acts 21:15–28:31). In *Jesus's trial* before Pilate the thrice-repeated Jewish charge, intended to place Jesus in the Zealot context (cf. Luke 23:2, 5, 14),[373] is juxtaposed to Pilate's thrice-repeated declaration of Jesus's innocence (cf. Luke 23:4, 14–15, 22). Pilate three times declares his intention to release Jesus (Luke 23:16, 20, 22), only to allow himself to be diverted each time by the outcry of the Sanhedrin and the people. In Luke's portrayal, Herod Antipas, a friend of the Romans, also strikingly confirms Jesus's innocence (Luke 23:15; cf. previously 9:7–9), as do those crucified with Jesus and the Roman centurion (23:41, 47). Thus the Jewish leaders and people seem to be solely responsible for the death of Jesus, so that there is great irony in the situation that Barabbas, who was in fact guilty of insurrection and murder, is released (Luke 23:18–19), while the innocent Jesus is crucified. In portraying matters in this way, Luke is obviously pursuing the tendency to *absolve the Romans and those associated with them (Herod Antipas)* and to place the guilt for Jesus's death on the Jews. This tendency can also be seen in the *legal proceedings against Paul.*[374] Paul is presented as a law-abiding Roman citizen (cf. Acts 25:8) whose legal rights are respected by the government court system (Acts 16:37ff.; 22:25ff.), which finally rescues him from the Jews (cf. Acts 23:10, 27) and grants him a rather gentlemanly custody in Rome (Acts 28:30–31). Paul is Luke's demonstration that "Christian preaching does not impinge on the power of the empire."[375] It is not the Roman government that persecutes Paul, but the Jews (cf. Acts 13:50; 17:5–7, 13; 21:27ff.). The Jews take illegal measures against Paul (cf. Acts 23:12–15; 25:3), or turn to the state to carry out their purposes against him (cf. Acts 18:12ff.; 24:1ff.; 25:5), but are constantly thwarted in this attempt. To be sure, the state in Luke's view must proceed against crime and sacrilege, but it is not the state's job to interfere in religious issues (cf. Acts 18:12–17). There are thus no grounds for either Gallio (Acts 18:15) or Festus (Acts 25:18, 25) to charge Paul with any crime. According to Roman law Paul was innocent and really should have been released (cf. Acts 25:25; 26:31–32), and only corruption and dysfunction in the

---

277–90; Freidrich Wilhelm Horn, "Die Haltung des Lukas zum römischen Staat im Evangelium und in der Apostelgeschichte," in *The Unity of Luke-Acts* (ed. J. Verheyden; BETL 142; Louvain: Leuven University Press, 1999), 203–24; Martin Meiser, "Lukas und die römische Staatsmacht," in *Zwischen den Reichen: Neues Testament und römische Herrschaft: Vorträge auf der Ersten Konferenz der European Association for Biblical Studies* (ed. Michael Labahn and Jürgen Zangenberg; TANZ 36; Tübingen: Francke, 2002), 175–93.

373. Horn, "Haltung des Lukas," 205.

374. On this point cf. Brian Rapske, *The Book of Acts and Paul in Roman Custody* (Book of Acts in Its First Century Setting 3; Grand Rapids: Eerdmans, 1994); Omerzu, *Der Prozess des Paulus.*

375. Hans Conzelmann, *Acts of the Apostles: A Commentary on the Acts of the Apostles* (Hermeneia; trans. James Limburg et al.; Philadelphia: Fortress, 1987), xlvii.

Roman legal system (cf. Acts 24:26ff.; 25:9) forced Paul to appeal to Caesar. In Rome, Paul was relatively free to move about and preach, and it is no accident that the last word of Luke's two volumes is ἀκωλύτως (unhindered). Other passages in Luke-Acts manifest this same positive attitude toward Rome. Jesus's parents follow the edict of the emperor without hesitation (Luke 2:1, 5), John the Baptist's sermon to various social classes (3:10–14) directs Roman military and administrative personnel to proper conduct in their vocation, the centurion beneath the cross "praises God" (Luke 23:47), and the first Gentile to be converted is an officer of the Roman army (Acts 10).

The tendency of Luke's presentation is clear: the Jewish leaders and people are *the* ones who persecute Jesus and the Christians (Luke develops the image already present in Mark 15:16–20; cf. further Acts 13:50; 17:5–7, 13; 21:17ff.), while the Roman authorities intervene when Christians are attacked by Jews and protect them (Acts 19:23–40; 23:29; 25:25; 26:31). The Romans and the family of Herod associated with Rome are presented in a positive light, while the Jews are portrayed negatively. What are the grounds for this (apologetic) construction?[376] Luke obviously wants to maintain some elbow room for his church in relation to the state, the space it needs in order to practice its worship and structure its congregational life. He counteracts potential conflicts with the government by showing that Christians conduct themselves with loyalty to the authorities and pose no danger to the state. After the events associated with the fire in Rome in 64 CE and the continuing agitation from the Jewish side, Luke attempts to specify his church's place in society.[377] He thus does not presuppose any situation of acute persecution[378] but rather addresses his call to fearless confession (cf. Luke 12:1–12)[379] to situations involving local Jewish repressions (cf. Acts 13:45, 50; 14:2, 5, 19; 16:19ff.; 17:5–6, 13; 18:12, 17; 19:9, 23–40) and to his own church's precarious life-setting between the conflicting forces of the synagogue and the Roman courts. It is to be noted

376. In view of the exegetical data, the concept of apologetics is unavoidable (cf. especially Conzelmann, *Theology of St. Luke*, 138–49) but at the same time is not adequate to describe Luke's stance. For the portrayal of legally relevant positions and the emphasis on law that Luke associates with them, cf. Lukas Bormann, "Die Verrechtlichung der frühesten christlichen Überlieferung im lukanischen Schrifttum," in *Religious Propaganda and Missionary Competition in the New Testament World: Essays Honoring Dieter Georgi* (ed. Lukas Bormann et al.; NovTSup 74; Leiden: Brill, 1994), 283–311.

377. Differently Wolter, "Obrigkeit," 289, who argues that Luke's statements are not made in the service of any sort of apologetic, "either in favor of the Christians over against the Roman state, or in favor of the Roman state over against readers of Luke-Acts. Instead, the individual episodes are consistently oriented to the relation of the main narrative characters to the Jews or Judaism, and Luke thus represents them to his Christian readers as constituent elements in the process of Christian-Jewish separation that was under way, a process that resulted in the parallel existence of the primarily Gentile church and Judaism."

378. Walter Schmithals' several publications assume a situation of persecution; for a critique of this view, cf. Horn, *Glaube und Handeln*, 216–20.

379. Cf. the analyses of Stegemann, *Zwischen Synagoge und Obrigkeit*, 40–90.

that Luke does not thereby argue that Christianity is the better Judaism and must therefore receive Roman protection. For the evangelist, Christianity is an independent entity, politically loyal to Rome in its own right. The new movement even appears as a new potentially elite group, for its leading representatives consistently act in ways both politically and ethically right. Luke's interest in the relation between right and religion, always constitutive for ancient thought, has yet another dimension: "Luke surveys the scene from an external perspective. He thus opens up the Jesus tradition to readers of the Roman and Greco-Hellenistic world in the broadest sense of the term, whether to Hellenistic Jews, to Greeks, or to Romans familiar with the ideas of the Hellenistic world."[380] Not only are the texts thus enriched with interesting and suspenseful details, but Luke also shows himself to be thoroughly acquainted with the political, legal, and religious world.

None of these interests of course prevent the evangelist from also including critical words (cf. Luke 3:19; 13:32–33: Herod Antipas as hostile to John the Baptist and Jesus; Luke 13:1, Pilate's violence), and in Acts 5:29 Peter can say, "We must obey God rather than any human authority." Luke understands the ambivalence of political power, for only in Luke's version of the temptation story is the devil a clear analogy to the Roman Caesar (Luke 4:6, "And the devil said to him, 'To you I will give their glory and all this authority; for it has been given over to me, and I give it to anyone I please'").[381]

Exemplary Life

In Luke, directions to the disciples also are transparent to the current situation of his church, i.e., already in the gospel the time of the church is always present in the way the story is told. First of all, the third evangelist demonstrates by the life of Jesus what a true Christian life looks like. Jesus's way to the Passion has prototypical character: "For who is greater, the one who is at the table or the one who serves? Is it not the one at the table? But I am among you as one who serves" (Luke 22:27). The motifs of compassion and justice are the twin foundations for the whole ethical structure, as shown by the essence of God's nature (Luke 6:36, "Be merciful, just as your Father is merciful"), and the model behavior of Zechariah (1:72, 74–75), the woman of Luke 7:47, and Zacchaeus (19:8–9). It is thus no accident that all the *example stories* in the New Testament are found in the Gospel of Luke.[382] The stories of the Rich Fool (Luke 12:16–21), of the Good Samaritan (10:25–37), of the Rich Man and Poor Lazarus (16:19–31) and the Pharisee and the Tax Col-

380. Lukas Bormann, *Recht, Gerechtigkeit und Religion im Lukasevangelium* (SUNT 24; Göttingen: Vandenhoeck & Ruprecht, 2001), 358.

381. On this point cf. Paul Mikat, "Lukanische Christusverkündigung und Kaiserkult: Zum Problem der christlichen Loyalität gegenüber dem Staat," in *Religionsrechtliche Schriften* (ASE 5; Berlin: Duncker & Humblot, 1974), 809–28.

382. On example stories, cf. Erlemann, *Gleichnisauslegung*, 81–82.

lector (18:9–14) are models of right and wrong conduct intended directly to motivate the church to step over cultural boundaries with compassion, not to base its life on material possessions, and to practice genuine humility in relation to both God and other human beings. Authentic humility, lowliness (Luke 9:46–48; 14:7–11; 18:9–14), and warnings against greed all belong together (cf. 1:51–52; 18:9ff.; 22:24ff.).[383] This basic orientation is united with the double command of love (Luke 10:26–27), the Decalogue (18:20), and the Old Testament tradition (16:29, 31, Moses and the prophets). The disciples are challenged to conduct their lives in a respectable manner (Luke 3:12–14), to share their material resources (3:10–12), to give to those who ask (6:30), not to judge others (6:37), and to forgive each other's wrongs (6:37b, "Forgive, and you will be forgiven"). By renouncing any claims for their own person, the disciples are like their Master and become his followers (cf. Luke 21:12, 17). By addressing the words about self-denial, cross bearing, and discipleship to "all," and adding the word "daily" to the saying about bearing the cross (9:23), Luke links the Passion with the practice of faith in everyday life. *Faith must correspond to action, saying with doing*, for to be a disciple is to produce fruit/results (6:46, "Why do you call me 'Lord, Lord,' and do not do what I tell you?"). In continuity with Jesus, the post-Easter way for both individual and church can only be the way of service and suffering.

8.4.7 Ecclesiology

Ecclesiology is another central element of Luke's salvation-history perspective, for he sees the church in direct relationship with the act of God in history. The evangelist wants to show how the church developed through the testimony of Jesus's witnesses and thus stands in unbroken continuity with Jesus's own history.[384] Foundational for this view is the transition from the story of Passion and Easter to the time of the church: according to Luke 24:47–49 and Acts 1:8, the risen and ascended Lord sends the Spirit on the apostles, which is the empowering act for the proclamation of the message of salvation throughout the world, i.e., *the evangelistic mission of the church and the assembling of the eschatological community of salvation stand under the presupposition of the continuing work of the exalted Lord through the Holy Spirit* (see above, §8.4.3). The Spirit is received in *baptism* (Acts 2:38), so that now Christian believers, like Jesus himself (Luke 4:18), are filled with the power of God and led by his Spirit.[385] Moreover, *table fellowship with Jesus* is the place where this bond with him is constantly renewed and realized, for just as the earthly Jesus invited his

383. Cf. here Horn, *Glaube und Handeln*, 204–15.

384. Cf. Reinmuth, *Anthropologie*, 120: "The way of Jesus is conceived as history that must be witnessed to before all people, in order that they may repent and be forgiven."

385. On Acts statements about baptism, cf. Friedrich Avemarie, *Die Tauferzählrlung der Apostelgeschichte* (WUNT 139; Tübingen: Mohr, 2002).

followers to eat with him and celebrated a farewell meal with them (Luke 9:16; 22:16), the Risen One makes himself known to them in the breaking of bread (Luke 24:30) and manifests the unity of the church in the eucharistic celebration (Acts 2:42).[386] Within this conceptual framework, Luke presents all the events and episodes that accord with his understanding of the continuity and unity of salvation history, omitting or reinterpreting events that appear to contradict these lines of thought.

The Church as People of God

Luke's ecclesiology is based on the concept of the gathering of the church as the people of God.[387] For Luke, the church comes into being as a process within the history of salvation, as an act of God, centered on the concept of its abiding continuity with Israel as the people of God (see above, §8.4.1). The message of salvation applies to Israel and occurs in Israel, while at the same time it results in a division within Israel, a separation that is already a theme in the prologue and reaches its climax in the Passion narrative. Even after the gospel has been rejected by the majority of Israel and the church has opened its doors to the Gentiles, the church continues to be the eschatological and fulfilled Israel—now, of course, an Israel composed of Gentiles and Jews. This means in effect that Luke claims most of the Jewish people have excluded themselves from the people of God (see above, §8.4.1).

Pentecost

The eschatological people of God, assembled under the guidance of the Holy Spirit, emerges visibly into history on Pentecost (Acts 2),[388] an event that represents not a completely new beginning but the spectacular fulfillment of Old Testament prophecies. The Spirit is given to the whole people of God, including the Gentiles who still stand outside Israel. According to Luke, the gathering of the people of God runs its course as an event in two phases, both determined by the Spirit, which are characterized as fulfillment of God's promises. At the center of the *founding phase* stands the earliest Jerusalem church: Luke portrays its beginnings as an epoch of unity—a unity in prayer, in eucharistic fellowship, and in teaching and acting. His depictions of social and economic relationships

386. On this point cf. Heinz Schürmann, "Der Abendmahlsbericht Lk 22,7–38 als Gottesdienstordnung, Gemeindeordnung, Lebensordnung," in *Ursprung und Gestalt: Erörterungen und Besinnungen zum Neuen Testament* (ed. Heinz Schürmann; KBANT 2; Düsseldorf: Patmos, 1970), 108–50; Joachim Wanke, *Beobachtungen zum Eucharistieverständnis des Lukas auf Grund der lukanischen Mahlberichte* (ETS 8; Leipzig: St-Benno-Verlag, 1973); Willibald Bösen, *Jesusmahl, Eucharistisches Mahl, Endzeitmahl: Ein Beitrag zur Theologie des Lukas* (SBS 67; Stuttgart: 1980).

387. Cf. Roloff, *Kirche im Neuen Testament*, 192–206.

388. On Pentecost in Acts, cf. J. Kremer, *Pfingstbericht und Pfingstgeschehen* (SBS 63/64; Stuttgart: Katholisches Bibelwerk, 1973).

within the earliest church also stand under the motif of unity, explicitly underscored by the summaries of Acts 2:42–46 and 4:32–35. In this way Luke wants to show that the apostles, led by the Spirit, have really gathered eschatological Israel. At the end of this gathering phase, Luke uses the word ἐκκλησία (church) for the first time. This centering on Israel is then extended in a broader phase by the coming in of the Gentiles, in which the "Godfearers" (cf. Acts 13:16, 26, 43, 50; 16:14; 17:4, 17; 18:7, 13; 19:27) play a very special role, for example, the centurion Cornelius (Acts 10:2, 22, 35).[389] In this phase, the beginning period of Acts 1–5 remains constantly in view, but now the Jews appear in a different light, for they repeatedly oppose the proclamation of the gospel and thus become enemies of the people of God (cf. Acts 12:1–5; 13:45; 14:4, 19; 17:5, 13; 18:6; 21:27). This view of the growth of the church through both continuity and change is programmatically pictured by Luke in the first part of the speech given by James in Acts 15:16–17: "'After this I will return, and I will rebuild the dwelling of David, which has fallen; from its ruins I will rebuild it, and I will set it up, so that all other peoples may seek the Lord—even all the Gentiles over whom my name has been called.' Thus says the Lord, who has been making these things known from long ago." For Luke, Gentile Christians and Jewish Christians do not live in the church as two peoples of God alongside each other but together form the one people of God, which owes its existence to God's faithfulness to his promise to Israel. At the beginning of Acts, Jerusalem is the place of Jesus's work and the origin of the church, but at the end of the narrative the holy city appears in an entirely different perspective. It is the place no longer of salvation but of disaster, for there Paul is taken prisoner and threatened with death by the lynch-justice of the Jews (Acts 21:27–36). Rome, meanwhile, appears in an ever more positive light (Acts 19:21; 23:11), ultimately becoming the real place for preaching the gospel (Acts 23:11). Neither the forces of nature (Acts 27:1–28:10) nor political and legal intrigues can prevent Paul, as authorized bearer of the gospel message, from reaching this goal. The reader is thus assured that with Paul's arrival in Rome, the purpose of God has also reached its goal, and the promise of the risen Jesus in Acts 1:8 has found its fulfillment.

The Twelve Apostles

For Luke, the twelve apostles are a prototype of the church, for they bear witness to the way of the earthly Jesus (Luke 6:12–16); they are representatives of Israel (22:30); the mission charge is directed to them (24:47); they become eyewitnesses of the ascension and exaltation (Luke 24:48; Acts 1:21–22); and they are the recipients of the Spirit (Luke 24:49; Acts 1:8).[390] The twelve apostles

389. Cf. here Bernd Wander, *Gottesfürchtige und Sympathisanten: Studien zum heidnischen Umfeld von Diasporasynagogen* (WUNT 104; Tübingen: Mohr, 1998).

390. On Luke's understanding of apostleship, cf. on the one hand Günter Klein, *Die zwölf Apostel: Ursprung und Gehalt einer Idee* (FRLANT 77; Göttingen: Vandenhoeck & Ruprecht,

are thus the designated and authorized witnesses of the Christ event and the definitive bearers of tradition. To a certain extent, they represent for Luke the fulfilled Israel, in that they symbolize the continuity between the time of Jesus and the church that is in the process of formation. In these functions, they can have no successors, for they are historically and theologically unique guarantors of the Jesus-tradition and prototypes of the later ecclesiastical offices. Thus, according to Acts 1:21–22, the one who is admitted to this circle as Judas's replacement must be "one of the men who have accompanied us during all the time that the Lord Jesus went in and out among us, beginning from the baptism of John until the day when he was taken up from us—one of these must become a witness with us to his resurrection." Matthias fulfills these criteria, and is thus selected (by the Spirit) for this office. Obviously, the Lukan concept of the twelve apostles serves to secure the picture outlined by Luke in 1:1–4: the Jesus tradition taught by the church is trustworthy. To accomplish this goal, Luke equates the pre-Easter circle of disciples with the Twelve (Luke 6:13, "And when day came, he called his disciples and chose twelve of them, whom he also named Apostles"), and identifies the Twelve with the post-Easter circle of the apostles. After Easter, the twelve apostles include the Jesus tradition in the church's missionary proclamation (Acts 2:22–23; 4:10ff.; 6:4) and make it the foundation of the Jerusalem church, as expressed in Acts 2:42, "they continued in the teaching of the Apostles." Luke clearly accents certain items in his concept of continuity, for it is the encounter with the risen and exalted Lord in Luke 24:47 and Acts 1:8 that first makes the Twelve active "witnesses" who hand on the traditions in continuity with Jesus's own life and teachings and apply them within the developing church. Since the risen Jesus instructed the apostles for "forty days" (Acts 1:3), they become for Luke the decisive bearers of the Jesus tradition beyond Easter and Pentecost. This means that the whole Jesus tradition is interpreted in the light of the resurrection.

Luke's Understanding of Paul

Within this conception, Luke cannot regard Paul as an apostle, since, as one called after Easter (Acts 9:1–19), he is not one who can be a bearer of the Jesus tradition from the very beginning.[391] On the one hand, Paul must then be placed in salvation history after the time of the calling of the "real" apostles; on the other hand, like them, he is also a "witness" of the Christ event (22:15; 26:16), and the effects of his own work exceed theirs by far, as especially the second half of Acts makes clear. With a deft narrative touch, Luke has Paul

1961), 114ff.; on the other side, cf. Jürgen Roloff, *Apostolat, Verkündigung, Kirche* (1st ed.; Gütersloh: Gütersloher Verlagshaus G. Mohn, 1965), 169–235.

391. The exceptions in Acts 14:4, 14 probably go back to pre-Lukan tradition; cf. Roloff, *Apostelgeschichte*, 211.

make a cameo appearance in Acts 8:3; thus Stephen, the church's first martyr, and Paul, its greatest martyr, appear in the same scene. The story of Paul is the real theological center of Acts.[392] Paul functions as representative of the second Christian generation, to whom Luke's own (third-generation) church owes its faith. Paul should by no means be demoted in contrast to the Twelve, for, like them, he represents a fundamental phase in the formation of the church. At the Apostolic Council, the apostles appear last (Acts 15:2, 4, 6, 22–23); thereafter they are not mentioned at all, for they have fulfilled their salvation-historical role for the unity of the church. As the narrative perspective is changed from Jerusalem to Rome, the apostles lose their significance, while Paul becomes the central character in the narrative.

Of foundational importance for Luke's ecclesiology is *Paul's farewell speech to the Ephesian elders at Miletus* (Acts 20:17–38).[393] Here the official ministers that lead the congregations of post-Pauline times are addressed, and a model of congregational structure is presupposed. The model of the essential nature and responsibilities of church leadership advocated by Paul is characterized primarily by the view that the elders are appointed as ἐπίσκοποι (bishops, overseers), and receive the commission "to shepherd the church of God" (20:28). Through the Spirit, God himself thus establishes the continuity of the church, and the official ministers are instruments of God's own acts. By having the Lukan Paul identify the πρεσβύτεροι (elders) from Ephesus (20:17) in their official capacity as overseers/bishops (20:28), he legitimizes the transition from the Palestinian understanding of eldership to the concepts of bishops and deacons of the Pauline churches of Asia Minor (cf. Phil. 1:1)—a process that was still under way as Luke writes. Luke does not explicitly mention deacons, although their ministry is presupposed in Acts 6:4, parallel to the ministry of the word exercised by the apostolic leaders of the church. Luke characterizes the pastoral ministry of overseers/bishops by the metaphor of "shepherding," exercised as a ministry for the unity of the church. This ministry takes shape in the leadership of the congregation and proclamation of the word, which ward off the attacks of false teachers and their doctrines (cf. 20:29–30).

The Miletus speech makes clear that Luke has implicitly transferred to Paul those functions previously exercised by the apostles: Paul is now the advocate

392. Roloff, "Paulusdarstellung," is the foundational work. Cf. also Karl Löning, "Paulinism in der Apostelgeschichte," in *Paulus in den neutestamentlichen Spätschriften: zur Paulusrezeption im Neuen Testament* (ed. Karl Kertelge; QD 89; Freiburg i.B.: Herder, 1981), 202–334; Ulrich Luz and Peter Lampe, "Nachpaulinsches Christentum und pagane Gesellschaft," in *Die Anfänge des Christentums: Alte Welt und neue Hoffnung* (ed. Jürgen Becker; Stuttgart: Kohlhammer, 1987), 186, according to whom Acts is to be read as "the story of Paul with an extensive introduction."

393. For analysis, cf. Hans-Joachim Michel, *Die Abschiedsrede des Paulus an die Kirche Apg 20,17–38: Motivgeschichte und theologische Bedeutung* (SANT 35; Munich: Kösel-Verlag, 1973); and F. Prast, *Presbyter und Evangelium in nachapostolischer Zeit* (FzB 29; Stuttgart: Verlag Katholisches Bibelwerk, 1979).

of the tradition and continuity in the church, and he is the one who actually fulfills the commission of the risen Jesus of Acts 1:8, and thus the true hero of Luke-Acts.

The Essential Nature of Ecclesiastical Office

The basic lines of Luke's conception of official church ministries have already become clear: The twelve apostles, as bearers of the tradition, are the indispensable link in the transition from Jesus to the church, since they are the ones who gather the people of God in Jerusalem (Acts 2:32; 3:15; 5:32). Moreover, from their seat in Jerusalem (8:1) they accompany the beginnings of the Gentile mission as it extends outward from Jerusalem (cf. 8:14–17; 11:18). However, Luke is not concerned only with showing that official ministries are significant in church leadership and that precedents for the exercise of such ministries are traceable to the earliest days of the church; he also wants to point out the theological elements of the church's structure. For Luke, the apostles become prototypical representatives of the kind of conduct normative for the bearers of church office, in that *they adopt Jesus's service to his own as the binding norm*: "But not so with you; rather the greatest among you must become like the youngest, and the leader like one who serves. For who is greater, the one who is at the table or the one who serves? Is it not the one at the table? But I am among you as one who serves" (Luke 22:26–27). Luke is emphatic that church office must not be misused as the means of dominating others but is to be understood as service within the community of faith. Jesus's own way of life thus forms the binding norm for the practice of every church office. Luke deals with this theme indirectly in numerous passages (cf., e.g., Luke 12:35–48; 17:7–10). Church leaders are to recognize that their office does not make them superior or empower them to lord it over others; rather, it always finds its goal in service for the church.

The Word of God

Luke attributes fundamental importance to the power of the word in Jesus's work.[394] In Acts 1:1 he describes the Gospel of Luke as the "first *word*" (πρῶτος λόγος), and in Luke 1:2 he calls the bearers of the tradition that he has received and is handing on "ministers of the *word*." The advent of Jesus means the proclamation of the *word* of God (Luke 5:1) and of the good news of the kingdom (16:16), in which the ministry of Jesus is, as always, transparent to the time of the church. This is seen in Luke's interpretation of the parable of the Sower, where the seed is explicitly identified as the word of God (8:11). The word appears in Luke 8:4–21 as the vital element of the church, and since the disciples play a decisive role in the handing on and spreading of the word,

394. Cf. Claus-Peter März, *Das Wort Gottes bei Lukas: Die lukanische Worttheologie als Frage an die neuere Lukasforschung* (ETS 11; Leipzig: Sankt-Benno-Verlag, 1974).

Luke defuses the saying about hardening in Mark 4:12. For him, proclaiming the word, accepting it, and putting it into practice in one's life all belong together, so that the Lukan Jesus can say, "My mother and my brothers are those who hear the word of God and do it" (Luke 8:21). The word of God is taught (Acts 16:6; 18:11), heard (Luke 5:1; 8:21; Acts 13:44; 19:10), and received (Acts 11:1; 15:36; 17:13) so that it can grow (Acts 6:7; 12:24). As the word of salvation (Acts 13:26) and grace (20:32), the word is directed by the Holy Spirit (16:6) to the teaching (18:11) and practice of the faith, for "Blessed . . . are those who hear the word of God and obey it!" (Luke 11:28).

WOMEN AS WITNESSES

Alongside the apostles and Paul, Luke is particularly interested in the role of women as witnesses of the saving event (see above, §8.4.2). The prologue with Mary, Elizabeth, and Anna makes this conspicuous; Luke's depiction of *Mary* has not only a biographical concern, but doubtless also a theological motivation.[395] She belongs to Israel and as a member of the chosen people is entrusted with God's promise (Luke 1:26–38). In her person and destiny Luke wants readers to see the Israel that, through faith in Jesus, abides in the continuity of the promise (Luke 1:45). Mary stands for the Israel that "continues to be Israel by becoming church."[396] She thus has an ecclesiological function, in that she trusts in God's word of promise and so becomes a prototype of Christian believers (cf. Acts 1:14). In addition to Mary and Elizabeth, Luke also draws portraits of other women in Luke-Acts. Especially noteworthy is the God-fearing woman Lydia (Acts 16:14–15), who joined the church in Philippi and, obviously as a person of means, supported its mission financially.[397] She thus represents a model that also stands behind Luke 8:1–3, which portrays women as traveling around with Jesus and supporting his work financially. In the gospel, Jesus repeatedly turns to women in unconventional ways (Luke 7:36–50), as teacher (10:38–42, Mary and Martha) and healer (8:40–56). He lifts up widows as models (18:1–8; 21:1–4), and several women are the first to hear and transmit the message of the resurrection (24:10).

8.4.8 Eschatology

Within the framework of his concept of salvation history, and in view of his historical situation, Luke rearranges the eschatological program into a new pattern, which he works out at different levels.

395. Cf. the comprehensive treatment by Jürgen Becker, *Maria: Mutter Jesu und erwählte Jungfrau* (BG 4; Leipzig: Evangelische Verlagsanstalt, 201), 144–96.
396. Roloff, *Kirche im Neuen Testament*, 195.
397. For a discussion of Lydia's importance in Acts, cf. Pilhofer, *Philippi*, 234–40.

The Time and Nature of the Parousia

Within this new arrangement, Luke makes the *ascension* fundamentally significant, for with this image—which is explosive, given the religious context of the emperor cult (see above, §8.4.2)—Luke introduces a deceleration of the eschatological timetable. Luke could not simply take over the first and second generation's expectation of the immediate parousia and hand it on without modification, for in view of the continuing extension of time, such a concept no longer held out promise for the future. The ascension clarified for the church three fundamental aspects of the continuing present and future of Jesus Christ:

1. The Crucified and Risen One, as their exalted Lord, had for forty days instructed the apostles, and through them the church, about the kingdom of God (Acts 1:3), so that they were equipped in the best possible way for the present and immediate future.
2. The exalted Lord had sent the Holy Spirit, who would remain with the church as the abiding power of God (Acts 1:8).
3. The one who had been taken to heaven by God in this way would come again in the same way.

On this basis it was possible for Luke to reinterpret the signs of the coming end, its target date, and the nature of the parousia, without abandoning the eschatological hope they represented. *The ascension remodeled the architecture of the final events, for there is only a minimal connection between sudden and catastrophic apocalyptic events and an expectation of the parousia understood in continuity with the ascension.* Rather, the ascension suggests that even the final event of history will exhibit that same goal-directed continuity in God's saving activity that Luke has portrayed throughout his twofold work.

Luke works out the details of this thematic complex on different levels; thus on the question of the *signs of the end*, he departs from traditional views, as comparing Mark 13:1–32 and Luke 21:5–33 makes clear. Luke removes events that Mark considers to be signs of the immediate end and places them in a different perspective. While in Mark 13:14 the fall of Jerusalem is associated with the "desolating sacrilege" (or "abomination of desolation"), Luke 21:20 speaks only of the armies that will surround Jerusalem. In place of deliverance from the eschatological tribulation of Mark 13:13, Luke has patient endurance that leads to life (Luke 21:19). While for Mark 13:10 the Gentile mission is a constituent element of the eschatological events, Luke omits this verse, since it does not fit his conception of history. For Luke, the end of history has by no means become insubstantial and devoid of content, but eschatology is no longer the pervasive and driving force of his theology. One can also see this in the way in which he minimizes speculations about the *date* of the parousia. Luke expresses a basic principle of his eschatology in Luke 17:20–21: "Once

Jesus was asked by the Pharisees when the kingdom of God was coming, and he answered, 'The kingdom of God is not coming with things that can be observed; nor will they say, "Look, here it is!" or "There it is!" For, in fact, the kingdom of God is among you.'" This statement simultaneously affirms the assurance that God's kingdom will come, that one cannot determine its time, and that it is somehow already present in the ministry of Jesus, a complex of views that corresponds to Acts 1:6–7, "So when they had come together, they asked him, 'Lord, is this the time when you will restore the kingdom to Israel?' He replied, 'It is not for you to know the times or periods that the Father has set by his own authority.'" Acts 3:21 points in the same general direction ("[Jesus] must remain in heaven until the time of universal restoration that God announced long ago through his holy prophets"). On the one hand, God has defined a period during which the risen Lord will remain in heaven, but, on the other hand, the extent of this period remains open. Luke also has in mind the correction of an eschatology that supposes the particular time of the end can be calculated when he places Luke 19:11 ("he went on to tell a parable, because he was near Jerusalem, and because they supposed that the kingdom of God was to appear immediately") just before the parable of the Pounds. The same is true of his expansion of Mark 13:6 in Luke 21:8 ("Beware that you are not led astray; for many will come in my name and say, 'I am he!' and, 'The time is near.' Do not go after them"). Luke replaces the summary of Jesus's preaching in Mark 1:15 with the inaugural sermon in Nazareth (cf. especially Luke 4:21), and corrects the statement of Mark 9:1 that the end would come in the first generation in Luke 9:27 (by omitting "has come with power"). This does not mean that Luke gives up hope for the future parousia,[398] but that he combines the unknown time of the Lord's return (cf. Luke 12:40, "You also must be ready, for the Son of Man is coming at an unexpected hour"; cf. 17:24, 26–30; Acts 1:7) with the call to patient endurance (cf. Luke 8:15, "But as for that in the good soil, these are the ones who, when they hear the word, hold it fast in an honest and good heart, and bear fruit with patient endurance") and the charge to remain alert (cf. Luke 12:35ff.; 21:34, 36). So also, the sayings about the nearness of the kingdom of God (Luke 10:9, 11) show that the evangelist does not in principle renounce the expectation of the imminent end but sees *responsible readiness* as the appropriate conduct in view of the *nature* of the parousia. It is not the parousia hope as such that Luke rejects, but only the calculation of particular times and dates! According to Acts 1:6–8, the final events will not occur before Christian missionaries have reached the ends of the earth. When this will be, and when in this context the events connected with the parousia will begin, cannot be determined in

398. Haenchen, *Acts*, 143: "He has decisively renounced all expectation of an imminent end." On the other hand, cf. Schneider, *Apostelgeschichte*, 142: "He vigorously holds fast to the parousia hope, but disputes that its date can be determined."

chronological terms. In positive terms: God arranges the epochs of history in such a way that the preaching of the gospel can proceed and the nations of the world can participate in the "salvation for Israel" (Luke 2:30; Acts 28:28).[399] Thus Luke attributes to the extension of time *an eminently positive function, namely that only thereby does God make provision for carrying out the divine plan of the saving acts of God in history*. Readers of Luke-Acts thus perceive the meaning of the historical period granted by God, and in view of Jesus's ascension they may hope for his return with confidence and without distress at its delay. The formation and growth of the church is thus for Luke neither directly nor indirectly a substitute for the expectation of the parousia.[400] Luke continues to maintain this hope, because he is convinced that the parousia will indeed occur after the preaching of the gospel to the nations of the world results in the gathering of the chosen people of God in the time and manner that God has determined (cf. Luke 2:30–31).

The Kingdom of God

Luke also needed to reinterpret the key eschatological concept of Jesus's own preaching, the kingdom of God, to preserve its theological potency. The importance of this expression for Luke's eschatology (and for his whole theology) is already apparent in the framing statements of Luke 4:43 and Acts 28:31: by introducing the whole story of Jesus's ministry with this term, and by repeating it in the last verse of his two-volume work, Luke assigns a key role to the concept of the kingdom of God in his comprehensive interpretation of the meaning of the Christ event in God's plan for history. This restructuring of the kingdom-of-God concept takes place on several levels:

1. Luke separates the kingdom-of-God concept from the connotations it had in early Judaism,[401] especially from its particularistic focus on Israel (and Jerusalem) and the corollary negative role of the Gentiles (cf. Luke 19:11; Acts 1:6–7; 28:23, 31).
2. The positive counterpart to this separation is the linking of the kingdom of God to Jesus Christ. This conception emerges at the very beginning, with Jesus's preaching of the gospel of the kingdom of God (Luke 4:43). Jesus's proclamation of the βασιλεία (rule, reign, kingdom) has

399. The statement of Michael Wolter, "Israels Zukunft und die Parusieverzögerung bei Lukas," in *Eschatologie und Schöpfung* (ed. M. Evang et al.; BZNW 89; Berlin: de Gruyter, 1997), 423, is on target: "The delay of the parousia is thus not a part of the problem but belongs to its solution."

400. But this was the influential thesis of Conzelmann, *Theology of St. Luke*, 135: "If Luke has definitely abandoned belief in the early expectation, what does he offer on the positive side as an adequate solution to the problem? An outline of the successive stages in redemptive history according to God's plan."

401. Cf. Wolter, "'Reich Gottes,'" 544–49.

the character of tangible reality, a reality that becomes visible in his miracles (cf. 11:20; 7:21).

3. After Jesus's death, resurrection, and ascension, the kingdom becomes the kingdom of the risen and exalted Lord (cf. Luke 19:12, 15), promised to him by the Father (22:29), and into which he enters (23:42).
4. Throughout the whole of Luke-Acts, the kingdom of God has an aspect of proclamation; thus the kingdom of God is the object of εὐαγγελίζομαι (Luke 4:43; 8:1; 16:16; Acts 8:12) and of κηρύσσω (Luke 9:2; Acts 20:25; 28:31). Jesus himself preaches the kingdom of God (Luke 4:43); he allows the Twelve to share in this preaching (Luke 8:1) and as the Risen One instructs them for forty days about the kingdom of God (Acts 1:3). The proclamation of the kingdom of God even takes on violent aspects (Luke 16:16). In Acts,[402] the kingdom of God is proclaimed beyond the borders of Israel (Acts 8:12), and Paul becomes its universal advocate (Acts 19:8; 20:25; 28:23, 31). In view of the mission of Jesus, the kingdom of God receives a christological stamp and the central content of the Christian message. Thus for Luke, preaching Christ is always preaching the kingdom of God, and vice versa! The third evangelist thereby achieves the motif of continuity, which is so important for him, for the kingdom of God determines not only the message of Jesus but also that of the later witnesses, because the risen Lord Jesus himself establishes this continuity (Acts 1:3). Seen in this perspective, the missionary message of the church is the consistent next chapter of the message of Jesus, both the earthly and risen Lord.[403]
5. Statements that establish the concept of continuity also serve to connect Luke's concept of the Spirit and the preaching of the kingdom of God. "Since the Risen One, who is also still present, speaks of the kingdom of God (Acts 1:3), but denies that this kingdom will be established soon, pointing instead to the promised coming of the Holy Spirit and the commission to carry the gospel to the whole world (1:6–8), Luke indicates that for the church, too, the kingdom of God is bound to the saving presence of Jesus."[404] Jesus remains present to the church in the proclamation of the kingdom of God directed by the Spirit. Luke thus sets before the eyes of his church the proclamation of the kingdom of God as a central and continuing task, made explicit by Paul's preaching of the kingdom of God in Rome (28:23, 31).

402. Cf. here A. Weiser, "'Reich Gottes' in der Apostelgeschichte," in *Der Treue Gottes trauen: Beiträge zum Werk des Lukas; für Gerhard Schneider* (ed. Claus Bussmann and Walter Radl; Freiburg i.B.: Herder, 1991), 127–35.

403. Cf. Wolter, "'Reich Gottes,'" 551–52.

404. Otto Merk, "Das Reich Gottes in den lukanischen Schriften," in *Wissenschaftsgeschichte und Exegese: Gesammelte Aufsätze zum 65. Geburtstag Otto Merks* (ed. Otto Merk; BZNW 95; Berlin: de Gruyter, 1998), 282.

6. Finally, even in its transcendent nature, the kingdom of God is directly real, because it is linked to Jesus. Thus one's earthly situation is a new criterion, already valid in the present, for belonging to the kingdom of God (cf. Luke 6:20, 24; 12:13–34; 14:15–24; 18:18–30). Those who withstand the afflictions of the present will enter into the kingdom of God (Acts 14:22).

Luke's restructuring of the kingdom-of-God concept is thus far more than a reworking of the parousia theme.[405] It bears on a central realm of Lukan theology, since it binds the preaching of the later witnesses directly to that of Jesus himself, and is thus one more building block in the continuity with the normative beginnings postulated by Luke's concept of continuity.

Individual Eschatology

Another important step in Luke's restructuring of eschatology is his effort to instruct his church as to how Christians, in view of the eschatological events but without believing that they are imminent, can continue to live in a responsible attitude of hope and expectation. Luke includes numerous texts, especially in his special materials, that deal with the destiny of the individual after death. In these the reader can perceive a movement in the direction of Hellenistic views. Thus ultimate salvation is individualized and the parousia becomes less important. An individualistic eschatology clearly comes to the fore in Luke 6:20–26; 12:4–5, 16–21, 33–34; 16:1–9, 19–31; 21:19; 23:39–43; Acts 1:25; 7:55–59; 14:22. In the case of the Rich Fool, his foolishness lies not in failing altogether to think about death but in failing to do anything about what comes after. Luke knows the language of eternal damnation, which is to be taken as a warning (Luke 3:9, 17; 9:24; 12:5; 17:26–27, 33–35), and knows about what happens to one in Hades (Luke 16:23).[406] Likewise, Luke devotes much space to the message of eternal salvation (cf. Luke 12:35–38; 13:28–29; 14:15–24; 22:16, 18, 30), speaks of "eternal homes" (16:9), of redemption (21:28), of eternal life (9:24; 10:25–28; 17:33; 18:18, 30), and of paradise (23:43). To be sure, Luke has no comprehensive scheme in which the differences between individual and general eschatology are resolved. The evangelist holds firmly to the future parousia as the beginning of the universal

405. Conzelmann speaks in this connection of removing events from an eschatological context and placing them in a merely historical perspective ("Ent-Eschatologisierung," literally "de-eschatologizing"; *Theology of St. Luke*, 36–38, 113–14). Cf. Grässer, *Parusieverzögerung*, 140–41, who also takes this line. To be sure, the theme of the delay of the parousia continues to be related to that of the theme of the kingdom of God by the questions about the time of the end in Luke 17:20–21; 19:11; and Acts 1:6–8.

406. Parallels to Luke 16:22 (Hades) and 23:43 (paradise) from Greek tomb inscriptions are discussed in Peres, *Grabinschriften*, 187–92. In summarizing, he states that "Luke appears to stand particularly close to Greek folk piety."

final events while at the same time emphasizing individual eschatology. In this way he lays before members of his church the possibility of orienting their lives to the final, universal end, which he does not directly tie to the end of each individual's life.

8.4.9 Setting in the History of Early Christian Theology

Luke's status as a historian as well as his theological achievement has been freshly appreciated in recent scholarship.[407] Luke's church apparently found itself in a severe crisis of self-identity and continuity with its past.[408] The relation to Israel, the problem of the delay of the parousia, the theme "rich and poor," the stance of the new "way" vis-à-vis Greco-Roman society, and its relation to the Roman state had to be rethought. Luke's goal in composing his history was multidimensional. In the first place, Luke wanted to clarify the present situation of his church historically and legitimate it theologically. In doing so, he argued that the transition of salvation from the Jews to the Gentiles as bearers of the promises to Israel was in accord with God's foreknowledge and will. Luke thought through the meaning of the increasing distance between Christianity and Judaism, because it threatened to put in question the continuity of the church with Israel in salvation history, and thus the validity of the promises to Israel. Luke wants his readers to become insightful about how the divine σωτηρία ("salvation"; Luke 1:69, 71, 77; 19:9; Acts 4:12; 7:25; 13:26, 47; 16:7; 27:34) came to the nations and thus ultimately to the (Christian) readers, and how it is now realized in the one "church" of Jews and Gentiles. Associated with this is an explicit advocacy of the theological legitimacy of the Gentile mission that did not require circumcision, as seen above all in the second half of Acts. Even if the two-volume work was not written primarily in order to overcome the problem of the delay of the parousia, Luke's thinking about the theology of history is inseparably bound up with this theme: the broadening of the historical perspective with the continued passing of time, in combination with Luke's concept of continuity, is also, of course, an attempt to decelerate the eschatological timetable and remove its threatening character. In all this, Luke wants to convey assurance, strengthen identity, and gain recruits for the Christian faith![409]

407. The older, primarily negative discussion is critically reviewed by Werner Georg Kümmel, "Lukas in der Anklage der heutigen Theologie," in *Heilsgeschehen und Geschichte* (ed. Werner Georg Kümmel et al.; MTS 3; 16 vols.; Marburg: Elwert, 1965), 87–100.

408. On this point cf. Eckhard Plümacher, "Acta-Forschung 1974–1982," *TRu* 48 (1983): 45ff.

409. Cf. K. Backhaus, "Lukas der Maler: Die Apostelgeschichte als intentionale Geschichte der christlichen Erstepoche," in *Historiographie und fiktionales Erzählen* (ed. G. Häfner; Biblisch-theologische Studien 86; Neukirchen: Neukirchener Verlag, 2007), 31: Luke "anchors the relational memory in the 'objective' depths of a beginning epoch, in order to show the ancient biblical origin

Along with this broadening of the historical-theological perspective through his composition of Luke-Acts, Luke also combines an openness to realms that early Christianity had, at the most, previously only touched on: (1) the evangelist has in view the educated people of his time (Luke 1:1–4; Acts 25:13–26:32), in that he (2) permits influences from urban culture to influence his narrative world (Acts 19:23–40) and (3) portrays Christian teaching in the context of and in dispute with contemporary magic and superstition (Acts 8:4–25; 13:8–12; 16:16–22)[410] and philosophy (Acts 17:16–34). The "new way" thus not only appears interested in current culture and able to dialogue with it; it is also in itself a new cultural religion with Jewish roots in the Roman Empire. By writing his two-volume work, Luke intentionally enters the forum of ancient historiography, gives a literary form to his and the church's new perception of its own history, and announces a claim to interpret the meaning of universal history.[411]

of his group in the context of a lively forum of competing religious self-definitions, to show the present relevance of memories of the founding generation, and to present its continuing attraction to the eyes of his contemporaries, and thus to give it a normative identity in its present."

410. On this point cf. Hans-Josef Klauck, *Magie und Heidentum in der Apostelgeschichte des Lukas* (SBS 167; Stuttgart: Verlag Katholisches Bibelwerk, 1996).

411. Cf. Schröter, "Lukas als Historiograph," 246.

9

The Fourth Transformation

The Gospel in the World

9.1 Social, Religious, and Political Developments

In the last third of the first century CE, early Christianity spread and began to stabilize itself, primarily in the Mediterranean basin, while also experiencing internal and external dangers. These struggles are important factors in shaping the theology of several documents from the later New Testament period.

Social Structures in the Churches

The continued success of the early Christian mission, especially in the cities of Asia Minor and Greece, brought about changes in the social structure of the congregations,[1] since the inclusion of people from various social strata brought these social distinctions into the church. From the very beginning, the Pauline house churches doubtless included some members of the upper class (cf. Erastus, the "city treasurer" of Rom. 16:23; members of the *familia Caesaris* [the emperor's household] in Phil. 4:22; Gaius in 1 Cor. 1:14, who is "host to the whole church"; Phoebe in Rom. 16:1–2; Stephanus in 1 Cor. 1:16; 16:15, 17; Philemon in Philem. 2).[2] They were owners of houses, some

1. For a survey, see Luz and Lampe, "Nachpaulinisches Christentum," 185–216.

2. For a history of research, cf. Ekkehard Stegemann and Wolfgang Stegemann, *The Jesus Movement: A Social History of Its First Century* (trans. O. C. Dean, Jr.; Minneapolis: Fortress, 1999), 288–91. Gehring, *Hausgemeinde und Mission*, 291–99; idem, *House Church*

of them with slaves, and were especially important as patrons who supported the church. The great majority of the church's membership, however, must have belonged to the lower social class (cf. 1 Cor. 1:26), including numerous slaves (cf. 1 Cor. 7:21–24; Gal. 3:28; Philemon; Rom. 16:22).[3] In the post-Pauline period, more and more wealthy people joined the new religion. We thus find comments about Christian homeowners (Col. 4:15; 2 Tim. 1:16; 4:19), upper-class women are mentioned (1 Tim. 2:9; 1 Pet. 3:3; Acts 17:4, 12), and the Roman church near the end of the century included not just rich people (*1 Clem.* 38.2) but members of the elite upper crust such as Claudius Ephebus, a member of the emperor's household (*1 Clem.* 65.1),[4] and even Flavia Domitilla, the wife of a Consul (cf. Dio Cassius, *Hist.* 67; Eusebius, *Hist. eccl.* 3.18.4).[5] Affluent members of the congregation bring their slaves with them into the assembly room (Eph. 6:5–9). The rich insist on places of honor in the worship service (James 2:2–4); they are snobbish (1 Tim. 6:17; James 4:16; Rev. 3:17–18); and their life is entirely directed by the profit motive (1 Tim. 6:6–10; Titus 1:7; 2 Tim. 3:2; James 4:13). At the same time, the congregation includes poor widows (1 Tim. 5:3–16) and slaves (1 Tim. 6:1–2; Eph. 6:5–8; Col. 3:11, 22–25; 1 Pet. 2:18–23). Instructions to the rich to get involved in the plight of the poor members of the congregation indirectly confirm the high percentage of the congregation that was in economic need (cf. 1 Tim. 5:10; 6:18–19; Eph. 4:28; Titus 3:14; James 1:27; 2:15–16; Acts 20:35). There were more women than men in the churches, for Christian women were often married to unbelieving men (cf. 1 Pet. 3:1–2; 2 Tim. 1:5). We must also note great disparities in educational level as well as some tension between urban and rural. Pauline Christianity was essentially an urban religion even until the end of the first century CE (cf. the Pastoral Epistles). At the same time, especially in Asia Minor, Christianity began to gain a foothold among the rural population, as 1 Peter—addressed to whole provincial districts—makes clear (cf. also Pliny, *Ep.* 10.96, "The plague of

and Mission, 165–71. Basic bibliography on the early Christian house churches (in addition to Gehring and studies of the household codes [*Haustafeln*]) is found in Hans-Josef Klauck, *Hausgemeinde und Hauskirche im frühen Christentum* (SBS 103; Stuttgart: Verlag Katholisches Bibelwerk, 1981); David L. Balch and Carolyn Osiek, *Families in the New Testament World: Households and House Churches* (Louisville: Westminster John Knox, 1997); Halvor Moxnes, *Constructing Early Christian Families: Family as Social Reality and Metaphor* (London: Routledge, 1997).

3. According to Leonhard Schumacher, *Sklaverei in der Antike: Alltag und Schicksal der Unfreien* (Beck's archäologische Bibliothek; Munich: Beck, 2001), 42, at the end of the first century CE slaves constituted ca. 15–20 percent of the population of the Roman Empire; in absolute numbers, this would be about 10 million persons.

4. Cf. Frank Kolb, *Rom: Die Geschichte der Stadt in der Antike* (3rd ed.; Munich: Beck, 2002), 632.

5. On this point, cf. Peter Lampe, *From Paul to Valentinus: Christians at Rome in the First Two Centuries* (trans. Michael Steinhauser; ed. Marshall D. Johnson; Minneapolis: Fortress, 2003), 198–205.

this superstition has spread not only in the cities, but through villages and the countryside").

The whole development is clearly characterized by increasing distance between particular groups in the congregations, resulting in social tensions within the church. Church leaders and teachers developed a variety of very different theological and socioethical strategies to resolve these problems. These approaches spanned the spectrum from adoption and adaptation of traditional household codes (in Colossians, Ephesians, and 1 Peter) to uncompromising critique of the rich (James).

Processes of Theological Clarification

As is the case with every new religious movement, so also in early Christianity there existed from the very beginning certain fundamental convictions: the one God of Israel had raised Jesus Christ from the dead, who would shortly return as judge of the world to save those who believe. This basic perspective included numerous undisputed theological and ethical insights, but some central issues remained unsettled and posed new challenges:[6]

1. Despite the guidelines provided by Paul in the previous generation, in numerous congregations the relations between Jews and Gentiles still needed clarification. There were issues regarding circumcision (Col. 2:11; 3:11; Eph. 2:11), particular doctrines deriving from Jewish and Hellenistic backgrounds (Col. 2:8; Titus 1:10–11), worship of angels (Col. 2:18), dietary regulations and calendar observances (Col. 2:16), and the Torah (1 Tim. 1:3–11; Eph. 2:15; James 2:8–12; 4:11). In particular, the Letter of James shows that for a long time, various views of the law had their advocates.
2. Likewise, clarification was needed regarding the timing of the parousia and individual resurrection. Both the eschatological schedule of 2 Thess. 2:1–12 and the apologetic statement cited in 2 Pet. 3:8 ("With the Lord one day is like a thousand years, and a thousand years are like one day") clearly indicate that the delay of the parousia continued to stir theological debate. Regarding the resurrection, the issue was focused on whether the resurrection had already occurred for the individual at the time of conversion, as advocated in Col. 3:1–4 and Eph. 2:6, an idea explicitly described as heretical in 2 Tim. 2:18.

6. The main lines of development are sketched by Ulrich B. Müller, *Zur frühchristlichen Theologiegeschichte: Judenchristentum und Paulinismus in Kleinasien an der Wende vom 1. zum 2. Jahrhundert nach Christus* (Gütersloh: Gütersloher Verlagshaus Mohn, 1976), passim; and Jürgen Becker, ed., *Die Anfänge des Christentums: Alte Welt und neue Hoffnung* (Stuttgart: Kohlhammer, 1987), 160ff.

3. The continuing growth of the church made the question of identifying a Christian way of life more and more urgent, as the treatment of several ethical questions clearly indicates (rich and poor: James 2:1–13; 4:13–5:6; 1 Tim. 6:17–19; respectable conduct in the eyes of society: Col. 4:5; Eph. 4:28–29; 2 Thess. 3:6, 11–12; sexual immorality: Eph. 5:1ff.; the conduct of church members in dealing with each other: 1 Tim. 5:1–16, 17–19; the rebuttal of charges and suspicions against Christians: 1 Pet. 2:12–17; 3:16; 4:4, 14–15; Luke 6:22–23; Acts 14:22).
4. As the congregations grew larger, leadership structures had to be created at different levels within the household and house churches. Two models shaped this developing process: (a) The household codes (Haustafeln; Col. 3:18–4:1; Eph. 5:22–6:9; 1 Pet. 2:18–3:7; 1 Tim. 2:8–15; Titus 2:2–10),[7] based on the ancient understanding of the οἶκος (household), determined the basic structural outline. The priority of the man, as husband and father, was accepted into such structures, at the same time being qualified by the obligation of mutual love and care. (b) The dominant concepts in the introduction of official clergy were the college of presbyters, the office of deacons, and the episcopal office (1 Tim. 3:1–7, 8–13; Titus 1:5–7).
5. Toward the end of the first century CE, competitive systems of Christian doctrine emerged, associated with the reproach "dangerous speculations" or the term Gnosis (knowledge, Gnosticism).[8] In this situation the development of ecclesiastical offices obviously facilitated the internal stability of the churches.

The Relation to the Religious State

As they threaded their way between distancing themselves from the world and accommodating themselves to it, the relation of the early Christian congregations to the state was of decisive importance. The Roman Empire was religiously constituted to its very core, for "The Roman emperor was divine. He had been this from the very beginning, since the time of Julius Caesar and Augustus; he was already divine during his lifetime, including in the western part of the Roman Empire, in Italy, in Rome itself."[9] The Roman emperor cult,

7. On the backgrounds of the household codes in the history of religions and early Christian history, see below, §10.1.6.

8. On the origin and worldview of Gnostic groups, cf. Hans-Josef Klauck, *The Religious Context of Early Christianity: A Guide to Graeco-Roman Religions* (trans. Brian McNeil; Minneapolis: Fortress, 2003), 430–504.

9. Clauss, *Kaiser und Gott*, 17. For the eastern part of the Roman Empire, cf. S. R. Price, *Rituals and Power: The Roman Imperial Cult in Asia Minor* (Cambridge: Cambridge University Press, 1984); Thomas Witulski, *Kaiserkult in Kleinasien: Die Entwicklung der kultisch-religiösen Kaiserverehrung in der römischen Provinz Asia von Augustus bis Antoninus Pius* (NTOA 63; Göttingen: Vandenhoeck & Ruprecht, 2007).

which grew out of the Hellenistic veneration for rulers, was by no means a matter of purely external ritual; it must be understood as a political-religious phenomenon that touched the lives of the inhabitants of the Roman Empire at many levels. The emperor cult was already attaining clear contours in the last years of Julius Caesar, who was already honored during his lifetime as a divine being. Temples were built in his honor, altars and statues were erected, and a special priesthood was instituted to serve them (cf. Suetonius, *Jul.* 76.1). After his death, he received "all divine and human honors" (*Jul.* 84.2), was solemnly acknowledged to have been received among the gods, and from then on was considered a god of the empire. Under Octavian/Augustus, there was a restoration of the Roman religion. Established rituals were reinstituted, and temples were restored and reopened. Augustus intentionally extended and upgraded the Caesar cult as a religio-political means of securing his rule. With explicit emphasis on continuity with his stepfather Julius Caesar, Augustus encouraged worship of himself as divine not only in the eastern part of the empire but also in Rome itself: "No honor was left for the gods, when Augustus chose to be himself worshiped with temples and statues, like those of the deities, and with flamens and priests" (Tacitus, *Ann.* 1.10.6). In order to express the divine honors due the Caesar, months were given new names and the time of the beginning of the new year was changed.[10] The Caesar received divine attributes: he was eternal, unconquerable; he provided for the empire, did not rest, was omnipresent.[11] Virgil celebrates the birth of Augustus as the beginning of the golden age (*Aen.* 6.791–97). Caesar appears on numberless inscriptions and coins as "God" or "Son of God," as one worshiped by both Greeks and Romans. The Caesars had themselves acclaimed as bringers of peace to the world, as its benefactors and saviors.[12] The emperor cult, with its veneration of the Caesar as a divine being (sometimes during his lifetime, always after his death), had numerous adherents in Rome but was especially popular in the provinces.[13] Different emperors promoted it to different degrees; while Tiberius, Claudius, Vespasian, and Titus were somewhat reserved, Caligula, Nero, and Domitian intensified the cult to promote their personal and political goals.[14]

Roman religion was not traditionally disposed toward conflict with other religions but attempted to integrate them.[15] Romans felt no responsibility or mission to convert other peoples to their own religion. It spread through dif-

10. Cf. the calendar edict to the "Greeks in Asia"; *OGIS* 458 = *NW* 1.2:246–47.

11. Cf. Clauss, *Kaiser und Gott*, 219–79.

12. Texts in *NW* 1.2:239–56.

13. On this point cf. Hubert Cancik and Konrad Hitzl, eds., *Die Praxis der Herrscherverehrung in Rom und seinen Provinzen* (Tübingen: Mohr, 2003).

14. As an absolutely classic example, cf. Nero's declaration of freedom to the Greeks in 67 CE, *SIG*[3] 814 (*NW* 1.2:249–50).

15. On this point cf. Jörg Rüpke, *Die Religion der Römer: Eine Einführung* (Munich: Beck, 2001).

fusion and was able to integrate other religious practices, at least in part. It's capacity for integration is seen especially in the vigorous expansion of oriental cults—even in the city of Rome.[16] The Romans practiced tolerance in religious issues, on the basic principle that the gods themselves could take care of offenses against their dignity (Cf. Tacitus, *Ann.* 1.73.4). The presupposition, of course, for this acceptance was that foreign religions did not violate the existing social conventions and did not have any destabilizing effects on Roman law and order.[17] The situation was entirely different with the two oriental religions that, by their radical monotheism, called in question the whole polytheistic religious foundation of the Roman political and social structure: Judaism and Christianity. At the beginning of the first century CE there were approximately thirty or forty thousand Jews in Rome;[18] despite repeated conflicts between the authorities and the Jews, Judaism was tolerated and accepted as an ancient and traditional religion.[19] Christianity, on the other hand, with its exclusive monotheism, its veneration of a crucified criminal as the Son of God, its aggressive mission, its distance from cultural rituals hallowed by tradition, and its refusal to sacrifice to the emperor was, in Roman eyes, a destabilizing factor. The no to the emperor cult was, from the Roman point of view, a no to the Roman state, for it disrupted the fundamental relation of the state to its gods.

Controversies

A new religious movement that makes exclusive claims about its own identity never forms without conflict. Controversies inevitably arose between Christianity and the Judaism within which it emerged and which provided the context for its early missionary success.[20] Paul's letters (1 Thess. 2:14–16;

16. Cf. Kolb, *Rom*, 607–20.

17. The Bacchanalian trials described in Livius 39 show clearly that the religious tolerance of the Romans ended at the point where they saw religious practice as a threat to public order. On the relation of Roman religion to other religions, cf. Ursula Berner, "Religio und Superstitio," in *Der Fremden wahrnehmen: Bausteine für eine Xenologie* (ed. Theo Sundermeier; SVR 5; Gütersloh: Gütersloher Verlagshaus, 1992), 45–64.

18. Cf. Kolb, *Rom*, 621: this was about 3.5 percent of the population.

19. Cf. Josephus, *Ant.* 14.190–260; 19.280–285, 286–291, 299–311; 20.10–14. The Jews were granted special privileges: the right of assembly, the right to pay the annual Jewish temple tax, their own internal legal provisions, Sabbath rest, keeping the food laws, no sacrifice to other gods, excused from participation in the emperor cult. Cf. Gerhard Delling, *Die Bewältigung der Diasporasituation durch das hellenistische Judentum* (Göttingen: Vandenhoeck & Ruprecht, 1987), 49–55; Günter Stemberger, "Die Juden im römischen Reich: Unterdrückung und Privilegien einer Minderheit," in *Christlicher Antijudaismus und jüdischer Antipaganismus: Ihre Motive und Hintergründe in den ersten drei Jahrhunderten* (ed. Herbert Frohnhofen; HTS 3; Hamburg: Steinmann & Steinmann, 1990), 6–22.

20. On this point cf. Bernd Wander, *Trennungsprozesse zwischen frühem Christentum und Judentum im 1. Jahrhundert nach Christus: Datierbare Abfolgen zwischen der Hinrichtung Jesu und der Zerstörung des Jerusalemer Tempels* (TANZ 16; Tübingen: Francke, 1994).

Gal. 6:12) and Acts (16:20–21; 17:5–9) provide evidence that, in the wake of the Claudius edict (49 CE), local Jewish communities took action against the young Christian movement. While ancient Judaism attempted to preserve its own religious and ethnic identity, formative Christianity deliberately and systematically transgressed ethnic, cultural, and religious boundaries. The new movement advocated *a universal concept of messianic redemption* that welcomed and included people of all nations. Not segregation, but acculturation (cf. 1 Cor. 9:20–22) and enculturation, as well as transethnic conceptions (cf. Gal. 3:26–28), definitively shaped the early Christian mission. Early Christianity created a new cognitive identity, which in part adopted previous cultural identities, at the same time profoundly transforming them. It offered the same attractive features as Judaism—a monotheistic faith and an exclusive ethos—but without restrictions and personal hurdles. The *early Christian concept of identity* integrated and transformed fundamental convictions of Judaism; but at the same time it abandoned the classic pillars of Judaism (election, Torah, temple, and land). The Christian proclamation obviously was deeply appealing to the God-fearers. As they joined the Christian movement, the synagogue lost men and women who had economic and political influence (cf. Acts 16:14–15; 17:4) and were therefore important links to pagan society. In many places, such conversions disturbed the already delicate balance between Jews and their Gentile context. From their perspective, the Jews had to regard the growing Christian movement as a destabilizing factor: it drew a considerable proportion of its membership from the penumbra of the synagogue. Moreover, since the Romans at first did not distinguish Christians and Jews, the new movement endangered the reasonable relation to the Roman state that Judaism had worked out. Not only did emerging early Christianity separate itself from Judaism, but Judaism also distanced itself from emerging early Christianity. Judaism could not afford to find itself directly connected to a movement instigated by a man executed by the Romans as a revolutionary but venerated as Son of God by his followers.[21]

A grave change in the church's situation came with the persecution of Christians in the city of Rome in 64 CE under Nero (cf. Tacitus, *Ann.* 15.44.2–5; Suetonius, *Nero* 16.2).[22] The Roman authorities now perceived the Christians to be an independent movement separate from Judaism. The fact that Nero could gain the applause of the populace by making Christians answerable for the fire at Rome, and that without even making a case against them, indicates that the whole city had already been aware of the movement and thought it deserving of

21. Cf. here F. Vittinghoff, "'Christianus sum': Das 'Verbrechen' von Außenseitern der römischen Gesellschaft," *Historia* 33 (1984): 336ff.

22. All relevant texts are readily available in Peter Guyot and Richard Klein, *Das frühe Christentum bis zum Ende der Verfolgungen: Eine Dokumentation* (Texte zur Forschung 60; Darmstadt: Wissenschaftliche Buchgesellschaft, 1993); Joseph Cullen Ayer, *A Sourcebook for Ancient Church History* (New York: Scribners, 1941; repr. Echo Library, 2008), 6–8.

punishment. Worshiping a crucified criminal as though he were a divine being, having strange texts and practicing rituals such as baptism and the eucharist that seemed weird to outsiders, their exclusive congregational organization, their support of needy members of their own community but their refusal to participate in the broader social and political life—all this very likely resulted in widespread suspicion and complaints against the group. Christians were perceived as culturally esoteric and politically dangerous. From Nero's time onward, the public confession "*Christianus sum*" (I am a Christian) was regarded as a capital crime. The basis for this was probably "that Christianity, 'founded' by an executed political rebel, and 'Christians,' as his followers and bearers of his name, had been considered criminals from the very beginning."[23]

The persecutions took on a new dimension during the rule of Domitian (born 51 CE, emperor 81–96 CE),[24] who began in 85 CE to insist on being addressed as "dominus et deus noster" ("our Lord and God"; Suetonius, *Dom.* 13.2).[25] Whether Domitian actually instituted a comprehensive persecution of Christians is a disputed point.[26] Probably intensification of the emperor cult, especially in Asia Minor, led to repressions that were more than purely local events. Christians' nonparticipation in the emperor cult, added to their general cultural role as outsiders, could have resulted in measures directed against the Christians, as Pliny the Younger, writing later (under Trajan), implies was already to some extent the case even for Domitian's time.[27] Within the New Testament, both 1 Peter (see below, §11.1) and Revelation (see below, chap. 13) probably reflect persecution of Christians under Domitian. First Peter presupposes a situation of actual conflict between the church and its environment, a situation that goes beyond local repression. According to 1 Pet. 4:15–16, Christians can be condemned before the court like murderers, thieves,

23. Vittinghoff, "'Christianus sum,'" 336.

24. Portraits of Domitian are provided in Leonard L. Thompson, *The Book of Revelation: Apocalypse and Empire* (Oxford: Oxford University Press, 1990), 96–115; and C. Urner, "Kaiser Domitian im Urteil antiker literarischer Quellen und moderner Forschung" (PhD diss., Universität Augsburg, 1993). Both scholars are concerned to reevaluate the previous (negative) image of Domitian.

25. Cf. also the texts in *NW* 1.2:854–55.

26. Cf. R. Freudenberger, "Christenverfolgen," *TRE* 8:25; Kurt Aland, "Das Verhältnis von Kirche und Staat in der Frühzeit," *ANRW* 2.23.1 (Berlin: de Gruyter, 1979), 224; Adela Yarbro Collins, *Crisis and Catharsis: The Power of the Apocalypse* (Philadelphia: Westminster, 1984), 69ff. The classical expression of the opposite position is Ethelbert Stauffer, *Christ and the Caesars: Historical Sketches* (trans. K. and R. Gregor Smith; Philadelphia: Westminster Press, 1955).

27. In addition to *Ep.* 10.96.6 (twenty years previously, some of those charged had renounced their faith), *Ep.* 10.96.5 should be noted. Here Pliny mentions his demand that the Christians prove their loyalty by sacrificing to the emperor and curse Christ, "For it is said that real Christians cannot be compelled to do such things." This presupposes that such a practice had been customary in Asia Minor for some time! According to Tacitus, *Ann.* 15.44 and Pliny, *Ep.* 10.96, Christians were charged with hatred of the human race, opposition to the state, atheism, superstition, cultic immorality, and damaging the economy.

or other criminals for their Christian confession alone (ὡς Χριστιανός).[28] The Christian community is being subjected to a purifying fire (cf. 1 Pet. 4:12); they are to withstand the devil, who is loose in the whole world and is afflicting all Christians with the same suffering (1 Pet. 5:8–9). The Christians addressed by Revelation see themselves as exposed to the same Roman claim to power that has exalted itself to divine heights, represented by the seer John's elaborate symbolic and linguistic forms. The seer describes the wrath of the Beast in mythological language (Rev. 13; 17), while the messages to the seven churches communicate the historical background: Christians are slandered and harassed (Rev. 2:9) and thrown into prison (Rev. 2:10), and one witness has already suffered martyrdom (Antipas in Rev. 2:13; cf. Rev. 6:9–11). The hour of testing is coming on the whole earth (Rev. 3:10).[29]

Finally, the exchange of letters between Pliny and Trajan between 111 and 113 CE indicates that for some time Christians have been subject to proceedings in which the *nomen ipsum* (name itself) was sufficient ground for charges.[30] Pliny and Trajan argue for the punishment of those Christians who had been charged and showed no inclination to change their mind when brought before the court. At the same time, their attitude shows a certain moderation, for Pliny reflects on the cases in which he himself has been involved, and Trajan considers anonymous charges as invalid. Moreover, it is possible that he reduces the minimum standards for loyalty to the Roman state. All the same, it remains clear that both Pliny and Trajan adopt and continue to practice a firm judgment that had already been made about the new movement: Christians are in principle guilty of a capital crime.

Strategies

Different New Testament documents represent different strategies for coming to terms with these complex problems at the end of the first century CE, but some common fundamental mechanisms can be discerned:

28. Cf. Pliny, *Ep.* 96.2–3: "I asked them whether they were Christians. Those who responded affirmatively I have asked a second and third time, under threat of the death penalty. If they persisted in their confession [Latin *perseverantes, related to "endurance,"* ὑπομονή, the central virtue for Christians in Revelation], I had them executed. For whatever they are actually advocating, it seems to me that obstinacy and stubbornness must be punished in any case" (trans. MEB).

29. A reflection of persecution of Christians under Domitian is probably found in Dio Cassius, *Hist.* 68.1–2, where it is reported, in the context of new developments in the time of the emperor Nerva: "Nerva also released all those who were on trial for *maiestas* [reviling the majesty of the emperor] and restored the exiles; moreover, he put to death all the slaves and freedmen who had conspired against their masters and allowed that class of persons to lodge no complaint whatsoever against their masters; and no persons were permitted to accuse anybody of *maiestas* or of adopting the Jewish mode of life."

30. For analysis of these letters, cf. Rudolf Freudenberger, *Das Verhalten der römischen Behörden gegen die Christen im 2. Jahrhundert* (2nd ed.; MBPAR 52; Munich: Beck, 1969).

1. The churches did not require any external changes in the status of their members. Instead, the awareness developed, along with the corresponding practice, that in Christ, and therefore in the church, all were equal. This consciousness and practice favored the integration of the churches into society.
2. The churches strove to level differences between poor and rich by requiring care for the social welfare of its members and through the commands of justice and love.
3. The churches did not strive for any particular changes in society itself, but attempted by their exemplary conduct to secure their own existence and to represent the Christian mission to the world.

9.2 Pseudepigraphy/Deuteronymity as a Historical, Literary, and Theological Phenomenon

New Testament pseudepigraphy, i.e., the publication of writings under the name of an author who did not in fact compose them, does not represent a phenomenon peculiar to early Christianity within the world of ancient literature. Numerous pseudepigraphical works are found in both Greco-Roman[31] and Jewish[32] literature.

Terminology

The words *pseudepigraphy* (ψευδεπίγραφος, false title, false ascription) and *pseudonymity* (ψευδώνυμος, false, incorrectly named) are often associated with value judgments resulting from the labels "false" and "lie" (ψευδής, false, lying). Whether particular cases are instances of forgery or of false attribution of names is a disputed point, so scholars have attempted to find a neutral terminology. The suggestion that we adopt the term *deuteronymity* (secondary authorship) seems to make sense:[33] an author claims a secondary (δεύτερος) name as a means of authorizing his or her cause. This is a legitimate procedure for authors in the Pauline school (see below, chap. 10), but not for other

31. On pseudepigraphy among Greek and Roman authors, cf. especially Wolfgang Speyer, *Die literarische Fälschung im heidnischen und christlichen Altertum: Ein Versuch ihrer Deutung* (HAW 1.2; Munich: Beck, 1971), 111–49.

32. On this point, cf. D. G. Meade, *Pseudonymity and Canon* (WUNT 39; Tübingen: Mohr, 1986), 17–85.

33. So Joachim Gnilka, *Der Kolosserbrief* (HTKNT 10; Freiburg: Herder, 1980), 23–24, adopted by Hahn, *Theologie*, 1:333–34. Alfred Zimmermann, "Unecht—und doch wahr? Pseudepigraphie im Neuen Testament als theologisches Problem," *ZNT* 12 (2003): 30, speaks of "imitative pseudepigraphy"; I. Howard Marshall, *The Pastoral Epistles* (ICC; Edinburgh: T&T Clark, 1999), 84, uses "allonymity" or "allepigraphy."

pseudepigraphical writings. It thus seems to me to be equally appropriate to use either pseudepigraphy or deuteronymity, and to decide from case to case which category is most suitable.

Historical Situation

New Testament pseudepigraphy/deuteronymity has clear temporal boundaries: most of the pseudepigraphical writings were composed between 60 and 100 CE, the authentic letters of Paul forming the early boundary and the authentic letters of Ignatius the later. Within the history of early Christianity, this is the period of radical change and reorientation. The first generation of witnesses had died; an organizational structure for the whole church did not yet exist; congregational offices were in the process of formation; the church was becoming fully aware of the problem of the delay of the parousia; the first extensive persecutions of the church were occurring; and, finally, in this period the church experienced both the painful separation from Judaism and internal disputes with false teachers within the church's own ranks. In addition, we may surmise from 2 Thess. 2:2 that opponents of what came to be mainstream Christianity were claiming Paul's authority by pseudepigraphical/deuteronymous writings. In this situation of reorientation and reinterpretation, pseudepigraphy was obviously for many early Christian groups the most effective means of influencing the way things were developing.[34]

In terms of social history, Paul's collaborative mission practice[35] and the existence of a Pauline school[36] were of great importance for the deutero-Pauline writings. In this manner the person of the apostle received a legitimizing and normative significance. With the exception of Romans, the opening lines of all the authentic Pauline letters refer to coauthors (1 Thess. 1:1; 1 Cor. 1:1; 2 Cor. 1:1; Gal. 1:2; Phil. 1:1; Philem. 1); they were composed by secretaries (Rom. 16:22) or scribes (1 Cor. 16:21; Gal. 6:11; Philem. 19). This means that, even though Paul is the primary author in each case, all the letters *also* have the character of collaborative works. Thus his followers could rightly claim the authority of Paul when they took up his ideas, developed them further, integrated oral traditions about him in their letters,[37] and brought the argument up to date in addressing the current situations

34. Cf. Karl Martin Fischer, "Anmerkungen zur Pseudepigraphie im Neuen Testament," *NTS* 23 (1977): 79ff. Wolter, "Die anonymen Schriften," 15, emphasizes the separation from Judaism as a supplementary factor that called for a new conception of the idea of tradition. Now Jesus "himself became the founder of a new tradition and the guarantor of a new identity, both of which were ultimately sanctioned by God himself" (ibid., 16).

35. On this point, cf. Ollrog, *Mitarbeiter*, 109ff.

36. Cf. Schnelle, *Apostle Paul*, 146–57.

37. On this point, cf. Angela Standhartinger, *Studien zur Entstehungsgeschichte und Intention des Kolosserbriefs* (NovTSup 94; Leiden: Brill, 1999), 91–152.

of the churches. It also seemed to the early Christian churches a thoroughly plausible idea that Paul would have written letters to his closest coworkers Timothy (cf. 1 Thess. 3:2; Rom. 16:21; Phil. 2:19–23) and Titus (cf. 2 Cor. 8:16). One could also expect that Paul would have written to the important churches in Ephesus (cf. 1 Cor. 15:32; 16:8; Acts 18:19, 21, 24; 19:1, 17, 26; 20:16–17) and Colossae, as well as a second letter to a church Paul himself had founded (2 Thessalonians). These letters could be "found" in various churches or published in collections along with authentic letters.[38] Finally, letters from such important figures as Peter and James would not have been perceived as anything unusual. Each had experienced an eventful history to which proper claim could be made.

All New Testament pseudepigraphical/deuteronymous letters were thus related to a very particular historical situation; they must be seen as a successful attempt of the third Christian generation's struggle to overcome its central problems. The goal of New Testament pseudepigraphy consisted not only in establishing the continuity of apostolic tradition in the time after the death of the apostles. Rather, the authority of the apostle was above all to be brought to bear in new words and language for the present. By appealing to the origins of the tradition, the authors grounded their claim in binding authority but with new interpretations directed to the problems that had arisen in the present. The secondary attribution to authors of the past thus always testifies to the significance of the primary authors!

The Literary Construction

Pseudepigraphy/deuteronymity is a constructive literary procedure oriented to intertextuality,[39] which serves to give direction and orientation as to how a person (e.g., Peter or James) or a document (e.g., Pauline letters) is to be read. As a rule, the goal of this procedure is to broaden the spectrum of the significance of a person or writing, or to make a more specific claim with regard to a particular issue. Placing a person or text within a changed herme-

38. Cf. the plausible suggestion of P. Trummer, "Corpus Paulinum—Corpus Pastorale," in *Paulus in den neutestamentlichen Spätschriften: Zur Paulusrezeption im Neuen Testament* (ed. Karl Kertelge; QD 89; Freiburg i.B.: Herder, 1981), 133: "As Pauline Pseudepigrapha, the Pastorals could only have been written and circulated in the course of a new edition of the previous corpus of Pauline letters. Despite the presence of credulity and the partly uncritical procedure of early Christian groups, a different origin would still have had to face a very perceptive critique and rejection."

39. On intertextuality, cf. Stefan Alkier, "Intertextualität—Annäherungen an ein texttheoretisches Paradigma," in *Heiligkeit und Herrschaft: Intertextuelle Studien zu Heiligkeitsvorstellungen und zu Psalm 110* (ed. Dieter Sänger; Biblisch-theologische Studien 55; Neukirchen-Vluyn: Neukirchener Verlag, 2003), 1–26. I presuppose the following concept of intertextuality: "intertextuality" means all forms of citations, allusions, and references within a text to another text, within a linguistic and cultural world of meaning.

neutical framework by means of a new text facilitates new readings and new meanings.[40] A new polyvalence is generated in regard to both the reference person/text and the new text, i.e., the goal is a broadening of understanding. Pseudepigraphic/deuteronymous writings identify themselves from the outset with a whole personal or literary world of meaning, for which they were written and within which they are to be received in a particular way.

Particular authors utilize the pseudepigraphic/deuteronymous form in quite different ways. While, for example, the Letter to the Hebrews only hints that it wants to be understood as a letter of Paul (13:23), the Pastorals represent a full-blown fictionalized Paul. Thus the letter openings and conclusions imitate the Pauline style in the way they address their recipients, with their greetings, mention of names, and relaying of personal information (cf. 1 Tim. 1:1–2; 6:21; 2 Tim. 1:1–5; 4:19–22; Titus 1:1–4; 3:12–15). Moreover, the author pictures the present life of Paul in detail (cf. 1 Tim. 1:20; 2 Tim. 4:13), even giving Paul's thoughts as he faces death (cf. 2 Tim. 4:6–8, 17–18). The apostle thereby receives legitimizing, normative significance. In the deutero-Paulines, the imitation Paul had called for takes on a literary form (cf. 1 Cor. 4:16). The elements of stylistic imitation, the fictive portrayal of his situation through chronological data or the picturing of his historical circumstances and the description of his personal situation—these features belong, in differing levels of intensity, to the authority claimed through the means of New Testament pseudepigraphy/deuteronymity. They are the stylistic means that communicate the necessary emphasis on the authoritative person (e.g., Paul or Peter). Thus the stylistic means chosen by the author and the situation for which the pseudepigraphical/deuteronymous author is writing condition each other. When, for example, in 1 Tim. 5:23 Paul advises Timothy to drink a little wine for the sake of his health, this personal advice is also directed against the rigorous ascetic practices (cf. also Col. 2:16) combated by the writer of the letter in 1 Tim. 4:3–9.

Pseudepigraphic/deuteronymous writings are set in a simulated communication situation, in order, by literary means both powerful and subtle, to address the concerns of the actual situation by reference to a person or writing.

The Theological Problematic

We must not base our theological evaluation on (contemporary) moral categories of forgery or fraud,[41] for New Testament pseudepigraphy/deutero-

40. Cf. here Annette Merz, *Die fiktive Selbstauslegung des Paulus: Intertextuelle Studien zur Intention und Rezeption der Pastoralbriefe* (NTOA 52; Göttingen: Vandenhoeck & Ruprecht, 2004), 35–71.

41. On this point, cf. Norbert Brox, *Falsche Verfasserangaben: Zur Erklärung der frühchristlichen Pseudepigraphie* (SBS 79; Stuttgart: KBW Verlag, 1975), 81ff.

nymity fits into its own historical context,[42] in which deception was not the goal.

In the last third of the first century CE, from the perspective of the authors of the pseudepigraphical writings, pseudepigraphy was the best means at their disposal for indicating authoritatively how the figures whose mantels they took up would solve newly arising problems. Their goal was not deception about authorship but that the message of the writings be heard by the addressees in a particular way. The moral category of forgery is thus inappropriate for understanding the intentions and goals of pseudepigraphy/deuteronymity,[43] for the truth of what the writings affirm does not depend on whether or not the purported authors actually composed the documents—an issue that, in any case, can never be absolutely resolved. It would therefore be more appropriate to speak of *borrowed authorial designation*, in which apostolic authority appears as the guarantor for the validity of the contents of the pseudepigraphical/deuteronymous documents.[44] In the New Testament, pseudepigraphy/deuteronymity must therefore be seen as the theologically legitimate and ecclesiologically necessary attempt to think through and preserve apostolic traditions in an act of hermeneutical anamnesis in the context of a changed situation, giving the responses called for by new situations and their questions. Thus the perspective of pseudepigraphical/deuteronymous writings is characteristically that of the whole church, for they originated from a sense of ecumenical responsibility.

42. For parallels, cf. especially the Cynic letters; the texts are available in Ludwig Köhler, *Die Briefe des Sokrates und der Sokratiker* (Leipzig: Liselotte, 1928), Philologus 20.2; Eike Müseler and Martin Sicherl, eds., *Die Kynikerbriefe* (2 vols.; SGKA 1 NF 6–7; Paderborn: Schöningh, 1994); Abraham J. Malherbe, *The Cynic Epistles: A Study Edition* (SBLSBS 12; Missoula, MT: Scholars Press, 1977).

43. Zimmermann, "Unecht," 34–35.

44. Cf. Brox, *Falsche Verfasserangaben*, 105, who emphasizes "the motif of participation in the considered past" in New Testament pseudepigraphy.

10

The Deutero-Pauline Letters

Paul's Thought Extended

The deutero-Pauline letters constitute the largest group of pseudepigraphic/deuteronymous writings in the New Testament. This is no accident, since through his intellectual accomplishment, his impressive life's work, and finally by his death as a martyr, Paul became a central figure in the process of early Christianity's self-identification. Moreover, Pauline theology was never a brittle, unchanging monolithic block but a system of thought that rested on fundamental convictions but was open to historical modifications and new theological challenges. Disciples of the apostle took up these tendencies already present in his thought and composed letters in his name that reflected further developments in Pauline theology for changed times, with the intention of creating a fresh hearing for the apostle's message. The deutero-Paulines took up and further developed the apostle's basic concerns in view of their specific historical and theological situation. So they are quite diverse: the letters of Colossians and Ephesians take up Paul's thought in a comprehensive way, modifying it and developing further; the Pastoral Epistles concentrate on individual concrete issues; and 2 Thessalonians is devoted almost exclusively to the parousia theme.

10.1 Colossians: Paul in Changing Times

The Letter to the Colossians is the first writing composed in Paul's (and Timothy's) name after the death of the apostle. Written by a coworker and disciple of the apostle ca. 70 CE, Colossians has a closer historical and theological continuity with the apostle's own work than any other post-Pauline document.[1] This proximity justifies us in designating Colossians as a deuteronymous writing intended to stabilize the endangered identity of the church through a careful further development of Pauline thought. The church in Colossae was obviously in danger of reactivating central elements of their previous religious practice—such as the veneration of stars and intermediary divine beings (angels), reverence and fear of demons, belief in fate, and practice of ascetic disciplines—in combination with their Christian faith. The author of Colossians considered this a relativizing of the saving effect of the Christ event, which he attempted to overcome by emphasizing the universal aspects of God's act in Jesus Christ. The whole argumentation of Colossians, with its characteristic intensive interweaving of Christology, soteriology, eschatology, and ecclesiology, all on the foundation of theology proper, serves this pragmatic goal.

10.1.1 Theology

Theology proper forms the functional and objectively factual presupposition for Colossians' argumentation, even though it is not dominant at the level of the surface of the text. God appears as the Father of Jesus Christ (Col. 1:3), whose grace has generated the word of truth, the gospel (1:5–6). Paul became a minister of this word, which God has kept hidden throughout the ages and generations (1:25) but now has revealed to the Gentiles: "Christ in you, the hope of glory" (1:27). Christ is the μυστήριον τοῦ θεοῦ ("God's mystery"), in whom are hidden all the treasures of wisdom and knowledge (2:3; cf. 1:27). God is the one who is to be praised for his act in Jesus Christ (3:16–17), and the church is to pray to God that even in prison the apostle will be able to declare the mystery of Christ (4:3).

The theological grounding of Christology is particularly evident in the way Col. 1:12–14 is related to 1:15–20 and 2:14–15.[2] The "Christ hymn" (see below, §10.1.2) is theologically grounded by 1:12–14: the acting subject of the whole event is God the Father, who has called believers out of darkness and transferred them into the kingdom of his Son. God is superior to all the powers, for God alone grants redemption and forgiveness of sins in Christ (Col. 1:14). God is the fullness of the universe; the hymn speaks of his visible manifestation. A second key text is Col. 2:14–15;[3] in the dispute with the

1. For introductory issues, see Schnelle, *New Testament Writings*, 281–99.

2. Cf. here Rudolf Hoppe, "Theo-logie in den Deuteropaulinen (Kolosser- und Epheserbrief)," in *Monotheismus und Christologie: Zur Gottesfrage im hellenistischen Judentum und im Urchristentum* (ed. Hans-Josef Klauck; QD 138; Freiburg i.B.: Herder, 1992), 163–85.

3. For an extensive analysis, cf. Rudolf Hoppe, *Der Triumph des Kreuzes: Studien zum Verhältnis des Kolosserbriefes zur paulinischen Kreuzestheologie* (SBB 28; Stuttgart: Verlag Katholisches Bibelwerk, 1994), 252–59.

Colossian "philosophy" (2:8, φιλοσοφία) the author of the letter again argues theologically: it is God who "forgave us all our trespasses, erasing the record that stood against us with its legal demands. He set this aside, nailing it to the cross. He disarmed the rulers and authorities and made a public example of them, triumphing over them in it." The military metaphor of the triumphal procession (cf. 2 Cor. 2:14) underscores the finality of the event: just as the commander of the army demonstrates his victory by the triumphal procession (cf. Plutarch, *Pomp.* 83.3), God documents for all time the defeat of the rulers and powers on the cross.

The pragmatic goal of the Letter to the Colossians is the demonstration of the comprehensive, all-embracing, almighty lordship of God in Jesus Christ. This is the reason Colossians adopts central concepts and terms of the common religious life of antiquity,[4] grounds them theologically and fills them with christological content, in order to remove the fascination from the Colossian "philosophy" as a competing interpretation of the world and life influencing the church's self-understanding. This "philosophy" apparently was based on an attractive, comprehensive combination of old and new interpretative models that facilitated a universal worldview. The Letter to the Colossians responds by portraying a symbolic universe that is universal in every respect, in which God's act provides the foundation for the dominance of its Christology.[5]

10.1.2 Christology

The meaning of the saving work of Jesus Christ for the whole cosmos stands at the center of the Christology of the Letter to the Colossians.[6] It includes almost all the central christological themes: preexistence, the mediation of

4. Cf., e.g., truth (1:5, 6, ἀλήθεια); philosophy (2:8, φιλοσοφία, only here in the New Testament); visible/invisible (1:16, ὁρατός; 1:15, 16, ἀόρατος); knowledge (1:9, 10; 2:2; 3:10, ἐπίγνωσις); power (1:11, 29, δύναμις; 1:13, 16; 2:10, 15, ἐξουσία); light (1:12, φῶς); secret, mystery (1:26, 27; 2:2; 4:3, μυστήριον); fullness (1:19; 2:9, πλήρωμα; 1:25; 2:10; 4:17, πληρόω); image, icon (1:15; 3:10, εἰκών); submission, self-abasement (2:18, 23; 3:12, ταπεινοφροσύνη); elements of the world, elemental spirits of the universe (2:8, 20, στοιχεῖα τοῦ κόσμου). A helpful comparison to the religious language of Colossians is provided by the pseudo-Aristotelian writing *De mundo* (περὶ κόσμου), which may have originated in the first century CE, and is an impressive witness to the predominant ancient worldview of this time.

5. On this point cf. Roland Gebauer, "Der Kolosserbrief als Antwort auf die Herausforderung des Synkretismus," in *Die bleibende Gegenwart des Evangeliums: Festschrift für Otto Merk* (ed. Roland Gebauer and Martin Meiser; MTS 76; Marburg: Elwert, 2003), 153–69.

6. Surveys of the Christology of Colossians is found in A. de Oliveira, "Christozentrik im Kolosserbrief," in *Christologie in der Paulus-Schule: Zur Rezeptionsgeschichte des paulinischen Evangeliums* (ed. Klaus Scholtissek; SBS 181; Stuttgart: Verlag Katholisches Bibelwerk, 2000), 71–103; Hurtado, *Lord Jesus Christ*, 504–10; a penetrating analysis is presented by George H. van Kooten, *Cosmic Christology in Paul and the Pauline School: Colossians and Ephesians in the Context of Graeco-Roman Cosmology, with a New Synopsis of the Greek Texts* (WUNT 2.171; Tübingen: Mohr, 2003), 59–146.

creation, the cross, reconciliation, death and resurrection, God's kingdom, the return of Christ.

Cosmic Christology

Christ is the firstborn of all creation; in him all things were created; all things have their continued existence through him and for him (cf. Col. 1:15–17). As Lord of creation and the one through whom all things were made, he rules over every created thing, visible and invisible. Christ is the head of every ruler and authority (2:10) and triumphs over the cosmic powers (2:15). The cosmos continues to exist by his power, and he determines the significance of other powers. Already in the present, the church participates in this lordship of Christ. Through his death, he reconciles the believers with God (1:22), and erases the charges that have been written out against them (2:14). Now Christ can be proclaimed as Lord of the cosmos also to the Gentiles (1:27). Colossians 3:11 expresses the Christology of the letter concisely and pointedly: "Christ is all and in all!" (τὰ πάντα καὶ ἐν πᾶσιν Χριστός).[7]

This concept of a cosmic Christology, characterized by thinking in terms of spheres and realms of lordship, has points of contact in affirmations of the authentic Pauline letters that also proclaim the cosmic lordship of Christ (cf. 1 Cor. 8:6; Phil. 2:9–11; 3:20–21). The author of Colossians, however, goes far beyond these traditional statements, making the cosmological dimensions the foundation and center of his Christology. The catalyst for doing so was probably the propagation of the christological perspectives represented by the competing "philosophy" in Colossae.[8] This "philosophy" seems to have been influenced by a combination of elements from Hellenistic Judaism, contemporary Stoicism, neo-Pythagoreanism, and Middle Platonism, as well as from the mystery cults, so that in history-of-religion terms, derivation from a single source appears to be impossible. The opponents in Colossae obviously prac-

7. In 1 Cor. 15:28, God is "all in all" (ὁ θεὸς τὰ πάντα ἐν πᾶσιν)!

8. Surveys of research and histories of interpretation are provided by Günther Bornkamm, "Die Häresie des Kolosserbriefes," in *Das Ende des Gesetzes: Paulusstudien* (ed. Günther Bornkamm; BEvT 16; Munich: Kaiser, 1961), 139–56 (the older discussion); Fred O. Francis and Wayne A. Meeks, eds., *Conflict at Colossae: A Problem in the Interpretation of Early Christianity Illustrated by Selected Modern Studies* (SBLSBS 4; Missoula, MT: Society of Biblical Literature, 1973); Eduard Schweizer, *Der Brief an die Kolosser* (EKKNT 12; Zürich: Benziger, 1976), 100–104; Michael Wolter, *Der Brief an die Kolosser: Der Brief an Philemon* (ÖTK 12; Gütersloh: Gütersloher Verlagshaus Gerd Mohn, 1993), 155–63; Ingrid Maisch, *Der Brief an die Gemeinde in Kolossä* (THKNT 12; Stuttgart: Kohlhammer, 2003), 30–40. On the key term τὰ στοιχεῖα τοῦ κόσμου, cf. Delling, "στοιχέω," 666–87; Josef Blinzler, *Lexikalisches zu dem Terminus* τὰ στοιχεῖα τοῦ κόσμου *bei Paulus* (AnBib 18; Rome: Pontifical Biblical Institute, 1963), 429–43; Lohse, *Colossians and Philemon*, 96–99; Eduard Schweizer, "Altes und Neues zu den 'Elementen der Welt' in Kol 2,20; Gal 4,3. 9," in *Wissenschaft und Kirche: Festschrift für Eduard Lohse* (ed. Kurt Aland and Siegfried Meurer; TAB 4; Bielefeld: Luther-Verlag, 1989), 111–18; D. Rusam, "Neue Belege zu den στοιχεῖα τοῦ κόσμου," *ZNW* 83 (1992): 119–25; Wolter, *Kolosser, Philemon*, 122–24.

ticed their rituals and taught their doctrines within the church. They did not understand themselves as heretics but regarded their philosophy as a legitimate expression of the Christian faith. The juxtaposition of τὰ στοιχεῖα τοῦ κόσμου (elemental spirits of the universe) with Christ in Col. 2:8 permits the inference that in the "philosophy" the στοιχεῖα were considered to be personal powers. They appear as rulers who want to exercise their power over human beings (cf. 2:10, 15). Probably the Colossians both feared and worshiped the powers in rituals that included ascetic practices, circumcision, attitudes of submission, and worship of angels. The purpose of such practices was to come to terms with the supposed demands of these heavenly powers. In each case there is a clear tendency to include these powers in the cosmic order alongside Christ and to pay them the proper respects.

The Hymn

On the levels of both composition and content, the hymn in Col. 1:15–20 is the foundational text that provides the basis for the debate with the rival teaching:[9]

15ὅς ἐστιν εἰκὼν τοῦ θεοῦ τοῦ ἀοράτου,	He is the image of the invisible God,
πρωτότοκος πάσης κτίσεως,	the firstborn of all creation;
16ὅτι ἐν αὐτῷ ἐκτίσθη τὰ πάντα	for in him all things were created
ἐν τοῖς οὐρανοῖς καὶ ἐπὶ τῆς γῆς,	in heaven and on earth,
τὰ ὁρατὰ καὶ τὰ ἀόρατα,	things visible and invisible,
εἴτε θρόνοι εἴτε κυριότητες	whether thrones or dominions
εἴτε ἀρχαὶ εἴτε ἐξουσίαι·	or rulers or powers—
τὰ πάντα δι' αὐτοῦ καὶ εἰς αὐτὸν ἔκτισται·	all things have been created through him and for him.
17καὶ αὐτός ἐστιν πρὸ πάντων	He himself is before all things,
καὶ τὰ πάντα ἐν αὐτῷ συνέστηκεν,	and in him all things hold together.
18καὶ αὐτός ἐστιν ἡ κεφαλὴ τοῦ σώματος	He is the head of the body,
τῆς ἐκκλησίας·	the church;
ὅς ἐστιν ἀρχή,	he is the beginning,
πρωτότοκος ἐκ τῶν νεκρῶν,	the firstborn from the dead,

9. In addition to the standard commentaries, on Col. 1:15–20 see especially Harald Hegermann, *Die Vorstellung vom Schöpfungsmittler im hellenistischen Judentum und Urchristentum* (TU 5.27; Berlin: Akademie-Verlag, 1961), 89–93; Christoph Burger, *Schöpfung und Versöhnung: Studien zum liturgischen Gut im Kolosser- und Epheserbrief* (WMANT 46; Neukirchen-Vluyn: Neukirchener Verlag, 1975), 3–53; Reinhard Deichgräber, *Gotteshymnus und Christushymnus in der frühen Christenheit: Untersuchungen zu Form, Sprache und Stil der frühchristlichen Hymnen* (SUNT 5; Göttingen: Vandenhoeck & Ruprecht, 1967), 143–55; Wengst, *Christologische Formeln*, 170–79; Franz Zeilinger, *Der Erstgeborene der Schöpfung: Untersuchungen zur Formalstruktur und Theologie des Kolosserbriefes* (Vienna: Herder, 1974), 179–205; Habermann, *Präexistenzaussagen*, 225–66; Christian Stettler, *Der Kolosserhymnus: Untersuchungen zu Form, traditionsgeschtlichem Hintergrund und Aussage von Kol 1,15–20* (WUNT 2.131; Tübingen: Mohr Siebeck, 2000), 75ff.

ἵνα γένηται ἐν πᾶσιν αὐτὸς πρωτεύων,	so that he might come to have first place in everything.
19 ὅτι ἐν αὐτῷ εὐδόκησεν πᾶν τὸ πλήρωμα κατοικῆσαι	For in him all the fullness of God was pleased to dwell,
20 καὶ δι' αὐτοῦ ἀποκαταλλάξαι τὰ πάντα εἰς αὐτόν,	and through him God was pleased to reconcile to himself all things,
εἰρηνοποιήσας διὰ τοῦ αἵματος τοῦ σταυροῦ αὐτοῦ,	by making peace through the blood of his cross,
εἴτε τὰ ἐπὶ τῆς γῆς εἴτε τὰ ἐν τοῖς οὐρανοῖς.	whether on earth or in heaven.

The traditional hymn begins in v. 15, where there is a sudden change of style.[10] While Col. 1:3–14 manifests typical elements of the letter's style (participial constructions, loosely attached infinitives, heaping up of synonyms and genitives, repetitions) these are lacking in 1:15–20.[11] In addition, there are linguistic peculiarities: ὁρατός (1:16), προτεύω (v. 18), and εἰρηνοποιέω (v. 20) are all hapax legomena in the New Testament. Neither θρόνος nor ἀρχή is found in the undisputed Pauline letters (v. 16). Paul himself speaks of the blood of Christ only when he is taking over traditional material (cf. Rom. 3:25; 1 Cor. 10:16; 11:25, 27), and the expression αἷμα τοῦ σταυροῦ αὐτοῦ (v. 20) has no parallel in the undisputed Pauline letters.

The division of the hymn into two strophes is indicated by the parallels ὅς ἐστιν in v. 15 and v. 18b. Moreover, πρωτότοκος πάσης κτίσεως in v. 15 corresponds to πρωτότοκος ἐκ τῶν νεκρῶν in v. 18b. Each relative clause is then followed by a causal ὅτι (vv. 16, 19). Verses 17 and 18a are each attached by a καὶ αὐτός, v. 20 by καὶ δι' αὐτοῦ. The hymn is divided into two strophes not only by formal markers, but by their respective contents. The first strophe speaks of the cosmological significance of the Christ event, while the second strophe focuses on its soteriological dimension. The epexegetical genitive τῆς ἐκκλησίας appended to ἡ κεφαλὴ τοῦ σώματος in v. 18a disturbs its structure, for it already introduces the soteriological-ecclesiological dimension into the first strophe. Moreover, this interpretative element corresponds to the understanding of the church as the body of Christ, as the author himself develops it, for example, in Col. 1:24. An additional interpretative element is found in the double prepositional phrase διὰ τοῦ αἵματος τοῦ σταυροῦ αὐτοῦ (v. 20). The reference to the cross event must be regarded as an addition by the author of Colossians, who binds the cosmic dimensions of the Christ event to the cross and thus to history.[12] There are undeniable parallels to the Philippians hymn; both here and there we find the traditional hymn related

10. On the variety of form-critical classifications of Col. 1:15–20 (hymn, Christ-song, Christ-psalm, didactic poem, Christ-encomium), cf. Maisch, *Kolossä*, 32ff.

11. Cf. H. Ludwig, "Der Verfasser des Kolosserbriefes: Ein Schüler des Paulus" (ThD diss., Georg August Universität, Göttingen, 1974), 32ff.

12. Cf. ibid., 79.

to its context by interpretative additions. The hymn has history-of-religions contacts with Hellenistic Judaism, where predicates here affirmed of Christ are connected to Wisdom.[13] The author takes up this Christian hymn, which probably originated in Asia Minor, and makes it the point of departure for his line of argument in a church in which hymnic traditions were of great importance (cf. Col. 3:16b).

The content of the hymn sets forth a *cosmic/universal Christology*: as image of the invisible God, Jesus Christ is creator, preserver, and reconciler of the cosmos. He was before all things, all things were created through him, and in him are reconciliation and peace. The hymn's dominant concepts of preexistence and mediation of creation, as well as the omnipresence, universal effectiveness, and exclusiveness of Jesus Christ are developed and supplemented in the body of the letter itself in a threefold manner:

1. By adding τῆς ἐκκλησίας in v. 18a, the letter fills the cosmological concept of the body with ecclesiological content. On the one hand, this takes up the Pauline concept of the church as the body of Christ (σῶμα Χριστοῦ, 1 Cor. 12), but on the other hand, the un-Pauline distinction between the "head" and the "body" takes on fundamental importance (Col. 2:19, "holding fast to the head, from whom the whole body, nourished and held together by its ligaments and sinews, grows with a growth that is from God"). This head-body distinction underscores the universal sovereignty of Christ (Col. 2:10, "and you have come to fullness in him, who is the head of every ruler and authority").
2. In v. 20b the interpretative addition διὰ τοῦ αἵματος τοῦ σταυροῦ αὐτοῦ (through the blood of his cross) introduces the Pauline theology of the cross (cf. 1 Cor. 1:18ff.): reconciliation and the establishment of peace result from the cross event.
3. Through these interpretative additions, the body of the letters facilitates a fusion between the cosmological dimensions of the traditional hymn and authentic Pauline thinking: fullness, reconciliation, and peace occur in the event of the cross and are present in the church as the body of Christ.

The basic ideas of the hymn also shape the affirmations in Colossians that develop Christology further, indicated linguistically above all by the adoption of the πᾶν/πάντα (all) vocabulary of the hymn (1:16, 17, 18, 19, 20) in 2:2, 9, 13, 19; 3:11, 17, 20, 22 and the hymn's ἐν αὐτῷ ("in him," 1:16, 17, 19) in 2:6, 7, 9, 10, 11, 12, 15. The hymn grounds the Christocentrism of the letter and thus already functions as part of the polemic (cf. the adoption of Col. 1:19

13. Cf. the documentation of this point in Lohse, *Colossians and Philemon*, 41–61.

in 2:9, and compare 2:10 with 1:16b, 17).[14] While the opponents proclaim a relationship between Christian faith and service to the principalities and powers, the author of Colossians opposes that teaching with his proclamation of *solus Christus*.[15] For the false teachers, Christ alone is not sufficient to attain the fullness of salvation. The author of Colossians addresses the church's anxiety about cosmic powers and the believers' uncertainty about their own place in the universe with the assurance of full salvation in Jesus Christ: "For in him the whole fullness of deity dwells bodily" (Col. 2:9).

The dispute with the Colossian "philosophy" provides the occasion for the explication of the Christology of Colossians, which represents *an independent development of Pauline Christology that was to have great influence.* Colossians does not take up Paul's doctrine of justification as expressed in Galatians and Romans (lacking are νόμος [law] and all words from the stem δικ- [righteous, just, justify]). Instead, the thought of Colossians is oriented to the spatial (the preposition ἐν [in] is found eighty-nine times; the term σῶμα [body], eight times) and participatory aspects of Paul's thought (cf. the σύν- [with] expressions in Col. 2:12, 13, 20; 3:3, 4). The author thus also positions himself in the context of contemporary philosophy,[16] for which the essence of the deity/deities and their relation to the universe, to time, and to the fullness of being was a central theme.[17] For Colossians, Jesus Christ is the one who redeems us from the enslaving powers, he is himself the true fullness of

14. Standhartinger, *Kolosserbriefs*, 284, minimizes the importance of the opposing teaching for shaping the thought of Colossians: "In my opinion, the authors of Colossians do not have in view a definite 'heresy' or 'philosophy' that is endangering the church." Instead, he emphasizes the influence of dualistic Jewish wisdom traditions on Colossians and thinks the theme of the letter is shaped by the problems for the church occasioned by the death of the apostle Paul.

15. Appropriately H. Löwe, "Bekenntnis, Apostelamt und Kirche im Kolosserbrief," in *Kirche: Festschrift für Günther Bornkamm zum 75. Geburtstag* (ed. Dieter Lührmann and Georg Strecker; Tübingen: Mohr, 1980), 310: "The author of the letter opposes the human traditions proclaimed as divine teaching (2:8) with the authentic *traditio divina* of Jesus Christ received as the baptismal confession (2:6)."

16. For the hymn Col. 1:15–20, cf. the documentation in Gnilka, *Kolosserbrief*, 59ff.; Schweizer, *Kolosser*, 56ff.; Wolter, *Kolosser, Philemon*, 76ff. On the Stoic "all" formula, cf. Eduard Norden, *Agnostos Theos: Untersuchungen zur Formengeschichte religiöser Rede* (Leipzig: Teubner, 1913), 240–50. Documentation for the Stoic and Middle Platonist theories of creation and "all" formulae are found in *NW* 2.1:313–16.

17. A survey of the contemporary physics of the Stoa and Middle Platonism is presented by Kooten, *Cosmic Christology*, 17–58. Of numerous examples, cf. Cicero, *Nat. d.* 2.115, which expresses awe at the arrangement of the stars: "But not only are these things marvelous, but nothing is more remarkable than the stability and coherence of the world, which is such that it is impossible even to imagine anything better adapted to endure. For all its parts in every direction gravitate with a uniform pressure towards the center." Cf. further Plutarch, *Mor.* 393A, where the existence of God is defined as the fullness of time and being: "But God is (if there be need to say so), and He exists for no fixed time, but for the everlasting ages which are immovable, timeless, and undeviating, in which there is no earlier nor later, no future nor past, no older nor younger; but He, being One, has with only one 'Now' completely filled 'Forever' [ἀλλ' εἷς ὢν ἑνὶ τῷ νῦν τὸ

all that is (1:19; 2:9), the one who sets the church in the realm of the freedom of faith and the new being (3:11).

10.1.3 Pneumatology

The Letter to the Colossians has no developed pneumatology (πνεῦμα occurs twice; πνευματικός also twice). Within the framework of the thanksgiving section (Col. 1:3–14), the conventional expression "he has made known your love to us in the Spirit" (1:8) occurs, and in 2:5 the author presents Paul as saying "For though I am absent in body, yet I am with you in spirit." This clear scaling back of interest in the Spirit, when compared to the authentic letters of Paul, is possibly related to the spatially oriented thinking of Colossians, with which dynamic elements such as the working of the Spirit can be only partially integrated. In addition, the incorporation of the apostle Paul into the thought world of tradition (see below, §10.1.7) no longer allows him to be portrayed in terms of elementary spiritual experiences (cf. 1 Thess. 5:19; 1 Cor. 14:1).

10.1.4 Soteriology

The starting point for the soteriology of the Letter to the Colossians is *the transfer of believers into a new realm of salvation by God*, who "has rescued us from the power of darkness and transferred us into the kingdom of his beloved Son" (Col. 1:13). In the Son, the church has "redemption, the forgiveness of sins" (1:14, ἀπολύτρωσιν, τὴν ἄφεσιν τῶν ἁμαρτιῶν). In Colossians, the cross becomes the place where the elementary spirits of the universe are deprived of their power (2:14–15), so that they no longer can affect the lives of believers.[18] On the cross, the *reconciliation* of the world takes place, and true peace comes into being through the blood of the Son (1:20). With the phrase διὰ τοῦ αἵματος τοῦ σταυροῦ αὐτοῦ (through the blood of his cross), Colossians brings a historical datum into the hymn's concept of universal reconciliation,[19] and

---

ἀεὶ πεπλήρωκεν]; and only when Being is after His pattern is it in reality Being, not having been nor about to be, nor has it had a beginning nor is it destined to come to an end."

18. Cf. Karrer, *Jesus Christus*, 110, "The central focus of soteriology is shifted to the conquest of those principalities and powers who could affect the lives of guilty human beings." On the background of Col. 2:14 in ancient practice regarding debt and repayment, cf. J. Luttenberger, "Der gekreuzigte Schuldschein: Ein Aspekt der Deutung des Todes Jesu im Kolosserbrief," *NTS* 51 (2005): 80–95.

19. On the Hellenistic background of the "reconciliation of all things," cf. Eduard Schweizer, "Zum hellenistischen Hintergrund der Vorstellung der 'Versöhnung des Alls,'" in *Neues Testament und Christologie im Werden: Aufsätze* (ed. Eduard Schweizer; Göttingen: Vandenhoeck & Ruprecht, 1982), 164–78 (he refers primarily to Philo); Wolter, *Kolosser, Philemon*, 87–88 (theories of rulership in antiquity).

thus preserves the concrete uniqueness of the event as irreplaceable.[20] In Col. 1:22 ("he has now reconciled in his fleshly body through death, so as to present you holy and blameless and irreproachable before him"), the letter's author incorporates the Pauline theology of the cross and concept of reconciliation,[21] thus signaling the centrality of this theme in his view: the crucified body of the earthly Jesus is the place where universal reconciliation occurred, and baptized believers now find themselves in the realm where this divine act is effective.[22] Here, Colossians stands close to Paul himself (cf. 2 Cor. 5:18–20; Rom. 5:10) but at the same time places its own characteristic accent: the acting subject in the reconciling event is not God, but Christ (cf. Eph. 2:16).[23]

Baptism

As for Paul (Rom. 6:1–11), so also for Colossians, *baptism* is the place where the universal saving event is appropriated by the individual Christian, the place where being transferred into the new realm of salvation occurs concretely in history (Col. 2:12, "When you were buried with him in baptism, you were also raised with him through faith in the power of God, who raised him from the dead").[24] As in Rom. 6:3–5, here we find the idea of a comprehensive participation of believers in the destiny of their Lord, to be sure with a fundamental difference: while Paul himself never speaks of the resurrection of believers as something that has already occurred—indeed, he explicitly avoids the idea, which is already implicit in the logic of the pre-Pauline tradition that stands behind Rom. 6:3b–4[25]—Colossians says that believers have not only died with Christ but also have already been resurrected with him. To be sure, the author is not thereby advocating an unreflective, exalted view of salvation that takes the believer out of this-worldly life, for the qualification "through

20. Cf. Maisch, *Kolossä*, 119–20.

21. Some exegetes see Col. 1:20, 22 as expressing the concept of atoning sacrifice. These include de Oliveira, "Christozentrik," 87–88; Andreas Dettwiler, "Das Verständnis des Kreuzes Jesu im Kolosserbrief," in *Kreuzestheologie im Neuen Testament* (ed. Andreas Dettwiler and Jean Zumstein; WUNT 151; Tübingen: Mohr, 2002), 103.

22. The comment of Wolter, *Kolosser, Philemon*, 94, is on target: "Those who have been reconciled are placed in the realm of salvation of the exalted Son."

23. Cf. ibid., 93; differently, e.g., Dettwiler, "Verständnis des Kreuzes," 95, who regards God as the acting subject of the reconciling act in this text too.

24. According to Petr Pokorný, *Colossians: A Commentary* (trans. Siegfried S. Schatzmann; Peabody, MA: Hendrickson, 1991), 27, the theology of Colossians is concentrated in the thesis of 2:12–13: "This thesis distinguishes Colossians and Ephesians from the rest of the Pauline letters and at the same time becomes the backbone of the theological argument."

25. On this point cf. Schnelle, *Gerechtigkeit und Christusgegenwart*, 80–81. Since the pre-Pauline tradition in Rom. 6:3b–4 had already spoken of the resurrection of believers as an element of past experience, we should assume that Colossians represents a traditional baptismal theology that existed prior to and alongside Paul, a theology like that of 2 Tim. 2:18 that affirmed realized eschatology in a comprehensive sense; differently Wolter, *Kolosser, Philemon*, 131–32, who assumes a direct reference to Rom. 6:4.

faith" (διὰ τῆς πίστεως) limits and more carefully defines the experience of present resurrection as the insight of faith. By taking up Col. 2:12 in 2:20 ("If with Christ you died to the elemental spirits of the universe, why do you live as if you still belonged to the world?"), the author again accents the certainty of salvation. A further agreement with Paul (cf. Rom. 6:1–3, 12–23) is found in the relation of baptism to the forgiveness of sins and the new life that then becomes possible (Col. 2:13, "And when you were dead in trespasses and the uncircumcision of your flesh, God made you alive together with him, when he forgave us all our trespasses"). As baptized believers, the Colossians are risen with Christ, who rules over all the powers of the universe, and they should live their lives in accord with this reality. The author addresses the readers' uncertainty and lack of self-assurance with a coherent soteriological concept: just as Christ is filled with the whole fullness of God (πᾶν τὸ πλήρωμα) and God dwells in him (Col. 2:9–10), so also the Colossians have come to fullness in him (ἐστὲ ἐν αὐτῷ πεπληρωμένοι), and thus are freed from the claims of any foreign powers. *The soteriology of Colossians is characterized throughout by the postulate that the change in rulership in all realms of being and time has already taken place.*

10.1.5 Anthropology

Colossians contains only incidental statements bearing on anthropology. The term σάρξ (flesh) is used in Col. 2:11, 13 as a designation for the "fleshly" existence of church members that has now been overcome, and in Col. 2:18, 23 to indicate that the life of the opponents is still "fleshly" (NRSV "human way of thinking" is literally "mind of the flesh"). The σῶμα (body) vocabulary is used in Colossians primarily in the christological-ecclesiological sense (see below, §10.1.7), but also in 2:11, 23 for the human body in a neutral sense. *Sin* (ἁμαρτία) occurs only in 1:14 and *trespass* (παράπτωμα) only in 2:13, in each case describing the saving act in which sins/transgressions have been overcome.

Faith has a central anthropological importance, but, characteristically for Colossians, it is found only as the noun πίστις (Col. 1:4, 23; 2:5, 7, 12), the verb πιστεύω being entirely absent—the result of the author's understanding of faith. The challenge to "continue securely established and steadfast in the faith" (Col. 1:23; 2:5, 7), in the immediate context of the Colossian "philosophy" (2:8), shows that in Colossians the focus is on faith as the content believed.[26] The author is clearly concerned with the content of Christian teaching, without thereby excluding faith as the believer's response and the life of faith. This content includes the cosmic dimensions of the Christ event as set forth in the hymn of Col. 1:15–20 and the soteriological consequence

26. Cf. Maisch, *Kolossä*, 129–30.

to be drawn from them, as formulated in 2:12: the present reality of the resurrection is experienced by faith, i.e., it is directed to the saving power of God manifest in God's act in Jesus Christ.

Closely bound up with the concept of faith is that of hope (ἐλπίς in Col. 1:5, 23, 27; as in the case of the faith terminology, so also here the verb is missing [ἐλπίζω]). Hope is understood in a spatial and static sense (1:5, "in heaven"; 1:23, "without shifting from the hope . . ."), directed to the gospel of Jesus Christ. Hope is the objective reality of salvation already present in the transcendent world; it is no longer oriented toward the future (cf. Rom. 8:24) but is a reality already prepared for believers in the heavenly world. Fundamental for the anthropology of Colossians is the adoption of the Pauline concept of the "new humanity," the "new self" (2 Cor. 5:17; Gal. 3:27, 28; 4:19; 6:15; Rom. 6:6; 13:14), formulated in Col. 3:9–10 as follows: "You have stripped off the old self [παλαιὸν ἄνθρωπον] with its practices and have clothed yourselves with the new self [καὶ ἐνδυσάμενοι τὸν νέον]." The adoption of the tradition of Gal. 3:28 in Col. 3:11, with only slight textual alteration, indicates the author's own standpoint: the status of the new self, the new humanity, is no longer defined by attributes taken from salvation history or culture but only by belonging to Jesus Christ. The ethical application of the tradition in Col. 3:12 shows that in Colossians, as in Paul, the new existence brings with it a new way of life. Because a real change of human existence has entered the world through God's act in Christ appropriated in baptism, the church can be addressed on the basis of this new reality.

10.1.6 Ethics

The theological-christological foundation of ethics is already indicated in the opening thanksgiving, where the author praises the church and prays for it, "that you may be filled with the knowledge of God's will in all spiritual wisdom and understanding, so that you may lead lives worthy of the Lord, fully pleasing to him, as you bear fruit in every good work and as you grow in the knowledge of God" (Col. 1:9b–10).[27] Very much like Paul (cf. Gal. 5:25), in Col. 2:6 the author insists that the new being must be expressed in a new way of living: "As you therefore have received Christ Jesus the Lord, continue to live your lives in him"; so also in Col. 3:13: "Just as the Lord has forgiven you, so you also must forgive." The specific position of Colossians on the relation between the basis of salvation and the life of the saved is clear in Col. 3:1–4, where the verbs that document what has already been accomplished—a

27. On the ethics of Colossians, cf. Eduard Lohse, "Christologie und Ethik im Kolosserbrief," in *Die Einheit des Neuen Testaments: Exegetische Studien zur Theologie des Neuen Testaments* (2nd ed.; Göttingen: Vandenhoeck & Ruprecht, 1973), 249–61; Schnackenburg, *Sittliche Botschaft*, 2:74–84 [The 1973 English translation of an earlier edition does not contain this section.—MEB]; Schrage, *Ethics*, 244–57.

change in rulership over the world and the resulting new reality (see below, §10.1.8)—are connected to two verbs in the imperative: "Seek the things that are above" (3:1) and "Set your minds on things that are above" (3:2). The definitive change that has already taken place in the world and in the believer's own life does not abolish personal responsibility but preserves it. Unlike the Corinthian Spirit-enthusiasts, the author of Colossians, despite his insistence on the present reality of salvation, proclaims no leapfrogging over the present reality of the world and life. The ethical admonitions he immediately adds underscore this point (Col. 3:5–17).[28] Pointedly juxtaposing the "once" and the "now" of Christian existence (3:7–8), they proceed through a catalog of vices to be avoided (3:5, 8) and a description of the new person in Christ (3:9–11) to a paean praising love as the supreme quality: "Above all, clothe yourselves with love, which binds everything together in perfect harmony" (3:14). *Love is the decisive ethical criterion, the characteristic quality of the new life.*

Finally, the *Haustafel* (household code)[29] that concludes the body of the letter (Col. 3:18–4:1) testifies to the fact that the life of the church is still interwoven with the realities of earthly life. The Roman *familia* was the fundamental model for the social order of the time;[30] it formed the center of all social relationships and all religious life, so of course the formative influence of this model would affect the early Christian churches. At the top of this social pyramid stands the *pater familias*, who represents the fundamental authority, but whose authority is at the same time involved in a variety of relationships. Paul himself already appears in an analogous role to that of the *pater familias* as the one who has begotten the congregations and is thus their father (1 Cor. 4:15). In the context of the concept of order prevalent in the ancient world,[31] the household code formulates the respective obligations of wife and husband,

28. For analysis, cf. Eduard Schweizer, "Gottesgerechtigkeit und Lasterkataloge bei Paulus (inkl. Kol und Eph)," in *Rechtfertigung: Festschrift für Ernst Käsemann zum 70. Geburtstag* (ed. Johannes Friedrich et al.; Göttingen: Vandenhoeck & Ruprecht, 1976), 453–77.

29. For a survey of research and a spectrum of interpretations, cf. Marlis Gielen, *Tradition und Theologie neutestamentlicher Haustafelethik: Ein Beitrag zur Frage einer christlichen Auseinandersetzung mit gesellschaftlichen Normen* (AMT 75; Frankfurt a.M.: Hain, 1990), 24–67, 105–203; Wolter, *Kolosser, Philemon*, 194–98; Ulrike Wagener, *Die Ordnung des "Hauses Gottes": Der Ort von Frauen in der Ekklesiologie und Ethik der Pastoralbriefe* (WUNT 2.65; Tübingen: Mohr, 1994), 15–65; Standhartinger, *Kolosserbriefs*, 247–75.

30. On this point, cf. Clarke, *Serve the Community*, 79–101.

31. The social model that stands behind the household code is elaborated in Aristotle, *Pol.* 1252ff.; for additional illustrative texts, cf. Cicero, *Off.* 1.17; civil rights prescriptions are found in Ulrich Manthe, ed., *Die Institutionen des Gaius* (TF 81; Darmstadt: Wissenschaftliche Buchgesellschaft, 2004), 1.52–107. The most important direct parallel is Seneca, *Ep.* 94.1: "One area of philosophy gives particular rules for every person without attempting to shape human life as a whole, but advises the husband how he should conduct himself toward his wife, the father on how he should raise his children, and the master on how he should direct his slaves" (trans. MEB); cf. further Epictetus, *Diatr.* 2.14.8; 2.17.31. On household management cf. the comprehensive treatment in G. Schöllgen, "Haus II," *RAC* 13:815–30.

children and parents, slaves and masters as a Christian text. The members of the Christian household are addressed as three pairs, in which a line that descends from the closest relationship (wife and husband) to that of slave and master can be perceived. In each case, the subordinate member of the pair is addressed first, both members are admonished to show mutual concern, and in each case there is the series of address, admonition, and basis for the instruction. The greater length of instruction to the slaves in 3:22–25 throws the neat reciprocal structure out of kilter, indicating problems in the church that called for special motivation. The reciprocal obligations are intended to make the congregation aware that they all have one Lord, who will reward them without partiality (Col. 3:24; 4:1).

The whole ethic of Colossians is stamped by the idea of the all-embracing lordship of Jesus Christ. In contrast to the opposing teachers, the church does not follow human traditions (Col. 2:22) but orients its life in love to the will and reality of God.

10.1.7 Ecclesiology

Two concepts determine the ecclesiology of the Letter to the Colossians: (1) Jesus Christ as cosmic Lord, and (2) the apostle Paul and the foundation of the church.[32]

Jesus Christ as Cosmic Lord

At the center of the letter's ecclesiology is the concept of the σῶμα (body), which is bound up with ideas of Christ's role in creating and ruling the cosmos (Col. 1:16–17).[33] While Paul used the body-of-Christ imagery in parenetic contexts (cf. especially 1 Cor. 12:12–27; Rom. 12:4–8),[34] in Colossians this imagery takes on cosmic importance. The fine-tuning of this image by the addition of τῆς ἐκκλησίας (of the church) in Col. 1:18a clarifies the ecclesiological focus: the church is the realm of the universal salvation made possible by Jesus Christ, permeated by his presence and authority (cf. Col. 1:18, 24; 2:17, 19; 3:15). This body is not primarily the local congregation, as in Paul, but

32. On this point cf. Eduard Schweizer, "Die Kirche als Leib Christi in den paulinischen Antilegomena," in *Neotestamentica: Deutsche und Englische Aufsätze, 1951–1963; German and English Essays, 1951–1963* (ed. Eduard Schweizer; Zürich: Zwingli Verlag, 1963), 293–316; Eduard Lohse, "Christusherrschaft und Kirche," in *Die Einheit des Neuen Testaments: Exegetische Studien zur Theologie des Neuen Testaments* (2nd ed.; Göttingen: Vandenhoeck & Ruprecht, 1973), 262–75; Roloff, *Kirche im Neuen Testament*, 223–31; Maisch, *Kolossä*, 40–47.

33. The history-of-religions materials are presented in Schweizer and Baumgärtel, "σῶμα," 7:1024–94; on Colossians, cf. 1074–77.

34. For Paul, cf. here Ernst Käsemann, "The Theological Problem Presented by the Motif of the Body of Christ," in *Perspectives on Paul* (Philadelphia: Fortress, 1971), 101–21; Schnelle, *Gerechtigkeit und Christusgegenwart*, 139–43, 243–45.

the universal church. Paul portrays Christ himself as the body of the church (cf. 1 Cor. 12:12–13; Rom. 12:4–5), but in Col. 1:18 Christ is the *head* of the body (contrast 1 Cor. 12:21). The author thus gives up Paul's picture, which was oriented to the concrete local situation, and takes up the cosmic idea of the worldwide body of the church, whose head is Christ. The interwoven relationship of charismatic gifts within the church is no longer the focus of discussion, but the relation between the head and the body that belongs to it. Jesus Christ, enthroned with God in heaven (Col. 3:1), is the head of the earthly body, the church, but this earthly church already fully participates in his cosmic lordship (Col. 2:10a). Filling the body-concept with ecclesiological content does not, however, exclude its cosmic dimension, for according to 2:10b Jesus Christ has become once and for all "the head of every ruler and authority," which means that not only the church but all that is stands under his lordship. Christ created the universe, reconciled it, and as its head exercises his lordship over it.[35] The church thus appears as the predetermined and chosen realm (Col. 1:24–27) where this lordship is visibly realized in an exceptional way.

Parallels for the head/body metaphor are found in the history of religions,[36] but the political dimension of this image is particularly important. The Roman Empire understood itself as the exemplary great imperial commonwealth that had been providentially provided by the gods to rule all other kingdoms.[37] Virgil sees the Romans as descendants of Hector, begotten by Mars and established by Romulus: "I set no boundaries to their power or temporal limits to their rule; I have conferred eternal rule on them" (*Aen.* 1.278–79 [trans. MEB]). Eternal Rome thus understood itself as the head of the earthly circle (Ovid, *Metam.* 15.434–35, "She therefore is changing her form by growth, and some day shall be the capital of the boundless world!"; Grattius, *Cyn.* 324, "Rome established as the head of the circle of the earth"). According to Seneca, *Clem.* 3.2.1, 3, the emperor Nero is "the head [from which comes] the health of the body . . . it will be diffused little by little throughout the whole body of the empire, and all things will be moulded into your likeness." When the Letter to the Colossians takes up the head-body imagery with its universal attributes and makes it central, it is also relativizing the Roman political ideology.

The extent to which the body imagery has become an independent theme in Colossians is seen in the idea of the "growth" of the body, an aspect of the metaphor not found in Paul. The church is challenged to orient itself to

35. This aspect is neglected in the treatment of Roloff, *Kirche im Neuen Testament*, 227, when he formulates: "In the present world situation, only the church is the body of Christ."

36. Cf. above all the idea mediated by Hellenistic Judaism of the one God who rules all the far reaches of the universe (e.g., Philo, *Migration* 220; *Flight* 108–113).

37. Relevant texts are found in B. Kytzler, ed., *Roma aeterna: Lateinische und griechische Romdichtung* (Munich: Artemis, 1972), 280–314.

its head, "from whom the whole body, nourished and held together by its ligaments and sinews, grows with a growth that is from God" (Col. 2:19). The body (the church) that belongs to the heavenly head (Christ) grows and permeates the whole cosmos. This happens through the preaching of the apostle Paul, through the acceptance of the gospel, through baptism, and through the thanksgiving and confession of the church at worship (3:16, "Let the word of Christ dwell in you richly; teach and admonish one another in all wisdom; and with gratitude in your hearts sing psalms, hymns, and spiritual songs to God"). *Above all this, however, stands the unbreakable living bond that connects the church to Christ, for the earthly body of Christ cannot exist apart from its heavenly head.*

The Apostle Paul and the Foundation of the Church

Paul himself always ascribed exceptional importance to his own person and message in the process of evangelism and the church formation (cf., e.g., 2 Cor. 3 and 5).[38] Colossians goes a step further, in that it regards the person of the apostle as having an explicit role in salvation history and makes this a theological theme.[39] The person of the apostle is now itself included as an element of the Pauline gospel; as bearer of the proclaimed message, the apostle himself is now part of the all-encompassing plan of God made before time began, the one in whose name it can be said, "I became its [the church's] servant according to God's commission that was given to me for you, to make the word of God fully known, the mystery that has been hidden throughout the ages and generations but has now been revealed to his saints" (Col. 1:25–26). As Paul proclaimed the gospel of Jesus Christ, so the central message of Colossians appears as the μυστήριον θεοῦ/Χριστοῦ (cf. 1:26, 27; 2:2; 4:3).[40] Behind this mystery, which was formulated before time began, was hidden throughout the ages, and is now revealed (thus, so to speak, simply bypassing Israel), stands the church. Now in the process of formation and expansion, it owes its existence in turn to the preaching of the apostle. Thus the person of the apostle and his suffering are also elements of the mystery (cf. Col. 1:24–29). As a minister of and to the body of Christ, Paul reveals to the church the mystery of the divine will; his person is no longer separable from the content of the gospel; his suffering (as apostle and martyr) even supplements or fulfills the afflictions of Jesus Christ for his church (Col. 1:24). Although not present in body, Paul is still present with the church in spirit (2:5)—the church that is to continue proclaiming Christ just as Paul had done (2:6). Any other proclamation is regarded as mere human doctrine (2:8), not apostolic

38. On this point, cf. Schröter, *Der versöhnte Versöhner*, passim.

39. On the reception of Paul in Colossians, cf. especially Helmut Merklein, "Paulinische Theologie in der Rezeption des Kolosser- und Epheserbriefes," in *Studien zu Jesus und Paulus* (2 vols.; WUNT 43, 105; Tübingen: Mohr, 1987–98), 1:409–47.

40. Cf. ibid., 412ff.

tradition. The gospel is no longer defined only in terms of its content, Jesus Christ; rather, it is essentially defined by the preaching of the apostle. Paul is not only the apostle to the Gentiles (1:27) but *the* apostle of the universal church (1:23b), who proclaims the gospel to "everyone" (1:28). The letter thus claims to be oriented likewise to the person, theology, and significance of the martyr-apostle. This "Paulinizing" of theology is intended to safeguard the identity of the christocentric gospel in the post-Pauline period.

10.1.8 Eschatology

The eschatology of Colossians[41] is structured on the basis of its Christology, and thus has a cosmological orientation from the outset.[42] Believers have died with Christ and are already risen with him (Col. 2:12–13; 3:1), so that other powers can no longer have any control over them. The powers belong to the realm "below," while Christians are to orient their lives to the realm "above," where Christ is (cf. 3:1–2).[43] The baptized believers' full participation in the death and resurrection of Jesus Christ and the associated eschatological conception are manifest above all in the σύν- (with) expressions in Col. 2:12, 13; 3:1. In contrast to Rom. 6:3–4, the past tense is already used with regard to the eschatological realities (cf. 2:12; 3:1, συνηγέρθητε, "you have been raised with").[44] For Paul, however, it is characteristic that the new reality in the Spirit (cf. 2 Cor. 1:22; 5:5; Rom. 8:23) is indeed already present but will not be comprehensively and completely revealed until the parousia (cf. in addition to Rom. 6:3–5, especially 1 Cor. 13:12; 2 Cor. 4:7; 5:7; 1 Cor. 15:20–23, 46). *Paul himself thus never speaks of the resurrection as something believers have already experienced, and, given his own theological presuppositions, cannot speak in this way, so that here a decisive difference must be seen between the eschatology of Colossians and Paul's own eschatology.* There is a fundamental difference between the two regarding the degree of participation in the reality of the resurrection.[45] For Paul, the Spirit

41. H. E. Lona, *Die Eschatologie im Kolosser- und Epheserbrief* (FzB 48; Würzburg: Katholisches Bibelwerk, 1984), 83–240, provides a comprehensive discussion of all issues (Colossians stands in the line begun by Paul, but follows a different conceptual approach).

42. Cf. Walter, "Hellenistische Eschatologie," 344ff.

43. Erich Grässer, "Kolosser 3,1–4 als Beispiel einer Interpretation secundum homines recipientes," in *Text und Situation: Gesammelte Aufsätze zum Neuen Testament* (ed. Erich Grässer; Gütersloh: Gütersloher Verlagshaus G. Mohn, 1973), 123–51, provides a penetrating analysis of Col. 3:1–4.

44. Continuity and discontinuity between Rom. 6 and Col. 3:1–4 are precisely worked out by Grässer in ibid., 129ff., and by Peter Müller, *Anfänge der Paulusschule: Dargestellt am zweiten Thessalonicherbrief und am Kolosserbrief* (ATANT 74; Zürich: Theologischer Verlag, 1988), 87–134.

45. Michael Dübbers, *Christologie und Existenz im Kolosserbrief: Exegetische und semantische Untersuchungen zur Intention des Kolosserbriefes* (WUNT 2.191; Tübingen: Mohr Siebeck, 2005), 238–42, attempts to minimize this fundamental difference, by classifying "risen

is the "firstfruits," the pledge of what is to come in the *future* eschatological events (Rom. 8:23; 2 Cor. 1:22; 5:5), while for Colossians these events are already spoken of in the past tense. The second big difference: *while Colossians postulates the present and lasting stability of the cosmos as a coherent reality in Christ, Paul does not expect the ultimate subjection of the cosmos until the parousia* (1 Cor. 15:23–28). To be sure, Colossians builds in cautionary measures against allowing Spirit-led enthusiasm to precipitate a leapfrogging over the present.[46] The Colossians already participate in a salvation that cannot be lost, but only in faith (Col. 2:12). Their resurrected life is an objective reality, but it is not yet revealed; it is hidden with Christ in God (cf. 3:3) and thus not available for this-worldly observation and demonstration. Statements of future eschatology are fading into the background in Colossians in favor of a spatial way of thinking, while at the same time being integrated into this spatial worldview, and are to be understood within its framework.[47] Their fundamental importance for the eschatology of Colossians is indicated by the way they hold fast to the conviction of the future act of God at the parousia of Christ (cf. Col. 3:4, 24–25). Judgment will be according to works, "and there is no partiality" (3:25). Affirmations of future eschatology are also constitutive for parenesis, for even though Christians already participate in the reality of salvation, they do not yet live in the heavenly realm "above." They should rather orient themselves to the salvation to be revealed in the future, and shape their lives accordingly.

These spatial dimensions permit Colossians to make the transition from Paul's temporal-linear thought to a conceptuality that on the one hand confirms the ultimate reality of salvation but on the other adjusts it in terms both spatial-temporal (life is hidden in Christ "above," and will be revealed with Christ) and ethical-temporal (living in accord with the new being is a criterion at the parousia and judgment).[48]

10.1.9 Setting in the History of Early Christian Theology

The Letter to the Colossians is the first witness for a comprehensive cosmic Christology in the New Testament. At the center of its thinking stands the all-surpassing and all-permeating reality and lordship of Jesus Christ, who rules all principalities and powers, a reality in which all baptized believers already fully participate in the present. This theological structure, with its Christology,

---

with him" as "metaphorical language . . . by which the author makes clear that the present life of the addressees is bound to the risen Christ and that their salvation is exclusively determined by him" (242). Paul also does this, but without speaking of being "risen with him"!

46. Cf. Merklein, "Rezeption," 426ff.; contra Klein, "Eschatologie," 286–87.

47. Cf. Lona, *Eschatologie*, 234: "Colossians does not eliminate the temporal aspect but integrates it into a christological concept."

48. On this point, cf. also Thomas Witulski, "Gegenwart und Zukunft in den eschatologischen Konzeptionen des Kolosser- und Epheserbriefes," *ZNW* 96 (2005): 211–42.

cosmology, and present-tense eschatology is a response to the challenge of the opposing "philosophy," at the same time representing a new, independent type of early Christian thought: the conceptuality of creation, lordship, and spatial orientation that is predominant in Colossians' theology marks out a Christian position within the prevailing ancient religious philosophy of rulership and nature. In ancient thought, it was self-evident that one should fit oneself into and subject oneself to the powers that determine fate; it was obvious, and wise, that one should pay tribute to the powers that determine one's destiny.[49] Moreover, it was a mark of an effective philosophical structure to be able to explain the cosmos and its phenomena in a way that was useful for interpreting human existence. Over against these obvious and highly attractive proposals of the opposing philosophy, the Letter to the Colossians posits the reality of the Christ event, which makes any additional attempt at securing one's salvation superfluous. Tacking on old religious practices will not intensify and secure the new identity; it rests exclusively in God's act in Christ to establish peace and reconciliation for the whole universe. Colossians succeeded in outlining an alternative model to that of the competing philosophy, but at the same time this model, by adopting and adapting spatial and rulership dimensions of its environment's thought world, facilitated the reception of this form of Christian thought in the Greco-Roman world.

In view of the reception of cosmological and ecclesiological elements of Pauline thought, it is worth noting some Pauline elements that Colossians does *not* pick up. The themes of the law, the relationship to Israel, and justification are missing.[50] The imagery of atonement and sacrifice clearly recedes, and spatial rather than temporal (salvation-historical) conceptions predominate. Finally, as the first "Pauline" writing after Paul, Colossians documents the transition to an expanded understanding of Paul himself. The person, status, work, and continuing effects of the apostle are pressed into service to oppose developments that, in the author's view, endanger the work of the apostle and the whole church.

10.2 Ephesians: Space and Time

The author of the Letter to the Ephesians, a member of the Pauline school, composed the document between 80 and 90 CE in Asia Minor.[51] Although his

49. Cf. Seneca, *Ep.* 107.11: "Lead, O Father of the high heavens, wherever you will; I do not hesitate to obey . . . Fate leads one, if one agrees; if one refuses, he is dragged along."

50. Merklein, "Rezeption," 432–35, rightly emphasizes that in Colossians (and Ephesians) ecclesiology takes the place of Paul's doctrine of justification: "If salvation means being placed in the saving realm of the church, then soteriology, which Paul had construed with the help of the doctrine of justification, is identified with ecclesiology. Or, better expressed: soteriology is driven by ecclesiology."

51. In introductory issues, cf. Schnelle, *New Testament Writings*, 299–314.

primary source for this composition was the Letter to the Colossians, Ephesians pursues its own theological goals. As a circular letter to the Pauline churches of Asia Minor, it attempts to save the endangered unity of the church, which is composed of Jewish Christians and Christians of Greco-Roman religious background, through the vision of the "new humanity" reconciled and united in Christ. In so doing, the letter utilizes a densely compact language and imagery that is unique in the New Testament.

10.2.1 Theology

The theological foundation for the letter (in the sense of "theology proper") is the opening liturgical blessing of Eph. 1:3–14, which succinctly designates *as salvation history* the beginning point of all theological thought: praise and thanks to God (1:3).[52] God had already chosen those who believe in Christ "before the foundation of the world" (1:4, πρὸ καταβολῆς κόσμου), he "destined" us "in advance" (1:5, προορίσας) for sonship (υἱοθεσίαν, NRSV "adoption as his children"), and revealed to them "the mystery of his will" (1:9, τὸ μυστήριον τοῦ θελήματος αὐτοῦ). God's grace in Christ is freely given to believers (1:6). It is God's will that everything in heaven and on earth be summed up in Christ (1:10), whom he has raised from the dead by his mighty power and installed at his right hand in the heavenly world (1:20). According to God's "purpose" (πρόθεσις), believers in Christ are appointed as heirs (1:11; cf. 3:11). God's actions in Christ for believers—acts that take place before creation and permeate the universe—constitute the basis of the argument for the whole of Ephesians, for grace, faith, and good works (2:8–10) are just as much gifts of God as are peace, mercy, and forgiveness (2:4; 4:32–5:2). Finally, it is God who acts in the event of the believer's being raised with Christ (2:4–6) and in the creation of the new humanity concretized in the "new self" (4:24). God is universally active as the Father "who is above all and through all and in all" (4:6). With great emphasis, the author of Ephesians praises the riches of God's grace (3:14–17), whose surpassing power rules over every "rule and authority and power" (1:19–21; 3:10). With his remarkable emphasis on God's prior activity for believers and the concomitant strengthened consciousness of election, the author evidently intends to address a feeling of insecurity within the churches.[53] God's eternal election applies not only to Jesus Christ but also to the community of baptized believers. Awareness of their election removes them from the randomness of being and comprehensively determines

52. On the analysis of Eph. 3:3–14, cf. Rudolf Schnackenburg, "Die grosse Eulogie Eph 1,3–14," *BZ* 21 (1977): 67–87.

53. This intention of Ephesians should be a warning against interpreting its theology within the framework of a static ontology, as largely done by Heinrich Schlier, *Der Brief an die Epheser: Ein Kommentar* (6th ed.; Düsseldorf: Patmos, 1968). Cf., e.g., p. 49: "Inasmuch as we are elected, and as elected are preexistent, we preexist already in Christ."

their threatened existence by grounding it in God's purpose.[54] God himself acts to fill believers "with all the fullness of God" (ἵνα πληρωθῆτε εἰς πᾶν τὸ πλήρωμα τοῦ θεοῦ); it is impossible to declare God's saving will and presence in more comprehensive terms! *God's eternal plan of salvation and its realization through Jesus Christ in the church are together the one great theme of the Letter to the Ephesians.*

10.2.2 Christology

The Christology of Ephesians is shaped in terms of a *spatial worldview*.[55] God as creator of the universe and Jesus Christ are enthroned over all in the heavenly realm, while the intermediate space between heaven and earth is dominated by aeons, angels, and demonic powers (Eph. 2:2; 6:12), and human beings and death are found in the lower realm. All the same, Jesus Christ fills the whole of reality, which Ephesians expresses incisively with the phrase τὰ πάντα (Eph. 1:10, 11, 23; 3:9; 4:10, 15).

Exaltation and Lordship

Within the framework of this worldview, the author of Ephesians develops his Christology of exaltation and lordship, orienting his thought by Col. 1:18–20, and interpreting Ps. 110:1 (Eph. 1:20–21), Ps. 8:7 (Eph. 1:22), and Ps. 68:18 (Eph. 4:7ff.) from this perspective. The risen Christ is seated at the right hand of God (Eph. 1:20; cf. 4:8, 10a); God, in accord with God's own eternal counsel, has placed all things under his feet (1:22a), and he fills the universe with the fullness of his life (1:23; 4:10b). Christ, enthroned as ruler over the universe, is the head of the church (cf. 1:22b; 5:23). Much more insistently than Colossians, Ephesians emphasizes that the church is the exclusive location where the lordship of Christ is already fully realized.[56] As the head, Christ determines and preserves the harmony of the members of the body (4:15–16), manifesting himself as the goal of all being, the point at which the history of the universe converges, for "he has made known to us the mystery of his will, according to his good pleasure that he set forth in Christ, as a plan for the fullness of time, to gather up all things in him, things in heaven and things on earth" (1:9–10). In Christ, the whole creation

54. On this point, cf. the good reflections of Hans Hübner, *An Philemon, an die Kolosser, an die Epheser* (HNT 12; Tübingen: Mohr, 1997), 141–43.

55. On the worldviews of antiquity, cf. the comprehensive treatment in Rainer Schwindt, *Das Weltbild des Epheserbriefes: Eine religionsgeschichtlich-exegetische Studie* (WUNT 148; Tübingen: Mohr, 2002), 135–350; on the worldview of Ephesians, cf. Franz Mussner, *Der Brief an die Epheser* (ÖTK 10; Gütersloh: Gütersloher Verlagshaus Gerd Mohn, 1982), 21–22; Andreas Lindemann, *Der Epheserbrief* (ZBK 8; Zürich: Theologischer Verlag, 1985), 121–23; Schwindt, *Weltbild*, 351–99.

56. Cf. Kooten, *Cosmic Christology*, 147–213.

reaches its goal. As reconciler and peacemaker he is head of the church, and as such also head of the cosmos. This event is not to be thought of in static terms. Despite its protological dimensions, its revealing unfolds as historical process:[57] in the cross and resurrection (2:14–16), in the proclamation of the apostle Paul (3:1–11), and in the present growth of the church (4:15, "But speaking the truth in love, we must grow up in every way into him who is the head, into Christ").

The noteworthy emphasis on the power of God/Christ in Eph. 1:22–23; 3:14–21; 6:10–20 is probably also conditioned by the religious milieu of the church in Ephesus. The religio-cultural situation in Ephesus was shaped by local cults, mystery religions, and the powerful and all-pervasive Artemis cult, with its many diverse practices (including magic).[58] Many new members of the church probably experienced a religious insecurity, not sure how they should live in response to these attractive alternatives. Ephesians proclaims to them: God's power in Jesus Christ stands over all the devilish forces and powers, the rulers of darkness and the evil spiritual beings in the heavenly realms (i.e., in the intermediate space between God's world and the human world; cf. Eph. 6:12).[59]

Christ as Mediator of Salvation

The liturgical blessing of Eph. 1:3–14 makes clear that for Ephesians the saving act of God occurs exclusively in and through Jesus Christ. God chose believers in him as the *preexistent one* (1:4, 9), and "in him" (ἐν ᾧ) they receive all the gifts of grace (1:7–8, 11–13). None of the other letters in the Pauline tradition, whether authentic or deutero-Pauline, make such frequent use of the expressions ἐν αὐτῷ (6 times), ἐν ᾧ (7 times), ἐν κυρίῳ (7 times), and ἐν Χριστῷ (14 times).[60] Believers are created (2:10, 15), redeemed (1:7), and reconciled (2:16) in Jesus Christ. In him they have peace (2:14, 17) and access to the Father (2:18). Christ "loved us and gave himself up for us, a fragrant offering and sacrifice to God" (5:2); he is the bridegroom who gave himself for the church in order to make her holy (5:25–26).

57. Cf. Helmut Merklein, "ἀνακεφαλαιόω," *EDNT* 1:82–83.

58. On the Artemis cult, cf. Winfried Elliger, *Ephesos: Geschichte einer antiken Weltstadt* (Stuttgart: Kohlhammer, 1985), 113–36; Clinton E. Arnold, *Ephesians, Power and Magic: The Concept of Power in Ephesians in Light of Its Historical Setting* (SNTSMS 63; Cambridge: Cambridge University Press, 1989), 20ff. On the debate between Christianity and the Artemis cult, see especially R. Oster, "The Ephesian Artemis as an Opponent of Early Christianity," *JAC* 19 (1976): 24–44. See also Peter Lampe, "Acta 19 im Spiegel der ephesischen Inschriften," *BZ* 19 (1992): 59–76; G. H. R. Horsley, "The Inscriptions of Ephesos and the New Testament," *NovT* 34 (1992): 105–68.

59. On the demonic powers in the argumentation of Ephesians, cf. Schwindt, *Weltbild*, 363–93.

60. On this point, cf. Joachim Gnilka, *Der Epheserbrief: Auslegung* (2nd ed.; HTKNT 10.2; Freiburg i.B.: Herder, 1977), 66–69.

As in no other New Testament writing, in Ephesians the goal of Jesus Christ as mediator of salvation is directed toward *unity*;[61] the unity of the church as the body of Christ (Eph. 1:22–23; 4:15–16), the unity of new individuals and the new humanity in Christ (2:15–16), and the unity of husband and wife (5:31). This unity is grounded in the unity of the one God (4:6) and "in the unity of the Spirit in the bond of peace" (4:3). The Ephesian Letter presents to the church a vision of the one universal body of Christ, which from God's perspective was already chosen before time began, which became visible in Jesus Christ on the cross, and which now is progressively actualized in the work of the Spirit.

10.2.3 Pneumatology

Pneumatology is a central theme of the Letter to the Ephesians.[62] The gift of the Spirit, conferred in baptism (Eph. 4:4), is interpreted in Eph. 1:13 as a "sealing" (cf. 2 Cor. 1:21–22), and its basic meaning is designated in Eph. 4:30: "And do not grieve the Holy Spirit of God, with which you were marked with a seal for the day of redemption." The Holy Spirit is the Spirit of God, which as pledge of the coming redemption (cf. 2 Cor. 1:22; 5:5) and as the "Spirit of wisdom and revelation" (Eph. 1:17) already determines the life of believers in the present: the Spirit whose guiding norms must not be violated. The declaration of Eph. 2:18—that through Jesus Christ "both of us [Jews and Gentiles] have access in one Spirit to the Father" in and through the one Spirit (ἐν ἑνὶ πνεύματι)—is of fundamental importance for the whole conception. As in Rom. 5:1–5, the Spirit opens access to God and makes concretely real the "new humanity" of Jews and Gentiles that is brought into being through Jesus Christ. The mention of Father, Son, and the one Spirit already resonates with later trinitarian thinking,[63] an anticipation that emerges even more clearly in Eph. 4:3–6: "the unity of the Spirit . . . one body and one Spirit . . . one Lord, one faith, one baptism . . . one God." *The reason there is one church is that the Spirit of the one God is effective in the life of the church, creating its unity!* The structure of the church is grounded in Christ and realized in the Spirit (Eph. 2:22), who now makes known the mystery of Christ to all people (3:5) by the word spoken through apostles and prophets, the word that is the "sword of the Spirit" (6:17). Finally, Eph. 5:8 is an instructive warning tinged with irony: "Do not get drunk with wine . . . but be filled with the Spirit."

61. Cf. E. Faust, *Pax Christi et Pax Caesaris* (NTOA 24; Göttingen: Vandenhoeck & Ruprecht, 1993), 471ff.; Ralph P. Martin, "The Christology of the Prison Epistles," in *Contours of Christology in the New Testament* (ed. Richard N. Longenecker; Grand Rapids: Eerdmans, 2005), 214–15.

62. Mussner, *Brief an die Epheser*, 27, rightly notes that the pneumatology of Ephesians has been much neglected in previous research.

63. Cf. Hübner, *Kolosser*, 179.

The letter's understanding of the Spirit is very close to Paul's in that it describes access to God, baptism, and centrally the unity of the church as gifts of the Spirit. Thus, within his partly static view of space and time (see below, §10.2.7 and §10.2.8) the author preserves a dynamic element that is of decisive importance for his understanding of the Spirit: *in and through the Spirit, God's space and time are opened up and made accessible.*[64]

10.2.4 Soteriology

The soteriology of Ephesians is shaped by its *protology*, which is especially dominant in the introductory liturgical blessing: the election of believers already occurred "*before* the foundation of the world" (Eph. 1:4); they were *pre*-destined to become God's children (1:5) according to God's purpose *pre*-formulated in Christ (1:9). In 1:11 the prefix προ- ("pre-," "prior") is found twice, in order to anchor salvation exclusively in the divine initiative of God's own prior will: "In Christ we have also obtained an inheritance, having been destined [προορισθέντες] according to the purpose [πρόθεσιν] of him who accomplishes all things according to his counsel and will." God's will, formulated before all time, becomes concrete reality through the believer's participation in the saving work of Christ through the sealing of the Spirit in baptism (1:13–14; 4:30). In Jesus Christ, believers have heard "the gospel of your salvation" (1:13) and have personal knowledge of "redemption through his blood, the forgiveness of our trespasses, according to the riches of his grace" (1:7; cf. 1:14; 2:13–14). Christ is "himself the savior of the body," his church (5:23, αὐτὸς σωτὴρ τοῦ σώματος).[65] Not the emperor, but Christ himself is the true bringer of peace and the reconciler (2:14–17; 4:3; 6:23). Ephesians is very close to Paul himself in the way the author develops his *doctrine of grace and justification*: "For by grace you have been saved through faith [Τῇ γὰρ χάριτί ἐστε σεσῳσμένοι διὰ πίστεως], and this is not your own doing; it is the gift of God—not the result of works [οὐκ ἐξ ἔργων], so that no one may boast" (2:8–9). The *grace of God*, which is the sole ground of redemption and salvation, is exuberantly praised in 1:6–7 and 2:5–6, so that the author can even speak of the resurrection and exaltation to the heavenly world as something believers have already experienced (see below, §10.2.8). Grace gave the apostle his office (3:2, 7–8) so that he could proclaim to the Gentiles the "mystery" of God (μυστήριον, 1:9; 3:3, 4, 9; 6:19): the good news of the saving grace and love of God manifest in Jesus Christ, but determined by God before the beginning of time.

What is the function of these strong soteriological statements in Ephesians? Quite obviously, the text-pragmatic aim of the letter is to strengthen the church,

64. Cf. Mussner, *Brief an die Epheser*, 27.

65. On the relation between soteriology and ecclesiology, see below, §10.2.7.

for whose members the problems of achieving unity out of their Jewish and Greco-Roman religious backgrounds clearly endanger their confidence in their election and thus their religious status. But, in addition to this obvious function, the intensity and density of soteriological motifs leave no doubt about the fact that the author wants to call attention to the reality of the new being of baptized believers. Predestination thus has not only a temporal but primarily an ontological dimension: the will of God is not subject to accident, to external influences, or arbitrariness.[66] God's initiative and decision has priority, and in every respect is prior to all human considerations; God's choice can and must be grounded only in himself. Ephesians confronts capricious fate and the helper gods of the local pantheon with the God who freely chooses in terms of his own love. But the question of whom God chooses remains closed to human knowledge, so that even in Ephesians statements about predestination are boundary statements that cannot be exploited for the construction of theological systems.

10.2.5 Anthropology

Ephesians portrays the new situation and the transformed being of baptized believers in a variety of ways. As Gentiles, as people who were physically uncircumcised, they were once far from God (Eph. 2:11–12), "But now in Christ Jesus you who once were far off have been brought near by the blood of Christ" (2:13; cf. 2:17–18). The christological foundation of Ephesians' anthropology is impressively manifest in its language about the "new humanity," the believer's "new self" or "new person."

The New Person

The person of Jesus Christ himself is the peace that makes the two into one, and so has broken down the dividing wall between Christians of Jewish background and those whose background is Greco-Roman religion (Eph. 2:14).[67] What had to be overcome, the "dividing wall" (2:14, μεσότοιχον), is the Torah (cf. 2:15a, and *Let. Aris.* 139!), whose segregating effects have been overcome in the one church of Jews and Gentiles.[68] Here Ephesians clearly goes beyond Paul's own critique of the Torah (cf. Rom. 3:31; 7:6–7) when it speaks of "destroying" or "abolishing" (καταργέω) the Torah along with its commandments and ordinances (Eph. 2:15a). Both the goal and result of this

66. Cf. Schlier, *Epheser*, 49–50: "As believers and saints, according to God's will and foreknowledge there was never a time when 'we' were not in Christ. If we are in him, we have always been in him."

67. For analysis of Eph. 2:14–16, cf. Faust, *Pax Christi*, 221ff., and Michael Gese, *Das Vermächtnis des Apostels* (WUNT 2.99; Tübingen: Mohr, 1997), 125–46.

68. Cf. Mussner, *Brief an die Epheser*, 75ff.; Rudolf Schnackenburg, *Die Brief an die Epheser* (EKKNT 10; Zürich: Benziger, 1982), 113–16. In contrast, Lindemann, *Epheserbrief*, 49, supposes that in 2:14–16 the author of Ephesians had "made use of a (non-Christian) Gnostic text."

event is that Christ "might create in himself one new humanity in place of the two, thus making peace" (2:15b). The "one new humanity" (εἷς καινὸς ἄνθρωπος) is the new existence, created in and through Christ (cf. Gal. 3:28; 2 Cor. 5:17), that transcends Jewish Christianity and Gentile Christianity; the new existence that is reconciled with God "in one body through the cross" (Eph. 2:16), that is, in the realm of the church.[69] The fact that this new humanity is actualized in the church does not mean that for the author of Ephesians ecclesiology has triumphed over anthropology and Christology.[70] Christ creates "in himself" the one new humanity; believers have come to know Christ (Eph. 4:20) and have abandoned their old way of life, their old selves (cf. Rom. 6:6), and have put on "the new self, created according to the likeness of God in true righteousness and holiness" (Eph. 4:24; cf. Gen. 1:27). Thus in Ephesians, too, theology and Christology continue to be the levels on which anthropology is worked out, even though they are more closely related to ecclesiology than is the case with Paul himself (see below, §10.2.7).

The "new humanity" has overcome sins (Eph. 2:1, 5), and no longer follows the passions of the flesh (2:3), because those who share this new humanity have been made alive together with Christ (Eph. 2:5; cf. Rom. 6:8). By the Spirit of God, the person who has been newly created in baptism (the "inner being," Eph. 3:16; cf. 2 Cor. 4:16) is to grow strong and thus live and act as one rooted and grounded in love (Eph. 3:17).

10.2.6 Ethics

Ephesians articulates a deep and abiding interest in ethics.[71] It is already clearly visible in the way ethical motifs are anchored in protology, for believers are "created in Christ Jesus for good works, which God prepared beforehand to be our way of life" (Eph. 2:10; cf. 1:4–5, 10).[72] The strong emphasis on

69. Cf. Faust, *Pax Christi*, 472: "The abolition of that which once separated corresponds positively to the new reality for both groups 'in Christ': here they have been recreated into *one* new humanity, which refers to the qualitative type of each individual, but not to the supposed collective-ecclesial macro-humanity."

70. To be sure, the interpretation of Gese, *Vermächtnis*, 137, tends in this direction.

71. Cf. Karl Martin Fischer, *Tendenz und Absicht des Epheserbriefes* (FRLANT 111; Göttingen: Vandenhoeck & Ruprecht, 1973), 147–72; Schrage, *Ethics*, 231–44; Ulrich Luz, "Überlegungen zum Epheserbrief und seiner Paränese," in *Vom Urchristentum zu Jesus: Für Joachim Gnilka* (ed. Hubert Frankemölle and Karl Kertelge; Freiburg: Herder, 1989), 376–96; Gerhard Sellin, "Die Paränese des Epheserbriefes," in *Gemeinschaft am Evangelium: Festschrift für Wiard Popkes zum 60. Geburtstag* (ed. Edwin Brandt et al.; Leipzig: Evangelische Verlagsanstalt, 1996), 281–300; Rudolf Hoppe, "Ekklesiologie und Paränese im Epheserbrief," in *Ethik als angewandte Ekklesiologie* (ed. Michael Wolter; SMBen; Rome: St. Paul's Abbey, 2005), 139–62.

72. Cf. Faust, *Pax Christi*, 471, who argues that believers participate in the conquest of the cosmic powers through Christ: "Thereby they are enabled to practice the new ethic of the good works which God prepared beforehand as the Christian way of life (2:10)."

the prior act of God is carried over into ethics;[73] God alone is the originator of good works, which God enables believers to do through the power of the Spirit conferred in baptism.[74] Following the exhortation that begins at 4:1 (παρακαλῶ, "I beg you"), the author continues his emphasis on the nature of the believer's new being as exclusively dependent on grace with a series of motivations and admonitions based on the presupposition that the believer's whole life actually participates in the reality of the saving event. The beginning point is the *concept of unity* that already dominates Eph. 2:14–18. That concept's theological and political implications (see below, §10.2.7) constitute the ethical foundation of Eph. 4:1–16.[75] The fundamental principle of ethics is to live in accord with this unity: "making every effort to maintain the unity of the Spirit in the bond of peace" (4:3; cf. 4:13, "the unity of the faith and the knowledge of the Son of God"). This concept of unity is underscored in Eph. 4:4–6 with unity formulae ("one body and one Spirit . . . one hope . . . one Lord, one faith, one baptism, one God"), and is directed via the head-body metaphor to the concept of love: "But speaking the truth in love, we must grow up in every way into him who is the head, into Christ" (4:15). The following parenesis begins with the contrast between the "old" and "new" self/humanity (4:17–24), which only then modulates into concrete commands: no lies and no anger; do not steal, but work; engage only in wholesome thoughts and speech (4:25–32).

The *central place of the concept of love* in the ethic of Ephesians emerges in 5:1–2: "Therefore be imitators of God, as beloved children, and live in love, as Christ loved us and gave himself up for us, a fragrant offering and sacrifice to God." The verse, which serves as a hinge connecting 4:25–32 and 5:2–20,[76] formulates the substance of the basic principle undergirding all the individual commands: God and Christ loved us (2:4; 3:17), so that each of us can lovingly support (and put up with) the others (4:2). No other letter in the Pauline tradition, whether authentic or deutero-Pauline, has such a concentration of references to ἀγάπη and ἀγαπάω ("love" as noun and verb, each occurring ten times in Ephesians), whether considered absolutely[77] or in relation to the length of each letter. The conventional list of individual commands (the list in Eph. 4:25–32; the "spiritual armor" of 6:10–20) should not distract the reader from the reality that the concept of love unites all that Ephesians has to say:[78]

73. Commentaries are typically nervous about the idea of the "preexistence" of the believer's good works and generally avoid it (cf., e.g., Mussner, *Brief an die Epheser*, 66), but the concept is thoroughly at home within the line of argument pursued in Eph. 2:8–10.

74. Cf. Schnackenburg, *Epheser*, 100.

75. Cf. Sellin, "Paränese," 294ff.

76. Cf. ibid., 294ff.

77. First Corinthians is only apparently an exception, for of the fourteen instances of ἀγάπη, nine are found in chapter 13.

78. Rom. 12:1–8 and 13:8–14 probably stand in the background of Eph. 4:1–5:20; cf. Luz, "Überlegungen zum Epheserbrief," 392–93.

it was because of God's great love for us that he raised Christ from the dead, and us with him (2:4–5), Christ now dwells in our hearts (3:17, 19), so that, as the body of Christ, the church "builds itself up in love" (4:16).

The concept of love also dominates the reinterpreted form of the Colossian *Haustafel*, which multiplies references to ἀγαπάω (once in Col. 3:18–4:1, six times in Eph. 5:21–6:9). On the one hand, the basic structure of the *Haustafel* is maintained (three groups of two, in the same order, with the weaker group addressed first), but on the other hand a characteristic expansion and elaboration interprets the basic anthropological reference to husband and wife in terms of the relation of Christ and the church (5:23–33).[79] Just as the husband is the head of the wife, so "Christ is the head of the church" (5:23b, ὁ Χριστὸς κεφαλὴ τῆς ἐκκλησίας); as Christ loves the church, so husbands should love their wives (5:25–30). The motif of love and marriage, facilitated christologically and realized ecclesiologically, is also apparent in 5:31–32, for it is in self-giving love and care for the other that Christ is the head of the church. Even more strongly than in Colossians, in 5:21–6:9 the concept of love is applied to the household as the sociopolitical unit that constitutes the unity of ancient society. It is precisely through the transfer of this idea of the relation between Christ and the church to life within the church that calls for Christians to understand every aspect of household life as the sphere of ἀγάπη.[80]

10.2.7 Ecclesiology

Ecclesiology is the dominant theme of Ephesians, placing its stamp on every aspect of the letter's line of argument.[81]

The Church as Body of Christ

Since his resurrection, Jesus Christ has been installed as the exalted ruler of the universe and head of his body, the church (Eph. 1:22, "And he has put all things under his feet and has made him the head over all things for the church, which is his body, the fullness of him who fills all in all"). The church thus appears throughout the letter as the realm of present salvation, with particular clarity as the framework for the marriage parenesis in Eph. 5:32, where in reference to Gen. 2:24 LXX the author declares: "This is a great mystery, and I am applying it to Christ and the church." The communion between Christ and the church is so direct and extensive that, while they can be distinguished, they cannot be separated: "for we are members of his body" (Eph. 5:30). The

79. For analysis, cf. Gielen, *Tradition und Theologie*, 204–315.

80. Cf. Schrage, *Ethics*, 253–55.

81. On ecclesiology, cf. Helmut Merklein, *Christus und die Kirche* (SBS 66; Stuttgart: Verlag Katholisches Bibelwerk, 1973); Roloff, *Kirche im Neuen Testament*, 231–49; Gese, *Vermächtnis*, 171ff.

church is Christ's partner, for on the cross Christ gave himself for her (2:16),[82] and he nourishes and cares for the church (5:29b). As the body of Christ (cf. also 4:3, 4, 12, 15) the church is also the heavenly building/temple (2:20–22; cf. 1 Cor. 3:9–17) and the "fullness" (πλήρωμα) of Christ (cf. Eph. 1:23; 3:19; 4:10, 13). The church is thus the exclusive realm in which the all-embracing fullness of Christ is effective and powerful. At the same time, the church participates in a dynamic process of growth (Eph. 2:21–22; 4:12, 15; cf. Col. 2:19) aligned to the "cornerstone" Jesus Christ and directed by him.

The metaphor of the church as the body of Christ is connected not only to the encouraging affirmation of present salvation, but also a claim to power, for we must read the head-body ecclesiology in the context of the political philosophy of the times, which was concerned (as, e.g., the fable of Menenius Agrippa illustrates) with the undivided lordship of the emperor (the head) over the Roman Empire (the body). The body-Christology of Ephesians presents a counterproposal. The claim to the cosmic lordship of Christ here poses an intentional contrast to the emperor cult.[83] With the head-body imagery, the author of Ephesians takes up an idea that has noteworthy parallels in Greco-Roman tradition[84] and Hellenistic Judaism (Philo),[85] stands in continuity with

82. While the term σῶμα ("body") in Col. 1:22 refers to the body of Jesus on the cross, the ἓν σῶμα of Eph. 2:16 refers to the church.

83. Cf. F. Mussner, "Epheserbrief," *TRE* 9:747: "It appears that a predilection for understanding salvation in present-tense terms was particularly present in the Christianity of Asia Minor, especially in reference to Christology, and precisely in terms of the Pantocrator Christ, apparently as an intentional contrast to the Caesar cult that flourished there." Cf. further Faust, *Pax Christi*, 475, according to whom the Roman emperor presented himself as the highest God who establishes peace on earth: "Against this background, the encomium tradition that echoes in the passage in 2:14–18 about Christ as the one who establishes peace can be well understood as a structurally parallel, alternative proposal to the emperor's claim as peacemaker for τὰ ἀμφότερα [both sides]: Christ integrates Jews and Gentiles in the common realm of peace that is his own body, which at the same time is a common *politeia* [citizenship] (2:19b). Christ does this in such a way that those who once were Jews no longer need claim or want a special position, for they already have a privileged position (2:19ff.)." Cf. Gerhard Sellin, "Epheserbrief," *RGG*[4] 1346: "Here, however, Ephesians is in competition with the Roman Empire. That the author is aware of this is indicated by the peroration of 6:10–20, where Paul's 'chains' are included in the context of the struggle with the 'world rulers of the present darkness' (6:19–20)."

84. Cf. Seneca, *Clem.* 1.3.5; 1.4.1–2 (the emperor guides the state as its mental principle, and is the guarantor of its unity and peace: "This gentleness of your attitude spreads further and gradually permeates the whole gigantic organism of the empire, and everything will be formed in your image. Good health proceeds from the head to all parts of the body; everything is vigorous and engaged, or languishing in drowsiness, depending on whether your spirit is living or powerless"); 2.2.1; Plutarch, *Num.* 20.8. For analysis of these and other texts, cf. Faust, *Pax Christi*, 290ff.

85. On Philo, cf. Hegermann, *Vorstellung*, 58ff., and the same author, Harald Hegermann, "Zur Ableitung der Leib-Christi-Vorstellung im Epheserbrief," *TLZ* 85 (1960): 839–42; Carsten Colpe, "Zur Leib-Christi-Vorstellung im Epheserbrief," in *Judentum—Urchristentum—Kirche: Festschrift für Joachim Jeremias* (ed. Walther Eltester; BZNW 26; Berlin: Töpelmann, 1960), 178ff.

Paul and the Letter to the Colossians,[86] but also—and primarily—serves his politico-ecclesiological theology of unity.

The Unity of the Church

The image of the church as body of Christ in Ephesians engages a current problem. The situation of the church or churches addressed is obviously characterized by tensions between Christians of Jewish and Greco-Roman backgrounds. The readers are directly addressed as Gentile Christians in Eph. 2:11; 3:1; 4:17, and their relation to Jewish Christians is the sole content of the instruction in 2:11–22, just as it is a dominant theme throughout. Ephesians projects the concept of one church, composed of Jewish Christians and Christians from Greco-Roman traditions, who together constitute the body of Christ. The author is here reacting to a current development within the churches of Asia Minor: Jewish Christians are already a minority, and Gentile Christians no longer see them as equal partners.[87] The unity of the church is the model that has been worked out and striven for, setting the pattern for the cosmic peace established by Christ.[88] This is the reason that the election of Israel is explicitly emphasized (differently from Colossians): "Remember that you were at that time without Christ, being aliens from the commonwealth of Israel, and strangers to the covenants of promise, having no hope and without God in the world" (2:12). Those who were "far off" have now been brought "near" (2:13); here the dominant idea is not incorporation in the chosen people of God, but reconciliation as the overcoming of hostility (2:14–18).[89] The truth of the matter is now: "So then you are no longer strangers and aliens, but you are citizens [συμπολῖται] with the saints and also members of the household [οἰκεῖοι] of God" (2:19).[90] With this political terminology the tensions that persist in society between Jews and people of Greco-Roman heritage are to a certain degree authoritatively confirmed. Against this background of an intensifying anti-Judaism both within the church and in society as a whole, Ephesians becomes the advocate of the equal inheritance of Jewish Christians within the body of Christ. The letter thus takes a stand against the growing tendencies of the churches

86. Cf. Gese, *Vermächtnis*, 175–84.

87. Cf. Fischer, *Epheserbriefes*, 79–94.

88. Cf. Gerhard Sellin, "Adresse und Intention des Epheserbriefes," in *Paulus, Apostel Jesu Christi: Festschrift für Günter Klein zum 70. Geburtstag* (ed. Michael Trowitzsch; Tübingen: Mohr, 1998), 186: "The primary theme of Ephesians is *unity*. This unity is present in the church, which abolishes the wall between Jews and Gentiles through the work of Paul."

89. Cf. Roloff, *Kirche im Neuen Testament*, 241–42.

90. Cf. Fischer, *Epheserbriefes*, 80: "The thesis of Ephesians is unambiguously clear: Israel is God's people and has God's covenant promises; the Gentiles have nothing. This is the point of departure. But then the inconceivable miracle happens, that Christ breaks down the wall between Gentiles and Jews, the law with its commandments, and thus opens up access to God in the one church (2:11ff.)."

in Asia Minor. To be sure, the Israel thematic is only perceived from the internal, churchly point of view, and no longer, as in Paul, as a problem of universal salvation history.[91]

Church Offices

In Ephesians, the offices and ministries of the church are understood as *gifts of the exalted Christ for establishing the unity of the church*, and they even take on a constitutive importance: "The gifts he gave were that some would be apostles, some prophets, some evangelists, some pastors and teachers, to equip the saints for the work of ministry, for building up the body of Christ, until all of us come to the unity of the faith and of the knowledge of the Son of God, to maturity, to the measure of the full stature of Christ" (Eph. 4:11–13). This list of church offices and ministries points to a markedly different church structure than what we find in Paul.[92] While apostles and prophets are also mentioned in 1 Cor. 12:28, the title for evangelists is missing. In 1 Cor. 12:28 the third slot is filled with "teachers," but in Eph. 4:11 they appear after the apostles, prophets, evangelists, and pastors. Since in Eph. 2:20 and 3:5 the apostles and prophets already appear as a fixed group, they must also be regarded here as a unit. They represent the church offices of the beginning period,[93] while the triad evangelists, pastors, and teachers embodies the church structure of the author's present.[94] The evangelists are probably the itinerant preachers, while pastors and teachers are responsible for preaching, instruction, and direction in the local congregations. The apostolic office is no longer directly functional but is regarded in terms of its theological significance: the apostles are the foundation of the church (2:20); to them the mystery of Christ was made known by revelation (cf. 3:5). The prophets probably no longer play an actual role in the life of the church; note the absence of charismatic ministries such as miracles, healing, and glossolalia in Ephesians. To be sure, Ephesians holds fast in principle to the Pauline conception of the charisms as gifts within the church (4:7–8), but it does not elaborate this principle in practice.

91. On this point, cf. Theo K. Heckel, "Kirche und Gottesvolk im Epheserbrief," in *Kirche und Volk Gottes: Festschrift für Jürgen Roloff zum 70. Geburtstag* (ed. Martin Karrer et al.; Neukirchen-Vluyn: Neukirchener Verlag, 2000), 163–75.

92. For analysis, cf. Helmut Merklein, *Das kirchliche Amt nach dem Epheserbrief* (SANT 33; Munich: Kösel, 1973), 57–117.

93. Differently Fischer, *Epheserbriefes*, 33: The author of Ephesians opposes the introduction of an episcopal church structure, "for him the apostles and prophets remain the only foundation for the church." As evidence for this thesis, he cites Eph. 4:11, which does not distinguish between the church's present leadership (evangelists, pastors, and teachers), and those of the past (apostles and prophets). "Exegetically, there is only one possibility: For Ephesians, the apostles and prophets are still the operative church offices, to whom he emphatically holds fast."

94. Cf. Roloff, *Kirche im Neuen Testament*, 247.

Paul as Apostle of the Church

In Eph. 3:1–13 Paul becomes the decisive bearer of revelation for the church (cf. Col. 1:24–29), in that he makes known to all people and powers what had been previously hidden: the mystery that God now grants salvation to all nations (Eph. 3:6–10). In the anamnesis of his person and work, the Pauline apostolate to the nations appears after his death as a dimension of salvation history (cf. Eph. 3:1; 4:1). Paul is the normative receiver and transmitter of God's revelation, the revelation that leads to the universal church of Jews and Gentiles. The grace communicated through Paul tears down the wall between these two divisions of humanity (cf. Eph. 3:3, 6) and makes possible the universal church, whose dimensions are thought through and developed in Ephesians. Christ is the cornerstone of the church, which is built on the foundation of the apostles and prophets (Eph. 2:20). Paul appears as the guarantor for the apostolic faith, the norm through which the church is related to Christ. There are no longer any traces of the disputes regarding Paul's own apostolic status (cf. 1 Cor. 9:1ff.) or of the severe conflicts between Jewish and Gentile Christians. Paul does not contend for his position, which already has a respected place in the church's history.[95] Thus the normative function of Paul is bound together with the letter's understanding of tradition. The apostles and prophets (above all, Paul himself) constitute the foundation and norm for what is Christian, which is no longer dependent on human trickery and deceitfulness (Eph. 4:14). Because the apostle is the messenger of the mystery of the gospel (6:20), this mystery can accordingly be proclaimed only by Paul. This recourse to Paul, and the pseudepigraphical character of Ephesians, necessarily result from the picture of Paul transmitted by the letter.[96]

Ecclesiology and Christology/Soteriology

The decisive consideration in evaluating the theological conception of Ephesians as a whole is the relation of ecclesiology and Christology/soteriology. Is the ecclesiology of Ephesians to be understood in the sense of an *ecclesia triumphans*, in which Christology/soteriology becomes a function of ecclesiology?[97] The dominance of ecclesiology is undeniable, but a christological basis for this ecclesiology is also clearly indicated:[98]

95. Merklein, "Rezeption," 32–33.

96. Gese, *Vermächtnis*, 275, emphasizes: "Among the post-Pauline letters, only Ephesians presents a compact presentation of Pauline theology as a whole, for which it also claims a timeless validity and authority. It is precisely this that justifies the claim that Ephesians is the theological legacy of the Pauline school."

97. Thus, tendentiously, Merklein, *Christus und die Kirche*, 63, who speaks of a "primacy of ecclesiology over soteriology"; Roloff, *Kirche im Neuen Testament*, 237: "Ecclesiology has become the presupposition of soteriology."

98. Cf. Mussner, *Brief an die Epheser*, 25.

1. In Ephesians, too, the saving event is anchored exclusively in the cross (Eph. 2:13, 14, 16).
2. In Eph. 5:23, Christ is the redeemer/savior of the church.
3. In the central section Eph. 2:11–22, Christ is the decisive acting subject who achieves reconciliation and establishes peace.
4. In Ephesians, the central ecclesiological expression ἐν Χριστῷ refers to the realm of salvation made possible and ruled by Christ, the realm in which those who are reconciled live in fellowship with God/Christ and with one another. The church is thus located in Christ, not the other way around.[99] The growth metaphor in Ephesians shows clearly that the church too is subject to growth and development.

The church is the realm of salvation opened up by Christ and ruled by him (cf. Eph. 1:22–23; 2:16; 4:15–16). There is no church apart from Christ, just as there is no Christ without the church. God reveals the divine wisdom to the powers through the church (3:10), and in 3:21 the church is even the object of a doxology. Nonetheless, it is also true that for Ephesians the church is consistently thought of in a way that begins with Christ, and always in reference to him, so that no one except Christ himself can rule over the church. As in no other New Testament writing, Ephesians emphasizes *the ecclesiological relevance of the gospel*, but without neglecting its christological foundation.

10.2.8 Eschatology

The understanding of the presence of salvation that prevails in ecclesiology also shapes the eschatology. In Ephesians the past tense is consistently used of the eschatological events (as also in Colossians), but even the believers' status in the heavenly world is spoken of as an event in past experience. Just as Christ has already won the struggle with the cosmic powers (cf. Eph. 1:20–23), the elect community already finds itself in the realm of salvation: the church as the body of Christ (cf. Eph. 1:9, 11, 19; 2:10; 3:11). Baptized believers are saved by grace (2:5, 6, 8), they have been "made alive together with Christ" (1:20, aorist συνεζωοποίησεν), are "raised with him" (aorist συνήγειρεν) and "seated with him in the heavenly places" (συνεκάθισεν, 2:5, 6). In contrast to Rom. 6:3–4 and Col. 2:12, Ephesians is unique in emphasizing the glorious status of baptized believers ("buried with him" is missing). As fellow citizens with the saints and members of the household of God (Eph. 2:19), they participate fully in redemption through the blood of Christ (cf. 1:7). Clear shifts from Paul's own eschatology are manifest in the receding of temporal categories and their replacement by spatial categories; the tension between present and future declines in significance. Paul's own strong emphasis on the presence

99. Cf. Gese, *Vermächtnis*, 171–75.

of salvation (cf., e.g., 2 Cor. 3:18; Rom. 8:29–30), the spatial orientation of Colossians, the hymnic tradition (cf. the prayers of Eph. 1:3–23 and 6:18–20 and the doxology of 3:14–19), and the experience of the sacramental presence of salvation leads in Ephesians to a theology in which it is not the future that determines the present, but the present that determines the future. Above all, however, the head-body imagery, with its spatial aspects and the theology of unity with which it is associated, calls for a strong emphasis on the present, for it is a matter of overcoming current divisions and (in view of the ruling Roman emperor) legitimating the universal, present lordship of Jesus Christ. In this conceptuality, the delay of the parousia no longer presents itself as a problem.

This does not mean, however, that the present-tense eschatology of Ephesians abolishes the significance of time and history in general.[100] Ephesians is not the advocate of a timeless ontology of the church and does not propose a mixture of heavenly and earthly realities. Heavenly realities, but not improved earthly conditions, are claimed for baptized believers. Because Christ is already seated at the right hand of God, the church knows that it already possesses transcendent salvation; that is to say, the firm relation to Christ is the factual basis of every statement about salvation.[101] Nor does Ephesians dissolve time into a formless ontology.[102] Thus baptized believers are challenged to withstand the threatening powers "on that evil day" (6:13). The coming judgment provides a motivation for parenesis (6:8); idolaters will not inherit the kingdom of God (5:5), for the wrath of God is coming on the disobedient (5:6). The age to come also stands under the lordship of Christ (1:21b). Ephesians reminds believers of their hope (1:18; 2:12; 4:4), speaking of the (coming) day of redemption (4:30), and salvation is the result of grace through faith (2:8a). As the body of Christ, the church is subject to a

100. On this point cf. Hübner, *Kolosser*, 165–68. Andreas Lindemann, *Die Aufhebung der Zeit: Geschichtsverständnis und Eschatologie im Epheserbrief* (SNT 12; Gütersloh: Gütersloher Verlagshaus Mohn, 1975), 248, argues Ephesians has no sense of history or of a particular situation: "For the author of Ephesians, time and history are 'in Christ'—that means for his theology, in the church—abolished. From such a present, there can be no real future."

101. This aspect is emphasized by Franz Mussner, *Christus, das All und die Kirche: Studien zur Theologie des Epheserbriefes* (2nd ed.; TTS 5; Trier: Paulinus-Verlag, 1968), 93, followed by Gese, *Vermächtnis*, 156: "Even if the heavenly life of the believer is already present, it nonetheless remains bound to Christ and fundamentally separate from all earthly fulfillments. The spatial differentiation clearly avoids an identification of the two realms, and there can be no talk of eliminating the eschatological reservation." Of course, in this way of posing the issue, the problem remains: how are we to conceptualize the presence of the heavenly in the earthly that Ephesians presupposes? It is not enough to point to baptism, the Spirit, and faith, for in Paul too they represent the presence of salvation.

102. Cf. Mussner, *Brief an die Epheser*, 28–30; Lona, *Eschatologie*, 241ff. Lona speaks of an "ecclesiological eschatology" in Ephesians: "The presence and future of salvation are spoken of only in relation to the reality of the church" (p. 442). Moreover, Eph. 1:13–14 and 4:30 show "that the emphasis on the presence of salvation is not contrasted with the future consummation."

process of growth and maturing (cf. 2:21–22; 3:19; 4:13, 16), which includes a perspective on the future.

Thus Ephesians too formulates an "eschatological reservation," though in a completely different way than Paul. The predominance of spatial dimensions carries with it a thought world oriented to static being rather than what is to come.

10.2.9 Setting in the History of Early Christian Theology

Ecclesiology emerges in no other New Testament writing so strongly as in the Letter to the Ephesians.[103] The church is not a historical accident but emerges in the world equipped with an exceptional dignity; it is elected and predestined. To be sure, its mission is perceived only under the perspective of unity: the ἐκκλησία is the church of Jesus Christ only as it is a unity. *The Letter to the Ephesians is the New Testament's great manifesto of Christian unity!* Both its protology (Eph. 1:3–14) and its present-tense eschatology are in the service of demonstrating that the primeval and present will of God in Jesus Christ is that the church, as the body of Christ under its head Jesus Christ, live out this intended unity of Jewish and Gentile believers. The letter's understanding of church office and ministry is likewise directly related to the issue of unity, for according to Eph. 4:13 establishing the unity of believers is the central task of church officials. What Paul himself did not succeed in doing, and what he left as his legacy to developing early Christianity, is accomplished in Ephesians: the proclamation of unity in the spiritual *politeia* of the body of Christ, a unity that transcends all previous dividing walls (2:19–22).

Even though Ephesians, with its cosmic ecclesiology and present-tense eschatology, is essentially different from Paul, the letter repeats and transmits in good scholastic style the central elements of Paul's doctrine of justification by faith alone: "by grace . . . through faith . . . not by works" (2:8–9). Thus Ephesians—seen from today's perspective—is a deeply ecumenical document that, so to speak, brings together "Catholic" and "Protestant" elements.[104]

The Christology of Ephesians also includes a potential for the future, for the cosmic lordship of Jesus Christ and his session at the right hand of God (Eph. 1:20) have universal peace and reconciliation as their goal (2:14–16). The life-giving power of Christ permeates and rules the universe (1:23), so that by his gospel of peace those who are far are brought near (2:13, 17). The "bond of peace" (4:3) is to unite believers in the unity of the one Spirit, and so represent God's new reality.

103. Roloff, *Kirche im Neuen Testament*, 231–32, speaks of a Copernican revolution: "While in the authentic Pauline letters it is always the Christ event that stands at the center, with the church always seen in relation to this, in the deutero-Pauline letters the church is the point of departure and the Christ event is interpreted in relation to it."

104. Cf. Mussner, *Brief an die Epheser*, 175–78.

10.3 Second Thessalonians: Date (of the End) as Problem

The Second Letter to the Thessalonians is a didactic and admonitory document written in the name of Paul in Macedonia or Asia Minor near the end of the first century CE.[105] It is intended to serve as a guide for how 1 Thessalonians is to be read.

Theology

At the center of the theology proper of 2 Thessalonians stands *God the Judge*. In view of the false eschatological teaching that threatens the church, the author both warns and motivates the church: the faithful community will be rewarded for its endurance of suffering, for "it is indeed just of God to repay with affliction those who afflict you, and to give relief to the afflicted as well as to us" (2 Thess. 1:6, 7a; cf. 1:8). The authentic call of the church is contrasted with the power of delusion that leads to lies—which is also sent from God (2:11–12). The eschatological final drama includes the advent of the Lawless One, who claims to be divine, and is in accord with God's saving plan that brings history to an end. God is thus simultaneously both director of the whole drama and an actor within it! This somewhat problematic line of reasoning is obviously intended to strengthen the threatened identity of the church. It may be sure of God's love (2:16; 3:5), while its opponents fall under God's judgment.

Christology/Eschatology

The Christology of 2 Thessalonians is an integral element of its eschatology.[106] The basic conceptuality is expressed in 2 Thess. 1:7b, which portrays the eschatological advent of the *parousia-kyrios* with the angels from heaven "when he comes to be glorified by his saints and to be marveled at on that day" (1:10). But when is "that day"? Second Thessalonians indicates that this was a bitterly contested question in the situation to which the writing was directed. A prophetic announcement of the presence of the day of the parousia (2:2c, ὡς ὅτι ἐνέστηκεν ἡ ἡμέρα τοῦ κυρίου [to the effect that the day of the Lord is already here]) apparently had triggered confusion and uncertainty within the church. The advocates of this present-tense eschatology appeal to insights revealed by the Spirit, to a saying of the apostle himself, and to an

105. On the introductory issues, cf. Schnelle, *New Testament Writings*, 315–26.

106. Cf. Müller, *Anfänge der Paulusschule*, 275–76; Gerhard Hotze, "Die Christologie des 2. Thessalonicherbriefes," in *Christologie in der Paulus-Schule: Zur Rezeptionsgeschichte des paulinischen Evangeliums* (ed. Klaus Scholtissek; SBS 181; Stuttgart: Verlag Katholisches Bibelwerk, 2000), 147–48.

(alleged or real) letter of Paul (cf. 2:2, 15). The claim that the final events are "already now" present cannot be combined without contradiction with the reality of the Christian community in continuing history, unless present reality is bypassed in a spiritualized eschatological euphoria. For the writer of the letter, the present, old age of human history continues. The day of the Lord's return has not yet come, and cannot have already arrived, for the old aeon is still ruled by God's adversary. The problem of the delay of the parousia is defused by an eschatological timetable in which the present is characterized as the continuing period of the Antichrist's activity, while the revelation of the ultimate lordship of Christ is still in the future.

The fundamental differences between the eschatological teachings in 1 Thess. 4:13–18 and 5:1–11 on the one hand, and 2 Thess. 2:1–12 and 1:5–10 on the other, are clearly obvious.[107] The eschatology of 1 Thessalonians is stamped by the expectation of the imminent parousia, which continues as the central aspect of all Paul's letters through his last one, the Letter to the Philippians (cf. Phil. 4:5b). In 2 Thess. 2:2 the author directs his writing against the motto ἐνέστηκεν ἡ ἡμέρα τοῦ κυρίου (the day of the Lord is already here) and then outlines a schedule of the eschatological events that cannot be combined with the way they are portrayed in 1 Thessalonians. In 1 Thess. 4:13–18, the central focus is on the coming of the Lord and the gathering of all Christians to be with him. The goal of the eschatological events is "being with the Lord forever" (1 Thess. 4:17). A completely different course of events is presented in 2 Thess. 2:1–12. Before the parousia of Christ, the "man of lawlessness" must appear, who reveals himself as God's adversary and sits in the place reserved for God (2 Thess. 2:4). The full epiphany of this adversary is still in the future (2 Thess. 2:6–7) but already has its effect in the present, deceiving the unbelievers. The adversary is presently restrained or hindered, but Christ will destroy him at the parousia, when those who persist in their unbelief will be judged. Both the problem of the delay of the parousia (2 Thess. 2:6–7) and the appearance of the eschatological adversary fundamentally differentiate the perspective of 2 Thess. 2:1–12 from that of 1 Thessalonians. While 1 Thess. 5:1 explicitly rejects speculations regarding the parousia, 2 Thess. 2:1–12 presents an eschatological schedule that not only allows observations and calculations, but requires them (cf. v. 5). While for Paul the advent of the risen Christ is always central (cf. 1 Thess. 4:16; 1 Cor. 15:23), in 2 Thess. 2:8 the climax of the parousia is the destruction of the Antichrist.

Adopting prophetic-apocalyptic motifs (cf. Dan. 11:36ff.; Isa. 11:4), the author designates the events of the coming apostasy, the advent of the man of lawlessness and his effects, as stages of the eschatological drama. They precede the parousia of Christ, so that the church itself can evaluate and judge whether

107. Cf. the extensive elaboration of this point in Müller, *Anfänge der Paulusschule*, 20–67.

or not the competing eschatology is in fact true. The revelation of the eschatological adversary is still future, so the parousia of Christ can neither be already present nor immediately imminent. At the same time, the church knows that the evil one is already at work in the present, and that it is God alone who is still restraining his final public appearance. The working of the evil one already qualifies the present as the time of decision with regard to the future.

The background of the doctrine opposed by 2 Thess. 2:1–12 is probably an elevated spiritual prophetism (cf. Mark 13:22; Matt. 7:15; 24:23–24) related to Old Testament and apocalyptic traditions (cf. Isa. 13:10; Ezek. 32:7–8; Joel 2:1–10; 4:15–16; *1 En.* 93.9; 102.2; *Jub.* 23.16ff.; Mark 13:7, 25).[108] For their declaration that the day of the Lord is already present, these early Christian prophets probably appealed to their gift of the prophetic Spirit and to a Pauline letter, which can only mean 1 Thessalonians.[109] In 1 Thess. 4:15, 17, Paul counts himself among those who will still be alive when the Lord returns, which will be very soon. These early Christian prophets possibly adopted this Pauline statement and understood it to mean that, since the apostle had died in the meantime, the day of the Lord he had anticipated must already be present. These prophets understood their eschatological conceptions as the consistent development of Paul's own thought, while at the same time abandoning his characteristic eschatological reservation. Thus when the author of 2 Thessalonians resists the teaching of these prophets, he does so in a way thoroughly in line with Paul's own view, though in the process adopting un-Pauline ideas and images.

In 2 Thess. 2:6–7 the author speaks of a power that presently restrains the final revelation of the Antichrist. "The Restrainer" (κατέχον 2:6, neuter; κατέχων 2:7, masculine) has the function of restraining the anti-God until a particular point in time. Here 2 Thessalonians takes up a tradition that probably goes back to Hab. 2:3:[110] "For there is still a vision for the appointed time; it speaks of the end, and does not lie. If it seems to tarry, wait for it; it will surely come, it will not delay." By using the apocalyptic motif of the Restrainer, the

108. E. E. Popkes, "Die Bedeutung des zweiten Thessalonicherbriefes für das Verständnis paulinischer und deuteropaulinischer Eschatologie," *BZ* 48 (2004): 45ff., argues that 2 Thessalonians engages the (predominantly) present-tense eschatology of Colossians and Ephesians, and with its firm adherence to future eschatology illustrates a split in the Pauline school. Against this thesis is above all the statements of 2 Thess. 2:2b (the letter mentioned there can only be 1 Thessalonians) and 2:2c (the eschatological slogans attacked there do not fit the eschatological conceptions of Colossians and Ephesians), as well as the background of 2 Thess. 2:1–12 in tradition history.

109. Cf. Wolfgang Trilling, *Der Zweite Brief an die Thessalonicher* (EKKNT 14; Neukirchen-Vluyn: Neukirchener Verlag, 1980), 76–77; Willi Marxsen, *Der zweite Brief an die Thessalonicher* (ZBK 11.2; Zürich: Theologischer Verlag, 1982), 80.

110. On this point cf. August Strobel, *Untersuchungen zum eschatologischen Verzögerungsproblem; auf Grund der spätjüdisch-urchristlichen Geschichte von Habakuk 2,2 ff* (NovTSup 2; Leiden: Brill, 1961), 98–116.

author emphasizes that God will finally bring about the promised end even if it seems to be delayed. The final events are subject to God's will and will take place according to his plan. The restraining power need not be understood as a particular person or in terms of world history (the Roman Empire),[111] for ultimately it is God himself who prevents the Antichrist from appearing until the appointed time. To be sure, a direct equation between the neuter κατέχον and God is not possible (cf. 2 Thess. 2:7b), but this identification appears as the logical consequence of the argumentation. The delay of the parousia corresponds to the will of God, for God is the only power that restrains it.[112]

What is the *real intention* of 2 Thessalonians? Did the author want only to refute a false understanding of 1 Thess. 4:13–5:11, or even replace 1 Thessalonians? If one affirms this latter thesis,[113] then 2 Thessalonians would have to be understood as a pseudepigraphical letter opposing another Pauline letter he considered to be a forgery. By making use of pseudepigraphy himself, the author would have attempted to displace the purported "first" letter of Paul to the Thessalonians.

This view, however, has weighty arguments against it: Would it have been possible to claim that 1 Thessalonians was a forgery forty years after it was written? On the contrary, the heavy dependence on 1 Thessalonians indicates that the author of 2 Thessalonians was persuaded that the letter he is using comes from Paul himself. The authority of the apostle assumed by the author throughout does not serve the purpose of correcting "Paul," but to ward off a false interpretation of the eschatological statements in 1 Thessalonians. Since Paul himself would not in fact have agreed with the eschatological slogans of the opponents, 2 Thessalonians, in its own situation, rightly claims to be defending Paul and to speak with his authority, even though it does this without repeating the authentic eschatological teaching of Paul.

Ethics

The letter's only ethical theme is also directly related to the polemic against the false teachers: dealing with the "disorderly." In 2 Thess. 3:6–15 the author

111. On individual issues and the history of interpretation, cf. Trilling, *Thessaloniker*, 94–105 and Paul Metzger, *Katechon: II Thess 2,1–12 im Horizont apokalyptischen Denkens* (BZNW 135; Berlin: de Gruyter, 2005), 15ff.

112. Cf. Trilling, *Thessaloniker*, 92; differently Metzger, *Katechon*, who understands the κατέχον to be the Roman Empire.

113. This thesis was argued by A. Hilgenfeld, "Die beiden Briefe an die Thessalonicher," *ZWT* 5 (1862): 225–64; and Heinrich Julius Holtzmann, "Zum zweiten Thessalonicherbrief," *ZNW* 2 (1901): 97–108. In more recent scholarship, among those who have advocated it are Andreas Lindemann, "Zum Abfassungszweck des zweiten Thessalonicherbriefes," *ZNW* 68 (1977): 39; Marxsen, *2 Thessalonicher*, 31ff.; Franz Laub, "Paulinische Autorität in nachpaulinischer Zeit," in *The Thessalonian Correspondence* (ed. Raymond F. Collins and Norbert Baumert; BETL 87; Louvain: University Press, 1990), 403–17.

refers to members of the church who live a disorderly life, do not work for a living, and engage in useless activities. On the one hand, the general nature of the statements and the parallels in 1 Thess. 5:13–14 might suggest that no actual abuses are going on (occasioned, for example, by the slogan of the false teachers of 2 Thess. 2:2). On the other hand, there may be some basis for supposing that some church members, acting on their conviction that the end of the world and history stood directly before them, had abandoned their normal way of life and its τάξις (order).[114]

The Picture of Paul

The whole argumentation of 2 Thessalonians rests on the person of Paul himself. The calling of the church into being is inseparably bound up with the Pauline gospel (2 Thess. 2:14). The church resists the false teachers by holding fast to the apostle's own teaching (2:5, 6; cf. 1:10b), and—like him—makes no place for evildoers (cf. 3:6). Alongside his authoritative word, the apostle's own lifestyle is intended to help the church to maintain its stability in the present confusions and to hold fast to the apostolic teaching. So also, the parenesis of 2 Thessalonians is stamped by a comprehensive appeal to the apostle. The teaching he has given the church serves as its ethical norm (cf. 2:15; 3:6, 14). Moreover, Paul himself appears as the model the church should follow (3:7–9). The apostle admonishes the church (3:4, 6, 10, 12) to live in holiness, in accord with God's election (2:13). This orientation to Paul cannot, of course, belie the fact that 2 Thessalonians (in contrast to Colossians and Ephesians) does not productively extend the development of Pauline theology for a changed situation.[115] The letter has a predominantly formalized language and argumentation; it obviously has only the one goal of correcting a false interpretation of Paul's eschatology.

10.4 The Pastoral Epistles: God's Philanthropy

The form of the Pastoral Epistles already indicates their changed perspective from that of the authentic Pauline letters (as well as from Colossians/Ephesians and 2 Thessalonians): they are not church letters but are addressed to Paul's personal coworkers who have responsibility for the church at large. In terms of both form and content, they obviously understand themselves to be supple-

114. Cf. Eckart Reinmuth, "Die Briefe an die Thessalonicher," in *Die Briefe an die Philipper, Thessalonicher und an Philemon* (ed. Nikolaus Walter et al.; NTD 8.2; Göttingen: Vandenhoeck & Ruprecht, 1998), 164.

115. Andreas Lindemann, *Paulus im ältesten Christentum: Das Bild des Apostels und die Rezeption der paulinischen Theologie in der frühchristlichen Literatur bis Marcion* (BHT 58; Tübingen: Mohr, 1979), 132–33.

mentary to the letters already circulated under the name of Paul. They were probably written in Ephesus ca. 100 CE[116] and published as part of an edition of the Corpus Paulinum.[117]

The designation "Pastoral Epistles" for 1 Timothy, 2 Timothy, and Titus was probably coined by the eighteenth-century Halle professor and exegete P. Anton,[118] who appropriately stated the intention of all three letters: their concern for establishing and equipping the church's pastoral ministerial offices. The directions for the proper practice of pastoral ministry have a universally valid character. Moreover, the Pastorals agree extensively in the church situation they presuppose and in their world of theological concepts. Their unifying element is the consistent demand for separation from and rejection of false teachers, the counterpart of their positive appeal to the person of the apostle Paul and the tradition of which he is the guarantor. In response to the threat to the Pauline identity of the churches that he addresses, the author of the Pastorals presents a personal and material continuity with Paul himself that looks to Paul as model and attains concrete form in the instructions given in his name.

10.4.1 Theology

The central predication for God in the Pastorals is σωτήρ (savior). The importance of this term is already signaled by its frequency; of twenty-four occurrences in the New Testament, ten are found in the Pastorals (six times in reference to God, four times referring to Jesus). Paul was called to be an apostle "according to the command of God our Savior" (1 Tim. 1:1; cf. Titus 1:3). The rationale for the command to pray for kings and rulers in 1 Tim. 2b–4 is "so that we may lead a quiet and peaceable life in all godliness and dignity. This is right and is acceptable in the sight of God our Savior, who desires everyone to be saved and to come to the knowledge of the truth." The universal perspective associated with the σωτήρ title is also visible in 1 Tim. 4:10b ("We have our hope set on the living God, who is the Savior of all people, especially of those who believe") and Titus 3:4 ("But when the goodness and loving-kindness of God our Savior appeared . . ."). The outstanding virtues of the Savior God are his mercy and love for all people (Titus 3:4–5; 1 Tim. 1:16) and his will

116. On introductory issues, cf. Schnelle, *New Testament Writings*, 326–48.

117. Cf. Trummer, "Corpus Pastorale," 133, who argues the author of the Pastorals was an unknown member of the Pauline school. He wrote and circulated the letters "in the course of publishing a new edition of the existing corpus."

118. Pauli Antonii, *Exegetische Abhandlung der Paulinschen Pastoral-Briefe Pauli an Timotheum und Titum, 1726 und 1727 öffentlich vorgetragen, nunmehr aber nach bisheriger Methode treulich mitgetheilet von Johann August Majer* (2 vols.; Halle: Weysenhaus, 1753–55); cf. Hermann von Lips, "Von den 'Pastoralbriefen' zum 'Corpus Pastorale,'" in *Reformation und Neuzeit: 300 Jahre Theologie in Halle* (ed. Udo Schnelle; Berlin: de Gruyter, 1994), 49–71.

that all be saved (Titus 2:11, "For the grace of God has appeared, bringing salvation to all"; cf. further 1 Tim. 2:4, 6; 4:10). The Father (1 Tim. 1:2; Titus 1:4), the one God (1 Tim. 2:5, εἷς θεός) saves believers "not according to our works but according to his own purpose and grace . . . given to us in Christ Jesus before the ages began" (2 Tim. 1:9). The revelatory schema expressed in 2 Tim. 1:9–10 expresses the basic approach of the Pastorals' theology of history: God's saving purpose, decided before history began, is now revealed "through the epiphany of our Savior Christ Jesus" (2 Tim. 1:10a; cf. Titus 1:1–4; Col. 1:24–29; Eph. 3:1–7).[119]

The adoption of the term σωτήρ as a key word in their theological and christological thought places the Pastorals in close relationship to Hellenistic ideas.[120] The semantic and conceptual field of the terms σωτήρ/σωτηρία/σῴζω also has an Old Testament/Hellenistic Jewish background (LXX; Philo; Josephus),[121] but in New Testament times it had primarily a politico-religious connotation: the Roman emperor is the benefactor and savior of the world who not only guarantees the Empire's political unity but maintains prosperity, well-being ("salvation"), and meaning for its citizens.[122] These cultural overtones are to be heard along with the title when God or Jesus Christ is called "Savior." The σωτήρ title was especially available and useful for the Pastorals in a Hellenistic context as a means of underscoring the universal perspective and unsurpassable character of the new religion and of facilitating the integration of Greco-Roman attributes of deity into its theology. The concept of the manifestation of the deity (ἐπιφάνεια, taking visible form, appearing) also was at home in the environs of the emperor cult; this conceptual model plays an important role especially in the Christology of the Pastorals (see below, §10.4.2), but also in its doctrine of God: "while we wait for the blessed hope and the manifestation of the glory of our great God and Savior, Jesus

119. On this point cf. Karl Löning, "Epiphanie der Menschenfreundlichkeit: Zur Rede von Gott im Kontext städtischer Öffentlichkeit," in *Und dennoch ist von Gott zu Reden (Festschrift für Herbert Vorgrimler)* (ed. Matthias Lutz-Bachmann; Freiburg i.B.: Herder, 1994), 107–24.

120. Cf. Franz Jung, ΣΩΤΗΡ*: Studien zur Rezeption eines hellenistischen Ehrentitles im Neuen Testament* (NTA NF 39; Münster: Aschendorff, 2002), 324–32.

121. On this point cf. ibid., 177–261.

122. Cf. the texts in *NW* 1.2:239–57, and the analyses in ibid., 45–176. Two examples of numerous instances: (1) Dio Chrysostom, *Or.* 1.84, which states following the narrative of Hercules' heroic works, "And therefore he is the Savior of the world and of all humanity" (καὶ διὰ τοῦτο τῆς γῆς καὶ τῶν ἀνθρώπων σωτῆρα εἶναι). (2) The speech of Nero preserved on an inscription is revealing in this regard. The speech was delivered in 67 CE in Corinth (cf. *NW* 1.2:249–50) at the dedication of the altar of Zeus Soter (τῷ Διὶ τῷ Σωτῆρι) to Nero, and the emperor appears as Lord of the World and the one and only Savior. Cf. C. Auffarth, "Herrscherkult und Christuskult," in *Die Praxis der Herrscherverehrung in Rom und seinen Provinzen* (ed. Hubert Cancik and Konrad Hitzl; Tübingen: Mohr, 2003), 283–317. On this topic, in addition to the work of F. Jung above, Adolf Deissmann, *Light from the Ancient East: The New Testament Illustrated by Recently Discovered Texts of the Graeco-Roman World* (trans. Lionel R. M. Strachan; New York: Doran, 1927) is still a very informative introduction (see 287–324).

Christ" (Titus 2:13).[123] Predications of deity from the realms of Hellenistic Judaism and Greco-Roman religion are found in 1 Tim. 1:17 ("To the King of the ages, immortal, invisible, the only God, be honor and glory forever and ever")[124] and 1 Tim. 6:16 ("It is he alone who has immortality and dwells in unapproachable light, whom no one has ever seen or can see; to him be honor and eternal dominion").[125]

The Pastorals present a thoroughly positive portrayal of God, which clearly stands very close to what contemporary philosophers such as Dio Chrysostom or Plutarch have to say about the ideal prince or king.[126] It is no accident that 1 Tim. 1:17 and 6:15 describe God as king, and that in form-critical terms the Pastorals resemble Hellenistic royal letters.[127] The qualities of God are the characteristics of the good king, and vice versa.[128] God is gracious (2 Tim. 1:9–10; Titus 2:11), merciful (Titus 3:5; 1 Tim. 1:13, 16), sympathetic to human beings (Titus 3:3–7); God has a saving plan (οἰκονομία, 1 Tim. 1:4) that includes leading human beings to insight through education (2 Tim. 2:25; 3:16; Titus 2:12).[129] Those who need improvement are not seen as lost sinners, but as people with defective knowledge who can be brought back to the right way. The repeated call for a quiet, exemplary piety that is thus a virtuous life (1 Tim. 2:2–3, 8–15; 3:2–4; 4:12; 5:3ff.; Titus 2:1ff.) fits into this picture, for it corresponds to the lives of the wise and philosophers.[130] Such a life does not call for asceticism, for "everything created by God is good, and nothing is to be rejected, provided it is received with thanksgiving" (1 Tim. 4:4; cf. 6:17). It is the will of God the creator that human beings live in harmony with the natural order of things.

The Pastorals advocate a universal picture of God that consciously makes contact with Greco-Roman imagery and portrays God as the ideal ruler, whose

123. For analysis, cf. Lorenz Oberlinner, *Die Pastoralbriefe* (HTKNT 11; 3 vols.; Freiburg: Herder, 1994–96), 137, who makes a good case that here Titus distinguishes between God and Jesus; on the Greek expression "great God," cf. the documentation in *NW* 2.2:1038–39.

124. Cf. *NW* 2.1:835–37.

125. Cf. *NW* 2.1:963–66.

126. Cf. Dio Chrysostom, *Or.* 32; Plutarch, *Princ. iner.* (to an uneducated prince) and *Praec. ger.* (political advice).

127. Cf. the comprehensive treatment in Michael Wolter, *Die Pastoralbriefe als Paulustradition* (FRLANT 146; Göttingen: Vandenhoeck & Ruprecht, 1988), 156–96. First Timothy and Titus present themselves as official didactic letters to individuals who themselves have official authority to instruct others.

128. Cf. Plutarch, *Mor.* 781A, where, within the framework of advice to a young prince, the conduct of God is compared to that of kings. Plutarch states, "those, however, who desire his (God's) virtues . . . truth and gentleness" (*NW* 2.2:1051).

129. Cf. Dio Chrysostom, *Or.* 32.16, which indicates that the Gods have created only one effective means against human ignorance: "Education and reason" (παιδείαν καὶ λόγον); cf. further *Or.* 4.29; 32.3; 33.22. Hercules is a model of the divine educator, for he had a good heart/soul, and his labors were interpreted allegorically as purification of the soul (cf. *Or.* 1.61; 4.31; 5.21; 60.8).

130. Cf. the texts in *NW* 2.1:842–47.

rule comes without violent force but through insight and education. God is a gentle, benevolent, healing and saving ruler, who establishes a new order of life and salvation in Jesus Christ, an order proclaimed by the apostle Paul. Paul's disciples now guard this order against false teaching.

10.4.2 Christology

At the center of the Pastorals' Christology stands the epiphany of Jesus Christ as savior of humanity. The key christological words are thus σωτήρ (Savior) and ἐπιφάνεια (appearance, taking visible form), which are applied to both God and Jesus Christ. This already indicates the Pastor's (i.e., the author of the Pastorals) basic approach, which proceeds from God to the unique status of Jesus Christ.

The Savior

The status of Jesus as "Savior" (2 Tim. 1:10; Titus 1:4; 2:13; 3:6) is bound to the divine predicate σωτήρ, for six of the ten instances of σωτήρ refer to God (see above, §10.4.1). Christology thus functions on the basis of knowledge and confession of God; at the same time, theology is filled with content in and through Christology.[131] The determining factor here is the universal saving will of God that has now come to historical form in Jesus Christ; in the epiphany of Jesus Christ, God appears in the world (Titus 1:4; 2:13). The σωτήρ Jesus Christ "has abolished death and brought life and immortality to light through the gospel" (2 Tim. 1:10). In baptism, God's mercy is poured out on believers through the savior Jesus Christ (Titus 3:6), "who gave himself a ransom for all" (1 Tim. 2:6a). The universal and soteriological connotation of the σωτήρ title places its stamp on the Christology of the Pastorals.

Jesus Christ's Appearance/Taking Visible Form in History

By using the word ἐπιφάνεια, the Pastor takes up another key term of Hellenistic religiosity.[132] This term designates "the deity's historically perceptible

131. On this point cf. Karoline Läger, *Die Christologie der Pastoralbriefe* (HTS 12; Münster: Lit, 1996), 119–26; Oberlinner, *Pastoralbriefe*, 155–56; Thomas Söding, "Das Erscheinen des Retters: Zur Christologie der Pastoralbriefe," in *Christologie in der Paulus-Schule: Zur Rezeptionsgeschichte des paulinischen Evangeliums* (ed. Klaus Scholtissek; SBS 181; Stuttgart: Verlag Katholisches Bibelwerk, 2000), 153ff.

132. On this point, cf. Elpidius Pax, ΕΠΙΦΑΝΕΙΑ: *Ein religionsgeschichtlicher Beitrag zur biblischen Theologie* (MThS 1/10; Munich: Zink, 1955); Dieter Lührmann, "Epiphaneia," in *Tradition und Glaube: Das frühe Christentum in seiner Umwelt; Festgabe für Karl Georg Kuhn zum 65. Geburtstag* (ed. Gert Jeremias et al.; Göttingen: Vandenhoeck & Ruprecht, 1971), 185–99; Lorenz Oberlinner, "Die 'Epiphaneia' des Heilswillens Gottes in Christus Jesus: Zur Grundstruktur der Christologie der Pastoralbriefe," *ZNW* 71 (1980): 192–213.

intervention in history for the sake of his worshipers."[133] That this term in the Pastorals is filled with christological content is clear from the fact the explicit subject is not God; it is Jesus Christ who "appears" (1 Tim. 6:14; 2 Tim. 1:10; 4:1, 8). In 2 Tim. 1:10 the word ἐπιφάνεια refers to the incarnation and the saving work of Jesus Christ as a whole, which is also the dominant meaning in 2 Tim. 4:8. In 1 Tim. 6:14 the spotlight is on the return of Jesus Christ (cf. 2 Thess. 2:8), connected in 2 Tim. 4:1 with Christ's role as judge. While the parousia is also in view in Titus 2:13, there ἐπιφάνεια refers primarily to God and thus to God's saving act. And finally, the simultaneous use of ἐπιφάνεια and σωτήρ in 2 Tim. 1:10 and Titus 2:13, the mention of the current gospel preaching in 2 Tim. 1:10–11, and the universal-soteriological affirmation in Titus 2:14 point to the fact that ἐπιφάνεια refers not to a specific individual event (e.g., the incarnation or the parousia) but to the saving event as a whole, in which God acts through Jesus Christ for the salvation of humanity.[134] The term ἐπιφάνεια signifies the comprehensive Christ event in all its saving, death-defeating dimensions, present and future.[135] The use of the verb ἐπιφαίνω (appear) in Titus 2:11 and 3:4 confirms these results, for the epiphany of God's love for humanity encompasses the whole Christ event.

Christological Traditions

The Pastorals draw central christological perspectives from a rich tradition in which especially the letters of Paul, but also the Synoptic tradition, stand in the background.[136] A traditional formulation of faith in the incarnation is found in 1 Tim. 1:15b, "Christ Jesus came into the world to save sinners" (cf. Mark 2:17; Luke 19:10). First Timothy 2:5–6 presents a confessional affirmation that includes differing traditional motifs:[137]

> There is one God;
> there is also one mediator between God and humankind,
> Christ Jesus, himself human,
> who gave himself a ransom for all [ἀντίλυτρον ὑπὲρ πάντων].

133. Lührmann, "Epiphaneia," 185, 195–96.

134. Läger, *Christologie*, 119: Ἐπιφάνεια designates "the whole spectrum of the compassionate divine turning toward humanity; not an individual, concrete datum, but the saving intervention of Christ in his incarnation, his present activity, and in that which is still to come." Cf. also Oberlinner, *Pastoralbriefe*, 157.

135. Thus there can be no talk of a "first" and "second" epiphany, as in, e.g., Jürgen Roloff, *Der erste Brief an Timotheus* (EKKNT 15; Neukirchen-Vluyn: Neukirchener Verlag, 1988), 364–65; Egbert Schlarb, *Die gesunde Lehre: Häresie und Wahrheit im Spiegel der Pastoralbriefe* (MTS 28; Marburg: Elwert, 1990), 166–71; Hanna Stettler, *Die Christologie der Pastoralbriefe* (WUNT 2.105; Tübingen: Mohr, 198), 331. For critique of this view, cf. Läger, *Christologie*, 116–18.

136. The Pastorals apparently presuppose that a small collection of Pauline letters had already been circulated; on this point cf. Lindemann, *Paulus im ältesten Christentum*, 134–49. A survey of all imaginable points of contact is given in Stettler, *Christologie*, 314–25.

137. For an extensive analysis, cf. Läger, *Christologie*, 38–43.

The fundamental confession of the one (Jewish) God (cf. 1 Cor. 8:6) is joined to the concept of the mediator, otherwise attested in the New Testament only in Hebrews (8:6; 9:15; 12:24). The mediator is explicitly the *human being* Jesus Christ, a clear accent against the false proto-Gnostic teaching that was becoming influential in the churches (see below, §10.4.7).[138] Also Jesus's representative giving of himself (cf. Mark 10:45) "for all" must be read against this background, for thereby the salvific significance of the death of Jesus is emphasized in a way that cannot be misunderstood. In clear proximity to Phil. 2:6–11, Rom. 1:3–4, and John 1:14, the hymnlike tripartite christological creedal statement of 1 Tim. 3:16 portrays the saving event:

> He was revealed in flesh, vindicated in spirit,
> seen by angels, proclaimed among Gentiles,
> believed in throughout the world, taken up in glory.[139]

The chiastic juxtaposition of earthly and heavenly reality is clearly recognizable, according to the pattern a-b/b-a/a-b (flesh-Spirit/angels-Gentiles/world-glory). The passive voice indicates the act of God (exception: line 3a), which corresponds to the basic approach of the theological Christology of the Pastorals. The first line designates the *incarnation*, and, like 2 Tim. 1:9–10 ("This grace was given to us in Christ Jesus before the ages began, but it has now been revealed through the appearing of our Savior Christ Jesus"), and presupposes the concept of the *preexistence* of Christ—although the christological title "Son" is absent from the Pastorals. The second line portrays the universal dimension of the Christ event between heaven and earth, the third line the *exaltation* to the heavenly world. In 2 Tim. 2:8 ("Remember Jesus Christ, raised from the dead, a descendant of David") the *resurrection* of Jesus is paired with his Davidic ancestry, as in Rom. 1:3, so that confession of the Risen One always includes the reference to the earthly Jesus. In Titus 3:5, the salvific self-offering of God in Jesus Christ is understood as a radical expression of his mercy: God's love for humanity appeared "not because of any works of righteousness that we had done, but according to his mercy, through the water of rebirth and renewal by the Holy Spirit." Titus 3:3–7 and 2 Tim. 1:8–10 reproduce, in concentrated form, the substance of the Pauline *doctrine of justification*: God justifies human beings by grace alone, without works of the law (cf. Gal. 2:16; Rom. 3:21ff.). Even works "of righteousness" can have no function in God's saving act! The connection between baptism and righteousness/justification in Titus 3:5 is also found in 1 Cor. 6:11 and Rom.

138. Cf. Oberlinner, *Pastoralbriefe*, 74.

139. Cf. here the analyses of Roloff, *Timotheus*, 192–97; Stettler, *Christologie*; Läger, *Christologie*, 43–54; Oberlinner, *Pastoralbriefe*, 162–69.

6. Titus 3:5 uses the philosophical term παλιγγενεσία (rebirth, regeneration)[140] to designate the renewal of the human person through the gift of the Spirit: in baptism God bestows new life "so that, having been justified by his grace [δικαιωθέντες τῇ ἐκείνου χάριτι], we might become heirs according to the hope of eternal life" (Titus 3:7).

God's Love for Humanity in Jesus Christ

The Pastorals present a surprisingly up-to-date Christology: God's gracious saving act in Jesus Christ is for all human beings.[141] The concept of God's benevolence to humanity (Titus 3:4, φιλανθρωπία, lit. "philanthropy") is developed in the context of the ancient city (cf. Titus 1:5b; 2 Tim. 4:10, 12, 20). The grace of God has appeared for the salvation of all human beings (Titus 2:11), grace that guides and educates "to renounce impiety and worldly passions, and in the present age to live lives that are self-controlled, upright, and godly" (Titus 2:12). This catalog of duties, typical in the ancient world, shows that in the Pastorals, Christology too is bound up with a concept of humanity and education, namely "to show every courtesy to everyone" (Titus 3:2). The universality of God's saving act is the expression of God's philanthropy, God's loving care for the human race; we are meant to share that loving care with everyone and thus manifest our own true humanity. The universality and the language of Christology are thus conscious elements of a conception that is obviously concerned with a cultural-religious capacity for appropriation and integration. Against this background, the loss of the theology of the cross in the Pastorals is no accident, for from the author's viewpoint it could be communicated to large segments of the educated Greco-Roman public only with great difficulty (cf. 1 Cor. 1:23).

10.4.3 Pneumatology

The Pastoral Epistles do not contain a developed pneumatology. In 2 Tim. 2:14 ("with the help of the Holy Spirit living in us") and Titus 3:5 ("through the water of rebirth and renewal by the Holy Spirit"), references to the Spirit are occasioned by the baptismal context. In 1 Tim. 3:16, πνεῦμα refers to God's act in Jesus Christ ("vindicated in spirit" or "through the Spirit"); in 1 Tim. 4:1 the Spirit appears as the divine bearer of revelation ("the Spirit

140. On the ideas of rebirth/regeneration in the thought of antiquity (especially in the mystery religions), cf. F. Back, "Wiedergeburt in der hellenistisch-römischen Zeit," in *Wiedergeburt* (ed. Reinhard Feldmeier; BTS 25; Göttingen: Vandenhoeck & Ruprecht, 2005), 45–73.

141. Roloff, *Timotheus*, 358–65, works out very precisely the differences between the Christology of the Pastorals and that of Paul (differences that are in fact present), but prevents himself from seeing new interpretative possibilities by assuming a certain decline and flattening (see ibid., 361).

expressly says").[142] This minimizing of the doctrine of the Spirit is consistent with the theological system of the Pastorals. Second Timothy 1:6–7 indicates that the gift of the Spirit is closely bound to ministerial office, so that the Spirit can no longer be understood as the comprehensive eschatological gift. To be sure, the πνεῦμα is not limited to those who hold ecclesiastical office (cf. Titus 3:5), but they are nonetheless the primary bearers of the Spirit (cf. also 2 Tim. 1:14; 1 Tim. 4:14).

The statement in 2 Tim. 3:16, which speaks of an inspiration of the "Scripture," i.e., of the Old Testament, is noteworthy: "All scripture is inspired by God [πᾶσα γραφὴ θεόπνευστος] and is useful for teaching, for reproof, for correction, and for training in righteousness." The emphasis is on the fact that God has inspired the Scripture, which qualifies it for its function within the Pastorals' concept of education.[143]

10.4.4 Soteriology

Both Christology (see above, §10.4.2) and theology (see above, §10.4.1) have already pointed to the *basic soteriological orientation* of the Pastorals: God's eternal plan is realized in Jesus Christ, whose saving epiphany conquered death and thus opens the way to eternal life.[144] This idea already dominates the opening verses of the letters (1 Tim. 1:12–17; 2 Tim. 1:3–14; Titus 1:1–4). The frequent use of σωτήρ (Savior) as a title for God (see above, §10.4.1) and Jesus Christ (see above, §10.4.2), as well as of σωτηρία (salvation) and σῴζω (save) underscores the central location of soteriology in the comprehensive theological conception of the Pastoral Epistles. Paul instructs Timothy "for salvation through the faith in Christ Jesus," for Paul himself had first experienced the saving grace of God (cf. 1 Tim. 1:15; 2 Tim. 4:18). Paul endures everything for the sake of the elect "so that they may also obtain the salvation that is in Christ Jesus" (2 Tim. 2:10). Within this universal concept, a soteriological quality is thus attributed to the *person of Paul himself*.[145] This is concisely formulated in Titus 1:3, "In due time he revealed his word through the proclamation with which I have been entrusted by the

142. The term πνεῦμα is used in the anthropological sense (rather than pneumatological) in 2 Tim. 1:7 ("God did not give us a spirit of cowardice") and 4:22 ("The Lord be with your spirit").

143. On this point cf. Alfons Weiser, *Der zweite Brief an Timotheus* (EKKNT 16.1; Neukirchen-Vluyn: Neukirchener Verlag, 2003), 286–97.

144. Cf. Abraham J. Malherbe, "'Christ Jesus Came into the World to Save Sinners': Soteriology in the Pastoral Epistles," in *Salvation in the New Testament: Perspectives on Soteriology* (ed. J. G. Van der Watt; NovTSup 121; Leiden: Brill, 2005), 331–58.

145. Cf. Karl Löning, "Gerechtfertigt durch seine Gnade (Tit 3,7): Zum Problem der Paulusrezeption in der Soteriologie der Pastoralbriefe," in *Der lebendige Gott: Studien zur Theologie des Neuen Testaments; Festschrift für Wilhelm Thüsing zum 75. Geburtstag* (ed. Thomas Söding; NTA NF 31; Münster: Aschendorff, 1996), 241–57.

command of God our Savior" (cf. 2 Tim. 1:10–11). Because the revelation of the salvific will of God takes place in the proclamation of the gospel, Paul appears as the "herald" or "proclaimer" (κῆρυξ) of the gospel, and thus as apostle and teacher of the churches (cf. 1 Tim. 2:7; 2 Tim. 1:11). He was appointed by God himself as teacher of the faith and of the truth (1 Tim. 1:7), so that as the prototypical former sinner who now proclaims the gospel, he embodies and guarantees its truth. Participation in this saving truth occurs through baptism (Titus 3:5, "He saved us . . . through the water of rebirth and renewal by the Holy Spirit") and through holding firm to the true teaching (1 Tim. 4:16, "Pay close attention to yourself and to your teaching; continue in these things, for in doing this you will save both yourself and your hearers"). Salvation is related to a process of recognition and knowledge, for it is God's will for "everyone to be saved and to come to the knowledge of the truth" (1 Tim. 2:4). In the overcoming and ignorance (1 Tim. 1:13; Titus 3:3) and recognition of the truth (1 Tim. 2:4; Titus 1:1; 2 Tim. 3:7), God's saving act takes place. Thus, in accord with the basic pedagogical orientation of the Pastorals, the preacher of the gospel should "correct opponents with gentleness. God may perhaps grant that they will repent and come to know the truth" (2 Tim. 2:25).

10.4.5 Anthropology

Significant differences exist between the anthropology of the Pastorals and that of Paul. While for Paul *sin* (ἡ ἁμαρτία in the singular) is a supra-personal power (see above, §6.5.2), ἁμαρτία appears in the Pastorals exclusively in the plural and refers to particular acts, whether of false ethical conduct (1 Tim. 5:22) or representing false teaching (1 Tim. 5:24; 2 Tim. 3:6–7). The verb ἁμαρτάνω (to sin) and the adjective and noun ἁμαρτωλός (sinner) are also used in this sense. Statements about the *law* diverge from Paul's own usage (see above, §6.5.3). The term νόμος occurs only twice in the Pastorals: "Now we know that the law is good, if one uses it legitimately. This means understanding that the law is laid down not for the innocent but for the lawless and disobedient, for the godless and sinful, for the unholy and profane, for those who kill their father or mother, for murderers, fornicators, sodomites, slave traders, liars, perjurers, and whatever else is contrary to the sound teaching" (1 Tim. 1:8–10). The law appears exclusively as a body of ethical material, which the "righteous" do not need.[146] For the Pastor, both the law and sin are ethical/moral categories to be measured by the norm of "sound teaching," that is to say, the proclamation of the gospel worked out in the dispute with false teaching (see below, §10.4.6).

146. Cf. Roloff, *Timotheus*, 74.

Faith

So also the *concept of faith* in the Pastorals is at some distance from that of Paul.[147] While for Paul faith is the direct gift of God that establishes a vital relationship between God and the believer (see above, §6.5.4), in the Pastorals the noun πίστις (thirty-two times) means primarily the "right faith" in contrast to heresy (cf. 1 Tim. 1:2, 4, 19; 2:7; 3:9, 13; 4:1, 6, 16; 5:8; 6:10, 12, 21; 2 Tim. 2:18; 3:8; 4:7; Titus 1:1, 4, 13; 2:2, 10) and as such characterizes the Christian's life. In the Pastorals πίστις (faith) and ἀγάπη (love) are used synonymously (1 Tim. 1:14; 2:15; 4:12; 6:11; 2 Tim. 1:13; 2:22; 3:10; Titus 2:2). "Faith" can be named in a list along with other virtues such as "good conscience" (1 Tim. 1:5, 19; 3:9), "modesty, love, and holiness" (1 Tim. 2:15), "purity" (1 Tim. 4:12), "righteousness, piety, patience, gentleness" (1 Tim. 6:11; see further 2 Tim. 1:13; 2:22; 3:10–11; Titus 2:2).[148] This formalizing of the concept of faith corresponds to the proximity of "faith" and "(sound) teaching" (διδασκαλία): "If you put these instructions before the brothers and sisters, you will be a good servant of Christ Jesus, nourished on the words of the faith and of the sound teaching that you have followed" (1 Tim. 4:6; cf. 2 Tim. 3:10). The content of faith becomes a body of teaching that is proclaimed; to depart from the faith thus means to depart from correct doctrine (cf. 1 Tim. 4:1).

Finally, for Paul it is inconceivable to think of the Christian faith as an item of family tradition, as the Pastor does in 1 Tim. 1:5 with regard to Timothy ("I am reminded of your sincere faith, a faith that lived first in your grandmother Lois and your mother Eunice and now, I am sure, lives in you"; cf. 2 Tim. 3:14–15) and in 2 Tim. 1:3a with regard to Paul himself ("I am grateful to God—whom I worship with a clear conscience, as my ancestors did").[149] However, the motif of faith as something in which one can be educated does fit organically into the

147. For analysis, cf. G. Kretschmar, "Der paulinische Glaube in den Pastoralbriefe," in *Glaube im Neuen Testament: Studien zu Ehren von Hermann Binder anlässlich seines 70. Geburtstags* (ed. Ferdinand Hahn and Hans Klein; BTS 7; Neukirchen-Vluyn: Neukirchener Verlag, 1982), 117–37.

148. On target is the comment of Otto Merk, "Glaube und Tat in den Pastoralbriefen," in *Wissenschaftsgeschichte und Exegese: Gesammelte Aufsätze zum 65. Geburtstag Otto Merks* (ed. Otto Merk; BZNW 95; Berlin: de Gruyter, 1998), 262: "Equipped with the attributes of good conduct, faith itself is a virtue."

149. For exegesis, cf. P. Trummer, *Die Paulustradition der Pastoralbriefe* (BET 8; Frankfurt: Lang, 1978), 125–27, 129. Second Timothy 1:5 clearly indicates the historical setting of the Pastorals: around the turn of the century, when one could already speak of Christian family traditions in which the faith was communicated. Cf. Merz, *Selbstauslegung*, 83. In my view, 2 Tim. 1:5 already makes it impossible to ascribe this letter (or Titus) to Paul, as J. Herzer would like to do. Cf. J. Herzer, "Abschied vom Konsens? Die Pseudepigraphie der Pastoralbriefe als Herausforderung an die neutestamentliche Wissenschaft," *TLZ* 129 (204), 1267–82. The problems are also exaggerated by Luke Timothy Johnson, who, commenting on 2 Timothy's understanding of faith, is unable to produce any examples in the undisputed letters of Paul for this understanding of faith and states, "And our analysis of 1 Timothy has shown some of the richness and complexity of pistis in that letter." This clearly begs the question, for 1 Timothy

concept of education and household repeatedly noted above: the household has become the place where the faith is transmitted and nurtured.

Closely related to the Pastor's understanding of faith is his use of the term *conscience*.[150] Thus it is specifically stated with regard to Timothy that he has "faith and a good conscience" (1 Tim. 1:19), and of deacons that they "must hold fast to the mystery of the faith with a clear conscience" (1 Tim. 3:9). In the Pastorals, the "good" conscience is not, as in Paul, a neutral court that makes judgments about the person's conduct, but the awareness that one is living in conformity with the stipulated teaching and expected conduct: "The aim of such instruction is love that comes from a pure heart, a good conscience, and sincere faith" (1 Tim. 1:5). That the content of the term "conscience" is determined by "sound teaching" is also indicated by language about a "pure" or "impure" conscience, in the context of polemics against the false teachers (1 Tim. 1:15; 1 Tim. 4:2).

These major differences from Paul in the way anthropology is understood are not accidental, but result from the changed historical situation and theological argumentation: the apostle's debates about the Torah already belong to the distant past, and in the acute threat posed by the false teaching (see below, §10.4.7) the understanding of faith as right doctrine necessarily gains increasing importance. The temporalization of the Christ event is connected with a strengthening of the internal forms of church organization and an ethicizing of what it means to be a Christian.

10.4.6 Ethics

The distinctive character of the ethics of the Pastoral Epistles is seen in the way that it decisively opens up the meaning of the Christ event in regard to the *contemporary ethos*.[151] The idea of εὐσέβεια ("reverence" or "piety"; Latin *pietas*)[152] becomes a key concept; of fifteen New Testament occurrences, ten are found in the Pastorals. As a central term of Greco-Roman religion and ethics,[153] εὐσέβεια had already been accepted into the language of Hellenistic Judaism (4 Maccabees; Philo; Josephus),[154] where it had come to mean conducting oneself

is just as unlikely to be from Paul as 2 Timothy! (See Luke Timothy Johnson, *The First and Second Letters to Timothy* [AB 35A; New York: Doubleday, 2001], 432.)

150. On this point cf. Eckstein, *Syneidesis*, 303–6; Roloff, *Timotheus*, 68–70.

151. For elaboration, cf. Schrage, *Ethics*, 257–68; Schnackenburg, *Sittliche Botschaft*, 2:95–109. [The 1973 English translation from an earlier edition does not contain this section.—MEB]

152. On this point, cf. W. Foerster, "εὐσεβής," *TDNT* 7:175–85; D. Kaufmann-Bühler, "Eusebeia," *RAC* 6:986–99; Angela Standhartinger, "Eusebeia in den Pastoralbriefen: Ein Beitrag zum Einfluss römischen Denkens auf das entstehende Christentum," *NovT* 48 (206), 51–82.

153. Cf. Xenophon, *Mem.* 4.8.11, where Socrates is portrayed as a pious and God-fearing man who is at the same time undaunted and just by human standards.

154. Cf. Weber, *Das Gesetz im hellenistischen Judentum*, 226–27; Weber, *Das "Gesetz" bei Philon*, 159–64, 213–19.

in accord with the will of God, respecting the values and order established in creation. The term occurs in this sense in 1 Tim. 2:2, which calls for intercessory prayer to be made "for kings and all who are in high positions, so that we may lead a quiet and peaceable life in all godliness and dignity [ἐν πάσῃ εὐσεβείᾳ καὶ σεμνότητι]." According to 1 Tim. 5:4, children and grandchildren should conduct their households in harmony with the established social order, supporting their widowed parents and grandparents. In 1 Tim. 6:11, εὐσέβεια is listed along with other virtues: "Pursue righteousness, godliness [εὐσέβεια], faith, love, endurance, gentleness" (cf. also 1 Tim. 6:6; Titus 2:12).[155] This is conduct that pleases God, and thus also is what human beings expect and approve. Several times the term εὐσέβεια is used in the sense of "faith" and "teaching" (1 Tim. 3:16; 4:7–8; 6:3, 5; 2 Tim. 3:5, 12; Titus 1:1). Most of the instances of σωφροσύνη (prudence, morality) and its derivatives are found, along with the ethical concept of faith as a virtue, in the Pastorals (ten of sixteen New Testament occurrences). Thus the bishop should be "temperate, sensible, respectable" (1 Tim. 3:2; cf. Titus 1:8), and so should the older men, the women, and the young men (Titus 2:2, 4, 5, 6). The statement in 2 Tim. 1:7 applies to all believers, that "God did not give us a spirit of cowardice, but rather a spirit of power and of love and of self-discipline [δυνάμεως καὶ ἀγάπης καὶ σωφρονισμοῦ]." Of course, the Pastor's concepts of virtue and education are interwoven, for divine grace moves or educates us "to renounce impiety and worldly passions, and in the present age to live lives that are self-controlled, upright, and godly" (Titus 2:12).[156] The virtue of σωφροσύνη is especially commended to women: they should "dress themselves modestly and decently in suitable clothing, not with their hair braided, or with gold, pearls, or expensive clothes" (1 Tim. 2:9). The catalogs of virtues in 1 Tim. 2:15; 4:12; 6:11; 2 Tim. 1:7; 2:22; 3:10 clearly indicate that the Pastorals also include ἀγάπη (love) as one of the virtues. To be sure, love "from a pure heart" is the "sum/aim of instruction" (1 Tim. 1:5), so that, while love does not occupy an exclusive place in the Pastor's ethic, it still plays an exceptional role.

The Pastorals' teaching about the virtuous life is embedded within the thought world of antiquity regarding the order of society; the Pastor's own view of the structures of the Christian household is shaped by this conceptual world, which is already given in his situation (cf. 1 Tim. 3:15, "that you

155. On this point, cf. Epictetus, *Ench.* 31: "Wherefore, whoever is careful to exercise desire and aversion as he should, is at the same time careful also about piety [εὐσέβεια]."

156. Comparable ideas are found, for example, in Dio Chrysostom, *Or.* 33.28, according to whom treasures count nothing in the eyes of God: "Prudence and reason alone bring salvation [ἀλλὰ σωφροσύνη καὶ νοῦς ἐστι τὰ σῴζοντα]. They make everyone who holds fast to them happy and well-pleasing to God." On the Stoic teaching about virtue, cf. *SVF* 4.264 (Stobaeus, *Anth.* 2.7.5B1: "There are four highest qualities: insight, prudence, courage, and righteousness [φρόνησιν, σωφροσύνην, ἀνδρείαν, δικαιοσύνην]." "Insight" refers to appropriate conduct, "prudence" to human drives, "courage" to steadfastness, and "righteousness" to a sense of proportion.

may know how one ought to behave in the household of God, which is the church of the living God"). Alongside catalogs of virtues (1 Tim. 3:2–4, 8–10, 11–12; 4:12; 6:11; Titus 3:2) and vices (1 Tim. 1:9–10; 6:4; 2 Tim. 3:2–4; Titus 3:3) are found specific instructions for the particular social levels within the "household." The *portrayal of women* in the Pastorals, in contrast to that of the authentic letters of Paul, does not reflect the model in which it is assumed women are coworkers who participate in the life of the church but is determined by the appeal to be subordinate.[157] Thus 1 Tim. 2:11–12 formulates the matter: "Let a woman learn in silence with full submission. I permit no woman to teach or to have authority over a man; she is to keep silent." To this is added a warrant from a theology of creation that sees the role of women as that of bearing children (1 Tim. 2:15; cf. 5:14). This restrictive argumentation is certainly bound up with the role of women in the context of the false teaching opposed in the Pastorals (cf. 2 Tim. 3:6; 1 Tim. 2:9–10; 3:11; Titus 2:3), for the ascetic practices advocated there (rejection of marriage and certain foods) are explicitly rejected on the basis of his theology of creation (1 Tim. 4:3–4). The parallels in contemporary household management are also important, for they make clear that the Pastorals are to be understood as part of a wider development.[158] The instructions for widows in 1 Tim. 5:3–16 are noteworthy. These women apparently constitute a sizeable group in the church,[159] and there was an account in the church treasury for the care of widows (cf. 1 Tim. 5:16). However, these funds were available only for women who had lived in accord with the rules set forth by the church. The misuse of this arrangement (cf. 1 Tim. 5:4–15) not only is evidence of the effectiveness of this support system but also reveals the conflicts around the question of who qualifies as a "widow" within the church. There was possibly a kind of official "status as a widow": women were provided for by the church and in return performed spiritual and social tasks in the congregation. This model was so attractive that it led to misuse and disputes. So also the parenesis to slaves in 1 Tim. 6:1–2 suggests that there were problems, for within the instructions that slaves

157. Cf. the comprehensive treatment by Wagener, *Ordnung*, 62ff. (she emphasizes the restrictive tendency of the Pastorals).

158. The pseudepigraphical letters of Pythagoras, almost contemporary with the Pastorals, state: "For that you are really interested in hearing what adorns a woman gives a justified hope that you are on the best way to a lasting marriage. The decent, freeborn woman must thus live together with her legal husband, adorned with modesty. She must wear a plain white dress, nothing expensive and luxurious . . . for the wife who strives for respectability must not concern herself with fancy clothes, but with directing the household . . . for the wishes of her husband must be the unwritten law for the respectable wife, and she must live by them" (trans. MEB from the German text of A. Städele, *Die Briefe des Pythagoras und der Pythagoreer* [BKP 115; Meisenheim: Hain, 1980], p. 161).

159. On this point cf. Ernst Dassmann, "Witwen und Diakonissen," in *Ämter und Dienste in den frühchristlichen Gemeinden* (ed. Ernst Dassmann; Bonn: Borengässer, 1994), 142–56; Wagener, *Ordnung*, 115–233.

should honor their masters, slaves who have Christian masters are explicitly addressed: "Those who have believing masters must not be disrespectful to them on the ground that they are members of the church; rather they must serve them all the more, since those who benefit by their service are believers and beloved" (1 Tim. 6:2). The change in theological status is not here related to a change in social status (as argued by Paul in his letter to Philemon), but the other way around: being a Christian brother is understood as increasing the obligation to be subject.[160]

Taken as a whole, the Pastorals propagate a style of life and piety characterized by a prudent and virtuous life in faith, works of love (Titus 3:8, 14), patience, modesty, hospitality, and comprehensive benevolence (cf. 1 Tim. 2:2; 4:7, 12; 6:6–11, 17–19; 2 Tim. 1:7; 2:22; 3:10; Titus 1:8; 2:1–2, 6, 11–13; 3:4–7). The author of the Pastorals orients his instruction to the conventional norms of his time;[161] his goal is the social integration of the congregations (cf. 1 Tim. 2:2). The bishop must have a good reputation not only among believers, but among non-Christians as well (1 Tim. 3:7); women may not teach (1 Tim. 2:12); slaves should stay in their place (1 Tim. 6:1; Titus 2:9); and Christians should be subject to the authorities (Titus 3:1). For the churches addressed by the Pastorals, there was apparently no conflict between the fundamental appeal back to the apostle Paul (see below, §10.4.7) and the adaptation/integration of pagan ethics; both were prerequisites for the identity and stability of the congregations. Nonetheless, the false teachers (see below, §10.4.7) attempted to give the churches a new identity that challenged the fundamental appeal back to Paul and propagated a view of the Christian faith that disengaged it from the world. Both social isolation and abandonment of tradition would have endangered the existence of the church. The Pastor counters this approach by focusing on a theology of the world as God's creation (1 Tim. 4:4–5) and by interlocking ethics closely with church structure.

10.4.7 Ecclesiology

Ecclesiology in its characteristic form of "order" and "teaching," is doubtless one of the major foci of the Pastorals. Of the twenty-one instances of διδασκαλία (teaching, doctrine) in the New Testament, fifteen are found in the Pastorals. It refers to Christian doctrine as a whole, especially in its contrast to the false doctrine opposed by the Pastor: the "sound" teaching (1 Tim. 1:10; 2 Tim. 4:3; Titus 1:9; 2:1), the "good" teaching (1 Tim. 4:6) that is in accord with godliness (1 Tim. 6:3). On the other side stand those who

160. Oberlinner, *Pastoralbriefe*, 265.

161. This (necessary and unavoidable) development does not justify a wholesale rejection of the ethic of the Pastorals as "bourgeois;" on this point cf. M. Reiser, "Bürgerliches Christentum in den Pastoralbriefen?" *Bib* 74 (1993): 27–44.

teach the "different" doctrine (1 Tim. 1:3) and have already "swerved from the truth" (2 Tim. 2:17–18; cf. 1 Tim. 1:19–20; 6:5; Titus 1:10–11; 2 Tim. 3:8). The use of διδασκαλία as a firm *terminus technicus* (1 Tim. 1:10; 4:6, 16; 6:1, 3; 2 Tim. 3:10; 4:3; Titus 1:9; 2:1, 10) reflects deep sociological and theological changes.

The Social Form of the Congregations

The congregations of the Pastoral Epistles are a socially complex phenomenon. Christian homeowners are mentioned several times (cf. 1 Tim. 3:4–5, 12; 5:4, 8; 2 Tim. 1:16; 4:19; cf. also 1 Tim. 5:13; 2 Tim. 3:6; Titus 1:11), and large houses with valuable furnishings were apparently not unusual (cf. 2 Tim. 2:20). So also women's jewelry (cf. 1 Tim. 2:9), the slaves of Christian masters (cf. 1 Tim. 6:2), warnings against acquisitiveness and love of money (cf. 1 Tim. 6:6–10; 2 Tim. 3:2; Titus 1:7), and the separate section devoted to instructions to the wealthy in 1 Tim. 6:17–19, all show that some members of the congregations addressed by the Pastorals belonged to the upper social class.[162]

The churches had considerable financial means at their disposal, for the elders (and certainly also the bishops, as the top ministerial officials)[163] were paid (cf. 1 Tim. 5:17–18; 3:1). Alongside the wealthy members, who apparently dominated congregational life, the Pastorals also mention slaves (cf. 1 Tim. 6:1; Titus 2:9–10) and widows (cf. 1 Tim. 5:3–16), handworkers (cf. 2 Tim. 4:14) and lawyers (cf. Titus 3:13), and give instructions on caring for the poor (cf. 1 Tim. 5:10). Also at work in the congregations are Christian teachers (cf. 1 Tim. 1:3, 7; 4:1; 6:3; 2 Tim. 4:3; Titus 1:11) who have triggered a crisis by their partially successful agitation. Leaders of the congregations are to ward off the potential slander of outsiders by their respectable behavior, pray for the civic authorities, and lead a blameless life (cf. 1 Tim. 2:2; Titus 3:1). The Pastor is just as concerned for the public reputation of congregational leaders (1 Tim. 3:1–13) as he is for the harmonious coexistence of the particular social groups within the church (cf. Titus 2:1–10).

The False Teaching

In the Pastoral Epistles there is a direct connection between the relatively large proportion of well-to-do members of the congregations, the success of the false teaching, the formation of a firm "teaching," and the establishment of an official ministry. The opposing teaching probably did not come into the churches from outside, for the advocates of this doctrine emerge openly in the congregational assemblies (cf. 2 Tim. 2:16, 25; 3:8; Titus 1:9; 3:9). They had experienced considerable success in the congregations; whole households

162. Cf. on this point Peter Dschulnigg, "Warnung vor Reichtum und Ermahnung der Reichen," *BZ* 37 (1993): 60–77.

163. Cf. Roloff, *Timotheus*, 308–9.

are receptive to the new teaching, which found many adherents among the wealthier women (cf. 2 Tim. 3:6). The naming of names in 1 Tim. 1:20; 2 Tim. 2:17; 4:14 also shows that the false teaching was advocated by elements of the church itself. The author of the Pastorals commands the churches to have nothing to do with this false teaching; what is required is not discussion, but distance (cf. 1 Tim. 6:20; 2 Tim. 2:14, 16, 23; 3:5; Titus 3:9–11). Extensive passages in the Pastorals read like official orders (e.g., 1 Tim. 2:1, 8, 12; 3:2, 7; Titus 2:1, 15; 2 Tim. 1:13–14; 2:1–2, 14, 22–23; Titus 3:10) that are to be followed in order to repress the false teaching.

This false teaching internal to the churches apparently combined very different elements. Thus the opposing teachers claim to purvey "gnosis" (γνῶσις, "knowledge"; cf. especially 1 Tim. 6:20–21; also 1 Tim. 4:3; 2 Tim. 3:7; Titus 1:16). The ascetic requirements of abstaining from marriage and from certain foods also suggest an early form of Christian Gnosticism (1 Tim. 4:3; cf. Irenaeus, *Against Heresies* 1.24.2; 28.1). Gnostic parallels are also found in the opponents' claim that the resurrection had already occurred (2 Tim. 2:18; cf. NHC 1/4 49.15–16). According to 1 Tim. 1:4; 4:7; 2 Tim. 4:4; Titus 1:14; 3:9, the false teaching also included myths and endless genealogies. Gnostic texts do in fact contain numerous mythological speculations.

The false teaching is also characterized by the inclusion of *Jewish elements*. Thus the opponents claim to be teachers of the law (1 Tim. 1:7; cf. Titus 1:9). According to Titus 1:10, the seductive teachers are "of the circumcision"; in Titus 1:14 their mythological speculations are designated μύθοι (myths). In history-of-religion terms, this opposing doctrine[164] is mostly categorized as a form of Jewish-Christian Gnosticism.[165] This thesis regards the Jewish elements as constitutive elements of the false teaching, and a Jewish origin of Gnosticism as such is often presupposed. To be sure, this assumption is strongly disputed, for central elements of Jewish faith (strict monotheism, God as creator, a positive view of creation) can hardly be combined with the basic orientation of Gnostic systems, which are generally hostile to the created world. If Jewish elements are regarded only as marginal phenomena of the false teaching, it could easily be understood as an *early form of Christian Gnosticism*[166] influenced by some Jewish elements that did not fundamentally affect its content. Clearly, the opponents, with their claim that the resurrection

164. For the history of research, cf. Schlarb, *Gesunde Lehre*, 73–82; the current state of the discussion is surveyed by Oberlinner, *Pastoralbriefe*, *Titus*, 52–73.

165. Cf., e.g., Martin Dibelius and Hans Conzelmann, *The Pastoral Epistles* (Hermeneia; trans. Philip Buttolph and Adela Yarbro; Philadelphia: Fortress, 1972), 66; Walter Schmithals, ed., *Neues Testament und Gnosis* (EdF 208; Darmstadt: Wissenschaftliche Buchgesellschaft, 1984), 93–94; Norbert Brox, *Die Pastoralbriefe: 1 Timotheus, 2 Timotheus, Titus* (5th ed.; RNT 7; Regensburg: Pustet, 1989), 33–34.

166. Cf. Roloff, *Timotheus*, 228–39; Wolter, *Pastoralbriefe*, 265–66; Helmut Merkel, *Die Pastoralbriefe* (NTD 9; Göttingen: Vandenhoeck & Ruprecht, 1991), 10, 13; Oberlinner, *Pastoralbriefe*, *Titus*, 63ff.; Weiser, *Der zweite Brief an Timotheus*, 217–18.

had already occurred, advocated a massively present-tense understanding of salvation,[167] which was probably related to their interpretation of baptism and the gift of the Spirit with which baptism was associated. The ascetic tendencies of the opponents' teaching indicate that the existing world is understood as the place of imprisonment, from which the Gnostic attempted to gain liberation through the redemptive knowledge of God. The creation and the creator God are evaluated negatively, for overcoming the hostile material world was the goal of the doctrine opposed by the Pastor. In contrast to this, 1 Tim. 4:4–5 emphasizes that the world is God's good creation, and nothing in it is to be rejected. The setting of the missionary work of the false teachers was primarily the small house churches (2 Tim. 3:6–9), which fits in with the esoteric character of Gnostic teaching.[168]

Seen against this background, it is not surprising that the author of the Pastorals responds by making "the household" the center of his ecclesiology—of course in a different sense from that of the false teachers.[169]

The Church as the Household of God, and Its Officials

The organizational structure for which the Pastoral Epistles strive is no longer formulated along the lines of the individual house church, but the ancient model of the household is used as the paradigm for the congregations in a particular location.[170] Through a new structure of official church leadership, the isolated house churches, threatened by the false teaching, are organized as a single united church presided over by one ἐπίσκοπος (bishop, president, supervisor), the one household of God in a particular place.[171] This concept is connected with the basic appeal back to Paul, as in the exemplary statement of 1 Tim. 3:15: "I am writing these instructions to you so that, if I am delayed, you may know how one ought to behave in the household of God [ἐν οἴκῳ θεοῦ], which is the church of the living God [ἐκκλησία θεοῦ ζῶντος], the pillar and bulwark of the truth" (cf. also 2 Tim. 2:20–21; Titus 1:7).

The retro-connection to Paul gives the office of ministerial leadership its authority in the church.[172] In Paul's absence, the ministry of the gospel entrusted to him (cf. 1 Tim. 1:12) is now actualized in the ministries of Timothy and

167. Cf. Schlarb, *Gesunde Lehre*, 93; Oberlinner, *Pastoralbriefe, Titus* 54, who also regards 2 Tim. 2:18 as the central point of the false teaching.

168. On the question of whether 1 Tim. 6:20 is an allusion to Marcion's "Antitheses," cf. Egbert Schlarb, "Miszell zu 1Tim 6,20," *ZNW* 77 (1986): 276–81.

169. On the οἶκος concept of the Pastorals, cf. especially Schlarb, *Gesunde Lehre*, 314–56; David C. Verner, *The Household of God: The Social World of the Pastoral Epistles* (SBLDS 71; Chico, CA: Scholars Press, 1983).

170. Cf. Roloff, *Kirche im Neuen Testament*, 255.

171. On this point cf. Ernst Dassmann, "Hausgemeinde und Bischofsamt," in *Ämter und Dienste in den frühchristlichen Gemeinden* (ed. Ernst Dassmann; Bonn: Borengässer, 1994), 74–95.

172. Cf. Roloff, *Timotheus*, 169–89; Merkel, *Pastoralbriefe*, 90–93.

Titus, as prototypes of the leaders in the church of the Pastor's time. Just as Paul was the one primarily entrusted with the truth of the gospel, so also the later leaders of the church have the task of preserving the tradition legitimated through Paul's own preaching (cf. 1 Tim. 6:20; 2 Tim. 1:14). In this process, the author of the Pastorals faced the task of combining two forms of church structure (both probably already existing in the churches),[173] and giving them a new interpretation. We thus find in the Pastorals statements about a presbyterial church structure led by elders (1 Tim. 5:17–19; Titus 1:5–6) as well as catalogs of qualifications and duties for bishops and deacons (1 Tim. 3:2–13; Titus 1:7–9). This fusion of the office of elder with that of the bishop and deacon is attested several times in Christian literature at the end of the first century CE (cf. Acts 14:23; 20:17; 1 Pet. 5:1–5; *1 Clem.* 40–44). The office of elder deriving from Jewish tradition[174] sees in the age and maturity of a person a decisive qualification for leadership. This office is never mentioned in the authentic letters of Paul, since for him one's age is not a charismatic gift, and all the functions and ministries of the church are derived from the authority of the Spirit (cf. 1 Cor. 12:28–31).[175] The Letter to the Philippians, from the late phase of Paul's ministry, documents the ministries of the ἐπίσκοπος and the διάκονος (cf. Phil. 1:1). The *episkopoi* apparently had a variety of responsibilities—primarily as leaders of the house churches. The *diakonoi* likewise exercised a variety of functions within the congregations, including assisting at the eucharist and in caring for the poor (cf. Mark 10:43–44; 2 Cor. 3:6; 4:1; 5:18). The parallel existence of these two forms of church order in the Pastorals raises the question of which form the Pastor himself is advocating. A merging of the two structural patterns was apparently not his goal, for only in Titus 1:5–9 do the two structures stand alongside each other, and there they are not really being combined. Instead, the author of the Pastorals favors

173. According to Roloff, *Timotheus*, 170, the Pastor is not introducing a new office, but his concern is "so far as possible, to integrate the offices and ministries already present into a united conception and to restructure them by reinterpreting them at a deeper level, so that they can face the challenges and tasks of the churches in his situation." In contrast, Merkel, *Pastoralbriefe*, 13, the tensions between the various statements in the Pastorals about ecclesiastical offices are "explained most simply on the assumption that the office of presbyter was already known among the churches, while the Pastor himself wants to introduce the episcopal/diaconate model." D.-A. Koch is critical of this model, and rejects the hypothesis of a "merging" of offices: "Neither was there a Pauline concept of an episcopal office, nor was the office of elder characteristic of the Jewish synagogues of the first and second centuries CE. The organization and structure of church offices of the Pastoral Epistles is thus a new design of the third Christian generation" (Dietrich-Alex Koch, "Die Einmaligkeit des Anfangs und die Fortdauer der Institution," in *Die kleine Prophetin Kirche leiten* [ed. M. Böttcher et al.; Wuppertal: Brockhaus, 2005], 167).

174. On this point, see the pre-70 Jerusalem inscription reproduced in Deissmann, *Light from the Ancient East*, 439–41; see also Acts 1:30; 14:23; 15:2, 4, 22–23; James 5:14, and Martin Karrer, "Das urchristliche Ältestenamt," *NovT* 32 (1990): 152–88.

175. On the fading away of language about the Spirit in the Pastorals, cf. Wolter, *Pastoralbriefe*, 41ff.

an episcopal structure combined with the diaconate.[176] According to 1 Tim. 3:1, the office of bishop is a good thing, for which one should legitimately strive. *The bishop is no longer only in charge of a single house church, but is responsible for leadership in all the congregations in a particular location,* surrounded by deacons and by elders who have accepted this responsibility. The desired new formation of the episcopal office and the gradual overcoming of the presbytery is illustrated by the ordination of Timothy in 1 Tim. 4:14. To be sure, the elders lay their hands on Timothy (according to 2 Tim. 1:6, Timothy was ordained by Paul), but he is ordained to be the ἐπίσκοπος of the whole church in his area. Ordination as a spiritual and legal-institutional act has the dual goals of establishing the authority of the one assuming ministerial office and the safeguarding of the tradition.[177]

If nothing else, the appearance of the false teaching and its success in the house churches accelerated the establishment of a functional office of ministerial leadership, for the ἐπίσκοπος is to be responsible for the whole church in a particular area (cf. 1 Tim. 5:1–21). The church as a sacred structure, an institution grounded on God and in which the only saving truth that has appeared in Jesus Christ is present (cf. 1 Tim. 3:15–16; 2 Tim. 2:19–21), must dissociate itself from false teaching. Nonetheless, legal categories do not grasp the essence of the episcopate, which is primarily a spiritual office, for the ability to teach is a qualification for such church leaders (1 Tim. 3:2; Titus 1:9). The bishop is addressed as the manager of God's household (Titus 1:7–9) who holds fast to right doctrine and withstands the opponents. *The bishop does not rule, but is the guarantor of the church's unity!*

As the apostle guided his churches through the gospel, so now the apostle's disciples, equipped with Paul's own instructions, assume this responsibility (cf. 1 Tim. 4:11, 13, 16; 2 Tim. 1:13; 2:24; 3:10, 14–17; Titus 2:1). Even in the apostle's absence, the gospel he preached and his untiring service to the churches continue as the norm for the ministry of his disciples, to which in turn the church leaders of the Pastor's time are to orient their own service to the churches. Like the Scriptures inspired by the Spirit (cf. 2 Tim. 3:16), the Pastorals make the claim to formulate, comprehensively and decisively, the obligatory will of the apostle Paul for the churches.

Paul as Model

What is generally true of the theology of the Pastoral Epistles is particularly valid for their ecclesiology: *the appeal back to the apostle and teacher*

176. Cf. Roloff, *Timotheus*, 175; Oberlinner, *Pastoralbriefe*, *Titus*, 91.

177. Cf. Hermann von Lips, *Glaube—Gemeinde—Amt: Zum Verständnis der Ordination in den Pastoralbriefen* (FRLANT 122; Göttingen: Vandenhoeck & Ruprecht, 1979), 279: "The importance of ordination as authorization and empowerment for the holder of ecclesiastical office is directed, on the one hand, at his official function and authority in the churches, and, on the other hand, at the preservation of the tradition by establishing an official line of continuity."

is foundational. Paul is the apostle of Jesus Christ appointed by God, *the* minister of the gospel, whose apostolate is a constituent element of the divine plan of salvation (cf. 1 Tim. 1:1; 2:7; Titus 1:1; 2 Tim. 1:1, 11). Paul's apostleship is valid for all peoples (cf. 1 Tim. 2:7; 2 Tim. 4:17), and Paul proclaims the gospel entrusted to him to them all (1 Tim. 1:11; 2:6–7; 2 Tim. 1:10–12; Titus 1:3). This gospel is the church's most precious treasure (cf. 1 Tim. 6:20–21; 2 Tim. 1:12, 14); it is παραθήκη (entrusted property), so it is the church's responsibility to preserve it. As its only legitimate proclaimer, Paul himself becomes part of the content of the message, so that *a soteriological dimension is attributed to his work*[178] (see above, §10.4.4). The apostle's fate becomes part of the Christian message, for in and through him God's saving purpose is paradigmatically fulfilled (cf., e.g., 1 Tim. 1:16, "But for that very reason I received mercy, so that in me, as the foremost, Jesus Christ might display the utmost patience, making me an example to those who would come to believe in him for eternal life"). Paul himself embodies the saving message, so that one can speak of a kerygmatizing of his person in the Pastorals.[179]

As the authorized preacher and content of the gospel, Paul in the Pastorals becomes the *guarantor of the tradition and its legitimate teacher.* He instructs the churches in sound teaching—described comprehensively by the terms διδασκαλία and παραθήκη—which appears in the Pastorals as proclamation of the gospel and ethical instruction for the Christian life.[180] While the heretical teachers are splitting churches by their advocacy of false doctrine, Timothy and Titus, and thus the churches addressed by the letters, hold fast to the original teaching and to the Scriptures (cf. 1 Tim. 1:3–7; 6:3–5; 2 Tim. 3:10–12, 15–16; Titus 1:10–2:15). As the prototypical believer, Paul is at the same time the example and role model for the churches (cf. 1 Tim. 1:15–16). The church is to follow the apostle in his teaching, his manner of life, in faith, and in suffering (cf. 2 Tim. 3:10–11; 1:13). Just as in the narrative world of the text Paul is the model for Timothy, so Timothy becomes the model for the churches (cf. 1 Tim. 4:12; 2 Tim. 3:10–11; Titus 2:7). Timothy and Titus are Paul's sons in the faith (cf. 1 Tim. 1:2, 18; 2 Tim. 1:2; 2:1; Titus 1:4) and represent the ideal type of postapostolic holders of ecclesiastical office. The Pauline model is thus present in the churches and in the Pastoral Epistles in the lives and ministries of the authorized bearers of church offices, though Paul's bodily presence among them will possibly be delayed (1 Tim. 3:15).

On the whole, the Pastorals present an extraordinarily powerful image of Paul, who enters the fray on behalf of his churches, fighting for them as

178. Cf. Wolter, *Pastoralbriefe*, 82; Läger, *Christologie*, 128.

179. Cf. Wolter, *Pastoralbriefe*, 52.

180. Cf. Gerhard Lohfink, "Paulinische Theologie in den Pastoralbriefen," in *Paulus in den neutestamentlichen Spätschriften: zur Paulusrezeption im Neuen Testament* (ed. Karl Kertelge; QD 89; Freiburg i.B.: Herder, 1981), 99.

preacher, teacher, pastor, and church organizer. This Paul is in equal parts apostle, ecclesiastical authority, founder of the church's identity, and ideal or model of a Christian life.[181] His exceptional status in the churches was not first promoted by the Pastor himself, who must have written in the context of a living Pauline tradition. The Pastorals attempt to resolve a problem that is faced by every Christian community, "namely, that of continuing its orientation to the normative beginnings in view of a changed historical situation, and thus facing the threat of losing its identity, a threat intensified by proposals for a new identity coming from outside the community."[182]

10.4.8 Eschatology

Eschatology is only a marginal theme in the Pastoral Epistles.[183] Christ's parousia becomes an epiphany that will occur at a time God has predetermined but not revealed (1 Tim. 6:14b–15, "keep the commandment without spot or blame until the manifestation of our Lord Jesus Christ, which he will bring about at the right time—he who is the blessed and only Sovereign, the King of kings and Lord of lords"). The primary feature of this appearance will be the judgment (2 Tim. 4:1, "In the presence of God and of Christ Jesus, who is to judge the living and the dead, and in view of his appearing and his kingdom"), a judgment to be conducted on the basis of one's works (cf. 1 Tim. 5:24–25; further, 2 Tim. 4:8; Titus 2:13).

Clearly an eschatological indeterminism prevails; the parousia of the Lord will occur "at the right time" (1 Tim. 6:15), which recedes into an undefined distance. This receding is related to the location of the author in the history of early Christian theology: on the one hand, he holds fast to the expectation of the future parousia, rejecting the slogan of the false teachers that the resurrection has already occurred (2 Tim. 2:18); on the other hand, he must accept the reality that time continues to extend itself indefinitely into the future. The author takes up both concerns, by incorporating the parousia into his theology of revelation with the comprehensive term ἐπιφάνεια (see above, §10.4.2), which intentionally permits a certain flexibility and imprecision. Moreover, he defines the truly load-bearing and enduring foundation of the church as the "sound teaching," as indicated by the interpretation of the apocalyptic motifs in 2 Tim. 4:1 by the didactic thoughts in 2 Tim. 4:2–3. Thus, ultimately, not what is undetermined but solely what endures characterizes the eschatology of the Pastorals.

181. On this point, cf. Benjamin Fiore, *The Function of Personal Example in the Socratic and Pastoral Epistles* (AnBib 105; Rome: Biblical Institute Press, 1986).

182. Cf. Wolter, *Pastoralbriefe*, 270.

183. Cf. Roloff, *Timotheus*, 213.

10.4.9 Setting in the History of Early Christian Theology

In modern discussions of the history of early Christian theology, the Pastoral Epistles have mostly been interpreted within the framework of a decadence theory of church history: Paul stands at the beginning, then follow Colossians and Ephesians (and 2 Thessalonians), until finally the Pastoral Epistles completely dissolve Pauline theology into contemporary morals and bourgeois social standards.[184] In several respects, this perspective represents an abridgement of the Pastorals' historical and theological achievement:

1. The Pastorals develop a comprehensive concept of education (cf. 1 Tim. 1:20; 2 Tim. 2:25; 3:16; Titus 2:12), which is at the same time a concept of human nature. At its center stands the love of God for humanity (cf. 1 Tim. 2:4; Titus 3:4, 11), which applies to all human beings and is for the help and healing of all. The goal of God's work is a tranquil life in righteousness and piety (2 Tim. 3:16; Titus 2:4).
2. Closely bound up with this concept is a sustained integration of Hellenistic virtues into the Pastorals' ethics. The Pastorals thereby not only achieve the historically indispensable opening for the integration of pagan ethics but also proclaim the self-evident integration of the human sciences and refinements of civilization into the new movement, thus making a universal claim: God's manifestation in Jesus Christ is also the revelation of what is truly human! And finally, the concept of Christian virtues is very attractive from the point of view of ethics.
3. The Pastorals' often-criticized doctrine of ecclesiastical office deserves a new interpretation. The office of bishop, in the process of formation in the Pastorals, is an essential instrument of a historically necessary and theologically legitimate securing of the community's identity. Every theory of organization recommends a changing and tightening of the organization whenever growth and the given circumstances, internal or external, make this necessary.
4. So also the tradition principle that prevails in the Pastorals appears in a different light when seen from the perspective of theories of identity

184. Thus Martin Dibelius speaks of an "Ideal of Good Christian Citizenship," Dibelius and Conzelmann, *Pastoral Epistles*, 39. Cf. further Siegfried Schulz, *Die Mitte der Schrift: Der Frühkatholizismus im Neuen Testament als Herausforderung an den Protestantismus* (Stuttgart: Kreuz-Verlag, 1976), 109: "And finally, if one looks at the history of the effects of this thesis of an early catholic understanding of ecclesiastical office, apostolic succession, tradition, and the ideal of Christian brotherliness, like that of the nature of a pious life . . . then one will not attempt to reproduce this early catholic development, and that precisely for Paul's sake. Rather, one must move backward [toward Paul himself]." But even Roloff, *Timotheus*, 380, also finds that the Pastorals have shortchanged Paul's doctrine of justification on essential points: "They no longer grasp the way in which Paul's doctrine of justification is suspended between the poles of sin, law and the works of the law on the one side, and Christ, grace, and faith on the other."

> and meaning. The creation and determination of tradition and traditions are fundamental factors of meaning-formation and stabilization; they obviate an overly hasty abandonment of previous convictions and ways of life. Learning by practice and repetition were and are the basic elements of every successful procedure for education and growth.

The Pastoral Epistles are to be taken seriously in their concern to stabilize Christianity in the predominantly urban churches of Asia Minor, in view of the strong internal (and probably also external) threats these churches were facing. They represent an important step toward the church structured in terms of official ministries and toward the formation of the biblical canon.

11

The Catholic Epistles

Voices in Dangerous Times

11.1 First Peter: Testing by Suffering

The First Letter of Peter occupies a special position within the New Testament, because it is the first witness to the fundamental conflict between emerging Christianity's christological monotheism and sacrally grounded ancient Roman society.[1] The letter deals with a theological theme of its time that will also become central for the Christianity of the twenty-first century: being a Christian minority in an increasingly hostile world.

11.1.1 Theology

The prescript (1 Pet. 1:1–2) functions as a hermeneutical basis for the whole letter, and clearly reveals its theological foundation (θεός, thirty-nine times) by addressing its readership as "chosen exiles." The designation of their status as resident aliens has both a sociological and theological meaning:[2] it describes

1. First Peter was probably written ca. 90 CE in Asia Minor; cf. Schnelle, *New Testament Writings*, 398–415.

2. Cf. Reinhard Feldmeier, *Die Christen als Fremde* (WUNT 64; Tübingen: Mohr, 1992), 124, who argues that the social rejection, and the resulting political rejection, have the same cause: "It is based on the exclusive religious fixation of the Christians which generates its own social and ethical reference system. This in turn places the Christian worldview in competition with the religious, social, and political views they had previously shared with society at large."

the social situation of the Christian community as outsiders, a foreign body within the social structure; at the same time their status as exiles corresponds theologically to their election by God, and thus has positive content. Because believers have been constituted by a divine act of new creation, they have been delivered from the vanity of their former lives; they have a new origin and are therefore "foreigners" in the world. Christian existence is lived out between divine election and social ostracism. Each dimension conditions the other, for the Christian community's conflicts with the surrounding world result from the act of God that separates them from the world and makes them into the people of God. The predicates "imperishable, undefiled, and unfading" in 1 Pet. 1:4 reflect the contemporary (Middle Platonic) mode of describing the deity through negation as totally other and independent of this world and human existence, localizing God and the divine inheritance in "heaven." Election is grounded in the "foreknowledge of God the Father" (1 Pet. 1:2), whose saving will is made known and effective in the resurrection of Jesus Christ from the dead, and who now continues to exercise that will in the divinely determined existence of the elected community, the church.[3]

This same theological thread continues with a liturgical blessing:[4] "Blessed be the God and Father of our Lord Jesus Christ! By his great mercy he has given us a new birth into a living hope through the resurrection of Jesus Christ from the dead" (1 Pet. 1:3). These opening words function to guide the recipients' attention back to God and the salvation he has inaugurated. God has changed their lives from the ground up, for they have been newly created and now live in the true hope. The present distress is made understandable by the assurance of God's saving act; thus the praise of God, God's reassuring promise of salvation, the readiness to suffer, and the knowledge of the real circumstances in which they live are all intertwined. The metaphor of rebirth (see below, §11.1.4) that is predominant in 1:3–2:3 has primarily a theological dimension: it designates the new, eschatological existence of Christians, who, now as transformed persons, do the will of God in a hostile environment (cf. 1 Pet. 2:12, 15, 16, 17; 4:2) and are thus categorically different from the surrounding world, so that suffering is an unavoidable and necessary consequence of their faith (cf. 2:19–20; 3:17; 4:14, 16, 17, 19). Just as God chose Jesus (2:4), destined him for undeserved suffering (2:21–25) and raised him from the dead (1:3, 21), so also believers have been chosen to be members of the elect people of God (2:9; 5:2) and may know that they have been granted to suffer—precisely this!—by the grace of God (4:10–11; 5:5–6, 10, 12). Jesus's own suffering and death were "in order to bring you to God" (3:18b).

3. The question of God's foreknowledge/predestination and omnipotence was also vigorously discussed in ancient philosophy; for arguments in defense of divine providence, see the writings of Seneca, *De providentia*, and Plutarch, *De sera numinis vindicta* (on the delay of divine punishment).

4. Cf. here Deichgräber, *Gotteshymnus*, 77–78.

Election by God for suffering is the central theological theme of 1 Peter. Although Christians are called to live a righteous life within the framework of their given social institutions, because of their relation to God they must suffer as strangers and aliens in the world. In God's eyes, this suffering is grace, in a different category from suffering caused by the sins one has committed (2:19–20; 3:14).

11.1.2 Christology

The basis and point of departure for 1 Peter's Christology is the resurrection of Jesus Christ from the dead (1 Pet. 1:3, 21). In the resurrection of Jesus Christ, God overcame sin and death and made possible the existence in which believers now live. As in Rom. 1:3–4, so also according to 1 Pet. 3:18 the resurrection takes place through the power of the Spirit of God: "For Christ also suffered for sins once for all, the righteous for the unrighteous, in order to bring you to God. He was put to death in the flesh, but made alive in the Spirit." Thus Jesus Christ was delivered over to death because he participated in the "flesh," but this was overcome because of his participation in the Spirit of God.

Related to the imagery of resurrection is an exceptional piece of tradition reflected in 1 Pet. 3:19–21 and 4:6: *Jesus's preaching to the spirits in prison* and his *preaching the gospel to the dead*, which 1 Pet. 3:22 combines as Christ's "descent into Hades" and his ascension (cf. Eph. 4:9–10). The *descent* to the spirits in prison makes clear that even the realms of guilt, death, and the past are not excluded from Christ's domain. The πνεύματα (spirits) in 1 Pet. 3:19 are probably not fallen angels[5] but "the souls of Noah's unrepentant contemporaries."[6] In the New Testament, κηρύσσω (proclaim, preach) consistently refers to the proclamation of salvation, πνεύματα occurs often as a designation for post-mortal existence,[7] and 1 Pet. 4:6 explicitly refers to proclaiming the gospel to the dead. The author of 1 Peter underscores the universality of the message of salvation, beginning with the appropriation of salvation in baptism and extending by way of the water motif to the unrepentant sinners of Noah's time.

5. For a comprehensive analysis, cf. Angelika Reichert, *Eine urchristliche praeparatio ad martyrium: Studien zur Komposition, Traditionsgeschichte und Theologie des 1. Petrusbriefes* (BET 22; Frankfurt a.M.: Lang, 1989), 213–47; cf. further Friedrich Spitta, *Christi Predigt an die Geister (1 Petr. 3,19 ff.): Ein Beitrag zur Neutestamentlichen Theologie* (Göttingen: Vandenhoeck & Ruprecht, 1890); Heinz-Jürgen Vogels, *Christi Abstieg ins Totenreich und das Läuterungsgericht an den Toten: Eine bibeltheologisch-dogmatische Untersuchung zum Glaubensartikel "descendit ad inferos"* (FTS 102; Freiburg: Herder, 1976).

6. Leonhard Goppelt, *A Commentary on 1 Peter* (trans. John E. Alsup; Grand Rapids: Eerdmans, 1993), 258; on the anthropological interpretation, cf. also Vogels, *Christi Abstieg*, 86; Reichert, *Praeparatio*, 247.

7. Cf. Heb. 12:23; for Jewish and pagan examples, see Reichert, *Praeparatio*, 239–43.

The *exaltation* of Jesus leads to his enthronement at the right hand of God, to total participation in divine power and rulership, as seen in the subjugation of all powers and forces of the universe under Christ. The motif of exaltation to the right hand of God has its closest parallel in Eph. 1:20 (cf. further Phil. 2:9–11; Matt. 28:18; John 3:14; 12:32ff.; Luke 24:49–51; Acts 1:8ff.) and its ultimate background in Ps. 110:1. Although located in opposite spatial realms, the descent to Hades and ascent to heaven are constitutive elements of one grand procession as Jesus moves from this world to the world of God. Jesus's installation as Lord of the universe outshines his suffering and death in this world.

The metaphorical language of Christ as the "living stone" (1 Pet. 2:4) is related to these motifs of Jesus's suffering and exaltation. Taking up the imagery of Isa. 28:16 and Ps. 118:22, the rejected Jesus Christ is portrayed as the cornerstone (1 Pet. 2:4–8) that supports the church and holds it together.[8] The church can see its own situation reflected in the predestined course of Jesus's life: they are purchased by the blood of Christ (cf. 1:19; 2:21–24; 3:18–22), the sinless one (2:22), who on the cross took upon himself the sins of humanity and overcame them (2:24). He thereby became the abiding model of suffering (2:21–24; 4:1, 13) in terms of which the church is to understand its situation and orient its own life. God took Jesus through his sufferings into God's own glory, and God promises to the suffering community of faith that they also will participate in the divine glory. This assurance leads to the insight that, before time began, God had already determined that at the end of time he would pour out the blood of Jesus Christ for the salvation of the church (1:19–21). The concept of *preexistence* is found not only in 1 Pet. 1:20 but also in 1:10–11, which speaks of the Spirit of Christ that was already at work in the Old Testament prophets.

The central christological-soteriological themes of the representative suffering, death, and resurrection of Jesus Christ are developed in the liturgical language of 1 Pet. 1:18–21; 2:21–25; and 3:18–22, texts that literary analysis and form-criticism have delineated and categorized in a variety of ways. The section 1:18–21 is a stylistic unity (vv. 18, 19, 21 are elevated prose, v. 20 rhythmic parallelism), but numerous indications suggest that the constituent elements of this text are from earlier tradition (v. 18: reference to Isa. 52:3; v. 19: Christ as the Passover lamb [cf. 1 Cor. 5:7; John 1:29; 19:36]; v. 20: the once-now schema [cf. Rom. 16:25–26; Col. 1:26; Eph. 3:5, 9; 2 Tim. 1:9–10]; v. 21: resurrection formula [cf. 2 Cor. 4:14; Gal. 1:1; Rom. 8:11]). A self-contained fragment of tradition is found in 1 Pet. 2:21–25.[9] Verse 21b is distinguished from the tradition both formally (participial style only here) and by its content. In the tradition used by 1 Peter, four relative clauses follow, three of which

8. For analysis, cf. Goppelt, *1 Peter*, 138–39; J. Herzer, *Petrus oder Paulus* (WUNT 103; Tübingen: Mohr, 1998), 143–57.

9. In addition to the standard commentaries, cf. here Deichgräber, *Gotteshymnus*, 140–43; Wengst, *Christologische Formeln*, 83–85.

begin with ὅς and one with οὗ (both are forms of the Greek relative pronoun "who"). Verse 25 is a pictorial interpretation of the text in prosaic style and probably derives from the author of the letter. Not only vv. 21b and 25, but also 23c[10] and 24b[11] are possibly insertions by the author. The reconstructed source is structured clearly. In terms of tradition history it is oriented to Isa. 53 LXX, and form-critically it can be designated a Christ-hymn. The purely soteriological statements of the source are interpreted parenetically by the author of the letter, in line with his thinking of Jesus as an example for Christians to follow. In 1 Pet. 3:18–22 we again have a reworking of traditional material, but it is not possible to reconstruct a coherent source.[12]

The Christology of 1 Peter, taken as a whole, very strongly emphasizes the soteriological and ethical dimensions of the Christ event,[13] so that it becomes the prototype and model of the Christian life (1 Pet. 2:21). The church is to pattern its own life after Jesus Christ's innocent suffering in fulfillment of God's will. In this way it can demonstrate its own participation in God's glory.

11.1.3 Pneumatology

The pneumatology of 1 Peter begins with the Spirit of God, who as the "Spirit of Christ" was already at work among the Old Testament prophets (1 Pet. 1:10–11). That Spirit raised Jesus Christ from the dead (3:18) and now rests on the church: "If you are reviled for the name of Christ, you are blessed, because the spirit of glory, which is the Spirit of God, is resting on you" (4:14). The Spirit of God thus shows itself to be the power that supports and preserves the church in its present troubles. The pneumatological aspects of Christ's preaching to the dead (3:19–20; 4:6) are unique in the New Testament. The plural πνεύματα in 3:19 probably refers to the souls of the dead who, when they accept the preaching of the gospel, are given life through the Spirit of God. This idea is taken up again in 4:6, "For this is the reason the gospel was proclaimed even to the dead, so that, though they had been judged in the flesh as everyone is judged, they might live in the spirit as God does." Just as Christ was made alive through the Spirit (3:18), so those who have already died can be brought into the realm where God's life-giving Spirit is effective. As the sufferings of Christ were proclaimed by the Old Testament prophets through the Spirit, so now the church, "sanctified by the Spirit to be obedient to Jesus Christ and to God" (1:2) can bear up under the sufferings of the present, as the counterpart to Jesus's own life and death.

10. Cf. Rudolf Bultmann, "Bekenntnis- und Liedfragmente im ersten Petrusbrief," in *Exegetica: Aufsätze zur Erforschung des Neuen Testaments* (ed. Erich Dinkler; Tübingen: Mohr, 1967), 296.

11. So Deichgräber, *Gotteshymnus*, 141.

12. Cf. Goppelt, *1 Peter*, 247–74.

13. Cf. de Jonge, *Christology*, 133–36.

11.1.4 Soteriology

Jesus's *representative suffering for others,* his death and resurrection, constitute the basis of 1 Peter's soteriology (1 Pet. 2:21, "Christ also suffered for you"; 3:18a, "Christ also suffered for [the forgiveness of] sins once for all"). God raised Jesus from the dead (1:21), so that the Sinless (2:22) and Righteous (3:18b) One could provide a new access to God (3:18c; cf. Rom. 5:1ff.). Believers have not been redeemed from their previous futile way of life by perishable things (1 Pet. 1:18–19) "but with the precious blood of Christ, like that of a lamb without defect or blemish." The ransom terminology (λυτρόω) and the imagery of the Passover lamb point to Isa. 52:3 LXX and comprehensively express the representative self-giving service of Jesus Christ for others.[14] The fundamental saving event is concisely formulated in 1 Pet. 2:24: "He himself bore our sins in his body on the cross, so that, free from sins, we might live for righteousness; by his wounds you have been healed."

The Hellenistic concept of rebirth/new birth as an overcoming of the fleeting, vain, and death-bound character of human life provides a central motif of 1 Peter's soteriology.[15] The verb ἀναγεννάω (cause to be born again) is lacking in the LXX and appears in the New Testament only in 1 Pet. 1:3, 23; it thus designates in a particular way the soteriological conceptuality of 1 Peter. This new begetting by the Spirit and the word gives the church access to participation in the fullness of the divine life: "You have been born anew, not of perishable but of imperishable seed, through the living and enduring word of God" (1:23). "Imperishability" in the linguistic usage of the pagan world is predicated only of God. In Epicurus[16] or Plutarch,[17] for example, imperishability differentiates the true being of God from the perishable being of humans. The attributes "undefiled" and "unfading" in 1 Pet. 1:4 point in this same direction: through the divine rebirth the elect are granted participation in the indestructible, imperishable power of the divine life. Rebirth is an event that occurs by God's mercy (1:3); it is grounded solely in God's own

14. For analysis, cf. Herzer, *Petrus oder Paulus*, 70–134.

15. On this point cf. Reinhard Feldmeier, *The First Letter of Peter: A Commentary on the Greek Text* (Waco: Baylor University Press, 2008), 127–30.

16. Cf. Cicero, *Nat. d.* 1.51, who presents Epicurus as teaching, "God is entirely inactive and free from all ties of occupation; he toils not neither does he labor, but he takes delight in his own wisdom and virtue, and knows with absolute certainty that he will always enjoy the pleasures at once consummate and everlasting." *Nat. d.* 1.45, "that which is blessed and eternal can neither know trouble itself nor cause trouble to another, and accordingly cannot feel either anger or favor, since all such things belong only to the weak . . . (since it is understood that anger and favor alike are excluded from the nature of a being at once blessed and immortal)."

17. As a leading advocate of a negative theology Plutarch describes the divine primarily in contrast to other realities, so that the divine reality is totally separate from perishability, and states: "Therefore it is characteristic of the imperishable and pure to be one and uncombined" (*E Delph.* 20).

essential being, the God who on his own initiative freely turns toward human beings and chooses the believers as his own people (2:9). Because God's word works as divine seed and is constantly generating a new relationship to God and granting a new life (cf. 1:23), the new birth is always a new beginning. Within the framework of the prevailing imagery of family and household, members of the church are addressed as "newborn children" who have tasted the goodness of God (2:2–3). In 1 Peter, the concept of rebirth or new birth is explicitly connected with *baptism*: "And baptism, which this [the waters of the flood] prefigured, now saves you—not as a removal of dirt from the body, but as an appeal to God for a good conscience" (3:21). Baptism is much more than an external washing; it is an internal cleansing of the person, an event that touches his or her innermost being and is fulfilled in the doing of good (2:20), in a good life (3:16) as the testimony of a good conscience. Rebirth/new birth are not simply identified with baptism as though they were totally congruent, but they are nonetheless inseparable.[18] Rebirth/new birth denotes the fundamental transformation that is the Christian life, which must become visible in the ritual of baptism.[19] The ritual location of rebirth is baptism.

The whole of 1 Peter's soteriology can be covered in two words: δι' ὑμᾶς (for your sake). The revolutionary turn from the old age to the new occurs in redemption through the blood of the lamb; God had already determined this course before time began, and it is for the sake of believers (1:20, "He was destined before the foundation of the world, but was revealed at the end of the ages *for your sake*"). The universality of this event is explicitly emphasized in 1 Pet. 4:6 by the proclamation to and for the dead, for whom provision has been made, just as for present and future generations, for the possibility of saving faith (1:5, 9).

11.1.5 Anthropology

The anthropology of 1 Peter is embedded in the thought world of the letter as a whole: the believer shares completely in God's saving work in Jesus Christ but is not thereby excluded from the troubles and attacks on one's faith that belong to life in this world. *Faith* is a saving event (1 Pet. 1:5a, "protected by the power of God through faith for a salvation ready to be revealed in the last time") but at the same time must demonstrate its reality in suffering (1:7a, "so that the genuineness of your faith . . . may be found to result in praise and glory and honor when Jesus Christ is revealed"). Faith is thus more than merely considering something to be true; it is the orientation of one's whole life to

18. Herzer, *Petrus oder Paulus*, 215–26, and Feldmeier, *Peter*, 127–28, differentiate too strongly between word/faith on the one side and baptism on the other, for the new reality takes concrete form in the ritual.

19. On baptism in 1 Peter, cf. especially F. Schröger, *Gemeinde im 1. Petrusbrief* (Passau: Passavia, 1981), 31–54.

God (1:21). Through faith, God's power can become effective in people, so that they can withstand being put to the test and endure inevitable suffering. These tests primarily take the form of hostility from the surrounding world and present the opportunity for faith to demonstrate its authenticity. In 1 Peter, faith is thus faith-under-attack (cf. 1:6; 4:12), faith that remains steadfast in trouble and consequently receives salvation.

This salvation is for the *soul*; no other New Testament document develops a comparably differentiated doctrine of the soul along the lines of Hellenistic tradition. Soteriology and anthropology are linked in 1 Pet. 1:9, where believers receive "the outcome of your faith, the salvation of your souls" (τὸ τέλος τῆς πίστεως [ὑμῶν] σωτηρίαν ψυχῶν). This expression, which occurs here for the first time in ancient literature, documents the great importance the concept of the soul has in 1 Peter. The ψυχή (soul) appears as the recipient of the divine saving action (1:9; 2:25, "You were going astray like sheep, but now you have returned to the shepherd and guardian of your souls"; 4:19, "Therefore, let those suffering in accordance with God's will entrust themselves [τὰς ψυχὰς αὐτῶν, 'their souls'] to a faithful Creator"). The soul purifies itself by obedience to the truth (1:22) and preserves itself in the struggle with "the desires of the flesh that wage war against the soul" (2:11). The beginnings of a dualistic anthropology are undeniable, for with the term ψυχή 1 Peter designates *the human self*, while "flesh" (σάρξ) belongs to the sphere of the perishable (1:24), of suffering (4:1) and death (3:18; 4:6). We see here a Hellenistic anthropology that, while it does not really think in dichotomous or trichotomous categories, still adopts a Hellenistic conceptuality that understands ψυχή as the human self in contrast to God and thus adopts something of the anthropological value system of the readers.[20] With this point of contact, there developed within early Christianity a doctrine of the soul with an integrative capacity in regard to ancient anthropological ideas.

The statements of 1 Peter about *sin* are also related to the themes of suffering, testing, and temptation (1 Pet. 4:1, "Whoever has suffered in the flesh has finished with sin"). While here ἁμαρτία (sin) appears in the singular and has a certain proximity to the Pauline understanding of sin, the references to "sins" in 2:20, 24; 3:18; 4:8 refer to concrete acts. The internal logic of 1 Peter's doctrine of sin is also seen in 2:22, 24: Christ committed no sinful act, and bore our sins on the cross, so that by his suffering we die to sin and live in righteousness (cf. 1 Pet. 3:18; Rom. 6:8, 11, 18).

In good Hellenistic tradition, *conscience* appears in 1 Pet. 2:19 and 3:16 as the internal court of self-evaluation; as a Christian conscience, it knows that the suffering of injustice is part and parcel of the Christian life (2:19; 3:16). The purification that takes place in baptism and rebirth does not affect the external surface of human life, but its innermost layers: the conscience (3:21). Thus the "inner self" is precious in God's sight (3:4).

20. On this point cf. Feldmeier, *Peter*, 87–92.

11.1.6 Ethics

The conception of ethics in 1 Peter can be grasped only when seen in the context of the sociopolitical situation of the churches to which the letter is addressed.[21] The crucial factor in understanding this situation is the interpretation of the *conflict situation* presupposed by 1 Peter's *suffering parenesis*. The linguistic data already signal the importance of this theme: of forty-two instances of πάσχω (suffer) in the New Testament, twelve are found in 1 Peter. The suffering of Christians in Asia Minor includes both local repressions as well as the more comprehensive actions against Christians that were already beginning. In 2:21–25; 3:18; 4:1, the sufferings of Christians are linked to the sufferings of Christ: the readiness of Christians to suffer for the faith is stamped by the *exemplary character* of Christ's own sufferings. Suffering appears in 1 Peter as a constituent element of Christian existence (2:21), the natural consequence of the believer's life in this world as a foreigner[22] (cf. 1:6–7; 5:10). Texts such as 2:19–20, 23; 3:14, 17; 4:15, 19 indicate the recipients of the letter live in the reality of *social discrimination*. Christians give public testimony to their faith, their ethos setting them apart from their social context (cf. 2:11–18; 3:1–4, 7, 15–16), and thereby evoke unjust sanctions. Some passages in 1 Peter, however, cannot be adequately explained in terms of social tensions. According to 4:15–16, Christians are condemned before the courts solely because they are Christians (ὡς Χριστιανός), along with murderers, thieves, and other criminals. Christians are subjected to a fiery ordeal that has broken in to their lives (cf. 4:12), and they are called to withstand the devil who ranges through the whole world subjecting all Christians to the same trial of suffering (5:8–9). Here, suffering has a different perspective and quality, for it is more than a matter of local harassments.[23] This points to the late period of Domitian's reign, who increasingly promoted the emperor cult in Asia Minor and the Greek provinces.[24] It was not a matter of direct measures taken by the Roman state

21. On the ethic of 1 Peter, see Schrage, *Ethics*, 268–78 and F. R. Prostmeier, *Handlungsmodelle im ersten Petrusbrief* (FzB 63; Stuttgart: Verlag Katholisches Bibelwerk, 1990), passim.

22. Cf. Feldmeier, *Christen als Fremde*, 192: "Christians are encouraged to live a model life precisely as foreigners."

23. Cf. Reichert, *Praeparatio*, 74–75; contra Norbert Brox, *Der Erste Petrusbrief* (EKKNT 21; Zürich: Benziger, 1979), 30: "The letter can be adequately explained from this 'everyday situation' of the early church."

24. In two central points, 1 Peter has parallels to the questions dealt with in the exchange of letters between Pliny the Younger (ca. 111–13 CE the imperial legate of Bithynia and Pontus) and the Emperor Trajan (98–117 CE): (1) Christians were persecuted solely on the basis that they belonged to the Christian group (nomen ipsum; cf. 1 Pet. 4:6; Pliny, *Ep.* 10.96.2); (2) The state did not actively search out Christians (Pliny, *Ep.* 10.96.2) who were apparently arrested on the basis of charges brought against them anonymously (*Ep.* 10.96.2, 5–6). This fits in with the whole situation of defamation and abuse to which the churches of 1 Peter were subject (e.g., 1 Pet. 2:12; 3:14; 4:4c, 12f, 16). Pliny's inquiry to the emperor already presupposes a legal procedure

that led to discrimination against Christians and actual persecution, but a revitalization of the emperor cult through local courts and the associated actions. Such actions are already hinted at in Acts, and later documented in Tacitus, *Ann.* 15.44, and Pliny, *Ep.* 10.96, based on objections against the new Christian movement that included cultural and social exclusiveness, hatred of the human race, opposition to the state, godlessness, superstition, cultic immorality, and damage to the economy.

The *newness of Christian existence* attains visible form when actions based on faith contrasts with the normal life of the world. Christians live lives of holiness (1 Pet. 1:14–15; 2:1–2) and brotherly love (1:22). They keep themselves apart from fleshly lusts (2:11–12), avoid the vices of the world in which they live (4:3), and lead a life devoted to righteousness and justice (4:1–2). Because a new being calls for a new way of living that corresponds to the new reality, believers are exposed to the insults and abuses of their environment (cf. 3:17). The fact that Christians live in a different way alienates the Gentiles (4:4) and evokes aggressive action. The *instructions on social ethics* in 1 Peter are directed to this context, and aim at an integration of the congregations into their social context while preserving their new identity. Especially the *catalog of socioethical duties* (2:13–17, 18, 25; 3:1–6, 7) shows that 1 Peter presupposes the realities of its social situation, while at the same time intending to implement within the churches the new Christian ethos of love and humility within the existing power structures. The exhortations and admonitions in 2:13–3:7 stand in the tradition of ancient and early Christian household codes and codes of social status.[25] In contrast to the typical characteristics of the early Christian *Haustafel* schema (see above, §10.1.6), 1 Peter has some distinguishing features:[26]

1. Instructions for Christian conduct toward the state are new.
2. The situation of the non-Christian household (οἶκος) is included.
3. The polarity of mutual instructions is omitted, with one exception (husbands-wives).
4. In the instructions to the individual groups of the household, the participial form substitutes for the imperative.

---

against Christians (partly arbitrary and thus in need of reform), and explicitly emphasizes that twenty years before—during the time of Domitian—some Christians had renounced their faith under duress (*Ep.* 96.6). In addition, there is evidence of the persecution of Christians during Domitian's last years in *1 Clem.* 1.1; Rev. 2:12–13; 13:11–18 (see below, §13.1).

25. For a recent comprehensive analysis, cf. Prostmeier, *Handlungsmodelle*, 141–448.

26. Designating 1 Pet. 2:13–3:7 as a *Haustafel,* "household code" or a "code of social status" does not do justice to the distinctive structure of this text, for not only are people of differing social status addressed (cf. 1 Pet. 2:13–17), and within the schema of the household code there are no instructions to masters, fathers, or children. It thus appears to be more appropriate to speak of a "catalog of socioethical duties"; Strecker, *New Testament Literature*, 81, speaks of 1 Peter's "socioethical teaching."

Two aspects are indispensable for interpreting this catalog of duties:

1. The fundamental orientation of the Christian ethic to respond to each other in love and humility, characterized by the verb ἀγαθοποιέω (to do good) in 1 Pet. 2:15, 20; 3:6, also determines the instruction about socioethical duties (cf. 1:22; 2:17; 3:8–9; 4:8ff.; 5:5–6). The inclusio in 2:12 and 3:11 underscores this comprehensive perspective. By including renunciation of revenge (2:23; 3:9) and suffering discipleship (2:21) as concrete expressions of this way of life, the importance of nonverbal testimony to unbelievers becomes clear (2:12; 3:1–2). By enduring unjust suffering, believers show their relationship to Christ. This becomes especially evident in the parenesis to slaves in 1 Pet. 2; subordination has as its goal the overcoming of evil by good.
2. Addressing Christians as "aliens" and "exiles/guests" (1 Pet. 2:11) places the whole of the Christian's everyday life under this sign. The position of Christians within social institutions cannot be understood apart from this redefinition of Christian existence. The church is challenged to orient its life to the way and example of its Lord, who is also their ethical example:[27] "For to this you have been called, because Christ also suffered for you, leaving you an example, so that you should follow in his steps" (2:21). Precisely what this does not mean is withdrawal from the institutions of society, but Christians, by their way of life and their good works, silence the charges made by their society (2:12, 15).

11.1.7 Ecclesiology

First Peter's ecclesiological conception is embedded in its theological construct as a whole.[28] The prescript of 1 Pet. 1:1 already serves a basic hermeneutical function, for by addressing the churches as "chosen exiles of the Diaspora" the author makes clear at the beginning his understanding of Christian existence and Christian community in the church: the world is not the Christian's homeland, and they can find no rest and security in it.[29] Christians live as a scattered people in a foreign land, even if they remain in the locale where they

27. According to Prostmeier, *Handlungsmodelle*, 480, the distinctive compositional procedure of the author of 1 Peter consists in his "characteristic combination of secular structures and secular competence with the Christian model in the form of 'table-like' exhortations and admonitions." The practical purpose of these admonitions is to prepare believers to witness for the Christian faith in their everyday life in the world. "The Christ-paradigm is both the condition for putting into practice the ethical possibilities that are simply given in the structures of the world, and the binding norm by which such possibilities are to be measured" (p. 512).

28. Cf. here Roloff, *Kirche im Neuen Testament*, 268–77; Herzer, *Petrus oder Paulus*, 158–95.

29. Cf. Schröger, *Gemeinde*, 234: "The church is represented as a people who are strangers in the world, but at home in heaven."

were born and raised. As people who have experienced a new birth in baptism, they live in the world but distanced from the world. This self-understanding is expressed ecclesiologically primarily by the concept of the people of God and by the household imagery.

By utilizing the *household imagery*, the author of 1 Peter takes up an important motif of New Testament ecclesiology, already found, for example, in 1 Cor. 3:9–11. The image of the household is introduced in 1 Pet. 2:5 in a characteristic way: "Like living stones, let yourselves be built into a spiritual house, to be a holy priesthood, to offer spiritual sacrifices acceptable to God through Jesus Christ." The church does not found itself, as though it were a religious association or club, but the imperative passive (οἰκοδομεῖσθε [let yourselves be built]) indicates that the church is constituted by the work of God through the Holy Spirit. The statement is grounded in 1 Pet. 2:6–8 by a combination of biblical quotations (Isa. 28:16; Ps. 118:22; Isa. 8:14) also found elsewhere in the New Testament.[30] As "household," the church appears as a special realm created and sanctified by God, in which believers, as a community of priests, live according to the will of God and offer up "spiritual sacrifices." The Lutheran concept of the general priesthood of all believers finds here one of its central exegetical supports. Directly related to the household imagery is the socioethical catalog of duties already discussed in §11.1.6.

The *concept of the people of God* is incorporated in 1 Pet. 2:9, "But you are a chosen race, a royal priesthood, a holy nation, God's own people, in order that you may proclaim the mighty acts of him who called you out of darkness into his marvelous light." In the background stand the honorary titles of Israel, here transferred to the Christian community (cf. Exod. 19:6; Isa. 43:20–21). To be sure, no reflection on salvation history is here included, for neither the promise to Abraham, the Israel thematic, nor the law (νόμος is entirely missing!) plays a role for these predominantly Gentile churches (cf. 1 Pet. 1:14, 18; 2:25; 4:3).[31] The theme is the relation of the church to the Gentile world, which in 1 Pet. 2:10, taking up Hos. 1:6, 9–10; 2:1, 25, is stated radically: "Once you were not a people, but now you are God's people; once you had not received mercy, but now you have received mercy." It is God's election alone that grounds the believers' new status, who now as aliens in the world find their new community and homeland in the church.

First Peter is the only non-Pauline writing that refers to a charismatic order (1 Pet. 4:7–11) in which important functions are not only service and the ministry of the word (4:10, 11), but also hospitality (4:9) and steadfast love (4:8). As in the Acts and the Pastoral Epistles, a presbyterial structure is pre-

30. Cf. Roloff, *Kirche im Neuen Testament*, 272–73.

31. Cf. ibid., 275, who points out that in 1 Pet. 3:6 Sarah and Abraham come into view only as ethical examples.

supposed (5:1–4). The primary responsibility of the presbyter is to shepherd the flock of God, i.e., here too church structure is developing in the direction of the episcopal office.[32] The direction of the local churches evidently lay in the hands of the presbyters, who were also understood to embody the charismatic gifts.[33]

11.1.8 Eschatology

The central eschatological theme of 1 Peter is *hope in suffering*. This hope is grounded in the resurrection of Jesus, through which Christians have received "a new birth into a living hope through the resurrection of Jesus Christ from the dead" (1 Pet. 1:3; cf. 1:13, 21). The resurrection of Jesus Christ from the dead delivered believers from the vanity and perishability of human existence; Jesus has ransomed them by his suffering and death (1:18–19), has healed and saved them (2:24; 4:18). This well-grounded hope appears as the very life principle of the person thus renewed, so that the church owes the world of nonbelievers information about its present hope (3:15, ἐν ὑμῖν ἐλπίς). Because the imperishable inheritance is already preserved in heaven (1:4), believers are able to endure their oppressive experience of suffering through this joyful hope. They accept responsibility for their obligations in family and society, set new standards within the church, and at the same time know that their true homeland is not in this world and live for the day when Jesus Christ will come again (cf. the eschatological motifs in the imagery of reward and punishment, 1:17; 3:7, 9–12; 4:5, 17; 5:1, 4).

Suffering appears not only as the consequence of their new Christian way of life within society, but is a constitutive element of Christian existence as such. Suffering occurs as a test of faith (1 Pet. 1:6; 4:12); whoever now suffers unjustly anticipates the future *judgment* of God. The disobedience to the gospel of God must shortly meet God in the judgment (1:11; 4:13; 5:1). Believers must wait in hope only a short time for eschatological salvation (cf. 1:5, 9, 10; 2:2), which will free them from the troubles of the present.[34] This joyful hope for the *parousia* (4:7, 17–18; 5:6) determines the present life of believers. Placed in the time between Easter and the parousia, they are not removed from the world and its troubles, but are equipped to overcome them.

Eschatology is fundamentally important for the theology of 1 Peter, for it interprets the present in the light of God's future, which has already broken in as *joy in suffering*.

32. Cf. ibid., 277.

33. Cf. on this point Schröger, *Gemeinde*, 110–24.

34. Eduard Schweizer, "Zur Christologie des ersten Petrusbriefes," in *Anfänge der Christologie: Festschrift für Ferdinand Hahn zum 65. Geburtstag* (ed. Cilliers Breytenbach et al.; Göttingen: Vandenhoeck & Ruprecht, 1991), 372, speaks of the eschatological hope in 1 Peter as a "stern weight [that keeps the vessel on course] toward the future."

11.1.9 Setting in the History of Early Christian Theology

The importance of 1 Peter for the history of early Christian theology is located in *the theological permeation of the individual and social dimensions of life by the theme of suffering*. The author wants to exhort, admonish, and strengthen the harassed Christians of Asia Minor (cf. 1 Pet. 5:12b). He has developed a twofold strategy for stabilizing their new Christian identity and assuring the survival of the churches in the hostile environment of Asia Minor.

1. The first place and most basic strategy is to utilize early Christian authorities to assure the churches of their legitimacy,[35] for 1 Peter places itself explicitly in the Petrine tradition and implicitly in the Pauline tradition. Both apostles are already models for the steadfast endurance of faith through suffering and death, and both had done missionary work in Asia Minor. The author chooses the pseudonym "Peter" because according to Acts 10 Peter was the founder of the Gentile mission, and because he was honored as one of the first martyrs in early Christianity.[36] His willingness to suffer and die made him the ideal author for this document. In addition, Paul then is intentionally made the indirect author of the letter, for the churches it addresses were located in his missionary territory, and, alongside Peter, he was *the* martyr of early Christianity. So also the reference to "Babylon"[37] in 1 Pet. 5:13 makes the claim that Peter wrote the document in Rome,[38] so underscoring these connections. The combined Petrine-Pauline traditions now resident in Rome (cf. *1 Clem.* 5.4; Ign. *Rom.* 4.3) and the proximity of 1 Peter to *1 Clement* strengthen the biographical-theological concern of 1 Peter: the churches should orient their life and faith to Peter and Paul, taking their readiness to suffer as a model for their own lives.

The Paulinism of 1 Peter should be understood as an element of the pseudepigraphical strategy of the writing, a strategy that combines "interpersonality" and intertextuality.[39] The geographical data in 1 Pet. 1:1, the heavy dependence on the Pauline letter formula, and the incorporation of Paul's coworkers Silvanus (cf. 1 Thess. 1:1; 2 Cor. 1:19; 2 Thess. 1:1; Acts 15:22, 27, 32, 40; 16:19–25, 29; 17:4, 10, 14–15; 18:5) and Mark (cf. Philem. 24; Col. 4:10; 2 Tim. 4:11; Acts 12:12, 25; 13:5, 13; 15:37, 39) compel the hearers/readers to

35. For the historical Peter, cf. Böttrich, *Petrus* and Hengel, *Der unterschätzte Petrus*.

36. Cf. K. M. Schmidt, *Mahnung und Erinnerung im Maskenspiel: Epistolographie, Rhetorik und Narrativik der pseudepigraphischen Petrusbriefe* (HBS 38; Freiburg: Herder, 2003), 295.

37. Babylon does not appear as a cipher for Rome until after 70 CE (cf. Rev. 14:8; 16:19; 17:5; 18:2, 10, 21); cf. also *Sib. Or.* 5.143; 5.159; *2 Bar.* 11.1; *4 Ezra* 3.1, 28, 31.

38. Brox, *Der Erste Petrusbrief*, 42, rightly emphasizes that "Babylon" in 1 Pet. 5:13 signifies only "that 1 Peter wants to represent itself as having been written in Rome, not necessarily that it was actually written there."

39. This question has previously been dealt with mostly under the history-of-traditions aspect; cf. the listing and (critical) evaluation of parallels in Schröger, *Gemeinde*, 212–16, 223–28; Goppelt, *1 Peter*, 28–30; Brox, *Der Erste Petrusbrief*, 47–51; Lindemann, *Paulus im ältesten Christentum*, 252–61; Herzer, *Petrus oder Paulus*, 22ff.

think of the figure of Paul. Central concepts and vocabulary of Pauline theology also shape the theology of 1 Peter: χάρις ("grace," 1:2, 10, 13; 2:19–20; 4:10; 5:10, 12), δικαιοσύνη ("righteousness," 2:24; 3:14), ἀποκάλυψις ("revelation," 1:7, 13; 4:13), ἐλευθερία ("freedom," 2:16; cf. Gal. 5:13), καλέω for the call to salvation (1 Pet. 1:15; 2:9, 21; 3:9; 5:10), and election (1:1; 2:9). The central concept of being ἐν Χριστῷ (in Christ) is found outside the Pauline tradition only in 3:16; 5:10, 14! Finally, the numerous contacts between the parenetic material in 1 Peter and Pauline parenesis are noteworthy, especially the agreements between 1 Pet. 2:13–17 and Rom. 13:1–7.

2. With the martyr figures Peter and Paul is linked the central and pervasive theological theme of 1 Peter:[40] the innocent suffering of Christian believers in a hostile world. Such sufferings are deeply troubling to the hard-pressed Christian community, but they are not alien to Christian identity, for since their call to be Christians, believers have been aliens in the world. This means that suffering is not only the consequence of the new and different conduct of Christians in society, but that suffering is a constitutive element of Christian existence as such. The righteous suffer for the unrighteous (1 Pet. 3:18), so that Christians can understand their suffering as a test of faith and an inner link with the suffering Christ.

11.2 James: Acting and Being

The Letter of James is an early Christian pseudepigraphical wisdom writing that presents itself as written by the Lord's brother James.[41] Written in the post-Pauline period between 80 and 100 CE, its goal is to redefine Jewish-Christian identity, which was undergoing a crisis during this period.

11.2.1 Theology

The basic thought world of the Letter of James is marked by a theocentric understanding of wisdom.[42] The point of departure and center is the idea,

40. Cf. Reichert, *Praeparatio*, 37–39, who points out that the exhortations of the first and second parts of the letter are linked to each other by their respective contents: (a) suffering as test (cf. 1 Pet. 1:6–7 and 3:17 with 4:12); (b) Jesus's suffering and that of Christians (cf. 1 Pet. 2:18ff.; 2:21; 4:1 with 4:13); (c) suffering is ultimately related to the will of God (cf. 1 Pet. 1:6; 3:17 with 4:19); (d) present suffering and future glory (cf. 1 Pet. 1:7 with 4:13; 5:4).

41. On introductory issues, cf. Schnelle, *New Testament Writings*, 383–97; surveys of research are provided by Matthias Konradt, "Theologie in der 'strohernen Epistel,'" *VuF* 44 (1999): 54–78; Karl-Wilhelm Niebuhr, "A New Perspective on James? Neuere Forschungen zum Jakobusbrief," *TLZ* 129 (2004): 1019–44.

42. Cf. Hubert Frankemölle, *Der Brief des Jakobus* (ÖTK 17.1.2; Gütersloh: Gütersloher Verlagshaus Gerd Mohn, 1994), 16; Hubert Frankemölle, "Das semantische Netz des Jakobusbriefes," *BZ* 34 (1990): 161–97.

taken from creation theology, of wisdom "from above" (cf. James 1:5, 17; 3:15, 17)[43] that is given to Christians in baptism as a new creation in the saving word of truth (1:18, 21);[44] it positions them to do the will of God as revealed in the law.[45] As the gift of God, the wisdom that comes "from above" renews human beings. It gives them what they need for expressing their faith in action and thus becoming righteous before God. James is essentially interested in giving his instructions for a successful life, for an integrated, unified life on a theocentric basis, a life that overcomes tensions and contradictions in thinking and acting.

This basic thought world combines numerous traditional Jewish and Hellenistic attributes of God. God is the one God (James 2:19, "You believe that God is one"; cf. 4:12), the creator (3:9), the unchanging "Father of lights, with whom there is no variation or shadow due to change" (1:17). The Hellenistic concept of God's immutability is combined with the doctrine, also from the Greek world,[46] that God is affectless, without emotions or feelings: "God cannot be tempted by evil and he himself tempts no one" (1:13b). God is the Lord of all life, to whom believers should be subject as they make their plans (4:7, 13–15). This claim is linked with the rejection of any kind of submission to the world (4:4, "Do you not know that friendship with the world is enmity with God? Therefore whoever wishes to be a friend of the world becomes an enemy of God"). The references to God as lawgiver and judge are anchored in traditional Old Testament–Jewish imagery (4:12, "There is one lawgiver and judge who is able to save and to destroy"). The judgment theme also appears in 2:13 and is combined in 2:5; 5:1–6 with God's taking up the cause of the poor and the letter's criticism of the rich.

The letter as a whole is dominated by statements about the *saving will of God*: God reveals himself as the one who gives wisdom to all, generously and ungrudgingly (James 1:5). Through his word, God generates the truth of a new reality (1:18). God loves social justice (1:27). This God allows his Spirit to dwell in us (4:5), and gives grace to the humble (4:6, 10). One can turn to God in petitionary prayer (1:6). God hears the cries of those who suffer (5:4).

43. On this point cf. Rudolf Hoppe, "Der Jakobusbrief als briefliches Zeugnis hellenistisch und hellenistisch-jüdisch geprägter Religiosität," in *Der neue Mensch in Christus: Hellenistische Anthropologie und Ethik im Neuen Testament* (ed. Hans Dieter Betz and Johannes Beutler; QD 190; Freiburg: Herder, 2001), 164–89.

44. It is especially the motif of new creation that speaks in favor of a reference to baptism in James 1:18, 21; cf. Franz Mussner, *Der Jakobusbrief: Auslegung* (HTKNT 13.1; Freiburg: Herder, 1964), 95–96.

45. Rudolf Hoppe, *Der theologische Hintergrund des Jakobusbriefes* (FzB 28; Würzburg: Echter-Verlag, 1977), 147, describes the theological conception of James as follows: "The hidden wisdom of God is shared through faith, which encourages people with eschatological promises; but the person must grasp the wisdom received by faith and constantly realize it anew."

46. Cf. Plato, *Resp.* 2.380B; Epicurus according to Diogenes Laertius, *Vit. phil.* 10.139; Plutarch, *Mor.* 1102D.

God gives the crown of life to all who love him, who keep his word and let it be effective in their lives (1:12). On the whole, one can speak "of a word-centered theology"[47] in James, for with the "word of truth" (1:18) believers are endowed with a power that enables them to translate faith into action.

11.2.2 Christology

It is at first remarkable that the name of Jesus Christ is mentioned only twice in James (1:1; 2:1). Other christological themes or attributes also appear only minimally, but in texts whose content and location give them special importance. The expression "James, a servant of God and of the Lord Jesus Christ" (1:1) affects how the whole letter is read, contains a high Christology, and establishes thoroughgoing coordination between Christology and theology proper. The very phrase that preserves the difference between God and Jesus Christ also ensures that they will be seen to belong together![48] So also in 2:1 numerous predicates are ascribed to Jesus, who appears as "Lord" and as the one who is "anointed in glory." For the Letter of James, Jesus has been taken into God's own glory: "He is the Lord [*Herr*], who in the glory [*Herrlichkeit*] of God determines the faith and actions of Christians."[49] The extraordinary predications in 1:1; 2:1 and the references to κύριος (Lord) Jesus in 5:7, 8, 15 underscore the fundamental importance of Christology for the letter's theology.[50] The use of the term κύριος for both God (1:7; 3:9; 4:10, 15; 5:4, 10, 11) and Jesus (1:1; 2:1; 5:7, 8, 14, 15) *indicates an intentional internal interweaving of Christology and theology proper*. Moreover, the internal linkage between Christology and the concept of faith or the parousia also point in this direction. The concept of faith is filled out christologically in 2:1 ("believe in our glorious Lord Jesus Christ") and 5:15 ("the prayer of faith will save the sick, and the Lord will raise him up").[51] In the midst of the statements about the parousia in 5:7–11 stands the expectation of the coming of the Lord Jesus

47. Matthias Konradt, "'Geboren durch das Wort der Wahrheit'—'gerichtet durch das Gesetz der Freiheit': Das Wort als Zentrum der theologischen Konzeption des Jakobusbriefes," in *Der Jakobusbrief: Beiträge zur Rehabilitierung der "strohernen Epistel"* (ed. Petra von Gemünden et al.; BVB 3; Münster: Lit-Verlag, 2003), 1.

48. Should θεοῦ (of God) in James 1:1 be taken as referring to Jesus, this text would represent a noteworthy *theological* confession (so, e.g., Martin Karrer, "Christus der Herr und die Welt als Stätte der Prüfung," *KD* 35 [1989]: 169). To be sure, the strict monotheism of James speaks against this (cf. 2:19; 4:12); for exegesis, cf. Frankemölle, *Jakobus*, 121–32.

49. Frankemölle, *Jakobus*, 173.

50. While in the older scholarship (e.g., M. Dibelius) the importance of Christology in James was disputed or minimized, more recent study perceives an independent Christology in James and gives it its proper significance. In this sense, cf. the works of C. Burchard, M. Karrer, and H. Frankemölle.

51. James 5:7–8, 14, suggest that the κύριος of James 5:15 also refers to Jesus Christ; cf. Mussner, *Jakobusbrief*, 221.

Christ. Finally, the reception of Jesus traditions documents an extraordinary interest in Christology, since their present epistolary context sets these traditions from and about the earthly Jesus within the hermeneutical horizon of the exalted (1:1) and returning (5:7–8) Lord.

We may list the following as common elements shared by James and the Jesus tradition, especially the Sermon on the Mount:[52] James 1:2–4/Matt. 5:48 par. (perfection); James 1:5/Matt. 7:7 par. (prayer for wisdom); James 1:22–23/ Matt. 7:24–26 par. (doers of the word, not merely hearers); James 2:5/Matt. 5:3 par. (the kingdom of God for the poor [in Spirit]); James 2:13/Matt. 5:7 (the reward for mercy); James 3:18/Matt. 5:9 (promise to peacemakers); James 4:13–15/Matt. 6:34 (renunciation of future planning); James 5:1/Luke 6:24 (woes to the rich); James 5:2/Matt. 6:20 par. (moths devour wealth); James 5:10/Matt. 5:12 par. (prophets as models of suffering); James 5:12/Matt. 5:33–37 (swearing prohibited). Agreements between James and the Sermon on the Mount stretch from the problem of wealth, through authentic piety, mercy, the right understanding of the law to respect for the will of God. They can hardly be explained either through literary dependence or by claiming that James the Lord's brother knew and reported the Jesus tradition.[53] It is better to see both James and the Sermon on the Mount as embedded in a common stream of tradition indebted to a Jewish Christianity strongly influenced by the wisdom tradition. In receiving this tradition, James accepts two goals:[54] he places his theology in a broad stream of early Christian tradition and gives it additional authority by means of the intentional echoes of Jesus's teaching. Unlike Matthew, however, he mostly does not identify these as coming from Jesus (not even in the prohibition of swearing). This reticence clearly indicates the pseudepigraphical character of the Letter of James: as an early Christian teacher (3:1), the author has no personal contacts with Jesus to draw upon.[55]

Faith in the exalted and returning Jesus Christ determines the Christology of James, which is by no means only a minor theme. It is still not to be denied, however, that James minimizes the independence of the person of Jesus Christ and lets it modulate into the glory of God (2:1) so as to avoid possible

52. For analysis of the texts, cf. Hoppe, *Hintergrund*, 123–45; Wiard Popkes, *Adressaten, Situation und Form des Jakobusbriefes* (SBS 125/126; Stuttgart: Verlag Katholisches Bibelwerk, 1986), 156–76.

53. So Martin Hengel, "The Letter of James as Anti-Pauline Polemic (1987)," in *The Writings of St. Paul* (ed. Wayne A. Meeks and John T. Fitzgerald; 2nd ed.; New York: Norton, 2007), 242–53, who assigns the Jesus traditions adopted by James to an early layer of tradition.

54. Cf. Wiard Popkes, "Traditionen und Traditionsbrüche im Jakobusbrief," in *The Catholic Epistles and the Tradition* (ed. Jacques Schlosser; BETL 176; Louvain: Leuven University Press, 2004), 167.

55. Contra Niebuhr, "New Perspective?" 1039–40, who under the heading "James and His 'Big Brother'" would like to see the Letter of James as testimony to Jesus that derives from his "closest relative."

problems with the role of the law in his soteriology. Moreover, the author of James fails to make explicit the christological potential suggested by the materials he incorporates. Thus he does not acknowledge the Jesus traditions as such, for example, lifting up Job (and not his "brother" Jesus!) as the model of suffering (James 5:11).[56] It is thus appropriate to speak of a Christology *in* James rather than *the* Christology *of* James.

11.2.3 Pneumatology

The Letter of James has no developed pneumatology.[57] James 4:5 takes up Gen. 2:7 to emphasize God's zealously watchful care for the Spirit "that he has made to dwell in us." Therefore Christians may not, and cannot, be too engaged with the world.[58] James 2:26 evinces an anthropological dimension of the πνεῦμα: "For just as the body without the spirit is dead, so faith without works is also dead." With this analogy, James takes up a motif common in antiquity[59] and incorporates it in his argument: one's faith and one's deeds naturally and necessarily supplement each other.

11.2.4 Soteriology

In the Letter of James, soteriology, anthropology, and ethics are closely interwoven. The basic soteriological conception is shaped not christologically but by the tradition of theocentric wisdom: the "wisdom from above" conferred by God (3:15, 17) enables the believers to follow the "perfect law of liberty" (1:25; 2:12) as a unity of faith and works.[60] For James, the law is a gift of God in the most comprehensive sense, but the law does not save;[61] it is God's act that saves: "In fulfillment of his own purpose he gave us birth by the word of truth, so that we would become a kind of first fruits of his creatures" (1:18; cf. 1:21, "Welcome with meekness the implanted word that has the power to save your souls"). This "word of truth" is identical with the "law of liberty"

56. In James 5:11, κύριος refers entirely to God; cf. Wiard Popkes, *Der Brief des Jakobus* (THKNT 14; Leipzig: Evangelische Verlagsanstalt, 2001), 330–31.

57. Cf. Christoph Burchard, *Der Jakobusbrief* (HNT 15.1; Tübingen: Mohr, 2000), 133: "James has nothing to say about the Spirit as the gift of eschatological salvation."

58. Cf. Hahn, *Theologie*, 1:402.

59. Cf., e.g., Plutarch, *Mor.* 137E: "Plato was right, therefore, in advising that there should be no movement of the body without the mind or of the mind without the body, but that we should preserve, as it were, the even balance of a well-matched team." For additional parallels, cf. Burchard, *Jakobusbrief*, 132–33.

60. The dual translation of ἔργα with *Werke/Taten* (works/deeds) attempts to grasp the multilayered aspect of the term; recent commentaries on James 2:14–26 translate variously (Frankemölle, *Werke*; Burchard and Popkes, *Taten*). [The translation generally renders Schnelle's original "Werke/Taten" as "works."—MEB]

61. Cf. Burchard, *Jakobusbrief*, 90.

(1:25),[62] which is thoroughly bound up with the aspect of doing/not doing (2:8–12; 4:11–12).[63] Thus James understands God's act as creating responsibility, calling for presenting one's whole self to God in response. Therefore, in the soteriological event, James attributes decisive importance to the *acting* associated with the law, the singular "work" or "deed" (ἔργον in 1:4, 25) or plural "works" or "deeds" (ἔργα in 2:14, 17–18, 20–21, 24–26; 3:3). His fundamental approach shows that James, unlike Paul (cf. Rom. 3:21), thinks this *action* of faith is of decisive and abiding importance. Those whose lives are divided (cf. δίψυχος in James 1:8; 4:8), those who doubt (1:6, 8), those who shift from one side to the other (4:8), the proud (1:11; 5:1–6) are thus challenged and motivated to restore the unity of their Christian existence. One's deeds will count in the judgment to come, so that one must always be aware of their consequences. According to James 2:8–13, the *judgment* will be strictly according to observance of the law (2:12–13, "So speak and so act as those who are to be judged by the law of liberty. For judgment will be without mercy to anyone who has shown no mercy; mercy triumphs over judgment."). With the phrase "law of liberty" James means primarily the "royal law," namely the command to love one's neighbor as oneself (Lev. 19:18 in James 2:8);[64] but believers are obligated to observe "the whole law" (ὅλον τὸν νόμον),[65] "For whoever keeps the whole law but fails in one point has become accountable for all of it" (James 2:10). Orientation to the love commandment does not overrule regarding all the commandments of the law as in principle equally important and relevant for salvation. Precisely because the whole law, as concentrated in the love commandment, constitutes the norm for Christian life, the final judgment will take place according to the standard set by the whole law (cf. 2:12–13; 3:1b; 4:12; 5:1, 9). In the final judgment, however, it is not the law that can save, but only God, who is lawgiver and judge (4:12a).

This soteriological concept is the expression of a self-conscious Jewish-Christian identity that directly links God's own mercy with human acts of mercy toward one's neighbor and makes judgments on the basis of the criterion of acting in accord with the law.[66] The decisive difference from Paul

62. Cf. ibid., 88.

63. The comment of Konradt, "Jakobusbrief," 12, is on target: "In contrast, faith without works is soteriologically useless."

64. Cf. Popkes, *Jakobus*, 180–81.

65. In order to defend themselves against the (unjustified) charge of rigorous nomism, recent commentaries weaken the positive significance of 2:10 for James's argumentation; Burchard, *Jakobusbrief*, 106, formulates "Thus not: 'violates all the commandments' . . . , but 'denies respect for all the commandments, even if he otherwise keeps them"; Popkes, *Jakobus*, 177, shifts the responsibility: "James does not advocate any such thing [sc. a rigorous nomism], but the addressees are charged with drawing a false conclusion."

66. The idea of complete devotion to the will of God is also widespread in Hellenism: "The morally elevated person thus always thinks . . . fulfill the will of God" (Epictetus, *Diatr.* 3.24, 95).

is actually in the concept of sin (see below, §11.2.5), since for James sin is an act one does, not a prior destructive power that causes the act: "If you show partiality, you commit sin [ἁμαρτίαν ἐργάζεσθε] and are convicted by the law as transgressors" (2:9; cf. 4:17). The law is not helplessly delivered over to the power of sin but has an indwelling positive energy that endures, grounding the Christian's life and overcoming its obstacles, so that it is anchored as a basic element in God's saving plan. For James, the freedom of the Christian life exists not as freedom from the law but as freedom within the law.

11.2.5 Anthropology

The Letter of James develops its thought primarily as anthropology and ethics in order to strengthen threatened Jewish-Christian identity.[67] James addresses people who are endangered from within, those who are threatened by their own being. His anthropology corresponds to this threat, directed to the unity and wholeness of the person (1:2–4; 3:2, 13–18).[68] This state of personal internal division (cf. 1:8; 4:8) is to be overcome so that the person may be whole, agreeing with himself or herself in word and deed. Personal fragmentation is expressed in doubts (1:6), in the yawning chasm between word and deed (1:22–27), in the misuse of the tongue (3:3–12), in love for the world (4:4ff.), in disdain for the will of God (2:1–13; 5:1ff.), in constant disputes (4:1–3), and in blurring the lines between a clear yes and no. This internal split in the self is due to evil desire (cf. 1:15; Rom. 7:5, 7–10). *External conflicts are thus the result of the internal conflict.*[69] Many members of the church are striving for social prestige and are thus inconsiderate in the way they treat their brothers and sisters in the church. It is not the wisdom "from above," but "earthly" wisdom that shapes the life of the person who is internally divided (cf. James 3:15). James sharply criticizes the idea of an autonomous self, oriented to this world, particularly manifest in the self-willed plans of those whose business dealings take them to distant places (4:13–17) and the unsocial conduct of owners of extensive holdings (5:1–6). Instead of ignoring

67. Cf. Frankemölle, *Jakobus*, 16: "The Letter of James is a theocentric writing with a very well thought-out theological conception that is singular in the New Testament. On this theocentric basis, James, like the Jewish wisdom teachers, devotes his entire effort to providing his readers with instructions for a successful life—in and despite all the ambivalences and conflicts within each person and among fellow Christians."

68. Cf. Hubert Frankemölle, "Gespalten oder ganz: Zur Pragmatik der theologischen Anthropologie des Jakobusbriefes," in *Kommunikation und Solidarität: Beiträge zur Diskussion des handlungstheoretischen Ansatzes von Helmut Peukert in Theologie und Sozialwissenschaften* (ed. Hans-Ulrich von Brachel and Norbert Mette; Freiburg, Schweiz: Edition Exodus, 1985), 160–78; Frankemölle, *Jakobus*, 305–20; Popkes, *Adressaten*, 191ff.

69. Cf. Petra von Gemünden, "Einsicht, Affekt und Verhalten: Überlegungen zur Anthropologie des Jakobusbriefes," in *Der Jakobusbrief: Beiträge zur Rehabilitierung der "strohernen Epistel"* (ed. Petra von Gemünden et al. (BVB 3; Münster: Lit-Verlag, 2003), 83–96.

God's rule of the world with their own false self-confidence, they should say, "If the Lord wishes, we will live and do this or that" (James 4:15). Christians cannot orient themselves to God and the world at the same time; self-seeking and love for the world stand against the will of God. According to the Letter of James, this internal division cannot be overcome by one's own efforts, from within oneself, but only through the heteronomous gift of God. Faith occurs through the creative act of God (1:6, 17–18; 2:5; 5:17)[70] and attains concrete form in a devout and steadfast attitude that resolutely struggles against evil desires and is completed and fulfilled in what one actually does. Both faith and wisdom demonstrate their reality in works, which in turn are oriented to the "royal law" (2:8) and the "perfect law of liberty" (1:25; 2:12). Since for James the love commandment is the goal and center of the law (cf. 2:8), there is an organic unity between the gift of wisdom, faith, and one's works.[71] Only the wisdom from above, and thus faith, makes possible the perfection that comes through fulfilling the law as expressed in the love commandment. The goal is unity of faith and works in a theonomous existence.[72]

Faith and Works

In the Letter of James, faith and the law are no more in opposition than are faith and works, but appear as two sides of the same coin. Love for God and neighbor and observance of the law constitute a perfect unity. The will of God, revealed completely in the law, overcomes the incomplete, biased, and divided activities of Christians.[73] *The differences between James and Paul are obvious*: while for Paul, sin is a supra-personal power that takes advantage of the law, drawing it into its own service and betraying human beings (cf. Rom. 7:7ff.), for James, sin can be overcome by observing the whole law (James 2:9; 4:17; 5:15b, 16, 20); i.e., sin in the Letter of James refers to a deed, an act against God's law.[74] Consequently, there exists for James no opposition between faith and works, but he presupposes such an opposition in his conversation partner.

Is this conversation partner Paul? The fact that the contrast πίστις/ἔργα (νόμου) is never found prior to Paul[75] suggests that the discussion in James

70. Cf. Burchard, *Jakobusbrief*, 56.

71. Appropriately ibid., "Faith must be accompanied by deeds, as encouraged and demanded by the law of liberty. They do not emerge from faith itself, although faith works along with them; instead, faith and deeds together constitute the whole, vital, Christian person."

72. Cf. Ulrich Luck, "Die Theologie des Jakobusbriefes," *ZTK* 81 (1984): 10–15.

73. On the law in James, cf. especially Hubert Frankemölle, "Gesetz im Jakobusbrief," in *Das Gesetz im Neuen Testament* (ed. Karl Kertelge and Johannes Beutler; QD 108; Freiburg: Herder, 1986), 175–221.

74. Cf. Burchard, *Jakobusbrief*, 74.

75. Cf. Hengel, "Anti-Pauline Polemic," 526 of German original; omitted from English translation; Friedrich Avemarie, "Die Werke des Gesetzes im Spiegel des Jakobusbriefes," *ZTK* 98 (2001): 291.

has Paul in view.[76] Moreover, James 2:10 appears to refer to Gal. 5:3 (ὅλον τὸν νόμον ["the whole law"] is found only here in the accusative [Matt. 22:40, the only other occurrence, is in the nominative]), and the allusion to Rom. 3:28 in James 2:24 is obvious because of the agreements in subject matter, in language, and in the rhetorical-polemical use of μόνον (alone).[77] Finally, there are points of contact in the Abraham theme (cf. Rom. 4:2/James 2:21) and in the quotation from Gen. 15:6 in Rom. 4:3 and James 2:23, which agree in departing from the LXX text in two points: Ἀβραάμ instead of Ἀβράμ, and the addition of δέ after ἐπίστευσεν.[78] To be sure, the polemic in James 2:14–26 does not strike home against Paul, since for Paul too there is no faith without works (one need only note Rom. 1:5; 13:8–10; Gal. 5:6). James could have intentionally misrepresented the Pauline position or simply misunderstood it. Perhaps he knew Galatians and Romans only indirectly, through oral or written intermediaries unknown to us. He is possibly arguing against Christians who practiced a faith without works and who appealed to Paul to justify their practice. Second Thessalonians 2:2 and 2 Tim. 2:18 document an elevated eschatological mood in some of the churches of the post-Pauline mission in Asia Minor and Greece, which possibly led to a position like that opposed by James. We need not impute to James a complete lack of understanding of Paul's own theology or a malicious misrepresentation of Pauline thought.

The possibility that James is referring to Paul and/or Pauline theology continues to be a very controversial point. One stream of scholarship regards the theology of James as having its own intellectual and conceptual presuppositions, which were not merely developed in reaction to Paul. Among those who interpret James in this way are H. Windisch, E. Lohse, U. Luck, H. Frankemölle, R. Heiligenthal, C. Burchard,[79] and M. Konradt.[80] H. Frankemölle even goes so

76. Cf. Popkes, "Traditionen," 161: "Decisively in favor of the view that James responds to traditions associated with Paul (not necessarily authentically Pauline) is, in my opinion, the circumstance that James reacts antithetically to positions that in this form are found in the writings of early Christianity only in Paul."

77. Cf. Hengel, "Anti-Pauline Polemic," 527n46 of German original: "It should no longer be debated that James 2:24 is directed against a Pauline polemical statement like Rom. 3:28."

78. Cf. Lindemann, *Paulus im ältesten Christentum*, 244–51; Lüdemann, *Opposition to Paul*, 140–49.

79. Cf. Hans Windisch and Herbert Preisker, *Die katholischen Briefe* (3rd ed.; HNT 15; Tübingen: Mohr, 1951), 15:20–21; Eduard Lohse, "Glaube und Werke," in *Die Einheit des Neuen Testaments: Exegetische Studien zur Theologie des Neuen Testaments* (2nd ed.; Göttingen: Vandenhoeck & Ruprecht, 1973), 290–91; Luck, "Jakobusbriefes," 27–28; Frankemölle, "Gesetz im Jakobusbrief," 196ff.; R. Heiligenthal, *Werke als Zeichen: Untersuchungen zur Bedeutung der menschlichen Taten im Frühjudentum, Neuen Testament und Frühchristentum* (WUNT 2.9; Tübingen: Mohr, 1983), 49–52; Burchard, *Jakobusbrief*, 125–26.

80. Cf. Matthias Konradt, "Der Jakobusbrief im frühchristlichen Kontext," in *The Catholic Epistles and the Tradition* (ed. Jacques Schlosser; BETL 176; Louvain: Leuven University Press, 2004), 189: "The genesis of the problematic engaged in 2:14ff. can be explained without looking any further than the general early Christianity language about saving faith, and thus

far as to state, "In the whole letter, James develops no doctrine of the law, and nowhere does the law become an actual theme; when it emerges, it is not itself the topic but a subsidiary function of whatever is the main topic."[81] In contrast to this point of view, numerous scholars hold fast to their perception of an anti-Pauline author engaging what he considers to be false Pauline teaching. According to A. Lindemann, the author of the Letter of James intended to "address and defeat Pauline theology, and with its own weapons."[82] M. Hengel labels James "a masterwork of early Christian polemic,"[83] namely, against Paul. According to F. Avemarie, James mounts an intensive assault against the Pauline doctrine of justification, with an explicit attack against the authentic Pauline understanding of ἔργα (νόμου), "works (of the law)."[84] According to some scholars (including M. Dibelius, W. G. Kümmel, P. Vielhauer, W. Schrage, F. Schnider, and M. Tsuji),[85] James does directly oppose Paul himself but only a hyper-Pauline understanding of his thought.

On the issue of the relation of James and Paul, two extremes are to be avoided: the letter as a whole is neither to be understood in terms of anti-Pauline polemic, nor can it be understood without any reference to Paul. Numerous topics have no connection to Paul and must be understood in terms of the letter's own train of thought and its basic concern to protect and reassure the Jewish Christianity's threatened self-identity and to give it a new foundation: the significance of the law, the essential meaning of faith, the relation of hearing and doing, the essence of wisdom, the relation of rich and poor, the ethical conduct of the church. At the same time, James 2:20–26 indisputably has Paul or Pauline disciples in view, for the linguistic and topical points of contact mentioned above are clear. In this limited section, we have a combination of intertextuality and interpersonality.[86] Hermeneutically, the interpretation of

---

without any specific reference to the Pauline sharpening of the issue in the antithesis of faith vs. works of the law."

81. Frankemölle, "Gesetz im Jakobusbrief," 202.

82. Lindemann, *Paulus im ältesten Christentum*, 249; cf. also Lüdemann, *Opposition to Paul*, 143: "In this passage James is thus combating a Pauline thesis."

83. Hengel, "Anti-Pauline Polemic," 525 of German original (the historical James versus Paul); cf. previously, e.g., Hans Lietzmann, *A History of the Early Church*, vol. 1, *The Beginnings of the Christian Church*; vol. 2, *The Founding of the Church Universal* (trans. Bertram Lee Woolf; Cleveland: World, 1963), 1:202, according to whom James is "a definite and conscious polemic against the teaching of Paul."

84. Cf. Avemarie, "Spiegel," 296ff.

85. Cf. Martin Dibelius and Heinrich Greeven, *A Commentary on the Epistle of James* (Hermeneia; trans. Michael Williams; Philadelphia: Fortress, 1976), 174–80; Wolfgang Schrage, "Die Briefe des Jakobus, Petrus, Judas," in *Die katholische Briefe* (ed. Horst Robert Balz; NTD 10; Göttingen: Vandenhoeck & Ruprecht, 1993), 35; Franz Schnider, *Der Jakobusbrief* (RNT 20; Regensburg: Pustet, 1987), 77; Manabu Tsuji, *Glaube zwischen Vollkommenheit und Verweltlichung: Eine Untersuchung zur literarischen Gestalt und zur inhaltlichen Kohärenz des Jakobusbriefes* (WUNT 2.93; Tübingen: Mohr, 1997), 154–71.

86. This is rightly emphasized by Avemarie, "Spiegel," 289.

the Letter of James cannot simply bracket Paul out of the equation, but at the same time Paul cannot simply determine the interpretation of James.

The Letter of James emphasizes the *natural and indissoluble unity* of faith and action; it advocates an integrative concept of faith, in which it is presupposed that faith includes hearing and doing the word. The position of the author is visible in James 2:22, where it is self-evident that faith and works work together, so that faith is completed by works. It is this completed faith that brings justification before God. This working together of faith and works should not be understood in the later sense of synergism prevalent in the history of dogma, for in James 2:22 faith remains the subject, as throughout James 2:14–16. It is not that faith is "supplemented," but that the essence of faith is defined as a stance that includes one's life as a whole. James is concerned with faith that justifies human beings before God, which is faith that generates works, demonstrates its reality through works, and is completed and perfected by works. This perfection is the goal of faith, and works serve this goal. In the act of baptism, God himself implants in human beings the word of truth (cf. James 1:18, 21), the word that is nothing other than the perfect law of liberty (James 1:25). Righteousness comes to be as the indissoluble unity of divine gift and human response (James 3:18, "A harvest of righteousness is sown [passive: σπείρεται] in peace for those who make peace").[87] The unity of hearing and doing corresponds to the perfection for which the Christian hopes.

11.2.6 Ethics

The Letter of James's basic concept of ethics is already apparent in its soteriology and anthropology (see above, §11.2.4 and §11.2.5): *living by the norm of the love commandment as the law's guiding principle is the visible expression of the unity of Christian existence.* On the one hand, the ethic of James is directly linked with the challenge to put the law into practice in one's life (1:22, 25; 4:11–12), but on the other hand, it is also true that here, too, Christians are always receivers (1:17). Thus terms such as "achievement ethic" or "works righteousness" are inappropriate for James's concept. It is rather a matter of working out how James actually argues his ethical points.[88] In the first place, we must note the characteristic alternation between imperative and indicative sections. Thus 1:2–18 is determined by the testing motif; a transition is effected by the direct address ἀδελφοί μου ἀγαπητοί (my beloved brothers and sisters), after which the content of 1:19–27 expands on the indicative statements about the "perfect gift . . . from above" and the "word of

87. Frankemölle, *Jakobus* 2:559, appropriately refers to an "anthropology of becoming."

88. A somewhat distanced and skeptical survey is given by Schrage, *Ethics*, 281–94; cf. further F. Mussner, "Die ethische Motivation im Jakobusbrief," in *Neues Testament und Ethik: Für Rudolf Schnackenburg* (ed. Helmut Merklein and Rudolf Schnackenburg; Freiburg: Herder, 1989), 416–23.

truth" in 1:17–18. On the whole, James 1 is shaped by the forms of traditional proverbial wisdom; individual sayings are assembled on the basis of common key words and interpreted by the author. James 2 and 3 contain units that are more extensive and more self-contained. The address ἀδελφοί (brothers and sisters) is characteristic (2:1, 14; 3:1), and the content of each unit is a diatribe-like treatment of a coherent theme. While the goal of the parenesis in 2:1–3:12 is the good way of life in the humility granted by divine wisdom (no partiality, the unity of faith and works, engaging the word), the appropriate question is then raised in 3:13–18 as to the source of such wisdom. In the immediate context, 4:1–12 represents a new subject (friendship with God or the world), but in the macro-context this section takes up again the theme of testing and temptation from 1:2–18. The admonitions in 4:13–17 against false self-confidence and the prophetic charges against the rich in 5:1–6 stand out from their context and represent independent traditions. With the typical address ἀδελφοί, the author once again introduces admonitions to be patient and the invitation to intercessory prayer in 5:7–20, which can be placed in the traditional category of proverbial parenesis.

On the whole, then, we can perceive a clear structure of the letter's train of thought even if we cannot find the basis on which each particular ethical instruction is argued. Both long-winded compositions (James 3:1–12) and short apodictic declarations (1:20, "Human anger does not produce God's righteousness"; the prohibition of oaths in 5:12; cf. Matt. 5:37) can serve as the means of forming the readers' capacity for ethical judgment.

In order to develop this capacity further, James chooses an original starting point: at the beginning stands the act of hearing (1:19) that is completed in the unity of speaking and acting, and thus will be able to stand in the judgment (2:12, "So speak and so act as those who are to be judged by the law of liberty"). Good words and thoughts are not adequate; what is required is concrete action oriented to the law. From this point of departure, the Letter of James—along with a few other New Testament writings—develops some beginning approaches to a social ethic that includes economic affairs, because the love commandment applies to all areas of life and definitively excludes anger (1:20).[89] The churches addressed by the letter are plagued by social tensions. Care for the needy is not functioning adequately (1:27; 2:15–16). Envy, arguing, and fighting prevail (3:13ff.; 4:1ff., 11–12; 5:9). Wealthy people are given preferential treatment in the worship services (2:1ff.), and the poor are put off with pious clichés (2:16). The wealthy trust in themselves rather than in God (4:13–17), and large landowners exploit their workers (5:1–6). Finally, the congregations are subjected to local legal discrimination (cf.

89. Cf. on this point cf. Petra von Gemünden, "Die Wertung des Zorns im Jakobusbrief auf dem Hintergrund des antiken Kontexts und seine Einordnung," in *Der Jakobusbrief: Beiträge zur Rehabilitierung der "strohernen Epistel"* (ed. Petra von Gemünden et al. (BVB 3; Münster: Lit-Verlag, 2003), 97–119.

2:6).[90] The numerous statements about poor and rich in James by no means derive from a spiritualized piety of the poor,[91] but this theme must have a background in the experience of the churches addressed by the letter, and the Letter of James aims at a change in their conduct.[92] The advocacy for the poor (1:27) against the rich (2:1–13; 4:13–5:6) corresponds to the will of God, for "Has not God chosen the poor in the world to be rich in faith and to be heirs of the kingdom that he has promised to those who love him?" (2:5). James is not aiming to settle accounts between the poor and the rich within the church in a way that levels the difference between them, nor does he portray the church as a household (οἶκος), but he does advocate solidarity within the church (2:14–16) and preaches the equality of church members (2:1–7).[93]

The tensions we recognize in the Letter of James fit into the social history of post-Pauline Christianity.[94] A development that had already begun in Paul's time continues: the integration of people from different social and economic levels, with differing social status. Even in Paul's time, the congregations he founded did not represent a homogeneous group but included people from all levels of society. In post-Pauline times, conflicts between these groups sharpened, since an increasing number of wealthy people joined the churches and the gap between rich and poor was widened. Thus the Pastoral Epistles call for self-sufficiency (cf. 1 Tim. 6:6–8) and explicitly warn against the consequences of love of money (1 Tim. 6:9, 10). It is hardly accidental that 1 Timothy concludes with a warning to the rich (1 Tim. 6:17–19). The author of Luke-Acts, by his warnings to the rich, also indicates that wealth and property had become a problem in the churches he addresses. The Letter to the Hebrews warns against the love of money (Heb. 13:5) and a slackening of faith (Heb. 2:1–4). Such lethargy is to be overcome by works of love (Heb. 6:10–12). Finally, the Revelation of John is an impressive witness for the sharp criticism from Jewish Christian circles against the dangers of wealth (cf. Rev. 3:17–19; 18:10ff., 15ff., 23–24). The sociological scene portrayed in James can thus be integrated into a larger development within Hellenistic post-Pauline Christianity, a development characterized by profound changes in the social stratification of church membership and disputes about faith and action associated with these changes.

90. Cf. here Schnider, *Jakobusbrief*, 61.

91. Contra Dibelius and Greeven, *James*, 134–36.

92. Cf. Schnider, *Jakobusbrief*, 57–58; Frankemölle, *Jakobus* 1:57–62, 251–59.

93. Cf. G. Garleff, *Urchristliche Identität im Matthäusevangelium, Didache und Jakobusbrief* (BVB 9; Münster: Lit-Verlag, 2004), 269; Gerd Theissen, "Nächstenliebe und Egalität," in *Der Jakobusbrief: Beiträge zur Rehabilitierung der "strohernen Epistel"* (ed. Petra von Gemünden et al., 120–42, who emphasizes with regard to James, "No New Testament author has so clearly understood the love commandment in terms of dealing with people impartially, at the same time formulating it in a way relatively open to outsiders" (120–21).

94. On this point, cf. Luz and Lampe, "Nachpaulinisches Christentum," 185–216.

James responded to these developments with an ethic primarily shaped by the wisdom tradition.[95] This ethic focuses on the idea of ethical perfection in humility and lowliness through fulfilling the law—a perfection made possible by the divine gift of wisdom.

11.2.7 Ecclesiology

Elders are incidentally mentioned in James 3:1 and 5:14; otherwise, the Letter of James does not present a developed ecclesiology. Because in the churches addressed by James responsible engagement with the word is of great importance, it appears that the office of teacher was attractive to many church members: "Not many of you should become teachers, my brothers and sisters, for you know that we who teach will be judged with greater strictness" (3:1). It was the task of the teacher to maintain the traditions from and about Jesus, interpreting them and handing them on; to interpret the Old Testament; and to formulate concrete ethical instructions for the life of the church.[96] The author of the letter was probably himself such a teacher (cf. the first-person plural in 3:1b), for his letter fulfills all the qualifications of a didactic writing. The thronging of church members to become teachers presupposes there was open access to this office, so that it became necessary to pay more attention to the question of qualifications and responsibilities (in view of the coming judgment).[97] The existence of elders is documented in 5:14: "Are any among you sick? They should call for the elders of the church [τοὺς πρεσβυτέρους τῆς ἐκκλησίας] and have them pray over them, anointing them with oil in the name of the Lord." The elders functioned as a collegium (cf. 1 Pet. 4:1ff.), and their office was considered to have a charismatic aspect: anointing the sick with oil (cf. Mark 6:13b; Luke 10:34). This was both a therapeutic and spiritual act, as indicated elsewhere by linking baptism to "the name of the Lord" (cf. 1 Cor. 6:11; Rom. 6:3) and the interpretation of baptism as "anointing" in 2 Cor. 1:21–22. The term ἐκκλησία appears only here in James, where it refers to the local congregation of believers, not to the church as a whole. According to James 1:5–6 and especially 5:15a, the power of prayer plays an important role: "The prayer of faith will save the sick, and the Lord will raise them up." Physical help and eschatological salvation lay equally in the hands of the Lord, who works through the prayer and ministry of the elders.

The ecclesiological statements of James, made rather incidentally and not conceptually elaborated, fit into a concept of ethics oriented to auton-

95. On the orientation of James to wisdom, cf. especially Hoppe, *Hintergrund*, passim; Ulrich Luck, "Weisheit und Leiden," *TLZ* 92 (1967): 253–58. Thus Frankemölle, *Jakobus*, 85, can state: "The Letter of James presents itself as a rereading of Jesus ben Sirach."

96. On the interpretation of James 3:1, cf. Zimmermann, *Lehrer*, 194–208.

97. Cf. Popkes, *Jakobus*, 220–21.

omy[98] over against the world and to equality and energetic faith within the congregation.[99]

11.2.8 Eschatology

The eschatological statements found in the Letter of James pertain to three areas:

1. Eschatology serves as a motivation for ethics; the ethical discussions in James 1:12, 26–27; 2:13, 26; 3:18; 4:12, 17; and 5:20 intentionally conclude in each case with a present or future outlook.
2. Closely related are the previously mentioned statements about judgment (see above, §11.2.4): God is the judge who can save or condemn whomever he will (4:12).
3. Also linked to the judgment theme is the parousia as an apparently current theme among the churches addressed by James. Cf. especially 5:7–8, "Be patient, therefore, beloved, until the coming of the Lord. The farmer waits for the precious crop from the earth, being patient with it until it receives the early and the late rains. You also must be patient. Strengthen your hearts, for the coming of the Lord is near [ἡ παρουσία τοῦ κυρίου ἤγγικεν]." The awareness of a delay of the parousia comes to expression in the call for patience, in the confidence and reassurance communicated by the agricultural imagery, as well as in the admonition not to grumble against one another,[100] "so that you may not be judged. See, the Judge is standing at the doors!" (5:9b). The coming Lord is also the Judge, and he will decide according to the deeds of each person (5:12; cf. 2:4, 6, 12–13; 3:1; 4:11–12).

11.2.9 Setting in the History of Early Christian Theology

Among the documents received in the New Testament canon, especially the Letter of James (alongside the Gospel of Matthew) advocates a decidedly

98. Gerd Theissen ("Ethos und Gemeinde im Jakobusbrief," in Petra von Gemünden et al., eds., *Der Jakobusbrief: Beiträge zur Rehabilitierung der "strohernen Epistel,"* 143–65), emphasizes autonomy as a basic concept of James's ecclesiology: "It is a church that orients itself autonomously on its *own* foundation: on the law of liberty. It is a church that receives instruction from its *own* teachers as to how it should live. It is a church that wants to translate its faith into the way it lives" (165).

99. Cf. Garleff, *Urchristliche Identität*, 315; possibly James is engaging in a polemic against patron-client structures in 2:1–7 (cf. 251ff.).

100. Differently Popkes, *Jakobus*, who sees no indication of a problem of the delay of the parousia in this text.

Jewish-Christian position.[101] The prescript already functions to signal this perspective, for the reference to the twelve tribes and the choice of the pseudonym "James" is intended to establish a consciousness of being in continuity with Israel. In early Christianity, James represents the view that Christian believers still needed to follow the guidance of the Torah (cf. Gal. 2:12–13; Acts 15:13–21). During a period in which the identity of Jewish Christians within post-Pauline Hellenistic Christianity was being threatened by social and theological conflicts, this James was a figure whose post-Easter authority could be claimed to preserve, strengthen, or reestablish this endangered sense of identity. The Letter of James attempts to do just that, on a theocentric basis, in order to preserve the unity of faith and works by a strong emphasis on anthropology and ethics. James wants to overcome the divided character of Christian existence; he is concerned about the wholeness and perfection of the Christian life. His reference point for this, however, is not the existence of the individual Christian, but the community of the church. Ethics and anthropology constitute the center of this identity-construction, which is marked by the quest for a faith oriented to true wisdom and the law, in the unity of being and doing, in which the law appears as the ordering of freedom in love.

Within the context of early Christianity, James emphatically creates a hearing for a basic issue: the continuity with Israel requires that the question of the law's significance and the related issue of the connection between faith and deeds be thought through theologically. Unlike Paul's opponents (cf. Gal. 5:3; Phil. 3:3), the Letter of James aims at a balanced resolution of the issue and does not call for circumcision of Christians from a Gentile background. By directly relating theology and social reality to each other, James advocates an ethical Christianity. He knows that in so doing he stands in continuity with Israel.

11.3 Hebrews: The God Who Speaks

The Letter to the Hebrews is among the New Testament's greatest riddles. Its historical situation is totally unclear, for the letter contains only vague references to the church situation and no clues at all as to the identity of its author. Pauline authorship, and composition in Rome, are presumably suggested by the letter's conclusion in Heb. 13:23–24. The authenticity of this letter's conclusion is doubtful however, and the genre of the writing and its history-of-religions connections are controversial topics.[102] So this rule applies

101. Cf. Garleff, *Urchristliche Identität*, 324.

102. The title Πρὸς Ἑβραίους is nowadays correctly regarded as secondary; cf. Erich Grässer, *An die Hebräer* (EKKNT 17.1–3; Neukirchen-Vluyn: Neukirchener Verlag, 1990), 1:41–45. For introductory issues, cf. Schnelle, *New Testament Writings*, 365–82. For thorough exegetical and theological treatment of the whole, cf. Harold W. Attridge, *The Epistle to the Hebrews*

to Hebrews more than to any other New Testament writing: the text must be understood on the basis of its own content.

11.3.1 Theology

The basis of the theological thought of Hebrews (in the sense of "theology proper") is *God's speaking*, that God is the God who speaks: "Long ago God spoke to our ancestors in many and various ways by the prophets, but in these last days he has spoken to us by a Son" (Heb. 1:1–2a). The gateway to the Letter to the Hebrews is the "word of God," as indicated by the framing of the first major section with theological affirmations about the word (1:1–2; 4:12, "Indeed, the word of God is living and active, sharper than any two-edged sword, piercing until it divides soul from spirit, joints from marrow; it is able to judge the thoughts and intentions of the heart"). A theology of the word is the guideline that begins with the prologue of 1:1–4 and proceeds throughout the entire writing,[103] seen especially in 1:5, 13; 2:1–4; 4:2, 12; 5:5, 12; 11:3; 12:25; 13:7. In Hebrews, God's word is an effective event, an eternal, creating, judging, and saving word. The event of the word of God takes place in heaven and on earth (12:22–29), and encompasses creation (4:3; 11:3), history (3:7–4:11; chap. 11), and judgment (4:13). In his speaking, God shows himself to be the just (6:10) and gracious God (12:15), the God who stands by his promises (6:17) and his covenant (7:22–25; 8:10; 9:20; 10:16; 12:24). God has foreseen and provided for the final perfection of believers (11:39–40) and raises the dead (11:19); at the same time, God is a consuming fire (12:29), who both helps and disciplines (12:7).

God's speaking as the fundamental dimension of his acting is emphasized in literary terms especially by the numerous *quotations from the LXX*, in an abundance and density unique in the New Testament, in most of which God himself is understood to be the speaker (ca. 22 times).[104] In addition to around 35 verbatim quotations, there are around 80 allusions to Old Testament texts. Hebrews cites the LXX exclusively; deviations from the standard LXX text can be explained by the author's use of differing LXX codices or his citing

(Hermeneia; Philadelphia: Fortress, 1989); and Craig R. Koester, *Hebrews* (AB 36; New York: Doubleday, 2001).

103. On this point, cf. Erich Grässer, "Das Wort als Heil," in *Aufbruch und Verheissung: Gesammelte Aufsätze zum Hebräerbrief; zum 65. Geburtstag mit einer Bibliographie des Verfassers* (ed. Erich Grässer et al.; BZNW 65; Berlin: de Gruyter, 1992), 129–42; Harald Hegermann, "Das Wort Gottes als aufdeckende Macht," in *Das Lebendige Wort: Beiträge zur kirchlichen Verkündigung: Festgabe für Gottfried Voigt zum 65. Geburtstag* (ed. Gottfried Voigt et al.; Berlin: Evangelische Verlagsanstalt, 1982), 83–98; David Wider, *Theozentrik und Bekenntnis: Untersuchungen zur Theologie des Redens Gottes im Hebräerbrief* (BZNW 87; Berlin: de Gruyter, 1997).

104. Michael Theobald, "Vom Text zum 'lebendigen Wort' (Hebr 4,12)," in *Jesus Christus als die Mitte der Schrift: Studien zur Hermeneutik des Evangeliums* (ed. Christof Landmesser et al.; BZNW 86; Berlin: de Gruyter, 1997), 751–90.

from memory.[105] He has a notable preference for the Psalter and likes to cite lengthy individual passages. Thus the only place in the New Testament where the whole of Jer. 31:31–34 is cited is Heb. 8:8–12; it is repeated in a shorter form in 10:15–18. The letter's prevailing usage of citing the texts without introductory formulae presents the quotations as *speech-acts*. The quotations not only witness to and illustrate God's sustained powerful speaking in history with Israel, and ultimately, in a way that can never be superseded, in Jesus Christ; they also perpetuate this speaking into the reader's present.

The effective literary-rhetorical device by which the author withdraws behind his message, simply beginning without a prescript,[106] is also in the service of his theology of the Word. This anonymity facilitates the direct hearing of the divine message without any intervening authority or mediating nuance. In Heb. 1:1–2, God is the exclusive subject who speaks, while the author places himself among the hearers (v. 2). This stylistic framework is linked to an immediate text-pragmatic interest, for the church is no longer hearkening to the saving message. Thus the author warns the readers, "See that you do not refuse the one who is speaking; for if they did not escape when they refused the one who warned them on earth, how much less will we escape if we reject the one who warns from heaven!" (12:25). If they remain unshaken, holding fast to the promise in faith and obedience, they are assured that, unlike the wilderness generation, they will enter the promised eschatological rest. The church must not abandon its faithful confidence (10:35), tired hands and weak knees must be strengthened (12:12), so that the conduct of believers does not occasion contempt for the death of Jesus Christ on the cross (6:6). God's speaking is thus directed to an immediate hearing within the church; it is to overcome doubt and lethargy, so that the confidence of faith again prevails among the hearers/readers (11:1).[107] This is what the Letter to the Hebrews aims to achieve, so that the letter itself, both in form (13:22, λόγος τῆς παρακλήσεως [word of exhortation]) and in content, functions as a constituent element of God's own speaking.

The appropriate response of the church to God's speaking is *confession*. The noun ὁμολογία ("confession": Heb. 3:1; 4:14; 10:23) and the verb ὁμολογέω ("confess," "declare one's faith": 11:13; 13:15), also found in the Pauline tradition (2 Cor. 9:13; Rom. 10:9; 1 Tim. 6:12–13; Titus 1:16), point in Hebrews not

105. For analysis, cf. Friedrich Schröger, *Der Verfasser des Hebräerbriefes als Schriftausleger* (BU 4; Regensburg: Pustet, 1968), 247–56. Formally, there are parallels to the interpretative methods of ancient Judaism; cf. the extensive catalog on pp. 256–99.

106. Cf. Martin Karrer, *Der brief an die Hebräer* (ÖTK 20; Gütersloh: Gütersloher Verlagshaus Mohn, 2002), 42–44.

107. Martin Karrer interprets Hebrews' theology of the word within the framework of liminal thinking: "Hebrews guides its readers across the threshold to the reality of God and trusts in the word as word to bring them further along this way to divine heights, beyond this initial threshold to live in the reality of the transcendent God" (ibid., 57).

so much to affirmation of prior texts and formulae[108] or to individual items of the faith, but to *attuning oneself to God's speaking and living in accord with this Word of God*. The Christian confession is always directed to the saving event as a whole, as indicated by Heb. 4:14, "Since, then, we have a great high priest who has passed through the heavens, Jesus, the Son of God, let us hold fast to our confession." The church is to get back in step, *to find its rhythm in accord with the Word of God*. To that end, Hebrews makes the Word of God the basis and midpoint of a theology that radiates outward in all directions, beginning with Christology.

11.3.2 Christology

God's speaking is the foundation for the Christology of Hebrews; theology proper is the ground of Christology, not the other way around. God's speaking "in the Son" (Heb. 1:2) takes place in the speaking of the Father to the Son, and in the presentation of the Son through the Father: "For to which of the angels did God ever say, 'You are my Son; today I have begotten you'"? (1:5). The Father confers unique status on the Son, who is the (preexistent) mediator of creation (1:2b, 10), the reflection of God's glory and the exact image of God's very being (1:3a). Only the Son shares the eternal being of the Father (1:11–12), different from all that is earthly and perishable, and "sustains all things by his powerful word" (1:3b). This global participation of the Son in the essential being of God reaches its apex in 1:8, 10, where the Son is addressed in the words of Scripture as "God" (θεός) and "Lord" (κύριος). "The Son does not belong among the many gods of the nations, nor is he, so to speak, a second, subordinate God under the one Lord. Instead, God attributes to the Son what God himself does and is."[109] The act of speaking and the medium of Scripture preserve the differentiation between Father and Son, but nonetheless, in no other New Testament writing is the Son so closely identified with the Father! This strong emphasis on the deity of Jesus Christ has several aspects:

1. Hebrews intends this conception to be a defense against a deficient angel Christology[110] (cf. Col. 2:18), which thinks of Jesus Christ as one of the angels, even if occupying the first place among them. This is the reason for the author's strong emphasis on the categorical superiority of Jesus

108. Heb. 1:3 possibly cites an early Christian hymn; in addition to the standard commentaries, cf. Habermann, *Präexistenzaussagen*, 267–99; one could also consider the possibility of a hymnic background for Heb. 5:7–10 and 7:1–3, 26. Cf. Heinrich Zimmermann, *Das Bekenntnis der Hoffnung: Tradition und Redaktion im Hebräerbrief* (BBB 47; Bonn: Hanstein, 1977), 44ff.; Grässer, *An die Hebräer*, 1:312ff., remains skeptical.

109. Karrer, *Hebräer*, 144.

110. On this point, cf. Stuckenbruck, *Angel Veneration*, 128–35.

over the angels (1:4–8, 13–14; 2:5, 16), expressed in a particularly appropriate way by the use of the term "Son" (fifteen times in Hebrews) as a primary christological title. All the same, Hebrews attributes a positive role to the angels, that of serving and helping those who are being saved (1:14).

2. The author wants to overcome the church's lethargy—a frequent topic of complaint in Hebrews—by pointing to the superior confidence in salvation assured by this high Christology. In 5:5c the author intentionally takes the Son predication of Ps. 2:7 LXX, already used in 1:5, and links it to the redemptive ministry of Jesus Christ in a way that shows his overwhelming superiority. Every earthly high priest must offer sacrifices to atone for his own sins (5:3), so that only the sinless Son of God, as God himself, is able to accomplish atonement and salvation for the believers.
3. The central theocentric feature of the Christology of Hebrews points to an intellectual milieu influenced by the thought world of Middle Platonism (see below, §11.3.8).[111] Plutarch, Maximus of Tyre, and Apuleius all testify to the strong influence in the late first and early second centuries of Middle Platonism, which advocated primarily a theology in which God can be described negatively, by what God is not. The strong emphasis on the absolute transcendence and total otherness of God—the categorical difference of the deity's mode of being from everything human—necessarily raised the question of how communication between such a God and humanity is possible at all. The whole of the Letter to the Hebrews is engaged with responding to this question!

From the reality of the speaking God, Hebrews develops a unique Christology of lofty divine exaltation, for *it is God himself who addresses the Son as "God" and grants him the divine name*,[112] so that he is totally and without reservation not only to be assigned to the heavenly realm, but is placed in the same category as the one God.

From this line of thought, based on a theology of the word, the author also develops a conception of cultic theology. The opening, which concentrates

111. Cf. James Thompson, *The Beginnings of Christian Philosophy: The Epistle to the Hebrews* (CBQMS 13; Washington, DC: Catholic Biblical Association of America, 1982); K. Backhaus, "Per Christum in Deum: Zur theozentrischen Funktion der Christologie im Hebräerbrief," in *Der lebendige Gott: Studien zur Theologie des Neuen Testaments* (ed. Thomas Söding; NTA 31; Münster: Aschendorff, 1996), 261ff.

112. Under these presuppositions, one can hardly locate Hebrews within an inner-Jewish discourse, as does Karrer, *Hebräer*, 90: "The Letter to the Hebrews—to say it pointedly—sees its Christianity as within Judaism." Knut Backhaus, *Der Neue Bund und das Werden der Kirche: Die Diatheke-Deutung des Hebräerbriefs im Rahmen der frühchristlichen Theologiegeschichte* (NTA 29; Münster: Aschendorff, 1996), 278ff., persuasively lists the arguments against locating Hebrews within a Jewish or Jewish-Christian discourse.

on the speaking God, leads to and climaxes in the key thesis statement about the atoning high priest in Heb. 2:17–18: "Therefore he had to become like his brothers and sisters in every respect, so that he might be a merciful and faithful high priest in the service of God, to make a sacrifice of atonement for the sins of the people. Because he himself was tested by what he suffered, he is able to help those who are being tested." After 5:1, this high-priestly Christology dominates the whole line of argument,[113] in which the motif of the overwhelming superiority of Christ in the history of revelation remains determinative: the high priest Jesus Christ performs his cultic priestly ministry not in an earthly temple but in the heavenly holy place; thus he is superior to all earthly cults. The major section of Hebrews framed by 4:14–16 and 10:19–23 clearly reveals the basic thesis of the high-priestly Christology: *the sinless, suffering Jesus, installed as high priest as the Son of God, passes through the heavens and thereby makes possible free access to God for believers.* There are no real antecedents for this concept in early Christianity;[114] the author of Hebrews was the first to apply this high-priestly imagery to Jesus Christ. In regard to contemporary history, the destruction of the Jerusalem temple is a presupposition for this imagery, for this brought the Old Testament Jewish cult to its earthly end. In regard to history-of-religions ideas, Philo's statements about the high priest provide material for understanding the office of high priest in a completely transcendent and universal way. (Cf. *Flight* 108, "We say, then, that the High Priest is not a man, but a Divine Word and immune from all unrighteousness whether intentional or unintentional"; *Spec. Laws* 1.230 affirms, contrary to Lev. 16:6, "The true high priest who is not falsely so-called is immune from sin, and if ever he slips, it will be something imposed on him not because of what he does himself, but because of some lapse common to the nation." Cf. further *Spec. Laws* 1.82–97, 228; 2.164; *Dreams* 1.214–216; *Flight* 106–118; *Moses* 2.109–135.)[115] The unique particularity of the high-priestly office of Jesus is elaborated by an appeal to Ps. 110:4 ("You are a priest forever according to the order of Melchizedek"; cf. Heb. 5:6, 10; 6:20) as an absolute superiority (cf. 7:11) of the eternal high priesthood of Melchizedek (cf. Gen. 14:18–20), in contrast to the Aaronite-Levitical priesthood. While

113. In addition to the standard commentaries, cf. especially Heinrich Zimmermann, *Die Hohepriester-Christologie des Hebräerbriefes* (Paderborn: Schöningh, 1964); William R. G. Loader, *Sohn und Hoherpriester: Eine traditionsgeschichtliche Untersuchung zur Christologie des Hebräerbriefes* (WMANT 53; Neukirchen-Vluyn: Neukirchener Verlag, 1981), passim; J. Kurianal, *Jesus Our High Priest* (EHS 23.693; Frankfurt: Lang, 1999).

114. Scholars frequently refer to the Stephen tradition (Acts 6:8ff.) and to Rom. 3:25, which, of course, do not portray Jesus as high priest; for the discussion, cf. Karrer, *Hebräer*, 85–91. The earliest parallel ideas are found in *1 Clem.* 36, 40.

115. In addition to theological speculations involving high-priestly imagery, there are numerous other parallels between Hebrews and Philo. On this point, in addition to the commentaries of Hegermann and Weiss, cf. especially Ronald Williamson, *Philo and the Epistle to the Hebrews* (ALGHJ 4; Leiden: Brill, 1970), who explores all the relevant parallels.

the Levitical high priest on the great Day of Atonement (cf. Lev. 16) must also offer sacrifice for his own sins (Heb. 5:3; 7:27; 9:7, 25; 13:11), Jesus is without sin (4:15) and therefore is the one person who can actually effect atonement. Thus, as Son of God (5:5–6), Jesus is high priest according to the order of Melchizedek (7:1–10), who, like Jesus (cf. 7:14), was not of Levitical ancestry but still received tithes from Abraham.[116]

In these contexts, the Letter to the Hebrews develops an independent conception:

1. The earthly Jesus, under the conditions of a truly human existence (Heb. 2:17–18; 4:15; 10:19–20) and in complete obedience to God (2:17; 3:1–2; 5:5–10) as a sinless fellow sufferer (4:15; 7:26–28), mediates between God and humanity, and is established by God as such an authentic high priest (2:17; 3:1–2; 5:5, "So also Christ did not glorify himself in becoming a high priest"; 6:20; 7:16, 21–22; 10:21).
2. By the offering of his own life (7:27; 10:10) and blood (9:11ff.; 10:19) on Good Friday as the Day of Atonement in the heavenly Holy of Holies (6:20; 8:1–3; 10:19–20), Jesus, as the sin offering for humanity, obtained their purification from sins and their redemption (9:11–15; 10:19–20, 22).
3. The Jesus who ascends to heaven thereby opens the way to God for his own (4:14–16; 5:9; 7:19; 10:19–21; 12:2).
4. As heavenly high priest, the exalted Christ serves as intercessor and advocate with God for the hard-pressed community of faith on earth (7:22–25; 8:1, 6; 9:24; 10:21).

For evaluating the Christology of Hebrews, it is critically important to note how the earthly existence and suffering of Jesus are integrated into this exalted cultic theological conception.[117] Is the imagery of the heavenly victory so powerfully dominant that Jesus's earthly existence becomes only a necessary transitional stage without decisive importance? Older exegesis sometimes answered this question in the affirmative, and Hebrews was seen as a preliminary form or evidence of a Christian Gnosticism.[118] Weighty considerations, however, speak against this view:

116. On the Melchizedek traditions in ancient Judaism, cf. Hans Friedrich Weiss, *Der Brief an die Hebräer* (15th ed.; KEK 13; Göttingen: Vandenhoeck und Ruprecht, 1991), 373–92.

117. Cf. here especially Jürgen Roloff, "Der mitleidende Hohepriester," in *Exegetische Verantwortung in der Kirche: Aufsätze* (ed. Martin Karrer; Göttingen: Vandenhoeck & Ruprecht, 1990), 144–67.

118. Cf. Ernst Käsemann, *The Wandering People of God: An Investigation of the Letter to the Hebrews* (trans. Roy A. Harrisville and Irving L. Sandberg; Minneapolis: Augsburg, 1984), 90ff.; Erich Grässer, "Hebräer, 1,1–4: Ein exegetischer Versuch," in *Text und Situation: Gesammelte Aufsätze zum Neuen Testament* (ed. Erich Grässer; Gütersloh: Gütersloher Verlagshaus G. Mohn, 1973), 224: "The life of Jesus and the cross retain their character as episodes: the

1. In Heb. 2:14a ("Since, therefore, the children share flesh and blood, he himself likewise shared the same things") we find, along with John 1:14, the clearest affirmation of the incarnation in the New Testament.
2. The argumentation of the whole letter is characterized by an interweaving of the heavenly and earthly event (Heb. 2:10/2:11–18; 4:14/4:15; 5:1–7/5:7–10; 9:11/9:12–15; 10:12). On earth Jesus exercised the office of high priest with his once-for-all sacrifice that he presented by his death on the cross as the eschatological act of atonement (9:11–28; 10:10). In his once-for-all death on the cross (cf. 7:27; 9:28; 10:10, 12, 14) the Son passed through the heavenly curtain, τοῦτ' ἔστιν τῆς σαρκὸς αὐτοῦ ("that is, through his flesh/body," 10:20), in order to enter into his heavenly ministry of making intercession for believers (cf. 7:25; 9:24; 4:16). Hebrews neither understands the exaltation to heaven as the decisive event that supersedes the cross, nor does it speak of an eternal self-offering of the Son; rather, the author of Hebrews succeeds in facilitating an understanding that "in terms of cultic theology brings together the Christ event of cross and exaltation as the saving event that includes earth and heaven, time and eternity"[119] (2:9, "We do see Jesus, who for a little while was made lower than the angels, now crowned with glory and honor because of the suffering of death, so that by the grace of God he might taste death for everyone"). In Hebrews, the cross and exaltation, the earthly and heavenly realms, collapse into each other, so that in the ἐφάπαξ (once-for-all) event, space and time are given a new quality.
3. The central motif of the compassionate solidarity of the bringer of salvation points to the cross as the place of salvation (Heb. 2:17–18; 5:7–10); the incarnation of Jesus is itself an act of saving solidarity. Jesus is the "pioneer of salvation" (ἀρχηγὸς τῆς σωτηρίας) who is made perfect through his sufferings, and who thus leads many children to glory (2:10).

The high-priestly Christology is grounded in the conviction that in the death of the sinless Jesus, death and the devil have been robbed of their power (Heb. 2:14b, "so that through death he might destroy the one who has the power of death, that is, the devil"), so that he alone and not the earthly (Jewish) high priest can effect the removal of sins. Like other forms of Christology, the high-priestly imagery portrays the *ministry of intercession* between God

---

goal is the exaltation"; cf. also Grässer, *An die Hebräer*, 1:135–36; for critique of the Gnostic interpretative model, cf. Weiss, *Hebräer*, 385.

119. Franz Laub, "'Ein für allemal hineingegangen in das Allerheiligste' (Hebr 9,12): Zum Verständnis des Kreuzestodes im Hebräerbrief," *BZ* 35 (1991): 80; Hermut Löhr, "Wahrnehmung und Bedeutung des Todes Jesu nach dem Hebräerbrief," in *Deutungen des Todes Jesu im Neuen Testament* (ed. J. Frey and J. Schröter; WUNT 181; Tübingen: Mohr, 2005), 455–76.

and humanity exercised by Jesus, who belongs at the same time to the earthly and heavenly realms.

11.3.3 Pneumatology

The Letter to the Hebrews does not contain a developed pneumatology, but the Spirit (of God) is included as an essential element in central lines of the letter's argument. The basic perspective is that the Holy Spirit comes from God, who distributes it according to his own will (Heb. 2:4). The Holy Spirit emerges in the context of God's speaking (3:7), and testifies to God's saving acts (10:15). Christ's reconciling act on the cross takes place through the "eternal Spirit" (9:14), the Spirit of God (cf. Rom. 1:3–4; 1 Tim. 3:16).[120] In the self-offering of Jesus Christ, it is God himself who acts; God brings him back from the dead (Heb. 13:20), installs him as the eternal high priest, and effects the believers' redemption. Therefore, all those who fall away from the faith vilify God and the Holy Spirit as they "trample the Son of God underfoot" (10:29 TNIV; cf. 6:4, 6).

11.3.4 Soteriology

The whole high-priestly Christology of the Letter to the Hebrews stands in the service of soteriology. The levitical high priesthood and the law do not have the power to bring humanity to their appointed goal: to participate in the holiness and glory of God's essential being and to have free access to God. The only one who can do this is the Son, who was made like his brothers and sisters in every respect, "so that he might be a merciful and faithful high priest in the service of God, to make a sacrifice of atonement for the sins of the people" (2:17). Jesus's capacity to sympathize with human beings (4:15; 2:17) is grounded in his own experience of anguish in suffering (5:7–10). Because Jesus himself suffered and was delivered over to the temptations of sin, but was not defeated by the power of sin, he is the only one who can truly cleanse from sin: "Because he himself was tested by what he suffered, he is able to help those who are being tested" (cf. 2:18; cf. further 1:3; 2:17; 4:15; 5:7–8). Soteriological deliverance is for Hebrews primarily the forgiveness of sins: the letter's whole soteriological conception is dependent on the two words χωρὶς ἁμαρτίας (without sin) in 4:15! Because Jesus was without sin, only he can take away sins. Jesus's sinlessness, however, is not only the result of his divine "nature," but is also the result of his struggle and conscious decision (cf. 12:2–3). *Sinlessness thus marks the incarnational and epiphanic difference between Jesus and all other human beings.* The lost human being,

120. Cf. Harald Hegermann, *Der Brief an die Hebräer* (THKNT 16; Berlin: Evangelische Verlagsanstalt, 1988), 180.

whose guilt and alienation from God cannot be overcome through the law, is delivered from the grasp off sin and led to perfection only through the blood of Jesus (7:11–19; 9:11–12). Hebrews thus develops a mediator soteriology:[121] in and through the event of the cross, Jesus becomes the mediator between the earthly and heavenly worlds of reality, making it possible for human beings to approach God with full assurance. As 10:19–20 states, "Therefore, my friends, since we have confidence to enter the sanctuary by the blood of Jesus, by the new and living way that he opened for us through the curtain (that is, through his flesh)." The consummation of Jesus's way has soteriological quality, for "by a single offering he has perfected for all time those who are sanctified" (10:14).

This is a message that must be *heard*: hearing and responding is the necessary human counterpart to the theology of the word that is the fundamental theme of Hebrews. Salvation, in fact, depends on this hearing, for it is in the act of responsive hearing that the saving act of God is revealed (Heb. 2:1, "Therefore we must pay greater attention to what we have heard, so that we do not drift away from it"; cf. 4:1–2, 12–13; 6:4–5).

11.3.5 Anthropology

Anthropology is a central theme of Hebrews, for in 2:4–18, the author's consideration of Ps. 8 and Gen. 1 extends the lofty Son Christology of Heb. 1 into a lofty anthropology. Human beings are only a little lower than the angels; God has placed everything under their feet (2:7–8). The children ("sons"), as God's creation, come from God just as does *the* Son. Human beings are directly related to Jesus (2:11), who does not insulate himself from human misery by wrapping himself in the holiness of the heavenly world; rather, he intentionally takes suffering upon himself so that he can restore human beings to their original grandeur. Here it becomes clear that in the Letter to the Hebrews, anthropology derives from Christology,[122] that the message of Hebrews is about the salvation of endangered humanity. Because Jesus, in giving himself over to death, completely identified himself with human beings and broke through the barrier of death (2:14–15), new assurance and freedom are opened up to human beings to overcome their subjection to death and to approach God with confidence (cf. παρρησία [boldness] in 4:16; 10:19, 35).

Sin

In Hebrews, the fundamental threat faced by humanity is bound up with the concept of sin. The work of the devil and death are concentrated in sin, for it is through sin that death invades and commandeers life, and sin receives its reward

121. Cf. Backhaus, "Per Christum," 269–70.
122. Cf. Karrer, *Hebräer*, 1:164.

in death. Sin is understood in a broad spectrum of ways:[123] the central idea is that by his death on the cross, Jesus has taken away sin and purified believers (Heb. 1:3, "When he had made purification for sins"; 2:17, "so that he might be a merciful and faithful high priest in the service of God, to make a sacrifice of atonement for the sins of the people"; 10:12, "But when Christ had offered for all time a single sacrifice for sins"; cf. 10:10, 14, 18). Here, sin appears as a power, a power that no earthly institution, including that of the high priest, is able to overcome (cf. 5:1, 3; 7:27; 10:6, 8; 13:11). Hebrews 10:4 formulates this programmatically: "For it is impossible for the blood of bulls and goats to take away sins." Hebrews thus speaks of the deceitfulness of sin (3:13), and insistently demands that sin be resisted (12:1, "Let us also lay aside every weight and the sin that clings so closely"; 12:4, "In your struggle against sin you have not yet resisted to the point of shedding your blood"). In 10:26, sin appears as something that can be avoided: "For if we willfully persist in sin after having received the knowledge of the truth, there no longer remains a sacrifice for sins." The positive corollary is reference to Jesus as the example in the struggle against sin (12:3). The author of Hebrews evidently attempts to combine two ideas that are (necessarily) not entirely free of contradiction, in order to renew the church's assurance of salvation and to motivate it in its continuing in the way of salvation: Jesus overcame sin on the cross, because only he is without sin (4:15; 7:26). At the same time, however, it is necessary to resist sin and to break through the negative connections between weakness, temptation, and sin. The christological and anthropological-ethical lines of thought perceive sin from different perspectives. While the former indicates that sin is fundamentally overcome in the Christ event, the latter registers its continuing existence as a real threat, as seen above all in the possibility of apostasy from salvation. Hebrews understands apostasy as sin in the absolute sense and urgently warns against it.

With the dissolution of the old cultic order, the *law* also lost its importance. Hebrews does not advocate an understanding of the law as a discrete topic but discusses the *law* only as an aspect of its cultic theology. It is definitively abolished, for the power of sin that separates from salvation cannot be overcome by the law. The law belongs to the category of externals, not to authentic life (7:16); it is not able to lead on to perfection (7:18–19a), because it is weak and unable to take away sins (10:1–2, 11).

Faith

Hebrews is the only New Testament writing to offer a definition of faith:[124] "Now faith is the assurance of things hoped for, the conviction of things not

123. For a detailed analysis, cf. Hermut Löhr, *Umkehr und Sünde im Hebräerbrief* (BZNW 73; Berlin: de Gruyter, 1994), 11–135.

124. On the concept of faith in Hebrews, cf. Erich Grässer, *Der Glaube im Hebräerbrief* (MTS 2; Marburg: Elwert, 1965), passim; Gerhard Dautzenberg, "Der Glaube im Hebräerbrief,"

seen" (11:1). The noun πίστις is found thirty-two times in Hebrews, a clear signal of the importance of this theme for the author's theology. Since the faith of the addressees is under severe attack, Hebrews emphasizes the steadfastness and resilience of authentic faith. At its core, faith is a confidence that relies on God's act in his Son and thus contains within itself its assurance in God and from God. Hebrews, like Philo, emphasizes the orientation of faith to the invisible, and thus to God himself. Faith is an absolute dependence on the invisible, the heavenly world, which in contrast to the earthly visible world is unchanging and imperishable. Believers can shelter their lives from the vicissitudes of the visible world only by aligning themselves, through faith, with the heavenly, unchanging world. The somewhat theoretical understanding of faith in Hebrews is also indicated by the fact that an object of faith is rarely named. Only in 6:1 does the author speak of "faith in God," and in 11:6 of faith that "God really is." The series of examples of faith in Heb. 11 is oriented to a pre-Christian history of the heroes of faith, at the end of which stands Jesus as the one who, as the pioneer and perfecter of faith, is now seated at God's right hand.

Unlike John and Paul, Hebrews does not define faith in strictly Christological terms; rather, faith describes primarily the attitude of people who endure testing, distinguish themselves by patience, and live by an unconditional assurance. Faith thus becomes something like a virtue or an ethical principle—but is not simply reduced to a virtue or principle.[125] The free access to God made possible through faith is in fact only made possible by Jesus Christ, who overcame the power of sin by his self-offering as the true high priest. Thus Heb. 10:22–23 can issue the challenge, "Let us approach with a true heart in full assurance of faith . . . Let us hold fast to the confession of our hope without wavering, for he who has promised is faithful." What faith hopes for is found in "the world to come" (2:5), the "city that is to come" (13:14), the eschatological Sabbath rest that is still to come, God's own rest (4:1ff.), "the promised eternal inheritance" (9:15). Hebrews' concept of faith thus stands clearly in continuity with the biblical and Jewish tradition, while at the same time all authentic human faith is grounded in the saving work of the high priest Jesus Christ. Only the suffering and death of Jesus is the basis of faith (2:17–18), for the assurance of faith is grounded in the confidence that Jesus has overcome the power of sin and thus the power of death.

The Conscience and the Soul

The Letter to the Hebrews has a marked psychological interest, for it treats thematically the innermost and deepest layers of human being. Of the thirty

BZ 17 (1973): 161–77; Dieter Lührmann, *Glaube im frühen Christentum* (Gütersloh: Güterloher Verlagshaus, 1976), 70–77; Weiss, *Hebräer*, 564–71.

125. Differently Grässer, *An die Hebräer*, 3:84–85, who interprets πίστις as the Christian virtue of steadfastness in the context "of an effort to conserve an acquired spiritual inheritance" (80).

instances of συνείδησις (conscience) in the New Testament, five are found in Hebrews. *Conscience is the location of human self-knowledge in regard to the will of God.* There is thus a crucial deficit in the old cultic order, in that its sacrifices could not really satisfy the uneasy conscience (Heb. 9:9), while the blood of Christ "purifies our conscience from dead works to worship the living God" (9:14). Because the conscience is the place where human beings become aware of their sins, those who come year by year with offerings seeking removal of their sins receive no satisfaction (10:2). In contrast, all who stand in the assurance of faith may come boldly to God with a clear conscience (10:22). A person's sins are present in the conscience; when sins are taken away, the conscience is also purified. The conscience as the organ and place of realistic self-evaluation leads the author of Hebrews to say in his concluding statements, "Pray for us; we are sure that we have a clear conscience" (13:18). Here συνείδησις appears in the sense common in the ancient world as the internal court of self-evaluation, which derives its criteria from a model pattern of how life should be lived.

The living center of the person, the inner self, is designated in Hebrews as the ψυχή ("soul"; six times).[126] According to Heb. 4:12, God's word penetrates the depths of human life, separating even soul and spirit, joints and marrow. The word of promise is an "anchor of the soul" (6:19), and those who remain steadfast in faith will "attain life" (10:39, εἰς περιποίησιν ψυχῆς, lit. "preserve their soul"). It is the teacher's task to keep watch over the souls of the community of faith (13:17), i.e., to work for the maintenance of their salvation. Thus Hebrews uses the term ψυχή to designate the innermost self, as the person stands before God; that "organ" that is at the same time receptive and vulnerable to God's word.

11.3.6 Ethics

In the "word from/about Christ" (Heb. 6:1), God himself speaks in the most direct immediacy, so that everything depends on whether and how one hears (2:1–4). To disdain this word would mean the irretrievable loss of unrepeatable grace: "See that you do not refuse the one who is speaking" (12:25a). In order to prevent this loss, Hebrews does not speak polemically to outsiders, but *encouragingly to insiders.* It is a matter of assessing and assuring the stability of the church he addresses, for its load-bearing pillars of faith have begun to shake. In regard to the message of salvation, the church has become "hard of hearing" and sluggish (cf. 5:11; 6:11, 12). Worship at-

126. Cf. also Hermut Löhr, "Anthropologie und Eschatologie im Hebräerbrief," in *Eschatologie und Schöpfung* (ed. M. Evang et al.; BZNW 89; Berlin: de Gruyter, 1997), 185: "The soul is that part of the human being that is exceptionally attuned to salvation and the last things. Salvation or damnation of the person as a whole is decided on the basis of the state of the soul."

tendance has declined (cf. 10:25), and the church needs to start over at the very beginning, relearning the first principles of the faith (cf. 5:12–6:2). Like the wilderness generation of Israel, the church is in danger of undervaluing God's grace (cf. 3:7–4:13; 12:15). Thus apostasy from the faith and the related problem of a second repentance was a current theme in the church (cf. 6:4–6; 10:26–29; 12:16–17; also 3:12; 12:15).[127] Here the soteriological, anthropological, and ethical argumentation of Hebrews becomes more dense: whoever denies the faith tramples the Son of God underfoot and profanes the blood of the covenant (10:29). The magnitude and once-for-all nature of the sacrifice of Jesus Christ is followed consistently by the warning not to disdain his saving work by apostasy. There can be no return for those who have fallen away; for that would nullify the meaning of Jesus's death on the cross (cf. 6:4–6; 10:26–29; 12:16–18). The once-for-all character of Jesus's sacrifice has its counterpart in the one baptism, but not in a second repentance. The ἐφάπαξ (once-for-all) nature of the saving event that is foundational for Christology and soteriology does not allow for a repetition of μετάνοια (repentance). In this context, the admonitions and warnings have primarily a positive, encouraging function,[128] for they call to memory the soteriological foundation that God has laid once and for all; they intend to strengthen the insight that the readers must not fall back from the status they have already reached. The passive formulation in 6:4–5 ("those who have once been enlightened . . .") shows that the repentance of which the author speaks is much more than a human change of mind; it is always and above all the granting of a grace that can be lost again.[129] But if the church, in faith and obedience to the promise, remains unshakably steadfast, it is promised—in contrast to the wilderness generation of Israel—that it will enter into God's eschatological rest. The church must not abandon its faith-filled confidence (10:35); the tired hands and weak knees must be strengthened (cf. 12:12), lest the death of Jesus Christ on the cross be mocked through their conduct (6:6). The later refinements and differentiations of penance theology are still far removed from the author of Hebrews,[130] who is concerned that the church ascertain its own faith, for its believers have already experienced a foretaste of eschatological salvation and nonetheless are in danger of abandoning the way they have already chosen.

The statements about a second repentance fit into the *ethical conception of Hebrews as a whole*, which is dominated by axioms (e.g., Heb. 2:1–4; 4:14–16; 10:19–21) that yield challenging and probing ethical corollaries (cf.

127. For analysis of the texts, in addition to the standard commentaries, see especially Goldhahn-Müller, *Die Grenze der Gemeinde*, 75–114.

128. Cf. Weiss, *Hebräer*, 347–51.

129. Cf. Löhr, *Umkehr*, 286ff.

130. On this point, cf. Goldhahn-Müller, *Die Grenze der Gemeinde*, 225–78.

Heb. 3:1; 4:1, 11; 10:22–24; 12:1–2, 12).[131] The author appeals to insight, but also to the emotions and to the fundamental convictions of the addressees, and thus contributes to the process of their ethical meaning-formation. He introduces examples (negative: the unbelief and disobedience of the wilderness generation, 3:7–19; 4:1–11; Esau, 12:16; positive: the faith and obedience of Jesus, 3:1–6; 5:1–10; the "cloud of witnesses" of chap. 11; an example from nature in 6:7–8). He formulates rhetorical questions (1:5, 10; 3:16–18; 7:11; 12:7, 9), and offers strengthening and enabling words of comfort to the community of faith (6:9–10, "Even though we speak in this way, beloved, we are confident of better things in your case, things that belong to salvation [σωτηρία]. For God is not unjust; he will not overlook your work and the love that you showed for his sake in serving the saints, as you still do."). The ethical statements of Hebrews can thus be described as paraclesis, inasmuch as "paraclesis also includes 'new' or deepening and clarifying explanations, which allow for reasoning, argumentation and the establishment of a theoretical foundation for a specific exhortation in a specific situation."[132] *While parenesis is comprised of brief and practical instructions, paraclesis is formulated with a theological basis, and is directed comprehensively to the intellect, to the heart, and to theological insight.* Only deepened theological perception, knowledge, and assent can reactivate insights that have been clouded over and generate new alignments and orientations.[133] The semantic data also speak for the classification *paraclesis*, since the noun παράκλησις appears in 6:18; 12:5; and 13:22 and the verb παρακαλέω in 3:13; 10:25; 13:19, 22; the author himself designates his writing a λόγος τῆς παρακλήσεως in 13:22, which might be translated "a word of helpful insight." Finally, 13:1–5, 7, 17–19 is composed entirely of brief admonitions directed to the current situation.

11.3.7 Ecclesiology

The paracletic (offering encouraging insight) theology of the Letter to the Hebrews, taken as a whole, has an ecclesiological dimension, for its goal is to generate a changed and renewed way of thinking and acting within the church. Because the life of the church is no longer permeated to its depths by the confession of faith it had once accepted, the danger of apostasy increases (cf. Heb. 2:1–4; 3:12–19; 4:1–13; 10:26–31; 12:14–17). The author wants to overcome the church's lack of confidence resulting from the weakness of its

131. For evidence and argument, cf. W. Übelacker, "Paraenesis or Paraclesis," in *Early Christian Paraenesis in Context* (ed. Troels Engberg-Pedersen and James M. Starr; BZNW 125; Berlin: de Gruyter, 2004), 327–46.

132. Cf. ibid., 348.

133. Cf. here also Seneca, *Ep.* 94, where Seneca gives an extensive discussion of his own views on the forms and foundations of ethical instruction.

faith and life. It belongs to the third generation of early Christianity (cf. 2:3; 3:14; 5:12; 6:10–12; 10:32–34), has endured persecutions (10:32–34; cf. also 6:10; 13:7), but has used up the energies of its beginnings. Thus the author especially emphasizes holding firmly to the confession of faith it has received from tradition (cf. 1:2; 2:3–4; 3:14; 4:14; 10:23; 13:7–9) and emphatically attempts to steer the church back to focusing on the Christ event as the all-embracing reality that determines its life.

The New Covenant

The author adopts the covenant concept as the basic ecclesiological metaphor; of thirty-three instances of διαθήκη (covenant) in the New Testament, seventeen occur in Hebrews, concentrated mainly in the central section (Heb. 7:1–10:18).[134] On the cross, Jesus established the better covenant (7:20–22) and is the mediator of a new covenant, which alone is able to bring redemption (9:15; cf. also 7:22; 8:6, 10; 10:16–18, 29; 12:24). The new covenant (καινὴ διαθήκη in 8:8; 9:15) surpasses the first covenant, because as the pioneer (2:10) and forerunner (6:20) of salvation, Jesus has already entered into the heavenly sanctuary and offered the true sacrifice (cf. 7:26; 8:1–2; 9:11, 24). Believers may follow Jesus in the confidence that, precisely through their own sufferings they attain the redemption achieved through the suffering of the Son. The author intentionally concludes his writing in 13:20 with the assurance that Jesus has put the "eternal covenant" into effect.

The author's covenant theology adopts the linguistic conventions of the Old Testament and early Judaism (cf. the reception of Jer. 31:31–34 and Exod. 24:8 in Heb. 8:8–12; 9:20; 10:16), while transforming its center and giving it a new interpretation. The author of Hebrews does not take into account the plurality of covenant traditions in the Old Testament but concentrates on the motifs of breaking the covenant and the blindness of the people of the old covenant. Neither does he take up the central connection between covenant and law.[135] The real link between Old Testament conceptions of the covenant and the covenant theology of Hebrews is found in its theocentricity: God is the origin, midst, and goal of the covenant.[136] At the same time, this theocentricity is filled with christological content and thus receives a new profile, for in Hebrews the center of the covenant concept is confessing Christ. In terms of text pragmatics, this term is an important element for the self-assessment and self-definition of a church that must redefine its own identity en route.

134. In addition to the foundational work of Backhaus, *Der neue Bund*, cf. especially Ulrich Luz, "Der alte und der neue Bund bei Paulus und im Hebräerbrief," *EvT* 27 (1967): 318–36; Grässer, "Bund," 1–134 (extensive treatment of all New Testament data); Weiss, *Hebräer*, 411–15.

135. Cf. Backhaus, *Der neue Bund*, 333.

136. Ibid., 350.

The Wandering People of God

An additional central ecclesiological metaphor is the image of the wandering people of God (cf. especially Heb. 3:7–4:11).[137] While the Israelite people who wandered in the wilderness cannot enter into the rest God had promised because of their disobedience, the consequences for the present must be drawn: "today" God's people must hear his voice and not harden their hearts (3:7–8). For Hebrews, the people of God are now composed of Christian believers who were previously Jews and those who were previously Gentiles, who now hear the same message once heard by the wilderness generation (4:2). The rest once promised to Israel is linked to the eschatological rest granted through Christ. Within the idea of the one people of God, there is a clear escalation, with the idea that the new people of God surpass the old, for the situation of the people of God in the time of the old covenant was different from that during the time of the new covenant. The imagery of the household in 3:4–6 expresses this dynamic: "For every house is built by someone, but the builder of all things is God. Now Moses was faithful in all God's house as a servant, to testify to the things that would be spoken later. Christ, however, was faithful over God's house as a son, and we are his house if we hold firm the confidence and the pride that belong to hope." Hebrews contains no reflections on the church/Israel relation from the perspective of salvation history, but the conception of the one people of God is combined with a theology of the word of God. This combination is crucial, since in every age the word of God, coming through God's own speaking, is what calls the people of God into being. Every generation stands before the challenge of responding to this word, allowing it to move them forward to the place of eschatological rest, which means to follow the path ultimately opened up by Christ. The promise applies solely to the wandering people of God of the new covenant (cf. 11:1–12:3), and everything depends on running "with perseverance the race that is set before us" (12:1). The church of Hebrews is determined by the reality that it is on its way toward a goal beyond this world and its history; it lives by the truth that "here we have no lasting city, but we are looking for the city that is to come" (13:14). In the present, the heavenly city of God is still closed; believers are not yet there, but they experience its reality through the unconditional promise of the word (12:22).

Hebrews makes no explicit reference to *church offices*, but within the church there are leaders (13:7, 17, 24) whose primary duty is to facilitate a hearing of the word of God in every situation of the community's life. They are to keep it from apostasy through encouragement and deeper involvement in this

137. Cf. here Erich Grässer, "Das wandernde Gottesvolk," in *Aufbruch und Verheissung: Gesammelte Aufsätze zum Hebräerbrief; zum 65. Geburtstag mit einer Bibliographie des Verfassers* (ed. Erich Grässer et al.; BZNW 65; Berlin: de Gruyter, 1992), 231–50; Roloff, *Kirche im Neuen Testament*, 282–87.

word. The teachers' authority derives solely from the word of God, which they help the church members to understand by the pastoral care that follows their preaching and teaching. According to 13:17, teachers are responsible for their commission and must render account to God. Terminological echoes of baptism (3:14; made explicit in 6:2) and the Lord's Supper (6:4–5; 9:20; 10:29; 13:9–10)[138] are present, but are not developed theologically. The church of Hebrews (ἐκκλησία in 2:12; 12:23) is exclusively a church of the word. It lives from the reality that this word is constantly given to it anew, and it is always in the situation of being able to penetrate more deeply into it. Jesus made this communion possible through his incarnation, and he opened up God's future to the church by his enthronement as heavenly high priest. The church may live in this assurance, since it is the "assembly of the firstborn who are enrolled in heaven" (12:23).

11.3.8 Eschatology

The eschatological statements of the Letter to the Hebrews must also be seen in the context of the paracletic orientation of the letter as a whole. The author takes up a variety of traditions, in part placing his own new stamp on them, in order to inculcate into his church a sense of the great responsibility they have for the salvation longed for but still to come, and to encourage them to hold fast to the salvation already experienced. His thought leads to an interweaving of spatial and temporal categories, without completely balancing the one against the other.

Resurrection and Parousia

According to Heb. 6:2, the resurrection hope is a basic element of the Christian faith, for the church had been instructed in the teachings about "repentance from dead works and faith toward God, instruction about baptisms, laying on of hands, resurrection of the dead, and eternal judgment." This hope is based on the resurrection of Jesus from the dead as *the* eschatological saving event: "Now may the God of peace, who brought back from the dead our Lord Jesus, the great shepherd of the sheep, by the blood of the eternal covenant . . ." (13:20). By his death Jesus destroyed the devil and thereby the power of death, so that now believers are no longer victims of slavery to death (2:14–16). To be sure, human beings will die and give account in the judgment (9:27; 10:27; 12:29), but for Jesus too life and death was a once-for-all event. God raised him from the dead, and believers may confidently hope that God will act for them in the same way. The author speaks of a different sort of resurrection in 11:5, 19, 35: for the witnesses of the old covenant, there was already a this-worldly, metaphorical resurrection, which, to be sure, is sharply

138. Cf. Weiss, *Hebräer*, 726–29.

distinguished from the eschatological resurrection, described in 11:35 as the "better resurrection."[139]

Jesus's *parousia* comes into view in Heb. 10:25 ("all the more as you see the Day approaching") and 10:37 ("in a very little while, the one who is coming will come and will not delay"). Hebrews 1:6 ("And again, when he brings the firstborn into the world, he says, 'Let all God's angels worship him'") probably also refers to the parousia, as indicated by the πάλιν (again) and the points of contact with 2:5 ("coming world"/angels).[140] Hebrews thinks of the parousia primarily in temporal terms but also links it with spatial categories, as indicated by 9:24–28. Jesus has gone into heaven, "now to appear in the presence of God on our behalf" (9:24b). On the cross he bore the sins of many, and he will now "appear a second time, not to deal with sin, but to save those who are eagerly waiting for him" (9:28).

Heavenly Realities

The worldview of Hebrews is essentially stamped by a dualistic order of being, according to which everything that is visible/changeable passes away, while the invisible/unchangeable is the truly real and abiding. Behind the visible world there stands, as its invisible pattern and prototype, the invisible heavenly world. Faith recognizes "that the worlds were prepared by the word of God, so that what is seen was made from things that are not visible" (Heb. 11:3; cf. also 4:3c). God is the creator of both worlds, but the only abiding reality is the heavenly world. The unshakable world of heaven—into which Christ entered at his exaltation, which is subject to him, and in which the believers also participate—is the central eschatological good (8:1, "Now the main point in what we are saying is this: we have such a high priest, one who is seated at the right hand of the throne of the Majesty in the heavens"). While the earthly cult in Jerusalem is only an "image" (or "sketch" or "copy") and "shadow" of the heavenly reality (8:5), the promise of the new covenant consists in the fact that believers, through the new high priest Jesus, have access to God in the heavenly Holy of Holies (10:19–23). While the wilderness generation failed because they were fixed on the visible (12:18–19, mountain, fire, storm), Jesus made it possible for believers, after their death, to participate in the heavenly festal assembly (12:22–23). In faith (cf. 3:1, the "heavenly call") and in worship (6:4, tasting the "heavenly gift"), the church is already privy to this reality. But everything depends on not rejecting the one who opens up this heavenly reality and makes it available: "Therefore, since we are receiving a kingdom that cannot be shaken, let us give thanks" (12:28a). Spatial dimensions serve as metaphors for the qualification of realms of being, in which it is characteristic

139. Cf. Löhr, "Anthropologie und Eschatologie," 187–89.

140. Cf. Wilfried Eisele, *Ein unerschütterliches Reich: Die mittelplatonische Umformung des Parusiegedankens im Hebräerbrief* (BZNW 116; Berlin: de Gruyter, 2003), 127–28.

of the thought of Hebrews that there is a combination of apocalyptic and Middle Platonic ideas. While numerous individual motifs derive from Jewish apocalyptic,[141] the dualistic pairs of earth and heaven, visible and invisible, perishable and abiding, shakable and unshakable, changeable and unchangeable, foreign land and homeland, time and eternity,[142] all point to an influence of Middle Platonism (cf., e.g., 8:5; 9:23; 11:3, 10, 13; 12:22–24, 25–29; 13:14).[143]

The Eschatological Rest

With an interpretation of Ps. 95:7–8, 11, the author of Hebrews in 3:7–4:11 portrays the believers' participation in the final events as "entering into the rest [κατάπαυσις] of God."[144] This expression refers to the place where God's promises are ultimately fulfilled; whoever enters that realm participates in the divine Sabbath rest (Heb. 4:4), resting as God himself did (4:10). Like the image of the "heavenly city" (11:10; 12:22; 13:14) or the "heavenly fatherland" (11:14, 16), the concept of eschatological rest as being totally in God's presence belongs to Hebrews' stock of metaphors for portraying the state of ultimate salvation. Κατάπαυσις is a theological designation for the goal to which the wandering people of God are en route. While this place is not simply to be identified with the Holy of Holies into which the high priest Jesus has already entered (6:20; 9:12; 10:19), 4:16 makes clear that "entering into that rest" and "approaching the throne of God" are closely related. Entering into this rest is the fulfillment of the eschatological promise of God that has remained the same through the ages, and though the wilderness generation failed to attain it, now it is a reality, through the leadership of Jesus the high priest, for those who have faith.

The multiplicity of eschatological motifs and statements shows that the author of Hebrews is concerned to work through the problem of the delay of the parousia as an independent issue.[145] He holds fast to the perspective of the imminent expectation but at the same time prefers spatial statements to temporal ones (under Middle Platonic influence), in order to more strongly emphasize the ontological status of the new being that transcends time.[146] This preference is already suggested by the way his Christology is conceived pri-

141. Cf., e.g., for Heb. 12:18–24 the exegesis of Weiss, *Hebräer*, 668–83.

142. Cf., e.g., Plutarch, *E Delph*. 19: "What, then, really is Being? It is that which is eternal, without beginning and without end, to which no length of time brings change."

143. For evidence and argument, cf. Eisele, *Unerschütterliches Reich*, 375–414. The Stoic concept of the true city should also be noted: "For the Stoics say that in the real sense, heaven is a city, while those here on earth are not true cities at all" (*SVF* 3.327).

144. Cf. here Otfried Hofius, *Katapausis: Die Vorstellung vom endzeitlichen Ruheort im Hebräerbrief* (WUNT 11; Tübingen: Mohr, 1970); Weiss, *Hebräer*, 268–73.

145. Cf. Weiss, *Hebräer*, 72–74.

146. Cf. Eisele, *Unerschütterliches Reich*, 132: "The traditional temporal schema of apocalyptic recedes behind spatial-ontological conceptions. In place of the already/not-yet, Hebrews places the dualism of shakable and unshakable, both of which already exist alongside each other."

marily in cultic terms, and therefore in spatial categories. The promised inheritance (1:14; 6:12; 9:15b), the "better hope" (7:19), the "confession of our hope" (10:23), and the "land he had been promised" (11:19) are all grounded in the once-for-all act of Jesus's self-offering, the Jesus who has now become the pioneer of salvation and has opened up and led the way into the heavenly sanctuary. In Hebrews, that which is still to come (13:14) does not refer to the content of faith and the present status of salvation, but to the preservation of salvation in the struggles for faith that immediately threaten the church. Believers are partners of Christ (3:14a), if they "hold our first confidence firm to the end" (3:14b).

11.3.9 Setting in the History of Early Christian Theology

In several respects, the Letter to the Hebrews occupies a special position within the New Testament writings.[147]

1. It is the witness to a theology of the word of God in the New Testament. God's speaking through the ages is the ground and the goal of all that is; in Jesus Christ as the founder and perfecter of salvation (Heb. 12:2) the saving event has happened at the end of the ages.
2. The Letter to the Hebrews is the witness of paracletic theology in the New Testament, for the author attempts to overcome the fatigue and weariness within the church, the fading away of its knowledge, the faintheartedness and feeling of nonredemption, by his deepened interpretation of the church's confession of faith—and that means through theology. Believers may follow Jesus in the confidence that precisely in their own sufferings they may attain perfection through the sufferings of the Son and participate in the redemption he has obtained for them. The assurance of salvation, and the experience of salvation in the present, are to overcome the stagnation of faith within the church, for the believing community may orient its life to the faithfulness of the God who speaks in the Son. From the greatness and once-for-all character of Jesus's sacrifice comes the consequent warning not to disdain his saving work through apostasy. Teaching and exhortation constantly alternate throughout Hebrews, each dependent on and reinforcing the other, such that the particular profile of Hebrews is to be seen in this consistent pointing of the teaching material to paraclesis.
3. The Letter to the Hebrews is the document of a theology by comparison in the New Testament: the saving act of the Son is developed in contrast to the old cultic order. Hebrews presents the superiority of the

147. On the achievements and limits of the theology of Hebrews, cf. Weiss, *Hebräer*, 767–86.

> new order of salvation in antithetical terms, such that the surpassing status of Jesus is seen especially in comparison to the angels and to the earthly high priest. The dualistic reading of the Old Testament under the influence of Jewish-Hellenistic and Middle Platonic traditions expresses a comprehensive process of reevaluation that is characterized by the idea of a qualitative superiority.

Within the history of early Christian theology, lines of connection between Hebrews and other streams of tradition can be discerned. Thus Heb. 1:1–4 manifests agreements with John 1:1–18; Phil. 2:6–11; Rom. 1:3–4; 1 Cor. 8:6; Col. 1:15ff. Like Paul (cf. Gal. 3; Rom. 4), the author of Hebrews also takes up the promise to Abraham (cf. Heb. 6:13–20; 11:8–19). The imagery of the atoning sacrifice is found both in Rom. 3:25 and Heb. 2:17–18, and, like Paul (cf. 2 Cor. 3), the author knows the antithesis first covenant–new covenant. At the same time, there are considerable differences between Paul's theology and that of Hebrews (law, justification, the concept of faith),[148] so that the author, despite Heb. 13:23–24, cannot be seen as a student of Paul. Rather, Hebrews represents an independent theology that, near the end of the first century CE, attempted to solve the problem of the church's weakening of faith by a combination of stock-taking, assurance, and warning.

11.4 Jude and 2 Peter: Identity through Tradition and Polemic against Heresy

As pseudepigraphical documents, Jude and 2 Peter are closely related, since 2 Peter incorporates almost all of Jude.[149] Both letters have the same goal, which each pursues in its own way: to rebut a competing doctrine and to safeguard their churches from its effects.

The Theological Conception of the Letter of Jude

The Letter of Jude is written in response to a current danger to the faith of the church(es) it addresses (Jude 3). Godless teachers (in the author's perspective) have crept into the church who "deny our master and Lord, Jesus Christ" (v. 4). The counterpolemic of the Letter of Jude functions consistently with traditional motifs, so we can hardly decide whether the author is dealing with itinerant preachers or members of the local congregation(s).[150] Their partici-

148. Cf. Lindemann, *Paulus im ältesten Christentum*, 233–40; K. Backhaus, "Der Hebräerbrief und die Paulus-Schule," *BZ* 37 (1993): 183–208.

149. For introductory issues, see Schnelle, *New Testament Writings*, 416–24.

150. Cf. Henning Paulsen, "Judasbrief," *TRE* 55.

pation in the congregational love-feasts (v. 12) speaks in favor of the latter possibility (cf. further vv. 19, 22, 23). The Letter of Jude attempts, at different levels, to strengthen the identity of his church. By writing in the name of the Lord's brother Jude, and by referring in the first verse to James the brother of the Lord (and thus to the Letter of James), an intertextual network is constructed that clearly suggests a perspective critical of Paul. This is probably related to the doctrine (and practice) of Spirit-enthusiasm apparently advocated by the opponents, possibly appealing to Paul and/or his disciples. They disdained the angelic powers (v. 8), saw themselves as filled with the Spirit (v. 19), and claimed that traditional prohibitions did not apply to them (vv. 7ff.). The numerous points of contact between Jude and Pauline/deutero-Pauline theology (Colossians in particular) likewise make clear that Jude (like 2 Peter) belongs in the milieu in which the heritage of Pauline theology was being debated.[151] So also, the address of the church as "called" (Jude 1) and "holy" ("saints") serves to mark off the faithful community from the false teachers, whose doctrine and immoral conduct lead to perdition (cf. vv. 4, 7–11). Finally, the Letter of Jude attributes a fundamental importance to the concept of tradition. The church is struggling for the faith that "was once for all entrusted to the saints" (v. 3). This faith is identical with what was "said before" by the apostles (v. 17), and constitutes the foundation of the church (v. 20). The threat from the false teaching calls for a formulation of the tradition and its enforcement, a concept particularly rooted in Jewish thought. Essential components of this tradition are apocalyptic speculations, and the traditions associated with the Enoch books,[152] but Hellenistic ideas are also included (v. 19b, the opponents are "worldly people [ψυχικοί], devoid of the Spirit"). To be sure, the concept of tradition is not made into a formal principle, but the church knows it has an obligation to preserve and stand by its heritage. The concluding doxology receives particular emphasis (v. 25), stressing the unity and uniqueness of the only God (μόνος θεός), the Savior. At the center of Jude's Christology stands the expectation of the coming Kyrios, who will appear with his angels for the final judgment (vv. 14–15). Christ will reveal his mercy to the church (v. 21), but the opponents will be punished for their godless works. Reverence for the angels was an assumed part of Christian faith for the author's church (vv. 6, 9, 14), while the opponents obviously disdained them, so that the role of angels

151. On this point, with (considerable) differences in their arguments, cf., e.g., Müller, *Theologiegeschichte*, 23–26; Richard Bauckham, *Jude, 2 Peter* (WBC; Waco: Word, 1983), 12; Gerhard Sellin, "Die Häretiker des Judasbriefes," *ZNW* 77 (1986): 224–25; Roman Heiligenthal, *Zwischen Henoch und Paulus: Studien zum theologiegeschichtlichen Ort des Judasbriefes* (TANZ 6; Tübingen: Francke, 1992), 128ff.; J. Frey, "Der Judasbrief zwischen Judentum und Hellenismus," in *Frühjudentum und Neues Testament im Horizont Biblischer Theologie* (ed. Wolfgang Kraus et al.; WUNT 162; Tübingen: Mohr Siebeck, 2003), 206–9 (Jude tendentiously advocates a position that Colossians argues against).

152. Cf. Heiligenthal, *Henoch und Paulus*, 89–94, who goes beyond these general considerations to argue that the bearers of the tradition in Jude were a group of Christian Pharisees.

in Christian worship seems to have been a focus of the controversy. Within the ethics of Jude, Jewish concepts of purity seem to have been important (cf. vv. 8, 12, 23). The church manifests holiness and the ideal of remaining unstained by impure contacts with the world and lives in a tense eschatological expectation: the rejection of false teaching that appears at the end time (cf. vv. 4, 11, 13, 15) is contrasted with the church's own salvation to eternal life (v. 21). In vv. 22–23, the church is given instructions for its dealing with deviant groups: the Lord's mercy to his church (v. 21) has its counterpart in the mercy extended to the wavering and to the deviants who are willing to repent, who are to be snatched from the coming fiery judgment.[153] Thus, for all its polemic, the Letter of Jude also reveals it has a basic orientation toward pastoral care.

The Theological Conception of the Second Letter of Peter

The author of 2 Peter is an educated Hellenistic (Jewish) Christian[154] who addresses a dispute in his church concerning the (delayed) parousia, presenting a way of resolving the problem. The intentional reference back to 1 Peter (2 Pet. 3:1) suggests that 2 Peter is directed to the same churches in Asia Minor to which 1 Peter was addressed.[155] The letter's Hellenistic conceptuality[156] and the type of dangers with which it is concerned also point to Gentile Christian churches with an influential Jewish Christian element. The churches are plagued by lack of clarity about ethical issues (cf., e.g., 2 Pet. 1:5, 10; 2:2; 3:14), controversies about interpretation of Scripture (cf. 1:20–21), and especially doubts about the traditional expectation of the parousia.

This situation was aggravated by false teachers whose theological profile, if one disregards the usual interchangeable stereotypical polemic,[157] appears as follows:

1. The opponents interpret Scripture in their own way (2 Pet. 1:20–21), and are thus explicitly called "false prophets" (2:1). The Scriptures they "falsely" interpret include letters of Paul (3:15–16).

153. On Jude 23b, cf. Paulsen, "Judasbrief," 85.

154. It is noteworthy that the author uses the religio-philosophical terminology of Hellenism without further ado. For analysis of the catalog of virtues presupposed by 2 Pet. 1:3–7, cf. Tord Fornberg, *An Early Church in a Pluralistic Society: A Study of 2 Peter* (ConBNT 9; Lund: Gleerup, 1977), 97–101.

155. Cf. Otto Knoch, *Der erste und zweite Petrusbrief, der Judasbrief* (RNT 8; Regensburg: Pustet, 1990), 199.

156. Cf. Fornberg, *Pluralistic Society*, 112ff., infers from the elevated Greek style of 2 Peter that the letter is addressed to churches in a somewhat sophisticated urban culture.

157. Cf. the catalog of typical motifs in Klaus Berger, "Streit um Gottes Vorsehung: Zur Position der Gegner im 2. Petrusbrief," in *Tradition and Re-interpretation in Jewish and Early Christian Literature: Essays in Honour of Jürgen C.H. Lebram* (ed. J. W. van Henten; StPB 36; Leiden: Brill, 1986), 122.

2. The opposing teachers obviously reject elements of traditional eschatological teaching (angels, parousia, final judgment, end of the world), and respond to these views with mocking skepticism (cf. 1:16; 3:3–5, 9).
3. The opponents "deny" the Lord (2:1), they "malign" and "slander" the truth and the heavenly powers (2:2, 10). They are proud and boisterous, and they proclaim a false doctrine of freedom (2:18a, 19).
4. The opponents throw wild parties in the daytime (2:13), and, from the author's perspective, lead an impure life (2:10, 18b, 20).

Apparently the death of the earlier generations of Christians and the delay of the parousia provide the basis for a skepticism that became widespread in the second century CE (cf. *1 Clem.* 23.3–4; *2 Clem.* 11.2–4),[158] which regarded the Jewish and Jewish Christian concepts of redemption and eschatological images as obsolete (cf. 2 Pet. 2:1, atonement Christology; 1:16, the traditional ideas of the parousia are μῦθοι ["myths"]). The opponents support their position by appeal to Paul's letters[159] and proclaim a *knowledge* of God guided by reason (cf. the emphatic use of γνῶσις in 1:5, 6; 3:18; ἐπίγνωσις in 1:2, 3, 8; 2:20), and a life of faith oriented to the concept of freedom.

The author of 2 Peter responds to the fundamental criticisms of his opponents on different labels. The choice of the pseudonym "Simon Peter" already signals his standpoint and intention: he understands himself to be a spokesperson for what is becoming the mainline Christian tradition and on its behalf claims ownership of the correct interpretation of the Scripture. Adoption of elements of the testamentary genre likewise serves the current debate, for the last words of a great leader before his death possess an uncontested authority. They can neither be taken back nor changed. On the fictive level of the letter, "Peter" claims to be in possession of the "prophetic word" (2 Pet. 1:19), and thus to be able to guarantee that the "day of the Lord" will certainly come. In order to demonstrate the dependability of God's promises, 2 Peter utilizes the idea that there is a typological correspondence between the judgment of the flood in Noah's day and the final judgment to come (3:5–7). He appeals to Ps. 90:4 (2 Pet. 3:8, "With the Lord one day is like a thousand years, and a thousand years are like one day"), and the motif

158. For the pagan realm, cf. the documentation (especially Plutarch, *Ser.*) in ibid., 124–25. The position of the opponents is explained primarily from the pagan environment by Fornberg, *Pluralistic Society*, 119–20; Jerome H. Neyrey, "The Form and Background of the Polemic in 2 Peter," *JBL* 99 (1980): 407–31; Bauckham, *Jude, 2 Peter*, 154–57; Berger, "Streit um Gottes Vorsehung," passim. Older research often categorized the opponents as Gnostics; for critique of this view, cf. Henning Paulsen, *Der Zweite Petrusbrief und der Judasbrief* (KEK 12.2; Göttingen: Vandenhoeck & Ruprecht, 1992), 95–96.

159. A list of possible references is provided by Knoch, *Der erste und zweite Petrusbrief, der Judasbrief*, 210–11.

of the thief (2 Pet. 3:10; cf. 1 Thess. 5:2; Matt. 24:29ff., 43; Rev. 3:3; 16:15). For 2 Peter, that the date of the Lord's return cannot be calculated, and the unshakable hope that it will certainly occur, are two features of the parousia hope that belong inseparably together. The reason the parousia has not yet occurred is named in 2 Pet. 3:9: God's patience still grants the possibility of repentance before the end. As the Lord of creation and history, God has not only a different perspective on time than we mortals, but the truth of the matter is that it is God's very kindness that is mocked by the false teachers! They thus reveal their true nature; they live in self-deception and sin (cf. 1:9; 2:10–12, 14, 18) and do not recognize that God's righteous judgment will certainly come upon them (cf. 2:3b, 12–13).

The Second Letter of Peter is directed to the right "knowledge of God and of Jesus our Lord" (2 Pet. 1:1–2). In him, God is revealed (1:17), and he is now the Lord of history (cf. 3:8–10, 15a, 18). The author emphasizes Jesus's divine nature (cf. 1:3–4; 3:18; cf. also 1:1, 11), for participation in the "divine nature" of Jesus Christ is the goal of the Christian life (1:4). The strong christological orientation of 2 Peter is also manifest in the double christological title, "our Lord and Savior Jesus Christ" (1:11; 2:20; 3:18), and in the correspondence between the beginning of the letter and its conclusion: the letter is framed by references to the κύριος (Lord) and σωτὴρ Ἰησοῦς Χριστός ("Savior Jesus Christ"; cf. 1:1–2; 3:18).

The Second Letter of Peter cannot simply be discredited by pronouncing the verdict "early Catholicism."[160] Rather, it teaches us to take seriously the patience of God for the salvation of as many people as possible. The letter directs the readers' view "toward acknowledging the development from the 'apostolic' to the 'catholic' church in the full sense of the word and to the serious effort to preserve all legitimate Christian traditions in the church and to let them have their effect."[161] Interpretation of 2 Peter cannot disregard its actual historical situation. The hermeneutical appropriation of the past and the comprehensive ethical discourse are effective means of developing a firm sense of Christian identity in a Hellenistic environment. By adopting the pseudonym "Peter," by referring to the Synoptic tradition (especially Matthew),[162] by appealing to 1 Peter (2 Pet. 3:1), and especially by invoking Paul (and his letters) in 2 Pet. 3:15–16, the author of 2 Peter makes a claim to the whole spectrum of Christian witnesses as supporting his interpretation of the delay of the parousia. In 2 Peter, the apostles Peter and Paul now step forth together as

160. So especially Ernst Käsemann, "An Apologia for Primitive Christian Eschatology," in *Essays on New Testament Themes* (SBT 41; London: SCM, 1964), 169–95.

161. Knoch, *Der erste und zweite Petrusbrief, der Judasbrief*, 231.

162. Cf. the catalog in Peter Dschulnigg, "Der theologische Ort des Zweiten Petrusbriefes," *BZ* 33 (1989): 168–76. According to Dschulnigg, the author of 2 Peter is located in the Jewish Christianity of the Gospel of Matthew, "whose theology the author defends throughout his letter" (177).

witnesses to the unity and truth of the faith.[163] In its Hellenistic context, ethics is given a key position in the letter's message. In fact, extended sections of the letter are nothing more or less than parenesis, focused on Hellenistic virtues advocated from the point of view of Christian faith: abstinence/self-control (ἐγκράτεια), patience/steadfastness (ὑπομονή), piety/fear of God (εὐσέβεια), and love (ἀγάπη). At the beginning of the second century CE, the dependability of the traditional testimony and loyalty to the beginnings of the faith have not lost their relevance for the author of 2 Peter.

163. Cf. Theo K. Heckel, "Die Traditionsverknüpfungen des Zweiten Petrusbriefes und die Anfänge einer neutestamentlichen biblischen Theologie," in *Die bleibende Gegenwart des Evangeliums: Festschrift für Otto Merk* (ed. Roland Gebauer and Martin Meiser; MTS 76; Marburg: Elwert, 2003), 193–95.

12

Johannine Theology

Introduction to the Christian Faith

The process of the formation of theology as creative meaning-formation through narrative can be grasped by a study of the Fourth Gospel in a way that is not available through any other New Testament author.[1] John stands at a decisive turning point; he sees clearly that Christians of his time (ca. 100 CE in Asia Minor)[2] can remain true to Jesus and the origins of the Christian faith only when they take the risk of reformulating language and thought for expressing the Christ event. It is thus just as important for the Fourth Evangelist to hark back to the historical Jesus as it is to reformulate the message from and about Jesus for his own time. Without the historical Jesus, whom the author is explicitly concerned to locate in the space-time world of history and geography (cf., e.g., John 1:28, 44; 2:1, 13; 3:22; 4:4; 5:2; 6:1; 7:1; 11:1), there is for John no Christian faith. But without repackaging in a new and different linguistic and conceptual format, this message from and about Jesus cannot realize its potential: it brings forth no "fruit" (cf. John 15:1–8). The language of the Fourth Gospel portrays a reality that does not admit of superficial expression in conceptual terms. This reality is cryptic and mysterious, because it creates a hearing for the mystery of God's own being and acts in a way that can be expressed only in images and symbols. It approaches its subject matter

1. Cf. Udo Schnelle, "Das Johannesevangelium als neue Sinnbildung," in *Theology and Christology in the Fourth Gospel* (ed. G. van Belle et al.; BETL 184; Louvain: Leuven University Press, 2005), 291–313.

2. On introductory issues, cf. Schnelle, *New Testament Writings*, 469–516 (John 1–20 as a literary and theological unit). Raymond Edward Brown and Francis J. Moloney, *An Introduction to the Gospel of John* (1st ed.; ABRL; New York: Doubleday, 2003), place the accents differently.

in a way that both stops short of the inexpressible reality and simultaneously facilitates understanding in a new way. John effectively utilizes this new development to receive God's revelation in and through Jesus and to extend it further in his gospel composition. In the evangelist's self-understanding, this process is not a matter of his own hermeneutical efforts. One might say that through the Paraclete, Jesus presents the Gospel of John as his own self-interpretation. The insight that came through post-Easter hindsight is for John both a theological program and a narrative perspective that makes it possible for the Fourth Evangelist to translate theological insights into narrated history. John thereby thinks through, more resolutely than any other New Testament author, the works and significance of Jesus Christ as an indestructible unity and translates fundamental theological insights into narrative, so that his gospel can be read as the first "Introduction to the Christian Faith" (see below, §12.9).

12.1 Theology

The term θεός (God) occurs eighty-two times in the Fourth Gospel, mostly in genitive constructions determined by Christology. This already indicates the theological program of the gospel: theology as Christology, without thereby minimizing the fundamental importance of theology in the proper sense.[3] The prologue of John 1:1–18 already signals a *theological protology*.[4] The foundation of the Johannine portrayal of God in the Old Testament is illustrated, for example, in the reference to Gen. 1:1 LXX in John 1:1–2, the concept of the "glory" of God (1:14; 5:44; 17:1, 24), the quotations in 2:17; 6:31, 45; 12:13, 38, 40, the expression "the one true God" in 17:3 (cf. 3:33), and the "I am" sayings (see below, §12.2.3). *The Gospel of John does not proclaim a new God but proclaims the one God in a new way.* It is about the one true and living God (6:57), whose love sent his Son into the world to save those who believe (3:16–17). No one has seen this invisible and transcendent God except for the Son, who now brings revelation from the Father (1 John 4:12a; John 1:18; 5:37; 6:46).

12.1.1 God as Father

By far the most frequent term for God in the Fourth Gospel is πατήρ ("Father," 112 times); no other New Testament document approaches this usage. In the Old Testament, "Father" is seldom used for God, though in the writings of ancient Judaism God is both addressed and described with this term

3. Cf. Brown and Moloney, *Introduction to John*, 249: "Thus Johannine Christology never replaces theology."

4. On reading the prologue from the perspective of theology, cf. D. R. Sadananda, *The Johannine Exegesis of God* (BZNW 121; Berlin: de Gruyter, 204), 151–217.

rather often;[5] it also appears regularly in the pagan world as an address to Zeus.[6] Thus Johannine Christians of different cultural backgrounds agree in their basic confession of God as πατήρ.

First of all, God is Father *in his relation to the Son*,[7] and Jesus in turn speaks of "his Father" (e.g., John 6:32, 57; 8:19, 54; 10:18, 25). The Father loves the Son (3:35; 14:21, 23; 15:9) and sends him (e.g., 3:16; 5:37; 6:29). The Father works (5:17, 19, 20, 36; 8:18; 14:10), validates the work of the Son (5:43), and testifies on behalf of the Son (5:37; 10:25). The Son does the will of the Father (4:34; 5:30; 6:38, 39, 40). The Father is the bearer of life and confers this power on the Son (5:25, 26; 6:57).[8] The Father has placed the believers in the hand of the Son (6:37, 44, 65; 13:3), for all that the Father has also belongs to the Son (16:5). The Father teaches the Son (8:28), who says only what he hears from the Father (8:38; 12:49, 50; 14:24). The Son accomplishes the Father's work (10:37; 14:31) and is honored by the Son (8:49). The Father judges (8:16), and has given all authority to the Son, who also judges (5:22b). Finally, the Father glorifies the Son, just as the Son glorifies the Father (8:54; 12:28; 17:1).

Within the Johannine familial imagery, believers are represented as "children of God"; on τέκνα (children), cf. 1 John 2:1, 12, 28; 3:7, 18; 4:4; 5:21; John 13:33; on τέκνα θεοῦ (children of God), cf. 2 John 1, 4, 13; 3 John 4; 1 John 3:1, 2, 10; 5:2; John 1:12; 11:52.[9] They are born/begotten of/by God (1 John 2:29; 3:9; 4:7; John 1:13; 3:3ff.) and belong to a different order of reality than those people who have only an earthly origin. John severs the existence of believers from all historical and biological presuppositions and propagates a universal *familia dei*. The new creation of human beings takes place in faith through the power of the Spirit in baptism (John 3:3, 5). The special status of believers in their orientation to the Father and the Son is also expressed by the honoring designations ἀδελφοί ("brothers"; 3 John 3, 5, 10; John 20:17; 21:23) and φίλοι ("friends"; 3 John 15; John 11:11; 15:14–15). The disciples are not strangers or slaves but brothers and friends of Jesus, for they fulfill the will of the Father.

The Conflict concerning the True Father

In the ancient world, genealogy was the basis of dignity and social status; it legitimized one's claims. The exclusive reference of the Father to the Son

5. Cf. Marianne Meye Thompson, *The God of the Gospel of John* (Grand Rapids: Eerdmans, 2001), 58–68; E. Zingg, *Das Reden von Gott als "Vater" im Johannesevangelium* (HBS 48; Freiburg i.B.: Herder, 2006), 304–8.

6. See above, §3.3.1; cf. further examples in *NW* 1.1.2 at Matt. 6:9.

7. On this point, cf. Sadananda, *Johannine Exegesis of God*, 59–80.

8. Cf. Marianne Meye Thompson, "The Living Father," in *God the Father in the Gospel of John* (ed. A. Reinhartz; Semeia 85; Atlanta: Society of Biblical Literature, 1999), 19–31.

9. On this point, cf. Dietrich Rusam, *Die Gemeinschaft der Kinder Gottes: Das Motiv der Gotteskindschaft und die Gemeinden der johanneischen Briefe* (BWANT 133; Stuttgart: Kohlhammer, 1993); Zingg, *Gott als "Vater,"* 314–17.

and the unique claim of the Son within Johannine theology could not remain without contradiction. The evangelist deals with this issue in the dispute about the true children of Abraham in John 8:37–47.[10] Jesus explicitly acknowledges the claim of the Ἰουδαῖοι (Jews) to be children of Abraham (8:37, "I know that you are descendants of Abraham; yet you look for an opportunity to kill me, because there is no place in you for my word"). Nevertheless, it is also true that "if God were your Father, you would love me, for I came from God and now I am here. I did not come on my own, but he sent me" (8:42). Being an authentic child of God or child of Abraham is a matter decided by one's faith or lack of faith in the Son of God. John seeks an explanation for the unbelief of the Jews and the resulting intention to kill Jesus. The unbelief of the Ἰουδαῖοι is not simply a result of their own decision; unbelief is traced back to the ultimate power of evil, the devil: "You are from your father the devil, and you choose to do your father's desires" (8:44a). John thus stands in the tradition of ancient Judaism, in which increasingly the experiences of evil that transcend human comprehension were attributed to an anti-divine transcendent power. To be sure, God remains the Lord of creation and history, but events that cannot be explained, or that cannot be fitted into God's saving plan, are explained by this transcendent antagonist. In the Fourth Gospel and in 1 John there are numerous such satanological statements: the devil is the Lord of this world (John 12:31; 14:30; 16:11; 1 John 5:19), he is the cause of the world's evil deeds (John 3:19; 7:7). Not only is he responsible for the betrayal of Jesus, entering and taking possession of Judas (cf. John 6:70; 13:2, 27), but every sort of sin originates from the devil (cf. 1 John 3:8). It is not the truth, but the lie, that signals the work of the devil. When Jesus's opponents want to kill him, this demonstrates that they have their being "from [their] father, the devil" (John 8:44). To understand this difficult verse, it is fundamentally important to recognize two items of Johannine theology:

1. "The Jews" are not intrinsically children of the devil, but become so under the influence of an alien, unavoidable power: the devil.
2. Jesus does not speak in general of the Jews as being children of the devil, but speaks in direct address (ὑμῶν, "your") exclusively against

10. Cf. here especially Erich Grässer, "Die antijüdische Polemik im Johannesevangelium," in *Der Alte Bund im Neuen: Exegetische Studien zur Israelfrage im Neuen Testament* (ed. Erich Grässer; WUNT 35; Tübingen: Mohr, 1985), 135–53; Udo Schnelle, "Die Juden im Johannesevangelium," in *Gedenkt an das Wort: Festschrift für Werner Vogler zum 65. Geburtstag* (ed. Christoph Kähler et al.; Leipzig: Evangelische Verlagsanstalt, 1999), 217–30; R. Bieringer et al., eds., *Anti-Judaism and the Fourth Gospel* (1st ed.; Louisville: Westminster John Knox, 2001); Manfred Diefenbach, *Der Konflikt Jesu mit den "Juden": Ein Versuch zur Lösung der johanneischen Antijudaismus-Diskussion mit Hilfe des antiken Handlungsverständnisses* (NTA 41; Münster: Aschendorff, 2002); Zingg, *Gott als "Vater,"* 107–31; Lars Kierspel, *The Jews and the World in the Fourth Gospel: Parallelism, Function, and Context* (WUNT 220; Tübingen: Mohr Siebeck, 2006), 13–110.

> those Ἰουδαῖοι who want to kill him, i.e., primarily against the leaders of the people.[11]

Moreover, the Fourth Gospel also makes very positive statements about the Jews (see below, §12.4.1).

Also linked with the Johannine understanding of "the Jews" is the observation that, for the Fourth Gospel, the Ἰουδαῖοι are only a subordinate aspect of *the primary anti-God reality, namely the cosmos, "the world."*[12] The Jews cannot be seen simply as *the* representatives of the unbelieving world; they are one (and not the only!) embodiment of the world. Within the narrative structure of the gospel, this antagonistic world is the result of the concrete historical situation of the work of Jesus and the beginnings of the Johannine community (conflicts with Jews).[13] Not only the Jews but also Pilate, and thus the Greco-Roman world, prove to be Jesus's opponents when they persist in unbelief. It is no longer belonging to a particular ethnic group that legitimates being called and appointed by the one true God, the Father; only one's response to Jesus Christ, who says, "I am the way, the truth, and the life; no one comes to the Father except through me" (John 14:6), can establish this relation with God.

12.1.2 God Works in the Son

The central theological concept in the Fourth Gospel is the work of the Father in the Son. It is not a matter of the Father's working through the Son, for the Son is far more than an instrument, messenger, or agent of the Father: the Son shares the Father's essential being.[14] The unity of Father and Son is the basis of the Johannine theology (in the sense of theology proper) and Christology (John 10:30). The Father reveals himself fully in the Son, who claims to be and to work in unity with the Father/God.

The Revelation Derives from the Father's Love

The revelation of the Father in the Son is grounded exclusively in God's love: "For God so loved the world that he gave his only Son, so that everyone

11. Cf. Diefenbach, *Konflikt*, 280.

12. The basic data is provided in Kierspel, *Jews and the World*, 111–213.

13. The concentration in chapters 5–11 and in the Passion story shows clearly that the use of Ἰουδαῖοι in the Gospel of John must be understood as a dramaturgical element. Cf. Udo Schnelle, *Das Evangelium nach Johannes* (THKNT 4; Leipzig: Evangelische Verlagsanstalt, 1998), 180–83.

14. Contra D. R. Sadananda, *The Johannine Exegesis of God* (BZNW 121; Berlin: de Gruyter, 2004), 64–65, who wants to minimize the ontological and functional unity of Father and Son through the concept of God's "self-emptying," and prefers to speak of a "divine Agent Christology" (280) or a "sub-ordinate Christology" (285). This does justice neither to the "I am" sayings (see below, §12.2.3) nor to the explicit qualification of Jesus as God (see below, §12.2.4).

who believes in him may not perish but may have eternal life" (John 3:16); cf. 1 John 4:9, "God's love was revealed among us in this way: God sent his only Son into the world so that we might live through him." Differently from Epicurus,[15] for example, the evangelist does not proceed on the basis of a divine disinterest in the world or from the absence of God from the world. The first reference to God's love in the Gospel of John indicates that the conceptual field of ἀγάπη/ἀγαπάω points to the love of God for the whole world. John could not make his position more clear, that in the sending of the Son, God expresses his love and mercy for the world![16]

The love of the Father for the Son (cf. John 3:35; 10:17) is an expression of their essential solidarity, so that the Father "shows the Son all that he himself is doing" (5:20). The Father loves him with an eternal love (17:26; 15:9), and Jesus abides in this love (15:10); through this love he receives his authority (3:35; 5:20). This love sustains him even when he completes his work by giving his life (10:17). The unity between God and Jesus is thus a unity of love. From the Father goes forth an encompassing movement of love, which includes the Son (3:35; 10:17; 15:9, 10; 17:23, 26) as well as the world (3:16) and the disciples (14:21, 23; 17:23, 26). This love continues its course in Jesus's love for God (14:31) and for the disciples (11:5; 13:1, 23, 34; 14:21, 23; 15:12, 13; 19:26) and in the love of the disciples for Jesus (14:15, 21, 23) and for each other (13:34, 35; 15:13, 17). Johannine thought is stamped at its innermost core by the concept of love; the love that proceeds from the Father continues in the works of the Son and the disciples, until finally, despite the unbelief of many, the world recognizes "that the world may know that you have sent me and have loved them even as you have loved me" (17:23). The narrative presentation of the Jesus-Christ-history in the Fourth Gospel is comprehensively shaped by a "dramaturgical Christology of the love of God."[17] It belongs to the essence of love that it does not want to remain by itself; love as a moving force, going forth from itself, determines the concept of love not only of John's theology proper, but it is also embodied in his Christology, and then from there proceeds to fill up every realm of Johannine thought.[18]

15. Cf. Cicero, *Nat. d.* 1.121: "Epicurus, however, in abolishing divine beneficence and divine benevolence, uprooted and exterminated all religion from the human heart. For while asserting the supreme goodness and excellence of the divine nature, he yet denies the god the attribute of benevolence."

16. Cf. the extensive analysis of E. E. Popkes, *Die Theologie der Liebe Gottes in den johanneischen Schriften* (WUNT 2.197; Tübingen: Mohr, 2005), 239–48, who rightly designates John 3:16 as the "foundational statement of the whole Gospel of John."

17. Ibid., 173.

18. Cf. ibid., 355: "The motifs embraced by the semantic field 'love' has a key function in understanding the Fourth Gospel. They stand in an interactive system of internal references through which the Fourth Gospel's train of thought comes impressively to light. This conception can be described as a 'dramaturgical Christology of the love of God,' since the love of God is embodied in the words and deeds of the incarnate Jesus."

Mutual Dynamic Immanence

The direct expression of the unity of being and work that exists between the Father and the Son is their mutual dynamic immanence.[19] Here too we can speak of a theological protology, for already in John 1:1–3 the being and work of the Logos is strictly related to the absolute beginning: God.[20] Jesus declares the reciprocal immanence of Father and Son, for example, in 10:38 ("so that you may know and understand that the Father is in me and I am in the Father") and 14:9 ("Have I been with you all this time, Philip, and you still do not know me? Whoever has seen me has seen the Father. How can you say, 'Show us the Father'? Do you not believe that I am in the Father and the Father is in me? The words that I say to you I do not speak on my own; but the Father who dwells in me does his works."). These statements concisely express the Johannine conception: because Jesus lives from the unity willed and granted by the Father, his words and deeds are a revelation of the Father himself. From this unity there follows a reciprocal knowledge (10:15) and full participation of each in the life of the other: all that the Father has, Jesus also has (16:15; 17:10). The Father is completely present in the Son, and the Son in the Father; at the same time, the two are essentially distinguished from each other: the Son does not become the Father, the Father continuously abides as the Father, who reveals himself in the Son. As Christ abides in God and God abides in him (14:10), thus the believer abides in Christ (John 6:56; 15:4–7; 1 John 2:6, 24; 3:6, 24). So also, God abides in the believer (1 John 4:16; 3:24) and the believer abides in God (1 John 2:24; 3:24; 4:16). Thus the unity of Christians with God or Jesus Christ is an extension of the fellowship between Father and Son (John 17:21, "As you, Father, are in me and I am in you, may they also be in us, so that the world may believe that you have sent me"; cf. further John 14:20; 17:11; 1 John 2:24; 5:20). As is the case with the Pauline ἐν Χριστῷ, so the Johannine concept of immanence includes a strong ethical dimension. In particular, the verb μένω (abide) communicates the practical expression of the "ontological" solidarity between God and Christ, for abiding in God or Christ corresponds to abiding in love (cf. John 15:9, 10; 1 John 2:10, 17; 3:15, 17; 4:12, 16).

Knowing God

Associated with the concept of immanence is another fundamental idea: if no one has ever seen God (John 1:18; 3:13; 5:37–38; 6:46; 8:19), and God's words and works can be experienced only through Jesus, then whoever knows

19. See the foundational study of Klaus Scholtissek, *In ihm sein und bleiben: Die Sprache der Immanenz in den johanneischen Schriften* (HBS 21; Freiburg: Herder, 2000).

20. Appropriately ibid., 193: "As the meta-text and hermeneutical key to the *Corpus Evangelii*, the Prologue to the Gospel of John is at the same time the meta-text of the Johannine language of immanence."

Jesus also knows the Father (8:19; 14:7), and whoever sees Jesus sees the Father (14:7, 9; 12:45). God does not remain transcendent and hidden, but lets himself be known in Jesus; it is only in the Son that the Father is visible on earth (cf. 8:19; 14:8).[21] In turn, John responds to fundamental questions of the philosophy of religion: Who is God? How and where can I come in contact with God? How can I recognize God? How can I get to know God? God's word can be heard on earth only in Jesus Christ, the essential being of God can be seen only in the Son. Such affirmations do not affirm an identity, but a paradox: Jesus is not the Father himself, and nevertheless it is only in Jesus that God appears and is present among human beings in time and history (8:24, 29, 58; 14:9; cf. 6:20). Thomas confesses his faith consistently with this: "My Lord and my God!" (20:28). "Knowing" God (cf., e.g., 1 John 2:3–5, 13–14; 3:1, 6; 4:6–8; John 1:10; 8:55; 14:7; 16:3) is for John identical with believing in Jesus Christ as God's Son (see below, §12.5.1), for the one who has seen him and believed in him knows God.

The Works of the Father in the Son

Johannine theology (and Christology) is stamped with a fundamental idea: *the will of the Father makes possible and legitimizes the work/works of the Son*. Jesus does not work alone, but the Father is in him and with him (John 8:16, 29; 16:32). The word ἔργον (work) in the singular appears twice as a comprehensive designation of Jesus's activity/ministry (4:34; 17:4),[22] with the second reference placing all of Jesus's work under the perspective of the Passion: "I glorified you on earth by finishing the work that you gave me to do." In completing the work that the Father had commissioned him to do on earth, Jesus is glorified by the Father. Therefore, the work of the Father too attains its goal in the necessity of the Son's suffering and death, which means that the work of God (not only of the Son) is accomplished on the cross (cf. 19:30). The plural ἔργα (works) is found twenty-seven times in the gospel; these works include, in the first place, Jesus's miracles. Clear reference is made to the σημεῖα (signs/miracles) in 5:20, 36; 6:29, 30; 7:3, 21; 9:3, 4; 10:25, 32ff.; 14:10–11; 15:24. As works of Jesus, the miracles have both a revelatory quality and a legitimizing function, and they are an obvious manifestation of the unity of the Son with the Father. As witnesses of the unity of Father and Son, ἔργα appear in 4:34; 5:36 ("The works that the Father has given me to complete . . . testify on my behalf that the Father has sent me"); 6:28–29; 9:4; 10:25, 32, 37; 14:10; 17:4. The Son does the ἔργα τοῦ θεοῦ, does the will of the one who sent him, and his works testify precisely to that reality. The words of Jesus can also appear as ἔργα; cf. 5:36–38; 8:28; 14:10; 15:22–24.

21. Cf. further, Rudolf Bultmann, "γινώσκω κτλ.," *TDNT* 1:711–13.

22. On this point, cf. Udo Schnelle, *Antidocetic Christology in the Gospel of John* (trans. Linda M. Maloney; Minneapolis: Fortress, 1992), 135–49.

The "ontological" and functional unity of Father and Son is concisely developed in John 5:17ff., for the Father authorizes the Son to exercise the same power over life and death that the Father himself has. In the encounter with Jesus, the step from death to life takes place, for in Jesus the saving reality of eternal life is already present (see below, §12.8). Jesus's claim and work are grounded solely in the will of the Father who sent him (see below, §12.2.2), which means that for John too Christology is thoroughly grounded in theology proper.

12.1.3 God as Light, Love, and Spirit

It is no accident that the three definitions of God in the New Testament are all found in the Johannine literature: God is light (1 John 1:5, ὁ θεὸς φῶς ἐστίν), God is love (1 John 4:16b, ὁ θεὸς ἀγάπη ἐστίν), and God is Spirit (John 4:24, πνεῦμα ὁ θεός). This corresponds to the double Johannine tendencies to fix ideas precisely and to adopt the religious symbolism of the milieu in order to facilitate understanding. In such symbolic Johannine statements, the subject and the predicate nominative are not interchangeable; symbols from the world of human religion are linked to God but may not be confused with God.[23]

Light is already a common symbol for God in the Old Testament (cf. Isa. 2:3, 5; 10:17; 45:7; Ps. 27:1; 104:2) and was widespread in the whole of antiquity.[24] Light comes from "above," is bright and pure and thus manifests qualities of the divine, just as darkness is firmly anchored in human experience as the place of danger. John takes up these elements and explicitly reworks them into his theological conception: "light" and "darkness" are constituted in view of the revelation of Jesus Christ (John 8:12, "I am the light of the world"; cf. 1:9; 9:5; 12:36, 46), human beings are not themselves the light, but they encounter the light and find themselves placed where the divine light shines upon them (cf. Ps. 36:10). Just as the light is a mark of revelation, the darkness testifies to its absence. Within the Johannine symbolic language, light as the epitome of revelation designates the realm of belonging to God, and thus of authentic life, while darkness stands for alienation from God, judgment, and death.

Beginning with the strong impulse of Jesus himself (see above, §3.5), the idea of love played a central role in the symbolic language of early Christianity from

23. Cf. Craig R. Koester, *Symbolism in the Fourth Gospel* (2nd ed.; Minneapolis: Fortress, 2003), 4: "A symbol is an image, an action, or a person that is understood to have transcendent significance. In Johannine terms, symbols span the chasm between what is 'from above' and what is 'from below' without collapsing that distinction."

24. Cf. the comprehensive treatment in Otto Schwankl, *Licht und Finsternis: Ein metaphorisches Paradigma in den johanneischen Schriften* (HBS 5; Freiburg i.B.: Herder, 1995); Koester, *Symbolism*, 123–54; Popkes, *Theologie der Liebe Gottes*, 229–39.

the very beginning. In the Gospel of John and in 1 John this idea is brought to its sharpest conceptual expression:[25] because the self-communication of God is understood as an all-embracing movement of love, God's self-definition as love is entirely consistent. God's love is the beginning point and center of a process that includes the Son just as it includes believers (see above, §12.1.2). This observation does not yet exhaust the meaning of the expression ὁ θεὸς ἀγάπη ἐστίν (1 John 4:16b), for first and foremost it says something about God himself: the being, essence, and working of God is entirely characterized by love. Transcending any concept of love as a human emotion, God's love is directed to the goal of taking up all creation into the unity of Father and Son, and thus of giving it true life.

The expression πνεῦμα ὁ θεός (John 4:24, "God is Spirit") is a climactic statement of Hellenistic religious history and of Johannine theology.[26] Because God is Spirit and thus can only be approached in prayer that is inspired by the Spirit, the Johannine understanding of worship is universal, allowing no discrimination based on religious-national status, social class, or gender. Samaritans, Greeks, and Jews can all participate in this worship, just as can both men and women. With the appearance of Jesus in this world, there arrives the true worship of God "in Spirit and truth," without bloody sacrifices, and corresponding to the nature of God who is love. The question of "where" God can be truly worshiped is no longer valid, for Jesus Christ is himself the new locus of salvation (cf. John 2:14–22).

Theology as the Basis of Johannine Thinking

For John, there is only *one God, who has revealed himself fully and once for all* in Jesus Christ and is with him in unity of essential being, will, and work.[27] The status of the Son as Son of God is not a matter of usurpation of the divine prerogatives (as in the objection of the Jews in John 5:18; 19:7) or of a compromise of monotheism but is rather a precise *expression and determination of the will of the Father*. The concept of the unity of Father and Son makes it possible for John, in his Jesus-Christ-history, to hold firmly to monotheism while at the same time dealing with the ("hierarchical") relation of Father and Son in the manner characteristic of his thought (see below, §12.3.3). John does not think in static terms but in dynamic, communicative relations: the love of the Father for the Son is the basis of their unity (cf., e.g., 3:35; 10:17), in the relation of the Son to the Father each is unreserv-

25. On the ethical dimension of the Johannine concept of love, see below, §12.6; for 1 John, cf. Georg Strecker, *The Johannine Letters: A Commentary on 1, 2, and 3 John* (Hermeneia; Minneapolis: Fortress, 1996), 174–80.

26. Cf. Philo, *Worse* 21; Seneca, *Ep.* 42.1–2, and additional texts in *NW* 1.2:226–34.

27. Cf. Ulrich Wilckens, "Monotheismus und Christologie," in *Der Sohn Gottes und seine Gemeinde: Studien zur Theologie der Johanneischen Schriften* (ed. Ulrich Wilckens; FRLANT 200; Göttingen: Vandenhoeck & Ruprecht, 2003), 126–35.

edly oriented to the other, which means that Christology is the appropriate development of theology.[28]

12.2 Christology

The *basis* of Johannine thinking is the unity in essential being, revelation, and work between Father and Son (cf. John 1:1; 17:20–22); John 10:30 is intentionally placed in the exact center of the Fourth Gospel ("I and the Father are one"). The *center* of Johannine theology is the incarnation of the preexistent Son of God, Jesus Christ.[29] Behind Jesus stands God himself; herein lies the deepest foundation for the truth of Jesus's claim. His work is entirely grounded in his unity with the Father, and only on the basis of this unity does he refer to his own status. *Jesus's proclamation of himself*, the most striking feature of Johannine Christology, grows out of this perfect unity with God and is its expression.

12.2.1 Preexistence and Incarnation

The statements affirming *preexistence*[30] speak of Jesus's heavenly prehistory, giving linguistic expression to Jesus's being[31] as before creation and unbounded by time, his participation in the eternity of God the Father (cf. John 1:1–3, 30; 6:62; 17:5, 24). No one has ever seen God, except for the Logos/Son (cf. 1:18; 3:11, 13, 32; 5:37–38; 6:46; 8:19); thus Jesus can say, "I came from the Father and have come into the world; again, I am leaving the world and am going to the Father" (16:28). Jesus comes from "above" (3:31; 8:14, 23), from heaven (3:13; 6:33, 38, 41–42, 46, 50, 62), and returns to the Father (13:33; 14:2, 28; 16:5). John concisely expresses this movement of descent and ascent, coming forth and going away, in the vocabulary of καταβαίνω/ἀναβαίνω ("come down"/"go up"; cf., e.g., 1:51; 3:13; 6:33, 62) and ἔρχομαι/ὑπάγω ("come"/"go away"; cf., e.g., 1:9, 11; 3:2; 8:14, 21; 13:3; 16:27–28). Moses (5:45–46), Abra-

28. Cf. C. K. Barrett, "Christocentric or Theocentric?" in *Essays on John* (ed. C. K. Barrett; Philadelphia: Westminster, 1982), 16: "The figure of Jesus does not (so John in effect declares) make sense when viewed as a national leader, a rabbi, or a θεῖος ἀνήρ; he makes sense when in hearing him you hear the Father, when looking at him you see the Father, and worship him."

29. Cf. Hans Weder, "Die Menschwerdung Gottes," in *Einblicke ins Evangelium: Exegetische Beiträge zur neutestamentlichen Hermeneutik; Gesammelte Aufsätze aus den Jahren 1980–1991* (ed. Hans Weder; Göttingen: Vandenhoeck & Ruprecht, 1992), 391, and Marianne Meye Thompson, *The Incarnate Word: Perspectives on Jesus in the Fourth Gospel* (Peabody, MA: Hendrickson, 1993), 117ff.

30. As parallels to the prologue as a whole, cf. especially Prov. 8:22–31; Sir. 1:1–10, 15; 24:3–31; Cleanthes, frg. 537; Cicero, *Tusc.* 5.5; all relevant texts are displayed in *NW* 1.2:1–15.

31. Habermann, *Präexistenzaussagen*, 403, speaks appropriately of a "precreator preexistence."

ham (8:58), and Isaiah (12:41) testify that, as the preexistent Son of God, Jesus has always belonged to God. His existence is subject to no temporal or spatial boundaries. After Jesus has performed God's will on earth and has completed God's work (4:34), he returns to the Father (7:33; 13:1, 3; 14:12; 12:28; 17:11). Preexistence has its counterpart in *postexistence*, into which Jesus enters when he returns to the Father (cf. 17:5).

Because God's reality cannot be perceived in earthly terms in any other way than through Jesus's words and works, from the very beginning the gospel's statements about preexistence point to Jesus of Nazareth and his works. Preexistence finds its goal in the *incarnation*, for it is God who in Jesus enters into the human world, inasmuch as God wills to reveal himself and effect the salvation of the world.[32] Preexistence and incarnation condition each other, for the preexistence statements underscore the claim of the human being Jesus, showing that his words are at the same time the words of God, his works are at the same time the works of God, that as a human being he is at the same time "from above." Preexistence and incarnation thus respond to the old question of religious philosophy, how and where there can ever be a point where transcendence and immanence meet. Jesus's true origin is God, from whom he has come forth; he thus comes from heaven, has descended to earth, and brings authentic knowledge of God. Consequently all his words, teachings, and works likewise have their origin in God—they are God's words, God's teaching, God's works.

This descending line from preexistence to incarnation and thus the *fundamentally incarnational character of Johannine theology* is already manifest in the prologue (John 1:1–18), the programmatic text that begins the gospel and provides the model for understanding it as a whole. At the beginning of a Jesus-Christ-history, a decision must be made about its character. The narrator's decision about how to begin the story provides direction as to how its hearers and readers will appropriate the story as a whole. The prologue presents this necessary preliminary knowledge and thus guides the reader's understanding.[33]

32. Entirely different is the view of Jürgen Becker, *Johanneisches Christentum* (Tübingen: Mohr, 2004), 131: "It is best to simply abandon the interpretative model 'incarnation' as the matrix for Johannine Christology"; similarly Ulrich B. Müller, "Zur Eigentümlichkeit des Johannesevangeliums: Das Problem des Todes Jesu," *ZNW* 88 (1997): 54; E. Straub, "Der Irdische als der Auferstandene: Kritische Theologie bei Johannes ohne ein Wort vom Kreuz," in *Kreuzestheologie im Neuen Testament* (ed. Andreas Dettwiler and Jean Zumstein; WUNT 151; Tübingen: Mohr, 2002), 255. In these authors, the postulate of the invalidity of incarnation as a key Johannine category is related to their view that the cross likewise is not central to John's theology.

33. The prologue fulfills in a masterful fashion the requirements set forth by Cicero for the beginning of a speech: "Every introduction will have to include either a statement of the whole of the matter that is to be put forward, or an approach to the case and a preparation of the ground, or else to possess some element of ornament and dignity" (*Or.* 2.320).

The Prologue as the History of God's Care for the World*

1 Ἐν ἀρχῇ ἦν ὁ λόγος,	1 In the beginning was the Logos,
καὶ ὁ λόγος ἦν πρὸς τὸν θεόν,	and the Logos was with God,
καὶ θεὸς ἦν ὁ λόγος.	and the Logos was God.
2 οὗτος ἦν ἐν ἀρχῇ πρὸς τὸν θεόν.	2 This one was in the beginning with God.
3 πάντα δι' αὐτοῦ ἐγένετο,	3 All things came into being through this one,
καὶ χωρὶς αὐτοῦ ἐγένετο οὐδὲ ἕν, ὃ γέγονεν.	and without this one not one thing came into being that has come into being.
4 ἐν αὐτῷ ζωὴ ἦν,	4 In him was life,
καὶ ἡ ζωὴ ἦν τὸ φῶς τῶν ἀνθρώπων·	and the life was the light of human beings.
5 καὶ τὸ φῶς ἐν τῇ σκοτίᾳ φαίνει,	5 The light shines in the darkness,
καὶ ἡ σκοτία αὐτὸ οὐ κατέλαβεν.	and the darkness did not apprehend it.
6 Ἐγένετο ἄνθρωπος, ἀπεσταλμένος παρὰ θεοῦ, ὄνομα αὐτῷ Ἰωάννης·	6 There was a man sent from God, whose name was John.
7 οὗτος ἦλθεν εἰς μαρτυρίαν	7 He came as a witness
ἵνα μαρτυρήσῃ περὶ τοῦ φωτός,	to testify to the light,
ἵνα πάντες πιστεύσωσιν δι' αὐτοῦ.	so that all might believe through him.
8 οὐκ ἦν ἐκεῖνος τὸ φῶς,	8 He himself was not the light,
ἀλλ' ἵνα μαρτυρήσῃ περὶ τοῦ φωτός.	but he came to testify to the light.
9 Ἦν τὸ φῶς τὸ ἀληθινόν,	9 The true light,
ὃ φωτίζει πάντα ἄνθρωπον,	which enlightens every human being,
ἐρχόμενον εἰς τὸν κόσμον.	was coming into the world.
10 ἐν τῷ κόσμῳ ἦν,	10 He was in the world,
καὶ ὁ κόσμος δι' αὐτοῦ ἐγένετο,	and the world came into being through him;
καὶ ὁ κόσμος αὐτὸν οὐκ ἔγνω.	yet the world did not know him.
11 εἰς τὰ ἴδια ἦλθεν,	11 He came to what was his own,
καὶ οἱ ἴδιοι αὐτὸν οὐ παρέλαβον.	and his own people did not accept him.
12 ὅσοι δὲ ἔλαβον αὐτόν,	12 But to all who received him,
ἔδωκεν αὐτοῖς ἐξουσίαν τέκνα θεοῦ γενέσθαι,	he gave power to become children of God,
τοῖς πιστεύουσιν εἰς τὸ ὄνομα αὐτοῦ,	to those who believed in his name,
13 οἳ οὐκ ἐξ αἱμάτων οὐδὲ ἐκ θελήματος σαρκὸς	13 who were born, not of blood or of the will of the flesh
οὐδὲ ἐκ θελήματος ἀνδρὸς ἀλλ' ἐκ θεοῦ ἐγεννήθησαν.	or of the will of man, but of God.
14 Καὶ ὁ λόγος σὰρξ ἐγένετο	14 And the Logos became flesh
καὶ ἐσκήνωσεν ἐν ἡμῖν,	and lived among us,
καὶ ἐθεασάμεθα τὴν δόξαν αὐτοῦ,	and we have seen his glory,
δόξαν ὡς μονογενοῦς παρὰ πατρός,	the glory as of a father's only son,
πλήρης χάριτος καὶ ἀληθείας.	full of grace and truth.
15 Ἰωάννης μαρτυρεῖ περὶ αὐτοῦ καὶ κέκραγεν λέγων·	15 John testified to him and cried out,

οὗτος ἦν ὃν εἶπον·	“This was he of whom I said,
ὁ ὀπίσω μου ἐρχόμενος ἔμπροσθέν μου γέγονεν,	‘He who comes after me ranks ahead of me
ὅτι πρῶτός μου ἦν	because he was before me.’”
16ὅτι ἐκ τοῦ πληρώματος αὐτοῦ ἡμεῖς πάντες ἐλάβομεν	16From his fullness we have all received,
καὶ χάριν ἀντὶ χάριτος·	grace upon grace.
17ὅτι ὁ νόμος διὰ Μωϋσέως ἐδόθη,	17For the law was given through Moses;
ἡ χάρις καὶ ἡ ἀλήθεια διὰ Ἰησοῦ Χριστοῦ ἐγένετο.	grace and truth came through Jesus Christ.
18Θεὸν οὐδεὶς ἑώρακεν πώποτε·	18No one has ever seen God.
μονογενὴς θεὸς ὁ ὢν εἰς τὸν κόλπον τοῦ πατρὸς	It is God the only Son, who is close to the Father’s heart,
ἐκεῖνος ἐξηγήσατο.	who has made him known.

*[The English translation reflects Schnelle’s German translation and his punctuation of the Greek text.—MEB]

The prologue to the Gospel of John is a story of loving care, for to direct one’s word to someone means to turn one’s attention to them: in Jesus Christ, the Logos/Word of God, God turns in loving care to human beings. The prologue develops the basic features of the Johannine symbolic universe,[34] at the very beginning definitively answering the central question posed by all cultures and religions, namely the issue of legitimization by genealogy and origin: the Logos Jesus Christ belongs to God from the very beginning. In the thought world of antiquity, the beginning of things is not available for human view and reflection; it belongs to God or the gods and their agents. For John, too, it is God who establishes being, time, and order. The manner of this beginning is presented in mythical terms that narrate what preceded the creation of the world. Reality was shaped with an integral temporal dimension, and the relation of the leading actors of the following drama are related to each other. *This inherent temporal dimension of the created world corresponds to a theological hierarchy characteristic of the whole gospel and represents a thoroughgoing christological priority*: God and the Logos who dwelt with him in the beginning are prior to all being, which is created, sustained, and determined by God through the Logos. The relation of God and the Logos

34. For interpretation of the prologue, cf. Ernst Käsemann, “The Structure and Purpose of the Prologue to John’s Gospel,” in *New Testament Questions of Today* (London: SCM, 1969); G. Richter, “Die Fleischwerdung des Logos im Johannesevangelium,” in *Studien zum Johannesevangelium* (ed. G. Richter; BU 13; Regensburg: Pustet, 1977), 149–98; Otfried Hofius, “Struktur und Gedankengang des Logos-Hymnus,” in *Johannesstudien* (ed. Otfried Hofius and H.-C. Kammler; WUNT 88; Tübingen: Mohr, 1996), 1–23; Schnelle, *Das Evangelium nach Johannes*, 34–55; W. Paroschi, *Incarnation and Covenant in the Prologue to the Fourth Gospel (John 1:1–18)* (EHS 23.820; Frankfurt: Lang, 2006).

represented in John 1:1 is intended to affirm the original and total participation of the Logos in the life of the one God,[35] who is the origin and ground of all being. God and the Logos are not equally causal but are contemporary and alike in kind and effect. God presents himself as Speaker: his word, however, is much more than mere communication: it is the life-giving word of the Creator. It is impossible to think of God apart from his Word; God not only communicates through his Word but reveals his essential life and being, allowing human beings, through faith in the Logos Jesus Christ, to participate in his life, so that the Logos is likewise the one who gives form to the divine reality, reveals and communicates it.

Each human being is the creation of the Logos (John 1:3) and bears the stamp of this origin.[36] For John, human beings are originally determined by the Word of God, for life understood as the specific attribute of being human is an attribute of the Logos (1:4). The Logos appears as the light "which enlightens every human being" (1:4b, 9b). John understands the human vitality of every person as a reflection of the light that belonged to the Logos from the very beginning. In the Logos this life is present, the Logos is the locus of life itself, and only the light of the Logos illuminates the life of human beings. The Logos wants to enlighten the life of humanity, and comes to them. This movement of the Logos characterizes the entire prologue.[37] The Logos shines in the darkness (1:5), comes into the world (1:9c), to his own property (1:11), and gives human beings the power to become children of God (1:12–13). The rejection (v. 11) and reception (v. 12) of the Logos structures the whole of the narrative events that follow. This is already clear from the fact that the prologue already includes the conflict between faith and unbelief that forms the plot, the conflict that both drives and differentiates the events of the narrative as a whole.

In John 1:14a the gracious movement of the Logos toward the world reaches its goal: καὶ ὁ λόγος σὰρξ ἐγένετο (and the Word became flesh). The Logos wants to be so close to human beings that he becomes human himself. The Creator himself becomes a creature; the light of all human beings becomes one of them. In the Gospel of John, σάρξ (flesh) describes the human creature of flesh and blood (cf. 1:13; 3:6; 6:51–56, 63; 8:15; 17:2), genuinely human. The Logos is now what he had not been previously: a true and real human being.[38]

35. The comment of T. Söding is on target: "Just as the Logos is by no means identified with ὁ θεός, the God and Father of Jesus, the Logos is nonetheless fully participant in his deity" (Thomas Söding, "'Ich und der Vater sind eins' [Joh 10,30]: Die johanneische Christologie vor dem Anspruch des Hauptgebotes Dtn 6,4f," *ZNW* 93 [2002]: 192).

36. Cf. Josef Blank, "Der Mensch vor der radikalen Alternative," *Kairos* 22 (1980): 151.

37. Cf. Hans Weder, "Der Mythos vom Logos," in *Mythos und Rationalität* (ed. Hans Heinrich Schmid; Gütersloh: Güterloher Verlagshaus, 1988), 53.

38. Contra Ernst Käsemann, *The Testament of Jesus: A Study of the Gospel of John in the Light of Chapter 17* (NTL; London: SCM, 1968), 13, who sees in John 1:14a merely "the backdrop for the Son of God proceeding through the world" (cf. also pp. 6, 10, 44).

The event of the incarnation of the preexistent Logos includes statements of both identity and essence: that Logos who was with God in the very beginning and is the creator of all being became a real, authentic human being. Although time and history owe their own being to God and the Logos, the Logos truly entered into time and history, without thereby being dissolved into it. The incarnation affirms the full participation of Jesus Christ in the creatureliness and historicalness of all being. God himself thereby becomes subject to truly human existence. Nevertheless, incarnation does not mean the surrender of Jesus's divinity; on the contrary, in the Fourth Gospel, Jesus's humanity is a predicate of his divinity. Jesus became human and at the same time remained God: God in the modality of the incarnation. He became human without reservation and distinction, a human being among other human beings. At the same time, he is God's Son, again without reservation or distinction.[39] Here the fundamental paradox of Johannine Christology is concentrated: the historical Jesus of Nazareth claims to be the unlimited and abiding presence of God. Thus, in the Gospel of John, the incarnation is not the expression of a humiliation in which the divine Son is divested of deity, but in the human being Jesus it is the God/Logos who appears. One might say that the incarnation is understood as a change of medium that makes possible a new work of God among and for human beings.

Through the meta-reflections in 1:12c, 13, 17, 18, John extends the range of the statements already made in his source. The Christ event has for him universal characteristics, exceeds any particularistic understanding of salvation, and must be understood as the unique self-exegesis of God. So also, the christocentric interpretation of the evangelist becomes visible, for the time of the law is abolished by the time of grace. John underscores this idea with his concept of ἀλήθεια (truth), which describes the uniqueness of Jesus's person not only in regard to his origin but primarily in regard to his soteriological function. The name of Jesus Christ appears in the prologue only in 1:17, and 1:18 underscores John's view that only Jesus can deliver revelation from God.

The Revelation of Glory and Truth

The prologue also introduces another central concept of Johannine Christology: the incarnation of the Preexistent One is directed to the revelation of the δόξα θεοῦ, "the glory of God" (cf. John 1:14c, "and we have seen his

39. Entirely different is the view of Klaus Wengst, *Das Johannesevangelium* (THKNT 4.1–2; Stuttgart: Kohlhammer, 2000, 2001), 1:61: "The statement that 'the Word became flesh' does not legitimize the beloved Christian way of speaking of the 'incarnation of God.' John speaks more precisely of the Word becoming flesh . . . God really communicates himself in the concrete existence of the human being Jesus of Nazareth, but it remains an indirect communication." This intentional minimizing of the Johannine Christology already falls apart at John 1:1 and 1:18; cf. also John 10:30; 20:28.

glory, the glory as of a father's only son").[40] "Seeing the glory" is said with regard to the σὰρξ γενόμενος (one who has become flesh), i.e., the event of the incarnation has the divine glory as its content. Jesus's belonging to God has no temporal or spatial boundaries, but is comprehensive and total, because it originated before time and the cosmos.[41] The term δόξα designates both the divine mode of being of Jesus Christ and his appearance in this world in a way that can be experienced by human beings. For John, Jesus is always and entirely in the realm of the one glory of God, but at the same time we can distinguish between a *preexistence glory* (17:5, 24c–d; 12:41), the appearance of the glory in the *incarnation* (1:14), the manifestation of the glory in *miracles* (2:11; 11:4, 40), and a *postexistence glory* (17:1b, 5, 10b, 22, 24c) into which Jesus returns through *his glorifying God on the cross* (7:39; 12:16). The entire event of Jesus's revelatory work means the glorifying of the Father through the Son and of the Son through the Father (cf. 8:54; 12:28; 13:31–32; 14:13), so that the departing Jesus says in 17:4–5, "I glorified you on earth by finishing the work that you gave me to do. So now, Father, glorify me in your own presence with the glory that I had in your presence before the world existed." The church, too, participates in the divine glory that Jesus already had before the foundation of the world, which he revealed in his earthly work, and in which he now dwells forever (17:22, "The glory that you have given me I have given them, so that they may be one, as we are one").[42]

Along with the imagery of the Logos, in the prologue John already takes up another central term of ancient philosophy,[43] the *concept of truth*.[44] In 1:14, 17, Jesus Christ appears as the locus of God's grace and truth, which means that truth has the character of event, a reality that can be experienced, and is thought of by John in personal terms. Truth is thus much more than, and completely different from, a consensus of subjective assumptions. As himself the truth, Jesus discloses to believers the meaning of his sending, reveals the Father to them, and thereby frees them from the powers of death, sin, and darkness. Jesus Christ is not only a witness to the truth[45] but is himself the truth. Freedom is thus the direct effect of believers' experience of truth: "You

40. On this point, cf. Wilhelm Thüsing, *Die Erhöhung und Verherrlichung Jesu im Johannesevangelium* (NTA 21/1, 2; Münster: Aschendorff, 1979), 227–29.

41. Δόξα as a designation for the divine epiphany is linked to Old Testament theophany traditions (cf., e.g., Exod. 16:10; 24:16–17; 33:18–19; 40:34–35); see also Wis. 7:25.

42. Cf. Thüsing, *Erhöhung*, 214–19.

43. Cf. here Y. Ibuki, *Die Wahrheit im Johannesevangelium* (BBB 39; Bonn: Hannstein, 1972).

44. Cf. the texts in *NW* 1.2:794–95. One example: Plato, *Leg.* 2.663E, "Truth, Stranger, is a noble thing and lasting, but a thing of which men are hard to be persuaded."

45. On the Hellenistic idea that truth is always a gift of God or the gods, which comes into being in the right use of reason, cf. Plutarch, *Is. Os.* 1: "For we believe that there is nothing more important for man to receive, or more ennobling for God of His grace to grant, than the truth."

will know the truth, and the truth will make you free" (8:32). The personal dimension of the Johannine concept of truth is clear in 14:6: "Jesus said to him, 'I am the way, and the truth, and the life. No one comes to the Father except through me.'" Jesus is the way, because he himself is the truth, and the one who grants life. The evangelist links authentic understanding of God exclusively to the person of Jesus; who God is can only be seen by looking at Jesus. John thus formulates an unsurpassable claim to exclusivity[46] that represents an *intrinsic claim to absoluteness*: the possibility of coming to know God and coming to God, the goal of every religious life and striving, is found only in Jesus Christ. Every religion, every movement, lives from its inherent capacity to persuade—when that capacity flags, its continued existence becomes impossible in the long run. The intrinsic claim to absoluteness means to believe and confess that Jesus is the one and only way to God. It means to take seriously Jesus's claim that he has opened up the one true way to God, and not to relativize it a priori. An extrinsic claim to absoluteness would be a claim that could and should be enforced under all circumstances, possibly including even violence. Johannine Christianity is far removed from this idea, for it is a religion of love; for John, truth and violence cannot belong together, but only truth and love. The exclusiveness of the manifestation of divine reality in Jesus Christ is critically directed against all competing claims. Truth and life, in the comprehensive sense, are not at human disposal, but available only through Jesus Christ. Because John does not understand truth abstractly, but thinks in personal terms, his concept of truth must be made more precise. God's saving work in Jesus Christ can, in John's view, be adequately understood as an act of God's love to human beings (cf. John 3:16; 1 John 4:8, 16), so that truth and love mutually interpret each other. The Johannine concept of absoluteness is nothing more or less than a variation of the absoluteness of divine love to humanity in Jesus Christ. In the Son, God turns to humanity in absolute love.

Miracle as Event of Gracious Divine Turning to the World

Jesus turns toward human beings above all in his miracles; the concept of perceptible signs is a central element of the Fourth Gospel's incarnation Christology.[47] John integrates seven miracle stories into his gospel, an expression

46. This claim is already inherent in the Old Testament concept of God; one need only note Exod. 20:2–3; Isa. 44:6; Deut. 6:4–5.

47. For analysis of the Johannine miracle tradition, cf. W. Nicol, *The Semeia in the Fourth Gospel: Tradition and Redaction* (NovTSup 32; Leiden: Brill, 1972); Hans-Peter Heekerens, *Die Zeichen-Quelle der johanneischen Redaktion: Ein Beitrag zur Entstehungsgeschichte des vierten Evangeliums* (SBS 113; Stuttgart: Verlag Katholisches Bibelwerk, 1984); Schnelle, *Antidocetic Christology*, 74–175; Wolfgang J. Bittner, *Jesu Zeichen im Johannesevangelium: Die Messias-Erkenntnis im Johannesevangelium vor ihrem jüdischen Hintergrund* (WUNT 26; Tübingen: Mohr, 1987); Christian Welck, *Erzählte Zeichen: Die Wundergeschichten des Johannesevangeli-*

of the number seven as representing fullness and completion, as in Gen. 2:2. Each type of miracle is found only once in John. The individual miracle stories, systematically apportioned throughout the public ministry of Jesus, illustrate a central aspect of Johannine Christology: *the saving divine presence in the Incarnate One, who as the mediator of creation created life at the beginning (John 1:3), is himself the Life (1:4), and is the giver of life to others.*[48] This creative, life-giving power is manifest in the greatness of the miracles; John raises the Synoptics' comparative to the superlative. Jesus not only changes water into wine, but fills six huge jars with a quantity of almost seven hundred liters (2:1–11). The healing of the son of a royal official from a distance in Capernaum no longer takes place within the same town, but Jesus is in Cana (4:46–54). The lame man at the Pool of Bethesda has been sick for thirty-eight years (5:1–9). At the miraculous feeding of the five thousand, all could take as much as they wanted, and still twelve large baskets full of bread were left over (6:1–15). Jesus not only walks on the sea and delivers the disciples from their trouble (6:16–20), he performs the additional miracle of relocating the boat to its intended destination (6:21). Jesus restores the sight of a man blind from birth (9:1–41). Lazarus has already been dead four days and his body is at the point of decomposing, when Jesus awakens him from the dead; even though he was bound hand and foot and his face had been covered by a cloth, Lazarus came forth from the grave at Jesus's command (11:1–44).

The Human Being Jesus

The miracles demonstrate their reality by their extraordinary dimensions and by the fact that they can be explicitly verified (cf. John 2:9–10; 4:51ff.; 5:2, 5; 6:13; 9:9, 20, 25, 39; 11:18, 39, 44) as the divine presence in the world. At the same time, both in the miracle stories and in other central narrative contexts, the humanity of Jesus is emphasized.[49] He attends a wedding celebration (2:1–11); he loves his friend Lazarus (11:3); he is deeply moved by the sorrow of others (11:33–34) and weeps at the grave of Lazarus (11:35). Jesus comes from Nazareth in Galilee (1:45–46; 4:44; 7:41, 52), and not from Bethlehem (cf. 7:42!); his parents are likewise known (1:45; 2:1, 3, 12; 6:42; 19:26), as are his brothers (2:12; 7:1–10). He has a mortal body (2:21) of flesh (6:51) and blood (19:34). He purifies the temple with great passion (2:14–22); his traveling on

---

ums literarisch untersucht; mit einem Ausblick auf Joh 21 (WUNT 69; Tübingen: Mohr, 1994); Michael Labahn, *Jesus als Lebensspender: Untersuchungen zu einer Geschichte der johanneischen Tradition anhand ihrer Wundergeschichten* (BZNW 98; Berlin: de Gruyter, 1999), passim. For a survey of the history of research, cf. Gilbert van Belle, *The Signs Source in the Fourth Gospel: Historical Survey and Critical Evaluation of the Semeia Hypothesis* (BETL 116; trans. Peter J. Judge; Louvain: Leuven University Press, 1994).

48. Cf. Labahn, *Lebensspender*, 501: In the Incarnate One, "God himself comes near to humanity with the gift of life."

49. On this point, cf. Thompson, *Incarnate Word*, 53–86.

foot makes him tired and thirsty (4:6–7). In view of the destiny set before him, (12:27; cf. 13:21) Jesus experiences inward turmoil or excitement (ταράσσω), and on the cross asks for a drink (19:28). Pilate allows his soldiers to torture him with the lash and thorns (19:1–2), and then somewhat officially declares, "Look, the man!" (19:5, ἰδοὺ ὁ ἄνθρωπος). A member of the execution squad makes it unmistakably clear that Jesus is in fact dead (19:38). At his burial, his body is prepared with aromatic spices to mask the anticipated stench of a corpse (19:39–40). The disciples, and then, finally, Thomas, can confirm with their own eyes that the body of the risen Jesus is identical with that of the earthly and crucified Jesus (20:20, 27).

The sharpening of the theological point is clear: in his saving act in behalf of the world, God binds himself entirely to this human being Jesus of Nazareth and his work. God himself speaks and acts in Jesus, and that in an exclusive and unsurpassable sense. God's word can be heard nowhere else (5:39–40), nowhere else are God's works to be experienced (3:35; 5:20–22) apart from the human being Jesus of Nazareth.

The Continuing Incarnation

John understands the incarnation of the Preexistent One as an event that is completed in regard to its foundational nature, but as an *abiding* event in its continuing effects. The Son of God who came "from above" has returned to the Father, but is nonetheless still present: in baptism and the eucharist. In the Gospel of John, space-time dimensions cannot be objectified in the this-worldly sense, but serve to portray Jesus's works in a way that transcends space and time. Baptism and eucharist testify to the abiding, saving presence of the one who came from heaven to reveal God and effect his saving work. Because the Son of Man who came "from above" (John 3:31; 8:14, 23) and has now gone back up is constantly linked to this heavenly reality (1:51), believers can and must be born anew/from above (ἄνωθεν) in order to enter the kingdom of God (3:3, 5).[50] Jesus Christ is the bread of life that has come down from heaven, the living bread who is present and given in the eucharist (6:26ff.). The essence of John's incarnational theology is articulated in pointed fashion in the eucharistic passage 6:51c–58. This passage was composed by the evangelist and added to the traditional speech about the bread of life in 6:30–35, 41–51b, in order to formulate a central christological statement:[51] the eucharist is the salvific locus of the presence of the incarnate, crucified, exalted, and glorified Jesus Christ, who grants believers participation in eternal life and thereby

50. On placing John 3 in its context, as well as the literary and theological unity of the text, cf. Thomas Popp, *Grammatik des Geistes: Literarische Kunst und theologische Konzeption in Johannes 3 und 6* (ABG 3; Leipzig: Evangelische Verlagsanstalt, 2001), 81–107; 206–20, 233–55.

51. For a comprehensive argument for the literary and theological unity of John 6, cf. ibid., 256–76.

allows them to share in the unity of Father and Son. The real death of Jesus presupposes his true humanity. It is this real death of a truly human being that makes possible the saving effect of his death, which continues to be present in baptism and eucharist as the gift of life (cf. 19:34b–35).

The Christological Schism

The incarnational thinking of the Fourth Gospel derives from the basic theological starting point and the internal logic of Johannine thinking, but at the same time is also the response to a controversy within the Johannine school.[52] In the story line of the gospel, the eucharistic section, with its emphasis on the irreducible unity of humanity and deity in the person of Jesus, triggers a schism among the disciples (John 6:60–71).[53] This division among the disciples in the narrative reflects a split within the Johannine school that had been ignited by a controversy about the soteriological significance of the earthly existence of Jesus, as seen especially in 1 John. The opponents who are resisted there had once been members of the Johannine community (cf. 1 John 2:19), but, in the view of the author, had denied the soteriological identity between the earthly Jesus and the heavenly Christ (cf. 1 John 2:22, Ἰησοῦς οὐκ ἔστιν ὁ Χριστός; cf. further the affirmations of identity in 1 John 4:15; 5:1, 5). It is evident that, for the opponents, only the Father and the heavenly Christ were relevant for salvation, but not the life, suffering, and death of the historical Jesus of Nazareth. In contrast, for the author of 1 John, those who reject the Son by teaching their false doctrine do not have the Father either. Moreover, the statement about the incarnation in 1 John 4:2 (cf. also 1 John 1:2; 3:8b) indicates that the opponents rejected the incarnation of the preexistent Son. The Passion of the historical Jesus of Nazareth (cf. 1 John 5:6b) had no more significance for them than his atoning death (cf. 1 John 1:9; 2:2; 3:16; 4:10). They made a strict distinction between the heavenly Christ, who alone had saving power, and the earthly Jesus, who only appeared to be an earthly being, and had no actual body of flesh and blood. The opponents "eliminated Jesus from their teaching, and denied the human side of the Redeemer."[54]

So also were the letters of Ignatius of Antioch (written between 110 and 117 CE) directed against a docetic Christology.[55] He charged his opponents

52. On this point, cf. Schnelle, *New Testament Writings*, 463–66.

53. Cf. here Ludger Schenke, "Das johanneische Schisma und die 'Zwölf' (Joh 6,60–71)," *NTS* 38 (1992): 105–21; Popp, *Grammatik*, 386–437.

54. P. Weigandt, "Der Doketismus im Urchristentum und in der theologischen Entwicklung des zweiten Jahrhunderts" (PhD diss., Ruprecht-Karls-Universität Heidelberg, 1961), 105; on docetism cf. also Pamela E. Kinlaw, *The Christ Is Jesus: Metamorphosis, Possession, and Johannine Christology* (SBLAB 18; Atlanta: Society of Biblical Literature, 2005), 74–93.

55. See the comprehensive analysis of the Ignatius texts in Wolfram Uebele, "*Viele Verführer sind in die Welt ausgegangen*"*: Die Gegner in den Briefen des Ignatius von Antiochien und in den Johannesbriefen* (BWANT 151; Stuttgart: Kohlhammer, 2001), 37–92.

with denying the bodily existence of Jesus Christ, for they did not confess that the Lord had a real body (Ign. *Smyrn.* 5.2). In contrast, Ignatius himself emphasizes that Jesus Christ was born of the virgin Mary, was baptized by John, and for our sakes was really nailed to the cross under Pontius Pilate (*Smyrn.* 1.1; cf. *Trall.* 9.1). The opponents understood that Jesus only appeared to suffer (cf. *Trall.* 10; *Smyrn.* 2; 4.2). In contrast, Ignatius himself explicitly emphasizes the suffering and death of Jesus Christ (cf. *Eph.* 7.2; 20.1; *Trall.* 9.1; 11.2; *Rom.* 6.1; *Smyrn.* 1.2; 6.2). If Jesus Christ lived on this earth only in τὸ δοκεῖν (in appearance), he did not really suffer and die, so the opponents must also deny his resurrection. Only by seeing such opponents in view can we understand the vehemence with which Ignatius emphasizes the resurrection of Jesus Christ in the flesh (cf. *Smyrn.* 1.2; 3.1; 7.1; *Trall.* 9.2; *Eph.* 20.1; *Magn.* 11). If the opponents deny the resurrection, then the eucharist is also without meaning, and the grace of Jesus Christ is belittled (*Smyrn.* 6.2). It is only consistent with this when the opponents do not attend the eucharistic services (cf. *Smyrn.* 6.2; 7.1).

The parallel between the way Ignatius and Polycarp resist their respective opponents (cf. Pol. *Phil.* 7.1) is particularly noteworthy, for it confirms that those opposed in 1 John were also advocates of a *docetic Christology.*[56] As a monophysite Christology, docetism disputed the soteriological significance of the embodiment of the Son of God; his time on earth and his suffering and death only *appeared* to affect him (δοκέω [appear, seem to be something]). While the opponents in fact allowed the person of the Redeemer to be split into parts, 1 John and especially the author of the Gospel of John emphasize the thoroughgoing soteriological unity of the earthly Jesus and the heavenly Christ (cf. John 1:14; 6:51–58; 19:34b–35).[57]

56. Cf. Rudolf Bultmann, *A Commentary on the Johannine Epistles* (trans. R. Philip O'Hara et al.; Hermeneia; Philadelphia: Fortress, 1973), 62; Weigandt, "Doketismus," 193ff.; Strecker, *Johannine Letters*, 131–41; Schnelle, *Antidocetic Christology*, 61–70; Martin Hengel, *The Johannine Question* (Philadelphia: Trinity, 1989), 68–72, 187; Uebele, *Gegner*, 147–63. Other positions on the question of identifying the opponents are advocated by Johannes Rinke, *Kerygma und Autopsie: Der christologische Disput als Spiegel johanneischer Gemeindegeschichte* (HBS 12; Freiburg: Herder, 1997); Hansjörg Schmid, *Gegner im 1. Johannesbrief? Zu Konstruktion und Selbstreferenz im johanneischen Sinnsystem* (BWANT 159; Stuttgart: Kohlhammer, 2002).

57. Among those who see antidocetic features in the Christology of the Fourth Gospel are Wilhelm Wilkens, *Die Entstehungsgeschichte des vierten Evangeliums* (Zollikon: Evangelischer Verlag AG., 1958), 171; Fritz Neugebauer, *Die Entstehungsgeschichte des Johannesevangeliums* (AT 1/36; Stuttgart: Calwer, 1968), 19–20; Schnelle, *New Testament Writings*, passim; Hengel, *Johannine Question*, 68–72; J. Frey, *Die johanneische Eschatologie* (WUNT 96, 110, 117; 3 vols.; Tübingen: Mohr, 1997–2000), 3:396–97; Popp, *Grammatik*, 365; Kinlaw, *The Christ Is Jesus*, 171; Popkes, *Theologie der Liebe Gottes*, 261; among those who are skeptical about an antidocetic perspective in the Fourth Gospel is Hartwig Thyen, *Das Johannesevangelium* (HNT 6; Tübingen: Mohr, 2005), 91.

12.2.2 The Sending of the Son

Another central element of Johannine Christology is represented by the *sending pronouncements*. Jesus is to be believed in, because God (the Father) sent him (John 5:36; 11:42; 17:8, 21, 23, 25). Jesus constantly refers to the Father who sent him (cf. 3:16; 5:23, 24, 30, 37; 6:29, 38, 39, 44, 57; 7:16, 18, 28, 29, 33; 8:16, 18, 26, 29, 42; 10:36; 12:44, 45, 49; 13:16, 20; 14:24; 15:21; 16:5; 17:3, 8, 18, 21, 23, 25; 20:21). The sending of Jesus itself becomes the content of faith, so that to come to know this is precisely the goal of the learning process in hearing/reading the gospel. Thus the sending of Jesus has an incomparably greater importance than the sending of John the Baptist (1:6, 33), who was also authorized for his mission by being sent by God, but who was still only a human being (cf. 5:34). His sending had no importance in itself, but only in reference to the sending of Jesus (3:28). In contrast, the sending of Jesus is itself the saving event (3:17; 17:3), for in this act God gives his Son to the world as a gift of love (3:16; 6:32).

The sending of the Son has its basis in the love of God, and its goal in the salvation of the world: "Indeed, God did not send the Son into the world to condemn the world, but in order that the world might be saved through him" (John 3:17; cf. 1 John 4:9–10).[58] *The Sent One not only represents the Sender, but the sending is as though the Sender himself has come; he not only brings a message, but is himself the message.* He acts in the place of the Sender; his acts have the same validity as those of the Sender: as the Sent One, Jesus speaks freely and openly the words of God (3:34; 12:49, 50; 14:24; cf. 14:10);[59] his teaching does not derive from himself, but from the one who sent him (7:16); it is from God (7:17). The same is true of the Son's authority to judge (5:30; 8:16). When Jesus works, he only does the work of the one who sent him; he acts in the name of the Sender (10:25), and not on his own authority (5:19, 30). He cannot do otherwise than what the Father himself does (5:19); the Father shows him all that he should do (5:20, 36). All this means: the One at work in what Jesus does is the Father himself (14:10). As the Sent One, Jesus has no independent will but seeks to do the will of the Sender (5:30), puts it into effect (4:34; 6:38ff.), follows his command (8:29; 10:18; 14:31), and completes his work (4:34; 17:4). The sending pronouncements thus express: in the human

58. The agreements with Gal. 4:4; Rom. 8:3, 32; and 1 John 4:9, 10, 14 point to a common background in the religious traditions of Jewish-Hellenistic wisdom literature (cf., e.g., Wis. 9:9–10, 17; Sir. 24:4, 12ff.; Philo, *Agriculture* 51; *Heir* 205; *Confusion* 63; *Flight* 12); additional texts in *NW* 1.2:156–63. Also to be noted is Epictetus, *Diatr.* 3.22.23–24, according to whom the true Cynic "must know that he has been sent by Zeus to men, . . . in order to show that in questions of good and evil they have gone astray, and are seeking the true nature of the good and the evil where it is not, but where it is they never think."

59. On the motif of παρρησία (open, bold, candid speaking), cf. Michael Labahn, "Die παρρησία des Gottessohnes," in *Kontexte des Johannesevangeliums* (ed. Albert Frey and Udo Schnelle; WUNT 175; Tübingen: Mohr, 2004), 321–63.

being Jesus, who speaks, teaches, and works, there is at the same time Another who is present, teaches, and works: God himself. Whoever believes that Jesus has been sent from God acknowledges this presence of God in Jesus.

All this already makes clear that the Johannine sending-Christology may not be considered in isolation but must be understood as an organic component of Johannine Christology as a whole. It assumes the preexistence and incarnation of the Son, just as it presupposes Jesus's death on the cross and his exaltation, for the sending does not take place in some timeless descent and ascent but is consummated on the cross.[60] Being with God and coming from God is the common foundation for the pronouncements about preexistence, incarnation, and sending.

The Witnesses of the Sending

Jesus's revelatory claim is grounded in his being sent by the Father. The Pharisees, however, misunderstand Jesus's self-revelation as testimony about himself that can be taken as self-promotion, and so from their perspective must be investigated (cf. John 7:14ff.). Jesus responds to this objection by emphasizing the veracity of his own testimony:[61] "My teaching is not mine but his who sent me" (7:16b). In the background stands the principle of Jewish law that the consistent testimony of two witnesses is true (cf. Num. 35:30; Deut. 17:6; 19:15). No one except Jesus himself can base his claim on this principle, for the relation of Father and Son is not a matter of externals, but is revealed in their intrinsic, total agreement. Not only the Father, but other witnesses also confirm Jesus's claim. Alongside the Baptist (John 1:6–8, 15, 19ff.) and the "works" (14:11), it is above all the Scripture that testifies to the validity of Jesus's claim to be the Revealer, for not only Moses (5:45–47) but also Abraham (8:56) and Isaiah (12:41) testify to him. The quotations and allusions from the Old Testament point to the fulfillment of God's will in Jesus Christ (1:23, 51; 2:17; 3:13; 6:31, 45; 7:18, 38, 42; 10:34; 12:13, 15, 27, 38, 40; 13:18; 15:25; 16:22; 17:12; 19:24, 28, 36, 37; 20:28).[62] This understanding of Scripture can only be the result of the Johannine christological hermeneutic. The first, and at the same time, the ultimate, revelation in Jesus Christ (cf.

60. Contra Müller, "Eigentümlichkeit," 39–40, who plays off the sending-Christology against the cross theology. Against the view that, within the framework of a predominantly sending Christology the death of Jesus would have no salvific importance, one can cite John 1:29, 36; 2:14–22; 3:14–16; 10:15, 17–18; 11:51–52; 12:27–32, and especially John 19:30: the cross as the place of ascension and glorification is at the same time the goal of Jesus's sending (for comprehensive grounding of this view, see below, §12.2.5).

61. On the witness motif, cf. Johannes Beutler, *Martyria* (FTS 10; Frankfurt: Knecht, 1972).

62. On the Johannine understanding of Scripture, cf. M. F. F. Menken, *Old Testament Quotations in the Fourth Gospel: Studies in Textual Form* (CBET 15; Kampen: Kok Pharos, 1996); Schuchard, *Scripture within Scripture*; Obermann, *Erfüllung der Schrift*; Kraus, "Johannes und das Alte Testament."

1:1–18) cannot contradict the revelation that comes through the Scripture. The highest and abiding meaning of the Scripture consists in its fundamental witness, so that, according to the Johannine understanding, the Scripture can only be rightly read as pointing to Jesus Christ and can be understood only from a perspective that begins with him. John by no means relativizes the status of Scripture but attributes to it an extraordinary importance within the framework of the temporal and objective priority of the Christ event: as a witness to Christ, the Scripture interprets and deepens the true knowledge of the Son of God.

The Tendency toward Dualism

The Gospel of John developed out of the post-Easter anamnesis of the Christ event effected by the Spirit (cf. 2:17, 22; 10:6; 12:16; 13:7; 14:26; 18:32; 20:9) and reflects on the human response to the incarnate Logos under the categories of acceptance and rejection.[63] If Jesus Christ is the Revealer sent from God, the possible responses to this event are only belief or unbelief, antithetically opposite options that totally determine the life of the individual who responds. *This dualizing tendency does not point to antithesis as an a priori principle of Johannine thought; rather, it follows logically from the Johannine understanding of revelation.* The concept of revelation has consequences in various theological areas, and this tendency is one of them. So we should not speak of "Johannine dualism" but rather of a "dualizing tendency" within Johannine thought.[64]

With the preposition ἐκ (out of, from), John precisely designates the "whence," and thereby also the essential nature, of human existence. Believers are ἐκ τοῦ θεοῦ (out of/from God); they hear God's Word (cf. John 8:47) and do the will of God (cf. 1 John 3:10; 4:6; 5:19). They are children of the light (John 12:36a), are born of (or begotten from) God (John 1:13) and of (or from) the truth (1 John 2:21; 3:19; John 18:37). On the other hand, unbelief is bound to this world. The nonbelievers (John 8:23) and the false teachers are ἐκ τοῦ κόσμου ("out of/from the world," 1 John 4:5). Their father is the devil (John

63. Concisely expressed by F. Mussner, "Die 'semantische Achse' des Johannesevangeliums: Ein Versuch," in *Vom Urchristentum zu Jesus: Für Joachim Gnilka* (ed. Hubert Frankemölle and Karl Kertelge; Freiburg: Herder, 1989), 252, who says regarding the author of the Gospel of John, "He reflects the story of Jesus as a story of faith and decision, and presents the conflicts in response to the Logos-Christ through opponents and helpers by the opposing linguistic pair 'accept'/'not accept.'"

64. The term "dualism" was already vehemently rejected by Josef Blank, *Krisis: Untersuchungen zur johanneischen Christologie und Eschatologie* (Freiburg i.B.: Lambertus, 1964), 342–43; for the history of research, see Popkes, *Theologie der Liebe Gottes*, 11–51; J. Frey, "Zu Hintergrund und Funktion des johanneischen Dualismus," in *Paulus und Johannes: Exegetische Studien zur paulinischen und johanneischen Theologie und Literatur* (ed. Dieter Sänger and Ulrich Mell; WUNT 198; Tübingen: Mohr Siebeck, 2006), who speak of "dualistic motifs/dualisms" in John.

8:44; cf. 1 John 3:8, 10), and they are oriented to what is "below" (John 8:23, εἶναι ἐκ τῶν κάτω). These distinctions derive from the Johannine concept of revelation itself, for the Revealer is "from above" (John 8:23, ἐγὼ ἐκ τῶν ἄνω εἰμί; 3:31, "The one who comes from above is above all; the one who is of the earth belongs to the earth and speaks about earthly things. The one who comes from heaven is above all."). Because the Revealer himself is not ἐκ τοῦ κόσμου, neither are his own from the world (cf. 17:16).

The Johannine concept is fundamentally different from Gnostic systems, in which believers belong to the upper sphere from the very beginning, and dualism has a protological function.[65] An antithesis (light/darkness) appears in the gospel for the first time in John 1:5. In order to understand it, the prior statement about creation (1:3–4) is extremely important. The creation precedes the "darkness," and thus is not considered, as in the Gnostic systems, a work of "darkness." "Light" and "darkness" are constituted as such in view of revelation, as positive response or rejection, so that the dualizing tendency in the Johannine writings, in contrast to that of the Gnostic writings, has no protological significance but must be understood as a function of Johannine Christology.[66] *God's gracious turning to the world in Jesus Christ precedes every dualism!*[67] In the Fourth Gospel, no anti-worldly dualism is temporally or factually prior to the revelatory event; rather, in response to the revelation, a separation occurs between the believing community and the world that has become hardened by its own unbelief.

The world (κόσμος, "cosmos") is by no means considered only in a negative light. The world of God and the world of human beings originally belong together. Already in the creation, the good temporally precedes the evil, for it is a work of the Logos who was in the beginning with God. God so loved the world that he sent his Son into the world (John 3:16; cf. 10:36; 1 John 4:9–10, 14); Jesus is the prophet and Son of God who comes into the world (John 6:14; 11:27). As the bread that came down from heaven, he gives life to the world (6:33; cf. 6:51), and he is the light of the world (9:5). Jesus came to save the

65. On this point, cf. Herbert Kohler, *Kreuz und Menschwerdung im Johannesevangelium: Ein exegetisch-hermeneutischer Versuch zur johanneischen Kreuzestheologie* (ATANT 72; Zürich: Theologischer Verlag, 1987), 137–39. So also, the appeal frequently made that the Johannine statements have parallels in the dualistic statements of the Qumran manuscripts does not stand up to close investigation; cf. J. Frey, "Licht aus den Höhlen: Der 'johanneische Dualismus' und die Texte von Qumran," in *Kontexte des Johannesevangeliums* (ed. Albert Frey and Udo Schnelle; WUNT 175; Tübingen: Mohr, 2004), 117–203. The older treatment of Frey, "Licht," is still well worth study.

66. Cf. Takashi Onuki, *Gemeinde und Welt im Johannesevangelium: Ein Beitrag zur Frage nach der theologischen und pragmatischen Funktion des johanneischen "Dualismus"* (WMANT 56; Neukirchen-Vluyn: Neukirchener Verlag, 1984), 41ff.

67. Entirely different is the view of Becker, *Johanneisches Christentum*, 142: "The evangelist's understanding of reality is thus characterized by a horizontal division that separates God and humanity by a great barrier."

world (cf. 3:17; 12:47): he is the σωτὴρ τοῦ κόσμου (John 4:42, "savior of the world"; cf. 1 John 2:2). With great intentionality, the departing Christ prays that the Father will *not* take the church out of the world (John 17:15), but that he will preserve it from the evil one. The church lives in the world, but is not ἐκ τοῦ κόσμου (cf. 15:29; 17:14). Jesus sends his disciples into the world (17:18), and the world is even described as having the capability of recognizing and believing in Jesus's mission (cf. 17:21, 23). The world in and of itself is not evaluated negatively, for it is unbelief that makes the cosmos into the ungodly world (cf. 16:9; 1:10; 7:7; 8:23; 9:39; chap. 14; chap. 17).[68]

Because the coming of the light has created a new situation for humanity, and because the quest for salvation can be resolved only through faith in Jesus Christ (cf. John 3:16–17; 12:46, and the ἐγώ εἰμί ["I am"] sayings in 6:35; 8:12; 10:7, 11; 11:25; 14:6; 15:1), all those who reject the message of Christ necessarily remain in darkness. The Johannine tendency to dualism calls for a decision and is at the same time its result, since the decision of human beings in response to the revelation of Christ determines their "whence" and "whither," their origin and destiny. Those who in faith let the saving act of God in Jesus Christ apply to themselves receive their new life as a rebirth "from above" in the power of the Spirit (cf. 3:3, 5), with a new foundation and a new orientation. On the other hand, those who do not believe continue in the realm of darkness and death. This tendency to dualism is the Johannine expression of the significance of the Christ event; it designates the eschatological dimensions of the demanded decision, because faith and unbelief already constitute, in the here and now, the ultimate decision for life or death (cf., e.g., 3:18, 36; 5:24).

The instances of dualizing thought that we see in John do not constitute a free-standing phenomenon following a history-of-religions dynamic of its own;[69] rather, they fit into an overarching line of argument: *the concept of love, which is prior to all the forms of Johannine dualizing, encloses them on every side and interprets them.*[70] While the dualistic tendency marks out a boundary line from case to case, Johannine thought as a whole is positively determined by the dynamic of the love of God for the world (John 3:16), for the Son (3:35; 10:17; 15:9, 10; 17:23, 26), and for the disciples (14:21, 23; 17:23, 26); the love of Jesus for God (14:31) and for the disciples (11:5; 13:1, 23, 34; 14:21, 23; 15:12, 13; 19:26); as well as the love of the disciples for Jesus (14:15, 21, 23) and for one another (13:34, 35; 15:13, 17). John's ultimate conviction

68. Cf. Rudolf Bultmann, *The Gospel of John: A Commentary* (trans. G. R. Beasley-Murray et al.; Philadelphia: Westminster, 1971), 54–55.

69. Cf. Frey, "Hintergrund," 70, who emphasizes the relevance of the dualistic motifs to the situation of the addressees and the embedding of these motifs in the Johannine dramaturgy: "The formative will of the Johannine author is thus to be evaluated more highly than the influence of his religious milieu."

70. The basic evidence and argument is provided by Popkes, *Theologie der Liebe Gottes*, passim.

is that the love that dynamically moves from the Father continues in the work of the Son and the disciples, until finally "the world may know that you have sent me and have loved them even as you have loved me" (17:23).

12.2.3 *The "I Am" Sayings*

The "I am" sayings are the center of Jesus's self-proclamation and are key sayings of the Johannine revelation theology and hermeneutic. In them, Jesus declares who he is, what he wants to be for humanity, and how people are to understand him. The "I am" sayings embody a uniquely concentrated combination of Christology and soteriology.[71] The sayings about the bread of life (John 6:35a); the light of the world (8:12); the door (10:7); the shepherd (10:11); the resurrection and the life (11:25); the way, the truth, and the life (14:6); and the vine (15:1) concisely signal the unique relationship of Father and Son. By intentionally adopting the Father's mode of revelatory speech (cf. Exod. 3:14 LXX; cf. further Exod. 3:6, 17; Isa. 43:10–11 LXX; 45:12 LXX), the Son himself becomes the medium of revelation.[72] Each saying expresses the life that has appeared in Christ; the "I am" sayings are words of life, for in five of the classic seven of the "I am" sayings, the key word "life" is present (ζωή, ψυχή). The ἐγώ εἰμι sayings have a metaphorical dimension, and are constituent elements of a whole complex of metaphorical language and material with which the author works and which is of decisive importance for interpreting the gospel (John 6; 8; 10; 11; 14; 15). No one can claim to be "the bread" or "the light" in the everyday sense of the words. At the same time, the definite article indicates that Jesus not only *brings* "the bread," "the light," and so on, but that he himself *is* this reality. In ἐγώ εἰμι the speaker modulates into what is spoken; he presents himself, manifests himself before the hearers/readers of the gospel as God. With the ἐγώ εἰμι sayings Jesus gives an answer to an implicit question: he reveals in the first place *who* he is, from which then follows *what* he is for the believers. Both aspects condition and supplement each other. Jesus can be "the bread," "the light," "the resurrection," and so on for the believers only because he *is* the Son of God. In a carefully planned structure, John clarifies the meaning of Jesus's messiahship in the seven "I am" sayings, using metaphors from the world of human experience. The "I am" sayings are summaries of the Johannine revelation theology,[73] in which the Son reveals himself, as the Father had done previously, with the words ἐγώ εἰμι.

71. The basic structure of the "I am" sayings is clearly recognizable: After the presentation (ἐγώ εἰμι), the metaphorical term with the article follows; then comes the invitation and promise. Cf. Siegfried Schulz, *Komposition und Herkunft der Johanneischen Reden* (BWANT 1; Stuttgart: Kohlhammer, 1960), 85–90.

72. "I am" sayings are found in Egyptian, Greek, and Jewish tradition; cf. *NW* 1.2:357–73.

73. John Ashton, *Understanding the Fourth Gospel* (New York: Oxford University Press, 1991), 186, appropriately designates the "I am" sayings as "miniature Gospels."

Christology in Visual Imagery

The "I am" sayings illustrate a basic principle of Johannine Christology: the presentation of christological affirmations in pictorial form.[74] Particularly for the Fourth Gospel, pictures are *the* central category for the communication of religious meaning.[75] This metonymic language utilizes symbols that are rooted in the Johannine school tradition,[76] symbols that have a referential character intended to disclose the essential character of God (see above, §12.1.3) or of Jesus Christ the Son: light (e.g., 1 John 1:5; John 1:4–5; 3:19; 8:12; 12:46); love (1 John 4:16; John 3:35; 17:26); Spirit (John 4:24); Jesus Christ as the "living water" (John 4:14; 7:37–39). This picture-language takes up metaphors that, in contrast to symbols, already on the direct level of the text call for a transcendent leap to a new level of meaning: Jesus as the bread of life (John 6), the true shepherd (John 10), the door (John 10), the grain of wheat (12:24), the vine (John 15). Moreover, John's pictorial language is characterized by spatial categories (above/below, coming/going away, sending), by titles and names (Father, Son, Logos, Lamb, Messiah, Christ, Lord) and by powerful pictorial narratives (cf. especially John 2:1–11; 3:1–11; 4:4–42; chap. 6; 8:12–20; chap. 9; chap. 10; 11:1–45).[77]

The goal of this pictorial, metonymic language is communication, recognition, and acceptance: the readers/hearers, through appropriate and positive pictures, metaphors, and pictorial language[78] drawn from their immediate life experience and their cultural background, are led ever more

74. In addition to the works of C. R. Koester and R. Zimmermann, see especially J. Frey, "Das Bild als Wirkungspotential," in *Bildersprache verstehen* (ed. Ruben Zimmermann; Übergänge 38; Munich: Fink, 2000), 331–61; J. G. Van der Watt, *Family of the King: Dynamics of Metaphor in the Gospel according to John* (BIS 47; Leiden: Brill, 2000).

75. On the ancient concept of pictorial imagery, cf. Ruben Zimmermann, *Christologie der Bilder im Johannesevangelium: Die Christopoetik des vierten Evangeliums unter besonderer Berücksichtigung von Joh 10* (WUNT 171; Tübingen: Mohr Siebeck, 2004), 61–74. Three aspects are constitutive: (1) a picture expresses a specific reality in between true being and nonbeing; (2) a picture always has a referential dimension in that it is always a picture "of something"; (3) pictures have a constitutive function in the cognitive process in that they are perceived and interpreted, i.e., the recipients of pictures have themselves a fundamental importance in this process. Zimmermann (102–3) proceeds on the basis of five basic types of imagery in the Gospel of John: metaphorical, symbolical, titular, narrative, and conceptual imagery. For the current discussion, cf. Jörg Frey et al., *Imagery in the Gospel of John: Terms, Forms, Themes, and Theology of Johannine Figurative Language* (WUNT 200; Tübingen: Mohr Siebeck, 2006).

76. On the definitions of "symbol" and "metaphor," see above, §3.4; cf. also the comprehensive theoretical discussion in Zimmermann, *Bilder*, 137–65.

77. Cf. ibid., 197–217.

78. The transfer of meaning called for by pictorial and metaphorical language is possible only when the imagery is perceived as embedded in the narrative as a whole (as emphasized by Van der Watt, *Family of the King*, 91–92) and the context of each image is considered. Within the Johannine world, it must be added that a transfer of meaning is possible only when the hearers/readers are able to read such pictures as pointing beyond their everyday world, i.e., in the power of the Spirit to perceive, for instance, that the meaning of the "shepherd" is Jesus Christ.

deeply into a true knowledge of Jesus Christ. To accomplish this purpose, the Johannine pictorial language makes use of a remarkable communications spectrum that ranges from individual motifs (e.g., Jesus as the temple, John 2:19–22), through combinations and connections (e.g., "Cana" in John 2–4 to form a ring composition), to a network of visual images (e.g., Jesus as "king" in 1:49; 12:13; 19:21). Pictorial terms such as light, life, and glory (often in interaction with their opposites) become leitmotifs that have a networking function both in smaller units of the text and through an extended sequence of passages. Through resumption, amplification, construction of inclusios, flashback, and substitution,[79] the evangelist attempts to intensify the meaning of his narrative by using pictorial language. In the Johannine picture-language, realities as they are known in everyday life constantly modulate to another level of reality that wants to be seen, recognized, and believed in; in such seeing, faith becomes an act of insight, recognition, and knowledge.[80]

12.2.4 Christological Titles

Christological titles are a central element of Johannine Christology, for they qualify Jesus of Nazareth in a particular way and concisely designate the content of the Christian faith: "But these [signs] are written so that you may come to believe that Jesus is the Messiah, the Son of God, and that through believing you may have life in his name" (John 20:31). The practical function of christological titles in the Gospel of John is illustrated in the correlation between prologue (1:1–18) and epilogue (20:30–31): the readers are introduced to the work with a christological title as its leitmotif, and they may be sure that they have understood the narrative if they can affirm the statement of faith that concludes the gospel with a christological title.[81]

Logos

It is hardly a coincidence that the absolute ὁ λόγος (Word, speech, thought, reason) is found as a christological title only in the realm of Johannine tradition (John 1:1, 14; Rev. 19:13; cf. 1 John 1:1). In John, as in Greek tradition generally, Logos is the divine principle of life and work; it designates the turning of God to humanity and the original unity of human thinking with God. The λόγος concept intentionally opens up a broad cultural vista: the worlds of

79. On these literary techniques, cf. Popp, *Grammatik*, 237–41, 444–46.

80. Cf. Zimmermann, *Bilder*, 44: "In this regard, Christology becomes an event of *seeing*, in which the multiplicity of images can still be perceived in the 'unity of visual perception,'" though not in the abstract conceptual unity of a coherent idea.

81. Sjef van Tilborg, *Reading John in Ephesus* (NovTSup 83; Leiden: Brill, 1996) has shown that there is no difficulty in explaining the deity of Jesus and all the central christological titles of the Fourth Gospel against the background of the imperial cult in Ephesus.

Greco-Roman philosophy and education[82] and of Hellenistic Judaism of the Alexandrian type.[83] As a key term of Greek educational history, the word λόγος activates a vast allusive potential that contributes to the generative collaboration of the hearer/reader in the process of understanding. The act of knowledge as it occurs in each particular cultural context is linked to the linguistic repertoire that is available for an author to activate. Concepts, terminology, and the normative aspects with which they are linked develop their force only within a linguistic community that already exists, a community that provides in advance the rules for understanding, acting, and making coherent judgments, a community that is constantly reformulating such rules.[84] By taking the key concept of Greco-Roman cultural history and making it into the leitmotif of his gospel (see above, §12.2.1), John is expressing a universal claim: the Logos Jesus Christ has come forth from his original unity with God, he is God's own creative power, he is the origin and goal of all being, and in the Logos Jesus Christ the religious and intellectual history of antiquity reaches its goal.

Son of God

The title ὁ υἱός (τοῦ θεοῦ) is found thirty-eight times in the gospel and is a key term in Johannine Christology (see above, §12.1.1 and §12.1.2). It is particularly appropriate for expressing the unique relationship between God and Jesus of Nazareth, and, on the basis of the unity of Father and Son in their essential being (cf. John 10:30), is to be understood relationally and functionally.[85] The title appears in its full revelatory sense for the first time in John 1:34 (the Baptist says, "I myself have seen and have testified that this is the Son of God") and then is developed more and more in the further course of the gospel.[86] The introduction of the title at this point

82. On the logos concept as a whole, cf. Bernhard Jendorff, *Der Logosbegriff: Seine philosophische Grundlegung bei Heraklit von Ephesos und seine theologische Indienstnahme durch Johannes den Evangelisten* (EHS 20.19; Frankfurt: Lang, 1976); Arno Schmidt, *Die Geburt des Logos bei den frühen Griechen* (Berlin: Logos-Verlag, 2002). Classically Diogenes Laertius, *Vit. phil.* 6.3, of Antisthenes, "He was the first to define statement (or assertion), by saying that a statement [λόγος] is that which sets forth what a thing was or is [λόγος ἐστὶν ὁ τὸ τί ἦν ἢ ἔστι δηλῶν]." Almost contemporary with the Gospel of John, Dio Chrysostom, for example, formulated: "This doctrine [ὁ δὲ λόγος], in brief, aims to harmonize the human race with the divine, and to embrace in a single term everything endowed with reason, finding in reason the only sure and indissoluble foundation for fellowship and justice" (*Or.* 36.31). See additional texts in *NW* 1.2:10–15.

83. Cf. here Burton L. Mack, *Logos und Sophia: Untersuchungen zur Weisheitstheologie im hellenistischen Judentum* (SUNT 10; Göttingen: Vandenhoeck & Ruprecht, 1973).

84. It is thus not possible to confine interpretation of the logos to a Hellenistic-Jewish background, as, e.g., F. Hahn would like to do (cf. Hahn, *Theologie*, 1:616–17).

85. Ferdinand Hahn, "υἱός," *EDNT* 3:385–86, rightly emphasizes that, while different traditions are associated with the Son title, the Johannine conception is to be regarded as an independent model.

86. Cf. especially the confessions of Nathanael (John 1:49) and of Martha (John 11:27).

reveals the careful composition of the evangelist: with the phrase ὁ υἱὸς τοῦ θεοῦ John points ahead to the concluding verse of the gospel (20:31), so that the title "Son of God" brackets the totality of Jesus's work from the call of the first disciples to their final commission and sending. The content of the title itself includes the revelatory work of the Son, to whom the Father has given authority over all things (3:35; 17:2), who alone brings revelatory knowledge from the Father (1:18; 6:46), who does the will of the Father (5:19–20), and who is sent into the world for its salvation (see above, §12.2.2). Whoever sees the Son and believes in him has eternal life (3:36; 6:40), has true freedom (8:32, 36), and sees and knows the Father as well (12:45; 14:9). It is not surprising that the charge of ditheism was ignited by the Son title (5:18; 10:33–39; 19:7). The Son title concisely expresses the unique revelatory power and authority and the exclusive saving function exercised by Jesus Christ alone.

Christ

The title/name Ἰησοῦς Χριστός (Jesus Christ) appears only in John 1:17 and 17:3 (but cf. 1 John 1:3; 2:1; 3:23; 4:2; 5:5, 20); the focus is on the absolute (ὁ) Χριστός, oriented to the Old Testament messianic expectation (seventeen times in the gospel; transliterated into Greek as Μεσσίας in John 1:41; 4:25). The Baptist explicitly rejects this title for himself (John 1:20, 25; 3:28). In contrast, the confessional statements in John 4:29; 7:26, 41; 10:24 ("This one is the Christ"); 11:27 (Martha "said to him, 'Yes, Lord, I believe that you are the Messiah, the Son of God, the one coming into the world'"); and 20:31 all make the positive claim that Jesus of Nazareth is the Messiah promised in the Old Testament. The questions associated with this claim are treated thematically: the Messiah's origin (4:25; 7:27, 41–42), miracles (7:31), and eternal existence (12:41). The use of Messiah and Son of God alongside each other in 11:27 and 20:31 shows clearly that for John, messiahship and divine sonship belong together.

King of Israel/King of the Jews

The royal motif frames the works and words of Jesus (cf. John 1:49; 12:13, 15; 18:33, 36, 37, 39; 19:3, 12, 14, 15, 19, 21): at the beginning stands Nathanael's confession that Jesus is the king of Israel (1:49), resumed in the acclamation during Jesus's procession into Jerusalem (12:13); the conclusion of the gospel is dominated by the motif of Jesus's royal dignity. Linked therewith is the expression βασιλεία τοῦ θεοῦ (kingdom of God) in 3:3, 5, with obvious reference to the hearing before Pilate (see below, §12.2.5). Just as Jesus's βασιλεία is not of this world (18:36), human beings must be born "from above/anew" in order to participate in salvation. In contrast to the masses that judge superficially (cf. 6:15), the readers of the gospel know of Jesus's true kingship, which exists only by his legitimation by the Father.

Kyrios

The title κύριος (Lord) occurs forty-three times in the Gospel of John, but does not attain its distinguishing Johannine profile until the post-Easter narratives. Prior to chapters 20–21, "Lord" is mostly used without the weightiness of a christological title (cf. chaps. 4; 11; and 13; in 13:13–14, κύριος is used as the equivalent of διδάσκαλος [teacher]; cf. also 15:15, 20). But in 20:2, 18, 20, 25, κύριος serves to designate the Risen One, climaxing in the confession of Thomas, "My Lord and my God" (20:28, ὁ κύριος μου καὶ ὁ θεός μου). The reference to "seeing the Lord" in 20:18, 20, 25 points to 1 Cor. 9:1 and shows that κύριος was also used in the tradition of the Johannine community as a specific designation for the risen Lord.

Son of Man

The Son of Man concept has been totally integrated into the way Johannine Christology is conceived as a whole. The link to the preexistence and sending motifs is clearly indicated in the references to the "descent" and "ascent" of the Son of Man (cf. John 1:51; 3:13–14; see further 6:27, 53 with 6:33, 38, 41–42, 50–51, 58) and the explicit affirmation of the preexistence of the Son of Man in 6:62 ("Then what if you were to see the Son of Man ascending to where he was before"). As the Son of Man who has descended from heaven and has ascended back to heaven, in John's understanding he already fulfills in the present his functions as judge (5:27), giver of life (6:27, 52, 62), and Messiah (8:28; 9:35; 12:23, 34; 13:31–32).[87] The pointedly clarifying addition of ὁ θεός (God) to πατήρ (Father) in 6:27 ("It is on him [the Son of Man] that God the Father has set his seal") thus points to the absolute priority of the Father, whose act in the Son of Man makes possible the salvation of humanity.

The Logos who comes from God also has continuous access to the heavenly world after his incarnation; as the Son of Man who is presently at work, he grants believers access to the heavenly world, and thus to God (John 1:51, "Very truly, I tell you, you will see heaven opened and the angels of God ascending and descending upon the Son of Man"). The internal networking of different motif complexes is seen in 3:13–14, where preexistence and sending are linked with the ascension and glorification of the Son of Man. The Johannine Son of Man sayings receive their particular stamp through their interpretation within the framework of John's theology of the cross and ascension (lifting up).[88] The anabasis of the Son of Man is interpreted in a specific Johannine way as "rising/raising/ascending/being lifted up"; as in 8:28 and 12:32, ὑψόω also in 3:13–14 means the crucifixion of Jesus.[89] As the serpent was lifted up

87. On this point, cf. Rudolf Schnackenburg, *The Gospel according to St. John* (3 vols.; New York: Seabury, 1980), 1:529–42.

88. Cf. Frey, *Eschatologie*, 3:260–80.

89. Cf. Thüsing, *Erhöhung*, 3–4.

in the wilderness, so also the lifting up of Jesus has saving power. The saving event does not first occur when Jesus ascends to heaven, but his being lifted up on the cross is already the saving event (see below, §12.2.5).

Alongside the christological titles that appear in large numbers throughout the gospel, there are also *christological predications* that emphasize particular aspects of Jesus's status and saving work.

Savior of the World

In the conversation with the Samaritan woman at the well (John 4:4–42), Jesus is designated, on an ascending scale, as a Jew (v. 9), as one more important than Jacob (v. 12), as prophet (v. 19), and as Messiah (vv. 25–26, 29), and then 4:42 declares οὗτός ἐστιν ἀληθῶς ὁ σωτὴρ τοῦ κόσμου (this is truly the Savior of the world). The term σωτήρ (savior) derives from the Hellenistic ruler cult (see above, §10.4.1) and in early Christianity was applied to Jesus (cf. Luke 2:11; Acts 5:31; 13:23; Phil. 3:20; 1 Tim. 4:10; 2 Tim. 1:10; Titus 1:4; 2:13; 3:6; Eph. 5:23; 2 Pet. 1:1, 11; 2:20; 3:2, 18; 1 John 4:14).[90] The semantic field σωτήρ/σωτηρία/σῴζω has a political-religious connotation in New Testament times: the Roman emperor is the benefactor and savior of the world who not only guarantees the political unity of the realm but grants its citizens prosperity, well-being, and meaning.[91] Here, too, John claims an absolute superlative, since for him Jesus Christ is the only savior, and he already gives eternal life in the present to those who believe.[92] The universal salvation of the world cannot be expected from political rulers but only from the crucified and risen Jesus Christ. At the same time, this predication expresses the self-understanding of the Johannine Christians: they understand themselves to be charged with a message to the whole world, because only Jesus is the Savior of the world (cf. John 3:16; 6:33; 12:47).

The Holy One of God

In John 6:69, Peter speaks in the name of the disciples who have not deserted Jesus, "We have come to believe and know that you are the Holy One [ἅγιος θεοῦ] of God." This christological predication that appears only here in the Fourth Gospel expresses, in a very concentrated manner, the unity of Father and Son. As the ἅγιος θεοῦ, Jesus participates in the innermost essence of God (cf. 10:30, 36; 14:10; 17:17, 19). For John, there is an intrinsic unity between the Son and the Father, constituted by the exclusive relationship of the Sent One to the Sender (cf. 17:18, 20), his working in the world as the Truth, his return to the Father, and the continuing presence of this event in the word, in the

90. On this point, cf. Craig R. Koester, "The Savior of the World," *JBL* 109 (1990): 665–80; Jung, ΣΩΤΗΡ, 45–176; Martin Karrer, "Jesus der Retter (Σωτήρ)," *ZNW* 93 (2002): 153–76.

91. Cf. the texts in *NW* 1.2:239–57.

92. Cf. Labahn, "Heiland der Welt," 147–73.

power of the Spirit, and in the gifts of the eucharist. In all these dimensions, Jesus is set apart as holy and is thus the "Holy One of God."

The Lamb of God

In the opening narrative section of the gospel, Jesus is twice called the ἀμνὸς θεοῦ (Lamb of God);[93] the revelatory declaration of the Baptist truly applies to him, and, as the first positive designation of his status, has a programmatic character: "Here is the Lamb of God who takes away the sin of the world!" (John 1:29). The variation in 1:36 ("Look, here is the Lamb of God") underscores the significance of this saying about Jesus. The lamb, as a contrasting image to superficial power and strength, shows that God's love comes to humanity in weakness and hiddenness. Paradoxically, the power of love is revealed in the powerlessness of the cross (see below, §12.2.5). Jesus appears in the form of lowliness, and nevertheless has the power from the Father to redeem the world.

Jesus as God

It is no accident that the clearest examples of the designation "God" for Jesus are found in the Johannine writings: cf. 1 John 5:20; John 1:1, 18; 20:28, and the objection of ditheism in John 5:18; 10:33 (cf. also Heb. 1:8–9; Titus 2:13; 2 Pet. 1:1; the interpretation of Rom. 9:5; James 1:1; Acts 20:28; 2 Thess. 1:2 is disputed). In the context of the Roman Caesar cult and local persecutions (cf. 1 John 5:21), 1 John 5:20 says about the Son of God, Jesus Christ, "He is the true God [ὁ ἀληθινὸς θεός] and eternal life." The author thereby places a clear accent against the claim of the Roman emperor's presentation of himself as God. A similar polemical context is evident in Thomas's confession in John 20:28, "My Lord and my God [ὁ κύριός μου καὶ ὁ θεός μου]." The connecting of ὁ κύριος and ὁ θεός points to Ps. 34:23 LXX, and has a striking parallel from the latter years of Domitian's reign, when he insisted on being addressed as "Dominus et Deus noster."[94] The harsh critique of ancient authors reveals how strongly this claim to lordship could influence people's lives and conduct.[95] When, against this background, the attributes claimed by the emperor are transferred to the crucified and risen Jesus Christ, a clear

93. Comprehensive analyses of the tradition are found in Martin Hasitschka, *Befreiung von Sünde nach dem Johannesevangelium: Eine bibeltheologische Untersuchung* (ITS 27; Innsbruck: Tyrolia-Verlag, 1989), 52–108 (votes for the concept of the Servant of the Lord); Thomas Knöppler, *Die theologia crucis des Johannesevangeliums: Das Verständnis des Todes Jesu im Rahmen der johanneischen Inkarnations- und Erhöhungschristologie* (WMANT 69; Neukirchen-Vluyn: Neukirchener Verlag, 1994), 67–88; Rainer Metzner, *Das Verständnis der Sünde im Johannesevangelium* (WUNT 122; Tübingen: Mohr, 2000), 153–56 (both see the Passover tradition in the background).

94. Suetonius, *Dom.* 13.2 (*NW* 1.2:855).

95. Cf. Dio Chrysostom, *Or.* 45.1; Martial, *Spect.* 10.72.1–3, where Martial describes the changes at the court with the new Emperor Trajan: "Flatteries . . . of a 'Lord and God' I have no

critique of the Caesar cult is implied.[96] To be sure, John 1:1, 18 show that using God-language for Jesus cannot simply be reduced to this polemical usage. It has its independent, objective grounding in the "ontological" unity of Father and Son (10:30), as stated in 1:1–2, "In the beginning was the Word, and the Word was with God, and the Word was God. He was in the beginning with God." The Logos dwelt from the very beginning with God, both God and the Logos are equally original, and God cannot be thought of apart from his Word (see above, §12.2.1). In v. 1c the Logos receives the predicate θεός. The Logos is neither simply identical with God, nor is there a second God alongside the highest God, but the Logos, as to its essential being, *is* God.[97] Philo indicates a clear distinction between his use of ὁ θεός and θεός: the one God alone receives the designation ὁ θεός.[98] John 1:1c deliberately positions the term θεός as the predicate nominative in order to express the essential divine being of the Logos and still at the same time to distinguish the Logos from the most high God. John 1:1c contains the climactic statement about the being and essence of the Logos,[99] who cannot be surpassed in status and importance. God is the locus of the Word; in the Word God speaks comprehensively out of his own being. Self-revelation and self-communication are here one and the same thing, for from the very beginning the Word was none other than Jesus Christ. Therefore, Jesus Christ alone may give the definitive self-revelation of God, and only to the Logos can the predicate be applied: μονογενὴς θεός (1:18, "only begotten God," NASB).

12.2.5 *Theology of the Cross*

At the center of recent discussion of Johannine thought stands the question whether John has a theology of the cross, and, if so, to what extent it shapes Johannine theology as a whole.[100] The substantive issue that stands behind this debate is whether the Johannine statements about Jesus's death are neutralized by being incorporated in and subordinated to a primary and comprehensive hermeneutical schema (e.g., dualism, sending Christology, the way of the Re-

---

intention of speaking" (*NW* 1.2:854; cf. further *Spect*. 5.8.1; 7.34.8; 8.2.6; 9.66.3; Dio Chrysostom, *Or.* 1.21).

96. The inscriptions at Ephesus include the term θεός for several emperors; cf. Tilborg, *Reading John*, 41–47.

97. Cf. Ernst Haenchen, *John*, vol. 1, *A Commentary on the Gospel of John: Chapters 1–6* (Hermeneia; trans. Robert W. Funk and Ulrich Busse; Philadelphia: Fortress, 1984), 1:110.

98. Cf. Philo, *Dreams* 1:229–230, 239–241; *Alleg. Interp.* 2.86.

99. Cf. Schnackenburg, *John* 1:234–35; Haenchen, *John*, 1:109.

100. A summary of recent research is given in Johanna Rahner, *"Er aber sprach vom Tempel seines Leibes": Jesus von Nazaret als Ort der Offenbarung Gottes im vierten Evangelium* (BBB 117; Bodenheim: Philo, 1998), 3–117, and J. Frey, "Die 'theologia crucifixi' des Johannesevangeliums," in *Kreuzestheologie im Neuen Testament* (ed. Andreas Dettwiler and Jean Zumstein; WUNT 151; Tübingen: Mohr, 2002), 169–91.

vealer from the Father and back), thereby becoming a separate and relatively minor topic,[101] or whether John too has thought through the meaning of the cross theologically and christologically, so that the cross has a foundational and lasting significance.[102] An additional question: What is "theology of the cross"? The current debate includes a variety of ways of determining and differentiating this issue,[103] but here we mean by "theology of the cross" only a theology that fulfills four conditions. Authentic cross theology must (1) explain the semantics of the σταυρός/σταυρόω terminology, (2) not only refer to the cross as the place of Jesus's death, but (3) make the cross the structuring narrative and material basis and center of a theological system, and (4) show in a theologically reflective way how cross and resurrection relate.

The Cross Perspective of the Gospel's Composition

The death of Jesus first comes explicitly into view in John 1:29, 36. As ἀμνὸς θεοῦ (Lamb of God), Jesus, through his atoning, representative death on the cross, saves the cosmos that has rebelled against God from its fallen, sinful status. Precisely at the point where the Johannine Jesus first steps onto the narrative stage, he appears as the Crucified One.[104] The end is already present at the beginning, and the hearers/readers know that the way of the preexistent and incarnate Logos leads to the cross. The narrative resumption of the imagery of "carrying" in 19:17 illustrates these connections: Jesus himself carries the cross to the place of execution, which is already in view in 1:5 ("The light shines in the darkness, and the darkness did not overcome it") and 1:11 ("He came to what was his own, and his own people did not accept him"). From the very beginning of the narrative, the cross is in view as the locus of Jesus's life-creating death, from which it determines and gives perspective to the whole Jesus-Christ-history.[105] Why does John use the word

101. Thus Bultmann, *Theology of the New Testament*, 2:53, states, "In John, Jesus's death has no preeminent importance for salvation." According to Käsemann, *Testament of Jesus*, 52, John lacks "the great Pauline paradox, that the power of the resurrection can be experienced only in the shadow of the cross," but instead, "death is the way to glory." Cf. further in this sense, Ulrich B. Müller, "Die Bedeutung des Kreuzestodes Jesu im Johannesevangelium," *KD* 21 (1975): 69; Becker, *Johanneisches Christentum*, 151; Straub, "Der Irdische," 264.

102. So, e.g., Schnelle, *Antidocetic Christology*, 173–75; Kohler, *Kreuz und Menschwerdung*, passim; Martin Hengel, "Die Schriftauslegung des 4. Evangeliums auf dem Hintergrund der urchristlichen Exegese," *JBTh* 4 (1989): 271ff.; Knöppler, *Theologia crucis*, passim; Frey, *Eschatologie*, 432ff.

103. On this point, cf. K. Haldimann, "Kreuz—Wort vom Kreuz—Kreuzestheologie," in *Kreuzestheologie im Neuen Testament* (ed. Andreas Dettwiler and Jean Zumstein; WUNT 151; Tübingen: Mohr, 2002), 1–25.

104. Whoever would like to minimize the significance of the cross in John must consider v. 29b secondary, and without adequate grounds; thus, e.g., Becker, *Johanneisches Christentum*, 152; Müller, "Eigentümlichkeit," 51–52.

105. On the interpretation of John 1:29 from the perspective of the theology of the cross, cf. also Metzner, *Verständnis der Sünde*, 197–207.

ἀμνός (the individual male sheep) only here?[106] The answer emerges within the framework of an interpretation focused on the theology of the cross: for the once-for-all event of the cross, the evangelist uses the term ἀμνός only *once* (cf. Isa. 53:7 LXX).

The narrative thread of John 1:29, 36 is taken up and strengthened in the Cana story at 2:1a ("on the third day") and in 2:4c ("My hour has not yet come"). For the recipients of the gospel, the "third day" can mean nothing else than the day of resurrection. The ὥρα (hour) of Jesus is the "hour" of the Passion (and glorification) of the preexistent Son of God. The theology of the cross (always hovering in the background) fills up the meaning of the wine miracle in a way that Mary's presence underscores: only here and in the scene at the foot of the cross (19:25–27) does Mary appear in the story, each time addressed as γύναι (woman).

In placing the *cleansing of the temple*[107] near the beginning of his narrative, the Fourth Evangelist is following a theological chronology. Since, in terms of actual history, the incident in the temple triggered the events that led to Jesus's death, and the dramaturgy of the content and structure of the Fourth Gospel is determined from the very beginning by the cross, the cleansing of the temple *necessarily* had to come at the beginning of Jesus's public ministry. John makes the motif of the theology of the cross explicit in 2:17, 22 with the hermeneutical concept of "remembering." The evangelist repeatedly refers to the death of Jesus with brief side comments from the narrator to the readers (cf. 11:13; 12:16, 33; 13:7; 18:32; 20:9), in which the motif of remembering or not yet understanding (in 12:16; 13:7; 20:9) clearly indicates the Johannine line of thought: Jesus's pre-Easter history is not understood until the Paraclete gives the post-Easter understanding (14:26). The image of destroying and rebuilding the temple in three days (2:19–22) can only be understood in terms of Jesus's resurrection by the post-Easter church. By introducing his hermeneutical concept of post-Easter remembering in the story of cleansing the temple (2:17), John is giving his readers/hearers a clear signal: the cleansing of the temple does not deal with some random incident in the life of Jesus but already presents an interpretation of the meaning of Jesus's mission as a whole. *The story of the temple cleansing thus has the character of a fundamental interpretation of the whole Christ event from the perspective of the theology of the cross!* Cross and resurrection are not merely mentioned but are thought through from a comprehensive theological perspective.

After some conceptual reflections in John 3:14–16; 10:15, 17–18; 11:51–52; 12:27–32, the emphasis on the real death of Jesus as making possible the eucharist (6:51c–58; see below, §12.7.2), and numerous allusions to the Pas-

106. Πρόβατα occurs seventeen times in John 1–20 in the sense of "flock of sheep."

107. Cf. Udo Schnelle, "Die Tempelreinigung und die Christologie des Johannesevangeliums," *NTS* 42 (1996): 359–73; Rahner, *Ort der Offenbarung*, 176–340.

sion story and its theology (2:23; 5:1; 6:4; 7:2, 10; 11:18, 55ff.; 12:1, 12), the *footwashing scene* in 13:1–20 emphatically directs the readers' view to the cross and resurrection (see below, §12.6.1). As prologue to the second main part of the gospel and portal to the Passion story, the story of the footwashing takes up the preceding allusions to the Passion and focuses the readers' perspective directly on the destiny of Jesus that immediately follows.[108] For John, the footwashing is the anticipation of Jesus's way to the cross, for in each case the action is dominated by Jesus's movement from above to below, in which Jesus serves human beings because of his love for them. Paradoxically, the power of the Son of God is revealed in the form of a servant, just as true life can come only through death. A counterpart to this story is found in the mocking scene of 19:1–5, where the king of the Jews is made a laughingstock by being crowned with thorns, clothed in a purple robe, and presented to the crowd.[109] Jesus leads his own into the new life in which people love one another as members of the family of God, the life that he himself lives and makes possible through his death on the cross. Incarnation, footwashing, and cross are all alike movements from above to below, into the depths of a truly human life, motivated by self-giving love. So also, the farewell discourses appear in the light of the love of God that leads Jesus to the cross. The new commandment of love is intentionally placed at the beginning (13:34–35), for only such love can overcome the pain of separation and establish the abiding relationship.

Finally, the *Passion narrative and the Easter stories* are oriented to the theology of the cross.[110] Different lines of the plot converge here and place their stamp on the gospel as a whole. In John in particular, the revelatory event that occurs in Jesus reaches its climax on the cross; here is where the Son fulfills the Father's will (cf. 13:1, 32; 14:31; 17:5; 18:11; 19:11, 23–24). In the hearing before Pilate, the disputed point is the nature of Jesus's kingship, such that the references to Jesus as βασιλεύς ("king"; 1:49; 12:13, 15; 18:33, 36, 37, 39; 19:3, 12, 14, 15, 19, 21)[111] take up and interpret the expression βασιλεία τοῦ θεοῦ ("kingdom of God") of 3:3, 5. There are clear points of contact between the Nicodemus conversation and the hearing before Pilate: the first dialogue with a Jew has its counterpart in the last dialogue with a Gentile, with Jesus's

108. The dimensions of the footwashing story that reflect the theology of the cross are emphasized by, e.g., Kohler, *Kreuz und Menschwerdung*, 192–98; Udo Schnelle, "Die johanneische Schule," in *Bilanz und Perspektiven gegenwärtiger Auslegung des Neuen Testaments: Symposion zum 65. Geburtstag von Georg Strecker* (ed. Friedrich W. Horn; BZNW 75; Berlin: de Gruyter, 1995), 215–16; Jean Zumstein, "Die johanneische Auffassung der Macht, gezeigt am Beispiel der Fußwaschung (Joh 13,1–17)," in *Kreative Erinnerung* (ed. Jean Zumstein; ATANT 78; Zürich: Theologischer Verlag, 2004), 174 (the footwashing is a "metaphor for the cross"); Thyen, *Johannesevangelium*, 586.

109. Cf. Kohler, *Kreuz und Menschwerdung*, 209.

110. M. Lang, *Johannes und die Synoptiker* (FRLANT 182; Göttingen: Vandenhoeck & Ruprecht, 1999), 305–42.

111. Cf. Frey, *Eschatologie*, 3:271–76.

dialogue partner in each case failing to recognize Jesus's essential identity and remaining stuck at the superficial earthly level. The *inscription on the cross* (cf. 19:19) holds up before all the world that Jesus's death as βασιλεύς is the presupposition and ground of the possibility of baptized believers' entering the kingdom of God. Just as Jesus's βασιλεία is not from this world (cf. 18:36), so human beings must be born "from above/anew" in order to participate in salvation.

The Jesus who has already been abused and mistreated carries his own cross (John 1:17; cf. 1:29) and sits naked on his throne: the cross. From the cross, Jesus establishes his new community, which, like Mary, is given into the care of the beloved disciple. The Johannine community was founded from the cross and beneath the cross (see below, §12.7.1). In the cross, the Scripture finds its fulfillment (19:28), and on the cross the Incarnate One declares τετέλεσται (19:30, "It is finished"). The thirsting, exhausted Jesus speaks his last word from the cross, in which τελέω (finish, fulfill) in 19:28, 30 refers back to the determining prepositional phrase εἰς τέλος of 13:1, which contains both temporal ("until the end") and qualitative ("entirely," "with perfect fulfillment") dimensions. The cross is the place where Jesus's love for his own attains its final goal and fulfillment; the way of the Revealer ends on the cross. The disciples' understanding of this event is compositionally worked out by intentional structural analogies between 6:19–20 and 20:19–23: in each scene the disciples find themselves in danger, and each time Jesus appears in a miraculous way to save them. While in the pre-Easter scene the disciples do not recognize Jesus walking on the sea, 20:20 clarifies that, in John as in Mark, Jesus's true identity cannot be grasped until he is seen as the Crucified and Risen One. The palpable reality of Jesus's death is emphasized in 19:34b–35 by the water and blood that comes forth from Jesus's side. In the Thomas pericope (20:24–29), the identification of the preexistent and incarnate Christ with the crucified and risen Jesus is made almost crudely obvious. Here the narrative ends, and at the same time is lifted to a higher level: "Blessed are those who have not seen, and yet believe" (20:29b).

Interpretation of the Crucifixion in Discursive Terms

One special Johannine narrative technique is filling familiar terms with new theological connotations in order to present central themes in compressed form, and thus achieve illuminating surprises and alienating, distancing effects. In connection with the cross and resurrection, these are above all Jesus's "hour" and his "lifting up" and "glorification."

With the term "hour" (ὥρα), John places the whole public ministry of Jesus under the perspective of the theology of the cross.[112] The evangelist speaks

112. John probably took up this motif from Mark 14:41: "He came a third time and said to them, 'Are you still sleeping and taking your rest? Enough! The hour has come; the Son of

of the hour of Jesus's glorification (John 12:23, 27–28; 17:1), the hour that testifies to Jesus's sending from the Father (13:1; 7:30; 8:20), the hour of accepting the Passion (12:27), and the hour that is coming (4:21, 23; 5:25; 16:2, 4, 25). In his debut at the Cana wedding, Jesus says to his mother without introduction or transition, "My hour has not yet come" (2:4c), referring to the hour of the crucifixion and glorification of the preexistent and incarnate Son of God.[113] As in 7:6, 8, 30; 8:20, οὔπω (not yet) separates the time before the Passion from the Passion itself. With this "not yet," John builds a narrative tension into the gospel that is not resolved until the announcement of "the" hour in 12:23 ("Jesus answered them, 'The hour has come for the Son of Man to be glorified'"). By "glorification," John designates the exaltation of Jesus into the divine realm, an act of God that occurs in the cross and resurrection (cf. 12:27–33). The motif of "the hour" is also stamped on the footwashing story (13:1). After the conclusion of his public ministry, Jesus knows about the coming hour of suffering that will lead to his glorification (cf. 12:23).

A distinctive mark of Johannine Christology is the designation of Jesus's death as *exaltation* (lifting up) and *glorification*.[114] John 3:13–14 already refers to the anabasis of the Son of Man as his "lifting up" ("No one has ascended into heaven except the one who descended from heaven, the Son of Man. And just as Moses lifted up the serpent in the wilderness, so must the Son of Man be lifted up."). With the word ὑψόω ("go up, ascend"; in passive, "be lifted up"), the Johannine symbolic language here points to the crucifixion of Jesus, as in 8:28; 12:32.[115] Like the lifting up of the serpent in the wilderness, so the lifting up of Jesus has a salvific function. The lifting up does not begin to be salvific only with the ascension into heaven; the lifting up on the cross is already saving. Elsewhere in the New Testament, the image of ascension is firmly bound with that of the resurrection, as in Phil. 2:9; Acts 2:33; 5:31. *John redefines the imagery by consistently thinking of the cross and resurrection as one image*. As the Crucified One, Jesus is "lifted up" in a double sense: *He is lifted up on the cross, and is at the same time with the Father; his being installed at the right hand of God is his being placed on the cross—his session takes place from the cross*.[116] This interpretation is supported above all by John 12:27–33, where being lifted up and being glorified interpret each other. With the comment from the narrator at v. 33 ("He said this to indicate the kind of

---

Man is betrayed into the hands of sinners.'" For exegesis of the text, cf. Knöppler, *Theologia crucis*, 102–15.

113. Cf. ibid., 103; Frey, *Eschatologie*, 2:182.

114. On this point, cf. J. Frey, "'Wie Mose die Schlange in der Wüste erhöht hat . . . ,'" in *Schriftauslegung im antiken Judentum und im Urchristentum* (ed. Martin Hengel and Hermut Löhr; WUNT 73; Tübingen: Mohr, 1994), 153–205; Knöppler, *Theologia crucis*, 154–73.

115. Cf. Thüsing, *Erhöhung*, 3ff.

116. On what actually happened in the procedure of capital punishment by crucifixion, cf. Kuhn, "Der Gekreuzigte," 303–34.

death he was to die"), the evangelist shows by ποίῳ θανάτῳ (by what kind of death) his understanding of cross, ascension, and glorification with a careful and precise use of language. *The point is not the death of Jesus in a general sense, but how Jesus died, namely on a cross!*[117] The status of ascended and glorified Lord is attained when Jesus is lifted up on the cross.[118]

It is particularly the case for John that the cross is the fundamental reality and abiding locus of salvation, and that Jesus can rightly be seen as returning to the Father only via the cross.[119] The lifting up of Jesus on the cross coincides with his exaltation to the Father (cf. John 13:31–32). The perspective of the high-priestly prayer underscores this idea: "Father, the hour has come; glorify your Son so that the Son may glorify you" (17:1; cf. vv. 4, 5, 22, 24). As the Son and the one sent from the Father, Jesus stands before the hour of the cross and of being "lifted up" (in both senses), in which the glory of the Father shines forth and overcomes the power of death. Precisely because John emphasizes the salvific meaning of the cross, in his gospel Jesus's Passion already modulates into the resurrection victory. This is why the Fourth Evangelist can understand the crucifixion as "exaltation" and "glorification." In this sense, the theology of the cross is the presupposition for the theology of glory.

Finally, the statements about *Jesus's actions for his own* reveal the significance of the cross as an important theme of Johannine Christology.[120] The evangelist picks up this theme especially in the Good Shepherd discourse of John 10: Jesus Christ is the Good Shepherd, the Messiah, the one who on the basis of his own love and in concord with the Father's will gives his life for his own. The expression τιθέναι τὴν ψυχὴν ὑπέρ (to give one's life for) is a central theological formula in the Fourth Gospel (10:11, 15, 17; 13:37–38; 15:13; cf. 1 John 3:16),[121] which emphasizes, in agreement with the Johannine Passion story, the idea of Jesus's voluntarily giving his own life in order to make life possible for those who believe in him. The adoption of the Hellenistic ethic of

117. Whoever wants to minimize the theological significance of Jesus's death on the cross in favor of a Johannine theology of glory must reduce the significance of John 12:33, either by passing over this text (so Becker, *Johanneisches Christentum*, 151), or by regarding it as only "superficial" (so Müller, "Eigentümlichkeit," 44).

118. The background in the history of traditions for the Johannine Christology of ascension/lifting up and glorification is provided by Isa. 52:13 LXX, where it is said of the Servant of the Lord, ἰδοὺ συνήσει ὁ παῖς μου καὶ ὑψωθήσεται καὶ δοξασθήσεται σφρόδρα; cf. Knöppler, *Theologia crucis*, 162–63. From the pagan context, cf. Artemidorus, *Onir.* 2.53; 4.49.

119. Contra Jürgen Becker, *Das Evangelium nach Johannes* (ÖTK 4.2; Gütersloh: Gütersloher Verlagshaus, 1979, 1981), 2:470: "It is not the cross, but the exaltation to heaven, that is the conclusion and goal of the sending, and the abiding basis in reality for redemption."

120. Cf. Knöppler, *Theologia crucis*, 201–16.

121. Contra Müller, "Kreuzestodes," 63, who states that in John 10:11, 15, "we have a speech formed in the tradition prior to John that does not yet grasp the authentic Johannine theology." Becker, *Evangelium nach Johannes*, 1:388, dismisses these texts with the comment, "None of these texts belong to the evangelist himself."

responsibility and friendship[122] in John 15:13 is worthy of note: "No one has greater love than this, to lay down one's life for one's friends." Jesus's love, expressed in radical self-giving for his own, is here placed in contact with a rich cultural tradition and opened up to interpretation in this wider context. The cross as the shameful instrument of execution of criminals here modulates into the means of heroic intervention on behalf of others, the loving act of the Father through the Son, and of the Son for his own. Just as Jesus loved those who believed in him with an exemplary devotion that did not stop short of death, so believers should love one another. Jesus's death for his friends is a representative death in their place, which makes new life possible and opens up the new being in love.

The four criteria for an authentic theology of the cross named at the beginning of this section have been thoroughly thought through by John on every level:[123] (1) the σταυρός/σταυρόω language (cross, crucify, crucifixion) has been concentrated in the Passion narrative (σταυρόω in 19:6, 10, 15, 16, 18, 20, 23, 32, 41; σταυρός in 19:17, 19, 25, 31). (2) Not only is reference made to the cross, but (3) in both the narrative story line and in the theological-conceptual structure of the composition, the cross forms the goal and culmination of the gospel, so that the sending and destiny of the Son of God is understood from this point of reference. (4) Finally, the distinctive Johannine interweaving of crucifixion and exaltation/glorification ("lifting up" in both senses), like the Thomas pericope, reveals an independent and creative reworking of the relation of cross and resurrection: the cross reveals the love of God as simultaneous weakness and power.

Cross and Resurrection

The close relationship between cross and resurrection in the Gospel of John has already become clear; narrative techniques are used to link this theme especially with the raising of Lazarus (11:1–44), the final decision of the Jewish leaders to put Jesus to death (11:53), the anointing in Bethany (12:1–11), and the procession into Jerusalem (12:12–19).[124] The *raising of Lazarus* is the climax

122. Cf. the texts in *NW* 1.2:592–98, 715–25. On the whole subject, cf. Klaus Scholtissek, "Eine größere Liebe als diese hat niemand, als wenn einer sein Leben hingibt für seine Freunde" (Joh 15,13)," in *Kontexte des Johannesevangeliums* (ed. Albert Frey and Udo Schnelle; WUNT 175; Tübingen: Mohr, 2004), 413–39.

123. Because it is a matter of Jesus's death *on* the cross, *theologia crucis* and *theologia crucifixi* belong together: it is Jesus Christ who dies; he dies on a particular place that is not interchangeable with any other: on the cross. Differently Frey, "Theologia crucifixi," 235: "It is not the cross (as an instrument of execution and 'shameful pillory'), but the glorified Crucified One *in person*, that plays the central role in Johannine thought."

124. On the key function of John 11–12 in the structure and technique of John's narrative drama, cf. Michael Labahn, "Bedeutung und Frucht des Todes Jesu im Spiegel des johanneischen Erzählaufbaus," in *The Death of Jesus in the Fourth Gospel* (ed. G. van Belle; BETL 200; Louvain: Leuven University Press, 2007), 431–56.

of Jesus's public ministry, and at the same time the trigger for the final decision of the Jewish leaders (11:53).[125] John intentionally places the greatest miracle story in the New Testament at this location in his narrative. For Jesus, this event definitively introduces the way to the cross, but the hearers/readers of the gospel likewise know: as Jesus awakened Lazarus from the dead, God will awaken Jesus, so that the Lazarus story is at the same time always a model for the story of Jesus's own destiny. In a twofold manner at the conclusion of the story, John presents the raising of Lazarus as a prototype of the resurrection of Jesus:

1. In the case of Lazarus, as with Jesus, the final resting place is a rock-hewn tomb (cf. John 11:38; 20:1).
2. In each case, it is stated that they were buried according to the Jewish customs; both heads were wrapped in a cloth (cf. 11:44/19:40).

At the same time, small details reveal the great differences between Lazarus and Jesus:

1. In the case of Lazarus, the tomb is still closed (11:38), while with Jesus, the stone has already been rolled away (20:1).
2. While the one, completely wrapped with strips of cloth, must be set free by others (11:43–44), the other sets himself free from the binding grave cloths (20:6–7), as evidenced by the neatly folded cloth that had been about Jesus's head.
3. Finally, the thrice repeated ὅν ἤγειρεν ἐκ τῶν νεκρῶν (whom he had raised from the dead) in 12:1, 9, 17 for Lazarus and ἠγέρθη ἐκ νεκρῶν in 2:22 for Jesus establishes a clear link between the raising of Lazarus and the resurrection of Jesus, for the verb ἐγείρω appears in the sense of "raised from the dead" only in these three places (and in the appendix, 21:14).

The *anointing in Bethany* (John 12:1–11)[126] and the triumphal entry into Jerusalem are in turn prolepses that strengthen the connecting lines between suffering, death, and resurrection, between the Lazarus pericope and the Passion/Easter event. The Passion event is already present in the deceitful conduct of Judas (12:4–6) and the decision to put Lazarus to death (12:10). The anointing is a barely concealed reference to Easter:

125. In addition to the standard commentaries, on John 11:1–44 cf. especially Labahn, *Lebensspender*, 378–465; W. E. Sproston North, *The Lazarus Story within the Johannine Tradition* (JSNTSup 212; Sheffield: Sheffield Academic, 2001); Frey, *Eschatologie*, 3:403–62.

126. Cf. M. Gruber, "Die Zumutung der Gegenseitigkeit: Zur johanneischen Deutung des Todes Jesu anhand einer pragmatisch-intratextuellen Lektüre der Salbungsgeschichte Joh 12, 1–8," in *The Death of Jesus in the Fourth Gospel* (ed. G. van Belle; BETL 200; Louvain: Leuven University Press, 2007), 647–60.

1. John 12:27 refers directly to the burial of Jesus in 19:38–42;
2. The anointing oil signifies the aroma of life and celebration,[127] a direct contrast to the stink of Lazarus's decaying body; i.e., it symbolizes the reality of the resurrection that is underscored by the refrain-like reference to the raising of Lazarus (12:1, 9, 17). Mary anoints a living person, who continues as the Living One, so that she can then wipe off the anointing oil.
3. The explicit reference to Jesus's departure to the Father in 12:8b anticipates the Farewell Discourse (John 13–17) and the whole Easter event.
4. Finally, the proverbial saying of John 12:24[128] makes the theme of Jesus's death and resurrection specific: "Very truly, I tell you, unless a grain of wheat falls into the earth and dies, it remains just a single grain; but if it dies, it bears much fruit." Jesus must die, if he is to bring forth "fruit"; it is only his death that can generate new life.

The dramatic sequence in John 11–12 should make it clear to the readers and hearers of the gospel that Jesus's way does not lead into the emptiness of death, but straight into his triumph of eternal life, while Lazarus must ultimately die. *Precisely in the place where references to Jesus's death are so frequent that they cannot be ignored, the reality of the resurrection comes unavoidably into view!* Conversely, the stories of the appearance of the Risen One in John 20 still bear the imprint of the Crucified One. In a wonderful manner, Thomas is allowed to confirm the identity of the risen Christ and the space-time earthly Jesus, and thereby comes to faith (20:24–29). He thus validates that, *in the bodily identity of the Crucified and Risen One, cross and resurrection modulate into each other!*

12.2.6 The Unity of Johannine Christology

The question of the structure of Johannine Christology involves determining the intellectual profile of the Fourth Evangelist as such. There can be no talk of a christological pattern that involves various concepts that run parallel or even against each other; rather, it is characteristic of Johannine Christology that it must be thought of holistically: *preexistence and incarnation, sending and lifting up/glorification on the cross all converge in the one concept of love.* According to 17:24–25, the love of the Father for the Son before the foundation of the world and the sending of the Son come together into a unity in the same way that the sending of the Son coalesces with his way to the cross because of God's love for the world (3:13–14, 16; 10:17; 13:1). It is hardly accidental

127. Cf. ibid., 650.
128. Cf. Epictetus, *Diatr.* 4.8.36–39.

that the first references in the gospel to the κόσμος (world) are linked to the concepts of preexistence and incarnation (1:9–10), cross (1:29), and sending (3:16). Like all the other major New Testament authors, John took up a number of different christological conceptions from the tradition and integrated them into an impressive whole: the Preexistent, Incarnate, and Sent One is for him none other than the Crucified and Risen One (cf. 20:24–29), for at the cross the movement of the Son to the Father and the Father to the Son collapse into each other.[129] Jesus Christ as the Preexistent and Incarnate One who is lifted up and glorified on the cross is the embracing personal answer to the question of a loving human life, lived according to the will of God.

The Johannine dualizings by no means smooth out the significance of the cross, for they are integrated into a comprehensive line of argument: the concept of love, which transforms the cross into a place of life, outflanks and interprets such dualizings (see above, §12.2.2). Jesus's way to the cross is in continuity with the whole of his life and work, in the continuity generated by love. Jesus defines love as the readiness to give one's life for one's friends. He dies as an example of such love, and so makes it possible for the gathering and salvation of the children of God.

12.3 Pneumatology

A deep stratum of Johannine theology is constituted by its pneumatology: "God is Spirit" (John 4:24); the Spirit descended and remains on Jesus Christ (1:32–33); believers are reborn from "water and Spirit" (3:3, 5) and experience the present guidance of the Paraclete. The Spirit creates the community of faith, reveals to believers the essential nature of Jesus Christ, separates them from the death-dealing sphere of the σάρξ (flesh), and empowers them for living a meaningful life in the loving context of the Christian family. The unity of believers with the Father and the Son is unity in love and in the Spirit.

12.3.1 Jesus Christ and the Believers as Bearers of the Spirit

In the Gospel of John, Jesus Christ appears as the bearer of the Spirit in the absolute sense. Jesus's baptism (John 1:29–34) manifests three distinctive features:

1. John the Baptist merely testifies to the baptism, which—according to the logic of the text—was enacted by God. No one except God can "baptize" the preexistent and incarnate Logos.

129. Kohler, *Kreuz und Menschwerdung*, 201–2.

2. It is entirely a matter of baptism in the Spirit (cf. Isa. 61:1 LXX), which is qualitatively superior to the water baptism of John.
3. The continual abiding of the Spirit on Jesus Christ is explicitly emphasized (John 1:32–33), so that his whole public life, his words and deeds, are understood as an event in the power of the Spirit.[130]

The Gift of the Spirit Received in Baptism

The Johannine community knows that it is included in continuity with this event of the Spirit, for its baptism takes place ἐξ ὕδατος καὶ πνεύματος (John 3:5, "of water and Spirit"), and only the Johannine community anchors its own baptismal practice in the life of Jesus (cf. 4:1).[131] For the evangelist, being begotten/born of water and Spirit, and therefore baptism, is a condition for participation in eschatological salvation. There is no other entrance into the kingdom of God except through baptism, for only baptism mediates the eschatological saving gift of the Spirit. There cannot be a natural transition into the kingdom of God, for "what is born of the flesh is flesh, and what is born of the Spirit is spirit" (3:6).

For John, one's essential being is determined by one's origin, so that the designation of one's origin, indicated by the preposition ἐκ (out of, from), is at the same time a statement about one's true being. Because the essential nature of a being is determined by its origin, like can only produce like. Since what has been generated from the world of flesh belongs essentially to the sphere of σάρξ (flesh), the sphere of the Pneuma (Spirit) is fundamentally separated from this world. For the *sarx*-person, there is no access to the kingdom of God; only through a new origin effected by God can human beings enter into the realm of God[132] (John 6:63a, "It is the spirit that gives life; the flesh is useless"). Thus pneuma does not refer only to a gift, but must be understood in a more comprehensive sense as a divine operative principle or creative power.

For John, the new birth thus designates a comprehensive new creation, which begins in baptism and leads to a life determined by the Spirit. This being-born/begotten by the Spirit is not something that is available at human disposal, but "the wind blows where it chooses, and you hear the sound of it, but you do not know where it comes from or where it goes. So it is with everyone who is born of the Spirit" (John 3:8). Such statements emphasize that the new birth is exclusively a divine possibility, not one of the options available as a matter of human choice. John preserves the *extra nos* (beyond us, not at our disposal) of the saving event and at the same time designates the

130. On this point, cf. Gary M. Burge, *The Anointed Community: The Holy Spirit in the Johannine Tradition* (Grand Rapids: Eerdmans, 1987), 50ff.

131. For analyses of the Johannine baptismal texts, cf. Schnelle, *Antidocetic Christology*, 177–93.

132. Felix Porsch, *Pneuma und Wort: Ein exegetischer Beitrag zur Pneumatologie des Johannesevangeliums* (FTS 16; Frankfurt a.M.: Knecht, 1974), 124–25.

place where human beings can be partakers in God's salvation: in the baptism of the Johannine community.

The *First Letter of John* likewise makes clear that in the Johannine school, baptism and the eucharist were understood as events in which the Spirit is at work (1 John 5:6–8). The Spirit testifies to and makes real the saving event that occurs in the sacraments. The life of the baptized person is lived out within the realm where the Spirit is at work. The Spirit given by God abides (μένω) in the believers and determines their lives: "By this we know that we abide in him and he in us, because he has given us of his Spirit" (4:13; cf. 3:24). So also the words of Jesus in the gospel are Spirit and life (cf. John 6:63b). Because the life-giving Spirit is present and effective in the words of Jesus, they grant life and are themselves life. The whole worship service of the Johannine community occurs as adoration and prayer to God in the Spirit, for "God is spirit, and those who worship him must worship in spirit and truth" (John 4:24).

Likewise, the *mission* of the Johannine school (see below, §12.7.4) is carried out in the power of the Spirit given by the Risen One to his disciples: "Jesus said to them again, 'Peace be with you. As the Father has sent me, so I send you.' When he had said this, he breathed on them and said to them, 'Receive the Holy Spirit'" (John 20:21b–22). What Jesus had promised in the Farewell Discourses, he fulfills by giving the Spirit, as the Risen One commissions them and sends them forth. John 7:39 explicitly names the resurrection and exaltation of Jesus as the condition for the gift of the Spirit: "Now he said this about the Spirit, which believers in him were to receive; for as yet there was no Spirit, because Jesus was not yet glorified." The Johannine community lives in the time after the exaltation of Jesus, so that all the gospel's statements about the Spirit are already experienced reality for them.

12.3.2 The Holy Spirit as Paraclete

The distinctive awareness of the Johannine Christians that they were bearers of the Holy Spirit is expressed in their concept of the Paraclete. The use of the term παράκλητος can probably best be explained in relation to the genre "farewell speech."[133] As a verbal adjective derived from παρακαλέω, used as a noun (with a passive meaning, lit. "called along side" one to help), the term παράκλητος is used in secular Greek in the sense of an attorney, counselor, or advocate at the court.[134] Since in the situation of the Farewell Discourses the preservation of continuity is an extension of the admonition

133. Cf. ibid., 124–25.

134. On the linguistic aspects, cf. Johannes Behm, "παράκλητος," *TDNT* 5:799–801. The relevant attempts to derive the term from a background in the history of religion (Gnosticism, the concept of precursor and fulfiller; the concept of intercessor, Qumran theology, the genre of farewell speeches) are summarized in Schnackenburg, *John*, 3:138–54; Burge, *Anointed Community*, 10–30.

and teaching of the earthly life of Jesus, John took up the term παράκλητος in this sense and extended it: the Paraclete receives above all a hermeneutical function. As teacher, witness, and interpreter, the Paraclete reveals to the community the significance of the person of Jesus Christ and leads believers into the future.

The Paraclete appears in the post-Easter situation of the community as the *Christus praesens*, the presence of the glorified Jesus Christ in his church.[135] The Paraclete, explicitly identified as the πνεῦμα ἅγιον (Holy Spirit) or πνεῦμα τῆς ἀληθείας ("Spirit of truth"; cf. John 14:17, 26; 15:26; 16:13) dwells and works in the church and will be with it forever (cf. 14:16–17). The Paraclete teaches the church and reminds it of what Jesus had said (cf. 14:26) and is thus *the church's memory*. The Paraclete testifies to and about Jesus (cf. 16:13–14), takes from the fullness of revelation in Jesus and gives it to the church: "All that the Father has is mine. For this reason I said that he [the Paraclete] will take what is mine and declare it to you" (16:15). The Paraclete thus facilitates the Spirit-effected interpretation of the Christ event as this interpretation is developed in the Gospel of John's comprehensive realization of this saving event. Ultimately, the Paraclete makes it impossible to separate the proclaiming Jesus from the proclaimed Christ. The glorified Jesus Christ himself speaks through the Paraclete, so that the gap between past and present is abolished. A fusion of horizons takes place, facilitated by the emphasis on the unity of the preexistent Christ who was and is present in this world, is now glorified, and will come again.[136] The whole of the Gospel of John is nothing more or less than an interpretation of the Christ event through the Paraclete, through whom the glorified Christ continues to speak and who legitimizes the Johannine tradition. The presence of the Spirit in the Christian community cannot be thought through more thoroughly than John has done.[137] The Spirit effects the transition into the realm of God; the worship and life of the Johannine community takes place in the Spirit; and Jesus is present with his own in the

135. To be sure, the exalted Christ and the Paraclete are not simply identical, as indicated by the differentiation in John 14:16 (ἄλλον παράκλητον [another Paraclete]); John 14:26 (ἐν τῷ ὀνόματί μου [in my name]); John 15:26c ("he will testify on my behalf"); and the sending of the Paraclete by Jesus in John 15:26a and 16:7e. The risen and exalted Lord works in and through the Paraclete, but he is not the Paraclete! Contra Bultmann, *John*, 617–18: "The prophecy of the Paraclete picks up the early Christian idea of Pentecost, and similarly that of Jesus's coming again takes up the primitive expectation of the Parousia; precisely in the coming of the Spirit, Jesus comes himself."

136. Foundational here is F. Mussner, *Die johanneische Sehweise* (QD 28; Freiburg: Herder, 1965), 56ff.

137. J.-A. Bühner accurately designates pneumatology as the deepest level of Johannine thought: "The interweaving of times and places that comes to its sharpest focus in the community's worship is enabled and empowered by the access to the heavenly world provided by the Spirit—an access granted to Jesus, which he passes along [to the community]" (J.-A. Bühner, "Denkstrukturen im Johannesevangelium," *ThB* [1982], 229).

Spirit, teaching them, reminding them of what he said, revealing to them what is to come, and protecting them from the world's hatred.

The Farewell Discourses

Symbolic universes can be constructed, succeed, and endure only when they have sufficient plausibility, capacity for appropriation and integration, and power for self-renewal. These components are all present in John's case, since he succeeds in establishing continuity, designating the abiding elements of the past that will endure into the future. This is the achievement of the Farewell Discourses, which are to be regarded as the particular theological and literary artifice of the Fourth Evangelist.[138] What appears on the narrative dramatic level as prediction of the future is at the same time a look at the past that shapes the readers' present. The Farewell Discourses deal with a fundamental theological problem of early Christianity: *the continuing presence of Jesus Christ in and with his community, though he is bodily absent*. They present this problem in a new genre within the gospels, and thematically treat the central problem of the harassed Johannine church: Why has Jesus gone away and left the believing community behind in a hostile world? The answer: If Jesus had not returned to the Father, the church would not have received the Holy Spirit, the Paraclete, through whom both Father and Son are present, and who stands by the believers in times of trouble. The Farewell Discourses both explain and comfort; they have an encouraging and consoling function,[139] in that they make the irreversibility of the event plausible, point out its extra benefits, and at the same time point the way for the believers' future life: a fearless abiding in love (cf. John 13:34–35; 14:1, 27; 15:9–17).

On the whole, the Farewell Discourses represent a composition that has been thought through as a coherent unit, stretched between the poles of the greatest internal unity (cf. John 13:31–38) and the greatest external danger (cf.

138. On the literary problems and theological dimensions of the Farewell Discourses, cf. Udo Schnelle, "Die Abschiedsreden im Johannesevangelium," *ZNW* 80 (1989): 64–79; M. Winter, *Das Vermächtnis Jesu und die Abschiedsworte der Väter* (FRLANT 161; Göttingen: Vandenhoeck & Ruprecht, 1994); Andreas Dettwiler, *Die Gegenwart des Erhöhten* (FRLANT 169; Göttingen: Vandenhoeck & Ruprecht, 1995); Christina Hoegen-Rohls, *Der nachösterliche Johannes: die Abschiedsreden als hermeneutischer Schlüssel zum vierten Evangelium* (Tübingen: Mohr, 1996), 82–229; Frey, *Eschatologie*, 3:102–239; K. Haldimann, *Rekonstruktion und Entfaltung: Exegetische Untersuchungen zu Joh 15 und 16* (BZNW 104; Berlin: de Gruyter, 2000); Johanna Rahner, "Vergegenwärtigende Erinnerung," *ZNW* 91 (2000): 72–90; Klaus Scholtissek, "Abschied und neue Gegenwart," *ETL* 75 (1999): 332–58; L. Scott Kellum, *The Unity of the Farewell Discourse: The Literary Integrity of John 13.31–16.33* (JSNTSup 256; London: Sheffield Academic, 2004); George L. Parsenios, *Departure and Consolation: The Johannine Farewell Discourses in Light of Greco-Roman Literature* (NovTSup 117; Leiden; Boston: Brill, 2005).

139. Cf. M. Lang, "Johanneische Abschiedsreden und Senecas Konsolationsliteratur," in *Kontexte des Johannesevangeliums* (ed. Albert Frey and Udo Schnelle; WUNT 175; Tübingen: Mohr, 2004), 365–412.

16:4b–15). It is also no accident that John speaks of the Paraclete exclusively in the Farewell Discourses, for the functions of the Paraclete are closely linked to the literary genre farewell discourse (authorization speech, literary testament). The genre of the farewell discourse also has a legitimizing function; the dying hero chooses his successor and equips him with the requisite charism.[140] In the Farewell Discourses, through the Paraclete the evangelist firmly anchors the community in the past in order to safeguard its endangered identity: the believers' communion with God and Jesus of Nazareth will not be broken. In both literary and theological-hermeneutical perspective, the Farewell Discourses are a constitutive element of the Johannine form of the gospel.

12.3.3 Trinitarian Thinking in the Gospel of John

A basic internal concern of John's rewriting of the Jesus-Christ-history is to clarify the relation between God the Father, Jesus Christ the Son, and the Spirit-Paraclete. This was made necessary by the theological logic that pressed for determining the status of the divine persons and their fields of operation. In addition, there was the charge of ditheism emanating from Judaism (cf. John 5:18; 10:33, 36; 19:7),[141] which struck at the very core of early Christian proclamation and thus also the Johannine symbolic universe. John responded to these perils by utilizing one of the basic functions of narrative discourse: *the establishing and clarifying of relationships*. Narratives can function to place persons and things in particular relationships and to establish causal connections that facilitate understanding. The establishing of relationships in 1:1 aims at an original and all-embracing participation of the Logos in the one God, the origin and ground of all being. John 1:18 develops the concept of the unique relation of Jesus to the Father in its historical dimensions. Jesus is the exegete of God, the sole Revealer of the Father. With the incarnation, Jesus's unique and immediate experience of God enters into history and is now palpably available to human beings as the revelation of the Son of God. As the counterpart to 1:18, 20:28 emphasizes the deity of Jesus, which was his from the very beginning, remained visible during his earthly life, and is an essential aspect of the appearances of the Risen One.

In John 5:17–30, the unity of Father and Son is realized as the unity of their will, acts, and revelation, concentrated in the encounter with Jesus Christ,

140. Cf. especially Deut. 31–34; Josh. 23–24; 1 Sam. 12; 1 Kings 2:1–10. For analysis, cf. Winter, *Vermächtnis Jesu*, 65–87. Additional examples of farewell discourses from Hellenistic Judaism and Greco-Roman contexts are provided in *NW* 1.2:655–64.

141. Cf. also Mark 14:61–64 par. According to Lev. 24:15–16, blasphemy is a capital crime, and execution is to be by stoning. According to Deut. 21:22–23, the corpse is to be hanged on a cross; cf. the extensive treatment of Darrell L. Bock, *Blasphemy and Exaltation in Judaism and the Final Examination of Jesus: A Philological-historical Study of the Key Jewish Themes Impacting Mark 14:61–64* (WUNT 2.106; Tübingen: Mohr, 1998).

who functions as the giver of life in unbroken continuity with the Father and in direct dependence on him. The subject matter of John 5 is then taken up in 10:30: "I and the Father are one." The statements of reciprocal immanence in 10:38 ("that you may know and understand that the Father is in me and I am in the Father") and 14:10 ("Jesus said to him [Philip] . . . 'Do you not believe that I am in the Father and the Father is in me?'") concisely express the Johannine conception. Because Jesus lives from the unity willed and granted by the Father, his words and works reveal the Father himself.[142] Jesus's belonging to God has no limitations, either temporally or in regard to essential nature; it is comprehensive and total, because it originated before time and the world (cf. 12:41; 17:5, 24c–d). Furthermore, Jesus's relation to the Father appears as the basis for his saving work, which began before all time and will endure into eternity. Finally, the "I am" sayings signal, in concentrated form, the unique relation of Father and Son. Whoever sees the Son sees the Father (12:45; 14:9); whoever hears the Son hears the Father (14:24); whoever believes in the Son believes in the Father (14:1); and whoever does not honor the Son does not honor the Father (5:23).

What about the texts that point to a *subordination of the Son*? Directly prior to John 10:30, the Johannine Jesus emphasizes, "My Father, who has given them to me, is greater than all" [ET of Luther Bible cited by author; cf. NRSV]. Jesus constantly refers to the Father who sent him (cf. 3:16; 5:23, 24, 30, 37; 6:29, 38, 39, 44, 57; 7:16, 18, 28, 29, 33; 8:16, 18, 26, 29, 42; 10:36; 12:44, 45, 49; 13:16, 20; 14:24; 15:21; 16:5; 17:3, 8, 18, 21, 23, 25; 20:21). The Father is the "only" God (5:44) and has given all authority to the Son, so that the Son can do nothing on his own authority (cf. 5:19–20; 6:37). The Son glorifies the Father (14:13b) and testifies directly in 14:28c, "The Father is greater than I." In 17:1, Jesus lifts his eyes to heaven and prays to his Father, the one, true God. Finally, John emphasizes throughout the true humanity of the preexistent Son of God (see above, §12.2.1).[143] He became "flesh" (1:14), subjected himself to the conditions of earthly existence, lived as a Jew (4:9), and is frequently designated as (ὁ) ἄνθρωπος ("human being"; cf. 5:12; 8:40; 9:11; 11:50; 18:17, 29).

How are these apparently conflicting, or at least tensive, series of statements to be incorporated into one system? We must avoid the two extremes of ditheism and subordinationism:

1. For John there is only the one God who has revealed himself in Jesus Christ (cf. John 10:30). Only the Father is the εἷς θεός (the one God)! The Father sends, authorizes, and empowers the Son, who acts only on

142. K. Scholtissek appropriately comments, "Jesus's own theocentricity makes it possible for the Father to make himself entirely present in the Son. Jesus does not represent the Father, he presents him" (Scholtissek, *Sein und Bleiben*, 371).

143. Cf. Söding, "'Ich und der Vater,'" 193–96.

the basis of this conferred authority. Thus the risen Jesus says to Mary Magdalene, "I am ascending to my Father and your Father, to my God and your God" (20:17). The objection that John has a ditheistic conception has no basis.

2. It must be affirmed just as clearly, however, that the concept of subordination as it was later developed in the history of dogma is not appropriate for expressing the Johannine understanding of the Son to the Father. The Son is much more than an agent of the Father; he not only participates in the essential being of the Father but is of the same essential being as the Father.

In the Gospel of John, therefore, we must speak of a unity of essential being between Father and Son, a unity that is realized in the unity of their will and work. *John advocates an exclusive monotheism in a binitarian form*: the worship of the one God is extended to the Son. Within this conception, the idea of *orientation toward* best grasps the way John intends the relation of Father and Son to be understood—the Son's whole being is determined by his orientation to the Father. Semantically, this concept is suggested by the preposition πρός (to, toward), which not only serves in 1:1–2 to name the relation of Father and Son, but designates a fundamental characteristic of the comprehensive Johannine system of thought: just as the Son is oriented to the Father, so human beings should be oriented to the Son, in order to find their true relationship to each other (17:11, "that they may be one as we are one"). The goal of this way of thinking about relationships is participation in the life of the other, an abiding unity in the differentiation. The Son returns to the Father (cf. 13:1) and receives believers to himself (14:3), so that they participate in the special relationship between Father and Son.

Out of the fullness of this unity, the Father and/or the Son sends the Spirit of truth, whose origin is oriented entirely to the Father and the Son. (John does not affirm a mutual indwelling.) In his works, the Spirit is entirely oriented to the Son, in that the Spirit constantly causes the revelatory event to be realized anew, so that the Son, and the Father who sent and authorized him, are always present. This presence is illuminated by the final Paraclete saying in John 16:13–15. The Paraclete is assigned the task of leading the Johannine community to a deeper understanding of the person of Jesus Christ.[144] In this work, the Paraclete constantly refers back to the exalted Jesus Christ, from whose fullness of revelation he "takes." There is only the one Paraclete, who represents Father and Son as the "Spirit of truth." Because for John the historical truth of revelation in Jesus Christ and the truth of God are one and the same, the work of the Spirit can only refer back to this foundational unity. At the same time, this revelation still has a future before it, a future shaped

144. Dettwiler, *Gegenwart*, 234.

by the work of the Paraclete. Here the trinitarian orientation of the basic conception of Johannine thought comes into view: the Father gives the word to the Son, which the Son embodies and reveals; in turn, the Spirit, as the one sent from the Father and the Son, makes this word effective in the post-Easter situation of the church.

It is pneumatology that first enables the Johannine understanding of the relation of Father and Son to become a comprehensive systematic whole. It presents John with the possibility of thinking together of realities that were mostly thought of separately, in antiquity as in the modern world: heaven and earth, space and time, history and the eschaton. Through the sending of the Paraclete, the Johannine community knew itself to be continuous with and included in the Father's conferral of the Spirit on the Son. John 14:16–17 already points to the Paraclete sayings as a focus of the Johannine way of relating Father and Son. The functional unity of Father and Son in the sending of the Paraclete is also expressed in 15:26, for here it is the Son who sends the Paraclete. God as Spirit, the pneumatically endowed Jesus, and the Paraclete-community are united in their common origin "from above." Within the framework of a basically trinitarian conception, the unity of believers with the Father and the Son appears as a unity in the Spirit and love (cf. 17:21–23), for the whole revelatory event is directed to the goal of the believers' participation in the communion of love that exists between Father and Son: "Those who love me will keep my word, and my Father will love them, and we will come to them and make our home with them" (14:23). Johannine thinking is trinitarian thinking!

12.4 Soteriology

Johannine thought, regardless of the specific topic, is always soteriological, since it is always concerned with God's saving act in Jesus Christ; everything in the Fourth Gospel modulates into soteriology, for whoever believes in Jesus *has* eternal life (e.g., John 3:15, 16, 36; 5:24; 6:40).[145] In the salvation of believers too Jesus works not in isolation but in common with the Father: he is the vine and the Father is the vine grower (15:1). Jesus's love for his own (13:13) is shared by the Father (14:21), who thus shares in the disciples' love for Jesus (14:23). Jesus and the Father both dwell in the disciples (14:23; cf. 14:20; 17:21–23), who are just as secure in Jesus's hand as they are in God's own hand (10:28–29). Jesus Christ has died and been raised "to gather into one the dispersed children of God" (11:52). Despite

145. A survey is provided by J. G. Van der Watt, "Salvation in the Gospel of John," in *Salvation in the New Testament* (ed. J. G. Van der Watt; NovTSup 121; Leiden: Brill, 2005), 101–28.

the constant interweaving of all Johannine themes with soteriology, it is still useful to highlight conceptual and thematic complexes that deal with soteriology in a particular way.

12.4.1 Conceptuality

The purpose of God's sending the Son and the revelation that occurred in him is not the judgment of the world, but its salvation (John 12:47, "I came not to judge the world, but to save the world"). God's saving will surpasses and overcomes the world's rejection, for its driving force is God's love for the world. Not a Roman emperor, but only Jesus Christ is "the savior of the world" (4:42, ὁ σωτὴρ τοῦ κόσμου), because his work is the work of the one true God, and thus brings the only true salvation (see above, §12.2.4). Alongside σῴζω (save) and σωτήρ (savior), the term σωτηρία (salvation) is also found in the Gospel of John: "Salvation is from the Jews" (4:22b, ἡ σωτηρία ἐκ τῶν Ἰουδαίων ἐστίν). This fundamental and unqualifiedly positive statement, "Salvation is from the Jews," is surprising, in view of the numerous negative statements about "the Jews" in the Fourth Gospel, and is often excised as a gloss.[146] Without any manuscript evidence, judging an element of the text to be a gloss is always problematic, so the question is posed as to whether 4:22b can really be integrated into Johannine theology. In the Johannine perspective, a new epoch began with the revelation of Jesus Christ, an epoch characterized by direct experience of God and unmediated worship of God (cf. 4:23–24). Wherever human beings truly honor God as their Father, where God is loved and trusted, there can be no strife about the true or false location of cultic worship, since for John, Jesus Christ is the new locus of salvation. This is why he can say that salvation comes from the Jews, for Jesus is a Jew, as explicitly emphasized in 4:9. This statement cannot be reduced to this christological provision, however, for by using the plural Ἰουδαίων, John adds another dimension to the statement: the Jews are and remain the bearers of the divine promissory testimony.[147] God has been faithful to his promises; in the Jew Jesus of Nazareth, salvation comes forth out of the Jewish people. John 4:22b is thus not a later gloss but is to be read as a *fundamental conviction and concentrated statement of Johannine soteriology*. The claim inherent in the divine promises made to the Jews is by no means negated by John; in the Jew Jesus of Nazareth, God remains true to his word of promise.[148]

146. One need note only Bultmann, *John*, 189n6; Becker, *Evangelium nach Johannes*, 1:207–8.

147. Cf. Ferdinand Hahn, "'Das Heil kommt von den Juden': Erwägungen zu Joh 4,22b," in *Die Verwurzelung des Christentums im Judentum* (ed. Ferdinand Hahn; Neukirchen: Neukirchener Verlag, 1996), 99–118; Schnelle, "Juden im Johannesevangelium," 224–30.

148. On the negative statements, see above, §12.1.1.

12.4.2 Predestination

The central problem of Johannine soteriology consists of the question whether salvation has been previously determined, independently of human decision, or the decision of faith plays the decisive role. How are human acts and the act of God related? How does John relate human responsibility and divine sovereignty?[149]

Determinism

A series of statements appears to suggest a Johannine doctrine of determinism or predestination. Thus John 6:44a says, "No one can come to me unless drawn by the Father who sent me." Not only the sending of the Son but also the response of faith appears here as a work effected by God (6:65, "For this reason I have told you that no one can come to me unless it is granted by the Father"). The effective principle is, "No one can receive anything except what has been given from heaven" (3:27). The Father has "given" his own to the Son, so that they now participate in eternal life (cf. 17:2, 6, 9). No one may tear believers out of the hand of the Son, for "what my Father has given me is greater than all else, and no one can snatch it out of the Father's hand" (10:29). None of Jesus's own are lost, except the traitor, who was predestined for this from the very beginning (cf. 6:64; 17:12). All whom God has given Jesus will see the glory of the Son (17:24). John formulates his basic position in 8:47, "Whoever is from God hears the words of God" (ὁ ὢν ἐκ τοῦ θεοῦ τὰ ῥήματα τοῦ θεοῦ ἀκούει). The unbelieving Jews are under the power of the devil, and therefore *cannot* understand Jesus's word (8:43, "Why do you not understand what I say? It is because you cannot [οὐ δύνασθε] accept my word."). Only his "own" hear the voice of the shepherd (10:3–4), while unbelievers do not belong to his sheep (10:26). "Not being able to hear" is the counterpart of the "not being able to see" of 9:39–41; if God does not grant the gift of faith, then one cannot believe. The natural human being, judging according to external appearance (cf. 7:24; 8:15), perceives Jesus to be only Joseph's son (cf. 6:42). Just as unbelief, understood as imprisonment in the world, means much more than an individual decision (cf. the adoption of the hardening imagery of Isa. 6:9–10 in John 12:40), so faith goes back ultimately to God's own initiative.[150] Only those who are of the truth hear the voice of the Son (cf. 18:37c). Only those come to the Son who have been given to the Son by the Father (cf. 6:37, 39; 10:29; 17:2, 9, 24). Jesus chooses his disciples out of the world, they do not choose him (cf. 15:16, 19). In Johannine understanding, faith is a work of God: "This is the work of God, that you believe in

149. A survey of research is given in Röhser, *Prädestination*, 179–92.

150. Bultmann, *Theology of the New Testament*, 2:25, "In the decision between faith and un-faith a man's being definitively constitutes itself, and from then on his Whence becomes clear."

him whom he has sent" (6:29). The believer must be born "anew/from above" (ἄνωθεν, 3:3, 5). Because human beings in their natural state belong to the sphere of the flesh (3:6) and cannot attain to God on their own resources, they receive a new origin from God.

The Freedom to Decide

If these statements point in the direction of predestination and determinism, the Gospel of John also contains numerous statements that challenge and call to decision. John 6:27a contains the imperative formulation, "Do not work for the food that perishes, but for the food that endures for eternal life." Immediately after the emphasis on the divine act in 6:44, 6:45c emphasizes the individual's responsibility to hear and respond. The Johannine Christ can command people to believe: "Believe me that I am in the Father and the Father is in me; but if you do not, then believe me because of the works themselves" (14:11; cf. 10:38; 14:1). John 8:12 is a call to decision: "I am the light of the world. Whoever follows me will never walk in darkness but will have the light of life" (cf. also 5:24; 6:35, and elsewhere). The Johannine Revealer specifically and directly calls people to believe in him: "I have come as light into the world, so that everyone who believes in me should not remain in the darkness" (12:46; cf. also 3:36). The invitation, like the promise or threat, is one of the fundamental forms of "I am" saying (see above, §12.2.3), and is prevalent in 12:44–50: here it is human decision and response to the revelation alone that decides human destiny. This happens positively as salvation through faith, negatively as self-judgment through unfaith (3:36b; 12:48). The whole gospel can be understood as a call for faith, for it was written "so that you may come to believe that Jesus is the Messiah, the Son of God" (20:31a).

A Persistent Tension

How are these two series of statements to be related to each other? For the Fourth Evangelist, neither faith nor unfaith is merely a matter of individual decision, for their "whence" lies outside the realm of human possibility.[151] Just as God effects faith, so unfaith comes from being imprisoned in the world through the work of the devil (cf. John 8:41–46; 13:2) or as the act of God that hardens people's hearts (cf. 12:37–41). According to John, God alone decides about salvation and damnation, preserving the act of God as something not at human disposal. At the same time, the prevenient act of God touches human existence, so that the decision for faith and persistence in disobedience as possible reactions that follow from God's act are also realities for the evangelist. The human being should allow himself or herself to be moved toward faith, for the saving will of God does not annul the human freedom

151. John also thereby emphasizes the "prevenience of grace" (Joachim Gnilka, *Neutestamentliche Theologie im Überblick* [NEchtB; Würzburg: Echter, 1989], 136).

to decide. The tension thus expressed is appropriate to the subject matter, because the two complexes of statements cannot be combined in a way that removes the contradiction.[152]

The concept that salvation is not a matter at human disposal, which is also constitutive for John, lets God appear as the sole acting subject in the saving event in all its dimensions. At the same time, the idea of human freedom and responsibility in response to God's initiating act calls for an emphasis on human decision in the face of the saving event. What appears as predestination on the level of theological reflection is, on the historical level, the by-product of later attempts to explain the experience that both faith and unfaith in fact exist. Such an attempt at explanation must necessarily collide with certain limits,[153] since human beings attempting such explanations are in a certain sense placing themselves in God's place, wanting insights into God's mysteries. Predestination statements are always theological boundary statements; they serve to preserve God's freedom, which is not at human disposal, and are not intended to make a priori objectifying statements about human salvation or damnation.

The decisive element for the soteriological program of the Fourth Evangelist is ultimately not the derivation of faith, but the promise of the Crucified and Risen One: "I did not lose a single one of those whom you gave me" (John 18:9; cf. 10:28; 17:12).

12.5 Anthropology

The concept of creation is foundational for Johannine anthropology; the world and human existence are traced back to the will of God and thought through from that point forward. The Logos Jesus Christ created all that is (John 1:3–4), then entered into the created world himself. The incarnation of God in Jesus Christ as revelation of the glory of life, truth, and grace in the Word means for John that truly human self-realization has been made possible as the way of love. Theology and Christology are thus the foundation of an-

152. Appropriately Roland Bergmeier, *Glaube als Gabe nach Johannes: Religions- und theologiegeschichtliche Studien zum prädestinatianischen Dualismus im vierten Evangelium* (BWANT 112; Stuttgart; Berlin: Kohlhammer, 1980), 231: "The evangelist thinks in predestinarian terms, but does not develop a doctrine of predestination that satisfies the laws of logic"; cf. further Hahn, *Theologie*, 1:676: "In this respect, both faith and unfaith are conditional upon God's act, but nevertheless also through human response to the encounter with the revelatory event."

153. It is no surprise that scholarly interpretations differ widely precisely on the subject of predestination. While Röhser, *Prädestination*, 253–54, disputes that there is a predestination doctrine in the Fourth Gospel, Hans-Christian Kammler, *Christologie und Eschatologie: Joh 5,17–30 als Schlüsseltext johanneischer Theologie* (WUNT 126; Tübingen: Mohr Siebeck, 2000), 148, argues strongly for a Johannine doctrine of predestination, according to which "the evangelist advocates a radical predestination to be understood in the sense of the *praedestinatio gemina*." Neither position does justice to the textual data and its exegesis.

thropology. When believers abide in the word of Jesus Christ, they participate in this fullness of life and overcome the power of sin; they themselves become truly human beings, in that they take up the love of the Son of God, so that each becomes truly human in relation to others. This positive anthropological perspective in John modulates into the concept of becoming "children of God" (τέκνα θεοῦ); as such, believers participate in the internal relationships of Father, Son, and Spirit.

12.5.1 Faith

No New Testament author has thought more intensively about the nature of faith than the evangelist John. The linguistic data already signify the importance of this topic: in John the verb πιστεύω (believe) occurs 98 times, while it appears in Matthew only 11 times, in Mark 14 times, and in Luke only 8 times.[154] In the majority of cases, πιστεύω is combined with εἰς (in, on), which indicates a fundamental characteristic of the Johannine understanding of faith: *for John, faith is bound to the person of Jesus Christ.*[155] At the same time, faith in Jesus Christ means for John "to believe in his word" (cf. John 4:41, 50; 5:24), "to believe Moses and the Scriptures" that testify to Jesus (5:46–47), and, above all, to believe in the one who sent him (cf. 5:24; 6:29; 11:42; 12:44; 17:8). Jesus appears as God's representative, so that "whoever sees me sees him who sent me" (12:45) and "whoever has seen me has seen the Father" (14:9). Thus Jesus can also say, "Believe in God, believe also in me" (14:1). *Faith in God and faith in Jesus Christ are identified, because Jesus Christ is the Son of God.* The whole Gospel of John was written "so that you may come to believe that Jesus is the Messiah, the Son of God, and that through believing you may have life in his name" (20:31).[156]

Faith and Miracle

As Jesus's whole ministry is a revelation and glorification of the Father through the Son, and the Son through the Father (cf. John 8:54; 12:28; 13:31–32; 14:13), so the miracle is the particular locus of this revelation. It is not merely a pointer to the δόξα (glory), but is itself an expression of this glory.[157] This revelation of Jesus's glory in the miracle evokes faith, since, for John, faith is directly linked to Jesus's works. In the story of the wedding feast at Cana, the

154. In 1 John, πιστεύω is found nine times; the noun πίστις is found only in 1 John 5:4.

155. Cf. Ferdinand Hahn, "Das Glaubensverständnis im Johannesevangelium," in *Glaube und Eschatologie: Festschrift für Werner Georg Kümmel zum 80. Geburtstag* (ed. Erich Grässer and Otto Merk; Tübingen: Mohr, 1985), 56–57.

156. Like John 1:1–18, John 20:31 is a guide to the hearers/readers intended to lead them to a proper understanding of the gospel as a whole. On the exegesis of John 20:30–31, cf. Neugebauer, *Entstehungsgeschichte*, 10–20.

157. Schnelle, *Antidocetic Christology*, 164–67.

evangelist elaborates his understanding of miracle and faith, using the disciples as an example (2:11, "Jesus did this, the first of his signs, in Cana of Galilee, and revealed his glory; and his disciples believed in him"). It is not the case that faith is there first and sees the event as miracle; rather, faith originates through the revelation of Jesus's glory in the miracle. Because the miracle has revelatory character and testifies powerfully to the unity of the Son with the Father, it is able to awaken faith. How directly miracle and faith belong together in the evangelist's view is seen in 10:40–42, in which the essential difference between Jesus and John is that John did no miracles. Thus the "many" can believe only in Jesus, not in John. John 11:15 likewise makes clear that faith originates through the miracle. Jesus is glad, for the sake of the disciples, that he was not present at the death of Lazarus, for now he can raise his friend from the dead, which will enable his disciples to come to faith. Here, miracle is not the incidental occasion for faith but is intentionally performed in order to evoke faith.[158]

For the evangelist John the miracle effects faith; seeing the σημεῖον (sign, miracle) is followed by πιστεύειν εἰς Ἰησοῦν Χριστόν (believing in Jesus Christ). This utterly nondualistic link between seeing and believing is made explicit in John 2:11, 23; 4:53; 6:14; 7:31; 9:35–38; 10:40–42; 11:15, 40, 45; 12:11; 20:8, 25, 27, 29a, so that it plays a central role in the way the Fourth Evangelist understands faith. Faith results from the miracle that has already occurred; faith does not make the miracle possible. John thus by no means sees faith in miracles as only a "preliminary, first-level faith"; the miracle generates not only a pointer to faith, or a second-rate or incomplete faith,[159] but faith in the full sense of the word: recognizing that Jesus Christ is the Son of God and accepting him as such. As faith originates in the encounter with Jesus, who reveals his glory in the miracle, so faith likewise comprehends Jesus's fleshly, this-worldly and heavenly existence. It is thus not the case that faith has only the "that" of the revelatory event as its content;[160] rather, the miracles describe, with a clarity and reality that can hardly be surpassed, the work of the Revealer in history. Seeing the miracle is thus not merely a spiritual perception, but a true seeing of something that is in fact visible.[161] In John, "know" and "see" are structural elements of faith.

158. There is no fundamental critique of miracles in John 2:24–25; 4:48; 6:30; 20:29b, for Jesus is rejecting only the mere demand or request for a miracle (4:48; 6:30), or the questionable faith of the crowds (2:24–25); cf. Bittner, *Zeichen*, 122–34.

159. Contra Bultmann, *Theology of the New Testament*, 2:73: "Genuine faith must not be confused with a seeming faith that is aroused by Jesus's 'signs.'" Among those who follow this evaluation are Hahn, "Glaubensverständnis," 54 (rejection of a false faith oriented to "what is visible and demonstrable"); Gnilka, *Überblick*, 132 ("superficial faith in miracles").

160. As in the classical thesis of Bultmann, *Theology of the New Testament*, 2:66: "John, that is, in his gospel presents only the fact [*das Dass*] of the Revelation without describing its content [*ihr Was*]."

161. In contrast, Bultmann, *John*, 66, designates the visibility of the Revealer as a "pietistic misunderstanding," and opines: "Accordingly in the Johannine portrayal of the incarnate Re-

Faith and Knowing/Seeing

For John, to believe in Jesus means the same as to "know" (γινώσκω) him.[162] Thus John 14:7 states, "If you know me, you will know my Father also. From now on you do know him and have seen him." Jesus says of himself, "I am the good shepherd. I know my own and my own know me" (10:14). Believers have come to know him (1 John 4:16; John 6:69); they recognize him and know who he is: the one sent by God, the Son of Man, the truth (cf. John 7:17; 8:28; 14:6, 17, 20; 17:7–8, 25; 1 John 2:4; 3:19; 5:20). Those who abide in Jesus's word have the promise, "you will know the truth, and the truth will make you free" (John 8:32). The Johannine "knowing" is not oriented to what may be seen by superficial observation but penetrates to the essential being of the one who is known. In Jesus of Nazareth, God's glory is revealed; he is the one sent from God as the savior of the world (4:42). Thus "know" in John means to acknowledge Jesus as Lord and thus to enter into a personal relationship with him. To know Jesus means to follow him (10:27, "My sheep hear my voice. I know them, and they follow me"). Thus knowing Jesus and accepting the Christian message lead to doing the will of God. Thus 1 John 2:3 states, "Now by this we may be sure that we know him, if we obey his commandments" (cf. also 1 John 2:4–5; 3:19, 24; 4:13). Love for brothers and sisters in the family of God is the mark of those who know God or the love of God (cf. 1 John 3:16; 4:7–8). In contrast, the one who sins does not know God (1 John 3:6). "Keeping of the word" (τηρεῖν τὸν λόγον, John 8:51; 14:23; 15:20; 17:6) and "abiding in the word" (μένειν ἐν τῷ λόγῳ, John 8:31) are essential to faith, because knowing the Revealer includes confessing faith in his word and his will.[163] Knowing is inseparable from believing, for faith is a faith that knows. In the relation of Father and Son, however, full and direct knowledge does replace faith: "just as the Father knows me and I know the Father" (John 10:15a; cf. 17:25).

A further central feature of the Johannine understanding of faith is that of "seeing" (ὁράω, βλέπω, θεωρέω).[164] Already in John 1:14, "seeing" the glory of the Incarnate One stands front and center, and then becomes a motif that permeates the whole gospel (cf. 11:40; 17:24). The first words of the Johannine Jesus are in the form of a question (1:38b, "What are you looking for?"), and an invitation (1:39a, "Come and *see*"). The hearers and readers of the

---

vealer there is no attempt to present him as a visible figure; to encounter the Revealer is not to be presented with a persuasive set of answers but only to be faced with a question."

162. On γινώσκω, cf. Strecker, *Johannine Letters*, 222–26.

163. Cf. here Jürgen Heise, *Bleiben: Menein in den Johanneischen Schriften* (HUT 8; Tübingen: Mohr, 1967), 44ff.

164. Extensive analyses of relevant texts are found in Clemens Hergenröder, *Wir schauten seine Herrlichkeit: Das Johanneische Sprechen vom Sehen im Horizont von Selbsterschliessung Jesu und Antwort des Menschen* (FzB 80; Würzburg: Echter Verlag, 1996), 56ff. Cf. also Schwankl, *Licht und Finsternis*, 330–47; Zimmermann, *Bilder*, 45–59.

Fourth Gospel are thereby challenged to enter into the world of the text, to seek its meaning, and, like the disciples in the story, to see Jesus Christ as the Messiah (1:41). As the narrative continues through and beyond the stories of the call of the disciples, encounter texts such as 4:1–42; 5:1–15; 7:25–28; 9:35–38; and 20:1–10, 11–18 are stamped with the motif of "seeking and finding" and the transition from "not knowing/not seeing" to faith. The evangelist thereby constructs a narrative line that incrementally develops his meaning, a line that is characterized by one basic idea: Jesus Christ reveals his identity to his own.[165] The Johannine concept of "seeing" is exemplified in the story of chapter 9: Jesus gives sight to the man born blind, who through faith becomes one who truly sees, while the Pharisees lapse into a crisis that subjects them to divine judgment because, persisting in unbelief, they become blind to the truth (9:39–41). John thus challenges his church to be like the blind man and respond in faith to Jesus's healing act. When they do, Jesus opens not only the eyes of the man born blind but the eyes of the church as well, giving it the gift of true sight. Like the disciples and Mary Magdalene (20:18, 25), they then confess: "I/we have seen the Lord." Sending and seeing are programmatically paired in 12:44–45: "Whoever believes in me believes not in me but in him who sent me. And whoever sees me sees him who sent me." With the macarism of 20:29 ("Blessed are those who have not seen and yet have come to believe"), John nuances and differentiates pre-Easter and post-Easter "seeing": the blessing is pronounced on later generations that no longer can come to faith through the direct seeing of the Risen One.[166] The reality that already existed in the time of the gospel writer is exemplified in the story of Thomas: one believes on the basis of the eyewitness tradition handed on in the church, without seeing the Risen One miraculously and directly, as Thomas saw him. The different temporal perspectives are decisive for interpreting the Thomas pericope. While 20:24–29a report an event that was only possible at the time of the epiphanies of the Risen One in the first generation of disciples, v. 29b directs the gaze to the future. Verse 29b is thus not criticizing or relativizing the previous seeing of Thomas but merely formulates what was already the case for the following generations, in contrast to the eyewitnesses. Direct seeing was limited to the generation of the eyewitnesses. But this seeing provided the foundation for the Johannine tradition; it continues to be important for the kerygma of the Johannine church. The absence of Jesus's body must not be misunderstood as the absence of his person. On the contrary, the stories of the empty tomb, and of the appearances to Mary Magdalene, the Twelve, and to Thomas, mean that immediately after Easter there was a different kind of "seeing" and faith. In this sense, the connection between seeing and faith

165. On this point cf. Peter Dschulnigg, *Jesus begegnen: Personen und ihre Bedeutung im Johannesevangelium* (Theologie 30; Münster: Lit, 2000).

166. For exegesis and interpretation, see Schnelle, *Das Evangelium nach Johannes*, 332–34.

is by no means limited to the life of Jesus but has contemporary importance in the proclamation of the church, which means that the Gospel of John is to be read and understood as a school in which one learns how to see.[167]

Unbelief

The sending of Jesus into the world evokes not only faith but unbelief as well. In view of the fact that the revelation has occurred, faith and unbelief are the fundamental possibilities of human existence. This state of affairs is formulated in a bluntly programmatic manner in John 12:37, "Although he had performed so many signs in their presence, they did not believe in him." Even Jesus's brothers did not believe in him (7:5), although they saw his works (7:3). The healing of the man born blind results in both faith and unbelief among the Jews (cf. 9:16). So also the raising of Lazarus leads many Jews to faith (11:45), but at the same time, Jesus's greatest miracle becomes the trigger that leads some to betray him (11:46). It is especially in the miracle stories that John demonstrates the essential nature of unbelief, for in view of the σημεῖα, unbelief denies the obvious fact of the matter: Jesus Christ is the Son of God. The core of unbelief is not ignorance or incapability but the intentional rejection of a blatantly obvious factual reality. Thus 6:36 states, "But I said to you that you have seen me and yet do not believe." Precisely because Jesus speaks the truth and is himself the truth, many do not believe in him (8:45, "But because I tell the truth, you do not believe me"). John knows of the enslavement of humanity to the powers of the world, knows that human beings close themselves off against the truth (cf. 5:47; 6:64; 8:46; 10:26; 16:9). Jesus's words and miracles, though they actualize divine revelation, do not work automatically or magically. They require a decision from the human side (see above, §12.4.2).

Faith as Saving Event

For John, faith is a saving event. Faith is not ineffectual, for the will of the Father is "that all who see the Son and believe in him may have eternal life; and I will raise them up on the last day" (John 6:40). Faith opens the way to the reality of salvation, eternal life, because it is directed to the One who is himself life (cf. 3:15–16; 5:24; 6:47; 11:25–26; 20:31). For the believer, judgment already belongs to the past, for faith saves from the coming wrath of the Judge (3:18, "Those who believe in him are not condemned; but those who do not believe are condemned already, because they have not believed in the name of the only Son of God"). Thus faith is not just something it might be nice to have; it decides between life and death. So the message of saving faith in Jesus Christ must be proclaimed to all people.

167. The comment of Schwankl, *Licht und Finsternis*, 397, is on target: "John has a partiality for the visual; he is the 'optical theologian' among the evangelists."

12.5.2 Eternal Life

The Christian's new being is designated by John with the comprehensive term ζωή (life) or ζωὴ αἰώνιος (eternal life). Thus the essential character of human life is first made known by faith: the life made possible by God. Life is first and foremost an attribute of the Father,[168] who gives life to the Son: "For just as the Father has life in himself, so he has granted the Son also to have life in himself" (John 5:26; cf. 6:57). The Son in turn receives from the Father the authority over all human beings, "to give eternal life to all whom you have given him" (17:2b). The preexistent Logos already had life in himself, the life that became the light of all human beings (1:4; 1 John 1:2). Here is manifest the characteristic Johannine fusion of different levels of time and space: it is not the resurrection that first makes possible the declaration that Jesus is life and gives life. Rather, Jesus comes forth from God as the epitome and embodiment of life; as the Preexistent One he is already the Incarnate, Crucified, and Risen One. The divine life of the cosmos is present in a concrete historical person.[169] It is precisely as the presupposition for the salvation of humanity from domination by death that the whole of the incarnation event has as its goal eternal life for those who believe (cf. John 3:16, 36a).

The knowledge of God and the one he has sent open up the way to eternal life (John 17:3) *and are at the same time its content*. True life is revealed only in the encounter with Jesus Christ that awakens faith, for in him the divine life-giving power broke into this world of death. Neither the philosophical way to knowledge of one's true self nor the Gnostic's faith in the ontological identity with a heavenly redeemer can free human beings from the realm of death.[170] For John, Jesus alone is the one who gives the water that becomes a spring of living water gushing up to eternal life (4:14). Streams of living water will flow from Jesus's body (7:38), namely the Spirit (cf. 7:39), the divine principle of life who grants the saving gift of eternal life. As the light of the world, Jesus is at the same time the light of life (8:12). He can say of himself that he is the resurrection and the life (11:25), and "I am the way, the truth, and the life" (14:6).

The healing of the son of a royal official in John 4:46–54 and, above all, the raising of Lazarus from the dead after four days (11:1–44) present Jesus as

168. On this point, cf. Franz Mussner, ΖΩΗ*: die Anschauung vom "Leben" im vierten Evangelium, unter Berücksichtigung der Johannesbriefe; ein Beitrag zur biblischen Theologie* (MTS 1.5; Munich: Karl Zink, 1952), 70ff.

169. Cf. ibid., 82ff.

170. Karl-Wolfgang Tröger, "Ja oder Nein zur Welt: War der Evangelist Johannes Christ oder Gnostiker?" *ThV* 7 (1976): 75, designates this fundamental difference between the Gospel of John and Gnosticism as follows: "The concept of identification is scrapped, and the redeemed person does not become the redeemer."

Lord over life and death.[171] Jesus makes life possible by calling the dead back to life or by overcoming the threats that limit the possibilities of life (the healing of the lame and blind in 5:1–9; 9:1–41). Hunger (6:1–15) and peril at sea (6:16–25) endanger life but are defeated by Jesus. Jesus Christ, the mediator of creation, preserves life and makes clear that the creation continues to be dependent on the Creator and under his control. The Creator's gift of life, which transcends temporal boundaries, is far above all that is transient and limited. Whoever has eternal life is no longer lost and does not come into judgment (cf. 10:28; 3:36; 5:24). Jesus's promise has only this content: eternal life (1 John 2:25). Jesus is the bread of life (John 6:35a). Whoever eats of this bread will never die (John 6:50) but lives forever (6:58).

The ancestors who ate the manna in the wilderness still finally died (John 6:49), but the true bread that comes down from heaven grants eternal life. The allusions to the Lord's Supper in the Bread of Life discourse (6:30–51) and the eucharistic section (6:51c–58) illustrate the sacramental dimension of the Johannine concept of life: in the common meal of the community the Risen One reveals himself as the essence of the believers' life and grants them participation in his own fullness of life (see below, §12.7.2). Similarly, already with John the Baptist, baptism is the quintessential life-giving event (3:3–5). The new birth in the power of the Spirit occurs as a vertical incursion into a person's previous life. The Spirit, as the living power of God, places the believer in a new reality. Physical death is a reality afterward as well as before, but it no longer hems life in as its ultimate boundary, so that John can tell the community, "We know that we have passed from death to life because we love one another" (1 John 3:14; cf. John 5:24). Whoever keeps Jesus's word "will never see death" (John 8:51; cf. 11:26). In the Son, the Father grants a life that can never be destroyed by biological death. As a communion with God that begins in the present, eternal life opens into a never-ending future. John promises believers not freedom from death but lasting, true life with God.

12.5.3 Sin

Word counts already point to the importance of the concept of sin for the Johannine tradition: the noun ἁμαρτία (sin) is found seventeen times in the Gospel of John; only Romans and Hebrews have a greater number of instances. The Synoptic Gospels, for example, lag far behind (Mark, six times; Matthew, seven times; Luke, twelve times). Moreover, ἁμαρτία is found an additional seventeen times in 1 John.

To begin with, note that sin vocabulary is found primarily in the debates about the miracles of John 5 and 9. Clearly the Johannine Jesus is not con-

171. This fundamental dimension of the Johannine miracle stories has been comprehensively explored by Labahn, *Lebensspender*.

cerned with determining who is or was a sinner; the point is that his coming exposes the essential nature of sin and overcomes it. This Johannine profile of sin is further developed in Jesus's debates with the Ἰουδαῖοι (Jews) and the world in the revelatory discourses in John 8, 15, and 16. The term ἁμαρτία is found six times in John 8, a clear indication of the explosive power of this theme. Sin is here defined more closely as incomprehension of the Ἰουδαῖοι when they encounter Jesus Christ—the one sent by God—and his way. This lack of understanding turns out to be itself unbelief, for *sin is unbelief vis-à-vis the one sent from God*. Further, sin means being enslaved to the world in such a way that that existence in sin and sinful acts mutually constitute and reinforce each other. Sin consists in the intentional rejection of a self-evident reality manifest in miracles and words: Jesus Christ is the sinless Son of God (cf. John 8:46). John sees the real basis for this refusal in the world's love for itself and its own. The world strives after its own glory and lacks love for God. While God turns to the world in loving compassion (cf. 3:16), the world responds only with rejection and hatred. Sin thus appears in John as love for oneself and as self-inflicted withdrawal from the love of God.

John's first and last statements about sin form a literary and theological bracket: John 1:29 and 20:23. For the world to receive the benefit of authentic life, sin must be overcome. The point at which the sin of the world and the ζωή (life) of God converge and meet is the cross. Johannine irony is visible in the background: on the cross, the Lamb of God takes away the sin of the world, while at the same time the world does away with the Lamb of God on the cross. John 10:23 links the work of Jesus and the work of the disciples within the perspective of the work of the Spirit and the liberation from sin: just as Jesus's sending is essential for taking away sin, so the sending of the disciples brings forgiveness of sins by the commissioning and authority of the Son.

The First Epistle of John shows that there were conflicts in the Johannine school on the subject of forgivable and unforgivable sins.[172] While 1 John 1:8–10 explicitly states that claiming to be without sin is contrary to the truth, 1 John 3:9 emphasizes that "those who have been born of God do not sin, because God's seed abides in them; they cannot sin, because they have been born of God." Being born of God and being united with Christ simply exclude the possibility of sin. There is a clear separation between the children of God and the children of the devil (1 John 3:10). However, 1 John 5:16–17 points in a different direction: "If you see your brother or sister committing what is not a mortal sin, you will ask, and God will give life to such a one—to those whose sin is not mortal. There is sin that is mortal; I do not say that you should pray about that. All wrongdoing is sin, but there is sin that is not mortal."

172. For analysis of the texts, cf. Goldhahn-Müller, *Die Grenze der Gemeinde*, 27–72.

Whoever sins is not in the realm of the Spirit and life but belongs to the realm of death. However, the author of 1 John takes account of the reality of church life, when he speaks of sins that do not lead to death. For these sins, one's brother or sister in the church may ask God for forgiveness. It is hardly accidental that neither the gospel nor the letters of John attempt to define these two categories of sin. The community thereby retains the freedom to decide from case to case the sins that occur within its life together, determining which offenses can be regarded as forgivable and which sins lead to death. With this conception, the essential opposition between sinful acts and the Christian life is maintained, while at the same time the imperative is all the more intensive: there are sins that so disrupt one's relation to God that even the baptized can fall back outside the realm of life.[173]

The Johannine understanding of sin exhibits a clear theological profile: sin is neither a legal nor a moral category. Instead, the predominant use of the word in the singular points to the fact that John understands sin in a general, comprehensive sense: *sin is unbelief, lack of faith*. This general character of the Johannine concept of sin does not permit it to be localized historically and applied only to the Ἰουδαῖοι.[174] On the contrary, in the Johannine perspective, all those who do not believe in the Revealer Jesus Christ find themselves in the realm of sin, whether they are Jews or Gentiles. The Johannine concept of faith permits a further inference: just as faith grants life, eternal life, so lack of faith, i.e., sin, separates from life. The true antonym of "sin" in the Gospel of John is "life"—eternal life.

Why does the world persist in unbelief when it encounters the saving message of God's act in Jesus Christ? In the Johannine view, the world succumbs to sin, understood as both the deeds that one intentionally does and the fate to which one is subject. John expresses his view of human responsibility in that he understands rejection of God's revelation as a voluntary refusal. At the same time, the act of sin reinforces the sin of the world and generates a fateful connection that leads both to being enslaved in and by the world and its demonic powers and to being hardened by God (John 12:39) and that finally results in eschatological death (8:21, 24). It is a vicious circle [German *Teufelskreis*, literally "devil's circle"] in the truest sense of the word. For John, this reality of unbelief is so oppressive precisely because at the cross, God has spoken the ultimate No to sin and the ultimate Yes to life. At the cross, sin is both exposed for what it is and overcome. Thus here too, in the Gospel of John, we can speak of the prevalence of salvation even in his understanding of sin.

173. On similarities and differences regarding the respective concepts of sin in 1 John and the Gospel of John, cf. Metzner, *Verständnis der Sünde*, 325–27.

174. So Bultmann, *Theology of the New Testament*, 2:27–28: "The sin of 'the Jews' is . . . their imperviousness to the Revelation which throws into question their self-security."

12.6 Ethics

Can one speak of a Johannine ethic in the conventional sense? Ernst Käsemann insists on a negative response to this question and emphasizes, "The object of Christian love for John is only what belongs to the community under the Word, or what is elected to belong to it, that is, the brotherhood of Jesus."[175] In this view, love is purely an inward-directed event of the divine word, an internal attitude, limited to the elect congregation, with no reference to the world and people outside the community of faith. Given that view, it would be correct to say that, in comparison with the Synoptics or Paul, the Gospel of John contains no concrete ethical instructions for life in this world. There are no statements of individual or social ethics; the political state no more comes into view than the problems of wealth and poverty, marriage and sexual conduct, or concrete directions for conduct in the church or outside it. Everything is concentrated in the single word "love." But what does John mean by this term ἀγάπη/ἀγαπάω (noun and verb forms of "love")? The answer to this question depends on how one grasps Johannine thought in its literary form as a gospel. Concentrating the problem to two verses (John 13:34–35) is inadequate, because it overlooks two presuppositions of the Johannine ethic that are also its integral components: (1) the ethical relevance of the literary genre "gospel," and (2) the significance of the basic structure of Johannine theology as a kind of thought that deals with fundamental principles.

The Ethical Relevance of the Literary Genre "Gospel"

Among the basic functions of narratives is the formation of the reader's orientation (see above, §1.3). Thus narratives always have a normative dimension; they are intended to establish an ethical orientation, to generate, change, or stabilize attitudes and ways of living one's life. Narratives that achieve their intended purpose, such as the gospels, always have an orienting function. Their structure provides room for reception and interpretation, makes possible transformations, and determines those guidelines that give the story line its character. *Thus the narrative genre of the Gospel of John already leads the reader to expect ethical orientation from it.* Its particular character cannot be grasped apart from the specific mode of Johannine thought.

Thinking That Deals with Fundamental Principles

John consistently thinks through the revelation of God in Christ in terms of its fundamental principles. He is concerned with the all-encompassing

175. Käsemann, *Testament of Jesus*, 65. Cf. Bultmann's prior discussion, Bultmann, *John*, 274.

foundations of human existence itself and the fundamental orientation of human actions as such. The Johannine love commandment must be interpreted in this context; *it is the center of the principled ethic of the Fourth Evangelist.* John thereby takes up a central impulse of Jesus's own preaching (cf. Matt. 5:44; Mark 12:28–34) and brings it to fulfillment: those who live on the basis of love and from its power do not need concrete commandments but know themselves to be linked to and bound by the basic principle of all being. Love unites one not only with one's true self and one's fellow human beings but also with the Ground of Being who upholds and sustains all things (cf. 1 John 4:8, ὁ θεὸς ἀγάπη ἐστίν [God is love]).

The concept of love is not a marginal phenomenon in the Fourth Gospel, for Johannine thought as a whole is characterized throughout by the idea of love.[176] When the evangelist takes up the ἀγάπη/ἀγαπάω ("love" as noun and verb) vocabulary for the first time in John 3:16, he connects the concept of incarnation with the concept of love from the outset: it is God's love for the world that sends the Son. The gospel was written in order to show that God's prevenient love enables and sustains all life in order to finally attain its goal when human beings come to faith (cf. 15:16, "You did not choose me but I chose you. And I appointed you to go and bear fruit, fruit that will last").

12.6.1 The Love Commandment

John places the love commandment in the context of Jesus's departure: "I give you a new commandment, that you love one another. Just as I have loved you, you also should love one another. By this everyone will know that you are my disciples, if you have love for one another" (John 13:34–35).[177] In the situation of Jesus's departure, the love command designates the means by which the disciples—and thus the church external to the text—can remain in communion with Jesus.[178] By expressing Jesus's own loving deeds in the form of familial love within the family of God, the believing community can continue to experience Jesus's once-for-all ministry.[179] The disciples may and must let themselves be swept up in the movement of love initiated by God; in this, Jesus and his disciples are united. The command of mutual love within the family of God as the central ethical instruction of the Johannine school

176. Cf. Popkes, *Theologie der Liebe Gottes*, 361: "The 'dramaturgical Christology of the love of God in the Gospel of John' embodies a high point of early Christian theological formation. It reflects and expresses in analogical language why it is that the life and death of Jesus can be understood as an event of the love of God."

177. Extensive analysis in ibid., 257–71.

178. Cf. Ulrich Wilckens, "Der Paraklet und die Kirche," in *Kirche: Festschrift für Günther Bornkamm zum 75. Geburtstag* (ed. Dieter Lührmann and Georg Strecker; Tübingen: Mohr, 1980), 187; Schnelle, "Abschiedsreden," 66; Frey, *Eschatologie*, 2:312–13.

179. Cf. Bultmann, *John*, 526.

(in addition to John 13:34–35, cf. 2 John 4–7; 1 John 2:7–11; 4:10, 19) reveals mutuality and analogy as its central ethical category: just as Jesus, in his prototypical and exemplary act, gave himself over to death for the sake of his own, so they should love one another in the same way. While in the Synoptic tradition the love command is derived from the Scripture in the form of a double commandment (cf. the adoption of Deut. 6:4, 5; Lev. 19:18 in Mark 12:30, 31), in the Gospel of John Jesus grounds the command in his own authority. This grounding corresponds to Johannine logic, for the Scripture itself already testifies to Jesus (cf. John 5:46); he is Lord of all, including the Scripture. The qualification *new* for the love command likewise derives from this fundamental thought pattern, for the newness of the command does not consist in its content as such but is derived solely from the one who commands it. Since the preexistent, incarnate, crucified, and risen Jesus Christ formulates the love command, it receives a new quality.

The Footwashing Scene as the Locus of Love

John intentionally chooses the footwashing scene to illustrate the *concrete content* of the love concept.[180] Footwashing was a menial service assigned to slaves, a concrete and dirty job,[181] by no means only a symbolic or liturgical act. Jesus himself gives his disciples a paradigm of Christian existence and the Christian way of life; he takes them up into the loving act of God that opens to them a new existence in mutual love within the fellowship of believers. What we have here is no merely intellectual act, a matter of ethical proclamations or requirements, *but a concrete act of Jesus*! For John, too, love is an event that cannot be kept to itself but can only be complete in action. The paradoxical form of this love is expressed in the narrative of John 13:4–5: the Lord washes his servants' feet. Love not only marks Jesus's essential being and character; in the footwashing scene love takes concrete form, becomes a determining event. While it is reported of Caligula that he intentionally humiliated Roman senators by commanding them to wash his feet,[182] Jesus proves his love in the free act of performing the most menial task of a slave for his disciples. In the footwashing scene, where love takes concrete form, Jesus reveals and enacts the fact that his being is from God.

180. On the footwashing, cf. Johannes Beutler, "Die Heilsbedeutung des Todes Jesu im Johannesevangelium nach Joh. 13,1–20," in *Der Tod Jesu: Deutungen im Neuen Testament* (ed. Johannes Beutler and Karl Kertelge; QD 74; Freiburg: Herder, 1976), 188–204; Kohler, *Kreuz und Menschwerdung*, 192–229; Christoph Niemand, *Die Fußwaschungserzählung des Johannesevangeliums* (StAs 114; Rome: Pontificio Ateneo S. Anselmo, 1993); Schnelle, "Johanneische Schule," 210–16; J. C. Thomas, *Footwashing in John 13 and the Johannine Community* (JSNTSup 61; Sheffield: Sheffield Academic, 1991); Zumstein, "Macht."

181. Cf. the documentation in *NW* 1.2:635–45.

182. Cf. Suetonius, *Cal.* 26; Dio Cassius, *Hist.* 59.27.1, which states of Caligula, "He used to kiss very few; for to most of the senators, even, he merely extended his hand or foot for homage."

This surprising exchange of roles evokes a deep lack of understanding, even dismay, from those who have been graced by Jesus's act (John 13:6–10a). Peter, in his unwillingness to understand that Jesus's lordship is fulfilled precisely in his role as servant, energetically resists Jesus's act. In the footwashing, Jesus draws near to needy people and purifies them (13:10). A reversal takes place here: both in ancient Judaism and in the pagan cults, human beings by their own actions undertake purification rites that are prerequisite to encountering the divine, but here God himself draws near to human beings and makes them pure. The human being must not, and cannot, contribute anything to this purification. Here God transforms human existence, giving it a new quality that corresponds to Jesus's act of footwashing: "So if I, your Lord and Teacher, have washed your feet, you also ought to wash one another's feet" (13:14). Jesus's act includes the obligation for the disciples to act in the same way (13:15, "For I have set you an example, that you also should do as I have done to you").[183] Jesus's act is here at the same time both prototype and example for human conduct. If Jesus were exclusively an example, then human beings would be thrown back on their own resources and would have to imitate the model as best they could under their own power. Such a state of affairs would run afoul of the movement of God's prevenient love. Human beings are incapable of imitating Jesus, because Jesus's acting is what grounds human existence, and human activity devolves out of his act. Human beings can, however, let themselves be taken up into the movement of love initiated by God, and in this they will become like Jesus (13:34–35). The footwashing scene tells believers their lives cannot correspond to Jesus's life without specific acts; *a purely verbal understanding of the concept of love falls short of Jesus's own deed!* Action is a fundamental component of the Johannine concept of love, which, precisely in its axiomatic structure, is extremely concrete.

Bearing Fruit

Another central aspect of the Johannine ethic is found in the metaphorical language of "bearing fruit" in the discourse about the true vine:[184] "I am the true vine, and my Father is the vinegrower. He removes every branch in me that bears no fruit. Every branch that bears fruit he prunes to make it bear more fruit" (John 15:1–2). The "bearing of fruit" is specifically concentrated on abiding in the word; through the encounter with the word of Jesus, believers are purified and enabled to bring forth fruit (15:3). The election of the disciples by Jesus (15:16) is the presupposition for bearing fruit, and this is the goal of their election. All the being, abilities, and doing of believers can

183. Seneca says about philosophy, "Philosophy teaches one to act, not talk" (*Ep.* 20.2: "facere docet philosophia, non dicere").

184. In addition to the standard commentaries, for interpretation cf. Pfeiffer, *Einweisung*, 265–303.

be realized only in their relation to Jesus; Jesus, the embodiment and epitome of life and love, makes it possible for his own to live in faith and love. On the other hand, separation from Jesus or indifference to him results in radical barrenness. The disciple who bears no fruit has already fallen away from the living connection with Jesus and has fallen into judgment (15:6). The Father is glorified not only by the departure of the Son (13:31–32) but also by the fruit-bearing of the disciples.

Being a true disciple of Jesus includes abiding in Jesus's word, living the life of prayer, and living one's life on the basis of the love of God revealed in Christ. This fundamental trait of Johannine thought is also developed in the discourse about the true vine, with clear references back to the footwashing under the aspect of love. The fruit-bearing called for in the vine discourse is nothing more or less than love. Thus the command to "abide in me" can also be expressed in the challenge, "Abide in my love" (cf. John 15:9–10). Love is fulfilled and becomes concrete in the keeping of the commandments (cf. 14:15, 21, 23). The plural ἐντολαί (commandments), like the giving of one's life for one's friends (15:13) and the reference back to the footwashing, shows that for John "bearing fruit" always includes the dimension of concrete action. The commandments manifest their obligatory character in deeds of love.

The striking concentration of instances of ἀγάπη/ἀγαπάω in the Farewell Discourses and their direct context (ἀγάπη occurs 7 times in the Gospel of John, of which 6 times are in the Farewell Discourses/context; ἀγαπάω occurs 37 times in the Gospel of John, of which 25 times are in the Farewell Discourses/context)[185] underscores the action dimension of the love commandment from the perspective of text pragmatics. In view of the concrete hostile actions of the world, the Johannine Christians are called to unity in love and thus to action. The structure of the gospel as a whole, characterized by a constant increasing of the dramatic element, leaves no doubt that the community of faith is expected to act in love, grounded in a love that radiates out into the world.

12.6.2 Narrative Ethics

Growing the love for God, for Jesus, and mutual love within the Christian family requires instruction and maintenance. In his gospel, the Fourth Evangelist elaborates the perils and successes of this process by means of individual narrative figures. In and with the narrative, he creates and fashions characters with identification potential,[186] who present models of ethical conduct. One

185. Cf. in addition: φίλος, 6 times in the Gospel of John and 3 times in the Farewell Discourses; φιλέω, 8 times in John 1–20 and 3 times in the Farewell Discourses.

186. On the narrative strategies used by the Fourth Evangelist, in addition to the foundational works of R. Alan Culpepper, *Anatomy of the Fourth Gospel: A Study in Literary Design* (New Testament Foundations and Facets; Philadelphia: Fortress, 1983), and M. W. G. Stibbe, *John as Storyteller* (Cambridge: Cambridge University Press, 1992), see especially Sjef van

of the first figures with whom the reader might identify is Nicodemus, a character in the story portrayed as on the way toward confessing the faith.[187] The evangelist introduces him as a person who has a sincere question (John 3:1–12), who then indirectly defends Jesus (7:50–51), until he finally steps out as one willing to make a public confession of his faith (19:39–40). Joseph of Arimathea and Nicodemus step forth out of concealment and publicly confess their faith in Jesus by their loving service, giving him an honorable burial. The process of developing faith, from its origin through confession and perseverance, is also narrated in the healing of the man born blind (John 9).[188] This miracle story is an illustration and demonstration of the christological affirmation of 8:12, legitimates Jesus's divine origin, and identifies him as the miracle worker sent from God (cf. 9:7c, 16, 33). While the Jews persist in unbelief, interpreting Jesus's handling of tradition as sinful (9:14, 16a), and even denying the factuality of the miracle, the man born blind proceeds by stages to knowledge, then confession of the divine origin of Jesus. His story reaches its climax in the confession πιστεύω (I believe) of 9:38. The exemplary function of the story of the man born blind is obvious; he receives his sight through Jesus's act, holds his ground against external pressures, and through his faith becomes one who truly sees. The Jews, on the other hand, lapse into a crisis because they persist in unbelief (9:39–41). The man born blind has received his sight in a double sense: he not only receives physical eyesight, but beyond that he recognizes that Jesus is from God and comes to faith in him. In contrast, the Pharisees only suppose they can see, for they do not recognize Jesus as the Revealer. Thus they are the ones who are truly blind, even though they have physical eyesight (cf. 9:40–41). In the story of the man born blind, John presents his community with a model of action and perseverance, and with this story challenges them to respond to Jesus's healing act in the same way as the man born blind. When that happens, Jesus opens the eyes not only of the man in the story, but of the church. *Seeing* means *believing*; *unbelief* is *blindness*.

The Lazarus pericope presents an additional constellation of narrative characters who feature a number of movements and perspectives.[189] Although Lazarus is already mentioned in the first verse, he first appears as a living person

---

Tilborg, *Imaginative Love in John* (BIS 2; Leiden: Brill, 1993); David R. Beck, *The Discipleship Paradigm: Readers and Anonymous Characters in the Fourth Gospel* (BIS 27; Leiden: Brill, 1997); James L. Resseguie, *The Strange Gospel: Narrative Designs and Point of View in John* (BIS 56; Leiden: Brill, 2001).

187. Cf. here Dschulnigg, *Jesus begegnen*, 106–21.

188. Cf. Michael Labahn, "Der Weg eines Namenlosen—vom Hilflosen zum Vorbild (Joh 9)," in *Die bleibende Gegenwart des Evangeliums: Festschrift für Otto Merk* (ed. Roland Gebauer and Martin Meiser; MTS 76; Marburg: Elwert, 2003), 63–80, and Matthias Rein, *Die Heilung des Blindgeborenen: (Joh 9); Tradition und Redaktion* (WUNT 2.73; Tübingen: Mohr, 1995).

189. For the narrative analysis, cf. Eckart Reinmuth, "Lazarus und seine Schwestern—was wollte Johannes erzählen?" *TLZ* 124 (1999): 127–37.

in the last verse of the story. Between the poles of this inclusio John works in miniature portraits that illustrate possible responses to Jesus.[190] While Martha hears of Jesus's coming and goes out to meet him, Mary lingers at the house, as fitting for a woman in mourning (cf. Ezek. 8:14). Through their conduct, the two women express different expectations: Martha apparently hopes that Jesus will be able to do something, even in the face of death, while for Mary the situation appears hopeless (John 11:20). After the revelatory saying of John 11:25–26, that Jesus, as the true giver of life, is the Lord of life and death, it is not only Martha who confesses her faith. A radical change also happens to Mary, who feels that she has been directly addressed, drops what she has been doing, and hurries to Jesus (11:29). Though different in terms of character, both sisters find their way to Jesus and thus abide in his love (11:5). Even the portrait of Jesus in this pericope manifests surprising features. Precisely as Lord over life and death, he is portrayed in his full humanity. He loves the sisters and their brother (11:5), cries over the death of Lazarus (11:35), and becomes angry in the face of unbelief (11:33). The community of hearers and readers external to the text understands the raising of Lazarus, who has throughout been abiding in the love of Jesus, not only as an anticipation of Jesus's own destiny; they can hope that Jesus will act for all believers just as he has acted for Lazarus.

The model disciple, and thus the example of discipleship par excellence with whom the hearers/readers might identify, is "the disciple whom Jesus loved" (John 13:23, ὃν ἠγάπα ὁ Ἰησοῦς). In the symposium setting of the Johannine Last Supper, the beloved disciple reclines on the breast of Jesus, just as Jesus was in the bosom of the Father (1:18). Thus the beloved disciple becomes the unique exegete of Jesus, who is the exclusive exegete of God! The "love" verbs ἀγαπάω (13:23; 19:26) and φιλέω (20:2) place the beloved disciple emphatically in the communion of love shared by the Father and the Son (cf., e.g., 3:35; 10:17; 15:9; 17:23–24). With great intentionality, John names the master-disciple "the disciple whom Jesus loved," for in his knowledge, faithfulness, persistence, and faith, he embodies as no other what it means to be a disciple in the love that unites him with the Son and the Father (see below, §12.7.1).

12.6.3 The Ethic of 1 John

In no other New Testament document are references to "love" so numerous as in 1 John, whether absolutely or relative to length (ἀγάπη, 18 times; ἀγαπάω, 28 times).[191] The basic orientation of the letter is similar to that of the gospel, in that the love of God both commands mutual love among members of the

190. Cf. Dschulnigg, *Jesus begegnen*, 195–219.

191. On the command of mutual love in the Johannine letters, cf. Popkes, *Theologie der Liebe Gottes*, 75–165.

church and makes it possible (1 John 4:10, "In this is love, not that we loved God but that he loved us and sent his Son to be the atoning sacrifice for our sins"; 4:19, "We love because he first loved us"; cf. 2:4ff.; 5:1–5 and other such texts). At the same time, the letter manifests a remarkably different profile:

1. It is characteristic of the letter that it interweaves the metaphors of love and light, a combination that does not occur in the gospel (1 John 2:10–11, "Whoever says, 'I am in the light,' while hating a brother or sister, is still in the darkness. Whoever loves a brother or sister lives in the light, and in such a person there is no cause for stumbling."). While in the gospel "light" is a christocentric term (cf. John 1:4–5; 3:19; 9:5; 12:36, 46), in 1 John a clearly theocentric conception predominates: God is light and love (cf. 1:5; 4:7–12, 19–21). Light as symbol of the divine fullness of life is linked with love as its visible form.
2. In 1 John, love is an integral component of a comprehensive communicative event: the one who knows God and is from God keeps his commandments and lives not in darkness but in the light, walking in love and truth, separated from both sin and the error of the antichrist.
3. The level on which this comprehensive event occurs is made an explicit theme in 1 John: "We know love by this, that he laid down his life for us—and we ought to lay down our lives for one another. How does God's love abide in anyone who has the world's goods and sees a brother or sister in need and yet refuses help? Little children, let us love, not in word or speech, but in truth and action" (3:16–18). Love, light, life, and truth are here most closely related: the beginning point is the love of Christ manifest in his giving his life for the brothers and sisters of the family of God. This model of Jesus's own way of life is applied to the Johannine community. The love of God is at stake in the situation where wealthy members of the church either ignore their needy brothers and sisters in the faith or actively come to their aid.

The Johannine school thus requires of its members a concrete, exemplary, social conduct implemented in the active support of needy members of the community of faith. These calls to action are far removed from a mere attitudinal ethic; a particular kind of social conduct is explicitly required, a love realized in deed.

Unity in Word and Deed

The ethical affirmations of the Johannine writings must be understood within a line of thought based on fundamental principles, a kind of thought directed toward a basic orientation of one's life, but still without giving hard and fast rules on individual issues. For John, ethics means a categorical stance toward how one lives one's life as a whole, a stance that transcends the level of individual acts.[192] This is no weakness, but the very strength of his concept of ethics, which understands love (both verb and noun) as the essential being of God and which expects a particular way of thinking and living to emerge from this basic approach. The ethical content of ἀγάπη/ἀγαπάω is revealed in Jesus's own acts, for which the footwashing scene provides at one and the same time the presupposition, enabling power, and normative content of the loving service the disciples themselves are to do. Abiding in Jesus, unity in the word, is also always a unity in deed, for at the beginning stands the loving service of Jesus on the cross, which can find its adequate counterpart and response only through actions performed in love and on the basis of love. Nothing is more concrete than love!

12.7 Ecclesiology

In exegetical study of the Gospel of John, ecclesiology was for a long time only a marginal topic. Wherever the references to baptism and the Lord's Supper in John 3:5; 6:51c–58; 19:34b–35 were considered secondary, and only a conceptually oriented Christology was considered worthy of hermeneutical attention, the theological question of the shape of Johannine ecclesiology was not raised in any substantive manner.[193] This perception is changed when the hermeneutical perspective and fundamental conceptuality of Johannine theology is taken seriously as a comprehensive whole:[194] in the post-Easter anamnesis under the guidance of the Paraclete, John thinks through the meaning of divine incarnation. According to John's convictions, the form of divine incursion into this world includes a place for the church.

12.7.1 Orientation Points: Paraclete and Beloved Disciple

The fundamental idea of historical continuity, important for every ecclesiology, is developed by John in a distinctive manner: the Paraclete and the beloved disciple link the present of the Johannine community with the originating event, and thus vouch for the authenticity of the unique Johannine theology.

192. Cf. also J. G. Van der Watt, "Ethics and Ethos in the Gospel according to John," *ZNW* 97 (2006): 166–75, who rightly sees the idea of love as realized in the realm of interpersonal relations, among which he counts especially the common meals, the footwashing, and the mission of the Johannine school.

193. Cf. Bultmann, *Theology of the New Testament*, "No specifically ecclesiological interest can be detected. There is no interest in cult or organization"; Käsemann, *Testament of Jesus*, 27, "One of the surprising features of the Fourth Gospel and perhaps the most surprising of all is that it does not seem to develop an explicit ecclesiology."

194. The lack of the word ἐκκλησία ("church") in the Gospel of John says nothing at all about the subject matter itself, for this word is also missing in Mark, but no one can deny a concept of the church to him!

The Paraclete

The ecclesiological dimension of Johannine theology is clearly revealed in the concept of the Paraclete (see above, §12.3.2). The coming of the Paraclete presupposes Jesus's departure and lasting presence with the Father (cf. John 16:7; also 7:39; 20:22), and the Johannine community is aware that its life continues through time (cf. 17:15). At the same time, the coming of the Paraclete uniquely reveals the self-understanding of the Johannine school: the Paraclete will abide with the community forever (14:16), reminds the community of what Jesus has said (14:26), and testifies to Jesus (15:26); he convicts the world of sin (16:8), announces the future to the disciples (16:13), and glorifies Jesus in the community of faith (16:14). Thus the Johannine school knows that its present and future are globally determined by the Father and the Son, who send the Paraclete (cf. 14:16, 25; 15:26; 16:7). Since the Paraclete not only keeps the words of Jesus in the church's memory, but teaches the community everything it needs to know about the future (14:26), the Johannine school claims to be in communion with the Father and the Son in a special way even in the time between Easter and the parousia.[195]

The Beloved Disciple

Just as the Paraclete determines the presence of the community and opens up the future to it, the beloved disciple[196] uniquely links the community with the past of the earthly work of Jesus. John links a variety of literary, theological, and historical strategies with the beloved disciple. In literary terms, the beloved disciple appears as the model disciple who implements movements in the narrative world of the text within which the hearers/readers can see themselves included and thereby realize their own discipleship. In John 1:37–40 and 18:15–18, the beloved disciple must be imported into the text, functioning as a "blank space" that must be filled so the text can function.[197] Theologically, the beloved disciple is above all the guarantor of the tradition and the ideal witness of the Christ event. The beloved disciple was called before Peter (1:37–40); he is both the hermeneut of Jesus and the spokesperson

195. Cf. Mussner, *Sehweise*, 56–63.

196. On the beloved disciple, cf. Alv Kragerud, *Der Lieblingsjünger im Johannesevangelium: Ein exegetischer Versuch* (Oslo: Osloer Universitätsverlag, 1959); Jürgen Roloff, "Der johanneische 'Lieblingsjünger' und der Lehrer der Gerechtigkeit," *NTS* 15 (1968/1969); J. Kügler, *Der Jünger, den Jesus liebte* (SBB 16; Stuttgart: Katholisches Bibelwerk, 1988); Richard Bauckham, "The Beloved Disciple as Ideal Author," *JSNT* 49 (1993): 21–44; L. Simon, *Petrus und der Lieblingsjünger im Johannesevangelium* (EHS 23.498; Frankfurt: Lang, 1994); R. Alan Culpepper, *John, the Son of Zebedee: The Life of a Legend* (Minneapolis: Fortress, 1999); James H. Charlesworth, *The Beloved Disciple* (Valley Forge, PA: Trinity, 1995); Michael Theobald, "Der Jünger, den Jesus liebte," in *Geschichte—Tradition—Reflexion: Festschrift für Martin Hengel zum 70. Geburtstag* (ed. Hubert Cancik et al.; 3 vols.; Tübingen: Mohr, 1996), 219–55.

197. Cf. Umberto Eco, *Lector in fabula: La cooperazione interpretativa nei testi narrativi* (Milano: Bompiani, 1979), 63–64.

for the circle of disciples (13:23–26a). In the hour of trial, he remains true to his Lord (18:15–18), and thus becomes the true witness beneath the cross and the exemplary follower of Jesus (19:25–27). The scene at the cross is the founding legend of the Johannine community: Mary represents the believers of all times, who, like herself, are entrusted to the care and direction of the beloved disciple. From the cross, Jesus establishes his church, which, like Mary, is given over to the custody of the beloved disciple. *Thus, in John, the hour of the crucifixion is the hour of the church's birth!* The beloved disciple confirms the real death of Jesus on the cross (19:34b, 35), and is the first to recognize the eschatological dimension of the Easter event (20:2–10). Typological and individual traits are concentrated in the figure of the beloved disciple,[198] as he is repeatedly introduced by the evangelist John.[199] By no means is the beloved disciple "a fiction pure and simple,"[200] for 21:22–23 presupposes his unexpected death, which occasions the final editor of the Gospel of John to add a brief correction to the personal history of the beloved disciple and his relation to Simon Peter. If the beloved disciple were only a literary fiction representing an ideal or theological principle, then both the competitive role with Peter in which he is consistently cast, as well as his role as acknowledged guarantor of the community's tradition, would not be persuasive.[201] Historically as well as theologically, the most plausible view is to regard the beloved disciple as the presbyter of 2 and 3 John, who, in turn, is identical with the presbyter John mentioned by Papias (cf. Eusebius, *Hist. eccl.* 3.39.4). As the founder of the Johannine school, the presbyter already appears in 2 and 3 John as a special bearer of tradition, a function taken up and extended by the author of the Fourth Gospel. By making the post-Easter founder of the Johannine school into the pre-Easter authentic eyewitness and guarantor of the tradition, the evangelist lets the beloved disciple represent the post-Easter Johannine disciples in his portrayal of the pre-Easter disciples! So the circle is complete: with the beloved disciple and the Paraclete, the evangelist executes a double modulation of temporal levels, forward and backward, in which Easter is at the same time the middle and beginning point. Thus the Johannine school knows itself to be bound in a unique way with both the earthly and exalted Jesus Christ.

198. Cf. Walter Grundmann, *Zeugnis und Gestalt des Johannes-Evangeliums; eine Studie zur denkerischen und gestalterischen Leistung des vierten Evangelisten* (AT 7; Stuttgart: Calwer, 1961), 18: "The beloved disciple is both individual and type; when the individual died, the type remains."

199. Cf. Theodor Lorenzen, *Der Lieblingsjünger im Johannesevangelium* (SBS 55; Stuttgart: KBW Verlag, 1971), 73.

200. Kragerud, *Lieblingsjünger*, 149.

201. On the most important suggestions for identifying the beloved disciple (John Son of Zebedee, the evangelist John, the Presbyter John, Lazarus, John Mark, Paul, the ideal representative of Gentile Christianity, an anonymous church teacher), cf. the surveys of Kügler, *Jünger*, 439–48, and Culpepper, *John, the Son of Zebedee*, 72–88.

12.7.2 Sacraments

The significance of baptism and the eucharist in the Gospel of John derives appropriately from the fundamental confession of Johannine faith: in Jesus Christ, God became human and is the presence of God. Baptism and eucharist give direct expression to this idea. In baptism, the transition from the sphere of the flesh to the divine realm of life takes place through the gift of the Spirit (3:5), the Spirit which comes forth from the incarnation, death, and glorification of Jesus Christ. With its baptismal practice, the Johannine school shows in a twofold manner that it is the legitimate successor that continues Jesus's work:

1. By baptizing, it continues the work of the historical Jesus (3:22, 26; 4:1).
2. At the same time, its baptism grants participation in the saving work of the exalted Jesus Christ.[202]

The basic incarnational character of Johannine theology is pointedly articulated in the *eucharistic section*, John 6:51c–58. This section was composed by the evangelist and appended to the traditional discourse on the Bread of Life of 6:30–35, 41–51b[203] as a way of formulating a central christological affirmation: in the eucharist, the Johannine school recognizes and acknowledges the identity of the exalted Son of Man with the incarnate and crucified Jesus. The Preexistent and Risen One is none other than the one who became truly human and who died on the cross, Jesus of Nazareth. Christological, soteriological, and ecclesiological moments are all concentrated precisely at the Lord's Supper, for, as the locus of the saving presence of the incarnate, crucified, and glorified Christ, the Lord's Supper allows believers to participate in the gift of eternal life. The reference to "blood and water" (αἷμα καὶ ὕδωρ) in 19:34b, and the testimony of the beloved disciple in 19:35, underscore this interpretation. That Jesus died a truly human death presupposes the incarnation, and, in turn, both incarnation and real death are what make possible the saving effect of the death of Jesus that become concretely real in baptism and the eucharist. The ecclesiological dimension of the Johannine portrayal of Christ is revealed precisely in the sacraments, for they are grounded in the life and death of the historical Jesus of Nazareth, while at the same time granting the gifts of the new creation (3:5) and eternal life (6:51c–58) in the sphere of the church.

So also from the point of view of ritual theory it is untenable to deny the Fourth Evangelist's interest in the sacraments. Rituals such as baptism and

202. On the Johannine understanding of baptism, cf. Schnelle, *Antidocetic Christology*, 177–93; Popp, *Grammatik*, 233ff.

203. On this point, cf. Popp, *Grammatik*, 360ff.

the eucharist, as compressions of reality, can stabilize and maintain collective identity. Their functions in the group's life-world consists in constructing a bridge to facilitate "crossing the boundaries to other realities."[204] Rituals, like symbols, are a central category of the communication of religious meaning,[205] and John makes use of them (cf. 3:5; 13:1–20) in order to give the central ideas of his symbolic universe a distinctive profile that cannot be misunderstood: the incarnate, crucified, and resurrected Jesus Christ is present in baptism and eucharist as the true giver of life.

12.7.3 Disciples

The whole group of disciples are prototypes, and thus identification figures of what it means to believe in Jesus.[206] They do not have to be called but follow Jesus of their own accord (John 1:37, 40–42); not until Philip does Jesus extend a call to discipleship (1:43). In John 1:35–51 the Johannine community external to the text recognizes in the call of the first disciples the beginnings of its own story, which is closely linked to the ministry of John the Baptist. John gives graphic pictures of how people seek and find their way to Jesus and then, through their own confession of faith in the Messiah, call others into discipleship. Verbs of movement and perception predominate; the encounter with Jesus cannot be without results! The call narratives of the disciples, as the first Johannine stories of the divine-human encounter, already illustrate that seeking and finding, as fundamental elements of religious life, find their fulfillment in Jesus. In the telling of these stories, the model of indirect call of new disciples already speaks directly to the evangelist's church, which finds itself in the situation of a mediated discipleship. The call stories of the disciples develop a dynamic that shapes the whole Gospel of John: on his revelatory way, Jesus Christ repeatedly encounters people and grants them access to the mystery of his person—which then applies to the hearers/readers external to the text.[207]

From the very beginning, Jesus's public work takes place in the presence of "the disciples" (John 2:1–10) and leads them to faith (2:11b, "and his disciples believed in him"). As those who accompany their Lord and witness his miracles

204. Schutz and Luckmann, *Structures*, 2:131.

205. Cf. on this point Clifford Geertz, *Dichte Beschreibung: Beiträge zum Verstehen kultureller Systeme* (Frankfurt: Suhrkamp, 1987), 44ff.

206. On this point, cf. Schnackenburg, *John*, 203–17; Klaus Scholtissek, "Kinder Gottes und Freunde Jesu: Beobachtungen zur johanneischen Ekklesiologie," in *Ekklesiologie des Neuen Testaments: Für Karl Kertelge* (ed. Rainer Kampling and Thomas Söding; Freiburg: Herder, 1996), 184–211; T. Nicklas, *Ablösung und Verstrickung: "Juden" und Jüngergestalten als Charaktere der erzählten Welt des Johannesevangeliums und ihre Wirkung auf den impliziten Leser* (RST 60; Frankfurt: Lang, 2001).

207. Cf. here Klaus Scholtissek, "'Mitten unter euch steht der, den ihr nicht kennt (Joh 1,26)," *MTZ* 48 (1997): 103–21; Dschulnigg, *Jesus begegnen*, 36–54, 82–89.

and discourses, the disciples also appear prominently in 2:22; 3:22; 4:27–38; 6:1–15, 16–25. Following the eucharistic section (6:51c–58), a schism breaks out among the disciples (6:60–66), followed by Peter's confession (6:66–71). Here the texts are transparent to the current situation in the Johannine community, for in the background of 6:60–66 stands a split within the Johannine school (cf. 1 John 2:19), ignited by the dispute about the salvific significance of the existence of the earthly Jesus—a dispute in which the eucharist apparently played an important role.[208] The description of Jesus's disciples as οἱ ἴδιοι (his own) in John 13:1 is programmatic, a term with which the Johannine community expressed its own special relation to its Lord: they belong to Jesus, he is their shepherd (10:11, 15), they number themselves among his own sheep (10:3, 4). The Johannine Christians do not follow outside intruders, but keep themselves unswervingly loyal to their shepherd. The operative reality is: "I know my own, and my own know me" (10:14b). Likewise, the other ecclesiological self-descriptions underscore the close communion between the Johannine Christians and their exalted Lord: οἱ φίλοι ("friends," 15:14), τέκνα θεοῦ ("children of God," 1:12; 11:52; 13:33), ἀδελφοί ("brothers and sisters," 20:17).

In the secure setting of a common meal (John 13:1–20), the Farewell Discourses[209] address Jesus's disciples primarily as "friends" (15:13, 14, 15). Among true friends, it is possible to speak the truth in all candor and thus cultivate friendship, so that the Farewell Discourses themselves function as a kind of friendship maintenance. The love commandment (13:34–35), the discourse about the true vine (15:1–8) with the motif of "abiding," the Paraclete sayings (14:16, 17, 26; 15:26; 16:7–11, 13–15), and the commissioning statements (17:18–23) underscore, each in its own way, the ecclesiological dimensions of the Farewell Discourses, for here the faith of the Johannine school at the time of the writing of the gospel comes to expression. It sees the text's promises to the disciples as fulfilled in its own midst, knows that it is guided by the Paraclete, and witnesses and proclaims God's saving act in Jesus Christ to the world.

12.7.4 Sending and Mission

In the scene in which Jesus sends forth his disciples (John 20:21–23) and in the Thomas pericope (20:24–29), the portrayal of the disciples and the gospel as a whole come to an appropriate conclusion, for here the presence of the

208. On this point, cf. Thomas Popp, "Die Kunst der Wiederholung: Repetition, Variation und Amplifikation im vierten Evangelium am Beispiel von Johannes 6:60–71," in *Kontexte des Johannesevangeliums* (ed. Albert Frey and Udo Schnelle; WUNT 175; Tübingen: Mohr, 2004), 559–92.

209. For an analysis of the ecclesiological aspects of John 15–17, cf. Onuki, *Gemeinde und Welt*, 117–82.

heavenly Lord modulates into the present situation of the church in the world. The church knows that it is charged with its mission by the risen Lord himself and given the authority to forgive sins or withhold forgiveness. In 20:21, the sending of the Son into the world makes possible and necessitates the sending of the disciples into the world.[210] It is not coincidental that the risen Jesus charges his disciples with mission, for with the conclusion of the earthly work of the Son, his sending is transferred to his disciples. By the gift of the Spirit, they are authorized and equipped for their task of forgiving sins, i.e., bringing people over from the realm of death into the realm of life. The risen Lord includes his disciples in the gift of life with which he himself has been endowed by the Father. Just as the Son received the gift of the Spirit from the Father (1:33; 3:34), so the church receives it from the Son (20:22).

Because Jesus's death and exaltation are the presupposition and rationale for the mission of the Johannine school, the "high-priestly prayer" of John 17 is particularly rich in statements about the sending of the disciples and theological perspectives on the church's mission.[211] In 17:15 Jesus explicitly asks the Father not to take the disciples, i.e., the later church, out of the world, and then in 17:18, "As you have sent me into the world, so I have sent them into the world." Here, Jesus's missionary commission to the disciples is essentially the extension of Jesus's own sending by the Father. Just as Jesus came into the world to awaken faith and bring salvation, so the disciples are also sent ἵνα ὁ κόσμος πιστεύῃ ὅτι σύ με ἀπέστειλας ("so that the world may believe that you have sent me," 17:21c). In 17:20 Jesus even prays for those who will come to faith through the preaching of the gospel, a clear reference to the missionary activity of the Johannine school.

In John 4:5–42, Jesus himself appears programmatically as a missionary.[212] He takes all the initiative, speaking to a Samaritan woman at Jacob's well (4:7b), revealing himself as the water of life (4:14b) and as the Messiah (4:26). The interchange leads to a mutual recognition between Jesus and the woman. As Jesus knows the woman's innermost being and discloses her past, so she comes to know the messianic significance of Jesus's person. This results in the Samaritans coming to Jesus (4:27–30), and through Jesus's own word they come to the all-important knowledge: "We know that this is truly the Savior of the world" (4:42). The harvest imagery of 4:38 points to the post-Easter missionary

210. For analysis, cf. Miguel Rodríguez Ruiz, *Der Missionsgedanke des Johannesevangeliums: Ein Beitrag zur johanneischen Soteriologie und Ekklesiologie* (FzB 55; Würzburg: Echter, 1987), 257–76.

211. For interpretation, cf. Rudolf Schnackenburg, "Strukturanalyse von Joh 17," *BZ* 17 (1973): 67–78, 196–202; H. Ritt, *Das Gebet zum Vater* (FzB 36; Stuttgart: Verlag Katholisches Bibelwerk, 1979); Ruiz, *Missionsgedanke*, 222–55; M. T. Sprecher, *Einheitsdenken aus der Perspektive von Joh 17* (EHS 23.495; Frankfurt: Lang, 1993).

212. Cf. here T. Okure, *The Johannine Approach to Mission* (WUNT 2.31; Tübingen: Mohr, 1989).

work of the disciples, which is in continuity with the sending and ministry of Jesus himself. The way Jesus relates to the Samaritan woman is a model that illustrates that both Christian missionaries and those to whom they are sent are challenged to cross over traditional religious and cultural boundaries. The woman of Samaria, who has become a believer, by proclaiming Jesus to the people of her own country, has also become a missionary herself (4:29) who gives her testimony to him (4:39). People are called by Jesus, gathered into the community of faith when they become believers, and then are themselves led to continue the Christian mission.

Post-Easter missionary activity is also evident in the curious reference to the Ἕλληνες (Greeks) in John 7:35–36; 12:20–22.[213] According to 12:20–22, some Greeks at the Passover festival want to see Jesus. They cannot approach him directly, however, but need the mediation of the disciples. At the time the Fourth Gospel was composed, the Johannine school obviously included native-born Greeks. This is also indicated by John 10:16, where Jesus speaks of sheep that do not belong to this fold, but which he wants to gather and include (cf. 11:52 with the motif of gathering "the scattered children of God"). So also, the fruit-bearing in 15:2ff.; 17:3, 9 is a missionary motif, for just as Jesus does the saving will of the Father, so also the disciples are doing this in their own mission. They will even do "greater works" than the Son (14:12). Just as the sending of the Son carries out the saving work of God, so also in the preaching of the Johannine school this same saving will of God for the world is at work. Thus those who receive the ones sent by Jesus receive the Lord himself (13:20). Finally, it is consistent with the Johannine concept of mission that Jesus himself baptizes (4:1), since his saving work is the prototype, basis, and norm of the church's own mission. The importance of the mission concept derives from the fundamental conviction of Johannine theology that in Jesus Christ, God has become a human being in order to open the way of salvation to humanity.

12.8 Eschatology

The theological evaluation of the Johannine understanding of time is a disputed topic. While older research frequently contrasted present and future eschatology, and regarded texts such as John 5:28–29; 6:39–40, 44, 54; 11:25–26; and 12:48 as belonging to a secondary editorial layer, in more recent exegesis an

213. On this point, cf. J. Frey, "Heiden—Griechen—Gotteskinder," in *Die Heiden: Juden, Christen und das Problem des Fremden* (ed. Reinhard Feldmeier and Ulrich Heckel; WUNT 70; Tübingen: Mohr, 1994), 228–68. On the importance of the Gentile mission in John, cf. also Ruiz, *Missionsgedanke*, 73–162. The Johannine letters presuppose both a vigorous mission by itinerant preachers of the Johannine school (cf. 2 John 7a; 3 John 3, 6, 8, 12; 1 John 4:1b) and a methodical, planned Gentile mission (3 John 5–8).

increasing number of voices are speaking in favor of including the statements of future eschatology as an authentic component of the Johannine conception.[214] Methodologically, the hermeneutical perspective of the Fourth Evangelist must, here as elsewhere, form the starting point of all such reflection: the Johannine post-Easter anamnesis. The gospel's dominant statements of present eschatology do not cover the whole spectrum of Johannine eschatology; on the contrary, the specifically Johannine approach also requires affirmations of future eschatology. The post-Easter anamnesis already takes place at some temporal distance from the events narrated in the gospel. From the point of view of the internal narrative level of the gospel, the Johannine Christians are already in the future, so that it is precisely statements of future eschatology in the narrative that can refer to their own present. Faith does not abolish the timeline, with its spectrum of temporal differences, but gives it a new quality and orientation.

12.8.1 The Present

The strong emphasis on the present results from the fundamental experience and conviction that the saving event in Jesus Christ does not merely belong to the past, but is immediately present in its soteriological dimension: in the sacraments and in the works of the Paraclete. Thus for John the levels of time and space collapse into each other.[215] The separated realms of the divine "above" and earthly "below" are united in Jesus Christ. The Revealer who comes "from above" truly enters into the earthly sphere. The believing community is itself involved and included in this mutual interpenetration of "spatial" realms. In baptism as rebirth "from above/anew" (John 3:3, 7), the believer's existence experiences a new orientation. In the eucharist the Johannine community receives the bread of life come from heaven. John 6:51a–b: "I am the living bread that came down from heaven. Whoever eats of this bread will live forever" (cf. 6:33, 50, 58). In the person of the Paraclete, the heavenly Revealer is still present in the church after the ascension; the fundamental distinction between heaven and earth is abrogated precisely by the presence of the Paraclete.

Present Eschatology

The interweaving of spatial categories corresponds in John to an interweaving of temporal levels; events traditionally regarded as future already reach back into the present. The dominance of *statements of present eschatology* in the Fourth

214. Extensive presentations and discussions of the individual positions are found in Frey, *Eschatologie*, vol. 1, passim; cf. further his treatment in J. Frey, "Eschatology in the Johannine Circle," in *Theology and Christology in the Fourth Gospel* (ed. G. van Belle et al.; BETL 184; Louvain: Leuven University Press, 2005), 47–82. Hahn, *Theologie*, 1:597, still argues for classifying John 5:28–29; 6:39–40, 44 as "deutero-Johannine supplements."

215. Cf. Bühner, "Denkstrukturen," 224ff.

Gospel is obvious. The saving reality of eternal life is already present in faith, which means that the step from death into life is not something that happens in the future, but something that for the believer has already taken place in the past (5:24, "Very truly, I tell you, anyone who hears my word and believes him who sent me has eternal life, and does not come under judgment, but has passed from death to life"). The operative reality is thus, "Whoever believes in the Son has eternal life; whoever disobeys the Son will not see life, but must endure God's wrath" (3:36; cf. also 6:47; 8:51; 11:25–26). Because the decision about the future has already been made in the present, believers have already passed through the judgment (3:18; 12:48).[216] Faith already confers full participation in life in the here and now, but whoever does not obey the Son will not see life, for the wrath of God remains on that person (cf. 5:14, 16). So also, the present intrudes into the past: "Before Abraham was, I am" (8:58). Moses already wrote about Jesus (5:46), and Jesus was already before the Baptist (1:15, 30).

Present eschatology corresponds to the primary incarnational feature of Johannine Christology: the decision about life and death is made in the present encounter with Jesus Christ. Believers thus know that, already in the present, they have been delivered from the realm of death, for their existence as new creation from water and Spirit is "from God," and no longer imprisoned in the world.

12.8.2 The Future

The whole spectrum of Johannine theology cannot be reduced to statements about the present.[217] As early as John 5:25, we can see that despite the predominantly present eschatology, John does not avoid or reject the future: "Very truly, I tell you, the hour is coming, and is now here [ἔρχεται ὥρα καὶ νῦν ἐστιν], when the dead will hear the voice of the Son of God, and those who hear will live." The apparent paradox of juxtaposing the expression "the hour is coming, and is now here" with the future forms of 5:25c (ἀκούσουσιν, ζήσουσιν) clearly reveals the bi-temporal thinking of the evangelist: Jesus's utterance of the saying within the narrative "now" of the text and the potential actualization of the saying cannot be located in the same tense. They require a temporal continuum.

Future Eschatology

The gospel contains further examples of statements expressing a future eschatology, as do the Johannine letters (cf. 2 John 7; 1 John 2:18, 25, 28;

216. On the Johannine concept of judgment, cf. Oliver Groll, *Finsternis, Tod und Blindheit als Strafe: Eine exegetische Untersuchung zu den Begriffen krinein, krisis und krima im Johannesevangelium* (EHS 23.781; Frankfurt: Lang, 2004).

217. Contra R. Bultmann and others, who see only the statements of present eschatology as "authentic" Johannine theology. As a key example of Bultmann's approach, see his exegesis of John 5:24–30 in Bultmann, *John*, 257–63.

3:2–3; 4:17), and historical-critical analysis and source-critical judgments cannot eliminate them. In the Farewell Discourses, whose real addressees are the later Christian reader/hearers external to the text,[218] John opens up a future for the Johannine community, and that precisely on the basis of their present experience of salvation, a future characterized both by the work of the Spirit and the expectation of the parousia. In accord with the will of the Father and the Son, they are to deliberately remain in the world (cf. John 17:15a, "I am not asking you to take them out of the world") where they are exposed to the threats and dangers of their time (cf., e.g., 15:18, "If the world hates you, be aware that it hated me before it hated you"). In this situation it may explicitly base its hope on the future act of the Father and the Son, as indicated by 14:2–3, "In my Father's house there are many dwelling places. If it were not so, would I have told you that I go to prepare a place for you? And if I go and prepare a place for you, I will come again and will take you to myself, so that where I am, there you may be also." Here we find two striking statements:

1. After his departure, Jesus prepares dwelling places for believers in heaven.
2. Jesus will come from heaven to take his own to himself.

This can refer only to the parousia of the risen and exalted Christ, as confirmed by the background of the statement in apocalyptic tradition (cf. *1 En.* 14.15–23; 39.4–8; 41.2; 48.1; 71.5–10, 16; *2 En.* 61.2; *Apoc. Abr.* 17.16; 29.15) and the New Testament parallels (esp. 1 Thess. 4:16–17). Decisive for this understanding of the tradition are its statements about time and space. The "house" is a religious metaphor for salvation in which the inhabitants of the heavenly house are delivered from the uncertainties of earthly existence; there they will live in the abiding security of the Father and the Son.[219] The strong future orientation of the saying is directed to helping the community deal with the negative experiences of the present through which the Johannine church is living. Present eschatology is clearly not an adequate answer to the troubles of the present and anxiety about the future. Both the distress of the present and the problem of death make it important and meaningful not to locate the presence of salvation exclusively in the present but to relate present and future together in a meaningful way.

The prospect of Christ's return serves to interpret and overcome the problems of the church's situation: its "sorrow" (λύπη in John 16:6, 20). Only the return of the Son makes possible for believers to have what will deliver them from the troubles of the present and the future: being with the Father forever.

218. On this point, cf. Schnelle, "Abschiedsreden," 66ff.

219. Documentation in *NW* 1.2:667–77; cf. further Euripides, *Alc.* 364–365; Seneca, *Nat.* 6.32.6.

This observation does not relativize the statements about present salvation but makes them more appropriate from the perspective of the reality of the church's present: the life of the believer in the present and the future is encompassed by the saving will and acts of God. The expectation of Christ's parousia, as expressed in 14:18–21, 28; 16:13e, 16, must also be seen in this perspective, for the promise that they will see the Son again is aimed at transforming the sorrow that oppresses the community into eschatological joy (cf. 16:20–22).[220]

The announcement of an *eschatological resurrection* in John 5:28–29; 6:39–40, 44, 54 also aims beyond the world of the narrative to address the hearers/readers. By faith, the Johannine Christians have already stepped out of the realm of death and into the realm of life; the decision made in the present has already decided the future. But faith does not effect the resurrection of the dead. No text in the Johannine writings states that believers are already raised from the dead. *The Johannine concept of life does not exclude the reality of physical death.*[221] On the contrary, the resurrection means the reawakening or re-creation of the body in the encounter with Jesus, to whom the Father has given the authority to raise human beings from the dead (cf. 5:21). This is illustrated, within the narrative world of the text, by the Lazarus pericope (11:1–44), in which Jesus appears as the Lord of life and death. In contrast to Jewish hopes for the future (cf. 11:24), Jesus emphatically states, "I am the resurrection and the life. Those who believe in me, even though they die, will live, and everyone who lives and believes in me will never die" (11:25–26). In the case of Lazarus, Jesus himself meets him and calls him back to life in space and time, so no future, eschatological resurrection is required. In contrast, the Johannine community finds itself in a fundamentally different situation: Jesus is with the Father, and believers will meet him only at the parousia. At his return Jesus will put into effect for believers the destiny that has already been decided, but has not yet become reality: the resurrection of the dead.

The Unity of Johannine Eschatology

Present and future eschatology are not antithetical for John but complementary: what is already firmly decided in the present also has a future reality.[222]

220. On this point, cf. Schnelle, "Abschiedsreden," 68–69, 75–76; Frey, *Eschatologie*, 3:166, 207–15.

221. In particular, the Johannine recoding of the vocabulary of life and death as faith and unbelief is not rescinded in 5:28–29, for those "in their graves" are physically dead, not eschatologically dead. They go on to meet a resurrection to life; i.e., despite their physical death they abide in the life-giving power of God/Jesus; cf. Schnelle, *Das Evangelium nach Johannes*, 122–23.

222. Among those who vote for the view that the substance of Johannine theology necessarily requires affirmations of future eschatology are L. van Hartingsveld, *Die Eschatologie des Johannesevangeliums: Eine Auseinandersetzung mit Rudolf Bultmann* (Assen: Prakke & Prakke, 1962), 48–50; Goppelt and Roloff, *Theology of the New Testament*, 2:303–5; C. K. Barrett, *The Gospel according to St. John* (2nd ed.; Philadelphia: Westminster, 1978), 67–70; Udo Schnelle, *The Human Condition: Anthropology in the Teachings of Jesus, Paul, and John*

Because eschatology is really a dimension of Christology (cf. 5:19–30),[223] statements of present eschatology and future eschatology do not contradict each other, for Jesus Christ is the true giver of life in both present and future. As Son of God, he wills authentic life for human beings; he intervenes for them and, already in the present, opens up full participation in eternal life for them, a life that is not ended by biological death. This fundamental conviction does not abolish the importance of the future, for in the future the resurrection of the dead will reveal what has already been decided in the present. An exclusively present eschatology would drop the future and ideologically inflate the importance of the present, thereby shortchanging the church. The distinctiveness of John's eschatological conception is part and parcel of Johannine thought as a whole: the relation of Father and Son means that both are Lord over time in both its chronological and kairological aspects.* The strong emphasis on the all-embracing presence of salvation emerges from the incarnation of the Son of God. The continuing work of the Paraclete means that, for the church, the saving acts of the Father and the Son encompass the future as well.

12.9 Setting in the History of Early Christian Theology

The Gospel of John, which represents the high point of the formation of early Christian theology, can be categorized as a "master narrative." One recent theorist says that a master narrative (*Meistererzählung*) gives people "an image of their affiliation, their collective identity: stories of the founding and success of the national group, stories of religious salvation."[224] When

(trans. O. C. Dean Jr.; Minneapolis: Fortress, 1996), 130–34; Joachim Gnilka, *Theologie des Neuen Testaments* (HTKNT 5; Freiburg: Herder, 1994), 298–99; Strecker, *Theology of the New Testament*, 496–98; Ulrich Wilckens, *Das Johannesevangelium* (NTD 4; Göttingen: Vandenhoeck & Ruprecht, 1998), 121; Frey, *Eschatologie*, 3:85–87 and passim; Ludger Schenke, *Johannes: Kommentar* (Düsseldorf: Patmos, 1998), 108–9; Wengst, *Johannesevangelium*, 202–3; Popkes, *Theologie der Liebe Gottes*, 101–2; Thyen, *Johannesevangelium*, 313–18, 528. The contrary position is advocated by, among others, Jürgen Becker, "Die Hoffnung auf ewiges Leben im Johannesevangelium," *ZNW* 91 (2000): 192–211.

223. On the interpretation of this key text, cf. Frey, *Eschatologie*, 3:322–400, who works out a careful and persuasive argument for the unity of present and future eschatology in John. The matter is differently accented by Kammler, *Christologie und Eschatologie*, who argues that John consistently advocates a strictly present eschatology. A mediating position is taken by Hans-Joachim Eckstein, "Die Gegenwart im Licht der erinnerten Zukunft: Zur modalisierten Zeit im Johannesevangelium," in *Der aus Glauben Gerechte wird leben* (ed. Hans-Joachim Eckstein; BVB 5; Münster: Lit, 2003), 204, who argues that present eschatology is the basic Johannine model but adjusts this view on the basis of his theory of time.

*[The terminology reflects the distinction often made between linear, chronological time (χρόνος) and special, fulfilled time (καιρός); but see James Barr, *Biblical Words for Time* (SBT 33; Naperville, IL: Allenson, 1962).—MEB]

224. Jörn Rüsen, "Kann gestern besser werden? Über die Verwandlung der Vergangenheit in Geschichte," in *Kann gestern besser werden?* (ed. Jörn Rüsen; Berlin: Kadmos, 2003), 29–30.

such a meaning-structure arises, its power depends on its content, or rather on the interplay of form and specific content: content that has the power to captivate is given a virtuoso performance. John was very well aware of the fundamental issues involved in representing the past through historical writing; he worked with his material and transposed it in theological and literary terms to produce his Jesus-Christ-history. It was clear to him that events of the past attain the status of history only when they are appropriated through the process of historical meaning-formation. The Fourth Gospel is the result of such a process of appropriation.

An Introduction to Christianity

The Gospel of John thus attains the quality of a primer in Christianity. John *unites two main streams of early Christian theological formation*:[225] while Paul presents a Jesus-Christ-history oriented to the kerygma, Mark develops a narrative Jesus-Christ-history. John unites both tendencies, in that *he consistently presents the memory of the earthly Jesus from the perspective of the exalted Lord*. He takes over the gospel genre, expands it in continuity with Paul[226] by way of his preexistence Christology, and intensifies (differently than Matthew and Luke) the theology of the cross that predominates in Mark and especially in Paul. The point of departure for this line of thought is (as already for Paul and Mark) the *character of the cross as disruptive discontinuity*. *Theologically*, the cross shatters all ancient concepts of deity, for it can no more be combined with Yahweh, the powerful God of history, than it can be integrated into any form of Greco-Roman theology. In terms of *narrative*, the cross breaks through the conventional structure of all events from beginning to end and opens a new narrative dimension through the resurrection. *The cross thus undergoes a broadening of its semantic field and an intensification of its literary-rhetorical*

225. Theissen, *Religion of the Earliest Churches*, 185: "This forms a synthesis of two developments which run towards each other. On the one hand we find in Paul belief in the Exalted One with divine status—and observe how individual recollections of the Earthly One are fragmentarily combined with this picture of Jesus, without the formation of a consecutive narrative. On the other hand, the tradition of the Earthly One formed in the Synoptic tradition and the first Gospels is increasingly permeated by the sovereignty of the Exalted One without belief in the preexistence of Jesus developing in the Synoptic Gospels. In the Gospel of John both strands of the development are fused. Everywhere the glory of the Exalted One shines through the activity of the Earthly One."

226. On the relation between John and Paul, cf. Rudolf Schnackenburg, "Paulinische und johanneische Christologie," in *Das Johannesevangelium* (ed. Rudolf Schnackenburg; HTKNT 4; 4 vols.; Freiburg: Herder, 1984), 102–18 (this section is not included in the English translation); Dieter Zeller, "Paulus und Johannes," *BZ* 27 (1983): 167–82; Rudolf Schnackenburg, "Ephesus: Entwicklung einer Gemeinde von Paulus zu Johannes," *BZ* 35 (1991): 41–64; Christina Hoegen-Rohls, "Johanneische Theologie im Kontext paulinischen Denkens?" in *Kontexte des Johannesevangeliums* (ed. Albert Frey and Udo Schnelle; WUNT 175; Tübingen: Mohr, 2004), 593–612.

function, in that it becomes the abbreviation of a total, complex event. Mark and John (like Paul before them) grasp this potential. Their conceptualizing and composing work transposes the historical and theological significance of the cross into their respective paradigmatic narratives.

In the Fourth Gospel the exalted status of the resurrected Lord permeates the portrayal of the earthly Jesus more strongly than in Mark. Compared to Paul, John goes beyond a high Christology structured and expressed primarily in terms of discursive language; he transforms it into a dramatic narrative about the pre-Easter Jesus.[227] He is clear about the perspectival nature of historical knowledge and understands that in the telling of his story the events and the creative appropriation (through the Paraclete) of the events are indissolubly interwoven. He broadens the linguistic and theological presentation of the Christ event in order to enable a new perspective that can strengthen his community's threatened identity.

The presentation of the Jesus-Christ-history in the genre "gospel" has the goal of making the event that really happened what it was from the very beginning and what it can always be, and doing this through the narrative mode. It is thus clear in the Fourth Gospel that in the debate between faith and unbelief one sees that form of narrative structure by which the event that occurred is both pushed forward and differentiated. The Gospel of John was written in order to show that God's unconditional love creates and sustains all life in order to reach its goal in the faith of human beings. Both prologue (1:1–18) and epilogue (20:30–31) formulate this fundamental insight. As the boundary markers of the work, they set it in a particular narrative framework and show how readers can enter the story world of the narrative, facilitating the increased understanding that can be attained through such an appropriate reading. John stage-manages his Jesus-Christ-history by a skillfully arranged series of dialogical and monological scenes. He constructs a systematic network in which the narrative sections are interrelated by the key characters and concepts. John presents his readers with the Jesus-Christ-history in new concepts, images, and narratives (cf. 1:2–11; 3:1–11; 4:4–42; 10:1–18; 13:1–20; 15:1–8; 20:11–18), and he introduces new characters, names, and groups into his Jesus-Christ-history (Nathanael, 1:45–49; Nicodemus, 1:1, 4, 9; 7:50; 19:39; the "Greeks," 7:35; 12:20ff.; Malchus, 18:20, 26; Annas, 18:13, 24).

Through the literary techniques of repetition, variation, and amplification, through quotations, number symbolism, and expressions with multiple layers of meaning, through symbolic sayings and speeches, wordplays and irony, through key words and concepts, John opens to his hearers/readers, as they make their way through the gospel, a symbolic universe oriented to incarnation, the Spirit,

227. Cf. Udo Schnelle, "Theologie als kreative Sinnbildung: Johannes als Weiterbildung von Paulus und Markus," in *Johannesevangelium, Mitte oder Rand des Kanons? Neue Standortbestimmungen* (ed. Klaus Berger et al.; QD 203; Freiburg i.B.: Herder, 2003), 119–45.

and the theology of the cross.[228] In a reflective, meditative mode, the evangelist circles around the primeval mystery of the incarnation of God in Jesus Christ and creates a new symbolic picture-language of faith, at the center of which stand symbols and metaphors that are at once simple and intuitive. This symbolic language works directly on the hearers/readers, since it simultaneously facilitates understanding at both the intellectual and emotional levels. John takes up the fundamental phenomena of religious life that are common across many different cultures—such as God and world, above and below, light and darkness, death and life, truth and lie, birth and rebirth, water, bread, hunger and thirst, eating and drinking—in order to fill them with new positive content in Jesus Christ. This metaphorical Christology reaches its high point in the "I am" sayings (see above, §12.2.3) and is so oriented that it illuminates the mystery of Jesus Christ without binding itself to a particular linguistic implementation. It thus facilitates and guides that thought process triggered by reading the gospel as an introduction to the basic issues of Christian faith.

The Gospel of John presents itself as an *introduction to Christianity* and the first *textbook of religious education* in early Christianity (20:30–31) by working through and answering *all the central questions* of the new symbolic universe. The prologue already links time and eternity to the Logos and delineates the unique relationship between God and the Logos Jesus Christ, who, as the Creator, is the source of all life. God's truth and glory are visible in him alone. From Jesus's own mouth, believers learn what birth and rebirth are (chap. 3), who it is that really satisfies the thirst for life, who it is that gives eternal life (chaps. 4; 6), and who, already in the present, is Lord of life and death (chaps. 5; 11). The way of the man born blind (chap. 9) provides a new orientation for the church, just as do the Good Shepherd discourse (chap. 10) and the Farewell Discourses (13:31–16:33). The latter formulate the theological value of Jesus's departure, and, like the high-priestly prayer (chap. 17), place the Passion events in a new perspective. Intentionally and sovereignly, Jesus goes the way that leads to the cross, for he knows the deepest meaning of this event and permits the disciples to participate in the reality of his death and life (20:24–29). Because the coming of the Paraclete depends on the departure of Jesus, only after Easter can the events prior to Easter, as well as the Easter event itself, be understood (cf. 20:29b, "Blessed are those who have not seen and yet have come to believe"). Only from this perspective can the significance of what happened in the past be perceived and understood. The presupposition for this tight line of argument is understanding the relation of Father, Son, and Spirit, which John, as the pioneering theologian in early Christianity, was the first to undertake in a comprehensive way. On the whole, John shows himself to be a master of interpretative integration. He takes up the very different streams of tradition and brings them together under the heading of God's love to humanity in Jesus Christ.

228. Cf. Popp, *Grammatik*, 457–91.

The Last Word in Appropriation and Integration

The systematic quality of Johannine theology is clearly seen in the fact that the gospel cannot be adequately portrayed as a debate with contemporary Judaism[229] or Gnostic streams of thought; neither can it be grasped by way of historical-critical separation into layers of tradition. None of these approaches has a sufficient grasp of the literary artistry and intellectual achievement of the Fourth Evangelist. Neither the (supposed) analysis and labeling of history-of-religions views (e.g., dualism) nor the (postulated) amendments and expansions of texts (e.g., in the Farewell Discourses) can provide the methodological point of departure for understanding the gospel. We must approach the extant text in terms of its own content and theology. Here it becomes apparent that the numerous internal intertwinings/emphases in the gospel are components/variations of its fundamental theological agenda: the revelation of the love of God in Jesus Christ as the love of God for the world and for believers, for whom abiding in God and Jesus Christ is implemented and fulfilled as abiding in love. Neither history-of-religions prejudgments nor the reductionistic application of source analysis do justice to this central meaning. On the whole, the Gospel of John occupies a key position within early Christianity: it not only concludes the formation of New Testament theology on the highest level, but also—in particular by its use of the concepts and terminology of the Logos, truth, and freedom—provides an opening for the Christian faith in Greco-Roman intellectual history. It thereby at the same time prepares the transition to the early catholic church.[230] The Johannine prologue's identification of Jesus Christ with the primary concept in the intellectual history of Greco-Roman culture puts forward an absolutely unique claim: the whole history of ancient religion and culture finds its consummation in the Logos Jesus Christ, the origin and goal of all that is. The apologists will take up and develop this claim before it ultimately becomes a major topic in the christological debates of the third and fourth centuries.

229. Cf. J. Frey, "Das Bild 'der Juden' im Johanneischen Gemeinde," in *Israel und seine Heilstraditionen im Johannessevangelium: Festgabe für Johannes Beutler SJ zum 70. Geburtstag* (ed. Michael Labahn et al.; Paderborn: Schöningh, 2004), 33–53. Frey emphasizes (as do Schnelle and Hengel) that the dispute with Judaism is not the key to the historical and theological world of the Fourth Gospel; differently, J. Louis Martyn, *History and Theology in the Fourth Gospel* (rev. and exp. ed.; Nashville: Abingdon, 1979) and Klaus Wengst, *Bedrängte Gemeinde und verherrlichter Christus: Ein Versuch über das Johannesevangelium* (4th ed.; Munich: Kaiser, 1992).

230. On this point, cf. Titus Nagel, *Die Rezeption des Johannesevangeliums im 2. Jahrhundert: Studien zur vorirenäischen Aneignung und Auslegung des vierten Evangeliums in christlicher und christlich-gnostischer Literatur* (ABG 2; Leipzig: Evangelische Verlagsanstalt, 2000).

13

Revelation

Seeing and Understanding

In antiquity, all religious life was fundamentally determined by ritually ordered cultic worship, which was thus a central element in the formation of every symbolic universe and the meaning of life itself. On this basis, the Revelation of John develops an impressive sacral architecture. By presenting a heavenly cultic reality within the framework of an apocalyptic vision of history, it provides a new interpretation for earthly events and experiences.[1] In the context of persecution of Christians in Asia Minor under Domitian (ca. 95 CE),[2] the author develops a theology in visionary pictures of the cultic reality in heaven and on earth, aiming to strengthen the threatened identity of his churches and to orient it by this new symbolic universe. At the same time, this cultic thought world grants participation in the event itself, for Revelation was written to be read out in the worship services (Rev. 1:3, "Blessed is the one who reads aloud the words of the prophecy, and blessed are those who hear and who keep what is written in it, for the time is near"; cf. 22:18). The goal is that the churches addressed will understand their present danger and experience God's

1. The variety of imagery and references to space and time bear traits from the realms of both Jewish and Hellenistic traditions; cf. the comprehensive treatment of Franz Tóth, *Der himmlische Kult: Wirklichkeitskonstruktion und Sinnbildung in der Johannesoffenbarung* (ABG 22; Leipzig: Evangelische Verlag, 2006), 48–156. The Hellenistic context, long underrated, has been rightly emphasized by Otto Böcher, "Hellenistisches in der Apokalypse des Johannes," in *Geschichte—Tradition—Reflexion: Festschrift für Martin Hengel zum 70. Geburtstag* (ed. Hubert Cancik et al.; Tübingen: Mohr, 1996), 473–92.

2. On introductory issues, cf. Schnelle, *New Testament Writings*, 517–38.

ultimate victory over evil.[3] The way Revelation is constructed also facilitates this interweaving of temporal levels, for the messages to the seven churches address the present (2–3) and the following visions (4–22) portray the future, with 1:9–20 introducing both main sections.[4] "Thus the introductory messages to the churches are a guide to the readers in how to understand the visions: the readers do not view the surface level of the factual world in which they live, but it becomes transparent to the deeper meaning from which they can truly live."[5] The Revelation is intended not to conceal but to reveal,[6] to make things visible and understandable; its goal is not speculative *fore*sight, but theological *in*sight.

13.1 Theology

The fundamental assurance presented by the Apocalypse is the insight that God, the Lord of history, upholds and finally determines all things.[7] The framing of the whole composition between Rev. 1:8 ("'I am the Alpha and the Omega,' says the Lord God, who is and who was and who is to come, the Almighty") and 21:6 ("I am the Alpha and the Omega, the Beginning and the End") clearly reveals the theocentric structure of Revelation: from the perspective of the reality of this God, both the believers' own present history and situation and their future in heaven and on earth become transparently clear. The Jewish Christian prophet John (1:2; 10:11; 19:10; 22:7, 9, 10, 18, 19) takes up specific Old Testament divine predications. For instance, the triadic formulae in 1:4, 8, 17; 2:8; 4:8; 11:17; 16:5; 21:6; 22:13 are variations of Exod. 3:14 and Isa. 44:6 and also have notable parallels

3. Revelation's cultic line of thought provides the point of contact for the concluding prayer for the coming of the Lord (22:21) and the responsive pronouncement of grace (cf. 1 Cor. 16:22, 23); cf. Jürgen Roloff, *The Revelation of John* (trans. John E. Alsup; Continental Commentary; Minneapolis: Fortress, 1993), 254.

4. Cf. Ferdinand Hahn, "Zum Aufbau der Johannesoffenbarung," in *Kirche und Bibel: Festgabe für Bischof Eduard Schick* (ed. Fulda Professoren der Phil.-Theol. Hochschule; Paderborn: Schöningh, 1979), 145–54. For the variety of possible structural arrangements of the Apocalypse, cf. Otto Böcher, ed., *Die Johannesapokalypse* (EF 41; Darmstadt: Wissenschaftliche Buchgesellschaft, 1980), 605–8 (605: "a logical structure of Revelation is not easy to recognize").

5. K. Backhaus, "Apokalyptische Bilder? Die Vernunft der Vision in der Johannes-Offenbarung," *EvT* 64 (2004): 424.

6. The verb ἀνοίγω (open) is found in no other New Testament document so frequently as in Revelation (27 times). Key passages are: 4:1 (opening of the heavenly door); 11:19 (opening of the heavenly sanctuary); 19:11 (opening of heaven for the final heavenly victory); cf. ibid., 426–27.

7. Appropriately K. Backhaus, "Die Vision vom ganz Anderen," in *Theologie als Vision: Studien zur Johannes-Offenbarung* (ed. Knut Backhaus; SBS 191; Stuttgart: Verlag Katholisches Bibelwerk, 2001), 26: "The seer argues for a theocentric understanding of Christian identity, which for him includes a refusal to be integrated into the Roman imperial world of Asia Minor."

in the pagan all-formulae.[8] In contrast to self-deifying earthly rulers, God appears as the παντοκράτωρ, the Almighty (Rev. 1:8; 4:8; 11:17; 16:7, 14; 19:6, 15; 21:22), i.e., as the One who truly is and rules.[9] Corresponding to Revelation's dynamic picture of God, the triadic formulations do not portray individual aspects of God's action but overlap and permeate each other, for the presence of God embraces and transcends all temporal dimensions. God's reign, which has already begun (11:17, "We give you thanks, Lord God Almighty, who are and who were, for you have taken your great power and begun to reign"), and the statements about his coming (1:4, 7–8; 4:8) are components of a view of history that comprehends God's rule in heaven and the execution of this rule on earth as a unity. God sits on his throne (7:10–11, 15–16; 11:16; 12:5; 21:5; 22:1, 3). His heaven spans the whole earth, his dominating power shines forth throughout the universe, and every being in heaven and on earth must worship him. The seer's thought is determined by God's function as ruler and judge, so that world history is interpreted as end history. God's creative act before all time (cf. 4:11; 10:6; 14:7) has its counterpart in God's eschatological act, so that the operative principle is: "See, I am making all things new" (21:5).[10] The devil, in his earthly form as the dragon (12:12–13), is allowed to threaten the church for only a short time, for God is coming (cf. 1:4, 8; 4:8; 22:6–7). God will soon destroy the embodiment of Satan in the Roman Empire and all the godless. At the end, God will remain faithful to the covenant people: "See, the home of God is among mortals. He will dwell with them as their God; they will be his peoples, and God himself will be with them" (21:3). Living in the presence of God will remove the tension between present troubles, the kingdom of God in process of realization, and the ultimate victory of God. A *political theology* is also involved, for John gives a clear No! to the political religion of the Caesar cult and the church's possible cooperation with it (cf. 2:14).[11] There is only one Lord, one God, who rules and who is to be worshiped.

8. On this point, cf. Gerhard Delling, "Zum gottesdienstlichen Stil der Johannes-Apokalypse," in *Studien zum Neuen Testament und zum hellenistischen Judentum: Gesammelte Aufsätze 1950–1968* (ed. Ferdinand Hahn et al.; Göttingen: Vandenhoeck & Ruprecht, 1970), 439–42; cf. also the texts in *NW* 2.2:1455–56, 1649–51, 1668.

9. For Old Testament background, cf. ibid., 442–48.

10. Cf. Traugott Holtz, "Gott in der Apokalypse," in *Geschichte und Theologie des Urchristentums: Gesammelte Aufsätze* (ed. Traugott Holtz et al.; WUNT 57; Tübingen: Mohr, 1991), 332: "Thus God, precisely because he is the Creator, always also the God who is present"; C. G. Müller, "Gott wird alle Tränen abwischen—Offb 21,4: Anmerkungen zum Gottesbild der Apokalypse," *TGl* 95 (2005): 292: "The assurance, 'See, I am making everything new,' occurs in the Apocalypse of John first and foremost in the threatened and endangered present." Cf. also M. Eugene Boring, "The Theology of Revelation: 'The Lord our God the Almighty Reigns,'" *Int* 40 (1986): 257–69; Richard Bauckham, "God in the Book of Revelation," *PIBA* 18 (1995): 40–53.

11. Cf. Thomas Söding, "Heilig, Heilig, Heilig: Zur politischen Theologie der Johannes-Apokalypse," *ZTK* 96 (1999): 53: "Over against this, John places *his* political theology with its absolute claim, superior power, true justice, and God alone as its final goal."

Thus the expression ὁ κύριος καὶ ὁ θεὸς ἡμῶν (our Lord and God) in Rev. 4:11 is formulated as a direct antithesis to the address Domitian required of his subjects, "dominus et deus noster" (see Suetonius, *Dom.* 13.2; see also Rev. 15:4; 19:10; 20:4; 22:9).[12] The fundamentally theocentric nature of Revelation's theology is the consistent result of John's concept of God, which focuses on power, lordship, and judgment (11:17; 15:3, 8; 19:1, 5–6, 15; 20:4; 22:5).[13] The seer John writes his work within the horizon of the kingdom of God, which has already broken in and is on the way to its ultimate victory. Everything in the universe is moving toward the final revelation of God's glory (21:11, 22–23). *The main theological theme of Revelation is the coming of God.* This theme determines all cultic events and is the transcendent reality that drives the narrative. God is the eschatological Coming One who has appeared in Jesus Christ for judgment and salvation. In the performance of ritual acts of worship, this reality of the coming and presence of God is redefined in a way that transcends both Jewish temple and Caesar cult.

The Apocalypse as a whole "is concerned to establish the validity and certitude of the lordship of God and Jesus as his anointed, the Lamb, which grants and guarantees salvation to those who belong to them."[14] The mythological language and imagery also are in the service of this concern; "The Dass, not the Was or Wie, is the focus of John's concern."[15] A linear conception of eschatological history does not do justice to this fundamental perspective, which is better conceived as a series of concentric circles, with the already inaugurated kingdom of God and of Jesus serving as both foundation and center of the seer's thought.

13.2 Christology

As elsewhere in the New Testament, so also in the Apocalypse: theology and Christology stand over against each other in a relationship of generative tension.[16] The foundation of Christology is the saving act of God in Jesus Christ,

12. Additional traits critical of the imperial cult are noted by Martin Karrer, "Stärken des Randes: Die Johannesoffenbarung," in *Das Urchristentum in seiner literarischen Geschichte: Festschrift für Jürgen Becker zum 65. Geburtstag* (ed. Ulrich Mell and Ulrich B. Müller; BZNW 100; New York: de Gruyter, 1999), 411–16; Tóth, *Kult,* 302–5; on the infrastructure of the Caesar cult in Rome and in Asia Minor, cf. Tóth, *Kult,* 82–120.

13. On the concept of judgment, cf. Holtz, "Gott in der Apokalypse," 340–42.

14. Martin Karrer, *Die Johannesoffenbarung als Brief: Studien zu ihrem literarischen, historischen und theologischen Ort* (FRLANT 140; Göttingen: Vandenhoeck & Ruprecht, 1986), 147.

15. M. Eugene Boring, "Narrative Christology in the Apocalypse," *CBQ* 54 (1992): 718.

16. On this point cf. Thomas Söding, "Gott und das Lamm, Theozentrik und Christologie in der Johannesapokalypse," in *Theologie als Vision: Studien zur Johannes-Offenbarung* (ed. Knut Backhaus; SBS 191; Stuttgart: Verlag Katholisches Bibelwerk, 2001), 77–120; and Richard

for it establishes eschatological salvation and delivers from the realm of the powers of this world that resist God (cf., e.g., Rev. 1:5b–6; 5:9–10; 7:15; 12:11). On the one hand, in Revelation Christ or the Lamb is clearly subordinate to God. At the beginning stands God's word, which the testimony of Christ and the church follow (1:2); Christ is the "faithful witness" (1:5; 3:14), but not the ultimate cause of the event; the vision of God in 4:1–11 precedes and is the basis for the vision of Christ in Rev. 5. So also all the decisive affirmations are first about God, and then transferred to Christ (cf. the Alpha-Omega predicate in 1:8 and 22:13; the motif of "coming" in 1:4 and 1:7);[17] God alone is the "Father" (1:6; 2:28; 3:5, 21; 14:1).[18] The "holy, holy, holy" formula is directed only to God (4:8); God is creator of heaven and earth (4:11; 10:6), while Christ is the first/beginning of creation (3:14); as "Pantocrator," God alone is lord of history and stands over all (e.g., 11:17; 15:3; 16:7). God sits on the throne, where he is joined by the Lamb (1:4–5; 3:21; 4:2; 5:6–7, 13; 6:16; 7:10, 17; 21:3; 22:1, 3); the Lamb receives the book with the "seven seals" from the One seated on the throne (5:7). God initiates the final act of the drama of salvation (20:1–8), and God alone conducts the final judgment (20:11–15).

On the other hand, this clear primacy of theology in Revelation has its counterpart in the comprehensive participation of Jesus in the work of God, yielding a Christology with a theocentric profile. The first sentence of Revelation already undertakes to state the relationship between God and Christ: "The revelation of Jesus Christ, which God gave him" (Rev. 1:1a). The *authorial genitive* Ἰησοῦ Χριστοῦ grounds a *christological* theology of revelation, which eventuates in the testimony of the seer and the churches (1:3). Doxologies refer not only to God, but to Jesus (1:5, 6); like God (4:9–10), so also Jesus is "the Living One" (1:18a); Jesus alone refers to God as "my Father" (2:28; 3:5, 21); "the Coming One" is a designation for God, but Jesus too is "the Coming One" (1:7; 2:5, 16, 25; 3:11; 16:15; 22:7, 12, 17, 20). God's handing over of historical power and the authority to judge to the Lamb (chaps. 5ff.) is always also a transfer of power and authority, so that Jesus Christ now acts in God's place (6:15–17); like God, Jesus too is "holy" (3:7); according to 5:13, worship and praise are due "to the One who sits on the throne, and to the Lamb"; as for God, the attribute "Alpha and Omega" applies also to Jesus (22:13). Jesus Christ is "king of kings/the nations" (1:5; 17:14; 19:15–16), just as is God (15:3); God and Christ act together, are fused into one acting subject (11:15; 22:3–4); and, finally, both God and the Lamb call forth the new Jerusalem (21:22; 22:3b–4).

This tension cannot be resolved in one direction or the other but corresponds to the dynamic of the work as a whole and is carried along and borne up by

---

Bauckham, *The Theology of the Book of Revelation* (NTTh; Cambridge: Cambridge University Press, 1993), passim.

17. Cf. ibid., 109.

18. Cf. also the expression "his anointed one" in Rev. 11:15; 12:10; 20:4, 6.

this dynamic. Thus Rev. 1:17; 2:28; 3:14b can be claimed for preexistence Christology,[19] but it is also true that the child is born from a woman, "But her child was snatched away and taken to God and to his throne" (12:5). Neither the thesis of an "equality of essence and unity in being,"[20] nor exaltation as a merely functional description[21] grasps the dynamic of Revelation's Christology, which can be appropriately described as *total participation of Jesus in God's rulership*: the deity of Jesus Christ and the primacy of the Father are both equally valid statements of the divine reality, without the distinction in persons being dissolved.[22]

Christological Titles

Jesus's unique role and status is expressed in the title "*Lamb*" (ἀρνίον used twenty-eight times as a title in Revelation),[23] which includes both Jesus's giving himself for his own and his status as ruler (Rev. 5:6).[24] The majestic dignity of the Lamb is based on his lowliness (5:6, 9, 12; 13:8, the slaughtered Lamb); the firstborn of the dead (1:5) is at the same time the slaughtered lamb. The aspect of the Lamb's lordship is expressed particularly by the image of the Lamb

19. Traugott Holtz, *Die Christologie der Apokalypse des Johannes* (2nd rev. and exp. ed.; TUGAL 85; Berlin: Akademie Verlag, 1971), 143–54, derives preexistence from the concept of exaltation; on the other hand, Otfried Hofius, "Das Zeugnis der Johannesoffenbarung von der Gottheit Jesu Christi," in *Neutestamentliche Studien* (ed. Otfried Hofius; WUNT 132; Tübingen: Mohr, 2000), 228–29, makes preexistence an attribute of Christ's essential unity with God. Martin Hengel, "Die Throngemeinschaft des Lammes mit Gott in der Johannesoffenbarung," *ThB* 27 (1996): 174, speaks of a preexistence Christology *in statu nascendi* (in a nascent state) which is presupposed by the concept of incarnation. In all this, one must be clear first of all that Revelation speaks neither of the preexistence nor or the incarnation of Christ.

20. So Hofius, "Gottheit Jesu Christi," 235.

21. For Holtz, *Christologie der Apokalypse*, 213 and elsewhere, the dominant form of Christology in Revelation is an exaltation Christology, indicated especially by the enthronement and the handing over of the book in Rev. 5; Ulrich B. Müller, *Die Offenbarung des Johannes* (ÖTK 19; Gütersloh: Gütersloher Verlagshaus, 1984), 55–56, speaks of a "functional unity . . . without any thought of an ontological equality with God."

22. Cf. Dieter Sänger, "'Amen, komm, Herr Jesus!' (Apk 22,20): Anmerkungen zur Christologie der Johannes-Apokalypse," in *Studien zur Johannesoffenbarung und ihrer Auslegung: Festschrift für Otto Böcher zum 70. Geburtstag* (ed. Friedrich Wilhelm Horn and Michael Wolter; Neukirchen-Vluyn: Neukirchener Verlag, 2005), 91.

23. On this point, cf. Holtz, *Christologie der Apokalypse*, 78–80; Müller, *Offenbarung*, 160–62; Peter Stuhlmacher, "Das Lamm Gottes—eine Skizze," in *Geschichte—Tradition—Reflexion: Festschrift für Martin Hengel zum 70. Geburtstag* (ed. Hubert Cancik et al.; Tübingen: Mohr, 1996), 530–41.

24. The translation is disputed; cf. Böcher, ed., *Johannesapokalypse*, 47; Karrer, "Stärken," 406–8, who translate ἀρνίον with "ram," in order to unite weakness with the power of the heavenly Messiah. In contrast, Otfried Hofius, "'Ἀρνίον—Widder oder Lamm?" in *Neutestamentliche Studien* (ed. Otfried Hofius; WUNT 132; Tübingen: Mohr, 2000), 241–50, consistently argues that ἀρνίον should consistently be translated "Lamb" in Revelation.

who shares God's throne (7:9–10; 21:22; 22:1, 3); the Lamb carries out God's judgment, and has military functions (6:16; 17:14); he stands as a conqueror on Mt. Zion (14:1); he redeems through his blood (7:14, 17; 12:11; 13:8; 14:4) and obtains life for the church (19:7, 9; 21:9, 27). In Revelation, too, death is the presupposition for his position as Lord (5:12, "Worthy is the Lamb that was slaughtered to receive power and wealth and wisdom and might and honor and glory and blessing").

Another central christological figure is the "one like the Son of Man" (Rev. 1:13; 14:14, ὅμοιον υἱὸν ἀνθρώπου).[25] He is introduced in the call vision in 1:11–12 and more fully described in the prolepsis of the final judgment in 14:14. The portrayal is oriented to Dan. 7:9, 13; 10:5–6 and finds its fulfillment in Christ's functions as ruler and judge in the figure of the "one like the Son of Man."[26] In Rev. 19:11–21 Christ appears as the *divine knight and warrior* who defeats the anti-God Beast. The classical christological titles are amazingly rare in Revelation. "Son of God" (υἱὸς θεοῦ) is found only in 2:18, while in 21:7 all church members are designated "sons" (interpreting 2 Sam. 7:14; NRSV "children"). Jesus appear as κύριος (Lord) in his ruling function in Rev. 11:8; 14:13; 17:14; 19:16; 22:20–21, while elsewhere κύριος always refers to God (11:4, 15, 17; 15:3–4; 16:7; 18:8; 19:6; 21:22; 22:5). So also, the Χριστός title (anointed, Messiah, Christ) expresses Jesus's exalted position (1:1, 2, the "revelation" of Jesus Christ; 1:5, the firstborn of the dead and Lord over the kings of the earth; 11:15; 12:10, Christ rules over the empires of the world and over Satan; 20:4, 6, the thousand-year reign). According to 19:13, Jesus bears the name "The Word of God" (ὁ λόγος τοῦ θεοῦ), by which no ontological claim is intended; rather, as the word of God, Christ "embodies the divine dealings."[27]

Narrative Christology

As in Revelation as a whole, so also its Christology is borne along by a movement: it begins with the presentation (Rev. 1:4–8) and commissioning (1:9–20), which already comprehensively present the theme of Christ's work of redemption. This prologue has its counterpart in the epilogue of 19:11–22:5,

25. For analysis, cf. M.-E. Herghelegiu, *Sieh, er kommt mit den Wolken: Studien zur Christologie der Johannesoffenbarung* (EHS 23.785; Frankfurt: Lang, 2004), 111–74.

26. The portrayal of the "one like the Son of Man" in the context of angels (cf. Rev. 14), as well as the analogies between angelology and Christology in Rev. 1:12–20; 10:1; 15:6 have repeatedly raised the issue of whether one can speak of an angel Christology in Revelation. On this subject, cf. Stuckenbruck, *Angel Veneration*, who shows that in Revelation some of the views of angel worship in ancient Judaism are incorporated, but at the same time they are criticized (Rev. 19:10; 22:8–9) and, in the form of the slaughtered Lamb, are surpassed.

27. Heinrich Kraft, *Die Offenbarung des Johannes* (HNT 16a; Tübingen: Mohr, 1974), 249.

which portrays the consummation of God's plan for history. The transfer of the Alpha-Omega predication from God (1:8) to Christ (22:13) and the motif of "coming" (1:7–8; 22:17, 20) clarify these connections. Surrounded by these heavenly realities, the churches of the seven messages of 2:1–3:22 suffer no loss from the oppressive reality in which they live but themselves appear in a different light that emanates from this heavenly reality. With the opening of heaven in 4:1, a new perspective is introduced that determines this whole major section until in 19:1 the heaven opens again to reveal the victory of the concluding final act.[28] The throne room vision of 4:1–5:14 has a key function,[29] in which the dominant theme is the reality of the kingdom of God and Christ that has already broken in to this world. The heavenly throne room is opened, so that (as in worship) there can be an encounter between believers and the reality of God/the Lamb. Christologically, the event of the cross stands at the central point, so that 1:5 is taken up by 5:9b–10, "You are worthy to take the scroll and to open its seals, for you were slaughtered and by your blood you ransomed for God saints from every tribe and language and people and nation; you have made them to be a kingdom and priests serving our God, and they will reign on earth." The "slaughtered Lamb" (5:6, 12; 13:8) stands at the center of Revelation's *theology of the cross*,[30] the Lamb whose blood by his death and resurrection purchases the people of God (see below, §13.4). The sacrificed Lamb and the risen and exalted Lord are identical (1:5), for it is Jesus's death on the cross that establishes his position as heavenly ruler and judge; as such, he is and remains the slaughtered Lamb (19:13). From this affirmation of salvation, in the indicative mode, the church may look forward in confidence to the revelation of the Coming One. The opening of the seven seals in 6:1–8:1 introduces the portrayal of the power of the Lamb that is now put into effect. Further visions are summarized in cycles of seven trumpets (8:2–14:20) and seven bowls (15:1–19:10). In the center of all this stands Jesus Christ, who functions as ruler, judge, and warrior. The plot is carried forward from 12:1 on by new actors, the woman (12:1) and the dragon (12:3), as emphatically presented in the following narrative. The Beast vision of Rev. 13 is designed as the counterpart of the savior-figure of the Lamb in Rev. 5. The vision of salvation in Rev. 14 and the appended series of plagues in 15:1–6 correspond to the sequence in Rev. 7 and 8–9. The Babylon-complex

28. Cf. Backhaus, "Apokalyptische Bilder," 426–27.

29. Cf. Roloff, *Revelation*, 66, who sees this text as the theological center of Revelation. On Rev. 5, cf. also Holtz, *Christologie der Apokalypse*, 27–54; Heinz Giesen, ed., *Studien zur Johannesapokalypse* (SBAB 29; Stuttgart: Katholisches Bibelwerk, 2000), 52–53. A comprehensive catalog of possible allusions to tradition in Rev. 4–5, with an extensive interpretation, is given by Gottfried Schimanowski, *Die himmlische Liturgie in der Apokalypse des Johannes: Die frühjüdischen Traditionen in Offenbarung 4–5 unter Einschluss der Hekhalotliteratur* (WUNT 154; Tübingen: Mohr, 2002), 197–318.

30. Cf. Thomas Knöppler, "Das Blut des Lammes," in *Deutungen des Todes Jesu im Neuen Testament* (ed. J. Frey and J. Schröter; WUNT 181; Tübingen: Mohr, 2005), 478ff.

of Rev. 17–18 concludes with the jubilation over the demonstration of God's royal power in 19:1–10. In turn, the new section begins at 19:11 and leads to the ultimate vision of the end at 22:5: the universal judgment of the world, the gathering of the elect, and the final re-creative act of God the creator. The conclusion of the book at 22:6–21 explicitly picks up the themes with which it began, pointing once again to Jesus as the originator of the book, and reveals that a eucharistic worship service is the space in which the visions coalesce with the realities in which the churches live.[31] The whole of the Apocalypse, both in structure and in its Christology, is determined by a movement directed toward a single goal: *the lordship of Christ is asserting itself over the universe despite the plagues and the eschatological adversary.*

The image of the installation of the crucified Christ as the savior, the lord over life and death, world and history, determines the Christology of Revelation.[32] By his total participation in God's ruling power, Christ carries out his saving and judging acts in the struggle with the anti-God powers. The primary christological metaphor of the Lamb thereby symbolizes both his lowliness and his exalted status. Traversing the visionary world of Revelation leads believers to the insight: Jesus Christ is both the present Lord and the future Coming One. The dominance of the anti-God powers is already broken, but only at the parousia will the exalted Christ fully implement God's power, ultimately and visibly, in the renewal of heaven and earth.

13.3 Pneumatology

Revelation's statements about the Spirit are to be read within the prophetic orientation of the work as a whole (Rev. 1:3; 22:7, "the words of this prophecy"),[33] in which 19:10c is a key text: "The testimony of Jesus is the spirit of prophecy" (ἡ γὰρ μαρτυρία Ἰησοῦ ἐστιν τὸ πνεῦμα τῆς προφητείας). The exalted Jesus Christ is the witness of the revelation given him by God (1:5; 3:14b; 22:20), who in turn delivers it to the seer John (1:1–2, 9). Thus John steps in alongside the heavenly witnesses as one of the earthly witnesses of God's eschatological act.[34] His Spirit-inspired prophecy grows out of Jesus's own testimony received and passed on in the Apocalypse. For the seer, "true words of God" (19:9) exist only in the power of the Spirit, the Spirit that proceeds from Jesus's own testimony and always refers back to it. This internal coherence is the basis of

31. Cf. Roloff, *Revelation*, 249.

32. Cf. ibid., 11.

33. On this point cf. Ferdinand Hahn, "Das Geistverständnis in der Johannesoffenbarung," in *Studien zur Johannesoffenbarung und ihrer Auslegung: Festschrift für Otto Böcher zum 70. Geburtstag* (ed. Friedrich Wilhelm Horn and Michael Wolter; Neukirchen-Vluyn: Neukirchener Verlag, 2005), 3–9.

34. Regarding other witnesses, cf. Rev. 2:18; 6:9; 12:11, 17; 17:6; 19:10b; 20:4.

all other statements about the Spirit in Revelation:[35] John is grasped by the Spirit and sees his vision in the power of the Spirit (ἐν πνεύματι; cf. 1:10; 4:2; 17:3; 21:10; 22:6), which means it is the power of the Spirit that makes possible the content of Revelation. The stereotyped formula, "what the Spirit says to the churches" in 2:7, 11, 17, 29; 3:6, 13, 22 refers to John's Spirit-generated auditory experiences. The prophet speaks in the name of the exalted Christ, who knows and reveals what is really going on in the churches. The direct working of the exalted Lord through the Spirit is also seen in 14:13, where the Spirit speaks the blessing on those who have died in the Lord. So also in 22:17, where the Spirit and the bride (as a metaphor of the church) pray for the coming of Jesus. Revelation 1:4; 3:1; 4:5; and 5:6 speak of the "seven spirits of God." As elsewhere in Revelation, the number seven refers to the fullness and wholeness of God's work (Gen. 2:7). The seven spirits belong to God's throne, and according to 5:6 are directly related to Christ and are sent forth to the earth.

On the whole, Revelation's statements about the Spirit are shaped by a single fundamental conception: the exalted Christ participates in the spiritual reality that emanates from God and thus enables the powerful, Spirit-inspired testimony of the prophet John.

13.4 Soteriology

At the soteriological center of Revelation stands the image of the *redeeming power of the blood of the Lamb*. This is already programmatically formulated in Rev. 1:5–6, ". . . and from Jesus Christ, the faithful witness, the firstborn of the dead, and the ruler of the kings of the earth. To him who loves us and freed us from our sins by his blood, and made us to be a kingdom, priests serving his God and Father, to him be glory and dominion forever and ever. Amen." The foundation for what follows is here laid in a threefold manner:[36] (1) Christ's love appears as the all-embracing motive for his actions (cf. 3:9, 19; 20:9), which (2) takes place in the redemption of his own through his blood, and (3) leads to the establishment of the people of God as a royal-priestly community. In 5:9, 1:5–6 is taken up and expanded with the *motif of ransom*: "You are worthy to take the scroll and to open its seals, for you were slaughtered and by your blood you ransomed for God saints from every

35. In Rev. 13:15 (the breath/spirit of the image of the Beast); 16:13, 14 (spirit of the dragon/devil); 18:2 (unclean spirits/demons), evil spirits are mentioned that function as negative counterparts to the reality of God's Spirit.

36. On this point, cf. Roloff, *Revelation*, 25–26; Herghelegiu, *Wolken*, 39–72; Knöppler, "Blut des Lammes," 486–87; a comprehensive discussion is found in J. A. du Rand, "Soteriology in the Apocalypse of John," in *Salvation in the New Testament* (ed. J. G. Van der Watt; NovTSup 121; Leiden: Brill, 2005), 465–504.

tribe and language and people and nation." Blood represents the concrete, once-for-all giving of Jesus's life on the cross; his life was the purchase price for salvation from the power of sin and the realm of the anti-God powers. Thus the 144,000 "have been redeemed from humankind as first fruits for God and the Lamb" (14:4b). Moreover, the blood-motif links this event with the Old Testament sacrificial system; references have been seen to Isa. 53,[37] to the Passover tradition,[38] and to the daily offering in the temple (the *tamid*; cf. Num. 28:3–8; Exod. 29:38–42).[39] The most probable reference is to the Passover tradition, since the connections with Isa. 53 are too weak; the tamid offering always required the sacrifice of two sheep, and no New Testament passage refers specifically to the tamid texts of the Old Testament. *The blood imagery expresses the atoning dimension of the crucifixion.*[40] Blood delivers from the power of sin (Rev. 1:5b), whitens the clothing of the witnesses (7:14), and the faithful witnesses conquer (temptations/the world) "through the blood of the Lamb" (12:11).

In Revelation, the eschatological events of course also have a soteriological quality, in particular the victory over the dragon (Rev. 12:7–12),[41] the establishment of the everlasting kingdom of God as the new creation (see below, §13.8), and the installation of the believers as priests for God (see below, §13.7). In the divine reality of eschatological salvation, believers will enter the gates of the heavenly Jerusalem (22:14). The church is assured that "Salvation [σωτηρία] belongs to our God who is seated on the throne, and to the Lamb" (7:10; cf. 12:10; 19:1).

13.5 Anthropology

At the interface between anthropology, soteriology, and eschatology in Revelation stands the *concept of life*.[42] Deliverance from the power of sin through the Lamb (Rev. 1:5) grants entrance into true, real, total life with God and Christ. The "Book of Life" (3:5; 17:8; 20:12, 15) is the "book of life of the Lamb that was slaughtered" (13:8; cf. 21:27). In this book, from the very beginning, the names of all those who did not apostatize and worship the Beast

37. Cf. Kraft, *Offenbarung des Johannes*, 108–10.

38. Cf. Holtz, *Christologie der Apokalypse*, 39–47; Roloff, *Revelation*, 78–79; Müller, *Offenbarung*, 162; Knöppler, "Blut des Lammes," 483–84.

39. Cf. Stuhlmacher, "Lamm Gottes," 532; Tóth, *Kult*, 218–24.

40. Knöppler, "Blut des Lammes," 503.

41. On this point, cf. Peter Busch, *Der gefallene Drache: Mythenexegese am Beispiel von Apokalypse 12* (TANZ 19; Tübingen: Francke Verlag, 1996).

42. Revelation does not contain a reflected, developed anthropology. Central concepts and terms are either missing entirely (νόμος [law], πιστεύω [believe], συνείδησις [conscience]) or are used only rarely (ἁμαρτία [sin], 3 times; πίστις [faith], 4 times) or without particularly incisive reference to the content of the term (σάρξ [flesh], σῶμα [body], καρδία [heart]).

have been entered (cf. Dan. 12:1). When they "conquer" and thus remain firm in their faith, Christians receive the "crown of life" (Rev. 2:10) and may eat from the "tree of life" in the eschatologically restored paradise (2:7; 22:2, 14, 19). The metaphor of "living water" (7:17; 21:6; 22:1, 17) is also linked with the paradise imagery. Life in its totally real sense, without the threat of the "second" eschatological death (2:11), is available only to those who do not deny the faith and live as faithful witnesses (2:13, 19; 13:10; 14:12).

13.6 Ethics

Revelation is a document thoroughly oriented to ethics. This orientation is already evident in its form, for the epistolary framework in Rev. 1:1–8 and 22:21 must be understood as the direct expression of the personal address to the readership inherent in the work as a whole.[43] The epistolary orientation as direct address and unmediated effort to influence the hearers/readers is seen clearly in the *messages to the seven churches* (2:1–3:22).[44] The churches regard themselves as exposed to internal and external dangers, with those internal to the churches being evaluated in a variety of different ways. External threats include not only the dangers of war (6:2–4),[45] inflated prices (6:5–6), and pressures on the churches from the Jews (2:9–10; 3:9), but also the domination of Asia Minor by the ungodly Beast (chaps. 13; 17; 18), the Roman emperor, and along with him the second Beast, the imperial priesthood (13:11–17; 16:13–14; 19:20). They propagate the ruler cult as a religious-political declaration of loyalty binding on all citizens. Christians are threatened (2:9) and thrown in prison (2:10), and one witness/martyr has already been killed (Antipas, in 2:13; cf. 6:9–11). The hour of testing is coming on the whole world (3:10). Internal dangers include false teachers who threaten the identity of the churches (cf. 2:2, 6, 14–15, 20ff.). But Revelation also speaks of the "lukewarmness" of faith (2:4–5; 3:15–16); a few congregations are powerless and "dead" (3:1). For the seer, there is an internal connection between these two types of danger, for in his eyes the silent assimilation to the forms of pagan religion was just as problematic as the churches' distancing themselves from the cults of the false gods, including the emperor cult. This silent assimilation placed the purity

43. Cf. Karrer, *Johannesoffenbarung als Brief*, 160; Müller, *Offenbarung*, 91–92.

44. On the messages to the churches, cf. Ferdinand Hahn, "Die Sendschreiben der Johannesapokalypse," in *Tradition und Glaube: Das frühe Christentum in seiner Umwelt: Festgabe für Karl Georg Kuhn zum 65. Geburtstag* (ed. Gert Jeremias et al.; Göttingen: Vandenhoeck & Ruprecht, 1971), 357–94; Hans-Josef Klauck, "Das Sendschreiben nach Pergamon und der Kaiserkult in der Johannesoffenbarung," *Bib* 73 (1992): 183–207.

45. Revelation 6:2 could refer to the Parthian incursions into Roman territory (cf. Rev. 9:13ff.; 16:12), and Rev. 6:3–4 to disputes within the Roman Empire; cf. Müller, *Offenbarung*, 167; Roloff, *Revelation*, 86.

of the eschatological congregation in question, for such accommodation appears as a sublimated form of apostasy.[46] Especially the polemic against the churches in Pergamum (2:12–17) and Thyatira (2:18–29), with the charge of eating food sacrificed to idols (2:14, 20), shows that there were movements in the congregations that argued for a moderate cooperation with the Caesar cult. This cult doubtless had great drawing power, as seen by its repeated portrayal as a seductive woman (17:1, 5; 19:2; 21:8; 22:15). In contrast, John emphasizes that only those who have kept themselves away from the earthly sacred meals of the pagan cults will eat of the hidden heavenly manna (cf. 2:17).

The seer's ethical concept is bound up with his attempt to preserve the identity of the community in the face of these dangers. This is the purpose of the *conquering sayings* and the *victory imagery*. In the conquering sayings (cf. Rev. 2:7, 11, 17, 26; 3:5, 12, 21, "To everyone who conquers/wins the victory, I will give . . ."),[47] the ethical conception of Revelation clearly emerges: the promise of the future victory of the kingdom of God motivates believers to hold firm to their faith in the temptations of the present. The patience and suffering of Christians is seen as the counterpart to Christ's own sufferings (cf. 2:3; 6:9), which in turn has as its positive counterpart the appointment of Christians to participate in the kingdom of God at the end of time (cf. 3:21; 20:4; 21:7, "Those who conquer will inherit these things, and I will be their God and they will be my children" [lit. "my son"]). The motif of "conquering/victory" (νικάω) links believers with the way of Christ (5:5; 17:14); world history as well as one's own life is understood as an unceasing struggle between God and the anti-God powers. At the end stands the victory of God/the Lamb, and thus also of the believers, over all that is anti-God (5:5; 12:11; 15:2; 17:14; 21:7).[48] In 12:11, both are most closely bound together: "But they have conquered him [Satan] by the blood of the Lamb and by the word of their testimony, for they did not cling to life even in the face of death." The *testimony/witness motif* also reveals the christological foundation for ethics,

46. Cf. Müller, *Offenbarung*, 113 and elsewhere; Klauck, "Sendschreiben nach Pergamon," 181: "The author of the Apocalypse considered the 'soft' emperor cult much more dangerous [than the explicit, hardline version], when, for example, someone merely went along with the crowd in a festival or participated in a meal of some social club that had religious overtones because he believed his vocational obligations did not permit him to avoid it, and that the issue of confession of his faith was not involved." From a text-pragmatic perspective, Klauck sees the main concern of the author expressed in the challenge of 18:4: "Come out of her [the great city Babylon], my people" (cf. Klauck, "Sendschreiben nach Pergamon," 212–17).

47. The clearest parallel from the history of religions to the conqueror motif is found in Epictetus, *Diatr.* 1.18.21–24; for analysis of the conqueror sayings, cf. Karrer, *Johannesoffenbarung als Brief*, 212–17.

48. On the victory motif, cf. Jens-W. Taeger, "'Gesiegt! O himmlische Musik des Wortes!': Zur Entfaltung des Siegesmotivs in den johanneischen Schriften," *ZNW* 85 (1994): 23–46; Jürgen Kerner, *Die Ethik der Johannes-Apokalypse im Vergleich mit der des 4. Esra: Ein Beitrag zum Verhältnis von Apokalyptik und Ethik* (BZNW 94; Berlin: de Gruyter, 1998), 47–52.

for the first and abiding witness is Jesus Christ himself (1:5; 3:14; 22:20). John sees himself as a witness in the succession of witnesses (1:2, 9; 19:10), and all Christians who suffer for the sake of their testimony are authentic witnesses (2:13; 6:9; 11:7; 12:11; 17:6; 19:10; 20:4),[49] for the dragon/devil makes war against "those who keep the commandments of God and hold the testimony of Jesus" (12:17). It is no accident that Antipas, as the first who witnesses by shedding his blood, receives the title borne by Jesus himself: "the faithful witness" (1:5; 2:13). Endurance and faithfulness even to death, considered as a basic ethical stance, are specifically regarded by John in a positive sense as *works* (ἔργα) of Christians (14:13, "Write this: 'Blessed are the dead who from now on die in the Lord.' 'Yes,' says the Spirit, 'they will rest from their labors, for their deeds [ἔργα; KJV, NKJV, NAB works] follow them'").[50] Such works must be clearly identified and manifest in the life of the church, for judgment will take place according to works (cf. 2:23; 18:6; 10:12–13; 22:12). The church is called to "repent" (μετανοέω in 2:5, 16, 21–22; 3:3, 19; 9:20–21; 16:9, 11) and do "the works they did at first" (2:5). The works of Christians are positively described in 2:19 and 13:10: *love, faithfulness, righteousness/justice, patience, service, and endurance*. It is worthy of note that no text links "works" to the Jewish law (νόμος does not occur in Revelation). Over against these good works stand the vice catalogs of 9:21; 21:8; 22:15, where the polemic against idolatry, magic, and immorality characterizes Christians who participate in the emperor cult as cowards, faithless, and liars who will not enter into eternal salvation.[51]

The seer develops a powerful ethic, *an ethic of resistance and endurance*, which excludes every opportunistic accommodation to prevailing culture. A clear line of demarcation is drawn between the ethical conduct of the majority of the population, who orient their lives to "idolatry," that is, the emperor cult,[52] and the ethics of the churches (Rev. 18:4). A clear ethical standpoint should not be confused with ethical rigorism,[53] for John advocates an ethic in

49. Cf. on this point H. E. Lona, "'Treu bis zum Tod,'" in *Neues Testament und Ethik: Für Rudolf Schnackenburg* (ed. Helmut Merklein and Rudolf Schnackenburg; Freiburg: Herder, 1989), 442–46; H. Roose, *"Das Zeugnis Jesu": Seine Bedeutung für die Christologie, Eschatologie und Prophetie in der Offenbarung des Johannes* (TANZ 32; Tübingen: Mohr, 2000).

50. Cf. Traugott Holtz, "Die 'Werke' in der Johannesoffenbarung," in *Geschichte und Theologie des Urchristentums: Gesammelte Aufsätze* (ed. Traugott Holtz et al.; WUNT 57; Tübingen: Mohr, 1991), 426–41.

51. On this point, cf. Otto Böcher, "Lasterkataloge in der Apokalypse des Johannes," in *Leben lernen im Horizont des Glaubens* (ed. Bernhard Buschbeck and Friedrich Lemke; LSTR 1; Landau/Pfalz: Seminar Evang. Theologie, 1986), 75–84; Heinz Giesen, "Lasterkataloge und Kaiserkult in der Offenbarung des Johannes," in *Studien zur Johannesoffenbarung und ihrer Auslegung: Festschrift für Otto Böcher zum 70. Geburtstag* (ed. Friedrich Wilhelm Horn and Michael Wolter; Neukirchen-Vluyn: Neukirchener Verlag, 2005), 210–31.

52. Wolter, "Christliches Ethos," 206.

53. Schulz, *Neutestamentliche Ethik*, 550–53, categorizes John as an ethical rigorist, as does Roloff, *Kirche im Neuen Testament*, 169–70.

which the churches' own identity is emphasized, an ethic that in his situation must necessarily be expressed in antithetical and dualistic terms, if a community whose identity is threatened will survive. The seer is a fellow sufferer in the persecution (1:9),[54] sharing with the churches the fate of a stigmatized minority, which at the same time lives in the assurance of the victory already achieved by Christ and participation in his heavenly kingship (2:26–28; 3:21; 22:7, 14).

13.7 Ecclesiology

In Revelation, ecclesiology, ethics, and eschatology are most closely bound together. Ecclesiology is developed on the basis of Christology (see above, §13.2), clearly visible in the epistolary opening section (Rev. 1:1–8) and the commissioning vision of 1:9–20, where the crucified and exalted Christ appears in the midst of his churches. The number seven expresses the fullness and perfection of the divine work of creation, and, in terms of ecclesiology, stands for the church in its wholeness as willed by God and made effective through Christ (1:20).[55]

The Church as the Locus of Christ's Lordship

Christ rules in his church through his word, as received and delivered by the seer in the messages to the seven churches (Rev. 2:1–3:22). At the same time, the lordship motif is expressed within the horizon of world history, so that ecclesiology takes on some universal traits. This is illustrated above all by the word group βασιλεύς ("king/emperor," 21 times in Revelation), βασιλεία ("rule, kingdom, empire," 9 times in Revelation), and βασιλεύω ("rule," 7 times in Revelation). Already in 1:5, the Crucified One appears as "ruler of the kings of the earth"; rulership of the world belongs to God "and his Messiah, and he will reign forever and ever" (11:15; cf. also 11:17; 15:3; 19:6, 16). In the eschatological battle against the kings and empires of this world (6:15; 9:11; 10:11; 16:10, 12; 17:2, 9, 12, 18; 18:3, 9; and elsewhere), the Lamb will be the conqueror, "for he is Lord of lords and King of kings, and those with him are called and chosen and faithful" (17:14b). Baptized believers already participate in this lordship of the Lamb in the here and now, for Christ, through his sacrificial death, has already made them rulers and priests (1:6, 9; 2:26–28; 5:10). This, however, will be revealed only in the future (cf. 5:10b, "they will reign

54. Klaus Scholtissek, "'Mitteilhaber an der Bedrängnis, der Königsherrschaft und der Ausdauer in Jesus' (Offb 1,9): Partizipatorische Ethik in der Offenbarung des Johannes," in *Theologie als Vision: Studien zur Johannes-Offenbarung* (ed. Knut Backhaus; SBS 191; Stuttgart: Verlag Katholisches Bibelwerk, 2001), 191ff., speaks appropriately of John's "participatory ethic."

55. Cf. Roloff, *Kirche im Neuen Testament*, 171–74.

on earth"; 20:6; 22:5), for the battle between God and Satan has already been decided (and, in principle, also on earth). However, with the motif of the fall of Satan (12:1–17), John illustrates that the anti-God power on earth is still powerfully present and threatening the church.[56] On earth, the rule of God is contrasted with the arrogant presumption of rulership claimed by the Beast, which threatens the church. To be sure, as baptized Christians the believers bear the seal of the living God (cf. 7:1–8; 3:12), but they are nonetheless exposed to the real power and seduction of the Beast, to the point of death as martyrs (2:13; 6:9–11; 13:9–10).

The Church as the Place of Holiness

In full view of this existential threat, the seer propagates the "holiness" of the church (ἅγιος, twenty-five times in Revelation).[57] Just as God (Rev. 4:8) and Jesus (3:7; 6:10) are holy, so also baptized believers are to be holy: they must prove themselves in the dispute with the anti-God power. War is waged against the saints/holy ones (13:7), and the blood of the saints is poured out (16:6; 17:6; 18:24). Therefore, patience, endurance, and faith are required (13:10; 14:12), in order that, after the victory (18:20; 20:9) they may receive their just reward (11:18; 22:11–12) and participate in the marriage supper of the Lamb (19:8). Holiness appears as the predicate of a consistent faith, so that not all the baptized are among the 144,000 written in the Book of Life, who will wear white garments and eat from the tree of life (3:5). The figure 144,000 as the total number of Christians in the end time is a round number, but also an unimaginably large symbolic number (7:4–8; 14:1–5): the 12 tribes of Israel, each with 12,000 members, including all the "undefiled" (14:4–5), those who are not "lukewarm" (3:15–16) or apostate, who do not worship the Beast or his image (20:4). The 144,000, however, is by no means limited to Israel or to Jewish Christians, as clearly seen in 5:9 and 7:9–17.[58] On the contrary, they represent the seer's universal church from all nations. To it belong all the elect who endure as tried and true, for they fight on the side of the Lamb and will participate in his ultimate victory (17:14). The martyrs (2:13; 6:9, 11; 13:10; 16:6; 17:6; 18:24; 20:4) represent the holy congregation in a special way, because one can see in their life and death what "endurance and faith" truly means (13:10). To them is promised participation in the thousand-year reign (20:4).

The particular locus of holiness is the *worship service*. The liturgical orientation of the work is apparent in Rev. 1:10 and 22:20: the seer receives his visions on the Lord's Day and refers to the eucharist in order to directly involve

56. Cf. ibid., 176–77.
57. On this point, cf. Söding, "Heilig," 63ff.
58. Cf. Roloff, *Revelation*, 98–99.

the congregation in the revelatory event (cf. 3:20). Hymnic pieces appearing at noticeable junctures in the composition (cf. 4:8ff.; 5:9ff.; 11:15ff.; 15:3–5; 16:5–6; 19:1ff.) praise God for the saving or judging events that have happened or are to come, and so direct the gaze of the distressed earthly congregation to the glory of God.[59] Another significant aspect: in worship, the community of faith realizes its new identity under the lordship of the Lamb and under the conscious, intentional rejection of the claims to lordship made by Babylon/Rome.[60] As the place where the new being is repeatedly practiced, worship is also a locus of resistance against the anti-God powers, and, since the Apocalypse was read out in worship, also a place of hearing, seeing, learning, and understanding/insight.[61] This model of a church united in solidarity in praise, prayer, and understanding/insight explains the noticeable silence about the official ecclesial structures that we must presuppose for the close of the first century in Asia Minor (the Pastorals; Ignatius).[62] John mentions only the prophetic office but without indicating that it had become institutionalized. His ecclesiology is stamped with the idea of an egalitarian church of brothers and sisters. The seer describes himself as a fellow brother (1:9; 19:10; 22:9), one who shares the present troubles of the churches. All members of the church are servants (cf. 2:20; 6:11; 7:23; 19:2, 5; 22:3), and even the angels are only fellow servants (cf. 22:9). Even Christ, in a brotherly manner, will share the throne with his fellow servants the Christians (cf. 3:21; 20:6; 21:7).

The Church as Ideal City

The central ecclesiological image of Revelation is the New Jerusalem that comes down from heaven (Rev. 21:1–22:5; cf. 3:12).[63] After the unholy city Rome/Babylon has been destroyed (18:1–24), its eschatological counterpart, the holy city New Jerusalem, appears as the new creation of God. The Jeru-

59. On this point, cf. Delling, "Zum gottesdienstlichen Stil," passim; Klaus-Peter Jörns, *Das hymnische Evangelium: Untersuchungen zu Aufbau, Funktion und Herkunft der hymnischen Stücke in den Johannesoffenbarung* (SNT 5; Gütersloh: Güterloher Verlagshaus, 1971); Deichgräber, *Gotteshymnus*, 44–59.

60. The "seven hills" in Rev. 17:9 are a clear reference to Rome.

61. Cf. Wengst, *Pax Romana*, 166; Wolter, "Christliches Ethos," 207–8.

62. Müller, *Theologiegeschichte*, 33–34, supposes that John intentionally ignored these structures, and thus wrote to the church angels, the heavenly representatives of the churches.

63. For analysis, cf. Dieter Georgi, "Die Visionen vom himmlischen Jerusalem in Apk 21 und 22," in *Kirche: Festschrift für Günther Bornkamm zum 75. Geburtstag* (ed. Dieter Lührmann and Georg Strecker; Tübingen: Mohr, 1980), 351–72; Jürgen Roloff, "Neuschöpfung in der Offenbarung des Johannes," *JBTh* 5 (1990): 119–38; P. Söllner, *Jerusalem, du hochgebaute Stadt. Eschatologisches und himmlisches Jerusalem im Frühjudentum und im frühen Christentum* (TANZ 25; Tübingen: Mohr, 1998); Ferdinand Hahn, "Das neue Jerusalem," in *Kirche und Volk Gottes: Festschrift für Jürgen Roloff zum 70. Geburtstag* (ed. Martin Karrer et al.; Neukirchen-Vluyn: Neukirchener Verlag, 2000), 284–94.

salem imagery, which was available to John from ancient Judaism[64] and New Testament tradition (Gal. 4:21–31), fits into the salvation-history continuity that he values so highly.[65] At the end of time, the idea of the city of God as the realization of the ideal rule of God and ideal communion of believers emerges in place of its transitory this-worldly prototype. In the process of filling in this picture, the seer makes some remarkable emphases: the description of the city (cf. Rev. 21:12ff.) is oriented above all to Ezekiel's vision of the post-exilic temple (Ezek. 40–48),[66] so that now the ideal city appears as God's abiding dwelling place.[67] In it there is no longer any temple, "for its temple is the Lord God the Almighty and the Lamb" (Rev. 21:22). In the New Jerusalem as the ideal city, life together with one's brothers and sisters in the presence of God becomes a reality. Already in the here and now, this future event makes its salvific reality present in the life of the church, which helps it resist the obvious and hidden dangers. This saving reality will emerge in full view at the end of time.

13.8 Eschatology

As appropriate to the apocalyptic genre, the eschatology of Revelation is richly developed. Within the mythically structured basic movement from present distress to ultimate victory in heaven and on earth, it is especially important to determine the relationship between present and future eschatology.

Present and Future Eschatology

The basis of Revelation's eschatology is constituted by the statements of the presence of salvation in Rev. 1:5b–6; 5:9–10; 14:3–4. Through the sacrificial death of the Lamb, Christians are participants in the kingdom of God

64. Cf. Tobit 13:16–18; 14:5; *1 En.* 90.28–29; *4 Ezra* 7.26, 44; 8.52; 9.26, and elsewhere.

65. Cf. Roloff, *Kirche im Neuen Testament*, 178–81, appropriately describes this multilayered result: On the one hand, explicit scriptural proofs are lacking, while, on the other hand, Israel's symbolism (e.g., twelve tribes, Zion, temple, Jerusalem) is adopted on a grand scale.

66. The seer's favorite Old Testament source for his imagery is the book of Ezekiel; cf. Beate Kowalski, *Die Rezeption des Propheten Ezechiel in der Offenbarung des Johannes* (SBB 52; Stuttgart: Verlag Katholisches Bibelwerk, 2004); Dieter Sänger and Michael Bachmann, eds., *Das Ezechielbuch in der Johannesoffenbarung* (BTS 76; Neukirchen-Vluyn: Neukirchener Verlag, 2004).

67. Georgi, "Apk 21," 354ff., is probably right in supposing that ideas about the ideal Hellenistic polis also stand in the background. A sketch of the new Jerusalem is presented in Otto Böcher, "Mythos und Rationalität," in *Mythos und Rationalität* (ed. Hans Heinrich Schmid; Gütersloh: Güterloher Verlagshaus, 1988), 169, who helpfully classifies and evaluates the number symbolism/numerical riddles, the mineralogy, astronomy/astrology, angels/demons as rational elements of world interpretation.

(1:9).[68] The future events do not themselves bring forth the fundamental turn of history but are the final revelation and validation of the power of God.[69] All the same, the church looks ahead to Christ's parousia, which will happen "soon" (2:16; 3:11), with great anticipation (1:7; 19:11). Because the Lamb has in truth already defeated the dragon, Christ can respond to the church's imploring "Come" (22:17) with the reassuring "Surely I am coming soon" (22:20; cf. 2:16; 3:11, 20; 4:8; 22:7, 12, 17, 20). The seer sees himself and his church standing directly at the turn from the present to the coming aeon, immediately before the *thousand-year reign of Christ* (20:4, the faithful witnesses "came to life and reigned with Christ a thousand years").[70] With the symbolic number one thousand and the concept of the *intermediate Messianic kingdom* John is not advocating a speculative "chiliasm" (from χίλιοι, thousand) but is emphasizing that prior to the ultimate end, the present world too will be permeated by Christ.[71] Following the thousand-year intermediate kingdom comes the last great battle, then the eternal Jerusalem (chaps. 21–22) in which the redeemed will be gathered. In the present, the Beast/city of Rome still rules, but for only "a little while" (17:10). In only "one hour" (18:10) judgment will fall on the great city, and it will be burned up (18:9).

It is clear that the future events already determine the present: the future salvation, grounded in the death of the Lamb, decisively shapes the eschatology of Revelation. *Despite the resistance of the world, what John is permitted to see as already fulfilled in the heavenly world is already beginning to assert itself in the present, and to prevail.*[72] Christians are already, in the here and now, citizens of the New Jerusalem (Rev. 7:4, 8; 21:12–13); they are sealed (7:1–8), their names are already registered in the Book of Life (13:8; 17:8), and the church is already the bride of the Messiah (21:2b, 9b). The events that

68. Cf. Holtz, *Christologie der Apokalypse*, 70: "The redemption of the church is present reality; it possesses in the present what was once promised to the Old Testament community as eschatological gift."

69. Karrer, *Johannesoffenbarung als Brief*, 136.

70. The concept of a thousand-year reign has both Hellenistic and Jewish roots; cf. Böcher, ed., *Johannesapokalypse*, 625–26; for interpretation of the concept, cf. Roloff, *Revelation*, 223–26.

71. Müller, *Offenbarung*, 341, rejects a purely symbolic understanding of the thousand-year intermediate kingdom and concludes that John's view is that "there is to be an earthly kingdom that stands in contrast to the defeated power of the Roman Empire"; on this theme, cf. further J. Frey, "Das apokalyptische Millennium," in *Deutungen zum christlichen Mythos der Jahrtausendwende* (ed. C. Bochinger; Gütersloh: Güterloher Verlagshaus, 1999), 10–72; Martin Karrer, "Himmel, Millennium und neuer Himmel in der Apokalypse," *JBTh* 10 (2005): 225–59.

72. In view of this conscious, intentional correlation of future and present, the thesis of Bruce J. Malina, *On the Genre and Message of Revelation: Star Visions and Sky Journeys* (Peabody, MA: Hendrickson, 1995), 266, that John, as an "astral prophet," advocates an exclusively present eschatology is entirely off the track: "It seems quite certain that ancient Mediterraneans were not future-oriented at all. In other words, there is nothing in the book of Revelation that refers to the future. Even the new Jerusalem is descending right now."

are now breaking over the church can therefore never prevail, if the church perseveres and recognizes how God's acts in history have been put into effect and are now coming to their ultimate fulfillment.

The Judgment

There is an unremitting movement toward judgment in Revelation. The judgment idea is already dominant in the presentation of the "one like the Son of Man," clearly discernible in the fiery eyes that penetrate everything (Rev. 1:14) and the sharp two-edged sword that proceeds from his mouth (1:16). The adoption of the sword motif in 2:26 and 19:15, 21 shows that Christ's judgment functions through his word (19:13), both in the church and in the world.[73] He does not announce to the churches a general judgment of wrath or destruction, but the threat of discipline is intended to bring them to repentance (2:5, 16; 3:3, 18).[74] The inauguration of the general judgment of wrath through the Lamb begins in Rev. 4–5 with the picture of the Almighty on his throne and the transfer of world rulership to the Lamb.[75] With the reception of the book with the seven seals (Rev. 5:7) from the hand of the One who sits on the throne, the Lamb is installed as world ruler, to whom all beings in the universe now bow in worship (5:8–14). The judgment is carried out in *three visionary cycles*, in which the final vision of each cycle opens up a new cycle. The seven seals are opened first (6:1–8:5), to which the seven trumpets are joined (8:6–11:19), and after an interlude in movement of the main plot (chaps. 12–13: struggle with the anti-God powers; chap. 14: the preservation of believers during the final events), then comes the final cycle, the seven bowls (15:1–16:21). In 15:1 the seven bowls are explicitly designated as the conclusion, "for with them the wrath of God is ended" (cf. 15:8). Corresponding to this caesura, the last bowl is on Babylon/Rome (16:17–21; cf. 14:28), whose fall is described in great detail in Rev. 17–18 and celebrated with great joy in 19:1–10.[76]

What still remains to be accomplished before the Son of Man's judgment of the hostile powers is ultimately complete (Rev. 19:12–16) is above all the destruction of the dragon/Satan himself, who had been thrown into the abyss

73. On the background in tradition history (Isa. 11:4; 49:2; *Pss. Sol.* 17.35; 18.15–16), cf. Holtz, *Christologie der Apokalypse*, 127.

74. Cf. Werner Zager, "Gericht Gottes in der Johannesapokalypse," in *Studien zur Johannesoffenbarung und ihrer Auslegung: Festschrift für Otto Böcher zum 70. Geburtstag* (ed. Friedrich Wilhelm Horn and Michael Wolter; Neukirchen-Vluyn: Neukirchener Verlag, 2005), 312–13.

75. For analysis, cf. Tóth, *Kult*, 288–94.

76. On the issue of whether and to what extent Rev. 13 and 17 are to be interpreted with reference to individual emperors and to be linked with the Nero redivivus myth, cf. Müller, *Offenbarung*, 297–300, and Hans-Josef Klauck, "Do They Never Come Back? Nero Redivivus and the Apocalypse of John," in *Religion und Gesellschaft im frühen Christentum: neutestamentliche Studien* (ed. Hans-Josef Klauck; WUNT 152; Tübingen: Mohr Siebeck, 2003), 268–89.

during the thousand-year earthly reign (20:1–3).[77] The binding of Satan introduces the intermediate messianic millennial kingdom, in which the martyrs will rule: "The rest of the dead did not come to life until the thousand years were ended. This is the first resurrection. Blessed and holy are those who share in the first resurrection. Over these the second death has no power, but they will be priests of God and of Christ, and they will reign with him a thousand years" (20:5–6). For the elect, the "first resurrection" is evidently the definitive *resurrection*,[78] while after the final destruction of Satan (20:7–10) there is a general judgment of the whole world (20:11–15) according to works (20:7–10), from which those whose names are written in the book of life will be raised.[79] This differentiation between a "first" and a later resurrection is intended to motivate the hearers/readers of Revelation to stand fast during the persecution so that they can participate in the "first" resurrection. With the descent of the heavenly Jerusalem in Rev. 21–22 the kingdom of God and the Lamb is ultimately realized. It is already shaping the present of the persecuted churches.

The basic eschatological conception of the seer can be clearly recognized: He writes his work within the horizon of the kingdom of God/the Lamb that has already broken in and is presently in the process of being fully realized. He advocates a linear view of history that runs from the present troubles to eschatological salvation. For him, history has a beginning and an end, an end that involves both an eschatological struggle and the concept of a new creation brought about by God: God's heavenly world will replace this earthly world and transform all things.

13.9 Setting in the History of Early Christian Theology

The Revelation of John only apparently portrays an event in distant worlds; the truth of the matter is the exact opposite, for it is entirely grounded in the present, this-worldly reality in which the churches to whom it is addressed live.[80] This immediacy explains its unique power and its enduring effects in the history of the church.[81] The reality in which the churches lived, like that

77. Cf. Plato, *Phaed.* 249A–B.

78. Cf. Roloff, *Revelation*, 11–12.

79. On the Jewish concept that only the righteous will be raised, cf. *Pss. Sol.* 3.12; *1 En.* 91.10; 92.3.

80. Cf. Backhaus, "Apokalyptische Bilder," 423: "The Revelation of John moves with nimble feet through the heavenly fields. And still it can be precisely located in earthly history."

81. On the history of Revelation's later influences and effects, cf. Gerhard Maier, *Die Johannesoffenbarung und die Kirche* (WUNT 25; Tübingen: Mohr, 1981); G. Kretschmar, *Die Offenbarung des Johannes: Die Geschichte ihrer Auslegung im 1. Jahrtausend* (CTM, B 9; Stuttgart: Kaiser, 1985); Arthur Wainwright, *Mysterious Apocalypse: Interpreting the Book of Revelation* (Nashville: Abingdon, 1993).

of society as a whole, was structured along religious, cultic lines. All the cities addressed in the messages to the seven churches were influenced by the emperor cult,[82] so it is to be expected that this reality of their life-world will be reflected in Revelation's view of reality. Just as evident is the deep rootedness of Revelation in Jewish ideas and imagery, for the whole document is interwoven with obvious allusions to Old Testament cultic motifs. In contrast to myth, which is narrative in the broadest sense of the term, the cult represents the epiphany of what is hoped for, prayed for, and expected, the revelation and inbreaking of the divine world into the human confines of time and space. By understanding the rituals of worship as fundamental existential phenomena that facilitate meaning-formation and assure one's orientation in the cosmos, the present community of salvation achieves participation in this event. At the same time, Revelation is a wisdom book[83] that assembles material used in ancient education and integrates it into the cultic-prophetic orientation of the book as a whole.

In and through the Apocalypse, the seer develops a cultic event that transcends earthly troubles and links it with the apocalyptic view of history. From the resulting perspective both world history and the threatened existence of the individual become comprehensible. Revelation takes fundamental elements of faith (trouble, endurance, faithfulness to the confession, struggle) and raises them to the level of reflective theological themes. The yield: solace and encouragement. By participating in the victory of God and the Lamb, and by anticipating the heavenly saving event whose donor and founder is God, the seer achieves a view of history that incorporates multiple images but conveys a single idea: it communicates to the threatened earthly community the assurance of heavenly victory.[84]

82. On the introduction of the ruler/Caesar cult in the cities of western Asia Minor by Augustus, cf. Dio Cassius, *Hist.* 51.20.

83. Cf. Otto Böcher, "Aspekte einer Hermeneutik der Johannesoffenbarung," in *Theologie in der Spätzeit des Neuen Testaments: Vorträge auf dem Symposion zum 75. Geburtstag von Kurt Niederwimmer* (ed. Wilhelm Pratscher et al.; Vienna: Universität Wien, 2005), 23–33.

84. Thus Bultmann's statement that "the Christianity of Revelation has to be termed a weakly Christianized Judaism" (*Theology of the New Testament*, 2:175) does not even come close to grasping the theological quality of John's achievement.

Bibliography

Achtemeier, Paul J. "'He Taught Them Many Things': Reflections on Marcan Christology." *Catholic Biblical Quarterly* 42 (1980): 465–81.

Ådna, Jostein. *Jesu Stellung zum Tempel: Die Tempelaktion und das Tempelwort als Ausdruck seiner messianischen Sendung*. Wissenschaftliche Untersuchungen zum Neuen Testament 2.119. Tübingen: Mohr Siebeck, 2000.

Agamben, Giorgio. *Die Zeit, die bleibt: Ein Kommentar zum Römerbrief*. Frankfurt: Suhrkamp, 2006.

Agersnap, Sören. *Baptism and the New Life: A Study of Romans 6:1–14*. Aarhus: Aarhus University Press, 1999.

Aland, Kurt. "Das Verhältnis von Kirche und Staat in der Frühzeit." In *Aufstieg und Niedergang der römischen Welt*, edited by Joseph Vogt et al., 2.23.1:60–246. Berlin: de Gruyter, 1979.

Albani, Matthias. *Der eine Gott und die himmlischen Heerscharen: Zur Begründung des Monotheismus bei Deuterojesaja im Horizont der Astralisierung des Gottesverständnisses im Alten Orient*. Arbeiten zur Bibel und ihrer Geschichte 1. Leipzig: Evangelische Verlagsanstalt, 2000.

Albertz, Martin. *Die synoptischen Streitgespräche: Ein Beitrag zur Formengeschichte des Urchristentums*. Berlin: Trowitzsch, 1921.

Alexander, Loveday. *The Preface to Luke's Gospel: Literary Convention and Social Context in Luke 1.1–4 and Acts 1.1*. Cambridge: Cambridge University Press, 1993.

———. "Reading Luke-Acts from Back to Front." In *The Unity of Luke-Acts*, edited by J. Verheyden, 419–46. Bibliotheca ephemeridum theologicarum lovaniensium 142. Louvain: Leuven University Press, 1999.

Alkier, Stefan. "Intertextualität—Annäherungen an ein texttheoretisches Paradigma." In *Heiligkeit und Herrschaft: Intertextuelle Studien zu Heiligkeitsvorstellungen und zu Psalm 110*, edited by Dieter Sänger, 1–26. Biblisch-theologische Studien 55. Neukirchen-Vluyn: Neukirchener Verlag, 2003.

———. *Wunder und Wirklichkeit in den Briefen des Apostels Paulus: Ein Beitrag zu einem Wunderverständnis jenseits von Entmythologisierung und Rehistorisierung*. Wissenschaftliche Untersuchungen zum Neuen Testament 134. Tübingen: Mohr, 2001.

Allison, Dale C. *The Intertextual Jesus: Scripture in Q*. Harrisburg, PA: Trinity, 2000.

Althaus, Paul. *Paulus und Luther über den Menschen: Ein Vergleich*. 3rd ed. Studien der Luther-Akademie 14. Gütersloh: Bertelsmann, 1958.

———. *Die Wahrheit des christlichen Osterglaubens*. Beiträge zur Förderung christlicher Theologie 42. Gütersloh: Bertelsmann, 1940.

Anton, Paul. *Exegetische Abhandlung der Pastoral-Briefe Pauli an Timotheum und Titum, 1726 und 1727 öffentlich vorgetragen, nunmehr aber nach bisheriger Methode treulich mitgetheilet von Johann August Majer*. 2 vols. Halle: Weysenhaus, 1753–55.

Arnold, Clinton E. *Ephesians, Power and Magic: The Concept of Power in Ephesians in Light of Its Historical Setting*. Society for New Testament Studies Monograph Series 63. Cambridge: Cambridge University Press, 1989.

Arnold, G. "Mk 1,1 und Eröffnungswendungen in lateinischen Schriften." *Zeitschrift für die neutestamentliche Wissenschaft und die Kunde der älteren Kirche* 68 (1977): 123–27.

Asher, Jeffrey R. *Polarity and Change in 1 Corinthians 15: A Study of Metaphysics, Rhetoric, and Resurrection*. Hermeneutische Untersuchungen zur Theologie 42. Tübingen: Mohr, 2000.

Ashton, John. *Understanding the Fourth Gospel*. New York: Oxford University Press, 1991.

Assmann, Aleida. *Zeit und Tradition: Kulturelle Strategien der Dauer*. Cologne: Böhlau, 1999.

Assmann, Jan. "Fünf Stufen auf dem Weg zum Kanon: Tradition und Schriftkultur im alten Israel und frühen Judentum." In *Religion und kulturelles Gedächtnis: Zehn Studien*, edited by Jan Assmann, 81–100. Munich: Beck, 2000.

Attridge, Harold W. *The Epistle to the Hebrews*. Hermeneia—A Critical and Historical Commentary on the Bible. Philadelphia: Fortress, 1989.

Auffarth, Christoph. "Herrscherkult und Christuskult." In *Die Praxis der Herrscherverehrung in Rom und seinen Provinzen*, edited by Hubert Cancik and Konrad Hitzl, 283–317. Tübingen: Mohr, 2003.

Aune, David E. *Prophecy in Early Christianity and the Ancient Mediterranean World*. Grand Rapids: Eerdmans, 1983.

Avemarie, Friedrich. *Die Tauferzählung der Apostelgeschichte*. Wissenschaftliche Untersuchungen zum Neuen Testament 139. Tübingen: Mohr, 2002.

———. *Tora und Leben: Untersuchungen zur Heilsbedeutung der Tora in der frühen rabbinischen Literatur*. Texts and Studies in Ancient Judaism 55. Tübingen: Mohr, 1996.

———. "Die Werke des Gesetzes im Spiegel des Jakobusbriefes." *Zeitschrift für Theologie und Kirche* 98 (2001): 282–309.

Bachmann, Michael. *Jerusalem und der Tempel*. Beiträge zur Wissenschaft vom Alten und Neuen Testament 109. Stuttgart: Kohlhammer, 1980.

Bachmann, Michael, and Johannes Woyke, eds. *Lutherische und neue Paulusperspektive: Beiträge zu einem Schlüsselproblem der gegenwärtigen exegetischen Diskussion*. Wissenschaftliche Untersuchungen zum Neuen Testament 182. Tübingen: Mohr Siebeck, 2005.

Back, F. "Wiedergeburt in der hellenistisch-römischen Zeit." In *Wiedergeburt*, edited by Reinhard Feldmeier, 45–73. Biblisch-theologische Schwerpunkte 25. Göttingen: Vandenhoeck & Ruprecht, 2005.

Backhaus, K. "Apokalyptische Bilder? Die Vernunft der Vision in der Johannes-Offenbarung." *Evangelische Theologie* 64 (2004): 421–37.

———. "'Dort werdet ihr ihn sehen' (Mk 16,7): Die redaktionelle Schlussnotiz des zweiten Evangeliums als dessen christologische Summe." *Theologie und Glaube* 76 (1986): 277–94.

———. "Entgrenzte Himmelsherrschaft: Zur Endekkung der paganen Welt im Matthäusevangelium." In *"Dies ist das Buch . . .": Das Matthäusevangelium (FS H. Frankemölle)*, edited by Rainer Kampling, 75–103. Paderborn: Schöningh, 2004.

———. "Evangelium als Lebensraum: Christologie und Ethik bei Paulus." In *Paulinische Christologie: Exegetische Beiträge; Hans Hübner zum 70. Geburtstag*, edited by Udo Schnelle et al., 9–31. Göttingen: Vandenhoeck & Ruprecht, 2000.

———. "Der Hebräerbrief und die Paulus-Schule." *Biblische Zeitschrift* 37 (1993): 183–208.

———. *Die "Jüngerkreise" des Täufers Johannes*. Paderborner theologische Studien 19. Paderborn: Schöningh, 1991.

———. "'Lösepreis für viele' (Mk 10,45)." In *Der Evangelist als Theologe*, edited by Thomas Söding, 91–118. Stuttgarter Bibelstudien 163. Stuttgart: Katholisches Bibelwerk, 1995.

———. "Lukas der Maler: Die Apostelgeschichte als intentionale Geschichte der christlichen Erstepoche." In *Historiographie und fiktionales Erzählen*, edited by G. Häfner, 30–66. Biblisch-theologische Studien 86. Neukirchen: Neukirchener Verlag, 2007.

———. "Per Christum in Deum: Zur theozentrischen Funktion der Christologie im Hebräerbrief." In *Der lebendige Gott: Studien zur Theologie des Neuen Testaments*, edited by Thomas Söding, 258–84. Neutestamentliche Abhandlungen, n.F., 31. Münster: Aschendorff, 1996.

———. "Die Vision vom ganz Anderen." In *Theologie als Vision: Studien zur Johannes-Offenbarung*, edited by Knut Backhaus. Stuttgarter Bibelstudien 191. Stuttgart: Verlag Katholisches Bibelwerk, 2001.

Backhaus, Knut. *Der Neue Bund und das Werden der Kirche: Die Diatheke-Deutung des Hebräerbriefs im Rahmen der frühchristlichen Theologiegeschichte*. Neutestamentliche Abhandlungen 29. Münster: Aschendorff, 1996.

Badiou, Alain. *Saint Paul: The Foundation of Universalism*. Translated by Ray Brassier. Stanford, CA: Stanford University Press, 2003.

Baer, Heinrich von. *Der Heilige Geist in den Lukasschriften*. Beiträge zur Wissenschaft vom Alten und Neuen Testament 39. Stuttgart: Kohlhammer, 1926.

Baird, William R. *History of New Testament Research: Volume Two: From Jonathan Edwards to Rudolf Bultmann*. Minneapolis: Fortress, 2002.

Balch, David L., and Carolyn Osiek. *Families in the New Testament World: Households and House Churches*. Louisville: Westminster John Knox, 1997.

Balla, P. *Challenges to New Testament Theology*. Wissenschaftliche Untersuchungen zum Neuen Testament 2.95. Tübingen: Mohr, 1997.

Balz, Horst Robert, Gerhard Krause, and Gerhard Müller. *Theologische Realenzyklopädie*. 33 vols. Berlin: de Gruyter, 1977–.

Balz, Horst Robert, and Gerhard Schneider, eds. *Exegetical Dictionary of the New Testament*. Translated by James W. Thompson and John W. Medendorp. 3 vols. Grand Rapids: Eerdmans, 1990.

Barnett, P. W. "The Jewish Sign Prophets—A.D. 40–47: Their Intentions and Origin." *New Testament Studies* 27 (1981): 679–97.

Barr, James. *Biblical Words for Time*. Studies in Biblical Theology 33. Naperville, IL: Allenson, 1962.

Barrett, C. K. "Christocentric or Theocentric?" In *Essays on John*, edited by C. K. Barrett, 1–18. Philadelphia: Westminster, 1982.

———. *The Gospel according to St. John*. 2nd ed. Philadelphia: Westminster, 1978.

Bartchy, S. Scott. "The Historical Jesus and Honor Reversal at Table." In *The Social Setting of Jesus and the Gospels*, edited by Wolfgang Stegemann et al., 175–83. Minneapolis: Fortress, 2002.

Barth, Gerhard. "Matthew's Understanding of the Law." In *Tradition and Interpretation in Matthew*, edited by Günther Bornkamm et al., translated by Percy Scott, 58–164. New Testament Library 30. Philadelphia: Westminster John Knox, 1963.

———. "Pistis in hellenistischer Religiosität." In *Neutestamentliche Versuche und Beobachtungen*, edited by Gerhard Barth, 169–94. Waltrop: Spenner, 1996.

———. *Der Tod Jesu Christi im Verständnis des Neuen Testaments*. Neukirchen-Vluyn: Neukirchener Verlag, 1992.

Barth, Karl. *Church Dogmatics*. Vol. 3.2, *The Doctrine of Creation*. Translated by Geoffrey W. Bromiley et al. Edinburgh: T&T Clark, 1960.

Barthes, Roland. *The Semiotic Challenge*. Translated by Richard Howard. New York: Hill and Wang, 1988.

Barthes, Roland, and Helmut Scheffel. *Mythen des Alltags*. Frankfurt: Suhrkamp, 2006 [1957].

Bauckham, Richard. "The Beloved Disciple as Ideal Author." *Journal for the Study of the New Testament* 49 (1993): 21–44.

———. "For Whom Were Gospels Written?" In *The Gospels for All Christians: Rethinking the Gospel Audiences*, edited by Richard Bauckham, 9–48. Grand Rapids: Eerdmans, 1998.

———. "God in the Book of Revelation." *Proceedings of the Irish Biblical Association* 18 (1995): 40–53.

———. *Jude, 2 Peter*. Word Biblical Commentary. Waco: Word, 1983.

———. *The Theology of the Book of Revelation*. New Testament Theology. Cambridge: Cambridge University Press, 1993.

Bauer, Karl-Adolf. *Leiblichkeit, das Ende aller Werke Gottes*. Gütersloh: Gütersloher Verlagshaus, 1971.

Bauer, Walter, et al., eds. *Orthodoxy and Heresy in Earliest Christianity*. Translated by Paul J. Achtemeier et al. 2nd ed. Philadelphia: Fortress, 1971.

Baumbach, G. *Jesus von Nazareth im Lichte der jüdischen Gruppenbildung*. Berlin: Evangelische Verlagsanstalt, 1971.

———. "Die Schöpfung in der Theologie des Paulus." *Kairos* 21 (1979): 196–205.

Baumgarten, Jörg. *Paulus und die Apokalyptik: Die Auslegung apokalyptischer Überlieferungen in den echten Paulusbriefen*. Wissenschaftliche Monographien zum Alten und Neuen Testament 44. Neukirchen-Vluyn: Neukirchener Verlag, 1975.

Baumotte, Manfred. *Die Frage nach dem historischen Jesus: Texte aus drei Jahrhunderten*. Reader Theologie. Gütersloh: Gütersloher Verlagshaus, 1984.

Beasley-Murray, George R. *Jesus and the Last Days: The Interpretation of the Olivet Discourse*. Peabody, MA: Hendrickson, 1993.

Beck, David R. *The Discipleship Paradigm: Readers and Anonymous Characters in the Fourth Gospel*. Biblical Interpretation Series 27. Leiden: Brill, 1997.

Becker, E.-M. "Kamelhaare . . . und wilder Honig." In *Die bleibende Gegenwart des Evangeliums: Festschrift für Otto Merk*, edited by Roland Gebauer and Martin Meiser, 13–28. Marburger Theologische Studien 76. Marburg: Elwert, 2003.

Becker, Eve-Marie. "Der jüdisch-römische Krieg (66–70 n. Chr.) und das Markus-Evangelium." In *Die antike Historiographie und die Anfänge der christlichen Geschichtsschreibung*, edited by Eve-Marie Becker, 213–36. Beihefte zur Zeitschrift für die neutestamentliche Wissenschaft und die Kunde der älteren Kirche 129. Berlin: de Gruyter, 2005.

Becker, Jürgen. *Auferstehung der Toten im Urchristentum*. Stuttgarter Bibelstudien 82. Stuttgart: KBW Verlag, 1976.

———. *Das Evangelium nach Johannes*. Ökumenischer Taschenbuchkommentar zum Neuen Testament 4/1, 4/2. 2 vols. Gütersloh: Gütersloher Verlagshaus, 1979, 1981.

———. "Das Gottesbild Jesu." In *Jesus Christus in Historie und Theologie (FS Hans Conzelmann)*, edited by Georg Strecker, 105–26. Tübingen: Mohr, 1975.

———. "Die Hoffnung auf ewiges Leben im Johannesevangelium." *Zeitschrift für die neutestamentliche Wissenschaft und die Kunde der älteren Kirche* 91 (2000): 192–211.

———. *Jesus of Nazareth*. Translated by James E. Crouch. New York: de Gruyter, 1998.

———. *Johanneisches Christentum*. Tübingen: Mohr, 2004.

———. *Johannes der Täufer und Jesus von Nazareth*. Biblische Studien 63. Neukirchen-Vluyn: Neukirchener Verlag, 1972.

———. *Maria: Mutter Jesu und erwählte Jungfrau*. Biblische Gestalten 4. Leipzig: Evangelische Verlagsanstalt, 2001.

———. *Paul: Apostle to the Gentiles*. Translated by O. C. Dean. Louisville: Westminster John Knox, 1993.

———, ed. *Die Anfänge des Christentums: Alte Welt und neue Hoffnung*. Stuttgart: Kohlhammer, 1987.

Becker, Michael. *Wunder und Wundertäter im frührabbinischen Judentum: Studien zum Phänomen und seiner Überlieferung im Horizont von Magie und Dämonismus*. Tübingen: Mohr, 2002.

Behrends, O., and W. Sellert, eds. *Nomos und Gesetz: Ursprünge und Wirkungen des griechischen Gesetzesdenkens, Göttingen 1995*. Abhandlungen der Akademie der Wissenschaften in Göttingen, Philologisch-Historische Klasse 3/209. Göttingen: Vandenhoeck & Ruprecht, 1995.

Belle, Gilbert van. *The Signs Source in the Fourth Gospel: Historical Survey and Critical Evaluation of the Semeia Hypothesis*. Translated by Peter J. Judge. Bibliotheca ephemeridum theologicarum lovaniensium 116. Louvain: Leuven University Press, 1994.

Bellen, Heinz, and Hans Volkmann. *Grundzüge der römischen Geschichte*. 8th ed. Grundzüge 4. Darmstadt: Wissenschaftliche Buchgesellschaft, 1982.

Bendemann, R. von. "Die Auferstehung von den Toten als 'Basic Story.'" *Glaube und Lernen* 15 (2000): 148–62.

———. "Die kritische Diastase von Wissen, Wollen und Handeln." *Zeitschrift für die neutestamentliche Wissenschaft und die Kunde der älteren Kirche* 95 (2000): 35–63.

———. "Paulus und Israel in der Apostelgeschichte des Lukas." In *Ja und Nein: Christliche Theologie im Angesicht Israels; Festschrift zum 70. Geburtstag von Wolfgang Schrage*, edited by Klaus Wengst et al., 291–303. Neukirchen-Vluyn: Neukirchener Verlag, 1998.

———. "'Trefflich hat der Heilige Geist durch Jesaja, den Propheten, gesprochen . . .' (Apg 28,25): Zur Bedeutung von Jesaja 6,9f. für die Geschichtskonzeption des lukanischen Doppelwerkes." In *Das Echo des Propheten Jesaja: Beiträge zu seiner vielfältigen Rezeption*, edited by N. C. Baumgart et al., 45–73. Lüneburger theologische Beiträge 1. Münster: Lit, 2004.

———. *Zwischen ΔΟΞΑ und ΣΤΑΥΡΟΣ: Eine exegetische Untersuchung der Texte des sogenannten Reiseberichts im Lukasevangelium*. Beihefte zur Zeitschrift für die neutestamentliche Wissenschaft und die Kunde der älteren Kirche 101. Berlin: de Gruyter, 2001.

Berger, Klaus. *Formgeschichte des Neuen Testaments*. Heidelberg: Quelle & Meyer, 1984.

———. *Die Gesetzesauslegung Jesu: Ihr historischer Hintergrund im Judentum und im Alten Testament*. Wissenschaftliche Monographien zum

Alten und Neuen Testament 40. Neukirchen-Vluyn: Neukirchener Verlag, 1972.

———. "Streit um Gottes Vorsehung: Zur Position der Gegner im 2. Petrusbrief." In *Tradition and Re-interpretation in Jewish and Early Christian Literature: Essays in Honour of Jürgen C. H. Lebram*, edited by J. W. van Henten, 121–35. Studia post-Biblica 36. Leiden: Brill, 1986.

Berger, Peter L. *The Sacred Canopy: Elements of a Sociological Theory of Religion*. Garden City, NY: Doubleday, 1967.

Berger, Peter L., and Thomas Luckmann. *The Social Construction of Reality: A Treatise in the Sociology of Knowledge*. New York: Random House, 1966.

Bergmeier, Roland. *Glaube als Gabe nach Johannes: Religions- und theologiegeschichtliche Studien zum prädestinatianischen Dualismus im vierten Evangelium*. Beiträge zur Wissenschaft vom Alten und Neuen Testament 112. Stuttgart and Berlin: Kohlhammer, 1980.

Berner, Ursula. "Religio und Superstitio." In *Der Fremden wahrnehmen: Bausteine für eine Xenologie*, edited by Theo Sundermeier. Studien zum Verstehen fremder Religionen 5. Gütersloh: Gütersloher Verlagshaus, 1992.

Best, Ernest. *Following Jesus: Discipleship in the Gospel of Mark*. Journal for the Study of the New Testament: Supplement Series 4. Sheffield: Department of Biblical Studies, University of Sheffield, 1981.

Betz, Hans Dieter. "The Concept of the 'Inner Human Being' (ὁ ἔσω ἄνθρωπος) in the Anthropology of Paul." *New Testament Studies* 46 (2000): 315–41.

———. *Essays on the Sermon on the Mount*. Translated by L. L. Welborn. Philadelphia: Fortress, 1985.

———. *Galatians: A Commentary on Paul's Letter to the Churches in Galatia*. Hermeneia—A Critical and Historical Commentary on the Bible. Philadelphia: Fortress, 1979.

———. *Paul's Concept of Freedom in the Context of Hellenistic Discussions about the Possibilities of Human Freedom: Protocol of the Twenty-sixth Colloquy, 9 January 1977*. Berkeley: The Center, 1977.

———. *The Sermon on the Mount: A Commentary on the Sermon on the Mount, including the Sermon on the Plain (Matthew 5:3–7:27 and Luke 6:20–49)*. Hermeneia—A Critical and Historical Commentary on the Bible. Minneapolis: Fortress, 1995.

———, ed. *Die Religion in Geschichte und Gegenwart: Handwörterbuch für Theologie und Religionswissenschaft*. 4th ed. 6 vols. Tübingen: Mohr, 1998.

Betz, Otto. "Rechtfertigung in Qumran." In *Rechtfertigung: Festschrift für Ernst Käsemann zum 70. Geburtstag*, edited by Johannes Friedrich et al., 81–108. Göttingen: Vandenhoeck & Ruprecht, 1976.

Beutler, Johannes. "Die Heilsbedeutung des Todes Jesu im Johannesevangelium nach Joh. 13,1–20." In *Der Tod Jesu: Deutungen im Neuen Testament*, edited by Johannes Beutler and Karl Kertelge, 188–204. Quaestiones disputatae 74. Freiburg: Herder, 1976.

———. *Martyria*. Frankfurter theologische Studien 10. Frankfurt: Knecht, 1972.

Bickermann, E. "Die römische Kaiserapotheose." *Archiv für Religionswissenschaft* 27 (1929): 1–34.

Bieberstein, Sabine. *Verschwiegene Jüngerinnen, vergessene Zeuginnen: Gebrochene Konzepte im Lukasevangelium*. Novum Testamentum et Orbis Antiquus 38. Göttingen: Vandenhoeck & Ruprecht, 1998.

Bieringer, F. "Traditionsgeschichtlicher Ursprung und theologische Bedeutung der ὑπέρ-Aussagen im Neuen Testament." In *The Four Gospels, 1992: Festschrift Frans Neirynck*, edited by Frans van Segbroeck et al., 1:219–48. 3 vols. Bibliotheca ephemeridum theologicarum lovaniensium 100. Louvain: Leuven University Press, 1992.

Bieringer, R., et al., eds. *Anti-Judaism and the Fourth Gospel*. Louisville: Westminster John Knox, 2001.

Birt, Theodor. *Das antike Buchwesen in seinem Verhältniss zur Litteratur*. Berlin: Hertz, 1882.

Bittner, Wolfgang J. *Jesu Zeichen im Johannesevangelium: Die Messias-Erkenntnis im Johannesevangelium vor ihrem jüdischen Hintergrund*. Wissenschaftliche Untersuchungen zum Neuen Testament 26. Tübingen: Mohr, 1987.

Black, C. Clifton. *The Disciples according to Mark: Markan Redaction in Current Debate*. Journal for the Study of the New Testament: Supplement Series 27. Sheffield: JSOT Press, 1989.

Blank, Josef. *Krisis: Untersuchungen zur johanneischen Christologie und Eschatologie*. Freiburg i.B.: Lambertus, 1964.

———. "Der Mensch vor der radikalen Alternative." *Kairos* 22 (1980): 296–311.

Blass, Friedrich, and A. Debrunner. *A Greek Grammar of the New Testament and Other Early Christian Literature*. Translated by Robert W. Funk. Chicago: University of Chicago Press, 1961.

Blinzler, Josef. *Lexikalisches zu dem Terminus τὰ στοιχεῖα τοῦ κόσμου bei Paulus*. Analecta biblica 18. Rome: Pontifical Biblical Institute, 1963.

Blischke, Folker. *Die Begründung und die Durchsetzung der Ethik bei Paulus*. Leipzig: Evangelische Verlagsanstalt, 2007.

Blumenberg, Hans. *Matthäuspassion*. 4th ed. Frankfurt: Suhrkamp, 1993.

Böcher, Otto. "Aspekte einer Hermeneutik der Johannesoffenbarung." In *Theologie in der Spätzeit des Neuen Testaments: Vorträge auf dem Symposion zum 75. Geburtstag von Kurt Niederwimmer*, edited by Wilhelm Pratscher et al., 23–33. Vienna: Universität Wien, 2005.

———. "Hellenistisches in der Apokalypse des Johannes." In *Geschichte—Tradition—Reflexion: Festschrift für Martin Hengel zum 70. Geburtstag*, edited by Hubert Cancik et al., 3:473–92. Tübingen: Mohr, 1996.

———. "Lasterkataloge in der Apokalypse des Johannes." In *Leben lernen im Horizont des Glaubens*, edited by Bernhard Buschbeck and Friedrich Lemke, 75–84. Landauer Schriften zur Theologie und Religionspädagogik 1. Landau/Pfalz: Seminar Evang. Theologie, 1986.

———. "Mythos und Rationalität." In *Mythos und Rationalität*, edited by Hans Heinrich Schmid, 163–71. Gütersloh: Güterloher Verlagshaus, 1988.

———, ed. *Die Johannesapokalypse*. Erträge der Forschung 41. Darmstadt: Wissenschaftliche Buchgesellschaft, 1980.

Bock, Darrell L. *Blasphemy and Exaltation in Judaism and the Final Examination of Jesus: A Philological-historical Study of the Key Jewish Themes Impacting Mark 14:61–64*. Wissenschaftliche Untersuchungen zum Neuen Testament 2.106. Tübingen: Mohr, 1998.

Böhm, Martina. *Samarien und die Samaritai bei Lukas: Eine Studie zum religionshistorischen und traditionsgeschichtlichen Hintergrund der lukanischen Samarientexte und zu deren topographischer Verhaftung*. Wissenschaftliche Untersuchungen zum Neuen Testament 2.111. Tübingen: Mohr, 1999.

Borg, Marcus J. *Jesus: A New Vision: Spirit, Culture, and the Life of Discipleship*. San Francisco: Harper & Row, 1987.

Boring, M. Eugene. *The Continuing Voice of Jesus: Christian Prophecy and the Gospel Tradition*. Louisville: Westminster John Knox, 1991.

———. "The Historical-Critical Method's 'Criteria of Authenticity': The Beatitudes in Q and Thomas as a Test Case." In *The Historical Jesus and the Rejected Gospels*, edited by Charles W. Hedrick, 9–44. Semeia 44. Atlanta: Society of Biblical Literature, 1988.

———. "The Language of Universal Salvation in Paul." *Journal of Biblical Literature* 105 (1986): 269–92.

———. "Mark 1:1–15 and the Beginning of the Gospel." In *How Gospels Began*, edited by Dennis E. Smith, 43–82. Semeia 52. Atlanta: Society of Biblical Literature, 1990.

———. *Mark: A Commentary*. New Testament Library. Louisville: Westminster John Knox, 2006.

———. "Matthew: Introduction, Commentary, and Reflections." In *The New Interpreter's Bible*, edited by Leander Keck, 8:87–505. Nashville: Abingdon, 1995.

———. "Narrative Christology in the Apocalypse." *Catholic Biblical Quarterly* 54 (1992): 702–23.

———. "Narrative Dynamics in 1 Peter: The Function of Narrative World." In *Reading 1 Peter with New Eyes: Methodological Reassessments of the Letter of First Peter*, edited by Robert L. Webb and Betsy Bauman-Martin. Library of New Testament Studies 364. Edinburgh: T&T Clark, 2007.

———. "Rhetoric, Righteousness, and the Sermon on the Mount." In *Listening to the Word: Studies in Honor of Fred B. Craddock*, edited by Gail R. O'Day and Thomas G. Long. Nashville: Abingdon, 1993. 53ff.

———. *Sayings of the Risen Jesus: Christian Prophecy in the Synoptic Tradition*. Society of New Testament Studies Monograph Series 46. Cambridge: Cambridge University Press, 1982.

———. "The Theology of Revelation: 'The Lord Our God the Almighty Reigns.'" *Interpretation* 40 (1986): 257–69.

———. "The 'Third Quest' and the Apostolic Faith." *Interpretation* 50 (1996): 341–54. Reprinted in *Gospel Interpretation: Narrative-Critical and Social-Scientific Approaches*, edited by Jack D. Kingsbury, 237–52. Harrisburg, PA: Trinity, 1998.

———. "The Unforgivable Sin Logion Mark 3:28–29/Matt 12:31–32/Luke 12:10: Formal Analysis and History of the Tradition." *Novum Testamentum* 17 (1976): 258–79.

Boring, M. Eugene, et al., eds. *Hellenistic Commentary to the New Testament*. Nashville: Abingdon, 1995.

Bormann, Lukas. *Recht, Gerechtigkeit und Religion im Lukasevangelium*. Studien zur Umwelt des Neuen Testaments 24. Göttingen: Vandenhoeck & Ruprecht, 2001.

———. "Die Verrechtlichung der frühesten christlichen Überlieferung im lukanischen Schrifttum." In *Religious Propaganda and Missionary Competition in the New Testament World: Essays Honoring Dieter Georgi*, edited by Lukas Bormann et al., 283–311. Supplements to Novum Testamentum 74. Leiden: Brill, 1994.

Bornkamm, Günther. "Der Auferstandene und der Irdische: Mt 28,16–20." In *Zeit und Geschichte: Dankesgabe an Rudolf Bultmann zum 80. Geburtstag*, edited by Erich Dinkler and Hartwig Thyen, 171–91. Tübingen: Mohr, 1964.

———. "Das Doppelgebot der Liebe." In *Geschichte und Glaube*, edited by Günther Bornkamm, 37–45. Beiträge zur evangelischen Theologie 53. Munich: Kaiser, 1968.

———. "End-Expectation and Church in Matthew." In *Tradition and Interpretation in Matthew*, edited by Günther Bornkamm et al., translated by Percy Scott, 15–51. New Testament Library. Philadelphia: Westminster John Knox, 1963.

———. "Faith and Reason in Paul's Epistles." *New Testament Studies* 4.2 (1958): 93–100.

———. "Die Häresie des Kolosserbriefes." In *Das Ende des Gesetzes: Paulusstudien*, edited by Günther Bornkamm, 139–56. Beiträge zur evangelischen Theologie 16. Munich: Kaiser, 1961.

———. *Jesus von Nazareth*. 9th ed. Stuttgart: Kohlhammer, 1971.

———. "Der köstlichere Weg." In *Das Ende des Gesetzes: Paulusstudien*, edited by Günther Bornkamm. Beiträge zur evangelischen Theologie 16. Munich: Kaiser, 1961.

———. "Zum Verständnis des Christus-Hymnus Phil 2,6–11." In *Studien zu Antike und Urchristentum*, edited by Günther Bornkamm. Beiträge zur evangelischen Theologie 28. Munich: Kaiser, 1970.

Bösen, Willibald. *Galiläa als Lebensraum und Wirkungsfeld Jesu*. Freiburg: Herder, 1985.

———. *Jesusmahl, Eucharistisches Mahl, Endzeitmahl: Ein Beitrag zur Theologie des Lukas*. Stuttgarter Bibelstudien 67. Stuttgart: 1980.

Böttrich, C. *Petrus: Fischer, Fels, und Funktionär*. Biblische Gestalten 2. Leipzig: Evangelische Verlagsanstalt, 2001.

Bousset, Wilhelm. *Kyrios Christos: Geschichte des Christusglaubens von den Anfängen des Christentums bis Irenaeus*. Göttingen: Vandenhoeck & Ruprecht, 1967. ET: *Kyrios Christos: A History of the Belief in Christ from the Beginnings of Christianity to Irenaeus*. Translated by John E. Steely. Nashville: Abingdon, 1970.

Bovon, François. *Das Evangelium nach Lukas*. Evangelisch-katholischer Kommentar zum Neuen Testament 3. 4 vols. Neukirchen-Vluyn: Neukirchener Verlag, 1989–2009.

———. "Gott bei Lukas." In *Lukas in Neuer Sicht: Gesammelte Aufsätze*, edited by François Bovon, translated by Elizabeth Hartmann et al., 98–119. Biblisch-theologische Studien 8. Neukirchen-Vluyn: Neukirchener Verlag, 1985.

———. *Luke 1: A Commentary on the Gospel of Luke 1:1–9:50*. Hermeneia—A Critical and Historical Commentary on the Bible. Minneapolis: Fortress, 2002.

Brandenburger, Egon. "Gerichtskonzeptionen im Urchristentum und ihre Voraussetzungen: Eine Problemstudie." In *Studien zur Geschichte und Theologie des Urchristentums*, edited by Egon Brandenburger. Stuttgarter biblische Aufsatzbände NT 15. Stuttgart: Verlag Katholisches Bibelwerk, 1993.

———. *Markus 13 und die Apokalyptik*. Forschungen zur Religion und Literatur des Alten und Neuen Testaments 134. Göttingen: Vandenhoeck & Ruprecht, 1984.

Braun, Herbert. "Die Indifferenz gegenüber der Welt bei Paulus und bei Epiktet." In *Gesammelte Studien zum Neuen Testament und seiner Umwelt*, edited by Herbert Braun, 159–67. Tübingen: Mohr, 1971.

Breytenbach, Cilliers. "Das Markusevangelium als traditionsgebundene Erzählung? Anfragen an die Markusforschung der achtziger Jahre." In *The Synoptic Gospels: Source Criticism and the New Literary Criticism*, edited by F. Neirynck and Camille Focant, 77–110. Bibliotheca ephemeridum theologicarum lovaniensium 110. Louvain: Leuven University Press, 1993.

———. *Nachfolge und Zukunftserwartung nach Markus: Eine methodenkritische Studie*. Abhandlungen zur Theologie des Alten und Neuen Testaments 71. Zürich: Theologischer Verlag, 1984.

———. "Versöhnung, Stellvertretung und Sühne." *New Testament Studies* 39 (1993): 59–79.

———. *Versöhnung: Eine Studie zur paulinischen Soteriologie*. Wissenschaftliche Monographien zum Alten und Neuen Testament 60. Neukirchen-Vluyn: Neukirchener Verlag, 1989.

Broadhead, Edwin Keith. *Teaching with Authority: Miracles and Christology in the Gospel of Mark*. Journal for the Study of the New Testament: Supplement Series 74. Sheffield: JSOT Press, 1992.

Brockhaus, Ulrich. *Charisma und Amt: Die paulinische Charismenlehre auf dem Hintergrund der frühchristlichen Gemeindefunktionen*. Wuppertal: Brockhaus, 1972.

Brodersen, Kai, ed. *Prognosis: Studien zur Funktion von Zukunftsvorhersagen in Literatur und Geschichte seit der Antike*. Antike Kultur und Geschichte 2. Münster: LIT, 2001.

Broer, Ingo. "'Der Herr ist wahrhaft auferstanden' (Lk 24,34): Auferstehung Jesu und historisch-kritische Methode; Erwägungen zur Entstehung des Osterglaubens." In *Auferstehung Jesu, Auferstehung der Christen: Deutungen des Osterglaubens*, edited by Ingo Broer and Lorenz Oberlinner. Quaestiones disputatae 105. Freiburg i.B.: Herder, 1986.

———. "Jesus und das Gesetz." In *Jesus und das jüdische Gesetz*, edited by Ingo Broer, 61–104. Stuttgart: Kohlhammer, 1992.

Broer, Ingo, and Jens-W. Taeger, eds. *Jesus und das jüdische Gesetz*. Stuttgart: Kohlhammer, 1992.

Brown, Raymond E. *The Death of the Messiah: From Gethsemane to the Grave: A Commentary on the Passion Narratives in the Four Gospels*. Anchor Bible Reference Library. 2 vols. New York: Doubleday, 1994.

———. *Jesus: God and Man*. Modern Biblical Reflections. New York: Macmillan, 1967.

Brown, Raymond E., et al., eds. *Peter in the New Testament*. Minneapolis: Augsburg, 1973.

Brown, Raymond Edward, and Francis J. Moloney. *An Introduction to the Gospel of John*. 1st ed. Anchor Bible Reference Library. New York: Doubleday, 2003.

Brox, Norbert. *Der Erste Petrusbrief*. Evangelisch-katholischer Kommentar Zum Neuen Testament 21. Zürich: Benziger, 1979.

———. *Falsche Verfasserangaben: Zur Erklärung der frühchristlichen Pseudepigraphie*. Stuttgarter Bibelstudien 79. Stuttgart: KBW Verlag, 1975.

———. *Die Pastoralbriefe: 1 Timotheus, 2 Timotheus, Titus*. 5th ed. Regensburger Neues Testament 7. Regensburg: Pustet, 1989.

Brucker, Ralph. *"Christushymnen" oder "epideiktische Passagen"?* Forschungen zur Religion und Literatur des Alten und Neuen Testaments 176. Göttingen: Vandenhoeck & Ruprecht, 1997.

Büchele, Anton. *Der Tod Jesu im Lukasevangelium: Eine redaktionsgeschichtliche Untersuchung zu Lk 23*. 1st ed. Frankfurter theologische Studien 26. Frankfurt a.M.: Knecht, 1978.

Büchsel, Friedrich. "'In Christus' bei Paulus." *Zeitschrift für die neutestamentliche Wissenschaft und die Kunde der älteren Kirche* (1949): 141–58.

Bühner, J.-A. "Denkstrukturen im Johannesevangelium." *Theologische Beiträge* (1982): 224–31.

———. "Jesus und die antike Magie: Bemerkungen zu M. Smith, Jesus der Magier." *Evangelische Theologie* 43 (1983): 156–75.

Bultmann, Rudolf. "Bekenntnis- und Liedfragmente im ersten Petrusbrief." In *Exegetica: Aufsätze zur Erforschung des Neuen Testaments*, edited by Erich Dinkler, 285–97. Tübingen: Mohr, 1967.

———. *A Commentary on the Johannine Epistles*. Hermeneia—A Critical and Historical Commentary on the Bible. Translated by R. Philip O'Hara et al. Philadelphia: Fortress, 1973.

———. *The Gospel of John: A Commentary*. Translated by G. R. Beasley-Murray et al. Philadelphia: Westminster, 1971.

———. *The History of the Synoptic Tradition*. Translated by John Marsh. New York: Harper & Row, 1963.

———. *Jesus and the Word*. Translated by Louise Pettibone Smith and Erminie Huntress Lantero. New York: Scribner, 1958.

———. *Jesus Christ and Mythology*. London: SCM, 1958.

———. "Karl Barth, 'The Resurrection of the Dead.'" In *Faith and Understanding*, edited by Robert W. Funk, translated by Louise Pettibone Smith, 66–94. London: SCM, 1969.

———. "New Testament and Mythology." In *Kerygma and Myth*, edited by Hans Bartsch Werner, 1–44. New York: Harper, 1961.

———. "The Primitive Christian Kerygma and the Historical Jesus." In *The Historical Jesus and the Kerygmatic Christ: Essays on the New Quest of the Historical Jesus*, edited by Carl E. Braaten and Roy A. Harrisville, translated by Carl E. Braaten and Roy A. Harrisville, 15–42. Nashville: Abingdon, 1964.

———. *Primitive Christianity in Its Contemporary Setting*. New York: Meridian Books, 1956.

———. *Theology of the New Testament*. Translated by Kendrick Grobel. 2 vols. New York: Scribner, 1951–55.

Bultmann, Rudolf, and Erich Dinkler, eds. *The Second Letter to the Corinthians*. Translated by Roy A. Harrisville. Minneapolis: Augsburg, 1985.

Burchard, Christoph. "Das doppelte Liebesgebot in der frühchristlichen Überlieferung." In *Studien zur Theologie, Sprache und Umwelt des Neuen Testaments*, edited by Christoph Burchard and Dieter Sänger. Wissenschaftliche Untersuchungen zum Neuen Testament 107. Tübingen: Mohr, 1998.

———. *Der dreizehnte Zeuge: Traditions- und kompositionsgeschichtliche Untersuchungen zu Lukas Darstellung der Frühzeit des Paulus*. Forschungen zur Religion und Literatur des Alten und Neuen Testaments 103. Göttingen: Vandenhoeck & Ruprecht, 1970.

———. *Der Jakobusbrief*. Handbuch zum Neuen Testament 15/1. Tübingen: Mohr, 2000.

———. "Jesus von Nazareth." In *Die Anfänge des Christentums: Alte Welt und neue Hoffnung*, edited by Jürgen Becker, 12–58. Stuttgart: Kohlhammer, 1987.

Burfeind, C. "Paulus *muß* nach Rom." *New Testament Studies* 46 (2000): 75–91.

Burge, Gary M. *The Anointed Community: The Holy Spirit in the Johannine Tradition*. Grand Rapids: Eerdmans, 1987.

Burger, Christoph. "Jesu Taten nach Matthäus 8 und 9." *Zeitschrift für Theologie und Kirche* 70 (1973): 272–87.

———. *Schöpfung und Versöhnung: Studien zum liturgischen Gut im Kolosser- und Epheserbrief*. Wissenschaftliche Monographien zum Alten und Neuen Testament 46. Neukirchen-Vluyn: Neukirchener Verlag, 1975.

Burkert, Walter. *Greek Religion*. Translated by John Raffan. Cambridge, MA: Harvard University Press, 1985.

Burridge, Richard A. *What Are the Gospels? A Comparison with Graeco-Roman Biography*. Society of New Testament Studies Monograph Series 70. Cambridge: Cambridge University Press, 1992.

Busch, Peter. *Der gefallene Drache: Mythenexegese am Beispiel von Apokalypse 12*. Texte und Arbeiten zum neutestamentlichen Zeitalter 19. Tübingen: Francke Verlag, 1996.

Busemann, R. *Die Jüngergemeinde nach Markus*. Bonner biblische Beiträge 57. Bonn: Hannstein, 1983.

Busse, Ulrich. *Das Nazaret-Manifest Jesu*. Stuttgarter Bibelstudien 91. Stuttgart: 1978.

Bussmann, Claus. *Themen der paulinischen Missionspredigt auf dem Hintergrund der spätjüdisch-hellenistischen Missionsliteratur*. Europäische Hochschulschriften 23.3. Bern: Lang, 1971.

Campenhausen, Hans von. *Der Ablauf der Osterereignisse und das leere Grab*. 4th ed. Sitzungsberichte der Heidelberger Akademie der Wissenschaften. Heidelberg: C. Winter, 1977.

———. *The Formation of the Christian Bible*. Translated by John Austin Baker. London: Adam & Charles Black, 1972.

Camponovo, Odo. *Königtum, Königsherrschaft und Reich Gottes in den frühjudischen Schriften*. Orbis Biblicus et Orientalis 58. Göttingen: Vandenhoeck & Ruprecht, 1984.

Cancik, Hubert, and Konrad Hitzl, eds. *Die Praxis der Herrscherverehrung in Rom und seinen Provinzen*. Tübingen: Mohr, 2003.

Capes, David B. *Old Testament Yahweh Texts in Paul's Christology*. Wissenschaftliche Untersuchungen zum Neuen Testament 2.47. Tübingen: Mohr, 1992.

Carlson, Stephen C. *The Gospel Hoax: Morton Smith's Invention of Secret Mark*. Waco: Baylor University Press, 2005.

Cassirer, Ernst. *An Essay on Man: An Introduction to a Philosophy of Human Culture*. New Haven: Yale University Press, 1992.

Charlesworth, James H., ed. *The Beloved Disciple*. Valley Forge, PA: Trinity, 1995.

———. *The Messiah: Developments in Earliest Judaism and Christianity*. Minneapolis: Fortress, 1992.

Clarke, Andrew D. *Serve the Community of the Church: Christians as Leaders and Ministers*. Grand Rapids: Eerdmans, 2000.

Clauss, Manfred. *Kaiser und Gott: Herrscherkult im römischen Reich*. Stuttgart: Teubner, 1999.

Coenen, L., and Klaus Haacker, eds. *Theologisches Begriffslexikon zum Neuen Testament*. 2 vols. Wuppertal: Brockhaus, 1997–2000.

Collins, Adela Yarbro. *Crisis and Catharsis: The Power of the Apocalypse*. Philadelphia: Westminster, 1984.

———. "Mark and His Readers: The Son of God among Jews." *Harvard Theological Review* 92 (1999): 393–408.

———. *Mark: A Commentary*. Hermeneia—A Critical and Historical Commentary on the Bible. Minneapolis: Fortress, 2007.

———. "The Son of God among Greeks and Romans." *Harvard Theological Review* 92 (2000): 85–100.

Collins, John J. *The Scepter and the Star: The Messiahs of the Dead Sea Scrolls and Other Ancient Literature*. New York: Doubleday, 1995.

Colpe, Carsten. "Zur Leib-Christi-Vorstellung im Epheserbrief." In *Judentum—Urchristentum—Kirche: Festschrift für Joachim Jeremias*, edited by Walther Eltester, 172–87. Beihefte zur Zeitschrift für die neutestamentliche Wissenschaft und die Kunde der älteren Kirche 26. Berlin: Töpelmann, 1960.

Combrink, H. J. B. "Salvation in Mark." In *Salvation in the New Testament: Perspectives on Soteriology*, edited by J. G. Van der Watt, 33–66. Supplements to Novum Testamentum 121. Leiden: Brill, 2005.

Conrad, Christoph, and Martina Kessel. *Geschichte Schreiben in der Postmoderne: Beiträge zur aktuellen Diskussion*. Stuttgart: Reclam, 1994.

Conzelmann, Hans. *1 Corinthians: A Commentary on the First Epistle to the Corinthians*. Hermeneia—A Critical and Historical Commentary on the Bible. Translated by James W. Leitch. Philadelphia: Fortress, 1975.

———. *Acts of the Apostles: A Commentary on the Acts of the Apostles*. Hermeneia—A Critical and Historical Commentary on the Bible. Translated by James Limburg et al. Philadelphia: Fortress, 1987.

———. "On the Analysis of the Confessional Formula 1 Corinthians 15:3–5." *Interpretation* 20 (1966): 15–25.

———. *An Outline of the Theology of the New Testament*. Translated by John Bowden. New York: Harper & Row, 1969.

———. "Present and Future in the Synoptic Tradition." *Journal for Theology and the Church* 5 (1968): 26–44.

———. *The Theology of St. Luke*. Translated by Geoffrey Buswell. New York: Harper & Row, 1961.

Crossan, John Dominic. *The Historical Jesus: The Life of a Mediterranean Jewish Peasant*. San Francisco: HarperSanFrancisco, 1991.

Crossan, John Dominic, and Jonathan L. Reed. *Excavating Jesus: Beneath the Stones, behind the Texts*. 1st ed. San Francisco: HarperSanFrancisco, 2001.

———. *In Search of Paul: How Jesus's Apostle Opposed Rome's Empire with God's Kingdom: A New Vision of Paul's Words and World*. New York: HarperSanFrancisco, 2004.

Crüsemann, Frank. *Die Tora: Theologie und Sozialgeschichte des alttestamentlichen Gesetzes*. Munich: Kaiser, 1992.

Culpepper, R. Alan. *Anatomy of the Fourth Gospel. A Study in Literary Design*. New Testament Foundations and Facets. Philadelphia: Fortress, 1983.

———. *John, the Son of Zebedee: The Life of a Legend*. Minneapolis: Fortress, 1999.

Dalferth, Ingolf U. *Der auferweckte Gekreuzigte: Zur Grammatik der Christologie*. Tübingen: Mohr, 1994.

———. "Die soteriologische Relevanz der Kategorie des Opfers." *Jahrbuch für Biblische Theologie* 6 (1991): 173–94.

———. "Theologie im Kontext der Religionswissenschaft." *Theologische Literaturzeitung* 126 (2001): 4–20.

———. "Volles Grab, leerer Glaube?" *Zeitschrift für Theologie und Kirche* 95 (1998): 379–409.

Dalman, Gustaf. *The Words of Jesus: Considered in the Light of Post-biblical Jewish Writings and the Aramaic Language*. Translated by David Miller Kay. Edinburgh: T&T Clark, 1909.

Dassmann, Ernst. "Hausgemeinde und Bischofsamt." In *Ämter und Dienste in den frühchristlichen Gemeinden*, edited by Ernst Dassmann, 74–95. Bonn: Borengässer, 1994.

———. "Witwen und Diakonissen." In *Ämter und Dienste in den frühchristlichen Gemeinden*, edited by Ernst Dassmann, 142–56. Bonn: Borengässer, 1994.

Dauer, Anton. *Beobachtungen zur literarischen Arbeitstechnik des Lukas*. Athenäums Monografien, Theologie 79. Frankfurt a.M.: Hain, 1990.

Dautzenberg, Gerhard. "Freiheit im hellenistischen Kontext." In *Der neue Mensch in Christus: Hellenistische Anthropologie und Ethik im Neuen Testament*, edited by Hans Dieter Betz and Johannes Beutler. Quaestiones disputatae 190. Freiburg: Herder, 2001.

———. "Der Glaube im Hebräerbrief." *Biblische Zeitschrift* 17 (1973): 161–77.

———. *Urchristliche Prophetie: Ihre Erforschung, ihre Voraussetzungen im Judentum und ihre Struktur im ersten Korintherbrief*. Beiträge zur

Wissenschaft vom Alten (und Neuen) Testament. Stuttgart: Kohlhammer, 1975.

Dechow, J. *Gottessohn und Herrschaft Gottes: Der Theozentrismus des Markusevangeliums*. Wissenschaftliche Monographien zum Alten und Neuen Testament 86. Neukirchen: Neukirchener Verlag, 2000.

Deichgräber, Reinhard. *Gotteshymnus und Christushymnus in der frühen Christenheit: Untersuchungen zu Form, Sprache und Stil der frühchristlichen Hymnen*. Studien zur Umwelt des Neuen Testaments 5. Göttingen: Vandenhoeck & Ruprecht, 1967.

Deines, Roland. *Die Gerechtigkeit der Tora im Reich des Messias*. Wissenschaftliche Untersuchungen zum Neuen Testament 177. Tübingen: Mohr, 204.

Deissmann, Adolf. *Light from the Ancient East: The New Testament Illustrated by Recently Discovered Texts of the Graeco-Roman World*. Translated by Lionel R. M. Strachan. New York: Doran, 1927.

———. *Die neutestamentliche Formel "in Christo Jesu."* Marburg: Elwert, 1892.

Delling, Gerhard. *Die Bewältigung der Diasporasituation durch das hellenistische Judentum*. Göttingen: Vandenhoeck & Ruprecht, 1987.

———. *Die Taufe im Neuen Testament*. Berlin: Evangelische Verlagsanstalt, 1963.

———. "Der Tod Jesu in der Verkündigung des Paulus." In *Studien zum Neuen Testament und zum hellenistischen Judentum: Gesammelte Aufsätze 1950–1968*, edited by Ferdinand Hahn et al., 336–46. Göttingen: Vandenhoeck & Ruprecht, 1970.

———. *Zeit und Endzeit: Zwei Vorlesungen zur Theologie des Neuen Testaments*. Neukirchen-Vluyn: Neukirchener Verlag, 1970.

———. *Das Zeitverständnis des Neuen Testaments*. Gütersloh: Bertelsmann, 1940.

———. "Zum gottesdienstlichen Stil der Johannes-Apokalypse." In *Studien zum Neuen Testament und zum hellenistischen Judentum: Gesammelte Aufsätze 1950–1968*, edited by Ferdinand Hahn et al., 425–50. Göttingen: Vandenhoeck & Ruprecht, 1970.

Deming, Will. *Paul on Marriage and Celibacy: The Hellenistic Background of 1 Corinthians 7*. 2nd ed. Grand Rapids: Eerdmans, 2003.

Dettwiler, Andreas. *Die Gegenwart des Erhöhten*. Forschungen zur Literatur des Alten und Neuen Testaments 169. Göttingen: Vandenhoeck & Ruprecht, 1995.

———. "Das Verständnis des Kreuzes Jesu im Kolosserbrief." In *Kreuzestheologie im Neuen Testament*, edited by Andreas Dettwiler and Jean Zumstein, 81–105. Wissenschaftliche Untersuchungen zum Neuen Testament 151. Tübingen: Mohr, 2002.

Dewey, Joanna. *Markan Public Debate: Literary Technique, Concentric Structure and Theology in Mark 2:1–3:6*. Society of Biblical Literature Dissertation Series 48. Chico, CA: Scholars Press, 1980.

Dibelius, Martin. *From Tradition to Gospel*. New York: Scribner, 1935.

———. "Paul on the Areopagus." In *Studies in the Acts of the Apostles*, edited by Martin Dibelius and Heinrich Greeven, 26–77. London: SCM, 1956.

———. "The Speeches in Acts and Ancient Historiography." In *Studies in the Acts of the Apostles*, edited by Martin Dibelius and Heinrich Greeven, 138–85. London: SCM, 1956.

Dibelius, Martin, and Hans Conzelmann. *The Pastoral Epistles*. Hermeneia—A Critical and Historical Commentary on the Bible. Translated by Philip Buttolph and Adela Yarbro. Philadelphia: Fortress, 1972.

Dibelius, Martin, and Heinrich Greeven. *A Commentary on the Epistle of James*. Hermeneia—A Critical and Historical Commentary on the Bible. Translated by Michael Williams. Philadelphia: Fortress, 1976.

Dibelius, Martin, and Eduard Lohse. "Lukas als Theologe der Heilsgeschichte." In *Das Lukas-Evangelium*, 64–90. Weg der Forschung 280. Darmstadt: Wissenschaftliche Buchgesellschaft, 1974.

Diefenbach, Manfred. *Die Komposition des Lukasevangeliums unter Berücksichtigung antiker Rhetorikelemente*. Frankfurter theologische Studien 43. Frankfurt a.M.: Knecht, 1993.

———. *Der Konflikt Jesu mit den "Juden": Ein Versuch zur Lösung der johanneischen Antijudaismus-Diskussion mit Hilfe des antiken Handlungsverständnisses*. Neutestamentliche Abhandlungen 41. Münster: Aschendorff, 2002.

Dihle, Albrecht. *Die goldene Regel: Eine Einführung in die Geschichte der antiken und frühchristlichen Vulgärethik*. Studienhefte zur Altertumswissenschaft 7. Göttingen: Vandenhoeck & Ruprecht, 1962.

Dobbeler, Axel von. "Die Restitution Israels und die Bekehrung der Heiden." *Zeitschrift für die neu-*

testamentliche Wissenschaft und die Kunde der älteren Kirche 91 (2000): 18–44.

Doble, Peter. *The Paradox of Salvation: Luke's Theology of the Cross*. Society for New Testament Studies Monograph Series. Cambridge: Cambridge University Press, 1996.

Doering, Lutz. *Schabbat: Sabbathalacha und -praxis im antiken Judentum und Urchristentum*. Texte und Studien zum antiken Judentum 78. Tübingen: Mohr, 1999.

Dohmen, Christoph, and Thomas Söding, eds. *Eine Bibel, zwei Testamente: Positionen biblischer Theologie*. Paderborn: Ferdinand Schöningh, 1995.

Dormeyer, Detlev. *Das Markusevangelium*. Darmstadt: Wissenschaftliche Buchgesellschaft, 2005.

———. *Das Markusevangelium als Idealbiographie von Jesus Christus, dem Nazarener*. Stuttgarter Bibelstudien 43. Stuttgart: Katholisches Bibelwerk, 1999.

Downing, Francis Gerald. *Cynics, Paul, and the Pauline Churches: Cynics and Christian Origins II*. London: Routledge, 1998.

———. "Ethical Pagan Theism." *New Testament Studies* 27 (1981): 544–63.

———. "The Jewish Cynic Jesus." In *Jesus, Mark and Q: The Teaching of Jesus and Its Earliest Records*, edited by Michael Labahn and Andreas Schmidt, 118–214. Journal for the Study of the New Testament: Supplement Series 214. Sheffield: Sheffield Academic Press, 2001.

Droysen, Johann Gustav. *Historik: Rekonstruktion der ersten vollständigen Fassung der Vorlesungen*. Stuttgart-Bad Cannstatt: Frommann-Holzboog, 1857.

———. *Outline of the Principles of History*. Translated by E. Benjamin Andrews. New York: Fertig, 1893.

Dschulnigg, Peter. *Jesus begegnen: Personen und ihre Bedeutung im Johannesevangelium*. Theologie 30. Münster: Lit, 2000.

———. "Der theologische Ort des Zweiten Petrusbriefes." *Biblische Zeitschrift* 33 (1989): 161–77.

———. "Warnung vor Reichtum und Ermahnung der Reichen." *Biblische Zeitschrift* 37 (1993): 60–77.

Dübbers, Michael. *Christologie und Existenz im Kolosserbrief: Exegetische und semantische Untersuchungen zur Intention des Kolosserbriefes*. Wissenschaftliche Untersuchungen zum Neuen Testament 2.191. Tübingen: Mohr Siebeck, 2005.

Dunn, James D. G. *Christology in the Making. A New Testament Inquiry into the Origins of the Doctrine of the Incarnation*. Philadelphia: Westminster, 1980.

———. *Jesus Remembered*. Christianity in the Making 1. Grand Rapids: Eerdmans, 2003.

———. *New Testament Theology: An Introduction*. Nashville: Abingdon, 2009.

———. *The Theology of Paul the Apostle*. Grand Rapids: Eerdmans, 1998.

———. *Unity and Diversity in the New Testament: An Inquiry into the Character of Earliest Christianity*. 3rd ed. London: SCM, 2006.

Du Rand, J. A. "Soteriology in the Apocalypse of John." In *Salvation in the New Testament: Perspectives on Soteriology*, edited by J. G.Van der Watt, 465–504. Supplements to Novum Testamentum 121. Leiden: Brill, 2005.

Du Toit, A. B. "Redefining Jesus: Current Trends in Jesus Research." In *Jesus, Mark and Q: The Teaching of Jesus and Its Earliest Records*, edited by Michael Labahn and Andreas Schmidt, 82–124. Journal for the Study of the New Testament: Supplement Series 214. Sheffield: Sheffield Academic Press, 2001.

Du Toit, D. S. *Der abwesende Herr. Strategien im Markusevangelium zur Bewältigung der Abwesenheit des Auferstandenen*. Wissenschaftliche Monographien zum Alten und Neuen Testament 111. Neukirchen: Neukirchener Verlag, 2006.

———. "'Gesalbter Gottessohn'—Jesus als letzter Bote Gottes: Zur Christologie des Markusevangeliums." In "*. . . Was ihr auf dem Weg verhandelt habt": Beiträge zur Exegese und Theologie des Neuen Testaments; Festschrift für Ferdinand Hahn zum 75. Geburtstag*, edited by Peter Müller et al., 37–50. Neukirchen-Vluyn: Neukirchener Verlag, 2001.

Dux, Günter. *Historisch-genetische Theorie der Kultur: Instabile Welten: Zur prozessualen Logik im kulturellen Wandel*. Weilerswist: Velbrück Wissenschaft, 2000.

———. "Wie der Sinn in die Welt kam und was aus ihm wurde." In *Historische Sinnbildung: Problemstellungen, Zeitkonzepte, Wahrnehmungshorizonte, Darstellungsstrategien*, edited by Klaus E. Müller and Jörn Rüsen, 195–217. Reinbek bei Hamburg: Rowohlt, 1997.

Ebel, Eva. *Die Attraktivität früher christlicher Gemeinden: Die Gemeinde von Korinth im Spiegel griechisch-römischer Vereine*. Wissenschaftliche

Untersuchungen zum Neuen Testament 2.178. Tübingen: Mohr Siebeck, 2004.

Ebeling, Gerhard. "The Question of the Historical Jesus and the Problem of Christology." In *Word and Faith*, edited by Gerhard Ebeling, 288–304. Philadelphia: Fortress, 1963.

Ebersohn, M. *Das Nächstenliebegebot in der synoptischen Tradition*. Marburger Theologische Studien 37. Marburg: Elwert, 1993.

Ebner, Martin. *Jesus, ein Weisheitslehrer? Synoptische Weisheitslogien im Traditionsprozess*. Herders biblische Studien 15. Freiburg i.B.: Herder, 1998.

———. "Kreuzestheologie im Markusevangelium." In *Kreuzestheologie im Neuen Testament*, edited by Andreas Dettwiler and Jean Zumstein, 153–58. Wissenschaftliche Untersuchungen zum Neuen Testament 151. Tübingen: Mohr, 2002.

———. *Leidenslisten und Apostelbrief: Untersuchungen zu Form, Motivik und Funktion der Peristasenkataloge bei Paulus*. Forschung zur Bibel 66. Würzburg: Echter Verlag, 1991.

Eckert, Jost. "Wesen und Funktion der Radikalismen in der Botschaft Jesu." *Münchener theologische Studien* 24 (1973): 301–25.

Eckstein, Hans-Joachim. *Der Begriff Syneidesis bei Paulus: Eine neutestamentlich-exegetische Untersuchung zum "Gewissensbegriff."* Wissenschaftliche Untersuchungen zum Neuen Testament 2.10. Tübingen: Mohr, 1983.

———. "Die Gegenwart im Licht der erinnerten Zukunft: Zur modalisierten Zeit im Johannesevangelium." In *Der aus Glauben Gerechte wird leben*, edited by Hans-Joachim Eckstein, 187–206. Beiträge zum Verstehen der Bibel 5. Münster: Lit, 2003.

Eco, Umberto. *Lector in fabula: La cooperazione interpretativa nei testi narrativi*. Milano: Bompiani, 1979.

Edwards, Richard Alan. *Matthew's Narrative Portrait of Disciples: How the Text-Connoted Reader Is Informed*. Harrisburg, PA: Trinity, 1997.

Egger, P. *"Crucifixus sub Pontio Pilato."* Neutestamentliche Abhandlungen 32. Münster: Aschendorff, 1997.

Ego, Beate, et al., eds. *Gemeinde ohne Tempel = Community without temple: Zur Substituierung und Transformation des Jerusalemer Tempels und seines Kults im Alten Testament, antiken Judentum und frühen Christentum*. Wissenschaftliche Untersuchungen zum Neuen Testament 118. Tübingen: Mohr Siebeck, 1999.

Eichrodt, Walther. *Theology of the Old Testament*. Old Testament Library. 2 vols. Philadelphia: Westminster, 1967.

Eisele, Wilfried. *Ein unerschütterliches Reich: Die mittelplatonische Umformung des Parusiegedankens im Hebräerbrief*. Beihefte zur Zeitschrift für die neutestamentliche Wissenschaft und die Kunde der älteren Kirche 116. Berlin: de Gruyter, 2003.

Eliade, Mircea. *Myth and Reality*. New York: Harper & Row, 1963.

Elliger, Winfried. *Ephesos: Geschichte einer antiken Weltstadt*. Stuttgart: Kohlhammer, 1985.

———. *Paulus in Griechenland: Philippi, Thessaloniki, Athen, Korinth*. Stuttgart: Verlag Katholisches Bibelwerk, 1987.

Elliott, N. "Paul and the Politics of Empire." In *Paul and Politics: Ekklesia, Israel, Imperium, Interpretation: Essays in Honor of Krister Stendahl*, edited by Richard A. Horsley. Harrisburg, PA: Trinity, 2000.

———. "Romans 13:1–7 in the Context of Imperial Propaganda." In *Paul and Empire: Religion and Power in Roman Imperial Society*, edited by Richard A. Horsley, 184–204. Harrisburg, PA: Trinity, 1997.

Eltester, Friedrich Wilhelm. *Eikon im Neuen Testament*. Beihefte zur Zeitschrift für die neutestamentliche Wissenschaft 23. Berlin: Töpelmann, 1958.

Erlemann, Kurt. *Endzeiterwartungen im frühen Christentum*. Tübingen: Francke, 1996.

———. *Gleichnisauslegung: Ein Lehr- und Arbeitsbuch*. Tübingen: Francke, 1999.

———. *Naherwartung und Parusieverzögerung im Neuen Testament: Ein Beitrag zur Frage religiöser Zeiterfahrung*. Texte und Arbeiten zum neutestamentlichen Zeitalter 17. Tübingen: Francke, 1995.

Ernst, Josef. *Johannes der Täufer: Interpretation, Geschichte, Wirkungsgeschichte*. Beihefte zur Zeitschrift für die neutestamentliche Wissenschaft und die Kunde der älteren Kirche 53. Berlin: de Gruyter, 1989.

———. "Wo Johannes taufte." In *Antikes Judentum und frühes Christentum: Festschrift für Hartmut Stegemann zum 65. Geburtstag*, edited by Bernd Kollmann et al., 350–63. Beihefte zur Zeitschrift für die neutestamentliche Wissenschaft 97. Berlin: de Gruyter, 1999.

Esler, Philip Francis *Community and Society in Luke-Acts*. Society for New Testament Studies

Monograph Series 57. Cambridge: Cambridge University Press, 1987.

———. *Galatians*. London: Routledge, 1998.

———. "Jesus and the Reduction of Intergroup Conflict." In *The Social Setting of Jesus and the Gospels*, edited by Wolfgang Stegemann et al., 185–206. Minneapolis: Fortress, 2002.

Evans, C. F. "The New Quest for Jesus and the New Research on the Dead Sea Scrolls." In *Jesus, Mark and Q: The Teaching of Jesus and Its Earliest Records*, edited by Michael Labahn and Andreas Schmidt, 163–83. Journal for the Study of the New Testament: Supplement Series 214. Sheffield: Sheffield Academic Press, 2001.

Evans, Craig A., and James A. Sanders, eds. *Luke and Scripture*. Minneapolis: Fortress, 1993.

Fantham, Elaine. *Literarisches Leben im antiken Rom: Sozialgeschichte der römischen Literatur von Cicero bis Apuleius*. Stuttgart: Metzler, 1998.

Fassbeck, Gabriele, ed. *Leben am See Gennesaret: Kulturgeschichtliche Entdeckungen in einer biblischen Region*. Zaberns Bildbände zur Archäologie. Munich: Von Zabern, 2002.

Faust, E. *Pax Christi et Pax Caesaris*. Novum Testamentum et Orbis Antiquus 24. Göttingen: Vandenhoeck & Ruprecht, 1993.

Fee, Gordon D. *The First Epistle to the Corinthians*. New International Commentary on the New Testament. Grand Rapids: Eerdmans, 1987.

———. *God's Empowering Presence: The Holy Spirit in the Letters of Paul*. Peabody, MA: Hendrickson, 1994.

Feldmeier, Reinhard. *Die Christen als Fremde*. Wissenschaftliche Untersuchungen zum Neuen Testament 64. Tübingen: Mohr, 1992.

———. *The First Letter of Peter: A Commentary on the Greek Text*. Waco: Baylor University Press, 2008.

———. *Die Krisis des Gottessohnes*. Wissenschaftliche Untersuchungen zum Neuen Testament 21. Tübingen: Mohr, 1987.

Feneberg, M. *Der Markusprolog: Studien zur Formbestimmung des Evangeliums*. Studien zum Alten und Neuen Testament 36. Munich: Kösel, 1974.

Fiedler, M. "'Gerechtigkeit' im Matthäusevangelium." *Theologische Versuche* 8 (1977): 63–75.

Fiedler, Peter. *Das Matthäusevangelium*. Theologischer Handkommentar zum Neuen Testament 1. Stuttgart: 2006.

Fiore, Benjamin. *The Function of Personal Example in the Socratic and Pastoral Epistles*. Analecta biblica 105. Rome: Biblical Institute Press, 1986.

Fischer, Karl Martin. "Anmerkungen zur Pseudepigraphie im Neuen Testament." *New Testament Studies* 23 (1977): 76–81.

———. *Das Ostergeschehen*. 2nd ed. Göttingen: Vandenhoeck & Ruprecht, 1980.

———. *Tendenz und Absicht des Epheserbriefes*. Forschungen zur Religion und Literatur des Alten und Neuen Testaments 111. Göttingen: Vandenhoeck und Ruprecht, 1973.

Fischer, L., ed. *Evangelisches Kirchenlexikon*. Göttingen: Vandenhoeck & Ruprecht, 2001.

Fitzmyer, Joseph A., SJ. "The 'Son of God' Document from Qumran." *Biblica* 74 (1993): 153–74.

Fleddermann, Harry T. *Q: A Reconstruction and Commentary*. Biblical Tools and Studies 1. Louvain: Peeters, 2005.

Flusser, David, and R. Steven Notley. *Jesus*. 3rd ed. Jerusalem: Hebrew University Magnes Press, 2001.

Fornberg, Tord. *An Early Church in a Pluralistic Society: A Study of 2 Peter*. Coniectanea Biblica: New Testament Series 9. Lund: Gleerup, 1977.

Forschner, Maximilian. "Das Gute und die Güter: Zur stoischen Begründung des Wertvollen." In *Über das Handeln im Einklang mit der Natur: Grundlagen ethischer Verständigung*, edited by Maximilian Forschner, 31–49. Darmstadt: Primus, 1998.

———. *Die stoische Ethik: Über den Zusammenhang von Natur-, Sprach- und Moralphilosophie im altstoischen System*. Stuttgart: Klett-Cotta, 1981.

Fortner, S. "Tiberias—Eine Stadt zu Ehren des Kaisers." In *Leben am See Gennesaret: Kulturgeschichtliche Entdeckungen in einer biblischen Region*, edited by Gabriele Fassbeck, 86–92. Zaberns Bildbände zur Archäologie. Munich: Von Zabern, 2002.

Fossum, J. E. *The Name of God and the Angel of the Lord*. Wissenschaftliche Untersuchungen zum Neuen Testament 36. Tübingen: Mohr, 1985.

Foster, P. *Community, Law and Mission in Matthew's Gospel*. Wissenschaftliche Untersuchungen zum Neuen Testament 177. Tübingen: Mohr, 2004.

Francis, Fred O., and Wayne A. Meeks, eds. *Conflict at Colossae: A Problem in the Interpretation of Early Christianity Illustrated by Selected Modern Studies*. Sources for Biblical Study 4. Missoula, MT: Society of Biblical Literature, 1973.

Frankemölle, Hubert. *Der Brief des Jakobus*. Ökumenischer Taschenbuchkommentar zum Neuen Testament 17/1.2. Gütersloh: Gütersloher Verlagshaus Gerd Mohn, 1994.

———. "Gesetz im Jakobusbrief." In *Das Gesetz im Neuen Testament*, edited by Karl Kertelge and Johannes Beutler, 175–221. Quaestiones disputatae 108. Freiburg: Herder, 1986.

———. "Gespalten oder ganz: Zur Pragmatik der theologischen Anthropologie des Jakobusbriefes." In *Kommunikation und Solidarität: Beiträge zur Diskussion des handlungstheoretischen Ansatzes von Helmut Peukert in Theologie und Sozialwissenschaften*, edited by Hans-Ulrich von Brachel and Norbert Mette, 305–20. Freiburg, Schweiz: Edition Exodus, 1985.

———. *Jahwebund und Kirche Christi*. Münster: Aschendorff, 1974.

———. *Matthäus: Kommentar*. Düsseldorf: Patmos, 1994.

———. "Das semantische Netz des Jakobusbriefes." *Biblische Zeitschrift* 34 (1990): 161–97.

Frenschkowski, Marco. "Kyrios in Context." In *Zwischen den Reichen: Neues Testament und römische Herrschaft: Vorträge auf der Ersten Konferenz der European Association for Biblical Studies*, edited by Michael Labahn and Jürgen Zangenberg, 95–118. Texte und Arbeiten zum neutestamentlichen Zeitalter 36. Tübingen: Francke, 2002.

———. *Offenbarung und Epiphanie*. Wissenschaftliche Untersuchungen zum Neuen Testament 2.79–80. 2 vols. Tübingen: Mohr, 1995.

Freudenberger, Rudolf. *Das Verhalten der römischen Behörden gegen die Christen im 2. Jahrhundert*. 2nd ed. Münchener Beiträge zur Papyrusforschung und antiken Rechtsgeschichte 52. Munich: Beck, 1969.

Frey, Jörg. "Das apokalyptische Millennium." In *Deutungen zum christlichen Mythos der Jahrtausendwende*, edited by C. Bochinger, 10–72. Gütersloh: Güterloher Verlagshaus, 1999.

———. "Das Bild als Wirkungspotential." In *Bildersprache verstehen*, edited by Ruben Zimmermann, 331–61. Übergänge 38. Munich: Fink, 2000.

———. "Das Bild 'der Juden' im Johanneischen Gemeinde." In *Israel und seine Heilstraditionen im Johannessevangelium: Festgabe für Johannes Beutler SJ zum 70. Geburtstag*, edited by Michael Labahn et al., 33–53. Paderborn: Schöningh, 2004.

———. "Eschatology in the Johannine Circle." In *Theology and Christology in the Fourth Gospel*, edited by G. van Belle et al., 47–82. Bibliotheca ephemeridum theologicarum lovaniensium 184. Louvain: Leuven University Press, 2005.

———. "Heiden—Griechen—Gotteskinder." In *Die Heiden: Juden, Christen und das Problem des Fremden*, edited by Reinhard Feldmeier and Ulrich Heckel, 228–68. Wissenschaftliche Untersuchungen zum Neuen Testament 70. Tübingen: Mohr, 1994.

———. "Der historische Jesus und der Christ des Glaubens." In *Der historische Jesus*, edited by J. Schröter and R. Bruckner. Beihefte zur Zeitschrift für die neutestamentliche Wissenschaft und die Kunde der älteren Kirche 114. Berlin: de Gruyter, 2002.

———. "Der historische Jesus und der Christus der Evangelien." In *Der historische Jesus*, edited by J. Schröter and R. Bruckner, 273–336. Beihefte zur Zeitschrift für die neutestamentliche Wissenschaft und die Kunde der älteren Kirche 114. Berlin: de Gruyter, 2002.

———. *Die johanneische Eschatologie*. Wissenschaftliche Untersuchungen zum Neuen Testament 96, 110, 117. 3 vols. Tübingen: Mohr, 1997–2000.

———. "Der Judasbrief zwischen Judentum und Hellenismus." In *Frühjudentum und Neues Testament im Horizont Biblischer Theologie*, edited by Wolfgang Kraus et al., 180–220. Wissenschaftliche Untersuchungen zum Neuen Testament 162. Tübingen: Mohr Siebeck, 2003.

———. "Das Judentum des Paulus." In *Paulus: Leben—Umwelt—Werk—Briefe*, edited by Oda Wischmeyer, 35–43. Tübingen: Francke, 2006.

———. "Licht aus den Höhlen: Der 'johanneische Dualismus' und die Texte von Qumran." In *Kontexte des Johannesevangeliums*, edited by Albert Frey and Udo Schnelle, 117–203. Wissenschaftliche Untersuchungen zum Neuen Testament 175. Tübingen: Mohr, 2004.

———. "Probleme der Deutung des Todes Jesu." In *Deutungen des Todes Jesu im Neuen Testament*, 3–50. Wissenschaftliche Untersuchungen zum Neuen Testament 181. Tübingen: Mohr, 2005.

———. "Die 'theologia crucifixi' des Johannesevangeliums." In *Kreuzestheologie im Neuen Testament*, edited by Andreas Dettwiler and Jean Zumstein, 219–39. Wissenschaftliche Untersuchungen zum Neuen Testament 151. Tübingen: Mohr, 2002.

———. "'Wie Mose die Schlange in der Wüste erhöht hat. . . .'" In *Schriftauslegung im antiken Judentum und im Urchristentum*, edited by Martin Hengel and Hermut Löhr, 153–205. Wissenschaftliche Untersuchungen zum Neuen Testament 73. Tübingen: Mohr, 1994.

———. "Zu Hintergrund und Funktion des johanneischen Dualismus." In *Paulus und Johannes: Exegetische Studien zur paulinischen und johanneischen Theologie und Literatur*, edited by Dieter Sänger and Ulrich Mell, 3–73. Wissenschaftliche Untersuchungen zum Neuen Testament 198. Tübingen: Mohr Siebeck, 2006.

Frey, Jörg, et al. *Imagery in the Gospel of John: Terms, Forms, Themes, and Theology of Johannine Figurative Language*. Wissenschaftliche Untersuchungen zum Neuen Testament 200. Tübingen: Mohr Siebeck, 2006.

Freyne, Seán. *Jesus, a Jewish Galilean: A New Reading of the Jesus-Story*. London: T&T Clark, 2004.

Frickenschmidt, Dirk. *Evangelium als Biographie: Die vier Evangelien im Rahmen antiker Erzählkunst*. Texte und Arbeiten zum neutestamentlichen Zeitalter 22. Tübingen: Francke, 1997.

Friedrich, Gerhard. "Die formale Struktur von Mt 28,18–20." *Zeitschrift für Theologie und Kirche* 80 (1983): 137–83.

———. "Glaube und Verkündigung bei Paulus." In *Glaube im Neuen Testament: Studien zu Ehren von Hermann Binder anlässlich seines 70. Geburtstags*, edited by Ferdinand Hahn and Hans Klein. Biblisch-theologische Studien 7. Neukirchen-Vluyn: Neukirchener Verlag, 1982.

———. *Die Verkündigung des Todes Jesu im Neuen Testament*. Biblisch-theologische Studien 6. Neukirchen-Vluyn: Neukirchener Verlag, 1982.

Friedrich, Johannes, et al. "Zur historischen Situation und Intention von Röm 13,1–7." *Zeitschrift für Theologie und Kirche* 73 (1976): 131–66.

Friese, Heidrun, ed. *Identities: Time, Difference, and Boundaries*. Making Sense of History 2. New York: Berghahn Books, 2001.

Fulda, D. "Sinn und Erzählung—Narrative Kohärenzansprüche der Kulturen." In *Handbuch der Kulturwissenschaften*, edited by Friedrich Jaeger, vol. 1, 251–65. Stuttgart: Metzler, 2004.

Furnish, Victor Paul. *II Corinthians*. Anchor Bible 32A. Garden City, NY: Doubleday, 1984.

———. *The Love Command in the New Testament*. Nashville: Abingdon, 1972.

Ganser-Kerperin, Heiner. *Das Zeugnis des Tempels: Studien zur Bedeutung des Tempelmotivs im lukanischen Doppelwerk*. Neutestamentliche Abhandlungen. Münster: Aschendorff, 2000.

Garleff, G. *Urchristliche Identität im Matthäusevangelium, Didache und Jakobusbrief*. Beiträge zum Verstehen der Bibel 9. Münster: Lit-Verlag, 2004.

Gathercole, Simon J. *Where Is Boasting? Early Jewish Soteriology and Paul's Response in Romans 1–5*. Grand Rapids: Eerdmans, 2002.

Gaukesbrink, Martin. *Die Sühnetradition bei Paulus: Rezeption und theologischer Stellenwert*. Forschung zur Bibel 32. Würzburg: Echter Verlag, 1999.

Gebauer, Roland. "Der Kolosserbrief als Antwort auf die Herausforderung des Synkretismus." In *Die bleibende Gegenwart des Evangeliums: Festschrift für Otto Merk*, edited by Roland Gebauer and Martin Meiser, 153–69. Marburger Theologische Studien 76. Marburg: Elwert, 2003.

Geertz, Clifford. *Dichte Beschreibung: Beiträge zum Verstehen kultureller Systeme*. Frankfurt: Suhrkamp, 1987.

———. "Thick Description: Toward an Interpretative Theory of Culture." In *The Interpretation of Cultures: Selected Essays*, edited by Clifford Geertz. New York: Basic Books, 1973.

Gehring, Roger W. *Hausgemeinde und Mission: Die Bedeutung antiker Häuser und Hausgemeinschaften-von Jesus bis Paulus*. Bibelwissenschaftliche Monographien 9. Giessen: Brunnen, 2000.

———. *House Church and Mission: The Importance of Household Structures in Early Christianity*. Peabody, MA: Hendrickson, 2004.

Geist, Heinz. *Menschensohn und Gemeinde: Eine redaktionskritische Untersuchung zur Menschensohnprädikation im Matthäusevangelium*. Forschung zur Bibel 57. Würzburg: Echter, 1986.

Gemünden, Petra von. "Einsicht, Affekt und Verhalten: Überlegungen zur Anthropologie des Jakobusbriefes." In *Der Jakobusbrief: Beiträge zur Rehabilitierung der "strohernen Epistel,"* edited by Petra von Gemünden et al., 83–96. Beiträge zum Verstehen der Bibel 3. Münster: Lit-Verlag, 2003.

———. "Die Wertung des Zorns im Jakobusbrief auf dem Hintergrund des antiken Kontexts und seine Einordnung." In *Der Jakobusbrief: Beiträge zur Rehabilitierung der "strohernen Epistel,"* edited by Petra von Gemünden et al., 97–119. Beiträge zum Verstehen der Bibel 3. Münster: Lit-Verlag, 2003.

Genette, Gérard. *Narrative Discourse: An Essay in Method*. Translated by Jane E. Lewin. Ithaca, NY: Cornell University Press, 1980.

Georgi, Dieter. "Die Visionen vom himmlischen Jerusalem in Apk 21 und 22." In *Kirche: Festschrift für Günther Bornkamm zum 75. Geburtstag*, edited by Dieter Lührmann and Georg Strecker, 351–72. Tübingen: Mohr, 1980.

Gergen, K. J. "Erzählung, moralische Identität und historisches Bewußtsein." In *Erzählung, Identität und historisches Bewußtsein: Die psychologische Konstruktion von Zeit und Geschichte*, edited by Jürgen Straub, 170–202. Frankfurt: Suhrkamp, 2000.

Gese, Michael. *Das Vermächtnis des Apostels*. Wissenschaftliche Untersuchungen zum Neuen Testament 2.99. Tübingen: Mohr, 1997.

Geyer, H.-G. "Die Auferstehung Jesu Christi: Ein Überblick über die Diskussion in der evangelischen Theologie." In *Die Bedeutung der Auferstehungsbotschaft für den Glauben an Jesus Christus*, edited by Viering, F. Berlin: Evangelische Verlagsanstalt, 1967.

Gielen, Marlis. *Der Konflikt Jesu mit den religiösen und politischen Autoritäten seines Volkes im Spiegel der matthäischen Jesusgeschichte*. Bonner biblische Beiträge 115. Bodenheim: Philo, 1998.

———. *Tradition und Theologie neutestamentlicher Haustafelethik: Ein Beitrag zur Frage einer christlichen Auseinandersetzung mit gesellschaftlichen Normen*. Athenäums Monografien, Theologie 75. Frankfurt a.M.: Hain, 1990.

Giesen, Heinz. *Christliches Handeln: Eine redaktionskritische Untersuchung zum δικαιοσύνη Begriff im Matthäus-Evangelium*. Europäische Hochschulschriften 23.181. Frankfurt: Lang, 1982.

———. "Lasterkataloge und Kaiserkult in der Offenbarung des Johannes." In *Studien zur Johannesoffenbarung und ihrer Auslegung: Festschrift für Otto Böcher zum 70. Geburtstag*, edited by Friedrich Wilhelm Horn and Michael Wolter, 210–31. Neukirchen-Vluyn: Neukirchener Verlag, 2005.

———, ed. *Studien zur Johannesapokalypse*. Stuttgarter biblische Aufsatzbände 29. Stuttgart: Katholisches Bibelwerk, 2000.

Gillespie, Thomas W. *The First Theologians: A Study in Early Christian Prophecy*. Grand Rapids: Eerdmans, 1994.

Gnilka, Joachim. *Der Epheserbrief: Auslegung*. 2nd ed. Herders theologischer Kommentar zum Neuen Testament 10/2. Freiburg i.B.: Herder, 1977.

———. *Das Evangelium nach Markus*. Evangelisch-katholischer Kommentar zum Neuen Testament 2. 2 vols. Zürich: Benziger, 1978–79.

———. *Der Kolosserbrief*. Herders theologischer Kommentar zum Neuen Testament 10. Freiburg: Herder, 1980.

———. *Das Matthäusevangelium*. 2 vols. Herders theologischer Kommentar zum Neuen Testament 1. Freiburg: Herder, 1986.

———. *Neutestamentliche Theologie im Überblick*. Neue Echter Bibel. Würzburg: Echter, 1989.

———. *Paulus von Tarsus, Apostel und Zeuge*. Herders theologischer Kommentar zum Neuen Testament 6. Freiburg: Herder, 1996.

———. *Theologie des Neuen Testaments*. Herders theologischer Kommentar zum Neuen Testament 5. Freiburg: Herder, 1994.

———. "Zum Gottesgedanken in der Jesusüberlieferung." In *Monotheismus und Christologie: Zur Gottesfrage im hellenistischen Judentum und im Urchristentum*, edited by Hans-Josef Klauck, 144–62. Quaestiones disputatae 138. Freiburg i.B.: Herder, 1992.

Goertz, Hans-Jürgen. *Umgang mit Geschichte: Eine Einführung in die Geschichtstheorie*. Reinbek: Rowohlt, 1995.

———. *Unsichere Geschichte: Zur Theorie historischer Referentialität*. Stuttgart: Reclam, 2001.

Goldhahn-Müller, Ingrid. *Die Grenze der Gemeinde: Studien zum Problem der Zweiten Busse in Neuen Testament unter Berücksichtigung der Entwicklung im 2. Jh. bis Tertullian*. Göttinger theologische Arbeiten 39. Göttingen: Vandenhoeck & Ruprecht, 1989.

Goppelt, Leonhard. *A Commentary on 1 Peter*. Translated by John E. Alsup. Grand Rapids: Eerdmans, 1993.

———. *Theologie des Neuen Testaments*. 3rd ed. Göttingen: Vandenhoeck & Ruprecht, 1976.

Goppelt, Leonhard, and Jürgen Roloff, ed. *Theology of the New Testament*. Translated by John E. Alsup. 2 vols. Grand Rapids: Eerdmans, 1981.

Grabner-Haider, Anton. *Paraklese und Eschatologie bei Paulus: Mensch und Welt im Anspruch der Zukunft Gottes*. Neutestamentliche Abhandlungen, n.F., 4. Münster: Aschendorff, 1968.

Grass, Hans. *Ostergeschehen und Osterberichte*. 2nd ed. Göttingen: Vandenhoeck & Ruprecht, 1961.

Grässer, Erich. "Der Alte Bund im Neuen." In *Der Alte Bund im Neuen: Exegetische Studien zur Israelfrage im Neuen Testament*, edited by Erich Grässer, 1–134. Wissenschaftliche Untersuchungen zum Neuen Testament 35. Tübingen: Mohr, 1985.

———. *An die Hebräer*. Evangelischer-katholischer Kommentar zum Neuen Testament 17/1–3. Neukirchen-Vluyn: Neukirchener Verlag, 1990.

———. "Die antijüdische Polemik im Johannesevangelium." In *Der Alte Bund im Neuen: Exegetische Studien zur Israelfrage im Neuen Testament*, edited by Erich Grässer, 135–53. Wissenschaftliche Untersuchungen zum Neuen Testament 35. Tübingen: Mohr, 1985.

———. *Der Glaube im Hebräerbrief*. Marburger theologische Studien 2. Marburg: Elwert, 1965.

———. "Hebräer, 1,1–4: Ein exegetischer Versuch." In *Text und Situation: Gesammelte Aufsätze zum Neuen Testament*, edited by Erich Grässer, 182–228. Gütersloh: Gütersloher Verlagshaus G. Mohn, 1973.

———. "Jesus und das Heil Gottes." In *Der Alte Bund im Neuen: Exegetische Studien zur Israelfrage im Neuen Testament*, edited by Erich Grässer, 181–200. Wissenschaftliche Untersuchungen zum Neuen Testament 35. Tübingen: Mohr, 1985.

———. "Kolosser 3,1–4 als Beispiel einer Interpretation secundum homines recipientes." In *Text und Situation: Gesammelte Aufsätze zum Neuen Testament*, edited by Erich Grässer. Gütersloh: Gütersloher Verlagshaus G. Mohn, 1973.

———. *Das Problem der Parusieverzögerung in den synoptischen Evangelien und in der Apostelgeschichte*. Beihefte zur Zeitschrift für die neutestamentliche Wissenschaft und die Kunde der älteren Kirche 22. Berlin: Töpelmann, 1957.

———. "Das wandernde Gottesvolk." In *Aufbruch und Verheissung: Gesammelte Aufsätze zum Hebräerbrief; zum 65. Geburtstag mit einer Bibliographie des Verfassers*, edited by Erich Grässer et al., 231–50. Beihefte zur Zeitschrift für die neutestamentliche Wissenschaft und die Kunde der älteren Kirche 65. Berlin: de Gruyter, 1992.

———. "Das Wort als Heil." In *Aufbruch und Verheissung: Gesammelte Aufsätze zum Hebräerbrief; zum 65. Geburtstag mit einer Bibliographie des Verfassers*, edited by Erich Grässer et al., 129–42. Beihefte zur Zeitschrift für die neutestamentliche Wissenschaft und die Kunde der älteren Kirche 65. Berlin: de Gruyter, 1992.

Groll, Oliver. *Finsternis, Tod und Blindheit als Strafe: Eine exegetische Untersuchung zu den Begriffen krinein, krisis und krima im Johannesevangelium*. Europäische Hochschulschriften 23.781. Frankfurt: Lang, 2004.

Gruber, M. "Die Zumutung der Gegenseitigkeit: Zur johanneischen Deutung des Todes Jesu anhand einer pragmatisch-intratextuellen Lektüre der Salbungsgeschichte Joh 12, 1–8." In *The Death of Jesus in the Fourth Gospel*, edited by G. van Belle, 647–60. Bibliotheca ephemeridum theologicarum lovaniensium 200. Louvain: Leuven University Press, 2007.

Grundmann, Walter. *Das Evangelium nach Lukas*. Theologischer Handkommentar zum Neuen Testament 3. Berlin: Evangelische Verlagsanstalt, 1971.

———. "Überlieferung und Eigenaussage im eschatologischen Denken des Paulus." *New Testament Studies* 8 (1961): 12–26.

———. *Zeugnis und Gestalt des Johannes-Evangeliums: Eine Studie zur denkerischen und gestalterischen Leistung des vierten Evangelisten*. Arbeiten zur Theologie 7. Stuttgart: Calwer, 1961.

Gubler, M. L. *Die frühesten Deutungen des Todes Jesu*. Orbis biblicus et orientalis 15. Göttingen: Vandenhoeck & Ruprecht, 1977.

Gutbrod, Walter. *Die paulinische Anthropologie*. Beiträge zur Wissenschaft vom Alten (und Neuen) Testament 67. Stuttgart-Berlin: Kohlhammer, 1934.

Guttenberger, G. *Die Gottesvorstellung im Markusevangelium*. Beihefte zur Zeitschrift für die neutestamentliche Wissenschaft und die Kunde der älteren Kirche 123. Berlin: de Gruyter, 2004.

Güttgemanns, Erhardt. *Der leidende Apostel und sein Herr: Studien zur paulinischen Christologie*. Göttingen: Vandenhoeck & Ruprecht, 1966.

Guyot, Peter, and Richard Klein. *Das frühe Christentum bis zum Ende der Verfolgungen: Eine Dokumentation*. Texte zur Forschung 60. Darmstadt: Wissenschaftliche Buchgesellschaft, 1993.

Haacker, Klaus. "Der 'Antinomismus' des Paulus im Kontext antiker Gesetzestheorie." In *Geschichte—Tradition—Reflexion: Festschrift für Martin Hengel zum 70. Geburtstag*, edited by Hubert Cancik et al. Tübingen: Mohr, 1996.

———. "Das Bekenntnis des Paulus zur Hoffnung Israels nach der Apostelgeschichte des Lukas." *New Testament Studies* 31 (1985): 437–51.

———. *Der Brief des Paulus an die Römer*. Theologischer Handkommentar zum Neuen Testament 6. Leipzig: Evangelische Verlagsanstalt, 1999.

Habermann, Jürgen. *Präexistenzaussagen im Neuen Testament*. Europäische Hochschulschriften 23.362. Frankfurt: Lang, 1990.

Haenchen, Ernst. *The Acts of the Apostles: A Commentary*. Philadelphia: Westminster, 1971.

———. *Die Apostelgeschichte*. 15th ed. Kritisch-exegetischer Kommentar über das Neue Testament. Göttingen: Vandenhoeck & Ruprecht, 1977.

———. *John 1. A Commentary on the Gospel of John Chapters 1–6*. Hermeneia—A Critical and Historical Commentary on the Bible. Translated by Robert W. Funk and Ulrich Busse. Philadelphia: Fortress, 1984.

Hafemann, Scott J. *Paul, Moses, and the History of Israel: The Letter/Spirit Contrast and the Argument from Scripture in 2 Corinthians 3*. Wissenschaftliche Untersuchungen zum Neuen Testament 81. Tübingen: Mohr, 1995.

Häfner, G. *Der verheißene Vorläufer*. Stuttgarter Biblische Beiträge 27. Stuttgart: Katholisches Bibelwerk, 1994.

Hagene, Sylvia. *Zeiten der Wiederherstellung: Studien zur lukanischen Geschichtstheologie als Soteriologie*. Neutestamentliche Abhandlungen, n.F., 42. Münster: Aschendorff, 2003.

Hahn, Ferdinand. "Das Geistverständnis in der Johannesoffenbarung." In *Studien zur Johannesoffenbarung und ihrer Auslegung: Festschrift für Otto Böcher zum 70. Geburtstag*, edited by Friedrich Wilhelm Horn and Michael Wolter, 3–9. Neukirchen-Vluyn: Neukirchener Verlag, 2005.

———. "Gibt es eine Entwicklung in den Aussagen über die Rechtfertigung bei Paulus?" *Evangelische Theologie* 53 (1993): 342–66.

———. "Das Glaubensverständnis im Johannesevangelium." In *Glaube und Eschatologie: Festschrift für Werner Georg Kümmel zum 80. Geburtstag*, edited by Erich Grässer and Otto Merk, 51–69. Tübingen: Mohr, 1985.

———. "'Das Heil kommt von den Juden': Erwägungen zu Joh 4,22b." In *Die Verwurzelung des Christentums im Judentum*, edited by Ferdinand Hahn, 99–118. Neukirchen: Neukirchener Verlag, 1996.

———. "Methodologische Überlegungen zur Rückfrage nach Jesus." In *Rückfrage Nach Jesus*, edited by Karl Kertelge, 11–77. Freiburg: Herder, 1974.

———. "Das neue Jerusalem." In *Kirche und Volk Gottes: Festschrift für Jürgen Roloff zum 70. Geburtstag*, edited by Martin Karrer et al., 284–94. Neukirchen-Vluyn: Neukirchener Verlag, 2000.

———. "Die Petrusverheißung Mt 16,18f." In *Exegetische Beiträge zum ökumenischen Gespräch*, edited by Ferdinand Hahn, 185–200. Göttingen: Vandenhoeck & Ruprecht, 1986.

———. "Das Problem alter christologischer Überlieferungen in der Apostelgeschichte unter besonderer Berücksichtigung von Acts 3,19–21." In *Les Actes des Apôtres*, edited by J. Kremer, 129–54. Bibliotheca ephemeridum theologicarum lovaniensium 48. Louvain: Leuven University Press, 1979.

———. "Die Sendschreiben der Johannesapokalypse." In *Tradition und Glaube: Das frühe Christentum in seiner Umwelt; Festgabe für Karl Georg Kuhn zum 65. Geburtstag*, edited by Gert Jeremias et al., 357–94. Göttingen: Vandenhoeck & Ruprecht, 1971.

———. "Taufe und Rechtfertigung." In *Rechtfertigung: Festschrift für Ernst Käsemann zum 70. Geburtstag*, edited by Johannes Friedrich et al., 95–124. Göttingen: Vandenhoeck & Ruprecht, 1976.

———. *Theologie des Neuen Testaments*. 2nd ed. 2 vols. Tübingen: Mohr, 2005.

———. *The Titles of Jesus in Christology: Their History in Early Christianity*. Translated by Harold Knight and George Ogg. New York: World, 1969.

———. "Das Zeugnis des Neuen Testaments in seiner Vielfalt und Einheit." *Kerygma und Dogma* 48 (2002): 240–60.

———. "Zum Aufbau der Johannesoffenbarung." In *Kirche und Bibel: Festgabe für Bischof Eduard Schick*, edited by Professoren der Phil.-Theol. Hochschule, Fulda, 145–54. Paderborn: Schöningh, 1979.

———. "Zum Verständnis von Röm 11,26a." In *Paul and Paulinism: Essays in Honour of C. K. Barrett*, edited by Morna Dorothy Hooker and S. G. Wilson. London: SPCK, 1982.

———, ed. *Der Erzähler des Evangeliums: Methodische Neuansätze in der Markusforschung*. Stuttgarter Bibelstudien 118/119. Stuttgart: Katholisches Bibelwerk, 1985.

Haldimann, K. "Kreuz—Wort vom Kreuz—Kreuzestheologie." In *Kreuzestheologie im Neuen Testament*, edited by Andreas Dettwiler and Jean Zumstein, 1–25. Wissenschaftliche Untersuchungen zum Neuen Testament 151. Tübingen: Mohr, 2002.

———. *Rekonstruktion und Entfaltung: Exegetische Untersuchungen zu Joh 15 und 16*. Beihefte zur Zeitschrift für die neutestamentliche Wissenschaft 104. Berlin: de Gruyter, 2000.

Hampel, Volker. *Menschensohn und historischer Jesus: Ein Rätselwort als Schlüssel zum messianischen Selbstverständnis Jesu*. Neukirchen-Vluyn: Neukirchener Verlag, 1988.

Hanhart, Robert. "Die Bedeutung der Septuaginta in neutestamentlicher Zeit." *Zeitschrift für Theologie und Kirche* 81 (1984): 395–416.

Harnack, Adolf von. *The Mission and Expansion of Christianity in the First Three Centuries*. Translated by James Moffatt. 2nd ed. New York: Putnam, 1908.

———. *The Sayings of Jesus: The Second Source of St. Matthew and St. Luke*. Translated by J. L. Wilkinson. New Testament Studies 2. London: Williams and Norgate, 1908.

———. *What Is Christianity?* Translated by Thomas Bailey Saunders. New York: Harper & Row, 1957.

Harnisch, Wolfgang. *Eschatologische Existenz: Ein exegetischer Beitrag zum Sachanliegen von 1. Thessalonicher 4,13–5,11*. Forschungen zur Religion und Literatur des Alten und Neuen Testaments 110. Göttingen: Vandenhoeck & Ruprecht, 1973.

———. *Die Gleichniserzählungen Jesu: Eine hermeneutische Einführung*. Göttingen: Vandenhoeck & Ruprecht, 1985.

Harrill, James Albert. *Slaves in the New Testament: Literary, Social, and Moral Dimensions*. Minneapolis: Fortress, 2006.

Harrison, James R. *Paul's Language of Grace in Its Graeco-Roman Context*. Wissenschaftliche Untersuchungen zum Neuen Testament 2.172. Tübingen: Mohr Siebeck, 2003.

Hartingsveld, L. van. *Die Eschatologie des Johannesevangeliums: Eine Auseinandersetzung mit Rudolf Bultmann*. Assen: Prakke & Prakke, 1962.

Hartmann, L. *Auf den Namen des Herrn Jesus*. Stuttgarter Bibelstudien 148. Stuttgart: Katholisches Bibelwerk, 192.

Hasitschka, Martin. *Befreiung von Sünde nach dem Johannesevangelium: Eine bibeltheologische Untersuchung*. Innsbrucker theologische Studien 27. Innsbruck: Tyrolia-Verlag, 1989.

Hatina, Thomas R. *In Search of a Context: The Function of Scripture in Mark's Narrative*. Journal for the Study of the New Testament: Supplement Series 232. London: Sheffield Academic Press, 2002.

Haufe, Günter. *Der erste Brief des Paulus an die Thessalonicher*. Theologischer Handkommentar zum Neuen Testament 12/1. Leipzig: Evangelische Verlagsanstalt, 1999.

Heckel, Theo K. *Der innere Mensch: Die paulinische Verarbeitung eines platonischen Motivs*. Wissenschaftliche Untersuchungen zum Neuen Testament 2.53. Tübingen: Mohr, 1993.

———. "Kirche und Gottesvolk im Epheserbrief." In *Kirche und Volk Gottes: Festschrift für Jürgen Roloff zum 70. Geburtstag*, edited by Martin Karrer et al., 163–75. Neukirchen-Vluyn: Neukirchener Verlag, 2000.

———. "Die Traditionsverknüpfungen des Zweiten Petrusbriefes und die Anfänge einer neutestamentlichen biblischen Theologie." In *Die bleibende Gegenwart des Evangeliums: Festschrift für Otto Merk*, edited by Roland Gebauer and Martin Meiser, 189–204. Marburger Theologische Studien 76. Marburg: Elwert, 2003.

Hedinger, H.-W. "Historik." In *Historisches Wörterbuch der Philosophie*, edited by Karlfried Gründer et al. Darmstadt: Wissenschaftliche Buchgesellschaft, 1974.

Heekerens, Hans-Peter. *Die Zeichen-Quelle der johanneischen Redaktion: Ein Beitrag zur Entstehungsgeschichte des vierten Evangeliums*. Stuttgarter Bibelstudien 113. Stuttgart: Verlag Katholisches Bibelwerk, 1984.

Hegermann, Harald. *Der Brief an die Hebräer*. Theologischer Handkommentar zum Neuen Testament 16. Berlin: Evangelische Verlagsanstalt, 1988.

———. *Die Vorstellung vom Schöpfungsmittler im hellenistischen Judentum und Urchristentum*. Texte und Untersuchungen zur Geschichte der altchristlichen Literatur 5/27. Berlin: Akademie-Verlag, 1961.

———. "Das Wort Gottes als aufdeckende Macht." In *Das Lebendige Wort: Beiträge zur kirchlichen Verkündigung: Festgabe für Gottfried Voigt zum 65. Geburtstag*, edited by Gottfried Voigt et al., 83–98. Berlin: Evangelische Verlagsanstalt, 1982.

———. "Zur Ableitung der Leib-Christi-Vorstellung im Epheserbrief." *Theologische Literaturzeitung* 85 (1960): 839–42.

Heidegger, Martin. *Being and Time*. Translated by John Macquarrie and Edward Robinson [from the 7th German edition]. Oxford: Blackwell, 1967.

Heil, Christoph. *Die Ablehnung der Speisegebote durch Paulus: Zur Frage nach der Stellung des Apostels zum Gesetz*. Bonner biblische Beiträge 96. Weinheim: Beltz Athenäum, 1994.

———. "Beobachtungen zur theologischen Dimension der Gleichnisrede Jesu in Q." In *The Sayings Source Q and the Historical Jesus*, edited by Andreas Lindemann, 49–59. Bibliotheca ephemeridum theologicarum lovaniensium 158. Louvain: Leuven University Press, 2001.

———. *Lukas und Q: Studien zur lukanischen Redaktion des Spruchevangeliums Q*. Beihefte zur Zeitschrift für die neutestamentliche Wissenschaft und die Kunde der älteren Kirche 111. Berlin: de Gruyter, 2003.

Heil, Christoph, et al., eds. *Q 12:8–12: Confessing or Denying—Speaking against the Holy Spirit—Hearings before Synagogues*. Documenta Q. Louvain: Peeters, 1997.

Heiligenthal, R. *Werke als Zeichen: Untersuchungen zur Bedeutung der menschlichen Taten im Frühjudentum, Neuen Testament und Frühchristentum*. Wissenschaftliche Untersuchungen zum Neuen Testament 2.9. Tübingen: Mohr, 1983.

Heiligenthal, Roman. *Der verfälschte Jesus: Eine Kritik moderner Jesusbilder*. Darmstadt: Primus, 1997.

———. *Zwischen Henoch und Paulus: Studien zum theologiegeschichtlichen Ort des Judasbriefes*. Texte und Arbeiten zum neutestamentlichen Zeitalter 6. Tübingen: Francke, 1992.

Heininger, Bernhard. *Metaphorik, Erzählstruktur und szenisch-dramatische Gestaltung in den Sondergutgleichnissen bei Lukas*. Neutestamentliche Abhandlungen, n.F., 24. Münster: Druckhaus Aschendorff, 1991.

Heise, Jürgen. *Bleiben: Menein in den Johanneischen Schriften*. Hermeneutische Untersuchungen zur Theologie 8. Tübingen: Mohr, 1967.

Henderson, Suzanne Watts. *Christology and Discipleship in the Gospel of Mark*. Society for New Testament Studies Monograph Series 135. Cambridge: Cambridge University Press, 2006.

Hengel, Martin. "Abba, Maranatha, Hosanna und die Anfänge der Christologie." In *Denkwürdiges Geheimnis: Beiträge zur Gotteslehre, Festschrift für Eberhard Jüngel zum 70. Geburtstag*, edited by Ingolf Ulrich Dalferth et al., 144–83. Tübingen: Mohr, 2004.

———. "Das Begräbnis Jesu bei Paulus und die leibliche Auferstehung aus dem Grabe." In *Auferstehung = Resurrection: The Fourth Durham-Tübingen Research Symposium: Resurrection, Transfiguration and Exaltation in Old Testament, Ancient Judaism and Early Christianity*, edited by Friedrich Avemarie and Hermann Lichtenberger, 119–83. Wissenschaftliche Untersuchungen zum Neuen Testament 135. Tübingen: Mohr, 2001.

———. *The Charismatic Leader and His Followers*. Translated by James Greig. New York: Crossroad, 1981.

———. *Crucifixion*. Translated by John Bowden. Philadelphia: Fortress, 1977.

———. "Jakobus, der Herrenbruder—der erste Papst?" In *Paulus und Jakobus: Kleine Schriften III*, edited by Martin Hengel, 549–82. Wissenschaftliche Untersuchungen zum Neuen Testament 141. Tübingen: Mohr, 2002.

———. "Jesus der Messias Israels." In *Der messianische Anspruch Jesu und die Anfänge der Christologie: Vier Studien*, edited by Martin Hengel and Anna Maria Schwemer, 1–80. Wissenschaftliche Untersuchungen zum Neuen Testament 138. Tübingen: Mohr Siebeck, 2001.

———. "Jesus und die Tora." *Theologische Beiträge* (1978): 152–72.

———. *The Johannine Question*. Philadelphia: Trinity, 1989.

———. "The Letter of James as Anti-Pauline Polemic (1987)." In *The Writings of St. Paul*, edited by Wayne A. Meeks and John T. Fitzgerald, 242–53. New York: Norton, 2007.

———. "Präexistenz bei Paulus?" In *Jesus Christus als die Mitte der Schrift: Studien zur Hermeneutik des Evangeliums*, edited by Christof Landmesser et al., 479–517. Beihefte zur Zeitschrift für die neutestamentliche Wissenschaft 86. Berlin: de Gruyter, 1997.

———. "Psalm 110 und die Erhöhung des Auferstandenen zur Rechten Gottes." In *Anfänge der Christologie: Festschrift für Ferdinand Hahn zum 65. Geburtstag*, edited by Cilliers Breytenbach et al., 43–74. Göttingen: Vandenhoeck & Ruprecht, 1991.

———. "Die Schriftauslegung des 4. Evangeliums auf dem Hintergrund der urchristlichen Exegese." *Jahrbuch für Biblische Theologie* 4 (1989): 249–88.

———. *The Septuagint as Christian Scripture: Its Prehistory and the Problem of Its Canon*. Old Testament Studies. Translated by Mark E. Biddle. Edinburgh: T&T Clark, 2002.

———. *The Son of God: The Origin of Christology and the History of Jewish-Hellenistic Religion*. Translated by John Bowden. Philadelphia: Fortress, 1976.

———. "Die Throngemeinschaft des Lammes mit Gott in der Johannesoffenbarung." *Theologische Beiträge* 27 (1996): 159–75.

———. *Der unterschätzte Petrus: Zwei Studien.* Tübingen: Mohr Siebeck, 2006.

———. *Victory over Violence: Jesus and the Revolutionists.* Translated by David E. Green. Philadelphia: Fortress, 1973.

———. *War Jesus Revolutionär?* Stuttgart: Calwer, 1970.

———. *The Zealots: Investigations into the Jewish Freedom Movement in the Period from Herod I until 70 A.D.* Translated by David Smith. Edinburgh: T&T Clark, 1989.

———. "Zur matthäischen Bergpredigt und ihrem jüdischen Hintergrund." In *Judaica et Hellenistica: Kleine Schriften I*, edited by Roland Deines, 219–92. Wissenschaftliche Untersuchungen zum Neuen Testament 90. Tübingen: Mohr, 1996.

———. "Zwischen Jesus und Paulus: Die 'Hellenisten,' die 'Sieben,' und Stephanus." *Zeitschrift für Theologie und Kirche* 72 (1975): 151–206.

Hengel, Martin, and Anna Maria Schwemer. *Paul between Damascus and Antioch: The Unknown Years.* Translated by John Bowden. Louisville: Westminster John Knox, 1997.

———. *Die Septuaginta zwischen Judentum und Christentum.* Wissenschaftliche Untersuchungen zum Neuen Testament 72. Tübingen: Mohr, 1994.

———, eds. *Königsherrschaft Gottes und himmlischer Kult: Im Judentum, Urchristentum und in der hellenistischen Welt.* Wissenschaftliche Untersuchungen zum Neuen Testament 55. Tübingen: Mohr, 1991.

Henten, J. W. van. "The Tradition-Historical Background of Romans 3,25: A Search for Pagan and Jewish Parallels." In *From Jesus to John: Essays on Jesus and New Testament Christology in Honour of Marinus de Jonge*, edited by Martinus C. de Boer. Journal for the Study of the New Testament: Supplement Series 84. Sheffield: JSOT Press, 1993.

Hergenröder, Clemens. *Wir schauten seine Herrlichkeit: Das Johanneische Sprechen vom Sehen im Horizont von Selbsterschliessung Jesu und Antwort des Menschen.* Forschung zur Bibel 80. Würzburg: Echter Verlag, 1996.

Herghelegiu, M.-E. *Sieh, er kommt mit den Wolken: Studien zur Christologie der Johannesoffenbarung.* Europäische Hochschulschriften 23.785. Frankfurt: Lang, 2004.

Hermann, Ingo. *Kyrios und Pneuma: Studien zur Christologie der paulinischen Hauptbriefe.* Studien zum Alten und Neuen Testament 2. Munich: Kösel-Verlag, 1961.

Herrenbrück, F. "Wer waren die Zöllner?" *Zeitschrift für die neutestamentliche Wissenschaft und die Kunde der älteren Kirche* 72 (1981): 178–94.

Herzer, J. "Abschied vom Konsens? Die Pseudepigraphie der Pastoralbriefe als Herausforderung an die neutestamentliche Wissenschaft." *Theologische Literaturzeitung* 129 (204): 1267–82.

———. *Petrus oder Paulus.* Wissenschaftliche Untersuchungen zum Neuen Testament 103. Tübingen: Mohr, 1998.

Hilgenfeld, A. "Die beiden Briefe an die Thessalonicher." *Zeitschrift für wissenschaftliche Theologie* 5 (1862): 225–64.

Hintermaier, J. *Die Befreiungswunder der Apostelgeschichte.* Bonner biblische Beiträge 143. Berlin: Philo, 2003.

Hirsch-Luipold, Rainer, ed. *Gott und die Götter bei Plutarch: Götterbilder—Gottesbilder—Weltbilder.* Religionsgeschichtliche Versuche und Vorarbeiten 54. Berlin: de Gruyter, 2005.

Hoegen-Rohls, Christina. "Johanneische Theologie im Kontext paulinischen Denkens?" In *Kontexte des Johannesevangeliums*, edited by Albert Frey and Udo Schnelle, 593–612. Wissenschaftliche Untersuchungen zum Neuen Testament 175. Tübingen: Mohr, 2004.

———. *Der nachösterliche Johannes: Die Abschiedsreden als hermeneutischer Schlüssel zum vierten Evangelium.* Tübingen: Mohr, 1996.

Hoffmann, Heinrich. *Das Gesetz in der frühjüdischen Apokalyptik.* Studien zur Umwelt des Neuen Testaments 23. Göttingen: Vandenhoeck & Ruprecht, 1999.

Hoffmann, Paul. "Herrscher in oder Richter über Israel? Mt 19,28/Lk 22,28–30 in der synoptischen Tradition." In *Ja und Nein: Christliche Theologie im Angesicht Israels; Festschrift zum 70. Geburtstag von Wolfgang Schrage*, edited by Klaus Wengst et al., 253–64. Neukirchen-Vluyn: Neukirchener Verlag, 1998.

———. "Die historisch-kritische Osterdiskussion von H. S. Reimarus bis zu Beginn des 20. Jahrhunderts." In *Zur neutestamentlichen Überlieferung von der Auferstehung Jesu*, edited by Paul Hoffmann, 15–67. Darmstadt: Wissenschaftliche Buchgesellschaft, 1988.

———. "Der Menschensohn in Lukas 12:8." *New Testament Studies* 44 (1998): 357–79.

———. "Der Petrus-Primat im Matthäusevangelium." In *Neues Testament und Kirche: Für Rudolf Schnackenburg [z. 60. Geburtsag am 5. Jan. 1974 von Freunden u. Kollegen gewidmet]*, edited by Joachim Gnilka, 94–114. Freiburg i.B.: Herder, 1974.

———. "QR und der Menschensohn." In *Tradition und Situation: Studien zur Jesusüberlieferung in der Logienquelle und den synoptischen Evangelien*, edited by Paul Hoffmann, 243–78. Neutestamentliche Abhandlungen, n.F., 28. Münster: Aschendorff, 1995.

———. *Studien zur Theologie der Logienquelle*. Neutestamentliche Abhandlungen, n.F., 8. Münster: Aschendorff, 1972.

———. *Die Toten in Christus: Eine religionsgeschichtliche und exegetische Untersuchung zur paulinischen Eschatologie*. Neutestamentliche Abhandlungen, n.F., 2. Münster: Aschendorff, 1966.

———. "Tradition und Situation: Zur 'verbindlichkeit' des Gebots der Feindesliebe in der synoptischen Tradition und in der gegenwärtigen Friedensdiskusion." In *Tradition und Situation: Studien zur Jesusüberlieferung in der Logienquelle und den synoptischen Evangelien*, edited by Paul Hoffmann, 15–30. Neutestamentliche Abhandlungen, n.F., 28. Münster: Aschendorff, 1995.

———. "Die Versuchungsgeschichte in der Logienquelle: Zur Auseinandersetzung der Judenchristen mit dem politischen Messianismus." In *Tradition und Situation: Studien zur Jesusüberlieferung in der Logienquelle und den synoptischen Evangelien*, edited by Paul Hoffmann, 193–207. Neutestamentliche Abhandlungen, n.F., 28. Münster: Aschendorff, 1995.

———, ed. *Zur neutestamentlichen Überlieferung von der Auferstehung Jesu*. Darmstadt: Wissenschaftliche Buchgesellschaft, 1988.

Hoffmann, Paul, and Christoph Heil. *Die Spruchquelle Q: Studienausgabe Griechisch und Deutsch*. Darmstadt: Wissenschaftliche Buchgesellschaft, 2002.

Hofius, Otfried. "Ἀρνίον—Widder oder Lamm?" In *Neutestamentliche Studien*, edited by Otfried Hofius, 241–50. Wissenschaftliche Untersuchungen zum Neuen Testament 132. Tübingen: Mohr, 2000.

———. "Christus als Schöpfungsmittler und Erlösungsmittler: Das Bekenntnis 1Kor 8,6 im Kontext der paulinischen Theologie." In *Paulinische Christologie: Exegetische Beiträge; Hans Hübner zum 70. Geburtstag*, edited by Udo Schnelle et al., 47–58. Göttingen: Vandenhoeck & Ruprecht, 2000.

———. *Der Christushymnus Philipper 2,6–11: Untersuchungen zu Gestalt und Aussage eines urchristlichen Psalms*. Wissenschaftliche Untersuchungen zum Neuen Testament 17. Tübingen: Mohr, 1976.

———. "Erwägungen zur Gestalt und Herkunft des paulinischen Versöhnungsgedankens." In *Paulusstudien*, edited by Otfried Hofius. Wissenschaftliche Untersuchungen zum Neuen Testament 51. Tübingen: Mohr, 1989.

———. "Jesu Zuspruch der Sündenvergebung." In *Neutestamentliche Studien*, edited by Otfried Hofius, 38–56. Wissenschaftliche Untersuchungen zum Neuen Testament 132. Tübingen: Mohr, 2000.

———. *Katapausis. Die Vorstellung vom endzeitlichen Ruheort im Hebräerbrief*. Wissenschaftliche Untersuchungen zum Neuen Testament 11. Tübingen: Mohr, 1970.

———. "Der Mensch im Schatten Adams." In *Paulusstudien II*, edited by Otfried Hofius, 107–10. Wissenschaftliche Untersuchungen zum Neuen Testament 143. Tübingen: Mohr, 2002.

———. "Struktur und Gedankengang des Logos-Hymnus." In *Johannesstudien*, edited by Otfried Hofius and H.-C. Kammler, 1–23. Wissenschaftliche Untersuchungen zum Neuen Testament 88. Tübingen: Mohr, 1996.

———. "Vergebungszuspruch und Vollmachtsfrage." In *Neutestamentliche Studien*, edited by Otfried Hofius, 57–69. Wissenschaftliche Untersuchungen zum Neuen Testament 132. Tübingen: Mohr, 2000.

———. "'Werke des Gesetzes': Untersuchungen zu der paulinischen Rede von den ἔργα νόμου." In *Paulus und Johannes: Exegetische Studien zur paulinischen und johanneischen Theologie und Literatur*, edited by Dieter Sänger and Ulrich Mell, 271–310. Wissenschaftliche Untersuchungen zum Neuen Testament 198. Tübingen: Mohr Siebeck, 2006.

———. "Das Zeugnis der Johannesoffenbarung von der Gottheit Jesu Christi." In *Neutestamentliche Studien*, edited by Otfried Hofius, 223–40. Wissenschaftliche Untersuchungen zum Neuen Testament 132. Tübingen: Mohr, 2000.

Holmén, T. "The Jewishness of Jesus in the 'Third Quest.'" In *Jesus, Mark and Q: The Teaching of Jesus and Its Earliest Records*, edited by Michael

Labahn and Andreas Schmidt, 143–62. Journal for the Study of the New Testament: Supplement Series 214. Sheffield: Sheffield Academic Press, 2001.

Holm-Nielsen, S. *Die Psalmen Salomos*. Jüdische Schriften aus hellenistisch-römischer Zeit 4.2. Gütersloh: Güterloher Verlagshaus, 1977.

Hölscher, L. *Neue Annalistik: Umrisse einer Theorie der Geschichte*. Göttingen: Wallstein, 2003.

Holtz, Traugott. *Die Christologie der Apokalypse des Johannes*. 2nd, rev. and expanded ed. Texte und Untersuchungen zur Geschichte der Altchristlichen Literatur 85. Berlin: Akademie Verlag, 1971.

———. "Gott in der Apokalypse." In *Geschichte und Theologie des Urchristentums: Gesammelte Aufsätze*, edited by Traugott Holtz et al., 329–46. Wissenschaftliche Untersuchungen zum Neuen Testament 57. Tübingen: Mohr, 1991.

———. *Untersuchungen über die alttestamentlichen Zitate bei Lukas*. Texte und Untersuchungen zur Geschichte der Altchristlichen Literatur 104. Berlin: Akadamie Verlag, 1968.

———. "Die 'Werke' in der Johannesoffenbarung." In *Geschichte und Theologie des Urchristentums: Gesammelte Aufsätze*, edited by Traugott Holtz et al., 347–61. Wissenschaftliche Untersuchungen zum Neuen Testament 57. Tübingen: Mohr, 1991.

Holtzmann, Heinrich Julius. "Zum zweiten Thessalonicherbrief." *Zeitschrift für die neutestamentliche Wissenschaft und die Kunde der älteren Kirche* 2 (1901): 97–108.

Hommel, Hildebrecht. "Das 7. Kapitel des Römerbriefes." In *Sebasmata: Studien zur antiken Religionsgeschichte und zum frühen Christentum*, edited by Hildebrecht Hommel. Tübingen: Mohr, 1983.

Hoppe, Rudolf. "Ekklesiologie und Paränese im Epheserbrief." In *Ethik als angewandte Ekklesiologie*, edited by Michael Wolter, 139–62. Série monographique de Benedictina: Section paulinienne. Rome: St. Paul's Abbey, 2005.

———. "Galiläa—Geschichte, Kultur, Religion." In *Jesus von Nazaret—Spuren und Konturen*, edited by Ludger Schenke, 42–58. Stuttgart: Kohlhammer, 2004.

———. "Der Jakobusbrief als briefliches Zeugnis hellenistisch und hellenistisch-jüdisch geprägter Religiosität." In *Der neue Mensch in Christus: Hellenistische Anthropologie und Ethik im Neuen Testament*, edited by Hans Dieter Betz and Johannes Beutler, 164–89. Quaestiones disputatae 190. Freiburg: Herder, 2001.

———. "Theo-logie in den Deuteropaulinen (Kolosser- und Epheserbrief)." In *Monotheismus und Christologie: Zur Gottesfrage im hellenistischen Judentum und im Urchristentum*, edited by Hans-Josef Klauck, 163–85. Quaestiones disputatae 138. Freiburg i.B.: Herder, 1992.

———. *Der theologische Hintergrund des Jakobusbriefes*. Forschung zur Bibel 28. Würzburg: Echter-Verlag, 1977.

———. *Der Triumph des Kreuzes: Studien zum Verhältnis des Kolosserbriefes zur paulinischen Kreuzestheologie*. Stuttgarter biblische Beiträge 28. Stuttgart: Verlag Katholisches Bibelwerk, 1994.

Horbury, William. "Jewish Messianism and Early Christology." In *Contours of Christology in the New Testament*, edited by Richard N. Longenecker, 3–24. Grand Rapids: Eerdmans, 2005.

———. *Jewish Messianism and the Cult of Christ*. London: SCM, 1998.

Horn, Freidrich Wilhelm. "1Korinther 15,56—ein exegetischer Stachel." *Zeitschrift für die neutestamentliche Wissenschaft und die Kunde der älteren Kirche* 82 (1991): 88–105.

———. *Das Angeld des Geistes: Studien zur paulinischen Pneumatologie*. Forschungen zur Religion und Literatur des Alten und Neuen Testaments 154. Göttingen: Vandenhoeck & Ruprecht, 1992.

———. "Christentum und Judentum in der Logienquelle." *Evangelische Theologie* 51 (1991): 344–64.

———. *Glaube und Handeln in der Theologie des Lukas*. Göttinger Theologische Arbeiten 26. Göttingen: Vandenhoeck & Ruprecht, 1983.

———. "Die Gütergemeinschaft der Urgemeinde." *Evangelische Theologie* 58 (1998): 370–83.

———. "Die Haltung des Lukas zum römischen Staat im Evangelium und in der Apostelgeschichte." In *The Unity of Luke-Acts*, edited by J. Verheyden, 203–44. Bibliotheca ephemeridum theologicarum lovaniensium 142. Louvain: Leuven University Press, 1999.

———. "Kyrios und Pneuma bei Paulus." In *Paulinische Christologie: Exegetische Beiträge; Hans Hübner zum 70. Geburtstag*, edited by Udo Schnelle et al., 59–75. Göttingen: Vandenhoeck & Ruprecht, 2000.

———, ed. *Das Ende des Paulus: Historische, theologische und literaturgeschichtliche Aspekte*.

Beihefte zur Zeitschrift für die neutestamentliche Wissenschaft 106. New York: de Gruyter, 2001.

Horsley, G. H. R. "The Inscriptions of Ephesos and the New Testament." *Novum Testamentum* 34 (1992): 105–68.

Horsley, Richard A. *Archaeology, History, and Society in Galilee: The Social Context of Jesus and the Rabbis*. Valley Forge, PA: Trinity, 1996.

———. *Jesus and Empire: The Kingdom of God and the New World Disorder*. Minneapolis: Fortress, 2003.

———. *Paul and Empire: Religion and Power in Roman Imperial Society*. Harrisburg, PA: Trinity, 1997.

———. *Paul and Politics: Ekklesia, Israel, Imperium, Interpretation; Essays in Honor of Krister Stendahl*. Harrisburg, PA: Trinity, 2000.

———. "Pneumatikos vs. Psychikos." *Harvard Theological Review* 69 (1976): 269–88.

Horsley, Richard A., and John S. Hanson. *Bandits, Prophets, and Messiahs: Popular Movements in the Time of Jesus*. Minneapolis: Winston, 1985.

Hossenfelder, Malte, ed. *Antike Glückslehren: Kynismus und Kyrenaismus, Stoa, Epikureismus und Skepsis: Quellen in deutscher Übersetzung mit Einführungen*. Stuttgart: Kröner, 1996.

Hotze, Gerhard. "Die Christologie des 2. Thessalonicherbriefes." In *Christologie in der Paulus-Schule: Zur Rezeptionsgeschichte des paulinischen Evangeliums*, edited by Klaus Scholtissek, 124–48. Stuttgarter Bibelstudien 181. Stuttgart: Verlag Katholisches Bibelwerk, 2000.

———. *Paradoxien bei Paulus: Untersuchungen zu einer elementaren Denkform in seiner Theologie*. Neutestamentliche Abhandlungen, n.F., 33. Münster: Aschendorff, 1997.

Hübner, Hans. *Biblische Theologie des Neuen Testaments*. 3 vols. Göttingen: Vandenhoeck & Ruprecht, 1990.

———. "Das ganze und das eine Gesetz: Zum Problemkreis Paulus und die Stoa." In *Biblische Theologie als Hermeneutik: Gesammelte Aufsätze/ Hans Hübner zum 65 Geburtstag*, edited by Antje Labahn and Michael Labahn, 9–26. Göttingen: Vandenhoeck & Ruprecht, 1995.

———. *Das Gesetz in der synoptischen Tradition: Studien zur These einer progressiven Qumranisierung und Judaisierung innerhalb der synoptischen Tradition*. 2nd ed. Göttingen: Vandenhoeck & Ruprecht, 1973.

———. *Gottes Ich und Israel: Zum Schriftgebrauch des Paulus in Römer 9–11*. Göttingen: Vandenhoeck & Ruprecht, 1984.

———. "Die paulinische Rechtfertigungstheologie als ökumenisch-hermeneutisches Problem." In *Worum geht es in der Rechtfertigungslehre? Das biblische Fundament der "Gemeinsamen Erklärung" von katholischer Kirche und Lutherischem Weltbund*, edited by Thomas Söding and Frank-Lothar Hossfeld, 76–105. Quaestiones disputatae 180. Freiburg: Herder, 1999.

———. *An Philemon, an die Kolosser, an die Epheser*. Handbuch zum Neuen Testament 12. Tübingen: Mohr, 1997.

Hübner, Hans, et al. *Vetus Testamentum in Novo*. Vol. 1.2, *Evangelium Johannis*. Göttingen: Vandenhoeck & Ruprecht, 2003.

———. *Vetus Testamentum in Novo*. Vol. 2, *Corpus Paulinum*. Göttingen: Vandenhoeck & Ruprecht, 1995.

Hübner, Kurt. *Die Wahrheit des Mythos*. Munich: Beck, 1985.

Hulmi, Sini. *Paulus und Mose: Argumentation und Polemik in 2 Kor 3*. Schriften der finnischen exegetischen Gessellschaft 77. Göttingen: Vandenhoeck & Ruprecht, 1999.

Hummel, Reinhart. *Die Auseinandersetzung zwischen Kirche und Judentum im Matthäusevangelium*. Beiträge zur evangelischen Theologie 33. Munich: Kaiser, 1963.

Hüneburg, M. "Jesus als Wundertäter." In *The Sayings Source Q and the Historical Jesus*, edited by Andreas Lindemann, 635–48. Bibliotheca ephemeridum theologicarum lovaniensium 158. Louvain: Leuven University Press, 2001.

———. *Jesus als Wundertäter in der Logienquelle*. Arbeiten zur Bibel und ihrer Geschichte 4. Leipzig: Evangelische Verlagsanstalt, 2001.

Hunzinger, C. H. "Die Hoffnung angesichts des Todes im Wandel der paulinischen Aussagen." In *Leben angesichts des Todes: Beiträge zum theologischen Problem des Todes. Helmut Thielicke zum 60. Geburtstag*, edited by Bernhardt Lohse, 69–88. Tübingen: Mohr, 1968.

Hurtado, Larry W. *Lord Jesus Christ: Devotion to Jesus in Earliest Christianity*. Grand Rapids: Eerdmans, 2003.

———. *One God, One Lord: Early Christian Devotion and Ancient Jewish Monotheism*. Philadelphia: Fortress, 1988.

———. "Son of God." In *Dictionary of Paul and His Letters*, edited by Gerald F. Hawthorne et al., 900–906. Downers Grove, IL: InterVarsity, 1993.

Ibuki, Y. *Die Wahrheit im Johannesevangelium.* Bonner biblische Beiträge 39. Bonn: Hannstein, 1972.

Iser, Wolfgang. *The Act of Reading: A Theory of Aesthetic Response.* Baltimore: Johns Hopkins University Press, 1978.

Jaeger, Werner Wilhelm. *Die Theologie der frühen griechischen Denker.* Darmstadt: Wissenschaftliche Buchgesellschaft, 1964.

Janowski, Bernd. *Sühne als Heilsgeschehen: Studien zur Sühnetheologie der Priesterschrift und zur Wurzel כפר im Alten Orient und im Alten Testament.* Wissenschaftliche Monographien zum Alten und Neuen Testament 55. Neukirchen-Vluyn: Neukirchener Verlag, 1982.

Janowski, J. Christine, et al., eds. *Stellvertretung: Theologische, philosophische und kulturelle Aspekte.* Neukirchen-Vluyn: Neukirchener Verlag, 2006.

Järvinen, A. "The Son of Man and His Followers: A Q Portrait of Jesus." In *Characterization in the Gospels: Reconceiving Narrative Criticism*, edited by David M. Rhoads and Kari Syreeni, 180–222. Journal for the Study of the New Testament: Supplement Series 184. London: T&T Clark, 2004.

Jaspers, Karl, and Rudolf Bultmann. *Myth and Christianity. An Inquiry into the Possibility of Religion without Myth.* New York: Noonday, 1958.

Jaspert, Bernd. *Sackgassen im Streit mit Rudolf Bultmann: Hermeneutische Probleme der Bultmannrezeption in Theologie und Kirche.* St. Ottilien: EOS Verlag Erzabtei St. Ottilien, 1985.

Jendorff, Bernhard. *Der Logosbegriff: Seine philosophische Grundlegung bei Heraklit von Ephesos und seine theologische Indienstnahme durch Johannes den Evangelisten.* Europäische Hochschulschriften 20.19. Frankfurt: Lang, 1976.

Jeremias, Joachim. *The Eucharistic Words of Jesus.* Translated by Norman Perrin. New York: Scribner, 1966.

———. *Jesus's Promise to the Nations.* Studies in Biblical Theology 24. Naperville, IL: Allenson, 1958.

———. *Neutestamentliche Theologie.* 3rd ed. Gütersloh: Gütersloher Verlagshaus G. Mohn, 1979.

———. *New Testament Theology.* Vol. 1, *The Proclamation of Jesus.* New York: Scribner, 1971.

———. *The Parables of Jesus.* 2nd rev. ed. New York: Scribner, 1972.

———. "Zu Philipper 2,7: ἑαυτὸν ἐκένωσεν." In *Abba: Studien zur neutestamentlichen Theologie und Zeitgeschichte.* Göttingen: Vandenhoeck & Ruprecht, 1966.

———. "Zur Gedankenführung in den paulinischen Briefen (4. Der Christushymnus Phil 2,6–11)." In *Abba: Studien zur neutestamentlichen Theologie und Zeitgeschichte.* Göttingen: Vandenhoeck & Ruprecht, 1966.

Jeremias, Jörg. *Das Königtum Gottes in den Psalmen: Israels Begegnung mit dem kanaanäischen Mythos in den Jahwe-König-Psalmen.* Forschungen zur Religion und Literatur des Alten und Neuen Testaments 141. Göttingen: Vandenhoeck & Ruprecht, 1987.

Jervell, Jacob. *Die Apostelgeschichte.* 17th ed. Kritische-exegetischer Kommentar über das Neue Testament 3. Göttingen: Vandenhoeck & Ruprecht, 1998.

———. *Imago Dei. Gen 1,26f. im Spätjudentum, in der Gnosis und in den paulinischen Briefen.* Forschungen zur Literatur des Alten und Neuen Testaments 76. Göttingen: Vandenhoeck & Ruprecht, 1960.

———. "Die Mitte der Schrift: Zum lukanischen Verständnis des Alten Testaments." In *Die Mitte des Neuen Testaments: Einheit und Vielfalt neutestamentlicher Theologie; Festschrift für Eduard Schweizer zum siebzigsten Geburtstag*, edited by Ulrich Luz and Hans Weder, 79–96. Göttingen: Vandenhoeck & Ruprecht, 1983.

Jewett, Robert. *Paul's Anthropological Terms: A Study of Their Use in Conflict Settings.* Arbeiten zur Geschichte des antiken Judentums und des Urchristentums 10. Leiden: Brill, 1971.

———. *Romans: A Commentary.* Hermeneia—A Critical and Historical Commentary on the Bible. Minneapolis: Fortress, 2007.

Jobes, Karen H., and Moisés Silva. *Invitation to the Septuagint.* Grand Rapids: Baker Academic, 2000.

Johnson, Luke Timothy. *The First and Second Letters to Timothy.* Anchor Bible 35A. New York: Doubleday, 2001.

Jones, F. Stanley. *"Freiheit" in den Briefen des Apostels Paulus: Eine historische, exegetische und religionsgeschichtliche Studie.* Göttinger theologische Arbeiten 34. Göttingen: Vandenhoeck & Ruprecht, 1987.

Jonge, Marinus de. *Christology in Context: The Earliest Christian Response to Jesus.* Philadelphia: Westminster, 1988.

Jörns, Klaus-Peter. *Das hymnische Evangelium: Untersuchungen zu Aufbau, Funktion und Herkunft der hymnischen Stücke in den Johannesoffenbarung*. Studien zum Neuen Testament 5. Gütersloh: Güterloher Verlagshaus, 1971.

Jung, Franz. ΣΩΤΗΡ: *Studien zur Rezeption eines hellenistischen Ehrentitels im Neuen Testament*. Neutestamentliche Abhandlungen, n.F., 39. Münster: Aschendorff, 2002.

Kähler, Christoph. *Jesu Gleichnisse als Poesie und Therapie: Versuch eines integrativen Zugangs zum kommunikativen Aspekt von Gleichnissen Jesu*. Wissenschaftliche Untersuchungen zum Neuen Testament 78. Tübingen: Mohr, 1995.

Kähler, Martin. *The So-Called Historical Jesus and the Historic, Biblical Christ*. Translated by Carl E. Braaten. Seminar Editions. Philadelphia: Fortress, 1964.

Kamlah, Ehrhard. *Die Form der katalogischen Paränese im Neuen Testament*. Wissenschaftliche Untersuchungen zum Neuen Testament 7. Tübingen: Mohr, 1964.

Kammler, Hans-Christian. *Christologie und Eschatologie: Joh 5,17–30 als Schlüsseltext johanneischer Theologie*. Wissenschaftliche Untersuchungen zum Neuen Testament 126. Tübingen: Mohr Siebeck, 2000.

———. "Die Prädikation Jesu Christi als 'Gott' und die paulinische Christologie." *Zeitschrift für die neutestamentliche Wissenschaft und die Kunde der älteren Kirche* 94 (2003): 164–80.

Kampling, Rainer. "Das Gesetz im Markusevangelium." In *Der Evangelist als Theologe*, edited by Thomas Söding, 119–50. Stuttgarter Bibelstudien 163. Stuttgart: Katholisches Bibelwerk, 1995.

———. *Israel unter dem Anspruch des Messiah: Studien zur Israelthematik im Markusevangelium*. Stuttgarter Biblische Beiträge 25. Stuttgart: Katholisches Bibelwerk, 1992.

Karrer, Martin. *Der brief an die Hebräer*. Ökumenischer Taschenbuchkommentar zum Neuen Testament 20. Gütersloh: Gütersloher Verlagshaus Mohn, 2002.

———. "Christliche Gemeinde und Israel: Beobachtungen zur Logienquelle." In *Gottes Recht als Lebensraum: Festschrift für Hans Jochen Boecker*, edited by Peter Mommer, 145–63. Neukirchen-Vluyn: Neukirchener Verlag, 1993.

———. "Christus der Herr und die Welt als Stätte der Prüfung." *Kerygma und Dogma* 35 (1989): 166–88.

———. *Der Gesalbte: Die Grundlagen des Christustitels*. Forschungen zur Religion und Literatur des Alten und Neuen Testaments 151. Göttingen: Vandenhoeck & Ruprecht, 1991.

———. "Himmel, Millennium und neuer Himmel in der Apokalypse." *Jahrbuch für Biblische Theologie* 10 (2005): 225–59.

———. *Jesus Christus im Neuen Testament*. Grundrisse zum Neuen Testament 11. Göttingen: Vandenhoeck & Ruprecht, 1998.

———. "Jesus der Retter (Σωτήρ)." *Zeitschrift für die neutestamentliche Wissenschaft und die Kunde der älteren Kirche* 93 (2002): 153–76.

———. *Die Johannesoffenbarung als Brief: Studien zu ihrem literarischen, historischen und theologischen Ort*. Forschungen zur Religion und Literatur des Alten und Neuen Testaments 140. Göttingen: Vandenhoeck & Ruprecht, 1986.

———. "Petrus im paulinischen Gemeindekreis." *Zeitschrift für die neutestamentliche Wissenschaft und die Kunde der älteren Kirche* 80 (1989): 210–31.

———. "Stärken des Randes: Die Johannesoffenbarung." In *Das Urchristentum in seiner literarischen Geschichte: Festschrift für Jürgen Becker zum 65. Geburtstag*, edited by Ulrich Mell and Ulrich B. Müller, 391–417. Beihefte zur Zeitschrift für die neutestamentliche Wissenschaft 100. New York: de Gruyter, 1999.

———. "'Und ich werde sie heilen': Das Verstockungsmotiv aus Jes 6,9f in Apg 28,26f." In *Kirche und Volk Gottes: Festschrift für Jürgen Roloff zum 70. Geburtstag*, edited by Martin Karrer et al., 255–71. Neukirchen-Vluyn: Neukirchener Verlag, 2000.

———. "Das urchristliche Ältestenamt." *Novum Testamentum* 32 (1990): 152–88.

———. "Von David zu Christus." In *König David—biblische Schlüsselfigur und europäische Leitgestalt: 19. Kolloquium (2000) der Schweizerischen Akademie der Geistes- und Sozialwissenschaften*, edited by W. Dietrich and H. Herkommer, 327–65. Freiburg, Schweiz: Universitätsverlag; Stuttgart: Kohlhammer, 2003.

Käsemann, Ernst. "An Apologia for Primitive Christian Eschatology." In *Essays on New Testament Themes*, 169–95. Studies in Biblical Theology 41. London: SCM, 1964.

———. *Commentary on Romans*. Translated by Geoffrey W. Bromiley. Grand Rapids: Eerdmans, 1980.

———. "Erwägungen zum Stichwort Versöhnungslehre im Neuen Testament." In *Zeit und Geschichte: Dankesgabe an Rudolf Bultmann zum 80. Geburtstag*, edited by Erich Dinkler and Hartwig Thyen, 47–59. Tübingen: Mohr, 1964.

———. *Das Neue Testament als Kanon*. Göttingen: Vandenhoeck & Ruprecht, 1970.

———. "The Problem of the Historical Jesus." In *Essays on New Testament Themes*, translated by W. J. Montague, 15–47. Studies in Biblical Theology 41. London: SCM, 1964.

———. "'The Righteousness of God' in Paul." In *New Testament Questions of Today*, edited by Ernst Käsemann, 168–82. New Testament Library. London: SCM, 1969.

———. "The Structure and Purpose of the Prologue to John's Gospel." In *New Testament Questions of Today*, 138–67. London: SCM, 1969.

———. *The Testament of Jesus. A Study of the Gospel of John in the Light of Chapter 17*. New Testament Library. London: SCM, 1968.

———. "The Theological Problem Presented by the Motif of the Body of Christ." In *Perspectives on Paul*, 101–21. Philadelphia: Fortress, 1971.

———. *The Wandering People of God: An Investigation of the Letter to the Hebrews*. Translated by Roy A. Harrisville and Irving L. Sandberg. Minneapolis: Augsburg, 1984.

Keck, Leander. *Who Is Jesus? History in the Perfect Tense*. Columbia: University of South Carolina Press, 2000.

Kehrer, Günter, et al., eds. *Handbuch religionswissenschaftlicher Grundbegriffe*. 5 vols. Stuttgart: Kohlhammer, 1988.

Kellum, L. Scott. *The Unity of the Farewell Discourse: The Literary Integrity of John 13.31–16.33*. Journal for the Study of the New Testament: Supplement Series 256. London: Sheffield Academic Press, 2004.

Kerner, Jürgen. *Die Ethik der Johannes-Apokalypse im Vergleich mit der des 4. Esra: Ein Beitrag zum Verhältnis von Apokalyptik und Ethik*. Beihefte zur Zeitschrift für die neutestamentliche Wissenschaft und die Kunde der älteren Kirche 94. Berlin: de Gruyter, 1998.

Kertelge, Karl. "Der dienende Menschensohn." In *Jesus und der Menschensohn: Für Anton Vögtle*, edited by Rudolf Pesch et al., 225–39. Freiburg i.B.: Herder, 1975.

———. "Das Doppelgebot der Liebe im Markusevangelium." *Trierer Theologische Zeitschrif* 103 (1994): 38–55.

———. "Jüngerschaft und Kirche: Grundlegung der Kirche nach Marcus." In *Der Evangelist als Theologe*, edited by Thomas Söding, 151–65. Stuttgarter Bibelstudien 163. Stuttgart: Katholisches Bibelwerk, 1995.

———. *Rechtfertigung bei Paulus: Studien zur Struktur und zum Bedeutungsgehalt des paulinischen Rechtfertigungsbegriffs*. Münster: Aschendorff, 1967.

Kierspel, Lars. *The Jews and the World in the Fourth Gospel: Parallelism, Function, and Context*. Wissenschaftliche Untersuchungen zum Neuen Testament 220. Tübingen: Mohr Siebeck, 2006.

Kilgallen, John J. *The Stephen Speech: A Literary and Redactional Study of Acts 7,2–53*. Analecta biblica 67. Rome: Biblical Institute Press, 1976.

Killunen, J. *Die Vollmacht im Widerstreit*. Annales Academiae Scientiarum Fennicae: Dissertationes humanarum litterarum 40. Helsinki: Soumalainen Tiedeakatemia, 1985.

Kim, Panim. "Heilsgegenwart bei Paulus: Eine religionsgeschichtlich-theologische Untersuchung zu Sündenvergebung und Geistgabe in den Qumrantexten sowie bei Johannes dem Täufer, Jesus und Paulus." Diss., Georg August Universität, Göttingen, 1996.

Kingsbury, Jack Dean. *Matthew as Story*. 2nd rev. and enlarged ed. Philadelphia: Fortress, 1988.

Kinlaw, Pamela E. *The Christ Is Jesus: Metamorphosis, Possession, and Johannine Christology*. Academia Biblica 18. Atlanta: Society of Biblical Literature, 2005.

Kittel, Gerhard, and Gerhard Friedrich, eds. *Theological Dictionary of the New Testament*. Translated by Geoffrey W. Bromiley. 10 vols. Grand Rapids: Eerdmans, 1964–76.

Klappert, Bertold, ed. *Diskussion um Kreuz und Auferstehung: Zur gegenwärtigen Auseinandersetzung in Theologie und Gemeinde*. 9th ed. Wuppertal: Aussaat Verlag, 1985.

Klauck, Hans-Josef. *Apocryphal Gospels: An Introduction*. Translated by Bryan McNeil. London and New York: T&T Clark, 2003.

———. "Do They Never Come Back? Nero Redivivus and the Apocalypse of John." In *Religion und Gesellschaft im frühen Christentum: Neutestamentliche Studien*, edited by Hans-Josef Klauck, 268–89. Wissenschaftliche Untersuchungen zum Neuen Testament 152. Tübingen: Mohr Siebeck, 2003.

———. "Ein Richter im eigenen Innern: Das Gewissen bei Philo von Alexandrien." In *Alte Welt und neuer Glaube: Beiträge zur Religionsgeschichte, Forschungsgeschichte und Theologie des Neuen Testaments*, edited by Hans-Josef Klauck, 33–58. Novum Testamentum et Orbis Antiquus 29. Göttingen: Vandenhoeck & Ruprecht, 1994.

———. "Die erzählerische Rolle der Jünger im Markusevangelium: Eine narrative Analyse." *Novum Testamentum* 24 (1982): 1–26.

———. "'Der Gott in dir' (Ep 41,1): Autonomie des Gewissens bei Seneca und Paulus." In *Alte Welt und neuer Glaube: Beiträge zur Religionsgeschichte, Forschungsgeschichte und Theologie des Neuen Testaments*, edited by Hans-Josef Klauck, 11–31. Novum Testamentum et Orbis Antiquus 29. Göttingen: Vandenhoeck & Ruprecht, 1994.

———. "Gütergemeinschaft in der klassischen Antike, in Qumran und im Neuen Testament." In *Gemeinde—Amt—Sakrament: Neutestamentliche Perspektiven*, edited by Hans-Josef Klauck, 69–100. Würzburg: Echter, 1989.

———. *Hausgemeinde und Hauskirche im frühen Christentum*. Stuttgarter Bibelstudien 103. Stuttgart: Verlag Katholisches Bibelwerk, 1981.

———. *Magie und Heidentum in der Apostelgeschichte des Lukas*. Stuttgarter Bibelstudien 167. Stuttgart: Verlag Katholisches Bibelwerk, 1996.

———. *The Religious Context of Early Christianity: A Guide to Graeco-Roman Religions*. Translated by Brian McNeil. Minneapolis: Fortress, 2003.

———. "Das Sendschreiben nach Pergamon und der Kaiserkult in der Johannesoffenbarung." *Biblica* 73 (1992): 153–82.

———. *Vorspiel im Himmel? Erzähltechnik und Theologie im Markusprolog*. Biblisch-Theologische Studien 32. Neukirchen: Neukirchener Verlag, 1997.

Klauck, Hans-Josef, and Balbina Bäbler. *Olympische Rede, oder, Über die erste Erkenntnis Gottes*. Texte zur Forschung. Darmstadt: Wissenschaftliche Buchgesellschaft, 2000.

Klauser, Theodor, et al., eds. *Reallexikon für Antike und Christentum: Sachwörterbuch zur Auseinandersetzung des Christentums mit der antiken Welt*. Stuttgart: Hiersemann, 1985.

Klehn, L. "Die Verwendung von ἐν Χριστῷ bei Paulus." *Biblische Zeitschrift* 74 (1994): 66–79.

Klein, Günter. "Lukas 1,1–4 als theologisches Programm." In *Das Lukas-Evangelium*, edited by G. Braumann, 170–203. Weg der Forschung 280. Darmstadt: Wissenschaftliche Buchgesellschaft, 1974.

———. *Die zwölf Apostel: Ursprung und Gehalt einer Idee*. Forschungen zur Literatur des Alten und Neuen Testaments 77. Göttingen: Vandenhoeck & Ruprecht, 1961.

Klein, Hans. *Das Lukasevangelium*. Kritisch-exegetischer Kommentar über das Neue Testament 1/3. Göttingen: Vandenhoeck & Ruprecht, 2006.

———. "Rechtfertigung aus Glauben als Ergänzung der Gerechtigkeit aus dem Gesetz." In *Ja und Nein: Christliche Theologie im Angesicht Israels; Festschrift zum 70. Geburtstag von Wolfgang Schrage*, edited by Klaus Wengst et al., 155–64. Neukirchen-Vluyn: Neukirchener Verlag, 1998.

Klinghardt, Matthias. *Gesetz und Volk Gottes*. Wissenschaftliche Untersuchungen zum Neuen Testament 2.32. Tübingen: Mohr, 1988.

———. "Sünde und Gericht von Christen bei Paulus." *Zeitschrift für die neutestamentliche Wissenschaft und die Kunde der älteren Kirche* 88 (1997): 56–80.

Kloppenborg Verbin, John S. *Excavating Q: The Historical Setting of the Sayings Gospel*. Minneapolis: Fortress, 2000.

———. *The Formation of Q: Trajectories in Ancient Wisdom Collections*. Studies in Antiquity and Christianity. Philadelphia: Fortress, 1987.

Klumbies, Paul-Gerhard. *Die Rede von Gott bei Paulus in ihrem zeitgeschichtlichen Kontext*. Göttingen: Vandenhoeck & Ruprecht, 1992.

Kmiecik, U. *Der Menschensohn im Markusevangelium*. Forschung zur Bibel 81. Würzburg: Echter Verlag, 1997.

Knoch, Otto. *Der erste und zweite Petrusbrief, der Judasbrief*. Regensburger Neues Testament 8. Regensburg: Pustet, 1990.

Knöppler, Thomas. "Beobachtungen zur lukanischen theologia resurrectionis." In ". . . *Was ihr auf dem Weg verhandelt habt": Beiträge zur Exegese und Theologie des Neuen Testaments; Festschrift für Ferdinand Hahn zum 75. Geburtstag*, edited by Peter Müller et al., 51–62. Neukirchen-Vluyn: Neukirchener Verlag, 2001.

———. "Das Blut des Lammes." In *Deutungen des Todes Jesu im Neuen Testament*, edited by J. Frey and J. Schröter, 477–511. Wissenschaftliche Untersuchungen zum Neuen Testament 181. Tübingen: Mohr, 2005.

———. *Sühne im Neuen Testament: Studien zum urchristlichen Verständnis der Heilsbedeutung des Todes Jesu*. Neukirchen-Vluyn: Neukirchener Verlag, 2001.

———. *Die theologia crucis des Johannesevangeliums: Das Verständnis des Todes Jesu im Rahmen der johanneischen Inkarnations- und Erhöhungschristologie*. Wissenschaftliche Monographien zum Alten und Neuen Testament 69. Neukirchen-Vluyn: Neukirchener Verlag, 1994.

Knorr-Cetina, K. *Die Fabrikation von Erkenntnis: Zur Anthropologie der Naturwissenschaft*. Frankfurt: Suhrkamp, 1991.

Koch, Dietrich-Alex. *Die Bedeutung der Wundererzählungen für die Christologie des Markusevangeliums*. Beihefte zur Zeitschrift für die neutestamentliche Wissenschaft und die Kunde der älteren Kirche 42. Berlin: de Gruyter, 1975.

———. "Crossing the Border: The 'Hellenists' and Their Way to the Gentiles." *Neotestamentica* 39 (2005): 289–312.

———. "Die Einmaligkeit des Anfangs und die Fortdauer der Institution." In *Die kleine Prophetin Kirche leiten*, edited by M. Böttcher et al. Wuppertal: Brockhaus, 2005.

———. *Die Schrift als Zeuge des Evangeliums: Untersuchungen zur Verwendung und zum Verständnis der Schrift bei Paulus*. Beiträge zur historischen Theologie 69. Tübingen: Mohr, 1986.

Koch, Klaus, and Martin Rösel. "Das Reich der Heiligen und des Menschensohns: Ein Kapitel politischer Theologie." In *Die Reiche der Welt und der kommende Menschensohn: Studien zum Danielbuch*, 140–72. Neukirchen-Vluyn: Neukirchener Verlag, 1995.

Koch, Stefan. *Rechtliche Regelung von Konflikten im frühen Christentum*. Wissenschaftliche Untersuchungen zum Neuen Testament 174. Tübingen: Mohr, 2004.

Kocka, J. "Angemessenheitskriterien historischer Argumente." In *Objektivität und Parteilichkeit*, edited by W. J. Mommsen and Jörn Rüsen, 469–75. Munich: Deutscher Taschenbuch-Verlag, 1977.

Koester, Craig R. *Hebrews*. Anchor Bible 36. New York: Doubleday, 2001.

———. "The Savior of the World." *Journal of Biblical Literature* 109 (1990): 665–80.

———. *Symbolism in the Fourth Gospel*. 2nd ed. Minneapolis: Fortress, 2003.

Kohle, K.-H. "Ethnizität und Tradition aus ethnologischer Sicht." In *Identitäten*, edited by Aleida Assmann and Heidrun Friese, 269–87. Frankfurt: Suhrkamp, 1999.

Kohler, Herbert. *Kreuz und Menschwerdung im Johannesevangelium: Ein exegetisch-hermeneutischer Versuch zur johanneischen Kreuzestheologie*. Abhandlungen zur Theologie des Alten und Neuen Testaments 72. Zürich: Theologischer Verlag, 1987.

Köhler, Ludwig. *Die Briefe des Sokrates und der Sokratiker*. Leipzig: Liselotte, 1928.

Köhler, Wolf-Dietrich. *Die Rezeption des Matthäusevangeliums in der Zeit vor Irenäus*. Wissenschaftliche Untersuchungen zum Neuen Testament 2.24. Tübingen: Mohr, 1987.

Kolakowski, Leszek. *Die Gegenwärtigkeit des Mythos*. Munich: Piper, 1984.

Kolb, Frank. *Rom: Die Geschichte der Stadt in der Antike*. 3rd ed. Munich: Beck, 2002.

Kollmann, Bernd. "Jesu Schweigegebote an die Dämonen." *Zeitschrift für die neutestamentliche Wissenschaft und die Kunde der älteren Kirche* 82 (1991): 267–73.

———. *Jesus und die Christen als Wundertäter: Studien zu Magie, Medizin und Schamanismus in Antike und Christentum*. Forschungen zur Religion und Literatur des Alten und Neuen Testaments 170. Göttingen: Vandenhoeck & Ruprecht, 1996.

———. *Joseph Barnabas: Leben und Wirkungsgeschichte*. Stuttgarter Bibelstudien 175. Stuttgart: Verlag Katholisches Bibelwerk, 1998.

———. *Ursprung und Gestalten der frühchristlichen Mahlfeier*. Göttinger theologische Arbeiten 43. Göttingen: Vandenhoeck & Ruprecht, 1990.

Konradt, Matthias. "'Geboren durch das Wort der Wahrheit'—'gerichtet durch das Gesetz der Freiheit': Das Wort als Zentrum der theologischen Konzeption des Jakobusbriefes." In *Der Jakobusbrief: Beiträge zur Rehabilitierung der "strohernen Epistel,"* edited by Petra von Gemünden et al., 1–15. Beiträge zum Verstehen der Bibel 3. Münster: Lit-Verlag, 2003.

———. *Gericht und Gemeinde: Eine Studie zur Bedeutung und Funktion von Gerichtsaussagen im Rahmen der paulinischen Ekklesiologie und Ethik im 1 Thess und 1 Kor*. Beihefte zur Zeitschrift für die neutestamentliche Wissenschaft und die Kunde der älteren Kirche 117. Berlin: de Gruyter, 2003.

———. "Der Jakobusbrief im frühchristlichen Kontext." In *The Catholic Epistles and the Tradition*, edited by Jacques Schlosser, 171–212. Bibliotheca ephemeridum theologicarum lovaniensium 176. Louvain: Leuven University Press, 2004.

———. "Die Sendung zu Israel und zu den Völkern im Matthäusevangelium im Lichte seiner narrativen Christologie." *Zeitschrift für Theologie und Kirche* (2004): 397–425.

———. "Theologie in der 'strohernen Epistel.'" *Verkündigung und Forschung* 44 (1999): 54–78.

Kooten, George H. van. *Cosmic Christology in Paul and the Pauline School: Colossians and Ephesians in the Context of Graeco-Roman Cosmology, with a New Synopsis of the Greek Texts.* Wissenschaftliche Untersuchungen zum Neuen Testament 2.171. Tübingen: Mohr, 2003.

Korn, M. *Die Geschichte Jesu in veränderter Zeit.* Wissenschaftliche Untersuchungen zum Neuen Testament 2.51. Tübingen: Mohr, 1993.

Kosch, D. *Die eschatologische Tora des Menschensohnes: Untersuchungen zur Rezeption der Stellung Jesu zur Tora in Q.* Novum Testamentum et Orbis Antiquus 12. Göttingen: Vandenhoeck & Ruprecht, 1989.

———. "Q und Jesus." *Biblische Zeitschrift* 36 (1992): 30–58.

Koselleck, R. "Standortbindung und Zeitlichkeit." In *Theorie der Geschichte*, edited by R. Koselleck et al., 17–46. Munich: Deutscher Taschenbuch-Verlag, 1977.

Koskenniemi, Erkki. *Apollonios von Tyana in der neutestamentlichen Exegese: Forschungsbericht und Weiterführung der Diskussion.* Wissenschaftliche Untersuchungen zum Neuen Testament 2.61. Tübingen: Mohr (Paul Siebeck), 1994.

Kowalski, Beate. *Die Rezeption des Propheten Ezechiel in der Offenbarung des Johannes.* Stuttgarter biblische Beiträge 52. Stuttgart: Verlag Katholisches Bibelwerk, 2004.

Kraft, Heinrich. *Die Offenbarung des Johannes.* Handbuch zum Neuen Testament 16a. Tübingen: Mohr, 1974.

Kragerud, Alv. *Der Lieblingsjünger im Johannesevangelium: Ein exegetischer Versuch.* Oslo: Osloer Universitätsverlag, 1959.

Kramer, Werner R. *Christ, Lord, Son of God.* Translated by Brian Hardy. Studies in Biblical Theology 50. London: SCM, 1966.

Kraus, Wolfgang. "Johannes und das Alte Testament." *Zeitschrift für die neutestamentliche Wissenschaft und die Kunde der älteren Kirche* 88 (1997): 1–23.

———. "Der Tod Jesu als Sühnetod bei Paulus." *Zeitschrift für die neutestamentliche Wissenschaft und die Kunde der älteren Kirche* 3 (1999): 20–30.

———. *Das Volk Gottes: Zur Grundlegung der Ekklesiologie bei Paulus.* Wissenschaftliche Untersuchungen zum Neuen Testament 85. Tübingen: Mohr, 1996.

———. *Zwischen Jerusalem und Antiochia: Die "Hellenisten," Paulus und die Aufnahme der Heiden in das endzeitliche Gottesvolk.* Stuttgarter Bibelstudien 179. Stuttgart: Katholisches Bibelwerk, 1999.

Kremer, J. "'Dieser ist der Sohn Gottes.'" In *Der Treue Gottes trauen: Beiträge zum Werk des Lukas; für Gerhard Schneider*, edited by Claus Bussmann and Walter Radl, 137–57. Freiburg i.B.: Herder, 1991.

———. *Pfingstbericht und Pfingstgeschehen.* Stuttgarter Bibelstudien 63/64. Stuttgart: Katholisches Bibelwerk, 1973.

———. "Weltweites Zeugnis für Christus in der Kraft des Geistes." In *Mission im Neuen Testament*, edited by Karl Kertelge, 145–63. Quaestiones disputatae 93. Freiburg i.B.: Herder, 1982.

Kretschmar, G. *Die Offenbarung des Johannes: Die Geschichte ihrer Auslegung im 1. Jahrtausend.* Calwer theologische Monographien: Reihe B, Systematische Theologie und Kirchengeschichte 9. Stuttgart: Kaiser, 1985.

———. "Der paulinische Glaube in den Pastoralbriefe." In *Glaube im Neuen Testament: Studien zu Ehren von Hermann Binder anlässlich seines 70. Geburtstags*, edited by Ferdinand Hahn and Hans Klein, 115–40. Biblisch-theologische Studien 7. Neukirchen-Vluyn: Neukirchener Verlag, 1982.

Krieger, K. St. "Pontius Pilatus—ein Judenfeind? Zur Problematik einer Pilatus-biographie." *Biblische Notizen* 78 (1995): 63–83.

Kristen, P. *Familie, Kreuz und Leben: Nachfolge Jesu nach Q und dem Markusevangelium.* Marburger Theologische Studien 42. Marburg: Elwert, 1995.

Krückemeier, Nils. "Der zwölfjahrige Jesus im Tempel (Luke 2:40–52) und die biographische Literatur der hellenistischen Antike." *New Testament Studies* 50 (2004): 307–19.

Kügler, J. *Der Jünger, den Jesus liebte.* Stuttgarter Biblische Beiträge 16. Stuttgart: Katholisches Bibelwerk, 1988.

Kuhn, Hans Wolfgang. "Der Gekreuzigte von Giv'at ha-Mivtar: Bilanz einer Entdeckung." In *Theologia crucis, signum crucis: Festschrift für Erich Dinkler zum 70. Geburtstag*, edited by Carl Andresen and Günter Klein, 303–34. Tübingen: Mohr, 1979.

———. "Jesus als Gekreuzigter in der frühchristlichen Verkündigung bis zur Mitte des 2. Jahrhunderts." *Zeitschrift für die neutestamentliche*

Wissenschaft und die Kunde der älteren Kirche 72 (1975): 1–46.

———. "Jesus vor dem Hintergrund der Qumrangemeinde." In *Grenzgänge: Menschen und Schicksale zwischen jüdischer, christlicher und deutscher Identität; Festschrift für Diethard Aschoff*, edited by Folker Siegert and Diethard Aschoff, 50–60. Münsteraner judaistische Studien 11. Münster: Lit, 2002.

———. "Die Kreuzesstrafe während der frühen Kaiserzeit." In *Aufstieg und Niedergang der römischen Welt: Geschichte und Kultur Roms im Spiegel der neueren Forschung*, edited by Joseph Vogt et al., 2.25.1:648–793. Berlin: de Gruyter, 1982.

Kuhn, Heinz-Wolfgang. *Ältere Sammlungen in Markusevangelium*. Studien zur Umwelt des Neuen Testaments 8. Göttingen: Vandenhoeck und Ruprecht, 1971.

Kuhn, Karl G. "Πειρασμός—ἁμαρτία—σάρξ im Neuen Testament und die damit zusammenhängenden Vorstellungen." *Zeitschrift für Theologie und Kirche* 49 (1952): 200–222.

Kuhn, Peter. *Offenbarungsstimmen im antiken Judentum: Untersuchungen zur Bat Qol und verwandten Phänomenen*. Texts and Studies in Ancient Judaism 20. Tübingen: Mohr, 1989.

Kümmel, Werner Georg. "Äussere und innere Reinheit des Menschen bei Jesus." In *Heilsgeschehen und Geschichte*, edited by Erich Grässer et al., 1:117–29. Marburger theologische Studien 1. Marburg: Elwert, 1965.

———. "Das Gesetz und die Propheten gehen bis Johannes." In *Das Lukas-Evangelium*, edited by G. Braumann, 398–415. Weg der Forschung 280. Darmstadt: Wissenschaftliche Buchgesellschaft, 1974.

———. "Lukas in der Anklage der heutigen Theologie." In *Heilsgeschehen und Geschichte*, edited by Werner Georg Kümmel et al., 87–100. Marburger theologische Studien 3. Marburg: Elwert, 1965.

———. *Promise and Fulfillment: The Eschatological Message of Jesus*. Studies in Biblical Theology 23. London: SCM, 1961.

———. *Römer 7 und das Bild des Menschen im Neuen Testament: Zwei Studien*. Theologische Bücherei 53. Munich: Kaiser, 1974.

Kümmel, Werner Georg, and Helmut Merklein. *Vierzig Jahre Jesusforschung (1950–1990)*. 2nd ed. Bonner biblische Beiträge 91. Weinheim: Beltz Athenäum, 1994.

Kurianal, J. *Jesus Our High Priest*. Europäische Hochschulschriften 23.693. Frankfurt: Lang, 1999.

Kurz, Gerhard. *Metapher, Allegorie, Symbol*. 4th ed. Göttingen: Vandenhoeck & Ruprecht, 1997.

Kytzler, B., ed. *Roma aeterna: Lateinische und griechische Romdichtung*. Munich: Artemis, 1972.

Laato, Timo. *Paulus und das Judentum: Anthropologische Erwägungen*. Åbo: Åbo Akademis Förlag, 1991.

Labahn, Antje, and Michael Labahn. "Jesus als Sohn Gottes bei Paulus." In *Paulinische Christologie: Exegetische Beiträge; Hans Hübner zum 70. Geburtstag*, edited by Udo Schnelle et al. Göttingen: Vandenhoeck & Ruprecht, 2000.

Labahn, Michael. "Bedeutung und Frucht des Todes Jesu im Spiegel des johanneischen Erzählaufbaus." In *The Death of Jesus in the Fourth Gospel*, edited by G. van Belle, 431–56. Bibliotheca ephemeridum theologicarum lovaniensium 200. Louvain: Leuven University Press, 2007.

———. "Der Gottessohn, die Versuchung und das Kreuz: Überlegungen zum Jesusporträt der Versuchungsgeschichte in Q 4,1–13." *Ephemerides theologicae lovanienses* 80 (2004): 402–22.

———. "'Heiland der Welt': Der gesandte Gottessohn und der römische Kaiser—ein Thema johanneischer Christologie." In *Zwischen den Reichen: Neues Testament und römische Herrschaft: Vorträge auf der Ersten Konferenz der European Association for Biblical Studies*, edited by Michael Labahn and Jürgen Zangenberg. Texte und Arbeiten zum neutestamentlichen Zeitalter 36. Tübingen: Francke, 2002.

———. *Jesus als Lebensspender: Untersuchungen zu einer Geschichte der johanneischen Tradition anhand ihrer Wundergeschichten*. Beihefte zur Zeitschrift für die neutestamentliche Wissenschaft und die Kunde der älteren Kirche 98. Berlin: de Gruyter, 1999.

———. "Jesus Exorzismen (Q 11,19–20)." In *The Sayings Source Q and the Historical Jesus*, edited by Andreas Lindemann, 617–33. Bibliotheca ephemeridum theologicarum lovaniensium 158. Louvain: Leuven University Press, 2001.

———. "Jesus und die Autorität der Schrift." In *Israel und seine Heilstraditionen im Johannesevangelium: Festgabe für Johannes Beutler SJ zum 70. Geburtstag*, edited by Michael Labahn et al., 185–206. Paderborn: Schöningh, 2004.

———. "Die παρρησία des Gottessohnes." In *Kontexte des Johannesevangeliums*, edited by Albert Frey and Udo Schnelle, 321–63. Wissenschaftliche Untersuchungen zum Neuen Testament 175. Tübingen: Mohr, 2004.

———. "Der Weg eines Namenlosen—vom Hilflosen zum Vorbild (Joh 9)." In *Die bleibende Gegenwart des Evangeliums: Festschrift für Otto Merk*, edited by Roland Gebauer and Martin Meiser, 63–80. Marburger Theologische Studien 76. Marburg: Elwert, 2003.

Läger, Karoline. *Die Christologie der Pastoralbriefe*. Hamburger theologische Studien 12. Münster: Lit, 1996.

Lampe, Peter. "Acta 19 im Spiegel der ephesischen Inschriften." *Biblische Zeitschrift* 19 (1992): 59–76.

———. *From Paul to Valentinus: Christians at Rome in the First Two Centuries*. Translated by Michael Steinhauser. Edited by Marshall D. Johnson. Minneapolis: Fortress, 2003.

———. "Das Spiel mit dem Petrusnamen—Matt. XVI.18." *New Testament Studies* 25 (1979): 227–45.

Landmesser, Christof. *Jüngerberufung und Zuwendung zu Gott*. Wissenschaftliche Untersuchungen zum Neuen Testament 133. Tübingen: Mohr, 2001.

Lang, F. "Erwägungen zur eschatologischen Verkündigung Johannes des Täufers." In *Jesus Christus in Historie und Theologie (FS Hans Conzelmann)*, edited by Georg Strecker, 459–73. Tübingen: Mohr, 1975.

Lang, Friedrich. *Die Briefe an die Korinther*. 17th ed. Das Neue Testament deutsch 7. Göttingen: Vandenhoeck & Ruprecht, 1994.

Lang, M. "Johanneische Abschiedsreden und Senecas Konsolationsliteratur." In *Kontexte des Johannesevangeliums*, edited by Albert Frey and Udo Schnelle, 365–412. Wissenschaftliche Untersuchungen zum Neuen Testament 175. Tübingen: Mohr, 2004.

———. *Johannes und die Synoptiker*. Forschungen zur Literatur des Alten und Neuen Testaments 182. Göttingen: Vandenhoeck & Ruprecht, 1999.

———. "Leben in der Zeit: Pragmatische Studien aus der römischen Sicht zur 'christlichen Lebenskunst' anhand des lukanischen Paulusbildes." ThD diss., Martin-Luther-Universität, Halle-Wittenberg, 2007.

Laub, Franz. "'Ein für allemal hineingegangen in das Allerheiligste' (Hebr 9,12): Zum Verständnis des Kreuzestodes im Hebräerbrief." *Biblische Zeitschrift* 35 (1991): 65–85.

———. "Paulinische Autorität in nachpaulinischer Zeit." In *The Thessalonian Correspondence*, edited by Raymond F. Collins and Norbert Baumert, 403–17. Bibliotheca ephemeridum theologicarum lovaniensium 87. Louvain: Leuven University Press, 1990.

Lehnert, V. A. "Die 'Verstockung Israels' und biblische Hermeneutik." *Zeitschrift für Neues Testament* 16 (1998): 13–19.

Leipoldt, Johannes. *Geschichte des neutestamentlichen Kanons*. 2 vols. Leipzig: Heinrichs, 1907–8.

Lessing, G. E. "On the Proof of the Spirit and Power." In *Lessing's Theological Writings*, edited and translated by Henry Chadwick, 51–56. Library of Modern Religious Thought 2. London: Adam & Charles Black, 1956.

Lichtenberger, Hermann. *Das Ich Adams und das Ich der Menschheit: Studien zum Menschenbild in Römer 7*. Wissenschaftliche Untersuchungen zum Neuen Testament 164. Tübingen: Mohr Siebeck, 2004.

———. "Messianische Erwartungen und messianische Gestalten in der Zeit des Zweiten Tempels." In *Messias-Vorstellungen bei Juden und Christen*, edited by Ekkehard Stegemann and Albert H. Friedlander, 9–20. Stuttgart: Kohlhammer, 1993.

———. *Studien zum Menschenbild in Texten der Qumrangemeinde*. Studien zur Umwelt des Neuen Testaments 15. Göttingen: Vandenhoeck & Ruprecht, 1980.

———. "Das Tora-Verständnis im Judentum zur Zeit des Paulus." In *Paul and the Mosaic Law*, edited by James D. G. Dunn. Grand Rapids: Eerdmans, 2001.

Lietzmann, Hans. *An die Römer*. 5th ed. Handbuch zum Neuen Testament 8. Tübingen: Mohr, 1971.

———. *A History of the Early Church*. Vol. 1, *The Beginnings of the Christian Church*. Vol. 2, *The Founding of the Church Universal*. Translated by Bertram Lee Woolf. Cleveland: World, 1963.

Limbeck, Meinrad. *Die Ordnung des Heils: Untersuchungen zum Gesetzesverständnis des Frühjudentums*. Düsseldorf: Patmos, 1971.

Lindemann, Andreas. *Die Aufhebung der Zeit: Geschichtsverständnis und Eschatologie im Epheserbrief*. Studien zum Neuen Testament 12. Gütersloh: Gütersloher Verlagshaus Mohn, 1975.

———. "Die biblischen Toragebote und die paulinische Ethik." In *Paulus, Apostel und Lehrer der Kirche: Studien zu Paulus und zum frühen Paulusverständnis*, edited by Andreas Lindemann, 91–114. Tübingen: Mohr, 1999.

———. *Der Epheserbrief.* Zürcher Bibelkommentare 8. Zürich: Theologischer Verlag, 1985.

———. *Der Erste Korintherbrief.* Handbuch zum Neuen Testament 9.1. Tübingen: Mohr, 2000.

———. "Die Osterbotschaft des Markus." *New Testament Studies* 26 (1979–80): 298–317.

———. *Paulus im ältesten Christentum: Das Bild des Apostels und die Rezeption der paulinischen Theologie in der frühchristlichen Literatur bis Marcion.* Beiträge zur historischen Theologie 58. Tübingen: Mohr, 1979.

———. "Zum Abfassungszweck des zweiten Thessalonicherbriefes." *Zeitschrift für die neutestamentliche Wissenschaft und die Kunde der älteren Kirche* 68 (1977): 35–47.

———. "Zur Religion des Urchristentums." *Theologische Rundschau* 67 (2002): 238–61.

Linnemann, Eta. *Parables of Jesus: Introduction and Exposition.* Translated by John Sturdy. 3rd ed. London: S.P.C.K., 1966.

Lips, Hermann von. *Glaube—Gemeinde—Amt: Zum Verständnis der Ordination in den Pastoralbriefen.* Forschungen zur Literatur des Alten und Neuen Testaments 122. Göttingen: Vandenhoeck & Ruprecht, 1979.

———. "Die 'Leiden des Apostels' als Thema paulinischer Theologie." In *". . . Was ihr auf dem Weg verhandelt habt": Beiträge zur Exegese und Theologie des Neuen Testaments; Festschrift für Ferdinand Hahn zum 75. Geburtstag*, edited by Peter Müller et al., 117–28. Neukirchen-Vluyn: Neukirchener Verlag, 2001.

———. "Von den 'Pastoralbriefen' zum 'Corpus Pastorale.'" In *Reformation und Neuzeit: 300 Jahre Theologie in Halle*, edited by Udo Schnelle, 107–24. Berlin: de Gruyter, 1994.

———. *Weisheitliche Traditionen im Neuen Testament.* Wissenschaftliche Monographien zum Alten und Neuen Testament 64. Neukirchen-Vluyn: Neukirchener Verlag, 1990.

List, E. "Sinn." In *Handbuch religionswissenschaftlicher Grundbegriffe*, edited by Günter Kehrer et al., 62–71. Stuttgart: Kohlhammer, 1988.

Loader, William R. G. *Sohn und Hoherpriester: Eine traditionsgeschichtliche Untersuchung zur Christologie des Hebräerbriefes.* Wissenschaftliche Monographien zum Alten und Neuen Testament 53. Neukirchen-Vluyn: Neukirchener Verlag, 1981.

Lohfink, Gerhard. *Die Himmelfahrt Jesu: Untersuchungen zu den Himmelfahrts- und Erhöhungstexten bei Lukas.* Studien zum Alten und Neuen Testament 26. Munich: Kösel, 1971.

———. "Paulinische Theologie in den Pastoralbriefen." In *Paulus in den neutestamentlichen Spätschriften: Zur Paulusrezeption im Neuen Testament*, edited by Karl Kertelge, 70–121. Quaestiones disputatae 89. Freiburg i.B.: Herder, 1981.

———. *Die Sammlung Israels.* Studien zum Alten und Neuen Testament 39. Munich: Kösel, 1975.

———. "Wem gilt die Bergpredigt?" *Theologische Quartalschrift* 163 (1983): 264–84.

Lohmeyer, Ernst. *Kyrios Jesus: Eine Untersuchung zur Phil. 2,5–11.* 2nd ed. Sitzungsberichte der Heidelberger Akademie der Wissenschaften 4. Heidelberg: Winter, 1961.

Löhr, Hermut. "Anthropologie und Eschatologie im Hebräerbrief." In *Eschatologie und Schöpfung*, edited by M. Evang et al., 169–99. Beihefte zur Zeitschrift für die neutestamentliche Wissenschaft 89. Berlin: de Gruyter, 1997.

———. *Umkehr und Sünde im Hebräerbrief.* Beihefte zur Zeitschrift für die neutestamentliche Wissenschaft und die Kunde der älteren Kirche 73. Berlin: de Gruyter, 1994.

———. "Wahrnehmung und Bedeutung des Todes Jesu nach dem Hebräerbrief." In *Deutungen des Todes Jesu im Neuen Testament*, edited by J. Frey and J. Schröter, 455–76. Wissenschaftliche Untersuchungen zum Neuen Testament 181. Tübingen: Mohr, 2005.

Lohse, Eduard. "Christologie und Ethik im Kolosserbrief." In *Die Einheit des Neuen Testaments: Exegetische Studien zur Theologie des Neuen Testaments*, 249–61. Göttingen: Vandenhoeck & Ruprecht, 1973.

———. "Christusherrschaft und Kirche." In *Die Einheit des Neuen Testaments: Exegetische Studien zur Theologie des Neuen Testaments*, 262–75. Göttingen: Vandenhoeck & Ruprecht, 1973.

———. *Colossians and Philemon: A Commentary on the Epistles to the Colossians and to Philemon.* Translated by William R. Poehlmann and Robert J. Karris. Hermeneia—A Critical and Historical Commentary on the Bible. Philadelphia: Fortress, 1971.

———. "Glaube und Werke." In *Die Einheit des Neuen Testaments: Exegetische Studien zur Theologie des Neuen Testaments*, 285–306. Göttingen: Vandenhoeck & Ruprecht, 1973.

———. "Jesu Worte über den Sabbat." In *Die Einheit des Neuen Testaments: Exegetische Studien zur Theologie des Neuen Testaments*, edited by Eduard Lohse, 62–72. Göttingen: Vandenhoeck & Ruprecht, 1973.

———. *Märtyer und Gottesknecht: Untersuchungen zur urchristlichen Verkündigung vom Sühntod Jesu Christi*. Forschungen zur religion und Literatur des Alten und Neuen Testaments 46. Göttingen: Vandenhoeck & Ruprecht, 1955.

———. "Taufe und Rechtfertigung bei Paulus." In *Die Einheit des Neuen Testaments*, 228–44. Göttingen: Vandenhoeck & Ruprecht, 1973.

Loisy, Alfred. *The Gospel and the Church*. Lives of Jesus Series. Philadelphia: Fortress, 1976.

Lona, H. E. *Die Eschatologie im Kolosser- und Epheserbrief*. Forschung zur Bibel 48. Würzburg: Katholisches Bibelwerk, 1984.

———. "'Treu bis zum Tod.'" In *Neues Testament und Ethik: Für Rudolf Schnackenburg*, edited by Helmut Merklein and Rudolf Schnackenburg, 442–46. Freiburg: Herder, 1989.

Löning, Karl. "Epiphanie der Menschenfreundlichkeit: Zur Rede von Gott im Kontext städtischer Öffentlichkeit." In *Und dennoch ist von Gott zu Reden (Festschrift für Herbert Vorgrimler)*, edited by Matthias Lutz-Bachmann, 107–24. Freiburg i.B.: Herder, 1994.

———. *Das Evangelium und die Kulturen. Heilsgeschichtliche und kulturelle Aspekte kirchlicher Realität in der Apostelgeschichte*. Aufsteig und Niedergang der römischen Welt 25.3. Berlin: de Gruyter, 1985.

———. "Gerechtfertigt durch seine Gnade (Tit 3,7): Zum Problem der Paulusrezeption in der Soteriologie der Pastoralbriefe." In *Der lebendige Gott: Studien zur Theologie des Neuen Testaments; Festschrift für Wilhelm Thüsing zum 75. Geburtstag*, edited by Thomas Söding, 241–57. Neutestamentliche Abhandlungen, n.F., 31. Münster: Aschendorff, 1996.

———. *Das Geschichtswerk des Lukas*. 2 vols. Stuttgart: Kohlhammer, 2006.

———. "Das Gottesbild der Apostelgeschichte im Spannungsfeld von Frühjudentum und Fremdreligionen." In *Monotheismus und Christologie: Zur Gottesfrage im hellenistischen Judentum und im Urchristentum*, edited by Hans-Josef Klauck, 88–117. Quaestiones disputatae 138. Freiburg i.B.: Herder, 1992.

———. "Paulinism in der Apostelgeschichte." In *Paulus in den neutestamentlichen Spätschriften: Zur Paulusrezeption im Neuen Testament*, edited by Karl Kertelge, 202–335. Quaestiones disputatae 89. Freiburg i.B.: Herder, 1981.

Lorenz, Chris. *Konstruktion der Vergangenheit: Eine Einführung in die Geschichtstheorie*. Translated by Annegret Böttner. Cologne: Böhlau, 1997.

Lorenzen, Theodor. *Der Lieblingsjünger im Johannesevangelium*. Stuttgarter Bibelstudien 55. Stuttgart: KBW Verlag, 1971.

Löwe, H. "Bekenntnis, Apostelamt und Kirche im Kolosserbrief." In *Kirche: Festschrift für Günther Bornkamm zum 75. Geburtstag*, edited by Dieter Lührmann and Georg Strecker, 299–314. Tübingen: Mohr, 1980.

Lübking, Hans-Martin. *Paulus und Israel im Römerbrief: Eine Untersuchung zu Römer 9–11*. Europäische Hochschulschriften 23.260. Frankfurt: Lang, 1986.

Luck, Georg, ed. *Magie und andere Geheimlehren in der Antike: Mit 112 neu übersetzten und einzeln kommentierten Quellentexten*. Stuttgart: Kröner, 1990.

Luck, Ulrich. "Die Theologie des Jakobusbriefes." *Zeitschrift für Theologie und Kirche* 81 (1984): 1–30.

———. "Weisheit und Leiden." *Theologische Literaturzeitung* 92 (1967): 253–58.

Luckmann, Thomas. "Kanon und Konversion." In *Kanon und Zensur*, edited by Aleida Assmann and Jan Assmann. Beiträge zur Archäologie der literarischen Kommunikation 2. Munich: Fink, 1987.

———. "Religion—Gesellschaft—Transzendenz." In *Krise der Immanenz: Religion an den Grenzen der Moderne*, edited by Hans-Joachim Höhn and Karl Gabriel, 112–27. Philosophie der Gegenwart. Frankfurt: Fischer, 1996.

———. *Die unsichtbare Religion*. 2nd ed. Frankfurt: Suhrkamp, 1993.

Lüdemann, Gerd. *Early Christianity according to the Traditions in Acts: A Commentary*. Translated by John Bowden. Minneapolis: Fortress, 1989.

———. *Opposition to Paul in Jewish Christianity*. Translated by M. Eugene Boring. Minneapolis: Fortress, 1989.

———. *Paulus und das Judentum*. Theologische Existenz Heute 215. Munich: Kaiser, 1983.

———. *The Resurrection of Jesus: History, Experience, Theology*. Minneapolis: Fortress, 1994.

———. *What Really Happened to Jesus: A Historical Approach to the Resurrection*. Louisville: Westminster John Knox, 1996.

Ludwig, H. "Der Verfasser des Kolosserbriefes: Ein Schüler des Paulus." ThD diss., Georg August Universität, Göttingen, 1974.

Lührmann, Dieter. "Biographie des Gerechten als Evangelium: Vorstellungen zu einem Markus-Kommentar." *Wort und Dienst* 14 (1976): 25–50.

———. "Epiphaneia." In *Tradition und Glaube: Das frühe Christentum in seiner Umwelt; Festgabe für Karl Georg Kuhn zum 65. Geburtstag*, edited by Gert Jeremias et al., 185–91. Göttingen: Vandenhoeck & Ruprecht, 1971.

———. *Glaube im frühen Christentum*. Gütersloh: Güterloher Verlagshaus, 1976.

———. *Das Markusevangelium*. Handbuch zum Neuen Testament 3. Tübingen: Mohr, 1987.

———. "Pistis im Judentum." *Zeitschrift für die neutestamentliche Wissenschaft und die Kunde der älteren Kirche* 64 (1973): 19–38.

———. *Die Redaktion der Logienquelle. Anhang: Zur weiteren Überlieferung der Logienquelle*. Wissenschaftliche Monographien zum Alten und Neuen Testament 33. Neukirchen-Vluyn: Neukirchener Verlag, 1969.

Luther, Martin. *Preface to James and Jude*. In vol. 35 of *Luther's Works*, edited by H. J. Grimm et al. St. Louis: Concordia, 1956.

Luttenberger, J. "Der gekreuzigte Schuldschein: Ein Aspekt der Deutung des Todes Jesu im Kolosserbrief." *New Testament Studies* 51 (2005): 80–95.

Luz, Ulrich. "Der alte und der neue Bund bei Paulus und im Hebräerbrief." *Evangelische Theologie* 27 (1967): 318–36.

———. "Der Antijudaismus im Matthäusevangelium als historisches und theologisches Problem." *Evangelische Theologie* 53 (1993): 310–27.

———. "Das 'Auseinandergehen der Wege': Über die Trennung des Christentums vom Judentum." In *Antijudaismus—christliche Erblast*, edited by Walter Dietrich et al., 56–73. Stuttgart: Kohlhammer, 1999.

———. "The Disciples in the Gospel according to Matthew." In *The Interpretation of Matthew*, edited by Graham Stanton, 98–128. Issues in Religion and Theology 3. London: SPCK, 1983.

———. *Das Geschichtsverständnis des Paulus*. Beiträge zur evangelischen Theologie; theologische Abhandlungen 49. Munich: Kaiser, 1968.

———. "Jesus und die Pharisäer." *Judaica* 38 (1982): 111–24.

———. *Matthew 1–7: A Commentary*. Translated by James E. Crouch. Hermeneia—A Critical and Historical Commentary on the Bible. Minneapolis: Fortress, 2007.

———. *Matthew 8–20: A Commentary*. Translated by James E. Crouch. Hermeneia—A Critical and Historical Commentary on the Bible. Minneapolis: Fortress, 2001.

———. *Matthew 21–28: A Commentary*. Translated by James E. Crouch. Hermeneia—A Critical and Historical Commentary on the Bible. Minneapolis: Fortress, 2005.

———. *The Theology of the Gospel of Matthew*. Translated by J. Bradford Robinson. Cambridge: Cambridge University Press, 1993.

———. "Eine thetische Skizze der matthäischen Christologie." In *Anfänge der Christologie: Festschrift für Ferdinand Hahn zum 65. Geburtstag*, edited by Cilliers Breytenbach et al., 221–35. Göttingen: Vandenhoeck & Ruprecht, 1991.

———. "Überlegungen zum Epheserbrief und seiner Paränese." In *Vom Urchristentum zu Jesus: Für Joachim Gnilka*, edited by Hubert Frankemölle and Karl Kertelge, 376–96. Freiburg: Herder, 1989.

———. "Die Wundergeschichten von Mt 8–9." In *Tradition and Interpretation in the New Testament: Essays in Honor of E. Earle Ellis for His 60th Birthday*, edited by Gerald F. Hawthorne and Otto Betz, 149–65. Grand Rapids: Eerdmans, 1987.

Luz, Ulrich, and Peter Lampe. "Nachpaulinsches Christentum und pagane Gesellschaft." In *Die Anfänge des Christentums: Alte Welt und neue Hoffnung*, edited by Jürgen Becker, 185–216. Stuttgart: Kohlhammer, 1987.

Maas, Wilhelm. *Unveränderlichkeit Gottes: Zum Verhältnis von griechisch-philosophischer und christlicher Gotteslehre*. Paderborner theologische Studien 1. Munich: Schöningh, 1974.

Mack, Burton L. *Logos und Sophia: Untersuchungen zur Weisheitstheologie im hellenistischen Judentum*. Studien zur Umwelt des Neuen Testaments 10. Göttingen: Vandenhoeck & Ruprecht, 1973.

———. *Who Wrote the New Testament? The Making of the Christian Myth*. San Francisco: HarperSanFrancisco, 1996.

Maier, Gerhard. *Die Johannesoffenbarung und die Kirche*. Wissenschaftliche Untersuchungen zum Neuen Testament 25. Tübingen: Mohr, 1981.

———. *Mensch und freier Wille: Nach der jüdischen Religionsparteien zwischen Ben Sira und Paulus.*

Wissenschaftliche Untersuchungen zum Neuen Testament 12. Tübingen: Mohr, 1971.

Maier, Johann. "Beobachtungen zum Konfliktpotential in neutestamentlichen Aussagen über den Tempel." In *Jesus und das jüdische Gesetz*, edited by Ingo Broer and Jens-W. Taeger, 172–213. Stuttgart: Kohlhammer, 1992.

———. *Zwischen den Testamenten: Geschichte und Religion in der Zeit des zweiten Tempels*. Neue Echter Bibel 3, Supplementary Series. Würzburg: Echter Verlag, 1990.

Maisch, Ingrid. *Der Brief an die Gemeinde in Kolossä*. Theologischer Kommentar zum Neuen Testament 12. Stuttgart: Kohlhammer, 2003.

Malherbe, Abraham J. "'Christ Jesus Came into the World to Save Sinners': Soteriology in the Pastoral Epistles." In *Salvation in the New Testament: Perspectives on Soteriology*, edited by J. G. Van der Watt, 331–58. Supplements to Novum Testamentum 121. Leiden: Brill, 2005.

———. *The Cynic Epistles: A Study Edition*. Society of Biblical Literature Sources for Biblical Study 12. Missoula, MT: Scholars Press, 1977.

Malina, Bruce J. *On the Genre and Message of Revelation: Star Visions and Sky Journeys*. Peabody, MA: Hendrickson, 1995.

Manthe, Ulrich, ed. *Die Institutionen des Gaius*. Texte zur Forschung 81. Darmstadt: Wissenschaftliche Buchgesellschaft, 2004.

Marcus, Joel. *The Way of the Lord: Christological Exegesis of the Old Testament in the Gospel of Mark*. Louisville: Westminster John Knox, 1992.

Marguerat, Daniel. "The Enigma of the End of Acts." In *The First Christian Historian: Writing the "Acts of the Apostles,"* edited by Daniel Marguerat, 205–30. Society for New Testament Studies Monograph Series 121. Cambridge: Cambridge University Press, 2002.

———. "The God of Acts." In *The First Christian Historian: Writing the "Acts of the Apostles,"* edited by Daniel Marguerat. Society for New Testament Studies Monograph Series 121. Cambridge: Cambridge University Press, 2002.

———. "Juden und Christen im lukanischen Doppelwerk." *Evangelische Theologie* 54 (1994): 241–64.

———. *Le jugement dans l'Évangile de Matthieu*. Le Monde de la Bible. Geneva: Labor et Fides, 1981.

Marshall, I. Howard. *The Pastoral Epistles*. International Critical Commentary. Edinburgh: T&T Clark, 1999.

Martin, Ralph P. "The Christology of the Prison Epistles." In *Contours of Christology in the New Testament*, edited by Richard N. Longenecker, 193–218. Grand Rapids: Eerdmans, 2005.

———. *Reconciliation: A Study of Paul's Theology*. New Foundations Theological Library. Atlanta: John Knox, 1981.

Martyn, J. Louis. *History and Theology in the Fourth Gospel*. Rev. and expanded ed. Nashville: Abingdon, 1979.

Marxsen, Willi. *The Resurrection of Jesus of Nazareth*. Philadelphia: Fortress, 1970.

———. *Der zweite Brief an die Thessalonicher*. Zürcher Bibelkommentare 11/2. Zürich: Theologischer Verlag, 1982.

März, Claus-Peter. "The theologische Interpretation der Jesus-Gestalt bei Lukas." In *Gedenkt an das Wort: Festschrift für Werner Vogler zum 65. Geburtstag*, edited by Christoph Kähler et al., 134–49. Leipzig: Evangelische Verlagsanstalt, 1999.

———. *Das Wort Gottes bei Lukas: Die lukanische Worttheologie als Frage an die neuere Lukasforschung*. Erfurter theologische Studien 11. Leipzig: Sankt-Benno-Verlag, 1974.

Mason, Steve. *Josephus and the New Testament*. Peabody, MA: Hendrickson, 1992.

Matera, Frank J. *New Testament Christology*. Louisville: Westminster John Knox, 1999.

Mayer, Bernhard. *Unter Gottes Heilsratschluss: Prädestinationsaussagen bei Paulus*. Forschung zur Bibel 15. Würzburg: Echter Verlag, 1974.

Mayer, Günter. *Die jüdische Frau in der hellenistisch-römischen Antike*. Stuttgart: Kohlhammer, 1987.

Mayordomo-Marín, Moisés. *Den Anfang hören: Leserorientierte Evangelienexegese am Beispiel von Matthäus 1–2*. Forschungen zur Religion und Literatur des Alten und Neuen Testaments 180. Göttingen: Vandenhoeck & Ruprecht, 1998.

———. *Argumentiert Paulus logisch? Eine Analyse vor dem Hintergrund antiker Logik*. Wissenschaftliche Untersuchungen zum Neuen Testament 188. Tübingen: Mohr Siebeck, 2005.

McDonald, Lee Martin, and James A. Sanders, eds. *The Canon Debate*. Peabody, MA: Hendrickson, 2002.

Meade, D. G. *Pseudonymity and Canon*. Wissenschaftliche Untersuchungen zum Neuen Testament 39. Tübingen: Mohr, 1986.

Meeks, Wayne A. *The Origins of Christian Morality: The First Two Centuries*. New Haven: Yale University Press, 1993.

Meier, John P. *A Marginal Jew: Rethinking the Historical Jesus*. Vol. 1, *The Roots of the Problem and the Person*. Anchor Bible Reference Library 1. New York: Doubleday, 1991.

———. *A Marginal Jew: Rethinking the Historical Jesus*. Vol. 2, *Mentor, Message, and Miracles*. The Anchor Bible Reference Library 2. New York: Doubleday, 1994.

Meiser, Martin. "Lukas und die römische Staatsmacht." In *Zwischen den Reichen: Neues Testament und römische Herrschaft: Vorträge auf der Ersten Konferenz der European Association for Biblical Studies*, edited by Michael Labahn and Jürgen Zangenberg, 175–93. Texte und Arbeiten zum neutestamentlichen Zeitalter 36. Tübingen: Francke, 2002.

Mell, Ulrich. *Die "anderen" Winzer: Eine exegetische Studie zur Vollmacht Jesu Christi nach Markus 11,27–12,34*. Wissenschaftliche Untersuchungen zum Neuen Testament 77. Tübingen: Mohr, 1994.

Melzer-Keller, Helga. *Jesus und die Frauen: Eine Verhältnisbestimmung nach den synoptischen Überlieferungen*. Herder's Biblical Studies 14. Freiburg i.B.: Herder, 1997.

Menken, M. F. F. *Old Testament Quotations in the Fourth Gospel: Studies in Textual Form*. Contributions to Biblical Exegesis and Theology 15. Kampen: Kok Pharos, 1996.

Menken, M. J. J. *Matthew's Bible: The Old Testament Text of the Evangelist*. Bibliotheca ephemeridum theologicarum lovaniensium 173. Louvain: Leuven University Press, 2004.

Merk, Otto. "Glaube und Tat in den Pastoralbriefen." In *Wissenschaftsgeschichte und Exegese: Gesammelte Aufsätze zum 65. Geburtstag Otto Merks*, edited by Otto Merk, 260–71. Beihefte zur Zeitschrift für die neutestamentliche Wissenschaft und die Kunde der älteren Kirche 95. Berlin: de Gruyter, 1998.

———. "Das Reich Gottes in den lukanischen Schriften." In *Wissenschaftsgeschichte und Exegese: Gesammelte Aufsätze zum 65. Geburtstag Otto Merks*, edited by Otto Merk, 272–91. Beihefte zur Zeitschrift für die neutestamentliche Wissenschaft und die Kunde der älteren Kirche 95. Berlin: de Gruyter, 1998.

Merkel, Helmut. *Die Pastoralbriefe*. Das Neue Testament Deutsch 9. Göttingen: Vandenhoeck & Ruprecht, 1991.

———. "Israel in lukanischen Werk." *New Testament Studies* 40 (1994): 371–98.

———. "Das Gesetz im lukanischen Doppelwerk." In *Schrift und Tradition: Festschrift für Josef Ernst zum 70. Geburtstag*, edited by Knut Backhaus and Franz Georg Untergassmair, 119–33. Paderborn: Schöningh, 1996.

Merklein, Helmut. *Christus und die Kirche*. Stuttgarter Bibelstudien 66. Stuttgart: Verlag Katholisches Bibelwerk, 1973.

———. "Die Einzigkeit Gottes als die sachliche Grundlage der Botschaft Jesu." In *Studien zu Jesus und Paulus*, 2:154–73. 2 vols. Wissenschaftliche Untersuchungen zum Neuen Testament 43, 105. Tübingen: Mohr, 1987–98.

———. *Der erste Brief an die Korinther*. Ökumenischer Taschenbuch-Kommentar zum Neuen Testament 7. Gütersloh: Gütersloher Verlagshaus, 1992.

———. "Erwägungen zur überlieferungsgeschichte der neutestamentlichen Abendmahlstraditionen." In *Studien zu Jesus und Paulus*, 1:157–80. 2 vols. Wissenschaftliche Untersuchungen zum Neuen Testament 43, 105. Tübingen: Mohr, 1987–98.

———. *Die Gottesherrschaft als Handlungsprinzip: Unters. zur Ethik Jesu*. Forschung zur Bibel 34. Würzburg: Echter-Verlag, 1978.

———. *Jesu Botschaft von der Gottesherrschaft: Eine Skizze*. Stuttgarter Bibelstudien 111. Stuttgart: Verlag Katholisches Bibelwerk, 1983.

———. *Das kirchliche Amt nach dem Epheserbrief*. Studien zum Alten und Neuen Testament 33. Munich: Kösel, 1973.

———. "Paulinische Theologie in der Rezeption des Kolosser- und Epheserbriefes." In *Studien zu Jesus und Paulus*, 1:409–47. 2 vols. Wissenschaftliche Untersuchungen zum Neuen Testament 43, 105. Tübingen: Mohr, 1987–98.

———. "Sinn und Zweck von Röm 13,1–7: Zur semantischen und pragmatischen Struktur eines umstrittenen Textes." In *Studien zu Jesus und Paulus*, 2:405–37. 2 vols. Wissenschaftliche Untersuchungen zum Neuen Testament 43, 105. Tübingen: Mohr, 1987–98.

———. "Der Theologe als Prophet." In *Studien zu Jesus und Paulus*, 2:377–404. 2 vols. Wissenschaftliche Untersuchungen zum Neuen Testament 43, 105. Tübingen: Mohr, 1987–98.

———. "Die Umkehrpredigt bei Johannes dem Täufer und Jesus von Nazareth." In *Studien zu Jesus und Paulus*, 1:109–26. 2 vols. Wissenschaftliche Untersuchungen zum Neuen Testament 43, 105. Tübingen: Mohr, 1987–98.

———. "Zum Verständnis des paulinischen Begriffs 'Evangelium.'" In *Studien zu Jesus und Paulus*, 1:279–95. 2 vols. Wissenschaftliche Untersuchungen zum Neuen Testament 43, 105. Tübingen: Mohr, 1987–98.

Merklein, Helmut, and Marlis Gielen. *Der erste Brief an die Korinther*. Ökumenischer Taschenbuch-Kommentar zum Neuen Testament 7. Gütersloh: Gütersloher Verlagshaus, 2005.

Merz, Annette. *Die fiktive Selbstauslegung des Paulus: Intertextuelle Studien zur Intention und Rezeption der Pastoralbriefe*. Novum Testamentum et Orbis Antiquus 52. Göttingen: Vandenhoeck & Ruprecht, 2004.

Metzger, Bruce M. *The Canon of the New Testament: Its Origin, Development, and Significance*. Oxford: Oxford University Press, 1987.

Metzger, Paul. *Katechon: II Thess 2,1–12 im Horizont apokalyptischen Denkens*. Beihefte zur Zeitschrift für die neutestamentliche Wissenschaft und die Kunde der älteren Kirche 135. Berlin: de Gruyter, 2005.

Metzner, Rainer. "Paulus und der Wettkampf: Die Rolle des Sports in Leben und Verkündigung des Apostels (1Kor 9:24–27; Phil 3:12–16)." *New Testament Studies* 46 (2000): 565–83.

———. *Das Verständnis der Sünde im Johannesevangelium*. Wissenschaftliche Untersuchungen zum Neuen Testament 122. Tübingen: Mohr, 2000.

Meyer, Rudolf. *Der Prophet aus Galiläa: Studie zum Jesusbild der drei ersten Evangelien*. Darmstadt: Wissenschaftliche Buchgesellschaft, 1970.

Meyer-Blanck, Michael. *Vom Symbol zum Zeichen: Symboldidaktik und Semiotik*. 2nd ed. Rheinbach: CMZ-Verlag, 2002.

Meyers, Eric. "Jesus and His Galilean Context." In *Archaeology and the Galilee*, edited by Douglas R. Edwards and C. Thomas McCollough, 57–66. Atlanta: Scholars Press, 1997.

Michel, Hans-Joachim. *Die Abschiedsrede des Paulus an die Kirche Apg 20,17–38: Motivgeschichte und theologische Bedeutung*. Studien zum Alten und Neuen Testament 35. Munich: Kösel-Verlag, 1973.

Michel, Otto. "Der Abschluß des Matthäus-Evangeliums." In *Das Matthäus-Evangelium*, edited by Joachim Lange. Weg der Forschung 525. Darmstadt: Wissenschaftliche Buchgesellschaft, 1980.

Mikat, Paul. "Lukanische Christusverkündigung und Kaiserkult: Zum Problem der christlichen Loyalität gegenüber dem Staat." In *Religionsrechtliche Schriften*, 809–28. Abhandlungen zum Staatskirchenrecht und Eherecht 5. Berlin: Duncker & Humblot, 1974.

Mineshige, Kiyoshi. *Besitzverzicht und Almosen bei Lukas: Wesen und Forderung des lukanischen Vermögensethos*. Wissenschaftliche Untersuchungen zum Neuen Testament 2.163. Tübingen: Mohr Siebeck, 2003.

Mittmann-Richert, Ulrike. *Magnifikat und Benediktus: Die ältesten Zeugnisse der judenchristlichen Tradition von der Geburt des Messias*. Wissenschaftliche Untersuchungen zum Neuen Testament 2.90. Tübingen: Mohr, 1996.

Mönning, B. H. "Die Darstellung des urchristlichen Kommunismus nach der Apostelgeschichte des Lukas." ThD diss., Georg August Universität, Göttingen, 1978.

Moxnes, Halvor. *Constructing Early Christian Families: Family as Social Reality and Metaphor*. London: Routledge, 1997.

———. "The Construction of Galilee as a Place for the Historical Jesus." *Biblical Theology Bulletin* 31 (2001): 26–37, 64–77.

———. *Putting Jesus in His Place: A Radical Vision of Household and Kingdom*. Louisville: Westminster John Knox, 2003.

Moxter, M. "Erzählung und Ereignis." In *Der historische Jesus*, edited by J. Schröter and R. Bruckner, 67–88. Beihefte zur Zeitschrift für die neutestamentliche Wissenschaft und die Kunde der älteren Kirche 114. Berlin: de Gruyter, 2002.

Moyise, Steve. *The Old Testament in the New*. Continuum Biblical Studies Series. New York: Continuum, 2001.

Moyise, Steve, and M. J. J. Menken, eds. *The Psalms in the New Testament*. London: T&T Clark, 2004.

Müller, C. G. "Gott wird alle Tränen abwischen—Offb 21,4: Anmerkungen zum Gottesbild der Apokalypse." *Theologie und Glaube* 95 (2005): 275–97.

———. *Mehr als ein Prophet: Die Charakterzeichnung Johannes des Täufers im lukanischen Er-*

zählwerk. Herder's Biblical Studies 31. Freiburg: Herder, 2001.

Müller, Karlheinz. "Beobachtungen zum Verhältnis von Tora und Halacha in frühjüdischen Quellen." In *Jesus und das jüdische Gesetz*, edited by Ingo Broer, 105–34. Stuttgart: Kohlhammer, 1992.

———. "Menschensohn und Messias." In *Studien zur frühjüdischen Apokalyptik*, edited by Karlheinz Müller, 279–322. Stuttgarter biblische Aufsatzbände 11. Stuttgart: Verlag Katholisches Bibelwerk, 1991.

Müller, Klaus E. "Möglichkeit und Vollzug jüdischer Kapitalgerichtsbarkeit." In *Der Prozess gegen Jesus: Historische Rückfrage und theologische Deutung*, edited by Karl Kertelge and Josef Blank. Quaestiones disputatae 112. Freiburg i.B.: Herder, 1988.

Müller, Peter. *Anfänge der Paulusschule: Dargestellt am zweiten Thessalonicherbrief und am Kolosserbrief*. Abhandlungen zur Theologie des Alten und Neuen Testaments 74. Zürich: Theologischer Verlag, 1988.

———. *In der Mitte der Gemeinde: Kinder im Neuen Testament*. Neukirchen-Vluyn: Neukirchener Verlag, 1992.

Müller, Ulrich B. "Die Bedeutung des Kreuzestodes Jesu im Johannesevangelium." *Kerygma und Dogma* 21 (1975): 49–71.

———. *Der Brief des Paulus an die Philipper*. Theologischer Handkommentar zum Neuen Testament 11.1. Leipzig: Evangelische Verlagsanstalt, 1993.

———. *Johannes der Täufer*. Leipzig: Evangelische Verlagsanstalt, 2002.

———. *Die Offenbarung des Johannes*. Ökumenischer Taschenbuch-Kommentar zum Neuen Testament 19. Gütersloh: Gütersloher Verlagshaus, 1984.

———. "Zur Eigentümlichkeit des Johannesevangeliums: Das Problem des Todes Jesu." *Zeitschrift für die neutestamentliche Wissenschaft und die Kunde der älteren Kirche* 88 (1997): 24–55.

———. *Zur frühchristlichen Theologiegeschichte: Judenchristentum und Paulinismus in Kleinasien an der Wende vom 1. zum 2. Jahrhundert nach Christus*. Gütersloh: Gütersloher Verlagshaus Mohn, 1976.

Müseler, Eike, and Martin Sicherl, eds. *Die Kynikerbriefe*. 2 vols. Studien zur Geschichte und Kultur des Altertums 1 NF 6–7. Paderborn: Schöningh, 1994.

Mussner, Franz. *Der Brief an die Epheser*. Ökumenischer Taschenbuchkommentar zum Neuen Testament 10. Gütersloh: Gütersloher Verlagshaus Gerd Mohn, 1982.

———. *Christus, das All und die Kirche: Studien zur Theologie des Epheserbriefes*. 2nd ed. Trierer theologische Studien 5. Trier: Paulinus-Verlag, 1968.

———. "Die ethische Motivation im Jakobusbrief." In *Neues Testament und Ethik: Für Rudolf Schnackenburg*, edited by Helmut Merklein and Rudolf Schnackenburg, 416–23. Freiburg: Herder, 1989.

———. "'Ganz Israel wird gerettet werden' (Röm 11,26)." *Kairos* 18 (1976): 241–55.

———. *Der Jakobusbrief: Auslegung*. Herders theologischer Kommentar zum Neuen Testament 13.1. Freiburg: Herder, 1964.

———. *Die johanneische Sehweise*. Quaestiones disputatae 28. Freiburg: Herder, 1965.

———. "Die 'semantische Achse' des Johannesevangeliums: Ein Versuch." In *Vom Urchristentum zu Jesus: Für Joachim Gnilka*, edited by Hubert Frankemölle and Karl Kertelge, 246–55. Freiburg: Herder, 1989.

———. ΖΩΗ*: Die Anschauung vom "Leben" im vierten Evangelium, unter Berücksichtigung der Johannesbriefe; ein Beitrag zur biblischen Theologie*. Münchener theologische Studien 1/5. Munich: Karl Zink, 1952.

Nagel, Titus. *Die Rezeption des Johannesevangeliums im 2. Jahrhundert: Studien zur vorirenäischen Aneignung und Auslegung des vierten Evangeliums in christlicher und christlich-gnostischer Literatur*. Arbeiten zur Bibel und ihrer Geschichte 2. Leipzig: Evangelische Verlagsanstalt, 2000.

Nanos, Mark D. *The Irony of Galatians: Paul's Letter in First-Century Context*. Minneapolis: Fortress, 2002.

Nauck, W. "Die Tradition und Komposition der Areopagrede." *Zeitschrift für Theologie und Kirche* 53 (1956): 11–52.

Nebe, Gottfried. *"Hoffnung" bei Paulus: Elpis und ihre Synonyme im Zusammenhang der Eschatologie*. Studien zur Umwelt des Neuen Testaments 16. Göttingen: Vandenhoeck & Ruprecht, 1983.

———. *Prophetische Züge im Bilde Jesu bei Lukas*. Beiträge zur Wissenschaft vom Alten und Neuen Testament 127. Stuttgart: Kohlhammer, 1989.

Neirynck, Frans. "The Miracle Stories in the Acts of the Apostles." In *Les Actes des Apôtres*, edited by J. Kremer, 169–213. Bibliotheca ephemeridum theologicarum lovaniensium 48. Louvain: Leuven University Press, 1979.

———. "Paul and the Sayings of Jesus." In *Evangelica II: 1982–1991*, edited by Frans van Segbroeck, 511–68. Bibliotheca ephemeridum theologicarum lovaniensium 99. Louvain: Leuven University Press, 1991.

———. "Recent Developments in the Study of Q." In *Logia: Les paroles de Jésus: The Sayings of Jesus: Mémorial Joseph Coppens*, edited by Joël Delobel and Tjitze Baarda, 29–75. Bibliotheca ephemeridum theologicarum lovaniensium 59. Louvain: Uitgeverij Peeters, 1982.

———. "The Symbol Q (Quelle)." In *Evangelica: Gospel Studies = Evangelica: Études d'Évangile: Collected Essays*, edited by Frans van Segbroeck, 683–89. Bibliotheca ephemeridum theologicarum lovaniensium 60. Louvain: Leuven University Press, 1982.

Nepper-Christensen, P. "Die Taufe im Matthäusevangelium." *New Testament Studies* 31 (1985): 189–207.

Nestle, Dieter. *Eleutheria: Studien zum Wesen der Freiheit bei den Griechen und im Neuen Testament*. Hermeneutische Untersuchungen zur Theologie 6. Tübingen: Mohr, 1967.

Neugebauer, Fritz. *Die Entstehungsgeschichte des Johannesevangeliums*. Arbeiten zur Theologie 1.36. Stuttgart: Calwer, 1968.

———. *In Christus = Ἐν Χριστῷ: Eine Untersuchung zum Paulinischen Glaubensverständnis*. Göttingen: Vandenhoeck & Ruprecht, 1961.

Neusner, Jacob. *From Politics to Piety: The Emergence of Pharisaic Judaism*. Englewood Cliffs, NJ: Prentice-Hall, 1973.

———. Introduction to *Understanding Rabbinic Judaism*, edited by Jacob Neusner, 5–26. New York: Ktav, 1974.

———. "Die pharisäischen rechtlichen Überlieferungen." In *Das pharisäische und talmudische Judentum: Neue Wege zu seinem Verständnis*, edited by Jacob Neusner and Hermann Lichtenberger, 43–51. Texte und Studien zum antiken Judentum 4. Tübingen: Mohr, 1984.

Neyrey, Jerome H. "The Form and Background of the Polemic in 2 Peter." *Journal of Biblical Literature* 99 (1980): 407–31.

Nickel, Rainer. *Wege zum Glück*. Sammlung Tusculum. Düsseldorf: Artemis & Winkler, 2003.

Nicklas, Tobias. *Ablösung und Verstrickung: "Juden" und Jüngergestalten als Charaktere der erzählten Welt des Johannesevangeliums und ihre Wirkung auf den impliziten Leser*. Regensburger Studien zur Theologie 60. Frankfurt: Lang, 2001.

Nicol, W. *The Semeia in the Fourth Gospel: Tradition and Redaction*. Supplements to Novum Testamentum 32. Leiden: Brill, 1972.

Niebuhr, Karl-Wilhelm. "Die Antithesen des Matthäus: Jesus als Toralehrer und die frühjüdische weisheitliche Torarezeption." In *Gedenkt an das Wort: Festschrift für Werner Vogler zum 65. Geburtstag*, edited by Christoph Kähler et al., 175–200. Leipzig: Evangelische Verlagsanstalt, 1999.

———. *Gesetz und Paränese: Katechismusartige Weisungsreihen in der frühjüdischen Literatur*. Wissenschaftliche Untersuchungen zum Neuen Testament 2.28. Tübingen: Mohr, 1987.

———. "A New Perspective on James? Neuere Forschungen zum Jakobusbrief." *Theologische Literaturzeitung* 129 (2004): 1019–44.

Niemand, Christoph. *Die Fußwaschungserzählung des Johannesevangeliums*. Studia Anselmiana 114. Rome: Pontificio Ateneo S. Anselmo, 1993.

Nilsson, Martin P. *A History of Greek Religion*. Translated by F. J. Fielden. Westport, CT: Greenwood, 1980.

Nissen, Andreas. *Gott und der Nächste im antiken Judentum: Untersuchungen zum Doppelgebot der Liebe*. Wissenschaftliche Untersuchungen zum Neuen Testament 15. Tübingen: Mohr, 1974.

Nolland, John. *The Gospel of Matthew: A Commentary on the Greek Text*. New International Greek Testament Commentary. Grand Rapids: Eerdmans, 2005.

Nolte, Georg, and Hans-Ludwig Schreiber, eds. *Der Mensch und seine Rechte: Grundlagen und Brennpunkte der Menschenrechte zu Beginn des 21. Jahrhunderts*. Göttingen: Wallstein, 2004.

Norden, Eduard. *Agnostos Theos: Untersuchungen zur Formengeschichte religiöser Rede*. Leipzig: Teubner, 1913.

North, W. E. Sproston. *The Lazarus Story within the Johannine Tradition*. Journal for the Study of the New Testament: Supplement Series 212. Sheffield: Sheffield Academic, 2001.

Nützel, J. M. "Hoffnung und Treue: Zur Eschatologie des Markusevangeliums." In *Gegenwart und kommendes Reich: Schülergabe Anton Vögtle zum 65. Geburtstag*, edited by Peter Fiedler and Dieter Zeller, 79–90. Stuttgarter biblische Beiträge 6. Stuttgart: Verlag Katholisches Bibelwerk, 1975.

Oberlinner, Lorenz. "Die 'Epiphaneia' des Heilswillens Gottes in Christus Jesus: Zur Grundstruktur der Christologie der Pastoralbriefe." *Zeitschrift für die neutestamentliche Wissenschaft und die Kunde der älteren Kirche* 71 (1980): 192–213.

———. *Die Pastoralbriefe*. 3 vols. Herders theologischer Kommentar zum Neuen Testament 11. Freiburg: Herder, 1994–96.

Obermann, Andreas. *Die christologische Erfüllung der Schrift im Johannesevangelium: Eine Untersuchung zur johanneischen Hermeneutik anhand der Schriftzitate*. Wissenschaftliche Untersuchungen zum Neuen Testament 2.83. Tübingen: Mohr, 1996.

Oegema, Gerbern S. *Der Gesalbte und sein Volk: Untersuchungen zum Konzeptualisierungsprozess der messianischen Erwartungen von dem Makkabäern bis Bar Koziba*. Schriften des Institutum Judaicum Delitzschianum 2. Göttingen: Vandenhoeck & Ruprecht, 1994.

Ogden, Schubert M., ed. *Existence and Faith: Shorter Writings of Rudolf Bultmann*. New York: Meridian Books, 1960.

Öhler, Markus. *Barnabas: Der Mann in der Mitte*. Biblische Gestalten 12. Leipzig: Evangelische Verlagsanstalt, 2005.

Okure, T. *The Johannine Approach to Mission*. Wissenschaftliche Untersuchungen zum Neuen Testament 2.31. Tübingen: Mohr, 1989.

Oliveira, A. de. "Christozentrik im Kolosserbrief." In *Christologie in der Paulus-Schule: Zur Rezeptionsgeschichte des paulinischen Evangeliums*, edited by Klaus Scholtissek, 72–103. Stuttgarter Bibelstudien 181. Stuttgart: Verlag Katholisches Bibelwerk, 2000.

Ollrog, Wolf-Henning. *Paulus und seine Mitarbeiter: Untersuchung zu Theorie und Praxis der paulinischen Mission*. Wissenschaftliche Monographien zum Alten und Neuen Testament 50. Neukirchen-Vluyn: Neukirchener Verlag, 1979.

Omerzu, Heike. *Der Prozess des Paulus: Eine exegetische und rechtshistorische Untersuchung der Apostelgeschichte*. Beihefte zur Zeitschrift für die neutestamentliche Wissenschaft 115. Berlin: de Gruyter, 2002.

———. "Das Schweigen des Lukas: Überlegungen zum offenen Ende der Apostelgeschichte." In *Das Ende des Paulus: Historische, theologische und literaturgeschichtliche Aspekte*, edited by Friedrich Wilhelm Horn, 128–44. Beihefte zur Zeitschrift für die neutestamentliche Wissenschaft 106. New York: de Gruyter, 2001.

Onuki, Takashi. *Gemeinde und Welt im Johannesevangelium: Ein Beitrag zur Frage nach der theologischen und pragmatischen Funktion des johanneischen "Dualismus."* Wissenschaftliche Monographien zum Alten und Neuen Testament 56. Neukirchen-Vluyn: Neukirchener Verlag, 1984.

———. *Jesus: Geschichte und Gegenwart*. Biblisch-theologische Studien 82. Neukirchen-Vluyn: Neukirchener Verlag, 2006.

Osten-Sacken, Peter von der. "Die Apologie des paulinischen Apostolats in 1Kor 15,1–11." In *Evangelium und Tora: Aufsätze zu Paulus*, edited by Peter von der Osten-Sacken, 131–49. Theologische Bücherei 77. Munich: Kaiser, 1987.

———. *Römer 8 als Beispiel paulinischer Soteriologie*. Göttingen: Vandenhoeck & Ruprecht, 1975.

Oster, R. "The Ephesian Artemis as an Opponent of Early Christianity." *Jahrbuch für Antike und Christentum* 19 (1976): 24–44.

Overman, J. Andrew. *Matthew's Gospel and Formative Judaism: The Social World of the Matthean Community*. Minneapolis: Fortress, 1990.

Paesler, Kurt. *Das Tempelwort Jesu: Die Tradition von Tempelzerstörung und Tempelerneuerung im Neuen Testament*. Forschungen zur Religion und Literatur des Alten und Neuen Testaments 184. Göttingen: Vandenhoeck & Ruprecht, 1999.

Pannenberg, Wolfhart. "Die Auferstehung Jesu—Historie und Theologie." *Zeitschrift für Theologie und Kirche* 91 (1994): 318–28.

———. *Jesus, God and Man*. Translated by Lewis L. Wilkins and Duane A. Priebe. 2nd ed. Philadelphia: Westminster, 1977.

———. *Systematic Theology*. Translated by Geoffrey W. Bromiley. 3 vols. Grand Rapids: Eerdmans, 1991.

Panzram, S. "Der Jerusalemer Tempel und das Rom der Flavier." In *Zerstörungen des Jerusalemer Tempels: Geschehen, Wahrnehmung, Bewältigung*, edited by Johannes Hahn and Christian Ronning, 166–82. Wissenschaftliche Untersuchungen zum Neuen Testament 142. Tübingen: Mohr Siebeck, 2002.

Paroschi, W. *Incarnation and Covenant in the Prologue to the Fourth Gospel (John 1:1–18)*. Europäische Hochschulschriften 23.820. Frankfurt: Lang, 2006.

Parsenios, George L. *Departure and Consolation: The Johannine Farewell Discourses in Light of Greco-Roman Literature*. Supplements to Novum Testamentum 117. Leiden: Brill, 2005.

Passow, Franz, et al. *Handwörterbuch der griechischen Sprache*. 5th ed. 4 vols. Leipzig: Vogel, 1841.

Patsch, Hermann. *Abendmahl und historischer Jesus*. Stuttgart: Calwer, 1972.

Paulsen, Henning. *Der Zweite Petrusbrief und der Judasbrief*. Kritisch-exegetischer Kommentar über das Neue Testament 12/2. Göttingen: Vandenhoeck & Ruprecht, 1992.

Pax, Elpidius. ΕΠΙΦΑΝΕΙΑ: *Ein religionsgeschichtlicher Beitrag zur biblischen Theologie*. Münchener theologische Studien 1/10. Munich: Zink, 1955.

Peres, Imre. *Griechische Grabinschriften und neutestamentliche Eschatologie*. Wissenschaftliche Untersuchungen zum Neuen Testament 157. Tubingen: Mohr Siebeck, 2003.

Perkins, Pheme. *Peter: Apostle for the Whole Church*. Columbia: University of South Carolina Press, 1994.

Perrin, Norman. *Jesus and the Language of the Kingdom*. Philadelphia: Fortress, 1976.

———. *Rediscovering the Teaching of Jesus*. New York: Harper & Row, 1967.

Pesch, Rudolf. *Das Markusevangelium*. Vol. 1, *Kommentar zu Kap. 1,1–8,26*. Vol. 2, *Kommentar zu Kap. 8,27–16,20*. 4th ed. Herders Theologischer Kommentar zum Neuen Testament. Freiburg i.B.: Herder, 1984.

Petersen, Norman R. "'Literarkritik,' the New Literary Criticism and the Gospel according to Mark." In *The Four Gospels, 1992: Festschrift Frans Neirynck*, edited by Frans van Segbroeck et al., 2:935–48. 3 vols. Bibliotheca ephemeridum theologicarum lovaniensium 100. Louvain: Leuven University Press, 1992.

Petracca, Vincenzo. *Gott oder das Geld: Die Besitzethik des Lukas*. Texte und Arbeiten zum neutestamentlichen Zeitalter 39. Tübingen: Francke, 2003.

Petzke, Gerd. *Die Traditionen über Apollonius von Tyana und das Neue Testament*. Studia ad Corpus Hellenisticum Novi Testamenti 1. Leiden: Brill, 1970.

Petzoldt, Martin. *Gleichnisse Jesu und christliche Dogmatik*. Göttingen: Vandenhoeck & Ruprecht, 1984.

Pfeiffer, Matthias. *Einweisung in das neue Sein: Neutestamentliche Erwägungen zur Grundlegung der Ethik*. Gütersloh: Gütersloher Verlagshaus, 2001.

Pfitzner, Victor C. *Paul and the Agon Motif. Traditional Athletic Imagery in the Pauline Literature*. Supplements to Novum Testamentum 16. Leiden: Brill, 1967.

Philonenko, Marc. *Das Vaterunser: Vom Gebet Jesu zum Gebet der Jünger*. Tübingen: Mohr, 2002.

Pilhofer, Peter. "Livius, Lukas, und Lukian: Drei Himmelfahrten." In *Die frühen Christen und ihre Welt: Greifswalder Aufsätze 1996–2001*, edited by Peter Pilhofer et al., 166–82. Wissenschaftliche Untersuchungen zum Neuen Testament 145. Tübingen: Mohr Siebeck, 2002.

———. *Philippi*. 2 vols. Wissenschaftliche Untersuchungen zum Neuen Testament 87, 119. Tübingen: Mohr, 1995–2000.

Piper, Ronald A. *Wisdom in the Q-tradition*. Cambridge: Cambridge University Press, 1989.

Plümacher, Eckhard. "Acta-Forschung 1974–1982." *Theologische Rundschau* 48 (1983): 1–56.

———. "Neues Testament und hellenistische Form: Zur literarischen Gattung der lukanischen Schriften." *Theologia Viatorum* 14 (1979): 109–23.

———. "Rom in der Apostelgeschichte." In *Geschichte und Geschichten: Aufsätze zur Apostelgeschichte und zu den Johannesakten*, edited by Eckhard Plümacher et al., 135–69. Wissenschaftliche Untersuchungen zum Neuen Testament 170. Tübingen: Mohr Siebeck, 2004.

Pohlenz, M. *Der hellenische Mensch*. Göttingen: Vandenhoeck & Ruprecht, 1947.

Pöhlmann, Wolfgang. *Der Verlorene Sohn und das Haus: Studien zu Lukas 15,11–32 im Horizont der antiken Lehre von Haus, Erziehung and Ackerbau*. Wissenschaftliche Untersuchungen zum Neuen Testament 68. Tübingen: Mohr, 1993.

Pokorný, Julius. *Indogermanisches etymologisches Wörterbuch*. 2 vols. Bern: Francke, 1959.

Pokorný, Petr. *Colossians: A Commentary*. Translated by Siegfried S. Schatzmann. Peabody, MA: Hendrickson, 1991.

Polag, Athanasius. *Die Christologie der Logienquelle*. 1st ed. Neukirchen-Vluyn: Neukirchener-Verlag, 1977.

———. "Die theologische Mitte der Logienquelle." In *Das Evangelium und die Evangelien: Vorträge vom Tübinger Symposium 1982*, edited by Peter Stuhlmacher, 103–11. Wissenschaftliche Untersuchungen zum Neuen Testament 28. Tübingen: Mohr, 1983.

Popkes, E. E. "Die Bedeutung des zweiten Thessalonicherbriefes für das Verständnis paulinischer und deuteropaulinischer Eschatologie." *Biblische Zeitschrift* 48 (2004): 39–64.

———. *Die Theologie der Liebe Gottes in den johanneischen Schriften*. Wissenschaftliche Untersuchungen zum Neuen Testament 2.197. Tübingen: Mohr, 2005.

———. "Die Umdeutung des Todes Jesu im koptischen Thomasevangelium." In *Deutungen des Todes Jesu im Neuen Testament*, edited by J. Frey and J. Schröter, 513–43. Wissenschaftliche Untersuchungen zum Neuen Testament 181. Tübingen: Mohr, 2005.

Popkes, Wiard. *Adressaten, Situation und Form des Jakobusbriefes*. Stuttgarter Bibelstudien 125/126. Stuttgart: Verlag Katholisches Bibelwerk, 1986.

———. *Der Brief des Jakobus*. Theologischer Handkommentar zum Neuen Testament 14. Leipzig: Evangelische Verlagsanstalt, 2001.

———. *Christus Traditus: Eine Untersuchung zum Begriff der Dahingabe im Neuen Testament*. Abhandlungen zur Theologie des Alten und Neuen Testaments 49. Zürich, Stuttgart: Zwingli Verlag, 1967.

———. *Paränese und Neues Testament*. Stuttgarter Bibelstudien 168. Stuttgart: Verlag Katholisches Bibelwerk, 1995.

———. "Traditionen und Traditionsbrüche im Jakobusbrief." In *The Catholic Epistles and the Tradition*, edited by Jacques Schlosser, 143–70. Bibliotheca ephemeridum theologicarum lovaniensium 176. Louvain: Leuven University Press, 2004.

Poplutz, Uta. *Athlet des Evangeliums: Eine motivgeschichtliche Studie zur Wettkampfmetaphorik bei Paulus*. Herder's Biblical Studies 43. Freiburg i.B.: Herder, 2004.

Popp, Thomas. *Grammatik des Geistes: Literarische Kunst und theologische Konzeption in Johannes 3 und 6*. Arbeiten zur Bibel und ihrer Geschichte 3. Leipzig: Evangelische Verlagsanstalt, 2001.

———. "Die Kunst der Wiederholung: Repetition, Variation und Amplifikation im vierten Evangelium am Beispiel von Johannes 6:60–71." In *Kontexte des Johannesevangeliums*, edited by Albert Frey and Udo Schnelle, 559–92. Wissenschaftliche Untersuchungen zum Neuen Testament 175. Tübingen: Mohr, 2004.

Porsch, Felix. *Pneuma und Wort: Ein exegetischer Beitrag zur Pneumatologie des Johannesevangeliums*. Frankfurter theologische Studien 16. Frankfurt a.M.: Knecht, 1974.

Porter, Stanley E. "Jesus and the Use of Greek in Galilee." In *Studying the Historical Jesus: Evaluations of the State of Current Research*, edited by Bruce Chilton and Craig A. Evans. New Testament Tools and Studies 19. Leiden: Brill, 1994.

Powell, Mark Allen. *What Is Narrative Criticism?* Minneapolis: Fortress, 1990.

Powers, Daniel G. *Salvation through Participation: An Examination of the Notion of the Believers' Corporate Unity with Christ in Early Christian Soteriology*. Contributions to Biblical Exegesis and Theology 29. Louvain: Peeters, 2001.

Prast, F. *Presbyter und Evangelium in nachapostolischer Zeit*. Forschung zur Bibel 29. Stuttgart: Verlag Katholisches Bibelwerk, 1979.

Pratscher, Wilhelm. *Der Herrenbruder Jakobus und die Jakobustradition*. Forschungen zur Religion und Literatur des Alten und Neuen Testaments 139. Göttingen: Vandenhoeck & Ruprecht, 1987.

Pregeant, Russell. *Knowing Truth, Doing Good: Engaging New Testament Ethics*. Minneapolis: Fortress, 2008.

Price, S. R. *Rituals and Power: The Roman Imperial Cult in Asia Minor*. Cambridge: Cambridge University Press, 1984.

Prostmeier, F. R. *Handlungsmodelle im ersten Petrusbrief*. Forschung zur Bibel 63. Stuttgart: Verlag Katholisches Bibelwerk, 1990.

Radl, Walter. *Paulus und Jesus im Lukanischen Doppelwerk: Untersuchungen zu Parallelmotiven im Lukasevangelium und in der Apostelgeschichte*. Europäische Hochschulschriften 23.49. Frankfurt: Lang, 1975.

———. *Der Ursprung Jesu: Traditionsgeschichtliche Untersuchungen zu Lukas 1–2*. Herder's Biblical Studies 7. Freiburg: Herder, 1996.

Rahner, Johanna. *"Er aber sprach vom Tempel seines Leibes": Jesus von Nazaret als Ort der Offenbarung Gottes im vierten Evangelium*. Bonner biblische Beiträge 117. Bodenheim: Philo, 1998.

———. "Vergegenwärtigende Erinnerung." *Zeitschrift für die neutestamentliche Wissenschaft und die Kunde der älteren Kirche* 91 (2000): 72–90.

Räisänen, Heikki. "Der Bruch des Paulus mit Israels Bund." In *The Law in the Bible and in Its Environment*, edited by Timo Veijola, 156–72. Göttingen: Vandenhoeck & Ruprecht, 1990.

———. "Jesus and the Food Laws." *Journal for the Study of the New Testament* 16 (1982): 79–100.

———. *The "Messianic Secret" in Mark*. Edinburgh: T&T Clark, 1990.

———. *Neutestamentliche Theologie? Eine religionswissenschaftliche Alternative*. Stuttgarter

Bibelstudien 186. Stuttgart: Verlag Katholisches Bibelwerk, 2000.

———. *Paul and the Law*. 2nd ed. Wissenschaftliche Untersuchungen zum Neuen Testament 29. Tübingen: Mohr, 1987.

———. "The Redemption of Israel." In *Luke-Acts: Scandinavian Perspectives*, edited by P. Luomanen, 94–114. Göttingen: Vandenhoeck & Ruprecht, 1991.

———. "Römer 9–11: Analyse eines geistigen Ringens." In *Aufstieg und Niedergang der römischen Welt*, edited by Joseph Vogt et al., 2.25.4:2891–2939. Berlin: de Gruyter, 1987.

———. "Sprachliches zum Spiel des Paulus mit Nomos." In *Glaube und Gerechtigkeit: In memoriam Rafael Gyllenberg (18.6.1893–29.7.1982)*, edited by Rafael Gyllenberg et al., 131–54. Schriften der Finnischen Exegetischen Gesellschaft 38. Helsinki: Suomen Eksegeettisen Seuran, 1983.

Ranke, Leopold von. "Geschichten der romanischen und germanischen Völker von 1494–1514." In *Leopold von Ranke's sämmtliche Werke*, edited by Alfred Wilhelm Dove and Theodor Wiedemann. Leipzig: Duncker & Humblot, 1875.

Rapske, Brian. *The Book of Acts and Paul in Roman Custody*. Book of Acts in Its First Century Setting 3. Grand Rapids: Eerdmans, 1994.

Rau, Eckhard. *Das geheime Markusevangelium: Ein Schriftfund voller Rätsel*. Neukirchen: Neukirchener Verlag, 2003.

———. *Von Jesus zu Paulus: Entwicklung und Rezeption der antiochenischen Theologie im Urchristentum*. Stuttgart: Kohlhammer, 1994.

Reed, Jonathan L. *Archaeology and the Galilean Jesus: A Re-examination of the Evidence*. Harrisburg, PA: Trinity, 2000.

Reichert, Angelika. *Eine urchristliche praeparatio ad martyrium: Studien zur Komposition, Traditionsgeschichte und Theologie des 1. Petrusbriefes*. Beiträge zur biblischen Exegese und Theologie 22. Frankfurt a.M.: Lang, 1989.

———. *Der Römerbrief als Gratwanderung: Eine Untersuchung zur Abfassungsproblematik*. Forschungen zur Religion und Literatur des Alten und Neuen Testaments 194. Göttingen: Vandenhoeck & Ruprecht, 2001.

Reim, Günter. *Studien zum alttestamentlichen Hintergrund des Johannesevangeliums*. Society for New Testament Studies Monograph Series 22. Cambridge: Cambridge University Press, 1974.

Rein, Matthias. *Die Heilung des Blindgeborenen: (Joh 9); Tradition und Redaktion*. Wissenschaftliche Untersuchungen zum Neuen Testament 2.73. Tübingen: Mohr, 1995.

Reinbold, Wolfgang. *Der Prozess Jesu*. Biblisch-theologische Schwerpunkte 28. Göttingen: Vandenhoeck & Ruprecht, 2006.

Reinmuth, Eckart. *Anthropologie im Neuen Testament*. Tübingen: Mohr, 2006.

———. "Die Briefe an die Thessalonicher." In *Die Briefe an die Philipper, Thessalonicher und an Philemon*, edited by Nikolaus Walter et al. Das Neue Testament Deutsch 8/2. Göttingen: Vandenhoeck & Ruprecht, 1998.

———. "Historik und Exegese—zum Streit um die Auferstehung Jesu nach der Moderne." In *Exegese und Methodendiskussion*, edited by Stefan Alkier and Ralph Brucker, 1–8. Texte und Arbeiten zum neutestamentlichen Zeitalter 23. Tübingen: Francke, 1998.

———. "Lazarus und seine Schwestern—was wollte Johannes erzählen?" *Theologische Literaturzeitung* 124 (1999): 127–37.

———. "Neutestamentliche Historik." *Theologische Literaturzeitung* 8 (2003): 47–55.

Reiser, Marius. "Bürgerliches Christentum in den Pastoralbriefen?" *Biblica* 74 (1993): 27–44.

———. *Jesus and Judgment: The Eschatological Proclamation in Its Jewish Context*. Translated by Linda M. Maloney. Minneapolis: Fortress, 1997.

Rese, Martin. *Alttestamentliche Motive in der Christologie des Lukas*. Studien zum Neuen Testament 1. Gütersloh: Güterloher Verlagshaus, 1969.

———. "Die Aussagen über Jesu Tod und Auferstehung in der Apostelgeschichte—ältestes Kerygma oder lukanische Theologumena?" *New Testament Studies* (1984): 335–53.

Resseguie, James L. *The Strange Gospel: Narrative Designs and Point of View in John*. Biblical Interpretation Series 56. Leiden: Brill, 2001.

Rhoads, David, et al. *Mark as Story: An Introduction to the Narrative of a Gospel*. 2nd ed. Minneapolis: Fortress, 1999.

Richter, G. "Die Fleischwerdung des Logos im Johannesevangelium." In *Studien zum Johannesevangelium*, edited by G. Richter, 149–98. Biblische Untersuchungen 13. Regensburg: Pustet, 1977.

Ricœur, Paul. *The Symbolism of Evil*. Boston: Beacon, 1967.

———. *Time and Narrative*. Translated by Kathleen McLaughlin and David Pellauer. 3 vols. Chicago: University of Chicago Press, 1984.

———. *Zufall und Vernunft in der Geschichte*. Tübingen: Gehrke, 1986.

Riedo-Emmenegger, Christoph. *Prophetisch-messianische Provokateure der Pax Romana: Jesus von Nazaret und andere Störenfriede im Konflikt mit dem Römischen Reich*. Novum Testamentum et Orbis Antiquus 56. Göttingen: Vandenhoeck & Ruprecht, 2005.

Riedweg, Christoph. *Pythagoras: Leben, Lehre, Nachwirkung; Eine Einführung*. Munich: Beck, 2002.

Riesner, Rainer. *Paul's Early Period: Chronology, Mission Strategy, Theology*. Translated by Douglas W. Stott. Grand Rapids: Eerdmans, 1998.

Rigaux, B. "Die 'Zwölf' in Geschichte und Kerygma." In *Der Historische und der kerygmatische Christus: Beiträge zum Christusverständnis in Forschung und Verkündigung*, edited by Helmut Ristow and Karl Matthiae, 468–86. Berlin: Evangelische Verlagsanstalt, 1960.

Riniker, Christian. *Die Gerichtsverkündigung Jesu*. Europäische Hochschulschriften 23.653. Bern: Lang, 1999.

Rinke, Johannes. *Kerygma und Autopsie: Der christologische Disput als Spiegel johanneischer Gemeindegeschichte*. Herder's Biblical Studies 12. Freiburg: Herder, 1997.

Rissi, Mathias. *Die Taufe für die Toten: Ein Beitrag zur paulinischen Tauflehre*. Abhandlungen zur Theologie des Alten und Neuen Testaments 42. Zürich: Zwingli Verlag, 1962.

Ritschl, Albrecht. "Instruction in the Christian Religion." In *Three Essays*. Translated by Phil Hefner, 220–91. Philadelphia: Fortress, 1972.

Ritt, H. *Das Gebet zum Vater*. Forschung zur Bibel 36. Stuttgart: Verlag Katholisches Bibelwerk, 1979.

———. "Wer war schuld am Tod Jesu." *Biblische Zeitschrift* 31 (1987): 165–75.

Robbins, Vernon K. *Jesus the Teacher: A Socio-Rhetorical Interpretation of Mark*. Philadelphia: Fortress, 1984.

Robinson, James M. "Basic Shifts in German Theology." *Interpretation* 16 (1962): 76–97.

———. *The Gospel of Jesus: In Search of the Original Good News*. San Francisco: HarperSanFrancisco, 2005.

———. "History of Q Research." In *The Critical Edition of Q: Synopsis including the Gospels of Matthew and Luke, Mark and Thomas with English, German, and French Translations of Q and Thomas*, edited by James M. Robinson et al., xix–lxxi. Hermeneia—A Critical and Historical Commentary on the Bible. Minneapolis: Fortress, 2000.

———. *The Problem of History in Mark*. Studies in Biblical Theology 11. London: SCM, 1962.

———. "Der wahre Jesus? Der historische Jesus im Spruchevangelium Q." *Zeitschrift für Neues Testament* 1 (1998): 17–26.

———. "Der wahre Jesus? Der historische Jesus im Spruchevangelium Q." In *The Sayings Gospel Q: Collected Essays*, edited by Christoph Heil and Jozef Verheyden, 17–26. Bibliotheca ephemeridum theologicarum lovaniensium 189. Louvain: Leuven University Press, 2005.

Robinson, James M., Paul Hoffmann, and John S. Kloppenborg, eds. *The Critical Edition of Q: Synopsis including the Gospels of Matthew and Luke, Mark and Thomas with English, German, and French Translations of Q and Thomas*. Hermeneia—A Critical and Historical Commentary on the Bible: Supplements. Minneapolis: Fortress, 2000.

Robinson, James M., and Helmut Koester. *Trajectories through Early Christianity*. Philadelphia: Fortress, 1971.

Robinson, John A. T. *The Human Face of God*. Philadelphia: Westminster, 1973.

Roetzel, Calvin J. *Judgement in the Community: A Study of the Relationship between Eschatology and Ecclesiology in Paul*. Leiden: Brill, 1972.

Rohde, Erwin. *Psyche: The Cult of Souls and Belief in Immortality among the Greeks*. Translated by W. B. Hillis. Freeport, NY: Books for Libraries, 1972.

Röhser, Günter. *Metaphorik und Personifikation der Sünde: Antike Sündenvorstellungen und paulinische Hamartia*. Tübingen: Mohr, 1987.

———. *Prädestination und Verstockung: Untersuchungen zur frühjüdischen, paulinischen und johanneischen Theologie*. Tübingen: Francke, 1994.

Rollmann, H., and W. Zanger. "Unveröffentlichte Briefe William Wredes zur Problematisierung des messianischen Selbstverständnisses Jesu." *Zeitschrift für neuere Theologiegeschichte/Journal for the History of Modern Theology* (2001): 274–322.

Roloff, Jürgen. "Anfänge der soteriologischen Deutung des Todes Jesu (Mk. X.45 und Lk. XXII.27)." In *Exegetische Verantwortung in der Kirche: Aufsätze*, edited by Jürgen Roloff and Martin

Karrer, 117–43. Göttingen: Vandenhoeck & Ruprecht, 1990.

———. *Die Apostelgeschichte*. Das Neue Testament Deutsch 5. Göttingen: Vandenhoeck & Ruprecht, 1981.

———. *Apostolat, Verkündigung, Kirche: Ursprung, Inhalt und Funktion des kirchlichen Apostelamtes nach Paulus, Lukas und den Pastoralbriefen*. 1st ed. Gütersloh: Gütersloher Verlagshaus G. Mohn, 1965.

———. *Der erste Brief an Timotheus*. Evangelisch-katholischer Kommentar zum Neuen Testament 15. Neukirchen-Vluyn: Neukirchener Verlag, 1988.

———. *Jesus*. Munich: Beck, 2000.

———. "Der johanneische 'Lieblingsjünger' und der Lehrer der Gerechtigkeit." *New Testament Studies* 15 (1968–69): 129–51.

———. *Das Kerygma und der irdische Jesus*. Göttingen: Vandenhoeck & Ruprecht, 1970.

———. *Die Kirche im Neuen Testament*. Grundrisse zum Neuen Testament 10. Göttingen: Vandenhoeck & Ruprecht, 1993.

———. "Der mitleidende Hohepriester." In *Exegetische Verantwortung in der Kirche: Aufsätze*, edited by Martin Karrer, 373–92. Göttingen: Vandenhoeck & Ruprecht, 1990.

———. "Neuschöpfung in der Offenbarung des Johannes." *Jahrbuch für Biblische Theologie* 5 (1990): 119–38.

———. "Die Paulusdarstellung des Lukas." *Evangelische Theologie* 39 (1979): 510–39.

———. "Die Paulus-Darstellung des Lukas." In *Exegetische Verantwortung in der Kirche: Aufsätze*, edited by Martin Karrer. Göttingen: Vandenhoeck & Ruprecht, 1990.

———. "Das Reich des Menschensohnes: Ein Beitrag zur Eschatologie des Mattäus." In *Eschatologie und Schöpfung* edited by M. Evang et al., 275–92. Beihefte zur Zeitschrift für die neutestamentliche Wissenschaft 89. Berlin: de Gruyter, 1997.

———. *The Revelation of John*. Translated by John E. Alsup. Minneapolis: Fortress, 1993.

Roose, H. *"Das Zeugnis Jesu": Seine Bedeutung für die Christologie, Eschatologie und Prophetie in der Offenbarung des Johannes*. Texte und Arbeiten zum neutestamentlichen Zeitalter 32. Tübingen: Mohr, 2000.

Rothfuchs, Wilhelm. *Die Erfüllungszitate des Matthaüs-Evangeliums: Eine biblisch-theologische Untersuchung*. Beiträge zur Wissenschaft vom Alten und Neuen Testament 88. Stuttgart: Kohlhammer, 1969.

Rowland, C. *The Open Heaven*. New York: Crossroad, 1982.

Rowland, C., and C. M. Tuckett, eds. *The Nature of New Testament Theology*. Oxford: Oxford University Press, 2006.

Ruiz, Miguel Rodríguez. *Der Missionsgedanke des Johannesevangeliums: Ein Beitrag zur johanneischen Soteriologie und Ekklesiologie*. Forschung zur Bibel 55. Würzburg: Echter, 1987.

Rüpke, Jörg. *Die Religion der Römer: Eine Einführung*. Munich: Beck, 2001.

Rusam, D. *Das Alte Testament bei Lukas*. Beihefte zur Zeitschrift für die neutestamentliche Wissenschaft und die Kunde der älteren Kirche 112. Berlin: de Gruyter, 2003.

———. "Neue Belege zu den στοιχεῖα τοῦ κόσμου." *Zeitschrift für die neutestamentliche Wissenschaft und die Kunde der älteren Kirche* 83 (1992): 119–25.

Rusam, Dietrich. *Die Gemeinschaft der Kinder Gottes: Das Motiv der Gotteskindschaft und die Gemeinden der johanneischen Briefe*. Beiträge zur Wissenschaft vom Alten und Neuen Testament 133. Stuttgart: Kohlhammer, 1993.

Rüsen, Jörn. "Faktizität und Fiktionalität der Geschichte—Was ist Wirklichkeit im historischen Denken?" In *Konstruktion von Wirklichkeit: Beiträge aus geschichtstheoretischer, philosophischer und theologischer Perspektive*, edited by Jens Schröter and Antje Eddelbüttel, 19–32. Theologische Bibliothek Töpelmann 127. Berlin: de Gruyter, 2004.

———. "Historische Methode und religiöser Sinn." In *Geschichte im Kulturprozeß*, edited by Jörn Rüsen, 9–41. Cologne: Böhlau, 2002.

———. *Historische Vernunft*. Grundzüge einer Historik 1. Göttingen: Vandenhoeck & Ruprecht, 1983.

———. "Kann gestern besser werden? Über die Verwandlung der Vergangenheit in Geschichte." In *Kann gestern besser werden?* edited by Jörn Rüsen. Berlin: Kadmos, 2003.

———. *Lebendige Geschichte: Formen und Funktionen des historischen Wissens*. Grundzüge einer Historik 3. Göttingen: Vandenhoeck & Ruprecht, 1989.

———. "Narrativität und Objektivität." In *Geschichte im Kulturprozeß*, edited by Jörn Rüsen, 99–124. Cologne: Böhlau, 2002.

———. *Rekonstruktion der Vergangenheit: Die Prinzipien der historischen Forschung*. Grundzüge einer Historik 2. Göttingen: Vandenhoeck & Ruprecht, 1986.

———. "Was heißt: Sinn der Geschichte?" In *Historische Sinnbildung: Problemstellungen, Zeitkonzepte, Wahrnehmungshorizonte, Darstellungsstrategien*, edited by Klaus E. Müller and Jörn Rüsen, 17–47. Reinbek bei Hamburg: Rowohlt, 1997.

———, ed. *Kann gestern besser werden?* Berlin: Kadmos, 2003.

———. *Western Historical Thinking: An Intercultural Debate*. New York: Berghahn Books, 2002.

Rüsen, Jörn, et al., eds. *Studies in Metahistory*. Pretoria: Human Sciences Research Council, 1993.

Rüsen, Jörn, and K.-J. Hölkeskamp. "Einleitung." In *Sinn (in) der Antike*, edited by K.-J. Hölkeskamp et al., 1–15. Mainz: Von Zabern, 2003.

Sabbe, Maurits. "The Cleaning of the Temple and the Temple Logion." In *Studia Neotestamentica: Collected Essays*, edited by Maurits Sabbe, 331–54. Bibliotheca ephemeridum theologicarum lovaniensium 98. Louvain: Leuven University Press, 1991.

Sadananda, D. R. *The Johannine Exegesis of God*. Beihefte zur Zeitschrift für die neutestamentliche Wissenschaft und die Kunde der älteren Kirche 121. Berlin: de Gruyter, 2004.

Saldarini, Anthony J. *Matthew's Christian-Jewish Community*. Chicago: University of Chicago Press, 1994.

———. "Reading Matthew without Anti-Semitism." In *The Gospel of Matthew in Current Study: Studies in Memory of William G. Thompson, SJ*, edited by David Edward Aune, 166–84. Grand Rapids: Eerdmans, 2001.

Sánchez, Héctor. *Das lukanische Geschichtswerk im Spiegel heilsgeschichtlicher Übergänge*. Paderborner theologische Studien 29. Paderborn: Schöningh, 2001.

Sanders, E. P. *The Historical Figure of Jesus*. New York: Penguin Books, 1993.

———. *Jesus and Judaism*. Philadelphia: Fortress, 1985.

———. *Paul and Palestinian Judaism: A Comparison of Patterns of Religion*. Philadelphia: Fortress, 1977.

Sänger, Dieter. "'Amen, komm, Herr Jesus!' (Apk 22,20): Anmerkungen zur Christologie der Johannes-Apokalypse." In *Studien zur Johannesoffenbarung und ihrer Auslegung: Festschrift für Otto Böcher zum 70. Geburtstag*, edited by Friedrich Wilhelm Horn and Michael Wolter, 71–92. Neukirchen-Vluyn: Neukirchener Verlag, 2005.

———. "Schriftauslegung im Horizont der Gottesherrschaft." In *Christlicher Glaube und religiöse Bildung: Frau Prof. Dr. Friedel Kriechbaum zum 60. Geburtstag am 13. August 1995*, edited by Hermann Deuser and Gerhard Schmalenberg, 75–109. Giessener Schriften zur Theologie und Religionspädagogik des Fachbereichs Evangelische Theologie und Katholische Theologie und deren Didaktik der Justus-Liebig-Universität 11. Giessen: Selbstverlag des Fachbereichs Evangelische Theologie und Katholische Theologie und deren Didaktik, 1995.

———. *Die Verkündigung des Gekreuzigten und Israel: Studien zum Verhältnis von Kirche und Israel bei Paulus und im frühen Christentum*. Wissenschaftliche Untersuchungen zum Neuen Testament 75. Tübingen: Mohr, 1994.

Sänger, Dieter, and Michael Bachmann, eds. *Das Ezechielbuch in der Johannesoffenbarung*. Biblisch-theologische Studien 76. Neukirchen-Vluyn: Neukirchener Verlag, 2004.

Sariola, Heikki. *Markus und das Gesetz: Eine redaktionskritische Untersuchung*. Annales Academiae Scientiarum Fennicae. Dissertationes humanarum litterarum 56. Helsinki: Suomalainen Tiedeakatemia, 1990.

Sato, Migaku. *Q und Prophetie*. Tübingen: Mohr, 1988.

Sauer, Jürgen. *Rückkehr und Vollendung des Heils: Eine Untersuchung zu den ethischen Radikalismen Jesu*. Theorie und Forschung 133. Regensburg: Roderer, 1991.

Schade, Hans-Heinrich. *Apokalyptische Christologie bei Paulus: Studien zum Zusammenhang von Christologie und Eschatologie in den Paulusbriefen*. Göttinger theologische Arbeiten 18. Göttingen: Vandenhoeck & Ruprecht, 1981.

Schäfer, Peter. *The History of the Jews in the Greco-Roman World*. New York: Routledge, 2003.

Schelbert, G. "Abba, Vater!" *Freiburger Zeitschrift für Philosophie und Theologie* 40 (1993): 259–81; 41 (1994): 526–31.

Schenke, Ludger. "Gibt es im Markusevangelium eine Präexistenzchristologie?" *Zeitschrift für die neutestamentliche Wissenschaft und die Kunde der älteren Kirche* 91 (2000): 45–71.

———. "Jesus als Weisheitlehrer im Markusevangelium." In *Die Weisheit—Ursprünge und Rezeption: Festschrift für Karl Löning zum 65. Geburtstag*, edited by Martin Fassnacht, 125–38. Neutestamentliche Abhandlungen 44. Münster: Aschendorff, 2003.

———. "Das johanneische Schisma und die 'Zwölf' (Joh 6,60–71)." *New Testament Studies* 38 (1992): 105–21.

———. *Johannes: Kommentar*. Düsseldorf: Patmos, 1998.

———. *Das Markus-Evangelium*. Stuttgart: Kohlhammer, 1988.

Schiefer-Ferrari, Markus. *Die Sprache des Leids in den paulinischen Peristasenkatalogen*. Stuttgarter Biblische Beiträge 23. Stuttgart: Katholisches Bibelwerk, 1991.

Schimanowski, Gottfried. *Die himmlische Liturgie in der Apokalypse des Johannes: Die frühjüdischen Traditionen in Offenbarung 4–5 unter Einschluss der Hekhalotliteratur*. Wissenschaftliche Untersuchungen zum Neuen Testament 154. Tübingen: Mohr, 2002.

Schlarb, Egbert. *Die gesunde Lehre: Häresie und Wahrheit im Spiegel der Pastoralbriefe*. Marburger theologische Studien 28. Marburg: Elwert, 1990.

———. "Miszell zu 1Tim 6,20." *Zeitschrift für die neutestamentliche Wissenschaft und die Kunde der älteren Kirche* 77 (1986): 276–81.

Schlatter, Adolf von. "Atheistische Methoden in der Theologie." In *Die Bibel Verstehen: Aufsätze zur biblischen Hermeneutik*, edited by Adolf Schlatter and Werner Neuer, 131–48. Giessen: Brunnen, 2002.

———. *Der Glaube im Neuen Testament*. 5th ed. Stuttgart: Calwer, 1963.

Schlier, Heinrich. *Der Brief an die Epheser: Ein Kommentar*. 6th ed. Düsseldorf: Patmos, 1968.

———. *Der Brief an die Galater*. 10th ed. Kritisch-exegetischer Kommentar über das Neue Testament 7. Göttingen: Vandenhoeck & Ruprecht, 1949.

———. *Grundzüge einer paulinischen Theologie*. Freiburg: Herder, 1978.

———. "Über Sinn und Aufgabe einer neutestamentlichen Theologie." In *Das Problem der Theologie des Neuen Testaments*, edited by Georg Strecker, 323–44. Weg der Forschung 367. Darmstadt: Wissenschaftliche Buchgesellschaft, 1975.

Schluep, Christoph. *Der Ort des Christus: Soteriologische Metaphern bei Paulus als Lebensregeln*. Zürich: Theologischer Verlag Zürich, 2005.

Schmeller, Thomas. *Brechungen: Urchristliche Wandercharismatiker im Prisma soziologisch orientierter Exegese*. Stuttgarter Bibelstudien 136. Stuttgart: Verlag Katholisches Bibelwerk, 1989.

———. "Der Erbe des Weinbergs." *Münchner theologische Zeitschrift* 46 (1995): 183–201.

Schmid, Hans Heinrich. *Gerechtigkeit als Weltordnung: Hintergrund und Geschichte der alttestamentlichen Gerechtigkeitsbegriffes*. Beiträge zur historischen Theologie 40. Tübingen: Mohr (Siebeck), 1968.

Schmid, Hansjörg. *Gegner im 1. Johannesbrief? Zu Konstruktion und Selbstreferenz im johanneischen Sinnsystem*. Beiträge zur Wissenschaft vom Alten und Neuen Testament 159. Stuttgart: Kohlhammer, 2002.

Schmidt, Arno. *Die Geburt des Logos bei den frühen Griechen*. Berlin: Logos-Verlag, 2002.

Schmidt, K. M. *Mahnung und Erinnerung im Maskenspiel: Epistolographie, Rhetorik und Narrativik der pseudepigraphischen Petrusbriefe*. Herder's Biblical Studies 38. Freiburg: Herder, 2003.

Schmidt, Karl Ludwig. *The Place of the Gospels in the General History of Literature*. Translated by Byron R. McCane. Columbia: University of South Carolina Press, 2002.

Schmidt, Werner H. *Königtum Gottes in Ugarit und Israel*. 2nd rev. ed. Berlin: Töpelmann, 1966.

Schmithals, Walter, ed. *Neues Testament und Gnosis*. Erträge der Forschung 208. Darmstadt: Wissenschaftliche Buchgesellschaft, 1984.

Schnackenburg, Rudolf. *Die Brief an die Epheser*. Evangelisch-katholischer Kommentar zum Neuen Testament 10. Zürich: Benziger, 1982.

———. "Ephesus: Entwicklung einer Gemeinde von Paulus zu Johannes." *Biblische Zeitschrift* 35 (1991): 41–64.

———. *The Gospel according to St. John*. 3 vols. New York: Seabury, 1980.

———. "Die grosse Eulogie Eph 1,3–14." *Biblische Zeitschrift* 21 (1977): 67–87.

———. *Jesus in the Gospels: A Biblical Christology*. Louisville: Westminster John Knox, 1995.

———. "Paulinische und johanneische Christologie." In *Das Johannesevangelium*, edited by Rudolf Schnackenburg, 4:102–18. Herders theologischer Kommentar zum Neuen Testament 4. Freiburg: Herder, 1984.

———. *Die Sittliche Botschaft des Neuen Testaments*. 2nd ed. 2 vols. Herders theologischer Kommentar zum Neuen Testament: Supplementband 2. Freiburg: Herder, 1986–88.

———. "Strukturanalyse von Joh 17." *Biblische Zeitschrift* 17.1 (1973): 67–78; 17.2 (1973): 196–202.

Schneider, Gerhard. *Die Apostelgeschichte*. Herders theologischer Kommentar zum Neuen Testament 5. Freiburg: Herder, 1980.

———. *Das Evangelium nach Lukas: Kapitel 1–10*. Ökumenischer Taschenbuch-Kommentar zum Neuen Testament 3.1. Gütersloh: Gütersloher Verlagshaus Gerd Mohn, 1977.

———. "'Der Menschensohn' in der lukanischen Christologie." In *Lukas, Theologe der Heilsgeschichte*, edited by Gerhard Schneider, 98–113. Bonner biblische Beiträge 59. Bonn: Hannstein, 1985.

———. *Verleugnung, Verspottung und Verhör Jesu nach Lukas 22,54–71: Studien zur lukanischen Darstellung der Passion*. Studien zum Alten und Neuen Testament 22. Munich: Kösel, 1969.

Schnelle, Udo. "Die Abschiedsreden im Johannesevangelium." *Zeitschrift für die neutestamentliche Wissenschaft und die Kunde der älteren Kirche* 80 (1989): 64–79.

———. *Antidocetic Christology in the Gospel of John*. Translated by Linda M. Maloney. Minneapolis: Fortress, 1992.

———. *Apostle Paul: His Life and Thought*. Translated by M. Eugene Boring. Grand Rapids: Baker Academic, 2005.

———. *Einführung in die neutestamentliche Exegese*. 6th ed. Göttingen: Vandenhoeck & Ruprecht, 2005.

———. "Der erste Thessalonicherbrief und die Entstehung der paulinischen Anthropologie." *New Testament Studies* 32 (1986): 207–24.

———. "Die Ethik des 1. Thessalonikerbriefes." In *The Thessalonian Correspondence*, edited by Raymond F. Collins, 295–305. Bibliotheca ephemeridum theologicarum lovaniensium 87. Louvain: Leuven University Press, 1990.

———. *Das Evangelium nach Johannes*. Theologischer Handkommentar zum Neuen Testament 4. Leipzig: Evangelische Verlagsanstalt, 1998.

———. "Gerechtigkeit in den Psalmen Salomos und bei Paulus." In *Jüdische Schriften in ihrem antik-jüdischen und urchristlichen Kontext*, edited by Hermann Lichtenberger and Gerbern S. Oegema. Studien zu den Jüdischen Schriften aus hellenistisch-römischer Zeit 1. Gütersloh: Gütersloher Verlagshaus, 2002.

———. *Gerechtigkeit und Christusgegenwart: Vorpaulinische und paulinische Tauftheologie*. Göttinger theologische Arbeiten 24. Göttingen: Vandenhoeck & Ruprecht, 1983.

———. "Das Gesetz bei Paulus." In *Biographie und Persönlichkeit des Paulus*, edited by Eve-Marie Becker and Peter Pilhofer, 245–70. Wissenschaftliche Untersuchungen zum Neuen Testament 187. Tübingen: Mohr Siebeck, 2005.

———. "Heilsgegenwart: Christologische Hoheitstitel bei Paulus." In *Paulinische Christologie: Exegetische Beiträge; Hans Hübner zum 70. Geburtstag*, edited by Udo Schnelle et al., 178–93. Göttingen: Vandenhoeck & Ruprecht, 2000.

———. "Der historische Abstand und der Heilige Geist." In *Reformation und Neuzeit: 300 Jahre Theologie in Halle*, edited by Udo Schnelle, 87–103. Berlin: de Gruyter, 1994.

———. *The History and Theology of the New Testament Writings*. Translated by M. Eugene Boring. Minneapolis: Fortress, 1998.

———. *The Human Condition: Anthropology in the Teachings of Jesus, Paul, and John*. Translated by O. C. Dean Jr. Minneapolis: Fortress, 1996.

———. "Die johanneische Schule." In *Bilanz und Perspektiven gegenwärtiger Auslegung des Neuen Testaments: Symposion zum 65. Geburtstag von Georg Strecker*, edited by Friedrich W. Horn, 198–217. Beihefte zur Zeitschrift für die neutestamentliche Wissenschaft und die Kunde der älteren Kirche 75. Berlin: de Gruyter, 1995.

———. "Das Johannesevangelium als neue Sinnbildung." In *Theology and Christology in the Fourth Gospel*, edited by G. van Belle et al., 291–313. Bibliotheca ephemeridum theologicarum lovaniensium 184. Louvain: Leuven University Press, 2005.

———. "Die Juden im Johannesevangelium." In *Gedenkt an das Wort: Festschrift für Werner Vogler zum 65. Geburtstag*, edited by Christoph Kähler et al., 217–30. Leipzig: Evangelische Verlagsanstalt, 1999.

———. "Die Tempelreinigung und die Christologie des Johannesevangeliums." *New Testament Studies* 42 (1996): 359–73.

———. "Theologie als kreative Sinnbildung: Johannes als Weiterbildung von Paulus und Markus." In *Johannesevangelium, Mitte oder Rand des Kanons? Neue Standortbestimmungen*, edited by Klaus

Berger et al., 119–45. Quaestiones disputatae 203. Freiburg i.B.: Herder, 2003.

———. "Transformation und Partizipation als Grundgedanken paulinischer Theologie." *New Testament Studies* 47 (1986): 58–75.

———. "Vom Verfolger zum Verkündiger: Inhalt und Tragweite des Damaskusgeschehens." In *Forschungen zum Neuen Testament und seiner Umwelt*, edited by Christoph Niemand, 299–323. Frankfurt: Lang, 2002.

———. *Wandlungen im paulinischen Denken*. Stuttgarter Bibelstudien 137. Stuttgart: Verlag Katholisches Bibelwerk, 1989.

Schnelle, Udo, and Georg Strecker. *Neuer Wettstein: Texte zum Neuen Testament aus Griechentum und Hellenismus*. Berlin: de Gruyter, 1996.

Schnider, Franz. *Der Jakobusbrief*. Regensburger Neues Testament 20. Regensburg: Pustet, 1987.

Schniewind, J. *Das Evangelium nach Matthäus*. 5th ed. Das Neue Testament Deutsch 1. Göttingen: Vandenhoeck & Ruprecht, 1950.

Scholtissek, Klaus. "Abschied und neue Gegenwart." *Ephemerides theologicae lovanienses* 75 (1999): 332–58.

———. "'Eine größere Liebe als diese hat niemand, als wenn einer sein Leben hingibt für seine Freunde' (Joh 15,13)." In *Kontexte des Johannesevangeliums*, edited by Albert Frey and Udo Schnelle, 413–39. Wissenschaftliche Untersuchungen zum Neuen Testament 175. Tübingen: Mohr, 2004.

———. *In ihm sein und bleiben: Die Sprache der Immanenz in den johanneischen Schriften*. Herders biblische Studien 21. Freiburg: Herder, 2000.

———. "Kinder Gottes und Freunde Jesu: Beobachtungen zur johanneischen Ekklesiologie." In *Ekklesiologie des Neuen Testaments: Für Karl Kertelge*, edited by Rainer Kampling and Thomas Söding, 184–211. Freiburg: Herder, 1996.

———. "'Mitteilhaber an der Bedrängnis, der Königsherrschaft und der Ausdauer in Jesus' (Offb 1,9): Partizipatorische Ethik in der Offenbarung des Johannes." In *Theologie als Vision: Studien zur Johannes-Offenbarung*, edited by Knut Backhaus. Stuttgarter Bibelstudien 191. Stuttgart: Verlag Katholisches Bibelwerk, 2001.

———. "'Mitten unter euch steht der, den ihr nicht kennt' (Joh 1,26)." *Münchner theologische Zeitschrift* 48 (1997): 103–21.

———. "Der Sohn Gottes für das Reich Gottes." In *Der Evangelist als Theologe*, edited by Thomas Söding, 63–90. Stuttgarter Bibelstudien 163. Stuttgart: Katholisches Bibelwerk, 1995.

———. *Die Vollmacht Jesu: Traditions- und redaktionsgeschichtliche Analysen zu einem Leitmotiv markinischer Christologie*. Neutestamentliche Abhandlungen 25. Münster: Aschendorff, 1992.

Schottroff, Luise. "Frauen in der Nachfolge Jesu in neutestamentlicher Zeit." In *Traditionen der Befreiung*, edited by Willy Schottroff and Wolfgang Stegemann, 91–133. Munich: Kaiser, 1980.

Schottroff, Luise, et al. *Essays on the Love Commandment*. Philadelphia: Fortress, 1978.

Schottroff, Luise, and Wolfgang Stegemann. *Jesus and the Hope of the Poor*. Translated by Matthew J. O'Connell. Maryknoll, NY: Orbis Books, 1986.

———. *Jesus von Nazareth Hoffnung der Armen*. Stuttgart: Kohlhammer, 1981.

Schrage, Wolfgang. "Die Briefe des Jakobus, Petrus, Judas." In *Die katholische Briefe*, edited by Horst Robert Balz. Das Neue Testament Deutsch 10. Göttingen: Vandenhoeck & Ruprecht, 1993.

———. *Der erste Brief an die Korinther*. 4 vols. Evangelisch-katholischer Kommentar zum Neuen Testament 7. Zürich: Benziger, 1991.

———. *The Ethics of the New Testament*. Translated by David E. Green. Philadelphia: Fortress, 1988.

———. "Die Frage nach der Mitte und dem Kanon im Kanon des Neuen Testaments, in der neueren Diskussion." In *Rechtfertigung: Festschrift für Ernst Käsemann zum 70. Geburtstag*, edited by Johannes Friedrich et al., 415–42. Göttingen: Vandenhoeck & Ruprecht, 1976.

———. *Unterwegs zur Einzigkeit und Einheit Gottes: Zum "Monotheismus" des Paulus und seiner alttestamentlich-frühjüdischen Tradition*. Biblisch-theologische Studien 48. Neukirchen-Vluyn: Neukirchener Verlag, 2002.

Schreiber, Stefan. "Caesar oder Gott (Mk 12,17)?" *Biblische Zeitschrift* 48 (2004): 65–85.

———. *Gesalbter und König: Titel und Konzeptionen der königlichen Gesalbtenerwartung in frühjüdischen und urchristlichen Schriften*. Beihefte zur Zeitschrift für die neutestamentliche Wissenschaft und die Kunde der älteren Kirche 105. Berlin: de Gruyter, 2000.

Schröger, F. *Gemeinde im 1. Petrusbrief*. Passau: Passavia, 1981.

Schröger, Friedrich. *Der Verfasser des Hebräerbriefes als Schriftausleger*. Biblische Untersuchungen 4. Regensburg: Pustet, 1968.

Schröter, Jens. *Das Abendmahl in der frühchristlichen Literatur: Frühchristliche Deutungen und Impulse für die Gegenwart*. Stuttgarter Bibelstudien 210. Stuttgart: Katholisches Bibelwerk, 2006.

———. "Die Bedeutung des Kanons für eine Theologie des Neuen Testaments." In *Aufgabe und Durchführung einer Theologie des Neuen Testaments*, edited by C. Breytenbach and J. Frey, 135–58. Wissenschaftliche Untersuchungen zum Neuen Testament 205. Tübingen: Mohr, 2007.

———. "Entscheidung für die Worte Jesu." *Bibel und Kirche* 54 (1999): 70–74.

———. *Erinnerung an Jesu Worte: Studien zur Rezeption der Logienüberlieferung in Markus, Q und Thomas*. Wissenschaftliche Monographien zum Alten und Neuen Testament 76. Neukirchen-Vluyn: Neukirchener Verlag, 1997.

———. "Die Frage nach dem historischen Jesus und der Charakter historischer Erkenntnis." In *The Sayings Source Q and the Historical Jesus*, edited by Andreas Lindemann, 207–54. Bibliotheca ephemeridum theologicarum lovaniensium 158. Louvain: Leuven University Press, 2001.

———. "Jesus der Menschensohn: Zum Ansatz der Christologie in Markus und Q." In *Jesus und die Anfänge der Christologie: Methodologische und exegetische Studien zu den Ursprüngen des christlichen Glaubens*, edited by Jens Schröter, 140–79. Biblisch-theologische Studien 47. Neukirchen-Vluyn: Neukirchener Verlag, 2001.

———. "Jesus im frühen Christentum: Zur neueren Diskussion über kanonisch und apokryph gewordene Jesusüberlieferungen." *Verkündigung und Forschung* 51 (2006): 25–41.

———. *Jesus von Nazareth: Jude aus Galiläa—Retter der Welt*. Biblische Gestalten 15. Leipzig: Evangelische Verlagsanstalt, 2006.

———. "Lukas als Historiograph." In *Die antike Historiographie und die Anfänge der christlichen Geschichtsschreibung*, edited by Eve-Marie Becker, 237–62. Beihefte zur Zeitschrift für die neutestamentliche Wissenschaft und die Kunde der älteren Kirche 129. Berlin: de Gruyter, 2005.

———. "Q et la christologie implicite." In *The Sayings Source Q and the Historical Jesus*, edited by Andreas Lindemann, 289–316. Bibliotheca ephemeridum theologicarum lovaniensium 158. Louvain: Leuven University Press, 2001.

———. *Der versöhnte Versöhner: Paulus als unentbehrlicher Mittler im Heilsvorgang zwischen Gott und Gemeinde nach 2 Kor 2,14–7,4*. Texte und Arbeiten zum neutestamentlichen Zeitalter 10. Tübingen: Francke, 1993.

Schröter, Jens, and H.-G. Bethge. "Das Evangelium nach Thomas." In *Nag Hammadi Deutsch*, edited by Hans-Martin Schenke et al., 151–81. Die griechischen christlichen Schriftsteller der ersten Jahrhunderte, n.F., 8. Berlin: de Gruyter, 2001.

Schuchard, Bruce G. *Scripture within Scripture: The Interrelationship of Form and Function in the Explicit Old Testament Citations in the Gospel of John*. Society of Biblical Literature Dissertation Series 133. Atlanta: Scholars Press, 1992.

Schulz, Siegfried. "Gottes Vorsehung bei Lukas." *Zeitschrift für die neutestamentliche Wissenschaft und die Kunde der älteren Kirche* 54 (1963): 104–16.

———. *Komposition und Herkunft der Johanneischen Reden*. Beiträge zur Wissenschaft vom Alten und Neuen Testament 1. Stuttgart: Kohlhammer, 1960.

———. *Die Mitte der Schrift: Der Frühkatholizismus im Neuen Testament als Herausforderung an den Protestantismus*. Stuttgart: Kreuz-Verlag, 1976.

———. *Neutestamentliche Ethik*. Zürich: Theologischer Verlag, 1987.

Schumacher, Leonhard. *Sklaverei in der Antike: Alltag und Schicksal der Unfreien*. Beck's archäologische Bibliothek. Munich: Beck, 2001.

Schunack, G. "Glaube in griechischer Religiosität." In *Antikes Judentum und frühes Christentum: Festschrift für Hartmut Stegemann zum 65. Geburtstag*, edited by Bernd Kollmann et al., 296–326. Beihefte zur Zeitschrift für die neutestamentliche Wissenschaft 97. Berlin: de Gruyter, 1999.

Schüpphaus, Joachim. *Die Psalmen Salomos: Ein Zeugnis Jerusalemer Theologie und Frömmigkeit in der Mitte des vorchristlichen Jahrhunderts*. Leiden: Brill, 1977.

Schürer, Emil. *The History of the Jewish People in the Age of Jesus Christ (175 B.C.–A.D. 135)*. 2nd English ed. 3 vols. Edinburgh: T&T Clark, 1973.

Schürmann, Heinz. "Der Abendmahlsbericht Lk 22,7–38 als Gottesdienstordnung, Gemeindeordnung, Lebensordnung." In *Ursprung und Gestalt: Erörterungen und Besinnungen zum Neuen Testament*, edited by Heinz Schürmann. Kommentare und Beiträge zum Alten und Neuen Testament 2. Düsseldorf: Patmos, 1970.

———. "Das 'eigentümlich Jesuanische' im Gebet Jesu: Besu Beten als Schlüssel für das Verständnis seiner Verkündigung." In *Jesus, Gestalt und Ge-*

heimnis: Gesammelte Beiträge, edited by Heinz Schürmann and Klaus Scholtissek, 45–63. Paderborn: Bonifatius, 1994.

———. *Der Einsetzungsbericht: Lk 22,19–20*. Neutestamentliche Abhandlungen, n.F., 4. Münster: Aschendorff, 1955.

———. "'Das Gesetz des Christus' Gal 6,2: Jesu Verhalten und Wort als letztgültige sittliche Norm nach Paulus." In *Studien zur neutestamentlichen Ethik*, edited by Heinz Schürmann and Thomas Söding, 53–77. Stuttgarter biblische Aufsatzbände 7. Stuttgart: Verlag Katholisches Bibelwerk, 1990.

———. *Das Lukasevangelium*. 2 vols. Herders theologischer Kommentar zum Neuen Testament 3. Freiburg: Herder, 1969.

———. "'Pro-Existenz' als christologischer Grundbegriff." In *Jesus, Gestalt und Geheimnis: Gesammelte Beiträge*, edited by Heinz Schürmann and Klaus Scholtissek, 286–315. Paderborn: Bonifatius, 1994.

———. "Das Zeugnis der Redequelle für die Basileia-Verkündigung Jesu." In *Gottes Reich—Jesu Geschick: Jesu ureigener Tod im Licht seiner Basileia-Verkündigung*, edited by Heinz Schürmann, 65–152. Freiburg: Herder, 1983.

———, ed. *Gottes Reich—Jesu Geschick: Jesu ureigener Tod im Licht seiner Basileia-Verkündigung*. Freiburg: Herder, 1983.

Schutz, Alfred. *The Phenomenology of the Social World*. Translated by George Walsh and Frederick Lehnert. London: Heinemann, 1972.

Schutz, Alfred, and Thomas Luckmann. *The Structures of the Life-World*. Translated by Richard M. Zaner and H. Tristram Engelhardt Jr. 2 vols. Northwestern University Studies in Phenomenology and Existential Philosophy. Evanston, IL: Northwestern University Press, 1973–83.

Schütz, Frieder. *Der leidende Christus: Die angefochtene Gemeinde und der Christuskerygma der lukanischen Schriften*. Beiträge zur Wissenschaft vom Alten (und Neuen) Testament 89. Stuttgart: Kohlhammer, 1969.

Schwankl, Otto. *Licht und Finsternis: Ein metaphorisches Paradigma in den johanneischen Schriften*. Herder's Biblical Studies 5. Freiburg i.B.: Herder, 1995.

———. *Die Sadduzäerfrage (Mk 12,18–27 parr): Eine exegetisch-theologische Studie zur Auferstehungserwartung*. Bonner biblische Beiträge 66. Frankfurt: Athenäum, 1987.

Schweitzer, Albert. *The Mystery of the Kingdom of God: The Secret of Jesus's Messiahship and Passion*. Translated by Walter Lowrie. New York: Schocken Books, 1964.

———. *The Mysticism of Paul the Apostle*. Translated by William Montgomery. London: A&C Black, 1931.

———. *Paul and His Interpreters: A Critical History*. New York: Schocken Books, 1964.

———. *The Quest of the Historical Jesus: A Critical Study of Its Progress from Reimarus to Wrede*. Translated by W. Montgomery et al. 3rd ("first complete") ed. Minneapolis: Fortress, 2000.

Schweizer, Eduard. "Altes und Neues zu den 'Elementen der Welt' in Kol 2,20; Gal 4,3. 9." In *Wissenschaft und Kirche: Festschrift für Eduard Lohse*, edited by Kurt Aland and Siegfried Meurer, 111–18. Texte und Arbeiten zur Bibel 4. Bielefeld: Luther-Verlag, 1989.

———. *Der Brief an die Kolosser*. Evangelisch-katholischer Kommentar zum Neuen Testament 12. Zürich: Benziger, 1976.

———. "Gesetz und Enthusiasmus bei Matthäus." In *Das Matthäus-Evangelium*, edited by Joachim Lange, 350–76. Weg der Forschung 525. Darmstadt: Wissenschaftliche Buchgesellschaft, 1980.

———. *The Good News according to Mark*. Translated by Donald H. Madvig. Richmond, VA: John Knox, 1970.

———. "Gottesgerechtigkeit und Lasterkataloge bei Paulus (inkl. Kol und Eph)." In *Rechtfertigung: Festschrift für Ernst Käsemann zum 70. Geburtstag*, edited by Johannes Friedrich et al., 453–77. Göttingen: Vandenhoeck & Ruprecht, 1976.

———. "Die Kirche als Leib Christi in den paulinischen Antilegomena." In *Neotestamentica: Deutsche und Englische Aufsätze, 1951–1963; German and English Essays, 1951–1963*, edited by Eduard Schweizer, 293–316. Zürich: Zwingli Verlag, 1963.

———. "Mark's Theological Achievement (1964)." In *The Interpretation of Mark*, edited by William R. Telford, 63–88. Studies in New Testament Interpretation. Edinburgh: T&T Clark, 1995.

———. "Observance of the Law and Charismatic Activity in Matthew." *New Testament Studies* 16 (1970): 213–30.

———. "The Question of the Messianic Secret in Mark (1965)." In *The Messianic Secret*, edited by C. M. Tuckett, 65–74. Issues in Religion and Theology 1. London: SPCK, 1983.

———. "Röm 1,3f und der Gegensatz von Fleisch und Geist bei Paulus." In *Neotestamentica:*

Deutsche und Englische Aufsätze, 1951–1963; German and English Essays, 1951–1963, edited by Eduard Schweizer, 180–89. Zürich: Zwingli Verlag, 1963.

———. "Zum hellenistischen Hintergrund der Vorstellung der 'Versöhnung des Alls.'" In *Neues Testament und Christologie im Werden: Aufsätze*, edited by Eduard Schweizer, 164–78. Göttingen: Vandenhoeck & Ruprecht, 1982.

———. "Zur Christologie des ersten Petrusbriefes." In *Anfänge der Christologie: Festschrift für Ferdinand Hahn zum 65. Geburtstag*, edited by Cilliers Breytenbach et al., 369–81. Göttingen: Vandenhoeck & Ruprecht, 1991.

Schwemer, Anna Maria. "Gott als König und seine Königsherrschaft in den Sabbatliedern aus Qumran." In *Königsherrschaft Gottes und himmlischer Kult: Im Judentum, Urchristentum und in der hellenistischen Welt*, edited by Martin Hengel and Anna Maria Schwemer, 45–118. Wissenschaftliche Untersuchungen zum Neuen Testament 55. Tübingen: Mohr, 1991.

Schwier, Helmut. *Tempel und Tempelzerstörung: Untersuchungen zu den theologischen und ideologischen Faktoren im ersten jüdisch-römischen Krieg (66–74 n. Chr.)*. Novum Testamentum et Orbis Antiquus 11. Göttingen: Vandenhoeck & Ruprecht, 1989.

Schwindt, Rainer. *Das Weltbild des Epheserbriefes: Eine religionsgeschichtlich-exegetische Studie*. Wissenschaftliche Untersuchungen zum Neuen Testament 148. Tübingen: Mohr, 2002.

Scott, Bernard Brandon. *Jesus, Symbol-Maker for the Kingdom*. Philadelphia: Fortress, 1981.

Scriba, Albrecht. *Echtheitskriterien der Jesus-Forschung: Kritische Revision und konstruktiver Neuansatz*. Theos 74. Hamburg: Kovac, 2007.

Seeley, D. "Jesus's Death in Q." *New Testament Studies* 38 (1992): 222–34.

Segal, Lynn. *The Dream of Reality: Heinz von Foerster's Constructivism*. 2nd ed. Berlin: Springer, 2001.

Seifrid, Mark A. "In Christ." In *Dictionary of Paul and His Letters*, edited by Gerald F. Hawthorne et al., 27–41. Downers Grove, IL: InterVarsity, 1993.

———. *Justification by Faith: The Origin and Development of a Central Pauline Theme*. Supplements to Novum Testamentum 68. Leiden: Brill, 1992.

Sellin, Gerhard. "Adresse und Intention des Epheserbriefes." In *Paulus, Apostel Jesu Christi: Festschrift für Günter Klein zum 70. Geburtstag*, edited by Michael Trowitzsch, 171–86. Tübingen: Mohr, 1998.

———. "Die Häretiker des Judasbriefes." *Zeitschrift für die neutestamentliche Wissenschaft und die Kunde der älteren Kirche* 77 (1986): 206–25.

———. "Die Paränese des Epheserbriefes." In *Gemeinschaft am Evangelium: Festschrift für Wiard Popkes zum 60. Geburtstag*, edited by Edwin Brandt et al., 28–300. Leipzig: Evangelische Verlagsanstalt, 1996.

———. *Der Streit um die Auferstehung der Toten: Eine religionsgeschichtliche und exegetische Untersuchung von 1. Korinther 15*. Forschungen zur Religion und Literatur des Alten und Neuen Testaments 138. Göttingen: Vandenhoeck & Ruprecht, 1986.

Sevenich-Bax, Elisabeth. *Israels Konfrontation mit den letzten Boten der Weisheit: Form, Funktion und Interdependenz der Weisheitselemente in der Logienquelle*. Münsteraner theologische Abhandlungen 21. Altenberge: Orlos, 1993.

Siber, Peter. *Mit Christus leben: Eine Studie zur paulinischen Auferstehungshoffnung*. Zürich: Theologischer Verlag, 1971.

Sim, David C. *The Gospel of Matthew and Christian Judaism: The History and Social Setting of the Matthean Community*. Edinburgh: T&T Clark, 1998.

Simon, L. *Petrus und der Lieblingsjünger im Johannesevangelium*. Europäische Hochschulschriften 23.498. Frankfurt: Lang, 1994.

Slenczka, Reinhard. "'Nonsense' (Lk 24,11)." *Kerygma und Dogma* 40 (1994): 170–81.

Smith, Dennis Edwin. *From Symposium to Eucharist: The Banquet in the Early Christian World*. Minneapolis: Fortress, 2003.

Smith, Morton. *Jesus the Magician*. San Francisco: Harper & Row, 1978.

Söding, Thomas. "Das Erscheinen des Retters: Zur Christologie der Pastoralbriefe." In *Christologie in der Paulus-Schule: Zur Rezeptionsgeschichte des paulinischen Evangeliums*, edited by Klaus Scholtissek, 149–92. Stuttgarter Bibelstudien 181. Stuttgart: Verlag Katholisches Bibelwerk, 2000.

———. "Die Freiheit des Glaubens." In *Frühjudentum und Neues Testament im Horizont Biblischer Theologie*, edited by Wolfgang Kraus et al., 113–34. Wissenschaftliche Untersuchungen zum Neuen Testament 162. Tübingen: Mohr Siebeck, 2003.

———. "Das Geheimnis Gottes im Kreuz Jesu." In *Das Wort vom Kreuz: Studien zur paulinischen*

Theologie, edited by Thomas Söding, 71–92. Wissenschaftliche Untersuchungen zum Neuen Testament 93. Tübingen: Mohr, 1997.

———. "Das Geheimnis Gottes im Kreuz Jesu (1Kor)." *Biblische Zeitschrift* 38 (1994): 174–94.

———. *Glaube bei Markus*. Stuttgarter Biblische Beiträge 12. Stuttgart: Katholisches Bibelwerk, 1987.

———. "Gott und das Lamm, Theozentrik und Christologie in der Johannesapokalypse." In *Theologie als Vision: Studien zur Johannes-Offenbarung*, edited by Knut Backhaus, 77–120. Stuttgarter Bibelstudien 191. Stuttgart: Verlag Katholisches Bibelwerk, 2001.

———. "Gottes Sohn von Anfang an: Zur Präexistenzchristologie bei Paulus und den Deuteropaulinen." In *Gottes ewiger Sohn: Die Präexistenz Christi*, edited by Rudolf Laufen, 57–93. Paderborn: Schöningh, 1997.

———. *Der Gottessohn aus Nazareth: Das Menschsein Jesu im Neuen Testament*. Freiburg i.B.: Herder, 2006.

———. "Heilig, Heilig, Heilig: Zur politischen Theologie der Johannes-Apokalypse." *Zeitschrift für Theologie und Kirche* 96 (1999): 49–76.

———. "'Ich und der Vater sind eins' (Joh 10,30): Die johanneische Christologie vor dem Anspruch des Hauptgebotes Dtn 6,4f." *Zeitschrift für die neutestamentliche Wissenschaft und die Kunde der älteren Kirche* 93 (2002): 177–99.

———. "'Die Kraft der Sünde ist das Gesetz' (1Kor 15,56): Anmerkungen zum Hintergrund und zur Pointe einer gesetzeskritischen Sentenz des Apostels Paulus." *Zeitschrift für die neutestamentliche Wissenschaft und die Kunde der älteren Kirche* 83 (1992): 74–84.

———. "Kriterium der Wahrheit? Zum theologischen Stellenwert der paulinischen Rechtfertigungslehre." In *Worum geht es in der Rechtfertigungslehre? Das biblische Fundament der "Gemeinsamen Erklärung" von katholischer Kirche und Lutherischem Weltbund*, edited by Thomas Söding and Frank-Lothar Hossfeld, 193–246. Quaestiones disputatae 180. Freiburg: Herder, 1999.

———. "Leben nach dem Evangelium." In *Der Evangelist als Theologe*, edited by Thomas Söding, 167–95. Stuttgarter Bibelstudien 163. Stuttgart: Katholisches Bibelwerk, 1995.

———. *Das Liebesgebot bei Paulus: Die Mahnung zur Agape im Rahmen der paulinischen Ethik*. Neutestamentliche Abhandlungen, n.F., 26. Münster: Aschendorff, 1995.

———. "Die Tempelaktion Jesu." *Trierer Theologische Zeitschrift* 101 (1992): 36–64.

———, ed. *Der Evangelist als Theologe: Studien zum Markusevangelium*. Stuttgarter Bibelstudien 163. Stuttgart: Katholisches Bibelwerk, 1995.

Sohm, Rudolf. "Begriff und Organisation der Ekklesia." In *Das Kirchliche Amt im Neuen Testament*, edited by Karl Kertelge. Wege der Forschung 439. Darmstadt: Wissenschaftliche Buchgesellschaft, 1977.

Söllner, P. *Jerusalem, du hochgebaute Stadt: Eschatologisches und himmlisches Jerusalem im Frühjudentum und im frühen Christentum*. Texte und Arbeiten zum neutestamentlichen Zeitalter 25. Tübingen: Mohr, 1998.

Sonntag, Holger. ΝΟΜΟΣ ΣΩΤΗΡ*: Zur politischen Theologie des Gesetzes bei Paulus und im antiken Kontext*. Texte und Arbeiten zum neutestamentlichen Zeitalter 34. Tübingen: Francke, 2000.

Speyer, Wolfgang. *Die literarische Fälschung im heidnischen und christlichen Altertum: Ein Versuch ihrer Deutung*. Handbuch der Altertumswissenschaft 1.2. Munich: Beck, 1971.

Spitta, Friedrich. *Christi Predigt an die Geister (1 Petr. 3,19 ff.): Ein Beitrag zur Neutestamentlichen Theologie*. Göttingen: Vandenhoeck & Ruprecht, 1890.

Sprecher, M. T. *Einheitsdenken aus der Perspektive von Joh 17*. Europäische Hochschulschriften 23.495. Frankfurt: Lang, 1993.

Städele, A. *Die Briefe des Pythagoras und der Pythagoreer*. Beiträge zur klassichen Philologie 115. Meisenheim: Hain, 1980.

Standhartinger, Angela. "Eusebeia in den Pastoralbriefen: Ein Beitrag zum Einfluss römischen Denkens auf das entstehende Christentum." *Novum Testamentum* 48 (2006): 51–82.

———. *Studien zur Entstehungsgeschichte und Intention des Kolosserbriefs*. Supplements to Novum Testamentum 94. Leiden: Brill, 1999.

Stark, Rodney. *The Rise of Christianity: A Sociologist Reconsiders History*. Princeton, NJ: Princeton University Press, 1996.

Stauffer, Ethelbert. *Christ and the Caesars: Historical Sketches*. Translated by K. Gregor Smith and R. Gregor Smith. Philadelphia: Westminster, 1955.

Stegemann, Ekkehard. "Zur Tempelreinigung im Johannesevangelium." In *Die Hebräische Bibel und ihre zweifache Nachgeschichte: Festschrift für Rolf Rendtorff zum 65. Geburtstag*, edited by Erhard Blum, 503–16. Neukirchen-Vluyn: Neukirchener Verlag, 1990.

Stegemann, Ekkehard, and Wolfgang Stegemann. *The Jesus Movement: A Social History of Its First Century*. Translated by O. C. Dean Jr. Minneapolis: Fortress, 1999.

Stegemann, Hartmut. "'Die des Uria.'" In *Tradition und Glaube: Das frühe Christentum in seiner Umwelt; Festgabe für Karl Georg Kuhn zum 65. Geburtstag*, edited by Gert Jeremias et al., 246–76. Göttingen: Vandenhoeck & Ruprecht, 1971.

———. "Der lehrende Jesus." *Neue Zeitschrift für systematische Theologie* 24 (1982): 3–20.

———. *The Library of Qumran, on the Essenes, Qumran, John the Baptist, and Jesus*. Grand Rapids: Eerdmans, 1998.

Stegemann, Wolfgang. "The Contextual Ethics of Jesus." In *The Social Setting of Jesus and the Gospels*, edited by Wolfgang Stegemann et al., 45–61. Minneapolis: Fortress, 2002.

———. *Zwischen Synagoge und Obrigkeit: Zur historischen Situation der lukanischen Christen*. Forschungen zur Religion und Literatur des Alten und Neuen Testaments 152. Göttingen: Vandenhoeck & Ruprecht, 1991.

Stegemann, Wolfgang, et al., eds. *The Social Setting of Jesus and the Gospels*. Minneapolis: Fortress, 2002.

Stemberger, Günter. *Jewish Contemporaries of Jesus: Pharisees, Sadducees, Essenes*. Translated by Allan W. Mahnke. Minneapolis: Fortress, 1995.

———. "Die Juden im römischen Reich: Unterdrückung und Privilegien einer Minderheit." In *Christlicher Antijudaismus und jüdischer Antipaganismus: Ihre Motive und Hintergründe in den ersten drei Jahrhunderten*, edited by Herbert Frohnhofen, 6–22. Hamburger theologische Studien 3. Hamburg: Steinmann & Steinmann, 1990.

Stendahl, Krister. *The School of St. Matthew and Its Use of the Old Testament*. Philadelphia: Fortress, 1968.

Stettler, Christian. *Der Kolosserhymnus: Untersuchungen zu Form, traditionsgeschtlichem Hintergrund und Aussage von Kol 1,15–20*. Wissenschaftliche Untersuchungen zum Neuen Testament 2/131. Tübingen: Mohr Siebeck, 2000.

Stettler, Hanna. *Die Christologie der Pastoralbriefe*. Wissenschaftliche Untersuchungen zum Neuen Testament 2/105. Tübingen: Mohr, 198.

Stibbe, M. W. G. *John as Storyteller*. Cambridge: Cambridge University Press, 1992.

Stolle, Volker. *Luther und Paulus: Die exegetischen und hermeneutischen Grundlagen der lutherischen Rechtfertigungslehre im Paulinismus Luthers*. Arbeiten zur Bibel und ihrer Geschichte 10. Leipzig: Evangelische Verlagsanstalt, 2002.

Storck, G. "Eschatologie bei Paulus." ThD diss., Georg August Universität, Göttingen, 1979.

Strack, Hermann, and Paul Billerbeck, eds. *Kommentar zum Neuen Testament aus Talmud und Midrasch*. 6 vols. Munich: Beck, 1924.

Straub, E. "Der Irdische als der Auferstandene: Kritische Theologie bei Johannes ohne ein Wort vom Kreuz." In *Kreuzestheologie im Neuen Testament*, edited by Andreas Dettwiler and Jean Zumstein, 239–64. Wissenschaftliche Untersuchungen zum Neuen Testament 151. Tübingen: Mohr, 2002.

Straub, Jürgen. *Erzählung, Identität und historisches Bewußtsein: Die psychologische Konstruktion von Zeit und Geschichte*. 2nd ed. Frankfurt: Suhrkamp, 2000.

———. "Geschichten erzählen, Geschichte bilden: Grundzüge einer narrativen Psychologie einer historischer Sinnbildung." In *Erzählung, Identität und historisches Bewußtsein: Die psychologische Konstruktion von Zeit und Geschichte*, edited by Jürgen Straub. Frankfurt: Suhrkamp, 2000.

———. "Temporale Orientierung und narrative Kompetenz." In *Geschichtsbewußtsein: Psychologische Grundlagen, Entwicklungskonzepte, empirische Befunde*, edited by Jörn Rüsen, 15–44. Cologne: Böhlau, 2001.

———. "Über das Bilden von Vergangenheit." In *Geschichtsbewußtsein: Psychologische Grundlagen, Entwicklungskonzepte, empirische Befunde*, edited by Jörn Rüsen, 45–113. Cologne: Böhlau, 2001.

Strauss, David Friedrich. *The Life of Jesus Critically Examined*. Introduction by Peter C. Hodgson, ed. Translated by George Eliot. Lives of Jesus Series. London: SCM, 1973.

———. *The Old Faith & the New*. Translated by Mathilde Blind. New York: Holt, 1873.

Strecker, Christian. "Das Geschichtsverständnis des Matthäus." In *Das Matthäus-Evangelium*, edited by Joachim Lange, 326–49. Weg der Forschung 525. Darmstadt: Wissenschaftliche Buchgesellschaft, 1980.

———. "Jesus and the Demoniacs." In *The Social Setting of Jesus and the Gospels*, edited by Wolfgang Stegemann et al., 117–34. Minneapolis: Fortress, 2002.

———. *Die liminale Theologie des Paulus: Zugänge zur paulinischen Theologie aus kulturanthropologischer Perspektive*. Göttingen: Vandenhoeck & Ruprecht, 1999.

Strecker, Georg. "Das Evangelium Jesu Christi." In *Eschaton und Historie: Aufsätze*, edited by Georg Strecker, 183–228. Göttingen: Vandenhoeck & Ruprecht, 1979.

———. *History of New Testament Literature*. Translated by Calvin Katter and Hans-Joachim Mollenhauer. Harrisburg, PA: Trinity, 1997.

———. *The Johannine Letters: A Commentary on 1, 2, and 3 John*. Hermeneia—A Critical and Historical Commentary on the Bible. Minneapolis: Fortress, 1996.

———. "Literarkritische Überlegungen zum εὐαγγέλιον-Begriff im Markusevangelium." In *Eschaton und Historie*, edited by Georg Strecker, 76–89. Göttingen: Vandenhoeck & Ruprecht, 1979.

———. "Redaktionsgeschichte als Aufgabe der Synoptikerexegese." In *Eschaton und Historie: Aufsätze*, edited by Georg Strecker, 9–32. Göttingen: Vandenhoeck & Ruprecht, 1979.

———. *The Sermon on the Mount: An Exegetical Commentary*. Translated by O. C. Dean. Nashville: Abingdon, 1988.

———. "Strukturen einer neutestamentlichen Ethik." *Zeitschrift für Theologie und Kirche* 75 (1978): 117–46.

———. *Theology of the New Testament*. Translated by M. Eugene Boring. New York: de Gruyter, 2000.

———. *Der Weg der Gerechtigkeit: Untersuchung zur Theologie des Matthäus*. 3rd ed. Forschungen zur Religion und Literatur des Alten und Neuen Testaments 82. Göttingen: Vandenhoeck & Ruprecht, 1971.

Strobel, August. *Untersuchungen zum eschatologischen Verzögerungsproblem: Auf Grund der spätjüdisch-urchristlichen Geschichte von Habakuk 2,2ff*. Supplements to Novum Testamentum 2. Leiden: Brill, 1961.

———. "Zum Verständnis von Röm 13." *Zeitschrift für die neutestamentliche Wissenschaft und die Kunde der älteren Kirche* 47 (1956): 67–93.

Stuckenbruck, Loren T. *Angel Veneration and Christology: A Study in Early Judaism and in the Christology of the Apocalypse of John*. Wissenschaftliche Untersuchungen zum Neuen Testament 2/70. Tübingen: Mohr, 1995.

Stuhlmacher, Peter. *Biblische Theologie des Neuen Testaments*. 2 vols. Göttingen: Vandenhoeck & Ruprecht, 1992–99.

———. *Gerechtigkeit Gottes bei Paulus*. Göttingen: Vandenhoeck & Ruprecht, 1965.

———. "Das Lamm Gottes—eine Skizze." In *Geschichte—Tradition—Reflexion: Festschrift für Martin Hengel zum 70. Geburtstag*, edited by Hubert Cancik et al., 530–41. Tübingen: Mohr, 1996.

———. *Das paulinische Evangelium*. Forschungen zur Religion und Literatur des Alten und Neuen Testaments 95. Göttingen: Vandenhoeck & Ruprecht, 1968.

Suhl, Alfred. *Die Funktion der alttestamentlichen Zitate und Anspielungen im Markusevangelium*. Gütersloh: Gütersloher Verlagshaus Gerd Mohn, 1965.

Synofzik, Ernst. *Die Gerichts- und Vergeltungsaussagen bei Paulus: Eine traditionsgeschichtliche Untersuchung*. Göttinger theologische Arbeiten 8. Göttingen: Vandenhoeck & Ruprecht, 1977.

Taeger, Jens-W. "'Gesiegt! O himmlische Musik des Wortes!': Zur Entfaltung des Siegesmotivs in den johanneischen Schriften." *Zeitschrift für die neutestamentliche Wissenschaft und die Kunde der älteren Kirche* 85 (1994): 47–52.

———. *Der Mensch und sein Heil: Studien zum Bild des Menschen und zur Sicht der Bekehrung bei Lukas*. Studien zum Neuen Testament 14. Gütersloh: G. Mohn, 1982.

Talbert, Charles H., ed. *Reimarus: Fragments*. Translated by Ralph S. Fraser. Edited by Leander Keck. Lives of Jesus Series 1. Philadelphia: Fortress, 1970.

Tannehill, Robert C. "The Disciples in Mark: The Function of a Narrative Role (1977)." In *The Interpretation of Mark*, edited by William R. Telford, 169–96. Studies in New Testament Interpretation. Edinburgh: T&T Clark, 1995.

———. "Israel in Luke-Acts." *Journal of Biblical Literature* 104 (1985): 69–85.

———. *The Narrative Unity of Luke-Acts: A Literary Interpretation*. 2 vols. Philadelphia: Fortress, 1986–90.

Taubes, Jacob, and Aleida Assmann. *The Political Theology of Paul*. Cultural Memory in the Present. Stanford, CA: Stanford University Press, 2004.

Teichmann, Frank. *Der Mensch und sein Tempel: Griechenland*. Stuttgart: Urachhaus, 1980.

Theissen, Gerd. "Das Doppelgebot der Liebe: Jüdische Ethik bei Jesus." In *Jesus als historische Gestalt: Beiträge zur Jesusforschung; Zum 60. Geburtstag von Gerd Theissen*, edited by Gerd Theissen and Annette Merz. Forschungen zur Religion und Literatur des Alten und Neuen Testaments 202. Göttingen: Vandenhoeck & Ruprecht, 2003.

———. "Ethos und Gemeinde im Jakobusbrief." In *Der Jakobusbrief: Beiträge zur Rehabilitierung der "strohernen Epistel,"* edited by Petra von Gemünden et al., 143–65. Beiträge zum Verstehen der Bibel 3. Münster: Lit-Verlag, 2003.

———. "Evangelienschreibung und Gemeindeleitung: Pragmatische Motive bei der Abfassung des Markusevangeliums." In *Antikes Judentum und frühes Christentum: Festschrift für Hartmut Stegemann zum 65. Geburtstag*, edited by Bernd Kollmann et al., 389–414. Beihefte zur Zeitschrift für die neutestamentliche Wissenschaft 97. Berlin: de Gruyter, 1999.

———. *The Gospels in Context: Social and Political History in the Synoptic Tradition*. Translated by Linda M. Maloney. Minneapolis: Fortress, 1991.

———. "Gruppenmessianismus: Überlegungen zum Ursprung der Kirche im Jüngerkreis Jesu." In *Jesus als historische Gestalt: Beiträge zur Jesusforschung; Zum 60. Geburtstag von Gerd Theissen*, edited by Gerd Theissen and Annette Merz, 225–81. Forschungen zur Religion und Literatur des Alten und Neuen Testaments 202. Göttingen: Vandenhoeck & Ruprecht, 2003.

———. "Hellenisten und Hebräer (Apg 6,1–6): Gab es eine Spaltung in der Urgemeinde?" In *Geschichte—Tradition—Reflexion: Festschrift für Martin Hengel zum 70. Geburtstag*, edited by Hubert Cancik et al., 323–43. Tübingen: Mohr, 1996.

———. *Die Jesusbewegung: Sozialgeschichte einer Revolution der Werte*. Gütersloh: Gütersloher Verlagshaus, 2004.

———. *Lokalkolorit und Zeitgeschichte in den Evangelien: Ein Beitrag zur Geschichte der synoptischen Tradition*. Freiburg: Universitätsverlag; Göttingen: Vandenhoeck & Ruprecht, 1989.

———. *The Miracle Stories of the Early Christian Tradition*. Translated by Francis McDonagh. Philadelphia: Fortress, 1983.

———. "Nächstenliebe und Egalität." In *Der Jakobusbrief: Beiträge zur Rehabilitierung der "strohernen Epistel,"* edited by Petra von Gemünden et al., 120–42. Beiträge zum Verstehen der Bibel 3. Münster: Lit-Verlag, 2003.

———. *Psychological Aspects of Pauline Theology*. Translated by John P. Galvin. Philadelphia: Fortress, 1987.

———. "Das Reinheitslogion Mk 7,15 und die Trennung von Juden und Christen." In *Jesus als historische Gestalt: Beiträge zur Jesusforschung; Zum 60. Geburtstag von Gerd Theissen*, edited by Gerd Theissen and Annette Merz, 73–89. Forschungen zur Religion und Literatur des Alten und Neuen Testaments 202. Göttingen: Vandenhoeck & Ruprecht, 2003.

———. *The Religion of the Earliest Churches: Creating a Symbolic World*. Translated by John Bowden. Minneapolis: Fortress, 1999.

———. "Röm 9–11—Eine Auseinandersetzung des Paulus mit Israel und sich selbst: Versuch einer psychologischen Auslegung." In *Fair Play: Diversity and Conflicts in Early Christianity; Essays in Honour of Heikki Räisänen*, edited by Heikki Räisänen et al. Supplements to Novum Testamentum 103. Leiden: Brill, 2002.

———. "Urchristlicher Liebeskommunismus." In *Text and Contexts: Biblical Texts in Their Textual and Situational Contexts; Essays in Honor of Lars Hartman*, edited by Tord Fornberg et al., 689–712. Oslo: Scandinavian University Press, 1995.

———. "Vom Davidssohn zum Weltherrscher: Pagane und jüdische Endzeiterwartungen im Spiegel des Matthäusevangeliums." In *Das Ende der Tage und die Gegenwart des Heils*, edited by E.-M. Becker and W. Fenske, 145–64. Arbeiten zur Geschichte des antiken Judentums und des Urchristentums 44. Leiden: Brill, 1999.

———. "Wanderradikalismus." In *Studien zur Soziologie des Urchristentums*, edited by Gerd Theissen, 79–105. Wissenschaftliche Untersuchungen zum Neuen Testament 19. Tübingen: Mohr, 1992.

Theissen, Gerd, and Annette Merz. *The Historical Jesus: A Comprehensive Guide*. Translated by John Bowden. Minneapolis: Fortress, 1998.

Theissen, Gerd, and Dagmar Winter. *The Quest for the Plausible Jesus: The Question of Criteria*. Translated by M. Eugene Boring. Louisville: Westminster John Knox, 2002.

Theobald, Michael. "'Ich sah den Satan aus dem Himmel stürzen': Überlieferungskritische Beobachtungen zu Lk 10,18–20." *Biblische Zeitschrift* 49 (2005): 174–90.

———. "Der Jünger, den Jesus liebte." In *Geschichte—Tradition—Reflexion: Festschrift für Martin Hengel zum 70. Geburtstag*, edited by Hubert Cancik et al., 219–55. Tübingen: Mohr, 1996.

———. *Der Römerbrief*. Darmstadt: Wissenschaftliche Buchgesellschaft, 2000.

———. "Vom Text zum 'lebendigen Wort' (Hebr 4,12)." In *Jesus Christus als die Mitte der Schrift: Studien zur Hermeneutik des Evangeliums*, edited by Christof Landmesser et al., 751–90. Beihefte zur Zeitschrift für die neutestamentliche Wissenschaft 86. Berlin: de Gruyter, 1997.

Thomas, J. C. *Footwashing in John 13 and the Johannine Community*. Journal for the Study of the New Testament: Supplement Series 61. Sheffield: Sheffield Academic, 1991.

Thompson, James. *The Beginnings of Christian Philosophy: The Epistle to the Hebrews*. The Catholic Biblical Quarterly Monograph Series 13. Washington, DC: Catholic Biblical Association of America, 1982.

Thompson, Leonard L. *The Book of Revelation: Apocalypse and Empire*. Oxford: Oxford University Press, 1990.

Thompson, Marianne Meye. *The God of the Gospel of John*. Grand Rapids: Eerdmans, 2001.

———. *The Incarnate Word: Perspectives on Jesus in the Fourth Gospel*. Peabody, MA: Hendrickson, 1993.

———. "The Living Father." In *God the Father in the Gospel of John*, edited by A. Reinhartz, 19–31. Semeia 85. Atlanta: Society of Biblical Literature, 1999.

Thompson, Michael B. *The New Perspective on Paul*. Grove Biblical Series 26. Cambridge: Grove Books, 2002.

Thüsing, Wilhelm. *Die Erhöhung und Verherrlichung Jesu im Johannesevangelium*. Neutestamentliche Abhandlungen 21.1, 2. Münster: Aschendorff, 1979.

———. *Gott und Christus in der paulinischen Soteriologie*. 3rd ed. Münster: Aschendorff, 1986.

———. *Die Neutestamentlichen Theologien und Jesus Christus*. 3 vols. Düsseldorf: Patmos, 1981–99.

———. *Per Christum in Deum: Studien zum Verhältnis von Christozentrik und Theozentrik in den paulinischen hauptbriefen*. 2nd ed. Neutestamentliche Abhandlungen, n.F., 1. Münster: Aschendorff, 1969.

Thyen, Hartwig. *Das Johannesevangelium*. Handbuch zum Neuen Testament 6. Tübingen: Mohr, 2005.

Tilborg, Sjef van. *Imaginative Love in John*. Biblical Interpretation Series 2. Leiden: Brill, 1993.

———. *Reading John in Ephesus*. Supplements to Novum Testamentum 83. Leiden: Brill, 1996.

Tillich, Paul. *Systematic Theology*. Vol. 1, *Reason and Revelation: Being and God*. Chicago: University of Chicago Press, 1951.

Tilly, Michael. *Einfuhrung in die Septuaginta*. 2004.

———. *Johannes der Täufer und die Biographie der Propheten: Die synoptische Täuferüberlieferung und das jüdische Prophetenbild zur Zeit des Täufers*. Beiträge zur Wissenschaft vom Alten und Neuen Testament 17. Stuttgart: Kohlhammer, 1994.

Tiwald, M. "Der Wanderradikalismus als Brücke zum historischen Jesus." In *The Sayings Source Q and the Historical Jesus*, edited by Andreas Lindemann, 523–34. Bibliotheca ephemeridum theologicarum lovaniensium 158. Louvain: Leuven University Press, 2001.

Tödt, H. E. *The Son of Man in the Synoptic Tradition*. Translated by Dorothea M. Barton. New Testament Library. Philadelphia: Westminster, 1965.

Tolmie, D. F. "Salvation as Redemption." In *Salvation in the New Testament: Perspectives on Soteriology*, edited by J. G. Van der Watt, 247–69. Supplements to Novum Testamentum 121. Leiden: Brill, 2005.

Toorn, K. van der, Bob Becking, and Pieter Willem van der Horst, eds. *Dictionary of Deities and Demons in the Bible*. Leiden: Brill, 1999.

Trilling, Wolfgang. *Das wahre Israel: Studien zur Theologie des Matthäus Evangeliums*. 3rd ed. Studien zum Alten und Neuen Testament 10. Munich: Kösel, 1964.

———. *Der Zweite Brief an die Thessalonicher*. Evangelisch-katholischer Kommentar zum Neuen Testament 14. Neukirchen-Vluyn: Neukirchener Verlag, 1980.

Trobisch, David. *The First Edition of the New Testament*. Oxford: Oxford University Press, 2000.

Troeltsch, Ernst. "Historical and Dogmatic Method in Theology." In *Religion in History*, edited by James Luther Adams and Ernst Troeltsch, 11–32. Translated by James Luther Adams and Walter E. Bense. Minneapolis: Fortress, 1991.

Tröger, Karl-Wolfgang. "Ja oder Nein zur Welt: War der Evangelist Johannes Christ oder Gnostiker?" *Theologia Viatorum* 7 (1976): 61–80.

Trummer, P. "Corpus Paulinum—Corpus Pastorale." In *Paulus in den neutestamentlichen Spätschriften: Zur Paulusrezeption im Neuen Testament*, edited by Karl Kertelge, 122–45. Quaestiones disputatae 89. Freiburg i.B.: Herder, 1981.

———. *Die Paulustradition der Pastoralbriefe*. Beiträge zur biblischen Exegese und Theologie 8. Frankfurt: Lang, 1978.

Trunk, Dieter. *Der messianische Heiler: Eine redaktions- und religionsgeschichtliche Studie zu den Exorzismen im Matthäusevangelium*. Herders biblische Studien 3. Freiburg: Herder, 1994.

Tsuji, Manabu. *Glaube zwischen Vollkommenheit und Verweltlichung: Eine Untersuchung zur literarischen Gestalt und zur inhaltlichen Kohärenz des Jakobusbriefes*. Wissenschaftliche Untersuchungen zum Neuen Testament 2.93. Tübingen: Mohr, 1997.

Tuckett, Christopher M. "Q 12,8 Once Again—'Son of Man' or 'I'?" In *From Quest to Q: Festschrift James M. Robinson*, edited by Jon Ma Asgeirsson et al., 171–88. Bibliotheca ephemeridum theologicarum lovaniensium 146. Louvain: Leuven University Press, 2000.

———. *Q and the History of Early Christianity*. Edinburgh: T&T Clark, 1996.

———. "The Temptation Narrative in Q." In *The Four Gospels, 1992: Festschrift Frans Neirynck*, edited by Frans van Segbroeck et al., 1:479–507. 3 vols. Bibliotheca ephemeridum theologicarum lovaniensium 100. Louvain: Leuven University Press, 1992.

Übelacker, W. "Paraenesis or Paraclesis." In *Early Christian Paraenesis in Context*, edited by Troels Engberg-Pedersen and James M. Starr, 319–52. Beihefte zur Zeitschrift für die neutestamentliche Wissenschaft und die Kunde der älteren Kirche 125. Berlin: de Gruyter, 2004.

Udoh, F. E. "Paul's View on the Law." *Novum Testamentum* 42 (2000): 214–37.

Uebele, Wolfram. *"Viele Verführer sind in die Welt ausgegangen": Die Gegner in den Briefen des Ignatius von Antiochien und in den Johannesbriefen*. Beiträge zur Wissenschaft vom Alten und Neuen Testament 151. Stuttgart: Kohlhammer, 2001.

Umbach, Helmut. *In Christus getauft, von der Sünde befreit: Die Gemeinde als sündenfreier Raum bei Paulus*. Göttingen: Vandenhoeck & Ruprecht, 1999.

Urner, C. "Kaiser Domitian im Urteil antiker literarischer Quellen und moderner Forschung." PhD diss., Universität Augsburg, 1993.

Vahrenhorst, M. *"Ihr sollt überhaupt nicht schwören": Matthäus im halachischen Diskurs*. Wissenschaftliche Monographien zum Alten und Neuen Testament 95. Neukirchen: Neukirchener Verlag, 2002.

Van der Watt, J. G. "Ethics and Ethos in the Gospel according to John." *Zeitschrift für die neutestamentliche Wissenschaft und die Kunde der älteren Kirche* 97 (2006): 147–76.

———. *Family of the King: Dynamics of Metaphor in the Gospel according to John*. Biblical Interpretation Series 47. Leiden: Brill, 2000.

———. *An Introduction to the Johannine Gospel and Letters*. London: T&T Clark, 2007.

———. "Salvation in the Gospel of John." In *Salvation in the New Testament: Perspectives on Soteriology*, edited by J. G. Van der Watt, 101–28. Supplements to Novum Testamentum 121. Leiden: Brill, 2005.

Vegge, Tor. *Paulus und das antike Schulwesen: Schule und Bildung des Paulus*. Beihefte zur Zeitschrift für die neutestamentliche Wissenschaft und die Kunde der älteren Kirche 134. Berlin: de Gruyter, 2006.

Vermès, Géza. "Hanina ben Dosa." In *Post-biblical Jewish studies*, edited by Géza Vermès, 178–214. Studies in Judaism in Late Antiquity 8. Leiden: Brill, 1975.

———. *Jesus the Jew: A Historian's Reading of the Gospels*. Philadelphia: Fortress, 1973.

———. *Die Passion: Die wahre Geschichte der letzten Tage im Leben Jesu*. Darmstadt: Primus, 2005.

Verner, David C. *The Household of God: The Social World of the Pastoral Epistles*. Society of Biblical Literature Dissertation Series 71. Chico, CA: Scholars Press, 1983.

Vielhauer, Philipp. *Geschichte der urchristlichen Literatur: Einleitung in das Neue Testament, die Apokryphen und die Apostolischen Väter*. Berlin: de Gruyter, 1975.

———. "Gottesreich und Menschensohn in der Verkündigung Jesu." In *Aufsätze zum Neuen Testament*, edited by Philipp Vielhauer, 55–91. Theologische Bücherei: Neudrucke und Berichte aus dem 20. Jahrhundert 31. Munich: Kaiser, 1965.

———. "On the 'Paulinism' of Acts." In *Studies in Luke-Acts*, edited by Leander Keck and J. Louis Martyn, 33–50. Nashville: Abingdon, 1966.

Viering, F. *Die Bedeutung der Auferstehungsbotschaft für den Glauben an Jesus Christus*. Berlin: Evangelische Verlagsanstalt, 1967.

Vittinghoff, F. "'Christianus sum': Das 'Verbrechen' von Außenseitern der römischen Gesellschaft." *Historia* 33 (1984): 331–57.

Vogel, Manuel. *Das Heil des Bundes: Bundestheologie im Frühjudentum und im frühen Christentum*. Texte und Arbeiten zum neutestamentlichen Zeitalter 18. Tübingen: Francke, 1996.

———. *Commentatio Mortis: 2Kor 5,1–10 auf dem Hintergrund antiker Ars Moriendi*. Forschungen zur Religion und Literatur des Alten und Neuen Testaments 124. Göttingen: Vandenhoeck & Ruprecht, 2006.

Vogels, Heinz-Jürgen. *Christi Abstieg ins Totenreich und das Läuterungsgericht an den Toten: Eine bibeltheologisch-dogmatische Untersuchung zum Glaubensartikel "descendit ad inferos."* Freiburger theologische Studien 102. Freiburg: Herder, 1976.

Vögtle, Anton. *Die "Gretchenfrage" des Menschensohnproblems: Bilanz und Perspektive*. Quaestiones disputatae 152. Freiburg i.B.: Herder, 1994.

Vollenweider, Samuel. *Freiheit als neue Schöpfung: Eine Untersuchung zur Eleutheria bei Paulus und in seiner Umwelt*. Forschungen zur Religion und Literatur des Alten und Neuen Testaments 147. Göttingen: Vandenhoeck & Ruprecht, 1989.

———. "Der Geist Gottes als Selbst der Glaubenden." *Zeitschrift für Theologie und Kirche* 93 (1996): 163–92.

———. "'Ich sah den Satan wie einen Blitz vom Himmel fallen' (Lk 10,18)." *Zeitschrift für die neutestamentliche Wissenschaft und die Kunde der älteren Kirche* 79 (1988): 187–203.

———. "Die Metamorphose des Gottessohnes." In *Das Urchristentum in seiner literarischen Geschichte: Festschrift für Jürgen Becker zum 65. Geburtstag*, edited by Ulrich Mell and Ulrich B. Müller, 107–31. Beihefte zur Zeitschrift für die neutestamentliche Wissenschaft 100. Berlin: de Gruyter, 1999.

———. "Politische Theologie im Philipperbrief?" In *Paulus und Johannes: Exegetische Studien zur paulinischen und johanneischen Theologie und Literatur*, edited by Dieter Sänger and Ulrich Mell, 457–69. Wissenschaftliche Untersuchungen zum Neuen Testament 198. Tübingen: Mohr Siebeck, 2006.

———. "Der 'Raub' der Gottgleichheit: Ein religionsgeschichtlicher Vorschlag zu Phil 2,6(–11)." *New Testament Studies* 45 (1999): 413–33.

———. "Zwischen Monotheismus und Engelchristologie." *Zeitschrift für Theologie und Kirche* 99 (2002): 21–44.

Vorster, Willem S. "Markus—Sammler, Redaktor, Autor oder Erzähler?" In *Der Erzähler des Evangeliums: Methodische Neuansätze in der Markusforschung*, edited by Ferdinand Hahn, 93–136. Stuttgarter Bibelstudien 118/119. Stuttgart: Verlag Katholisches Bibelwerk, 1985.

Vos, Johannes Sijko. *Traditionsgeschichtliche Untersuchungen zur Paulinischen Pneumatologie*. Assen: Van Gorcum, 1973.

Voss, Florian. *Das Wort vom Kreuz und die menschliche Vernunft: Eine Untersuchung zur Soteriologie des 1. Korintherbriefes*. Forschungen zur Religion und Literatur des Alten und Neuen Testaments 199. Göttingen: Vandenhoeck & Ruprecht, 2002.

Vouga, François. "Habt Glauben an Gott." In *Text and Contexts: Biblical Texts in Their Textual and Situational Contexts: Essays in Honor of Lars Hartman*, edited by Tord Fornberg et al., 93–109. Oslo: Scandinavian University Press, 1995.

Wagener, Ulrike. *Die Ordnung des "Hauses Gottes": Der Ort von Frauen in der Ekklesiologie und Ethik der Pastoralbriefe*. Wissenschaftliche Untersuchungen zum Neuen Testament 2.65. Tübingen: Mohr, 1994.

Wainwright, Arthur. *Mysterious Apocalypse: Interpreting the Book of Revelation*. Nashville: Abingdon, 1993.

Walaskay, W. *"And So We Came to Rome": The Political Perspective of St. Luke*. Society for New Testament Studies Monograph Series 49. Cambridge: Cambridge University Press, 1983.

Walker, R. *Die Heilsgeschichte im ersten Evangelium*. Forschungen zur Religion und Literatur des Alten und Neuen Testaments 91. Göttingen: Vandenhoeck & Ruprecht, 1967.

Walter, Nikolaus. "Hellenistische Eschatologie bei Paulus." *Theologische Quartalschrift* 176 (1996).

———. "Leibliche Auferstehung? Zur Frage der Hellenisierung der Auferweckungshoffnung bei Paulus." In *Paulus, Apostel Jesu Christi: Festschrift für Günter Klein zum 70. Geburtstag*, edited by Günter Klein and Michael Trowitzsch, 109–27. Tübingen: Mohr, 1998.

Walter, Nikolaus, et al., eds. *Die Briefe an die Philipper, Thessalonicher und an Philemon*. Das Neue Testament Deutsch 8.2. Göttingen: Vandenhoeck & Ruprecht, 1998.

Wander, Bernd. *Gottesfürchtige und Sympathisanten: Studien zum heidnischen Umfeld von Diasporasynagogen*. Wissenschaftliche Untersuchungen zum Neuen Testament 104. Tübingen: Mohr, 1998.

———. *Trennungsprozesse zwischen frühem Christentum und Judentum im 1. Jahrhundert nach Christus: Datierbare Abfolgen zwischen der Hinrichtung Jesu und der Zerstörung des Jerusalemer Tempels*. Texte und Arbeiten zum neutestamentlichen Zeitalter 16. Tübingen: Francke, 1994.

Wanke, Joachim. *Beobachtungen zum Eucharistieverständnis des Lukas auf Grund der lukanischen Mahlberichte*. Erfurter theologische Studien 8. Leipzig: Sankt-Benno-Verlag, 1973.

———. *Die Emmauserzahlüng: Eine redaktionsgeschichtliche Untersuchung*. Erfurter theologische Studien 31. Leipzig: Sankt-Benno-Verlag, 1973.

Waschke, Ernst-Joachim. *Der Gesalbte: Studien zur alttestamentlichen Theologie*. Beihefte zur Zeitschrift für die alttestamentliche Wissenschaft 306. Berlin: de Gruyter, 2001.

Wasserberg, G. *Aus Israel's Mitte—Heil für die Welt*. Beihefte zur Zeitschrift für die neutestamentliche Wissenschaft und die Kunde der älteren Kirche 82. Berlin: de Gruyter, 1998.

Watzlawick, Paul. *The Invented Reality: How Do We Know What We Believe We Know? Contributions to Constructivism*. New York: Norton, 1984.

Weber, Reinhard. "Christologie und 'Messiasgeheimnis': Ihr Zusammenhang und Stellenwert in den Darstellungsintentionen des Markus." *Evangelische Theologie* 43 (1983): 108–25.

———. "Die Geschichte des Gesetzes und des Ich in Römer 7,7–8,4." *Neue Zeitschrift für systematische Theologie* 29 (1987): 147–79.

———. *Das Gesetz im hellenistischen Judentum: Studien zum Verständnis und zur Funktion der Thora von Demetrios bis Pseudo-Phokylides*. Arbeiten zur Religion und Geschichte des Urchristentums 10. Frankfurt: Lang, 2000.

———. *Das "Gesetz" bei Philon von Alexandrien und Flavius Josephus: Studien zum Verständnis und zur Funktion der Thora bei den beiden Hauptzeugen des hellenistischen Judentums*. Arbeiten zur Religion und Geschichte des Urchristentums 11. Frankfurt: Lang, 2001.

Wechsler, Andreas. *Geschichtsbild und Apostelstreit: Eine forschungsgeschichtliche und exegetische Studie über den antiochenischen Zwischenfall (Gal 2,11–14)*. Beihefte zur Zeitschrift für die neutestamentliche Wissenschaft 62. Berlin: de Gruyter, 1991.

Wedderburn, A. J. M. "Eine neuere Paulusperspektive?" In *Biographie und Persönlichkeit des Paulus*, edited by E.-M. Becker and Peter Pilhofer, 46–64. Wissenschaftliche Untersuchungen zum Neuen Testament 187. Tübingen: Mohr Siebeck, 2005.

Weder, Hans. "Die Energie des Evangeliums: Hermeneutische Überlegungen zur Wirklichkeit des Wortes." *Zeitschrift für Theologie und Kirche* 9 (1995): 94–119.

———. "'Evangelium Jesu Christi' (Mk 1,1) und 'Evangelium Gottes' (Mk 1,14)." In *Die Mitte des Neuen Testaments: Einheit und Vielfalt neutestamentlicher Theologie; Festschrift für Eduard Schweizer zum siebzigsten Geburtstag*, edited by Ulrich Luz and Hans Weder, 399–411. Göttingen: Vandenhoeck & Ruprecht, 1983.

———. *Gegenwart und Gottesherrschaft: Überlegungen zum Zeitverständnis bei Jesus und im frühen Christentum*. Biblisch-theologische Studien 20. Neukirchen-Vluyn: Neukirchener Verlag, 1993.

———. "Gesetz und Sünde: Gedanken zu einem qualitativen Sprung im Denken des Paulus." In *Einblicke ins Evangelium: Exegetische Beiträge zur neutestamentlichen Hermeneutik; Gesammelte Aufsätze aus den Jahren 1980–1991*, edited by Hans Weder, 171–82. Göttingen: Vandenhoeck & Ruprecht, 1992.

———. *Die Gleichnisse Jesu als Metaphern: Traditions- und redaktionsgeschichtliche Analysen und Interpretationen*. Göttingen: Vandenhoeck & Ruprecht, 1978.

———. *Das Kreuz Jesu bei Paulus: Ein Versuch, über den Geschichtsbezug des christlichen Glaubens nachzudenken*. Göttingen: Vandenhoeck & Ruprecht, 1981.

———. "Die Menschwerdung Gottes." In *Einblicke ins Evangelium: Exegetische Beiträge zur neutestamentlichen Hermeneutik; Gesammelte Aufsätze aus den Jahren 1980–1991*, edited by Hans Weder, 363–400. Göttingen: Vandenhoeck & Ruprecht, 1992.

———. "Der Mythos vom Logos." In *Mythos und Rationalität*, edited by Hans Heinrich Schmid, 44–80. Gütersloh: Güterloher Verlagshaus, 1988.

———. "Die Normativität der Freiheit." In *Paulus, Apostel Jesu Christi: Festschrift für Günter*

Klein zum 70. Geburtstag, edited by Michael Trowitzsch, 129–45. Tübingen: Mohr, 1998.

———. *Die "Rede der Reden": Eine Auslegung der Bergpredigt heute*. 2nd ed. Zürich: Theologischer Verlag, 1987.

———. "Wunder Jesu und Wundergeschichten." *Verkündigung und Forschung* 29 (1984): 25–49.

Wehnert, Jürgen. "Die Auswanderung der Jerusalemer Christen nach Pella—historisches Faktum oder theologische Konstruktion?" *Zeitschrift für Kirchengeschichte* 102 (1991): 231–55.

———. *Die Reinheit des christlichen Gottesvolkes aus Juden und Heiden: Studien zum historischen und theologischen Hintergrund des sogenannten Aposteldekrets*. Forschungen zur Religion und Literatur des Alten und Neuen Testaments 173. Göttingen: Vandenhoeck & Ruprecht, 1997.

Weigandt, P. "Der Doketismus im Urchristentum und in der theologischen Entwicklung des zweiten Jahrhunderts." PhD diss., Ruprecht-Karls-Universität Heidelberg, 1961.

Weiher, Anton, ed. *Homerische Hymnen: Griechisch und deutsch*. 6th ed. Sammlung Tusculum. Munich: Artemis, 1989.

Weischedel, Wilhelm. *Der Gott der Philosophen: Grundlegung einer philosophischen Theologie im Zeitalter des Nihilismus*. 3rd ed. Darmstadt: Wissenschaftliche Buchgesellschaft, 1994.

Weiser, A. "'Reich Gottes' in der Apostelgeschichte." In *Der Treue Gottes trauen: Beiträge zum Werk des Lukas; für Gerhard Schneider*, edited by Claus Bussmann and Walter Radl, 127–35. Freiburg i.B.: Herder, 1991.

Weiser, Alfons. *Die Apostelgeschichte*. Ökumenischer Taschenbuch-Kommentar zum Neuen Testament 5. Würzburg: Echter Verlag, 1981.

———. *Die Knechtsgleichnisse der synoptischen Evangelien*. Studien zum Alten und Neuen Testament 29. Munich: Kösel, 1971.

———. *Der zweite Brief an Timotheus*. Evangelisch-katholischer Kommentar zum Neuen Testament 16.1. Neukirchen-Vluyn: Neukirchener Verlag, 2003.

Weiss, Hans Friedrich. *Der Brief an die Hebräer*. 15th ed. Kritisch-exegetischer Kommentar über das Neue Testament 13. Göttingen: Vandenhoeck und Ruprecht, 1991.

———. *Kerygma und Geschichte*. Berlin: Akademie Verlag, 1983.

Weiss, Johannes. *Earliest Christianity: A History of the Period A.D. 30–150*. Translated by Frederick C. Grant. 2 vols. New York: Harper, 1937–59.

———. *Jesus's Proclamation of the Kingdom of God*. Translated by Richard H. Hiers and David Larrimore Holland. Lives of Jesus Series. Philadelphia: Fortress, 1971.

Weiss, W. *"Eine neue Lehre in Vollmacht."* Beihefte zur Zeitschrift für die neutestamentliche Wissenschaft und die Kunde der älteren Kirche 52. Berlin: de Gruyter, 1989.

Welck, Christian. *Erzählte Zeichen: Die Wundergeschichten des Johannesevangeliums literarisch untersucht; mit einem Ausblick auf Joh 21*. Wissenschaftliche Untersuchungen zum Neuen Testament 69. Tübingen: Mohr, 1994.

Wellhausen, Julius. *Kritische Analyse der Apostelgeschichte*. Berlin: Weidmann, 1914.

Welzer, Harald. "Das soziale Gedächtnis." In *Das soziale Gedächtnis: Geschichte, Erinnerung, Tradierung*, edited by Harald Welzer, 9–21. Hamburg: Hamburger Edition, 2001.

Wengst, Klaus. *Bedrängte Gemeinde und verherrlichter Christus: Ein Versuch über das Johannesevangelium*. 4th ed. Munich: Kaiser, 1992.

———. *Christologische Formeln und Lieder des Urchristentums*. Gütersloh: Gütersloher Verlagshaus, 1972.

———. "Gesetz und Gnade." In *Ja und Nein: Christliche Theologie im Angesicht Israels; Festschrift zum 70. Geburtstag von Wolfgang Schrage*, edited by Klaus Wengst et al., 171–82. Neukirchen-Vluyn: Neukirchener Verlag, 1998.

———. *Das Johannesevangelium*. Theologischer Kommentar zum Neuen Testament 4.1–2. Stuttgart: Kohlhammer, 2000–2001.

———. *Pax Romana: And the Peace of Jesus Christ*. Philadelphia: Fortress, 1987.

Wenschkewitz, H. "Die Spiritualisierung der Kultusbegriffe." *Angelos* 4 (1932): 74–151.

Westerholm, Stephen. *Perspectives Old and New on Paul: The "Lutheran" Paul and His Critics*. Grand Rapids: Eerdmans, 2004.

Wetter, Gillis Petersson. *Charis: Ein Beitrag zur Geschichte des ältesten Christentums*. Untersuchungen zum Neuen Testament 5. Leipzig: Brandstetter, 1913.

Wheelwright, Philip Ellis. *The Burning Fountain: A Study in the Language of Symbolism*. 2nd ed. Bloomington: Indiana University Press, 1968.

White, Joel R. "Baptized on account of the Dead." *Journal of Biblical Literature* 116 (1997): 487–99.

Wibbing, Siegfried. *Die Tugend- und Lasterkataloge im Neuen Testament und ihre Traditionsgeschichte unter besonderer Berücksichtigung der Qumran-Texte*. Beihefte zur Zeitschrift für die neutestamentliche Wissenschaft 25. Berlin: Töpelmann, 1959.

Wider, David. *Theozentrik und Bekenntnis: Untersuchungen zur Theologie des Redens Gottes im Hebräerbrief*. Beihefte zur Zeitschrift für die neutestamentliche Wissenschaft und die Kunde der älteren Kirche 87. Berlin: de Gruyter, 1997.

Wiefel, Wolfgang. *Das Evangelium nach Matthäus*. Theologischer Handkommentar zum Neuen Testament 1. Berlin: Evangelische Verlagsanstalt, 1998.

———. "Die Hauptrichtung des Wandels im eschatologischen Denken des Paulus." *Theologische Zeitschrift* 30 (1974): 65–81.

Wilckens, Ulrich. "Die Auferstehung Jesu: Historisches Zeugnis—Theologie—Glaubenserfahrung." *Pastoraltheologie* 85 (1996): 102–12.

———. *Der Brief an die Römer*. Neukirchener-Vluyn: Neukirchener Verlag, 1978.

———. *Das Johannesevangelium*. Das Neue Testament Deutsch 4. Göttingen: Vandenhoeck & Ruprecht, 1998.

———. *Die Missionsreden der Apostelgeschichte*. Wissenschaftliche Monographien zum Alten und Neuen Testament 5. Neukirchen: Neukirchener Verlag, 1974.

———. "Monotheismus und Christologie." In *Der Sohn Gottes und seine Gemeinde: Studien zur Theologie der Johanneischen Schriften*, edited by Ulrich Wilckens, 126–35. Forschungen zur Literatur des Alten und Neuen Testaments 200. Göttingen: Vandenhoeck & Ruprecht, 2003.

———. "Der Paraklet und die Kirche." In *Kirche: Festschrift für Günther Bornkamm zum 75. Geburtstag*, edited by Dieter Lührmann and Georg Strecker, 185–283. Tübingen: Mohr, 1980.

———. *Resurrection: Biblical Testimony to the Resurrection; An Historical Examination and Explanation*. Translated by A. M. Stewart. Atlanta: John Knox, 1978.

———. *Theologie des Neuen Testaments*. Band 1, *Geschichte der urchristlichen Theologie*. Teilband 1, *Geschichte des Wirkens Jesu in Galiläa*. 2nd rev. ed. 4 vols. Neukirchen-Vluyn: Neukirchener Verlag, 2005.

———. *Theologie des Neuen Testaments*. Band 1, *Geschichte der urchristlichen Theologie*. Teilband 2, *Jesu Tod und Auferstehung und die Entstehung der Kirche aus Juden und Heiden*. 4 vols. Neukirchen-Vluyn: Neukirchener Verlag, 2003.

———. "Der Ursprung der Überlieferung der Erscheinungen des Auferstandenen." In *Zur neutestamentlichen Überlieferung von der Aufersteung Jesu*, edited by Paul Hoffmann, 139–93. Darmstadt: Wissenschaftliche Buchgesellschaft, 1988.

Wilkens, Wilhelm. *Die Entstehungsgeschichte des vierten Evangeliums*. Zollikon: Evangelischer Verlag, 1958.

Williamson, Ronald. *Philo and the Epistle to the Hebrews*. Arbeiten zur Literatur und Geschichte des hellenistischen Judentums 4. Leiden: Brill, 1970.

Windisch, Hans. "Das Problem des paulinischen Imperativs." *Zeitschrift für die neutestamentliche Wissenschaft und die Kunde der älteren Kirche* 23 (1924): 265–81.

———. *Taufe und Sünde im ältesten Christentum bis auf Origenes: Ein Beitrag zur altchristlichen Dogmengeschichte*. Tübingen: Mohr, 1908.

———. *Der zweite Korintherbrief*. 9th ed. Kritisch-exegetischer Kommentar über das Neue Testament 6. Göttingen: Vandenhoeck & Ruprecht, 1924.

Windisch, Hans, and Herbert Preisker. *Die katholischen Briefe*. 3rd ed. Handbuch zum Neuen Testament 15. Tübingen: Mohr, 1951.

Wink, Walter. "Jesus as Magician." *Union Seminary Quarterly Review* 30 (1974): 3–14.

Winninge, Mikael. *Sinners and the Righteous: A Comparative Study of the Psalms of Solomon and Paul's Letters*. Coniectanea biblica: New Testament Series 26. Stockholm: Almqvist & Wiksell, 1995.

Winter, M. *Das Vermächtnis Jesu und die Abschiedsworte der Väter*. Forschungen zur Religion und Literatur des Alten und Neuen Testaments 161. Göttingen: Vandenhoeck & Ruprecht, 1994.

Wischmeyer, Oda. "Das Gebot der Nächstenliebe bei Paulus." *Biblische Zeitschrift* 30 (1986): 153–87.

———. *Der höchste Weg: Das 13. Kapitel des 1. Korintherbriefes*. Studien zum Neuen Testament 13. Gütersloh: Gütersloher Verlagshaus, 1981.

Wise, Michael O., et al., eds. *The Dead Sea Scrolls: A New English Translation*. New York: HarperCollins, 1996.

Witherington, Ben. *Jesus the Sage: The Pilgrimage of Wisdom*. Minneapolis: Fortress, 1994.

Witulski, Thomas. "Gegenwart und Zukunft in den eschatologischen Konzeptionen des Kolosser- und Epheserbriefes." *Zeitschrift für die neutestament-*

liche Wissenschaft und die Kunde der älteren Kirche 96 (2005): 211–42.

———. *Kaiserkult in Kleinasien: Die Entwicklung der kultisch-religiösen Kaiserverehrung in der römischen Provinz Asia von Augustus bis Antoninus Pius*. Novum Testamentum et Orbis Antiquus 63. Göttingen: Vandenhoeck & Ruprecht, 2007.

Wolff, Christian. *Der erste Brief des Paulus an die Korinther*. Theologischer Handkommentar zum Neuen Testament 7. Leipzig: Evangelische Verlagsanstalt, 1996.

Wolff, Hans Walter. *Anthropology of the Old Testament*. Philadelphia: Fortress, 1974.

Wolter, Michael. "Der Apostel und seine Gemeinden als Teilhaber am Leidensgeschick Jesu Christi." *New Testament Studies* 36 (1990): 535–57.

———. *Der Brief an die Kolosser; Der Brief an Philemon*. Ökumenischer Taschenbuchkommentar zum Neuen Testament 12. Gütersloh: Gütersloher Verlagshaus Gerd Mohn, 1993.

———. "Christliches Ethos nach der Offenbarung des Johannes." In *Studien zur Johannesoffenbarung und ihrer Auslegung: Festschrift für Otto Böcher zum 70. Geburtstag*, edited by Friedrich Wilhelm Horn and Michael Wolter. Neukirchen-Vluyn: Neukirchener Verlag, 2005.

———. "Die ethische Identität christlicher Gemeinden in neutestamentlicher Zeit." In *Marburger Jahrbuch Theologie*, vol. 13, *Woran orientiert sich Ethik?* edited by Wilfried Härle and Reiner Preul, 61–90. Marburger Theologische Studien 67. Marburg: Elwert, 2001.

———. "Ethos und Identität in paulinischen Gemeinden." *New Testament Studies* 43 (1997): 430–44.

———. "'Gericht' und 'Heil' bei Jesus von Nazareth und Johannes dem Täufer." In *Der historische Jesus*, edited by J. Schröter and R. Bruckner, 355–92. Beihefte zur Zeitschrift für die neutestamentliche Wissenschaft und die Kunde der älteren Kirche 114. Berlin: de Gruyter, 2002.

———. "Israels Zukunft und die Parusieverzögerung bei Lukas." In *Eschatologie und Schöpfung*, edited by M. Evang et al., 405–26. Beihefte zur Zeitschrift für die neutestamentliche Wissenschaft 89. Berlin: de Gruyter, 1997.

———. "Die Juden und die Obrigkeit bei Lukas." In *Ja und Nein: Christliche Theologie im Angesicht Israels; Festschrift zum 70. Geburtstag von Wolfgang Schrage*, edited by Klaus Wengst et al., 277–90. Neukirchen-Vluyn: Neukirchener Verlag, 1998.

———. "Das lukanische Doppelwerk als Epochengeschichte." In *Die Apostelgeschichte und die hellenistische Geschichtsschreibung*, edited by Cilliers Breytenbach and Jens Schröter, 253–84. Ancient Judaism and Early Christianity 57. Leiden: Brill, 2004.

———. *Die Pastoralbriefe als Paulustradition*. Forschungen zur Religion und Literatur des Alten und Neuen Testaments 146. Göttingen: Vandenhoeck & Ruprecht, 1988.

———. *Rechtfertigung und zukünftiges Heil: Untersuchungen zu Röm 5,1–11*. Beihefte zur Zeitschrift für die neutestamentliche Wissenschaft 43. Berlin: de Gruyter, 1978.

———. "'Reich Gottes' bei Lukas." *New Testament Studies* 41 (1995): 541–63.

Wong, K. C. *Interkulturelle Theologie und multikulturelle Gemeinde im Matthäusevangelium*. Novum Testamentum et Orbis Antiquus 22. Göttingen: Vandenhoeck & Ruprecht, 1992.

Wördemann, Dirk. *Das Charakterbild im bios nach Plutarch und das Christusbild im Evangelium nach Markus*. Studien zur Geschichte und Kultur des Altertums 1/19. Paderborn: Schöningh, 2002.

Wrede, William. *The Messianic Secret*. Translated by James C. G. Greig. Library of Theological Translations. London: James Clarke, 1971.

———. *Paul*. Translated by Edward Lummis. Boston: American Unitarian Association, 1908.

———. "Über Aufgabe und Methode der sogenannten Neutestamentlichen Theologie." In *Das Problem der Theologie des Neuen Testaments*, edited by Georg Strecker, 81–154. Weg der Forschung 367. Darmstadt: Wissenschaftliche Buchgesellschaft, 1975.

Wright, N. T. *Jesus and the Victory of God*. Christian Origins and the Question of God 2. Minneapolis: Fortress, 1996.

———. *Paul in Fresh Perspective*. Minneapolis: Fortress, 2005.

———. "Paul's Gospel and Caesar's Empire." In *Paul and Politics: Ekklesia, Israel, Imperium, Interpretation: Essays in Honor of Krister Stendahl*, edited by Richard A. Horsley, 160–83. Harrisburg, PA: Trinity, 2000.

———. *What Saint Paul Really Said: Was Paul of Tarsus the Real Founder of Christianity?* Grand Rapids: Eerdmans, 1997.

Würthwein, Ernst. *The Text of the Old Testament: An Introduction to the Biblia Hebraica*. Translated by Erroll F. Rhodes. Grand Rapids: Eerdmans, 1979.

Yieh, Yueh-Han. *One Teacher: Jesus's Teaching Role in Matthew's Report*. Wissenschaftliche Monographien zum Neuen Testament 2/124. Tübingen: Mohr, 204.

Zager, Werner. "Gericht Gottes in der Johannesapokalypse." In *Studien zur Johannesoffenbarung und ihrer Auslegung: Festschrift für Otto Böcher zum 70. Geburtstag*, edited by Friedrich Wilhelm Horn and Michael Wolter, 310–27. Neukirchen-Vluyn: Neukirchener Verlag, 2005.

———. *Gottesherrschaft und Endgericht in der Verkündigung Jesu: Eine Untersuchung zur markinischen Jesusüberlieferung einschliesslich der Q-Parallelen*. Beihefte zur Zeitschrift für die neutestamentliche Wissenschaft und die Kunde der älteren Kirche 82. Berlin: de Gruyter, 1996.

Zahn, Theodor. *Geschichte des Neutestamentlichen Kanons*. 2 vols. Leipzig: Deichert, 1888–92.

Zahrnt, Heinz. *The Historical Jesus*. Translated by J. S. Bowden. New York: Harper & Row, 1963.

Zeilinger, Franz. *Der Erstgeborene der Schöpfung: Untersuchungen zur Formalstruktur und Theologie des Kolosserbriefes*. Vienna: Herder, 1974.

Zeller, Dieter. *Der Brief an die Römer*. Regensburger Neues Testament. Regensburg: Pustet, 1985.

———. *Charis bei Philon und Paulus*. Stuttgarter Bibelstudien 142. Stuttgart: Verlag Katholisches Bibelwerk, 1990.

———. "Der eine Gott und der eine Herr Jesus Christus." In *Der lebendige Gott: Studien zur Theologie des Neuen Testaments; Festschrift für Wilhelm Thüsing zum 75. Geburtstag*, edited by Thomas Söding, 34–49. Neutestamentliche Abhandlungen, n.F., 31. Münster: Aschendorff, 1996.

———. "Gibt es religionsgeschichtliche Parallelen zur Taufe für die Toten (1Kor 15,29)?" *Zeitschrift für die neutestamentliche Wissenschaft und die Kunde der älteren Kirche* 98 (2007): 68–76.

———. "Jesu weisheitliche Ethik." In *Jesus von Nazaret—Spuren und Konturen*, edited by Ludger Schenke. Stuttgart: Kohlhammer, 2004.

———. "Jesus, Q, und die Zukunft Israels." In *The Sayings Source Q and the Historical Jesus*, edited by Andreas Lindemann, 351–69. Bibliotheca ephemeridum theologicarum lovaniensium 158. Louvain: Leuven University Press, 2001.

———. "Die Menschwerdung des Sohnes Gottes im Neuen Testament und die antike Religionsgeschichte." In *Menschwerdung Gottes—Vergöttlichung von Menschen*, edited by Dieter Zeller, 141–76. Novum Testamentum et Orbis Antiquus 7. Göttingen: Vandenhoeck & Ruprecht, 1988.

———. "New Testament Christology in Its Hellenistic Reception." *New Testament Studies* 46 (2001): 312–33.

———. "Paulus und Johannes." *Biblische Zeitschrift* 27 (1983): 167–82.

———. *Die weisheitlichen Mahnsprüche bei den Synoptiker*. Würzburg: Echter Verlag, 1977.

———. "Der Zusammenhang der Eschatologie in der Logienquelle." In *Gegenwart und kommendes Reich: Schülergabe Anton Vögtle zum 65. Geburtstag*, edited by Peter Fiedler and Dieter Zeller, 67–77. Stuttgarter biblische Beiträge 6. Stuttgart: Verlag Katholisches Bibelwerk, 1975.

Zimmermann, Alfred. *Die urchristlichen Lehrer: Studien zum Tradentenkreis der Didaskaloi im frühen Urchristentum*. Wissenschaftliche Untersuchungen zum Neuen Testament 2/12. Tübingen: Mohr, 1984.

———. "Unecht—und doch wahr? Pseudepigraphie im Neuen Testament als theologisches Problem." *Zeitschrift für Neues Testament* 12 (2003): 27–38.

Zimmermann, Heinrich. *Das Bekenntnis der Hoffnung: Tradition und Redaktion im Hebräerbrief*. Bonner biblische Beiträge 47. Bonn: Hanstein, 1977.

———. *Die Hohepriester-Christologie des Hebräerbriefes*. Paderborn: Schöningh, 1964.

Zimmermann, Johannes. *Messianische Texte aus Qumran: Königliche, priesterliche und prophetische Messiasvorstellungen in den Schriftfunden von Qumran*. Wissenschaftliche Untersuchungen zum Neuen Testament 2/104. Tübingen: Mohr, 1998.

Zimmermann, Ruben. *Christologie der Bilder im Johannesevangelium: Die Christopoetik des vierten Evangeliums unter besonderer Berücksichtigung von Joh 10*. Wissenschaftliche Untersuchungen zum Neuen Testament 171. Tübingen: Mohr Siebeck, 2004.

———. "Jenseits von Indikativ und Imperativ." *Theologische Literaturzeitung* 132 (2007): 259–84.

Zingg, E. *Das Reden von Gott als "Vater" im Johannesevangelium*. Herders biblische Studien 48. Freiburg i.B.: Herder, 2006.

Zumstein, Jean. "Die johanneische Auffassung der Macht, gezeigt am Beispiel der Fußwaschung (Joh 13,1–17)." In *Kreative Erinnerung*, edited by Jean Zumstein, 161–76. Abhandlungen zur Theologie des Alten und Neuen Testaments 78. Zürich: Theologischer Verlag, 2004.

Index of Subjects

Index of Greek Words and Phrases

Index of Modern Authors

Index of Ancient Sources

1. Old Testament

Hosea

Joel

Amos

Obadiah

Micah

Habakkuk

Zephaniah

Zechariah

Malachi

2. Old Testament Apocrypha/ Deutero-canonicals

Baruch

1 Maccabees

2 Maccabees

3 Maccabees

4 Maccabees

Sirach

Tobit

Wisdom of Solomon

3. New Testament

Matthew

Mark

Q (Sayings Source; Lukan numbering)

John

Acts

1 Corinthians

2 Corinthians

Galatians

Ephesians

Philippians

Colossians

1 Thessalonians

2 Thessalonians

1 Timothy

2 Timothy

Titus

Philemon

Hebrews

1 Peter

2 Peter

4. Old Testament Pseudepigrapha

Apocalypse of Abraham

Assumption of Moses

2 Baruch (Syriac Apocalypse)

1 Enoch (Ethiopic Apocalypse)

2 Enoch (Slavonic Apocalypse)

4 Ezra

Jubilees

Letter of Aristeas

Psalms of Solomon

Sibylline Oracles

5. Dead Sea Scrolls

6. Mishnah, Talmud, and Related Literature

7. Apostolic Fathers

8. New Testament Apocrypha/Pseudepigrapha

9. Other Ancient Writers